DATA STRUCTURES AND PROBLEM SOLVING USING C++

Second Edition

MARK ALLEN WEISS
Florida International University

ADDISON-WESLEY

An imprint of Addison Wesley Longman, Inc.

Reading, Massachusetts • Harlow, England • Menlo Park, California
Berkeley, California • Don Mills, Ontario • Sydney • Bonn • Amsterdam
Tokyo • Mexico City

Acquisitions Editor: Susan Hartman
Project Editor: Katherine Harutunian
Production Management: Shepherd, Inc.
Composition: Shepherd, Inc.
Cover Design: Diana Coe
Cover Photo: © Mike Shepherd/Photonica

Library of Congress Cataloging-in-Publication Data

Weiss, Mark Allen.
Data structures and problem solving using C++ / Mark Allen Weiss--2nd ed.
p. cm.
ISBN 0-201-61250-X
1. C++ (Computer program language) 2. Data structures (Computer science) 3. Problem solving--Data processing. I. Title
QA76.73.C153 W646 2000
005.13'3--dc21

99-047375

3 4 5 6 7 8 RRD 05 06 07 08

Contents

Part I: Objects and C++

Part V: Advanced Data Structures

Appendices

Preface

This book is designed for a two-semester sequence in computer science, beginning with what is typically known as Data Structures (CS-2) and continuing with advanced data structures and algorithm analysis.

The content of the CS-2 course has been evolving for some time. Although there is some general consensus concerning topic coverage, considerable disagreement still exists over the details. One uniformly accepted topic is principles of software development, most notably the concepts of encapsulation and information hiding. Algorithmically, all CS-2 courses tend to include an introduction to running-time analysis, recursion, basic sorting algorithms, and elementary data structures. An advanced course is offered at many universities that covers topics in data structures, algorithms, and running-time analysis at a higher level. The material in this text has been designed for use in both levels of courses, thus eliminating the need to purchase a second textbook.

Although the most passionate debates in CS-2 revolve around the choice of a programming language, other fundamental choices need to be made, including

- whether to introduce object-oriented design or object-based design early,
- the level of mathematical rigor,
- the appropriate balance between the implementation of data structures and their use, and
- programming details related to the language chosen.

My goal in writing this text was to provide a practical introduction to data structures and algorithms from the viewpoint of abstract thinking and problem solving. I tried to cover all of the important details concerning the data structures, their analyses, and their C++ implementations, while staying away from data structures that are theoretically interesting but not widely used. It is impossible to cover in a single course all the different data structures, including their uses and the analysis, described in this text. So, I designed the textbook to allow instructors flexibility in topic coverage. The instructor will need to decide on an appropriate balance between practice and theory and then choose those topics that best fit the course. As I discuss later in this Preface, I organized the text to minimize dependencies among the various chapters.

A Unique Approach

My basic premise is that software development tools in all languages come with large libraries, and many data structures are part of these libraries. I envision an eventual shift in emphasis of data structures courses from implementation to use. In this book I take a unique approach by separating the data structures into their specification and subsequent implementation and take advantage of an already existing data structures library, the Standard Template Library (STL).

A subset of the STL suitable for most applications is discussed in a single chapter (Chapter 7) in Part II. Part II also covers basic analysis techniques, recursion, and sorting. Part III contains a host of applications that use the STL's data structures. Implementation of the STL is not shown until Part IV, once the data structures have already been used. Because the STL is part of C++ (older compilers can use the textbook's STL code instead—see *Code Availability*, xxix), students can design large projects early on, using existing software components.

Despite the central use of the STL in this text, it is neither a book on the STL nor a primer on implementing the STL specifically; it remains a book that emphasizes data structures and basic problem-solving techniques. Of course, the general techniques used in the design of data structures are applicable to the implementation of the STL, so several chapters in Part IV include STL implementations. However, instructors can choose the simpler implementations in Part IV that do not discuss the STL protocol. Chapter 7, which presents the STL, is essential to understanding the code in Part III. I attempted to use only the basic parts of the STL.

Many instructors will prefer a more traditional approach in which each data structure is defined, implemented, and then used. Because there is no dependency between material in Parts III and IV, a traditional course can easily be taught from this book.

Prerequisites

Students using this book should have knowledge of either an object-oriented or procedural programming language. Knowledge of basic features, including primitive data types, operators, control structures, functions (methods), and input and output (but not necessarily arrays and classes) is assumed.

Students who have taken a first course using C++ or Java may find the first two chapters "light" reading in some places. However, other parts are definitely "heavy" with C++ details that may not have been covered in introductory courses.

Students who have had a first course in another language should begin at Chapter 1 and proceed slowly. They also should consult Appendix A which discusses some language issues that are somewhat C++ specific. If a student would like also to use a C++ reference book, some recommendations are given in Chapter 1, pages 38–39.

Knowledge of discrete math is helpful but is not an absolute prerequisite. Several mathematical proofs are presented, but the more complex proofs are preceded by a brief math review. Chapters 8 and 19–24 require some degree of mathematical sophistication. The instructor may easily elect to skip mathematical aspects of the proofs by presenting only the results. All proofs in the text are clearly marked and are separate from the body of the text.

Summary of Changes in the Second Edition

1. Much of Part I was rewritten. In Chapter 1, primitive arrays are no longer presented (a discussion of them was moved to Appendix D); vectors are used instead, and `push_back` is introduced. Pointers appear later in this edition than in the first edition. In Chapter 2, material was significantly rearranged and simplified. Chapter 3 has additional material on templates. In Chapter 4, the discussion on inheritance was rewritten to simplify the initial presentation. The end of the chapter contains the more esoteric C++ details that are important for advanced uses.
2. An additional chapter on design patterns was added in Part I. Several object-based patterns, including Functor, Wrapper, and Iterator, are described, and patterns that make use of inheritance, including Observer, are discussed.
3. The Data Structures chapter in Part II was rewritten with the STL in mind. Both generic interfaces (as in the first edition) and STL interfaces are illustrated in the revised Chapter 7.

4. The code in Part III is based on the STL. In several places, the code is more object-oriented than before. The Huffman coding example is completely coded.
5. In Part IV, generic data structures were rewritten to be much simpler and cleaner. Additionally, as appropriate, a simplified STL implementation is illustrated at the end of the chapters in Part IV. Implemented components include `vector`, `list`, `stack`, `queue`, `set`, `map`, `priority_queue`, and various function objects and algorithms.

C++

Using C++ presents both advantages and disadvantages. The C++ class allows the separation of interface and implementation, as well as the hiding of internal details of the implementation. It cleanly supports the notion of abstraction. The advantage of C++ is that it is widely used in industry. Students perceive that the material they are learning is practical and will help them find employment, which provides motivation to persevere through the course. One disadvantage of C++ is that it is far from a perfect language pedagogically, especially in a second course, and thus additional care needs to be expended to avoid bad programming practices. A second disadvantage is that C++ is still not a stable language, so the various compilers behave differently.

It might have been preferable to write the book in a language-independent fashion, concentrating only on general principles such as the theory of the data structures and referring to C++ code only in passing, but that is impossible. C++ code is complex, and students will need to see complete examples to understand some of its finer points. As mentioned earlier, a brief review of parts of C++ is provided in Appendix A. Part I of the book describes some of C++'s more advanced features relevant to data structures.

Several parts of the language stand out as requiring special consideration: templates, inheritance, exceptions, namespaces and other recent C++ additions, and the Standard Library. I approached this material in the following manner.

- *Templates:* Templates are used extensively. Some instructors may have reservations with this approach because it complicates the code, but I included them because they are fundamental concepts in any sophisticated C++ program.
- *Inheritance:* I use inheritance relatively sparingly because it adds complications, and data structures are not a strong application area

for it. This edition contains less use of inheritance than in the previous edition. However, there is a chapter on inheritance, and part of the design patterns chapter touches on inheritance-based patterns. For the most part, instructors who are eager to avoid inheritance can do so, and those who want to discuss inheritance will find sufficient material in the text.

- *Exceptions:* Exception semantics have been standardized and exceptions seem to work on many compilers. However, exceptions in C++ involve ugly code, significant complications (e.g., if used in conjunction with templates), and probably require discussing inheritance. So I use them sparingly in this text. A brief discussion of exceptions is provided, and in some places exceptions are thrown in code when warranted. However, I generally do not attempt to catch exceptions in any Part III code (most of the Standard Library does not attempt to throw exceptions).
- *Namespaces:* Namespaces, which are a recent addition to C++, do not work correctly on a large variety of compilers. I do not attempt to use namespaces and I import the entire `std` namespace when necessary (even though not great style, it works on the largest number of compilers). Appendix A discusses the namespace issues.
- *Recent language additions:* The `bool` data type is used throughout. The new `static_cast` operator is used in preference to the old-style cast. Finally, I use `explicit` when appropriate. For the most part, other additions are not used (e.g., I generally avoid using `typename`).
- *Standard Library:* As previously mentioned, the STL is used throughout, and a safe version (that does extra bounds checking) is available online (and implemented in Part IV). We also use the `string` class and the newer `istringstream` class that are part of the standard library.

Text Organization

In this text I introduce C++ and object-oriented programming (particularly abstraction) in Part I. I discuss arrays, pointers and some other C++ topics and then go on to discuss the syntax and use of classes, templates, and inheritance. The material in these chapters was substantially rewritten. New to this edition is an entire chapter on design patterns.

In Part II I discuss Big-Oh and algorithmic paradigms, including recursion and randomization. An entire chapter is devoted to sorting, and a separate chapter contains a description of basic data structures. I use the STL in presenting the interfaces and running times of the data structures. At this point in the text, the instructor may take several approaches to present the remaining material, including the following two.

1. Discuss the corresponding implementations (either the STL versions or the simpler versions) in Part IV as each data structure is described. The instructor can ask students to extend the classes in various ways, as suggested in the exercises.
2. Show how the STL class is used and cover implementation at a later point in the course. The case studies in Part III can be used to support this approach. As complete implementations are available on every modern C++ compiler (or on the Internet for older compilers), the instructor can use the STL in programming projects. Details on using this approach are given shortly.

Part V describes advanced data structures such as splay trees, pairing heaps, and the disjoint set data structure, which can be covered if time permits or, more likely, in a follow-up course.

Chapter-by-Chapter Text Organization

Part I consists of five chapters that describe some advanced features of C++ used throughout the text. Chapter 1 describes arrays, strings, pointers, references, and structures. Chapter 2 begins the discussion of object-oriented programming by describing the class mechanism in C++. Chapter 3 continues this discussion by examining templates, and Chapter 4 illustrates the use of inheritance. Several components, including strings and vectors, are written in these chapters. Chapter 5 discusses some basic design patterns, focusing mostly on object-based patterns such as function objects, wrappers and adapters, iterators, and pairs. Some of these patterns (most notably the wrapper pattern) are used later in the text.

Part II focuses on the basic algorithms and building blocks. In Chapter 6 a complete discussion of time complexity and Big-Oh notation is provided, and binary search is also discussed and analyzed. Chapter 7 is crucial because it covers the STL and argues intuitively what the running time of the supported operations should be for each data structure. (The implementation of these data structures, in both STL-style and a simplified version, is not provided until Part IV. The STL is available on recent compilers.) Chapter 8 describes recursion by first introducing the notion of proof by induction. It also discusses divide-and-conquer, dynamic programming, and backtracking. A section describes several recursive numerical algorithms that are used to implement the RSA cryptosystem. For many students, the material in the second half of Chapter 8 is more suitable for a follow-up course. Chapter 9 describes, codes, and analyzes several basic sorting algorithms, including the insertion sort, Shellsort, mergesort, and quicksort, as well as indirect sorting. It also proves the classic lower bound for sorting and discusses the related problems of selection. Finally, Chapter 10 is a short chapter that discusses random numbers, including their generation and use in randomized algorithms.

Part III provides several case studies, and each chapter is organized around a general theme. Chapter 11 illustrates several important techniques by examining games. Chapter 12 discusses the use of stacks in computer languages by examining an algorithm to check for balanced symbols and the classic operator precedence parsing algorithm. Complete implementations with code are provided for both algorithms. Chapter 13 discusses the basic utilities of file compression and cross-reference generation, and provides a complete implementation of both. Chapter 14 broadly examines simulation by looking at one problem that can be viewed as a simulation and then at the more classic event-driven simulation. Finally, Chapter 15 illustrates how data structures are used to implement several shortest path algorithms efficiently for graphs.

Part IV presents the data structure implementations. Implementations that use simple protocols (`insert`, `find`, `remove` variations) are provided. In some cases, STL implementations that tend to use more complicated C++ syntax are presented. Some mathematics is used in this part, especially in Chapters 19–21, and can be skipped at the discretion of the instructor. Chapter 16 provides implementations for both stacks and queues. First these data structures are implemented using an expanding array; then they are implemented using linked lists. The STL versions are discussed at the end of the chapter. General linked lists are described in Chapter 17. Singly linked lists are illustrated with a simple protocol, and the more complex STL version that uses doubly linked lists is provided at the end of the chapter. Chapter 18 describes trees and illustrates the basic traversal schemes. Chapter 19 is a detailed chapter that provides several implementations of binary search trees. Initially, the basic binary search tree is shown, and then a binary search tree that supports order statistics is derived. AVL trees are discussed but not implemented; however, the more practical red–black trees and AA-trees are implemented. Then the STL `set` and `map` are implemented. Finally, the B-tree is examined. Chapter 20 discusses hash tables and implements the quadratic probing scheme, after examination of a simpler alternative. Chapter 21 describes the binary heap and examines heapsort and external sorting. The STL `priority_queue` is implemented in this chapter.

Part Chapter V contains material suitable for use in a more advanced course or for general reference. The algorithms are accessible even at the first-year level; however, for completeness sophisticated mathematical analyses were included that are almost certainly beyond the reach of a first-year student. Chapter 22 describes the splay tree, which is a binary search tree that seems to perform extremely well in practice and is also competitive with the binary heap in some applications that require priority queues. Chapter 23 describes priority queues that support merging operations and provides an implementation of the pairing heap. Finally, Chapter 24 examines the classic disjoint set data structure.

The appendices contain additional C++ reference material. Appendix A describes tricky C++ issues, including some unusual operators, I/O, and recent language changes. Appendix B lists the operators and their precedence. Appendix C summarizes some C++ libraries. Appendix D describes primitive arrays and strings for those who want details of what is going on under the hood of the `vector` and `string` classes.

Chapter Dependencies

Generally speaking, most chapters are independent of each other. However, the following are some of the notable dependencies.

- *Part I:* The first three chapters should be covered in their entirety first. I recommend a brief discussion of inheritance in Chapter 4. Some instructors will want to cover all of inheritance, but it is possible to get by with just the basics of inheritance and avoid some of the more difficult C++ issues that inheritance involves. Some of the object-based patterns (e.g., wrappers and function objects) in Chapter 5 can be discussed shortly after templates, or later in the course as the need arises. Some of these patterns are used in the chapter on sorting and in Part IV.
- *Chapter 6* (*Algorithm Analysis*): This chapter should be covered prior to Chapters 7 and 9. Recursion (Chapter 8) can be covered prior to this chapter, but the instructor will have to gloss over some details about avoiding inefficient recursion.
- *Chapter 7* (*STL*): This chapter can be covered prior to, or in conjunction with, material in Part III or IV.
- *Chapter 8* (*Recursion*): The material in Sections 8.1–8.3 should be covered prior to discussing recursive sorting algorithms, trees, the tic-tac-toe case study, and shortest-path algorithms. Material such as the RSA cryptosystem, dynamic programming, and backtracking (unless tic-tac-toe is discussed) is otherwise optional.
- *Chapter 9* (*Sorting*): This chapter should follow Chapters 6 and 8. However, it is possible to cover Shellsort without Chapters 6 and 8.

Shellsort is not recursive (hence there is no need for Chapter 8), and a rigorous analysis of its running time is too complex and is not covered in the book (hence there is little need for Chapter 6).

- *Chapters 16 and 17* (*Stacks/Queues/Lists*): These chapters may be covered in either order. However, I prefer to cover Chapter 16 first, because I believe that it presents a simpler example of linked lists.
- *Chapters 18 and 19* (*Trees/Search trees*): These chapters can be covered in either order or simultaneously.

Separate Entities

The other chapters have little or no dependencies:

- *Chapter 10* (*Randomization*): The material on random numbers can be covered at any point as needed.
- *Part III* (*Case Studies*): Chapters 11–15 can be covered in conjunction with, or after, the STL (in Chapter 7), and in roughly any order. There are a few references to earlier chapters. These include Section 11.2 (tic-tac-toe), which references a discussion in Section 8.7, and Section 13.2 (cross-reference generation), which references similar lexical analysis code in Section 12.1 (balanced symbol checking).
- *Chapters 20 and 21* (*Hashing/Priority Queues*): These chapters can be covered at any point.
- *Part V* (*Advanced Data Structures*): The material in Chapters 22–24 is self-contained and is typically covered in a follow-up course.

Mathematics

I have attempted to provide mathematical rigor for use in CS-2 courses that emphasize theory and for follow-up courses that require more analysis. However, this material stands out from the main text in the form of separate theorems and, in some cases, separate sections (or subsections). Thus it can be skipped by instructors in courses that deemphasize theory.

In all cases, the proof of a theorem is not necessary to the understanding of the theorem's meaning. This is another illustration of the separation of an interface (the theorem statement) from its implementation (the proof). Some inherently mathematical material, such as Section 8.4 (*Numerical Applications of Recursion*), can be skipped without affecting comprehension of the rest of the chapter.

Course Organization

A crucial issue in teaching the course is deciding how the materials in Parts II–IV are to be used. The material in Part I should be covered in depth, and the student should write one or two programs that illustrate the design, implementation, and testing of classes and generic classes—and perhaps object-oriented design, using inheritance. Chapter 6 discusses Big-Oh notation. An exercise in which the student writes a short program and compares the running time with an analysis can be given to test comprehension.

In the separation approach, the key concept of Chapter 7 is that different data structures support different access schemes with different efficiency. Any case study (except the tic-tac-toe example that uses recursion) can be used to illustrate the applications of the data structures. In this way, the student can see the data structure and how it is used but not how it is efficiently implemented. This is truly a separation. Viewing things this way will greatly enhance the ability of students to think abstractly. Students can also provide simple implementations of some of the STL components (some suggestions are given in the exercises in Chapter 7) and see the difference between efficient data structure implementations in the existing STL and inefficient data structure implementations that they will write. Students can also be asked to extend the case study, but, again, they are not required to know any of the details of the data structures.

Efficient implementation of the data structures can be discussed afterward, and recursion can be introduced whenever the instructor feels it is appropriate, provided it is prior to binary search trees. The details of sorting can be discussed at any time after recursion. At this point, the course can continue by using the same case studies and experimenting with modifications to the implementations of the data structures. For instance, the student can experiment with various forms of balanced binary search trees.

Instructors who opt for a more traditional approach can simply discuss a case study in Part III after discussing a data structure implementation in Part IV. Again, the book's chapters are designed to be as independent of each other as possible.

Exercises

Exercises come in various flavors; I have provided four varieties. The basic *In Short* exercise asks a simple question or requires hand-drawn simulations of an algorithm described in the text. The *In Theory* section asks questions that either require mathematical analysis or asks for theoretically interesting solutions to problems. The *In Practice* section contains simple programming questions, including questions about syntax or particularly tricky lines of code. Finally, the *Programming Projects* section contains ideas for extended assignments.

Pedagogical Features

- Margin notes are used to highlight important topics.
- The *Objects of the Game* section lists important terms along with definitions and page references.

- The *Common Errors* section at the end of each chapter provides a list of commonly made errors.
- References for further reading are provided at the end of most chapters.

Code Availability

The code in the text is fully functional and has been tested on numerous platforms. It is available from my home page `http://www.fiu.edu/~weiss`. Be sure to browse the `README` file for information on compiler dependencies and bug fixes. The *On the Internet* section at the end of each chapter lists the filenames for the chapter's code.

Instructor's Resource Guide

An *Instructor's Guide* that illustrates several approaches to the material is available. It includes samples of test questions, assignments, and syllabi. Answers to select exercises are also provided. Instructors should contact their Addison Wesley Longman local sales representative for information on its availability or send an e-mail message to `aw.cse@awl.com`. This guide is not available for sale and is available to instructors only.

Acknowledgments

Many, many people have helped me in the preparation of this book. Many have already been acknowledged in the first edition and the related title, *Data Structures and Problem Solving Using Java*. Others, too numerous to list, have sent e-mail messages and pointed out errors or inconsistencies in explanations that I have tried to fix in this version.

For this book, I would like to thank all of the folks at Addison Wesley Longman: my editor, Susan Hartman, and associate editor, Katherine Harutunian, helped me make some difficult decisions regarding the organization of the C++ material and were very helpful in bringing this book to fruition. My copyeditor, Jerrold Moore, and proofreaders, suggested numerous rewrites that improved the text. Diana Coe did a lovely cover design. As always, Michael Hirsch has done a superb marketing job. I would especially like to thank Pat Mahtani, my production editor, and Lynn Steines at Shepherd, Inc. for their outstanding efforts coordinating the entire project.

I also thank the reviewers, who provided valuable comments, many of which have been incorporated into the text:

Zhengxin Chen, University of Nebraska at Omaha
Arlan DeKock, University of Missouri–Rolla
Andrew Duchowski, Clemson University
Seth Copen Goldstein, Carnegie Mellon University
G. E. Hedrick, Oklahoma State University
Murali Medidi, Northern Arizona University
Chris Nevison, Colgate University
Gurpur Prabhu, Iowa State University
Donna Reese, Mississippi State University
Gurdip Singh, Kansas State University
Michael Stinson, Central Michigan University
Paul Wolfgang, Temple University

Some of the material in this text is adapted from my textbook *Efficient C Programming: A Practical Approach* (Prentice-Hall, 1995) and is used with permission of the publisher. I have included end-of-chapter references where appropriate.

My World Wide Web page, `http://www.cs.fiu.edu/~weiss`, will contain updated source code, an errata list, and a link for receiving bug reports.

M. A. W.
Miami, Florida
September, 1999

Part I

Objects and C++

Chapter 1

Arrays, Pointers, and Structures

In this chapter we discuss three features contained in many programming languages: *arrays, pointers*, and *structures*. Sophisticated C++ programming makes heavy use of pointers to access objects. Arrays and structures store several objects in one collection. An array stores only one type of object, but a structure can hold a collection of several distinct types.

In this chapter, we show:

- why these features are important;
- how the `vector` is used to implement arrays in C++;
- how the `string` is used to implement strings in C++;
- how basic pointer syntax and *dynamic memory allocation* are used; and
- how pointers, arrays, and structures are passed as parameters to functions.

1.1 What Are Pointers, Arrays, and Structures?

A pointer is an object that can be used to access another object. A pointer provides *indirect* access rather than *direct* access to an object. People use pointers in real-life situations all the time. Let us look at some examples.

- When a professor says, "Do Problem 1.1 in the textbook," the actual homework assignment is being stated indirectly.
- A classic example of indirect access is looking up a topic in the index of a book. The index tells you where you can find a full description.
- A street address is a pointer. It tells you where someone resides. A forwarding address is a pointer to a pointer.

- A *uniform resource locator* (URL), such as `http://www.cnn.com`, is a pointer. The URL tells you where a target Web page is. If the target Web page moves, the URL becomes stale, and points to a page that no longer exists.

A *pointer* stores an address where other data reside.

In all these cases a piece of information is given out indirectly by providing a pointer to the information. In C++ a pointer is an object that stores an address (i.e., a location in memory) where other data are stored. An address is expected to be an integer, so a pointer object can usually be represented internally as an `(unsigned) int`.[1] What makes a pointer object more than just a plain integer is that we can access the datum being pointed at. Doing so is known as *dereferencing* the pointer.

An *aggregate* is a collection of objects stored in one unit.

An *array* stores a collection of identically-typed objects.

An **aggregate** is a collection of objects stored in one unit. The **array** is the basic mechanism for storing a collection of identically-typed objects. A different type of aggregate type is the structure, which stores a collection of objects that need not be of the same type. As a somewhat abstract example, consider the layout of an apartment building. Each floor might have a one-bedroom unit, a two-bedroom unit, a three-bedroom unit, and a laundry room. Thus each floor is stored as a structure, and the building is an array of floors.

1.2 Arrays and Strings

In C++ we can declare and use arrays in two basic ways. The primitive method is to use the built-in array. The alternative is to use a `vector`. The syntax for both methods is more or less the same; however, the `vector` is much easier and slightly safer to use than the primitive array and is preferred for most applications. The major philosophical difference between the two is that the `vector` behaves as a first-class type (even though it is implemented in a library), whereas the primitive array is a second-class type. Similarly, C++ provides primitive strings (which are simply primitive arrays of `char`) and the much-preferred `string`. In this section we examine what is meant by first-class and second-class types and show you how to use the `vector` and `string`.

1.2.1 First-Class Versus Second-Class Objects

***First-class objects* can be manipulated in all the "usual ways" without special cases and exceptions.**

Computer Scientists who study programming languages often designate certain language constructs as being *first-class objects* or *second-class objects*. The exact definition of these terms is somewhat imprecise, but the general idea is that **first-class objects** can be manipulated in all the "usual ways"

1. This fact is of little use in normal programming practice and in languages besides C, C++, and low-level assembly languages. It is used (often dangerously) by old-style C++ programmers.

without special cases and exceptions, whereas second-class objects can be manipulated in only certain restricted ways.

What are the "usual ways?" In the specific case of C++, they might include things like copying. Recall that an array stores a collection of objects. We would expect a copy of an array to copy the entire collection; this is not the case for the primitive array. We might also expect an array to know how many objects are in its collection. In other words, we would expect that the size of the array is part of its being. Again, this is not true for primitive arrays. (The reason for this is that arrays in C++ are little more than pointer variables, rather than their own first-class type.) We might also expect that when allocated arrays are no longer needed (for instance the function in which they are declared returns), then the memory that these arrays consumes is automatically reclaimed. This is true sometimes and false at other times for arrays, making for tricky coding.

Primitive arrays and strings are not first-class objects.

The primitive string may be considered even lower than a second-class object because it suffers all the second-class behavior of arrays. In addition, its comparison operators (for instance, == and <) do not do what we would normally expect them to do and thus have to be handled as a special case.

Throughout the text, we use a `vector` and a `string` to provide first-class treatment for arrays and strings.[2] The `vector` and `string` classes are now part of the Standard Library and thus are part of C++. However, many compilers do not yet support them. We provide our own versions of `vector` (Section 3.4.2) and `string` (Section 2.6), and in the process, illustrate how their second-class counterparts are manipulated. Our `vector` and `string` are implemented by wrapping the second-class behavior of the built-in types in a *class*.[3] This implementation is an acceptable use of the second-class type because the complicated second-class implementation details are hidden and never seen by the user of the first-class objects. As we demonstrate in Chapter 2, the class allows us to define new types. Included in these types are functions that can be applied to objects of the new type.

Throughout the text, we use a `vector` and a `string` to provide first-class treatment for arrays and strings.

The `vector` and `string` classes in the Standard Library treat arrays and strings as first-class objects. A `vector` knows how large it is. Two `string` objects can be compared with ==, <, and so on. Both `vector` and

---

2. The `vector` class contains the basic primitive array operations plus additional features. Thus it behaves more like a data structure than a simple array. However, its use is much safer than the primitive C++ array. The `vector` is part of the *Standard Template Library* (STL).
3. Appendix D contains further discussion of primitive arrays and strings if you want to see these details early. However, you must read Section 1.3 first. A less detailed discussion is given in Sections 2.6 and 3.4.2, which contain descriptions that are sufficient to show how the `string` and `vector` are implemented.

string can be copied with =. Except in special cases, you should avoid using the built-in C++ array and string.

The **string** is a class, or the library type used for first-class strings. The **vector** is a class template, or the library type used for first-class arrays. We discuss classes in Chapter 2 and class templates in Chapter 3. A recurring theme in this text is that using a library routine does not require knowing anything about its underlying implementation. However, you may need to know how the second-class counterparts are manipulated because occasionally you must resort to the primitive versions. It turns out that both string and vector are implemented by providing an interface that hides the second-class behavior of the built-in types.

1.2.2 Using the **vector**

To use the standard vector, your program must include a library header file with

```
#include <vector>
```

A *using* directive may be needed if one has not already been provided.

The *array indexing operator* [] provides access to any object in the array.

Just as a variable must be declared before it is used in an expression and initialized before its value is used, so must an array. A vector is declared by giving it a name, in accordance with the usual identifier rules, and by telling the compiler what type the elements are. A size can also be provided; if it is not, the size is zero, but vector will need to be resized later.

Each object in the collection of objects that an array denotes can be accessed by use of the **array indexing operator []**. We say that the [] operator *indexes* the array, meaning that it specifies which of the objects is to be accessed.

Arrays are indexed starting at zero.

In C++, arrays are always indexed starting at zero. Thus the declaration

```
vector<int> a(3); // 3 int objects: a[0], a[1], and a[2]
```

sets aside space to store three integers—namely, a[0], a[1], and a[2]; no index range checking is performed in the Standard Library's vector, so an access out of the array index bounds is not caught by the compiler (in this case, the legal array indices range from 0 to 2, inclusive). Although no explicit run-time error may be generated, undefined and occasionally mysterious behavior would occur. The vector that we implement in Section 3.4.2 allows the programmer to turn on index range checking so that this error causes the program to terminate immediately with a message. (Range checking can be done by using at; a.at(i) is the same as a[i], except that an error is signalled if i is out-of-bounds.)

The size of the `vector` can always be obtained with the `size` function. For the preceding code fragment example, `a.size()` returns 3. Note the syntax: The dot operator is used to call the vector's `size` function.

The size of the `vector` can always be obtained with the `size` operator.

The size of a `vector` can always be changed by calling `resize`. Thus an alternative declaration for the `vector a` could have been

```
vector<int> a;   // 0 int objects
a.resize( 3 );   // 3 int objects: a[0], a[1], and a[2]
```

Figure 1.1 illustrates the use of the `vector`. The program in Figure 1.1 repeatedly chooses numbers between 1 and 100, inclusive. The output is the number of times that each number has occurred.[4]

Line 17 declares an array of integers that count the occurrences of each number. Because arrays are indexed starting at zero, the `+ 1` is crucial if we want to access the item in position `DIFFERENT_NUMBERS`. Without it we would have an array whose indexible range was 0 to 99, and thus any access to index 100 might be to memory that was assigned to another object. Incorrect results could occur, depending on the implementation details of `vector`; we might find that the program would work perfectly on some platforms but would give wrong answers on others.

You must always be sure to declare the correct array size. Off-by-one errors are common and very difficult to spot.

The rest of the program is relatively straightforward. The routine `rand`, declared in `stdlib.h`, gives a (somewhat) random number; the manipulation at line 25 places it in the range 1 to 100, inclusive. The results are output at lines 28 to 30.

The C++ standard specifies that the scope of `i` on line 20 ends with the `for` loop. (In other words, `i` should not be visible at line 24). This is different from the original language specification, and some older compilers (and even some newer compilers) see `i` as being in scope at line 24. Thus we use different names for the loop counters.[5]

1.2.3 Resizing a `vector`

One limitation of primitive arrays is that, once they have been declared, their size can never change. Often this is a significant restriction. We know, however, that we can use `resize` to change the size of a `vector`. The technique used illustrates some of the efficiency issues that we address in this text.

---

4. The *using* directive, shown at line 4, is a recent addition to C++ and is discussed in Appendix A.5. Other significant additions are presented in Section A.6.
5. Note also that the STL vector has an initialization shorthand that we have not used. We could have written
   `vector<int> numbers( DIFFERENT_NUMBERS + 1, 0 );`
   to initialize all entries to zero and thus avoided the first `for` loop.

```
#include <stdlib.h>
#include <iostream>
#include <vector>
using namespace std;

// Generate numbers (from 1-100).
// Print number of occurrences of each number.
int main( )
{
    const int DIFFERENT_NUMBERS = 100;

      // Prompt for and read number of games.
    int totalNumbers;
    cout << "How many numbers to generate?: ";
    cin >> totalNumbers;

    vector<int> numbers( DIFFERENT_NUMBERS + 1 );

      // Initialize the vector to zeros.
    for( int i = 0; i < numbers.size( ); i++ )
        numbers[ i ] = 0;

      // Generate the numbers.
    for( int j = 0; j < totalNumbers; j++ )
        numbers[ rand( ) % DIFFERENT_NUMBERS + 1 ]++;

      // Output the summary.
    for( int k = 1; k <= DIFFERENT_NUMBERS; k++ )
        cout << k << " occurs " << numbers[ k ]
                  << " time(s)\n";

    return 0;
}
```

Figure 1.1 Simple demonstration of arrays.

What happens is that pointers (which we discuss later in this chapter) are used to give the illusion of an array that can be resized. To understand the algorithm does not require any knowledge of C++: all this detail is hidden inside the implementation of `vector`.

The basic idea is shown in Figure 1.2. There, `arr` is representing a 10-element `vector`. Somewhere, buried in the implementation then, memory is allocated for 10 elements. Suppose that we would like to expand this memory to 12 elements. The problem is that array elements must be stored in contiguous memory and that the memory immediately following `arr` might already be taken. So we do the following:

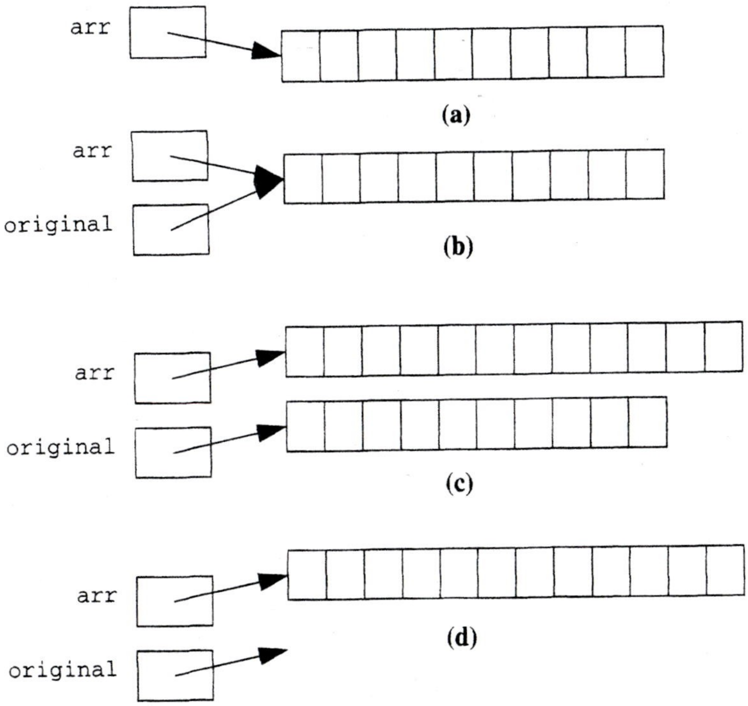

Figure 1.2 Array expansion, internally: (a) At the starting point, `arr` represents 10 integers; (b) after step 1, `original` represents the same 10 integers; (c) after steps 2 and 3, `arr` represents 12 integers, the first 10 of which are copied from `original`; and (d) after step 4, the 10 integers are freed.

1. We remember where the memory for the 10-element array is (the purpose of `original`).
2. We create a new 12-element array and have `arr` use it.
3. We copy the 10 elements from `original` to `arr`; the two extra elments in the new `arr` have some default value.
4. We inform the system that the 10-element array can be reused as it sees fit.

Always expand the array to a size that is some multiplicative constant times as large. Doubling is a good choice.

A moment's thought will convince you that this is an expensive operation because we copy all the elements from the originally allocated array to the newly allocated array. If, for instance, this array expansion is in response to reading input, expanding every time we read a few elements would be inefficient. Thus, when array expansion is implemented, we always make it some *multiplicative* constant times as large. For instance, we might expand to make it twice as large. In this way, when we expand the array from N items to $2N$ items, the cost of the N copies can be apportioned over the next N items that can be inserted into the array without an expansion. As a result, this dynamic expansion is only negligibly more expensive than starting with a fixed size, but it is much more flexible.

To make things more concrete, Figure 1.3 shows a program that reads an unlimited number of integers from the standard input and stores the result in a dynamically expanding array. The function declaration for `getInts` tells us that the `vector` is the parameter. The `&` in the function declaration before `array` specifies that it is a reference to the actual parameter, rather than a copy

```
#include <iostream>
#include <vector>
using namespace std;

// Read an unlimited number of ints with no attempts at error
// recovery; fill the vector parameter with the data; its size
// after the return tells how many items were read.
void getInts( vector<int> & array )
{
    int itemsRead = 0;
    int inputVal;

    cout << "Enter any number of integers: ";
    while( cin >> inputVal )
    {
        if( itemsRead == array.size( ) )
            array.resize( array.size( ) * 2 + 1 );
        array[ itemsRead++ ] = inputVal;
    }
    array.resize( itemsRead );
}

int main( )
{
    vector<int> array;

    getInts( array );
    for( int i = 0; i < array.size( ); i++ )
        cout << array[ i ] << endl;

    return 0;
}
```

Figure 1.3 Code to read an unlimited number of `int`s and write them out, using array-doubling.

of it. Thus all changes in the formal parameter are reflected in the actual argument. We discuss reference parameters in more detail in Section 1.5.

At the start of `getInts`, `itemsRead` is set to `0`. We repeatedly read new items at line 14. If the array is full, as indicated by a successful test at line 16, then the array is expanded at line 17. We resize to roughly twice the size of the old. We add 1 so that the initial doubling converts an array of 0 size to an array of size 1. At line 18 the actual input item is assigned to the array, and the number of items read is incremented. At line 20 we resize the array to match the number of items that were read. An alternative is to have `itemsRead` be an additional reference parameter that is eventually set to the new array size. When the input fails (for whatever reason), we merely return. The `main` routine calls `getInts`, passing a `vector`. The initial size of this `vector` happens to be 0.

1.2.4 `push_back`: `size` and `capacity`

The technique used in Figure 1.3 is so common that the `vector` has built-in functionality to mimic it. The basic idea is that the `vector` maintains not only a size, but also a capacity; the capacity is the amount of memory that it has reserved. The capacity of the `vector` is really an internal detail, not something that you need worry about.

The `push_back` function increases the size by 1, adds a new item to the array at the appropriate position, expanding capacity if needed.

The `push_back` function increases the size by one, and adds a new item into the array at the appropriate position. This is a trivial operation if capacity has not been reached. If it has, the capacity is automatically expanded, using the strategy described in Section 1.2.3.[6] Typically, we start the `vector` with a size of `0`.

The code in Figure 1.4 shows how `push_back` is used in `getInts`; it is clearly much simpler than the `getInts` function in Figure 1.3. Line 13 resizes the `vector` to no elements. This may or may not reduce its capacity, depending on the internal implementation of `vector`. Note that if we do not resize, then new items will be placed at the end of the `vector`; thus items that were in the vector when `getInts` was called will still be there.

1.2.5 Parameter-Passing Mechanisms

Suppose that we want to pass a `vector` to a routine that finds the maximum value in the array. The natural declaration for the routine would be

```
int findMax( vector<int> a );
```

6. Some compilers do not double the capacity, but instead expand by a small constant amount, thereby causing poor performance.

```
#include <stdlib.h>
#include <iostream>
#include <vector>
using namespace std;

// Read an unlimited number of ints with no attempts at error
// recovery; fill the vector parameter with the data; its size
// after the return tells how many items were read.
void getInts( vector<int> & array )
{
    int inputVal;

    array.resize( 0 );
    cout << "Enter any number of integers: ";
    while( cin >> inputVal )
        array.push_back( inputVal );
}
```

Figure 1.4 Code to read an unlimited number of `ints` and write them out using `push_back`.

Call by value **is the default parameter-passing mechanism. The actual argument is copied into the formal parameter.**

This function declaration has a fundamental problem: The default parameter-passing mechanism is **call by value,** whose semantics dictate that a copy be made of the actual argument and used as the formal parameter for every call to `findMax`. Because a could be large, this operation is expensive, so call by value is unsuitable. An alternative is to pass the parameter using **call by reference:**

```
int findMax( vector<int> & a );
```

The *call by reference parameter-passing mechanism* avoids a copy. However, it allows changes to the parameters.

Now we can avoid the overhead of a copy. This routine is still not perfect, however, because the declaration tells the reader, and also the compiler, that the actual argument might be changed as result of the call to `findMax`. When the parameter was passed by value, we were guaranteed that the actual parameter would not be altered. To obtain equivalent behavior, we use a third form of parameter passing, **call by constant reference:**

```
int findMax( const vector<int> & a );
```

The *call by constant reference parameter-passing mechanism* avoids a copy and guarantees that the actual parameter will not be changed.

The constant reference guarantees that

- the overhead of a copy is avoided and that
- the actual parameter is unchanged by the function call.

Choosing a parameter-passing mechanism is an easily overlooked chore of the programmer. After all, the program is often correct no matter which mechanism is used. Nevertheless, in C++ choosing a parameter-passing mechanism carefully is important for efficiency, readability, and program maintenance alike.

- Call by reference is required for objects that may be altered by the function.
- Call by value is appropriate for small objects that should not be altered by the function.
- Call by constant reference is appropriate for large objects that should not be altered by the function.

As we show later, in some more complex cases call by value must be avoided. The program can fail to compile if a wrong decision is made.

Because `string` and `vector` represent large objects, call by value is generally inappropriate. Instead, when these objects are parameters to a function, they are usually passed by reference or constant reference, depending on whether the function is expected to alter the value of the parameter.

1.2.6 Primitive Arrays of Constants

Occasionally, we revert to primitive arrays when we have global constants. The reason is a convenient notational shorthand, illustrated by the following declaration of `DAYS_IN_MONTH`:

```
const int DAYS_IN_MONTH[ ] = { 31, 28, 31, 30, 31, 30,
                               31, 31, 30, 31, 30, 31 };
```

Here, the size of the primitive array is automatically initialized, and its size is deduced by the number of initializers that are present. If this array is global, the number of items can be determined by dividing the amount of memory used by the primitive array `sizeof(DAYS_IN_MONTH)` by the amount of memory used by one item in the primitive array `sizeof (DAYS_IN_MONTH[0])`, as in

```
const int NUM_MONTHS = sizeof(DAYS_IN_MONTH) /
                       sizeof(DAYS_IN_MONTH[0]);
```

1.2.7 Multidimensional Arrays

A *multidimensional array* is an array that is accessed by more than one index. A `matrix` class can be used to implement two-dimensional arrays.

Sometimes access to arrays needs to be based on more than one index. A **multidimensional array** is an array that is accessed by more than one index, and its primitive version is second-class. There is no first-class version in the STL. In Section 3.5, we implement a two-dimensional array with first-class behavior, called a **`matrix`**. The sizes of its indices are specified, and each element is accessed by placing each index in its own pair of brackets. For example, the declaration

```
matrix<int> x( 2, 3 );    // x has two rows and three columns
```

defines the two-dimensional array `x`, with the first index ranging from 0 to 1 and the second index ranging from 0 to 2 (for a total of six objects). The `matrix` sets aside six memory locations for these objects: `x[0][0]`, `x[0][1]`, `x[0][2]`, `x[1][0]`, `x[1][1]`, and `x[1][2]`.

1.2.8 The Standard Library `string` Type

To use the Standard Library `string` type, you must have the include directive:

```
#include <string>
```

As the `string` is a first-class object, input, output, copying, and comparisons work as you would expect. Thus `str1==str2` is `true` if and only if the values of the strings are the same.

Each character of the `string` can be accessed by using the array indexing operator (as usual, indices start at zero). The `string` provides many useful functions.

`s.length()` returns the length of `s`; `+` and `+=` perform string concatenation.

If `s` is a `string`, then `s.length()` returns its length (i.e., the number of characters in its representation), and `s.c_str()` returns a primitive string. A primitive string is occasionally needed to interact with other parts of the libraries. For instance, to open a file, a primitive string must be passed. Finally, the `+` and `+=` operators for `strings` are defined to perform string concatenation (one string is tacked onto the end of another). Figure 1.5 illustrates these operations.

```
#include <iostream>
#include <string>
using namespace std;

int main( )
{
    string a = "hello";
    string b = "world";
    string c;                   // Should be ""

    c = a + " ";                // Should be "hello "
    c += b;                     // Should be "hello world"

      // Print c the easy way.
    cout << "c is: " << c << endl;

      // Print c the primitive way.
    cout << "c is: " << c.c_str( ) << endl;

      // Print c character-by-character.
    cout << "c is: ";
    for( int i = 0; i < c.length( ); i++ )
        cout << c[ i ];
    cout << endl;

    return 0;
}
```

Figure 1.5 Illustration of some `string` functions.

1.3 Pointer Syntax in C++

To have a pointer point at an object, we need to know the target object's memory address (that is, where it is stored). For (almost) any object `obj`, its memory address is given by applying the unary address-of operator `&`. Thus `&obj` is the memory location that stores `obj`.[7]

The unary *address-of operator &* returns the address of an object.

We can declare that an object `ptr` points at an `int` object by saying

```
int *ptr;
```

The value represented by `ptr` is an address. As with integer objects, this declaration does not initialize `ptr` to any particular value, so using `ptr`

7. Objects stored by using the `register` storage class cannot be the target of the address-of operator.

before assigning anything to it invariably produces bad results (e.g., a program crash). Suppose that we also have the declarations

```
int x = 5;
int y = 7;
```

We can make `ptr` point at `x` by assigning to `ptr` the memory location where `x` is stored. Thus

```
ptr = &x;                // LEGAL
```

sets `ptr` to point at `x`. Figure 1.6 illustrates this in two ways. In part (a) a memory model shows where each object is stored. In part (b) an arrow is used to indicate pointing.

The unary *dereferencing operator* * accesses data through a pointer.

The value of the data being pointed at is obtained by the unary **dereferencing operator** `*`. In Figure 1.6 `*ptr` will evaluate to 5, which is the value of the pointed-at variable `x`. To dereference something that is not a pointer is illegal. The `*` operator is the opposite of `&` (e.g., `*&x=5` is the same as `x=5` as long as `&x` is legal). Dereferencing works not only for reading values from an object, but also for writing new values to the object. Thus, if we say

```
*ptr = 10;               // LEGAL
```

we have changed the value of `x` to 10. Figure 1.7 shows the changes that result and the problem with pointers: Unrestricted alterations are possible, and a runaway pointer can overwrite all sorts of variables unintentionally.

We could also have initialized `ptr` at declaration time by having it point to `x`:

```
int x = 5;
int y = 7;
int *ptr = &x;           // LEGAL
```

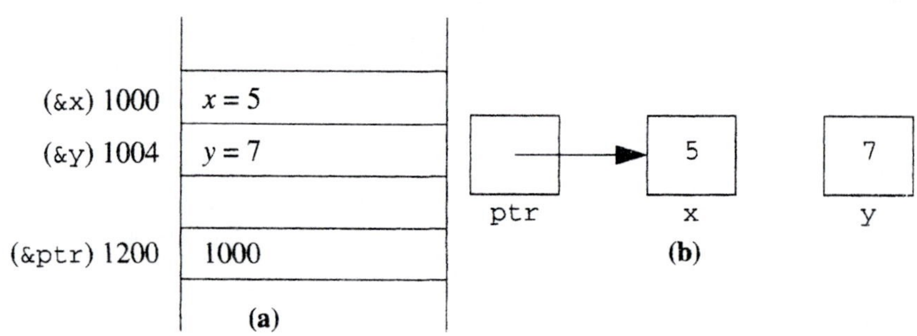

Figure 1.6 Pointer illustration.

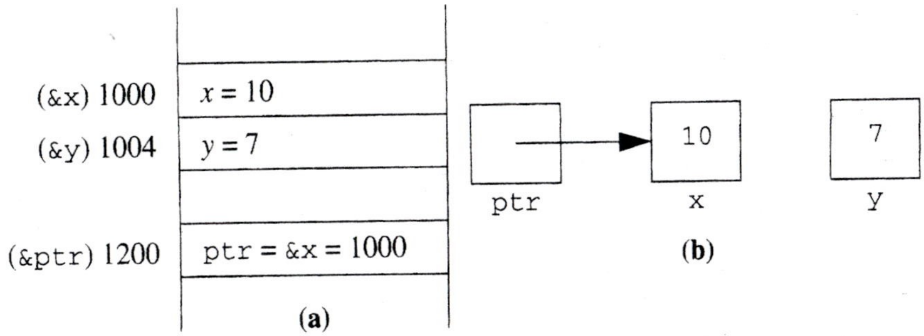

Figure 1.7 Result of `*ptr=10`.

The declaration says that `x` is an `int` initialized to 5, `y` is an `int` initialized to 7, and `ptr` is a pointer to an `int` and is initialized to point at `x`. Let us look at what could have gone wrong. The following declaration sequence is incorrect:

```
int *ptr = &x;          // ILLEGAL: x is not declared yet
int x = 5;
int y = 7;
```

Here we are using `x` before it has been declared, so the compiler will complain. Here is another common error:

```
int x = 5;
int y = 7;
int *ptr = x;           // ILLEGAL: x is not an address
```

In this case we are trying to have `ptr` point at `x`, but we have forgotten that a pointer holds an address. Thus we need an address on the right side of the assignment. The compiler will complain that we have forgotten the `&`, but its error message may initially appear cryptic.

Continuing with this example, suppose that we have the correct declaration but with `ptr` uninitialized:

```
int x = 5;
int y = 7;
int *ptr;               // LEGAL but ptr is uninitialized
```

Pointers must be pointing at an object before dereferencing.

What is the value of `ptr`? As Figure 1.8 shows, the value is undefined because it was never initialized. Thus the value of `*ptr` is also undefined. However, using `*ptr` when `ptr` is undefined is worse because `ptr` could hold an address that makes absolutely no sense, thus causing a program crash if it is dereferenced. Even worse, `ptr` could be pointing at an address

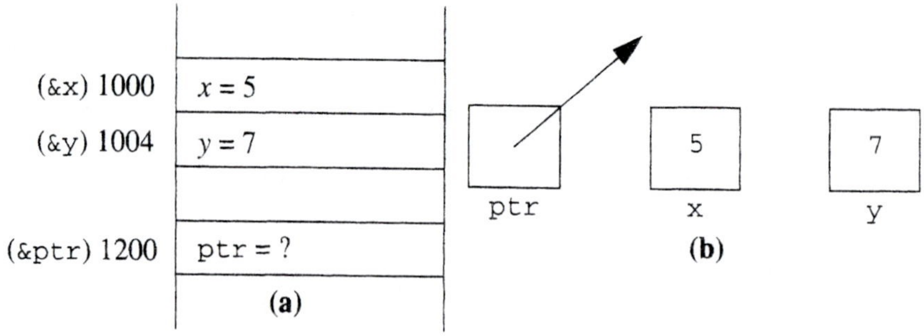

Figure 1.8 Uninitialized pointer.

that is accessible, in which case the program will not crash immediately, but it will be erroneous. If `*ptr` is the target of an assignment, then we would be accidentally changing some other data, which could result in a crash at a later point. This is a tough error to detect because the cause and symptom may be widely separated in time.

We have already shown the correct syntax for the assignment:

```
ptr = &x;                    // LEGAL
```

Suppose that we forget the address-of operator. Then the assignment

```
ptr = x;                     // ILLEGAL: x is not an address
```

rightly generates a compiler error. There are two ways to make the compiler be quiet. One is to use the address-of operator on the right-hand side, as in the correct syntax. The other method is erroneous:

```
*ptr = x;                    // Semantically incorrect
```

Always draw a picture at the first sign of pointer trouble.

The compiler is quiet because the statement says that the `int` to which `ptr` is pointing should get the value of `x`. For instance, if `ptr` is `&y`, then `y` is assigned the value of `x`. This assignment is perfectly legal, but it does not make `ptr` point at `x`. Moreover, if `ptr` is uninitialized, dereferencing it is likely to cause a run-time error, as discussed above. This error is obvious from Figure 1.8. The moral is: Always draw a picture at the first sign of pointer trouble.

Using `*ptr=x` instead of `ptr=&x` is a common error for two reasons. First, because it silences the compiler, programmers feel comfortable about using the incorrect semantics. Second, it looks somewhat like the syntax used for initialization at declaration time. The difference is that the

`*` at declaration time is not a dereferencing `*` but rather is just an indication that the object is a pointer type.

The *NULL pointer* has value 0 and should never be dereferenced. It is used to state that a pointer is pointing nowhere.

Some final words before we get to some substantive uses of these ideas: First, sometimes we want to state explicitly that a pointer is pointing nowhere, as opposed to an undefined location. The **NULL pointer** points at a memory location that is guaranteed to be incapable of holding anything. Consequently, a `NULL` pointer cannot be dereferenced. The symbolic constant `NULL` is defined in several header files, and either it or an explicit zero can be used. The choice is a matter of preference, although some programmers can get surprisingly testy when someone's choice does not agree with theirs. Pointers are best initialized to the `NULL` pointer because in many cases they have no default initial values (these rules apply to other predefined types as well).

Second, a dereferenced pointer behaves just like the object that it is pointing at. Thus, after the following three statements, the value stored in `x` is `15`:

```
x = 5;
ptr = &x;
*ptr += 10;
```

However, we must be cognizant of precedence rules because (as we discuss in Section D.1.3) performing arithmetic not only on the dereferenced values, but also on the (underereferenced) pointers themselves is possible.[8] For example, the following two statements are very different:

```
*ptr += 1;
*ptr++;
```

In the first statement the += operator is applied to `*ptr`, but in the second statement the ++ operator is applied to `ptr`. The result of applying the ++ operator to `ptr` is that `ptr` will be changed to point at a memory location one memory unit larger than it used to. (We discuss these semantics in Section D.3.)

Third, if `ptr1` and `ptr2` are pointers to the same type, then

```
ptr1 = ptr2;
```

sets `ptr1` to point to the same location as `ptr2`, whereas

```
*ptr1 = *ptr2;
```

8. This capability is an unfortunate consequence of C++'s very liberal rules, which allow arithmetic on pointers, making use of the fact that pointers are internally stored as integers. We discuss the reasoning for this in Appendix D but avoid using pointer arithmetic in the text. Nonetheless, you need to know that it exists in case you accidentally wander into that part of the language (owing to a programming error on your part).

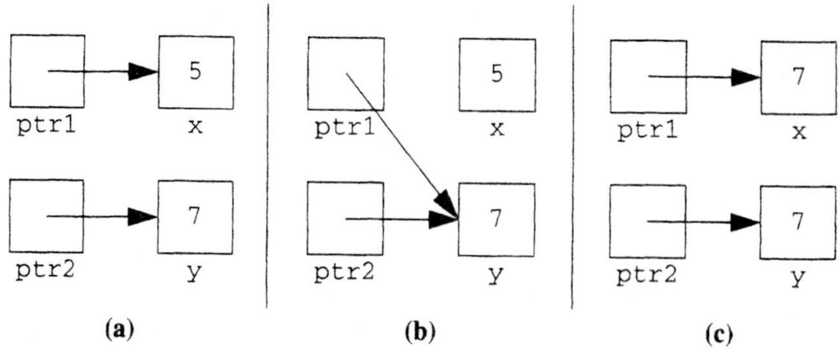

Figure 1.9 (a) Initial state; (b) `ptr1=ptr2` starting from initial state; (c) `*ptr1=*ptr2` starting from initial state.

When you use pointers, you must know whether you are working with addresses or the dereferenced pointers.

assigns the dereferenced `ptr1` the value of the dereferenced `ptr2`. Figure 1.9 shows that these statements are quite different. Moreover, when the wrong form is used mistakenly, the consequences might not be obvious immediately. In the previous examples, after the assignment, `*ptr1` and `*ptr2` are both 7. Similarly, the expression

```
ptr1 == ptr2
```

is true if the two pointers are pointing at the same memory location, whereas

```
*ptr1 == *ptr2
```

is true if the values stored at the two indicated addresses are equal. Using the wrong form is a common mistake.

The requirement that `ptr1` and `ptr2` point to the same type is a consequence of the fact that C++ is strongly typed: Different types of pointers cannot be mixed without an explicit type conversion, unless the user provides an implicit type conversion.

Finally, when pointers are declared, placement of the * and the white space that surrounds it are unimportant to the compiler. Pick a style that you like.

1.4 Dynamic Memory Management

Thus far, all local variables that we have used are *automatic variables*. This (little-used) term tells us that local variables are created when they are reached in the function and that they are destroyed when they are no longer in scope (e.g., when the function returns). Sometimes, objects need to be created in a different way. This different way is called *dynamic memory allocation*.

1.4.1 The **new** Operator

Objects can be created dynamically by calling `new`. The **new operator** dynamically allocates memory and returns a pointer to the newly created object.

The new operator dynamically allocates memory. The result of new is a pointer to a newly created object.

Figure 1.10 illustrates the issues involved in dynamic memory allocation. However, this example is a poor use of dynamic memory; an automatic `string` should be used instead. We use it here only to illustrate dynamic memory allocation in a simple context. A more reasonable application (but no code) is shown in Section 1.6.2.

In Figure 1.10, line 9 creates a new `string` object dynamically. Note that `strPtr` is a pointer to a `string`, so the `string` itself is accessed by `*strPtr`, as shown on lines 10–13. The parentheses are needed at line 11 because of precedence rules.

1.4.2 Garbage Collection and **delete**

In some languages, when an object is no longer referenced, it is subject to automatic garbage collection. The programmer does not have to worry about it. C++ does not have garbage collection. When an object allocated by `new` is no longer referenced, the **delete operator** must be applied to the object (through a pointer). Otherwise, the memory that it consumes is lost (until the program terminates), which is known as a **memory leak**. Unfortunately, memory leaks are common occurrences in many C++ programs. Fortunately,

When an object that is allocated by new is no longer referenced, the delete operator must be applied to the object (through a pointer).

```
 1 #include <iostream>
 2 #include <string>
 3 using namespace std;
 4
 5 int main( )
 6 {
 7     string *strPtr;
 8
 9     strPtr = new string( "hello" );
10     cout << "The string is: " << *strPtr << endl;
11     cout << "Its length is: " << (*strPtr).length( ) << endl;
12     *strPtr += " world";
13     cout << "Now the string is " << *strPtr << endl;
14
15     delete strPtr;
16
17     return 0;
18 }
```

Figure 1.10 Illustration of dynamic memory allocation.

many sources of memory leaks can be automatically removed with care, as we will see later in the text.

One important rule is not to use `new` when an *automatic variable* can be used instead. An automatic variable is automatically cleaned up (hence its name). You should never use `delete` on an object that was not created by `new`; if you do, run-time havoc is likely to result. The `delete` operator is illustrated at line 15.

1.4.3 Stale Pointers, Double Deletion, and More

One reason that programmers can get in trouble when using pointers is that one object may have several pointers pointing at it. Consider the following code:

```
string *s = new string( "hello" ); // s points at new string
string *t = s;                     // t points there, too
delete t;                          // The object is gone
```

Nobody would deliberately write these three lines of code next to each other; assume that they are scattered in a complex function. Prior to the call to `delete`, we have one dynamically allocated object that has two pointers pointing to it.

A *stale pointer* is a pointer whose value no longer refers to a valid object.

After the call to `delete`, the values of `s` and `t` (i.e., where they are pointing) are unchanged. However, as illustrated in Figure 1.11, they are now stale. A **stale pointer** is a pointer whose value no longer refers to a valid object. Dereferencing `s` and `t` can lead to unpredictable results. What makes things especially difficult is that, although `t` is obviously stale, the fact that `s` is stale is much less obvious, if, as assumed, these statements are scattered in a complex function. Furthermore, in some situations, the memory that was occupied by the object is unchanged until a later call to `new` claims the memory, which can give the illusion that there is no problem.

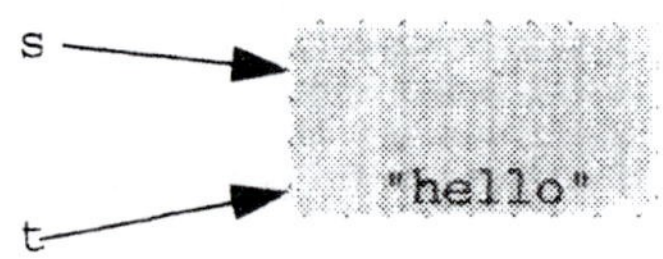

Figure 1.11 Stale pointers: Because of the call to `delete t`, pointers `s` and `t` are now pointing at an object that no longer exists; a call to `delete s` would now be an illegal double deletion.

A second problem is the so-called double-delete. A **double-delete** occurs when we attempt to call `delete` on the same object more than once. It would occur if we now made the call

```
delete s;                          // Oops -- double delete
```

because `s` is stale and the object that it points to is no longer valid. Trouble in the form of a run-time error is likely to result.

A *double-delete* occurs when we attempt to call `delete` on the same object more than once. Trouble in the form of a run-time error is likely to result.

These are the perils of dynamic memory allocation. We must be certain never to call `delete` more than once on an object—and then only after we no longer need it. If we don't call `delete` at all, we get a memory leak. And if we have a pointer variable and intend to call `delete`, we must be certain that the object being pointed at was created by a call to `new`. When we have functions calling functions calling other functions, keeping track of everything is not so easy.

Finally, pointers can go stale even if no dynamic allocation is performed. Consider the code in Figure 1.12.

For no good reason (except to illustrate the error), we have the function `stupid` return a pointer to a `string`. If `stupid` calls `new` to create a `string`, then the caller will be responsible for calling `delete`. Rather than burdening the caller, we mistakenly decided to have `stupid` use an automatic `string`, and return its address. The program compiles but may or may not work; it contains an error. The problem is that the value that `stupid` returns is a pointer. But the pointer is pointing at `s`, which no longer exists because it is an automatic variable and `stupid` has returned. When returning pointers, be sure that you have something to point to and that the something exists after the return has been completed.

```
string *stupid( )
{
    string s = "stupid";
    return &s;
}

int main( )
{
    cout << *stupid( ) << endl;
    return 0;
}
```

Figure 1.12 A stale pointer: the pointee, `s`, does not exist after `stupid` returns.

1.5 Reference Variables

A *reference type* is an alias and may be viewed as a pointer constant that is always dereferenced implicitly.

In addition to the pointer type, C++ has the reference type. A **reference type** is an alias for another object and may be viewed as a pointer constant that is always dereferenced implicitly. For instance, in the following code, `cnt` becomes a synonym for a longer, hard-to-type variable:

```
int longVariableName = 0;
int & cnt = longVariableName;

cnt += 3;
```

Reference variables must be initialized at declaration time. Reference parameters are used to achieve call by reference instead of call by value.

Reference variables must be initialized when they are declared. They cannot be changed to reference another variable because an attempted reassignment via

```
cnt = someOtherObject;
```

assigns to the object `longVariableName` the value of `someOtherObject`. This approach is a poor use of reference variables but accurately reflects how they are used in a more general setting in which the scope of the reference variable is different from that of the object being referenced. One important case is that a reference variable can be used as a formal parameter, which acts as an alias for an actual argument. We previously discussed this case in the context of passing `vectors` (see Section 1.2.5). Let us revisit parameter passing.

Figure 1.13 illustrtes a `swapWrong` procedure that does not work because of call-by-value restrictions. Two correct alternatives are shown: The first is a routine that uses the traditional C method of passing pointers to avoid call-by-value restrictions; the second is a functionally identical routine that uses C++ reference parameters.

The differences between reference and pointer types are summarized as follows.

- In the function declaration, reference parameters are used instead of pointers.
- In the function definition, reference parameters are implicitly dereferenced, so no `*` operators are needed (their placement would generate a syntax error).

```
#include <iostream>
using namespace std;

// Does not work.
void swapWrong( int a, int b )
{
    int tmp = a;
    a = b;
    b = tmp;
}

// C Style -- using pointers.
void swapPtr( int *a, int *b )
{
    int tmp = *a;
    *a = *b;
    *b = tmp;
}

// C++ Style -- using references.
void swapRef( int & a, int & b )
{
    int tmp = a;
    a = b;
    b = tmp;
}

// Simple program to test various swap routines.
int main( )
{
    int x = 5;
    int y = 7;

    swapWrong( x, y );
    cout << "x=" << x << " y=" << y << endl;
    swapPtr( &x, &y );
    cout << "x=" << x << " y=" << y << endl;
    swapRef( x, y );
    cout << "x=" << x << " y=" << y << endl;

    return 0;
}
```

Figure 1.13 Call-by-reference parameters versus call-by-pointer parameters.

- In the function call to `swapRef`, no `&` is needed because an address is implicitly passed by virtue of the fact that the corresponding formal parameters are references.
- The code involving the use of reference parameters is much more readable.

Reference variables are like pointer constants in that the value they store is the address of the object they refer to. They are different in that an automatic invisible dereference operator is applied to the reference variable. This difference translates into a notational convenience, especially because it allows parameters to be passed by reference without the excess baggage of the `&` operator on the actual arguments and the `*` operator that tends to clutter up C programs.

Pointers can be passed by reference. As a result, a function can change where a pointer is pointing.

By the way, pointers, can be passed by reference. This method is used to allow a function to change *where* a pointer, passed as a parameter, is pointing. A pointer that is passed with call by value cannot be changed to point to a new location (because the formal parameter stores only a copy of the *where* value). We use this approach in Chapter 19 where we discuss this tricky issue in more detail.

Another important issue is the choice between passing parameters by value or by reference. In Section 1.2.5 we discussed it in the context of `vectors`, but it applies for all types of parameters.

1.6 Structures

Recall that an array is a collection of identically typed objects. The array has two major benefits: First, we can index the array and thus we can loop over each item in the array; second, when using functions, we can pass the name of the array, thus using only one parameter to send the aggregate.

A *structure* stores a collection of generally dissimilar objects.

A different type of aggregate type is the structure. A **structure** stores a collection of objects that need not be of the same type. Because the objects in the collection are not constrained to be of the same type, we cannot simply loop over them as we would in an array.

Each *member* of the structure can be accessed by applying the *dot (.) member operator.*

Each object in the structure is a **member** and is accessed by applying the **dot member operator**. The basic structure declaration is given by using the keyword `struct`, providing the name of the structure type and giving a brace-enclosed list of its members. For example,

```
struct Student
{
    string firstName;
    string lastName;
    int studentNum;
    double gradePointAvg;
};
```

Figure 1.14 shows that `Student` is a structure consisting of four different objects. If we have the declaration

```
Student s;
```

the grade point average is given by `s.gradePointAvg`. Figure 1.15 illustrates how a `struct` is declared, how its constituent data members are accessed, and how it can be passed as a parameter to a function. Note that structures usually are not passed by using call by value because the overhead of call by value can be expensive. The parameter-passing mechanism is determined in accordance with the discussion in Section 1.2.5.

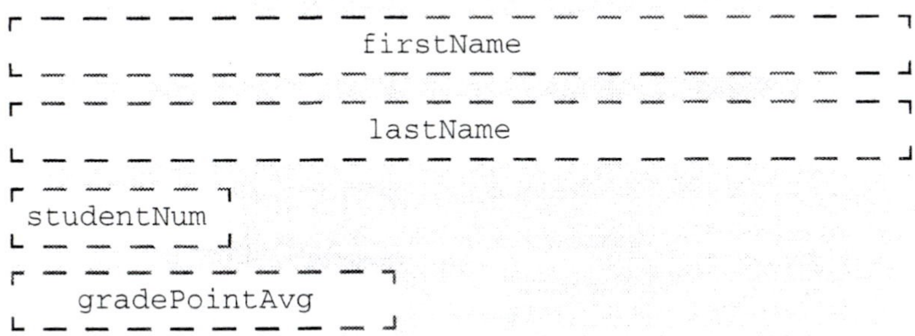

Figure 1.14 `Student` structure.

```
// Print the student information.
void printInfo( const Student & s )
{
    cout << "ID is "   << s.studentNum << endl;
    cout << "Name is " << s.firstName << " "
                       << s.lastName << endl;
    cout << "GPA is "  << s.gradePointAvg << endl;
}

// Simple main.
int main( )
{
    Student mary;

    mary.lastName = "Smith";
    mary.firstName = "Mary";
    mary.gradePointAvg = 4.0;
    mary.studentNum = 123456789;

    printInfo( mary );

    return 0;
}
```

Figure 1.15 Program to illustrate the declaration of a structure, access of its data members, and parameter passing.

The structure in C++ has been extended from its C counterpart.

The structure in C++ has been greatly extended from its C counterpart to allow functions as members, as well as restrictions on access to the members. This difference between C and C++ represents a major philosophical change. We discuss this change in the Chapter 2. For now let us stick with the basics of structures.

1.6.1 Pointers to Structures

In our discussion of advanced programming techniques, we show that frequently we need to declare a pointer to a structure and access the members of the pointed at structure. Suppose that we have

```
Student *ptr = &s;  // ptr points at structure s
```

The -> operator is used to access members of a pointed-at structure.

Then we can access the grade point average by `(*ptr).gradePointAvg`. The parentheses are absolutely necessary because the member operator, being a postfix operator, has higher precedence than the prefix dereferencing operator. The parentheses become annoying after awhile, so C++ provides an additional postfix operator, the **-> operator**, which accesses members of a pointed-at structure. Thus `ptr->gradePointAvg` gives the same access as before.

1.6.2 Exogenous Versus Indigenous Data and Shallow Versus Deep Copying

As we demonstrate in Chapter 2, C++ allows the user to define operators on structures. For instance the user can write the routine with the declaration

```
bool operator<( const Student & lhs, const Student & rhs );
```

which returns `true` if the first (left-hand side) `Student` is less than the second (right-hand side), according to some user-defined criterion. (Throughout this text, we use **lhs and rhs** for *left-hand side* and *right-hand side*, respectively.) Using the class mechanism discussed throughout the text, we could include this function as a structure member—much like a data member.

Throughout this text, we use *lhs* and *rhs* for *left-hand side* and *right-hand side*, respectively.

The copy assignment operator = and the equality operator == can also be defined, but if we do nothing, a default definition is used for copying and equality comparisons become illegal. Specifically, by default a structure copy is implemented as a member-by-member copy. In other words, each member is copied from one structure to the other.

A problem with this mechanism is illustrated by the following declaration:

```
struct Teacher
{
    string *firstName;
    string *lastName;
    int     employeeNum;
};
```

Suppose that we have

```
Teacher s, t;
```

If we assume that `t` has been initialized, then the assignment `s=t` is a member-by-member copy. However, the first two members are merely pointers, so only the addresses are copied. The result is that `s.firstName` is now sharing memory with `t.firstName`; these are not independent copies of the string. If the call

```
delete t.firstName
```

is made later to recycle the dynamically allocated memory, `s` is in serious trouble. This problem is illustrated in Figure 1.16, which highlights the difference between indigenous and exogenous data.

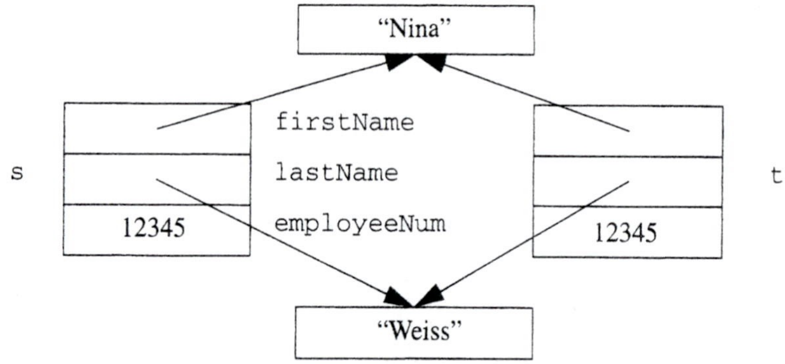

Figure 1.16 Illustration of a shallow copy in which only pointers are copied.

Indigenous data **are completely contained by the structure.**

Indigenous data are completely contained by the structure. For instance, in the `Student` structure, the `firstName` and `lastName` members are strings and are completely self-contained. The disadvantage of representing an object indigenously is that the size of the object is fixed, is usually large, and thus is expensive to copy.

Exogenous data **are not part of the structure but are accessed through a pointer.**

Exogenous data, by contrast, reside outside the structure and are accessed through a pointer. The advantage of exogenous data is that common data can be shared among several instances; when the default assignment operator is used, the copy is only a copy of pointers and not the pointed-at values. Often this behavior is desirable. For instance, it is the default behavior in the computer language Java.

A *shallow copy* is a copy of pointers rather than data being pointed at.

A copy of pointers rather than the data being pointed at is known as a **shallow copy.** Similarly, the equality comparisons for exogenous data are shallow by default because they only compare addresses. Although a shallow copy is correct on occasion, allowing a shallow copy when it is unwarranted can lead to havoc.

A *deep copy* is a copy of the data being pointed at rather than the pointers.

To get a **deep copy,** in which the pointed-at values are copied, we generally need to allocate some additional memory and then copy the dereferenced pointers. Doing so requires rewriting the copy assignment operator. Details on implementing this procedure are presented in the next several chapters. Normally, we also need to supply a deep comparison operator to implement a deep test. (Of course, we may need to go back to using indigenous data if we find that we are doing mostly deep operations.)

1.6.3 Noncontiguous Lists: Linked Lists

We close this chapter by discussing, in very general terms, one of the techniques we use when we discuss data structures. Earlier we showed that, by using the dynamically expanding array, we can read in an arbitrary number of input items. This technique has one serious problem.

Suppose that we are reading 1000-byte records and we have 1,000,000 bytes of memory available. Also suppose that, at some point, the array holds 400 records and is full. Then to double, we create an array of 800 records, copy over 400 records, and then delete the 400 records. The problem is that, in this intermediate step, we have both a 400- and an 800-record array in use and that the total of 1200 records exceeds our memory limit. In fact, we can run out of memory after using only roughly one third of the available memory.

A *linked list* stores data with a cost of one pointer per item.

A solution to this problem is to allow the list of records to be stored non-contiguously. For each record we maintain a structure that stores the record and a pointer, `next`, to the next structure in the list. The last structure has a `NULL next` pointer. We keep a pointer to both the first and last structures in the list. A basic example is shown in Figure 1.17. The resulting structure is the classic **linked list,** which stores data with a cost of one pointer per item. The structure definition is

```
struct Node
{
    Object item;    // Some element
    Node  *next;
};
```

At any point we can print the list by using the iteration

```
for( Node *p = first; p != NULL; p = p->next )
     printItem( p->item );
```

and at any point we can add a new last item `x`, as in

```
last->next = new Node;  // Attach a new Node
last = last->next;      // Adjust last
last->item = x;         // Place x in the node
last->next = NULL;      // It's the last, so make next NULL
```

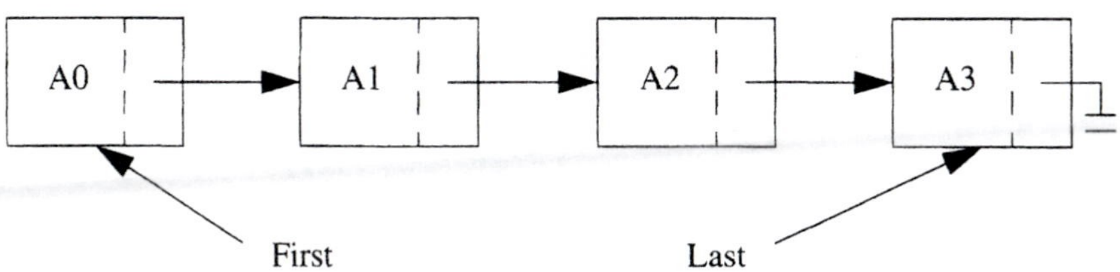

Figure 1.17 Illustration of a simple linked list.

An arbitrary item can no longer be found in one access. Instead, we must scan down the list. This difference is similar to that of accessing an item on a compact disk (one access) or a tape (sequential). On the other hand, inserting a new element between two existing elements requires much less data movement in a linked list than in an array.

We present a more detailed description of the linked list in Chapters 16 and 17.

Summary

In this chapter we examined the basics of pointers, arrays, and structures. The pointer variable emulates the real-life indirect answer. In C++ it is an object that stores the address where some other data reside. The pointer is special because it can be dereferenced, thus allowing access to those other data. The `NULL` pointer holds the constant `0`, indicating that it is not currently pointing at valid data. A reference parameter is an alias. It is like a pointer constant, except that the compiler implicitly dereferences it on every access. Reference variables allow three forms of parameter passing: call by value, call by reference, and call by constant reference. Choosing the best form for a particular application is an important part of the design process.

An array is a collection of identically typed objects. In C++ there is a primitive version with second-class semantics (discussed in Chapter 3 and Appendix D). A `vector` is also part of the standard library. In both cases, no index range checking is performed, and out-of-bounds array accesses can corrupt other objects. Because primitive arrays are second-class, they cannot be copied by using the assignment operator. Instead they must be copied element by element; however, a `vector` can be copied in a single assignment statement. A `vector` can be expanded as needed by calling `resize`.

Structures are also used to store several objects, but unlike arrays, the objects need not be identically typed. Each object in the structure is a member, and is accessed by the `.` member operator. The `->` operator is used to access a member of a structure that is accessed indirectly through a pointer.

We also noted that a list of items can be stored noncontiguously by using a linked list. The advantage is that less space is used for large objects than in the array-doubling technique. The penalty is that access of the *i*th item is no longer constant-time but requires examination of *i* structures.

Objects of the Game

-> operator Allows access to members of a pointed at structure. (p. 28)

address-of operator & Returns the address of an object. (p. 15)

aggregate A collection of objects stored in one unit. (p. 4)

array Stores a collection of identically-typed objects. (p. 4)

array indexing operator `[]` Provides access to any object in the array. (p. 6)

call by constant reference Parameter-passing mechanism that avoids a copy and guarantees that the actual parameter will not be changed. (p. 12)

call by reference Parameter-passing mechanism that avoids a copy but allows changes to the actual parameter. (p. 12)

call by value The default parameter-passing mechanism in which the actual argument is copied into the formal parameter. (p. 12)

deep copy A copy of the data being pointed at rather than the pointers. (p. 30)

`delete` operator Recycles dynamically allocated memory that is no longer needed. (p. 21)

dereferencing operator `*` Used to access the value of data being pointed at. (p. 16)

dot (.) member operator Allows access to each member of the structure. (p. 26)

double-delete An occurrence when we attempt to call `delete` on the same object more than once. Trouble in the form of a run-time error is likely to result. (p. 23)

exogenous data Not part of the structure but are accessed through a pointer. (p. 30)

first-class object An object that can be manipulated in all the "usual ways" without special cases and exceptions. (p. 4)

indigenous data Completely contained by the structure. (p. 30)

`lhs` and `rhs` Left-hand side and right-hand side, respectively. (p. 29)

linked list Stores data with a cost of one pointer per item. (p. 31)

`matrix` A type discussed in Chapter 3 that provides a first-class two-dimensional array. (p. 14)

member An object contained in a structure. (p. 26)

memory leak Memory allocated by `new` is not automatically recycled; failure to recycle causes a memory leak. (p. 21)

multidimensional array An array that is accessed by more than one index. (p. 14)

`new` operator Dynamically allocates memory. (p. 21)

`NULL` pointer Has value 0 and can never be dereferenced; it is used to state that a pointer is pointing nowhere. (p. 19)

pointer Stores an address where other data resides. (p. 4)

reference type An alias that may be viewed as a pointer constant that is always dereferenced implicitly. (p. 24)

shallow copy A copy of pointers rather than the data being pointed at. (p. 30)

stale pointer A pointer whose value no longer refers to a valid object. (p. 22)

`string` The library type used for first-class strings. (p. 6)

structure Stores a collection of objects that are generally dissimilar. (p. 26)

`vector` The library type used for first-class arrays. (p. 6)

Common Errors

1. If `ptr` is uninitialized, the assignment `*ptr=x` is likely to cause problems. Always be sure that a pointer is pointing at an object before attempting to dereference the pointer.
2. In a declaration, `*ptr=&x` initializes `ptr` to point at `x`. In an assignment statement, `*ptr=&x` is wrong (unless `ptr` is a pointer to a pointer) because the left-hand side is the dereferenced value rather than the pointer. The `*` in the declaration is not a dereferencing operator; instead, it is part of the type.
3. A common error is mixing up the pointer and the value being pointed at. That is, `ptr1==ptr2` is true if both pointers are pointing at the same memory location, but `*ptr1==*ptr2` is true if the values stored at the indicated addresses are equal.
4. Because of precedence rules, `*ptr++` increments `ptr`, not `*ptr`.
5. In C++, arrays are indexed from `0` to `n-1`, inclusive, where `n` is the array size. However, range checking is not performed.
6. In C++, primitive arrays cannot be copied or compared because the array name is merely an address.
7. Two-dimensional arrays are indexed as `A[i][j]`, not `A[i,j]`.
8. Dereferencing a pointer immediately after `delete` has been applied to it is an error (even though it will usually appear to work).
9. Large objects should not be passed using call by value. Use call by constant reference instead.

10. To avoid double deletion, beware of shallow copies when deep copies are needed.
11. Do not return a pointer or reference to a local (automatic) variable. Doing so has the same effect as Error 8.

On the Internet

The available files for this chapter are listed below. Everything is self-contained, and nothing is used later in the text.

ArrayDemo.cpp Contains the source code for the example in Figure 1.1.

GetInts.cpp Contains the source code for the examples in Figures 1.3 and 1.4. If `RESIZE` is defined, `getInts` from Figure 1.3 is used; otherwise, Figure 1.4 is used.

TestString.cpp Contains the source code for the example in Figure 1.5.

TestSwap.cpp Contains the source code for the swap examples in Figure 1.13.

Exercises

In Short

1.1. Name and illustrate five operations that can be applied to pointers.

1.2. Consider

```
int a, b;
int *ptr;       // A pointer
int **ptrPtr;   // A pointer to a pointer

ptr = &a;
ptrPtr = &ptr;
```

a. Is this code legal?
b. What are the values of `*ptr` and `**ptrPtr`?
c. Using no other objects besides those already declared, how can you alter `ptrPtr` so that it points at a pointer to `b` without directly touching `ptr`?

d. Is the following statement legal?

```
ptrPtr = ptr;
```

1.3. a. Is `*&x` always equal to `x`? If not, give an example.
b. Is `&*x` always equal to `x`? If not, give an example.

1.4. For the declarations

```
int a = 5;
int *ptr = &a;
```

what are the values of the following?

a. `ptr`
b. `*ptr`
c. `ptr == a`
d. `ptr == &a`
e. `&ptr`
f. `*a`
g. `*&a`
h. `**&ptr`

1.5. Give the type of each identifier declared here and the types of the expressions. Is any expression illegal?

a. `struct S { int a; S *b; };`
b. `S z;`
c. `S *x;`
d. `vector<S> y(10);`
e. `vector<S *> u(10);`
f. `x->a`
g. `x->b`
h. `z.b`
i. `z.a`
j. `*z.a`
k. `(*z).a`
l. `x->b-z.b`
m. `y->a`
n. `y[1]`
o. `y[1].a`
p. `y[1].b`
q. `u[2]`
r. `*u[2]`
s. `u[2]->a`
t. `u[2]->b`
u. `u[10]`

v. `&z`

w. `&x`

x. `u`

y. `y`

1.6. Draw a picture that illustrates the results after processing of each of the following statements, which are executed sequentially.

a. `int a = 3;`

b. `int & b = a;`

c. `int & c = b;`

d. `b = 5;`

e. `c = 2;`

1.7. Is the following code legal? Why or why not?

```
int a = 3;
const int & b = a;
```

1.8. What is wrong with omitting spacing in `*x/*y`?

In Practice

1.9. Use a linked list to read an arbitrary number of strings. After the strings have been read, output all strings that are lexicographically larger than the last string read from the input.

1.10. Repeat Exercise 1.9, using a `vector` with the `push_back` operation.

1.11. A *checksum* is the 32-bit integer that is the sum of the ASCII characters in a file. Two identical files have the same checksum. Write a program to compute the checksum of a file that is supplied as a command-line argument.

Programming Projects

1.12. Write a program that outputs the number of characters, words, and lines in the files that are supplied as command-line arguments.

1.13. Some personal computers come with a game called Minesweeper. The game is played on a grid, and some squares on the grid contain mines. Write a program that reads a file that contains the number of rows and columns in the grid and then the grid. The grid will have squares marked `o`; those are mines. Other squares do not have mines and will have `?`. Your output will output the grid. Mines will still have **o**s. Squares that do not have mines will be replaced by a number that indicates the number of adjacent mines

```
5 5
?o???
o??o?
??o?o
oo?o?
?o???
```

Figure 1.18 Sample input for Exercise 1.13.

```
2o211
o33o2
34o4o
oo4o2
3o311
```

Figure 1.19 Sample output for Exercise 1.13.

(the maximum will be 8). For example, is a sample input file, and Figure 1.19 is the corresponding output.

References

The base C++ language is described in [5] but is now standardized. Currently, the standard is available online for a price of $18.00, and a hard copy version of the standard is also available for $175.00. You can purchase either at `http://webstore.ansi.org/ansidocstore/default.asp` (but be aware that this pointer may go stale).

A description of the thinking behind the design of C++, as well as proposed extensions, is discussed in [11].

A host of C++ books are now available at various levels. For those with little programming experience, a popular choice is [4]. Books appropriate for those with a background in another programming language include [6], [8], [9], and [10]. Advanced features of C++, including more details on some of the issues discussed in later chapters of this text, can be found in [1], [3], and [7]. Answers to many C++ questions are presented in [2]. Answers to the questions in [6] are given in [12].

Some of the material in this chapter is adapted from the presentation in [13].

1. T. Cargill, *C++ Programming Style*, Addison-Wesley, Reading, Mass., 1992.
2. M. P. Cline and G. A. Lomow, *C++ FAQs*, 2d ed., Addison-Wesley, Reading, Mass., 1999.

3. J. O. Coplien, *Advanced C++*, Addison-Wesley, Reading, Mass., 1992.

4. H. M. Deitel and P. J. Deitel, *C++: How to Program*, 2d ed., Prentice-Hall, Englewood Cliffs, N.J., 1998.

5. M. A. Ellis and B. Stroustrup, *Annotated C++ Reference Manual*, Addison-Wesley, Reading, Mass., 1990.

6. J. Lajoie and S. Lippman, *C++ Primer*, 3d ed., Addison-Wesley, Reading, Mass., 1998.

7. S. Meyers, *Effective C++*, 2d ed., Addison-Wesley, Reading, Mass., 1998.

8. I. Pohl, *Object-Oriented Programming Using C++*, 2d ed., Addison-Wesley, Reading, Mass., 1997.

9. I. Pohl, *C++ for C Programmers*, 3d ed., Addison-Wesley, Reading, Mass., 1999.

10. B. Stroustrup, *The C++ Programming Language*, 3d ed., Addison-Wesley, Reading, Mass., 1997.

11. B. Stroustrup, *The Design and Evolution of C++*, Addison-Wesley, Reading, Mass., 1994.

12. C. L. Tondo and B. P. Leung, *C++ Primer Answer Book*, Addison-Wesley, Reading, Mass., 1999.

13. M. A. Weiss, *Efficient C Programming: A Practical Approach*, Prentice-Hall, Englewood Cliffs, N.J., 1995.

Chapter 2

Objects and Classes

In this chapter we begin a discussion of object-oriented programming and show why C++ is more than just C with a few bells and whistles added. The basic mechanism for accomplishing object-oriented programming in C++ is the *class*.

In this chapter, we show:

- how C++ uses the class to achieve *encapsulation* and *information hiding;*
- how classes are implemented; and
- several examples of classes, including classes used to manipulate rational numbers and strings

2.1 What Is Object-Oriented Programming?

Object-oriented programming appears to be emerging as the dominant paradigm. In this section we discuss some of the things that C++ provides in the way of object-oriented support and mention some of the principles of object-oriented programming.

At the heart of object-oriented programming is the object. An **object** is an entity—an instance of a data type—that has structure and state. Each object defines operations that may access or manipulate that state. One feature of object-oriented programming is that user-defined types should behave the same way as predefined (or built-in) types. When we work with any of the basic data types in a language, such as the integer, character, or floating-point number, we take certain things for granted.

An *object* is an entity that has structure and state. Each object defines operations that may access or manipulate that state.

- We can declare new objects, possibly with initialization.
- We can copy or test for equality.

- We can perform input and output on these objects.
- If the object is an automatic variable, then when the function it is declared in terminates the object goes away.
- We can perform type conversions when appropriate, and the compiler complains when they are inappropriate.

An object is also an *atomic unit:* Its parts cannot be dissected by the general users of the object.

Additionally, we view the object as an **atomic unit,** whose parts cannot be dissected by the general user. Most of us would not even think of fiddling with the bits that represent a floating-point number and would find it completely ridiculous to try to increment some floating-point object by altering its internal representation ourselves.

***Information hiding* makes implementation details, including components of an object, inaccessible.**

The atomicity principle is known as **information hiding.** In other words, the user does not have direct access to the parts of the object nor their implementations; they can be accessed only indirectly by functions supplied with the object. We can view each object as coming with the warning "Do not open—no user-serviceable parts inside." In real life most people who try to fix things that have such a warning wind up doing more harm than good. In this respect programming mimics the real world. The grouping of data and the operations that apply to them to form an aggregate, while hiding implementation details of the aggregate, is known as **encapsulation.**

***Encapsulation* is the grouping of data and the operations that apply to them to form an aggregate, while hiding implementation details of the aggregate.**

A second important goal of object-oriented programming is to support code reuse. Just as engineers use components over and over in their designs, programmers should be able to reuse objects rather than repeatedly reimplementing them. When we have an implementation of the exact object that we need to use, doing so is a simple matter. The challenge is to use an existing object when the object needed is not an exact match but is merely very similar.

C++ provides several mechanisms to support this goal. One is the *template* mechanism: If the implementation is identical except for the basic type of the object, a template can be used to describe the basic functionality. For instance, a procedure can be written to swap two items; the logic is independent of the types of objects being swapped, and so a template can be used. (We discuss templates in Chapter 3.)

The *inheritance* mechanism allows us to extend the functionality of an object. In other words, we can create new types with extended properties of the original type. Inheritance goes a long way toward our goal of code reuse.

Another important object-oriented principle is *polymorphism*. A polymorphic object can hold objects of several different types. When operations are applied to the polymorphic type, the operation appropriate to the actual stored type is automatically selected. In C++ polymorphism is implemented as part of inheritance. Polymorphism allows us to implement new types (classes) that share common logic. The use of inheritance to create these hierarchies distinguishes **object-oriented programming** from *object-based programming,* which involves the use of encapsulation and information hiding but not inheritance. (We discuss inheritance and polymorphism in Chapter 4.)

The use of inheritance to create hierarchies distinguishes *object-oriented programming* from *object-based programming.*

In this chapter we describe how C++ uses classes to achieve encapsulation and information hiding. A **class** is the same as a structure except that, by default, all members are inaccessible to the general user of the class. Because functions that manipulate the object's state are members of the class, they are accessed by use of the dot member operator (.)—just like any other structure member—and thus are called **member functions.** These functions are also called **methods.**

A *class* is the same as a structure except that, by default, all members are inaccessible.

In object-oriented terminology, when we make a call to a member function, we are passing a message to the object. Besides syntax and improved support for principles such as information hiding, the most obvious difference between object-oriented programming in C++ and typical C procedural programming is philosophical: In C++ the object is in charge.

Functions can be supplied as additional members; these *member functions* manipulate the object's state.

2.2 Basic `class` Syntax

In this section we discuss the basic syntax of C++ classes. More complicated issues are discussed in later sections of this chapter.

2.2.1 Class Members

To recap briefly, a class in C++ consists of its *members*. These members can be either data or functions. The functions are called *member functions*. Each instance of a class is an *object*. Each object contains the data components specified in the class (unless the data components are `static`, a detail that can be safely ignored for now). A member function is used to act on an object. Member functions are also called *methods.*[1]

As an example, Figure 2.1 presents the `IntCell` class. In this class, each instance of `IntCell`—an `IntCell` object—contains a single data member, `storedValue`. Everything else in this particular class is a method.

1. We use the terms *member function* and *method* synonymously.

```
// A class for simulating an integer memory cell.

class IntCell
{
  public:

      // Construct the IntCell. Initial value is 0.
    IntCell( )
      { storedValue = 0; }

      // Construct the IntCell. Initial value is initialValue.
    IntCell( int initialValue )
      { storedValue = initialValue; }

      // Return the stored value.
    int read( )
      { return storedValue; }

      // Change the stored value to x.
    void write( int x )
      { storedValue = x; }

  private:
    int storedValue;
};
```

Figure 2.1 A complete declaration of an `IntCell` class.

In our example, there are four methods. Two of these methods are `read` and `write`. The other two are special methods known as *constructors*. Let us look at some key features of this class declaration.

A *public member* is visible to all routines and may be accessed by any method in any class.

First, note the labels `public` and `private`. These labels determine visibility of class members. In this example, everything except the `storedValue` data member is `public`; `storedValue` is `private`. A **`public` member** is visible to all routines and may be accessed by any method in any class. A **`private` member** is not visible to nonclass routines and may be accessed only by methods in its class (an exception to this rule is discussed in Section 2.3.4). Typically, data members are declared `private`, thus restricting access to internal details of the class, while methods intended for general use are made `public`. Restricting access is also known as *information hiding*. Figure 2.2 shows the viewpoint from outside the class.

Figure 2.2 IntCell members: read and write are accessible, but storedValue is hidden.

By using private data members, we can change the internal representation of the object, without affecting other parts of the program that use the object. We can do so because the object is accessed through the public member functions, whose viewable behavior remains unchanged. The users of the class do not need to know the internal details of how the class is implemented. In many cases having this access leads to trouble. For instance, in a class that stores dates by month, day, and year, if we make the month, day, and year private, we prohibit an outsider from setting these data members to illegal dates, such as February 29, 2001. Methods strictly for internal use can (and should) be private. In fact, in a class, all members are private by default, so the initial public is required.

A *private member* is not visible to nonclass routines and may be accessed only by methods in its class.

Second, there are two constructors. A **constructor** is a method that describes how an instance of the class is created. If no constructor is explicitly defined, one that initializes the data members using language defaults is automatically generated.

A *constructor* describes how an object is declared and initialized.

The IntCell class defines two constructors. The first is called if no parameter is specified. The second is called if an int parameter is provided and uses that int to initialize the storedValue member. If the declaration of an IntCell object does not match any of the known constructors, the compiler complains.

If the initialization does not match any constructors, the compiler complains.

2.2.2 Extra Constructor Syntax and Accessors

Although the class works as written, some extra syntax can make the code better. Four changes are shown in Figure 2.3 (we omit comments for brevity).

Default Parameters

The IntCell constructor illustrates the *default parameter*. As a result, two IntCell constructors are still defined. One accepts an initialValue. The other is the zero-parameter constructor, which is implied because the one-parameter constructor says that initialValue is optional by having a default value. The default value of 0 signifies that 0 is used if no parameter is provided. Default parameters can be used in any function, but they are most commonly used in constructors.

```
1  // A class for simulating an integer memory cell.
2
3  class IntCell
4  {
5    public:
6      explicit IntCell( int initialValue = 0 )
7        : storedValue( initialValue ) { }
8      int read( ) const
9        { return storedValue; }
10     void write( int x )
11       { storedValue = x; }
12
13   private:
14     int storedValue;
15 };
```

Figure 2.3 `IntCell` class with revisions.

Initializer List

The `IntCell` constructor uses an initializer list (Figure 2.3, line 7) prior to the body of the constructor. The **initializer list** is used to specify nondefault initialization of each data member in an object directly. In Figure 2.3, there is hardly a difference, but using initializer lists instead of an assignment statement in the body saves time when the data members are class types that have complex initializations. In some cases it is required. For instance, if a data member is `const` (meaning that it cannot be changed after the object has been constructed), then the data member's value can be initialized only in the initializer list. Also, if a data member is itself a class type that does not have a zero-parameter constructor, then it must be initialized in the initializer list. We discuss these details in Section 2.3.1.

The `explicit` Constructor

The `IntCell` constructor is `explicit`. You should generally make all one-parameter constructors `explicit` to avoid behind the scenes type conversions. Otherwise, C++'s somewhat lenient rules allow type conversions without explicit casting operations. Usually, this behavior is unwanted—it destroys strong typing and can lead to hard-to-find bugs. Consider the following:

```
IntCell obj;      // obj is an IntCell
obj = 37;         // Should not compile: type mismatch
```

This code fragment constructs an `IntCell` object `obj` and then performs an assignment statement. But the assignment statement should not work, because the right-hand side of the assignment operator is not another `IntCell`. Instead, `obj`'s `write` method should have been used. However, C++ has lenient rules. Normally, a one-parameter constructor defines an implicit type conversion, in which a temporary object is created that makes an assignment (or parameter to a function) compatible. In this case, the compiler would attempt to convert

```
obj = 37;          // Should not compile: type mismatch
```

to

```
IntCell temp = 37;
obj = temp;
```

Note that the one-parameter constructor can be used to construct `temp`. The use of `explicit` means that a one-parameter constructor cannot be used to generate an implicit temporary. Thus, because `IntCell`'s constructor is declared `explicit`, the compiler will correctly complain of a type mismatch.

In Sections 2.3.2 and 2.6, we present cases in which the lenient rules are helpful. That usually occurs in the context of operator overloading (e.g., having == make sense).

The `explicit` keyword is new, and not all compilers support it. However, the preprocessor can be used to replace all occurrences of `explicit` with white space,[2] so there's no reason not to put `explicit` in your code.

Constant Member Function

A method that examines but does not change the state of its object is an **accessor.** A member function that changes the state of an object is a **mutator** (it *mutates* the state of the object). In the typical class that stores a collection of objects, for instance, `isEmpty` is an accessor, and `makeEmpty` is a mutator.

A method that does not change the state of its object is an *accessor.*

In C++, we can mark each member function as being an accessor or a mutator. Doing so is an important part of the design process and should not be viewed as simply a comment. Indeed, not doing so has important semantic consequences. For instance, mutators cannot be applied to constant objects. By default, all member functions are mutators. To make a member function an accessor, we must add the keyword `const` after the closing parenthesis that ends the parameter type list. The result is a constant member

A *constant member function* is a function that does not change any class data members.

2. Use the statement
```
#define explicit
```

function. A **constant member function** is a function that does not change any class data members.

The function *signature* includes the types of paremeters, including `const` and `&` directives, but not the return type.

The const-ness (whether the `const` is or is not present after the closing parenthesis) is part of the signature, and `const` can have many different meanings. The function declaration can have `const` in three different contexts. Only the `const` after a closing parenthesis signifies an accessor. The other uses are in parameter passing (Section 1.2.5) and the return type (see, for instance, Section 2.2.4). The function **signature** includes the types of parameters, including `const` and `&` directives, but not the return type.

In the `IntCell` class `read` is clearly an accessor: It does not change the state of the `IntCell`. Thus it is made a constant member function at line 8. If a member function is marked as an accessor but has an implementation that changes the value of any data member, a compiler error is generated.[3]

2.2.3 Separation of Interface and Implementation

The *interface* describes what can be done to an object. The *implementation* represents the internal processes by which the interface specifications are met.

The class presented in Figure 2.3 contains all the correct syntactic constructs. However, in C++, separating the class interface from its implementation is more common. The **interface** lists the class and its members (data and functions) and describes what can be done to an object. The **implementation** represents the internal processes by which the interface specifications are met.

If a class had many function members and these functions were nontrivial, having to write all the function definitions inside the class declaration would be unreasonable. The more typical mechanism is to provide the member function declarations in the class declaration and then define them later, using a normal function syntax augmented with the class name and scope operator `::`. This mechanism separates the class *interface* from the class *implementation*, which is a recurring theme throughout this text.

Because the interface represents the class design and tells us what can be done to an object, the syntax of C++ allows the class declaration to specify the properties of its member functions. In conjunction with good naming conventions, this approach can greatly reduce the amount of commenting that is necessary. Even so, the interface should be accompanied by comments that specify what may be done to objects of the class. As far as the class user is concerned, the internal details of how the implementation does these tasks are not important. In this separation, a change in the implementation can be confined to the source file that contains the implementation. Because this source file does not need to be `#included` by the users of the

---

3. Data members can be marked `mutable` to indicate that const-ness should not apply to them. This feature is new and is not supported on all compilers.

class (only the interface needs to be seen), separating the implementation from the interface can lead to easier program maintainence by reducing compile times and source file dependencies. Further, the implementation source code need not be distributed by the program designers. It can be precompiled and left in libraries.

Figure 2.4 shows the class interface for `IntCell`, Figure 2.5 shows the implementation, and Figure 2.6 shows a `main` routine that uses the `IntCell`.

Preprocessor Commands

Use `#ifndef` and `#endif` to enclose the contents of a header file and prevent multiple inclusion.

The interface is typically placed in a file that ends with `.h`. Source code that requires knowledge of the interface must `#include` the interface file, which here means that both the implementation file and the file that contains `main` have the `#include` directive. Occasionally, a complicated project will have files that contain other files, and there is the danger that an interface might be read twice in the course of compiling a file. This action can be illegal. To guard against it, each header file uses the preprocessor to define a symbol when the class interface is read, as shown on the first two lines in Figure 2.4. The symbol name, `_IntCell_H_`, should not appear in any other file; usually we construct it from the filename. The first line of the interface file tests if the symbol is undefined. If so, the file is processed. Otherwise, by skipping to the `#endif`, the file is not processed because we know that we have already read the file.

```
#ifndef _IntCell_H_
#define _IntCell_H_

// A class for simulating an integer memory cell.

class IntCell
{
  public:
    explicit IntCell( int initialValue = 0 );
    int read( ) const;
    void write( int x );

  private:
    int storedValue;
};

#endif
```

Figure 2.4 `IntCell` class interface, in the file *IntCell.h*.

```
#include "IntCell.h"

// Construct the IntCell with initialValue.
IntCell::IntCell( int initialValue )
  : storedValue( initialValue )
{
}

// Return the stored value.
int IntCell::read( ) const
{
    return storedValue;
}

// Store x.
void IntCell::write( int x )
{
    storedValue = x;
}
```

Figure 2.5 `IntCell` class implementation in file *IntCell.cpp*.

```
#include "IntCell.h"

int main( )
{
    IntCell m;    // Or, IntCell m( 0 ); but not IntCell m( );

    m.write( 5 );
    cout << "Cell contents: " << m.read( ) << endl;

    return 0;
}
```

Figure 2.6 Program that uses `IntCell` in file *TestIntCell.cpp*.

Scope Operator

The *scope operator* `::` is used to refer to the scope. In a class member function the scope is the class.

In the implementation file, which typically ends in `.cpp`, `.cc`, or `.C`, each member function must identify the class that it is part of. Otherwise, it would be assumed that the function is in the global scope (and many errors would result). The syntax is `ClassName::member`. The **scope operator** `::` is used to refer to the scope. In a class member function, as here, the scope is the class.

Signatures Must Match Exactly

The signature of an implemented member function must match exactly the signature listed in the class interface. Recall that whether a member function is an accessor (via the `const` at the end) or a mutator is part of the signature. Thus an error would result if, for example, the `const` was omitted from (exactly) one of the `read` signatures in Figures 2.4 and 2.5. Note that default parameters are specified in the interface and are omitted in the implementation.

`const` member function declarations are part of the signature.

Objects Are Declared Like Primitive Types

In C++, an object is declared just like a primitive type. On the one hand, the following are legal declarations of an `IntCell` object:

```
IntCell obj1;          // Zero parameter constructor
IntCell obj2( 12 );    // One parameter constructor
```

On the other hand, the following are incorrect:

```
IntCell obj3 = 37;     // Constructor is explicit
IntCell obj4( );       // Function declaration
```

The declaration of `obj3` is illegal because the one-parameter constructor is `explicit`. It would be legal otherwise. (In other words, a declaration that uses the one-parameter constructor must use the parentheses to signify the initial value.) The declaration for `obj4` states that it is a function (defined elsewhere) that takes no parameters and returns an `IntCell`.

2.2.4 The Big Three: Destructor, Copy Constructor, and `operator=`

In C++, classes come with three special functions already written for you: the *destructor*, *copy constructor*, and `operator=`. In many cases you can accept the default behavior provided by the compiler. Sometimes you cannot.

Destructor

The **destructor** is called whenever an object goes out of scope or is subjected to a `delete`. Typically, the only responsibility of the destructor is to free any resources that were allocated by the constructor or other member functions during the use of the object. That includes calling `delete` for any corresponding `new`s, closing any files that were opened, and so on. The default simply applies the destructor to each data member.

The *destructor* tells how an object is destroyed when it exits scope and frees resources when an object exits scope.

Copy Constructor

The *copy constructor* is called when an object is passed or returned by value.

A special constructor required to construct a new object, initialized to a copy of the same type of object, is the **copy constructor.** For any object, such as an `IntCell` object, a copy constructor is called

- for a declaration with initialization, such as

  ```
  IntCell B = C;
  IntCell B( C );
  ```

  but not

  ```
  B = C;        // Assignment operator, discussed later
  ```

- when an object is passed using call by value (instead of by `&` or `const &`), which, as mentioned in Section 1.2.5, usually should not be done anyway.
- when an object is returned by value (instead of by `&` or `const &`)

The first case is the simplest to understand because the constructed objects were explicitly requested. The second and third cases construct temporary objects that are never seen by the user. Even so, a construction is a construction, and in both cases we are copying an object into a newly created object.

By default, the copy constructor is a member-by-member application of copy constructors.

By default the copy constructor is implemented by applying copy constructors to each data member in turn. For data members that are primitive types (e.g., `int`, `double`, or pointers), simple assignment is done, as for the `storedValue` data member in our `IntCell` class. For data members that are themselves class objects, the copy constructor for each data member's class is applied to that data member.

The `operator=`

The *copy assignment operator* `operator=` is used to copy objects.

The **copy assignment operator,** `operator=`, is used to copy objects. It is called when = is applied to two objects after have both been previously constructed. The expression `lhs=rhs` is intended to copy the state of `rhs` into `lhs`. By default the `operator=` is implemented by applying `operator=` to each data member in turn.

Problems with the Defaults

If we examine the `IntCell` class, we see that the defaults are perfectly acceptable and so we do not have to do anything, which is often the case. If a class consists of data members that are exclusively primitive types and objects for which the defaults make sense, the class defaults usually do make sense. Thus a class whose data members are `int`, `double`, `vector<int>`, `string`, and even `vector<string>` can accept the defaults.

The main problem occurs in a class that contains a data member that is a pointer. Let us sketch the problem and a solution now and provide more specifics when we implement the `string` class in Section 2.6.

Suppose that the class contains a single data member that is a pointer. This pointer points at a dynamically allocated object. The default destructor for pointers does nothing (for good reason—recall that we must call `delete` ourselves). Furthermore, the copy constructor and `operator=` both copy not the objects being pointed at, but simply the value of the pointer. Thus we simply have two class instances that contain pointers that point to the same object. As discussed in Section 1.6.2, this condition is a so-called shallow copy. Typically, we would expect a deep copy, in which a clone of the entire object is made. Thus, when a class contains pointers as data members and deep semantics are important, we typically must implement the destructor, `operator=`, and copy constructor ourselves.

For `IntCell`, the signatures of these operations are

Assignment operators generally return constant references.

```
~IntCell( );                          // destructor
IntCell( const IntCell & rhs );       // copy constructor
const IntCell & operator=( const IntCell & rhs );
```

Although the defaults for `IntCell` are acceptable, we can write the implementations anyway, as shown in Figure 2.7. For the destructor, after the body has been executed, the destructors are called for the data members, so the default is an empty body. For the copy constructor, the default is an initializer list of copy constructors, followed by execution of the body.

The default destructor is a member-by-member application of destructors.

`operator=` is the most interesting. Line 15 is an alias test, to make sure that we are not copying to ourselves. Assuming that we are not, we apply `operator=` to each data member (at line 16). We then return a reference to the current object, at line 17, so assignments can be chained, as in `a=b=c`. (The return is actually a constant reference so that the nonsensical `(a=b)=c` is disallowed by the compiler). Let us look at the uses of the keyword `this` in more detail.

An additional keyword in C++, the pointer **`this`** points at the current object. Think of the pointer `this` as a homing device that, at any instant in time, tells you where you are. Consequently, `*this` is the current object, and returning `*this` achieves the desired result. Under no circumstances will the compiler knowingly allow you to modify `this`. The return at line 17 uses `*this`. The other use of `this` is at line 15.

The *pointer* `this` points at the current object. It is used to return a constant reference for assignment operators and also to test for aliasing.

```
IntCell::~IntCell( )
{
    // Does nothing since IntCell contains only an int data
    // member. If IntCell contained any class objects their
    // destructors would be called.
}

IntCell::IntCell( const IntCell & rhs )
  : storedValue( rhs.storedValue )
{
}

const IntCell & IntCell::operator=( const IntCell & rhs )
{
    if( this != &rhs )    // Standard alias test
        storedValue = rhs.storedValue;
    return *this;
}
```

Figure 2.7 The defaults for the Big Three.

Aliasing **is a special case that occurs when the same object appears in more than one role.**

The expression `a=a` is logically a nonoperation (a no-op). In some cases, although not here, failing to treat it as a special case can result in the destruction of `a`. For example, consider a program that copies one file to another. A normal algorithm begins by truncating the target file to zero length. If no check is performed to verify that the source and target file are indeed different, then the source file will be truncated—hardly a desirable feature. Thus when copying, the first thing you should do is check for this special case, known as **aliasing**, which occurs when the same object appears in more than one role.

Either implement a good copy constructor or disable it. Placing the declaration in the private section disables the copy constructor.

In the routines that we write, if the defaults make sense, we always accept them. However, if the defaults do not make sense, we need to implement the destructor, and `operator=`, and the copy constructor. When the default does not work, we can generally implement the copy constructor by mimicking normal construction and then calling `operator=`. Another often used option is to give a reasonable working implementation of the copy constructor but then place it in the `private` section, to disallow call by value.

When the Defaults Do Not Work

The most common situation in which the defaults do not work occurs when a data member is a pointer type and the pointee is allocated by some object member function (e.g., the constructor). For example, suppose that we

```
class IntCell
{
  public:
    explicit IntCell( int initialValue = 0 )
      { storedValue = new int( initialValue ); }

    int read( ) const;
      { return *storedValue; }
    void write( int x );
      { *storedValue = x; }

  private:
    int *storedValue;
};
```

Figure 2.8 The data member is a pointer; the defaults are no good.

```
int f( )
{
      IntCell a( 2 );
      IntCell b = a;
      IntCell c;

      c = b;
      a.write( 4 );
      cout << a.read( ) << endl << b.read( ) << endl
           << c.read( ) << endl;
      return 0;
}
```

Figure 2.9 Simple function that exposes problems in Figure 2.8.

implement the `IntCell` by dynamically allocating an `int`, as shown in Figure 2.8. For simplicity, we do not separate the interface and implementation.

Problems with this approach are exposed in Figure 2.9. First, the output is three `4`s, even though logically only `a` should be `4`. The problem is that the default `operator=` and copy constructor copy the pointer `storedValue`. Thus `a.storedValue`, `b.storedValue`, and `c.storedValue` all point at the same `int` value. These copies are shallow: that is, the pointers rather than the pointees are copied. A second less obvious problem is a memory leak. The `int` initially allocated by `a`'s constructor remains allocated and needs to be reclaimed. The `int` allocated by `c`'s constructor is no longer referenced by any pointer variable. It also needs to be reclaimed, but we no longer have a pointer to it.

To fix these problems, we implement the Big Three. The result (with the interface and implementation separated) is shown in Figure 2.10. Generally

```
class IntCell
{
  public:
    explicit IntCell( int initialValue = 0 );

    IntCell( const IntCell & rhs );
    ~IntCell( );
    const IntCell & operator=( const IntCell & rhs );

    int read( ) const;
    void write( int x );

  private:
    int *storedValue;
};

IntCell::IntCell( int initialValue )
{
    storedValue = new int( initialValue );
}

IntCell::IntCell( const IntCell & rhs )
{
    storedValue = new int( *rhs.storedValue );
}

IntCell::~IntCell( )
{
    delete storedValue;
}

const IntCell & IntCell::operator=( const IntCell & rhs )
{
    if( this != &rhs )
        *storedValue = *rhs.storedValue;
    return *this;
}

int IntCell::read( ) const
{
    return *storedValue;
}

void IntCell::write( int x )
{
    *storedValue = x;
}
```

Figure 2.10 Data member is a pointer; Big Three need to be written.

speaking, if a destructor is necessary to reclaim memory, the defaults for copy assignment and copy construction are not acceptable.

If the class contains data members that do not have the ability to copy themselves, the default `operator=` will not work. We show some examples of this lack later in the text, starting with the `string` class in Section 2.6.

2.2.5 Default Constructor

If no user-declared constructors are provided for a class, a default constructor is automatically generated. The default takes no parameters and is essentially a member-by-member application of each member's no-parameter constructor, with language defaults for the primitive members.

The default constructor is a member-by-member application of a no-parameter constructor.

2.3 Additional C++ Class Features

Now that we have discussed the basics of classes, we examine some additional related issues, including

- a second look at the distinction between initialization and assignment,
- implicit type conversions for classes,
- more details of operator overloading,
- input and output, including the friend concept, and
- private global variables (known as private static class members).

To illustrate these concepts, we design a class called `Rational` that manipulates rational numbers. A properly designed rational number class allows us to use rational numbers as easily as any of the built-in types, such as integers, doubles, or characters. Extending the types to which an operator can be applied is known as **operator overloading.** In Figure 2.11, the program reads a sequence of rational numbers and outputs their average and maximum. If we replace the word `Rational` with `double` (and use `int` for `IntType` at lines 24 and 27), the program requires no other changes to compile and run.

Extending the types to which an operator can be applied is known as *operator overloading.*

Examining `main`, we can see the use of an explicit type conversion (the comparison at line 24 and the division at line 27, in which an `IntType` is converted to a `Rational`). The other notable feature is the overloading of the input and output stream operators on lines 15, 17, 25, and 27.

Figures 2.12 and 2.13 show the interface for the `Rational` class. We attempted to give a complete listing of the operations that might be expected. However, providing actual implementations of all these operations does

```
#include "Rational.h"
#include <iostream>
using namespace std;

// Rational number test program.
int main( )
{
    Rational x;
    Rational sum = 0;
    Rational max = 0;
    int n = 0;

    cout << "Type as many rationals as you want" << endl;

    while( cin >> x )
    {
        cout << "Read " << x << endl;
        sum += x;
        if( x > max )
            max = x;
        n++;
    }
    cout << "Read " << n << " rationals << endl;
    if( max > IntType( 0 ) )
        cout << "Largest positive number is " << max << endl;
    if( n > 0 )
        cout << "Average is " << sum / IntType( n ) << endl;

    return 0;
}
```

Figure 2.11 Simple `main` routine for using rational numbers.

require a substantial amount of coding, so in the discussion that follows, we implement a representative subset of the member functions.

Recall that a rational number consists of a numerator and a denominator. The data members of the class are `numer` and `denom`, representing the numerator and denominator, respectively. We use `IntType` to represent their type. The type `IntType` could be an `int`, although that restricts the range of rationals that can be represented, especially as intermediate calculations could easily overflow an `int`. (In Exercise 2.26 you are asked to implement a general `IntType`, which is a lot more work than it seems.) Some systems come with an equivalent class.

We maintain the invariant that the denominator is never negative and that the rational number is expressed in the lowest form. Thus, the result of 8/–12 would be represented with a numerator of –2 and a denominator of 3.

```
// Rational class interface: support operations for rationals.
//
// CONSTRUCTION: with (a) no initializer, or (b) an integer
//     that specifies the numerator, or (c) two integers
//     specifying numerator and denominator, or
//     (d) another Rational.
//
// ***************PUBLIC OPERATIONS*********************
// =, +=, -=, /=, *=            --> Usual assignment
// +, -, /, *                   --> Usual binary arithmetic
// <, <=, >, >=, ==, !=         --> Usual relational and equality
// ++, --, +, -, !              --> Usual prefix, postfix, unary
// >> and <<                    --> Input and output
// double toDouble( )           --> Return double equivalent

#include <iostream>
using namespace std;

typedef long IntType;     // Better method is in Chapter 3

class Rational
{
  public:
      // Constructors
    Rational( const IntType & numerator = 0 )
      : numer( numerator ), denom( 1 ) { }
    Rational( const IntType & numerator,
              const IntType & denominator )
      : numer( numerator ), denom( denominator )
            { fixSigns( ); reduce( ); }
    Rational( const Rational & rhs )
      : numer( rhs.numer ), denom( rhs.denom ) { }

      // Destructor
    ~Rational( ) { }

      // Assignment Ops (implementation in Figure 2.15)
    const Rational & operator= ( const Rational & rhs );
    const Rational & operator+=( const Rational & rhs );
    const Rational & operator-=( const Rational & rhs );
    const Rational & operator/=( const Rational & rhs );
    const Rational & operator*=( const Rational & rhs );

      // Math Binary Ops (implementation in Figure 2.16)
    Rational operator+( const Rational & rhs ) const;
    Rational operator-( const Rational & rhs ) const;
    Rational operator/( const Rational & rhs ) const;
    Rational operator*( const Rational & rhs ) const;
```

Figure 2.12 The `Rational` class interface (part 1).

```
      // Relational & Equality Ops (implemented in Figure 2.17)
    bool operator< ( const Rational & rhs ) const;
    bool operator<=( const Rational & rhs ) const;
    bool operator> ( const Rational & rhs ) const;
    bool operator>=( const Rational & rhs ) const;
    bool operator==( const Rational & rhs ) const;
    bool operator!=( const Rational & rhs ) const;

      // Unary Operators (implemented in Figures 2.18 and 2.19)
    const Rational & operator++( );       // Prefix
    Rational operator++( int );           // Postfix
    const Rational & operator--( );       // Prefix
    Rational operator--( int );           // Postfix
    const Rational & operator+( ) const;
    Rational operator-( ) const;
    bool operator!( ) const;

      // Member Function
    double toDouble( ) const    // Do the division
      { return static_cast<double>( numer ) / denom; }

      // I/O friends: privacy is waived (see Figure 2.20)
    friend ostream & operator<< ( ostream & out,
                                  const Rational & value );
    friend istream & operator>> ( istream & in,
                                  Rational & value );

  private:
      // A rational number is represented by a numerator and
      // denominator in reduced form
    IntType numer;                    // The numerator
    IntType denom;                    // The denominator

    void fixSigns( );                 // Ensures denom >= 0
    void reduce( );                   // Ensures lowest form
};
```

Figure 2.13 The `Rational` class interface (part 2).

We allow `denom` to be 0, to represent either `infinity` or `-infinity` (even if `numer` is also `0`). These invariants are maintained internally by applying `fixSigns` and `reduce`, as appropriate. Those routines are shown in Figure 2.14. The `gcd` routine computes the greatest common divisor of two integers (the first of which might be negative). For instance `gcd(35,45)` is `5`. Computing the greatest common divisor is an interesting problem in its own right and is discussed in Section 8.4.

```
void Rational::fixSigns( )
{
    if( denom < 0 )
    {
        denom = -denom;
        numer = -numer;
    }
}

void Rational::reduce( )
{
    IntType d = 1;

    if( denom != 0 && numer != 0 )
        d = gcd( numer, denom );

    if( d > 1 )
    {
        numer /= d;
        denom /= d;
    }
}
```

Figure 2.14 Private member routines to keep `Rationals` in normalized format.

The remainder of this section is devoted to examining C++ features that are used in this class—namely, initialization lists, type conversions, operator overloading, and input and output.

2.3.1 Initialization Versus Assignment in the Constructor Revisited

Line 25 of the `Rational` class interface (see Figure 2.12) initializes as

```
Rational( const IntType & numerator = 0 )
  : numer( numerator ), denom( 1 ) { }
```

Recall that the sequence preceding the braces is the initializer list. Alternatively, the constructor could be written as

```
Rational( const IntType & numerator = 0 )
  { numer = numerator; denom = 1; }
```

Simple initialization of class members using initializer lists is preferable to assignment in the constructor.

The difference between the two is as follows. The form in the class interface, which uses an initializer list to specify data member initialization, initializes `numer` and `denom` using the one `int`-parameter constructor. Because the body of the constructor is empty, no further operations are performed. The alternative form initializes `numer` and `denom` by using the no-parameter constructor. The reason is that any member not specified in the initializer list is initialized using a zero-parameter constructor. The copy assignment operator is then called to perform the two assignments that are in the body of the `Rational` constructor. Imagine that `IntType` is itself a class that represents arbitrary precision integers. In that case the alternative form is wasteful because it first initializes `numer` and `denom` to `0`s, only to overwrite them with assignment copies. This procedure could have important repercussions, such as requiring the costly expansion of a dynamically allocated block of memory (we demonstrate this requirement in the `string` class in Section 2.6).

Members are initialized in the order they are declared, not in the order they are encountered in the initialization list. Generally, it is best to avoid writing code that depends on this fact.

Because initialization of each class member should usually be done with its own constructor, when possible you should use explicit initializer lists. Note, however, that this form is intended for simple cases only. If the initialization is not simple (e.g., if it allocates memory or error checks are needed), use an assignment. Among other things, the order of evaluation of the initializer list is given by the order in which class data members are listed. In our case, `numer` is initialized before `denom` only because it appears earlier in the listing of data members (of course, this does not apply to assignments in the body of the constructor). If the initialization of `numer` depended on the initialization of `denom` being done first, we would have to switch their declaration order. If we were to do this, we would need to comment that there is an order dependency. If possible, you should avoid order dependencies.

Initializer Lists Can Be Mandatory

An initializer list is required in three common situations.

1. If any data member does not have a zero-parameters constructor, the data member must be initialized in the initializer list.
2. Constant data members must be initialized in the initializer list. A constant data member can never be assigned to after the object is constructed. An example might be the social security number in an `Employee` class. Each `Employee` has his or her own social security number data member, but presumably the social security number never changes.

3. A data member that is a reference variable (for instance an `istream &`) must be initialized in the constructor.

2.3.2 Type Conversions

C++ has rules that allow the mixing of types. For instance, if `i` is an `int` and `d` is a `double`, `d=i` is allowed. This is known as an **implicit type conversion** because it is performed without the use of an explicit type conversion operator. A temporary `tmp` is created from `i` and then is used as the right-hand side of the assignment. Some languages do not allow implicit type conversion because of the danger of accidental usage and weakening the notion of strong typing. However, forcing all type conversions to be explicit tends to load code with conversions, sometimes unnecessarily.

A *type conversion* creates a temporary object of a new type.

A **type conversion** creates a temporary object of a new type. In C++ the rules for type conversion follow this general principle: If you can construct an object of type `t1` by providing an object of another type `t2`, then a type conversion from `t2` to `t1` is guaranteed to follow the same semantics. In the case of the `Rational` class, any appearance of an `IntType` object is implicitly converted to a (temporary) `Rational` when needed, as in the previously cited examples in `main` (Figure 2.11, lines 24 and 27). The temporary is created by executing the constructor. If you do not want implicit type conversions, declare your one-parameter constructors to be `explicit`.

A constructor defines an automatic type conversion.

A technical point: In our case, even though a conversion is defined for `int` to `IntType` and one is defined from `IntType` to `Rational`, transitivity does not hold. Thus these two conversions do not imply a third conversion from `int` to `Rational`. This lack of transitivity is why the type conversion from `int` to `IntType` is performed in Figure 2.11 at lines 24 and 27. We could attempt to provide a constructor for `Rational` that takes an `int`, which would solve our problems by providing the third type conversion. However, if `IntType` is an `int`, that approach provides two identical constructors, and the compiler will complain about the ambiguity.

Conversions are not transitive.

We can also define a type conversion by overloading `operator()`. For instance, we can specify a type conversion from `Rational` to `int` by writing the member function

Conversions can also be defined as member functions, but do not overdo them or ambiguity can result.

```
operator int ( ) const
  { return denom == 1 ? numer : int( longDecimal( ) ); }
```

```
1 const Rational & Rational::operator=( const Rational & rhs )
2 {
3     if( this != &rhs )
4     {
5         numer = rhs.numer;
6         denom = rhs.denom;
7     }
8     return *this;
9 }
10
11 const Rational & Rational::operator+=( const Rational & rhs )
12 {
13     numer = numer * rhs.denom + rhs.numer * denom;
14     denom = denom * rhs.denom;
15     reduce( );
16
17     return *this;
18 }
```

Figure 2.15 Assignment operators (two of five) for the `Rational` class.

Overloading the type conversion operator in this way is not recommended. Too many implicit conversions can easily get you in trouble; again, ambiguity can result. We present an example of this problem in Section 9.9.

2.3.3 Operator Overloading

We examine the operators in the same order given in the class interface. Many of the operators, such as the assignment operators, use no new principles. Two of them are shown in Figure 2.15. However, we do have to be careful. For example, lines 13 and 14 cannot be interchanged. For the corresponding /= operator, we need to use temporaries.

A binary arithmetic operator usually returns an object by value because the result is stored in a temporary. It can be implemented by calling the corresponding assignment operator.

The next group of operators are the *binary arithmetic operators.* A binary arithmetic operator usually returns an object by value because the result is stored in a temporary. It also can be implemented by calling the corresponding assignment operator. A simple implementation is provided in Figure 2.16 for the addition operator. Note how we use a previously defined operator, an excellent general technique.

An interesting technical issue here is the return type. As usual, we have three choices: We can return by value, by reference, or by constant reference. A return by reference is certainly wrong: We cannot allow expressions such as `(a+b)=c` because `a+b` is not a named object; the assignment could at best be meaningless.

```
Rational Rational::operator+( const Rational & rhs ) const
{
    Rational answer( *this );  // Initialize answer with *this
    answer += rhs;             // Add the second operand
    return answer;             // Return answer by copy
}
```

Figure 2.16 Mathematical binary operators (one of four) for the `Rational` class.

```
bool Rational::operator==( const Rational & rhs ) const
{
    return numer * rhs.denom == denom * rhs.numer;
}
```

Figure 2.17 Relational and equality operators (one of six) for the `Rational` class.

Because the `+=` operator returns a `const &` and a copy takes more time than a constant reference return, we appear to be doing the wrong thing. Why not return a constant reference? The answer is that the reference would refer to an automatic object, and when the procedure returns, the object is destroyed (by the destructor). Thus `answer` cannot be referenced. Returning a pointer to an automatic variable is a common C mistake. Analogously, returning a reference to an automatic variable ordinarily would be a common C++ mistake, but most C++ compilers flag the error at compile time.

What if we use a `static` local variable for `answer`? There are two problems—one is easy to fix, and one isn't easy to fix. The easy-to-fix problem is that the initialization is performed only once (the object is created only once). We can fix it with an additional assignment statement. The real problem is that for any four rationals, an expression such as

```
( r1 + r2 ) == ( r3 + r4 )
```

is always true because the values being compared are references to the same `static` object. Thus we see that what we have done is the only correct approach. Hence a statement such as

```
r1 = r2 + r3;
```

must call a copy constructor to copy `answer` into a temporary variable and then call a copy assignment operator to copy the temporary into `r1`. Many compilers optimize out the temporary and thus the copy constructor.

Next, are the equality and relational operators. A typical routine is shown in Figure 2.17. For the equality operators `==` and `!=`, we can do better by

```
const Rational & Rational::operator++( )  // Prefix form
{
    numer += denom;
    return *this;
}

Rational Rational::operator++( int )      // Postfix form
{
    Rational tmp = *this;
    numer += denom;
    return tmp;
}
```

Figure 2.18 Prefix and postfix operators (two of four) for the `Rational` class.

avoiding the expensive (and potentially overflowing) multiplication and directly comparing numerators and denominators. We leave this for you to do as an exercise (see Exercise 2.16), with a warning that you have to be careful when the numerator or denominator is 0.

Prefix and postfix ++ and -- operators have different semantics. The prefix member function is specified by an empty parameter list. The postfix form has an unused `int` parameter.

We continue with the ++ and -- operators and examine the incrementing operator. In C++ there are two kinds: prefix (before the operand) and postfix (after the operand). Both add 1 to an object, but the result of the expression (which is meaningful if used in a larger expression) is the new value in the prefix form and the original value in the postfix form. As they are completely different in semantics and precedence, we need to write separate routines for each form. They have the same name, so they must have different signatures to be distinguished. We give them different signatures by specifying an empty parameter list for the prefix form and a single (anonymous) `int` parameter for the postfix form. Then `++x` calls the zero-parameter `operator++`; and `x++` calls the one-parameter `operator++`. The `int` parameter is never used; it is present only to give a different signature.

The prefix and postfix forms shown in Figure 2.18 add 1 by increasing `numer` by the value of `denom`. In the prefix form we can then return `*this` by constant reference, as for the assignment operators. The postfix form requires that we return the initial value of `*this`, and thus we use a temporary. Because of the temporary, we have to return by value instead of reference. Even if the copy constructor for the return is optimized away, the use of the temporary suggests that, in many cases, the prefix form will be faster than the postfix form.

The three remaining unary operators have straightforward implementations, as shown in Figure 2.19. `operator!` returns true if the object is zero by applying `!` to the numerator. Unary `operator+` evaluates to the current object; a constant reference return can be used here. `operator-` returns the negative of the current object by creating a new object whose numerator is

```
1  bool Rational::operator!( ) const
2  {
3      return !numer;
4  }
5
6  const Rational & Rational::operator+( ) const
7  {
8      return *this;
9  }
10
11 Rational Rational::operator-( ) const
12 {
13     return Rational( -numer, denom );
14 }
```

Figure 2.19 Additional unary operators (three of three) for the `Rational` class.

the negative of the current object. The return must be by copy because the new object is a local variable. However, a trap lurks in `operator-`. If the word `Rational` is omitted from line 13, the comma operator evaluates `(-numer, denom)` as `denom`, and then an implicit conversion gives the rational `denom/1`, which is returned.

What Can Be Overloaded?

In C++, all but four operators can be overloaded. The four nonoverloadable operators are `.`, `.*`, `?:`, and `sizeof`. Operator precedence cannot be changed. That is, `a+b*c` is always `a+(b*c)`. Arity (whether an operator is unary or binary) cannot be changed so, for example, we cannot write a unary `/` operator or a binary `~` operator. Finally, only existing operators can be overloaded, and new operators cannot be created.

2.3.4 Input and Output and Friends

The remaining operators in the `Rational` class are `<<` and `>>`, which, as discussed in Appendix A, are used for output and input. When we make the call

```
cout << r1;   // Output Rational r1
```

the `operator<<` takes an `ostream` and a `Rational` as parameters. Both parameters are passed by reference. The `operator<<` returns a reference to an `ostream` so that output calls can be concatenated. A similar situation occurs for the `operator>>`, the only significant difference being that the `Rational` parameter is not a constant reference.

Input and output can be defined by overloading << and >>.

Consequently, we arrive at the following prototypes for `operator<<` and `operator>>`:

```
ostream & operator<<( ostream & out, const Rational & r );
istream & operator>>( istream & in,        Rational & r );
```

These are not member functions because, when they are called, a `Rational` is not the controlling object. The only class that these could possibly be members of would be the `ostream` or `istream` class, in which case the first parameter would not be present. For example, `ostream` has a member function for `int` output:

```
ostream & operator<<( int value );
```

Needless to say, we cannot add member functions to `ostream` every time we design a new class. Consequently, the input and output functions for `Rational` are stand-alone functions and are not members of any class. They are declared in global scope and are used just like any other function.

Figure 2.20 shows the implementation of these functions. Note again that no scope resolution operator is attached to their names. The input routine reads a fraction or a single integer, as appropriate, and then normalizes the fraction. We have not attempted any of the error checking required in a serious implementation. Likewise, the output routine is fairly simple and works by calling the preexisting output routines as needed.[4]

***Friends* are functions that are exempt from the usual private access restrictions.**

You may have noticed something strange in Figure 2.20: If `numer` and `denom` are private data members, how can a nonmember function access it? Under normal circumstances it cannot. To get around that restriction, we specified in the class interface (at lines 71 to 74 in Figure 2.13) that these functions are **friends,** which are exempt from the usual privte access restrictions. Notice that only the class can give additional access, and so this does not violate information-hiding principles. In general, classes should not have too many friends. Section 2.4.1 discusses an alternate strategy and Exercise 2.32 asks you to rewrite the `Rational` class to avoid the use of friends.

2.4 Some Common Idioms

In this section we discuss three idioms:

1. a technique that allows us to write global functions without using `friend` declarations;

4. Input and output are discussed in Section A.2.

```
istream & operator>>( istream & in, Rational & value )
{
    in >> value.numer;
    value.denom = 1;

    char ch;
    in.get( ch );

    if( !in.eof( ) )
    {
        if( ch == '/' )
        {
            in >> value.denom;
            value.fixSigns( );
            value.reduce( );
        }
        else
            in.putback( ch );  // unread ch
    }

    return in;
}

ostream & operator<<( ostream & out, const Rational & value )
{
    if( value.denom != 0 )
    {
        out << value.numer;
        if( value.denom != 1 )
            out << '/' << value.denom;
        return out;
    }

      // Messy code for denom == 0
    if( value.numer == 0 )
        out << "indeterminate";
    else
    {
        if( value.numer < 0 )
            out << '-';
        out << "infinity";
    }
    return out;
}
```

Figure 2.20 I/O friends for the `Rational` class.

2. use of static data members, which are data shared among all instances of the class; and
3. enum, which is a way to store integer class constants.

2.4.1 Avoiding Friends

As we discussed at the end of Section 2.3, classes should have as few friends as possible. We can get by with few friend functions if the class's public member functions have enough flexibility, which typically is the case.

Two functions that are prime candidates for friendship are the input and output functions. The input function can often be rewritten by reading basic data, using the data to construct an object, and then copying the object into the reference parameter that is to be the target. For example, here is how we can write `operator>>` for the `IntCell` class:

```
istream & operator>> ( istream & in, IntCell & val )
{
    int x;

    in >> x;
    if( !in.fail( ) )
        val = IntCell( x );

    return in;
}
```

Output can often be performed by calling accessors. However, a more common technique is to add the public member function `print` to the class. `print` outputs in exactly the format required by `operator<<`. The signature of the `print` member function is

```
  public:
    void print( ostream & out = cout ) const;
```

We can then implement `operator<<` by calling `print`:

```
ostream & operator<< ( ostream & out, const IntCell & x )
{
    x.print( out );
    return out;
}
```

A complete example of this procedure is shown in Figure 2.28.

2.4.2 Static Class Members

A *static class member* is essentially a global variable visible only to class members.

Suppose that we have an object that we want all the members of the `Rational` class to share. For instance, suppose that we want to keep track of the number of `Rational` objects that are currently active. What we need is essentially a single global variable because any class member will be local to the instance of each object, whereas all the `Rational` instances will share and have access to the global object. Unfortunately, a global variable also allows access to everyone else, violating information hiding principles. In C++ we can declare a static class member.[5] A **static class member** is essentially a global variable visible only to class members (if declared private) and whose scope is the same as a class member, not a data member. In other words, there is one static member per class instead of one data member per object.

Our example would work as follows. In the private section of the `Rational` class, we declare

```
private:
  static int activeInstances;
```

We could then increment `activeInstances` in the constructor and decrement it in the destructor. In the program, where we normally place definitions of global objects, we need to place the defining declaration

```
int Rational::activeInstances = 0;
```

2.4.3 The **enum** Trick for Integer Class Constants

Occasionally we need a classwide constant. For instance, consider the constant `ios::in`. Here, `in` is a constant that is shared among all instances of the class `ios`. We can always simply use the same syntax as in Section 2.4.2, putting the word `const` in front of the type (in both the class interface and defining declaration).

If the object is an integral type, two shorthand options are available. First, we can avoid the defining declaration by providing the value in the interface, as in

```
public:
  static const int RED = 0;
  static const int BLACK = 1;
```

5. A static class member is different from a static local variable. A static local variable is a variable that exists inside a function but has lifetime that extends for the entire program. Think of it as a global variable that is accessible only from inside the function in which is declared.

Unfortunately, this is a recent language addition and does not work on all compilers. An alternative is the `enum` trick, which we use in Exercise 2.23:

```
public:
  enum { RED = 0, BLACK = 1 };
```

2.5 Exceptions

When we design classes for use by others (or even just ourselves), we are often confronted with a problem: How can class methods report error conditions back to the user of the class?

One possibility is to have the method print an error message and then continue on. This solution is not a reasonable because it is likely to allow the program to keep running while in a bad state. Alternatively, we can print a message and terminate the program, which is often a rather drastic solution to put in a library routine. For instance if you are trying to load a Web page and the page cannot be found, you would not want that to cause your browser to exit automatically. So you want the method to inform the caller that an error has occurred and let the caller decide what to do. The caller then has the option of terminating the program, attempting error recovery, or passing the problem up the chain to its caller. So how does a method tell the caller that there is a problem?

Several techniques have been popular in the past. One technique is to set a variable to indicate failure. For instance, in the I/O package, the `istream` classes will set a class variable to indicate an I/O failure. Calls to the `fail`, `good`, `bad`, and `eof` methods simply query the state of this variable. However, this solution has several weaknesses, two of which are that the programmer can easily forget to test the state of the variable, leading to unpredictable results, and that the programmer must clear the error state before continuing.

Another popular technique is to have a method return an error code, but this solution also has several weaknesses. First, the programmer can ignore the return value, leading to unpredictable results. (For example, many C programmers routinely ignore the return value of `printf`, leading to problems when I/O errors occurred on output.) Second, there may be no natural return value. For instance, if a method performs division, what return value can be used to signal a divide by zero error?

A third alternative is to pass an additional parameter by reference to store the error condition. This option solves the problem of running out of unique return values, but it leaves intact the possibility that errors might be ignored. The fourth option is to use exceptions.

An **exception** is an object that stores information transmitted outside the normal return sequence. An exception is propagated back through the calling sequence until some routine *catches* it. An exception is used to signal *exceptional* occurrences, such as errors.

An *exception* is an object that stores information transmitted outside the normal return sequence and is used to signal exceptional occurrences, such as errors.

Any object (for instance an `int`) can be an exception object; however, defining a class that stores the exception's transmitted information is more common. The `throw` statement is used to propagate an exception, as in

```
throw 3;                // Throw an int object with value 3
throw IntCell( 3 );     // Throw an IntCell with state 3
throw IntCell( );       // Throw an IntCell with state 0
```

An exception object can be allowed to propagate uncaught. In that case, the program terminates.[6] For truly exceptional occurrences, such as being out of memory, or using an out-of-range index for a `vector` or `string` this action is reasonable. In fact, our implementation of the `string` and `vector` classes both throw an exception when that occurs (unfortunately, the Standard Library implementations do no error checking).

In this text, we use exceptions only for programming errors. Thus we do not need to catch exceptions. Other applications could require catching exceptions and performing some error recovery. In those cases, a more careful design of the exception objects is required, as is an understanding of the syntax for catching exceptions. The design of these exception objects typically involves *inheritance*. Thus, we defer additional discussion of exception handling until we cover inheritance in Chapter 4.[7]

Although the theory of exceptions is nice (and they are handled well in other languages, such as Java), exceptions were a late addition to C++. Consequently, they are not properly integrated into the C++ libraries (the I/O libraries do not use exceptions), and unexpected interactions occur between exceptions and other language features, most notably templates. This is why we use exceptions only to signal errors that we expect to be unrecoverable.

2.6 A string Class

Recall from Chapter 1 that C++ has two types of strings. The first is the **primitive string,** or *C-style string* (inherited from the C programming language), which is a null-terminated array of characters. The second is a `string` class

6. If the exception is not caught, the standard function `terminate` is called; typically, `terminate` stops the program abnormally. A replacement for `terminate` can be installed.
7. Sections 4.1, 4.2.2, and 4.2.3 illustrate concepts of inheritance by discussing how exception classes are written and used.

that was added to the language as part of the Standard Library. If your compiler has a `string` class you should use it; it will probably be very efficient. Otherwise, you have to choose between the C-style string or providing your own.

A C-style string uses an array of characters to represent a string. A special character, the **null terminator,** ends a string; it is represented by `'\0'`. Thus the string `"abc"` is stored in an array of `char`, with the first four positions containing `'a'`, `'b'`, `'c'`, and `'\0'`. Anything following the null terminator is not considered part of the string. Because an array name is just a pointer, C-style strings cannot be manipulated like first-class objects. Instead, to copy strings we must use the function `strcpy`. The user must guarantee that the target array is large enough to store the string being copied into it; otherwise, runtime errors that are difficult to debug are likely to result. This approach makes manipulating C-style strings tedious and error-prone. To compare C-style strings, we use `strcmp`. We can access individual characters in the string by array indexing, but the index is unchecked.

The `string` class can be implemented by storing a primitive array (`buffer`) as a data member. Recall that a primitive array is a second-class object, implemented as a pointer to a block of memory large enough to store the array objects. Because the primitive array is represented as a pointer, the size of the array is unknown and needs to be maintained in a separate variable, `bufferLength`.

Memory for the array is obtained by calling the `new[]` operator. This call occurs in the constructor and the assignment operators `operator=` and `operator+=`. The memory needs to be reclaimed by calling `delete[]`. This call occurs in the destructor and in both assignment operators. (Note that calls to `new[]` are always matched by calls to `delete[]`.)

For concrete syntax, refer back to Section 1.2.3, where we described abstractly how to expand primitive array `arr` from size 10 to size 12. Recall that we had the following series of operations shown again as Figure 2.21.

1. We remember where the memory for the 10-element array is (the purpose of `original`).
2. We create a new 12-element array and have `arr` use it.
3. We copy the 10 elements from `original` to `arr`; the two extra elements in the new `arr` have some default value.
4. We inform the system that the 10-element array can be reused as it sees fit.

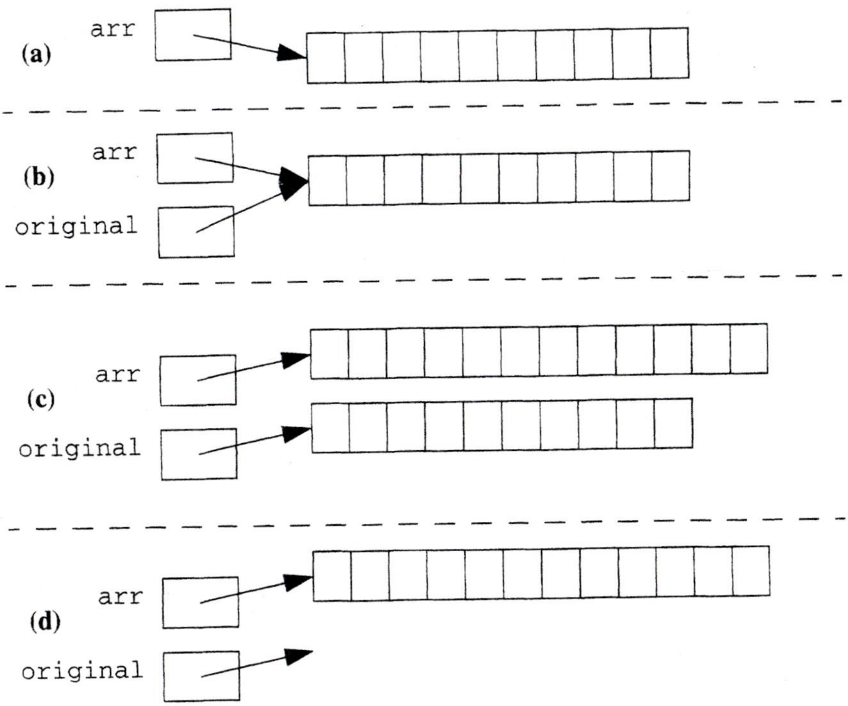

Figure 2.21 Array expansion, internally: (a) At the starting point, `arr` represents 10 integers; (b) after step 1, `original` represents the same 10 integers; (c) after steps 2 and 3, `arr` represents 12 integers, the first 10 of which are copied from `original`; and (d) after step 4, the 10 integers are freed.

These four steps translate as follows:

```
int *original = arr;                // Step 1
arr = new int[ 12 ];                // Step 2
for( int i = 0; i < 10; i++ )       // Step 3
    arr[ i ] = original[ i ];
delete [ ] original;                // Step 4
```

Our `string` class interface is shown in Figure 2.22. To avoid conflicts with the `string.h` header file, we store the interface in `mystring.h`. As promised, three data members store the C-style string, the length of the string, and the size of the array that stores the string. The array size is at least 1 larger than the string length, but it could be more. We provide two accessors (`c_str` and `length`) that return the C-style string and string length. `operator+=` appends `rhs` to the current string. A set of nonclass functions are also provided for I/O and comparison. The I/O functions are not class members because the `string` is not a first parameter. `operator[]` is used to access

```
#ifndef _MY_STRING_H_
#define _MY_STRING_H_

#include <iostream.h>    // Old-style.h file

class string
{
  public:
    string( char ch );                              // Constructor
    string( const char *cstring = "" );             // Constructor
    string( const string & str );                   // Copy constructor
    ~string( )                                      // Destructor
      { delete [ ] buffer; }

    const string & operator= ( const string & rhs );  // Copy
    const string & operator+=( const string & rhs );  // Append

    const char *c_str( ) const          // Return C-style string
      { return buffer; }
    int length( ) const                 // Return string length
      { return strLength; }

    char   operator[]( int k ) const;// Accessor operator[]
    char & operator[]( int k );      // Mutator operator[]

  private:
    int strLength;            // length of string (# of characters)
    int bufferLength;         // capacity of buffer
    char *buffer;             // storage for characters
};

ostream & operator<<( ostream & out, const string & str );
istream & operator>>( istream & in, string & str );
istream & getline( istream & in, string & str,
                   char delim = '\n' );

bool operator==( const string & lhs, const string & rhs );
bool operator!=( const string & lhs, const string & rhs );
bool operator< ( const string & lhs, const string & rhs );
bool operator<=( const string & lhs, const string & rhs );
bool operator> ( const string & lhs, const string & rhs );
bool operator>=( const string & lhs, const string & rhs );

#endif
```

Figure 2.22 *mystring.h.*

```
#include <string.h>
#include "mystring.h"

string::string( const char * cstring )
{
    if( cstring == NULL )                    // If NULL pointer
        cstring = "";                        //   use empty string
    strLength = strlen( cstring );           // Get length of cstring
    bufferLength = strLength + 1;            // Set length with '\0'
    buffer = new char[ bufferLength ];  // Allocate prim string
    strcpy( buffer, cstring );               // Do the copy
}

string::string( char ch )
{
    strLength = 1;
    bufferLength = strLength + 1;
    buffer = new char[ bufferLength ];
    buffer[ 0 ] = ch;
    buffer[ 1 ] = '\0';
}

string::string( const string & str )
{
    strLength = str.length( );               // Get length of str
    bufferLength = strLength + 1;            // Set length with '\0'
    buffer = new char[ bufferLength ];  // Allocate prim string
    strcpy( buffer, str.buffer );            // Do the copy
}
```

Figure 2.23 *string.cpp* (part 1): Constructors.

individual characters in the string. There are two versions; we explain why there are when we discuss their implementation.

The comparison functions are deliberately not implemented as class members. Implementing them outside the class allows the left-hand side of the comparison operator to be a C-style string or a `string`. If one of the operands for a comparison operator is a C-style string, a temporary `string` will be constructed (by calling the `string` constructor, which is deliberately not declared `explicit`). Thus, if `str1` and `str2` are `strings`, `str1==str2`, `str1=="ab"`, `"ab"==str2` are legal. If the comparison functions were class members (in which case we would write only the `rhs` parameter), `"ab"==str2` would not be legal.

The constructors are shown in Figure 2.23 and are relatively straightforward: They initialize the three data members. The assignment operators (Figure 2.24) are much more tricky because they involve two issues. First,

```
const string & string::operator=( const string & rhs )
{
    if( this != &rhs )                               // Alias test
    {
        if( bufferLength < rhs.length( ) + 1 ) // If no room
        {
                // Reclaim old array, compute new size,
                // allocate new array
            delete [ ] buffer;
            bufferLength = rhs.length( ) + 1;
            buffer = new char[ bufferLength ];
        }
        strLength = rhs.length( );               // Set new length
        strcpy( buffer, rhs.buffer );            // Do the copy
    }
    return *this;                         // Return reference to self
}

const string & string::operator+=( const string & rhs )
{
    if( this == &rhs )                    // Alias test: if s+=s
    {
        string copy( rhs );               // Make a copy of rhs
        return *this += copy;             // Append copy; avoid alias
    }

    int newLength = length( ) + rhs.length( );
    if( newLength >= bufferLength )     // If not enough room
    {
          // Begin the expansion: Allocate more room; use
          // 2x space so repeated calls to += are efficient
        bufferLength = 2 * ( newLength + 1 );
        char *oldBuffer = buffer;     // Save ptr for old array
        buffer = new char[ bufferLength ]; // Alloc new array
        strcpy( buffer, oldBuffer );        // Do the copy
        delete [ ] oldBuffer;               // Reclaim old array
    }

    strcpy( buffer + length( ), rhs.buffer ); // Append rhs
    strLength = newLength;                      // Set new length
    return *this;                         // Return reference to self
}
```

Figure 2.24 *string.cpp* (part 2): Assignment operators.

```
char & string::operator[ ]( int k )
{
    if( k < 0 || k >= strLength )
        throw StringIndexOutOfBoundsException( );
    return buffer[ k ];
}

char string::operator[ ]( int k ) const
{
    if( k < 0 || k >= strLength )
        throw StringIndexOutOfBoundsException( );
    return buffer[ k ];
}
```

Figure 2.25 *string.cpp* (part 3): Indexing operators.

we may need to expand `buffer` if the resulting string will not fit. Second, we must be careful to handle aliasing. Omitting the alias test for `operator+=` could create a stale pointer (i.e., a pointer to memory that has already been deleted) for `str+=str` if a resize of `buffer` is required.

The use of `operator+=` is time consuming if a sequence of concatenations that cause resizing are present. To avoid this problem, we sacrifice space and make the new buffer twice as large as it needs to be. This logic is the same as that used in array-doubling (see Section 1.2.3).

The array indexing operators are shown in Figure 2.25. If the index is out of bounds, a `StringIndexOutOfBounds` exception object is thrown. This class is one of many exception classes provided in the online code, and we discuss its design at various points in Section 4.2. The main issue for the array indexing operator is the return type.

We know that `operator[]` should return an entity of type `char`. Should we use return by value, by reference, or by constant reference? Immediately we eliminate return by constant reference because the returned entity is a primitive type and thus is small. Thus we are down to return by reference or by value. Let us consider the following method (ignore the possibility of aliasing or incompatible sizes, neither of which affects the algorithm).

```
void reverseCopy( const string & from, string & to )
{
    int len = from.size( );

    to = from;
    for( int i = 0; i < len; i++ )
        to[ i ] = from[ len - 1 - i ];
}
```

```
ostream & operator<<( ostream & out, const string & str )
{
    return out << str.c_str( );
}

istream & operator>>( istream & in, string & str )
{
    char ch;
    str = "";
    in >> ch;

    if( !in.fail( ) )
    {
        do
        {
            str += ch;
            in.get( ch );
        } while( !in.fail( ) && !isspace( ch ) );

        if( isspace( ch ) )   // put whitespace back on stream
            in.putback( ch );
    }

    return in;
}

istream & getline( istream & in, string & str, char delim )
{
    char ch;
    str = "";    // empty string; build one char at-a-time

    while( in.get( ch ) && ch != delim )
        str += ch;

    return in;
}
```

Figure 2.26 *string.cpp* (part 4): I/O functions.

In the `reverseCopy` function, we attempt to copy each `char` in `from` into the corresponding position in `string to`. (Ignore the fact that this is not the best way to do it.) Clearly, if `operator[]` returns a value, then `to[i]` cannot appear on the left-hand side of the assignment statement. Thus `operator[]` should return a reference. But then even though `from` is a constant `string` an expression such as `from[i]=to[i]` would still compile because `from[i]` would be a simple reference and thus modifiable. Oops!

```
bool operator==( const string & lhs, const string & rhs )
{
    return strcmp( lhs.c_str( ), rhs.c_str( ) ) == 0;
}

bool operator!=( const string & lhs, const string & rhs )
{
    return strcmp( lhs.c_str( ), rhs.c_str( ) ) != 0;
}

bool operator<( const string & lhs, const string & rhs )
{
    return strcmp( lhs.c_str( ), rhs.c_str( ) ) < 0;
}

bool operator<=( const string & lhs, const string & rhs )
{
    return strcmp( lhs.c_str( ), rhs.c_str( ) ) <= 0;
}

bool operator>( const string & lhs, const string & rhs )
{
    return strcmp( lhs.c_str( ), rhs.c_str( ) ) > 0;
}

bool operator>=( const string & lhs, const string & rhs )
{
    return strcmp( lhs.c_str( ), rhs.c_str( ) ) >= 0;
}
```

Figure 2.27 *string.cpp* (part 5): Comparison operators.

So what we really need is for `operator[]` to return a constant reference for `from`—but also a value for `to`. In other words, we need two versions of `operator[]` that differ only in their return types. Although that is not allowed, there is a loophole: Member function const-ness (i.e., whether a function is an accessor or a mutator) is part of the signature, so we can have the accessor version of `operator[]` return a value and have the mutator version return the simple reference. Then all is well—which is why we have two versions of `operator[]`.

Figure 2.26 shows the I/O operators. There is no limit on the length of the input. Note that, because these functions are not class members, they cannot and do not access any private data.

The comparison operators are shown in Figure 2.27. They simply call `strcmp` on the C-style strings. Again we must use an accessor to get the C-style strings because `buffer` is a private data member and these operators are not class members.

An inefficiency of the `string` class is its reliance on implicit type conversions. That is, if a C-style string (or string constant) is passed to the comparison operators or assignment operators, a temporary is generated. This action can add significant overhead to running time. A solution to this problem is to write additional functions that take a C-style string as a parameter. Thus we could add global functions

```
bool operator>=( const char * lhs, const string & rhs );
bool operator>=( const string & lhs, const char * rhs );
```

and class member functions

```
    const string & operator= ( const char * rhs );
    const string & operator+=( const char * rhs );
```

It might also be worthwhile to add an overloaded `operator+=` that accepts a single `char` as a parameter to avoid those type conversions.

2.7 Recap: What Gets Called and What Are the Defaults?

In this section we summarize what gets called in various circumstances. First, for initialization we have the following examples:

```
string r;           // string( )
string s = "Hello"; // string( const char * )
string t = s;       // string( const string & )
```

Next, we have cases where there are exact matches:

```
r = t;              // operator=( const string & )
s += r;             // operator+=( const string & )
r[0] = 'J';         // operator[] followed by character copy
```

In this case, the nonconstant `operator[]` is used. Here is an example that involves an implicit call to a constructor to create a temporary object:

```
if( r == "Jello" )  // string( const char * ) to
                    // create temporary; then operator==
```

Note, however, that newer versions of the compiler will not perform this conversion if the corresponding formal parameter is a (nonconstant) reference. In other words, if we have

```
bool operator==( const string & lhs, string & rhs );
```

`"Jello"` fails to match `rhs`. The reason is that the declaration of `==` is stating that `rhs` may be altered, which does not make sense if `rhs` is merely a temporary copy of `"Jello"`. Furthermore, for operators that are class members, the first actual parameter must be an exact match.

The copy constructor is also called if a `string` is passed by value to a function expecting a string or is returned by copy. Thus if the declaration for `==` was

```
bool operator==( string lhs, string rhs );
```

then `r` would be copied to `lhs` by a call to the `string` copy constructor, and `"Jello"` would be copied to `rhs` by a call to the `string(const char *)` constructor.

Other examples in which a `string` constructor is called are

```
vector<string> array( 100 );          // 100 calls
string *ptr1 = new string;            // 1 call
string *ptr2 = new string( "junk" ); // 1 call
string *ptr3 = new string( s );      // 1 call
string *ptr4 = new string[ 100 ];    // 100 calls
```

but not

```
string *ptr = new string( 100 );     // No string(int)
string & ref = s;                    // 0 call: reference
```

If any of the members required are placed in the private section, the corresponding operations become illegal. The operators most commonly placed in the private section are the copy constructor and `operator=`.

You also need to understand what happens when you fail to provide a default constructor, copy constructor, destructor, or `operator=`. If you do not provide any constructors, a default zero-parameter constructor is created. It performs a member-by-member construction of the class data members. If you provide a `string( const char * )` constructor but no `string( )` constructor, you merely disallow uninitialized `string` definitions.

If you do not provide a copy constructor, a default copy constructor is created. It performs member-by-member copy construction. Note that if the copy constructor is disabled for some member, this approach generates a compiler error.

If you do not provide a destructor, a default destructor is created and performs member-by-member destruction (in inverse order of the member declarations).

Finally, if you do not provide `operator=`, a default is created and performs member-by-member copying, using each member's `operator=`. As with the copy constructor, if `operator=` is disabled for some member, a compiler error is generated.

2.8 Composition

Once we have some classes, we can use objects of these classes as data members of other classes. This practice is called *composition*.

As an example, Figure 2.28 illustrates a few methods of the `Employee` class. Once the classes that define the data members have implemented `operator<<`, writing `operator<<` for our new class is a simple matter. We could easily have added other data members. For instance, if a `Date` class is written, we can add a `hired` data member of type `Date`.

```
class Employee
{
  public:
    void setValue( const string & n, double s )
      { name = n; salary = s; }

    void print( ostream & out = cout ) const
      { out << name << " (" << salary << ")"; }

    // Other general accessors and mutators, not shown
  private:
    string name;
    double salary;
};

// Define an output operator for Employee.
ostream & operator<< ( ostream & out, const Employee & rhs )
{
    rhs.print( out );
    return out;
}

int main( )
{
    vector<Employee> v( 3 );

    v[ 0 ].setValue( "Bill Clinton", 200000.00 );
    v[ 1 ].setValue( "Bill Gates", 2000000000.00 );
    v[ 2 ].setValue( "Billy the Marlin", 60000.00 );

    for( int i = 0; i < v.size( ); i++ )
        cout << v[ i ] << endl;

    return 0;
}
```

Figure 2.28 Illustration of composition.

Summary

In this chapter we described the C++ class construct. The class is the C++ mechanism used to create new types. Through it we can

- define construction and destruction of objects,
- define copy semantics,
- define input and output operations,
- overload almost all operators,
- define implicit and explicit type conversion operations (sometimes a bad thing), and
- provide for information hiding and atomicity.

The class consists of two parts: the interface and the implementation. The interface tells the user of the class what the class does. The implementation does it. The implementation frequently contains proprietary code and in some cases is distributed only in precompiled form.

Information hiding can be enforced by using the `private` section in the interface. Initialization of objects is controlled by the constructor functions, and the destructor function is called when an object goes out of scope. The destructor typically performs clean up work, closing files and freeing memory. Finally, when implementing a class, the use of `const` and correct parameter passing mechanisms, as well as the decision about whether to accept a default for the Big Three, write our own Big Three, or completely disallow copying is crucial for not only efficiency but also in some cases, correctness.

Objects of the Game

`#endif` and `#ifndef` Are used to enclose the contents of a header file and prevent multiple inclusion. (p. 49)

accessor A method that examines but does not change the state of its object. (p. 47)

aliasing A special case that occurs when the same object appears in more than one role. (p. 54)

atomic unit An object, whose parts cannot be dissected by the general users of the object. (p. 42)

class The same as a structure except that, by default, all members are inaccessible to the general user of the class. (p. 43)

constant member function A function that does not change any class data members. (p. 47)

constructor A method that describes how an object is declared and initialized, that is, created. The default constructor is a member-by-member application of a no-parameter constructor. (p. 45)

copy assignment operator, `operator=` Used to copy objects. (p. 52)

copy constructor Called when an object is passed or returned by value or initialized with an object of the same class. By default, the copy constructor is a member-by-member application of copy constructors. (p. 52)

destructor Called when an object exits scope and frees resources allocated by the constructor or other member functions during the use of the object. The default destructor is a member-by-member application of destructors. (p. 51)

encapsulation The grouping of data and the operations that apply to them to form an aggregate while hiding implementation details of the aggregate. (p. 42)

exception An object that stores information that is transmitted outside the normal return sequence and is used to signal *exceptional* occurrences, such as errors. (p. 73)

friends Functions that are exempt from the usual private access restrictions. (p. 68)

implementation Represents the internal processes by which the interface specifications are met. (p. 48)

implicit type conversion A type conversion performed without the use of an explicit type conversion operator. (p. 63)

information hiding Makes implementation details, including components of an object, inaccessible. (p. 42)

initializer list Specifies nondefault initialization of each data member in an object directly. (p. 62)

input and output stream operators Can be defined by overloading << and >>. (p. 68)

interface Describes what can be done to an object. (p. 48)

member functions Functions supplied as additional members that manipulate the object's state; also known as a *method*. (p. 43)

methods Another name for *member functions*. (p. 43)

mutator A method that changes the state of an object. (p. 47)

null terminator The special character that ends a primitive string; it is represented by `'\0'`. (p. 74)

object An entity that has structure and state and defines operations that may access or manipulate that state; an instance of a class. (p. 41)

object-based programming Uses the encapsulation and information hiding features of objects but does not use inheritance. (p. 43)

object-oriented programming Distinguished from object-based programming by the use of inheritance to form hierarchies of classes. (p. 43)

operator overloading Extending the types to which an operator can be applied. (p. 57)

primitive string A null-terminated array of characters. You must allocate an extra spot for the null terminator. (p. 74)

private member A member that is not visible to nonclass routines and may be accessed only by methods in its class. (p. 45)

public member A member that is visible to all routines and may be accessed by any method in any class. (p. 44)

scope operator `::` Used to refer to the scope. In a class member function, the scope is the class. (p. 50)

signature Includes the types of parameters in the function, including `const` and `&` directives, but not the return type. (p. 48)

static class member Essentially a global variable visible only to class members. (p. 71)

`this` A pointer that points at the current object. It is used to return a constant reference for assignment operators and also to test for aliasing. (p. 53)

type conversion Creates a temporary object of a new type. A constructor defines an automatic type conversion. (p. 63)

Common Errors

1. Forgetting that the class interface ends with a semicolon can lead to strange error messages.
2. The declaration `Rational r( );` does not call the zero-parameter constructor. Instead it is a declaration that function `r` accepts no parameters and returns a `Rational`.
3. The default copy is a shallow copy. If data members are pointers to dynamically allocated objects, the default generally is unacceptable and should either be changed or disabled.
4. Failure to test for aliasing in assignment operators can lead to errors.

5. The class member function definitions must be preceded by a class name and scope operator. Otherwise, they will not be recognized as class members. Exported class objects (e.g., `ios::in`) also require the class name and scope operator.
6. A common programming error is using the incorrect parameter-passing mechanism.
7. Forgetting to free memory in a destructor can lead to memory leaks.
8. Several errors are associated with the input and output routines (>> and <<) for classes. First, they may need to be friends. If they are not friends, the declarations must be placed in the interface file after the class declaration. A stream reference should be returned in both cases. A common error is to use `cin` or `cout` instead of the stream passed as a parameter.
9. The interface should be enclosed by an `#ifndef / #endif` pair to avoid double scanning.
10. Constant class members can be initialized only in the constructor initializer list (they cannot be assigned to).
11. Reference class members can be initialized only in the constructor initializer list.
12. All instances of `const` (except in the return type) are parts of the signature. Specifying a function as a constant member in the interface but not in the implementation generates an error—that the nonmember function was not declared in the interface. Similar rules apply with parameters.
13. Private members cannot be accessed outside the class. By default, class members are private.
14. Type conversions can lead to trouble. One problem is that they can lead to ambiguities when exact matches are not found and approximate matches are examined. Additionally, in some cases substantial overhead is required for accepting implicit conversions.
15. Exact matches are needed for reference parameters. Some compilers give only cryptic warnings.
16. If a declaration for a constructor or destructor is provided, an implementation must also be provided. Otherwise, the compiler will complain when the object is declared. If a declaration for a member function is provided, the implementation may be omitted if no attempt is made to use the member function. This approach allows incremental implementation of the class.

17. Functions that return new objects (e.g., `operator+`) must return them by copy. Functions that return existing objects (e.g., `operator+=`) should use constant reference returns unless a reference return is warranted.
18. The pointer `this` is a pointer constant and may not be altered.
19. Using inline functions can lead to many errors. Public inline functions must be defined in the interface file, and some compilers will not allow them in certain cases (e.g., if they throw an exception). Public inline functions should be avoided unless they can be proved to yield a substantial speed benefit.
20. Prefix and postfix `++` are different operators. Using one form when only the other form is implemented by the class is an error.
21. For static class members, in addition to the class declaration a single definition should be provided outside the class.

On the Internet

The `string` class is used in several other routines. Consequently, there is no `main` to test it. The files that are available are

IntCell.h	Interface file for the `IntCell` class, as shown in Figure 2.4.
IntCell.cpp	Implementation file for the `IntCell` class, as shown in Figure 2.5.
TestIntCell.cpp	Test routine file for the `IntCell` class, as shown in Figure 2.6.
BuggyIntCell.cpp	The incorrect `IntCell` shown in Figures 2.8 and 2.9.
DeepIntCell.cpp	The correct `IntCell` shown in Figure 2.10.
Rational.h	Interface file for the `Rational` class.
Rational.cpp	Implementation of the `Rational` class.
RatMain.cpp	Test routine for the `Rational` class, as shown in Figure 2.11.
mystring.h	Interface file for the `string` class, as shown in Figure 2.22.
string.cpp	Casual implementation of the `string` class.

Exercises

In Short

2.1. What is *information hiding?* What is *encapsulation?* How does C++ support these concepts?

2.2. Explain the public and private sections of the class.

2.3. Describe the roles of the constructor and destructor.

2.4. What is the difference between a copy constructor and a copy assignment operator?

2.5. If a class provides no constructor and no destructor, what is the result?

2.6. When is it acceptable not to provide a destructor? `operator=`? copy constructor?

2.7. Explain the benefits and liabilities of inline functions.

2.8. What restrictions are placed on operator overloading?

2.9. What is a friend function?

2.10. For a class `ClassName`, what declarations are needed to perform input and output? Where are the function definitions placed?

2.11. In the following code fragment, which functions are called at each line and what is the semantic meaning?

```
Rational a;
Rational b = 3;
Rational c( 4, 3 );
Rational d( 0 );
Rational e = ( 4, 3 );
Rational f( );
Rational *g = new Rational( 4, 3 );
Rational *h = new Rational( 5 );
Rational *i = new Rational[ 5 ];
vector<Rational> j( 10 );
vector<Rational> k[ 10 ];
```

2.12. For the definitions of `g`, `h`, and `i` in Exercise 2.11, what needs to be done to avoid a memory leak?

2.13. What does the `sizeof` operator do when applied on a class that has private members?

In Theory

2.14. Some compilers complain if a class's members are all private and it has no friends. Why?

2.15. Why can't the following be used to indicate the copy constructor for the `Rational` class ?

```
Rational( Rational rhs );
```

In Practice

2.16. Add the following improvements to the `Rational` class.

a. Rewrite `operator==` and `operator!=` to avoid multiplications.

b. Implement $\frac{N1}{D1} \times \frac{N2}{D2}$ as $\frac{N1}{D2} \times \frac{N2}{D1}$. Reduce $\frac{N1}{D2}$ and then $\frac{N2}{D1}$ prior to the multiplication. The result need not be reduced. Why? What is the advantage of this scheme?

c. What other operations are affected by this rearrangement?

d. Overload `^` to perform exponentiation. What are some of the problems that can occur? What is the value of `1+2^3` when `^` is overloaded for exponentiation?

2.17. Additional routines are required for the `string` class so that temporaries are not created when a `char *` is involved.

a. For the class interface presented in Figure 2.22, how many additional routines are needed?

b. Implement some subset of these routines.

2.18. Define `operator()` (with two parameters) to return a substring. For example, the output resulting from

```
string s = "abcd";
cout << s( 1, 2 );
```

is `bc` (after all of the implicit conversions are applied).

a. What is the return type?

b. Implement the substring operator.

c. Is there a substantial difference between the following two alternatives?

```
// Alternative 1
string subStr = s( 1, 2 );
```

```
  // Alternative 2
string subStr;
subStr = s( 1, 2 );
```

2.19. Let `s` be a `string`.

a. Is the typical C mistake `s='a'` caught by the compiler? Why or why not?

b. What functions are called in `s+='a'`?

2.20. Suppose that we add a constructor allowing the user to specify the initial size for the internal buffer. Describe an implementation of this constructor and then explain what happens when the user attempts to declare a `string` with a buffer size of 0.

2.21. Add operations to allow the copy assignment of a single `char` and concatenation of `char`. Make them efficient; do not simply call existing routines.

2.22. A *combination lock* has the following basic properties: The combination (a sequence of three numbers) is hidden; the lock can be opened by providing the combination; and the combination can be changed but only by someone who knows the current combination. Design a class with public member functions `open` and `changeCombo` and private data members that store the combination. The combination should be set in the constructor. Disable copying of combination locks.

Programming Projects

2.23. Implement a simple `Date` class. You should be able to represent any date from January 1, 1800, through December 31, 2500, subtract two dates, increment a date by a number of days, and compare two dates by using <. A `Date` is represented internally as the number of days since some starting time, which here is the first day of 1800, making most operations except for I/O trivial.

The rule for leap years is: A year is a leap year if it is divisible by 4, and not divisible by 100 unless it is also divisible by 400. Thus 1800, 1900, and 2100 are not leap years, but 2000 is. The input operation must check the validity of the input. The output operation must check the validity of the `Date`. The `Date` could be bad if a + or − operator caused it to go out of range.

Figure 2.29 gives a class specification skeleton for the `Date` class. Several items are missing, including `public` and `private` keywords, `const` and `&`, and `I/O` interfaces. Before you begin coding the interface, you must make some decisions:

```
class Date
{
    enum { FIRST_YEAR = 1800, MAX_YEAR = 2500 };

    int totalDays;                    // Days since 1/1/1800

      // Constructor.
    Date( int y = FIRST_YEAR, int m = 1, int d = 1 );

      // Assignment operator (instead of +)
    Date operator+=( int days );

      // Binary operators.
    int operator- ( Date right );
    bool operator<( Date right );
};
```

Figure 2.29 Class specification *skeleton* for `Date` (Exercise 2.23).

- where to use `const` and/or `&` (think about this very carefully);
- whether you are willing to accept the defaults for the copy assignment and copy constructor operators;
- how you will interface for input and output; and
- what should and should not be private.

Once you have decided on the interface, you can do an implementation. The difficult part is converting between the internal and external representations of a date. What follows is a possible algorithm. Set up two arrays that are static data members (the defining declarations are placed where globals would be).

```
static int Date::DAYS_TILL_FIRST_OF_MONTH [ ] =
  { 0, 31, 59, ... };
static int Date::DAYS_TILL_JAN1 [ ] =
  { ...                 };
```

The first array, `DAYS_TILL_FIRST_OF_MONTH`, will contain the number of days until the first of each month in a nonleap year. Thus it contains 0, 31, 59, 90, and so on. The second array, `DAYS_TILL_JAN1`, will contain the number of days until the first of each year, starting with `FIRST_YEAR`. Thus it contains 0, 365, 730, 1095, 1460, 1826, and so on because 1800 is not a leap year but 1804 is. You should have your program initialize this array once. If you choose this algorithm, you will need to add corresponding static class declarations in the interface. In any of the member functions you will be able to access these arrays as you would any member. For nonmember friends, you will have to use the scope resolution operator. For nonmember nonfriends, these items will not be visible. You can then use the array to convert from the internal to external representations.

2.24. Implement an `INT` class. Use a single `int` as the private data. Support all the operations that can be applied to an `int` and allow both initialization by an `int` and no initialization. Explain whether you need or can accept the default copy constructor, destructor, and copy assignment operator.

2.25. Continue Exercise 2.24.

a. Modify the += operator (and by inference the binary + operator) to detect overflow. To do so, change the internal representation to an `unsigned int`, and store a sign bit separately. Print a warning message if an overflow is detected (or throw an exception if you can).
b. Modify the -= operator to detect overflow.
c. Modify the /= operator to detect division by 0.
d. Modify the unary minus operator to detect overflow (there is only one case wherein this happens).
e. Modify the bit shift operators to print an illegal message if the second parameter is either negative or not smaller than the number of bits in an `unsigned int`.

2.26. Suppose that you want to modify the *= operator to detect overflow. Redo Exercise 2.25 by changing the internal representation to use two data members: One stores the leading bits, and the other stores the trailing bits. For example, for 32 bit integers, $X = 2^{16} H + L$, where H and L are 16 bits each.

2.27. Implement a complete `IntType` class. Maintain an `IntType` as a sufficiently large array. For this class the difficult operation is division, followed closely by multiplication. Begin by writing the class interface. Once again, you need to decide on an internal representation, the operations to be supported, how to pass parameters, whether you are willing to accept the default for copy assignment and copy construction, how you will provide I/O, how you will provide an implicit conversion from an `int` to an `IntType`, and what should and should not be private. Do not even think about writing an actual implementation until you have thought through the interface design. Only then should you begin the task of writing the actual algorithms to implement the class.

2.28. Implement a `Complex` number class. Recall that a complex number consists of a real and an imaginary part. Support the same operations as the `Rational` class, when meaningful (e.g., `operator<` is not meaningful). Add member functions to extract the real and imaginary parts.

2.29. Implement a `Fuzzy` class. Fuzzy logic defines *true, false,* and *maybe*. The *AND* operator returns the weaker of its two parameters, and the *OR* operator returns the stronger. Define constants `Fuzzy::TRUE`, `Fuzzy::FALSE`, and `Fuzzy::MAYBE` and support `&&`, `||`, `!` (for *NOT*), and I/O operations. Also provide a type conversion to `int` so that the `Fuzzy` can be used to express a condition (in an `if`, `while`, and so on).

2.30. Implement some of the following improvements to the `string` class.

a. Add `!` (which is false if the string is zero length).
b. Add the `*` and `*=` operators to expand into multiple copies. For instance, if `s` is equal to `"ab"`, then `s*=3` turns `s` into `"ababab"`.
c. Add the left shift operator, which shifts the string `x` positions. Can you think of a way to alter the class implementation to make shifting a fast operation?
d. Add `lowerCase` and `upperCase` member functions.

2.31. Index range checking costs the user time and space but greatly improves software reliability. Write a program that reads a large dictionary, storing each word in a `string`. Then access each character in the array of strings. Measure the time cost of range checking by running the program twice—once with range checking on and again with it disabled. Also measure the difference in space usage. Use a preprocessor conditional to disable range checking on access.

2.32. Add `setValue` and `print` member functions to the `Rational` class. Then rewrite `operator>>` and `operator<<` so that they are not friends of `Rational`.

References

More information on implementation of the `IntType` class is available in [2]. An example of a production quality `string` class is given in [1]. Tips on the correct use of `const` and references, as well as many advanced topics, are discussed in [3].

1. B. Flamig, *Practical Data Structures in C++*, John Wiley & Sons, New York, 1993.
2. D. E. Knuth, *The Art of Computer Programming, Vol. 2: Seminumerical Algorithms,* 3d ed., Addison-Wesley, Reading, Mass., 1997.
3. S. Meyers, *Effective C++*, 2d ed., Addison-Wesley, Reading, Mass., 1998.

Chapter 3

Templates

An important goal of object-oriented program is to support code reuse. In this chapter we introduce one mechanism, the C++ *template*, that is used to further this goal. The **template** allows us to write routines that work for arbitrary types without having to know, as we write the routines, what these types will be. Although this approach is supported somewhat by the use of the `typedef` facility, the template is more powerful than the `typedef`.

In this chapter, we show:

- what a template is and how it differs from the `typedef`,
- how to write some useful function templates,
- how to write class templates, and
- what the limitations of templates are.

3.1 What Is a Template?

Consider the problem of finding the largest item in an array of items. A simple algorithm is the sequential scan, in which we examine each item in order, keeping track of the maximum. As is typical of many algorithms, the sequential scan algorithm is *type-independent.* That is, the logic of this algorithm does not depend on the type of items stored in the array. The same logic works for an array of integers, floating-point numbers, or any type for which comparison can be meaningfully defined.

Throughout this text, we describe algorithms and data structures that are type-independent. Swapping, sorting, and searching are classic examples of type-independent algorithms. When we write C++ code for a type-independent algorithm or data structure, we would prefer to write the code once, rather than recode it for each different type.

In this chapter we describe how to write type-independent algorithms (also known as generic algorithms) in C++. We use a *template* to write these algorithms. We begin by discussing function templates and then examine class templates.

3.2 Function Templates

The ***typedef*** is a simple mechanism to allow generic routines. However, it is unsuitable if we want routines with two different types.

Suppose that we want to write a `swap` routine in Figure 1.13 for `doubles` instead of `ints`. The logic is identical; we just need to change the type declarations. One way to do so is to write the `swap` routine for an arbitrary `Object` and then issue the appropriate `typedef`. The **`typedef`** is a simple mechanism to allow generic routines, as shown in Figure 3.1.

Suppose, however, that we want to use `swap` for both `int` and `double`. Certainly this use would be acceptable because the two `swap` routines would have different signatures. However, the `typedef` would not work because `Object` cannot assume both `int` and `double` simultaneously. Fortuitously, C++ provides templates that make it possible to write a routine that can be used for both types.

A *function template* is a design for a function.

A **function template** is not an actual function; instead, it is a design, or pattern, for what could become an actual function. For example, a template for a `swap` routine is shown in Figure 3.2. This design is expanded (much like a preprocessor macro) as needed to provide an actual routine. If a call to `swap` with two `int` parameters is made, the compiler will generate a routine from this template, using lines 4–9, with `int` replacing `Object`.

Instantiation of a template with a particular type, logically creates a new function.

This expansion *instantiates* the function template. In other words, **instantiation** of a template with a particular type logically creates a new function. The compiler must now verify that the instantiation is legal C++. Some of the checking may have been performed when the template was defined. For example, missing semicolons and unbalanced parentheses are easy to check, but some checks cannot be performed that early. For instance, `operator=` might be disallowed for the instantiated type, and that check could only be performed at the point of instantiation. In that case the `swap` operation could not work. If the instantiated type does not have a copy constructor but does have `operator=`, we could rewrite the `swap` template in Figure 3.2 to avoid the copy constructor. Thus there is occasionally a tradeoff between requiring more operations to be supported by the template parameter and code compactness (and/or efficiency).

Only one instantiation is created for each parameter-type combination.

Figure 3.3 shows the `swap` template in use. Each call to `swap` with previously unseen parameter types generates new instantiations. Thus if there are two calls to `swap(int,int)` and one call to `swap(double,double)`, then there are two instantiations of the `swap` template: one with `Object` of `int` and another with `Object` of `double`. (Note: `swap` is part of the STL, so some compilers may object. The online code uses the name `Swap` to avoid potential conflicts.)

```
typedef double Object;

// Standard swap routine.
void swap( Object & lhs, Object & rhs )
{
    Object tmp = lhs;
    lhs = rhs;
    rhs = tmp;
}
```

Figure 3.1 The swap routine, using typedefs.

```
// swap function template.
// Object: must have copy constructor and operator=.
template <class Object>
void swap( Object & lhs, Object & rhs )
{
    Object tmp = lhs;
    lhs = rhs;
    rhs = tmp;
}
```

Figure 3.2 The swap function template.

```
// Exercise the swap function template.
int main( )
{
    int x = 5;
    int y = 7;
    double a = 2;
    double b = 4;

    swap( x, y );    // Instantiates swap with int
    swap( x, y );    // Uses already instantiated swap with int
    swap( a, b );    // Instantiates swap with double
    cout << x << " " << y << endl;
    cout << a << " " << b << endl;
//  swap( x, b );    // Illegal: no match

    return 0;
}
```

Figure 3.3 Using the swap function template.

3.3 A Sorting Function Template

Swapping is a classic example of a routine that is type-independent and thus well suited for a template implementation. In this section we write a function template that sorts and show how a `main` routine uses it.

Our simple program reads a sequence of integers (until the end of input or bad input is detected), sorts them, and outputs them. If we change our minds and decide that we want a sequence of floating-point numbers or `string` objects, then we expect only a one-word change (at one location) in the entire program.[1] Sorting is accomplished by a simple sort function template.

***Insertion sort* is a simple sorting algorithm that is appropriate for small inputs.**

Sorting is implemented by an algorithm known as insertion sort. **Insertion sort** is a simple sorting algorithm that is appropriate for small inputs. It is generally considered to be a good solution if only a few elements need sorting because it is such a short algorithm and the time required to sort is not likely to be an issue. However, if we are dealing with a large amount of data, insertion sort is a poor choice because it is too time consuming. In that case better algorithms should be used, as discussed in Chapter 9. The insertion sort algorithm is coded in Figure 3.4. We use this routine in Section 4.3.

Insertion sort works as follows. In the initial state the first element, considered by itself, is sorted. In the final state all elements (assume that there are N), considered as a group, are to have been sorted. Figure 3.5 shows that the basic action of insertion sort is to sort the elements in positions `0` through `p` (where `p` ranges from 1 through $N - 1$). In each stage `p` increases by 1. That is what the outer loop at line 7 in Figure 3.4 is controlling.

When the body of the `for` loop is entered at line 9, we are guaranteed that the elements in array positions `0` through `p-1` have already been sorted and that we need to extend this to positions `0` to `p`. Figure 3.6 gives us a closer look at what has to be done, detailing only the relevant part of the array. At each step the element in boldface type needs to be added to the previously sorted part of the array. We can easily do that by placing it in a temporary variable and sliding all the elements that are larger than it one position to the right. Then we can copy the temporary variable into the former position of the leftmost relocated element (indicated by lighter shading on the following line). We keep a counter `j`, which is the position to which the temporary variable should be written back. Every time an element is slid, `j` decreases by 1. Lines 9–14 implement this process.

1. Of course, this minimal change would also be true of the `typedef`. If our program were more complex and required two types of sorts, the `typedef` would be inadequate.

```
// insertionSort: sort items in array a.
// Comparable: must have copy constructor, operator=,
//   and operator<.
template <class Comparable>
void insertionSort( vector<Comparable> & a )
{
    for( int p = 1; p < a.size( ); p++ )
    {
        Comparable tmp = a[ p ];
        int j;

        for( j = p; j > 0 && tmp < a[ j - 1 ]; j-- )
            a[ j ] = a[ j - 1 ];
        a[ j ] = tmp;
    }
}
```

Figure 3.4 Insertion sort template.

Array Position	**0**	**1**	**2**	**3**	**4**	**5**
Initial State	8	5	9	2	6	3
After a[0..1] is sorted	5	8	9	2	6	3
After a[0..2] is sorted	5	8	9	2	6	3
After a[0..3] is sorted	2	5	8	9	6	3
After a[0..4] is sorted	2	5	6	8	9	3
After a[0..5] is sorted	2	3	5	6	8	9

Figure 3.5 Basic action of insertion sort (shaded part is sorted).

Array Position	**0**	**1**	**2**	**3**	**4**	**5**
Initial State	8	**5**				
After a[0..1] is sorted	5	8	**9**			
After a[0..2] is sorted	5	8	9	**2**		
After a[0..3] is sorted	2	5	8	9	**6**	
After a[0..4] is sorted	2	5	6	8	9	**3**
After a[0..5] is sorted	2	3	5	6	8	9

Figure 3.6 A closer look at the action of insertion sort (dark shading indicates the sorted area; light shading is where the new element was placed).

Always check the boundary cases.

We must verify that this insertion sort works in two boundary cases. First, in Figure 3.6, if the boldface element already is the largest in the group, it is copied to the temporary variable and then back immediately—and thus is correct. If the boldface element is the smallest in the group, the entire group moves over, and the temporary is copied into array position 0. We just need to be careful not to run past the end of the array. Thus we can be sure that, when the outer `for` loop terminates, the array has been sorted.

Now that we have the support functions, we can write `main`. The code for it is shown in Figure 3.7.

The instantiated type does not always make sense. In that case an error may be noticed at the instantiation point, or in some cases the code is legal but erroneous.

We can use templates to have sorting at our fingertips for any type. However, the instantiated type does not always make sense. Let us look at some different types.

1. `double`: No problem; a two-line change in `main` and everything works well.
2. `Rational`: No problem; a two-line change in `main` and everything works well.
3. `char *` (primitive strings): Serious problem; the `operator=` and `operator<` do not make sense, so the program won't work. Specifically, we cannot just read into a `char *` object without first setting

```
#include <iostream>
#include <vector>
using namespace std;

// Read an arbitrary number of items, sort and print them.
int main( )
{
    vector<int> array;          // The array
    int x;                      // An item to read

    cout << "Enter items to sort: " << endl;
    while( cin >> x )
        array.push_back( x );

    insertionSort( array );

    cout << "Sorted items are: " << endl;
    for( int i = 0; i < array.size( ); i++ )
        cout << array[ i ] << endl;

    return 0;
}
```

Figure 3.7 The `main` routine to read some integers, sort them, and output them.

aside memory. Assuming that we have done so, the sort won't work because `operator<` for two `char *` objects compares their memory locations.

4. `string`: A possible efficiency problem; the algorithm will work, but it could be overly expensive to use because of repeated calls to `operator=` and excessive `string` copies. We discuss a solution to this problem in Chapter 9 (it involves moving pointers rather than the actual `string` objects). Note that many `string` implementations optimize `string` copies by using an extra level of pointers, in which case there is no inefficiency problem.
5. A type for which `operator<` or some other needed operator is not defined: This lack of definition generates an error at link time. At that point, the linker will notice that `operator<` has not been implemented. Note that this occurs even if `operator>` is implemented.
6. A type for which `operator=` is disallowed via placement in the private section: This generates an error at compile time when the template is instantiated.

As a result, good practice requires placing in a comment a list of the conditions that must be satisfied by the template parameter. Throughout this text, we use `Object` and `Comparable` as template types. For `Object`, we assume that zero-parameter constructors and both a copy constructor and copy assignment operator are available. For `Comparable`, we require that, in addition to the properties satisfied by `Object`, the `operator<` also be available. If additional operations are needed, we specify them in a comment. On occasion we omit long comments to save space, if they are merely restating the assumptions we present here.

3.4 Class Templates

Classes can be templated, but the syntax is onerous.

In this section we show how to create and use class templates. As `vector` is actually a class template, we have already been using class templates. At the end of this chapter, we provide an implementation of `vector`. But first, we use a simpler example to illustrate the syntax and show how to template the `IntCell` class from Section 2.2.

3.4.1 A `MemoryCell` Template

Figure 3.8 shows a template version of the `IntCell` class previously depicted in Figure 2.1. Here, we use the more generic name, `MemoryCell`. In

```
1 // MemoryCell template class interface:
2 //   simulate one Object RAM.
3 //
4 // Object: must have zero-parameter constructor and operator=
5 // CONSTRUCTION: with (a) no initializer, or
6 //                    (b) an Object, or
7 //                    (c) another MemoryCell
8 // ******************PUBLIC OPERATIONS*********************
9 // Object read( )          --> Return stored value
10 // void write( Object x )  --> Place x as stored value
11
12 template <class Object>
13 class MemoryCell
14 {
15   public:
16     explicit MemoryCell( const Object & initVal = Object( ) )
17       : storedValue( initVal ) { }
18
19       // Public member functions
20     const Object & read( ) const
21       { return storedValue; }
22     void write( const Object & x )
23       { storedValue = x; }
24
25   private:
26     Object storedValue;
27 };
```

Figure 3.8 Complete declaration of the `MemoryCell` class.

this version we do not separate the interface and implementation in order to illustrate the most basic syntax. We revise this code shortly to do so because, as we discussed in Section 2.3, such separation is usually preferable.

A class template must have the `template` specification prior to the interface. Objects of a class template type must be instantiated with the template parameters.

The class template syntax is similar to the function template syntax; we merely add a template specification (shown on line 12 in Figure 3.8). Note that `write` accepts a parameter passed by constant reference and that `read` returns its parameter by constant reference. When possible, constant references should be used instead of call/return by value because, if `Object` is a large object, making a copy could be inefficient (or illegal if the copy constructor for `Object` is either disabled or not defined). Do not use constant reference returns blindly, however. Remember that you cannot return a reference to an automatic variable. Figure 3.9 shows a simple `main` that uses the class template.

```
// Exercise the MemoryCell class.
int main( )
{
    MemoryCell<int> m;

    m.write( 5 );
    cout << "Cell contents are " << m.read( ) << endl;

    return 0;
}
```

Figure 3.9 A simple test routine to show how `MemoryCell` objects are accessed.

You need to take note of two features of this routine. First, in the commented description of the interface, we do not specify whether a function is a constant member or how parameters are passed. To do so would merely duplicate information clearly specified in the interface code. Second, `Object` must have a zero-parameter constructor because the default constructor is used for `MemoryCell`, and it is a member-by-member call of the zero-parameter constructors.

If we implement class templates as a single unit, there is little syntax baggage. Many class templates, in fact, are implemented this way because currently separate compilation of templates does not work well on many platforms. Therefore, in many cases, the entire class with its implementation must be placed in a `.h` file. Popular implementations of the STL follow this strategy.

However, eventually, separate compilation will work, and separating the class template's interface and implementation as for classes in Chapter 2 will be better. Unfortunately, this approach adds some syntax baggage.

Each member function must be declared as a template.

Figure 3.10 shows the interface for the class template. That part is, of course, simple enough because it is identical to the entire class that we have already shown in Figure 3.9, with the inline implementations removed. For the implementation, we have a collection of function templates. Thus each function must include the template line, and when we use the scope operator, the name of the class must be instantiated with the template argument. In Figure 3.11, then, the name of the class is `MemoryCell<Object>`.

Figure 3.12 gives a layout of the general format used. Boldface items are to be typed exactly as shown. Although the syntax seem innocuous enough, it can get fairly substantial. For instance, to define `operator=` in the interface requires no extra baggage. In the implementation, we would have the horrendous code shown in Figure 3.13.

```
// Memory cell interface; same as in Figure 3.8.

template <class Object>
class MemoryCell
{
  public:
    explicit MemoryCell( const Object & initVal = Object( ) );
    const Object & read( ) const;
    void write( const Object & x );

  private:
    Object storedValue;
};
```

Figure 3.10 The `MemoryCell` class template interface.

```
// Implementation of the class members.

#include "MemoryCell.h"

template <class Object>
MemoryCell<Object>::MemoryCell( const Object & initVal )
  : storedValue( initVal )
{
}

template <class Object>
const Object & MemoryCell<Object>::read( ) const
{
    return storedValue;
}

template <class Object>
void MemoryCell<Object>::write( const Object & x )
{
    storedValue = x;
}
```

Figure 3.11 The `MemoryCell` class template implementation.

```
// Typical template interface.
template <class Object>
class ClassName
{
  public:
    // Public members
  private:
    // Private members
};


// Typical member implementation.
template <class Object>
ReturnType
ClassName<Object>::MemberName( Parameter List ) /* const */
{
      // Member body
}
```

Figure 3.12 Typical layout for template interface and member functions.

```
template <class Object>
const MemoryCell<Object> &
MemoryCell<Object>::operator=( const MemoryCell<Object> & rhs )
{
    if( this != &rhs )
        storedValue = rhs.storedValue;
    return *this;
}
```

Figure 3.13 Illustration of template syntax for `operator=`.

Typically, the declaration part of the more complex functions no longer fit on one line and need to be split as in Figure 3.13.

Even if the interface and implementation of the class template are separated, few compilers will automatically handle separate compilation correctly. The simplest, most portable, solution is to add an `#include` directive at the end of the interface file to import the implementation. It is added to the online code (for class templates only). Alternative solutions involve adding explicit instantiations for each type as a separate `.cpp` file. These details change rapidly, so you should consult the compiler's documentation to find the proper alternative.

3.4.2 Implementing the **vector** Class Template

We can use templates to design a safe, dynamically expanding array.

Our next example is a complete class that supports arrays in the manner of most programming languages. It provides index range checking, allows copying between identically typed arrays, and supports dynamically changing array sizes. Because the `string` class in Section 2.6 supported similar operations, the only new item is the use of templates in this class.

Our `vector` class supports array indexing, resizing, and copying and performs index range checking (the STL version does not). Because crucial functions are inlined, you can expect this version to be as efficient as the STL version, except for the overhead of index range checking. The class uses the symbol `NO_CHECK`, which if defined, causes the range checking code not to be compiled. All compilers provide options to define symbols as part of the compilation command; check your compiler's documentation for details. All code in the text makes use of the `vector` class. However you can use the STL version or this version; all member functions in this `vector` class are present in the STL version.

The `vector` class is implemented by storing a primitive array (`objects`) as a data member. Recall once again that a primitive array is a second-class object, implemented as a pointer to a block of memory large enough to store the array objects. Because the primitive array is represented as a pointer, the size of the array is unknown and needs to be maintained in a separate variable (`theCapacity`). Memory for the array is obtained by calling the `new[]` operator, which occurs in the constructor, the assignment operator, and the `reserve` operation. The memory needs to be reclaimed by `delete[]`, which occurs in the destructor and the assignment and `reserve` operations (for assignment, the old array is reclaimed *before* allocation of the new array; in `reserve`, the old array is reclaimed *after* allocation of the new array).

The class interface, shown in Figure 3.14, includes implementations of the functions that are one-liners, so as to avoid the overhead of function calls. The compiler can aggressively inline these functions. Normally, doing so is not worthwhile, but fast `vector` operations are certain to be crucial in any application. The remaining member functions are shown in Figure 3.15.

3.5 Templates of Templates: A **matrix** Class

As mentioned in Section 1.2.7, the C++ library does not provide first-class multidimensional arrays. However, we can write quickly a reasonable class to support two-dimensional arrays. We call this class a `matrix`. The basic idea is to use a `vector` of `vectors`. The code for the `matrix` class is shown in Figure 3.16.

```
// vector class interface. Supports construction with
// initial size (default is 0), automatic destruction,
// access of the current size, array indexing via [], deep
// copy, and resizing. Index range checking is performed
// unless NO_CHECK is defined.

template <class Object>
class vector
{
  public:
    explicit vector( int initSize = 0 )
      : theSize( initSize ), theCapacity( initSize )
      { objects = new Object[ theCapacity ]; }
    vector( const vector & rhs ) : objects( NULL )
      { operator=( rhs ); }
    ~vector( )
      { delete [ ] objects; }

    Object & operator[]( int index )
    {
                                                #ifndef  NO_CHECK
        if( index < 0 || index >= size( ) )
            throw ArrayIndexOutOfBoundsException( );
                                                #endif
        return objects[ index ];
    }

    const Object & operator[]( int index ) const
    {
                                                #ifndef NO_CHECK
        if( index < 0 || index >= size( ) )
            throw ArrayIndexOutOfBoundsException( );
                                                #endif
        return objects[ index ];
    }

    const vector & operator= ( const vector & rhs );
    void resize( int newSize );
    void reserve( int newCapacity );
    void push_back( const Object & x );
    int size( ) const
      { return theSize; }
    int capacity( ) const
      { return theCapacity; }

  private:
    int theSize;
    int theCapacity;
    Object * objects;
};
```

Figure 3.14 The *vector.h* file.

```
#include "vector.h"

template <class Object>
const vector<Object> &
vector<Object>::operator=( const vector<Object> & rhs )
{
    if( this != &rhs )                              // Alias test
    {
        delete [ ] objects;                         // Reclaim old
        theSize = rhs.size( );                      // Copy size
        theCapacity = rhs.capacity( );              //  and capacity
        objects = new Object[ capacity( ) ];        // Allocate
        for( int k = 0; k < size( ); k++ )          // Copy items
            objects[ k ] = rhs.objects[ k ];
    }
    return *this;                          // Return reference to self
}

template <class Object>
void vector<Object>::push_back( const Object & x )
{
    if( theSize == theCapacity )                   // If no room
        reserve( 2 * theCapacity + 1 );            //  Make room
    objects[ theSize++ ] = x;                      // Add x
}

template <class Object>
void vector<Object>::resize( int newSize )
{
    if( newSize > theCapacity )                   // If expanding
        reserve( newSize * 2 );                   //   Get space
    theSize = newSize;                            // Set size
}

template <class Object>
void vector<Object>::reserve( int newCapacity )
{
    Object *oldArray = objects;                    // Save old
    int numToCopy = newCapacity < theSize ?        // Compute # to
                    newCapacity : theSize;         //   copy

    objects = new Object[ newCapacity ];          // Allocate new
    for( int k = 0; k < numToCopy; k++ )          // Copy items
        objects[ k ] = oldArray[ k ];

    theSize = numToCopy                           // Set size
    theCapacity = newCapacity;                    // Set capacity

    delete [ ] oldArray;                          // Reclaim old
}
```

Figure 3.15 The *vector.cpp* file.

```
template <class Object>
class matrix
{
  public:
    matrix( int rows, int cols ) : array( rows )
    {
        for( int i = 0; i < rows; i++ )
            array[ i ].resize( cols );
    }

      // Copy constructor -- not really needed.
    matrix( const matrix & rhs ) : array( rhs.array ) { }

    const vector<Object> & operator[]( int row ) const
      { return array[ row ]; }
    vector<Object> & operator[]( int row )
      { return array[ row ]; }

    int numrows( ) const
      { return array.size( ); }
    int numcols( ) const
      { return numrows( ) > 0 ? array[ 0 ].size( ) : 0; }

    void push_back( const vector<Object> & newRow )
      { array.push_back( newRow ); }

  private:
    vector< vector<Object> > array;
};
```

Figure 3.16 A complete `matrix` class.

3.5.1 The Data Members, Constructor, and Basic Accessors

Be sure that you have space between > and > when instantiating layers of templates.

The matrix is represented by an `array` data member declared to be a `vector` of `vector<Object>`. Note that, in the declaration of `array`, white space *must* separate the two > characters; otherwise, the compiler will interpret the >> token as a shift operation. In other words, we must write

```
vector<vector<Object> > array;    // white space needed
```

The constructor first constructs `array`, as having `rows` entries each of type `vector<Object>`. Since each entry of `array` is constructed with the zero-parameter constructor, it follows that each entry of array is a `vector<object>` of size 0. Thus we have `rows` zero-length vectors of `Object`.

The body of the constructor is then entered and each row is resized to have cols columns. Thus the constructor terminates with what appears to be a two-dimensional array. The numrows and numcols accessors are then easily implemented as shown. We also provide a push_back method that adds a new row; it is trivially implemented by a call to the underlying vector's push_back.

3.5.2 **operator[]**

The idea of operator[] is that, if we have a matrix m, then m[i] should return a vector corresponding to row i of matrix m. If it does, m[i][j] gives the entry in position j for vector m[i], using the normal vector indexing operator. Thus the matrix operator[] is to return a vector<Object>, not an Object.

We use the now standard trick of writing both an accessor and a mutator version of operator[] that differ in their return types. The accessor version of operator[] returns a constant reference, and the mutator version returns the simple reference.

3.5.3 Destructor, Copy Assignment, and Copy Constructor

The destructor, operator=, and copy constructor defaults are all acceptable because the only data member is a vector, for which the Big-Three are meaningfully defined. Thus we have all the code needed for a fully functioning matrix class. Some compilers that have template bugs may require a trivial implementation of the copy constructor. For that reason only, a copy constructor is provided.

3.6 Fancy Templates

Our discussion of templates has only scratched the surface. The template facility of C++ has recently been expanded. Many of the new additions are used to implement the STL. Unfortunately, many also do not work everywhere. We discuss three advanced features, but only the first works on most platforms.

3.6.1 Multiple Template Parameters

The proposed template facility allows multiple instantiation parameters, such as

```
template <class KeyType, class ValueType>
class Map
{
    ...
};
```

Here the `Map` template requires two types for instantiation. For instance, to declare a `Map` that takes a city name (which is a `string`) as the item to search for and returns a zip code (which is an `int`) as the lookup value, we can declare

```
Map<string,int> zipCodes;
```

In fact, `map` (lowercase `m`) is part of the STL, and we provide an implementation of it in Part IV.

3.6.2 Default Template Parameters

Just as functions can have default parameters, templates can have default template types. Here is an example:

```
template <class KeyType, class ValueType=string>
class Map
{
    ...
};
```

We can now make the following declarations:

```
Map<int,int> m1;    // KeyType==int, ValueType==int
Map<int> m2;        // KeyType==int, ValueType==string
```

Default template parameters are widely used in the STL. Unfortunately, not all compilers support them.

3.6.3 The Reserved Word `typename`

A recent addition to the C++ Standard allows the use of the new reserved word `typename` instead of `class` in the template parameter list. In other words, we can write

```
template <typename Object>
class MemoryCell
{
    ...
};
```

Everything else is the same. The logic is that `class` is misleading because the template can be expanded with both class types and primitive types. However, not all compilers support `typename`, and the language designer suggests sticking with `class`. Who are we to argue?

There is a second use of `typename`, and it is shown in Figure 7.6, and discussed in Chapter 7, footnote 3.

3.7 Bugs Associated with Templates

We close our discussion of templates with some warnings. Templates are a relatively recent addition to the language, and not all the details have been completely worked out. Many compilers have bugs or unimplemented features that are a direct consequence of templates. We will describe some of the bugs that were noticed in the preparation of this text (note that some, or possibly none, might apply in your case).

3.7.1 Bad Error Messages and Inconsistent Rules

The rules on when templates need instantiation seem to change frequently, and compiler writers are having a hard time keeping up with the changes. You may find that your compiler is accepting old syntax, and when you port to another system it will complain that you have forgotten an explicit instantiation or, in some cases, provided an instantiation that you should not have. Some compilers do not accept current syntax, such as the explicit instantiation of a function template call.

3.7.2 Template-Matching Algorithms

Sometimes, the matching algorithm breaks when templates are involved. The most common example is that of function templates.

3.7.3 Nested Classes in a Template

Not all compilers support the nesting of classes in class templates. If yours does not, you will have to unnest the classes and make the original outer class a friend of the original inner class. Because some compilers do not support nested classes in templates, we use them sparingly in our code.

3.7.4 Static Members in Class Templates

Many compilers fail to handle correctly static methods and data members in class templates. As a result, we avoid their use in our code.

Summary

In this chapter we provided a brief discussion of the C++ template facilities. Templates allow us to write general classes and functions, thus helping us achieve the goal of code reuse. We use templates throughout the text.

In Chapter 4 we look at another important mechanism for code reuse: inheritance.

Objects of the Game

insertion sort A simple sorting algorithm that is appropriate for small inputs. (p. 100)

instantiation Replacement of generic types of a template with a specific type or types, which logically creates a new function or class. (p. 98)

template A template is a design for code and allows us to write routines that work for arbitrary types without having to know what these types will be. (p. 98)

`typedef` A simple mechanism to allow generic routines. (p. 98)

Common Errors

1. The template line must precede the template class interface and each member function definition.
2. A common error is forgetting an instantiation of a template, which occurs frequently in member function definitions. The definition shown in Figure 3.12 is typical of the instantiations that are required.
3. When instantiating a class template with an object that is itself a class template, white space must be used to separate successive `>`s. Otherwise, `>>` is interpreted as a shift operator.
4. When writing class templates, you must be especially careful about parameter-passing mechanisms. Avoid passing unknown types by copying. Use either reference or constant reference types. Always assume that you are working with a large object.

5. Sometimes when a template is instantiated, an ambiguity develops. For instance, if we have two constructors, `T(int)` and `T(Object)`, for class template `T` and `Object` is an `int`, we have an ambiguity. When designing classes, be sure that no ambiguities can develop.
6. When a class template is instantiated, all needed operations must be available. For instance, the insertion sort template needs to have `operator<` defined for whatever `Comparable` is instantiated. Otherwise, an error will be detected at link time. Clearly state what conditions must be satisfied by the template parameters.
7. If a class template uses call by value and the instantiated type has a disabled copy constructor, a compile-time error will be detected.
8. All the errors that occur for classes also occur for class templates.
9. Be aware of the limitations of your compiler. Many compilers still have buggy template implementations.
10. Generally, function templates do not separately compile.

On the Internet

The available files are:

FuncTemplates.cpp	Illustrates the `swap` funcion template.
InsSort.cpp	Contains `insertionSort` and `main`, shown in Figures 3.4–3.7.
MemoryCell.h	Contains the `MemoryCell` class (template)[2] interface shown in Figure 3.10.
MemoryCell.cpp	Contains the `MemoryCell` class implementation.
TestMemoryCell.cpp	Contains a program to test `MemoryCell`.
vector.h	Contains the `vector` class interface shown in Figure 3.14. (The actual class is slightly more complex, as described in Chapter 7.)
vector.cpp	Contains the `vector` class implementation.
matrix.h	Contains the `matrix` class shown in Figure 3.16.

2. Throughout the text often we will omit the word **template** for brevity, when the meaning is implied.

Exercises

In Short

3.1. Write a function template to sort three `Comparable` objects.

3.2. When templates are used, what types of errors are detected when the function template is scanned? What errors are detected when the function is instantiated?

3.3. Describe the syntax for class templates.

In Practice

3.4. Write function templates `min` and `max`, each of which accepts two parameters.

3.5. Write function templates `min` and `max`, each of which accepts a `vector`.

3.6. In many situations `operator<` is defined for an object, but you also need `operator>`. Assume that `operator==` is unavailable. Explore the possibility of writing an `operator>` template that calls `operator<`.

3.7. A `SingleBuffer` class supports `get` and `put`. The `SingleBuffer` stores a single item and a data member that indicates whether the `SingleBuffer` is logically empty. A `put` may be applied only to an empty buffer and inserts an item to the buffer. A `get` may be applied only to a nonempty buffer and deletes and returns the contents of the buffer. Write a class template to implement `SingleBuffer`. Throw an exception to signal an error. What is the return type of `get` and why?

Programming Projects

3.8. Implement an insertion sort that takes a primitive array and its size as a single parameter.

3.9. Implement a routine that reads an arbitrary number of `Object`s and stores them in a `vector`.

3.10. Add a `resize` member function and a zero-parameter constructor to the `matrix` class.

3.11. Write a class template for the `Rational` class in Chapter 2. The numerator and denominator should have a generic type.

3.12. Modify the `vector` class as follows.

a. Add a function that returns a reference to the internal array.
b. Add a constructor that takes a primitive array and a size.
c. Allow the `vector` to be constructed with a lower and upper bound that represent the valid index range. The size of the array is `upper-lower+1`.
d. Add a function, `fill`, that fills all entries with a given value.

Chapter 4

Inheritance

As mentioned in Chapter 2, an important goal of object-oriented programming is code reuse. Just as engineers use components over and over in their designs, programmers should be able to reuse objects rather than repeatedly reimplementing them. In Chapter 3 we described one mechanism for reuse provided by C++: the template. Templates are appropriate if the basic functionality of the code is type-independent. The other mechanism for code reuse is *inheritance*. Inheritance allows us to extend the functionality of an object. In other words, we can create new types with extended (or restricted) properties of the original type. Inheritance goes a long way toward meeting the goal for code reuse.

In this chapter, we show:

- how the general principles of inheritance and the object-oriented concept of polymorphism relate to code reuse,
- how inheritance is implemented in C++,
- how a collection of classes can be derived from a single abstract class, and
- how run-time binding decisions, rather than compile-time linking decisions, can be made for these classes.

4.1 What Is Inheritance?

On one level *inheritance* is the fundamental object-oriented principle governing the reuse of code among related classes. Inheritance models the IS-A relationship. In an **IS-A relationship,** the derived class *is a* (variation of the) base class. For example, a Circle IS-A Shape and a Car IS-A Vehicle. However, an Ellipse IS-NOT-A Circle. Inheritance relationships form *hierarchies*. For instance, we can extend Car to other classes, as a ForeignCar IS-A Car (and pays tariffs) and a DomesticCar IS-A Car (and does not pay tariffs), and so on.

In an *IS-A relationship*, the derived class is a (variation of the) base class.

In a *HAS-A relationship*, the derived class has a (instance of the) base class. Composition is used to model HAS-A relationships.

Another type of relationship is a HAS-A (or IS-COMPOSED-OF) relationship. In a **HAS-A relationship,** the derived class has a (instance of the) base class. This type of relationship does not possess the properties that would be natural in an inheritance hierarchy. An example of a HAS-A relationship is that a car HAS-A steering wheel. Generally, HAS-A relationships should not be modeled by inheritance. Instead, they should be modeled with the technique of *composition*, in which the components are simply made private data fields.

The C++ language itself makes some use of inheritance in implementing its class libraries. Two examples are exceptions and files.

- *Exceptions*. C++ defines in `<stdexcept>` the class `exception`. There are several kinds of exceptions, including `bad_alloc` and `bad_cast`. Figure 4.1 illustrates some of the classes in the `exception` hierarchy. Each is a separate class, but for all of them, the `what` method can be used to return a (primitive) string that details an error message.
- *I/O*. As shown in Figure 4.2, the streams hierarchy (`istream`, `ifstream`, etc.) uses inheritance. The streams hierarchy is more complex than shown.

In addition, systems such as Visual C++ and Borland CBuilder provide class libraries that can be used to design graphical user interfaces (GUIs). These libraries, which define components such as buttons, choice-lists, text-areas, and windows (all in different flavors), make heavy use of inheritance.

In all cases, the inheritance models an IS-A relationship. A button IS-A component. A `bad_cast` IS-A `exception`. An `ifstream` IS-A `istream` (but not vice-versa!). Because of IS-A relationships, the fundamental property

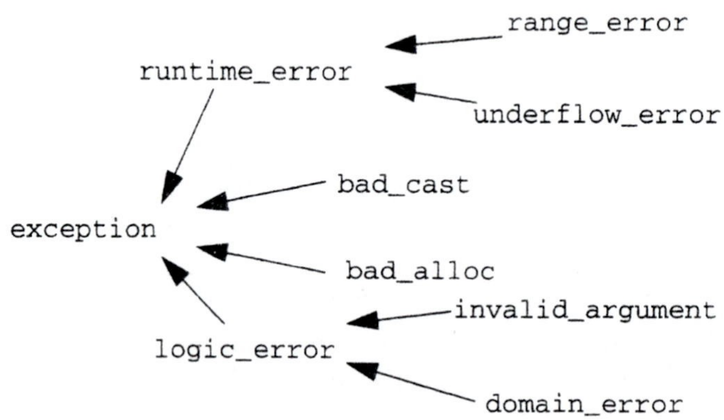

Figure 4.1 Part of the `exception` hierarchy.

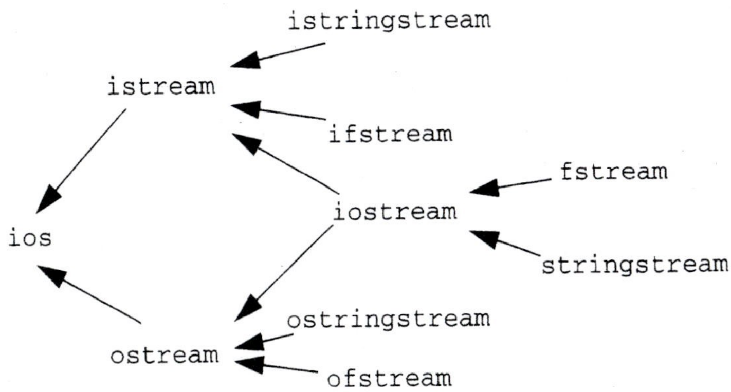

Figure 4.2 Part of the streams hierarchy.

of inheritance guarantees that any method that can be performed by `istream` can also be performed by `ifstream` and that an `ifstream` object can always be referenced by an `istream` reference. Note that the reverse is not true. This is why I/O operations are typically written in terms of `istream` and `ostream`.

Because `what` is a method available in the `exception` class, if we need to catch various exceptions (see Figure 4.1) we can use a `catch` handler and write:[1]

```
catch( const exception & e ) { cout << e.what( ) << endl; }
```

If `e` references a `bad_cast` object, the call to `e.what()` makes sense. The reason is that an `exception` object supports the `what` method, and a `bad_cast` IS-A `exception`, meaning that it supports at least as much as `exception`. Depending on the circumstances of the class hierarchy, the `what` method could be invariant or it could be *specialized* for each different class. When a method is invariant over a hierarchy—that is, it always has the same functionality for all classes in the hierarchy—we avoid having to rewrite an implementation of a class method.

1. Exceptions are handled by `try/catch` blocks. An illustration of the syntax is shown later in this chapter in Figure 4.7. Code that might throw the exception is placed in a `try` block, and the exception is handled in a `catch` block. Because the exception object is passed into the `catch` block, any public methods defined for the exception object can be used on it and any public data defined in the exception object can be examined.

In *polymorphism* a variable can reference objects of several different types. When operations are applied to the variable, the operation appropriate to the referenced object is automatically selected.

The call to `what` also illustrates an important object-oriented principle known as **polymorphism,** which is the ability of a reference variable to reference objects of several different types. When operations are applied to the variable, the operation that is appropriate to the actual referenced object is automatically selected. The same is true for pointer variables (recall that a reference really is a pointer). In the case of an `exception` reference, a run time decision is made: The `what` method for the object that `e` actually references at run time is the one used. This action is known as *dynamic,* or *late, binding*. Unfortunately, although dynamic binding is the preferred behavior, it is not the default in C++. This language flaw leads to complications.

***Inheritance* allows the derivation of classes from a base class without disturbing the implementation of the base class.**

Inheritance is the process of deriving a class from a *base class* without disturbing the implementation of the base class. The **base class** is the foundation for inheritance. A **derived class** is a completely new class that inherits all the properties of the base class, with all the public methods available to the base class becoming public methods—with identical implementations—of the derived class. The derived class can then add data members and additional methods and change the meaning of the inherited methods. However, the base class is completely unaffected by any changes that are made in the derived class. Thus, in designing the derived class, breaking the base class is impossible, which greatly simplifies the task of software maintenance.

A *derived class* is a completely new class that inherits the properties, public methods, and implementations of the class from which it was derived.

A derived class is type compatible with its base class. In other words, a reference variable of the base class type may reference an object of the derived class, but not vice versa (and similarly for pointers). Sibling classes (i.e., classes derived from a common class) are not type compatible.

If *X* IS-A *Y*, then *X* is a *subclass* of *Y* and *Y* is a *superclass* of *X*. These relationships are transitive.

As mentioned earlier, the use of inheritance typically generates a hierarchy of classes. Figure 4.1 illustrated a small part of the `exception` hierarchy. Note that `range_error` is indirectly, rather than directly, derived from `exception`. This fact is transparent to the user of the classes because IS-A relationships are transitive. In other words, if *X* IS-A *Y* and *Y* IS-A *Z*, then *X* IS-A *Z*. The `exception` hierarchy highlights the typical design approach of factoring commonalities into base classes and then specializing in the derived classes. In this hierarchy, we say that the derived class is a *subclass* of the base class and the base class is a *superclass* of the derived class. These relationships are transitive.

The arrows in the hierarchy diagrams reflect the modern convention of pointing toward the top (or *root*) of the hierarchy. The stream hierarchy illustrates some fancier design decisions. Among other things, commonality among `istream` and `ostream` is factored out and placed in `ios`. Also, `iostream` inherits from both `istream` and `ostream`, illustrating multiple inheritance.

In the next several sections we examine the following issues.

- What syntax is used to derive a new class from an existing base class?
- How does this derivation affect public or private status?
- How do we specialize a method?
- How do we factor common differences into an abstract class and then create a hierarchy?
- How do we specify that dynamic binding be used?
- How can we—and should we—derive a new class from more than one class (*multiple inheritance*)?

4.2 Inheritance Basics

Public inheritance models an IS-A relationship.

Private inheritance models a HAS-A relationship.

Because a derived class inherits all the properties of a base class, it can then add data members, disable functions, alter functions, and add new functions, becoming a completely new class. A typical layout for inheritance is shown in Figure 4.3, with C++ tokens shown in boldface. The form of inheritance described here and used almost exclusively throughout the text is **public inheritance,** the process by which all public members of the base class remain public in the derived class. Note that the word `public` after the colon on line 1 signifies public inheritance. Without it, we have **private inheritance,** the process occasionally used to implement a HAS-A relationship; even public members of the base class remain hidden. What we want, though, is public inheritance because it models an IS-A relationship. Let us briefly describe a derived class.

- Generally all data are private, so we just add additional data members in the derived class by specifying them in the private section.

```
 1 class Derived : public Base
 2 {
 3     // Any members that are not listed are inherited unchanged
 4     // except for constructor, destructor,
 5     // copy constructor, and operator=
 6   public:
 7     // Constructors, and destructors if defaults are not good
 8     // Base members whose definitions are to change in Derived
 9     // Additional public member functions
10   private:
11     // Additional data members (generally private)
12     // Additional private member functions
13     // Base members that should be disabled in Derived
14 };
```

Figure 4.3 General layout of public inheritance.

The derived class inherits all member functions from the base class. It may accept them, disallow them, or redefine them. Additionally, it can define new functions.

- Any base class member functions not specified in the derived class are inherited unchanged, with the following exceptions: constructor, destructor, copy constructor, and `operator=`. For them the typical defaults apply, with the inherited portion considered to be a member. Thus by default a copy constructor is applied to the inherited portion (considered to be a single entity) and then member by member. We present more specifics in Section 4.2.6.
- Any base class member function that is declared in the derived class' private section is disabled in the derived class.[2]
- Any base class member function declared in the derived class's public section requires an overriding definition that will be applied to objects of the derived class.
- Additional member functions can be added in the derived class.

4.2.1 Visibility Rules

Recall that any member declared with private visibility is accessible only to methods of the class. Thus any private members in the base class are not accessible to the derived class.

Occasionally, we want the derived class to have access to the base class members. There are several options. One is to use public access. However, it allows access to other classes in addition to derived classes. Another is to use a friend declaration, but this approach is also poor design and would require friend declaration for each derived class.

A *protected class member* is private to every class except a derived class.

If we want to allow access only to derived classes, we can make members protected. A **protected class member** is private to every class except a derived class. However, declaring data members as protected or public violates the spirit of encapsulation and information hiding and is generally done only as a matter of programming expediency. A better alternative usually is to write accessor and mutator methods. But, if a protected declaration allows you to avoid convoluted code, then using it is not unreasonable. In this text, we use protected data members precisely for this reason. We also use protected methods in this text, which allows a derived class to inherit an internal method without making it accessible outside the class hierarchy. Figure 4.4 shows the visibility of members in certain situations.

2. This is bad style because it violates the IS-A relationship: The derived class can no longer do everything that the base class can.

Public Inheritance Situation	Public	Protected	Private
Base class member function accessing *M*	Yes	Yes	Yes
Derived class member function accessing *M*	Yes	Yes	No
`main`, accessing *B.M*	Yes	No	No
`main`, accessing *D.M*	Yes	No	No
Derived class member function accessing *B.M*	Yes	No	No
B is an object of the base class; *D* is an object of the publicly derived class; *M* is a member of the base class.			

Figure 4.4 Access rules that depend on *M*'s visibility in the base class.

4.2.2 The Constructor and Base Class Initialization

Constructors should be defined for each derived class. If no constructor is written, a single zero-parameter default constructor is generated. This constructor will call the base class zero-parameter constructor for the inherited portion and then apply the default initialization for any additional data members.

If no constructor is written, a single zero-parameter default constructor is generated that calls the base class zero-parameter constructor for the inherited portion and then applies the default initialization for any additional data members.

Constructing a derived class object by first constructing its inherited portion is standard practice. In fact, it is done by default even if an explicit derived class constructor is given. This action is natural because encapsulation means that the inherited portion is a single entity, and the base class constructor tells us how to initialize this single entity.

Base class constructors can be explicitly called by name in the initializer list. Thus the default constructor for a derived class, in reality, is

```
Derived( ) : Base( )
{
}
```

The base class initializer can be called with parameters that match a base class constructor. As an example, Figure 4.5 illustrates the `UnderflowException` class that could be used in implementing data

A base class initializer is used to call the base class constructor.

```
class UnderflowException : public underflow_error
{
  public:
    UnderflowException( const string & msg = "" )
      : underflow_error( msg.c_str( ) ) { }
};
```

Figure 4.5 Constructor for the new exception class `Underflow` that uses base class initializer list.

structures. The `UnderflowException` is thrown when an attempt is made to extract something from an empty data structure. An `UnderflowException` object is constructed by providing an optional string. The `underflow_error` class specification requires a primitive string, so we need to use an initializer list. As the `UnderflowException` object adds no data members, the construction method is simply to use the `underflow_error` constructor to construct the inherited portion.

If the base class initializer is not provided, an automatic call to the base class constructor with no parameters is generated. If there is no such base class constructor, a compiler error results. Thus, in this case, initializer lists might be mandatory.

4.2.3 Adding Members

Because a derived class inherits from its base class the behavior of the base class, all methods defined for the base class are now defined for the derived class. In this section we examine the consequences of adding extra methods and data members.

Our `vector` class in Section 3.4.2 throws an exception if an out-of-bounds index is detected. The only information that it passes back is that an error has occurred. Let us look at an alternative that we could have used (note that `exception` and `<stdexcept>` are relatively new language additions, which is why we elected not to use them in the remainder of this text). The alternative stores information about what went wrong inside the exception object, providing accessors to get this information. However, it still IS-A `exception`, meaning that it can be used any place that an `exception` can be used. The new class is shown in Figure 4.6.

The `BadIndex` class has one constructor and three methods (in addition to defaults for copying and destruction that we ignore for now). The constructor accepts two parameters. It initializes the inherited `exception` portion by using a zero-parameter constructor. It then uses the two parameters to store the index that caused the error and the size of the `vector`. Presumably, the `vector` has code such as

```
// See Figure 3.14
Object & operator[]( int index )
{
    if( index < 0 || index >= size( ) )
        throw BadIndex( index, size( ) );
    return objects[ index ];
}
```

```
// Example of a derived class that adds new members.

class BadIndex : public exception
{
  public:
    BadIndex( int idx, int sz )
      : index( idx ), size( sz ) { }

    int getIndex( ) const
      { return index; }
    int getSize( ) const
      { return size; }

  private:
    int index;
    int size;
};
```

Figure 4.6 The `BadIndex` class, derived from the `exception` class.

The three methods available for `BadIndex` are `getIndex`, `getSize`, and `what`. The behavior of `what` is unchanged from the `exception` class.

Besides the new functionality, `BadIndex` has two data members in addition to the data members inherited from `exception`. What data were inherited from `exception`? The answer is, We do not know (unless we look at the `exception` class design). Moreover, if the inherited data are private, they are inaccessible. However, we do not need to know. Furthermore, our design works regardless of the underlying data representation in `exception`. Thus changes to the private implementation of `exception` will not require any changes to `BadIndex`.

Figure 4.7 shows how the `BadIndex` class could be used. If there is a `BadIndex` exception thrown, it is caught at lines 11-15, and information about it can be printed by calling the exception's public member functions. Note that, as a `BadIndex` IS-A `exception`, at line 11 we could catch it with an `exception` reference.[3] We could also apply the `what` method to get some information. However, we could not apply the `getIndex` and `getSize` methods because they are not defined for all `exception` objects.

Because the predefined `exception` class is a recent language addition, the online code has a collection of exceptions rooted at class `DSException`.

3. Even though the `BadIndex` object is an automatic variable in `operator[]`, it can be caught by reference because thrown objects are guaranteed longer lifetimes than normal function arguments.

```
// Use the BadIndex exception.
int main( )
{
    NewVector<int> v( 10 );

    try
    {
        for( int i = 0; i <= v.size( ); i++ )    // off-by-one
            v[ i ] = 0;
    }
    catch( const BadIndex & e )
    {
        cout << e.what( ) << ", index=" << e.getIndex( )
             << ", size=" << e.getSize( ) << endl;
    }

    return 0;
}
```

Figure 4.7 Using the `BadIndex` class.

4.2.4 Overriding a Method

The derived class method must have the same or compatible return type and signature.

We can override methods from the base class in the derived class by simply providing a derived class method with the same signature. A derived class method must have the same or compatible return type (the notion of a compatible return type is new and is discussed in Section 4.4.4.)

Partial overriding involves calling a base class method with the scope operator.

Sometimes we want the derived class method to invoke the base class method to augment a base class method rather than doing something entirely different. This is known as **partial overriding**. The `scope` operator can be used to call a base class method. Here is an example:

```
class Workaholic : public Worker
{
  public:
    void doWork( )
    {
        Worker::doWork( );   // Work like a Worker
        drinkCoffee( );      // Take a break
        Worker::doWork( );   // Work like a Worker some more
    }
};
```

4.2.5 Static and Dynamic Binding

Figure 4.8 illustrates the fact that we can declare `Worker` and `Workaholic` objects in the same scope because the compiler can deduce which `doWork` method to apply. Here, `w` is a `Worker` and `wh` is a `Workaholic`, so the determination of which `doWork` is used in the two calls at line 4 is computable at compile time. We call the decision made at compile time about which function to use to resolve an overload **static binding/overloading.**

In *static binding*, the decision about which function to use to resolve an overload is made at compile time.

However, the code in Figure 4.9 is more complicated. If `x` is zero, we create a `Worker` object; otherwise, we create a `Workaholic` object. Recall that, as a `Workaholic` IS-A `Worker`, a `Workaholic` can be accessed by a pointer to a `Worker`. Any method that we might call for `Worker` will have a meaning for `Workaholic` objects. Hence, public inheritance automatically defines a type conversion from a pointer to a derived class to a pointer to the base class. Thus we can declare that `wptr` is a pointer to the base class `Worker` and then dynamically allocate either a `Worker` or `Workaholic` object for it to point at. When we get to line 9, which `doWork` gets called?

```
1   Worker w;
2   Workaholic wh;
3       ...
4   w.doWork( ); wh.doWork( );
```

Figure 4.8 The `Worker` and `Workaholic` classes, with calls to `doWork` that are done automatically and correctly.

```
1   Worker *wptr;
2   cin >> x;
3   if( x != 0 )
4       wptr = new Workaholic( );
5   else
6       wptr = new Worker( );
7
8       ...
9   wptr->doWork( );        // Which doWork is used?
```

Figure 4.9 The `Worker` and `Workaholic` objects accessed though a pointer to a `Worker`; which version of `doWork` is used depends on whether `doWork` is declared virtual in `Worker`.

If a member function is declared to be virtual, *dynamic binding* is used. The decision about which function to use to resolve an overload is made at run time, if it cannot be determined at compile time.

The decision about which `doWork` to use can be made at compile time or at run time. If the decision is made at compile time (static binding), we must use `Worker`'s `doWork` because that is the type of `*wptr` at compile time. If `wptr` is actually pointing at `Workaholic`, this decision is wrong. Because the type of object that `wptr` is actually pointing at can be determined only as the program runs, this decision must be made at run time. A run-time decision to apply the method corresponding to the actual referenced object is called **dynamic binding.** As discussed earlier in this chapter, it is almost always the preferred course of action.

However a run-time decision incurs some run-time overhead because it requires that the program maintain extra information and that the compiler generate code to perform the test. This overhead was once thought to be significant and, although other languages such as Smalltalk and Objective C use dynamic binding by default, C++ does not.

In general, if a function is redefined in a derived class, it should be declared virtual in the base class.

Static binding is used for a *nonvirtual function* when the function is invariant over the inheritance hierarchy.

Instead, you must ask for it by specifying that the function is virtual. A **virtual function** uses dynamic binding if a compile-time binding decision is impossible to make. A nonvirtual function will always use static binding. The default, as we implied earlier, is that functions are nonvirtual. This condition is unfortunate because we now know that the overhead is relatively minor. As a result, a nonvirtual function should be used only when the function is invariant over the inheritance hierarchy.

Virtualness is inherited, so it can be indicated in the base class. Thus if the base class declares that a function is virtual (in its declaration), the decision can be made at run time; otherwise, it is made at compile time. For example, in the `exception` class, the `what` method is virtual. The derived classes require no further action to have dynamic binding apply for `what` method calls.

Consequently, for the program fragment in Figure 4.9, the answer to our earlier question depends entirely on whether we declared `doWork` as virtual in the `Worker` class (or higher in the hierarchy). Note that if `doWork` is not virtual in the `Worker` class (or higher in the hierarchy), but is later made virtual in `Workaholic`, then accesses through pointers and references to `Worker` will still use static binding. To make a run-time decision, we would have to place the keyword `virtual` at the start of the `doWork` declaration in the `Worker` class interface (the rest of the class is omitted for brevity):

```
class Worker
{
  public:
    virtual void doWork( );
};
```

As a general rule, if a function is overridden in a derived class, it should be declared `virtual` in the base class to ensure that the correct function is selected when a pointer to an object is used.

To summarize: Static binding is used by default, and dynamic binding is used for virtual functions if the binding cannot be resolved at compile time. However, a run-time decision is needed only when an object is accessed through a pointer or reference to a base class.

4.2.6 The Default Constructor, Copy Constructor, Copy Assignment Operator, and Destructor

Two issues surround the default constructor, copy constructor, and copy assignment operator: First, if we do nothing, are these operators private or public? Second, if they are public, what are their semantics?

The public/private status of the default constructor, copy constructor, and copy assignment operator, like all other members is inherited.

We assume public inheritance and that these functions were public in the base class. What happens if we omit them from the derived class? We know that they will be public, but what will their semantics be? For classes we know that defaults exist for the simple constructor, the copy constructor, and the copy assignment operator. Specifically, the default is to apply the appropriate operation to each member in the class. Thus, as we have shown, if a copy assignment operator is not specified in a class, it is defined as a member-by-member copy. The same rules apply to inherited classes. For instance,

```
const BadIndex & operator=( const BadIndex & rhs );
```

is not explicitly defined, so it is implemented by a call to `operator=` for the base class, followed by copying of any additional data members.

If a default destructor, copy constructor, or copy assignment operator is publicly inherited but not defined in the derived class, then by default the operator is applied to each member.

What is true in terms of visibility for any member function is, in effect, true for these operators. Thus, if `operator=` is disabled by being placed in the private section in the base class, it is still disabled. The same holds for the copy constructor and default constructor. The reasoning, however, is slightly different. In effect, `operator=` is disabled because a public default `operator=` is generated. However, by default, `operator=` is applied to the inherited portion and then member by member. Because `operator=` for the base class is disabled, the first step becomes illegal. Thus placing default constructors, copy constructors, and `operator=` in the private section of the base class has the effect of disabling them in the derived class (even though technically they are public in the derived class).

4.2.7 Constructors and Destructors: Virtual or Not Virtual?

Constructors are never virtual.

The answer to the question of whether constructors and destructors should be virtual or not virtual is that constructors are never virtual and that destructors should always be made virtual if they are being used in a base class and should be nonvirtual otherwise. The reasoning is as follows.

In an inheritance hierarchy the destructor should always be virtual.

For constructors a `virtual` label is meaningless. We can always determine at compile time what we are constructing. As a result, declaring a constructor virtual is forbidden by the Standard. Destructors need to be `virtual` to ensure that the destructor for the actual object is called. Otherwise, if the derived class consists of some additional members that have dynamically allocated memory, that memory will not be freed by the base class destructor. In a sense the destructor is no different from any other member function. For example, in Figure 4.10, suppose that the base class contains `strings` `name1` and `name2`. Automatically, its destructor calls the destructors for these strings, so we are tempted to accept the default. In the derived class we have an additional `string`, `newName`. Its destructor automatically calls `newName`'s destructor and then the base class destructor. So everything appears to work.

However, if the destructor for the base class is used for an object of the derived class, only those items that are inherited are destroyed. The destructor for the additional data member `newName` cannot possibly be called because the destructor for the base class is oblivious to `newName`'s existence.

Thus, even if the default destructor seems to work, it actually does not work if there is inheritance. In an inheritance hierarchy, then, the base class constructor should always be virtual. Even if it is a trivial destructor, it should be written anyway, with a virtual declaration and empty body. When the destructor is virtual, we are certain that a run-time decision will be used to choose the destructor appropriate to the object being deleted.

Figure 4.11 shows the class interface for `exception`. Note how the destructor is virtual.

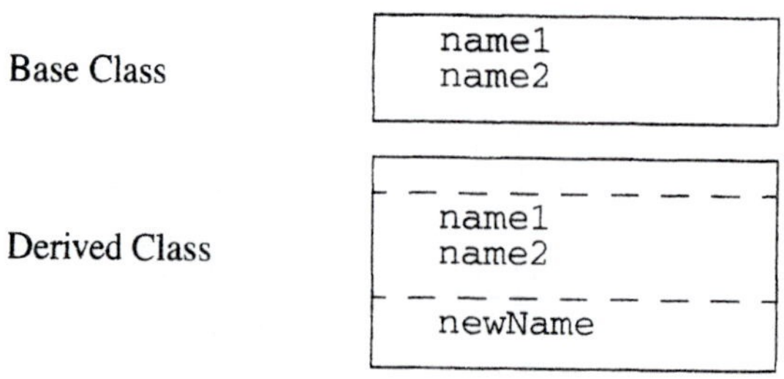

Figure 4.10 Calling the base class destructor does not free memory associated with `newName`.

```
// Interface for class exception in <exception>.

class exception
{
  public:
    exception( );
    exception( const exception & rhs );

    virtual ~exception( );

    const exception & operator=( const exception & rhs );

    virtual const char * what( );

  private:
    // implementation-defined
};
```

Figure 4.11 Interface for the class `exception`.

4.2.8 Abstract Methods and Classes

So far, we have shown that some methods are invariant over a hierarchy and that other methods can have their meanings changed over the hierarchy. A third possibility is that a method is meaningful for the derived classes and that an implementation must be provided for the derived classes; however, that implementation is not meaningful for the base class. In this case, we can declare the base class method to be *abstract*.

An *abstract method* has no meaningful definition and is thus always defined in the derived class.

An **abstract method** is declared in the base class and always defined in the derived class. It says (in the base class), what all class objects in the hierarchy can do and must eventually implement. It does not provide a default implementation, so each derived class must provide its own implementation.

A class that has at least one abstract method is called an **abstract class.** Because the behavior of an abstract class is not completely defined, abstract classes can never be instantiated. When a derived class fails to override an abstract method with an implementation, the method remains abstract in the derived class. As a result, the derived class remains abstract, and the compiler reports an error if an attempt to instantiate the abstract derived class is made.

An example is an abstract class `Shape`, which we use in a larger example later in this chapter. We derive specific shapes, such as `Circle` and `Rectangle`, from `Shape`. We can then derive a `Square` as a special `Rectangle`. Figure 4.12 shows the class hierarchy that results.

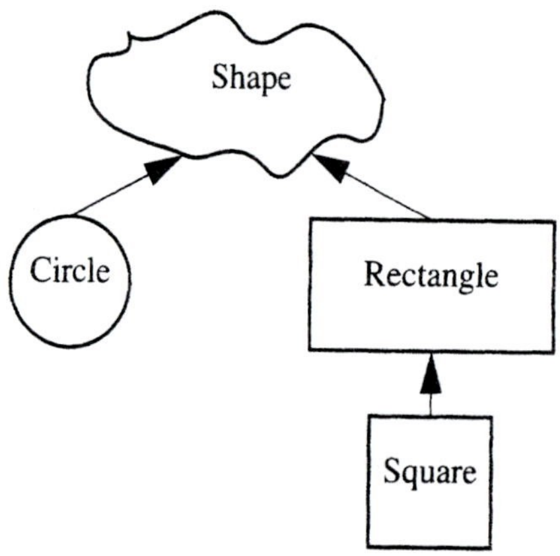

Figure 4.12 The hierarchy of shapes used in an inheritance example.

The `Shape` class can have data members that are common to all classes. In a more extensive example, they could include the coordinates of the object's extremities. The class declares and provides a definition for methods, such as `positionOf`, that are independent of the actual type of object; `positionOf` would be an invariant method. It also declares methods that apply for each particular type of object. Some of these methods make no sense for the abstract class `Shape`. For instance, computing the area of an abstract object is difficult; the `area` method could be an abstract method.

A class with at least one abstract method is an *abstract class*.

Because the existence of at least one abstract method makes the base class abstract, its creation is disallowed. In other words, a `Shape` object cannot itself be created; only the derived objects can. However, as usual, a `Shape` can point to or reference any concrete derived object, such as a `Circle` or `Rectangle`. Thus

```
Shape *a, *b;
a = new Circle( 3.0 );        // Legal
b = new Shape( "circle" );    // Illegal
```

An abstract class object can never be constructed. However, we still provide a constructor that can be called by derived classes.

Figure 4.13 shows the code for the abstract class `Shape`. At line 30, we declare a `string` that stores the type of shape. This method is used only for the derived classes. The member is private, so the derived classes do not have direct access to it. The rest of the class specifies a collection of methods.

The constructor never actually gets called directly because `Shape` is an abstract class. We need a constructor, however, so that the derived class can call it to initialize the private members. The `Shape` constructor sets the internal `name` data member. Note the virtual destructor, in accordance with the discussion in Section 4.2.7.

```
1  // Abstract base class for shapes.
2  //
3  // CONSTRUCTION: is not allowed; Shape is abstract.
4  //
5  // ******************PUBLIC OPERATIONS*********************
6  // double area( )              --> Return the area (abstract)
7  // bool operator< ( rhs )      --> Compare 2 Shape objects by area
8  // void print( out = cout)     --> Standard print method
9
10 #include <iostream>
11 #include <string>
12 using namespace std;
13
14 class Shape
15 {
16   public:
17     Shape( const string & shapeName = "" )
18       : name( shapeName ) { }
19     virtual ~Shape( ) { }
20
21     virtual double area( ) const = 0;
22
23     bool operator< ( const Shape & rhs ) const
24       { return area( ) < rhs.area( ); }
25
26     virtual void print( ostream & out = cout ) const
27       { out << name << " of area " << area( ); }
28
29   private:
30     string name;
31 };
```

Figure 4.13 The abstract base class `Shape`.

An abstract method is also known as a *pure virtual function* in C++.

Line 21 of Figure 4.13 declares the abstract method `area`. A method is declared abstract by specifying that it is `virtual` and by supplying `= 0` in the interface in place of an implementation. Because of the syntax, an abstract method is also known as a **pure virtual function** in C++. As with all virtual methods, a run-time decision selects the appropriate `area` in a derived class. The `area` method is an abstract method because no meaningful default could be specified for an inherited class that chose not to define its own.

The comparison method shown at lines 23 to 24 is not abstract because it can be meaningfully applied for all derived classes. In fact, its definition is invariant throughout the hierarchy of shapes, so we did not make it virtual.

```
// Output routine for Shape.
ostream & operator<< ( ostream & out, const Shape & rhs )
{
    rhs.print( out );
    return out;
}
```

Figure 4.14 Output routine for `Shape`, which includes its name and area.

The `print` method, shown at lines 26 and 27, prints out the name of the shape and its area. Although it appears to be invariant now, we make it virtual just in case we change our mind later on. The code for `operator<<` is written in Figure 4.14.

Before continuing, let us summarize the three types of member functions.

1. *Nonvirtual functions.* Overloading is resolved at compile time. To ensure consistency when pointers to objects are used, we generally use a nonvirtual method only when the function is invariant over the inheritance hierarchy (i.e., when the method is never redefined). Constructors are always nonvirtual, as mentioned in Section 4.2.7.
2. *Virtual functions.* Overloading is resolved at run time. The base class provides a default implementation that may be overridden by the derived classes. Destructors should be virtual, as mentioned in Section 4.2.7.
3. *Pure virtual functions.* Overloading is resolved at run time. The base class provides no implementation and is abstract. The absence of a default requires either that the derived classes provide an implementation or that the derived classes themselves be abstract.

4.3 Example: Expanding the `Shape` Class

In this section we implement the derived `Shape` classes and show how they are used in a polymorphic manner. The following problem is used:

SORTING SHAPES

READ N SHAPES (CIRCLES, SQUARES, OR RECTANGLES) AND OUTPUT THEM SORTED BY AREA.

The implementation of the derived classes, shown in Figure 4.15, is short and illustrates almost nothing that we have not already discussed. The only new item is `Square`, which is derived from `Rectangle`, which itself is

```
// Circle, Square, Rectangle class interfaces;
//     all based on Shape.
//
// CONSTRUCTION: with (a) no initializer or (b) radius (for
//     circle), side length (for square), length and width
//     (for rectangle).
// ******************PUBLIC OPERATIONS*********************
// double area( )        --> Implements Shape pure virtual area

const double PI = 3.1415927;

class Circle : public Shape
{
  public:
    Circle( double rad = 0.0 )
      : Shape( "circle" ), radius( rad ) { }
    double area( ) const
      { return PI * radius * radius; }

  private:
    double radius;
};

class Rectangle : public Shape
{
  public:
    Rectangle( double len = 0.0, double wid = 0.0 )
      : Shape( "rectangle" ), length( len ), width( wid ) { }
    double area( ) const
      { return length * width; }

  private:
    double length;
    double width;
};

class Square : public Rectangle
{
  public:
    Square( double side = 0.0 )
      : Rectangle( side, side ) { }
};
```

Figure 4.15 Complete Circle, Rectangle, and Square classes.

derived from `Shape`. This derivation is done exactly like all the others. In implementing these classes, we must

1. provide a new constructor;
2. examine each virtual function to decide whether we are willing to accept its defaults (for each virtual function whose defaults we do not like, we must write a new definition);
3. write a definition for each pure virtual function; and
4. write additional member functions if appropriate.

For each class, we provide a simple constructor that allows initialization with basic dimensions (e.g., radius for circles and side lengths for rectangles and squares). We first initialize the inherited portion by calling the base class initializer. Each class is required to provide an `area` method because `Shape` has declared that it is an abstract method. If the `area` method is not provided for some class, an error will be detected at compile time. The reason is that, if an implementation of `area` is missing, a derived class will itself be abstract. Note that `Square` can inherit the `area` method from `Rectangle`, so it does not provide a redefinition. Note also that its name internally is now `"rectangle"`.

We can only declare arrays of pointers to base classes because the size of the base class is usually smaller than the size of the derived class. It can never be larger.

Now that we have written the classes, we are ready to solve the original problem. What we would like to do is declare an array of `Shape`s. But we cannot declare one `Shape`, much less an array of them, for two reasons. First, `Shape` is an abstract base class, so a `Shape` object does not exist. Even if `Shape` was not abstract, which would be the case if it defined an `area` function, we still could not reasonably declare an array of `Shape`s. The reason is that the basic `Shape` has one data member, `Circle` adds a second data member, `Rectangle` adds a third data member, and so on. The basic `Shape` is not large enough to hold all of the possible derived types, so we need an array of pointers to `Shape`. In Figure 4.16, we attempt this approach; however, it does not quite work because we get in trouble at the sorting stage.

Let us examine the logic in Figure 4.16 and then correct the deficiency. First, we read the objects. At line 17 we are actually reading a character and then the dimensions of some shape, creating a shape, and finally assigning a pointer to point at the newly created shape. Figure 4.17 shows a bare-bones implementation. So far so good.

We then call `insertionSort` to sort the shapes. Recall that we already have an `insertionSort` template from Section 3.3. Because `array` is an array of pointers to shapes, we expect that it will work as long as we provide a comparison routine with the declaration

```
int operator<( const Shape * lhs, const Shape * rhs );
```

```
#include <iostream>
#include <vector>
using namespace std;

// main: read shapes and output in increasing order of area.
// Error checks omitted for brevity. DOES NOT WORK.
int main( )
{
    int numShapes;
    cin >> numShapes;
    vector<Shape *> array( numShapes );   // Array of Shape *

      // Read the shapes
    for( int i = 0; i < numShapes; i++ )
    {
        cout << "Enter a shape: ";
        cin >> array[ i ];
    }

    insertionSort( array );

    cout << "Sorted by increasing size:" << endl;
    for( int j = 0; j < numShapes; j++ )
        cout << *array[ j ] << endl;

    return 0;
}
```

Figure 4.16 The `main` routine to read shapes and output them in increasing order of area. Does not work.

Unfortunately, that does not work because `insertionSort` uses the `operator<` that already exists for pointers. That operator compares the addresses being pointed at, which guarantees that the array will be unaltered (because `a[i]` is always stored at a lower address than `a[j]` if `i<j`).

If a class is instantiated with pointer types, shallow operations are used.

To make this approach work, we need to define a new class that hides the fact that the objects we are storing and sorting are pointers, as shown in Figure 4.18. The `PtrToShape` object stores the pointer to a `Shape` and provides a comparison function that compares `Shapes` rather than pointers. It does this by dereferencing both pointers and calling the `Shape operator<` on the resulting `Shape` objects. Note that we make excessive calculations to compute areas. Avoiding this excess is left for you to do as Exercise 4.13. Note also that, in general, we must call `delete` to reclaim the memory consumed by the `Shape` objects.

Deep comparison semantics can be obtained by designing a class to store the pointer.

The `PtrToShape` class also overloads the unary `*` operator so that a `PtrToShape` object looks just like a pointer to a `Shape`. We can add more

```
// Create an appropriate Shape object based on input.
// The user types 'c', 's', or 'r' to indicate the shape
// and then provides dimensions when prompted.
// A zero-radius circle is returned for any error.
istream & operator>>( istream & in, Shape * & s )
{
    char ch;
    double d1, d2;

    in.get( ch );          // First character represents shape
    switch( ch )
    {
      case 'c':
        in >> d1;
        s = new Circle( d1 );
        break;

      case 'r':
        in >> d1 >> d2;
        s = new Rectangle( d1, d2 );
        break;

      case 's':
        in >> d1;
        s = new Square( d1 );
        break;

      case '\n':
        return in >> s;          // Newline; try again

      default:
        cerr << "Needed one of c, r, or s" << endl;
        s = new Circle;        // Radius is 0
        break;
    }

    return in;
}
```

Figure 4.17 A simple input routine for reading a pointer to a `Shape`.

```
struct PtrToShape
{
    Shape *ptr;

    bool operator< ( const PtrToShape & rhs ) const
      { return *ptr < *rhs.ptr; }

    const Shape & operator*( ) const
      { return *ptr; }
};

// main: read shapes and output in increasing order of area.
// Error checks omitted for brevity.
int main( )
{
    int numShapes;
    cout << "Enter number of shapes: ";
    cin >> numShapes;

      // Read the shapes
    vector<PtrToShape> array( numShapes );

    for( int i = 0; i < numShapes; i++ )
    {
        cout << "Enter a shape (c, r, or s with dimensions): ";
        cin >> array[ i ].ptr;
    }

    insertionSort( array );
    cout << "Sorted by increasing size:" << endl;
    for( int j = 0; j < numShapes; j++ )
        cout << *array[ j ] << endl;

    for( int k = 0; k < numShapes; k++ )
        delete array[ k ].ptr;

    return 0;
}
```

Figure 4.18 The `main` routine reads shapes and outputs them in increasing order of area.

members to hide information better, but we prefer to keep things as short as possible. The idea of wrapping a pointer inside a class is a common design pattern, which we look at in Section 5.3.

4.4 Tricky C++ Details

Inheritance in C++ has numerous subtle points. We discuss some of them in this section.

4.4.1 Static Binding of Parameters

In C++, the parameters to a method are always deduced statically, at compile time.

Dynamic binding means that the member function that is appropriate for the object being operated on is used. However, it does not mean that the absolute best match is performed for all parameters. Specifically, in C++, the parameters to a method are always deduced statically, at compile time.

Consider the code in Figure 4.19. In the `whichFoo` method, a call is made to `foo`. But which `foo` is called? We expect the answer to depend on the run-time types of `arg1` and `arg2`.

```
class Derived;    // Incomplete declaration

class Base
{
  public:
    virtual void foo( const Base & x );       // METHOD A
    virtual void foo( const Derived & x );    // METHOD B
};

class Derived : public Base
{
  public:
    virtual void foo( const Base & x );       // METHOD C
    virtual void foo( const Derived & x );    // METHOD D
};

void whichFoo( Base & arg1, Base & arg2 )
{
    arg1.foo( arg2 );
}
```

Figure 4.19 An illustration of static binding for parameters.

Because parameters are always matched at compile time, the type to which `arg2` is actually referencing does not matter. The `foo` that we match is

```
virtual void foo( const Base & x );    // METHOD A or C
```

The only issue is whether to use the `Base` or `Derived` version. That is the decision made at run-time when the object that `arg1` references is known.

Static binding has important ramifications. Consider the following situation in which we overload the output operator for both a base class and derived class:

```
ostream & operator<< ( ostream & out, const Base & x );
ostream & operator<< ( ostream & out, const Derived & x );
```

Suppose that we now try to call the output function:

```
Base *b = new Derived;
cout << *b << endl;
```

Because parameters are statically deduced, output (unfortunately) uses the `operator<<` that takes a `Base` parameter.

However, recall that we have been recommending that the class define a `print` method and then implement `operator<<` by calling the `print` method. If we use this approach, we need only to write `operator<<` for the base class:

```
ostream & operator<< ( ostream & out, const Base & x )
{
    x.print( out );     // print is deduced at run time
    return out;
}
```

Now the base class and derived class each provide their own version of the `print` method. The `operator<<` is called for all `Base` and `Derived` objects. However, when that happens, the call to `print` uses dynamic binding!

4.4.2 Default Parameters

Changing the default value in a derived class is unsafe.

Default parameters are statically bound, meaning that they are deduced at compile time. Changing the default value in a derived class is unsafe because doing so can create an inconsistency with virtual functions, which are bound at run time.

4.4.3 Derived Class Methods Hide Base Class Methods

An annoying feature of C++ is illustrated in Figure 4.20. In the code, we have a base class and a derived class. The base class declares a function named `bar` with zero parameters. The derived class adds a function named `bar` with one parameter.

In `test`, we illustrate the various calls that can be made. At line 15, we attempt to call the zero-parameter `bar` through a `Base` reference. We expect this call to work and it does. Note that the actual object being acted on could be a `Derived` object. At the next line, we attempt to call the one-parameter `bar` through a `Base` reference. Because this function is not defined for `Base` objects, the call must fail—and indeed, the line does not compile. The one-parameter `bar` must be called through a `Derived` reference, as shown on line 17.

So far, so good. Now comes the unexpected part. If we call the zero-parameter `bar` with a `Derived` reference, the code does not compile. This result is unexpected because the code at line 15 compiles and a `Derived` IS-A `Base`.

What has happened appears to be a language flaw. When a method is declared in a derived class, it hides all methods of the same name in the base class. Thus `bar` is no longer accessible through a `Derived` reference, even though it would be accessible through a `Base` reference:

```
Base & tmp = arg2; tmp.bar( );    // Legal!
```

```
 1 class Base
 2 {
 3   public:
 4     virtual void bar( );              // METHOD A
 5 };
 6
 7 class Derived : public Base
 8 {
 9   public:
10     void bar( int x );                // METHOD B
11 };
12
13 void test( Base & arg1, Derived & arg2 )
14 {
15     arg1.bar( );      // Compiles, as expected.
16     arg1.bar( 4 );    // Does not compile, as expected.
17     arg2.bar( 4 );    // Compiles, as expected.
18     arg2.bar( );      // Does not compile. Not expected.
19 }
```

Figure 4.20 An illustration of hiding.

There are two ways around this problem. One way is to override the zero-parameter `bar` in `Derived`, with an implementation that calls the `Base` class version. In other words, in `Derived` we add

```
void bar( ) { Base::bar( ); }    // In class Derived
```

The other method is newer and does not work on all compilers. In it we introduce the base class member function into the derived class scope with a `using` declaration:

```
using Base::bar;                  // In class Derived
```

The most important reason you should be aware of this rule is that many compilers will issue a warning when you hide a member function. A signature indicates whether a function is an accessor, so if the base class function is an accessor (a constant member function) and the derived class function is not, you have usually made an error, and this warning is how the compiler might let you know about it. Pay attention to these warnings.

4.4.4 Compatible Return Types for Overridden Methods

Return types present an important difficulty. Consider the following operator, defined in a base class:

```
virtual const Base & operator++( );
```

The derived class inherits it as

```
const Base & operator++( );
```

but that is not really what we want. If we have a return type in the derived class, it ought to be a constant reference to the derived type, not to the base type. Thus the `operator++` inherited is not the one we want. Instead, we would like to override `operator++` with

```
const Derived & operator++( );
```

Recall that overriding a function means writing a new function with the same signature. Under original C++ rules, the return type of the new and overridden function had to match exactly.

If the original return type is a pointer (or reference) to *B*, the new return type may be a pointer (or reference) to *D*, provided *D* is a publicly derived class of *B*.

Under the new rules, the return type may be **relaxed.** This means if the original return type is a pointer (or reference) to *B*, the new return type may be a pointer (or reference) to *D*, provided *D* is a publicly derived class of *B*. This condition corresponds to our normal expectation of IS-A relationships.

4.4.5 Private Inheritance

Private inheritance means that even public members of the base class are hidden.

Private inheritance means that even public members of the base class are hidden. That seems like a silly idea, doesn't it? In fact it is, if we are talking about implementing an IS-A relationship. Private inheritance is thus generally used to implement a HAS-A relationship (that is, a derived class *D* has or uses a base class *B*).

***Composition* is preferred to private inheritance. In composition, class *B* is said to be composed of class *A* (and other objects).**

In many cases we can get by without using inheritance. Instead, we can use **composition,** making an object of class *B* a member of class *D* and, if necessary, making *D* a friend of *B*. Composition is preferable to private inheritance, but occasionally the latter is more expedient or slightly faster (because it avoids a layer of function calls). For the most part, you should avoid private inheritance unless it greatly simplifies some coding logic or can be justified on performance grounds. However, in Section 5.3.3, we demonstrate an appropriate and typical use of private inheritance.

Although the default is private inheritance, it should be avoided.

Recall that by default, private inheritance is used. If we omitted the keyword `public` on line 3 of Figure 4.6, we would have private inheritance. In that case the public member functions of `exception` would still be inherited, but they would be private members of `BadIndex` and could not be called by users of `BadIndex`. Thus the `what` method would not be visible. The type compatibility of base class and derived class pointers and references described earlier does not apply for nonpublic inheritance. Thus, in the following code, a `BadIndex` exception would not be caught:

```
catch( const exception & e ) { cout << e.what( ) << endl; }
```

4.4.6 Friends

Friendship is not inherited.

Are friends of a class still friends in a derived class? The answer is no. For example, suppose that *F* is a friend of class *B*, and *D* is derived from *B*. Suppose also that *D* has nonpublic member *M*. Then, in class *D*, *F* does not have access to *M*. However, the inherited portion of *B* is accessible to *F* in class *D*. Figure 4.21 summarizes the results. Note that *D* can declare that *F* is also a friend, in which case all of *D*'s members would be visible.

4.4.7 Call by Value and Polymorphism Do Not Mix

Consider the following statement. Assume that `BadIndex` is publicly inherited from `exception` and suppose that it has overridden the `what` method:

```
catch( exception e ) { cout << e.what( ) << endl; }
```

Public Inheritance Situation	Public	Protected	Private
F accessing *B.MB*	Yes	Yes	Yes
F accessing *D.MD*	Yes	No	No
F accessing *D.MB*	Yes	Yes	Yes
B is an object of the base class; *D* is an object of the publicly derived class; *MB* is a member of the base class. *MD* is a member of the derived class. *F* is a friend of the base class (but not the derived class).			

Figure 4.21 Friendship is not inherited.

Note that `e` is passed by using call by value. Now suppose that a `BadIndex` exception has been thrown. Which `what` method gets called? The answer is not what we want.

When we use call by value, the actual argument is always copied into the formal parameter. Thus the `BadIndex` object is copied into `e` by using `e`'s `operator=`, so only the `exception` component of `BadIndex` is copied. The loss of inherited data when a derived class object is copied into a base class object is known as **slicing.** In any event, the type of `e` is `exception`, and so it is the `exception` class's `what` method that is called, and it is acting on a trimmed portion of the `BadIndex` object. The moral of the story: Polymorphism and call by value do not mix.

Slicing **is the loss of inherited data members when a derived class object is copied into a base class object.**

4.5 Multiple Inheritance

In all the inheritance examples presented so far, we derived one class from a single base class. In **multiple inheritance** a class may be derived from more than one base class. For example, in the `iostream` library, an `iostream` (which allows both reading and writing) is derived from both an `istream` and an `ostream`. As a second example, a university has several classes of people, including students and employees. But some people are both students and employees. The `StudentEmployee` class could be derived from both the `Student` class and the `Employee` class; each of those classes could be derived from the abstract base class `UniversityPerson`.

Multiple inheritance **is the process of deriving a class from several base classes. (We do not use multiple inheritance in this text.)**

In multiple inheritance the new class inherits members from all its base classes. This result leads to some immediate problems that you need to watch for.

- Suppose that `UniversityPerson` has class members `name` and `ssn` and that they are inherited by `Student` and `Employee`. However, as

StudentEmployee inherits the data members from both Student and Employee, we get two copies of name and ssn unless we use virtual inheritance, as in

```
class Student : virtual public UniversityPerson {...};
class Employee :virtual public UniversityPerson {...};
class StudentEmployee : public Student,
                        public Employee {...};
```

- What if Student and Employee have member functions that are augmented to Employee but have the same signatures? For instance, the credit function, not given in UniversityPerson, is added to Student to mean the number of credit hours for which a student is currently registered. For employees the function returns the number of vacation days still left. Consider the following:

```
UniversityPerson *p = new StudentEmployee;
cout << p->Student::credits( );    // OK
cout << p->Employee::credits( );   // OK
cout << p->credits( );             // Ambiguous
```

- Suppose that UniversityPerson defines a virtual member function f that and Student redefines it. However, Employee and StudentEmployee do nothing. Then, for p defined in the preceding example, is p->f() ambiguous? In that example the answer is no because UniversityPerson is a virtual base class with respect to Student; consequently, Student::f( ) is said to *dominate* UniversityPerson::f( ), and there is no ambiguity. Ambiguity would occur if we did not use virtual inheritance for Student.

Does all this make your head spin? Most of these problems tend to suggest that multiple inheritance is a tricky feature that requires careful analysis before you use it. Generally speaking, multiple inheritance is not needed nearly as often as you might suspect, but when it is needed it is extremely important. Although the rules for multiple inheritance are carefully defined in the language standard, it is also an unfortunate fact that many compilers have bugs associated with this feature (especially in conjunction with other features).

We will not use multiple inheritance in this text. The most common (and safe) way to use multiple inheritance is to inherit only from classes that define no data members and no implementations. Such classes specify protocols only, and most of the ambiguity problems described above go away.

You should avoid general use of multiple inheritance in C++ until you are extremely comfortable with simple inheritance and virtual functions;

many object-oriented languages (such as Smalltalk, Object Pascal, Objective C, and Ada) do not support multiple inheritance, so you can live without it.

Summary

Inheritance is a powerful feature that allows the reuse of code. However, be sure that functions applied to objects created at run time through the `new` operator are bound at run time. This feature is known as dynamic binding, and the use of virtual functions is required to ensure that run-time decisions are made. Reread this chapter as often as necessary to ensure that you understand the distinctions among nonvirtual functions (in which the same definition applies throughout the inheritance hierarchy and thus compile-time decisions are correct), virtual functions (in which the default provided in the base class can be overwritten in the derived class; run-time decisions are made if needed), and pure virtual functions (which have no default definition).

In this chapter we also described the programming technique of wrapping a variable inside a class (Figure 4.18) and mentioned the occasional usefulness of private inheritance. These techniques are two examples of design patterns that we encounter over and over again. In Chapter 5 we discuss some common design patterns.

Objects of the Game

abstract class A class with at least one pure virtual function. (p. 134)

abstract method A method that has no meaningful definition and is thus always defined in the derived class. (p. 133)

base class The foundation for inheritance. (p. 122)

composition Mechanism preferred to private inheritance when an IS-A relationship does not hold. In composition, an object of class *B* is said to be *composed* of an object of class *A* (and other objects). (p. 146)

derived class A completely new class that inherits all the properties of a base class, with all the public methods and identical implementations of the base class. (p. 122)

dynamic binding A run-time decision to apply the method corresponding to the actual referenced object. Used when a member function is declared to be virtual and the correct method cannot be determined at compile time. (p. 130)

HAS-A relationship The derived class has a (property of the) base class. (p. 120)

inheritance The process of deriving a class from a base class without disturbing the implementation of the base class. It also allows the design of class hierarchies, such as `exception`. (p. 122)

IS-A relationship The derived class is a (variation of the) base class. (p. 119)

multiple inheritance The process of deriving a class from several base classes. (p. 147)

nonvirtual function Used when the function is invariant over the inheritance hierarchy. Static binding is used for nonvirtual functions. (p. 129)

partial overriding The act of augmenting a base class method to perform additional, but not entirely different, tasks. The scope operator is used to call a base class method. (p. 128)

polymorphism The ability of a reference or pointer variable to reference or point to objects of several different types. When operations are applied to the variable, the operation that is appropriate to the actual referenced object is automatically selected. (p. 122)

private inheritance The process occasionally used to implement a HAS-A relationship. Even public members of the base class are hidden. (p. 146)

protected class member Accessible by a derived class but private to every other class. (p. 124)

public inheritance The process by which all public members of the base class remain public in the derived class. Public inheritance models an IS-A relationship. (p. 123)

pure virtual function An abstract method. (p. 135)

slicing The loss of inherited data when a derived class object is copied into a base class object. (p. 147)

static binding/overloading The decision about which function to use made at compile time. (p. 129)

virtual function A function for which dynamic binding is used. It should be used if the function is redefined in the inheritance hierarchy. (p. 130)

Common Errors

1. Inheritance is private by default. A common error is to omit the keyword `public`, which is needed to specify public inheritance.

2. If a base class member function is redefined in a derived class, it should be made virtual. Otherwise, the wrong function could be called when accessed through a pointer or reference.
3. Base class destructors should be declared as virtual functions. Otherwise, the wrong destructor may get called in some cases.
4. Constructors can never be declared virtual.
5. Objects of an abstract base class cannot be instantiated.
6. If the derived class fails to implement any inherited pure virtual function, the derived class becomes abstract and cannot be instantiated, even if it makes no attempts to use the undefined pure virtual function.
7. Never redefine a default parameter for a virtual function. Default parameters are bound at compile time, which can create an inconsistency with virtual functions that are bound at run time.
8. To access a base class member, the scope resolution must be used. Otherwise, the scope is the current class.
9. Friendship is not inherited.
10. In a derived class, the inherited base class members can be initialized only as an aggregate in a constructor's initializer list. If these members are public or protected, they may later be read or assigned to individually.
11. A common error is to declare a virtual destructor in an abstract base class but not provide an implementation (`virtual~Base()` or `virtual~Base()=0`). Both are wrong because the derived class destructor needs to call the base class destructor. If nothing needs to be done, then use `{}` as the definition.
12. If a constructor declaration is provided in the base class, provide the definition, too, for the same reason as in the destructor case.
13. The return type in a derived class cannot be redefined to be different from the base class unless they are both pointer or both reference types, and the new return type is type-compatible with the original.
14. If the base class has a constant member function *F* and the derived class attempts to define a nonconstant member function *F* with an otherwise identical signature, the compiler will warn that the derived *F* hides the base *F*. Heed the warning and find a way to work around it.

On the Internet

Three self-contained files and a set of exception classes are available.

Except.h	Contains the exception hierarchy.
Shape.cpp	The `Shape` example.
StaticBinding.cpp	Contains the code in Figure 4.19 illustrating that parameters are statically bound.
Hiding.cpp	Contains the code shown in Figure 4.20, illustrating how methods are hidden.

Exercises

In Short

4.1. Explain the rules for when to use virtual and nonvirtual functions.

4.2. Which members of an inherited class can be used in the derived class? What members become public for users of the derived class?

4.3. What is the default type of inheritance?

4.4. What is private inheritance? What is composition?

4.5. Consider the program presented in Figure 4.22.

a. Which accesses are illegal?
b. Make `main` a friend of class `Base`. Which accesses are illegal?
c. Make `main` a friend of both `Base` and `Derived`. Which accesses are illegal?
d. Write a three-parameter constructor for `Base`. Then write a five-parameter constructor for `Derived`.
e. The class `Derived` consists of five integers. Which are accessible to the class `Derived`?
f. The class `Derived` is passed a `Base` object. Which of the `Base` object members can the `Derived` class access?

4.6. Explain polymorphism.

4.7. Explain dynamic binding and when it is used.

4.8. What is a pure virtual function?

4.9. When should a constructor be virtual?

4.10. When should a destructor be virtual?

4.11. What is meant by parameters being statically bound?

```
class Base
{
  public:
    int bPublic;
  protected:
    int bProtect;
  private:
    int bPrivate;
};

class Derived : public Base
{
  public:
    int dPublic;
  private:
    int dPrivate;
};

int main( )
{
    Base b;
    Derived d;

    cout << b.bPublic << " " << b.bProtect << " " << b.bPrivate
         << " " << d.dPublic << " " << d.dPrivate << endl;

    return 0;
}
```

Figure 4.22 Program to test visibility.

In Practice

4.12. For the `Shape` example in Section 4.3 modify `readShape` and `main` by throwing and catching an exception (instead of creating a circle of radius zero) when an input error is detected.

Programming Projects

4.13. Rewrite the `Shape` hierarchy to store the area as a data member and have it computed by the constructor. Make `area` a nonvirtual function that returns only the value of this data member.

4.14. Add the concept of a position to the `Shape` hierarchy by including coordinates as data members. Then add a `distance` member function.

4.15. Write an abstract base class for `Date` and its derived class `GregorianDate`.

4.16. Implement a taxpayer hierarchy that consists of a `TaxPayer` abstract class and the nonabstract classes `SinglePayer` and `MarriedPayer`.

References

For more information on inheritance, see [5], in particular, in which the guidelines for use of virtual, pure virtual, and nonvirtual functions appear. You might also want to check out [6], which explains the design of C++. The `Shape` class is taken from [7].

The books [1], [2] [3], and [4] describe the general principles of object-oriented software development.

1. G. Booch, *Object-Oriented Design and Analysis with Applications,* 2d ed., Benjamin/Cummings, Redwood City, Calif., 1994.
2. D. de Champeaux, D. Lea, and P. Faure, *Object-Oriented System Development,* Addison-Wesley, Reading, Mass., 1993.
3. I. Jacobson, M. Christerson, P. Jonsson, and G. Overgaard, *Object-Oriented Software Engineering: A Use Case Driven Approach* (rev. 4th printing), Addison-Wesley, Reading, Mass., 1992.
4. B. Meyer, *Object-Oriented Software Construction,* Prentice-Hall, Englewood Cliffs, N.J., 1988.
5. S. Meyers, *Effective C++,* 2d ed., Addison-Wesley, Reading, Mass., 1998.
6. B. Stroustrup, *The Design and Evolution of C++*, Addison-Wesley, Reading, Mass., 1994.
7. M. A. Weiss, *Efficient C Programming: A Practical Approach*, Prentice-Hall, Englewood Cliffs, N.J., 1995.

Chapter 5

Design Patterns

In earlier chapters, we emphasized that a central goal of object-oriented programming is the support of code reuse. In this chapter we examine the tangential, but equally important, concept of idea reuse: the reuse of basic programming and design technique, rather than the reuse of actual code. Many of these techniques are known as *design patterns*.

In this chapter, we show:

- the importance of design patterns;
- several examples of object-based design patterns, including the Functor, Adapter, Wrapper, Iterator, Composite, and Observer patterns;
- some sophisticated C++ programming tricks; and
- a brief discussion of object-oriented (inheritance-based) design patterns.

5.1 What Is a Pattern?

A *design pattern* describes a problem that occurs over and over in software engineering and then describes the solution in a sufficiently generic manner as to be applicable in a wide variety of contexts.

Although software design and programming are often difficult challenges, many experienced software engineers argue that software engineering really has only a relatively small set of basic problems. Perhaps this is an understatement, but it is true that many basic problems are encountered over and over in software projects. Software engineers who are familiar with these problems, and in particular, the efforts of other programmers in solving these problems, have the advantage of not needing to "reinvent the wheel."

The idea of a design pattern is to document a problem and its solution so that others can take advantage of the collective experience of the entire software engineering community. Writing a pattern is much like writing a recipe for a cookbook; many common patterns have been written and, rather than expending energy reinventing the wheel, programmers can use these patterns to write better programs. Thus a **design pattern** describes a problem that occurs over and over in software engineering and then describes the solution in a sufficiently generic manner as to be applicable in a wide variety of contexts.

Like a recipe, design patterns usually follow a format. There are several formats for designing a pattern. Typically, a design pattern consists of

1. the pattern name;
2. the problem, including a specification of the problem the pattern solves, an explanation of why this problem is important, some applications of the problem, and examples of known uses;
3. the solution, including a description of the classes in the patterns, possibly with a structure diagram, a generic (language independent) implementation of the pattern, with language-specific issues as appropriate, and sample code; and
4. consequences, including the results and trade-offs of using the pattern and a discussion of related patterns.

In this chapter, we discuss several patterns that are commonly used in object-based data structures. Our pattern specifications are not as formal as those just mentioned, but where reasonable, we provide some code and pointers to the use of the pattern elsewhere in the text. Toward the end of the chapter, we present some object-oriented patterns.

5.2 The Functor (Function Objects)

In Chapter 3, we showed how function templates can be used to write generic algorithms. As an example, the function template in Figure 5.1 can be used to find the maximum item in an array.

However, the template has an important limitation: It works only for objects that have an `operator<` function defined, and it uses that `operator<` as the basis for all comparison decisions. In many situations this approach is not feasible. As an example, consider the `Rectangle` class in Figure 5.2.

The `Rectangle` class does not have an `operator<`. The main reason that it doesn't is the number of plausible alternatives, so deciding on a good meaning for `operator<` is difficult. We could base the comparison on area, perimeter, length, width, and so on. As we showed in the `Shape` example in Section 4.3, once we have written `operator<` as a member function, we are stuck with it.

Even without `operator<` as a member function, we could still write a two-parameter nonmember `operator<` and separate the comparison from the `Rectangle` class. Thus each time we write a new program, we can specify a

```cpp
// Generic findMax for Comparables; uses natural order.
// Precondition: a.size( ) > 0.
template <class Comparable>
const Comparable & findMax( const vector<Comparable> & a )
{
    int maxIndex = 0;

    for( int i = 1; i < a.size( ); i++ )
        if( a[ maxIndex ] < a[ i ] )
            maxIndex = i;

    return a[ maxIndex ];
}
```

Figure 5.1 A generic `findMax` algorithm, which works only for `Comparable` objects and uses their natural order.

```cpp
// A simple rectangle class.

class Rectangle
{
  public:
    Rectangle( int len = 0, int wid = 0 )
      : length( len ), width( wid ) { }

    int getLength( ) const
      { return length; }

    int getWidth( ) const
      { return width; }

    void print( ostream & out = cout ) const
      { out << "Rectangle " << getLength( ) << " by "
            << getWidth( ); }

  private:
    int length;
    int width;
};

ostream & operator<< ( ostream & out, const Rectangle & rhs )
{
    rhs.print( out );
    return out;
}
```

Figure 5.2 The `Rectangle` class, which does not have a meaningful `operator<` function.

version of `operator<` for it. This approach is a slight improvement, but we can write only one `operator<` for a program. What if we want to have `findMax`, for example, work with several different comparison alternatives?

The solution to the problem is to pass the comparison function as a second parameter to `findMax` and have `findMax` use the comparison function instead of assuming the existence of an `operator<`. Thus `findMax` will now have two parameters: a `vector` of `Object` (which need not have any `operator<` defined), and a comparison function.

The main issue left is how to pass the comparison function. Some languages, including C++, allow parameters to be functions (actually they are pointers to functions). However, this solution often is inefficient and is not available in all object-oriented languages.

Instead, a solution that works in all object-oriented languages is to use a function object.

The *function object* contains a method specified by the generic algorithm. An instance of the class is passed to the algorithm.

The **function object**—also call a **functor**—often contains no data but does contain a single method with a given name specified by the generic algorithm (in this case `findMax`). The object, which is simply an instance of the single-method class is then passed to the algorithm, which in turn calls the single method of the function object. We can design different comparison functions by simply declaring new classes. Each new class contains a different implementation of the agreed-upon single method. An example is shown in Figure 5.3.

***Functor* is another name for a function object.**

The method `findMax` now takes two parameters, the second of which is the function object. As shown on line 11, `findMax` expects the function object to implement a method named `isLessThan`. (Specifically, it is expecting that `isLessThan` takes two parameters, both of type compatible with `Object`, for whatever `Object` turns out to be.) As the name of the function object parameter is `comp`, line 11 calls the comparison function by `comp.isLessThan`. What is the type of `comp`? It can be any type (that has an `isLessThan` method), so we know that its type is a second template parameter. We use the symbolic name `Comparator` to signify its role. (`Functor` would work also, but `Comparator` is a more specific name for this function object.)

Once we've written `findMax`, it can be called in `main`. To do so, we need to pass to `findMax` a `vector` of `Rectangle` objects and a function object that has an `isLessThan` method. We implement a new class `LessThanByWidth`, which contains the required method. That method returns a Boolean, indicating whether the first rectangle is less than the second rectangle on the basis of widths. The `main` method simply passes an *instance* of `LessThanByWidth` to `findMax`.

```
// Generic findMax, with a function object.
// Uses a named method in the function object.
// Precondition: a.size( ) > 0.
template <class Object, class Comparator>
const Object & findMax( const vector<Object> & a,
                        Comparator comp )
{
    int maxIndex = 0;

    for( int i = 1; i < a.size( ); i++ )
        if( comp.isLessThan( a[ maxIndex ], a[ i ] ) )
            maxIndex = i;

    return a[ maxIndex ];
}


// Compare object: ordering by length.
class LessThanByWidth
{
  public:
    bool isLessThan( const Rectangle & lhs,
                     const Rectangle & rhs ) const
      { return lhs.getWidth( ) < rhs.getWidth( ); }
};

int main( )
{
    vector<Rectangle> a;
    ...
    cout << findMax( a, LessThanByWidth( ) ) << endl;
    ...
}
```

Figure 5.3 Example of a function object that does not use function call operator overloading.

Function objects can be passed by using call by value. Their calls can be inlined.

Observe that the `LessThanByWidth` object has no data members, which, as we've already stated, is usually true of function objects. Therefore function objects are often passed by using call by value. Observe also that when the `findMax` template is expanded, the type of `comp` is known. Hence the definition of `comp.isLessThan` is also known. An aggressive compiler can perform the inline optimization of replacing the function call to `comp.isLessThan` with the actual definition. In many cases, the ability of the compiler to perform this inline optimization can significantly decrease running time.

```
1  // Generic findMax, with a C++-style function object.
2  // Precondition: a.size( ) > 0.
3  template <class Object, class Comparator>
4  const Object & findMax( const vector<Object> & a,
5                          Comparator isLessThan )
6  {
7      int maxIndex = 0;
8
9      for( int i = 1; i < a.size( ); i++ )
10         if( isLessThan( a[ maxIndex ], a[ i ] ) )
11             maxIndex = i;
12
13     return a[ maxIndex ];
14 }
```

Figure 5.4 The method `findMax` with a C++-style function object.

The function object technique is an illustration of a pattern encountered over and over, not just in C++, but in any language that has objects. In C++, an additional coding trick makes the code look much better in the generic algorithm and only slightly worse in the function object's class.

The better looking `findMax` is shown in Figure 5.4. It contains two basic changes.

- Line 10 now has the call to `isLessThan`, apparently without a controlling object.
- The method `isLessThan` is the parameter to `findMax`.

It appears that we are passing the method directly to `findMax` and bypassing the function object. But that is not what is actually happening. Instead, we used the C++ trick of overloading the function call operator in the function object itself. That is, because `isLessThan` is an object, line 10, which reads as

```
if( isLessThan( a[ maxIndex ], a[ i ] ) )
```

is actually interpreted as

```
if( isLessThan.operator() ( a[ maxIndex ], a[ i ] ) )
```

The `operator()` is the function call operator.

The `operator()` is the function call operator, much like `operator[]` is the array indexing operator. With this piece of C++ syntax, we can implement various function objects in Figure 5.5. In Figure 5.6, we show a simple `main` that places some `Rectangle` objects in a `vector` and then, using the function objects of types defined in Figure 5.5, finds the maximum `Rectangle`, first on the basis of length and then on the basis of area.

```
// Compare object: ordering by length.
class LessThanByLength
{
  public:
    bool operator( ) ( const Rectangle & lhs,
                       const Rectangle & rhs ) const
      { return lhs.getLength( ) < rhs.getLength( ); }
};


// Compare object: ordering by area.
class LessThanByArea
{
  public:
    bool operator( ) ( const Rectangle & lhs,
                       const Rectangle & rhs ) const
      { return lhs.getLength( ) * lhs.getWidth( ) <
               rhs.getLength( ) * rhs.getWidth( ); }
};
```

Figure 5.5 Use of two C++-style function objects to compare `Rectangle` objects.

```
#include <iostream>
#include <vector>
using namespace std;

// main: create four rectangles.
// find the max, using two different criteria.
int main( )
{
    vector<Rectangle> a;

    a.push_back( Rectangle( 1, 10 ) );
    a.push_back( Rectangle( 10, 1 ) );
    a.push_back( Rectangle( 5, 5 ) );
    a.push_back( Rectangle( 4, 6 ) );

    cout << "Largest length:\n\t"
         << findMax( a, LessThanByLength( ) ) << endl;
    cout << "Largest area:\n\t"
         << findMax( a, LessThanByArea( ) ) << endl;

    return 0;
}
```

Figure 5.6 Sample program that illustrates `findMax` with two different comparison functions.

5.3 Adapters and Wrappers

When we implement algorithms, we often run into a language typing problem: We have an object of one type, but the language syntax requires an object of a different type. Sometimes a type conversion works, but often we need a little more.

For instance, in Section 4.3, we showed that sorting pointers to shapes did not quite work because `operator<` is already defined for pointers. Consequently, we needed to define a new class that stored the pointer and defined a meaningful `operator<`.

A *wrapper class* stores a primitive type and adds operations that the primitive type does not support or does not support correctly.

This technique illustrates the basic theme of a **wrapper class,** which typically stores a primitive type and adds operations that the primitive type either does not support or does not support correctly. A similar concept is an **adapter class,** which is typically used when the interface of a class is not exactly what is needed and provides a wrapping effect while changing the interface (in a manner similar to electrical adapters).

An *adapter class* is used when the interface of a class is not exactly what is needed.

One difference between wrappers and adapters is that often an adapter is implemented by private inheritance. Implementation via private inheritance often is not available for wrapper classes that wrap a primitive (and therefore a nonclass) type. In this section we illustrate some uses of wrapper classes and also provide an example of an adapter class.

5.3.1 Wrapper for Pointers

Here, we illustrate two wrapper templates for pointers. Our first template is based on the `Shape` example in Section 4.3. We use it when we discuss indirect sorting in Section 9.9. The second example illustrates a casual implementation of the newly standardized `auto_ptr` class. This wrapper is used to add limited destructorlike behavior to pointers.

Pointers for Sorting

The `Pointer` stores, as a data member, a pointer to a `Comparable`.

Our first wrapper is the class template `Pointer`, shown in Figure 5.7. The `Pointer` stores, as a data member, a pointer to a `Comparable`. We can then provide a comparison operator for the `Pointer` type.

The data member `pointee` is declared in the `private` section at line 17. The constructor for the `Pointer` class requires an initial value for `pointee` (which defaults to `NULL` if omitted), shown at line 7.

```
1 // Class that wraps a pointer variable for sorting.
2
3 template <class Comparable>
4 class Pointer
5 {
6   public:
7     explicit Pointer( Comparable *rhs = NULL )
8       : pointee( rhs ) { }
9     bool operator<( const Pointer & rhs ) const
10      { return *pointee < *rhs.pointee; }
11    operator Comparable * ( ) const
12      { return pointee; }
13    Comparable * get( ) const
14      { return pointee; }
15
16  private:
17    Comparable *pointee;
18 };
```

Figure 5.7 The `Pointer` class, which wraps a pointer variable for sorting.

Classes that encapsulate the behavior of a pointer are called **smart pointer classes.** This class is smarter than a plain pointer because it automatically initializes itself to `NULL` if no initial value is provided.

Classes that encapsulate the behavior of a pointer are called *smart pointer classes.*

Implementing `operator<` is identical to the approach used in the `PtrToShape` class in Figure 4.18. As was done there, we just apply the < operator to the `Comparable` objects that are being pointed at. Note that this is *not* circular logic. The (template) `operator<` at line 9 in the class `Pointer` compares two `Pointer` types; the call at line 10 compares two `Comparable` types.

Line 11 shows bizarre C++ syntax at its finest: the type conversion operator. This method defines a type conversion from `Pointer<Comparable>` to `Comparable *`. The implementation is simple enough: We just return `pointee` at line 12, allowing us to get at the pointer. Although we could have used a named member function, such as `get`, at line 13, this type conversion simplifies the `largeObjectSort` algorithm presented later in Figure 9.9.

These type conversions are great when they work, but they can cause unexpected problems. Consider the code in Figure 5.8. We provided `operator!=`, and to avoid any suspicious compiler bugs, we wrote it as a real function instead of a function template.

Type conversions can cause unexpected problems.

```
1 // Define != for two Pointer<int> objects.
2 bool operator!= ( const Pointer<int> & lhs,
3                   const Pointer<int> & rhs )
4 {
5     return lhs < rhs || rhs < lhs;
6 }
7
8 int main( )
9 {
10     int *p = new int( 3 );
11     Pointer<int> q( new int( 4 ) );
12
13     if( q != p )  // Compare pointed-at objects???
14         cout << "q and p are different" << endl;
15     return 0;
16 }
```

Figure 5.8 Ambiguity with dual-direction type conversions.

Suppose that the constructor at line 7 in Figure 5.7 was not declared with `explicit`. In this case line 13 in Figure 5.8 would not compile because an ambiguity would be created. We can either convert `q` to an `int *` and use the `!=` operator defined for primitive pointer variables, or we can promote `p` to a `Pointer<int>`, using the constructor, and then use the `!=` defined for `Pointer<int`. This ambiguity is a direct consequence of the fact that two types have implicit conversions to each other. This is a **dual-direction** implicit conversion.

Avoid dual-direction implicit conversions in any nontrivial class.

There are lots of ways out of this quandary (for instance, you can make the `Pointer` constructor `explicit` as was done in Figure 5.7). You should generally avoid dual-direction implicit conversions in any nontrivial class. If you always use `explicit` or never use type conversion operators, you won't have this problem.

Auto-pointers

The recently adopted C++ standard contains a new wrapper class called the **`auto_ptr`**, which helps automatically delete dynamically allocated objects. This class is intended to help solve three common C++ pointer problems.

The `auto_ptr` wraps a pointer, and its destructor calls `delete`.

Recall that, if an object is dynamically allocated by a call to `new`, it must eventually be freed by a call to `delete`. Otherwise, we can have a memory (or other resource) leak. The `auto_ptr` helps do this task automatically by wrapping the pointer inside the `auto_ptr` class and then having the `auto_ptr` destructor call `delete`. The `auto_ptr` class is designed for three scenarios.

Scenario 1: We need to `delete` a local dynamically allocated object.

In the first scenario, inside a function a local pointer variable allocates, via `new`, an object that has local scope only. When the function returns, the object is expected to be freed by a call to `delete`. Typical code looks like:

```
void func( )
{
    Object *obj = new Object( ... );
     ...
    delete obj;
}
```

This code seems simple enough, but some dangers are lurking. If `func` has multiple returns, we must ensure that `delete` is always reached. And if `func` throws an uncaught exception, the `delete` never occurs. However, as destructors are always called when a function exits (even if via an uncaught exception), if the pointer is wrapped inside an object whose destructor calls `delete`, the memory will be reclaimed.

Scenario 2: We need to `delete` an object created and returned from a completed function call.

The second scenario is a function that allocates an object and returns a pointer to it. The caller is now expected to call `delete` when it no longer needs the object. Typical code looks like:

```
Object *func1( )
{
    Object *obj1 = new Object( ... );
     ...
    return obj1;
}


void func( )
{
    Object *obj = func1( );
     ...
    delete obj;
}
```

This scenario has problems similar to those of the first scenario (we must be sure to reach the `delete` in all cases), except that we must ensure that `delete` is not called in `func1`.

Scenario 3: We need to `delete` a dynamically allocated object created by the calling function.

A third scenario is a function that allocates an object and then calls another function, with the expectation that the other function will clean up, as in

```
void func( Object *obj )
{
      ...
    delete obj;
}


void func1( )
{
    Object *obj1 = new Object( ... );
      ...
    func( obj1 );
      ...
}
```

Do not use `auto_ptr` for more than intended by its designers.

Here `func1` creates an object, sends a pointer to it to `func` and expects `func` to eventually call `delete`. These tasks are all that `auto_ptr` is expected to be used for. Fancier automatic garbage collection requires more sophisticated logic.

The basic property of the `auto_ptr` wrapper is as follows. It wraps the pointer variable (thus storing the value of the pointer as the `pointee` data member). It also indicates whether it is the owner of the pointer (as a Boolean `isOwner`). If it is the owner, then when its destructor is called it must apply the `delete` operator to the pointer. When a copy is performed, ownership is transferred.

The destructor calls `delete` if it owns the pointee.

Figure 5.9 illustrates our version, the `AutoPointer`. The basic constructor is shown starting at line 7. It simply sets `pointee` and `isOwner`. The destructor calls the private member function `free`, which itself calls `delete` if the `AutoPointer` is the owner (of `pointee`). Lines 37 and 38 implement some of the same logic used in the `Pointer` class earlier in this section. The code in lines 33 to 36 implements the dereferencing operator (which is the equivalent of `*pointee`) and `->` (which is the equivalent of `pointee`).

The `release` method gives up ownership of the pointee.

Only three other methods are left: `release`, the copy constructor, and `operator=`. The `release` method (lines 39 and 40) gives up ownership, but otherwise behaves like `get`. It can be called when control is transferred by a copy operation.

Thus, in the copy constructor at lines 10 and 11, instead of copying the pointer value with `pointee=rhs.pointee`, we use `rhs.pointee.release()` on the right-hand side. `rhs`'s ownership is

```
// Class that wraps a local pointer variable.

template <class Object>
class AutoPointer
{
  public:
    explicit AutoPointer( Object *rhs = NULL )
      : isOwner( rhs != NULL ), pointee( rhs ) { }

    AutoPointer( AutoPointer & rhs ) : isOwner( rhs.isOwner )
      { pointee = rhs.release( ); }

    ~AutoPointer( )
      { free( ); }

    const AutoPointer & operator= ( AutoPointer & rhs )
    {
        if( this != &rhs )
        {
            Object *other = rhs.get( );
            if( other != pointee )      // Different pointees, so
            {
                free( );                // Give up current pointer
                isOwner = rhs.isOwner;  // Assume ownership
            }
            else if( rhs.isOwner )      // Same pointers
                isOwner = true;         // If rhs owned it, now I do
            pointee = rhs.release( );   // Copy pointee, rhs drops ownership
        }
        return *this;
    }

    Object & operator* ( ) const
      { return *get( ); }
    Object * operator-> ( ) const
      { return get( ); }
    Object * get( ) const
      { return pointee; }
    Object * release( )
      { isOwner = false; return pointee; }

  private:
    Object *pointee;
    bool    isOwner;

    void free( )
      { if( isOwner ) delete pointee; }
};
```

Figure 5.9 The `auto_ptr` class (we use the name `AutoPointer`).

relinquished by the call to `release` and transferred to the newly constructed object via the initializer list.

The most complicated routine is the copy assignment operator, shown at lines 16–31. The main complication is that, before copying into the target, we must call `delete` on the target's current `pointee` if the target owns it (and the target's current `pointee` is different from the new `pointee`).

The code is extremely tricky; almost any change breaks it. After taking care of aliasing (line 18), we have two basic cases. Either both pointees are the same or they are different. If they are different, then the target pointee is freed (line 23), we assume ownership if `rhs` had ownership (line 24), and then we copy the pointee (line 28). Note carefully, that at line 28, `rhs` always gives up ownership if it had it. Otherwise, the pointees are different. In that case, if `rhs` had ownership, we take it over (line 27) prior to copying the pointee (line 28) (and relinquishing ownership). Note also that if the current `AutoPointer` had ownership at the start, then it still does.

***Member templates* allow us to declare member function templates, using additional template types.**

The main difference between this implementation and the implementation in the C++ standard is behavior under inheritance. Specifically, let us consider the classes `Base` and `Derived`, as usual. Although a `Derived*` value can be copied into a `Base*` value, an `AutoPointer<Derived>` object cannot be copied into a `AutoPointer<Base>` object in our implementation. Adding this functionality requires using **member templates,** which allow us to declare member function templates, using additional template types. For instance, the copy constructor would look like:

```
template <class OtherObject>
AutoPointer( AutoPointer<OtherObject> & rhs )
  : isOwner( rhs.isOwner ) { pointee = rhs.release( ); }
```

The main difference between this implementation and the implementation in the C++ standard is behavior under inheritance.

In this scenario, we define the construction (no longer a copy constructor) of an `AutoPointer` of one type with an `AutoPointer` of any other type. However, the assignment statement will generate a compiler error if the underlying pointees are not type compatible.

Although this is a neat solution, member templates unfortunately are a recent language addition that is not supported on all compilers.

5.3.2 A Constant Reference Wrapper

A reference variable must reference an object. Sometimes this requirement is unfortunate.

Reference variables in C++ are different from pointer variables in several ways. One important difference is that, whereas pointer variables can point at either an object or `NULL`, a reference variable must reference an object. Sometimes this requirement is unfortunate. For instance, when we search for an object in an arbitrary container, we may want to return a reference to it. But what if the object is not found?

```
// Class that wraps a constant reference variable.
// Useful for return value from a container find method.

template <class Object>
class Cref
{
  public:
    Cref( ) : obj( NULL ) { }
    explicit Cref( const Object & x ) : obj( &x ) { }

    const Object & get( ) const
    {
        if( isNull( ) )
            throw NullPointerException( );
        else
            return *obj;
    }

    bool isNull( ) const
      { return obj == NULL; }

  private:
    const Object *obj;
};
```

Figure 5.10 Constant reference wrapper.

The solution, as usual, is to wrap the behavior of a reference variable inside a class. Our class, `Cref`, shown in Figure 5.10, mimics a constant reference variable. (Alternatively, we could implement a simple reference class and even use inheritance to make the reference and constant reference classes type compatible; we leave this for you to do as Exercise 5.18.) The implementation is short.

`Cref` wraps the behavior of a reference variable inside a class.

We store a pointer to the referenced object as a private data member. The pointer is initialized in the constructor, but it is `NULL` if `Cref` is constructed with no parameters. We provide a `get` method that returns the constant reference and an `isNull` method that returns `true` if the null reference is being represented.

`Cref` provides an `isNull` method that returns `true` if the null reference is being represented.

5.3.3 Adapters: Changing an Interface

The adapter pattern is used to change the interface of an existing class to conform to another. Sometimes it is used to provide a simpler interface, either with fewer methods or easier-to-use methods. At other times it is used

The adapter pattern is used to change the interface of an existing class to conform to another.

```
// A class for simulating a memory cell.

template <class Object>
class StorageCell : private MemoryCell<Object>
{
  public:
    explicit StorageCell( const Object & initialValue
                                                   = Object( ) )
      : MemoryCell<Object>( initialValue ) { }

    const Object & get( ) const
      { return read( ); }
    void put( const Object & x )
      { write( x ); }
};
```

Figure 5.11 An adapter class that changes the `MemoryCell` interface to use `get` and `put`.

simply to change some method names. In either case, the implementation technique is similar.

For example, in our `MemoryCell` class in Section 3.4 we use `read` and `write`. But what if we wanted the interface to use `get` and `put` instead? There are two reasonable alternatives. One is to use composition. Doing so, however means, for instance, that a call to `get` will then call `read`, thus adding an extra layer of overhead. The other alternative is to use private inheritance.

We use private inheritance to implement the new class, `StorageCell`, in Figure 5.11. Its methods are implemented by calls to the base class methods. As discussed in Section 4.4.5, in private inheritance, public methods in the base class are private in the derived class. Thus, as Figure 5.12 illustrates, the only visible methods are the `StorageCell` constructor, `get`, and `put`.

5.4 Iterators

An *iterator* is the object that controls iteration of a collection.

Consider the problem of printing the elements in a collection. Typically, the collection is an array, so assuming that the object `v` is an expanded `vector` template, its contents are easily printed with code like

```
for( int i = 0; i < v.size( ); i++ )
    cout << v[ i ] << endl;
```

```
int main( )
{
    StorageCell<int>    m1;
    StorageCell<string> m2( "hello" );

    m1.put( 37 );
    m2.put( m2.get( ) + " world" );
    cout << m1.get( ) << endl << m2.get( ) << endl;

    // The next line does not compile if uncommented.
    // cout << m1.read( ) << endl;
    return 0;
}
```

Figure 5.12 An illustration of private inheritance, in which the `MemoryCell` methods are no longer visible.

In this loop, `i` is an iterator. An **iterator** is the object used to control the iteration of a collection. However, using the integer `i` as an iterator constrains the design: We can store the collection only in an arraylike structure. A more flexible alternative is to design an iterator class that encapsulates a position inside a collection. The iterator class provides methods to step through the collection.

The key is the concept of programming to an interface: We want the code that performs access of the container to be as independent of the type of the container as possible. To get this code we only use methods that are common to all containers and their iterators.

When we program to an interface, we write code that uses the most abstract methods. These methods are then applied to actual concrete types.

Of the many different possible iterator designs, we describe three here, in increasing order of complexity. Iterators are a core component of the STL, and their design is similar (but of course, slightly more complex) to our second design in Section 5.4.2. In Chapter 7, we discuss STL iterators. They are used throughout the case studies in Part III, and some implementations of these iterators and the collections that they iterate are provided in Part IV.

5.4.1 Iterator Design 1

In our first iterator design we use only three methods. The container class is required to provide a `getIterator` method, which returns an appropriate iterator for the collection. The iterator class has the other two methods: `hasNext` returns `true` if the iteration has not yet been exhausted; and `next` returns the next item in the collection (and in the process, advances the notion of the current position). This iterator interface matches one that is provided in the Java programming language.

The `getIterator` method returns an appropriate iterator for the collection.

```
int main( )
{
    MyVector<int> v;

    v.push_back( 3 );
    v.push_back( 2 );

    cout << "Vector contents: " << endl;

    VectorIterator<int> itr = v.getIterator( );
    while( itr.hasNext( ) )
        cout << itr.next( ) << endl;

    return 0;
}
```

Figure 5.13 The `main` method to illustrate iterator design 1.

```
template <class Object>
class VectorIterator;

// Same as the vector, but has a getIterator method.
// No extra data, no overridden methods, so non-virtual
// destructor in original vector is OK!

template <class Object>
class MyVector : public vector<Object>
{
  public:
    explicit MyVector( int size = 0 )
      : vector<Object>( size ) { }

    VectorIterator<Object> getIterator( ) const
      { return VectorIterator<Object>( this ); }
};
```

Figure 5.14 The `MyVector` class, designs 1 and 2.

To illustrate the implementation of this design, we write the collection and iterator class templates, `MyVector` and `VectorIterator`, respectively. We show their use in Figure 5.13 and the code for `MyVector` in Figure 5.14. To simplify matters, we inherit from the `vector` class. The only difference between `MyVector` and `vector` is its `getIterator` method. (The use of inheritance here has nothing to do with the iterator pattern.)

```
1 // A passive iterator class. Steps through its MyVector.
2
3 template <class Object>
4 class VectorIterator
5 {
6   public:
7     VectorIterator( const MyVector<Object> *v )
8       : owner( v ), count( 0 ) { }
9
10    bool hasNext( ) const
11      { return count != owner->size( ); }
12
13    const Object & next( )
14      { return (*owner)[ count++ ]; }
15
16  private:
17    const MyVector<Object> *owner;
18    int count;
19 };
```

Figure 5.15 Implementation of the `VectorIterator`, design 1.

The `getIterator` method simply returns a new iterator; note that the iterator must have information about the container that it is iterating over. Thus the iterator is constructed with a pointer to the `vector`. The only other method in `MyVector` is the constructor, which simply calls the base class constructor. Because we are using public inheritance, it would be proper to change the `vector` class's destructor to be virtual, if possible. However, in this case it does not matter because `MyVector` adds no extra data members. As a result, this case turns out to be a nice example of public inheritance.

The iterator is constructed with a pointer to the container that it iterates over.

Lines 1 and 2 represent an incomplete class declaration. This particular declaration states that `VectorIterator` is a class template, but it does not provide the class definition. However, this declaration is enough to make line 16 compile. An **incomplete class declaration** is used to inform the compiler of a class and is necessary when two or more classes refer to each circularly.

An *incomplete class declaration* is necessary when two or more classes refer to each circularly.

Figure 5.15 shows the code for `VectorIterator`. The iterator keeps both a variable (`count`) that represents the current position in the vector and a pointer to the vector. The implementation of the constructor and two member functions is straightforward. The constructor directly initializes the data members in the initializer list, `hasNext` simply compares the current position with the vector size, and `next` uses the current position to index the array (and then advances the current position). Note the use of `const` throughout—to ensure that this iterator makes no attempt to modify the container.

5.4.2 Iterator Design 2

The second design puts more functionality in the iterator.

A limitation of our first iterator design is the relatively limited interface. Resetting the iterator to the beginning is impossible, and the `next` method couples access of an item with advancing. Our second design, shown in Figure 5.16, puts more functionality in the iterator but leaves the `MyVector` class unchanged.

The STL iterator has some commonality with our second design, but there also are some important differences.

The STL iterator has some commonality with our second design, but there also are some important differences. It is similar in that the methods to advance and retrieve are separate. It is different in that the STL iterator can make changes to the underlying collection.

Another difference is that the STL iterator does not have `isValid` or `reset` methods. Instead, the container has a method to return an invalid iterator and a method to return an iterator representing the starting point. We can test whether an iterator is in an invalid state by comparing it with the invalid iterator given by the container. We can reset the iterator by copying the starting point iterator into it. The STL also makes extensive use of operator overloading. For example, `advance` is replaced with `operator++`. Details of using STL iterators are presented in Chapter 7.

5.4.3 Inheritance-Based Iterators and Factories

In the iterators that we have designed so far we have managed to abstract the concept of iteration into an iterator class. This approach is good, because it means that, if the collection changes from an array-based collection to something else, we do not need to change the basic code, as in lines 38 and 39 in Figure 5.16.

This is a significant improvement, but changes from an array-based collection to something else also require that we change all the declarations of the iterator. For instance, in Figure 5.16, we would need to change line 33. We discuss an alternative to doing that in this section.

An inheritance-based iteration scheme defines an iterator abstract base class. Clients program to this interface.

Our basic idea is to define an abstract base class `Iterator`. Corresponding to each different kind of container is an iterator that implements the `Iterator` protocol. In our example, this approach gives three classes: `MyVector`, `Iterator`, and `VectorIterator`. The relationship that holds is `VectorIterator` IS-A `Iterator`. The reason we use this approach is that each container can now create an appropriate iterator but pass it back as an abstract `Iterator`. To iterate through the container, we must use only methods defined in the abstract `Iterator` class. The technique of using classes by writing in terms of the most abstract interface is known as **programming to an interface.**

```
// A passive iterator class. Steps through its MyVector.

template <class Object>
class VectorIterator
{
  public:
    VectorIterator( const MyVector<Object> *v )
      : owner( v ), count( 0 ) { }

    void reset( )
      { count = 0; }

    bool isValid( ) const
      { return count < owner->size( ); }

    void advance( )
      { count++; }

    const Object & retrieve( ) const
      { return (*owner)[ count ]; }

  private:
    const MyVector<Object> *owner;
    int count;
};

int main( )
{
    MyVector<int> v;

    v.push_back( 3 );
    v.push_back( 2 );
    VectorIterator<int> itr = v.getIterator( );

    for( int i = 0; i < 2; i++ )
    {
        cout << "Vector contents: " << endl;
        for( itr.reset( ); itr.isValid( ); itr.advance( ) )
            cout << itr.retrieve( ) << endl;
    }

    return 0;
}
```

Figure 5.16 A new `VectorIterator`, with some additional functionality, and a test program.

```
template <class Object>
class Iterator;

template <class Object>
class VectorIterator;

// Same as the vector, but has a getIterator method.
// No extra data, no overridden methods, so non-virtual
// destructor in original vector is OK!

template <class Object>
class MyVector : public vector<Object>
{
  public:
    explicit MyVector( int size = 0 )
      : vector<Object>( size ) { }

    Iterator<Object> *getIterator( ) const
      { return new VectorIterator<Object>( this ); }
};
```

Figure 5.17 An inheritance-based iterator design, in which `getIterator` returns a pointer to an iterator.

The inheritance-based scheme introduces pointers (or references). The iterators are now allocated by `new`.

Figure 5.17 shows the new `MyVector`, which returns a pointer to an `Iterator` object that is dynamically constructed by calling `new`. Because `VectorIterator` IS-A `Iterator`, we can safely do so. Note that the use of inheritance and polymorphism require that we introduce pointers or references. Doing so muddies the code a bit, which is one reason why the STL is template based, rather than inheritance based.

A *factory method* creates a new concrete instance but returns it by using a pointer (or reference) to the abstract class.

Because `getIterator` creates and returns a new `Iterator` object, whose actual type is unknown, it is commonly called a *factory method*. In general, a **factory method** creates a new concrete instance but returns it by using a pointer (or reference) to the abstract class. The iterator classes are shown in Figure 5.18. First, we have the abstract class `Iterator`, which serves simply to establish the protocol by which all subclasses of `Iterator` can be accessed. The protocol is specified with pure virtual functions. As usual, we have a virtual destructor. In order to keep the code short, we use the simplest protocol—that seen in design 1 (Section 5.4.1).

This version of `VectorIterator` is essentially identical to the original implementation shown in Figure 5.15, except that it is a derived class of `Iterator`.

```
// A passive iterator class protocol.
// Steps through its container.

template <class Object>
class Iterator
{
  public:
    virtual ~Iterator( ) { }

    virtual bool hasNext( ) const = 0;
    virtual const Object & next( ) = 0;
};


// A concrete implementation of the iterator.
// Could have been nested inside of MyVector!

template <class Object>
class VectorIterator : public Iterator<Object>
{
  public:
    VectorIterator( const MyVector<Object> *v )
      : owner( v ), count( 0 ) { }

    bool hasNext( ) const
      { return count != owner->size( ); }

    const Object & next( )
      { return (*owner)[ count++ ]; }

  private:
    const MyVector<Object> *owner;
    int count;
};
```

Figure 5.18 The iterator abstract class and a concrete implementation.

Figure 5.19 demonstrates how the inheritance-based iterators are used. At line 10, the declaration of `itr:` is now a pointer to an `Iterator`. Nowhere in `main` is there any mention of the actual `VectorIterator` type. In fact, we could have written `VectorIterator` as a nested class in the private section of `MyVector`. The fact that a `VectorIterator` exists does not affect any clients of the `MyVector` class. This is a neat design and illustrates nicely the idea of hiding an implementation and programming to an interface.

Nowhere in `main` is there any mention of the actual iterator type.

The changes to `main` are relatively minimal. Lines 11 and 12 change because we must use `operator->` instead of the dot operator.

```
1  int main( )
2  {
3      MyVector<int> v;
4
5      v.push_back( 3 );
6      v.push_back( 2 );
7
8      cout << "Vector contents: " << endl;
9
10     Iterator<int> *itr = v.getIterator( );
11     while( itr->hasNext( ) )
12         cout << itr->next( ) << endl;
13
14     delete itr;
15
16     return 0;
17 }
```

Figure 5.19 An illustration of the use of iterators in inheritance-based design.

The dynamically allocated iterator must be reclaimed by calling `delete`.

Line 14 illustrates a disadvantage: The dynamically allocated iterator must be reclaimed by calling `delete`. Remembering to do so all the time is annoying. However, if we examine this situation closely, we can see a classic application of scenario #2 for the `auto_ptr`. Recall from Section 5.3.1 (page 165) that in this scenario an object is allocated inside a function (in this case, `getIterator`) and is returned to the caller. The caller is responsible for handling `delete`, which is exactly the situation in Figure 5.19. Thus although inconvenient, there is some support in the language to make our life easier.

By the way, recall that at the end of Section 5.3.1 (beginning on page 168), we explained that our version of `AutoPointer` differed from the STL `auto_ptr` because that version allows any compatible pointers to be wrapped, whereas our version requires an exact type match. We also explained that member templates could be used to loosen the requirement of an exact type match. Looking at how `auto_ptr` would be used here, we see that we would need to do the following.

1. In Figure 5.19, line 10, `itr` would be an `auto_ptr`, and line 14 would disappear.
2. In Figure 5.17, `getIterator` would be rewritten to return an `auto_ptr` (line 18), and the result of `new` would be wrapped inside an `auto_ptr` (line 19).

These changes to `getIterator` give the implementation that replaces lines 18–19 of Figure 5.17.

```
auto_ptr<Iterator<Object> > getIterator( ) const
  { return auto_ptr<Iterator<Object> >( new
                    VectorIterator<Object>( this ) ); }
```

The construction of an `auto_ptr<Iterator<Object> >`, with a `VectorIterator<Object>` pointer, implies that we need the STL version.

5.5 Composite (Pair)

In most languages, a function can return only a single object. What do we do if we need to return two or more objects? There are two possibilities: One is to use reference variables; the other is to combine the objects into a single `struct` (or `class`). The most common situation in which multiple objects need to be returned is the case of two objects. So a common design pattern, the Composite pattern, stores two objects in one entity. We return them as a **pair.**

A common design pattern is to return two objects as a *pair*.

In addition to the situation just described, pairs are useful for implementing maps and dictionaries. In both these abstractions, we maintain key-value pairs: Pairs are added to the map or dictionary; we then search for a key, returning its value. One common way to implement a map is to use a set, in which we have a collection of items and search for a match. If the items are pairs—and the match criterion is based exclusively on the key component of the pair—we can easily write an adapter class that constructs a map on the basis of the set. We explore this idea in more detail in Chapter 19.

Pairs are useful for implementing key-value pairs in maps and dictionaries.

The STL defines a `pair` class. An implementation is shown in Figure 5.20. Note that it is a class only in the technical sense; the data members are public.

The STL defines a `pair` class.

5.6 Observer

Our last pattern is the **Observer pattern,** the use of which involves a *subject* and a set of *observers;* the observers are informed whenever something interesting happens to the subject. The number of observers can vary as the application runs and can be large.

The *Observer pattern* involves a subject and a set of observers. The observers are informed whenever something interesting happens to the subject.

A simplistic example of an Observer pattern is a windowing operating system, such as Windows or Mac O/S. When a window is created or maximized, it covers other windows. The windows that are covered are now observers in the sense that they want to be informed when the newly created

```
// Class (more like a struct) that stores
// a pair of objects.

template <class Type1, class Type2>
class pair
{
  public:
    Type1 first;
    Type2 second;
    pair( const Type1 & f = Type1( ),
          const Type2 & s = Type2( ) )
      : first( f ), second( s ) { }
};
```

Figure 5.20 The `pair` class (basically the same as the STL version).

window is minimized or destroyed—or simply moved—as this action might require that the previously hidden windows be redrawn.

Another example might be a class that wraps pointers. Several wrapper objects may be sharing a pointee that is pointing at some dynamically allocated object. If one instance of the wrapper calls `delete` on the dynamically allocated object, the other wrappers have stale pointers, which gives undefined behavior that can be hard to detect. A solution is that when the `delete` is performed, we inform all the wrappers that are looking at that deleted object, perhaps setting their pointees to `NULL` to ensure defined behavior.

Figure 5.21 contains an abstract base class `Observer` and a base class (which could be abstract, but is not) for the observee `Subject`.

The `Observer` abstract class specifies a protocol: when something interesting happens, `Observer` is told about it by having its `update` method called.

The `Observer` abstract class specifies a protocol: when something interesting happens, `Observer` is told about it by having its `update` method called. A subclass can override `update` to handle the interesting occurrence. For instance, in our windowing example, the observer windows will have their `update` method called when the window that was covering it is no longer in the way. The `update` method could redraw an appropriate portion of the screen.

The `Subject` class defines methods to add an observer, remove an observer, and notify all observers that something has happened.

The `Subject` class is not abstract (but see Exercise 5.7). Instead it defines methods to add an observer, remove an observer, and notify all observers that something has happened. It does so by keeping an internal list of all registered observers (possibly in a `vector`). The implementations of `addObserver` and `removeObserver` are in the online code.

An illustration of the Observer pattern in action is shown in Figure 5.22. There we have a subject, which is a `Timer` object, and we have `Echo` objects, which are the interested observers. The `Timer` object has a `tick` method; whenever the `tick` method is called, any `Echo` objects that are

```
class Subject;

class Observer
{
  public:
    virtual ~Observer( ) { }
    virtual void update( Subject *observee ) = 0;
};

class Subject
{
  public:
    virtual ~Subject( ) { }

      // Add obs to the set of observers; see online code.
    virtual void addObserver( Observer *obs );

      // Remove obs from the set of observers.
    virtual void removeObserver( Observer *obs );

      // Call the update method for all observers.
    virtual void notifyAll( )
    {
        for( int i = 0; i < observers.size( ); i++ )
            observers[ i ]->update( this );
    }

  private:
    vector<Observer *> observers;
};
```

Figure 5.21 Abstract classes for `Observer` and a base class for the observee `Subject`.

observing the `Timer` object are notified, and their `update` method is called. In our example, the `update` method simply prints a message, allowing us to see that the notification occurred.

The `Timer` class is often used to implement callback functions. A **callback function** is a function that is registered to be called at a later time. In the Observer pattern `update` is such a function.

A *callback function* is a function that is registered to be called at a later time.

Here, the `update` method in the various `Echo` objects are called back when `tick` occurs. In a typical application, we have a set of actions that are to occur regularly, perhaps every hour. Each action registers itself with the `Timer`, and when the clock strikes a new hour, all registered actions are executed.

```
1 // Timer class: tick method calls notify.
2
3 class Timer : public Subject
4 {
5   public:
6     void tick( )
7       { notifyAll( ); }
8 };
9
10
11 // Echo class: this in an observer.
12 // It is constructed with a Timer object; when
13 // the Timer object ticks, update is
14 // automatically called.
15
16 class Echo : public Observer
17 {
18   public:
19     Echo( int id, Timer *t ) : myId( id ), observee( t )
20       { observee->addObserver( this ); }
21
22     ~Echo( )
23       { observee->removeObserver( this ); }
24
25     void update( Subject *s )
26       { if( observee == s ) cout << myId << endl; }
27
28   private:
29     int myId;
30     Subject *observee;
31 };
```

Figure 5.22 Concrete classes: `Echo` observes a `Timer` object and reacts when the `Timer`'s `tick` method is called,

A `Timer` object simply calls its inherited `notifyAll` whenever `tick` is executed. `Echo` objects are constructed by providing a `Timer` object.

Thus, a `Timer` object simply calls its inherited `notifyAll` whenever `tick` is executed. The `Echo` class is somewhat more complicated. `Echo` objects are constructed by providing a `Timer` object. In other words, an observer is constructed by passing in the subject that it is observing. The observer is then added to the subject's list of interested parties (line 20). When the observer is no longer active, it is removed from the subject's list. This task is handled in the `Echo` destructor. As mentioned earlier, we then provide the required implementation for the `Observer` protocol, which in our case means that we implement `update`. Our `update` simply prints a message.

```
1 // A test program.
2 void testEcho12( Timer & t )
3 {
4     Echo e1( 1, &t );
5     Echo e2( 2, &t );
6
7     cout << "Expecting 1 and 2 to respond." << endl;
8     t.tick( );
9     cout << "1 and 2 disappear." << endl;
10 }
11
12 int main( )
13 {
14     Timer t;
15
16     testEcho12( t );    // 1 and 2 should respond
17
18     Echo e3( 3, &t );
19     Echo e4( 4, &t );
20
21     Timer other;
22     Echo e5( 5, &other );   // registered with other, not t
23
24     cout << "Only 3 and 4 are currently observable." << endl;
25     cout << "Expecting 3 and 4 to respond." << endl;
26     t.tick( );
27
28     return 0;
29 }
```

Figure 5.23 Program to test the `Timer` and `Echo` classes.

A program that tests this process is shown in Figure 5.23. First we declare a `Timer` object `t`. Occasionally, we call `t.tick()`, and when we do, any `Echo` object actively registered with `t` has its `update` method called.

Thus, when `testEcho12` is called, because `e1` and `e2` are both constructed with `t` as their subject, when `t`'s `tick` method is called, we get output for objects `e1` and `e2`. When `testEcho12` returns, `e1` and `e2` no longer exist and their destructors ensure that they are no longer registered as observers for `t`. Then `e3`, `e4`, and `e5` are constructed as new observers. Note, however, that `e5` is listening for `other.tick()`. Thus when `t`'s `tick` method is called at line 26, only `e3` and `e4` respond.

Summary

In this chapter we described several common design patterns that we use throughout the text. Although we concentrated mostly on object-based design patterns, some of the patterns toward the end of the chapter emphasize the central role that inheritance plays in many patterns. Unfortunately, because of memory management issues, inheritance complicates our implementations, and as a result, we use it sparingly. However, these patterns can give you a feel for the power of inheritance and the techniques that it introduces.

This chapter concludes the first part of the text, which provided an overview of C++ and object-oriented programming. We now go on to look at algorithms and the building blocks of problem-solving programming.

Objects of the Game

adapter class Typically used when the interface of another class is not exactly what is needed and provides a wrapping effect while changing the interface. (p. 162)

`auto_ptr` A new class in the STL that helps automatically `delete` dynamically allocated objects. (p. 164)

callback function A function that is registered to be called at a later time. (p. 181)

Composite pattern Stores two or more objects in one entity. (p. 179)

design pattern Describes a problem that occurs over and over in software engineering and then describes the solution in a sufficiently generic manner as to be applicable in a wide variety of contexts. (p. 155)

dual-direction implicit conversion The circumstance in which implicit conversions between two types are defined in both directions, which often leads to ambiguities and thus should be avoided. (p. 164)

factory method Creates a new concrete instance but returns it by using a pointer (or reference) to the abstract class. (p. 176)

function object An object passed to a generic function with the intention of having its single method used by the generic function. (p. 158)

Functor A function object. (p. 158)

incomplete class declaration Used to inform the compiler of the existence of a class and is necessary when two or more classes refer to each circularly. (p. 173)

Iterator An object used to control iteration of a collection. (p. 170)

member templates Allow declaration of member function templates, using different template types. (p. 168)

Observer pattern Involves a *subject* and a set of *observers;* the observers are informed whenever something interesting happens to the subject. (p. 179)

Pair The composite pattern storing two objects as an entity. (p. 179)

programming to an interface The technique of using classes by writing in terms of the most abstract interface and attempting to hide even the name of the concrete class that is being operated on. (p. 174)

smart pointer classes Classes that encapsulate the behavior of a pointer. (p. 163)

Wrapper class Typically used to store a primitive type and add operations that the primitive type either does not support or does not support correctly. (p. 162)

Common Errors

1. When writing `operator()`, remember that you still must have a parameter list.
2. When you send a function object as a parameter, you must send a constructed object, not simply the name of the class.
3. Using dual-direction implicit type conversions is dangerous because they can lead to ambiguities.
4. Using `auto_ptr` in a setting more complex than it was designed for leads to trouble because the pointee will be destroyed if ownership is transferred to an owner that exits scope earlier than you think it will.
5. The Adapter pattern often implies private rather than public inheritance. If you are changing rather than simply augmenting the class interface, you do not want public inheritance.
6. Many design patterns that have cooperating classes require incomplete class declarations because the class declarations refer to each other circularly.
7. In C++, inheritance-based design patterns tend to require that you deal with reclaiming dynamically allocated objects, often leading to memory leaks, stale pointers, and other assorted bugs.
8. Using too few classes can be a sign of poor design. Often adding a class can clean up the design.

On the Internet

Rectangle.cpp	Contains the `Rectangle` example shown in Figures 5.2, and 5.4–5.6.
Wrapper.h	Contains both the `Cref` and `Pointer` classes.
Ambiguity.cpp	Illustrates the problem with dual-direction implicit type conversions, shown in Figure 5.8. To see the problem, you must remove the `explicit` directive in the `Pointer` constructor in **Wrapper.h.** To see the fix, you must be using a compiler that understands `explicit` (some simply ignore it).
AutoPointer.cpp	Contains an implementation of `AutoPointer`, shown in Figure 5.9, and a test program.
StorageCell.h	Contains the `StorageCell` adapter, shown in Figure 5.11.
TestStorageCell.cpp	Tests the `StorageCell` adapter, as shown in Figure 5.12.
Iterator1.cpp	Contains the complete iterator class and a test program, as shown in Section 5.4.1.
Iterator2.cpp	Contains the complete iterator class and a test program, as shown in Section 5.4.2.
Iterator3.cpp	Contains the complete iterator class and a test program, as shown in Section 5.4.3.
pair.h	Contains the `pair` class shown in Figure 5.20.
Observer.cpp	Contains the complete set of classes and a test program for the Observer pattern discussed in Section 5.6.

Exercises

In Short

5.1. What is a design pattern?

5.2. Describe how function objects are implemented in C++.

5.3. Explain the Adapter and Wrapper patterns. How do they differ?

5.4. What are two common ways to implement adapters? What are the trade-offs between these implementation methods?

5.5. Describe in general the
a. Iterator pattern.
b. Observer pattern.

5.6. Give an example of the Observer pattern that is not discussed in the text. Use a real-life example rather than a programming example.

In Theory

5.7. A class is abstract if it has at least one abstract method. The `Subject` class presented in Figure 5.21 is therefore not abstract. A little-known feature of C++ allows abstract methods to have an implementation; this feature is primarily used on the destructor. Verify that this feature exists by making the `Subject` destructor a pure virtual function while leaving its implementation in tact.

In Practice

5.8. Templates can be used to write generic function objects.
a. Write a class template function object named `less`. In the class template, overload `operator()` to call the `operator<` for its two `Comparable` parameters.
b. Rewrite the `findMax` function template in Figure 5.1 to call the `findMax` function template shown in Figure 5.4. Your rewrite may contain only one line in the function body: a call to the two-parameter `findMax` that sends a compatible function object from part (a).
c. Instead of writing a separate one-parameter `findMax`, can you simply rewrite the two-parameter `findMax` function template shown in Figure 5.4 to accept a default parameter that is a compatible function object from part (a)? Verify your answer by compiling code.

5.9. Write a generic `countMatches` function that takes two parameters. The first parameter is an array of `int`. The second parameter is a function object that returns a Boolean.
a. The method `countMatches` returns the number of array items for which the function object returns true. Implement `countMatches`.
b. Test `countMatches` by writing a function object `EqualsZero` that overloads `operator()` to accept one parameter and returns

true if the parameter is zero. Use an EqualsZero function object to test countMatches.

c. Rewrite countMatches (and EqualsZero) by using templates.

5.10. Although the function objects that we looked at store no data, that is not a requirement.

a. Write a function object EqualsK that contains one data member, k. The EqualsK object is constructed with a single parameter (default is zero) used to initialize k. Its one parameter operator() returns true if the parameter equals k.

b. Use EqualsK to test countMatches in Exercise 5.9 (if you did part (c), make EqualsK a template).

5.11. Add operator* and operator-> to the Pointer class template in Figure 5.7.

5.12. Is it safe to apply insertionSort (Figure 3.4) to a vector of auto_ptr objects?

5.13. The StorageClass adapter is implemented by private inheritance. Redo the implementation shown in Figure 5.11, using composition. Test your program by calling a significant number of StorageClass methods. Is there a significant difference in speed?

5.14. Add both the previous and hasPrevious methods to

a. Iterator design #1 (Section 5.4.1).

b. Iterator design #3 (Section 5.4.3).

5.15. In Java, iterator design #1 (Section 5.4.1) is an Enumeration. Assume that only design #2 has been written and that you want to write an iterator that follows the Enumeration interface.

a. What pattern describes the problem that you are trying to solve?

b. Write the class, using the name Enumeration, in terms of the iterator defined in design #2. Add a getEnumeration method to MyVector to do so.

5.16. Redo iterator design #3 (Section 5.4.3), using nested classes.

5.17. This exercise illustrates the idea of programming to an interface. Recall from Section 4.4.1 (and other chapters) that we often implement operator<< by calling a class's print method.

a. Write an abstract class Printable having one named method: print.

b. Should Printable define any other member functions? Why or why not? (*Hint:* recall Section 4.2.7.)

c. Implement an overloaded `operator<<` that takes a `Printable` object as a second parameter.
d. Suppose that `Shape` is a class. Describe the properties that `Shape` must have in order to have the overloaded method in part (b) called for all `Shape` objects.
e. An alternative scheme is simply to make `operator<<` a function template. Compare and contrast the two approaches. Is there any difference between them?

Programming Projects

5.18. Suppose that, in addition to a `Cref` class, we want a `Ref` class (that gives a simple reference). Keep in mind that `Ref<Obj>` and `Cref<Obj>` should be type-compatible in one direction. Recall that any function that is expecting a constant reference can receive either a constant reference or a reference, but not vice versa. This condition suggests that there should be an inheritance relationship between `Ref` and `Cref`.

a. Which class is the base class and which is the derived class?
b. One of the two classes will need to overload `get` with both an accessor and mutator version. Which one?
c. Implement the `Ref` and `Cref` classes.
d. Since `Cref<Base>` and `Cref<Derived>` are also type-compatible, if your compiler supports member templates, modify your classes to work when the template types are related by inheritance. See the discussion at the end of Section 5.3.2.

5.19. A reference-counted pointer class keeps track of how many pointers are pointing at the pointee. It does not `delete` the pointee until there are no more pointers to it. To implement the class you will need a second class, `RefCount`.

a. Write a class template called `RefCount` that stores a pointer to the pointee and a count of how many pointers are looking at the pointee. It should provide a method to add to the count and to decrement the count. If the count goes to 0, it can `delete` the pointee and then set the pointer to `NULL` (just to be safe). Carefully provide a constructor and, if you feel it to be appropriate, an implementation of the Big Three. The semantics of these methods may depend on how you implement the rest of this design.
b. Write a class template called `RefPointer` that stores a pointer to a `RefCount` object. If you construct it with a plain pointer, a new `RefCount` object is created, with count 1. If you construct

it with a copy constructor, it shares the `RefCount` object but adds 1 to the count in the `RefCount` object. If destructed, it drops the count in the `RefCount` object. You will need to work out the details for what happens in `operator=`. In addition to `get`, `RefPointer` should provide overloaded operators, such as `operator*`, `operator->`, and perhaps a one-way type conversion.

References

The classic reference on design patterns is [2]. It describes 23 standard patterns, many of which are inheritance based. Reference [1] provides C++ implementations for several patterns and coins the term *functor*.

1. J. O. Coplien, *Advanced C++ Programming Styles and Idioms*, Addison-Wesley, Reading, Mass., 1992.
2. E. Gamma, R. Helm, R. Johnson, and J. Vlissides, *Elements of Reusable Object-Oriented Software*, Addison-Wesley, Reading, Mass., 1995.

Part II Algorithms and Building Blocks

Chapter 6

Algorithm Analysis

In Part I we examined how object-oriented programming can help in the design and implementation of large systems. We did not examine performance issues. Generally, we use a computer because we need to process a large amount of data. When we run a program on large amounts of input, we must be certain that the program terminates within a reasonable amount of time. The amount of running time is almost always independent of the programming language or even the methodology we use (such as procedural versus object-oriented).

An **algorithm** is a clearly specified set of instructions a computer follows to solve a problem. Once an algorithm is given for a problem and determined to be correct, the next step is to determine the amount of resources, such as time and space, that the algorithm will require. This step is called *algorithm analysis*. An algorithm that requires several gigabytes of main memory is not useful for most current machines, even if it is completely correct.

In this chapter, we show:

- how to estimate the time required for an algorithm,
- how to use techniques that drastically reduce the running time of an algorithm,
- how to use a mathematical framework that more rigorously describes the running time of an algorithm, and
- how to write a simple *binary search* routine.

6.1 What Is Algorithm Analysis?

More data means that the program takes more time.

The amount of time that any algorithm takes to run almost always depends on the amount of input that it must process. We expect, for instance, that sorting 10,000 elements requires more time than sorting 10 elements. The running time of an algorithm is thus a function of the input size. The exact

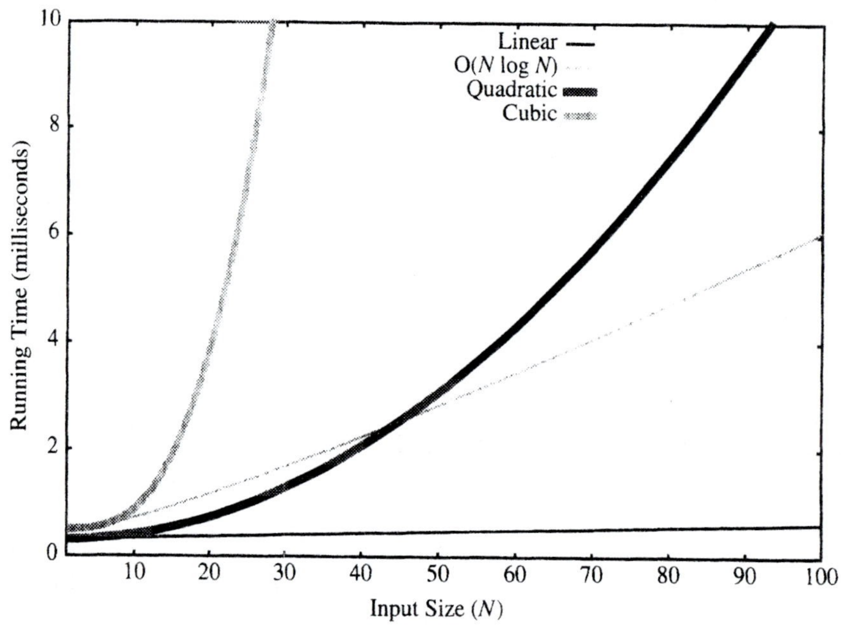

Figure 6.1 Running times for small inputs.

value of the function depends on many factors, such as the speed of the host machine, the quality of the compiler, and in some cases, the quality of the program. For a given program on a given computer, we can plot the running time function on a graph. Figure 6.1 illustrates such a plot for four programs. The curves represent four common functions encountered in algorithm analysis: linear, $O(N \log N)$, quadratic, and cubic. The input size N ranges from 1 to 100 items, and the running times range from 0 to 10 milliseconds. A quick glance at Figure 6.1 and its companion, Figure 6.2, suggests that the linear, $O(N \log N)$, quadratic, and cubic curves represent running times in order of decreasing preference.

An example is the problem of downloading a file from the Internet. Suppose that there is an initial 2-sec delay (to set up a connection), after which the download proceeds at 1.6 K/sec. Then if the file is N kilobytes, the time to download is described by the formula $T(N) = N/1.6 + 2$. This is a *linear function*. Downloading an 80K file takes approximately 52 sec, whereas downloading a file twice as large (160K) takes about 102 sec, or roughly twice as long. This property, in which time essentially is directly proportional to the amount of input, is the signature of a *linear algorithm*, which is the most efficient algorithm. In contrast, as these first two graphs show, some of the nonlinear algorithms lead to large running times. For instance, the linear algorithm is much more efficient than the cubic algorithm.

Of the common functions encountered in algorithm analysis, linear represents the most efficient algorithm.

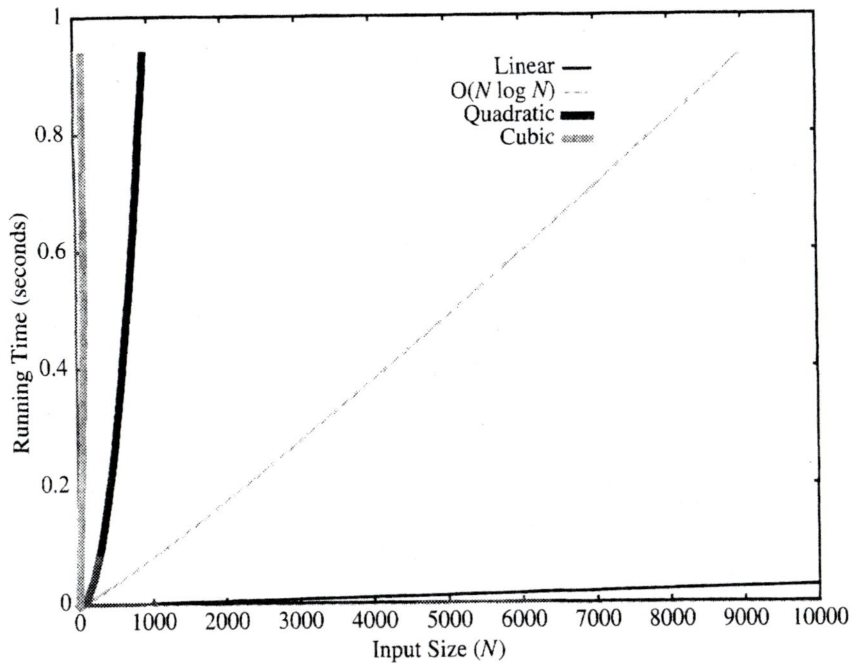

Figure 6.2 Running times for moderate inputs.

In this chapter we address several important questions:

- Is it always important to be on the most efficient curve?
- How much better is one curve than another?
- How do you decide which curve a particular algorithm lies on?
- How do you design algorithms that avoid being on less-efficient curves?

A *cubic function* is a function whose dominant term is some constant times N^3. For example, $10N^3 + N^2 + 40N + 80$ is a cubic function. Similarly, a quadratic function has a dominant term that is some constant times N^2, and a linear function has a dominant term that is some constant times N. The expression $O(N \log N)$ represents a function whose dominant term is N times the logarithm of N. The logarithm is a slowly growing function; for instance, the logarithm of 1,000,000 (with the typical base 2) is only 20. The logarithm grows more slowly than a square or cube (or any) root. We discuss the logarithm in more depth in Section 6.5.

The growth rate of a function is most important when N is sufficiently large.

Either of two functions may be smaller than the other at any given point, so claiming, for instance, that $F(N) < G(N)$ does not make sense. Instead, we measure the functions' rates of growth. This approach is justified for three reasons. First, for cubic functions such as the one shown in Figure 6.2, when N is 1000 the value of the cubic function is almost entirely determined by the cubic term. In the function $10N^3 + N^2 + 40N + 80$, for $N = 1000$, the value of the function is 10,001,040,080, of which 10,000,000,000 is due to the $10N^3$ term. If we were to use only the cubic term to estimate the entire function, an error of about 0.01 percent would result. For sufficiently large N, the value of a function is largely determined by its dominant term (the meaning of *sufficiently large* varies by function).

The second reason for measuring the functions' growth rates is that the exact value of the leading constant of the dominant term is not meaningful for different machines (although the relative values of the leading constant for identically growing functions might be). For instance, the quality of the compiler could have a large influence on the leading constant. The third reason is that small values of N generally are not important. For $N = 20$, Figure 6.1 shows that all algorithms terminate within 5 ms. The difference between the best and worst algorithm is less than a blink of the eye.

***Big-Oh* notation is used to capture the most dominant term in a function.**

We use **Big-Oh** notation to capture the most dominant term in a function and to represent the growth rate. For instance, the running time of a quadratic algorithm is specified as $O(N^2)$ (pronounced "order en-squared"). Big-Oh notation also allows us to establish a relative order among functions by comparing dominant terms. We discuss Big-Oh notation more formally in Section 6.4.

For small values of N (e.g., those less than 40), Figure 6.1 shows that one curve may be initially better than another, which doesn't hold for larger values of N. For example, initially the quadratic curve is better than the $O(N \log N)$ curve, but as N gets sufficiently large, the quadratic algorithm loses its advantage. For small amounts of input, making comparisons between functions is difficult because leading constants become very significant. The function $N + 2500$ is larger than N^2 when N is less than 50. Eventually, the linear function is always less than the quadratic function. Most important, for small input sizes the running times are generally inconsequential, so we need not worry about them. For instance, Figure 6.1 shows that when N is less than 25, all four algorithms run in less than 10 ms. Consequently, when input sizes are very small, a good rule of thumb is to use the simplest algorithm.

Figure 6.2 clearly demonstrates the differences between the various curves for large input sizes. A linear algorithm solves a problem of size 10,000 in a small fraction of a second. The $O(N \log N)$ algorithm uses roughly 10 times as much time. Note that the actual time differences depend on the constants involved and thus might be more or less. Depending on these constants, an $O(N \log N)$ algorithm might be faster than a linear algorithm for fairly large input sizes. For equally complex algorithms, however, linear algorithms tend to win out over $O(N \log N)$ algorithms.

This relationship is not true, however, for the quadratic and cubic algorithms. Quadratic algorithms are almost always impractical when the input size is more than a few thousand, and cubic algorithms are impractical for input sizes as small as a few hundred. To see how this works, try to run the `insertionSort` algorithm given in Section 3.3 for 1,000,000 items. Be prepared to wait a long time because an insertion sort is a quadratic algorithm. The sorting algorithms discussed in Chapter 9 run in *subquadratic* time (i.e., better than $O(N^2)$), thus making sorting large arrays practical.

Quadratic algorithms are impractical for input sizes exceeding a few thousand.

Cubic algorithms are impractical for input sizes as small as a few hundred.

The most striking feature of these curves is that the quadratic and cubic algorithms are not competitive with the others for reasonably large inputs. We can code the quadratic algorithm in highly efficient machine language and do a poor job coding the linear algorithm, and the quadratic algorithm will still lose badly. Even the most clever programming tricks cannot make an inefficient algorithm fast. Thus, before we waste effort attempting to optimize code, we need to optimize the algorithm. Figure 6.3 shows the functions that commonly describe algorithm running times in order of increasing growth rate.

Function	Name
c	Constant
$\log N$	Logarithmic
$\log^2 N$	Log-squared
N	Linear
$N \log N$	$N \log N$
N^2	Quadratic
N^3	Cubic
2^N	Exponential

Figure 6.3 Functions in order of increasing growth rate.

6.2 Examples of Algorithm Running Times

In this section we examine three problems. We also sketch possible solutions and determine what kind of running times the algorithms will exhibit, without providing detailed programs. The goal in this section is to provide you with some intuition about algorithm analysis. In Section 6.3 we provide more details on the process and in Section 6.4 formally approach an algorithm analysis problem.

We look at the following problems in this section:

MINIMUM ELEMENT IN AN ARRAY

GIVEN AN ARRAY OF N ITEMS, FIND THE SMALLEST ITEM.

CLOSEST POINTS IN THE PLANE

GIVEN N POINTS IN A PLANE (THAT IS, AN X–Y COORDINATE SYSTEM), FIND THE PAIR OF POINTS THAT ARE CLOSEST TOGETHER.

COLINEAR POINTS IN THE PLANE

GIVEN N POINTS IN A PLANE (THAT IS, AN X–Y COORDINATE SYSTEM), DETERMINE IF ANY THREE FORM A STRAIGHT LINE.

The minimum element problem is fundamental in computer science. It can be solved as follows.

1. Maintain a variable `min` that stores the minimum element.
2. Initialize `min` to the first element.
3. Make a sequential scan through the array and update `min` as appropriate.

The running time of this algorithm will be $O(N)$, or linear, because we repeat a fixed amount of work for each element in the array. A linear algorithm is as good as we can hope for. The reason is that we have to examine every element in the array, a process that requires linear time.

The closest points problem is a fundamental problem in graphics that can be solved as follows.

1. Calculate the distance between each pair of points.
2. Retain the minimum distance.

This calculation is expensive, however, because there are $N(N-1)/2$ pairs of points.[1] Thus there are roughly N^2 pairs of points. Examining all these pairs and finding the minimum distance among them takes quadratic time. A better algorithm runs in $O(N \log N)$ time and works by avoiding the computation of all distances. There is also an algorithm that is expected to take $O(N)$ time. These last two algorithms use subtle observations to provide faster results and are beyond the scope of this text.

The colinear points problem is important for many graphics algorithms. The reason is that the existence of colinear points introduces a degenerate case that requires special handling. It can be directly solved by enumerating all groups of three points. This solution is even more computationally expensive than that for the closest points problem because the number of different groups of three points is $N(N-1)(N-2)/6$ (using reasoning similar to that used for the closest points problem). This result tells us that the direct approach yields a cubic algorithm. A more clever strategy (also beyond the scope of this text) solves the problem in quadratic time (and further improvement is an area of continuously active research).

In Section 6.3 we look at a problem that illustrates the differences among linear, quadratic, and cubic algorithms. We also show how the performance of these algorithms compares to a mathematical prediction. Finally, after discussing the basic ideas, we examine Big-Oh notation more formally.

6.3 The Maximum Contiguous Subsequence Sum Problem

In this section, we consider the following problem:

MAXIMUM CONTIGUOUS SUBSEQUENCE SUM PROBLEM

GIVEN (POSSIBLY NEGATIVE) INTEGERS $A_1, A_2, \ldots, A_N$, FIND (AND IDENTIFY THE SEQUENCE CORRESPONDING TO) THE MAXIMUM VALUE OF $\sum_{k=i}^{j} A_k$. THE MAXIMUM CONTIGUOUS SUBSEQUENCE SUM IS ZERO IF ALL THE INTEGERS ARE NEGATIVE.

As an example, if the input is {–2, **11**, **–4**, **13**, –5, 2}, the answer is 20, which represents the contiguous subsequence encompassing items 2 through 4 (shown in boldface type). As a second example, for the input {1, –3, **4**, **–2**, **–1**, **6**}, the answer is 7 for the subsequence encompassing the last four items.

1. Each of N points can be paired with $N-1$ points, for a total of $N(N-1)$ pairs. However, this pairing double counts pairs A, B and B, A, so we must divide by two.

Programming details are considered after the algorithm design.

In C++, arrays begin at 0, so a C++ program would represent the input as a sequence A_0, ..., A_{N-1}. This is a programming detail and not part of the algorithm design.

Always consider emptiness.

Before discussing the algorithms for this problem, we need to comment on the degenerate case, in which all input integers are negative. The problem statement gives a maximum contiguous subsequence sum of 0 for this case. You might wonder why we do this, rather than just returning the largest (i.e., the smallest in magnitude) negative integer in the input. The reason is that the empty subsequence, consisting of zero integers, is also a subsequence, and its sum is clearly 0. Because the empty subsequence is contiguous, there is always a contiguous subsequence whose sum is 0. This result is analogous to the empty set being a subset of any set. Be aware that emptiness is always a possibility and that in many instances it is not a special case at all.

There are lots of drastically different algorithms (in terms of efficiency) that can be used to solve the maximum contiguous subsequence sum problem.

The maximum contiguous subsequence sum problem is interesting mainly because there are so many algorithms to solve it—and the performance of these algorithms varies drastically. In this section we discuss three such algorithms. The first is an obvious exhaustive search algorithm, but it is very inefficient. The second is an improvement on the first, which is accomplished by a simple observation. The third is a very efficient, but not obvious, algorithm. We prove that its running time is linear.

In Chapter 8 we present a fourth algorithm, which has $O(N \log N)$ running time. That algorithm is not as efficient as the linear algorithm, but it is much more efficient than the other two. It also is typical of the kinds of algorithms that result in $O(N \log N)$ running times. The graphs shown in Figures 6.1 and 6.2 are representative of these four algorithms.

6.3.1 The Obvious $O(N^3)$ Algorithm

A brute force algorithm is generally the least efficient but simplest method to code.

The simplest algorithm is a direct exhaustive search, or a *brute force algorithm,* as shown in Figure 6.4. Lines 10 and 11 control a pair of loops that iterate over all possible subsequences. For each possible subsequence, the value of its sum is computed at lines 13–15. If that sum is the best sum encountered, we update the value of `maxSum`, which is eventually returned at line 25. Two `int`s—`seqStart` and `seqEnd` (which are passed by reference)—are also updated whenever a new best sequence is encountered.

The direct exhaustive search algorithm has the merit of extreme simplicity; the less complex an algorithm is, the more likely it is to be programmed correctly. However, exhaustive search algorithms are usually not as efficient as possible. In the remainder of this section we show that the running time of the algorithm is cubic. We count the number of times (as a function of the input size) the expressions in Figure 6.4 are evaluated. We require only a

```
1 // Cubic maximum contiguous subsequence sum algorithm.
2 // seqStart and seqEnd represent the actual best sequence.
3 template <class Comparable>
4 Comparable maxSubsequenceSum( const vector<Comparable> & a,
5                int & seqStart, int & seqEnd )
6 {
7     int n = a.size( );
8     Comparable maxSum = 0;
9
10    for( int i = 0; i < n; i++ )
11        for( int j = i; j < n; j++ )
12        {
13            Comparable thisSum = 0;
14            for( int k = i; k <= j; k++ )
15                thisSum += a[ k ];
16
17            if( thisSum > maxSum )
18            {
19                maxSum = thisSum;
20                seqStart = i;
21                seqEnd = j;
22            }
23        }
24
25    return maxSum;
26 }
```

Figure 6.4 A cubic maximum contiguous subsequence sum algorithm.

Big-Oh result, so once we have found a dominant term, we can ignore lower order terms and leading constants.

The running time of the algorithm is entirely dominated by the innermost `for` loop in lines 14 and 15. Four expressions there are repeatedly executed:

1. the initialization `k = i`,
2. the test `k <= j`,
3. the increment `thisSum += a[ k ]`, and
4. the adjustment `k++`.

A mathematical analysis is used to count the number of times that certain statements are executed.

The number of times that expression 3 is executed makes it the dominant term among the four expressions. Note that each initialization is accompanied by at least one test. We are ignoring constants, so we may disregard the cost of the initializations; the initializations cannot be the single dominating cost of the algorithm. Because the test given by expression 2 is unsuccessful exactly once per loop, the number of unsuccessful tests performed by expression 2 exactly equals the number of initializations. Consequently, it is not dominant. The number of successful tests at expression 2, the number of increments performed by expression 3, and the number of adjustments at expression 4 are identical. Thus the number of increments (i.e., the number of times that line 15 is executed) is a dominant measure of the work performed in the innermost loop.

The number of times line 15 is executed exactly equals the number of ordered triplets (i, j, k) that satisfy $1 \le i \le k \le j \le N$.[2] The reason is that the index i runs over the entire array, j runs from i to the end of the array, and k runs from i to j. A quick and dirty estimate is that the number of triplets is somewhat less than $N \times N \times N$, or N^3, because i, j, and k can each assume one of N values. The additional restriction $i \le k \le j$ reduces this number. A precise calculation is somewhat difficult to obtain and is performed in Theorem 6.1.

The most important part of Theorem 6.1 is not the proof, but rather the result. There are two ways to evaluate the number of triplets. One is to evaluate the sum $\sum_{i=1}^{N} \sum_{j=i}^{N} \sum_{k=i}^{j} 1$. We could evaluate this sum inside out (see Exercise 6.9). Instead, we will use an alternative.

Theorem 6.1 *The number of integer ordered triplets (i, j, k) that satisfy $1 \le i \le k \le j \le N$ is $N(N+1)(N+2)/6$.*

Proof *Place the following $N + 2$ balls in a box: N balls numbered 1 through N, one unnumbered red ball, and one unnumbered blue ball. Remove three balls from the box. If a red ball is drawn, number it as the lowest of the numbered balls drawn. If a blue ball is drawn, number it as the highest of the numbered balls drawn. Note that if you draw both a red and a blue ball, then the effect is to have three balls identically numbered. Order the three balls. Each such order corresponds to a triplet solution to the equation in Theorem 6.1. The number of possible orders is the number of distinct ways to draw three balls without replacement from a collection of $N + 2$ balls. This problem is similar to that of selecting three points from a group of N that we evaluated in Section 6.2, so we immediately obtain the stated result.*

2. In C++, the indices run from 0 through $N - 1$. We have used the algorithmic equivalent 1 through N to simplify the analysis.

The result of Theorem 6.1 is that the innermost `for` loop accounts for cubic running time. The remaining work in the algorithm is inconsequential because it is done, at most, once per iteration of the inner loop. Put another way, the cost of lines 17–22 is inconsequential because it is done only as often as the initialization of the inner `for` loop, rather than as often as the repeated body of the inner `for` loop. Consequently, the algorithm is $O(N^3)$.

We do not need precise calculations for a Big-Oh estimate. In many cases, we can use the simple rule of multiplying the size of all the nested loops. Note that consecutive loops do not multiply.

The previous combinatoric argument allows us to obtain precise calculations on the number of iterations in the inner loop. But, for a Big-Oh calculation, that really isn't necessary; we need to know only that the leading term is some constant times N^3. Looking at the algorithm, we see a loop that is potentially of size N inside a loop that is potentially of size N inside another loop that is potentially of size N. This configuration tells us that the triple loop has the potential for $N \times N \times N$ iterations. This potential is only about six times greater than our precise calculation of what actually occurs. Constants are ignored anyway, so we can adopt the general rule that, when we have nested loops, we should multiply the cost of the innermost statement by the size of each loop in the nest to obtain an upper bound. In most cases, the upper bound will not be a gross overestimate.[3] Thus a program with three nested loops, each running sequentially through large portions of an array, is likely to exhibit $O(N^3)$ behavior. Note that three consecutive (nonnested) loops exhibit linear behavior; it is nesting that leads to a combinatoric explosion. Consequently, to improve the algorithm, we need to remove a loop.

6.3.2 An Improved $O(N^2)$ Algorithm

When we remove a loop from an algorithm, we generally lower the running time.

When we remove a loop from an algorithm, we generally lower the running time. But how do we remove a loop? Obviously, we cannot always do so. However, the preceding algorithm has many unnecessary computations. The inefficiency that the improved algorithm corrects is the unduly expensive computation in the inner `for` loop in Figure 6.4. The improved algorithm makes use of the fact that $\sum_{k=i}^{j} A_k = A_j + \sum_{k=i}^{j-1} A_k$. In other words, suppose that we have just calculated the sum for the subsequence $i, \ldots, j-1$. Then computing the sum for the subsequence $i, \ldots, j$ should not take much longer because we need only one more addition. However, the cubic algorithm throws away this information. If we use this observation, we obtain the improved algorithm shown in Figure 6.5. We have two rather than three nested loops, and the running time is $O(N^2)$.

3. Exercise 6.16 illustrates a case in which the multiplication of loop sizes yields an overestimate in the Big-Oh result.

```
// Quadratic maximum contiguous subsequence sum algorithm.
// seqStart and seqEnd represent the actual best sequence.
template <class Comparable>
Comparable maxSubsequenceSum( const vector<Comparable> & a,
                              int & seqStart, int & seqEnd )
{
    int n = a.size( );
    Comparable maxSum = 0;

    for( int i = 0; i < n; i++ )
    {
        Comparable thisSum = 0;
        for( int j = i; j < n; j++ )
        {
            thisSum += a[ j ];

            if( thisSum > maxSum )
            {
                maxSum = thisSum;
                seqStart = i;
                seqEnd = j;
            }
        }
    }

    return maxSum;
}
```

Figure 6.5 A quadratic maximum contiguous subsequence sum algorithm.

6.3.3 A Linear Algorithm

If we remove another loop, we have a linear algorithm.

The algorithm is tricky. It uses a clever observation to step quickly over large numbers of subsequences that cannot be the best.

To move from a quadratic algorithm to a linear algorithm, we need to remove yet another loop. However, unlike the reduction illustrated in Figures 6.4 and 6.5, where loop removal was simple, getting rid of another loop is not so easy. The problem is that the quadratic algorithm is still an exhaustive search; that is, we are trying all possible subsequences. The only difference between the quadratic and cubic algorithms is that the cost of testing each successive subsequence is a constant $O(1)$ instead of linear $O(N)$. Because a quadratic number of subsequences are possible, the only way we can attain a subquadratic bound is to find a clever way to eliminate from consideration a large number of subsequences, without actually computing their sum and testing to see if that sum is a new maximum. This section shows how this is done.

First, we eliminate a large number of possible subsequences from consideration. We let $A_{i,j}$ be the subsequence encompassing elements from i to j and let $S_{i,j}$ be its sum.

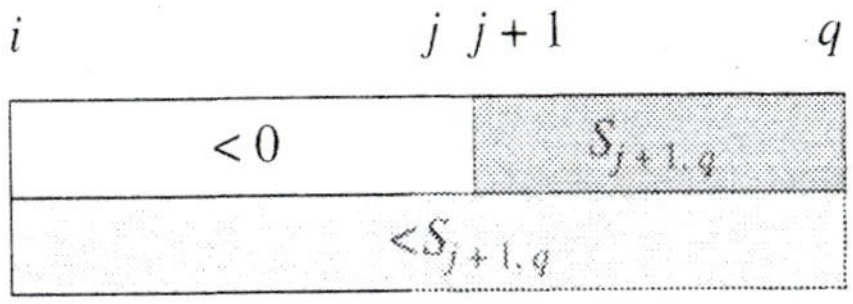

Figure 6.6 The subsequences used in Theorem 6.2

Theorem 6.2

Let $A_{i,j}$ be any sequence with $S_{i,j} < 0$. If $q > j$, then $A_{i,q}$ is not the maximum contiguous subsequence.

Proof

The sum of A's elements from i to q is the sum of A's elements from i to j added to the sum of A's elements from $j+1$ to q. Thus we have $S_{i,q} = S_{i,j} + S_{j+1,q}$. Because $S_{i,j} < 0$, we know that $S_{i,q} < S_{j+1,q}$. Thus $A_{i,q}$ is not a maximum contiguous subsequence.

An illustration of the sums generated by *i*, *j*, and *q* is shown on the first two lines in Figure 6.6. Theorem 6.2 demonstrates that we can avoid examining several subsequences by including an additional test: If `thisSum` is less than 0, we can `break` from the inner loop in Figure 6.5. Intuitively, if a subsequence's sum is negative, it cannot be part of the maximum contiguous subsequence. The reason is that we can get a large contiguous subsequence by not including it. This observation by itself is not sufficient to reduce the running time below quadratic. A similar observation also holds: All contiguous subsequences that border the maximum contiguous subsequence must have negative (or 0) sums (otherwise, we would include them). This observation also does not reduce the running time to below quadratic. However, a third observation, illustrated in Figure 6.7, does, and we formalize it with Theorem 6.3.

Theorem 6.3

For any i, let $A_{i,j}$ be the first sequence, with $S_{i,j} < 0$. Then, for any $i \le p \le j$ and $p \le q$, $A_{p,q}$ either is not a maximum contiguous subsequence or is equal to an already seen maximum contiguous subsequence.

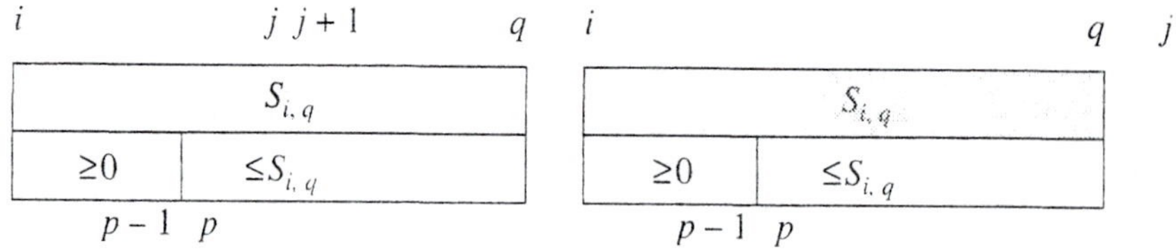

Figure 6.7 The subsequences used in Theorem 6.3. The sequence from *p* to *q* has a sum that is, at most, that of the subsequence from *i* to *q*. On the left-hand side the sequence from *i* to *q* is itself not the maximum (by Theorem 6.2). On the right-hand side, the sequence from *i* to *q* has already been seen.

Proof *If* $p = i$*, then Theorem 6.2 applies. Otherwise, as in Theorem 6.2, we have* $S_{i,q} = S_{i,p-1} + S_{p,q}$*. Because j is the lowest index for which* $S_{i,j} < 0$*, it follows that* $S_{i,p-1} \geq 0$*. Thus* $S_{p,q} \leq S_{i,q}$*. If* $q > j$ *(shown on the left-hand side in Figure 6.7), then Theorem 6.2 implies that* $A_{i,q}$ *is not a maximum contiguous subsequence, so neither is* $A_{p,q}$*. Otherwise, as shown on the right-hand side in Figure 6.7, the subsequence* $A_{p,q}$ *has a sum equal to, at most, that of the already seen subsequence* $A_{i,q}$*.*

If we detect a negative sum, we can move *i* all the way past *j*.

If an algorithm is complex, a correctness proof is required.

Theorem 6.3 tells us that, when a negative subsequence is detected, not only can we `break` the inner loop, but we can also advance `i` to `j + 1`. Figure 6.8 shows that we can rewrite the algorithm to use only a single loop. Clearly, the running time of this algorithm is linear: At each step in the loop, we advance `j`, so the loop iterates at most *N* times. The correctness of this algorithm is much less obvious than for the previous algorithms, which is typical. That is, algorithms that use the structure of a problem to beat an exhaustive search generally require some sort of correctness proof. We proved that the algorithm (although not the resulting C++ program) is correct by using a short mathematical argument. The purpose is not to make the discussion entirely mathematical, but rather to give a flavor of the techniques that might be required in advanced work.

6.4 General Big-Oh Rules

Now that we have presented the basic ideas of algorithm analysis, we can adopt a slightly more formal approach. In this section we outline the general rules for using Big-Oh notation. Although we use Big-Oh notation almost exclusively throughout this text, we also define three other types of algorithm notation that are related to Big-Oh and used occasionally later on in the text.

```
// Linear maximum contiguous subsequence sum algorithm.
// seqStart and seqEnd represent the actual best sequence.
template <class Comparable>
Comparable maxSubsequenceSum( const vector<Comparable> & a,
                              int & seqStart, int & seqEnd )
{
    int n = a.size( );
    Comparable thisSum = 0;
    Comparable maxSum = 0;

    for( int i = 0, j = 0; j < n; j++ )
    {
        thisSum += a[ j ];

        if( thisSum > maxSum )
        {
            maxSum = thisSum;
            seqStart = i;
            seqEnd = j;
        }
        else if( thisSum < 0 )
        {
            i = j + 1;
            thisSum = 0;
        }
    }
    return maxSum;
}
```

Figure 6.8 A linear maximum contiguous subsequence sum algorithm.

DEFINITION: (Big-Oh) $T(N)$ is $O(F(N))$ if there are positive constants c and N_0 such that $T(N) \le cF(N)$ when $N \ge N_0$.

DEFINITION: (Big-Omega) $T(N)$ is $\Omega(F(N))$ if there are positive constants c and N_0 such that $T(N) \ge cF(N)$ when $N \ge N_0$.

DEFINITION: (Big-Theta) $T(N)$ is $\Theta(F(N))$ if and only if $T(N)$ is $O(F(N))$ and $T(N)$ is $\Omega(F(N))$.

DEFINITION: (Little-Oh) $T(N)$ is $o(F(N))$ if and only if $T(N)$ is $O(F(N))$ and $T(N)$ is not $\Theta(F(N))$.

The first definition, *Big-Oh* notation, states that there is a point N_0 such that for all values of N that are past this point, $T(N)$ is bounded by some multiple of $F(N)$. This is the sufficiently large N mentioned earlier. Thus, if the running time $T(N)$ of an algorithm is $O(N^2)$, then, ignoring constants, we are guaranteeing that at some point we can bound the running time by a quadratic function. Note that, if the true running time is linear, then the statement that the running time is $O(N^2)$ is technically correct because the inequality holds. However, $O(N)$ would be the more precise claim.

Big-Oh is similar to less than or equal to, when growth rates are being considered.

If we use the traditional relational operators to compare growth rates, then the first definition says that the growth rate of $T(N)$ is less than or equal to that of $F(N)$.

***Big-Omega* is similar to greater than or equal to when growth rates are being considered.**

The second definition, $T(N) = \Omega(F(N))$, called **Big-Omega,** says that the growth rate of $T(N)$ is greater than or equal to that of $F(N)$. For instance, we might say that any algorithm that works by examining every possible subsequence in the maximum subsequence sum problem must take $\Omega(N^2)$ time because a quadratic number of subsequences are possible. This is a lower bound argument that is used in more advanced analysis. Later in the text, we give one example of this argument and demonstrate that any general-purpose sorting algorithm requires $\Omega(N \log N)$ time.

***Big-Theta* is similar to equal to when growth rates are being considered.**

The third definition, $T(N) = \Theta(F(N))$, called **Big-Theta,** says that the growth rate of $T(N)$ equals the growth rate of $F(N)$. For instance, the maximum subsequence algorithm shown in Figure 6.5 runs in $\Theta(N^2)$ time. In other words, the running time is bounded by a quadratic function, and this bound cannot be improved because it is also lower bounded by another quadratic function. When we use Big-Theta notation, we are providing not only an upper bound on an algorithm but also assurances that the analysis that leads to the upper bound is as good (tight) as possible. In spite of the additional precision offered by Big-Theta, however, Big-Oh is more commonly used, except by researchers in the algorithm analysis field.

***Little-Oh* is similar to less than when growth rates are being considered.**

The final definition, $T(N) = o(F(N))$, called **Little-Oh,** says that the growth rate of $T(N)$ is strictly less than the growth rate of $F(N)$. This function is different from Big-Oh because Big-Oh allows the possibility that the growth rates are the same. For instance, if the running time of an algorithm is $o(N^2)$, it is guaranteed to be growing at a slower rate than quadratic (i.e., it is a **subquadratic algorithm**). Thus a bound of $o(N^2)$ is a better bound than $\Theta(N^2)$. Figure 6.9 summarizes these four definitions.

Throw out leading constants, lower order terms, and relational symbols when using Big-Oh.

A couple of stylistic notes are in order. First, including constants or low-order terms inside a Big-Oh is bad style. Do not say $T(N) = O(2N^2)$ or $T(N) = O(N^2 + N)$. In both cases, the correct form is $T(N) = O(N^2)$. Second, in any analysis that requires a Big-Oh answer, all sorts of shortcuts are possible. Lower order terms, leading constants, and relational symbols are all thrown away.

Now that the mathematics have formalized, we can relate it to the analysis of algorithms. The most basic rule is that *the running time of a loop is at most the running time of the statements inside the loop (including tests) times the number of iterations*. As shown earlier, the initialization and testing

Mathematical Expression	Relative Rates of Growth
$T(N) = O(F(N))$	Growth of $T(N)$ is $\leq$ growth of $F(N)$.
$T(N) = \Omega(F(N))$	Growth of $T(N)$ is $\geq$ growth of $F(N)$.
$T(N) = \Theta(F(N))$	Growth of $T(N)$ is = growth of $F(N)$.
$T(N) = o(F(N))$	Growth of $T(N)$ is < growth of $F(N)$.

Figure 6.9 Meanings of the various growth functions.

of the loop condition is usually no more dominant than are the statements encompassing the body of the loop.

The running time of statements inside a group of nested loops is the running time of the statements (including tests in the innermost loop) multiplied by the sizes of all the loops. The running time of a sequence of consecutive loops is the running time of the dominant loop. The time difference between a nested loop in which both indices run from 1 to N and two consecutive loops that are not nested but run over the same indices is the same as the space difference between a two-dimensional array and two one-dimensional arrays. The first case is quadratic. The second case is linear because $N + N$ is $2N$, which is still $O(N)$. Occasionally, this simple rule can overestimate the running time, but in most cases it does not. Even if it does, Big-Oh does not guarantee an exact asymptotic answer—just an upper bound.

The analyses performed thus far involved use of a **worst-case bound,** which is a guarantee over all inputs of some size. Another form of analysis is the **average-case bound,** in which the running time is measured as an average over all the possible inputs of size N. The average might differ from the worst case if, for example, a conditional statement that depends on the particular input causes an early exit from a loop. We discuss average-case bounds in more detail in Section 6.8. For now, simply note that, because one algorithm has a better worst-case bound than another algorithm, nothing is implied about their relative average-case bounds. However, in many cases average-case and worst-case bounds are closely correlated. When they are not, the bounds are treated separately.

A *worst-case bound* is a guarantee over all inputs of some size.

In an *average-case bound,* the running time is measured as an average over all of the possible inputs of size *N*.

The last Big-Oh item we examine is how the running time grows for each type of curve, as illustrated in Figures 6.1 and 6.2. We want a more quantitative answer to this question: If an algorithm takes $T(N)$ time to solve a problem of size N, how long does it take to solve a larger problem? For instance, how long does it take to solve a problem when there is 10 times as much input? The answers are shown in Figure 6.10. However, we want to

	Figure 6.4	Figure 6.5	Figure 18.18	Figure 6.8
N	$O(N^3)$	$O(N^2)$	$O(N \log N)$	$O(N)$
10	0.000009	0.000004	0.000006	0.000003
100	0.002580	0.000109	0.000045	0.000006
1,000	2.281013	0.010203	0.000485	0.000031
10,000	NA	1.2329	0.005712	0.000317
100,000	NA	135	0.064618	0.003206

Figure 6.10 Observed running times (in seconds) for various maximum contiguous subsequence sum algorithms.

answer the question without running the program and hope that our analytical answers agree with the observed behavior.

We begin by examining the cubic algorithm. We assume that the running time is reasonably approximated by $T(N) = cN^3$. Consequently, $T(10N) = c(10N)^3$. Mathematical manipulation yields

$$T(10N) = 1000cN^3 = 1000T(N).$$

If the size of the input increases by a factor of f, the running time of a cubic program increases by a factor of roughly f^3.

Thus the running time of a cubic program increases by a factor of 1000 (assuming that N is sufficiently large) when the amount of input is increased by a factor of 10. This relationship is roughly confirmed by the increase in running time from $N = 100$ to 1000 shown in Figure 6.10. Recall that we do not expect an exact answer—just a reasonable approximation. We would also expect that for $N = 10{,}000$, the running time would increase another 1000-fold. The result would be that a cubic algorithm requires roughly 35 minutes of computation time. In general, if the amount of input increases by a factor of f, the cubic algorithm's running time increases by a factor of f^3.

If the size of the input increases by a factor of f, the running time of a quadratic program increases by a factor of roughly f^2.

We can perform similar calculations for quadratic and linear algorithms. For the quadratic algorithm, we assume that $T(N) = cN^2$. It follows that $T(10N) = c(10N)^2$. When we expand, we obtain

$$T(10N) = 100cN^2 = 100T(N).$$

So when the input size increases by a factor of 10, the running time of a quadratic program increases by a factor of approximately 100. This relationship is also confirmed in Figure 6.10. In general, an f-fold increase in input size yields an f^2-fold increase in running time for a quadratic algorithm.

Finally, for a linear algorithm, a similar calculation shows that a 10-fold increase in input size results in a 10-fold increase in running time. Again, this relationship has been confirmed experimentally. Note, however, that for a linear program the term *sufficiently large* means a somewhat higher input size than for the other programs. The reason is that of the overhead of 0.000003 sec is used in all cases. For a linear program, this term is still significant for moderate input sizes.

If the size of the input increases by a factor of *f*, the running time of a linear program also increases by a factor of *f*. It is the preferred running time for an algorithm.

The analysis used here does not work with logarithmic terms. When an $O(N \log N)$ algorithm is presented with 10 times as much input, the running time increases by a factor slightly larger than 10. Specifically, we have $T(10N) = c(10N)\log(10N)$. When we expand, we obtain

$$T(10N) = 10cN \log (10N) = 10cN \log N + 10cN \log 10 = 10T(N) + c'N.$$

Here $c' = 10c \log 10$. As N gets very large, the ratio $T(10N)/T(N)$ gets closer and closer to 10 because $c'N/T(N) \approx (10 \log 10)/\log N$ gets smaller and smaller with increasing N. Consequently, if the algorithm is competitive with a linear algorithm for very large N, it is likely to remain competitive for slightly larger N.

Does all this mean that quadratic and cubic algorithms are useless? The answer is no. In some cases, the most efficient algorithms known are quadratic or cubic. In others, the most efficient algorithm is even worse (exponential). Furthermore, when the amount of input is small, any algorithm will do. Frequently the algorithms that are not asymptotically efficient are nonetheless easy to program. For small inputs, that is the way to go. Finally, a good way to test a complex linear algorithm is to compare its output with an exhaustive search algorithm. In Section 6.8 we discuss some other limitations of the Big-Oh model.

6.5 The Logarithm

The list of typical growth rate functions includes several entries containing the logarithm. A **logarithm** is the exponent that indicates the power to which a number (the base) is raised to produce a given number. In this section we look in more detail at the mathematics behind the logarithm. In Section 6.6 we show its use in a simple algorithm.

We begin with the formal definition and then follow with more intuitive viewpoints.

The *logarithm* of *N* (to the base 2) is the value *X* such that 2 raised to the power of *X* equals *N*. By default, the base of the logarithm is 2.

DEFINITION: For any $B, N > 0$, $\log_B N = K$ if $B^K = N$.

In this definition, B is the base of the logarithm. In computer science, when the base is omitted, it defaults to 2, which is natural for several reasons, as we show later in the chapter. We prove one mathematical theorem, Theorem 6.4, to show that, as far as Big-Oh notation is concerned, the base is unimportant and also to show how relations that involve logarithms can be derived.

Theorem 6.4 *The base does not matter. For any constant $B > 1$, $\log_B N = O(\log N)$.*

Proof *Let $\log_B N = K$. Then $B^K = N$. Let $C = \log B$. Then $2^C = B$. Thus $B^K = (2^C)^K = N$. Hence, we have $2^{CK} = N$, which implies that $\log N = CK = C \log_B N$. Therefore $\log_B N = (\log N)/(\log B)$, thus completing the proof.*

In the rest of the text, we use base 2 logarithms exclusively. An important fact about the logarithm is that it grows slowly. Because $2^{10} = 1024$, $\log 1024 = 10$. Additional calculations show that the logarithm of 1,000,000 is roughly 20 and that the logarithm of 1,000,000,000 is only 30. Consequently, performance of an $O(N \log N)$ algorithm is much closer to a linear $O(N)$ algorithm than to a quadratic $O(N^2)$ algorithm for even moderately large amounts of input. Before we look at a realistic algorithm whose running time includes the logarithm, let us look at a few examples of how the logarithm comes into play.

BITS IN A BINARY NUMBER

How many bits are required to represent N consecutive integers?

The number of bits required to represent numbers is logarithmic.

A 16-bit `short` integer represents the 65,536 integers in the range –32,768 to 32,767. In general, B bits are sufficient to represent 2^B different integers. Thus the number of bits B required to represent N consecutive integers satisfies the equation $2^B \geq N$. Hence we obtain $B \geq \log N$, so the minimum number of bits is $\lceil \log N \rceil$. (Here $\lceil X \rceil$ is the ceiling function and represents the smallest integer that is at least as large as X. The corresponding floor function $\lfloor X \rfloor$ represents the largest integer that is at least as small as X.)

REPEATED DOUBLING

Starting from $X = 1$, how many times should X be doubled before it is at least as large as N?

Suppose that we start with \$1 and double it every year. How long would it take to save a million dollars? In this case, after 1 yr we would have \$2; after 2 yr, \$4; after 3 yr, \$8, and so on. In general, after K years we would have 2^K dollars, so we want to find the smallest K satisfying $2^K \geq N$. This is the same equation as before, so $K = \lceil \log N \rceil$. After 20 yr, we would have more than a million dollars. The **repeated doubling principle** holds that, starting from 1, we can repeatedly double only $\lceil \log N \rceil$ times until we reach N.

The *repeated doubling principle* holds that, starting at 1, we can repeatedly double only logarithmically many times until we reach *N*.

REPEATED HALVING

STARTING FROM $X = N$, IF N IS REPEATEDLY HALVED, HOW MANY ITERATIONS MUST BE APPLIED TO MAKE N SMALLER THAN OR EQUAL TO 1?

If the division rounds up to the nearest integer (or is real, not integer, division), we have the same problem as with repeated doubling, except that we are going in the opposite direction. Once again the answer is $\lceil \log N \rceil$ iterations. If the division rounds down, the answer is $\lfloor \log N \rfloor$. We can show the difference by starting with $X = 3$. Two divisions are necessary, unless the division rounds down, in which case only one is needed.

The *repeated halving principle* holds that, starting at *N*, we can halve only logarithmically many times. This process is used to obtain logarithmic routines for searching.

Many of the algorithms examined in this text contain logarithms, introduced because of the **repeated halving principle,** which holds that, starting at N, we can halve only logarithmically many times. In other words, an algorithm is $O(\log N)$ if it takes constant ($O(1)$) time to cut the problem size by a constant fraction (usually 1/2). This condition follows directly from the fact that there will be $O(\log N)$ iterations of the loop. Any constant fraction will do because the fraction is reflected in the base of the logarithm, and Theorem 6.4 tells us that the base does not matter.

The *N*th *harmonic number* is the sum of the reciprocals of the first *N* positive integers. The growth rate of the harmonic number is logarithmic.

All the remaining occurrences of logarithms are introduced (either directly or indirectly) by applying Theorem 6.5. This theorem concerns the Nth **harmonic number,** which is the sum of the reciprocals of the first N positive integers, and states that the Nth harmonic number, H_N, satisfies $H_N = O(\log N)$. The proof uses calculus, but you do not need to understand the proof to use the theorem.

Theorem 6.5

Let $H_N = \sum_{i=1}^{N} 1/i$. Then $H_N = \Theta(\log N)$. A more precise estimate is $\ln N + 0.577$.

Proof *The intuition of the proof is that a discrete sum is well approximated by the (continuous) integral. The proof uses a construction to show that the sum H_N can be bounded above and below by $\int \frac{dx}{x}$, with appropriate limits. Details are left as Exercise 6.18.*

6.6 Static Searching Problem

An important use of computers is to look up data. If the data are not allowed to change (e.g., it is stored on a CD-ROM), we say that the data are static. A **static search** accesses data that are never altered. The static searching problem is naturally formulated as follows.

STATIC SEARCHING PROBLEM

GIVEN AN INTEGER X AND AN ARRAY A, RETURN THE POSITION OF X IN A OR AN INDICATION THAT IT IS NOT PRESENT. IF X OCCURS MORE THAN ONCE, RETURN ANY OCCURRENCE. THE ARRAY A IS NEVER ALTERED.

An example of static searching is looking up a person in the telephone book. The efficiency of a static searching algorithm depends on whether the array being searched is sorted. In the case of the telephone book, searching by name is fast, but searching by phone number is hopeless (for humans). In this section, we examine some solutions to the static searching problem.

6.6.1 Sequential Search

A *sequential search* steps through the data sequentially until a match is found.

When the input array has not been sorted, we have little choice but to do a linear **sequential search** that steps through the array sequentially until a match is found. The complexity of the algorithm is analyzed in three ways. First, we provide the cost of an unsuccessful search. Then, we give the worst-case cost of a successful search. Finally, we find the average cost of a successful search. Analyzing successful and unsuccessful searches separately is typical. Unsuccessful searches usually are more time consuming than are successful searches (think about the last time you lost something in your house). For sequential searching, the analysis is straightforward.

A sequential search is linear.

An unsuccessful search requires the examination of every item in the array, so the time will be $O(N)$. In the worst case, a successful search, too, requires the examination of every item in the array because we might not find a match until the last item. Thus the worst-case running time for a successful search is also linear. On average, however, we search only half an array. That is, for every successful search in position i, there is a corresponding successful search in position $N - 1 - i$ (assuming we start numbering from 0). However,

$N/2$ is still $O(N)$. As mentioned earlier in the chapter, all these Big-Oh terms should correctly be Big-Theta terms. However, the use of Big-Oh is more popular.

6.6.2 Binary Search

If the input array is sorted, we can use the *binary search,* which is performed from the middle of the array rather than the end.

If the input array has been sorted, we have an alternative to the sequential search, the **binary search,** which is performed from the middle of the array rather than the end. We keep track of `low` and `high`, which delimit the portion of the array in which an item, if present, must reside. Initially, the range is from 0 to $N - 1$. If `low` is larger than `high`, we know that the item is not present, so we return `NOT_FOUND`. Otherwise, we let `mid` be the halfway point of the range (rounding down if the range has an even number of elements) and compare the item we are searching for with the item in position `mid`. If we find a match, we are done and can return. If the item we are searching for is less than the item in position `mid`, then it must reside in the range `low` to `mid-1`. If it is greater, then it must reside in the range `mid+1` to `high`. In Figure 6.11, lines 16 to 19 alter the possible range,

```
 1 // Performs the standard binary search
 2 // using two comparisons per level.
 3 // Returns the index where item is found, or NOT_FOUND.
 4 template <class Comparable>
 5 int binarySearch( const vector<Comparable> & a,
 6                   const Comparable & x )
 7 {
 8     int low = 0;
 9     int high = a.size( ) - 1;
10     int mid;
11 
12     while( low <= high )
13     {
14         mid = ( low + high ) / 2;
15 
16         if( a[ mid ] < x )
17             low = mid + 1;
18         else if( a[ mid ] > x )
19             high = mid - 1;
20         else
21             return mid;
22     }
23 
24     return NOT_FOUND;     // NOT_FOUND = -1
25 }
```

Figure 6.11 Basic binary search, using three-way comparisons.

essentially cutting it in half. By the repeated halving principle, we know that the number of iterations will be $O(\log N)$.

The binary search is logarithmic because the search range is halved in each iteration.

For an unsuccessful search, the number of iterations in the loop is $\lfloor \log N \rfloor + 1$. The reason is that we halve the range in each iteration (rounding down if the range has an odd number of elements); we add 1 because the final range encompasses zero elements. For a successful search, the worst case is $\lfloor \log N \rfloor$ iterations because in the worst case we get down to a range of only one element. The average case is only one iteration better because half the elements require the worst case for their search, a quarter of the elements save one iteration, and only one in 2^i elements save i iterations from the worst case. The mathematics involves computing the weighted average by calculating the sum of a finite series. The end result, however, is that the running time for each search is $O(\log N)$. In Exercise 6.20 you are asked to complete the calculation.

For reasonably large values of N, the binary search outperforms the sequential search. For instance, if N is 1000, then on average a successful sequential search requires 500 comparisons. The average binary search, using the previous formula, requires $\lfloor \log N \rfloor - 1$, or eight iterations for a successful search. Each iteration uses 1.5 comparisons on average (sometimes, 1; other times, 2), so the total is 12 comparisons for a successful search. The binary search wins by even more in the worst case or when searches are unsuccessful.

Optimizing the binary search can cut the number of comparisons roughly in half.

If we want to make the binary search even faster, we need to make the inner loop tighter. A possible strategy is to remove the (implicit) test for a successful search from that inner loop and shrink the range to one item in all cases. Then we can use a single test outside the loop to determine whether the item is in the array or cannot be found, as shown in Figure 6.12. If the item we are searching for in Figure 6.12 is no larger than the item in the `mid` position, it is in the range that includes the `mid` position. When we break the loop, the subrange is 1, and we can test to see whether we have a match.

In the revised algorithm, the number of iterations is always $\lfloor \log N \rfloor$ because we always shrink the range by half, possibly by rounding down. Thus the number of comparisons used is always $\lfloor \log N \rfloor + 1$.

Binary search is surprisingly tricky to code. Exercise 6.6 illustrates some common errors.

Note that, for small N, such as values smaller than 6, the binary search might not be worth using. It uses roughly the same number of comparisons for a typical successful search, but it has the overhead of line 13 in each iteration. Indeed, the last few iterations of the binary search progress slowly. We can adopt a hybrid strategy in which the binary search loop terminates when the range is small and applies a sequential scan to finish. Similarly, people search a phone book nonsequentially. Once they have narrowed the range to

```
// binarySearch: Return position of x in sorted array a
//    or NOT_FOUND if item is not found.
template <class Comparable>
int binarySearch( const vector<Comparable> & a,
                  const Comparable & x )
{
    int low = 0;
    int high = a.size( ) - 1;
    int mid;

    while( low < high )
    {
        mid = ( low + high ) / 2;

        if( a[ mid ] < x )
            low = mid + 1;
        else
            high = mid;
    }
    return ( low == high && a[ low ] == x ) ? low : NOT_FOUND;
}
```

Figure 6.12 Binary search, using two-way comparisons.

a column, they perform a sequential scan. The scan of a telephone book is not sequential, but it also is not a binary search. Instead it is more like the algorithm discussed in the next section.

6.6.3 Interpolation Search

The binary search is very fast at searching a sorted static array. In fact, it is so fast that we would rarely use anything else. A static searching method that is sometimes faster, however, is an **interpolation search,** which has better Big-Oh performance on average than binary search but has limited practicality and a bad worst case. For an interpolation search to be practical, two assumptions must be satisfied.

1. Each access must be very expensive compared to a typical instruction. For example, the array might be on a disk instead of in memory, and each comparison requires a disk access.
2. The data must not only be sorted, but it must also be fairly uniformly distributed. For example, a phone book is fairly uniformly distributed. If the input items are {1, 2, 4, 8, 16, … }, the distribution is not uniform.

These assumptions are quite restrictive, so you might never use an interpolation search. But it is interesting to see that there is more than one way to solve a problem and that no algorithm, not even the classic binary search, is the best in all situations.

The interpolation search requires that we spend more time to make an accurate guess of where the item might be. The binary search always uses the midpoint. However, searching for *Hank Aaron* in the middle of the phone book would be silly; somewhere near the start clearly would be more appropriate. Thus, instead of `mid`, we use `next` to indicate the next item that we will try to access.

Here's an example of what might work well. Suppose that the range contains 1000 items, the low item in the range is 1000, the high item in the range is 1,000,000, and we are searching for an item of value 12,000. If the items are uniformly distributed, we expect to find a match somewhere near the twelfth item. The applicable formula is

$$next = low + \left\lceil \frac{x - a[low]}{a[high] - a[low]} \times (high - low - 1) \right\rceil.$$

The subtraction of 1 is a technical adjustment that performs well in practice. Clearly, this calculation is more costly then the binary search calculation. It involves an extra division (the division by 2 in the binary search is really just a bit shift, just as dividing by 10 is easy for humans), multiplication, and four subtractions. These calculations may need to be done with floating-point operations. One iteration may be slower than the complete binary search. However, if the cost of these calculations is insignificant when compared to the cost of accessing an item, speed is immaterial; we care only about the number of iterations.

***Interpolation search* has a better Big-Oh bound on average than does binary search but has limited practicality and a bad worst case.**

In the worst case, where data are not uniformly distributed, the running time could be linear and every item might be examined. In Exercise 6.19 you are asked to construct such a case. However, if we assume that the items are reasonably distributed, as with a phone book, the average number of comparisons is $O(\log \log N)$. In other words, we apply the logarithm twice in succession. For $N = 4{,}000{,}000{,}000$, $\log N$ is about 32 and $\log \log N$ is roughly 5. Of course, there are some hidden constants in Big-Oh notation, but the extra logarithm can lower the number of iterations considerably, so long as a bad case does not crop up. Proving the result rigorously, however, is quite complicated.

6.7 Checking an Algorithm Analysis

Once we have performed an algorithm analysis, we want to determine whether it is correct and as good we can possibly make it. One way to do so is to code the program and see if the empirically observed running time matches the running time predicted by the analysis.

When N increases by a factor of 10, the running time goes up by a factor of 10 for linear programs, 100 for quadratic programs, and 1000 for cubic programs. Programs that run in $O(N \log N)$ take slightly more than 10 times as long to run under the same circumstances. These increases can be hard to spot if the lower order terms have relatively large coefficients and N is not large enough. An example is the jump from $N = 10$ to $N = 100$ in the running time for the various implementations of the maximum contiguous subsequence sum problem. Differentiating linear programs from $O(N \log N)$ programs, based purely on empirical evidence, also can be very difficult.

Another commonly used trick to verify that some program is $O(F(N))$ is to compute the values $T(N)/F(N)$ for a range of N (usually spaced by factors of two), where $T(N)$ is the empirically observed running time. If $F(N)$ is a tight answer for the running time, the computed values converge to a positive constant. If $F(N)$ is an overestimate, the values converge to zero. If $F(N)$ is an underestimate, and hence wrong, the values diverge.

Suppose that we write a program to perform N random searches, using the binary search algorithm. Because each search is logarithmic, we expect the total running time of the program to be $O(N \log N)$. Figure 6.13 shows the actual observed running time for the routine for various input sizes on a real (but extremely slow) computer. The last column is most likely the converging

N	CPU Time T (milliseconds)	T/N	T/N^2	$T/(N \log N)$
10,000	100	0.01000000	0.00000100	0.00075257
20,000	200	0.01000000	0.00000050	0.00069990
40,000	440	0.01100000	0.00000027	0.00071953
80,000	930	0.01162500	0.00000015	0.00071373
160,000	1960	0.01225000	0.00000008	0.00070860
320,000	4170	0.01303125	0.00000004	0.00071257
640,000	8770	0.01370313	0.00000002	0.00071046

Figure 6.13 Empirical running time for N binary searches in an N-item array.

column and thus confirms our analysis, whereas the increasing numbers for T/N suggest that $O(N)$ is an underestimate and the quickly decreasing values for T/N^2 suggest that $O(N)^2$ is an overestimate.

Note in particular that we do not have definitive convergence. One problem is that the clock that we used to time the program ticks only every 10 ms. Note also that there is no great difference between $O(N)$ and $O(N \log N)$. Certainly an $O(N \log N)$ algorithm is much closer to being linear than being quadratic. Finally, note that the machine in this example has enough memory to store 640,000 objects (in the case of this experiment, integers). If your machine does not have this much memory, you will not be able to reproduce these results.

6.8 Limitations of Big-Oh Analysis

Big-Oh analysis is a very effective tool, but it does have limitations. As already mentioned, its use is not appropriate for small amounts of input. For small amounts of input, use the simplest algorithm. Also, for a particular algorithm, the constant implied by the Big-Oh may be too large to be practical. For example, if one algorithm's running time is governed by the formula $2N \log N$ and another has a running time of $1000N$, the first algorithm would most likely be better, even though its growth rate is larger. Large constants can come into play when an algorithm is excessively complex. They also come into play because our analysis disregards constants and thus cannot differentiate between things like memory access (which is cheap) and disk access (which typically is many thousand times more expensive). Our analysis assumes infinite memory, but in applications involving large data sets, lack of sufficient memory can be a severe problem.

Worst case is sometimes uncommon and can be safely ignored. At other times, it is very common and cannot be ignored.

Sometimes, even when constants and lower order terms are considered, the analysis is shown empirically to be an overestimate. In this case, the analysis needs to be tightened (usually by a clever observation). Or the average-case running time bound may be significantly less than the worst-case running time bound, and so no improvement in the bound is possible. For many complicated algorithms the worst-case bound is achievable by some bad input, but in practice it is usually an overestimate. Two examples are the sorting algorithms Shellsort and quicksort (both described in Chapter 9).

Average-case analysis is almost always much more difficult than worst-case analysis.

However, worst-case bounds are usually easier to obtain than their average-case counterparts. For example, a mathematical analysis of the average-case running time of Shellsort has not been obtained. Sometimes, merely defining what *average* means is difficult. We use a worst-case analysis because it is expedient and also because, in most instances, the worst-case analysis is very meaningful. In the course of performing the analysis, we frequently can tell whether it will apply to the average case.

Summary

In this chapter we introduced algorithm analysis and showed that algorithmic decisions generally influence the running time of a program much more than programming tricks do. We also showed the huge difference between the running times for quadratic and linear programs and illustrated that cubic algorithms are, for the most part, unsatisfactory. We examined an algorithm that could be viewed as the basis for our first data structure. The binary search efficiently supports static operations (i.e., searching but not updating), thereby providing a logarithmic worst-case search. Later in the text we examine dynamic data structures that efficiently support updates (both insertion and deletion).

In Chapter 7 we discuss some of the data structures and algorithms included in C++'s STL. We also look at some applications of data structures and discuss their efficiency.

Objects of the Game

average-case bound Measurement of running time as an average over all the possible inputs of size *N*. (p. 209)

Big-Oh The notation used to capture the most dominant term in a function; it is similar to less than or equal to when growth rates are being considered. (p. 196)

Big-Omega The notation similar to greater than or equal to when growth rates are being considered. (p. 208)

Big-Theta The notation similar to equal to when growth rates are being considered. (p. 208)

binary search The search method used if the input array has been sorted and is performed from the middle rather than the end. The binary search is logarithmic because the search range is halved in each iteration. (p. 215)

harmonic number The *N*th harmonic number is the sum of the reciprocals of the first *N* positive integers. The growth rate of the harmonic numbers is logarithmic. (p. 213)

interpolation search A static searching algorithm that has better Big-Oh performance on average than binary search but has limited practicality and a bad worst case. (p. 218)

linear-time algorithm An algorithm that causes the running time to grow as $O(N)$. If the size of the input increases by a factor of f, then the running time also increases by a factor of f. It is the preferred running time for an algorithm. (p. 211)

Little-Oh The notation similar to less than when growth rates are being considered. (p. 208)

logarithm The exponent that indicates the power to which a number is raised to produce a given number. For example, the logarithm of N (to the base 2) is the value X such that 2 raised to the power of X equals N. (p. 211)

repeated doubling principle Holds that, starting at 1, repeat doubling can occur only logarithmically many times until N is reached. (p. 213)

repeated halving principle Holds that, starting at N, repeated halving can occur only logarithmically many times until 1 is reached. This process is used to obtain logarithmic routines for searching. (p. 213)

sequential search A linear search method that steps through an array until a match is found. (p. 214)

static search Accesses data that are never altered. (p. 214)

subquadratic algorithm An algorithm whose running time is strictly slower than quadratic, which can be written as $o(N^2)$. (p. 208)

worst-case bound A guarantee over all inputs of some size. (p. 209)

Common Errors

1. For nested loops, the total time is affected by the product of the loop sizes. For consecutive loops, it is not.
2. Do not just blindly count the number of loops. A pair of nested loops that each run from 1 to N^2 accounts for $O(N^4)$ time.
3. Do not write expressions such as $O(2N^2)$ or $O(N^2 + N)$. Only the dominant term, with the leading constant removed, is needed.
4. Use equalities with Big-Oh, Big-Omega, and so on. Writing that the running time is $> O(N^2)$ makes no sense because Big-Oh is an upper bound. Do not write that the running time is $< O(N^2)$; if the intention is to say that the running time is strictly less than quadratic, use Little-Oh notation.
5. Use Big-Omega, not Big-Oh, to express a lower bound.
6. Use the logarithm to describe the running time for a problem solved by halving its size in constant time. If more than constant time is required to halve the problem, the logarithm does not apply.
7. The base of the logarithm is irrelevant for the purposes of Big-Oh. To include it is an error.

On the Internet

The three maximum contiguous subsequence sum algorithms, as well as a fourth taken from Section 8.5, are available, along with a `main` that conducts the timing tests. Also provided is a binary search algorithm.

MaxSum.cpp Contains four algorithms for the maximum subsequence sum problem.

BinarySearch.cpp Contains the binary search shown in Figure 6.12 and a test program. Included in the test program is a test of the STL equivalent.

Exercises

In Short

6.1. Balls are drawn from a box as specified in Theorem 6.1 in the combinations given in (a)–(d). What are the corresponding values of i, j, and k?
  a. Red, 5, 6
  b. Blue, 5, 6
  c. Blue, 3, Red
  d. 6, 5, Red

6.2. Why isn't an implementation based solely on Theorem 6.2 sufficient to obtain a subquadratic running time for the maximum contiguous subsequence sum problem?

6.3. Suppose that $T_1(N) = O(F(N))$ and $T_2(N) = O(F(N))$. Which of the following are true:
  a. $T_1(N) + T_2(N) = O(F(N))$
  b. $T_1(N) - T_2(N) = O(F(N))$
  c. $T_1(N) / T_2(N) = O(1)$
  d. $T_1(N) = O(T_2(N))$

6.4. Group the following into equivalent Big-Oh functions:

$$x^2, \quad x, \quad x^2 + x, \quad x^2 - x, \quad \text{and} \quad (x^3 / (x - 1)).$$

6.5. Programs A and B are analyzed and are found to have worst-case running times no greater than $150N \log N$ and N^2, respectively. Answer the following questions, if possible.
  a. Which program has the better guarantee on the running time for large values of N ($N > 10{,}000$)?

b. Which program has the better guarantee on the running time for small values of N ($N < 100$)?
c. Which program will run faster *on average* for $N = 1000$?
d. Can program B run faster than program A on *all* possible inputs?

6.6. For the binary search routine shown in Figure 6.11, describe the consequences of each of the following replacement code fragments.
a. Line 12: using the test `low < high`
b. Line 14: assigning `mid = low + high / 2`
c. Line 17: assigning `low = mid`
d. Line 19: assigning `high = mid`

In Theory

6.7. For the typical algorithms that you use to perform calculations by hand, determine the running time to
a. add two N-digit integers.
b. multiply two N-digit integers.
c. divide two N-digit integers.

6.8. In terms of N, what is the running time of the following algorithm to compute X^N:

```
double power( double x, int n )
{
    double result = 1.0;

    for( int i = 0; i < n; i++ )
        result *= x;
    return result;
}
```

6.9. Directly evaluate the triple summation that precedes Theorem 6.1. Verify that the answers are identical.

6.10. For the quadratic algorithm, determine precisely how many times the innermost statement is executed.

6.11. An algorithm takes 0.5 ms for input size 100. How long will it take for input size 500 (assuming that low-order terms are negligible) if the running time is
a. linear.
b. $O(N \log N)$.
c. quadratic.
d. cubic.

6.12. An algorithm takes 0.5 ms for input size 100. How large a problem can be solved in 1 min (assuming that low-order terms are negligible) if the running time is

a. linear.
b. $O(N \log N)$.
c. quadratic.
d. cubic.

6.13. Complete Figure 6.10 with estimates for the running times that were too long to simulate. Interpolate the running times for all four algorithms and estimate the time required to compute the maximum contiguous subsequence sum of 10,000,000 numbers. What assumptions have you made?

6.14. Order the following functions by growth rate: N, $\sqrt{N}$, $N^{1.5}$, N^2, $N \log N$, $N \log \log N$, $N \log^2 N$, $N \log (N^2)$, $2/N$, 2^N, $2^{N/2}$, 37, N^3, and $N^2 \log N$. Indicate which functions grow at the same rate.

6.15. For each of the following program fragments,

a. give a Big-Oh analysis of the running time.
b. implement the code and run for several values of N.
c. compare your analysis with the actual running times.

```
// Fragment #1
for( int i = 0; i < n; i++ )
    sum++;

// Fragment #2
for( int i = 0; i < n; i += 2 )
    sum++;

// Fragment #3
for( int i = 0; i < n; i++ )
    for( int j = 0; j < n; j++ )
        sum++;

// Fragment #4
for( int i = 0; i < n; i++ )
    sum++;
for( int j = 0; j < n; j++ )
    sum++;

// Fragment #5
for( int i = 0; i < n; i++ )
    for( int j = 0; j < n * n; j++ )
        sum++;
```

```
// Fragment #6
for( int i = 0; i < n; i++ )
    for( int j = 0; j < i; j++ )
        sum++;

// Fragment #7
for( int i = 0; i < n; i++ )
    for( int j = 0; j < n * n; j++ )
        for( int k = 0; k < j; k++ )
            sum++;
```

6.16. Occasionally, multiplying the sizes of nested loops can give an overestimate for the Big-Oh running time. This result happens when an innermost loop is infrequently executed. Repeat Exercise 6.15 for the following program fragment:

```
for( int i = 1; i < n; i++ )
    for( int j = 0; j < i * i; j++ )
        if( j % i == 0 )
            for( int k = 0; k < j; k++ )
                sum++;
```

6.17. In a recent court case, a judge cited a city for contempt and ordered a fine of \$2 for the first day. Each subsequent day, until the city followed the judge's order, the fine was squared (i.e., the fine progressed as follows: \$2, \$4, \$16, \$256, \$65,536, . . .).

a. What would be the fine on day N?

b. How many days would it take for the fine to reach D dollars? (A Big-Oh answer will do.)

6.18. Prove Theorem 6.5. (*Hint*: Show that $\sum_{i=2}^{N} \frac{1}{i} < \int_1^N \frac{dx}{x}$. Then show a similar lower bound.)

6.19. Construct an interpolation search that examines every element in the input array.

6.20. Analyze the cost of an average successful search for the binary search algorithm in Figure 6.11.

In Practice

6.21. Give an efficient algorithm to determine if an integer i exists such that $A_i = i$ in an array of increasing integers. What is the running time of your algorithm?

6.22. A prime number has no factors besides 1 and itself. Do the following.

a. Write a program to determine whether a positive integer N is prime. In terms of N, what is the worst-case running time of your program?
b. Let B equal the number of bits in the binary representation of N. What is the value of B?
c. In terms of B, what is the worst-case running time of your program?
d. Compare the running times to determine whether a 20-bit number and a 40-bit number are prime.

6.23. An important problem in numerical analysis is to find a solution to the equation $F(X)$ for some arbitrary F. If the function is continuous and has two points, *low* and *high*, such that $F(low)$ and $F(high)$ have opposite signs, then a root must exist between *low* and *high* and can be found by either a binary search or an interpolation search. Write a function that takes as parameters F, *low*, and *high* and solves for a zero. What must you do to ensure termination?

6.24. A majority element in an array A of size N is an element that appears more than $N/2$ times (thus there is at most one such element). For example, the array

$$3, 3, 4, 2, 4, 4, 2, 4, 4$$

has a majority element (4), whereas the array

$$3, 3, 4, 2, 4, 4, 2, 4$$

does not. Give an algorithm that finds a majority element if one exists or reports that one does not exist. What is the running time of your algorithm? (*Hint:* There is an $O(N)$ solution.)

6.25. The input is an $N \times N$ matrix of numbers that is already in memory. Each individual row is increasing from left to right. Each individual column is increasing from top to bottom. Give an $O(N)$ worst-case algorithm that decides if a number X is in the matrix.

6.26. Design efficient algorithms that take an array of positive numbers `a`, and determine

a. the maximum value of `a[j]+a[i]`, for `j ≥ i`.
b. the maximum value of `a[j]-a[i]`, for `j ≥ i`.
c. the maximum value of `a[j]*a[i]`, for `j ≥ i`.
d. the maximum value of `a[j]/a[i]`, for `j ≥ i`.

Programming Projects

6.27. The Sieve of Eratosthenes is a method used to compute all primes less than N. Begin by making a table of integers 2 to N. Find the smallest integer, i, that is not crossed out. Then print i and cross out i, $2i$, $3i$, ... When $i > \sqrt{N}$, the algorithm terminates. The running time is $O(N \log \log N)$. Write a program to implement the Sieve and verify the running time. How difficult is differentiating the running time from $O(N)$ and $O(N \log N)$?

6.28. The equation $A^5 + B^5 + C^5 + D^5 + E^5 = F^5$ has exactly one integral solution that satisfies $0 < A \le B \le C \le D \le E \le F \le 75$. Write a proram to find the solution. (*Hint:* First, precompute all values of X^5 and store them in an array. Then, for each tuple (A, B, C, D, E), you only need to verify that some F exists in the array. (There are several ways to check for F, one of which is to use a binary search. Other methods might prove to be more efficient.)

6.29. Implement the maximum contiguous subsequence sum algorithms to obtain data equivalent to the data shown in Figure 6.10. Compile the programs with the highest optimization settings.

References

The maximum contiguous subsequence sum problem is from [5]. References [4], [5], and [6] show how to optimize programs for speed. Interpolation search was first suggested in [14] and was analyzed in [13]. References [1], [8], and [17] provide a more rigorous treatment of algorithm analysis. The three-part series [10], [11], and [12], newly updated, remains the foremost reference work on the topic. The mathematical background required for more advanced algorithm analysis is provided by [2], [3], [7], [15], and [16]. An especially good reference for advanced analysis is [9].

1. A. V. Aho, J. E. Hopcroft, and J. D. Ullman, *The Design and Analysis of Computer Algorithms,* Addison-Wesley, Reading, Mass., 1974.
2. M. O. Albertson and J. P. Hutchinson, *Discrete Mathematics with Algorithms,* John Wiley & Sons, New York, 1988.
3. Z. Bavel, *Math Companion for Computer Science,* Reston Publishing Company, Reston, Va., 1982.
4. J. L. Bentley, *Writing Efficient Programs,* Prentice-Hall, Englewood Cliffs, N.J. 1982.

5. J. L. Bentley, *Programming Pearls,* Addison-Wesley, Reading, Mass., 1986.
6. J. L. Bentley, *More Programming Pearls,* Addison-Wesley, Reading, Mass., 1988.
7. R. A. Brualdi, *Introductory Combinatorics,* North-Holland, New York, N.Y. 1977.
8. T. H. Cormen, C. E. Leiserson, and R. L. Rivest, *Introduction to Algorithms,* MIT Press, Cambridge, Mass., 1990.
9. R. L. Graham, D. E. Knuth, and O. Patashnik, *Concrete Mathematics,* Addison-Wesley, Reading, Mass., 1989.
10. D. E. Knuth, *The Art of Computer Programming, Vol 1: Fundamental Algorithms,* 3d ed., Addison-Wesley, Reading, Mass., 1997.
11. D. E. Knuth, *The Art of Computer Programming, Vol 2: Seminumerical Algorithms,* 3d ed., Addison-Wesley, Reading, Mass., 1997.
12. D. E. Knuth, *The Art of Computer Programming, Vol 3: Sorting and Searching,* 2d ed., Addison-Wesley, Reading, Mass., 1998.
13. Y. Pearl, A. Itai, and H. Avni, "Interpolation Search—A log log *N* Search," *Communications of the ACM* **21** (1978), 550–554.
14. W. W. Peterson, "Addressing for Random Storage," *IBM Journal of Research and Development* **1** (1957), 131–132.
15. F. S. Roberts, *Applied Combinatorics,* Prentice-Hall, Englewood Cliffs, N.J. 1984.
16. A. Tucker, *Applied Combinatorics,* 2d ed., John Wiley & Sons, New York, 1984.
17. M. A. Weiss, *Data Structures and Algorithm Analysis in C++*, 2d ed., Addison-Wesley, Reading, Mass., 1999.

Chapter 7

The Standard Template Library

Many algorithms require the use of a proper representation of data to achieve efficiency. This representation and the accompanying operations are known as a *data structure*. Each data structure allows arbitrary insertion but differs in how it allows access to members in the group. Some data structures allow arbitrary access and deletions, whereas others impose restrictions, such as allowing access only to the most recently or least recently inserted item in the group.

The recently adopted C++ Standard requires all implementations to provide a supporting library known as the *Standard Template Library* (known simply as the *STL*). The STL provides a collection of data structures and provides some generic algorithms, such as sorting. As its name suggests, the STL makes heavy use of templates.

Our primary goal here is to describe, in general terms, some examples and applications of data structures. Our secondary goal is to describe the basics of the STL, so that we can use it in Part III. We do not discuss the theory behind an efficient STL implementation until Part IV, at which point we provide simplified implementations of some core STL components. But delaying the discussion of the STL's implementation until after we use it is not a problem. We do not need to know *how* something is implemented so long as we know that it *is* implemented.

In this chapter, we show:

- common data structures, their allowed operations, and their running times;
- some applications of these data structures; and
- the organization of the STL and its integration with the rest of the C++ programming language.

7.1 Introduction

A *data structure* is a representation of data and the operations allowed on that data.

Data structures allow us to achieve an important object-oriented programming goal: component reuse. The data structures described in this section (and implemented later in Part IV) have recurring uses. When each data structure has been implemented once, it can be used over and over in various applications.

A **data structure** is a representation of data and the operations allowed on that data. Many, but by no means all, of the common data structures store a collection of objects and then provide methods to add a new object to, remove an existing object from, or access a contained object in the collection.

Data structures allow us to achieve component reuse.

In this chapter we examine some of the fundamental data structures and their applications. Using a high-level protocol, we describe typical operations that are usually supported by the data structures and briefly describe their uses. When possible, we give an estimate of the cost of implementing these operations correctly. This estimate is often based on analogy with noncomputer applications of the data structure. Our high-level protocol usually supports only a core set of basic operations. Later, when describing the basics of how the data structures can be implemented (in general there are multiple competing ideas), we can more easily focus on language-independent algorithmic details if we restrict the set of operations to a minimum core set.

As an example, Figure 7.1 illustrates a generic protocol that many data structures tend to follow (`Cref`, written in Section 5.3.2, wraps a constant `Object` reference, so that we can abstract a null reference.) We do not actually use this protocol directly in any code. However, you could use this class as a starting point for an inheritance-based hierarchy of data structures.

```
// Collection protocol.

template <class Object>
class Collection
{
  public:
    virtual ~Collection( ) { }

    virtual void insert( const Object & x ) = 0;
    virtual void remove( const Object & x ) = 0;
    virtual Cref<Object> find( const Object & x ) const = 0;

    virtual bool isEmpty( ) const = 0;
    virtual void makeEmpty( ) = 0;
};
```

Figure 7.1 A generic protocol for many data structures.

Then, we give a description of the STL interface provided for these data structures. By no means does the STL necessarily represent the best way of doing things. However, it represents the one library for data structures and algorithms guaranteed to be available on all compilers that implement the Standard. Its use also illustrates some of the core issues that must be dealt with once the theory is taken care of.

The STL is the one library for data structures and algorithms guaranteed to be available on all compilers that implement the Standard.

We defer consideration of efficient implementation of data structures to Part IV. At that point we provide some competing implementations for data structures that follow the simple protocols developed in this chapter. We also provide one implementation for the basic STL components described in this chapter. Thus we are separating the interface of STL (i.e., what the STL does), from its implementation (i.e., how the STL does it). This approach—the separation of the interface and implementation—is part of the object-oriented paradigm. The user of the data structure needs to see only the available operations, not the implementation. Recall this is the encapsulation and information hiding part of object-oriented programming.

The rest of this chapter is organized as follows. First, we discuss two fundamental data structures, namely the stack and queue. Our discussion is STL-independent. Then we discuss the interface for containers and iterators in the STL. Next, we describe some STL algorithms. Finally, we examine some other data structures that are supported in the STL.

7.2 Stacks and Queues

In this section we describe two containers: the stack and the queue. Both have simple interfaces and very efficient implementations. Even so, as you will see, they are very useful data structures.

7.2.1 Stacks

A **stack** is a data structure in which all access is restricted to the most recently inserted element. It behaves much like a stack of bills, stack of plates, or stack of newspapers. The last item added to the stack is placed on the top and is easily accessible, whereas items that have been in the stack for a while are more difficult to access. Thus the stack is appropriate if we expect to access only the top item; all other items are inaccessible.

A *stack* restricts access to the most recently inserted item.

In a stack the three natural operations of `insert`, `remove`, and `find` are renamed `push`, `pop`, and `top`. These basic operations are illustrated in Figure 7.2.

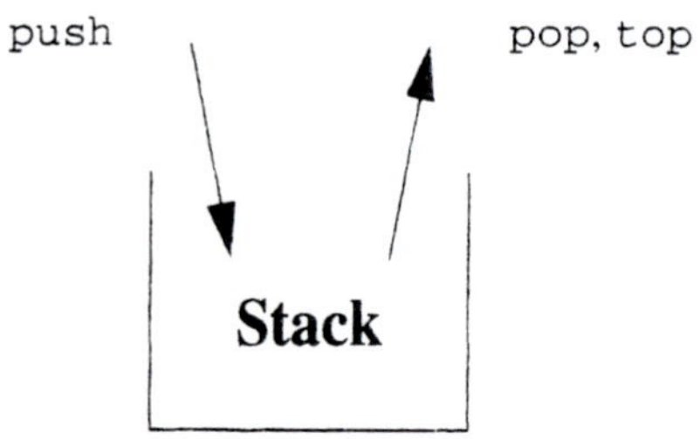

Figure 7.2 Stack model: Input to a stack is by `push`, output is by `top`, and deletion is by `pop`.

```
// Stack protocol.

template <class Object>
class Stack
{
  public:
    virtual ~Stack( ) { }    // Destructor

    virtual void push( const Object & x ) = 0;    // Insert
    virtual void pop( ) = 0;                      // Remove
    virtual const Object & top( ) const = 0;      // Find

    virtual bool isEmpty( ) const = 0;
    virtual void makeEmpty( ) = 0;
};
```

Figure 7.3 Protocol for the abstract stack class.

The C++ class template shown in Figure 7.3 illustrates the typical protocol, which is similar to the protocol in the STL. By pushing items and then popping them, we can use the stack to reverse the order of things.

Stack operations take a constant amount of time.

Each stack operation should take a constant amount of time, independent of the number of items in the stack. By analogy, finding today's newspaper in a stack of newspapers is fast, no matter how deep the stack is. However, arbitrary access in a stack is not efficiently supported, so we do not list it as an option in the protocol.

What makes the stack useful are the many applications for which we need to access only the most recently inserted item. An important use of stacks is in compiler design.

7.2.2 Stacks and Computer Languages

Compilers check programs for syntax errors. Often, however, a lack of one symbol (e.g., a missing `*/` or `}`) causes the compiler to spill out numerous lines of diagnostics without identifying the real error. Other compilers are simply quiet: some will tell you that `_main` is undefined, even though the real problem is a missing closing brace.

A useful tool in this situation is a program that checks on whether everything is balanced, that is, every `{` corresponds to a `}`, every `[` to a `]`, and so on. The sequence `[()]` is legal, but `[(])` is not—so simply counting the numbers of each symbol is insufficient. (Assume for now that we are processing only a sequence of tokens and won't worry about problems such as the character constant `'{'` not needing a matching `'}'`.)

A stack can be used to check for unbalanced symbols.

A stack is useful for checking unbalanced symbols because we know that when a closing symbol such as `)` is seen, it matches the most recently seen unclosed `(`. Therefore, by placing opening symbols on a stack, we can easily check that a closing symbol makes sense. Specifically, we have the following algorithm.

1. Make an empty stack.
2. Read symbols until the end of the file.
   a. If the token is an opening symbol, push it onto the stack.
   b. If it is a closing symbol and if the stack is empty, report an error.
   c. Otherwise, pop the stack. If the symbol popped is not the corresponding opening symbol, report an error.
3. At the end of the file, if the stack is not empty, report an error.

In Section 12.1 we will develop this algorithm to work for (almost) all C++ programs. Details include error reporting, processing of comments, strings, and character constants, as well as escape sequences.

The stack is used to implement function calls in most procedural languages.

The algorithm used to check balanced symbols suggests a way to implement function calls. The problem is that, when a call is made to a new function, all the variables local to the calling function need to be saved by the system; otherwise, the new function would overwrite the calling routine's variables. Furthermore, the current location in the calling routine must be saved so that the new function knows where to go after it is done. The variables have generally been assigned by the compiler to machine registers, and conflicts will certainly arise. The reason that this problem is similar to balancing symbols is because a function call and a function return are essentially the same as an open parenthesis and a closed parenthesis, so the same ideas should apply. This indeed is the case: As discussed in Section 8.3, the stack is used to implement function calls in most procedural languages.

The *operator precedence parsing* algorithm uses a stack to evaluate expressions.

A final important application of the stack is the evaluation of expressions in computer languages. In the expression `1+2*3`, at the point that the `*` is encountered, we have already read the operator `+` and the operands `1` and `2`. Does `*` operate on `2`, or `1+2`? Precedence rules tell us that `*` operates on `2`, which is the most recently seen operand. After we see the `3`, we can evaluate `2*3` as `6` and then apply the `+` operator. This process suggests that operands and intermediate results should be saved on a stack. It also suggests that the operators be saved on the stack (as the `+` is held until the higher precedence `*` is evaluated). An algorithm that uses a stack to evaluate expressions is **operator precedence parsing.** We describe it in detail in Section 12.2.

7.2.3 Queues

The *queue* restricts access to the least recently inserted item.

Another simple data structure is the **queue,** which restricts access to the least recently inserted item. In many cases being able to find and/or remove the most recently inserted item is important. But in an equal number of cases, it is not only unimportant, but it is actually the wrong thing to do. In a multiprocessing system, for example, when jobs are submitted to a printer, we expect the least recent or most senior job to be printed first. This order is not only fair, but it also is required to guarantee that the first job does not wait forever. Thus you can expect to find printer queues on all large systems.

The basic operations supported by queues are

- `enqueue`, or insertion at the back of the line;
- `dequeue`, or removal of the item from the front of the line; and
- `getFront`, or access of the item at the front of the line.

Figure 7.4 illustrates these queue operations. Historically, `dequeue` and `getFront` have been combined into one operation, but we keep them separate here. Because C++ allows function overloading, we could simultaneously define two forms of `dequeue`: one that gives the front item and one that does not.

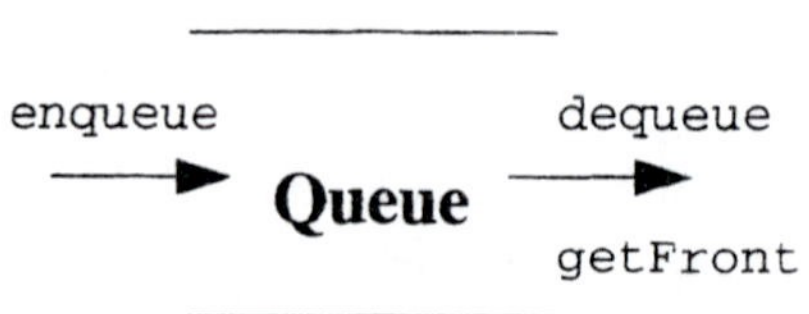

Figure 7.4 Queue model: Input is by `enqueue`, output is by `getFront`, and deletion is by `dequeue`.

```
//Queue protocol.

template <class Object>
class Queue
{
  public:
    virtual ~Queue( ) { }    // Destructor

    virtual void enqueue( const Object & x ) = 0;   // Insert
    virtual void dequeue( ) = 0;                     // Remove
    virtual const Object & getFront( ) const = 0;   // Find

    virtual bool isEmpty( ) const = 0;
    virtual void makeEmpty( ) = 0;
};
```

Figure 7.5 Protocol for the abstract queue class

Queue operations take a constant amount of time.

Figure 7.5 illustrates a possible protocol for queues. Because queue operations and stack operations are restricted similarly, we expect that they should also take a constant amount of time per query. That is indeed the case. All basic queue operations take $O(1)$ time. We present several applications of queues in the case studies.

7.3 Containers and Iterators

In this section we describe the basics of the STL iterators and how they interact with containers. Recall from Section 5.4, that an iterator is an object that is used to traverse a collection of objects. In the STL such a collection is called a *container.* Recall also, that the iterator maintains a notion of a current position in the container and provides basic operations such as the ability to advance to the next position and access the item in the current position.

The STL iterators are very flexible, in that sometimes they allow changes to the underlying container, but at other times they do not. The iterator syntax is based heavily on making it appear that an iterator is a primitive (pointer) type rather than a class type. Thus, instead of having named member functions, as in the design in Section 5.4.2, the STL iterators make heavy use of operator overloading.[1]

1. Operator overloading gives the STL iterators the same look and feel as a pointer variable used in pointer hopping, as discussed in Section D.3.

7.3.1 Containers

A *container* represents a group of objects, known as its elements.

A **container** represents a group of objects, known as its *elements.* Some implementations, such as vectors and lists, are unordered; others, such as sets and maps, are ordered. Some implementations allow duplicates; others do not. All containers support the following operations.

`bool empty( ) const`
returns `true` if the container contains no elements and `false` otherwise.

`iterator begin( ) const`
returns an `iterator` that can be used to begin traversing all locations in the container.

The *end marker* is a position one past the last element in the container.

`iterator end( ) const`
returns an `iterator` that represents the **end marker,** a position past the last element in the container.

`int size( ) const`
returns the number of elements in the container.

The most interesting of these methods are those that return an `iterator`. We describe the operations that can be performed by an `iterator` in Section 7.3.2.

7.3.2 The `iterator`

An *iterator* is an object that allows access to and iteration through the elements in a container.

As described in Section 5.4, an **iterator** is an object that allows access to and iteration through all the elements in a container. We discussed the use of the `Iterator` class in the context of read-only vectors in Section 5.4.

In the STL, there are actually many types of `iterators`. However, we can always count on the following operations being available for any iterator type.

`itr++`
advances the iterator `itr` to the next location. Both the prefix and postfix forms are allowable, but the precise return type (whether it is a constant reference or a reference) can depend on the type of iterator.

A `const_iterator` must be used to traverse `const` containers.

`*itr`
returns a reference to the object stored at iterator `itr`'s location. The reference returned may or may not be modifiable, depending on the type of iterator.[2] For instance, the **`const_iterator`**, which must be used to

2. The reference may be only modifiable (i.e., `*itr` may not appear on the right-hand side). These are output iterators, but we won't have occasion to make use of them. Instead, we restrict our discussion to forward iterators, bidirectional iterators, and random access iterators.

traverse const containers, has an operator* that returns a const reference, thus not allowing *itr to be on the left-hand side of an assignment.

itr1==itr2
returns true if iterators itr1 and itr2 refer to the same location and false otherwise.

itr1!=itr2
returns true if iterators itr1 and itr2 refer to a different location and false otherwise.

Each container defines several iterators. For instance, vector<int> defines vector<int>::iterator and vector<int>::const_iterator. (There are also reverse iterators that we do not discuss.) The const_iterator must be used instead of an iterator if the container is nonmodifiable.

As an example, the routine shown in Figure 7.6 prints the elements of any container, provided that the element has operator<< defined for it. If the container is an ordered set, its elements are output in sorted order.[3]

***Bidirectional iterators* support operator--.**

Some iterators have more power than the **forward iterator** shown in Figure 7.6. Because we do not cover the full STL, we restrict our discussion to the iterators that occur in the text. The *forward iterator* allows forward traversal through a container, via operator++. If the iterator also supports operator--, that is, it supports both forward and backward traversal through a container, it is said to be a **bidirectional** iterator. Generally speaking, in Part IV we write the code for the forward iterator and leave the bidirectional support as an exercise for you to do.

```
1 // Print the contents of Container c.
2 template <class Container>
3 void printCollection( const Container & c )
4 {
5     typename Container::const_iterator itr;
6     for( itr = c.begin( ); itr != c.end( ); ++itr )
7         cout << *itr << endl;
8 }
```

Figure 7.6 Routine for printing the contents of any Container.

3. typename is used to signal that Container::const_iterator is a type; thus line 5 is a declaration.

A *random access iterator* efficiently supports arbitrary advancing and retreating in a collection.

Some iterators that support even more are called *random access iterators*. With a **random access iterator,** we can efficiently advance or retreat an arbitrary amount in a collection. In other words, the + and - operators are defined so that `itr+100` advances 100 positions. Iterator subtraction is also allowed, so `itr1-itr2` measures a separation distance.[4]

The type of iterators available depend upon the container. Some containers export random access interators, while others export bidirectional iterators. The iterators are the bridge between the containers and the algorithms. A container will provide the maximally capable iterator reasonable, and an algorithm will require a minimally capable iterator reasonable.

7.4 STL Algorithms

The STL provides numerous general purpose algorithms that operate on many of the containers. We examine only a few of these algorithms, with the intention of showing the general ideas that pervade the STL, while documenting the specific algorithms to be used in Part III.

The material in Section 5.2 is an essential prerequisite to this section.

The STL algorithms make heavy use of function objects. Consequently, the material in Section 5.2 is an essential prerequisite to this section.

7.4.1 STL Function Objects

***Unary function objects* accept one parameter. *Binary function objects* accept two parameters.**

The function objects needed for the STL follow the convention described in Section 5.2. Specifically, these function objects are instances of classes that have implemented the function call operator, `operator()`. Some have function call operators that accept only one parameter and are called **unary function objects.** Others have function call operators that accept two parameters and are called **binary function objects.** In the file `<functional>`, the STL provides several function object templates. We describe those used in this text.

Binary Comparison Objects

For many algorithms, such as sorting, a default ordering is used. This ordering is to call `operator<` if the underlying collection has such an operator defined in it. The function object template that encapsulates `operator<` is `less`. Because `less` has a short implementation, as shown in Figure 7.7, seeing the implementation helps to illustrate the behavior.

---

4. Again, it is worth noting that pointers used in pointer hopping (Appendix D.3) satisfy the requirements of a random access iterator and that `const` pointers satisfy the properties of a random access `const_iterator`.

```
// The less function template.

template <class Object>
class less
{
  public:
    bool operator() ( const Object & lhs, const Object & rhs ) const
      { return lhs < rhs; }
};
```

Figure 7.7 Implementation of the `less` function template.

Each comparison operator has a function object template. These operators are `less`, `greater`, `equal_to`, `not_equal_to`, `greater_equal`, and `less_equal`.

Each comparison operator has a function object template.

Unary Binder Adapters

Consider the problem of finding in a collection of items the first item that satisfies some property. For instance, we might want to find the first item that is less than 50. If we write a generic algorithm to solve this problem, we pass to the algorithm information about the container plus a function object that would express the property that we would like to satisfy. In this context, the function object is called a *predicate*. A **predicate** is a function object that returns a Boolean. A predicate that takes a single parameter (a particular item in the collection) and returns a Boolean, indicating whether the item satisfies the property is a **unary predicate.**

A *predicate* is a function object that returns a Boolean.

Although we could write the predicate ourselves (it is actually a simplified version of `less`), we want somehow to be able to reuse `less`. To do so, we can use a **unary binder adapter** to generate a unary function from a binary function by making constant one of the parameters to the binary function.

A *unary binder adapter* is used to generate a unary function from a binary function by making constant one of the parameters to the binary function.

The function `bind2nd` takes two parameters—`function`, which is a binary function and `secondVal`—and returns a new function. The new function uses `function`, with `secondVal` as the second parameter in the binary function. If the function is a predicate, which is typical, the new predicate is a unary predicate.

For instance, the result of `bind2nd(less<int>(),5)` is a new unary predicate. If this new object is `f1`, any call `f1(x)` is interpreted as `less<int>()(x,5)`. A similar function is `bind1st`, which can be used to return a new predicate, with the first value bound. The result of `bind1st(less<int>(),5)` is a new unary predicate. If this new object is `f2`, any call `f2(x)` is interpreted as `less<int>()(5,x)`. We show how to use these binders in Section 7.4.2. Their implementation is left as Exercise 7.20.

The **find_if** Algorithm

find_if returns an iterator that represents the first object that satisfies a predicate.

Our discussion of unary binder adapters suggested an application in which we perform a search, basing matches on a predicate. This is precisely what `find_if` does.

```
Iterator find_if( Iterator begin, Iterator end,
                  Predicate pred )
```

returns an iterator representing the first object that satisfies `pred`. The search range is from `begin` to `end`, not including `end`. If no match is found, `end` is returned.

To illustrate how `find_if` is used, let us suppose that `v` is a `vector<int>` and that we want to find the first occurrence of an item that is less than 50. We can easily define a function object class that expresses this condition:

```
class LessThan50
{
  public:
    bool operator() ( int x ) const
      { return x < 50; }
};
```

We need to declare an iterator, `itr`, which is of type `vector<int>::iterator`. At the end of the following code fragment, `itr` will either be `v.end()` or it will be located at an item that is less than 50:

```
itr = find_if( v.begin( ), v.end( ), LessThan50( ) );
```

Alternatively we can use a unary binder adapter:

```
itr = find_if( v.begin( ), v.end( ),
                          bind2nd( less<int>( ), 50 ) );
```

Again, we provide an implementation of an STL component, shown in Figure 7.8, to illustrate what is going on. The `find_if` algorithm is heavily templated and is written in terms of basic iterator operations. As a result, it works for any forward iterator. Note that it is not written in terms of any container: rather it is written in terms of the container's iterator. Many of the STL algorithms look just like this one. Again, we observe the principle of programming to an interface.

```
template <class ForwardIterator, class UnaryPredicate>
ForwardIterator find_if( const ForwardIterator & begin,
                         const ForwardIterator & end,
                         UnaryPredicate isMatch )
{
    for( ForwardIterator itr = begin; itr != end; ++itr )
        if( isMatch( *itr ) )
            break;

    return itr;
}
```

Figure 7.8 Implementation of `find_if`.

7.4.2 Binary Search

The `find` algorithm is a specialized version of `find_if` that returns the location (in an iterator) of the first occurrence of some value `x`. It is easily implemented by calling `find_if` with an appropriate predicate (see Exercise 7.11).

Clearly, `find_if` and thus `find` must take linear time because they use sequential search. However, if the collection is sorted, we can use binary search. But, recall that binary search also requires a random access iterator: The underlying assumption is that the collection is arraylike and that an item in any position can be accessed in constant time.

The `lower_bound` function template uses binary search and returns an iterator corresponding to the first position that contains a value at least as large as the object being searched for.

The STL implementation of the binary search is `lower_bound`. As usual, a pair of iterators that define the search space must be passed. We also pass the value being searched for. Optionally, we pass a comparison function; the default is `less<Object>`. The `lower_bound` function template returns an iterator corresponding to the *first position* that contains a value at least as large as the object being searched for. The presence of the object in the search space can easily be tested for, by comparing the object being searched for with the object referenced by the iterator. If the object is larger than all others in the collection, the end marker is returned.

The implementation is almost identical to the code shown in Figure 6.12 and is shown in Figure 7.9. A default parameter cannot be used because it would be the only instance in which the third template parameter is used. That would make deducing the template expansion impossible for the compiler. Instead, we have to write two separate function templates and have one call the other (see line 6). In the primary routine, the main complication is at line 21. Iterators cannot be averaged by adding them and then dividing by 2. Instead, to compute a midpoint, we compute `low` and `high`'s separation distance and add half the separation distance to `low`. This line of code requires use of the

```
template <class RandomIterator, class Comparable>
RandomIterator lower_bound( const RandomIterator & begin
                            const RandomIterator & end,
                            const Comparable & x )
{
    return lower_bound( begin, end, x, less<Comparable>( ) );
}

template <class RandomIterator, class Object, class Compare>
RandomIterator lower_bound( const RandomIterator & begin,
                            const RandomIterator & end,
                            const Object & x,
                            Compare lessThan )
{
    RandomIterator low = begin;
    RandomIterator mid;
    RandomIterator high = end;

    while( low < high )
    {
        mid = low + ( high - low ) / 2;

        if( lessThan( *mid, x ) )
            low = mid + 1;
        else
            high = mid;
    }
    return low;
}
```

Figure 7.9 Implementation of `lower_bound`.

random access iterator. If `lower_bound` is passed iterators that do not support iterator subtraction, a compiler error will result if we attempt to expand the template. We use the `lower_bound` function template in Section 11.1.

7.4.3 Sorting

The STL provides a sort algorithm. It is called by passing a pair of iterators and an optional predicate that implements the less-than test. The sort algorithm requires random access iterators.

`template <class RandomIterator>`
`void sort( RandomIterator begin, RandomIterator end )`
rearranges the elements in the specified range to be in sorted order, using the natural order.

```
template <class RandomIterator, class Comparator>
void sort( RandomIterator begin, RandomIterator end,
           Comparator lessThan )
```

rearranges the elements in the specified range to be in sorted order, using `lessThan`.

7.5 Implementation of vector with an Iterator

The `vector` class shown in Section 3.4.2 was not iterator-aware. The online version of `vector` is iterator-aware. That is, we omitted portions of the online implementation when we discussed the `vector` implementation. In this section we briefly sketch what was omitted.

STL iterators are not bounds-checked.

Like all of the iterators in the STL, the online code implements an unsafe iterator. For instance, `*itr` when `itr` is already at the end marker is not explicitly detected by the STL as an error. Neither is `++itr`, under the same circumstances. Of course, an error is likely to occur, terminating your program abnormally. However, the STL will not give you any help in tracking down the problem.

Our `vector` class, as described in Section 3.4.2, performed error checks on array indexing. We can also add error checks for the iterators. We do so for all the iterators discussed in Part IV. We leave making the `vector` iterators safe as an exercise in Part IV.

A `vector<Object>` defines `vector<Object>::iterator` and `vector<Object>::const_iterator`. This task is most conveniently done with a `typedef`, as shown in Figure 7.10. Because pointer hopping pointers satisfy the properties of a random access iterator, we can use pointer types as the iterator!

Consequently, lines 9 and 10 define `iterator` as an `Object *` and `const_iterator` as `const Object *`. We then need to provide implementations of `begin` and `end`, which return iterators, as done at lines 12 to 20. Note that we provide both accessor and mutator versions. The accessor returns a `const_iterator`, and the mutator returns an `iterator`.

This code contains most of the logic used in designing a safe iterator class. To do so, we would first need to write two new class templates, `VectorIterator` and `ConstVectorIterator`, and change the typedefs at lines 9 and 10 to reference them. Next, we would have to change the bodies of `begin` and `end` to return constructed iterators (by calling appropriate constructors for the two new classes). We would construct the iterators by passing a position (`0` for `begin`, `size()` for `end`) and `this` (most likely, these constructors would be not be public, and we would use appropriate friend declarations). We would pass two parameters so that the iterator can store both a current position and a pointer to the `vector` that it is iterating

```
template <class Object>
class vector
{
  public:
    // Constructors, and other member functions.
    // See Figure 3.14, lines 11 to 44

      // Iterator stuff: not bounds checked
    typedef Object * iterator;
    typedef const Object * const_iterator;

    iterator begin( )
      { return &objects[ 0 ]; }
    const_iterator begin( ) const
      { return &objects[ 0 ]; }

    iterator end( )
      { return &objects[ size( ) ]; }
    const_iterator end( ) const
      { return &objects[ size( ) ]; }

  private:
    int theSize;
    int theCapacity;
    Object * objects;
};
```

Figure 7.10 Adding unsafe iterators to the `vector` class.

over. That way it can ensure that it is at a valid position. Also, when two iterators are subtracted, the first iterator can verify that the second iterator refers to the same `vector`.

The two iterator classes must then provide overloaded operators, such as two versions of `operator++`, two versions of `operator--`, up to two versions of `operator*`, `operator==`, `operator!=`, `operator+`, and various `operator-`, all of which can have extensive error checking.

There is one additional major detail: Because an `iterator` can be used anywhere a `const_iterator` can be used (but not vice versa), it follows that there is an IS-A relationship. As a result, `ConstVectorIterator` is a base class and `VectorIterator` is a derived class. Needless to say, that introduces quite a few additional details. You will have to wait until Chapter 17 to see how it all gets resolved (in the context of another container).

7.6 Sequences and Linked Lists

In Section 1.6.3 we presented a basic linked list. In a **linked list** we store items noncontiguously rather than in the usual contiguous array. The advantage of doing so is twofold. First, an insertion into the middle of the list does not require moving all the items that follow the insertion point. Data movement is very expensive in practice, and the linked list allows insertion with only a constant amount of assignment statements. Second, if the array size is not known in advance, we must use the array-doubling technique. In the course of expanding the array from size S to $2S$, we need $3S$ units of available memory. After the expansion has been completed, we still need $2S$ units of memory, meaning that we have to waste lots of memory. If the data items are large, we would rather have only the overhead of a pointer per item. The basic linked list is shown in Figure 7.11.

The linked list is used to avoid large amounts of data movement. It uses a small amount of space per item.

Note that, if we allow access only at `first`, we have a stack and that, if we allow insertions only at `last` and access only at `first`, we have a queue. Typically we need more general operations, such as finding or removing any named item in the list. We also need to be able to insert a new item at any point. These requirements are far more than either a stack or a queue allows.

Access to the list is achieved by an iterator class. The list class has operations that reflect the state of the list. All other operations are in the iterator class.

To access items in the linked list, we need a pointer to the corresponding node. Clearly, however, granting this access is a violation of information hiding principles. We need to ensure that any access to the list through a pointer is safe, which is where the iterator comes in.

7.6.1 The `list` Class

The STL provides three sequence implementations, but only two are generally used: an array-based version and a linked-list based version. The array-based version may be appropriate if insertions are performed only at the high end of the array (using `push_back`), for the reasons discussed in Section 1.2.4. The

The `list` class implements a linked list.

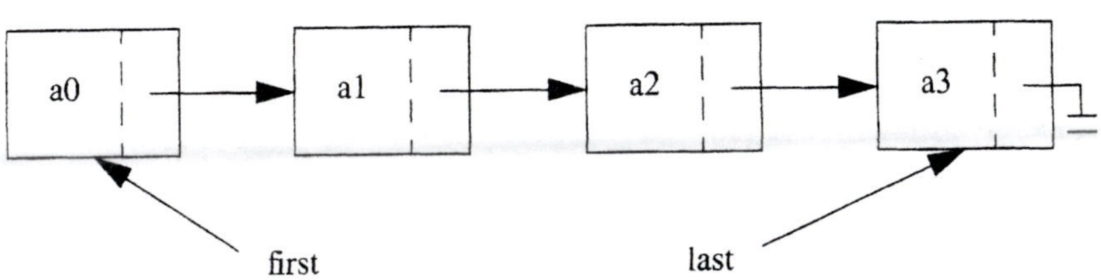

Figure 7.11 A simple linked list.

STL doubles the array if an insertion at the high-end would exceed an internal capacity. Although this procedure gives good Big-Oh performance, for large objects that are expensive to construct, a list version would be preferable in order to minimize calls to the constructors. The `list` class implements a linked list.

The basic trade-off between `vector` and `list` is that random access iterators are available only for `vector`, whereas insertion and removal from the middle of a container is efficiently supported only for `list`.

Insertions and deletions toward the middle of the sequence are inefficient in `vector`. A `vector` allows direct access by the index, but a `list` does not. Thus the `list` class can always be safely used unless indexing is needed. The `vector` class may still be a better choice if insertions occur only at the end and the objects being inserted are not overly expensive to construct. Additional operations on sequences include the following.

`void push_back( const Object & element )`
appends `element` at the end of this sequence.

`void push_front( const Object & element )`
prepends `element` to the front of this sequence. It is not available for `vector` because it is too inefficient. However, a `deque` is available that is like a `vector` (in that it supports `operator[]` in constant time), but it supports double-ended access.

`Object & front( )`
returns the first element in this sequence. An accessor version is also defined.

`Object & back( )`
returns the last element in this sequence. An accessor version is also defined.

`void pop_front( )`
removes the first element from this sequence. It is available only for `list` and `deque`.

`void pop_back( )`
removes the last element from this sequence.

`iterator insert( iterator pos, const Object & obj )`
inserts `obj` prior to the element in the position referred to by `pos`. This operation takes constant time for a `list`, but takes time proportional to the distance from `pos` to the end of the sequence for a `vector`. Returns the position of the newly inserted item.

`iterator erase( iterator pos )`
removes the object at the position referred to by `pos`. Elements in the sequence are logically moved as required. This operation is done in constant time for a `list`, but it takes time proportional to the distance from `pos` to the end of the sequence for a `vector`. Returns the position of the element that followed `pos` prior to the call to `erase`.

```
#include <stack>
#include <iostream>
#include <vector>
using namespace std;

// Do some inserts and removes.
int main( )
{
    stack<int,vector<int> > s;

    s.push( 1 ); s.push( 2 ); s.push( 3 );

    cout << "Contents are: " << endl;
    for( ; !s.empty( ); s.pop( ) )
        cout << s.top( ) << endl;

    return 0;
}
```

Figure 7.12 Routine to demonstrate the STL `stack`; the output is `3 2 1`.

7.6.2 Stacks and Queues

The STL provides `stack` and `queue` classes, but they simply use a sequence container (`list`, `vector`, or `deque`) to call the appropriate functions. Thus they are adapters (as described in Section 5.3.3). Both `stack` and `queue` are templates that require the specification of both the type of object in the container and the type of container. There is a default container, but using the default requires a compiler that understands default template parameters. As an example, Figure 7.12 shows how to use a stack of integers having a `vector` as the underlying container. The idea of the client having to specify the underlying implementation of a data structure seems to run counter to the principle of programming to an interface. However, that is necessary only because some compilers do not yet fully understand templates.

The STL provides `stack` and `queue` classes, but they use a sequence container (`list`, `vector`, or `deque`) to call the appropriate functions.

The `queue` does not use standard names such as `enqueue` and `dequeue`. Instead it uses `push`, `pop`, and `top`. Thus there is no compelling reason to use the `queue`; these names are more misleading than the names in the `list` class. Seemingly, then, only the `stack` is worth using.

The `queue` does not use standard names such as `enqueue` and `dequeue`.

7.7 Sets

In Section 6.6 we examined the static searching problem and demonstrated that, if the items are presented in sorted order, we can support the `find` operation in logarithmic worst-case time. This approach involves static searching because, once we have been presented with the items, we cannot add or remove items. Suppose, however, that we do want to add and remove items. The STL data structure that allows us to do so is the `set`.

The `set` is an ordered container that allows no duplicates.

The `set` is an ordered container that allows no duplicates.[5] We discuss the underlying implementation in Chapter 19. In addition to the usual `begin`, `end`, `size`, and `empty`, the `set` provides the following operations.

`pair<iterator,bool> insert( const Object & element )`
adds `element` to the set if it is not already present. The `bool` component of the return value is `true` if the set did not already contain `element`; otherwise, it is `false`. The `iterator` component of the return value is the location of `element` in the set.

`iterator find( const Object & element ) const`
returns an `iterator` containing the location of `element` in the set or `end()` if `element` is not in the set.

`int erase( const Object & element )`
removes `element` from the set if it is present. Returns the number of elements removed (either 0 or 1).

By default, ordering uses the `less<Object>` function object, which itself is implemented by calling `operator<` for the `Object`. An alternative ordering can be specified by instantiating the `set` template with a function object type.[6] As an example, Figure 7.13 illustrates how a `set` that stores strings in decreasing order is constructed. The call to `printCollection` will output elements in decreasing sorted order.

We are hoping that the worst-case cost of the `find`, `insert`, and `erase` operations is $O(\log N)$ because that would match the bound obtained for the static binary search. Unfortunately, for the simplest implementation of the `set`, that is not the case. The average case is logarithmic, but the worst case is $O(N)$ and occurs frequently. However, by applying some algorithmic tricks, we can obtain a more complex structure that does indeed have $O(\log N)$ cost per operation. The STL `set` is guaranteed to have this performance, and in Chapter 19 we discuss how to obtain it using the *binary search tree* and its variants, and provide an implementation of the `set`, with a forward iterator.

5. The `multiset` allows duplicates, but we do not discuss it here.
6. Some compilers do not support default template parameters. For those compilers, the function object type must be explicitly provided. In this text we always explicitly provide a function object type.

```
#include <iostream>
#include <set>
#include <functional>
#include <string>
using namespace std;

int main( )
{
    set<string, greater<string> > s;   // Use reverse order

    s.insert( "joe" );
    s.insert( "bob" );
    printCollection( s );    // Figure 7.6

    return 0;
}
```

Figure 7.13 Illustration of `set`, using reverse order.

We mention in closing that the iterator returned by the set is not a random access iterator. However, it is possible to make the set iterator a slightly slow $O(\log N)$ random access iterator, while preserving the running time of the other operations. In other words, by careful modification of the binary search tree, we can access the Kth smallest item in logarithmic time.

Using a binary search tree, we can access the *K*th smallest item. The cost is logarithmic average-case time for a simple implementation and logarithmic worst-case time for a more careful implementation.

7.8 Maps

A **`map`** is used to store a collection of ordered entries that consists of *keys* and their *values* and maps keys to values. Keys must be unique, but several keys can be mapped to the same values.[7] Thus values need not be unique.

A `map` is used to store a collection of ordered entries that consists of keys and their values and maps keys to values.

A `map` behaves like a `set` instantiated with a `pair` (see Section 5.5), whose comparison function refers only to the key.[8] Thus it supports `begin`, `end`, `size`, and `empty`, but the underlying iterator is a (key, value) pair. Thus for an iterator `itr`, `*itr` is of type `pair<KeyType,ValueType>`. The `map` also supports `insert`, `find`, and `erase`. For `insert`, we must provide a `pair<KeyType, ValueType>` object. Although `find` requires only a key, the iterator it returns references a `pair`. Using only these operations is hardly worthwhile because the syntactic baggage can be excessive.

7. The `multimap` allows duplicate keys, but we do not discuss it here.
8. Like a `set`, an optional template parameter can be used to specify a comparison function that differs from `less<KeyType>`.

Fortunately the `map` class has an important extra operation: The array-indexing operation is overloaded as follows.

`ValueType & operator[]( const KeyType & key )`
Return the value to which `key` is mapped by `map`. If `key` is not mapped, it becomes mapped to a default `ValueType` generated by applying a zero-parameter constructor (or a default value of zero for the primitive types).

Because the `map` can be directly implemented with a `set`, both have the same performance properties.

An *associative array* uses array indexing: The index is the key, and the result of the index is the value.

This type of syntax is sometimes known as an **associative array,** which uses array indexing: The index is the key, and the result of the index is the value. In Figure 7.14, `people` maps a `string` to an `int`. Hence `"Tim"` is initially `3` and then `5`, which is output by the first print statement. `"Bob"` is not in the `map` prior to the print statement, but the call to `operator[]` puts it in the `map` with a default value of `0`. Thus `0` is (perhaps unintentionally) output by the second print statement. To know whether `"Bob"` was in the `map`, we first would have needed to call `find` and then check to see whether the returned iterator was equal to `end()`. Once we have called `find` and because we have an iterator `itr`, to find the value we should use `(*itr).second`[9] to avoid a second search. We demonstrate this technique in Chapter 15.

```
#include <iostream>
#include <map>
#include <string>
using namespace std;

int main( )
{
    map<string,int,less<string> > people;

    people[ "Tim" ] = 3;
    people[ "Tim" ] = 5;
    cout << "Tim's value is " << people[ "Tim" ] << endl;
    cout << "Bob's value is " << people[ "Bob" ] << endl;

    return 0;
}
```

Figure 7.14 Illustration of the `map` class. Tim's value is 5. Bob's value is 0.

9. Although `itr->second` appears to be equivalent to `(*itr).second`, the equivalence holds only if the iterator class overloads `operator->`. The Standard requires that STL iterators do so, but many compilers do not yet conform to this aspect of the Standard.

7.9 Priority Queues

The *priority queue* supports access of the minimum item only.

Although jobs sent to a printer are generally placed on a queue, that might not always be the best thing to do. For instance, one job might be particularly important, so we might want to allow that job to be run as soon as the printer is available. Conversely, when the printer finishes a job and several 1-page jobs and one 100-page job are waiting, it might be reasonable to print the long job last, even if it is not the last job submitted. (Unfortunately, most systems do not do this, which can be particularly annoying at times.)

Similarly, in a multiuser environment the operating system scheduler must decide which of several processes to run. Generally, a process is allowed to run only for a fixed period of time. A poor algorithm for such a procedure involves use of a queue. Jobs are initially placed at the end of the queue. The scheduler repeatedly takes the first job on the queue, runs it until either it finishes or its time limit is up, and places it at the end of the queue if it does not finish. Generally, this strategy is not appropriate because short jobs must wait and thus seem to take a long time to run. Clearly, users that are running an editor should not see a visible delay in the echoing of typed characters. Thus short jobs (i.e., those using fewer resources) should have precedence over jobs that have already consumed large amounts of resources. Furthermore, some resource-intensive jobs, such as jobs run by the system administrator, might be important and should also have precedence.

If we give each job a number to measure its priority, the smaller number (pages printed, resources used) tends to indicate greater importance. Thus we want to be able to access the smallest item in a collection of items and remove it from the collection. To do so we use the `findMin` and `deleteMin` operations. The data structure that supports these operations is the **priority queue** and supports access of the minimum item only. Figure 7.15 illustrates the basic priority queue operations.

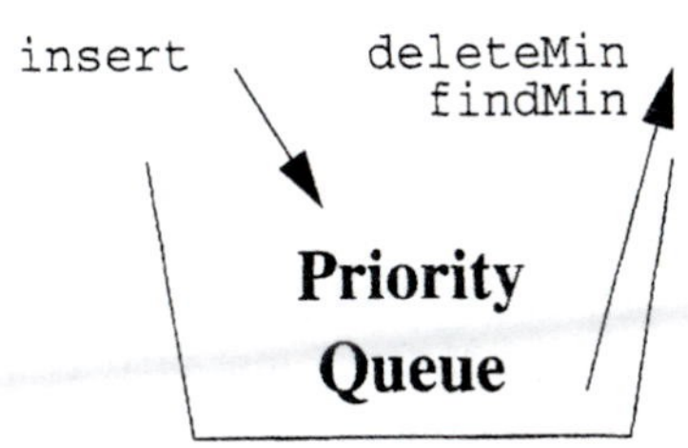

Figure 7.15 Priority queue model: Only the minimum element is accessible.

```
// PriorityQueue protocol (not the STL version).

template <class Comparable>
class PriorityQueue
{
  public:
    virtual ~PriorityQueue( ) { }    // Destructor

    virtual void insert( const Comparable & x ) = 0; // Insert
    virtual void deleteMin( ) = 0;                   // Remove
    virtual void deleteMin( Comparable & min ) = 0;  // Remove
    virtual const Comparable & findMin( ) const = 0; // Find

    virtual bool isEmpty( ) const = 0;
    virtual void makeEmpty( ) = 0;
};
```

Figure 7.16 Protocol for typical priority queues (but not the STL version).

A typical priority queue protocol is shown in Figure 7.16. Note that `deleteMin` has two forms: One form removes the smallest item, and the second form removes the smallest item but passes that item back to the caller.

The STL protocol is somewhat different, as we discuss shortly. Because the priority queue allows duplicates, it cannot be implemented by a `set`. It can be implemented by a `multiset`, but that turns out to be overkill because a multiset supports many more operations than required by a priority queue. The penalty for the overkill is typically somewhat slower performance.

The *binary heap* implements the priority queue in logarithmic time per operation with little extra space.

As the priority queue supports only the `deleteMin` and `findMin` operations, we might expect performance that is a compromise between the constant-time queue and the logarithmic time set. Indeed, this is the case: The basic priority queue supports all operations in logarithmic worst-case time, uses only an array, supports insertion in constant average time, and is simple to implement and is known as the **binary heap.** This structure is one of the most elegant data structures known. In Chapter 21 we provide details on the implementation of priority queues.

An important use of priority queues is *event-driven simulation.*

An important application of the priority queue is *event-driven simulation*. Consider, for example, a system such as a bank in which customers arrive and wait in line until one of *K* tellers is available. Customer arrival is governed by a probability distribution function, as is the service time (the amount of time it takes a teller to provide complete service to one customer). We are interested in statistics such as how long on average a customer has to wait or how long a line might be.

With certain probability distributions and values of K, we can compute these statistics exactly. However, as K gets larger, the analysis becomes considerably more difficult, so the use of a computer to simulate the operation of the bank is appealing. In this way the bank's officers can determine how many tellers are needed to ensure reasonably smooth service. An event-driven simulation consists of processing events. The two events here are (1) a customer arriving and (2) a customer departing, thus freeing up a teller. At any point we have a collection of events waiting to happen. To run the simulation, we need to determine the *next* event, this is the event whose time of occurrence is minimum. Hence we use a priority queue that extracts the event of minimum time to process the event list efficiently. We present a complete discussion and implementation of event-driven simulation in Section 14.2.

The STL priority queue uses `push`, `top`, and `pop` and accesses the maximum, rather than the minimum, item.

We close by mentioning that the STL priority queue uses different conventions than presented here. First, a priority queue must be specified by several template parameters, leading to an often tortuous declaration because default template parameters do not always work correctly. Second, the priority queue does not use standard names such as `insert`, `findMin`, and `deleteMin`. Instead, it uses `push`, `top`, and `pop` and thus easily wins the award for worst method names in a widely used library. Finally, it accesses the maximum, rather than the minimum, item. The following is a summary of the operations.

```
template <class Object, class Container, class Less>
class priority_queue
```
requires the specification of the type of object being stored, the type of container storing it (typically a vector of object), and the class that defines the function object for comparison. The function object is used to implement the internal meaning of less than.

```
void push( const Object & element )
```
adds `element` to the container.

```
const Object & top( ) const
```
returns the *largest item* in the container.

```
void pop( )
```
removes the *largest item* from the container.

On the surface, `priority_queue` is sufficiently complicated that an example is warranted, which we provide in Figure 7.17. We begin with the include directives. Priority queues are in the header file `<queue>`, and as we have to specify that a `vector` is used and also have to provide the comparison function objects, we have a few extra header files.

```
1 #include <queue>
2 #include <iostream>
3 #include <string>
4 #include <vector>
5 #include <functional>
6 using namespace std;
7
8 // Empty the priority queue and print its contents.
9 template <class PriorityQueue>
10 void dumpContents( const string & msg, PriorityQueue & pq )
11 {
12     cout << msg << ":" << endl;
13     while( !pq.empty( ) )
14     {
15         cout << pq.top( ) << endl;
16         pq.pop( );
17     }
18 }
19
20 // Do some inserts and removes (done in dumpContents).
21 int main( )
22 {
23     priority_queue<int,vector<int>,greater<int> > minPQ;
24     priority_queue<int,vector<int>,less<int>    > maxPQ;
25
26     minPQ.push( 4 ); minPQ.push( 3 ); minPQ.push( 5 );
27     maxPQ.push( 4 ); maxPQ.push( 3 ); maxPQ.push( 5 );
28
29     dumpContents( "minPQ", minPQ );   // 3 4 5
30     dumpContents( "maxPQ", maxPQ );   // 5 4 3
31
32     return 0;
33 }
```

Figure 7.17 Routine that demonstrates the STL `priority_queue`; the comment shows expected order of output.

The `dumpContents` method accesses a priority queue and empties it, printing its contents. The first parameter, `msg`, is used to print the name of the priority queue or any other interesting message. Note that, again, we are programming to an interface: this template works regardless of how the `priority_queue` template has been expanded.

The `main` method creates two priority queues, throws some items into each of them, and then dumps the contents. Recall that by default (or with a `less` function object), the priority queue produces the maximum item. So, if we reverse the order of comparison, we get minimums. The comments at lines 29 and 30 show the output that we expect to receive.

Summary

In this chapter we examined the basic data structures used throughout this text. We provided generic protocols and explained what the running time should be for each data structure. We also described the interface provided by the STL. In later chapters we show how these data structures are used and eventually give an implementation of each data structure that meets the time bounds we have claimed here. Figure 7.18 summarizes the results obtained.

Chapter 8 describes an important problem-solving tool known as *recursion.* Recursion allows many problems to be efficiently solved with short algorithms and is central to the efficient implementation of a sorting algorithm and several data structures.

Objects of the Game

associative array A map that uses array indexing: the index is the key, and the result of the index is the value. (p. 252)

bidirectional iterator An iterator that allows both forward and backward traversal through a container. (p. 239)

binary function objects Function objects that accept two parameters. (p. 240)

binary heap Implements the priority queue in logarithmic time per operation with little extra space. (p. 253)

Data Structure	Access	Comments
Stack	Most recent only, `pop`, $O(1)$	Very very fast
Queue	Least recent only, `dequeue`, $O(1)$	Very very fast
Linked list	Any item	$O(N)$
Ordered set	Any item by name or rank, $O(\log N)$	Average case easy to do; worst case requires effort
Priority queue	`findMin`, $O(1)$, `deleteMin`, $O(\log N)$	`insert` is $O(1)$ on average $O(\log N)$ worst case

Figure 7.18 Summary of some data structures.

binary search tree A data structure that supports insertion, removal, and searching. We can also use it to access the *K*th smallest item. The cost is logarithmic average-case time for a simple implementation and logarithmic worst-case time for a more careful implementation. (p. 250)

`const_iterator` The type of iterator that must be used to traverse `const` containers. (p. 238)

container A representation of a group of objects, known as its *elements*. (p. 238)

data structure A representation of data and the operations allowed on that data, permitting component reuse. (p. 232)

end marker A position past the last element in a container. (p. 238)

forward iterator An iterator that allows forward traversal through a container. In the full STL, a forward iterator must satisfy requirements of two other iterators, known as *input* and *output iterators*. (p. 239)

iterator An object that allows access to and iteration through the elements in a container. (p. 238)

linked list A data structure used to avoid large amounts of data movement. It uses a small amount of extra space per item. (p. 247)

`list` The STL class that implements a linked list. (p. 247)

`map` An STL class used to store a collection of ordered entries consisting of keys and their values and maps keys to values. (p. 251)

operator precedence parsing An algorithm that uses a stack to evaluate expressions. (p. 236)

predicate A function object that returns a Boolean. (p. 241)

priority queue A data structure that supports access of the minimum item only. (p. 253)

queue A data structure that restricts access to the least recently inserted item. (p. 236)

random access iterator An iterator that efficiently supports arbitrary advancing and retreating in a collection. (p. 240)

`set` An ordered STL container that allows no duplicates. (p. 250)

stack A data structure that restricts access to the most recently inserted item. (p. 233)

unary binder adapter An adapter that is used to generate a unary function from a binary function by making constant one of the parameters to the binary function. (p. 241)

unary function objects Function objects that accept one parameter. (p. 240)

Common Errors

1. Do not worry about low-level optimizations until after you have concentrated on basic design and algorithmic issues.
2. The iterator returned by `end( )` is one-past the last element in the container. You cannot safely apply `operator*` to it.
3. A constant collection cannot be accessed by an iterator; you must use a `const_iterator`.
4. When you send a function object as a parameter, you must send a constructed object, not simply the name of the class.
5. It is an error to access or delete from an empty stack, queue, or priority queue. The class implementer must ensure that the error is detected. Unfortunately, the STL classes do not do so.
6. When using a `map`, if you are not sure whether a key is in the map, you may need to use `find` and check whether the returned iterator matches the end marker.
7. A priority queue is not a queue. It just sounds like it should be.

On the Internet

In writing the code in this chapter, we made use of the STL. If your compiler does not support the STL, you can still use the subset implemented in Part IV and contained in the online code (we list those files as we have occasion to implement them in Part IV). You need to `#include` the same files, except with a `.h` extension. For instance, to use the `map`, `#include "map.h"`. Except for the `vector` iterator, all iterators are bounds-checked, so you may prefer to use this version even if your compiler supports the STL. Further details on using these classes and avoiding naming conflicts with preexisting STL classes are provided in the `README` file in the online bundle. Some (but not all) of the code demos from this chapter are available online.

functional.h	Implements the `less` function predicate template and a few others.
algorithm.h	Contains an implementation of `lower_bound`.
SimpleSetDemo.cpp	Contains the code in Figures 7.6 and 7.13.
TestPQ.cpp	Contains the priority queue demonstrated in Figure 7.17.

Exercises

In Short

7.1. Show the results of the following sequence: `add(4)`, `add(8)`, `add(1)`, `add(6)`, `remove()`, and `remove()` when the `add` and `remove` operations correspond to the basic operations in a

a. stack.
b. queue.
c. priority queue.

In Theory

7.2. Suppose that you want to support the following three operations exclusively: `insert`, `findMax`, and `deleteMax`. How fast do you think these operations can be performed?

7.3. Can all the following be supported in logarithmic time: `insert`, `deleteMin`, `deleteMax`, `findMin`, and `findMax`?

7.4. Which of the data structures in Figure 7.18 lead to sorting algorithms that could run in less than quadratic time?

7.5. Show that the following operations can be supported in constant time simultaneously: `push`, `pop`, and `findMin`. Note that `deleteMin` is not part of the repertoire. (*Hint*: Maintain two stacks—one to store items and the other to store minimums as they occur.)

7.6. A double-ended queue supports insertions and deletions at both the front and end of the line. What is the running time per operation?

In Practice

7.7. Write a routine that uses the STL to print out the items in a collection in reverse order. Do not use reverse iterators.

7.8. A deletion in a linked list or a binary search tree leaves the following problem: If an element is deleted, what happens to the iterators that are referencing that element? Discuss some alternatives. (*Hint:* One alternative is to make use of the Observer pattern in Section 5.6.)

7.9. Show how to implement a `stack` efficiently by using a `list` as a data member.

7.10. Show how to implement a `queue` efficiently by using a `list` as a data member.

7.11. In the implementation of `find`, what predicate should `find` use to call `find_if`?

Programming Projects

7.12. A queue can be implemented by using an array. The queue elements are stored in consecutive array positions, with the front item always in position 0. Note that this is not the most efficient method. Do the following.

a. Describe the algorithms for `getFront`, `enqueue`, and `dequeue`.
b. What is the Big-Oh running time for each of `getFront`, `enqueue`, and `dequeue`, using these algorithms?
c. Write an implementation that uses these algorithms and the protocol shown in Figure 7.5.
d. Write an implementation that uses these algorithms and the STL queue protocol.

7.13. The operations supported by the `set` can also be implemented by using an array. The array elements are stored in sorted order in consecutive array positions. Thus `find` can be implemented by a binary search. Do the following.

a. Describe the algorithms for `insert` and `remove`.
b. What is the running time for these algorithms?
c. Write an implementation that uses these algorithms and the protocol shown in Figure 7.1.

7.14. A priority queue can be implemented by using a sorted array (as in Exercise 7.13). Do the following.

a. Describe the algorithms for `findMin`, `deleteMin`, and `insert`.
b. What is the Big-Oh running time for each of `findMin`, `deleteMin`, and `insert`, using these algorithms?
c. Write an implementation that uses these algorithms and the STL priority queue interface, with a comparison function as a template parameter.

7.15. A priority queue can be implemented by storing items in an unsorted array and inserting items in the next available location. Do the following.

a. Describe the algorithms for `findMin`, `deleteMin`, and `insert`.

b. Using these algorithms, what is the Big-Oh running time for each of `findMin`, `deleteMin`, and `insert`?
c. Write an implementation that uses these algorithms and the STL priority queue interface, with a comparison function as a template parameter.

7.16. By adding an extra data member to the priority queue class shown in Exercise 7.15, you can implement both `insert` and `findMin` in constant time. The extra data member maintains the array position where the minimum is stored. However, `deleteMin` is still expensive. Do the following.

a. Describe the algorithms for `insert`, `findMin`, and `deleteMin`.
b. What is the Big-Oh running time for `deleteMin`?
c. Write an implementation that uses these algorithms and the STL priority queue interface, with a comparison function as a template parameter.

7.17. By maintaining the invariant that the elements in the priority queue are sorted in nonincreasing order (i.e., the largest item is first, and the smallest is last), you can implement both `findMin` and `deleteMin` in constant time. However, `insert` is expensive. Do the following.

a. Describe the algorithms for `insert`, `findMin`, and `deleteMin`.
b. What is the Big-Oh running time for `insert`?
c. Write an implementation that uses these algorithms and the STL priority queue interface, with a comparison function as a template parameter.

7.18. A double-ended priority queue allows access to both the minimum and maximum elements. In other words, all the following are supported: `findMin`, `deleteMin`, `findMax`, and `deleteMax`. Do the following.

a. Describe the algorithms for `findMin`, `deleteMin`, `findMax`, `deleteMax`, and `insert`.
b. What is the Big-Oh running time for each of `findMin`, `deleteMin`, `findMax`, `deleteMax`, and `insert`, using these algorithms?
c. Write an implementation that uses these algorithms.

7.19. A median heap supports the operations `insert`, `findKth`, and `removeKth`. The last two find and remove, respectively, the *K*th smallest element. The simplest implementation maintains the data in sorted order. Do the following.

a. Describe the algorithms that can be used to support median heap operations.
b. What is the Big-Oh running time for each of the basic operations using these algorithms?
c. Write an implementation that uses these algorithms.

7.20. Implement `bind2nd` as follows (for simplicity assume the function parameter is a predicate function).

a. Define a class template `Bind2ndClass` that stores a predicate and bound object as data members.
b. Add a two-parameter constructor that initializes the data members.
c. Provide a one-parameter implementation of `operator()` that calls the predicate with `operator()`'s parameter and the bound object.
d. Implement `bind2nd` by returning an instantiated `Bind2ndClass` object.

7.21. Write a program that reads strings from input and outputs them sorted, by length, shortest string first. If a subset of strings have the same length, output them in alphabetical order.

7.22. Implement the `PriorityQueue` protocol shown in Figure 7.16 by adapting the `priority_queue` STL class. You may use either composition or private inheritance. If your compiler does not support the STL, use the `priority_queue` class provided in the online code (in `queue.h` and `queue.cpp`).

7.23. The `fill` function template takes a pair of forward iterators (`begin` and `end`) and a value, and places `value` in all positions in range specified by the iterators (as usual, `end` is one past the last affected item). Implement `fill`.

7.24. The `min_element` function template takes a pair of forward iterators (`begin` and `end`) and returns an iterator that refers to the minimum element in the range specified by the iterators (as usual, `end` is one past the last affected item). Optionally, you can use a function object to specify a less-than function. Implement (the two versions of) `min_element`.

7.25. The `adjacent_find` function template takes a pair of iterators (`begin` and `end`) and a binary predicate (`pred`). It returns an iterator referring to the first element such that `pred` returns true when applied to the element and its predecessor. By default, `pred` is `equal_to<Object>`. Implement (the two versions of) `adjacent_find`.

References

References for the theory that underlies these data structures are provided in Part IV. The STL is described in [1] and most recent C++ books (see the references in Chapter 1).

1. D. R. Musser and A. Saini, *C++ Programming with the Standard Template Library*, Addison-Wesley, Reading, Mass., 1996.

Chapter 8

Recursion

A function that is partially defined in terms of itself is called *recursive*. Like many languages, C++ supports recursive functions. Recursion, which is the use of recursive functions, is a powerful programming tool that in many cases can yield both short and efficient algorithms. In this chapter we explore how recursion works, thus providing some insight into its variations, limitations, and uses. We begin our discussion of recursion by examining the mathematical principle on which it is based: *mathematical induction*. Then we give examples of simple recursive functions and prove that they generate correct answers.

In this chapter, we show:

- the four basic rules of recursion;
- numerical applications of recursion, leading to implementation of an encryption algorithm;
- a general technique called *divide and conquer;*
- a general technique, called *dynamic programming,* that is similar to recursion but uses tables instead of recursive function calls; and
- a general technique, called *backtracking,* that amounts to a careful exhaustive search

8.1 What Is Recursion?

A **recursive function** is a function that either directly or indirectly makes a call to itself. This action may seem to be circular logic: How can a function F solve a problem by calling itself? The key is that the function F calls itself on a different, generally simpler, instance. The following are some examples.

A *recursive function* is a function that directly or indirectly makes a call to itself.

- In C++ the source file is processed by replacing all `#include` directives with the contents of the *include* file. However, *include* files may themselves have `#include` directives. This situation is easily handled with recursion: To process a file, we replace all `#include` directives with the contents of the recursively processed *include* file. Any nested includes are automatically handled. Note that, if a file attempts to include itself, either directly or indirectly, an infinite loop results.

- Files on a computer are generally stored in directories. Users may create subdirectories that store more files and directories. Suppose that we want to examine every file in a directory *D*, including all files in all subdirectories (and subsubdirectories, and so on). We do so by recursively examining every file in each subdirectory and then examining all files in the directory *D* (discussed in Chapter 18).
- Suppose that we have a large dictionary. Words in dictionaries are defined in terms of other words. When we look up the meaning of a word, we might not always understand the definition, so we might have to look up words in the definition. Likewise, we might not understand some of those, so we might have to continue this search for a while. As the dictionary is finite, eventually either we come to a point where we understand all the words in some definition (and thus understand that definition and can retrace our path through the other definitions), we find that the definitions are circular and that we are stuck, or some word we need to understand is not defined in the dictionary. Our recursive strategy to understand words is as follows: If we know the meaning of a word we are done; otherwise, we look the word up in the dictionary. If we understand all the words in the definition, we are done. Otherwise, we figure out what the definition means by recursively looking up the words that we do not know. This procedure terminates if the dictionary is well defined, but it can loop indefinitely if a word is circularly defined.
- Computer languages are frequently defined recursively. For instance, an arithmetic expression is an object, a parenthesized expression, two expressions added to each other, and so on.

Recursion is a powerful problem-solving tool. Many algorithms are most easily expressed in a recursive formulation. Furthermore, the most efficient solutions to many problems are based on this natural recursive formulation. But you must be careful not to create circular logic that would result in infinite loops.

In this chapter we discuss the general conditions that must be satisfied by recursive algorithms and give several practical examples. It shows that sometimes algorithms that are naturally expressed recursively must be rewritten without recursion.

8.2 Background: Proofs by Mathematical Induction

In this section we discuss proof by mathematical *induction*. (Throughout this chapter we omit the word *mathematical* when describing this technique.) **Induction** is commonly used to establish theorems that hold for positive integers. We start by proving a simple theorem, Theorem 8.1. This particular theorem can be easily established by using other methods, but often a proof by induction is the simplest mechanism.

***Induction* is an important proof technique used to establish theorems that hold for positive integers.**

Theorem 8.1

For any integer $N \geq 1$, the sum of the first N integers, given by $\sum_{i=1}^{N} i = 1 + 2 + \cdots + N$, equals $N(N+1)/2$.

Obviously, the theorem is true for $N = 1$ because both the left-hand and right-hand sides evaluate to 1. Further checking shows that it is true for $2 \leq N \leq 10$. However, the fact that the theorem holds for all N that are easy to check by hand does not imply that it holds for all N. Consider, for instance, numbers of the form $2^{2^k} + 1$. The first five numbers (corresponding to $0 \leq k \leq 4$ are 3, 5, 17, 257, and 65,537. These numbers are all prime. Indeed, at one time mathematicians conjectured that all numbers of this form are prime. That is not the case. We can easily check by computer that $2^{2^5} + 1 = 641 \times 6{,}700{,}417$. In fact, no other prime of the form $2^{2^k} + 1$ is known.

A proof by induction is carried out in two steps. First, as we have just done, we show that the theorem is true for the smallest cases. We then show that if the theorem is true for the first few cases, it can be extended to include the next case. For instance, we show that a theorem that is true for all $1 \leq N \leq k$ must be true for $1 \leq N \leq k + 1$. Once we have shown how to extend the range of true cases, we have shown that it is true for all cases. The reason is that we can extend the range of true cases indefinitely. We use this technique to prove Theorem 8.1.

A proof by induction shows that the theorem is true for some simple cases and then shows how to extend the range of true cases indefinitely.

Proof (of Theorem 8.1)

Clearly, the theorem is true for $N = 1$. Suppose that the theorem is true for all $1 \leq N \leq k$. Then

$$\sum_{i=1}^{k+1} i = (k+1) + \sum_{i=1}^{k} i. \qquad \textbf{(8.1)}$$

By assumption, the theorem is true for k, so we may replace the sum on the right-hand side of Equation 8.1 with $k(k+1)/2$, obtaining

Proof (of Theorem 8.1 continued)

$$\sum_{i=1}^{k+1} i = (k+1) + (k(k+1)/2) \qquad \textbf{(8.2)}$$

Algebraic manipulation of the right-hand side of Equation 8.2 now yields

$$\sum_{i=1}^{k+1} i = (k+1)(k+2)/2$$

This result confirms the theorem for the case k + 1. Thus by induction, the theorem is true for all integers $N \geq 1$.

In a proof by induction, the *basis* is the easy case that can be shown by hand.

Why does this constitute a proof? First, the theorem is true for $N = 1$, which is called the *basis*. We can view it as being the basis for our belief that the theorem is true in general. In a proof by induction the **basis** is the easy case that can be shown by hand. Once we have established the basis, we use **inductive hypothesis** to assume that the theorem is true for some arbitrary k and that, under this assumption, if the theorem is true for k, then it is true for $k + 1$. In our case, we know that the theorem is true for the basis $N = 1$, so we know that it also is true for $N = 2$. Because it is true for $N = 2$, it must be true for $N = 3$. And as it is true for $N = 3$, it must be true for $N = 4$. Extending this logic, we know that the theorem is true for every positive integer beginning with $N = 1$.

The *inductive hypothesis* assumes that the theorem is true for some arbitrary case and that, under this assumption, it is true for the next case.

Let us apply proof by induction to a second problem, which is not quite as simple as the first. First, we examine the sequence of numbers 1^2, $2^2 - 1^2$, $3^2 - 2^2 + 1^2$, $4^2 - 3^2 + 2^2 - 1^2$, $5^2 - 4^2 + 3^2 - 2^2 + 1^2$, and so on. Each member represents the sum of the first N squares, with alternating signs. The sequence evaluates to 1, 3, 6, 10, and 15. Thus, in general, the sum seems to be equal to the sum of the first N integers, which, as we know from Theorem 8.1, would be $N(N+1)/2$. Theorem 8.2 proves this result.

Theorem 8.2

The sum $\sum_{i=N}^{1} (-1)^{N-i} i^2 = N^2 - (N-1)^2 + (N-2)^2 - \cdots$ is $N(N+1)/2$.

Proof

The proof is by induction.

Basis: Clearly, the theorem is true for $N = 1$.

Inductive hypothesis: First we assume the theorem is true for k:

$$\sum_{i=k}^{1} (-1)^{k-i} i^2 = \frac{k(k+1)}{2}.$$

Proof (continued)

Then we must show that it is true for k + 1; namely, that

$$\sum_{i=k+1}^{1} (-1)^{k+1-i} i^2 = \frac{(k+1)(k+2)}{2}.$$

We write

$$\sum_{i=k+1}^{1} (-1)^{k+1-i} i^2 = (k+1)^2 - k^2 + (k-1)^2 - \cdots. \quad \textbf{(8.3)}$$

If we rewrite the right-hand side of Equation 8.3, we obtain

$$\sum_{i=k+1}^{1} (-1)^{k+1-i} i^2 = (k+1)^2 - (k^2 - (k-1)^2 + \cdots),$$

and a substitution yields

$$\sum_{i=k+1}^{1} (-1)^{k+1-i} i^2 = (k+1)^2 - \left(\sum_{i=k}^{1} (-1)^{k-i} i^2\right). \quad \textbf{(8.4)}$$

If we apply the inductive hypothesis, then we can replace the summation on the right-hand side of Equation 8.4, obtaining

$$\sum_{i=k+1}^{1} (-1)^{k+1-i} i^2 = (k+1)^2 - k(k+1)/2. \quad \textbf{(8.5)}$$

Simple algebraic manipulation of the right-hand side of Equation 8.5 then yields

$$\sum_{i=k+1}^{1} (-1)^{k+1-i} i^2 = (k+1)(k+2)/2,$$

which establishes the theorem for $N = k + 1$. *Thus, by induction, the theorem is true for all* $N \geq 1$.

8.3 Basic Recursion

A recursive function is defined in terms of a smaller instance of itself. There must be some base case that can be computed without recursion.

Proofs by induction show us that, if we know that a statement is true for a smallest case and can show that one case implies the next case, then we know the statement is true for all cases.

Sometimes mathematical functions are defined recursively. For instance, let $S(N)$ be the sum of the first N integers. Then $S(1) = 1$, and we can write $S(N) = S(N - 1) + N$. Here we have defined the function S in terms of a smaller instance of itself. The recursive definition of $S(N)$ is virtually identical to the closed form $S(N) = N(N + 1)/2$, with the exception that the recursive definition is only defined for positive integers and is less directly computable.

```
1 // Recursive routine to compute sum of first n integers.
2 int s( int n )
3 {
4     if( n == 1 )
5         return 1;
6     else
7         return s( n - 1 ) + n;
8 }
```

Figure 8.1 Recursive evaluation of the sum of the first N integers.

Sometimes writing a formula recursively is easier than writing it in closed form. Figure 8.1 shows a straightforward implementation of the recursive function. If $N = 1$, we have the basis, for which we know that $S(1) = 1$. We take care of this case at lines 4 and 5. Otherwise, we follow the recursive definition $S(N) = S(N - 1) + N$ precisely at line 7. It is hard to imagine that we could implement the recursive function any more simply than this, so the natural question is, Does it actually work?

The answer, except as noted shortly, is that this routine works. Let us examine how the call to `s(4)` is evaluated. When the call to `s(4)` is made, the test at line 4 fails. We then execute line 7, where we evaluate `s(3)`. Like any other function, this evaluation requires a call to `s`. In that call we get to line 4, where the test fails; thus we go to line 7. At this point we call `s(2)`. Again, we call `s`, and now `n` is 2. The test at line 4 still fails, so we call `s(1)` at line 7. Now we have `n` equal to 1, so `s(1)` returns 1. At this point `s(2)` can continue, adding the return value from `s(1)` to 2; thus `s(2)` returns 3. Now `s(3)` continues, adding the value of 3 returned by `s(2)` to `n`, which is 3; thus `s(3)` returns 6. This result enables completion of the call to `s(4)`, which finally returns 10.

Note that, although `s` seems to be calling itself, in reality it is calling a *clone* of itself. That clone is simply another function with different parameters. At any instant only one clone is active; the rest are pending. It is the computer's job, not yours, to handle all the bookkeeping. If there were too much bookkeeping even for the computer, then it would be time to worry. We discuss these details later in the chapter.

The *base case* is an instance that can be solved without recursion. Any recursive call must make progress toward a base case.

A **base case** is an instance that can be solved without recursion. Any recursive call must progress toward the base case in order to terminate eventually. We thus have our first two (of four) fundamental **rules of recursion.**

1. *Base case:* Always have at least one case that can be solved without using recursion.
2. *Make progress:* Any recursive call must progress toward a base case.

Our recursive evaluation routine does have a few problems. One is the call `s(0)`, for which the function behaves poorly.[1] This behavior is natural because the recursive definition of $S(N)$ does not allow for $N < 1$. We can fix this problem by extending the definition of $S(N)$ to include $N = 0$. Because there are no numbers to add in this case, a natural value for $S(0)$ would be 0. This value makes sense because the recursive definition can apply for $S(1)$, as $S(0) + 1$ is 1. To implement this change, we just replace `1` with `0` on lines 4 and 5. Negative N also causes errors, but this problem can be fixed in a similar manner (and is left for you to do as Exercise 8.2).

A second problem is that the return value may be too large to fit in an `int`, but that is not an important issue here. A third problem, however, is that if the parameter `n` is large, but not so large that the answer does not fit in an `int`, the program can crash or hang. Our system, for instance, cannot handle $N \geq 74{,}754$.

The reason is that, as we have shown, the implementation of recursion requires some bookkeeping to keep track of the pending recursive calls, and for sufficiently long chains of recursion, the computer simply runs out of memory. We explain this condition in more detail later in the chapter. This routine also is somewhat more time consuming than an equivalent loop because the bookkeeping also uses some time.

Needless to say, this particular example does not demonstrate the best use of recursion because the problem is so easy to solve without recursion. Most of the good uses of recursion do not exhaust the computer's memory and are only slightly more time consuming than nonrecursive implementations. However, recursion almost always leads to more compact code.

8.3.1 Printing Numbers in Any Base

A good example of how recursion simplifies the coding of routines is number printing. Suppose that we want to print out a nonnegative number N in decimal form but that we do not have a number output function available. However, we can print out one digit at a time. Consider, for instance, how we would print the number `1369`. First we would need to print `1`, then `3`, then `6`, and then `9`. The problem is that obtaining the first digit is a bit sloppy: Given a number `n`, we need a loop to determine the first digit of `n`. In contrast is the last digit, which is immediately available as `n%10` (which is `n` for `n` less than 10).

Recursion provides a nifty solution. To print out `1369`, we print out `136`, followed by the last digit, `9`. As we have mentioned, printing out the last

1. A call to `s(-1)` is made, and the program eventually crashes because there are too many pending recursive calls. The recursive calls are not progressing toward a base case.

digit using the % operator is easy. Printing out all but the number represented by eliminating the last digit also is easy, because it is the same problem as printing out n/10. Thus, it can be done by a recursive call.

The code shown in Figure 8.2 implements this printing routine. If n is smaller than 10, line 5 is not executed and only the one digit n%10 is printed; otherwise, all but the last digit are printed recursively and then the last digit is printed.

Note how we have a base case (n is a one-digit integer), and because the recursive problem has one less digit, all recursive calls progress toward the base case. Thus we have satisfied the first two fundamental rules of recursion.

This printing routine is already provided, so it may seem like a silly exercise. However, the iostream classes supply only octal, decimal, and hexadecimal formats. To make our printing routine useful, we can extend it to print in any base between 2 and 16. This modification is shown in Figure 8.3.

We introduced a string to make the printing of a through f easier. Each digit is now output by indexing to the DIGIT_TABLE string. The printInt routine is not robust. If base is larger than 16, the index to DIGIT_TABLE could be out of bounds. If base is 0, an arithmetic error results when division by 0 is attempted at line 8.

```
1 // Print n as a decimal number.
2 void printDecimal( int n )
3 {
4     if( n >= 10 )
5         printDecimal( n / 10 );
6     cout.put( '0' + n % 10 );
7 }
```

Figure 8.2 A recursive routine for printing *N* in decimal form.

```
 1 // Print n in any base.
 2 // Assumes 2 <= base <= 16.
 3 void printInt( int n, int base )
 4 {
 5     static string DIGIT_TABLE = "0123456789abcdef";
 6
 7     if( n >= base )
 8         printInt( n / base, base );
 9     cout << DIGIT_TABLE[ n % base ];
10 }
```

Figure 8.3 A recursive routine for printing *N* in any base.

The most interesting error occurs when `base` is 1. Then the recursive call at line 8 fails to make progress because the two parameters to the recursive call are identical to the original call. Thus the system makes recursive calls until it eventually runs out of bookkeeping space (and exits less than gracefully).

Failure to progress means that the program does not work.

We can make the routine more robust by adding an explicit test for `base`. The problem with this strategy is that the test would be executed during each of the recursive calls to `printInt`, not just during the first call. Once `base` is valid in the first call, to retest it is silly because it does not change in the course of the recursion and thus must still be valid. One way to avoid this inefficiency is to set up a driver routine. A **driver routine** tests the validity of `base` and then calls the recursive routine, as shown in Figure 8.4. The use of driver routines for recursive programs is a common technique.

A *driver routine* tests the validity of the first call and the calls the recursive routine.

```
const string DIGIT_TABLE = "0123456789abcdef";
const int    MAX_BASE    = DIGIT_TABLE.length( );

// Print n in base base, recursively.
// Precondition: n >= 0, 2 <= base <= MAX_BASE.
void printIntRec( int n, int base )
{
    if( n >= base )
        printIntRec( n / base, base );
    cout << DIGIT_TABLE[ n % base ];
}

// Driver routine.
void printInt( int n, int base )
{
    if( base <= 1 || base > MAX_BASE )
        cerr << "Cannot print in base " << base << endl;
    else
    {
        if( n < 0 )
        {
            cout << "-";
            n = -n;
        }
        printIntRec( n, base );
    }
}
```

Figure 8.4 A robust number printing program.

8.3.2 Why It Works

Recursive algorithms can be proven correct with mathematical induction.

In Theorem 8.3 we show, somewhat rigorously, that the `printDecimal` algorithm works. Our goal is to verify that the algorithm is correct, so the proof is based on the assumption that we have made no syntax errors.

Theorem 8.3 *The algorithm `printDecimal` shown in Figure 8.2 correctly prints `n` in base 10.*

Proof *Let k be the number of digits in `n`. The proof is by induction on k.*

Basis: If $k = 1$, then no recursive call is made, and line 6 correctly outputs the one digit of `n`.

Inductive Hypothesis: Assume that `printDecimal` works correctly for all $k \geq 1$ digit integers. We show that this assumption implies correctness for any $k + 1$ digit integer `n`. Because $k \geq 1$, the `if` statement at line 4 is satisfied for a $k + 1$ digit integer `n`. By the inductive hypothesis, the recursive call at line 5 prints the first k digits of `n`. Then the call at line 6 prints the final digit. Thus if any k digit integer can be printed, then so can a $k + 1$ digit integer. By induction, we conclude that `printDecimal` works for all k, and thus all `n`.

The proof of Theorem 8.3 illustrates an important principle. When designing a recursive algorithm, we can always assume that the recursive calls work (if they progress toward the base case) because, when a proof is performed, this assumption is used as the inductive hypothesis.

At first glance such an assumption seems strange. However, recall that we always assume that function calls work, and thus the assumption that the recursive call works is really no different. Like any function, a recursive routine needs to combine solutions from calls to other functions to obtain a solution. However, other functions may include easier instances of the original function.

This observation leads us to the third fundamental rule of recursion.

3. *"You gotta believe":* Always assume that the recursive call works.

Rule 3 tells us that when we design a recursive function, we do not have to attempt to trace the possibly long path of recursive calls. As we showed earlier, this task can be daunting and tends to make the design and verification more difficult. A good use of recursion makes such a trace almost impossible to understand. Intuitively, we are letting the computer handle the bookkeeping that, were we to do ourselves, would result in much longer code.

The third fundamental rule of recursion: Always assume that the recursive call works. Use this rule to design your algorithms.

This principle is so important, that we state it again: *Always assume that the recursive call works.*

8.3.3 How It Works

Recall that the implementation of recursion requires additional bookkeeping on the part of the computer. Said another way, the implementation of any function requires bookkeeping and a recursive call is not particularly special (except that it can overload the computer's bookkeeping limitations by calling itself too many times).

The bookkeeping in a procedural language is done by using a stack of *activation records*. Recursion is a natural by-product.

C++, like other languages such as Pascal, Ada, and Java, implements functions by using an internal stack of activation records. An **activation record** contains relevant information about the function, including, for instance, the values of the parameters and local variables. The actual contents of the activation record is system dependent.

The stack of activation records is used because functions return in reverse order of their invocation. Recall that stacks are great for reversing the order of things. In the most popular scenario, the top of the stack stores the activation record for the currently active function. When function *G* is called, an activation record for *G* is pushed onto the stack, which makes *G* the currently active function. When a function returns, the stack is popped and the activation record that is the new top of the stack contains the restored values.

Function calling and function return sequences are stack operations.

As an example, Figure 8.5 shows a stack of activation records that occurs in the course of evaluating `s(4)`. At this point, we have the calls to `main`, `s(4)`, and `s(3)` pending and we are actively processing `s(2)`.

The space overhead is the memory used to store an activation record for each currently active function. Thus, in our earlier example where `s(74754)` crashes, the system has room for roughly 74,754 activation records. (Note that `main` generates an activation record itself.) The pushing and popping of the internal stack also represents the overhead of executing a function call, which is what is saved when an inline directive is honored.

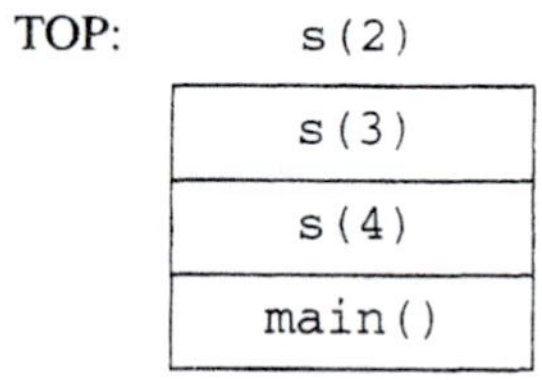

Figure 8.5 A stack of activation records.

Recursion can always be removed by using a stack. This is occasionally required to save space.

The close relation between recursion and stacks tells us that recursive programs can always be implemented iteratively with an explicit stack. Presumably our stack will store items that are smaller than an activation record, so we can also reasonably expect to use less space. The result is slightly faster but longer code. Modern optimizing compilers have lessened the costs associated with recursion to such a degree that, for the purposes of speed, removing recursion from an application that uses it well is rarely worthwhile.

8.3.4 Too Much Recursion Can Be Dangerous

Do not use recursion as a substitute for a simple loop.

In this text we give many examples of the power of recursion. However, before we look at those examples, you should recognize that recursion is not always appropriate. For instance, the use of recursion in Figure 8.1 is poor because a loop would do just as well. A practical liability is that the overhead of the recursive call takes time and limits the value of n for which the program is correct. A good rule of thumb is that you should never use recursion as a substitute for a simple loop.

The *i*th *Fibonacci number* is the sum of the two previous Fibonacci numbers.

A much more serious problem is illustrated by an attempt to calculate the Fibonacci numbers recursively. The **Fibonacci numbers** $F_0, F_1, \ldots, F_i$ are defined as follows: $F_0 = 0$ and $F_1 = 1$; the ith Fibonacci number equals the sum of the (ith – 1) and (ith – 2) Fibonacci numbers; thus $F_i = F_{i-1} + F_{i-2}$. From this definition we can determine that the series of Fibonacci numbers continues: 1, 2, 3, 5, 8, 13, 21, 34, 55, 89, ...

Do not do redundant work recursively; the program will be incredibly inefficient.

The Fibonacci numbers have an incredible number of properties, which seem always to crop up. In fact, one journal, *The Fibonacci Quarterly*, exists solely for the purpose of publishing theorems involving the Fibonacci numbers. For instance, the sum of the squares of two consecutive Fibonacci numbers is another Fibonacci number. The sum of the first N Fibonacci numbers is one less than F_{N+2} (see Exercise 8.9 for some other interesting identities).

Because the Fibonacci numbers are recursively defined, writing a recursive routine to determine F_N seems natural. This recursive routine, shown in Figure 8.6, works but has a serious problem. On our relatively fast machine,

```
1 // Compute the Nth Fibonacci number.
2 // Bad algorithm.
3 long fib( int n )
4 {
5     if( n <= 1 )
6         return n;
7     else
8         return fib( n - 1 ) + fib( n - 2 );
9 }
```

Figure 8.6 A recursive routine for Fibonacci numbers: A bad idea.

it takes nearly a minute to compute F_{40}, an absurd amount of time considering that the basic calculation requires only 39 additions.

The underlying problem is that this recursive routine performs redundant calculations. To compute `fib(n)`, we recursively compute `fib(n-1)`. When the recursive call returns, we compute `fib(n-2)` by using another recursive call.[2] But we have already computed `fib(n-2)` in the process of computing `fib(n-1)`, so the call to `fib(n-2)` is a wasted, redundant calculation. In effect, we make two calls to `fib(n-2)` instead of only one.

Normally, making two function calls instead of one would only double the running time of a program. However, here it is worse than that: Each call to `fib(n-1)`and each call to `fib(n-2)` makes a call to `fib(n-3)`; thus there are actually three calls to `fib(n-3)`. In fact, it keeps getting worse: Each call to `fib(n-2)` or `fib(n-3)` results in a call to `fib(n-4)`, so there are five calls to `fib(n-4)`. Thus we get a compounding effect: Each recursive call does more and more redundant work.

The recursive routine `fib` is exponential.

Let $C(N)$ be the number of calls to `fib` made during the evaluation of `fib(n)`. Clearly $C(0) = C(1) = 1$ call. For $N \geq 2$, we call `fib(n)`, plus all the calls needed to evaluate `fib(n-1)` and `fib(n-2)` recursively and independently. Thus $C(N) = C(N-1) + C(N-2) + 1$. By induction, we can easily verify that for $N \geq 3$ the solution to this recurrence is $C(N) = F_{N+2} + F_{N-1} - 1$. Thus the number of recursive calls is larger than the Fibonacci number we are trying to compute, and it is exponential. For $N = 40$, $F_{40} =$ 102,334,155, and the total number of recursive calls is more than 300,000,000. No wonder the program takes forever. The explosive growth of the number of recursive calls is illustrated in Figure 8.7.

2. Technically, C++ does not guarantee the order of evaluation, so at line 8, `fib(n-2)` could be evaluated prior to `fib(n-1)`. However, this does not affect the total number of recursive calls.

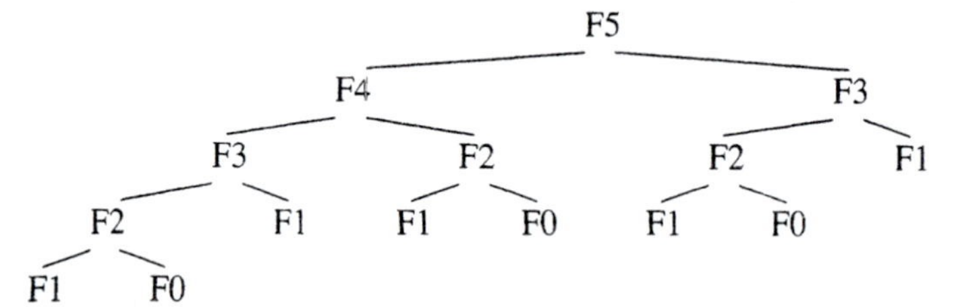

Figure 8.7 A trace of the recursive calculation of the Fibonacci numbers.

The fourth fundamental rule of recursion: Never duplicate work by solving the same instance of a problem in separate recursive calls.

This example illustrates the fourth and final basic rule of recursion.

4. *Compound interest rule:* Never duplicate work by solving the same instance of a problem in separate recursive calls.

8.3.5 Preview of Trees

The *tree* is a fundamental structure in computer science. Almost all operating systems store files in trees or treelike structures. Trees are also used in compiler design, text processing, and searching algorithms. We discuss trees in detail in Chapters 18 and 19. We also make use of trees in Sections 12.2.4 (expression trees) and 13.1 (Huffman codes).

One definition of the tree is recursive: Either a tree is empty or it consists of a root and zero or more nonempty subtrees $T_1, T_2, \ldots, T_k$, each of whose roots are connected by an edge from the root, as illustrated in Figure 8.8. In certain instances (most notably, the *binary trees* discussed in Chapter 18), we may allow some of the subtrees to be empty.

A *tree* consists of a set of nodes and a set of directed edges that connect them.

Nonrecursively, then, a **tree** consists of a set of nodes and a set of directed edges that connect pairs of nodes. Throughout this text we consider only rooted trees. A rooted tree has the following properties.

Parents and children are naturally defined. A directed edge connects the *parent* to the *child*.

- One node is distinguished as the root.
- Every node c, except the root, is connected by an edge from exactly one other node p. Node p is c's *parent*, and c is one of p's *children*.
- A unique path traverses from the root to each node. The number of edges that must be followed is the *path length*.

Parents and children are naturally defined. A directed edge connects the **parent** to the **child.**

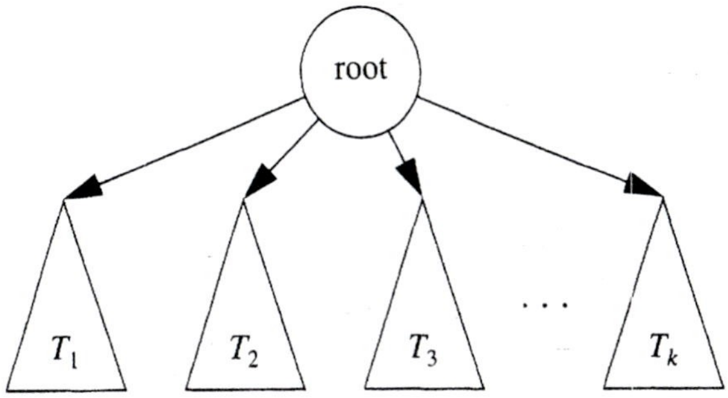

Figure 8.8 A tree viewed recursively.

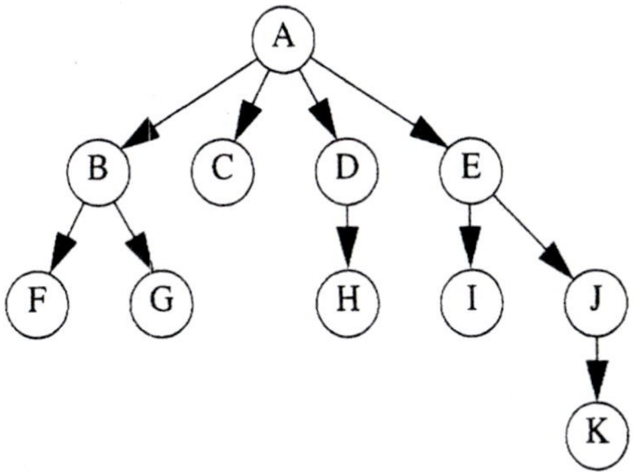

Figure 8.9 A tree.

Figure 8.9 illustrates a tree. The root node is A: A's children are B, C, D, and E. Because A is the root, it has no parent; all other nodes have parents. For instance, B's parent is A. A node that has no children is called **leaf.** The leaves in this tree are C, F, G, H, I, and K. The length of the path from A to K is 3 (edges); the length of the path from A to A is 0 (edges).

***A leaf* has no children.**

8.3.6 Additional Examples

Perhaps the best way to understand recursion is to consider examples. In this section, we look at four more examples of recursion. The first two are easily implemented nonrecursively, but the last two show off some of the power of recursion. The last two examples draw recursive pictures; unfortunately, C++ does not have a standard way of doing graphics. Consequently, the code for those examples is in Java. The code is identical, syntactically, to C++ code, and thus the Java syntax should not get in the way of understanding the examples.

```
// Evaluate n!
long factorial( int n )
{
    if( n <= 1 )      // base case
        return 1;
    else
        return n * factorial( n - 1 );
}
```

Figure 8.10 Recursive implementation of the `factorial` function.

Factorials

Recall that $N!$ is the product of the first N integers. Thus we can express $N!$ as N times $(N-1)!$. Combined with the base case $1! = 1$, this information immediately provides all that we need for a recursive implementation. It is shown in Figure 8.10.

Binary Search

In Section 6.6.2 we described the binary search. Recall that in a binary search, we perform a search in a sorted array A by examining the middle element. If we have a match, we are done. Otherwise, if the item being searched for is smaller than the middle element, we search in the subarray that is to the left of the middle element. Otherwise, we search in the subarray that is to the right of the middle element. This procedure presumes that the subarray is not empty; if it is, the item is not found.

This description translates directly into the recursive method shown in Figure 8.11. The code illustrates a thematic technique in which the public driver routine makes an initial call to a recursive routine and passes on the return value. Here, the driver sets the low and high points of the subarray, namely, `0` and `a.size( )-1`.

In the recursive method, the base case at lines 15 and 16 handles an empty subarray. Otherwise, we follow the description given previously by making a recursive call on the appropriate subarray (line 21 or 23) if a match has not been detected. When a match is detected, the matching index is returned at line 25.

Note that the running time, in terms of Big-Oh, is unchanged from the nonrecursive implementation because we are performing the same work. In practice, the running time would be expected to be slightly larger because of the hidden costs of recursion.

```
// Performs the standard binary search using two comparisons
// per level. This is a driver that calls the recursive method.
template <class Comparable>
int binarySearch( const vector<Comparable> & a,
                  const Comparable & x )
{
    return binarySearch( a, x, 0, a.size( ) - 1 );
}

// Recursive routine.
template <class Comparable>
int binarySearch( const vector<Comparable> & a,
                  const Comparable & x, int low, int high )
{
    if( low > high )
        return NOT_FOUND;

    int mid = ( low + high ) / 2;

    if( a[ mid ] < x )
        return binarySearch( a, x, mid + 1, high );
    else if( x < a[ mid ] )
        return binarySearch( a, x, low, mid - 1 );
    else
        return mid;
}
```

Figure 8.11 A binary search routine, using recursion.

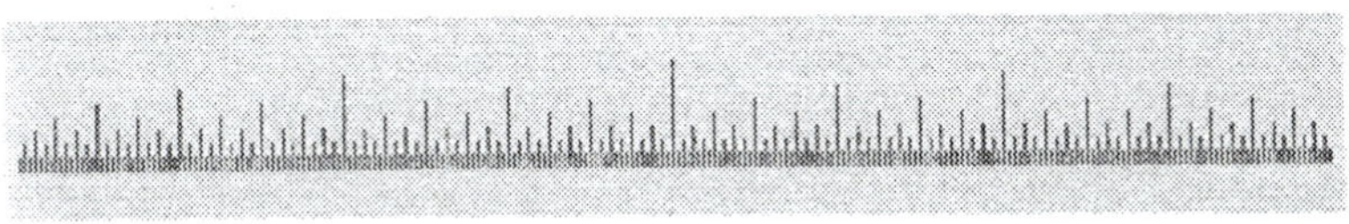

Figure 8.12 A recursively drawn ruler.

Drawing a Ruler

Figure 8.12 shows the result of running a Java program that draws ruler markings. Here, we consider the problem of marking 1 inch. In the middle is the longest mark. In Figure 8.12, to the left of the middle is a miniaturized version of the ruler and to the right of the middle is a second miniaturized version. This result suggests a recursive algorithm that first draws the middle line and then draws the left and right halves.

```
1 // Java code to draw Figure 8.12.
2 void drawRuler( Graphics g, int left, int right, int level )
3 {
4     if( level < 1 )
5         return;
6
7     int mid = ( left + right ) / 2;
8
9     g.drawLine( mid, 80, mid, 80 - level * 5 );
10
11    drawRuler( g, left, mid - 1, level - 1 );
12    drawRuler( g, mid + 1, right, level - 1 );
13 }
```

Figure 8.13 A recursive method for drawing a ruler.

You do not have to understand the details of drawing lines and shapes in Java to understand this program. You simply need to know that a `Graphics` object is something that gets drawn to. The `drawRuler` method in Figure 8.13 is our recursive routine. It uses the `drawLine` method, which is part of the `Graphics` class. The method `drawLine` draws a line from one (x, y) coordinate to another (x, y) coordinate, where coordinates are offset from the top-left corner.

Our routine draws markings at `level` different heights; each recursive call is one level deeper (in Figure 8.12 there are eight levels). It first disposes of the base case at lines 4 and 5. Then the midpoint mark is drawn at line 9. Finally, the two miniatures are drawn recursively at lines 11 and 12. In the online code, we include extra code to slow down the drawing. In that way, we can see the order in which the lines are drawn by the recursive algorithm.

Fractal Star

Shown in Figure 8.14(a) is a seemingly complex pattern, called a *fractal star,* which we can easily draw by using recursion. The entire canvas is initially gray (not shown), the pattern is formed by drawing white squares onto the gray background. The last square drawn is over the center. Figure 8.14(b) shows the drawing immediately before the last square is added. Thus prior to the last square being drawn, four miniature versions have been drawn, one in each of the four quadrants. This pattern provides the information needed to derive the recursive algorithm.

As with the previous example, the method `drawFractal` uses a Java library routine. In this case, `fillRect` draws a rectangle; its upper left-hand corner and dimensions must be specified. The code is shown in Figure 8.15.

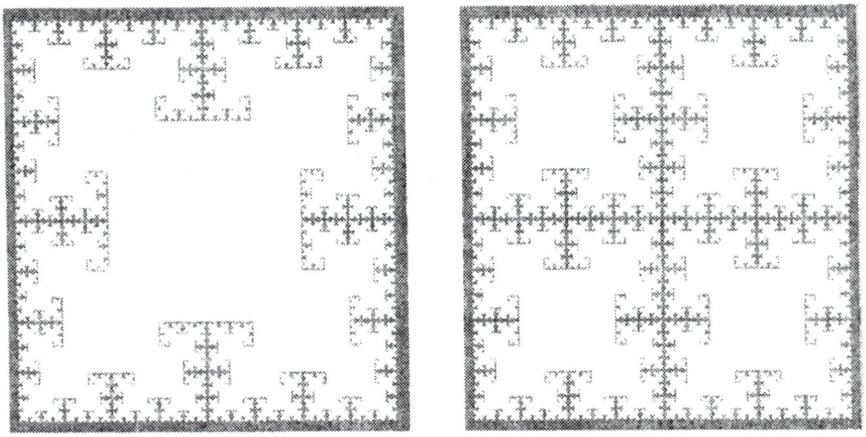

(a) (b)

Figure 8.14 (a) A fractal star outline drawn by the code shown in Figure 8.15. (b) The same star immediately before the last square is added.

```
// Draw picture in Figure 8.14.
void drawFractal( Graphics g, int xCenter,
                  int yCenter, int boundingDim )
{
    int side = boundingDim / 2;

    if( side < 1 )
        return;

      // Compute corners.
    int left =   xCenter - side / 2;
    int top =    yCenter - side / 2;
    int right =  xCenter + side / 2;
    int bottom = yCenter + side / 2;

      // Recursively draw four quadrants.
    drawFractal( g, left, top, boundingDim / 2 );
    drawFractal( g, left, bottom, boundingDim / 2 );
    drawFractal( g, right, top, boundingDim / 2 );
    drawFractal( g, right, bottom, boundingDim / 2 );

      // Draw central square, overlapping quadrants.
    g.fillRect( left, top, right - left, bottom - top );
}
```

Figure 8.15 Code for drawing fractal star outline shown in Figure 8.14.

The parameters to `drawFractal` include the center of the fractal and the overall dimension. From this, we can compute, at line 5, the size of the large central square. After handling the base case at lines 7 and 8, we compute the boundaries of the central rectangle. We can then draw the four miniature fractals at lines 17 to 20. Finally, we draw the central square at line 23. Note that this square must be drawn after the recursive calls. Otherwise, we obtain a different picture (In Exercise 8.26 you are asked to describe the difference).

8.4 Numerical Applications

In this section we look at three problems drawn primarily from number theory. Number theory used to be considered an interesting but useless branch of mathematics. However, in the last 30 years, an important application for number theory has emerged: data security. We begin the discussion with a small amount of mathematical background and then show recursive algorithms to solve three problems. We can combine these routines in conjunction with a fourth algorithm that is more complex (described in Chapter 10), to implement an algorithm that can be used to encode and decode messages. To date, nobody has been able to show that the encryption scheme described here is not secure.

Here are the four problems we examine.

1. *Modular exponentiation:* Compute $X^N (\text{mod } P)$.
2. *Greatest common divisor:* Compute $\gcd(A, B)$.
3. *Multiplicative inverse:* Solve $AX \equiv 1 (\text{mod } P)$ for X.
4. *Primality testing:* Determine whether N is prime (deferred to Chapter 10).

The integers we expect to deal with are all large, requiring at least 100 digits each. Therefore we must have a way to represent the class `HugeInt`, along with a complete set of algorithms for the basic operations of addition, subtraction, multiplication, division, and so on. Implementing the `HugeInt` efficiently is no trivial matter, and in fact there is an extensive literature on the subject. Some libraries (for instance the one that comes with g++) provide the `Integer` class for this purpose.

The functions that we write are templated to work with some `HugeInt` class, for which we assume that the normal arithmetic operations are overloaded. By instantiating with `int`, you can test the basic algorithms.Those described here work with large objects but still execute in a reasonable amount of time.

8.4.1 Modular Arithmetic

The problems in this section, as well as the implementation of the hash table data structure (Chapter 20), require the use of the C++ `%` operator. The `%` operator, denoted as `operator%`, computes the remainder of two integral types.[3] For example, `13%10` evaluates to 3, as does `3%10`, and `23%10`. When we compute the remainder of a division by 10, the possible results range from 0 to 9. This range makes `operator%` useful for generating small integers.

If two numbers A and B give the same remainder when divided by N, we say that they are congruent modulo N, written as $A \equiv B \pmod{N}$. In this case, it must be true that N divides $A - B$. Furthermore, the converse is true: If N divides $A - B$, then $A \equiv B \pmod{N}$. Because there are only N possible remainders—0, 1, ..., $N - 1$— we say that the integers are divided into congruence classes modulo N. In other words, every integer can be placed in one of N classes, and those in the same class are congruent to each other, modulo N. We use three important theorems in our algorithms (we leave the proof of these facts as Exercise 8.10).

1. If $A \equiv B \pmod{N}$, then for any C, $A + C \equiv B + C \pmod{N}$.
2. If $A \equiv B \pmod{N}$, then for any D, $AD \equiv BD \pmod{N}$.
3. If $A \equiv B \pmod{N}$, then for any positive P, $A^P \equiv B^P \pmod{N}$.

These theorems allow certain calculations to be done with less effort. For instance, suppose that we want to know the last digit in 3333^{5555}. Because this number has more than 15,000 digits, it is expensive to compute the answer directly. However, what we want is to determine $3333^{5555} \pmod{10}$. As $3333 \equiv 3 \pmod{10}$, we need only to compute $3^{5555} \pmod{10}$. As $3^4 = 81$, we know that $3^4 \equiv 1 \pmod{10}$, and raising both sides to the power of 1388 tells us that $3^{5552} \equiv 1 \pmod{10}$. If we multiply both sides by $3^3 = 27$, we obtain $3^{5555} \equiv 27 \equiv 7 \pmod{10}$, thereby completing the calculation.

8.4.2 Modular Exponentiation

In this section we show how to compute $X^N \pmod{P}$ efficiently. We can do so by initializing `result` to 1 and then repeatedly multiplying `result` by X, applying the `%` operator after every multiplication. Using `operator%` in this way instead of just the last multiplication makes each multiplication easier because it keeps `result` smaller.

---

3. C++ does not specify what happens when negative numbers are involved. We assume that they are not.

```
1 // Compute x^n ( mod p ).
2 // HugeInt: must have copy constructor, operator=,
3 //      conversion from int, *, /, %, ==, and !=.
4 //      Assumes p is not zero and power( 0, 0, p ) is 1.
5 template <class HugeInt>
6 HugeInt power( const HugeInt & x, const HugeInt & n,
7                const HugeInt & p )
8 {
9     if( n == 0 )
10        return 1;
11
12    HugeInt tmp = power( ( x * x ) % p, n / 2, p );
13
14    if( n % 2 != 0 )
15        tmp = ( tmp * x ) % p;
16
17    return tmp;
18 }
```

Figure 8.16 Modular exponentiation routine.

After N multiplications, `result` is the answer that we are looking for. However, doing N multiplications is impractical if N is a 100-digit `HugeInt`. In fact, if N is 1,000,000,000, it is impractical on all but the fastest machines.

A faster algorithm is based on the following observation. That is, if N is even, then

$$X^N = (X \cdot X)^{\lfloor N/2 \rfloor},$$

and if N is odd, then

$$X^N = X \cdot X^{N-1} = X \cdot (X \cdot X)^{\lfloor N/2 \rfloor}.$$

(Recall that $\lfloor X \rfloor$ is the largest integer that is smaller than or equal to X.) As before, to perform modular exponentiation, we apply a `%` after every multiplication.

The recursive algorithm shown in Figure 8.16 represents a direct implementation of this strategy. Lines 9 and 10 handle the base case: X^0 is 1, by definition.[4] At line 12, we make a recursive call based on the identity stated in the preceding paragraph. If N is even, this call computes the desired answer; if N is odd, we need to multiply by an extra X (and use `operator%`).

4. We define $0^0 = 1$ for the purposes of this algorithm. We also assume that N is nonnegative and P is positive.

This algorithm is faster than the simple algorithm proposed earlier. If $M(N)$ is the number of multiplications used by `power`, we have $M(N) \le M\lfloor N/2 \rfloor + 2$. The reason is that if N is even, we perform one multiplication, plus those done recursively, and that if N is odd, we perform two multiplications, plus those done recursively. Because $M(0) = 0$, we can show that $M(N) < 2 \log N$. The logarithmic factor can be obtained without direct calculation by application of the halving principle (see Section 6.5), which tells us the number of recursive invocations of `power`. Moreover, an average value of $M(N)$ is $(3/2)\log N$, as in each recursive step N is equally likely to be even or odd. If N is a 100-digit number, in the worst case only about 665 multiplications (and typically only 500 on average) are needed.

Exponentiation can be done in logarithmic number of multiplications.

A C++ note: `HugeInts` are passed by constant reference to avoid the copy. However, we return by copy. We could attempt to avoid these excessive copies, but doing so is not worth the effort. The reason is that, for each return, we know we have done a multiplication and mod operation, and the costs of these operations greatly exceed the overhead of the copy. Thus optimizing by attempting to use reference return values or global variables is not likely to achieve any significant time improvements.

Do not over optimize. You are likely to break your program.

8.4.3 Greatest Common Divisor and Multiplicative Inverses

Given two nonnegative integers A and B, their greatest common divisor, gcd(A, B), is the largest integer D that divides both A and B. For instance, gcd(70, 25) is 5. In other words, the **greatest common divisor (gcd)** is the largest integer that divides two given integers.

The *greatest common divisor* (gcd) of two integers is the largest integer that divides both of them.

We can easily verify that $\gcd(A, B) \equiv \gcd(A - B, B)$. If D divides both A and B, it must also divide $A - B$; and if D divides both $A - B$ and B, then it must also divide A.

This observation leads to a simple algorithm in which we repeatedly subtract B from A, transforming the problem into a smaller one. Eventually A becomes less than B, and then we can switch roles for A and B and continue from there. At some point B will become 0. Then we know that $\gcd(A, 0) \equiv A$, and as each transformation preserves the gcd of the original A and B, we have our answer. This algorithm is called *Euclid's algorithm* and was first described more than 2,000 years ago. Although correct, it is unusable for `HugeInts` because a huge number of subtractions are likely to be required.

A computationally efficient modification is that the repeated subtractions of B from A until A is smaller than B is equivalent to the conversion of A to precisely $A \bmod B$. Thus $\gcd(A, B) \equiv \gcd(B, A \bmod B)$. This recursive definition, along with the base case in which $B = 0$, is used directly to obtain the routine shown in Figure 8.17. To visualize how it works, note that in the previous example we used the following sequence of recursive calls to

```
// Returns the greatest common divisor of a and b.
template <class HugeInt>
HugeInt gcd( const HugeInt & a, const HugeInt & b )
{
    if( b == 0 )
        return a;
    else
        return gcd( b, a % b );
}
```

Figure 8.17 Computation of greatest common divisor.

deduce that the gcd of 70 and 25 is 5: gcd(70, 25) $\Rightarrow$ gcd(25,20) $\Rightarrow$ gcd(20, 5) $\Rightarrow$ gcd(5, 0) $\Rightarrow$ 5.

The number of recursive calls used is proportional to the logarithm of A, which is the same order of magnitude as the other routines that we have presented in this section. The reason is that, in two recursive calls, the problem is reduced at least in half. The proof of this is left for you to do as Exercise 8.11.

The greatest common divisor and multiplicative inverse can also be calculated in logarithmic time by using a variant of Euclid's algorithm.

The gcd algorithm is used implicitly to solve a similar mathematical problem. The solution $1 \le X < N$ to the equation $AX \equiv 1 (\text{mod } N)$ is called the **multiplicative inverse** of A, mod N. Also assume that $1 \le A < N$. For example, the inverse of 3, mod 13 is 9; that is, $3 \cdot 9$ mod 13 yields 1.

The ability to compute multiplicative inverses is important because equations such as $3i \equiv 7 (\text{mod } 13)$ are easily solved if we know the multiplicative inverse. These equations arise in many applications, including the encryption algorithm discussed at the end of this section. In this example, if we multiply by the inverse of 3 (namely 9), we obtain $i \equiv 63 (\text{mod } 13)$, so $i = 11$ is a solution. If

$$AX \equiv 1 (\text{mod } N), \quad \text{then} \quad AX + NY = 1 (\text{mod } N)$$

is true for any Y. For some Y, the left-hand side must be exactly 1. Thus the equation

$$AX + NY = 1$$

is solvable if and only if A has a multiplicative inverse.

Given A and B, we show how to find X and Y satisfying

$$AX + BY = 1.$$

We assume that $0 \le |B| < |A|$ and then extend the `gcd` algorithm to compute X and Y.

First, we consider the base case, $B \equiv 0$. In this case we have to solve $AX = 1$, which implies that both A and X are 1. In fact, if A is not 1, there is no multiplicative inverse. Hence A has a multiplicative inverse modulo N only if $\gcd(A, N) = 1$.

Otherwise, B is not zero. Recall that $\gcd(A, B) \equiv \gcd(B, A \bmod B)$. So we let $A = BQ + R$. Here Q is the quotient and R is the remainder, and thus the recursive call is $\gcd(B, R)$. Suppose that we can recursively solve

$$BX_1 + RY_1 = 1.$$

Since $R = A - BQ$, we have

$$BX_1 + (A - BQ)Y_1 = 1,$$

which means that

$$AY_1 + B(X_1 - QY_1) = 1.$$

Thus $X = Y_1$ and $Y = X_1 - \lfloor A/B \rfloor Y_1$ is a solution to $AX + BY = 1$. We code this observation directly as `fullGcd` in Figure 8.18. The method `inverse` just calls `fullGcd`, passing X and Y by reference. The only detail left is that the value given for X may be negative. If it is, line 33 of `inverse` will make it positive. We leave a proof of that fact for you to do as Exercise 8.14. The proof can be done by induction.

8.4.4 The RSA Cryptosystem

Number theory is used in cryptography because factoring appears to be a much harder process than multiplication.

For centuries, number theory was thought to be a completely impractical branch of mathematics. Recently, however, it has emerged as an important field because of its applicability to cryptography.

The problem we consider has two parts. Suppose that Alice wants to send a message to Bob but that she is worried that the transmission may be compromised. For instance, if the transmission is over a phone line and the phone is tapped, somebody else may be reading the message. We assume that, even if there is eavesdropping on the phone line, there is no maliciousness (i.e., damage to the signal)—Bob gets whatever Alice sends.

***Encryption* is used to transmit messages so that they cannot be read by other parties.**

A solution to this problem is to use **encryption,** an encoding scheme to transmit messages that cannot be read by other parties. Encryption consists of two parts. First, Alice *encrypts* the message and sends the result, which is no longer plainly readable. When Bob receives Alice's transmission, he *decrypts* it to obtain the original. The security of the algorithm is based on

```
// Given a and b, assume gcd( a, b ) = 1.
// Find x and y such that a x + b y = 1.
// HugeInt: must have copy constructor,
//     zero-parameter constructor, operator=,
//     conversion from int, *, /, +, -, %, ==, and >.
template <class HugeInt>
void fullGcd( const HugeInt & a, const HugeInt & b,
                  HugeInt & x, HugeInt & y )
{
    HugeInt x1, y1;

    if( b == 0 )
    {
        x = 1;          // If a != 1, there is no inverse
        y = 0;          // We omit this check
    }
    else
    {
        fullGcd( b, a % b, x1, y1 );
        x = y1;
        y = x1 - ( a / b ) * y1;
    }
}

// Solve a x == 1 ( mod n ).
// Assume that gcd( a, n ) = 1.
template <class HugeInt>
HugeInt inverse( const HugeInt & a, const HugeInt & n )
{
    HugeInt x, y;

    fullGcd( a, n, x, y );
    return x > 0 ? x : x + n;
}
```

Figure 8.18 A routine for determining multiplicative inverse.

the fact that nobody else besides Bob should be able to perform the decryption, including Alice (if she did not save the original message).

The *RSA cryptosystem* is a popular encryption method.

Thus Bob must provide Alice with a method of encryption that only he knows how to reverse. This problem is extremely challenging. Many proposed algorithms can be compromised by subtle code-breaking techniques. One method, described here, is the **RSA cryptosystem** (named after the initials of its authors), an elegant implementation of an encryption strategy.

Here we give only a high-level overview of encryption, showing how the methods written in this section interact in a practical way. The references contain pointers to more detailed descriptions, as well as proofs of the key properties of the algorithm.

First, however, note that a message consists of a sequence of characters and each that character is just a sequence of bits. Thus a message is a sequence of bits. If we break the message into blocks of B bits, we can interpret the message as a series of very large numbers. Thus the basic problem is reduced to encrypting a large number and then decrypting the result.

Computation of the RSA Constants

The RSA algorithm begins by having the receiver determine some constants. First, two large primes p and q are randomly chosen. Typically, these would be at least 100 or so digits each. For the purposes of this example, suppose that p = 127 and q = 211. Note that Bob is the receiver and thus is performing these computations. Note, also, that primes are plentiful. Bob can thus keep trying random numbers until two of them pass the primality test (discussed in Chapter 10).

Next, Bob computes $N = pq$ and $N' = (p-1)(q-1)$, which for this example gives N = 26,797 and N' = 26,460. Bob continues by choosing any $e > 1$ such that gcd(e, N'). In mathematical terms, he chooses any e that is relatively prime to N'. Bob can keep trying different values of e by using the routine shown in Figure 8.17 until he finds one that satisfies the property. Any prime e would work, so finding e is at least as easy as finding a prime number. In this case, e = 13,379 is one of many valid choices. Next, d, the multiplicative inverse of e, mod N' is computed by using the routine shown in Figure 8.18. In this example, d = 11,099.

Once Bob has computed all these constants, he does the following. First, he destroys p, q, and N'. The security of the system is compromised if any one of these values is discovered. Bob then tells anybody who wants to send him an encrypted message the values of e and N, but he keeps d secret.

Encryption and Decryption Algorithms

To encrypt an integer M, the sender computes $M^e \pmod N$ and sends it. In our case, if M = 10,237, the value sent is 8,422. When an encrypted integer R is received, all Bob has to do is compute $R^d \pmod N$. For R = 8,422, he gets back the original M = 10,237 (which is not accidental). Both encryption and decryption can thus be carried out by using the modular exponentiation routine given in Figure 8.16.

The algorithm works because the choices of e, d, and N guarantee (via a number theory proof beyond the scope of this text) that $M^{ed} = M \pmod N$, so long as M and N share no common factors. As the only factors of N are two 100-digit primes, it is virtually impossible for that to occur.[5] Thus decryption of the encrypted text gets the original back.

5. You are more likely to win a typical state lottery 13 weeks in a row. However, if M and N have a common factor, the system is compromised because the gcd will be a factor of N.

What makes the scheme seem secure is that knowledge of d is apparently required in order to decode. Now N and e uniquely determine d. For instance, if we factor N, we get p and q and can then reconstruct d. The caveat is that factoring is apparently very hard to do for large numbers. Thus the security of the RSA system is based on the belief that factoring large numbers is intrinsically very difficult. So far it has held up well.

In *public key cryptography*, each participant publishes the code others can use to send encrypted messages but keeps the decrypting code secret.

This general scheme is known as **public key cryptography,** by which anybody who wants to receive messages publishes encryption information for anybody else to use but keeps the decryption code secret. In the RSA system, e and N would be computed once by each person and listed in a publicly readable place.

The RSA algorithm is widely used to implement secure e-mail, as well as secure Internet transactions. When you see a closed lock () at the bottom of a Netscape Navigator Web page, a secure transaction is being performed via cryptography. The method actually employed is more complex than described here. One problem is that the RSA algorithm is somewhat slow for sending large messages.

In practice, RSA is used to encrypt the key used by a single-key encryption algorithm, such as DES.

A faster method is called *DES*. Unlike the RSA algorithm, DES is a single-key algorithm, meaning that the same key serves both to encode and decode. It is like the typical lock on your house door. The problem with single-key algorithms is that both parties need to share the single key. How does one party ensure that the other party has the single key? That problem can be solved by using the RSA algorithm. A typical solution is that, say, Alice will randomly generate a single key for DES encryption. She then encrypts her message by using DES, which is much faster than using RSA. She transmits the encrypted message to Bob. For Bob to decode the encrypted message, he needs to get the DES key that Alice used. A DES key is relatively short, so Alice can use RSA to encrypt the DES key and then send it in a second transmission to Bob. Bob next decrypts Alice's second transmission, thus obtaining the DES key, at which point he can decode the original message. These types of protocols, with enhancements, form the basis of most practical encryption implementations.

8.5 Divide-and-Conquer Algorithms

A *divide-and-conquer algorithm* is a recursive algorithm that is generally very efficient.

An important problem-solving technique that makes use of recursion is divide-and-conquer. A **divide-and-conquer algorithm** is an efficient recursive algorithm that consist of two parts:

- *divide,* in which smaller problems are solved recursively (except, of course, base cases); and

- *conquer,* in which the solution to the original problem is then formed from the solutions to the subproblems.

In *divide and conquer,* the recursion is the *divide,* the overhead is the *conquer.*

Traditionally, routines in which the algorithm contains at least two recursive calls are called divide-and-conquer algorithms, whereas routines whose text contains only one recursive call are not. Consequently, the recursive routines presented so far in this chapter are not divide-and-conquer algorithms. Also, the subproblems usually must be disjoint (i.e., essentially nonoverlapping), so as to avoid the excessive costs seen in the sample recursive computation of the Fibonacci numbers.

In this section we give an example of the divide-and-conquer paradigm. First we show how to use recursion to solve the maximum subsequence sum problem. Then we provide an analysis to show that the running time is $O(N \log N)$. Although we have already used a linear algorithm for this problem, the solution here is thematic of others in a wide range of applications, including the sorting algorithms, such as mergesort and quicksort, discussed in Chapter 9. Consequently, learning the technique is important. Finally, we show the general form for the running time of a broad class of divide-and-conquer algorithms.

8.5.1 The Maximum Contiguous Subsequence Sum Problem

In Section 6.3 we discussed the problem of finding, in a sequence of numbers, a contiguous subsequence of maximum sum. For convenience, we restate the problem here.

MAXIMUM CONTIGUOUS SUBSEQUENCE SUM PROBLEM

GIVEN (POSSIBLY NEGATIVE) INTEGERS $A_1, A_2, \ldots, A_N$, FIND (AND IDENTIFY THE SEQUENCE CORRESPONDING TO) THE MAXIMUM VALUE OF $\sum_{k=i}^{j} A_k$. THE MAXIMUM CONTIGUOUS SUBSEQUENCE SUM IS ZERO IF ALL THE INTEGERS ARE NEGATIVE.

The maximum contiguous subsequence sum problem can be solved with a divide-and-conquer algorithm.

We presented three algorithms of various complexity. One was a cubic algorithm based on an exhaustive search: We calculated the sum of each possible subsequence and selected the maximum. We described a quadratic improvement that takes advantage of the fact that each new subsequence can be computed in constant time from a previous subsequence. Because we have $O(N^2)$ subsequences, this bound is the best that can be achieved with an approach that directly examines all subsequences. We also gave a linear-time algorithm that works by examining only a few subsequences. However, its correctness is not obvious.

First Half				Second Half				
4	−3	5	−2	−1	2	6	−2	Values
4*	0	3	−2	−1	1	7*	5	Running sums

Running sum from the center (*denotes maximum for each half).

Figure 8.19 Dividing the maximum contiguous subsequence problem into halves.

Let us consider a divide-and-conquer algorithm. Suppose that the sample input is {4, −3, 5, −2, −1, 2, 6, −2}. We divide this input into two halves, as shown in Figure 8.19. Then the maximum contiguous subsequence sum can occur in one of three ways.

- *Case 1:* It resides entirely in the first half.
- *Case 2:* It resides entirely in the second half.
- *Case 3:* It begins in the first half but ends in the second half.

We show how to find the maximums for each of these three cases more efficiently than by using an exhaustive search.

We begin by looking at case 3. We want to avoid the nested loop that results from considering all $N/2$ starting points and $N/2$ ending points independently. We can make so by replacing two nested loops by two consecutive loops. The consecutive loops, each of size $N/2$, combine to require only linear work. We can make this substitution because any contiguous subsequence that begins in the first half and ends in the second half must include both the last element of the first half and the first element of the second half.

Figure 8.19 shows that we can calculate, for each element in the first half, the contiguous subsequence sum that ends at the rightmost item. We do so with a right-to-left scan, starting from the border between the two halves. Similarly, we can calculate the contiguous subsequence sum for all sequences that begin with the first element in the second half. We can then combine these two subsequences to form the maximum contiguous subsequence that spans the dividing border. In this example, the resulting sequence spans from the first element in the first half to the next-to-last element in the second half. The total sum is the sum of the two subsequences, or $4 + 7 = 11$.

This analysis shows that case 3 can be solved in linear time. But what about cases 1 and 2? Because there are $N / 2$ elements in each half, an exhaustive search applied to each half still requires quadratic time per half; specifically, all we have done is eliminate roughly half of the work, and half of quadratic is still quadratic. In cases 1 and 2 we can apply the same strategy—that of dividing into more halves. We can keep dividing those quarters further and further until splitting is impossible. This approach is succinctly stated as follows: *Solve cases 1 and 2 recursively.* As we demonstrate later, doing so lowers the running time below quadratic because the savings compound throughout the algorithm. The following is a summary of the main portion of the algorithm:

1. recursively compute the maximum contiguous subsequence sum that resides entirely in the first half;
2. recursively compute the maximum contiguous subsequence sum that resides entirely in the second half;
3. compute, via two consecutive loops, the maximum contiguous subsequence sum that begins in the first half but ends in the second half; and
4. choose the largest of the three sums.

A recursive algorithm requires specifying a base case. When the size of the problem reaches one element, we do not use recursion. The resulting C++ function is coded in Figure 8.20.

The general form for the recursive call is to pass the input array along with the left and right borders, which delimit the portion of the array being operated on. A one-line driver routine sets this action up by passing the borders 0 and $N - 1$ along with the array.

Lines 10 and 11 handle the base case. If `left==right`, there is one element, and it is the maximum contiguous subsequence if the element is nonnegative (otherwise, the empty sequence with sum 0 is maximum). Lines 13 and 14 perform the two recursive calls. These calls are always on a smaller problem than the original; thus we progress toward the base case. Lines 16 to 21 and then 23 to 28 calculate the maximum sums that touch the center border. The sum of these two values is the maximum sum that spans both halves. The routine `max3` (not shown) returns the largest of the three possibilities.

```
// Recursive maximum contiguous subsequence sum algorithm.
template <class Comparable>
Comparable maxSubSum( const vector<Comparable> & a,
                      int left, int right )
{
    Comparable maxLeftBorderSum = 0, maxRightBorderSum = 0;
    Comparable leftBorderSum = 0, rightBorderSum = 0;
    int center = ( left + right ) / 2;

    if( left == right )         // Base Case.
        return a[ left ] > 0 ? a[ left ] : 0;

    Comparable maxLeftSum  = maxSubSum( a, left, center );
    Comparable maxRightSum = maxSubSum( a, center + 1, right );

    for( int i = center; i >= left; i-- )
    {
        leftBorderSum += a[ i ];
        if( leftBorderSum > maxLeftBorderSum )
            maxLeftBorderSum = leftBorderSum;
    }

    for( int j = center + 1; j <= right; j++ )
    {
        rightBorderSum += a[ j ];
        if( rightBorderSum > maxRightBorderSum )
            maxRightBorderSum = rightBorderSum;
    }

    return max3( maxLeftSum, maxRightSum,
                 maxLeftBorderSum + maxRightBorderSum );
}

// Public driver.
template <class Comparable>
Comparable maxSubsequenceSum( const vector<Comparable> & a )
{
    return a.size( ) > 0 ? maxSubSum( a, 0, a.size() - 1 ) : 0;
}
```

Figure 8.20 A divide-and-conquer algorithm for the maximum contiguous subsequence sum problem.

8.5.2 Analysis of a Basic Divide-and-Conquer Recurrence

Intuitive analysis of the maximum contiguous subsequence sum divide-and-conquer algorithm: We spend *O*(*N*) per level.

The recursive maximum contiguous subsequence sum algorithm works by performing linear work to compute a sum that spans the center border and then performing two recursive calls. These calls collectively compute a sum that spans the center border, do further recursive calls, and so on. The total work performed by the algorithm is then proportional to the scanning done over all the recursive calls.

Figure 8.21 graphically illustrates how the algorithm works for $N = 8$ elements. Each rectangle represents a call to `maxSubSum`, and the length of the rectangle is proportional to the size of the subarray (and hence the cost of the scanning of the subarray) being operated on by the invocation. The initial call is shown on the first line: The size of the subarray is N, which represents the cost of the scanning for the third case. The initial call then makes two recursive calls, yielding two subarrays of size $N/2$. The cost of each scan in case 3 is half the original cost, but as there are two such recursive calls, the combined cost of these recursive calls is also N. Each of those two recursive instances themselves make two recursive calls, yielding four subproblems that are a quarter of the original size. Thus the total of all case 3 costs is also N.

Eventually, we reach the base case. Each base case has size 1, and there are N of them. Of course, there are no case 3 costs in this instance, but we charge 1 unit for performing the check that determines whether the sole element is positive or negative. The total cost then, as illustrated in Figure 8.21, is N per level of recursion. Each level halves the size of the basic problem, so the halving principle tells us that there are approximately $\log N$ levels. In fact, the number of levels is $1 + \lceil \log N \rceil$ (which is 4 when N equals 8). Thus we expect that the total running time is $O(N \log N)$.

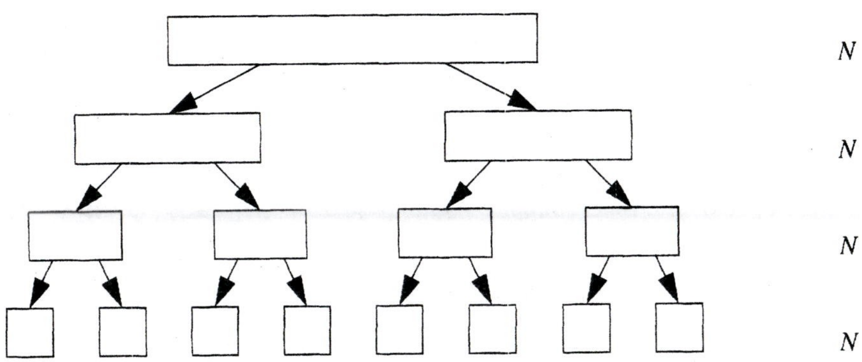

Figure 8.21 Trace of recursive calls for recursive maximum contiguous subsequence sum algorithm for $N = 8$ elements.

This analysis gives an intuitive explanation of why the running time is $O(N \log N)$. In general, however, expanding a recursive algorithm to examine behavior is a bad idea; it violates the third rule of recursion. We next consider a more formal mathematical treatment.

Note that the more formal analysis holds for all classes of algorithms that recursively solve two halves and use linear additional work.

Let $T(N)$ represent the time required to solve a maximum contiguous subsequence sum problem of size N. If $N = 1$, the program takes some constant amount of time to execute lines 10 to 11, which we call 1 unit. Thus $T(1) = 1$. Otherwise, the program must perform two recursive calls and the linear work involved in computing the maximum sum for case 3. The constant overhead is absorbed by the $O(N)$ term. How long do the two recursive calls take? Because they solve problems of size $N/2$, we know that they must each require $T(N/2)$ units of time; consequently, the total recursive work is $2T(N/2)$. This analysis gives the equations

$$T(1) = 1;$$
$$T(N) = 2T(N/2) + O(N).$$

Of course, for the second equation to make sense, N must be a power of 2. Otherwise, at some point $N/2$ will not be even. A more precise equation is

$$T(N) = T(\lfloor N/2 \rfloor) + T(\lceil N/2 \rceil) + O(N).$$

To simplify the calculations, we assume that N is a power of 2 and replace the $O(N)$ term with N. These assumptions are minor and do not affect the Big-Oh result. Consequently, we need to obtain a closed form solution for $T(N)$ from

$$T(1) = 1 \quad \text{and} \quad T(N) = 2T(N/2) + N. \tag{8.6}$$

This equation is illustrated in Figure 8.21, so we know that the answer will be $N \log N + N$. We can easily verify the result by examining a few values: $T(1)$, $T(2) = 4$, $T(4) = 12$, $T(8) = 32$, and $T(16) = 80$. We now prove this analysis mathematically in Theorem 8.4, using two different methods.

Theorem 8.4 *Assuming that N is a power of 2, the solution to the equation $T(N) = 2T(N/2) + N$, with initial condition $T(1) = 1$, is $T(N) = N \log N + N$.*

Proof (Method 1)

For sufficiently large N, we have $T(N/2) = 2T(N/4) + N/2$ because we can use Equation 8.6 with $N/2$ instead of N. Consequently, we have

$$2T(N/2) = 4T(N/4) + N.$$

Substituting this into Equation 8.6 yields

$$T(N) = 4T(N/4) + 2N. \tag{8.7}$$

If we use Equation 8.6 for $N/4$ and multiply by 4, we obtain

$$4T(N/4) = 8T(N/8) + N,$$

which we can substitute into the right-hand side of Equation 8.7 to obtain

$$T(N) = 8T(N/8) + 3N.$$

Continuing in this manner, we obtain

$$T(N) = 2^k T(N/2^k) + kN.$$

Finally, using $k = \log N$ (which makes sense because then $2^k = N$), we obtain

$$T(N) = NT(1) + N \log N = N \log N + N.$$

Although this proof method appears to work well, it can be difficult to apply in more complicated cases because it tends to give very long equations. Following is a second method that appears to be easier because it generates equations vertically that are more easily manipulated.

Proof (Method 2) *We divide Equation 8.6 by N, yielding a new basic equation:*

$$\frac{T(N)}{N} = \frac{T(N/2)}{N/2} + 1.$$

This equation is now valid for any N that is a power of 2, so we may also write the following equations:

$$\begin{aligned}\frac{T(N)}{N} &= \frac{T(N/2)}{N/2} + 1;\\ \frac{T(N/2)}{N/2} &= \frac{T(N/4)}{N/4} + 1;\\ \frac{T(N/4)}{N/4} &= \frac{T(N/8)}{N/8} + 1;\\ &\dots\\ \frac{T(2)}{2} &= \frac{T(1)}{1} + 1.\end{aligned} \tag{8.8}$$

A *telescoping sum* generates large numbers of canceling terms.

Now we add the collective in Equation 8.8. That is, we add all the terms on the left-hand side and set the result equal to the sum of all the terms on the right-hand side. The term $T(N/2)\,/\,(N/2)$ appears on both sides and thus cancels. In fact, virtually all the terms appear on both sides and cancel. This is called a ***telescoping sum.*** *After everything is added, the final result is*

$$\frac{T(N)}{N} = \frac{T(1)}{1} + \log N$$

because all the other terms cancel and there are log *N equations. Thus all the 1s at the end of these equations sum to* log *N. Multiplying through by N gives the final answer, as before.*

Note that, if we had not divided through by N at the start of the solution, the sum would not have telescoped. Deciding on the division required to ensure a telescoping sum requires some experience and makes the method a little more difficult to apply than the first alternative. However, once you have found the correct divisor, the second alternative tends to produce scrap work that fits better on a standard sheet of paper, leading to fewer mathematical errors. In contrast, the first method is more of a brute-force approach.

Note that whenever we have a divide-and-conquer algorithm that solves two half-sized problems with linear additional work, we always have $O(N \log N)$ running time.

8.5.3 A General Upper Bound for Divide-and-Conquer Running Times

The general formula given in this section allows the number of subproblems, the size of the subproblems, and the amount of additional work to assume general forms. The result can be used without understanding of the proof.

The analysis in Section 8.5.2 showed that, when a problem is divided into two equal halves that are solved recursively—with $O(N)$ overhead, the result is an $O(N \log N)$ algorithm. What if we divide a problem into three half-sized problems with linear overhead, or seven half-sized problems with quadratic overhead? (See Exercise 8.17.) In this section we provide a general formula to compute the running time of a divide-and-conquer algorithm. The formula requires three parameters:

- A, which is the number of subproblems;
- B, which is the relative size of the subproblems (for instance $B = 2$ represents half-sized subproblems); and
- k, which is representative of the fact that the overhead is $\Theta(N^k)$.

The formula and its proof is presented as Theorem 8.5. The proof of the formula requires familiarity with geometric sums. However, knowledge of the proof is not needed for you to use the formula.

Theorem 8.5

The solution to the equation $T(N) = AT(N/B) + O(N^k)$, *where* $A \geq 1$ *and* $B > 1$, *is*

$$T(N) = \begin{cases} O(N^{\log_B A}) & \text{for } A > B^k; \\ O(N^k \log N) & \text{for } A = B^k; \\ O(N^k) & \text{for } A < B^k. \end{cases}$$

Before proving Theorem 8.5, let us look at some applications. For the maximum contiguous subsequence sum problem, we have two problems, two halves, and linear overhead. The applicable values are $A = 2$, $B = 2$, and $k = 1$. Hence the second case in Theorem 8.5 applies, and we get $O(N \log N)$, which agrees with our previous calculations. If we recursively solve three half-sized problems with linear overhead, we have $A = 3$, $B = 2$, and $k = 1$, and the first case applies. The result is $O(N^{\log_2 3}) = O(N^{1.59})$. Here, the overhead does not contribute to the total cost of the algorithm. Any overhead smaller than $O(N^{1.59})$ would give the same running time for the recursive algorithm. An algorithm that solved three half-sized problems but required quadratic overhead would have $O(N^2)$ running time because the third case would apply. In effect, the overhead dominates once it exceeds the $O(N^{1.59})$ threshold. At the threshold the penalty is the logarithmic factor shown in the second case. We can now prove Theorem 8.5.

Proof (of Theorem 8.5)

Following the second proof of Theorem 8.4, we assume that N is a power of B and let $N = B^M$. Then $N/B = B^{M-1}$ and $N^k = (B^M)^k = (B^k)^M$. We assume that $T(1) = 1$ and ignore the constant factor in $O(N^k)$. Then we have the basic equation

$$T(B^M) = AT(B^{M-1}) + (B^k)^M.$$

If we divide through by A^M, we obtain the new basic equation

$$\frac{T(B^M)}{A^M} = \frac{T(B^{M-1})}{A^{M-1}} + \left(\frac{B^k}{A}\right)^M.$$

Now we can write this equation for all M, obtaining

$$\begin{aligned}
\frac{T(B^M)}{A^M} &= \frac{T(B^{M-1})}{A^{M-1}} + \left(\frac{B^k}{A}\right)^M;\\
\frac{T(B^{M-1})}{A^{M-1}} &= \frac{T(B^{M-2})}{A^{M-2}} + \left(\frac{B^k}{A}\right)^{M-1};\\
\frac{T(B^{M-2})}{A^{M-2}} &= \frac{T(B^{M-3})}{A^{M-3}} + \left(\frac{B^k}{A}\right)^{M-2};\\
&\cdots\\
\frac{T(B^1)}{A^1} &= \frac{T(B^0)}{A^0} + \left(\frac{B^k}{A}\right)^1.
\end{aligned} \tag{8.9}$$

If we add the collective denoted by Equation 8.9, once again virtually all the terms on the left-hand side cancel the leading terms on the right-hand side, yielding

$$\begin{aligned}
\frac{T(B^M)}{A^M} &= 1 + \sum_{i=1}^{M}\left(\frac{B^k}{A}\right)^i\\
&= \sum_{i=0}^{M}\left(\frac{B^k}{A}\right)^i.
\end{aligned}$$

Thus

Proof (continued)

$$T(N) = T(B^M) = A^M \sum_{i=0}^{M} \left(\frac{B^k}{A}\right)^i. \quad \textbf{(8.10)}$$

If A > B^k, then the sum is a geometric series with a ratio smaller than 1. Because the sum of an infinite series would converge to a constant, this finite sum is also bounded by a constant. Thus we obtain

$$T(N) = O(A^M) = O(N^{\log_B A}). \quad \textbf{(8.11)}$$

If $A = B^k$, then each term in the sum in Equation 8.10 is 1. As the sum contains $1 + \log_B N$ terms and $A = B^k$ implies $A^M = N^k$,

$$T(N) = O(A^M \log_B N) = O(N^k \log_B N) = O(N^k \log N).$$

Finally, if $A < B^k$, then the terms in the geometric series are larger than 1. We can compute the sum using a standard formula, thereby obtaining

$$T(N) = A^M \frac{\left(\frac{B^k}{A}\right)^{M+1} - 1}{\frac{B^k}{A} - 1} = O\left(A^M \left(\frac{B^k}{A}\right)^M\right) = O((B^k)^M) = O(N^k),$$

proving the last case of Theorem 8.5.

8.6 Dynamic Programming

Dynamic *programming* solves subproblems nonrecursively by recording answers in a table.

A problem that can be mathematically expressed recursively can also be expressed as a recursive algorithm. In many cases, doing so yields a significant performance improvement over a more naive exhaustive search. Any recursive mathematical formula could be directly translated to a recursive algorithm, but often the compiler may not do justice to the recursive algorithm and an inefficient program results. That is the case for the recursive computation of the Fibonacci numbers described in Section 8.3.4. To avoid this recursive explosion, we can use **dynamic programming** to rewrite the recursive algorithm as a nonrecursive algorithm that systematically records the answers to the subproblems in a table. We illustrate this technique with the following problem.

CHANGE-MAKING PROBLEM

For a currency with coins C_1, C_2, ..., C_N (cents) what is the minimum number of coins needed to make K cents of change?

Greedy algorithms make locally optimal decisions at each step. This is the simple, but not always the correct, thing to do.

U.S. currency has coins in 1-, 5-, 10-, and 25-cent denominations (ignore the less-frequently occurring 50-cent piece). We can make 63 cents by using two 25-cent pieces, one 10-cent piece, and three 1-cent pieces, for a total of six coins. Change-making in this currency is relatively simple: We repeatedly use the largest coin available to us. We can show that for U.S. currency this approach always minimizes the total number of coins used, which is an example of so-called greedy algorithms. In a **greedy algorithm,** during each phase, a decision is made that appears to be optimal, without regard for future consequences. This "take what you can get now" strategy is the source of the name for this class of algorithms. When a problem can be solved with a greedy algorithm, we are usually quite happy: Greedy algorithms often match our intuition and make for relatively painless coding. Unfortunately, greedy algorithms do not always work. If the U.S. currency included a 21-cent piece, the greedy algorithm would still give a solution that uses six coins, but the optimal solution uses three coins (all 21-cent pieces).

The question then becomes one of how to solve the problem for an arbitrary coin set. We assume that there is always a 1-cent coin so that the solution always exists. A simple strategy to make K cents in change uses recursion as follows.

1. If we can make change using exactly one coin, that is the minimum.
2. Otherwise, for each possible value i we can compute the minimum number of coins needed to make i cents in change and $K - i$ cents in change independently. We then choose the i that minimizes this sum.

A simple recursive algorithm for change making is easily written but inefficient.

For example, let us see how we can make 63 cents in change. Clearly, one coin will not suffice. We can compute the number of coins required to make 1 cent of change and 62 cents of change independently (these are 1 and 4, respectively). We obtain these results recursively, so they must be taken as optimal (it happens that the 62 cents is given as two 21-cent pieces and two 10-cent pieces). Thus we have a method that uses five coins. If we split the problem into 2 cents and 61 cents, the recursive solutions yield 2 and 4, respectively, for a total of six coins. We continue trying all the possibilities, some of which are shown in Figure 8.22. Eventually, we see a split into 21 cents and 42 cents, which is changeable in one and two coins, respectively, thus allowing change to be made in three coins. The last split we need to try is 31 cents and 32 cents. We can change 31 cents in two coins,

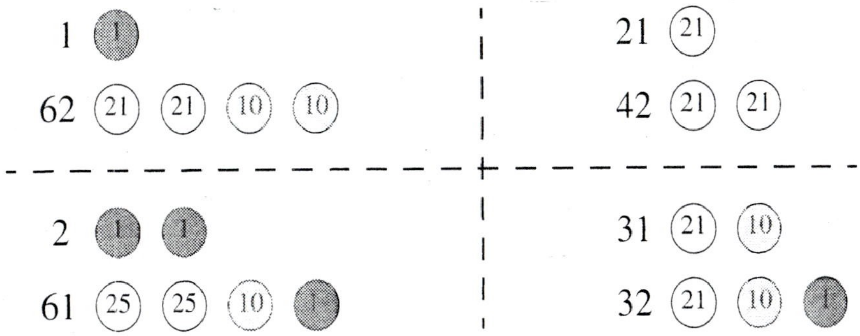

Figure 8.22 Some of the subproblems solved recursively in Figure 8.23.

```
// Return minimum number of coins to make change.
// Simple recursive algorithm that is very inefficient.
int makeChange( const vector<int> & coins, int change )
{
    int minCoins = change;

      // Look for exact match with any single coin.
    for( int i = 0; i < coins.size( ); i++ )
        if( coins[ i ] == change )
            return 1;

      // No match; solve recursively.
    for( int j = 1; j <= change / 2; j++ )
    {
        int thisCoins = makeChange( coins, j )
                      + makeChange( coins, change - j );
        if( thisCoins < minCoins )
            minCoins = thisCoins;
    }

    return minCoins;
}
```

Figure 8.23 A simple but inefficient recursive procedure for solving the coin-changing problem.

and we can change 32 cents in three coins for a total of five coins. But the minimum remains three coins.

Again, we solve each of these subproblems recursively, which yields the natural algorithm shown in Figure 8.23. If we run the algorithm to make small change, it works perfectly. But like the Fibonacci calculations, this

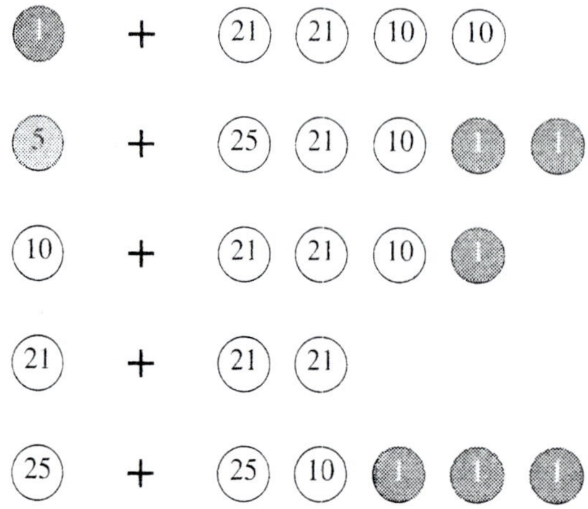

Figure 8.24 An alternative recursive algorithm for the coin-changing problem.

algorithm requires too much redundant work, and it will not terminate in a reasonable amount of time for the 63-cent case.

Our alternative recursive change-making algorithm is still inefficient.

An alternative algorithm involves reducing the problem recursively by specifying one of the coins. For example, for 63 cents, we can give change in the following ways, as shown in Figure 8.24.

- One 1-cent piece plus 62 cents recursively distributed
- One 5-cent piece plus 58 cents recursively distributed
- One 10-cent piece plus 53 cents recursively distributed
- One 21-cent piece plus 42 cents recursively distributed
- One 25-cent piece plus 38 cents recursively distributed

Instead of solving 62 recursive problems, as in Figure 8.22, we get by with only 5 recursive calls, one for each different coin. Again, a naive recursive implementation is very inefficient because it recomputes answers. For example, in the first case we are left with a problem of making 62 cents in change. In this subproblem, one of the recursive calls made chooses a 10-cent piece and recursively solves for 52 cents. In the third case we are left with 53 cents. One of its recursive calls removes the 1-cent piece and also recursively solves for 52 cents. This redundant work again leads to excessive running time. If we are careful, however, we can make the algorithm run reasonably fast.

The trick is to save answers to the subproblems in an array. This dynamic programming technique forms the basis of many algorithms. A large answer depends only on smaller answers, so we can compute the optimal way to change 1 cent, then 2 cents, then 3 cents, and so on. This strategy is shown in the function in Figure 8.25.

```
1 // Dynamic programming algorithm for change-making problem.
2 // As a result, the coinsUsed array is filled with the minimum
3 // number of coins needed for change from 0->maxChange and
4 // lastCoin contains one of the coins needed to make the change.
5 void makeChange( const vector<int> & coins, int maxChange,
6                  vector<int> & coinsUsed, vector<int> & lastCoin )
7 {
8     int differentCoins = coins.size( );
9     coinsUsed.resize( maxChange + 1 );
10    lastCoin.resize( maxChange + 1 );
11
12    coinsUsed[ 0 ] = 0; lastCoin[ 0 ] = 1;
13    for( int cents = 1; cents <= maxChange; cents++ )
14    {
15        int minCoins = cents, newCoin = 1;
16        for( int j = 0; j < differentCoins; j++ )
17        {
18            if( coins[ j ] > cents )   // Can't use coin j
19                continue;
20            if( coinsUsed[ cents - coins[ j ] ] + 1 < minCoins )
21            {
22                minCoins = coinsUsed[ cents - coins[ j ] ] + 1;
23                newCoin  = coins[ j ];
24            }
25        }
26
27        coinsUsed[ cents ] = minCoins;
28        lastCoin[ cents ]  = newCoin;
29    }
30 }
```

Figure 8.25 A dynamic programming algorithm for solving the change-making problem by computing optimal change for all amounts from 0 to `maxChange` and maintaining information to construct the actual coin sequence.

First, at line 12 we observe that 0 cents can be changed using zero coins. The `lastCoin` array is used to tell us which coin was last used to make the optimal change. Otherwise, we attempt to make `cents` cents worth of change, for `cents` ranging from 1 to the final `maxChange`. To make `cents` worth of change, we try each coin in succession as indicated by the `for` statement beginning at line 16. If the amount of the coin is larger than the amount of change we are trying to make, there is nothing to do. Otherwise, we test at line 20 to determine whether the number of coins used to solve the subproblem plus the one coin combine to be fewer than the minimum number of coins used thus far; if so, we perform an update at lines 22 and 23. When the loop ends for the current number of `cents`, the minimums can be inserted in the arrays, which is done at lines 27 and 28.

At the end of the algorithm, `coinsUsed[i]` represents the minimum number of coins needed to make change for `i` cents (`i==maxChange` is the particular solution that we are looking for). By tracing back through `lastCoin`, we can figure out the coins needed to achieve the solution. The running time is that of two nested `for` loops and is thus $O(NK)$, where N is the number of different denominations of coins and K is the amount of change that we are trying to make.

8.7 Backtracking

A *backtracking algorithm* uses recursion to try all the possibilities.

In this section we set out the last application of recursion. We show how to write a routine to have the computer select an optimal move in the game Tic-Tac-Toe. The interface for a `TicTacToe` class is shown in Figure 8.26. The class has a data object `board` that represents the current game position.[6] A host of trivial member functions are specified, including routines to clear the board, to test whether a square is occupied, to place something on a square, and to test whether a win has been achieved. The implementation details are provided in the online code.

The challenge is to decide, for any position, what the best move is. The routine used is `chooseMove`. The general strategy involves the use of a backtracking algorithm. A **backtracking algorithm** uses recursion to try all the possibilities.

The *minimax strategy* is used for Tic-Tac-Toe. It is based on the assumption of optimal play by both sides.

The basis for making this decision is `positionValue`, which is shown in Figure 8.27. The method `positionValue` returns `HUMAN_WIN`, `DRAW`, `COMPUTER_WIN`, or `UNCLEAR`, depending on what the board represents.

The strategy used is the **minimax strategy,** which is based on the assumption of optimal play by both players. The value of a position is a `COMPUTER_WIN` if optimal play implies that the computer can force a win. If the computer can force a draw but not a win, the value is `DRAW`; if the human player can force a win, the value is `HUMAN_WIN`. We want the computer to win, so we have `HUMAN_WIN < DRAW < COMPUTER_WIN`.

For the computer, the value of the position is the maximum of all the values of the positions that can result from making a move. Suppose that one move leads to a winning position, two moves lead to a drawing position, and six moves lead to a losing position. Then the starting position is a winning position because the computer can force the win. Moreover, the move that leads to the winning position is the move to make. For the human player we use minimum instead of the maximum.

---

6. Tic-tac-toe is played on a three-by-three board. Two players alternate placing their symbols on squares. The first to get three squares in a row, column, or a long diagonal wins.

```
class TicTacToe
{
  public:
    enum Side { HUMAN, COMPUTER, EMPTY };
    enum PositionVal{ HUMAN_WIN, DRAW, UNCLEAR, COMPUTER_WIN };

      // Constructor.
    TicTacToe( ) : board( 3, 3 ) { clearBoard( ); }

      // Find optimal move.
    int chooseMove( Side s, int & bestRow, int & bestColumn );
      // Play move, including checking legality
    bool playMove( Side s, int row, int column );

      // Simple supporting routines.
    void clearBoard( );                    // Make the board empty
    void getMove( );            // Get move from human; update board
    bool boardIsFull( ) const;  // Return true if board is full
    bool isAWin( Side s ) const;    // True if board shows a win
    const matrix<int> & getBoard( ) const    // Return the board
      { return board; }

  private:
    matrix<int> board;

      // Play a move, possibly clearing a square. No checks.
    void place( int row, int column, int piece = EMPTY )
      { board[ row ][ column ] = piece; }

      // Test if a square is empty.
    bool squareIsEmpty( int row, int column ) const
      { return board[ row ][ column ] == EMPTY; }

      // Compute static value of position (win, draw, etc.).
    int positionValue( ) const;
};
```

Figure 8.26 Interface for class `TicTacToe`.

```
// Return the static value of the current position.
int TicTacToe::positionValue( ) const
{
    return isAWin( COMPUTER ) ? COMPUTER_WIN :
           isAWin( HUMAN )    ? HUMAN_WIN    :
           boardIsFull( )     ? DRAW         : UNCLEAR;
}
```

Figure 8.27 Supporting routine for evaluating positions.

This approach suggests a recursive algorithm to determine the value of a position. Keeping track of the best move is a matter of bookkeeping once the basic algorithm to find the value of the position has been written. If the position is a terminal position (i.e., we can see right away that tic-tac-toe has been achieved or the board is full without tic-tac-toe), the position's value is immediate. Otherwise, we recursively try all moves, computing the value of each resulting position, and choose the maximum value. The recursive call then requires that the human player evaluate the value of the position. For the human player the value is the minimum of all the possible next moves because the human player is trying to force the computer to lose. Thus the recursive function `chooseMove`, shown in Figure 8.28 takes a parameter `s`, which indicates whose turn it is to move.

Lines 11 and 12 handle the base case of the recursion. If we have an immediate answer, we can return. Otherwise, we set some values at lines 14 to 21, depending on which side is moving. The code in lines 28 to 38 is executed once for each available move. We try the move at line 28, recursively evaluate the move at line 29 (saving the value), and then undo the move at line 30. Lines 33 and 34 test to determine whether this move is the best seen so far. If so, we adjust `value` at line 36 and record the move at line 37. At line 41 we return the value of the position; the move is stored in the parameters `bestRow` and `bestColumn`, which are passed by reference.

***Alpha–beta pruning* is an improvement to the minimax algorithm.**

Although the routine shown in Figure 8.28 optimally solves tic-tac-toe, it performs a lot of searching. Specifically, to choose the first move on an empty board, it makes 549,946 recursive calls (this number is obtained by running the program). By using some algorithmic tricks, we can compute the same information with fewer searches. One such technique is known as **alpha–beta pruning,** which is an improvement to the minimax algorithm. We describe this technique in detail in Chapter 11. Application of alpha–beta pruning reduces the number of recursive calls to only 18,297.

Summary

In this chapter we examined recursion and showed that it is a powerful problem-solving tool. Following are its fundamental rules, which you should never forget.

1. *Base cases:* Always have at least one case that can be solved without using recursion.
2. *Make progress:* Any recursive call must progress toward the base case.
3. *"You gotta believe":* Always assume that the recursive call works.

```
// Routine to compute optimal tic-tac-toe move.
int TicTacToe::chooseMove( Side s, int & bestRow,
                                  int & bestColumn )
{
    Side opp;               // The other side
    int reply;              // Value of opponent's reply
    int dc;                 // Placeholder
    int simpleEval;         // Result of an immediate evaluation
    int value;

    if( ( simpleEval = positionValue( ) ) != UNCLEAR )
        return simpleEval;

    if( s == COMPUTER )
    {
        opp = HUMAN; value = HUMAN_WIN;
    }
    else
    {
        opp = COMPUTER; value = COMPUTER_WIN;
    }

      // Search for a move.
    for( int row = 0; row < 3; row++ )
        for( int column = 0; column < 3; column++ )
            if( squareIsEmpty( row, column ) )
            {
                place( row, column, s );    // Try a move; then
                reply = chooseMove( opp, dc, dc );// Evaluate;
                place( row, column, EMPTY );       // then undo

                  // If s gets a better position; update
                if( s == COMPUTER && reply > value ||
                    s == HUMAN && reply < value )
                {
                    value = reply;
                    bestRow = row; bestColumn = column;
                }
            }

    return value;
}
```

Figure 8.28 A recursive routine for finding an optimal tic-tac-toe move.

4. *Compound interest rule:* Never duplicate work by solving the same instance of a problem in separate recursive calls.

Recursion has many uses, some of which we discussed in this chapter. Three important algorithm design techniques that are based on recursion are divide-and-conquer, dynamic programming, and backtracking.

In Chapter 9 we examine sorting. The fastest known sorting algorithm is recursive.

Objects of the Game

activation record The method by which the bookkeeping in a procedural language is done. A stack of activation records is used. (p. 275)

alpha–beta pruning An improvement to the minimax algorithm. (p. 310)

backtracking An algorithm that uses recursion to try all possibilities. (p. 308)

base case An instance that can be solved without recursion. Any recursive call must progress toward a base case. (p. 270)

basis In a proof by induction, the easy case that can be shown by hand. (p. 268)

divide-and-conquer algorithm A type of recursive algorithm that is generally very efficient. The recursion is the *divide* part, and the combining of recursive solutions is the *conquer* part. (p. 292)

driver routine A routine that tests the validity of the first case and then calls the recursive routine. (p. 273)

dynamic programming A technique that avoids the recursive explosion by recording answers in a table. (p. 303)

encryption An encoding scheme used in the transmitting of messages that cannot be read by other parties. (p. 289)

Fibonacci numbers A sequence of numbers in which the ith number is the sum of the two previous numbers. (p. 276)

greatest common divisor (gcd) The greatest common divisor of two integers is the largest integer that divides both of them. (p. 287)

greedy algorithm An algorithm that makes locally optimal decisions at each step—a simple but not always correct thing to do. (p. 304)

induction A proof technique used to establish theorems that hold for positive integers. (p. 267)

inductive hypothesis The hypothesis that a theorem is true for some arbitrary case and that, under this assumption, it is true for the next case. (p. 268)

leaf In a tree, a node with no children. (p. 279)

minimax strategy A strategy used for Tic-Tac-Toe and other strategic games, which is based on the assumption of optimal play by both players. (p. 308)

multiplicative inverse The solution $1 \le X < N$ to the equation $AX \equiv 1 (\text{mod } N)$. (p. 288)

public key cryptography A type of cryptography in which each participant publishes the code others can use to send the participant encrypted messages but keeps the decrypting code secret. (p. 292)

recursive function A function that directly or indirectly makes a call to itself. (p. 269)

RSA cryptosystem A popular encryption method. (p. 290)

rules of recursion 1. *Base case:* Always have at least one case that can be solved without using recursion. (p. 270); 2. *Make progress:* Any recursive call must progress toward a base case. (p. 270); 3. *"You gotta believe":* Always assume that the recursive call works. (p. 274); 4. *Compound interest rule:* Never duplicate work by solving the same instance of a problem in separate recursive calls. (p. 278)

telescoping sum A procedure that generates large numbers of canceling terms. (p. 300)

tree A widely used data structure that consists of a set of nodes and a set of edges that connect pairs of nodes. Throughout the text, we assume the tree is rooted. (p. 278)

Common Errors

1. The most common error in the use of recursion is forgetting a base case.
2. Be sure that each recursive call progresses toward a base case. Otherwise, the recursion is incorrect.
3. Overlapping recursive calls must be avoided because they tend to yield exponential algorithms.
4. Using recursion in place of a simple loop is bad style.
5. Recursive algorithms are analyzed by using a recursive formula. Do not assume that a recursive call takes linear time.

6. Violating copyright laws is another bad error. RSA is patented, but some uses are allowed. See the References section for more information.

On the Internet

Most of the chapter's code is provided, including a Tic-Tac-Toe program. An improved version of the Tic-Tac-Toe algorithm that uses fancier data structures is discussed in Chapter 11. The following are the filenames.

RecSum.cpp	The routine shown in Figure 8.1 with a simple `main`.
PrintInt.cpp	The routine given in Figure 8.4 for printing a number in any base, plus a `main`.
BinarySearchRec.cpp	Virtually the same as **BinarySearch.cpp** (in Chapter 7), but with the `binarySearch` shown in Figure 8.11.
Ruler.java	The routine shown in Figure 8.13, ready to run. It contains code that forces the drawing to be slow.
FractalStar.java	The routine given in Figure 8.15, ready to run. It contains code that allows the drawing to be slow.
Math.cpp	The math routines presented in Section 8.4, the primality testing routine, and a `main` that illustrates the RSA computations.
MaxSum.cpp	The four maximum contiguous subsequence sum routines.
MkChnge.cpp	The routine shown in Figure 8.25, with a simple `main`.
TicTacSlow.cpp	The Tic-Tac-Toe algorithm, with a primitive `main`.

Exercises

In Short

8.1. What are the four fundamental rules of recursion?

8.2. Modify the program given in Figure 8.1 so that zero is returned for negative `n`. Make the minimum number of changes.

8.3. Following are four alternatives for line 12 of the routine `power` (in Figure 8.16). Why is each alternative wrong?

```
HugeInt tmp = power( x * x, n/2, p );
HugeInt tmp = power( power( x, 2, p ), n/2, p );
HugeInt tmp = power( power( x, n/2, p ), 2, p );
HugeInt tmp = power( x, n/2, p ) * power( x, n/2, p ) % p;
```

8.4. Show how the recursive calls are processed in the calculation 2^{63}mod 37.

8.5. Compute gcd(1995, 1492).

8.6. Bob chooses p and q equal to 37 and 41, respectively. Determine acceptable values for the remaining parameters in the RSA algorithm.

8.7. Show that the greedy change-making algorithm fails if 5-cent pieces are not part of United States currency.

In Theory

8.8. Prove by induction the formula

$$F_N = \frac{1}{\sqrt{5}}\left(\left(\frac{1+\sqrt{5}}{2}\right)^N - \left(\frac{1-\sqrt{5}}{2}\right)^N\right)$$

8.9. Prove the following identities relating to the Fibonacci numbers.

a. $F_1 + F_2 + \cdots + F_N = F_{N+2} - 1$

b. $F_1 + F_3 + \cdots + F_{2N-1} = F_{2N}$

c. $F_0 + F_2 + \cdots + F_{2N} = F_{2N+1} - 1$

d. $F_{N-1}F_{N+1} = (-1)^N + F_N^2$

e. $F_1F_2 + F_2F_3 + \cdots + F_{2N-1}F_{2N} = F_{2N}^2$

f. $F_1F_2 + F_2F_3 + \cdots + F_{2N}F_{2N+1} = F_{2N+1}^2 - 1$

g. $F_N^2 + F_{N+1}^2 = F_{2N+1}$

8.10. Show that if $A \equiv B (\text{mod } N)$, then for any C, D, and P, the following are true.

a. $A + C \equiv B + C (\text{mod } N)$

b. $AD \equiv BD (\text{mod } N)$

c. $A^P = B^P (\text{mod } N)$

8.11. Prove that if $A \geq B$, then $A \text{ mod } B < A/2$. (*Hint:* Consider the cases $B \leq A/2$ and $B > A/2$ separately.) How does this result show that the running time of `gcd` is logarithmic?

8.12. Prove by induction the formula for the number of calls to the recursive function `fib` in Section 8.3.4.

8.13. Prove by induction that if $A > B \geq 0$ and the invocation `gcd(a,b)` performs $k \geq 1$ recursive calls, then $A \geq F_{k+2}$ and $B \geq F_{k+1}$.

8.14. Prove by induction that in the extended gcd algorithm, $|X| < B$ and $|Y| < A$.

8.15. Write an alternative gcd algorithm, based on the following observations (arrange that $A > B$).

a. $\gcd(A, B) = 2 \gcd(A/2, B/2)$ if A and B are both even.
b. $\gcd(A, B) = \gcd(A/2, B)$if A is even and B is odd.
c. $\gcd(A, B) = \gcd(A, B/2)$ if A is odd and B is even.
d. $\gcd(A, B) = \gcd((A + B)/2, (A - B)/2)$ if A and B are both odd.

8.16. Solve the following equation. Assume that $A \geq 1$, $B > 1$, and $P \geq 0$.

$$T(N) = AT(N/B) + O(N^k \log^P N).$$

8.17. Strassen's algorithm for matrix multiplication multiplies two $N \times N$ matrices by performing seven recursive calls to multiply two $N/2 \times N/2$ matrices. The additional overhead is quadratic. What is the running time of Strassen's algorithm?

In Practice

8.18. The `printInt` method shown in Figure 8.4 may incorrectly handle the case where $N =$ `INT_MIN`. Explain why and fix the method.

8.19. Write a recursive method that returns the number of 1s in the binary representation of N. Use the fact that this number equals the number of 1s in the representation of $N/2$, plus 1, if N is odd.

8.20. Implement the one comparison per level binary search recursively.

8.21. The maximum contiguous subsequence sum algorithm given in Figure 8.20 gives no indication of the actual sequence. Modify it so that it fills reference parameters `seqStart` and `seqEnd`, as in Section 6.3.

8.22. For the change-making problem, give an algorithm that computes the number of different ways to give exactly K cents in change.

8.23. The *subset sum problem* is as follows: Given N integers $A_1, A_2, \ldots, A_N$ and an integer K, is there a group of integers that sums exactly to K? Give an $O(NK)$ algorithm to solve this problem.

8.24. Give an $O(2^N)$ algorithm for the subset sum problem described in Exercise 8.23. (*Hint:* Use recursion.)

8.25. Write the routine with the declaration

```
void permute( const string & str );
```

that prints all the permutations of the characters in the string `str`. If `str` is `"abc"`, then the strings output are `abc`, `acb`, `bac`, `bca`, `cab`, and `cba`. Use recursion.

8.26. Explain what happens if in Figure 8.15 we draw the central square before making the recursive calls.

Programming Projects

8.27. The binomial coefficients $C(N, k)$ can be defined recursively as $C(N, 0) = 1$, $C(N, N) = 1$ and, for $0 < k < N$, $C(N, k) = C(N-1, k) + C(N-1, k-1)$. Write a function and give an analysis of the running time to compute the binomial coefficients

a. recursively.

b. by using dynamic programming.

8.28. Implement the RSA cryptosystem with a library `HugeInt` class. If one is not available, write your own.

8.29. Improve the `TicTacToe` class by making the supporting routines more efficient.

8.30. Let A be a sequence of N distinct sorted numbers $A_1, A_2, \ldots, A_N$ with $A_1 = 0$. Let B be a sequence of $N(N-1)/2$ numbers, defined by $B_{i,j} = A_i - A_j$ $(i < j)$. Let D be the sequence obtained by sorting B. Both B and D may contain duplicates. *Example:* $A = 0, 1, 5, 8$. Then $D = 1, 3, 4, 5, 7, 8$. Do the following.

a. Write a program that constructs D from A. This part is easy.

b. Write a program that constructs some sequence A that corresponds to D. Note that A is not unique. Use a backtracking algorithm.

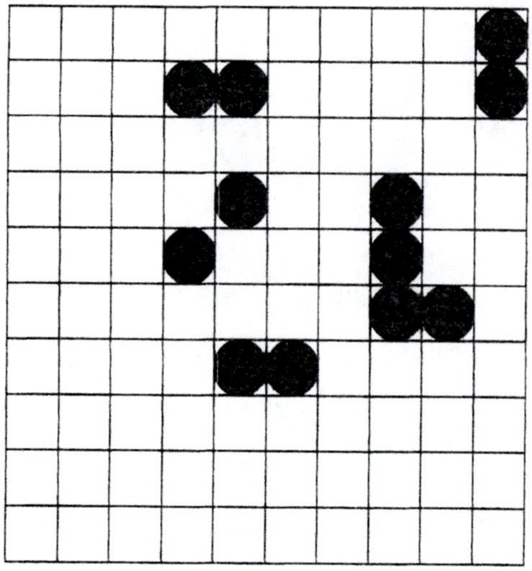

Figure 8.29 Grid for Exercise 8.31

8.31. Consider an $N \times N$ grid in which some squares are occupied. Two squares belong to the same group if they share a common edge. In Figure 8.29 there is one group of four occupied squares, three groups of two occupied squares, and two individual occupied squares. Assume that the grid is represented by a two-dimensional array. Write a program that

a. computes the size of a group when a square in the group is given.
b. computes the number of different groups.
c. lists all groups.

8.32. Write a program that expands a C++ source file's `#include` directives (recursively). Do so by replacing lines of the form

```
#include "filename"
```

with the contents of `filename`.

References

Much of this chapter is based on the discussion in [4]. A description of the RSA algorithm, with proof of correctness, is presented in [1], which also devotes a chapter to dynamic programming. The RSA algorithm is patented, and its commercial use requires payment of a licensing fee. However, an implementation of RSA, namely, *PGP* (pretty good privacy), is widely available, and free noncommercial use is allowed. See [3] for more details. The shape-drawing examples are adapted from [2].

1. T. H. Cormen, C. E. Leiserson, and R. L. Rivest, *Introduction to Algorithms,* MIT Press, Cambridge, Mass., 1990.
2. R. Sedgewick, *Algorithms in C++*, Addison-Wesley, Reading, Mass., 1992.
3. W. Stallings, *Protect Your Privacy: A Guide for PGP Users,* Prentice-Hall, Englewood Cliffs, N.J., 1995.
4. M. A. Weiss, *Efficient C Programming: A Practical Approach,* Prentice-Hall, Englewood Cliffs, N.J., 1995.

Chapter 9

Sorting Algorithms

Sorting is a fundamental application for computers. Much of the output eventually produced by a computation is sorted in some way, and many computations are made efficient by invoking a sorting procedure internally. Thus sorting is perhaps the most intensively studied and important operation in computer science.

In this chapter we discuss the problem of sorting an array of elements. We describe and analyze the various sorting algorithms. The sorts in this chapter can be done entirely in main memory, so the number of elements is relatively small (less than a few million). Sorts that cannot be performed in main memory and must be done on disk or tape are also quite important. We discuss this type of sorting, called *external sorting,* in Section 21.7.

This discussion of sorting is a blend of theory and practice. We present several algorithms that perform differently and show how an analysis of an algorithm's performance properties can help us make implementation decisions that are not obvious.

In this chapter, we show:

- that the insertion sort, previously shown in Figure 3.4, runs in quadratic time;
- how to code Shellsort, which is a simple and efficient algorithm that runs in subquadratic time;
- how to write the slightly more complicated $O(N \log N)$ mergesort and quicksort algorithms;
- that $\Omega(N \log N)$ comparisons are required for any general-purpose sorting algorithm; and
- how pointers can be used to sort large objects without incurring the excessive overhead associated with data movement.

9.1 Why Is Sorting Important?

Recall from Section 6.6 that searching a sorted array is much easier than searching an unsorted array. This is especially true for people. That is, finding a person's name in a phone book is easy, for example, but finding a phone number without knowing the person's name is virtually impossible. As a result, any significant amount of computer output is generally arranged in some sorted order so that it can be interpreted. The following are some more examples.

- Words in a dictionary are sorted (and case distinctions are ignored).
- Files in a directory are often listed in sorted order.
- The index of a book is sorted (and case distinctions are ignored).
- The card catalog in a library is sorted by both author and title.
- A listing of course offerings at a university is sorted, first by department and then by course number.
- Many banks provide statements that list checks in increasing order by check number.
- In a newspaper, the calendar of events in a schedule is generally sorted by date.
- Musical compact disks in a record store are generally sorted by recording artist.
- In the programs printed for graduation ceremonies, departments are listed in sorted order and then students in those departments are listed in sorted order.

An initial sort of the data can significantly enhance the performance of an algorithm.

Not surprisingly, much of the work in computing involves sorting. However, sorting also has indirect uses. For instance, suppose that we want to decide whether an array has any duplicates. Figure 9.1 shows a simple function that requires quadratic worst-case time. Sorting provides an alternative algorithm. That is, if we sort a copy of the array, then any duplicates will be adjacent to each other and can be detected in a single linear-time scan of the array. The cost of this algorithm is dominated by the time to sort, so if we can sort in subquadratic time, we have an improved algorithm. The performance of many algorithms is significantly enhanced when we initially sort the data.

The vast majority of significant programming projects use a sort somewhere, and in many cases, the sorting cost determines the running time. Thus we want to be able to implement a fast and reliable sort.

```
// Return true if a has duplicates; false otherwise.
template <class Comparable>
bool duplicates( const vector<Comparable> & a )
{
    const int n = a.size( );

    for( int i = 0; i < n; i++ )
        for( int j = i + 1; j < n; j++ )
            if( a[ i ] == a[ j ] )
                return true;    // Duplicate found

    return false;               // No duplicates found
}
```

Figure 9.1 A simple quadratic algorithm for detecting duplicates.

<table>
<tr><th>Operator</th><th>Definition</th></tr>
<tr><td><code>operator> (a, b)</code></td><td><code>return b < a;</code></td></tr>
<tr><td><code>operator>=(a, b)</code></td><td><code>return !(a < b);</code></td></tr>
<tr><td><code>operator<=(a, b)</code></td><td><code>return !(b < a);</code></td></tr>
<tr><td><code>operator!=(a, b)</code></td><td><code>return a < b || b < a;</code></td></tr>
<tr><td><code>operator==(a, b)</code></td><td><code>return !(a < b || b < a);</code></td></tr>
</table>

Figure 9.2 Deriving the relational and equality operators from `operator<`.

9.2 Preliminaries

The algorithms we describe in this chapter are all interchangeable. Each is passed an array containing the elements.

***A comparison-based sorting algorithm* makes ordering decisions only on the basis of comparisons.**

We require the existence of `operator<`, which can be used to place a consistent ordering on the input.[1] As shown in Figure 9.2, once one of the relational operators has been defined, all the relational and equality operators can also be meaningfully defined. Besides the copy assignment operator, these are the only operations allowed on the input data. An algorithm that makes ordering decisions only on the basis of comparisons is called a **comparison-based sorting algorithm.** In this chapter, N is the number of elements being sorted.

1. As shown in Section 5.2, changing the sorting interface by requiring a `Comparator` function object is straightforward.

9.3 Analysis of the Insertion Sort and Other Simple Sorts

The insertion sort is quadratic in the worst and average cases. It is fast if the input has already been sorted.

We discussed the simplest sort, the *insertion sort,* in Section 3.3. The implementation in Figure 9.3 repeats Figure 3.4 for convenience. Because of the nested loops, each of which can take N iterations, the insertion sort algorithm is $O(N^2)$. Furthermore, this bound is achievable because input in reverse order really does take quadratic time. A precise calculation shows that the tests at line 12 in Figure 9.3 can be executed at most $P + 1$ times for each value of P. Summing over all P gives a total time of

$$\sum_{P=1}^{N-1}(P+1) = \sum_{i=2}^{N} i = 2+3+4+\dots+N = \Theta(N^2).$$

However, if the input is presorted, the running time is $O(N)$ because the test at the top of the inner `for` loop always fails immediately. Indeed, if the input is almost sorted (we define *almost sorted* more rigorously shortly), the insertion sort will run quickly. Thus the running time depends not only on the amount of input, but also on the specific ordering of the input. Because of this wide variation, analyzing the average-case behavior of this algorithm is worthwhile. The average case turns out to be $\theta(N^2)$ for the insertion sort as well as a variety of other simple sorting algorithms.

An inversion measures unsortedness.

An **inversion** is a pair of elements that are out of order in an array. In other words, it is any ordered pair (i, j) having the property that $i < j$ but $A_i > A_j$. For example, the sequence {8, 5, 9, 2, 6, 3} has 10 inversions that correspond to the pairs (8, 5), (8, 2), (8, 6), (8, 3), (5, 2), (5, 3), (9, 2), (9, 6),

```
1  // InsertionSort: sort items in array a.
2  // Comparable: must have copy constructor, operator=,
3  //    and operator<.
4  template <class Comparable>
5  void insertionSort( vector<Comparable> & a )
6  {
7      for( int p = 1; p < a.size( ); p++ )
8      {
9          Comparable tmp = a[ p ];
10         int j;
11
12         for( j = p; j > 0 && tmp < a[ j - 1 ]; j-- )
13             a[ j ] = a[ j - 1 ];
14         a[ j ] = tmp;
15     }
16 }
```

Figure 9.3 The insertion sort template.

(9, 3), and (6, 3). Note that the number of inversions equals the total number of times that line 13 in Figure 9.3 is executed. This condition is always true because the effect of the assignment statement is to swap the two items `a[j]` and `a[j-1]`. (We avoid the actual excessive swapping by using the temporary variable, but nonetheless it is an abstract swap.) Swapping two elements that are out of place removes exactly one inversion, and a sorted array has no inversions. Thus, if there are I inversions at the start of the algorithm, we must have I implicit swaps. As $O(N)$ other work is involved in the algorithm, the running time of the insertion sort is $O(I + N)$, where I is the number of inversions in the original array. Thus the insertion sort runs in linear time if the number of inversions is $O(N)$.

We can compute precise bounds on the average running time of the insertion sort by computing the average number of inversions in an array. However, defining *average* is difficult. We can assume that there are no duplicate elements (if we allow duplicates, it is not even clear what the average number of duplicates is). We can also assume that the input is some arrangement of the first N integers (as only relative ordering is important); these arrangements are called *permutations*. We can further assume that all these permutations are equally likely. Under these assumptions we can establish Theorem 9.1.

Theorem 9.1

The average number of inversions in an array of N distinct numbers is $N(N-1)/4$.

Proof

For any array A of numbers, consider A_r, *which is the array in reverse order. For example, the reverse of array 1, 5, 4, 2, 6, 3 is 3, 6, 2, 4, 5, 1. Consider any two numbers (x, y) in the array, with* $y > x$. *In exactly one of A and* A_r, *this ordered pair represents an inversion. The total number of these pairs in an array A and its reverse* A_r *is* $N(N-1)/2$. *Thus an average array has half this amount, or* $N(N-1)/4$ *inversions.*

Theorem 9.1 implies that insertion sort is quadratic on average. It also can be used to provide a very strong lower bound about any algorithm that exchanges adjacent elements only. This lower bound is expressed as Theorem 9.2.

Theorem 9.2 *Any algorithm that sorts by exchanging adjacent elements requires $\Omega(N^2)$ time on average.*

Proof *The average number of inversions is initially $N(N-1)/4$. Each swap removes only one inversion, so $\Omega(N^2)$ swaps are required.*

The *lower-bound proof* shows that quadratic performance is inherent in any algorithm that sorts by performing adjacent comparisons.

This proof is an example of a **lower-bound proof.** It is valid not only for the insertion sort, which performs adjacent exchanges implicitly, but also for other simple algorithms such as the bubble sort and the selection sort, which we do not describe here. In fact, it is valid over an entire *class* of algorithms, including undiscovered ones, that perform only adjacent exchanges.

Unfortunately, any computational confirmation of a proof applying to a class of algorithms would require running all algorithms in the class. That is impossible because there are infinitely many possible algorithms. Hence any attempt at confirmation would apply only to the algorithms that are run. This restriction makes the confirmation of the validity of lower-bound proofs more difficult than the usual single-algorithm upper bounds that we are accustomed to. A computation could only *disprove* a lower-bound conjecture; it could never prove it in general.

Although this lower-bound proof is rather simple, proving lower bounds is in general much more complicated than proving upper bounds. Lower-bound arguments are much more abstract than their upper-bound counterparts.

This lower bound shows us that, for a sorting algorithm to run in subquadratic or $o(N^2)$ time, it must make comparisons and, in particular, exchanges between elements that are far apart. A sorting algorithm progresses by eliminating inversions. To run efficiently, it must eliminate more than just one inversion per exchange.

9.4 Shellsort

Shellsort is a subquadratic algorithm that works well in practice and is simple to code. The performance of Shellsort is highly dependent on the increment sequence and requires a challenging (and not completely resolved) analysis.

The first algorithm to improve on the insertion sort substantially was *Shellsort,* which was discovered in 1959 by Donald Shell. Though it is not the fastest algorithm known, **Shellsort** is a subquadratic algorithm whose code is only slightly longer than the insertion sort, making it the simplest of the faster algorithms.

Shell's idea was to avoid the large amount of data movement, first by comparing elements that were far apart and then by comparing elements that were less far apart, and so on, gradually shrinking toward the basic insertion sort. Shellsort uses a sequence $h_1, h_2, \ldots, h_t$ called the *increment sequence.*

Any increment sequence will do as long as $h_1 = 1$, but some choices are better than others. After a phase, using some increment h_k, we have $a[i] \le a[i + h_k]$ for every i where $i + h_k$ is a valid index; all elements spaced h_k apart are sorted. The array is then said to be h_k-sorted.

For example, Figure 9.4 shows an array after several phases of Shellsort. After a 5-sort, elements spaced five apart are guaranteed to be in correct sorted order. In the figure, elements spaced five apart are identically shaded and are sorted relative to each other. Similarly, after a 3-sort, elements spaced three apart are guaranteed to be in sorted order, relative to each other. An important property of Shellsort (which we state without proof) is that an h_k-sorted array that is then h_{k-1}-sorted remains h_k-sorted. If this were not the case, the algorithm would likely be of little value because work done by early phases would be undone by later phases.

In general, an h_k-sort requires that, for each position i in $h_k, h_{k+1}, \ldots, N - 1$, we place the element in the correct spot among $i, i - h_k, i - 2h_k$, and so on. Although this order does not affect the implementation, careful examination shows that an h_k-sort performs an insertion sort on h_k independent subarrays (shown in different shades in Figure 9.4). Therefore, not surprisingly, in Figure 9.6, which we come to shortly, lines 7 to 15 represent a *gap insertion sort*. In a gap insertion sort, after the loop has been executed, elements separated by a distance of `gap` in the array are sorted. For instance, when `gap` is 1, the loop is identical, statement by statement, to an insertion sort. Thus Shellsort is also known as **diminishing gap sort.**

A diminishing gap sort is another name for Shellsort.

As we have shown, when `gap` is 1 the inner loop is guaranteed to sort the array `a`. If `gap` is never 1, there is always some input for which the array cannot be sorted. Thus Shellsort sorts so long as `gap` eventually equals 1. The only issue remaining, then, is to choose the increment sequence.

Shell suggested starting `gap` at $N/2$ and halving it until it reaches 1, after which the program can terminate. Using these increments, Shellsort represents a substantial improvement over the insertion sort, despite the fact that it nests three `for` loops instead of two, which is usually inefficient. By altering the sequence of gaps, we can further improve the algorithm's performance. A

Shell's increment sequence is an improvement over the insertion sort (although better sequences are known).

Original	**81**	**94**	**11**	**96**	**12**	**35**	**17**	**95**	**28**	**58**	**41**	**75**	**15**
After 5-sort	35	17	11	28	12	41	75	15	96	58	81	94	95
After 3-sort	28	12	11	35	15	41	58	17	94	75	81	96	95
After 1-sort	11	12	15	17	28	35	41	58	75	81	94	95	96

Figure 9.4 Shellsort after each pass if the increment sequence is {1, 3, 5}.

N	Insertion Sort	Shellsort		
		Shell's increments	Odd gaps only	Dividing by 2.2
10,000	575	10	11	9
20,000	2,489	23	23	20
40,000	10,635	51	49	41
80,000	42,818	114	105	86
160,000	174,333	270	233	194
320,000	NA	665	530	451
640,000	NA	1,593	1,161	939

Figure 9.5 Running time (milliseconds) of the insertion sort and Shellsort for various increment sequences.

summary of Shellsort's performance with three different choices of increment sequences is shown in Figure 9.5.

9.4.1 Performance of Shellsort

The running time of Shellsort depends heavily on the choice of increment sequences, and in general the proofs can be rather involved. The average-case analysis of Shellsort is a long-standing open problem except for the most trivial increment sequences.

In the worst case, Shell's increments give quadratic behavior.

When Shell's increments are used, the worst case is $O(N^2)$. This bound is achievable if N is an exact power of 2, all the large elements are in even-indexed array positions, and all the small elements are in odd-indexed array positions. When the final pass is reached, all the large elements will still be in the even-indexed array positions, and all the small elements will still be in the odd-indexed array positions. A calculation of the number of remaining inversions shows that the final pass will require quadratic time. The fact that this is the worst that can happen follows from the fact that an h_k-sort consists of h_k insertion sorts of roughly N/h_k elements. Thus the cost of each pass is $O(h_k(N/h_k)^2)$, or $O(N^2/h_k)$. When we sum this cost over all the passes, we obtain $O(N^2\Sigma h_k)$. The increments are roughly a geometric series, so the sum is bounded by a constant. The result is a quadratic worst-case running time. We can also prove via a complex argument that when N is an exact power of 2 the average running time is $O(N^{3/2})$. Thus, on average, Shell's increments give a significant improvement over insertion sort.

```
1 // Shellsort.
2 template <class Comparable>
3 void shellsort( vector<Comparable> & a )
4 {
5     for( int gap = a.size( ) / 2; gap > 0;
6             gap = gap == 2 ? 1 : static_cast<int>( gap / 2.2 ) )
7         for( int i = gap; i < a.size( ); i++ )
8         {
9             Comparable tmp = a[ i ];
10            int j = i;
11
12            for( ; j >= gap && tmp < a[ j - gap ]; j -= gap )
13                a[ j ] = a[ j - gap ];
14            a[ j ] = tmp;
15        }
16 }
```

Figure 9.6 Shellsort implementation.

If consecutive increments are relatively prime, the performance of Shellsort is improved.

A minor change to the increment sequence can prevent the quadratic worst case from occurring. If we divide gap by 2 and it becomes even, we can add 1 to make it odd. We can then prove that the worst case is not quadratic but only $O(N^{3/2})$. Although the proof is complicated, the basis for it is that in this new increment sequence, consecutive increments share no common factors (whereas in Shell's increment sequence they do). Any sequence that satisfies this property (and whose increments decrease roughly geometrically) will have a worst-case running time of at most $O(N^{3/2})$.[2] The average performance of the algorithm with these new increments is unknown but seems to be $O(N^{5/4})$, based on simulations.

Dividing by 2.2 gives excellent performance in practice.

A third sequence, which performs well in practice but has no theoretical basis, is to divide by 2.2 instead of 2. This divisor appears to bring the average running time to below $O(N^{5/4})$—perhaps to $O(N^{7/6})$—but this case is completely unresolved. For 100,000 to 1,000,000 items, it typically improves performance by about 25 to 35 percent over Shell's Increments, although nobody knows why. A Shellsort implementation with this increment sequence is coded in Figure 9.6. The complicated code at line 6 is necessary to avoid setting gap to 0. If that happens, the algorithm is broken because we never see a 1-sort. Line 6 ensures that, if gap is about to be set to 0, it is reset to 1.[3]

2. To appreciate the subtlety involved, note that subtracting 1 instead of adding 1 does not work. For instance, if N is 186, the resulting sequence is 93, 45, 21, 9, 3, 1, which all share the common factor 3.
3. The newer syntax for compile-time casting is `static_cast`. It is preferable to the older forms because seeing that a cast is being performed is easier.

The entries in Figure 9.5 compare the performance of insertion sort and Shellsort, with various gap sequences. These results were obtained on a reasonably fast machine. We could easily conclude that Shellsort, even with the simplest gap sequence, provides a significant improvement over the insertion sort, at a cost of little additional code complexity. A simple change to the gap sequence can further improve performance. More improvement is possible (see in Exercise 9.24). Some of these improvements have theoretical backing, but no known sequence markedly improves the program shown in Figure 9.6.

Shellsort is a good choice for moderate amounts of input.

The performance of Shellsort is quite acceptable in practice, even for N in the tens of thousands. The simplicity of the code makes it the algorithm of choice for sorting up to moderately large input. It is also a fine example of a very simple algorithm with an extremely complex analysis.

9.5 Mergesort

***Mergesort* uses divide-and-conquer to obtain an $O(N \log N)$ running time.**

Recall from Section 8.5 that recursion can be used to develop subquadratic algorithms. Specifically, a divide-and-conquer algorithm in which two half-size problems are solved recursively with an $O(N)$ overhead results in an $O(N \log N)$ algorithm. Mergesort is such an algorithm. It offers a better bound, at least theoretically, than the bounds claimed for Shellsort.

The mergesort algorithm involves three steps.

1. If the number of items to sort is 0 or 1, return.
2. Recursively sort the first and second halves separately.
3. Merge the two sorted halves into a sorted group.

Merging of sorted arrays can be done in linear time.

To claim an $O(N \log N)$ algorithm, we need only to show that the merging of two sorted groups can be performed in linear time. In this section we show how to merge two input arrays, A and B, placing the result in a third array, C. We then provide a simple implementation of mergesort. The merge routine is the cornerstone of most external sorting algorithms, as demonstrated in Section 21.7.

9.5.1 Linear-Time Merging of Sorted Arrays

The basic merge algorithm takes two input arrays, A and B, an output array, C, and three counters, *Actr*, *Bctr*, and *Cctr*, which are initially set to the beginning of their respective arrays. The smaller of *A[Actr]* and *B[Bctr]* is copied to the next entry in C, and the appropriate counters are advanced. When either input array is exhausted, the rest of the other array is copied to C.

An example of how the merge routine works is provided for the following input:

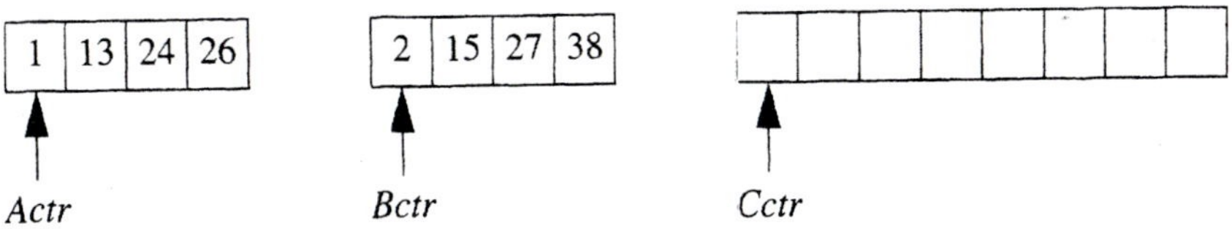

If array A contains 1, 13, 24, 26 and B contains 2, 15, 27, 38, the algorithm proceeds as follows. First, a comparison is made between 1 and 2, 1 is added to C, and 13 and 2 are compared:

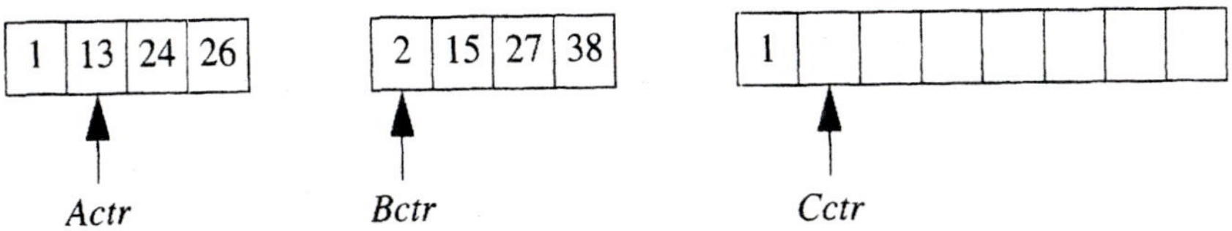

Then 2 is added to C, and 13 and 15 are compared:

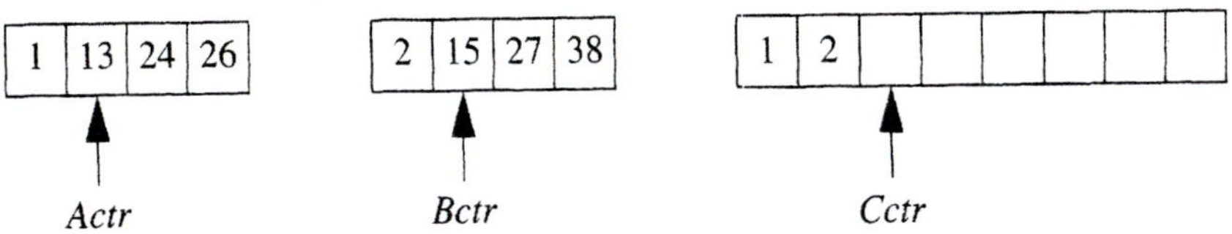

Next, 13 is added to C, and 24 and 15 are compared:

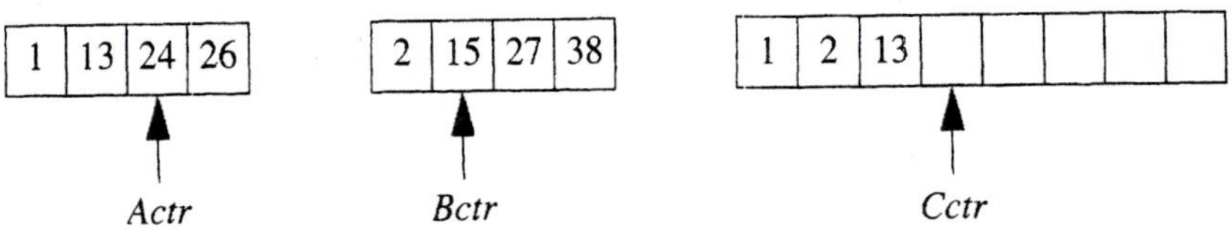

The process continues until 26 and 27 are compared:

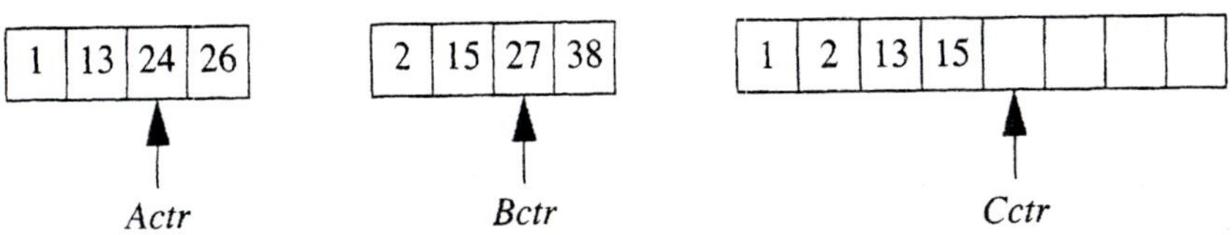

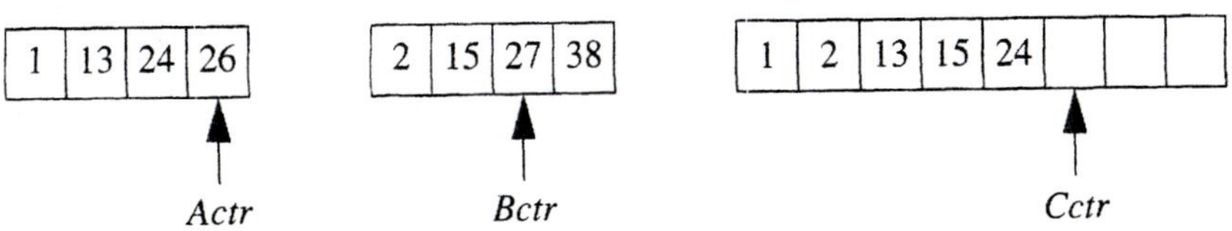

Then 26 is added to *C*, and the *A* array is exhausted:

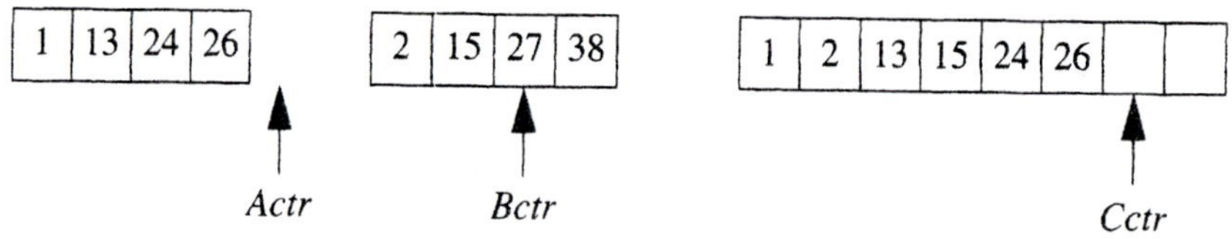

Finally, the remainder of the *B* array is copied to *C*:

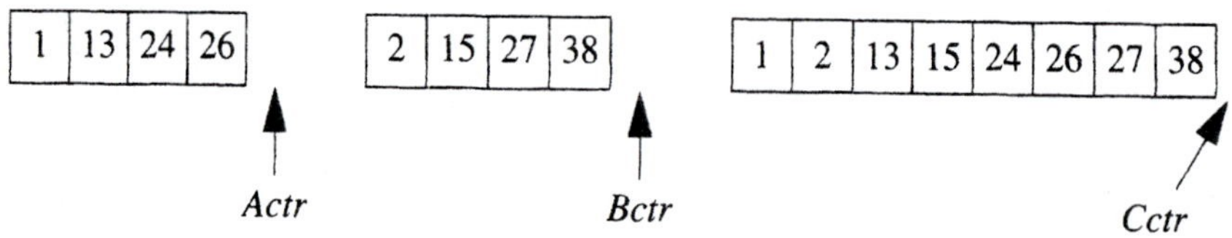

The time needed to merge two sorted arrays is linear because each comparison advances *Cctr* (thus limiting the number of comparisons). As a result, a divide-and-conquer algorithm that uses a linear merging procedure runs in $O(N \log N)$ worst-case time. This running time also represents the average-case and best-case times because the merging step is always linear.

An example of the mergesort algorithm would be sorting the 8-element array 24, 13, 26, 1, 2, 27, 38, 15. After recursively sorting the first four and last four elements, we obtain 1, 13, 24, 26, 2, 15, 27, 38. Then we merge the two halves, obtaining the final array 1, 2, 13, 15, 24, 26, 27, 38.

9.5.2 The Mergesort Algorithm

Mergesort uses linear extra memory, which is a practical liability.

A straightforward implementation of mergesort is shown in Figure 9.7. The one-parameter, nonrecursive `mergeSort` is a simple driver that declares a temporary array and calls recursive `mergeSort` with the boundaries of the array. The `merge` routine follows the description given in Section 9.5.1. It uses the first half of the array (indexed from `left` to `center`) as *A*, the second half (indexed from `center+1` to `right`) as *B*, and the temporary as *C*. Figure 9.8 implements the `merge` routine. The temporary is then copied back into the original array.

```
// Internal method that makes recursive calls.
// a is an array of Comparable items.
// tmpArray is an array to place the merged result.
// left is the left-most index of the subarray.
// right is the right-most index of the subarray.
template <class Comparable>
void mergeSort( vector<Comparable> & a,
                vector<Comparable> & tmpArray, int left, int right )
{
    if( left < right )
    {
        int center = ( left + right ) / 2;
        mergeSort( a, tmpArray, left, center );
        mergeSort( a, tmpArray, center + 1, right );
        merge( a, tmpArray, left, center + 1, right );
    }
}

// Mergesort algorithm (driver).
template <class Comparable>
void mergeSort( vector<Comparable> & a )
{
    vector<Comparable> tmpArray( a.size( ) );
    mergeSort( a, tmpArray, 0, a.size( ) - 1 );
}
```

Figure 9.7 Basic `mergeSort` routines.

Although mergesort's running time is $O(N \log N)$, it is hardly ever used for main memory sorts. The problem is that merging two sorted lists uses linear extra memory. The additional work involved in copying to the temporary array and back, throughout the algorithm, slows the sort considerably. This copying can be avoided by judiciously switching the roles of `a` and `tmpArray` at alternate levels in the recursion.

Excessive copying can be avoided with more work, but the linear extra memory cannot be removed without excessive time penalties.

A variant of mergesort can also be implemented nonrecursively. For serious internal sorting applications, however, the algorithm of choice is quicksort.

```
// Internal method that merges two sorted halves of a subarray.
// a is an array of Comparable items.
// tmpArray is an array to place the merged result.
// leftPos is the left-most index of the subarray.
// rightPos is the index of the start of the second half.
// rightEnd is the right-most index of the subarray.
template <class Comparable>
void merge( vector<Comparable> & a,
            vector<Comparable> & tmpArray,
            int leftPos, int rightPos, int rightEnd )
{
    int leftEnd = rightPos - 1;
    int tmpPos = leftPos;
    int numElements = rightEnd - leftPos + 1;

      // Main loop
    while( leftPos <= leftEnd && rightPos <= rightEnd )
        if( a[ leftPos ] <= a[ rightPos ] )
            tmpArray[ tmpPos++ ] = a[ leftPos++ ];
        else
            tmpArray[ tmpPos++ ] = a[ rightPos++ ];

    while( leftPos <= leftEnd )     // Copy rest of first half
        tmpArray[ tmpPos++ ] = a[ leftPos++ ];

    while( rightPos <= rightEnd )   // Copy rest of second half
        tmpArray[ tmpPos++ ] = a[ rightPos++ ];

      // Copy tmpArray back
    for( int i = 0; i < numElements; i++, rightEnd-- )
        a[ rightEnd ] = tmpArray[ rightEnd ];
}
```

Figure 9.8 The `merge` routine.

9.6 Quicksort

***Quicksort* is a fast divide-and-conquer algorithm, when properly implemented. In practice it is the fastest comparison-based sorting algorithm.**

As its name implies, **quicksort** is a fast divide-and-conquer algorithm; in practice it is the fastest sorting algorithm known. Its average running time is $O(N \log N)$. Its speed is mainly due to a very tight and highly optimized inner loop. It has quadratic worst-case performance, which can be made statistically unlikely to occur with a little effort. On the one hand, the quicksort algorithm is relatively simple to understand and prove correct because it relies on recursion. On the other hand, it is a tricky algorithm to implement because minute changes in the code can make significant differences in running time. We first describe the algorithm in broad terms. We then provide an analysis that shows its best-, worst-, and average-case running times. We use this analysis to make decisions about how to implement certain details in C++, such as the handling of duplicate items.

9.6.1 The Quicksort Algorithm

The basic algorithm *Quicksort*(S) consists of the following four steps.

The basic quicksort algorithm is recursive. Details include choosing the pivot, deciding how to partition, and dealing with duplicates. Wrong decisions give quadratic running times for a variety of common inputs.

1. If the number of elements in S is 0 or 1, then return.
2. Pick *any* element v in S. It is called the *pivot*.
3. *Partition* $S - \{v\}$ (the remaining elements in S) into two disjoint groups: $L = \{x \in S - \{v\} | x \leq v\}$ and $R = \{x \in S - \{v\} | x \geq v\}$.
4. Return the result of *Quicksort*(L) followed by v followed by *Quicksort*(R).

The *pivot* divides array elements into two groups: those smaller than the pivot and those larger than the pivot.

Several points stand out when we look at these steps. First, the base case of the recursion includes the possibility that S might be an empty set. This provision is needed because the recursive calls could generate empty subsets. Second, the algorithm allows any element to be used as the pivot. The **pivot** divides array elements into two groups: elements that are smaller than the pivot and elements that are larger than the pivot. The analysis performed here shows that some choices for the pivot are better than others. Thus, when we provide an actual implementation, we do not use just any pivot. Instead we try to make an educated choice.

In the *partition* step every element except the pivot is placed in one of two groups.

In the partition step, every element in S, except for the pivot, is placed in either L (which stands for the left-hand part of the array) or R (which stands for the right-hand part of the array). The intent is that elements that are smaller than the pivot go to L and that elements larger than the pivot go to R. The description in the algorithm, however, ambiguously describes what to do with elements equal to the pivot. It allows each instance of a duplicate to go into either subset, specifying only that it must go to one or the other. Part of a good C++ implementation is handling this case as efficiently as possible. Again, the analysis allows us to make an informed decision.

Figure 9.9 shows the action of quicksort on a set of numbers. The pivot is chosen (by chance) to be 65. The remaining elements in the set are partitioned into two smaller subsets. Each group is then sorted recursively. Recall that, by the third rule of recursion, we can assume that this step works. The sorted arrangement of the entire group is then trivially obtained. In a C++ implementation, the items would be stored in a part of an array delimited by `low` and `high`. After the partitioning step, the pivot would wind up in some

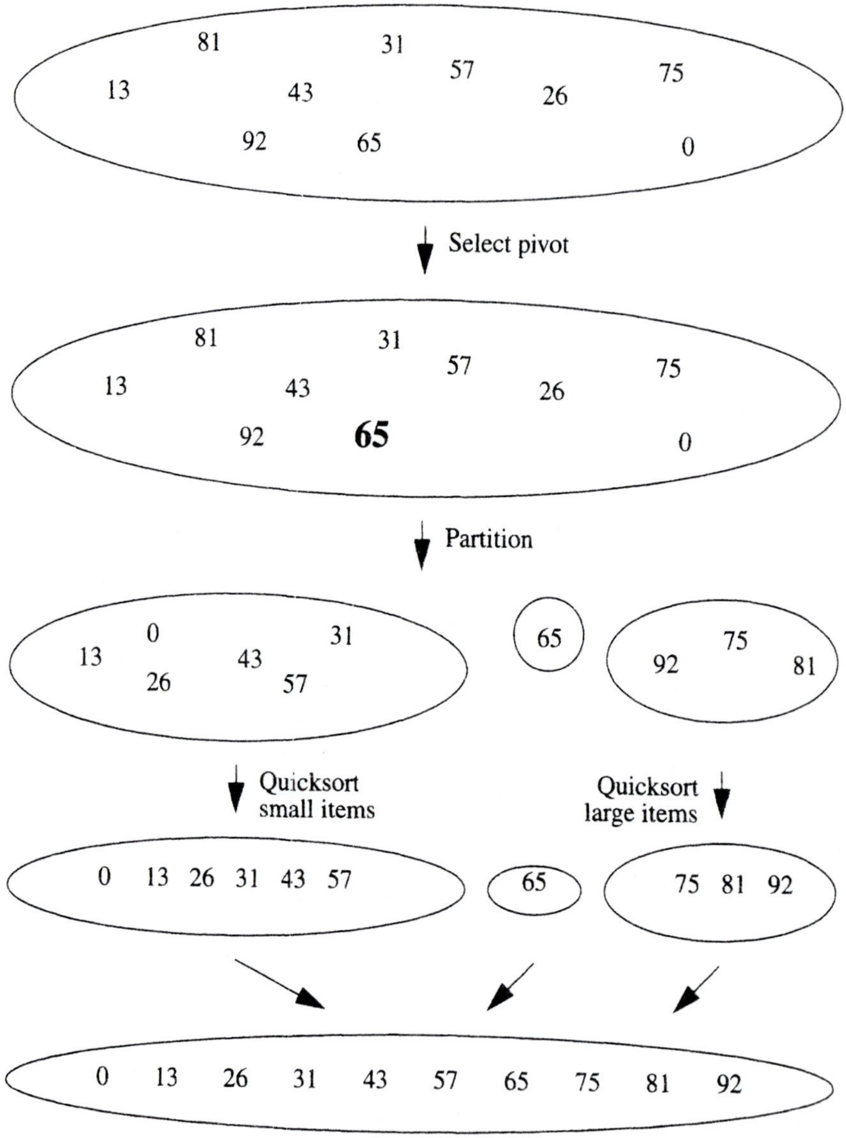

Figure 9.9 The steps of quicksort.

array cell `p`. The recursive calls would then be on the parts from `low` to `p-1` and then `p+1` to `high`.

Because recursion allows us to take the giant leap of faith, the correctness of the algorithm is guaranteed as follows.

- The group of small elements is sorted, by virtue of the recursion.

- The largest element in the group of small elements is not larger than the pivot, by virtue of the partition.
- The pivot is not larger than the smallest element in the group of large elements, by virtue of the partition.
- The group of large elements is sorted, by virtue of the recursion.

Although the correctness of the algorithm is easily established, why it is faster than mergesort is not clear. Like mergesort, it recursively solves two subproblems and requires linear additional work (in the form of the partitioning step). Unlike mergesort, however, quicksort subproblems are not guaranteed to be of equal size, which is bad for performance. However, quicksort is faster than mergesort because the partitioning step can be performed significantly faster than the merging step can. In particular, the partitioning step can be performed without using an extra array, and the code to implement it is very compact and efficient. This advantage makes up for the lack of equally sized subproblems.

Quicksort is fast because the partitioning step can be performed quickly and in place.

9.6.2 Analysis of Quicksort

The algorithm description leaves several questions unanswered: How do we choose the pivot? How do we perform the partition? What do we do if we see an element that is equal to the pivot? All these questions can dramatically affect the running time of the algorithm. We perform an analysis to help us decide how to implement the unspecified steps in quicksort.

Best Case

The best case for quicksort is that the pivot partitions the set into two equally sized subsets and that this partioning happens at each stage of the recursion. We then have two half-sized recursive calls plus linear overhead, which matches the performance of mergesort. The running time for this case is $O(N \log N)$. (We have not actually proved that this is the best case. Although such a proof is possible, we omit the details here.)

The best case occurs when the partition always splits into equal subsets. The running time is $O(N \log N)$.

Worst Case

Since equally sized subsets are good for quicksort, you might expect that unequally sized subsets are bad. That indeed is the case. Let us suppose that, in each step of the recursion, the pivot happens to be the smallest element. Then the set of small elements L will be empty, and the set of large elements R will have all the elements except the pivot. We then have to recursively call quicksort on subset R. Suppose also that $T(N)$ is the running time to quicksort N elements and we assume that the time to sort 0 or 1 element is just 1 time unit.

The worst case occurs when the partition repeatedly generates an empty subset. The running time is $O(N^2)$.

Suppose further that we charge N units to partition a set that contains N elements. Then for $N > 1$, we obtain a running time that satisfies

$$T(N) = T(N-1) + N. \tag{9.1}$$

In other words, Equation 9.1 states that the time required to quicksort N items equals the time to sort recursively the $N - 1$ items in the subset of larger elements plus the N units of cost to perform the partition. This assumes that in each step of the iteration we are unfortunate enough to pick the smallest element as the pivot. To simplify the analysis, we normalize by throwing out constant factors and solve this recurrence by telescoping Equation 9.1 repeatedly:

$$\begin{aligned} T(N) &= T(N-1) + N; \\ T(N-1) &= T(N-2) + (N-1); \\ T(N-2) &= T(N-3) + (N-2); \\ &\cdots \\ T(2) &= T(1) + 2. \end{aligned} \tag{9.2}$$

When we add everything in Equation 9.2, we obtain massive cancellations, yielding

$$T(N) = T(1) + 2 + 3 + \cdots + N = \frac{N(N+1)}{2} = O(N^2). \tag{9.3}$$

This analysis verifies the intuition that an uneven split is bad. We spend N units of time to partition and then have to make a recursive call for $N - 1$ elements. Then we spend $N - 1$ units to partition that group, only to have to make a recursive call for $N - 2$ elements. In that call we spend $N - 2$ units performing the partition, and so on. The total cost of performing all the partitions throughout the recursive calls exactly matches what is obtained in Equation 9.3. This result tells us that, when implementing the selection of the pivot and the partitioning step, we do not want to do anything that might encourage the size of the subsets to be unbalanced.

Average Case

The average case is $O(N \log N)$. Although this seems intuitive, a formal proof is required.

The first two analyses tell us that the best and worst cases are widely different. Naturally, we want to know what happens in the average case. We would expect that, as each subproblem is half the original on average, the $O(N \log N)$ would now become an average-case bound. Such an expectation, although correct for the particular quicksort application we examine here, does not constitute a formal proof. Averages cannot be thrown around lightly. For example, suppose that we have a pivot algorithm guaranteed to select only the smallest or largest element, each with probability 1/2. Then the average size of the small group of elements is roughly $N/2$, as is the average size of the large group of elements (because each is equally likely to have 0 or $N-1$ elements). But the running time of quicksort with that pivot selection is always quadratic because we always get a poor split of elements. Thus we must carefully assign the label *average.* We can argue that the group of small elements is as likely to contain 0, 1, 2, ..., or $N-1$ elements, which is also true for the group of large elements. Under this assumption we can establish that the average-case running time is indeed $O(N \log N)$.

Because the cost to quicksort N items equals N units for the partitioning step plus the cost of the two recursive calls, we need to determine the average cost of each of the recursive calls. If $T(N)$ represents the average cost to quicksort N elements, the average cost of each recursive call equals the average—over all possible subproblem sizes—of the average cost of a recursive call on the subproblem:

The average cost of a recursive call is obtained by averaging the costs of all possible subproblem sizes.

$$T(L) = T(R) = \frac{T(0) + T(1) + T(2) + \cdots + T(N-1)}{N}. \qquad (9.4)$$

Equation 9.4 states that we are looking at the costs for each possible subset size and averaging them. As we have two recursive calls plus linear time to perform the partition, we obtain

$$T(N) = 2\left(\frac{T(0) + T(1) + T(2) + \cdots + T(N-1)}{N}\right) + N. \qquad (9.5)$$

To solve Equation 9.5, we begin by multiplying both sides by N, obtaining

The average running time is given by $T(N)$. We solve Equation 9.5 by removing all but the most recent recursive value of T.

$$NT(N) = 2(T(0) + T(1) + T(2) + \cdots + T(N-1)) + N^2. \qquad (9.6)$$

We then write Equation 9.6 for the case $N-1$, with the idea being that we can greatly simplify the equation by subtraction. Doing so yields

$$(N-1)T(N-1) = 2(T(0) + T(1) + \cdots + T(N-2)) + (N-1)^2 \qquad (9.7)$$

Now, if we subtract Equation 9.7 from Equation 9.6, we obtain

$$NT(N) - (N-1)T(N-1) = 2T(N-1) + 2N - 1.$$

We rearrange terms and drop the insignificant -1 on the right-hand side, obtaining

$$NT(N) = (N+1)T(N-1) + 2N. \qquad (9.8)$$

Once we have $T(N)$ in terms of $T(N-1)$ only, we attempt to telescope.

We now have a formula for $T(N)$ in terms of $T(N-1)$ only. Again the idea is to telescope, but Equation 9.8 is in the wrong form. If we divide Equation 9.8 by $N(N+1)$, we get

$$\frac{T(N)}{N+1} = \frac{T(N-1)}{N} + \frac{2}{N+1}.$$

Now we can telescope:

$$\begin{aligned}
\frac{T(N)}{N+1} &= \frac{T(N-1)}{N} + \frac{2}{N+1};\\
\frac{T(N-1)}{N} &= \frac{T(N-2)}{N-1} + \frac{2}{N};\\
\frac{T(N-2)}{N-1} &= \frac{T(N-3)}{N-2} + \frac{2}{N-1};\\
&\cdots\\
\frac{T(2)}{3} &= \frac{T(1)}{2} + \frac{2}{3}.
\end{aligned} \tag{9.9}$$

If we add all the equations in Equation 9.9, we have

$$\begin{aligned}
\frac{T(N)}{N+1} &= \frac{T(1)}{2} + 2\left(\frac{1}{3} + \frac{1}{4} + \cdots + \frac{1}{N} + \frac{1}{N+1}\right)\\
&= 2\left(1 + \frac{1}{2} + \frac{1}{3} + \cdots + \frac{1}{N+1}\right) - \frac{5}{2}\\
&= O(\log N).
\end{aligned} \tag{9.10}$$

We use the fact that the *N*th harmonic number is *O*(log*N*).

The last line in Equation 9.10 follows from Theorem 6.5. When we multiply both sides by $N + 1$, we obtain the final result:

$$T(N) = O(N \log N). \tag{9.11}$$

9.6.3 Picking the Pivot

Now that we have established that quicksort will run in $O(N \log N)$ time on average, our primary concern is to ensure that the worst case does not occur. By performing a complex analysis, we can compute the standard deviation of quicksort's running time. The result is that, if a single random permutation is presented, the running time used to sort it will almost certainly be close to the average. Thus we must see to it that degenerate inputs do not result in bad running times. Degenerate inputs include data that have already been sorted and data that contain only N completely identical elements. Sometimes it is the easy cases that give algorithms trouble.

A Wrong Way

The popular, uninformed choice is to use the first element (i.e., the element in position `low`) as the pivot. This selection is acceptable if the input is random, but if the input has been presorted or is in reverse order, the pivot provides a poor partition because it is an extreme element. Moreover, this behavior will continue recursively. As we demonstrated earlier in the chapter, we would end up with quadratic running time to do absolutely nothing. Needless to say, that would be embarrassing. *Never* use the first element as the pivot.

Picking the pivot is crucial to good performance. Never choose the first element as pivot.

Another popular alternative is to choose the larger of the first two distinct keys[4] as the pivot, but this selection has the same bad effects as choosing the first key. Stay away from any strategy that looks only at some key near the front or end of the input group.

A Safe Choice

A perfectly reasonable choice for the pivot is the middle element (i.e., the element in array cell `(low+high)/2`). When the input has already been sorted, this selection gives the perfect pivot in each recursive call. Of course, we could construct an input sequence that forces quadratic behavior for this strategy (see Exercise 9.8). However, the chances of randomly running into a case that took even twice as long as the average case is extremely small.

The middle element is a reasonable but passive choice.

Median-of-Three Partitioning

Choosing the middle element as the pivot avoids the degenerate cases that arise from nonrandom inputs. Note that this is a passive choice, however. That is, we do not attempt to choose a good pivot. Instead, we merely try to avoid picking a bad pivot. Median-of-three partitioning is an attempt to pick a better than average pivot. In **median-of-three partitioning,** the median of the first, middle, and last elements is used as the pivot.

In *median-of-three partitioning,* the median of the first, middle, and last elements is used as the pivot. This approach simplifies the partitioning stage of quicksort.

The median of a group of N numbers is the $\lceil N/2 \rceil$th smallest number. The best choice for the pivot clearly is the median because it guarantees an even split of the elements. Unfortunately, the median is hard to calculate, which would slow quicksort considerably. So, we want to get a good estimate of the median without spending too much time doing so. We can obtain such an estimate by sampling—the classic method used in opinion polls. That is, we pick a subset of these numbers and find their median. The larger the sample, the more accurate is the estimate. However the larger sample takes longer to evaluate. A sample size of 3 gives a small improvement in the average running time of quicksort and also simplifies the resulting partitioning code by

4. In a complex object, the *key* is usually the part of the object on which the comparison is based.

eliminating some special cases. Large sample sizes do not significantly improve performance and thus are not worth using.

The three elements used in the sample are the first, middle, and last elements. For instance, with input 8, 1, 4, 9, 6, 3, 5, 2, 7, 0, the leftmost element is 8, the rightmost element is 0, and the center element is 6; thus the pivot would be 6. Note that for already sorted items, we keep the middle element as the pivot, and in this case, the pivot is the median.

9.6.4 A Partitioning Strategy

There are several commonly used partitioning strategies. The one that we describe in this section gives good results. The simplest partitioning strategy consists of three steps. In Section 9.6.6 we show the improvements that occur when median-of-three pivot selection is used.

Step 1: Swap the pivot with the element at the end.

The first step in the partitioning algorithm is to get the pivot element out of the way by swapping it with the last element. The result for our sample input is shown in Figure 9.10. The pivot element is shown in the darkest shade at the end of the array.

For now we assume that all the elements are distinct and leave for later what to do in the presence of duplicates. As a limiting case, our algorithm must work properly when *all* the elements are identical.

Step 2: Run `i` from left to right and `j` from right to left. When `i` encounters a large element, `i` stops. When `j` encounters a small element, `j` stops. If `i` and `j` have not crossed, swap their items and continue. Otherwise, stop this loop.

In step 2, we use our partitioning strategy to move all the small elements to the left in the array and all the large elements to the right. *Small* and *large* are relative to the pivot. In Figures 9.10–9.15, white cells are those that we know are correctly placed. The lightly shaded cells are not necessarily correctly placed.

We search from left to right, looking for a large element, using a counter `i`, initialized at position `low`. We also search from right to left, looking for a small element, using a counter `j`, initialized to start at `high-1`. Figure 9.11 shows that the search for a large element stops at 8 and the search for a small element stops at 2. These cells have been lightly shaded. Note that, by skipping past 7, we know that 7 is not small and thus is correctly placed. Thus it is a white cell. Now, we have a large element, 8, on the left-hand side of the array and a small element, 2, on the right-hand side of the array. We must swap these two elements to place them correctly, as shown in Figure 9.12.

As the algorithm continues, `i` stops at large element 9 and `j` stops at small element 5. Once again, elements that `i` and `j` skip during the scan are guaranteed to be correctly placed. Figure 9.13 shows the result: The ends of the array (not counting the pivot) are filled with correctly placed elements.

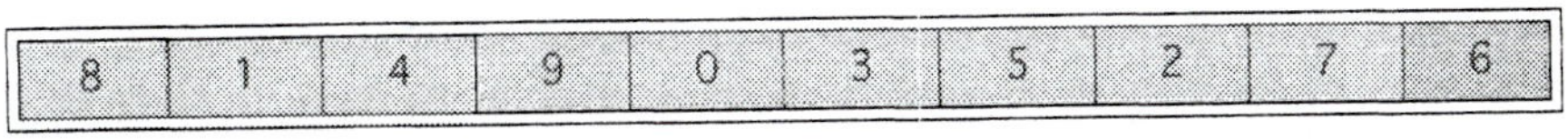

Figure 9.10 Partitioning algorithm: Pivot element 6 is placed at the end.

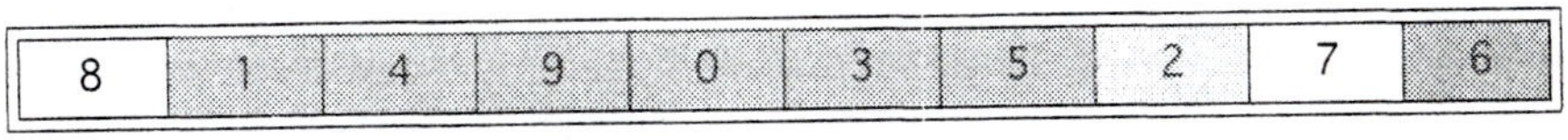

Figure 9.11 Partitioning algorithm: `i` stops at large element 8; `j` stops at small element 2.

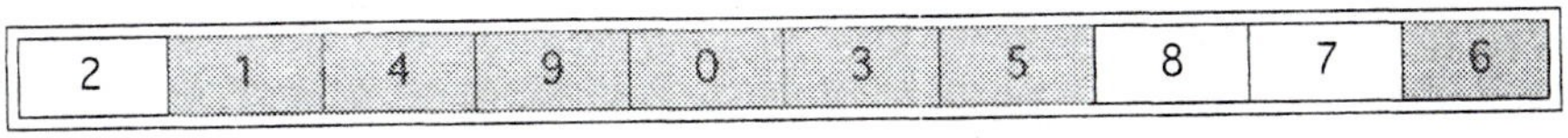

Figure 9.12 Partitioning algorithm: The out-of-order elements 8 and 2 are swapped.

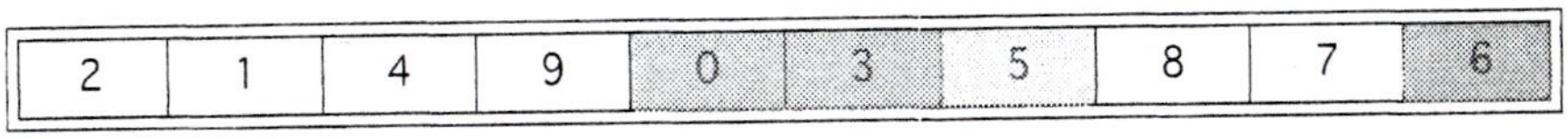

Figure 9.13 Partitioning algorithm: `i` stops at large element 9; `j` stops at small element 5.

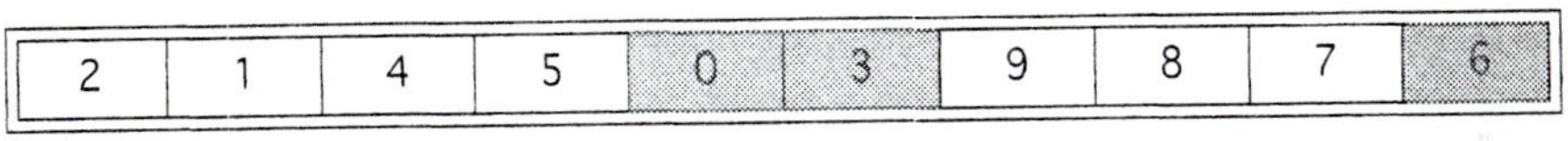

Figure 9.14 Partitioning algorithm: The out-of-order elements 9 and 5 are swapped.

Next, swap the elements that `i` and `j` are indexing, as shown in Figure 9.14. The scan continues, with `i` stopping at large element 9 and `j` stopping at small element 3. However, at this point `i` and `j` have crossed positions in the array. Consequently, a swap would be useless. Hence Figure 9.15 shows that the item being accessed by `j` is already correctly placed and should not move.

Step 3: Swap the element in position `i` with the pivot.

Figure 9.15 shows that all but two items are correctly placed. Wouldn't it be nice if we could just swap them and be done? Well, we can. All we need to do is swap the element in position `i` and the element in the last cell (the pivot), as shown in Figure 9.16. The element that `i` is indexing clearly is large, so moving it to the last position is fine.

Note that the partitioning algorithm requires no extra memory and that each element is compared exactly once with the pivot. When the code is written, this approach translates to a very tight inner loop.

2	1	4	5	0	3	9	8	7	6

Figure 9.15 Partitioning algorithm: `i` stops at large element 9; `j` stops at small element 3.

2	1	4	5	0	3	6	8	7	9

Figure 9.16 Partitioning algorithm: Swap pivot and element in position `i`.

9.6.5 Keys Equal to the Pivot

One important detail that we must consider is how to handle keys that are equal to the pivot. Should `i` stop when it encounters a key equal to the pivot, and should `j` stop when it encounters a key equal to the pivot? Counters `i` and `j` should do the same thing; otherwise, the partitioning step is biased. For instance, if `i` stops and `j` does not, all keys that are equal to the pivot wind up on the right-hand side.

Let us consider the case in which all elements in the array are identical. If both `i` and `j` stop, many swaps will occur between identical elements. Although these actions seem useless, the positive effect is that `i` and `j` cross in the middle, so when the pivot is replaced the partition creates two nearly equal subsets. Thus the best-case analysis applies, and the running time is $O(N \log N)$.

If neither `i` nor `j` stops, then `i` winds up at the last position (assuming of course that it does stop at the boundary), and no swaps are performed. This result seems great until we realize that the pivot is then placed as the last element because that is the last cell that `i` touches. The result is widely uneven subsets and a running time that matches the worst-case bound of $O(N^2)$. The effect is the same as using the first element as a pivot for presorted input: It takes quadratic time to do nothing.

Counters `i` and `j` must stop when they encounter an item equal to the pivot to guarantee good performance.

We conclude that doing the unnecessary swaps and creating even subsets is better than risking widely uneven subsets. Therefore we have both `i` and `j` stop if they encounter an element equal to the pivot. This action turns out to be the only one of the four possibilities that does not take quadratic time for this input.

At first glance, worrying about an array of identical elements may seem silly. After all, why would anyone want to sort 5000 identical elements? However, recall that quicksort is recursive. Suppose that there are 100,000 elements, of which 5000 are identical. Eventually quicksort could make the recursive call on only the 5000 identical elements. Then, ensuring that 5000 identical elements can be sorted efficiently really is important.

9.6.6 Median-of-Three Partitioning

When we do median-of-three partitioning, we can do a simple optimization that saves a few comparisons and also greatly simplifies the code. Figure 9.17 shows the original array.

Recall that median-of-three partitioning requires that we find the median of the first, middle, and last elements. The easiest way to do so is to sort them in the array. The result is shown in Figure 9.18. Note the resulting shading: The element that winds up in the first position is guaranteed to be smaller than (or equal to) the pivot, and the element in the last position is guaranteed to be larger than (or equal to) the pivot. This outcome tells us four things.

Computing the median-of-three involves sorting three elements. Hence we can give the partitioning step a head start and also never worry about running off the end of the array.

- We should not swap the pivot with the element in the last position. Instead, we should swap it with the element in the next-to-last position, as shown in Figure 9.19.
- We can start `i` at `low+1` and `j` at `high-2`.
- We are guaranteed that, whenever `i` searches for a large element, it will stop because in the worst case it will encounter the pivot (and we stop on equality).
- We are guaranteed that, whenever `j` searches for a small element, it will stop because in the worst case it will encounter the first element (and we stop on equality).

All of these optimizations are incorporated into the final C++ code.

8	1	4	9	6	3	5	2	7	0

Figure 9.17 Original array.

0	1	4	9	6	3	5	2	7	8

Figure 9.18 Result of sorting three elements (first, middle, and last).

0	1	4	9	7	3	5	2	6	8

Figure 9.19 Result of swapping the pivot with next-to-last element.

9.6.7 Small Arrays

Sort 10 or fewer items by insertion sort. Place this test in the recursive quicksort routine.

Our final optimization concerns small arrays. Is using a high-powered routine such as quicksort worthwhile when there are only 10 elements to sort? The answer is of course not. A simple routine, such as the insertion sort, probably is faster for small arrays. The recursive nature of quicksort tells us that we would generate many calls that have only small subsets. Thus testing the size of the subset is worthwhile. If it is smaller than some cutoff, we apply insertion sort; otherwise, we use quicksort.

A good cutoff is 10 elements, although any cutoff between 5 and 20 is likely to produce similar results. The actual best cutoff is machine dependent. Using a cutoff saves us from degenerate cases. For example, finding the median of three elements does not make much sense when there are not three elements.

In the past, many thought that an even better alternative was to leave the array slightly unsorted by doing absolutely nothing when the subset size was below the cutoff. Because the insertion sort is so efficient for nearly sorted arrays, we could show mathematically that running a final insertion sort to clean up the array was faster than running all the smaller insertion sorts. The savings were roughly the overhead of the insertion sort function calls.

Now, function calls are not as expensive as they used to be. Furthermore a second scan of the array for the insertion sort is expensive. Because of a technique called *caching,* we are better off doing the insertion sort on the small arrays. Localized memory accesses are faster than nonlocalized accesses. On many machines, touching memory twice in one scan is faster than touching memory once in each of two separate scans.

The idea of combining a second sorting algorithm when recursive calls to quicksort seem inappropriate can also be used to guarantee an $O(N \log N)$ worst-case for quicksort. In Exercise 9.19 you are asked to explore combining quicksort and mergesort to get quicksort's average-case performance almost all the time with mergesort's worst-case guarantee. In practice, instead of mergesort we use another algorithm, namely *heapsort,* which we discuss in Section 21.6.

9.6.8 C++ Quicksort Routine

We use a driver to set things up.

The actual implementation of quicksort is shown in Figure 9.20. The one-parameter `quicksort`, declared at lines 42 to 46, is merely a driver that calls the recursive `quicksort`. Thus we discuss only the implementation of the recursive `quicksort`.

At line 6 we test for small subarrays and call the insertion sort (not shown) when the problem instance is below some specified value given by

```
// Internal quicksort method that makes recursive calls.
// Uses median-of-three partitioning and a cutoff.
template <class Comparable>
void quicksort( vector<Comparable> & a, int low, int high )
{
    if( low + CUTOFF > high )
        insertionSort( a, low, high );
    else
    {
          // Sort low, middle, high
        int middle = ( low + high ) / 2;
        if( a[ middle ] < a[ low ] )
            swap( a[ low ], a[ middle ] );
        if( a[ high ] < a[ low ] )
            swap( a[ low ], a[ high ] );
        if( a[ high ] < a[ middle ] )
            swap( a[ middle ], a[ high ] );

          // Place pivot at position high - 1
        Comparable pivot = a[ middle ];
        swap( a[ middle ], a[ high - 1 ] );

          // Begin partitioning
        int i, j;
        for( i = low, j = high - 1; ; )
        {
            while( a[ ++i ] < pivot ) { }
            while( pivot < a[ --j ] ) { }
            if( i < j )
                swap( a[ i ], a[ j ] );
            else
                break;
        }
        swap( a[ i ], a[ high - 1 ] );  // Restore pivot

        quicksort( a, low, i - 1 );     // Sort small elements
        quicksort( a, i + 1, high );    // Sort large elements
    }
}

// Quicksort algorithm (driver).
template <class Comparable>
void quicksort( vector<Comparable> & a )
{
    quicksort( a, 0, a.size( ) - 1 );
}
```

Figure 9.20 Quicksort with median-of-three partitioning and cutoff for small arrays.

the constant `CUTOFF`. Otherwise, we proceed with the recursive procedure. Lines 11 to 17 sort the low, middle, and high elements in place. In keeping with our previous discussion, we use the middle element as the pivot and swap it with the element in the next-to-last position at lines 20 and 21. We then do the partitioning phase. We initialize the counters `i` and `j` to 1 past their true initial values because the prefix increment and decrement operators will immediately adjust them before the array accesses at lines 27 and 28. When the first `while` loop at line 27 exits, `i` will be indexing an element that is greater than or possibly equal to the pivot. Likewise, when the second loop ends, `j` will be indexing an element that is less than or possibly equal to the pivot. If `i` and `j` have not crossed, these elements are swapped and we continue scanning. Otherwise, the scan is terminated and the pivot is restored at line 34. The sort is finished when the two recursive calls are made at lines 36 and 37.

The inner loop of quicksort is very tight and efficient.

The fundamental operations occur at lines 27 through 30. The scans consist of simple operations: increments, array accesses, and simple comparisons, accounting for the "quick" in quicksort. To ensure that the inner loops are tight and efficient, we want to be sure that the swap at line 30 comprises the three assignments that we expect and does not incur the overhead of a function call. Thus we declare that the `swap` routine is an inline function, or in some cases, we write the three assignments explicitly (e.g., if the compiler exercises its right to ignore the inline request).

Quicksort is a classic example of using an analysis to guide program implementation.

Although the code looks straightforward now, that is only because of the analysis we performed prior to coding. Additionally, some traps are still lurking (see Exercise 9.15). Quicksort is a classic example of using an analysis to guide a program implementation.

9.7 Quickselect

***Selection* is finding the *k*th smallest element of an array.**

A problem closely related to sorting is **selection,** or finding the kth smallest element in an array of N items. An important special case is finding the median, or the $N/2$th smallest element. Obviously, we can sort the items, but as selection requests less information than sorting, we hope that selection would be a faster process. That turns out to be true. By making a small change to quicksort, we can solve the selection problem in linear time on average, giving us the algorithm quickselect. The steps for *Quickselect(S, k)* are as follows.

1. If the number of elements in S is 1, presumably k is also 1, so we can return the single element in S.
2. Pick any element v in S. It is the pivot.

3. Partition $S - \{v\}$ into L and R, exactly as was done for quicksort.
4. If k is less than or equal to the number of elements in L, the item we are searching for must be in L. Call *Quickselect*(L, k) recursively. Otherwise, if k is exactly equal to 1 more than the number of items in L, the pivot is the kth smallest element, and we can return it as the answer. Otherwise, the kth smallest element lies in R, and it is the $(k - |L| - 1)$th smallest element in R. Again, we can make a recursive call and return the result.

Quickselect makes only one recursive call, compared to quicksort's two. The worst case of quickselect is identical to that of quicksort and is quadratic. It occurs when one of the recursive calls is on an empty set. In such cases quickselect does not save much. We can show that the average time is linear, however, by using an analysist similar to that used for quicksort (see Exercise 9.9).

***Quickselect* is used to perform a selection. It is similar to quicksort but makes only one recursive call. The average running time is linear.**

The implementation of quickselect, shown in Figure 9.21, is simpler than our abstract description implies. Except for the extra parameter, k, and the recursive calls, the algorithm is identical to quicksort. When it terminates, the kth smallest element is in its correct position in the array. As the array begins at index 0, the fourth smallest element is in position 3. Note that the original ordering is destroyed. If this situation is undesirable, we can have the driver routine pass a copy of the array instead.

Using median-of-three partitioning makes the chance of the worst case occurring almost negligible. By carefully choosing the pivot, we can ensure that the worst case never occurs and that the running time is linear even in the worst-case scenario. The resulting algorithm is entirely of theoretical interest, however, because the constant that the Big-Oh notation hides is much larger than the constant obtained in the normal median-of-three implementation.

The linear worst-case algorithm is a classic result even though it is impractical.

9.8 A Lower Bound for Sorting

Although we have $O(N \log N)$ algorithms for sorting, it is not clear that this is as good as we can do. In this section we prove that any algorithm for sorting that uses only comparisons requires $\Omega(N \log N)$ comparisons (and hence time) in the worst case. In other words, *any algorithm that sorts by using element comparisons must use at least roughly* $N \log N$ *comparisons for some input sequence.* We can use a similar technique to show that this condition holds on average.

Any comparison-based sorting algorithm must use roughly $N \log N$ comparisons on average and in the worst case.

```
// Internal selection method that makes recursive calls.
// Uses median-of-three partitioning and a cutoff of 10.
// Places the kth smallest item in a[k-1].
// a is an array of Comparable items.
// low is the left-most index of the subarray.
// high is the right-most index of the subarray.
// k is the desired rank (1 is minimum) in the entire array.
template <class Comparable>
void quickSelect( vector<Comparable> & a,
                  int low, int high, int k )
{
    if( low + CUTOFF > high )
        insertionSort( a, low, high );
    else
    {
          // Sort low, middle, high
        int middle = ( low + high ) / 2;
        if( a[ middle ] < a[ low ] )
            swap( a[ low ], a[ middle ] );
        if( a[ high ] < a[ low ] )
            swap( a[ low ], a[ high ] );
        if( a[ high ] < a[ middle ] )
            swap( a[ middle ], a[ high ] );

          // Place pivot at position high - 1
        Comparable pivot = a[ middle ];
        swap( a[ middle ], a[ high - 1 ] );

          // Begin partitioning
        int i, j;
        for( i = low, j = high - 1; ; )
        {
            while( a[ ++i ] < pivot ) { }
            while( pivot < a[ --j ] ) { }
            if( i < j )
                swap( a[ i ], a[ j ] );
            else
                break;
        }
        swap( a[ i ], a[ high - 1 ] );  // Restore pivot

          // Recurse; only this part changes
        if( k <= i )
            quickSelect( a, low, i - 1, k );
        else if( k > i + 1 )
            quickSelect( a, i + 1, high, k );
    }
}
```

Figure 9.21 Quickselect with median-of-three partitioning and cutoff for small arrays.

Must every sorting algorithm work by using comparisons? The answer is no. However, algorithms that do not involve the use of general comparisons are likely to work only for restricted types, such as integers. Although we may often need to sort only integers (see Exercise 9.16), we cannot make such sweeping assumptions about the input of a general-purpose sorting algorithm. We may assume only the given—namely, that, because the items need to be sorted, any two items can be compared.

The proofs are abstract; we show the worst-case lower bound.

Next, we prove one of the most fundamental theorems in computer science, as Theorem 9.3. Recall first that the product of the first N positive integers is $N!$. The proof is an existence proof, which is somewhat abstract. It shows that some bad input must always exist.

Theorem 9.3

Any algorithm that sorts by using element comparisons only must use at least $\lceil \log (N!) \rceil$ comparisons for some input sequence.

Proof

We may regard the possible inputs as any of the permutations of 1, 2, …, N because only the relative order of the input items matters, not their actual values. Thus the number of possible inputs is the number of different arrangements of N items, which is exactly N!. Let P_i be the number of permutations that are consistent with the results after the algorithm has processed i comparisons. Let F be the number of comparisons processed when the sort terminates. We know the following: (a) $P_0 = N!$ because all permutations are possible before the first comparison; (b) $P_F = 1$ because, if more than one permutation were possible, the algorithm could not terminate with confidence that it produced the correct output; (c) there exists a permutation such that $P_i \geq P_{i-1}/2$ because, after a comparison, each permutation goes into one of two groups: the still-possible group and the no-longer-possible group. The larger of these two groups must have at least half the permutations. Furthermore, there is at least one permutation for which we can apply this logic throughout the comparison sequence. The action of a sorting algorithm is thus to go from the state P_0, in which all N! permutations are possible, to the final state P_F, in which only one permutation is possible, with the restriction that there exists an input such that in each comparison only half of the permutations can be eliminated. By the halving principle, we know that at least $\lceil \log (N!) \rceil$ comparisons are required for that input.

How large is $\lceil \log (N!) \rceil$? It is approximately $N \log N - 1.44N$.

9.9 Indirect Sorting

Although we can use templates to write sorting routines that are easily reused for different objects, we have thus far ignored an important consideration. Recall that large objects are very expensive to copy. Thus when writing templated routines we always pass an unknown `Comparable` object by reference (or constant reference). Sorting presents a different problem: Sorting large structures is algorithmically identical to sorting integers, but the data movement is extremely expensive. Changes may need to be made to avoid the overhead of unnecessary copies.

If we can reduce the number of copies (i.e., assignments of `Comparable` objects in the quicksort), we can significantly improve the running time for large objects.

9.9.1 Using Pointers to Reduce `Comparable` Copies to 2*N*

Large objects are expensive to move. *Indirect sorting* constructs an array of pointers and moves the pointers during most of the algorithm. At the end of the algorithm, the array of large objects is then rearranged to match the pointers.

In principle, the solution to our problem is simple. We use a technique called **indirect sorting** to create an array of pointers to `Comparable` and rearrange the pointers; once we know where the elements should go, we place them there without the overhead of the intermediate copies. Rearranging the items elegantly requires an algorithm known as *in-situ permutation*. Doing it in C++ requires a lot of syntax, all of which we have mentioned earlier but used infrequently.

The first step of the algorithm creates an array of pointers. Let `a` be the array to sort and `p` be the array of pointers. Initially `p[i]` points at the object stored in `a[i]`. Next, we sort `p[i]`, using the value of the object being pointed at to determine ordering. The objects in array `a` do not move, but the pointers in array `p` are rearranged. Figure 9.22 shows how the array of pointers looks after the sorting stage.

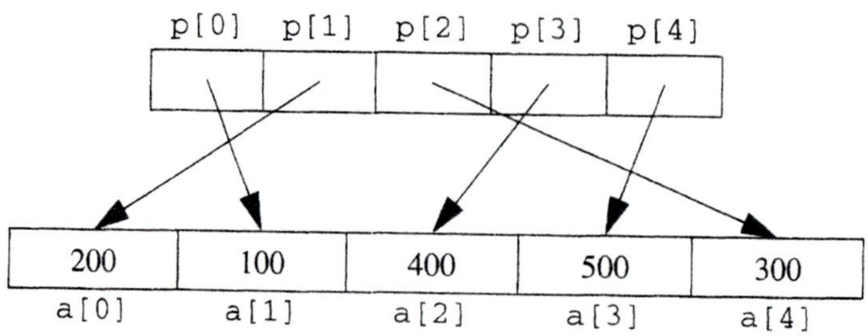

Figure 9.22 Using an array of pointers to sort.

We must still rearrange the array `a`. The simplest way is to declare a second array of `Comparable`, which we call `copy`. We can write the correct sorted order into `copy` and then write from `copy` back into `a`. The cost of doing so is an extra array and a total of $2N$ `Comparable` copies.

The simplest rearrangement strategy uses an extra array of large objects.

9.9.2 Avoiding the Extra Array

The algorithm in Section 9.9.1 has a potentially important problem. By using `copy`, we doubled the space requirement. We can assume that N is large (otherwise, we would use insertion sort) and that the size of a `Comparable` object is large (otherwise, we would not bother using a pointer implementation). Thus we can reasonably expect that we are operating near the memory limits of our machine. Although we can expect to use an extra `vector` of pointers, we cannot necessarily expect an extra `vector` of `Comparable` objects to be available. Thus we need to rearrange the array `a` in place, without resorting to an extra array.

A second consequence of our decision to use `copy` is that a total of $2N$ `Comparable` copies are used. Although this situation is an improvement over the original algorithm, we can improve the algorithm even more. In particular, in the following improvement, we never use more than $3N/2$ `Comparable` copies, and on almost all inputs we use only a few more than N. Not only do we save space, but also we save time. Before stepping through the code, let us get a general idea of what needs to be done. Surprisingly, we have already done it before.

A more complex strategy performs the rearrangement in place and typically moves each object only once.

To get an idea of what we have to do, let us start with $i = 2$. With `p[2]` pointing at `a[4]`, we know that we need to move `a[4]` to `a[2]`. First, we must save `a[2]`, or we will not be able to place it correctly later. Thus we have `tmp=a[2]` and then `a[2]=a[4]`. When `a[4]` has been moved to `a[2]`, we can move something into `a[4]`, which is essentially vacant. By examining `p[4]`, we see that the correct statement is `a[4]=a[3]`. Now we need to move something into `a[3]`. With `p[3]` pointing at `a[2]`, we know that we want to move `a[2]` there. But `a[2]` has been overwritten at the start of this rearrangement; as its original value is in `tmp`, we finish with `a[3]=tmp`. This process shows that, by starting with `i` equal to 2 and following the `p` array, we form a cyclic sequence 2, 4, 3, 2, which corresponds to

```
tmp    = a[ 2 ];
a[ 2 ] = a[ 4 ];
a[ 4 ] = a[ 3 ];
a[ 3 ] = tmp;
```

We have rearranged three elements while using only four `Comparable` copies and one extra `Comparable` of storage. Actually, we have described

```
1 // Sort objects -- even large ones --
2 // with only N + ln N Comparable moves on average.
3 template <class Comparable>
4 void largeObjectSort( vector<Comparable> & a )
5 {
6     vector<Pointer<Comparable> > p( a.size( ) );
7     int i, j, nextj;
8
9     for( i = 0; i < a.size( ); i++ )
10        p[ i ] = &a[ i ];
11
12    quicksort( p );
13
14      // Shuffle items in place
15    for( i = 0; i < a.size( ); i++ )
16        if( p[ i ] != &a[ i ] )
17        {
18            Comparable tmp = a[ i ];
19            for( j = i; p[ j ] != &a[ i ]; j = nextj )
20            {
21                nextj = p[ j ] - &a[ 0 ];
22                a[ j ] = *p[ j ];
23                p[ j ] = &a[ j ];
24            }
25            a[ j ] = tmp;
26            p[ j ] = &a[ j ];
27        }
28 }
```

Figure 9.23 An algorithm for sorting large objects.

this method before. Recall that the innermost loop of the insertion sort saves the current element `a[i]` in a `tmp` object. We then assign `a[j]=a[j-1]`, to move lots of elements 1 unit to the right. Finally, we assign `a[j]=tmp` to place the original element. We are doing exactly the same thing here, except that instead of sliding the elements over by 1 unit, we are using `p` to guide the rearrangement.

This algorithm is implemented in the `largeObjectSort` function template shown in Figure 9.23. We use the `Pointer` wrapper class shown in Figure 5.7. First, we initialize the array of pointers, `p`, at lines 9 and 10, and then we sort them at line 12. The rest of the algorithm requires rearranging the objects in `a`, according to the order in `p`.

At line 15 we search sequentially for a position `i` that contains the wrong element. When we find such an `i` (the test at line 16 succeeds), we do the sequence of assignments that we just described. We also update the `p` array when we assign to `a[j]`. We can obtain the index that `p[j]` represents by using pointer subtraction (Section D.3.2). If `p1` and `p2` point at two elements in the same array, then `p1-p2` is their separation distance, as an `int`. Thus `p[j]-&a[0]` is the index of the object that `p[j]` points at. This tricky piece of C++ is used at line 21. Note also that `*p[j]`, at line 22, is the same as `a[nextj]`.

The analysis requires counting the number of cycles in the permutations.

In general, we have a collection of cycles that are to be rearranged. In Figure 9.22 there are two cycles: One involves two elements, and the other involves three. Rearranging a cycle of length L uses $L + 1$ `Comparable` copies, as we have shown. Cycles of length 1 represent elements that have been correctly placed and thus use no copies. This approach improves the previous algorithm because now a sorted array does not incur any `Comparable` copies.

For an array of N elements, we let C_L be the number of cycles of length L. The total number of `Comparable` copies, M, is given by

$$M = N - C_1 + (C_2 + C_3 + \cdots + C_N). \tag{9.12}$$

The best thing that can happen is that we have no `Comparable` copies because there are N cycles of length 1 (i.e., every element is correctly placed). The worst thing that can happen is that we have $N/2$ cycles of length 2, in which case Equation 9.12 tells us that $M = 3N/2$ `Comparable` copies are performed. That can happen if the input is 2, 1, 4, 3, 6, 5, and so on. What is the expected value of M? We need only compute the expected value of C_L for each L (see Exercise 9.12, in which you are asked to argue that this value is $1/L$). Doing so gives the value of M:

$$\begin{aligned} M &= N - 1 + \frac{1}{2} + \frac{1}{3} + \cdots + \frac{1}{N} \\ &= N - 2 + 1 + \frac{1}{2} + \frac{1}{3} + \cdots + \frac{1}{N} \\ &= N - 2 + H_N. \end{aligned}$$

The result obtained by using a known estimate for the term H_N (see Theorem 6.5) is that the average number of `Comparable` copies is given by $N + \ln N - 1.423$. A random arrangement of the input yields only a very small number of cycles.

Summary

For most general internal sorting applications, an insertion sort, Shellsort, or quicksort is the method of choice. The decision regarding which to use depends on the size of the input.

Insertion sort is appropriate for very small amounts of input. Shellsort is a good choice for sorting moderate amounts of input. With a proper increment sequence, it gives excellent performance and uses only a few lines of code. Quicksort gives the best performance but is trickier to code. Asymptotically, it has almost certain $O(N \log N)$ performance with a careful implementation, and we showed that this outcome is essentially as good as we can expect. In Section 21.6 we discuss another popular internal sort, *heapsort*.

When sorting large objects, we must minimize data movement. We showed how to use pointers to do so with almost no extra moves. When sorting input that does not fit entirely in main memory, we need to use different techniques. The general technique, discussed in Section 21.7, makes use of the merge algorithm discussed in Section 9.5.

To test and compare the merits of the various sorting algorithms, we need to be able to generate random inputs. Randomness is an important topic in general, and we discuss it in Chapter 10.

Objects of the Game

comparison-based sorting algorithm An algorithm that makes ordering decisions only on the basis of comparisons. (p. 323)

diminishing gap sort Another name for Shellsort. (p. 327)

indirect sorting An algorithm that constructs an array of pointers and moves the pointers during most of the algorithm to match the sorted order. At the end of the algorithm, the array of large objects is then rearranged to match the pointers. (p. 352)

inversion A pair of elements that are out of order in an array. Used to measure unsortedness. (p. 324)

lower-bound proof for sorting Confirms that any comparison-based sorting algorithm must use at least roughly $N \log N$ comparisons on average and in the worst case. (p. 349)

median-of-three partitioning The median of the first, middle, and last elements is used as the pivot. This approach simplifies the partitioning stage of quicksort. (p. 341)

mergesort A divide-and-conquer algorithm that obtains an $O(N \log N)$ sort. (p. 330)

partition The step of quicksort that places every element except the pivot in one of two groups, one consisting of elements that are smaller than or equal to the pivot and one consisting of elements that are larger than or equal to the pivot. (p. 335)

pivot For quicksort, an element that divides an array into two groups; one that is smaller than the pivot and one that is larger than the pivot. (p. 335)

quickselect An algorithm used to perform a selection that is similar to quicksort but makes only one recursive call. The average running time is linear. (p. 349)

quicksort A fast divide-and-conquer algorithm when properly implemented; in practice it is the fastest comparison-based sorting algorithm known. (p. 334)

selection The process of finding the *k*th smallest element of an array. (p. 348)

Shellsort A subquadratic algorithm that works well in practice and is simple to code. The performance of Shellsort is highly dependent on the increment sequence and requires a challenging (and not completely resolved) analysis. (p. 326)

Common Errors

1. The sorts coded in this chapter begin at array position 0, not position 1.
2. Using the wrong increment sequence for Shellsort is a common error. Be sure that the increment sequence terminates with 1 and avoid sequences that are known to give poor performance.
3. Quicksort has many traps. The most common errors deal with sorted inputs, duplicate elements, and degenerate partitions.
4. For small inputs an insertion sort is appropriate, but using it for large inputs is wrong.

On the Internet

All the sorting algorithms and an implementation of quickselect are in a single file.

Duplicate.cpp	Contains the routine in Figure 9.1 and a test program.
Sort.h	Contains all the sorting algorithms and the selection algorithm.
TestSort.cpp	Contains a program that tests all the sorting methods.

Exercises

In Short

9.1. Sort the sequence 8, 1, 4, 1, 5, 9, 2, 6, 5 by using
a. insertion sort.
b. Shellsort for the increments {1, 3, 5}.
c. mergesort.
d. quicksort, with the middle element as pivot and no cutoff (show all steps).
e. quicksort, with median-of-three pivot selection and a cutoff of 3.

9.2. A sorting algorithm is *stable* if elements with equal keys are left in the same order as they occur in the input. Which of the sorting algorithms in this chapter are stable and which are not? Why?

9.3. Explain why the elaborate quicksort in the text is better than randomly permuting the input and choosing the middle element as pivot.

In Theory

9.4. When all keys are equal, what is the running time of
a. insertion sort.
b. Shellsort.
c. mergesort.
d. quicksort.

9.5. When the input has been sorted, what is the running time of
a. insertion sort.
b. Shellsort.
c. mergesort.
d. quicksort.

9.6. When the input has been sorted in reverse order, what is the running time of
a. insertion sort.
b. Shellsort.
c. mergesort.
d. quicksort.

9.7. Suppose that we exchange elements `a[i]` and `a[i+k]`, which were originally out of order. Prove that at least 1 and at most $2k - 1$ inversions are removed.

9.8. Construct a worst-case input for quicksort with
   a. the middle element as pivot.
   b. median-of-three pivot partitioning.

9.9. Show that the quickselect has linear average performance. Do so by solving Equation 9.5 with the constant 2 replaced by 1.

9.10. Using Stirling's formula, $N! \geq (N/e)^N \sqrt{2\pi N}$, derive an estimate for $\log(N!)$.

9.11. Prove that any comparison-based algorithm used to sort four elements requires at least five comparisons for some input. Then show that an algorithm that sorts four elements using at most five comparisons does indeed exist.

9.12. Let p be any position in the array containing N elements. For the rearrangement procedure shown in Section 9.9.2, in parts (a)–(c)
   a. show that the probability that p is in a cycle of length 1 is $1/N$.
   b. show that the probability that p is in a cycle of length 2 is also $1/N$.
   c. show that the probability that p is in a cycle of any length $1 \leq L \leq N$ is $1/N$.
   d. Based on part (c), deduce that the expected number of cycles of length L is $1/L$. (*Hint:* Each element contributes $1/N$ to the number of cycles of length L, but a simple addition overcounts cycles.)

9.13. When implementing quicksort, if the array contains lots of duplicates, you may find it best to perform a three-way partition (into elements less than, equal to, and greater than the pivot) and make smaller recursive calls. Assume that you can use three-way comparisons.
   a. Give an algorithm that performs a three-way in-place partition of an N element subarray using only $N-1$ three-way comparisons. If there are d items equal to the pivot, you may use d additional `Comparable` swaps, above and beyond the two-way partitioning algorithm. (*Hint:* As `i` and `j` move toward each other, maintain the five groups of elements shown.)

```
EQUAL   SMALL       UNKNOWN        LARGE        EQUAL
            i                   j
```

   b. Prove that, using the algorithm in part (a), sorting an N-element array that contains only d different values takes $O(d\,N)$ time.

9.14. Suppose that both arrays A and B are sorted and contain N elements. Give an $O(\log N)$ algorithm to find the median of $A \cup B$.

In Practice

9.15. A student alters the `quicksort` routine in Figure 9.20 by making the following changes to lines 25 to 28. Is the result equivalent to the original routine?

```
for( i = low + 1, j = high - 2; ; )
{
    while( a[ i ] < pivot )
        i++;
    while( pivot < a[ j ] )
        j--;
```

9.16. If you know more information about the items being sorted, you can sort them in linear time. Show that a collection of N 16-bit integers can be sorted in $O(N)$ time. (*Hint:* Maintain an array indexed from 0 to 65,535.)

9.17. The quicksort in the text uses two recursive calls. Remove one of the calls as follows.

a. Rewrite the code so that the second recursive call is unconditionally the last line in quicksort. Do so by reversing the `if/else`, and returning after the call to `insertionSort`.

b. Remove the tail recursion by writing a `while` loop and altering `low`.

9.18. Continuing from Exercise 9.17, after part (a),

a. perform a test so that the smaller subarray is processed by the first recursive call and the larger subarray is processed by the second recursive call.

b. remove the tail recursion by writing a `while` loop and altering `low` or `high`, as necessary.

c. prove that the number of recursive calls is logarithmic in the worst-case.

9.19. Suppose that the recursive quicksort receives an `int` parameter, `depth`, from the driver that is initially approximately $2 \log N$.

a. Modify the recursive quicksort to call `mergeSort` on its current subarray if the level of recursion has reached `depth`. (*Hint:* decrement `depth` as you make recursive calls; when it is 0, switch to mergesort.

b. Prove that the worst-case running time of this algorithm is $O(N \log N)$.
c. Conduct experiments to determine how often `mergeSort` gets called.
d. Implement this technique in conjunction with tail recursion removal in Exercise 9.17.
e. Explain why the technique in Exercise 9.18 would no longer be needed.

9.20. An array contains N numbers, and you want to determine whether two of the numbers sum to a given number K. For instance, if the input is 8, 4, 1, 6 and K is 10, the answer is yes (4 and 6). A number may be used twice. Do the following.
a. Give an $O(N^2)$ algorithm to solve this problem.
b. Give an $O(N \log N)$ algorithm to solve this problem. (*Hint:* Sort the items first. After doing so, you can solve the problem in linear time.)
c. Code both solutions and compare the running times of your algorithms.

9.21. Repeat Exercise 9.20 for four numbers. Try to design an $O(N^2 \log N)$ algorithm. (*Hint:* Compute all possible sums of two elements, sort these possible sums, and then proceed as in Exercise 9.20.)

9.22. Repeat Exercise 9.20 for three numbers. Try to design an $O(N^2)$ algorithm.

9.23. In Exercise 6.28 you were asked to find the single integral solution to $A^5 + B^5 + C^5 + D^5 + E^5 = F^5$ with $0 < A \le B \le C \le D \le E \le F \le N$, where N is 75. Use the ideas explored in Exercise 9.21 to obtain a solution relatively quickly by sorting all possible values of $A^5 + B^5 + C^5$ and $F^5 - (D^5 + E^5)$, and then seeing if a number in the first group is equal to a number in the second group. In terms of N, how much space and time does the algorithm require?

Programming Projects

9.24. Compare the performance of Shellsort with various increment sequences, as follows. Obtain an average time for some input size N by generating several random sequences of N items. Use the same input for all increment sequences. In a separate test obtain the average number of `Comparable` comparisons and `Comparable` copies. Set the number of repeated trials to be large but doable within 1 hour of CPU time. The increment sequences are

a. Shell's original sequence (repeatedly divide by 2).
b. Shell's original sequence, adding 1 if the result is nonzero but even.
c. Gonnet's sequence shown in the text, with repeated division by 2.2.
d. Hibbard's increments: 1, 3, 7, ..., $2^k - 1$.
e. Knuth's increments: 1, 4, 13, ..., $(3^k - 1)/2$.
f. Sedgewick's increments: 1, 5, 19, 41, 109, ..., with each term having the form of either $9 \cdot 4^k - 9 \cdot 2^k + 1$ or $4^k - 3 \cdot 2^k + 1$.

9.25. Code both Shellsort and quicksort and compare their running times. Use the best implementations in the text and run them on
a. integers.
b. real numbers of type `double`.
c. strings.

9.26. Many implementations of quicksort use primitive arrays and pointer hopping (see Appendix D) as an alternative to the normal array-indexing mechanism. In Section D.3.4 we argue that pointer hopping is not always a good idea. Implement quicksort by using both techniques on primitive arrays (you will need to pass the number of items to sort to the driver routine) and determine which is faster on average for sorting 100,000 integers.

9.27. Write a template indirect sort, using the techniques in Section 9.9.2. In the template, use a function object to pass the underlying sorting algorithm to your indirect sort function.

9.28. Write a function that removes all duplicates in an array A of N items. Return the number of items that remain in A. Your function must run in $O(N \log N)$ average time (use quicksort as a preprocessing step).

9.29. Exercise 9.2 addressed stable sorting. Write a function template that performs a stable quicksort. To do so, create an array of records; each record is to contain a data item and its initial position in the array (you can use a `pair` object; see Section 5.5). Then sort the array; if two records have identical data items, use the initial position to break the tie. After the array of records has been sorted, rearrange the original array.

9.30. Redo Exercise 9.29 by using pointers to avoid excessive data movement.

9.31. Write a simple sorting utility, `sort`. The `sort` command takes a file name as a parameter, and the file contains one item per line. By default the lines are considered strings and are sorted by normal lexicographic order (in a case-sensitive manner). Add two options: The `-c` option means that the sort should be case insensitive; the `-n` option means that the lines are to be considered integers for the purpose of the sort.

References

The classic reference for sorting algorithms is [5]. Another reference is [3]. The Shellsort algorithm first appeared in [8]. An empirical study of its running time was done in [9]. Quicksort was discovered by Hoare [4]; that paper also includes the quickselect algorithm and details many important implementation issues. A thorough study of the quicksort algorithm, including analysis for the median-of-three variant, appears in [7]. A detailed C implementation that includes additional improvements is presented in [1]. Exercise 9.19 is based on [6]. The $\Omega(N \log N)$ lower bound for comparison-based sorting is taken from [2]. The presentation of Shellsort and indirect sorting is adapted from [10].

1. J. L. Bentley and M. D. McElroy, "Engineering a Sort Function," *Software—Practice and Experience* **23** (1993), 1249–1265.
2. L. R. Ford and S. M. Johnson, "A Tournament Problem," *American Mathematics Monthly* **66** (1959), 387–389.
3. G. H. Gonnet and R. Baeza-Yates, *Handbook of Algorithms and Data Structures*, 2d ed., Addison-Wesley, Reading, Mass., 1991.
4. C. A. R. Hoare, "Quicksort," *Computer Journal* **5** (1962), 10–15.
5. D. E. Knuth, *The Art of Computer Programming, Volume 3: Sorting and Searching,* 2d. ed., Addison-Wesley, Reading, Mass., 1998.
6. D. R. Musser, "Introspective Sorting and Selection Algorithms," *Software—Practice and Experience* **27** (1997), 983–993.
7. R. Sedgewick, *Quicksort*, Garland, New York, 1978. (Originally presented as the author's Ph.D. dissertation, Stanford University, 1975.)
8. D. L. Shell, "A High-Speed Sorting Procedure," *Communications of the ACM* **2** 7 (1959), 30–32.
9. M. A. Weiss, "Empirical Results on the Running Time of Shellsort," *Computer Journal* **34** (1991), 88–91.
10. M. A. Weiss, *Efficient C Programming: A Practical Approach,* Prentice-Hall, Englewood Cliffs, N.J., 1995.

Chapter 10

Randomization

Many situations in computing require the use of random numbers. For example, modern cryptography, simulation systems, and, surprisingly, even searching and sorting algorithms rely on random number generators. Yet good random number generators are difficult to implement. In this chapter we discuss the generation and use of random numbers.

In this chapter, we show:

- how random numbers are generated,
- how random permutations are generated, and
- how random numbers allow the design of efficient algorithms, using a general technique known as the *randomized algorithm.*

10.1 Why Do We Need Random Numbers?

Random numbers are used in many applications. In this section we discuss a few of the most common ones.

Random numbers have many important uses, including cryptography, simulation, and program testing.

One important application of random numbers is in program testing. Suppose, for example, that we want to test whether a sorting algorithm written in Chapter 9 actually works. Of course, we could provide some small amount of input, but if we want to test the algorithms for the large data sets they were designed for, we need lots of input. Providing sorted data as input tests one case, but more convincing tests would be preferable. For instance, we would want to test the program by perhaps running 5000 sorts for inputs of size 1000. To do so requires writing a routine to generate the test data, which in turn requires the use of random numbers.

A *permutation* of 1, 2, ..., *N* is a sequence of *N* integers that includes each of 1, 2, ..., *N* exactly once.

Once we have the random number inputs, how do we know whether the sorting algorithm works? One test is to determine whether the sort arranged the array in nondecreasing order. Clearly, we can run this test in a linear-time sequential scan. But how do we know that the items present after the sort are the same as those prior to the sort? One method is to fix the items in an arrangement of 1, 2, ..., N. In other words, we start with a random *permutation* of the first N integers. A **permutation** of 1, 2, ..., N is a sequence of N integers that includes each of 1, 2, ..., N exactly once. Then, no matter what permutation we start with, the result of the sort will be the sequence 1, 2, ..., N, which is also easily tested.

In addition to helping us generate test data to verify program correctness, random numbers are useful in comparing the performance of various algorithms. The reason is that, once again, they can be used to provide a large number of inputs.

Another use of random numbers is in simulations. If we want to know the average time required for a service system (e.g., teller service in a bank) to process a sequence of requests, we can model the system on a computer. In this computer simulation we generate the request sequence with random numbers.

Still another use of random numbers is in the general technique called the *randomized algorithm,* wherein a random number is used to determine the next step performed in the algorithm. The most common type of randomized algorithm involves selecting from among several possible alternatives that are more or less indistinguishable. For instance, in a commercial computer chess program, the computer generally chooses its first move randomly rather than playing deterministically (i.e., rather than always playing the same move). In this chapter we look at several problems that can be solved more efficiently by using a randomized algorithm.

10.2 Random Number Generators

***Pseudorandom numbers* have many properties of random numbers. Good random-number generators are hard to find.**

How are random numbers generated? True randomness is impossible to achieve on a computer, because any numbers obtained depend on the algorithm used to generate them and thus cannot possibly be random. Generally, it is sufficient to produce **pseudorandom numbers,** or numbers that *appear* to be random because they satisfy many of the properties of random numbers. Producing them is much easier said than done.

Suppose that we need to simulate a coin flip. One way to do so is to examine the system clock. Presumably, the system clock maintains the number of seconds as part of the current time. If this number is even, we can return 0 (for heads); if it is odd, we can return 1 (for tails). The problem is that this strategy does not work well if we need a sequence of random numbers. One second is a long time, and the clock might not change at all while the program is running, generating all 0s or all 1s, which is hardly a random sequence. Even if the time were recorded in units of microseconds (or smaller) and the program were running by itself, the sequence of numbers generated would be far from random because the time between calls to the generator would be essentially identical on every program invocation.

What we really need is a *sequence* of pseudorandom numbers, that is, a sequence with the same properties as a random sequence. Suppose that we want random numbers between 0 and 999, uniformly distributed. In a **uniform distribution,** all numbers in the specified range are equally likely to occur. Other distributions are also widely used. The class interface shown in Figure 10.1 supports several distributions. Most distributions can be derived

In a *uniform distribution*, all numbers in the specified range are equally likely to occur.

```
// Random class interface: random number generation.
//
// CONSTRUCTION: with (a) no initializer or (b) an integer
//      that specifies the initial state of the generator.
// *****************PUBLIC OPERATIONS*********************
//      Return a random number according to some distribution
// int randomInt( )                      --> Uniform, 1 to 2^31-1
// double randomReal( )                  --> Uniform 0..1
// int randomInt( int low, int high )    --> Uniform low..high
// int poisson( double expectedVal )     --> Poisson
// double negExp( double expectedVal )   --> Neg exponential

class Random
{
  public:
    Random( int initVal = 1 ) : state( initVal ) { }

      // Uniform distributions
    int randomInt( );              // 1 to 2^31-1   (Coded below)
    double randomReal( );          // >0.0 to <1.0 (Online code)
    int randomInt( int low, int high );      // (Online code)

      // Nonuniform distributions
    int poisson( double expectedVal );       // (Section 10.3)
    double negExp( double expectedVal );     // (Section 10.3)

  private:
    int state;

    static const int A;
    static const int M;
    static const int Q;
    static const int R;
};
```

Figure 10.1 Interface for the Random class that generates random numbers.

from the uniform distribution so that is the one we consider first. The following properties hold if the sequence 0, ..., 999 is a true uniform distribution.

- The first number is equally likely to be 0, 1, 2, ..., 999.
- The ith number is equally likely to be 0, 1, 2, ..., 999.
- The expected average of all the generated numbers is 499.5.

Typically a random sequence, rather than one random number, is required.

These properties are not particularly restrictive. For instance, we could generate the first number by examining a system clock that was accurate to 1 ms and then using the number of milliseconds. We could generate subsequent numbers by adding 1 to the preceding number, and so on. Clearly, after 1000 numbers are generated, all the previous properties hold. However, stronger properties do not.

Two stronger properties that would hold for uniformly distributed random numbers are the following.

- The sum of two consecutive random numbers is equally likely to be even or odd.
- If 1000 numbers are randomly generated, some will be duplicated. (Roughly 368 numbers will never appear.)

Our numbers do not satisfy these properties. Consecutive numbers always sum to an odd number, and our sequence is duplicate-free. We say then that our simple pseudorandom number generator has failed two statistical tests. All pseudorandom number generators fail some statistical tests, but the good generators fail fewer tests than the bad ones. (See Exercise 10.14 for a common statistical test.)

The *linear congruential generator* is a good algorithm for generating uniform distributions.

In this section we describe the simplest uniform generator that passes a reasonable number of statistical tests. By no means is it the best generator. However, it is suitable for use in applications wherein a good approximation to a random sequence is acceptable. The method used is the linear congruential generator, which was first described in 1951. The **linear congruential generator** is a good algorithm for generating uniform distributions. It is a random-number generator in which numbers $X_1, X_2, \ldots$ are generated that satisfy

$$X_{i+1} = AX_i (\bmod M). \tag{10.1}$$

Equation 10.1 states that we can get the $(i+1)$th number by multiplying the ith number by some constant A and computing the remainder when the result is divided by M. In C++ we would have

```
x[ i + 1 ] = A * x[ i ] % M;
```

We specify the constants A and M shortly. Note that all generated numbers will be smaller than M. Some value X_0 must be given to start the sequence. This initial value of the random number generator is the **seed.** If $X_0 = 0$, the sequence is not random because it generates all zeros. But if A and M are carefully chosen, any other seed satisfying $1 \le X_0 < M$ is equally valid. If M is prime, X_i is never 0. For example, if $M = 11$, $A = 7$ and the seed $X_0 = 1$, the numbers generated are

The *seed* is the initial value of the random number generator.

$$7, 5, 2, 3, 10, 4, 6, 9, 8, 1, 7, 5, 2, \ldots \quad \textbf{(10.2)}$$

Generating a number a second time results in a repeating sequence. In our case the sequence repeats after $M - 1 = 10$ numbers. The length of a sequence until a number is repeated is called the **period** of the sequence. The period obtained with this choice of A is clearly as good as possible because all nonzero numbers smaller than M are generated. (We must have a repeated number generated on the 11th iteration.)

The length of a sequence until a number is repeated is called its *period.* A random number generator with period *P* generates the same sequence of numbers after *P* iterations.

If M is prime, several choices of A give a full period of $M - 1$, and this type of random number generator is called a **full-period linear congruential generator.** Some choices of A do not give a full period. For instance, if $A = 5$ and $X_0 = 1$, the sequence has a short period of 5:

A *full-period linear congruential generator* has period *M* – 1.

$$5, 3, 4, 9, 1, 5, 3, 4, \ldots \quad \textbf{(10.3)}$$

If we choose M to be a 31-bit prime, the period should be significantly large for most applications. The 31-bit prime $M = 2^{31} - 1 = 2{,}147{,}483{,}647$ is a common choice. For this prime, $A = 48{,}271$ is one of the many values that gives a full-period linear congruential generator. Its use has been well studied and is recommended by experts in the field. As we show later in the chapter, tinkering with random number generators usually means breaking, so you are well advised to stick with this formula until told otherwise.

Implementing this routine seems simple enough. If `state` represents the last value computed by the `randomInt` routine, the new value of `state` should be given by

Because of overflow, we must rearrange calculations.

```
state = ( A * state ) % M;       // Incorrect
```

Unfortunately, on most machines this computation is done on 32-bit integers, and the multiplication is certain to overflow. Although C++ allows overflow—and we could argue that the result is part of the randomness—overflow is unacceptable because we would no longer have the guarantee of a full period. However, a slight reordering allows the computation to proceed without overflow. Specifically, if Q and R are the quotient and remainder of M/A, then we can rewrite Equation 10.1 as

$$X_{i+1} = A(X_i(\text{mod } Q)) - R\lfloor X_i/Q \rfloor + M\delta(X_i), \qquad \textbf{(10.4)}$$

and the following conditions hold (see Exercise 10.5).

- The first term can always be evaluated without overflow.
- The second term can be evaluated without overflow if $R < Q$.
- $\delta(X_i)$ evaluates to 0 if the result of the subtraction of the first two terms is positive; it evaluates to 1 if the result of the subtraction is negative.

Stick with these numbers until you are told otherwise.

For the values of M and A, we have $Q = 44{,}488$ and $R = 3399$. Consequently, $R < Q$ and a direct application now gives an implementation of the `Random` class for generating random numbers. The resulting code is shown in Figure 10.2. The class works so long as `int` is capable of holding M. The routine `randomInt` returns the value of the state.

Two additional member functions are provided in the interface given in Figure 10.1. One generates a random real number in the open interval from 0 to 1, and the other generates a random integer in a specified closed interval (see the online code).

Finally, the `Random` class provides a generator for nonuniform random numbers when they are required. In Section 10.3 we provide the implementation for the member functions `poisson` and `negExp`.

You might be tempted to assume that all machines have a random number generator at least as good as the one shown in Figure 10.2. Sadly, that is not the case. Many libraries have generators based on the function

```
// Implementation of some of the Random class.
const int Random::A = 48271;
const int Random::M = 2147483647;
const int Random::Q = M / A;
const int Random::R = M % A;

// randInt returns the next random number and updates state.
int Random::randomInt( )
{
    int tmpState = A * ( state % Q ) - R * ( state / Q );
    if( tmpState >= 0 )
        state = tmpState;
    else
        state = tmpState + M;

    return state;
}
```

Figure 10.2 Random number generator that works if `INT_MAX` is at least $2^{31} - 1$.

$$X_{i+1} = (AX_i + C) \bmod 2^B,$$

where B is chosen to match the number of bits in the machine's integer, and C is odd. These libraries, like the `randomInt` routine in Figure 10.2, also return the newly computed `state` directly, instead of (for example) a value between 0 and 1. Unfortunately, these generators always produce values of X_i that alternate between even and odd—obviously an undesirable property. Indeed, the lower k bits cycle with a period of 2^k (at best). Many other random number generators have much smaller cycles than the one we provided. These generators are not suitable for any application requiring long sequences of random numbers.

Finally, it may seem that we can get a better random number generator by adding a constant to the equation. For instance, we might conclude that

$$X_{i+1} = (48{,}271 X_i + 1) \bmod (2^{31} - 1)$$

would somehow be more random. However, when we use this equation, we see that

$$(48{,}271 \cdot 179{,}424{,}105 + 1) \bmod (2^{31} - 1) = 179{,}424{,}105.$$

Hence, if the seed is 179,424,105, the generator gets stuck in a cycle of period 1, illustrating how fragile these generators are.

10.3 Nonuniform Random Numbers

The *Poisson distribution* models the number of occurrences of a rare event and is used in simulations.

Not all applications require uniformly distributed random numbers. For example, grades in a large course are generally not uniformly distributed. Instead, they satisfy the classic bell curve distribution, more formally known as the *normal* or *Gaussian distribution*. A uniform random number generator can be used to generate random numbers that satisfy other distributions.

An important nonuniform distribution that occurs in simulations is the **Poisson distribution,** which models the number of occurrences of a rare event. Occurrences that happen under the following circumstances satisfy the Poisson distribution.

1. The probability of one occurrence in a small region is proportional to the size of the region.
2. The probability of two occurrences in a small region is proportional to the square of the size of the region and is usually small enough to be ignored.

3. The event of getting k occurrences in one region and the event of getting j occurrences in another region disjoint from the first region are independent. (Technically this statement means that you can get the probability of both events simultaneously occurring by multiplying the probability of individual events.)
4. The mean number of occurrences in a region of some size is known.

If the mean number of occurrences is the constant a, the probability of exactly k occurrences is $a^k e^{-a}/k!$.

The Poisson distribution generally applies to events that have a low probability of a single occurrence. For example, consider the event of purchasing a winning lottery ticket in Florida, where the odds of winning the jackpot are 14,000,000 to 1. Presumably the picked numbers are more or less random and independent. If a person buys 100 tickets, the odds of winning become 140,000 to 1 (the odds improve by a factor of 100), so condition 1 holds. The odds of the person holding two winning tickets are negligible, so condition 2 holds. If someone else buys 10 tickets, that person's odds of winning are 1,400,000 to 1, and these odds are independent of the first person's, so condition 3 holds. Suppose that 28,000,000 tickets are sold. The mean number of winning tickets in this situation is 2 (the number we need for condition 4). The actual number of winning tickets is a random variable with an expected value of 2, and it satisfies the Poisson distribution. Thus the probability that exactly k winning tickets have been sold is $2^k e^{-2}/k!$, which gives the distribution shown in Figure 10.3. If the expected number of winners is the constant a, the probability of k winning tickets is $a^k e^{-a}/k!$.

To generate a random unsigned integer according to a Poisson distribution that has an expected value of a, we can adopt the following strategy (whose mathematical justification is beyond the scope of this book): Repeatedly generate uniformly distributed random numbers in the interval (0, 1) until their product is smaller than (or equal to) e^{-a}. The code shown in Figure 10.4 does just that, using a mathematically equivalent technique that is less sensitive to overflow. The code adds the logarithm of the uniform random numbers until their sum is smaller than (or equal to) $-a$.

Winning Tickets	0	1	2	3	4	5
Frequency	0.135	0.271	0.271	0.180	0.090	0.036

Figure 10.3 Distribution of lottery winners if the expected number of winners is 2.

```
#include <math.h>

// Return random number according to Poisson distribution.
int Random::poisson( double expectedValue )
{
    double limit = -expectedValue;
    double sum = log( randomReal( ) );
    int count;

    for( count = 0; sum > limit; count++ )
        sum += log( randomReal( ) );
    return count;
}
```

Figure 10.4 Generation of a random number according to the Poisson distribution.

```
// Return random number according to neg-exp distribution.
double Random::negExp( double expectedValue )
{
    return - expectedValue * log( randomReal( ) );
}
```

Figure 10.5 Generation of a random number according to the negative exponential distribution.

Another important nonuniform distribution is the **negative exponential distribution,** shown in Figure 10.5, which has the same mean and variance and is used to model the time between occurrences of random events. We use it in the simulation application shown in Section 14.2.

The *negative exponential distribution* has the same mean and variance. It is used to model the time between occurrences of random events.

Many other distributions are commonly used. Our main purpose here is to show that most can be generated from the uniform distribution. Consult any book on probability and statistics to find out more about these functions.

10.4 Generating a Random Permutation

Consider the problem of simulating a card game. The deck consists of 52 distinct cards, and in the course of a deal, we must generate cards from the deck, without duplicates. In effect, we need to shuffle the cards and then iterate through the deck. We want the shuffle to be fair. That is, each of the 52! possible orderings of the deck should be equally likely as a result of the shuffle.

```
1 // Generate a random permutation of 1..n.
2 void permute( vector<int> & a )
3 {
4     Random r( (int) time( 0 ) ); // State set by time
5     const int n = a.size( );
6
7     for( int i = 0; i < n; i++ )
8         a[ i ] = i + 1;
9
10    for( int j = 1; j < n; j++ )
11        swap( a[ j ], a[ r.randomInt( 0, j ) ] );
12 }
```

Figure 10.6 A permutation routine.

***A random permutation* can be generated in linear time, using one random number per item.**

This type of problem involves the use of a **random permutation.** In general, the problem is to generate a random permutation of 1, 2, ..., N, with all permutations being equally likely. The randomness of the random permutation is, of course, limited by the randomness of the pseudorandom number generator. Thus all permutations being equally likely is contingent on all the random numbers being uniformly distributed and independent. We demonstrate that random permutations can be generated in linear time, using one random number per item.

A routine, `permute`, to generate a random permutation is shown in Figure 10.6. In the `permute` routine the first loop initializes the permutation with 1, 2, ..., N. The second loop performs a random shuffling. In each iteration of the loop, we swap `a[j]` with some array element in positions `0` to `j` (it is possible to perform no swap).

The correctness of `permute` is subtle.

Clearly, `permute` generates shuffled permutations. But are all permutations equally likely? The answer is both yes and no. The answer, based on the algorithm, is yes. There are $N!$ possible permutations, and the number of different possible outcomes of the $N - 1$ calls to `randomInt` at line 11 is also $N!$ The reason is that the first call produces 0 or 1, so it has two outcomes. The second call produces 0, 1, or 2, so it has three outcomes. The last call has N outcomes. The total number of outcomes is the product of all these possibilities because each random number is independent of the previous random numbers. All we have to show is that each sequence of random numbers corresponds to only one permutation. We can do so by working backward (see Exercise 10.6).

However, the answer is actually no—all permutations are not equally likely. There are only $2^{31} - 2$ initial states for the random number generator, so there can be only $2^{31} - 2$ different permutations. This condition could be a problem in some situations. For instance, a program that generates 1,000,000 permutations (perhaps by splitting the work among many computers) to measure the performance of a sorting algorithm almost certainly generates some permutations twice—unfortunately. Better random number generators are needed to help the practice meet the theory.

Note that rewriting the call to `swap` with the call to `r.randomInt (0,n-1)` does not work, even for three elements. There are $3! = 6$ possible permutations, and the number of different sequences that could be computed by the three calls to `randomInt` is $3^3 = 27$. Because 6 does not divide 27 exactly, some permutations must be more likely than others.

10.5 Randomized Algorithms

Suppose that you are a professor who is giving weekly programming assignments. You want to ensure that the students are doing their own programs or, at the very least, that they understand the code that they are submitting. One solution is to give a quiz on the day each program is due. However, these quizzes take time from class and doing so might be practical for only roughly half the programs. Your problem is to decide when to give the quizzes.

Of course, if you announce the quizzes in advance, that could be interpreted as an implicit license to cheat for the 50 percent of the programs that will not get a quiz. You could adopt the unannounced strategy of giving quizzes on alternate programs, but students would quickly figure out that strategy. Another possibility is to give quizzes on what seem like the important programs, but that would likely lead to similar quiz patterns from semester to semester. Student grapevines being what they are, this strategy would probably be worthless after one semester.

One method that seems to eliminate these problems is to flip a coin. You make a quiz for every program (making quizzes is not nearly as time consuming as grading them), and at the start of class, you flip a coin to decide whether the quiz is to be given. This way neither you nor your students can know before class whether a quiz will be given. Also, the patterns do not repeat from semester to semester. The students can expect a quiz to occur with 50 percent probability, regardless of previous quiz patterns. The disadvantage of this strategy is that you could end up giving no quizzes during an entire semester. Assuming a large number of programming assignments, however, this is not likely to happen unless the coin is suspect. Each semester the expected number of quizzes is half the number of programs, and with high probability, the number of quizzes will not deviate much from this.

A *randomized algorithm* uses random numbers rather than deterministic decisions to control branching.

This example illustrates the **randomized algorithm,** which uses random numbers, rather than deterministic decisions, to control branching. The running time of the algorithm depends not only on the particular input, but also on the random numbers that occur.

The worst-case running time of a randomized algorithm is almost always the same as the worst-case running time of the nonrandomized algorithm. The important difference is that a good randomized algorithm has no bad inputs—only bad random numbers (relative to the particular input). This difference may seem only philosophical, but actually it is quite important, as we show in the following example.

The running time of a randomized algorithm depends on the random numbers that occur, as well as the particular input.

Let us say that your boss asks you to write a program to determine the median of a group of 1,000,000 numbers. You are to submit the program and then run it on an input that the boss will choose. If the correct answer is given within a few seconds of computing time (which would be expected for a linear algorithm), your boss will be very happy, and you will get a bonus. But if your program does not work or takes too much time, your boss will fire you for incompetence. Your boss already thinks that you are overpaid and is hoping to be able to take the second option. What should you do?

The quickselect algorithm described in Section 9.7 might seem like the way to go. Although the algorithm (see Figure 9.21) is very fast on average, recall that it has quadratic worst-case time if the pivot is continually poor. By using median-of-three partitioning, we have guaranteed that this worst case will not occur for common inputs, such as those that have been sorted or that contain a lot of duplicates. However, there is still a quadratic worst case, and as Exercise 9.8 showed, the boss will read your program, realize how you are choosing the pivot and be able to construct the worst case. Consequently, you will be fired.

Randomized quickselect is statistically guaranteed to work in linear time.

By using random numbers, you can statistically guarantee the safety of your job. You begin the quickselect algorithm by randomly shuffling the input by using lines 10 and 11 in Figure 10.6.[1] As a result, your boss essentially loses control of specifying the input sequence. When you run the quickselect algorithm, it will now be working on random input, so you expect it to take linear time. Can it still take quadratic time? The answer is yes. For any original input, the shuffling may get you to the worst case for quickselect, and thus the result would be a quadratic-time sort. If you are unfortunate enough to have this happen, you lose your job. However, this event is statistically impossible. For a million items, the chance of using even twice as much time as the average would indicate is so small that you

1. You need to be sure that the random number generator is sufficiently random and that its output cannot be predicted by the boss.

can essentially ignore it. The computer is much more likely to break. Your job is secure.

Instead of using a shuffling technique, you can achieve the same result by choosing the pivot randomly instead of deterministically. Take a random item in the array and swap it with the item in position `low`. Take another random item and swap it with the item in position `high`. Take a third random item and swap it with the item in the middle position. Then continue as usual. As before, degenerate partitions are always possible, but they now happen as a result of bad random numbers, not bad inputs.

Let us look at the differences between randomized and nonrandomized algorithms. So far we have concentrated on nonrandomized algorithms. When calculating their average running times, we assume that all inputs are equally likely. This assumption does not hold, however, because nearly sorted input, for instance, occurs much more often than is statistically expected. This situation can cause problems for some algorithms, such as quicksort. But when we use a randomized algorithm, the particular input is no longer important. The random numbers are important, and we get an *expected* running time, in which we average over all possible random numbers for any particular input. Using quickselect with random pivots (or a shuffle preprocessing step) gives an $O(N)$ expected time algorithm. That is, *for any input,* including already sorted input, the running time is expected to be $O(N)$, based on the statistics of random numbers. On the one hand an expected time bound is somewhat stronger than an average-case time bound because the assumptions used to generate it are weaker (random numbers versus random input) but it is weaker than the corresponding worst-case time bound. On the other hand, in many instances solutions that have good worst-case bounds frequently have extra overhead built in to assure that the worst case does not occur. The $O(N)$ worst-case algorithm for selection, for example, is a marvelous theoretical result but is not practical.

Some randomized algorithms work in a fixed amount of time but randomly make mistakes (presumably with low probability). These mistakes are *false positives* or *false negatives.*

Randomized algorithms come in two basic forms. The first, as already shown, always gives a correct answer but it could take a long time, depending on the luck of the random numbers. The second type is what we examine in the remainder of this chapter. Some randomized algorithms work in a fixed amount of time but randomly make mistakes (presumably with low probability) called **false positives** or **false negatives.** This technique is commonly accepted in medicine. False positives and false negatives for most tests are actually fairly common, and some tests have surprisingly high error rates. Furthermore, for some tests the errors depend on the individual, not random numbers, so repeating the test is certain to produce another false result. In randomized algorithms we can rerun the test on the same input using different random numbers. If we run a randomized algorithm 10 times and get 10 positives—and if a single false positive is an unlikely occurrence (say, 1 chance in 100)—the probability of 10 consecutive false positives (1 chance in 100^{10} or one hundred billion billion) is essentially zero.

10.6 Randomized Primality Testing

Recall that in Section 8.4 we described some numerical algorithms and showed how they could be used to implement the RSA encryption scheme. An important step in the RSA algorithm is to produce two prime numbers p and q. We can find a prime number by repeatedly trying successive odd numbers until we find one that is prime. Thus the issue boils down to determining whether a given number is prime.

Trial division **is the simplest algorithm for primality testing. It is fast for small (32-bit) numbers but cannot be used for larger numbers.**

The simplest algorithm for primality testing is **trial division.** In this algorithm, an odd number greater than 3 is prime if it is not divisible by any other odd number smaller than or equal to $\sqrt{N}$. A direct implementation of this strategy is shown in Figure 10.7.

Trial division is reasonably fast for small (32-bit) numbers, but it is unusable for larger numbers because it could require the testing of roughly $\sqrt{N}/2$ divisors, thus using $O(\sqrt{N})$ time.[2] What we need is a test whose running time is of the same order of magnitude as the `power` routine in Section 8.4.2. A well-known theorem, called **Fermat's Little Theorem,** looks promising. We state and provide a proof of it in Theorem 10.2 for completeness, but the proof is not needed for an understanding of the primality-testing algorithm.

Theorem 10.1 *Fermat's Little Theorem: If P is prime and $0 < A < P$, then $A^{P-1} \equiv 1 (\bmod P)$.*

Proof *Consider any $1 \leq k < P$. Clearly, $Ak \equiv 0 (\bmod P)$ is impossible because P is prime and is greater than A and k. Now consider any $1 \leq i < j < P$. $Ai \equiv Aj (\bmod P)$ would imply $A(j-i) \equiv 0 (\bmod P)$, which is impossible by the previous argument because $1 \leq j-i < P$. Thus the sequence $A, 2A, \ldots, (P-1)A$, when considered (mod P), is a permutation of $1, 2, \ldots, P-1$. The product of both sequences (mod P) must be equivalent (and non-zero), yielding the equivalence $A^{P-1}(P-1)! \equiv (P-1)! (\bmod P)$ from which the theorem follows.*

2. Though $\sqrt{N}$ may seem small, if N is a 100-digit number, then $\sqrt{N}$ is still a 50-digit number; tests that take $O(\sqrt{N})$ time are thus out of the question for the `HugeInt` type.

```
// Return true if odd integer n is prime.
template <class HugeInt>
bool isPrime( const HugeInt & n )
{
    for( HugeInt i = 3; i * i <= n; i += 2 )
        if( n % i == 0 )
            return false;      // Not prime

    return true;               // Prime
}
```

Figure 10.7 Primality testing by trial division.

***Fermat's Little Theorem* is necessary but not sufficient to establish primality.**

If the converse of Fermat's Little Theorem were true, then we would have a primality-testing algorithm that would be computationally equivalent to modular exponentiation (i.e., $O(\log N)$). Unfortunately, the converse is not true. For example, $2^{340} \equiv 1 (\bmod 341)$, but 341 is composite (11×31).

To do the primality test, we need an additional theorem, Theorem 10.2.

Theorem 10.2

If P is prime and $X^2 \equiv 1 (\bmod P)$, then $X \equiv \pm 1 (\bmod P)$.

Proof

Because $X^2 - 1 \equiv 0 (\bmod P)$ implies $(X-1)(X+1) \equiv 0 (\bmod P)$ and P is prime, then $X - 1$ or $X + 1 \equiv 0 (\bmod P)$.

A combination of Theorems 10.1 and 10.2 is useful. Let A be any integer between 2 and $N-2$. If we compute $A^{N-1} (\bmod N)$ and the result is not 1, we know that N cannot be prime; otherwise, we would contradict Fermat's Little Theorem. As a result, A is a value that proves that N is not prime. We say then that A is a **witness to N's compositeness.** Every composite number N has some witnesses A, but for some numbers, called the *Carmichael numbers*, these witnesses are hard to find. We need to be sure that we have a high probability of finding a witness no matter what the choice of N is. To improve our chances, we use Theorem 10.2.

In the course of computing A^i, we compute $(A^{\lfloor i/2 \rfloor})^2$. So we let $X = A^{\lfloor i/2 \rfloor}$ and $Y = X^2$. Note that X and Y are computed automatically as part of the `power` routine. If Y is 1 and if X is not $\pm 1 (\bmod N)$, then by Theorem 10.2, N cannot be prime. We can return 0 for the value of A^i when that condition is detected, and N will appear to have failed the test of primality implied by Fermat's Little Theorem.

If the algorithm declares a number not to be prime, it is not prime with 100 percent certainty. Each random attempt has at most a 25 percent false positive rate.

The routine `witness`, shown in Figure 10.8, computes $A^i (\text{mod } P)$, augmented to return 0 if a violation of Theorem 10.2 is detected. If `witness` does not return 1, then A is a witness to the fact that N cannot be prime. Lines 14 through 16 make a recursive call and produce X. We then compute X^2, as is normal for the `power` computation. We check whether Theorem 10.2 is violated, returning 0 if it is. Otherwise, we complete the `power` computation.

The only remaining issue is correctness. If our algorithm declares that N is composite, then N *must* be composite. If N is composite, are all $2 \le A \le N - 2$ witnesses? The answer, unfortunately, is no. That is, some choices of A will trick our algorithm into declaring that N is prime. In fact, if we choose A randomly, we have at most a 1/4 chance of failing to detect a composite number and thus making an error. Note that this outcome is true for *any* N. If it were obtained only by averaging over all N, we would not have a good enough routine. Analogous to medical tests, our algorithm generates false positives at most 25 percent of the time for any N.

Some composites will pass the test and be declared prime. A composite is very unlikely to pass 20 consecutive independent random tests.

These odds do not seem very good because a 25 percent error rate generally is considered very high. However, if we independently use 20 values of A, the chances that none of them will witness a composite number is $1/4^{20}$, which is about one in a million million. Those odds are much more reasonable and can be made even better by using more trials. The routine `isPrime`, which is also shown in Figure 10.8, uses five trials.[3]

Summary

In this chapter we described how random numbers are generated and used. The linear congruential generator is a good choice for simple applications, so long as care is taken in choosing the parameters A and M. Using a uniform random number generator, we can derive random numbers for other distributions, such as the Poisson and negative exponential distributions.

Random numbers have many uses, including the empirical study of algorithms, the simulation of real-life systems, and the design of algorithms that probabilistically avoid the worst case. We use random numbers in other parts of this text, notably in Section 14.2 and Exercise 21.20.

This concludes Part II of the book. In Part III we look at some simple applications, beginning with a discussion of games in Chapter 11 that illustrates three important problem-solving techniques.

3. These bounds are typically pessimistic, and the analysis involves number theory that is much too involved for this text.

```
// Probabilistic primality testing routine.
// If witness does not return 1, n is definitely composite.
// Do this by computing a^i ( mod n ) and looking for
// non-trivial square roots of 1 along the way.
// HugeInt: must have copy constructor, operator=,
//     conversion from int, *, /, -, %, ==, and !=.
template <class HugeInt>
HugeInt witness( const HugeInt & a, const HugeInt & i,
                                    const HugeInt & n )
{
    if( i == 0 )
        return 1;

    HugeInt x = witness( a, i / 2, n );
    if( x == 0 )    // If n is recursively composite, stop
        return 0;

      // n is not prime if we find a nontrivial square root of 1
    HugeInt y = ( x * x ) % n;
    if( y == 1 && x != 1 && x != n - 1 )
        return 0;

    if( i % 2 == 1 )
        y = ( a * y ) % n;

    return y;
}

// Make NUM_TRIALS calls to witness to check if n is prime.
template <class HugeInt>
bool isPrime( const HugeInt & n )
{
    const int NUM_TRIALS = 5;

    for( int counter = 0; counter < NUM_TRIALS; counter++ )
        if( witness( randomHugeInt( 2, n - 2 ), n - 1, n ) != 1 )
            return false;

    return true;
}
```

Figure 10.8 A randomized test for primality.

Objects of the Game

false positives /false negatives Mistakes randomly made (presumably with low probability) by some randomized algorithms that work in a fixed amount of time. (p. 377)

Fermat's Little Theorem States that if P is prime and $0 < A < P$, then $A^{P-1} \equiv 1 \pmod{P}$. It is necessary but not sufficient to establish primality. (p. 379)

full-period linear congruential generator A random number generator that has period $M - 1$. (p. 369)

linear congruential generator A good algorithm for generating uniform distributions. (p. 368)

negative exponential distribution A form of distribution used to model the time between occurrences of random events. Its mean equals its variance. (p. 373)

period The length of the sequence until a number is repeated. A random number generator with period P generates the same random sequence of random numbers after P iterations. (p. 369)

permutation A permutation of 1, 2, ..., N is a sequence of N integers that includes each of 1, 2, ..., N exactly once. (p. 365)

Poisson distribution A distribution that models the number of occurrences of a rare event. (p. 371)

pseudorandom numbers Numbers that have many properties of random numbers. Good generators of pseudorandom numbers are hard to find. (p. 366)

random permutation A random arrangement of N items. Can be generated in linear time using one random number per item. (p. 374)

randomized algorithm An algorithm that uses random numbers rather than deterministic decisions to control branching. (p. 376)

seed The initial value of a random number generator. (p. 369)

trial division The simplest algorithm for primality testing. It is fast for small (32-bit) numbers but cannot be used for larger numbers. (p. 378)

uniform distribution A distribution in which all numbers in the specified range are equally likely to occur. (p. 367)

witness to compositeness A value of A that proves that a number is not prime, using Fermat's Little Theorem. (p. 379)

Common Errors

1. Using an initial seed of zero gives bad random numbers.
2. Inexperienced users occasionally reinitialize the seed prior to generating a random permutation. This action guarantees that the same permutation will be repeatedly produced, which is probably not intended.
3. Many random number generators are notoriously bad; for serious applications in which long sequences of random numbers are required, the linear congruential generator is also unsatisfactory.
4. The low-order bits of linear congruential generators are known to be somewhat nonrandom, so avoid using them. For example, `randomInt()%2` is often a bad way to flip a coin.
5. When random numbers are being generated in some interval, a common error is to be slightly off at the boundaries and either allow some number outside the interval to be generated or not allow the smallest number to be generated with fair probability.
6. Many random permutation generators do not generate all permutations with equal likelihood. As discussed in the text, our algorithm is limited by the random number generator.
7. Tinkering with a random number generator is likely to weaken its statistical properties.

On the Internet

Most of the code in this chapter is available.

Random.h	Contains the class interface for `Random`, as shown in Figure 10.1.
Random.cpp	Contains the `Random` class implementation.
Permute.cpp	Contains the `permute` routine shown in Figure 10.6.
Math.cpp	Contains the primality-testing routine shown in Figure 10.8 and the math routines presented in Section 8.4.

Exercises

In Short

10.1. For the random-number generator described in the text, determine the first 10 values of `state`, assuming that it is initialized with a value of 1.

10.2. Show the result of running the primality-testing algorithm for $N = 561$ with values of A ranging from 2 to 5.

10.3. If 42,000,000 Florida lottery tickets are sold, what is the expected number of winners? What are the odds that there will be no winners? One winner?

10.4. Why can't zero be used as a seed for the linear congruential generator?

In Theory

10.5. Prove that Equation 10.4 is equivalent to Equation 10.1 and that the resulting program in Figure 10.2 is correct.

10.6. Complete the proof that each permutation obtained in Figure 10.6 is equally likely.

10.7. Suppose that you have a biased coin that comes up heads with probability p and tails with probability $1 - p$. Show how to design an algorithm that uses the coin to generate a 0 or 1 with equal probability.

In Practice

10.8. Write a program that calls `randomInt` (that returns an `int` in the specified interval) 100,000 times to generate numbers between 1 and 1000. Does it meet the stronger statistical tests given in Section 10.2?

10.9. Run the Poisson generator shown in Figure 10.4 1,000,000 times, using an expected value of 2. Does the distribution agree with Figure 10.3?

10.10. Consider a two-candidate election in which the winner received a fraction p of the vote. If the votes are counted sequentially, what is the probability that the winner was ahead (or tied) at every stage of the election? This problem is the so-called *ballot problem*. Write a program that verifies the answer, p. (*Hint:* Simulate an election of 10,000 voters. Generate random arrays of $10{,}000p$ ones and $10{,}000(1 - p)$ zeros. Then verify in a sequential scan that the difference between 1s and 0s is never negative.

Programming Projects

10.11. An alternative permutation algorithm is to fill the array `a` from `a[0]` to `a[n-1]`, as follows. To fill `a[i]`, generate random numbers until you get one that has not been used previously. Use an array of Booleans to perform that test. Give an analysis of the expected running time (this is tricky) and then write a program that compares this running time with both your analysis and the routine shown in Figure 10.6.

10.12. Suppose that you want to generate a random permutation of N distinct items drawn from the range 1, 2, ..., M. (The case $M = N$, of course, has already been discussed). Floyd's algorithm does the following. First, it recursively generates a permutation of $N - 1$ distinct items drawn from the range $M - 1$. It then generates a random integer in the range 1 to M. If the random integer is not already in the permutation we add it; otherwise, we add M.

a. Prove that this algorithm does not add duplicates.
b. Prove that each permutation is equally likely.
c. Give a recursive implementation of the algorithm.
d. Give an iterative implementation of the algorithm.

10.13. A *random walk* in two dimensions is the following game played on the x–y coordinate system. Starting at the origin, (0, 0), each iteration consists of a random step either 1 unit left, up, right, or down. The walk terminates when the walker returns to the origin. The probability of this happening is 1 in two dimensions but less than 1 in three dimensions.) Write a program that performs 100 independent random walks and computes the average number of steps taken in each direction.

10.14. A simple and effective statistical test is the *chi-square test*. Suppose that you generate N positive numbers that can assume one of M values (for example, we could generate numbers between 1 and M, inclusive). The number of occurrences of each number is a random variable with mean $\mu = N/M$. For the test to work, you should have $\mu > 10$. Let f_i be the number of times i is generated. Then compute the chi-square value $V = \sum(f_i - \mu)^2/u$. The result should be close to M. If the result is consistently more than $2\sqrt{M}$ away from M (i.e., more than once in 10 tries), then the generator has failed the test. Implement the chi-square test and run it on your implementation of the `randomInt` member function (with `low` = 1 and `high` = 100).

References

A good discussion of elementary random number generators is provided in [3]. The permutation algorithm is due to R. Floyd, and is presented in [1]. The randomized primality-testing algorithm is taken from [2] and [4]. More information on random numbers is available in any good book on statistics or probability.

1. J. Bentley, "Programming Pearls," *Communications of the ACM* **30** (1987), 754–757.
2. G. L. Miller, "Riemann's Hypothesis and Tests for Primality," *Journal of Computer and System Science* **13** (1976), 300–317.
3. S. K. Park and K. W. Miller, "Random Number Generators: Good Ones Are Hard to Find," *Communications of the ACM* **31** (1988) 1192–1201. (See also *Technical Correspondence* in **36** (1993) 105–110, which provides the value of A used in Figure 10.2.)
4. M. O. Rabin, "Probabilistic Algorithms for Testing Primality," *Journal of Number Theory* **12** (1980), 128–138.

Part III

Applications

Chapter 11

Fun and Games

In this chapter we introduce three important algorithmic techniques and show how to use them by implementing programs to solve two recreational problems. The first problem is the *word search puzzle* and involves finding words in a two-dimensional grid of characters. The second is optimal play in the game of Tic-Tac-Toe.

In this chapter, we show:

- how to use the binary search algorithm to incorporate information from unsuccessful searches and to solve large instances of a word search problem in under 1 sec,
- how to use the *alpha–beta pruning* algorithm to speed up the recursive algorithm presented in Section 8.7, and
- how to use maps to increase the speed of the tic-tac-toe algorithm.

11.1 Word Search Puzzles

The *word search puzzle* requires searching for words in a two-dimensional grid of letters. Words may be oriented in one of eight directions.

The input to the **word search puzzle** problem is a two-dimensional array of characters and a list of words, and the object is to find the words in the grid. These words may be horizontal, vertical, or diagonal in any direction (for a total of eight directions). As an example, the grid shown in Figure 11.1 contains the words `this`, `two`, `fat`, and `that`. The word `this` begins at row 0, column 0—the point (0, 0)—and extends to (0, 3); `two` goes from (0, 0) to (2, 0); `fat` goes from (3, 0) to (1, 2); and `that` goes from (3, 3) to (0, 0). (Additional, mostly shorter, words are not listed here.)

	0	1	2	3
0	t	h	i	s
1	w	a	t	s
2	o	a	h	g
3	f	g	d	t

Figure 11.1 A sample word search grid.

11.1.1 Theory

The brute-force algorithm searches each word in the word list.

We can use any of several naive algorithms to solve the word search puzzle problem. The most direct is the following brute-force approach:

```
for each word W in the word list
    for each row R
        for each column C
            for each direction D
                check if W exists at row R, column C
                in direction D
```

An alternative algorithm searches from each point in the grid in each direction for each word length and looks for the word in the word list.

Because there are eight directions, this algorithm requires eight word/row/column ($8WRC$) checks. Typical puzzles published in magazines feature 40 or so words and a 16×16 grid, which involves roughly 80,000 checks. That number is certainly easy to compute on any modern machine. Suppose, however, that we consider the variation in which only the puzzle board is given and the word list is essentially an English dictionary. In this case, the number of words might be 40,000 instead of 40, resulting in 80,000,000 checks. Doubling the grid would require 320,000,000 checks, which is no longer a trivial calculation. We want an algorithm that can solve a puzzle of this size in a fraction of a second (not counting disk I/O time) so we must consider an alternative algorithm:

```
for each row R
    for each column C
        for each direction D
            for each word length L
                check if L chars starting at row R column C
                            in direction D form a word
```

The lookups can be done by a binary search.

This algorithm rearranges the loop to avoid searching for every word in the word list. If we assume that words are limited to 20 characters, the number of checks used by the algorithm is $160\,RC$. For a 32×32 puzzle, this number is roughly 160,000 checks. The problem, of course, is that we must now decide whether a word is in the word list. If we use a linear search, we lose. If we use a good data structure, we can expect an efficient search. If the word list is sorted, which is to be expected for an online dictionary, we can use a binary search (shown in Figure 6.12) and perform each check in roughly $\log W$ string comparisons. For 40,000 words, doing so involves perhaps 16 comparisons per check, for a total of less than 3,000,000 string comparisons. This number of comparisons can certainly be done in a few seconds and is a factor of 100 better than the previous algorithm.

We can further improve the algorithm based on the following observation. Suppose that we are searching in some direction and see the character sequence `qx`. An English dictionary will not contain any words beginning with `qx`. So is it worth continuing the innermost loop (over all word lengths)? The answer obviously is no: If we detect a character sequence that is not a prefix of any word in the dictionary, we can immediately look in another direction. This algorithm is given by the following pseudocode:

If a character sequence is not a prefix of any word in the dictionary, we can terminate searching in that direction.

```
for each row R
    for each column C
        for each direction D
            for each word length L
                check if L chars starting at row R column
                            C in direction D form a word
                if they do not form a prefix,
                    break;    // the innermost loop
```

The only remaining algorithmic detail is the implementation of the prefix test: Assuming that the current character sequence is not in the word list, how can we decide whether it is a prefix of some word in the word list? The answer turns out to be simple. Recall from Section 7.4.2 that the `lower_bound` STL function returns the position of the smallest element that is at least as large as the target. The caller can easily check on whether a match is found. If a match is not found, verifying that the character sequence is a prefix of some word in the list also is easy, because, if it is, it must be a prefix of the word in the returned position (in Exercise 11.3 you are asked to prove this outcome).

Prefix testing can also be done by binary search.

11.1.2 C++ Implementation

Our C++ implementation follows the algorithm description almost verbatim. We design a `Puzzle` class to store the grid and word list, as well as the corresponding input streams. The class interface is shown in Figure 11.2. The public part of the class consists of a constructor and a single member function, `solvePuzzle`. The private part includes the data members and supporting routines.

Our implementation follows the algorithm description.

```
// Puzzle class interface: solve word search puzzle.
//
// CONSTRUCTION: with no initializer.
// *****************PUBLIC OPERATIONS*********************
// int SolvePuzzle( )   --> Print all words found in the
//                          puzzle; return number of matches

#include <fstream>
#include <string>
#include <vector>
#include <algorithm>
#include "matrix.h"
using namespace std;

class Puzzle
{
  public:
    Puzzle( );
    int solvePuzzle( ) const;

  private:
    matrix<char> theBoard;
    vector<string> theWords;
    ifstream puzzleStream;
    ifstream wordStream;

    void openFile( const string & message, ifstream & inFile );
    void readPuzzle( );
    void readWords( );
    int solveDirection( int baseRow, int baseCol,
                        int rowDelta, int colDelta ) const;
};
```

Figure 11.2 The `Puzzle` class interface.

The constructor opens and reads the data files. We skimp on error checks for brevity.

Figure 11.3 gives the code for the constructor. It merely opens and reads the two files corresponding to the grid and the word list. The supporting routine `openFile`, shown in Figure 11.4, repeatedly prompts for a file until an open is successful. The `readWords` routine, shown in Figure 11.5, reads the word list. The code includes an error check to ensure that the word list has been sorted. Similarly, `readPuzzle`, shown in Figure 11.6, reads the grid and is also concerned with error handling. We need to be sure that we can handle missing puzzles, and we want to warn the user if the grid is not rectangular. Note that we use the `matrix push_back` method to add a new row. However, `push_back` needs a `vector` (not a `string`), which we get by calling `toVec`.

```
// Constructor for Puzzle class.
// Prompts for and reads puzzle and dictionary files.
Puzzle::Puzzle( ) : theBoard( 0, 0 )
{
    openFile( "Enter puzzle file", puzzleStream );
    openFile( "Enter dictionary name", wordStream );
    readPuzzle( );
    readWords( );
}
```

Figure 11.3 The `Puzzle` class constructor.

```
// Print a prompt and open a file.
// Retry until open is successful.
void Puzzle::openFile( const string & mesg, ifstream & inFile )
{
    string name;

    do
    {
        inFile.clear( );
        cout << mesg << ": ";
        cin >> name;
        inFile.open( name.c_str( ) );
    } while( !inFile );
}
```

Figure 11.4 The `openFile` routine for opening either the grid or word list file.

```
// Routine to read the dictionary.
// Error message is printed if dictionary is not sorted.
void Puzzle::readWords( )
{
    string thisWord;
    int numEntries = 0;

    for( ; wordStream >> thisWord; numEntries++ )
    {
        theWords.push_back( thisWord );

        if( numEntries != 0 && theWords[ numEntries ] <
                              theWords[ numEntries - 1 ] )
        {
            cerr << "Dictionary is not sorted... skipping << endl;
            continue;
        }
    }
}
```

Figure 11.5 The `readWords` routine for reading the word list.

```
// Return a vector<char> containing characters in str.
vector<char> toVec( const string & str )
{
    vector<char> v( str.length( ) );

    for( int i = 0; i < str.length( ); i++ )
        v[ i ] = str[ i ];
    return v;
}

// Routine to read the grid.
// Checks to ensure that the grid is rectangular.
void Puzzle::readPuzzle( )
{
    string oneLine;

    if( getline( puzzleStream, oneLine ).eof( ) )
        return;

    int columns = oneLine.length( );
    theBoard.push_back( toVec( oneLine ) );

    while( !( getline( puzzleStream, oneLine ) ).eof( ) )
    {
        if( oneLine.length( ) != columns )
            cerr << "Puzzle is not rectangular" << endl;
        else
            theBoard.push_back( toVec( oneLine ) );
    }
}
```

Figure 11.6 The `readPuzzle` routine for reading the grid.

We use two loops to iterate over the eight directions.

The `solvePuzzle` routine shown in Figure 11.7 nests the row, column, and direction loops and then calls the private routine `solveDirection` for each possibility. The return value is the number of matches found. We give a direction by indicating a column direction and then a row direction. For instance, south is indicated by `cd=0` and `rd=1` and northeast by `cd=1` and `rd=-1`; `cd` can range from `-1` to `1` and `rd` from `-1` to `1`, except that both cannot be `0` simultaneously. All that remains to be done is to provide `solveDirection`, which is coded in Figure 11.8. The `solveDirection` routine constructs a string by starting at the base row and column and extending in the appropriate direction.

We also assume that one-letter matches are not allowed (because any one-letter match would be reported eight times). At lines 23 through 26, we iterate

```
// Routine to solve the word search puzzle.
// Performs checks in all eight directions.
int Puzzle::solvePuzzle( ) const
{
    int matches = 0;

    for( int r = 0; r < theBoard.numrows( ); r++ )
        for( int c = 0; c < theBoard.numcols( ); c++ )
            for( int rd = -1; rd <= 1; rd++ )
                for( int cd = -1; cd <= 1; cd++ )
                    if( rd != 0 || cd != 0 )
                        matches += solveDirection( r, c, rd, cd );

    return matches;
}
```

Figure 11.7 The `solvePuzzle` routine for searching in all directions from all starting points.

and extend the string while ensuring that we do not go past the grid's boundary. At line 28 we tack on the next character, using `operator+=`, and perform a binary search at line 31. If we do not have a prefix, we can stop looking and return. Otherwise, we know that we have to continue after checking at line 36 for a possible exact match. Line 44 returns the number of matches found when the call to `solveDirection` can find no more words. A simple `main` program is shown in Figure 11.9.

11.2 The Game of Tic-Tac-Toe

The *minimax strategy* examines lots of positions. We can get by with less without losing any information.

Recall from Section 8.7 a simple algorithm, known as the **minimax strategy,** allows the computer to select an optimal move in a game of Tic-Tac-Toe. This recursive strategy involves the following decisions.

1. A **terminal position** can immediately be evaluated, so if the position is terminal return its value.
2. Otherwise, if it is the computer's turn to move, return the maximum value of all positions reachable by making one move. The reachable values are calculated recursively.
3. Otherwise, it is the human player's turn to move. Return the minimum value of all positions reachable by making one move. The reachable values are calculated recursively.

```
// Return true if prefix is a prefix of word.
bool isPrefix( const string & prefix, const string & word )
{
    if( word.length( ) < prefix.length( ) )
        return false;

    for( int i = 0; i < prefix.length( ); i++ )
        if( prefix[ i ] != word[ i ] )
            return false;

    return true;
}

// Search the grid from a starting point and direction.
int Puzzle::solveDirection( int baseRow, int baseCol,
                            int rowDelta, int colDelta ) const
{
    string word;
    int numMatches = 0;

    word = theBoard[ baseRow ][ baseCol ];

    for( int i = baseRow + rowDelta, j = baseCol + colDelta;
            i >= 0 && j >= 0 && i < theBoard.numrows( )
                              && j < theBoard.numcols( );
                i += rowDelta, j += colDelta )
    {
        word += theBoard[ i ][ j ];

        vector<string>::const_iterator itr;
        itr = lower_bound( theWords.begin( ), theWords.end( ), word );

        if( itr == theWords.end( ) || !isPrefix( word, *itr ) )
            break;

        if( *itr == word )
        {
            numMatches++;
            cout << "Found " << word << " at " <<
                baseRow << " " << baseCol << " to " <<
                i << " " << j << endl;
        }
    }
    return numMatches;
}
```

Figure 11.8 Implementation of a single search.

```
// Simple main routine for word search puzzle problem.
int main( )
{
    Puzzle p;
    cout << "Found " << p.solvePuzzle( ) << " matches" << endl;
    return 0;
}
```

Figure 11.9 A simple `main` routine for the word search puzzle problem.

11.2.1 Alpha–Beta Pruning

A *refutation* is a countermove that proves that a proposed move is not an improvement over moves previously considered. If we find a refutation, we do not have to examine any more moves and the recursive call can return.

Although the minimax strategy gives an optimal tic-tac-toe move, it performs a lot of searching. Specifically, to choose the first move, it makes roughly a half-million recursive calls. One reason for this large number of calls is that the algorithm does more searching than necessary. Suppose that the computer is considering five moves: C_1, C_2, C_3, C_4, and C_5. Suppose also that the recursive evaluation of C_1 reveals that C_1 forces a draw. Now C_2 is evaluated. At this stage, we have a position from which it would be the human player's turn to move. Suppose that in response to C_2, the human player can consider H_{2a}, H_{2b}, H_{2c}, and H_{2d}. Further, suppose that an evaluation of H_{2a} shows a forced draw. Automatically, C_2 is at best a draw and possibly even a loss for the computer (because the human player is assumed to play optimally). Because we need to improve on C_1, we do not have to evaluate any of H_{2b}, H_{2c}, and H_{2d}. We say that H_{2a} is a *refutation,* meaning that it proves that C_2 is not a better move than what has already been seen. Thus we return that C_2 is a draw and keep C_1 as the best move seen so far, as shown in Figure 11.10. In general, then, a **refutation** is a countermove that proves that a proposed move is not an improvement over moves previously considered.

***Alpha–beta pruning* is used to reduce the number of positions evaluated in a minimax search. Alpha is the value that the human player has to refute, and beta is the value that the computer has to refute.**

We do not need to evaluate each node completely; for some nodes, a refutation suffices and some loops can terminate early. Specifically, when the human player evaluates a position, such as C_2, a refutation, if found, is just as good as the absolute best move. The same logic applies to the computer. At any point in the search, `alpha` is the value that the human player has to refute, and `beta` is the value that the computer has to refute. When a search is done on the human player's side, any move less than `alpha` is equivalent to `alpha`; when a search is done on the computer side, any move greater than `beta` is equivalent to `beta`. This strategy of reducing the number of positions evaluated in a minimax search is commonly called **alpha–beta pruning.**

As Figure 11.11 shows, alpha–beta pruning requires only a few changes to `chooseMove`. Both `alpha` and `beta` are passed as additional parameters.

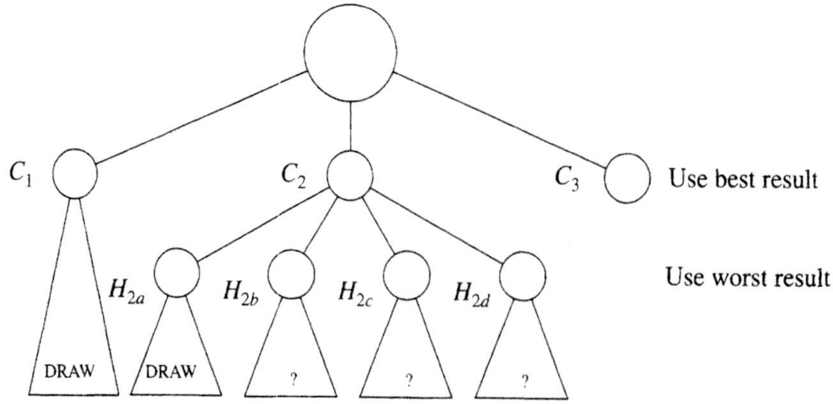

Figure 11.10 Alpha–beta pruning: After H_{2a} is evaluated, C_2, which is the minimum of the H_2's, is at best a draw. Consequently, it cannot be an improvement over C_1. We therefore do not need to evaluate H_{2b}, H_{2c}, and H_{2d} and can proceed directly to C_3.

Initially, `chooseMove` is started with `alpha` and `beta` representing `HUMAN_WIN` and `COMPUTER_WIN`, respectively. Lines 17 and 21 reflect a change in the initialization of `value`. The move evaluation is only slightly more complex than originally shown in Figure 8.26. The recursive call at line 29 includes the parameters `alpha` and `beta`, which are adjusted at line 36 or 38 if needed. The only other change is at line 41, which provides for an immediate return when a refutation is found.

Alpha–beta pruning works best when it finds refutations early.

To take full advantage of alpha–beta pruning, game programs usually try to apply heuristics to place the best moves early in the search. This approach results in even more pruning than we would expect from a random search of positions. In practice, alpha–beta pruning limits the searching to $O(\sqrt{N})$ nodes, where N is the number of nodes that would be examined without alpha–beta pruning, resulting in a huge savings. The tic-tac-toe example is not ideal because there are so many identical values. Even so, the initial search is reduced to roughly 18,000 positions.

11.2.2 Transposition Tables

A *transposition table* stores previously evaluated positions.

Another commonly employed practice is to use a table to keep track of all positions that have been evaluated. For instance, in the course of searching for the first move, the program will examine the positions shown in Figure 11.12. If the values of the positions are saved, the second occurrence of a position need not be recomputed; it essentially becomes a terminal position. The data

```
// Routine to compute optimal tic-tac-toe move.
int TicTacToe::chooseMove( Side s, int & bestRow,
                           int & bestColumn,
                           int alpha, int beta )
{
    Side opp;              // The other side
    int reply;             // Value of opponent's reply
    int dc;                // Placeholder
    int simpleEval;        // Result of an immediate evaluation
    int value;

    if( ( simpleEval = positionValue( ) ) != UNCLEAR )
        return simpleEval;

    if( s == COMPUTER )
    {
        opp = HUMAN; value = alpha;
    }
    else
    {
        opp = COMPUTER; value = beta;
    }

    for( int row = 0; row < 3; row++ )
        for( int column = 0; column < 3; column++ )
            if( squareIsEmpty( row, column ) )
            {
                place( row, column, s );
                reply = chooseMove( opp, dc, dc, alpha, beta );
                place( row, column, EMPTY );

                if( s == COMPUTER && reply > value ||
                    s == HUMAN && reply < value )
                {
                    if( s == COMPUTER )
                        alpha = value = reply;
                    else
                        beta = value = reply;

                    bestRow = row; bestColumn = column;
                    if( alpha >= beta )
                        return value;   // Refutation
                }
            }

    return value;
}
```

Figure 11.11 The `chooseMove` routine for computing an optimal tic-tac-toe move, using alpha–beta pruning.

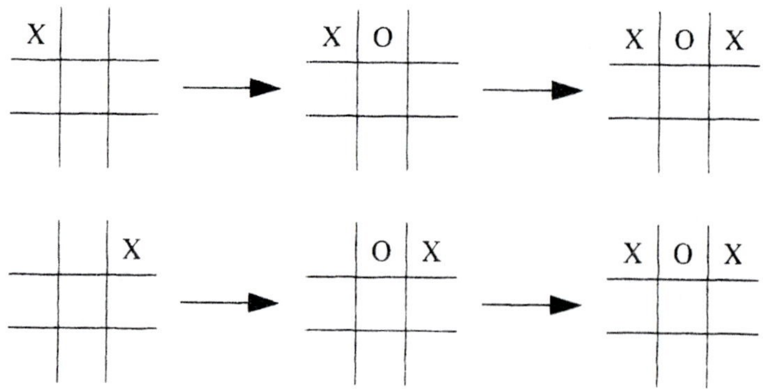

Figure 11.12 Two searches that arrive at identical positions.

structure that records and stores previously evaluated positions is called a **transposition table;** it is implemented as a map of positions to values.[1]

A map is used to implement the transposition table. Often the underlying implementation is a hash table.

We do not need an ordered map, but as the STL `map` is ordered—and is the only one available to us—we use it. More commonly, an unordered map, with a data structure called a *hash table* as the underlying implementation, is used to implement the transposition table. We discuss hash tables in Chapter 20.

To implement the transposition table we first define a `Position` class, as shown in Figure 11.13, which we use to store each position. Values in the board will be `HUMAN`, `COMPUTER`, or `EMPTY` (defined shortly in the `TicTacToe` class, as shown in Figure 11.15). The `map` requires that we define a default constructor, copy semantics, and `operator<` that can be used by the `map` to provide some total order. Note that `operator<` is not directly used by our code. However, if `operator<` is not meaningful (i.e., it does not provide a total order), the map searches can loop indefinitely. We also provide a constructor that can be initialized with a matrix representing the board.

We do not store positions that are at the bottom of the recursion in the transposition table.

Except for `operator<`, is shown in Figure 11.14, these routines are trivial (copy semantics are automatic!). The constructors and copy operators are not particularly efficient because they require copying a matrix. For larger game problems that is a serious consideration. A related issue concerns whether including all positions in the transposition table is worth-

1. We discussed this generic technique, which avoids repeated recursive calls by storing values in a table, in a different context in Section 8.6. This technique is also known as *memoizing*. The term *transposition table* is slightly misleading because fancier implementations of this technique recognize and avoid searching not only exactly identical positions, but also symmetrically identical postions.

```
#include "matrix.h"

// A minimal Position class for use with transposition table.
struct Position
{
    matrix<int> board;
    Position( ) : board( 3, 3 ) { }
    Position( const matrix<int> & theBoard )
      : board( theBoard ) { }
    bool operator< ( const Position & rhs ) const;
};
```

Figure 11.13 The `Position` class interface.

```
// Comparison operator, guarantees a total order.
bool Position::operator<( const Position & rhs ) const
{
    for( int i = 0; i < 3; i++ )
        for( int j = 0; j < 3; j++ )
            if( board[ i ][ j ] != rhs.board[ i ][ j ] )
                return board[ i ][ j ] < rhs.board[ i ][ j ];
    return false;
}
```

Figure 11.14 The `Position` class `operator<` used for the transposition table in the tic-tac-toe algorithm.

while. The overhead of maintaining the table suggests that positions near the bottom of the recursion ought not be saved because

- there are so many, and
- the point of alpha–beta pruning and transposition tables is to reduce search times by avoiding recursive calls early in the game; saving a recursive call very deep in the search does not greatly reduce the number of positions examined because that recursive call would examine only a few positions anyway.

The chooseMove method has additional parameters, all of which have defaults.

We show how this technique applies to the game of Tic-Tac-Toe when we implement the transposition table. The changes needed in the `TicTacToe` class interface are shown in Figure 11.15. The additions are the new data member at line 6 and the new declaration for `chooseMove` at lines 16 through 18. We now pass `alpha` and `beta` (as in alpha–beta pruning) and also the

```
typedef map<Position,int,less<Position> > MapType;

class TicTacToe
{
  private:
    MapType transpositions;

  public:
    enum Side { HUMAN, COMPUTER, EMPTY };
    enum PositionVal { HUMAN_WIN, DRAW, UNCLEAR, COMPUTER_WIN };

    TicTacToe( ) : board( 3, 3 )
      { clearBoard( ); }    // Constructor

      // Find optimal move
    int chooseMove( Side d, int & bestRow, int & bestColumn,
                    int alpha = HUMAN_WIN,
                    int beta = COMPUTER_WIN, int depth = 0 );
    ...
};
```

Figure 11.15 Changes to the `TicTacToe` class to incorporate transposition table and alpha–beta pruning.

`depth` of the recursion, which is zero by default. Presumably, the initial call to `chooseMove` involves only the first three parameters, and the last three parameters are assigned their default values.

Figures 11.16 and 11.17 show the new `chooseMove`. At line 12, we declare a `Position` object, `thisPosition`. When the time comes it will be placed in the transposition table. This technique is not the most efficient because it involves making a copy of the board, but it is simple. Moreover, a profiler shows that it is not excessively time consuming. The constant object `TABLE_DEPTH` tells us how deep in the search to allow positions to be placed in the transposition table. By experimenting we found that `depth` 5 was optimal. Allowing positions at `depth` 6 to be saved hurt because the extra cost of maintaining the larger transposition table was not offset by the fewer examined positions.

The code has a few little tricks but nothing major.

Lines 18 to 25 are new. If we are in the first call to `chooseMove`, we initialize the transposition table. Otherwise, if we are at an appropriate depth, we determine whether the current position has been evaluated; if it has, we return its value. The code has two tricks. First, we can transpose only at `depth` 3 or higher, as Figure 11.12 suggests. The only other difference is

```
1 // Routine to compute optimal tic-tac-toe move.
2 typedef MapType::const_iterator MapItr;
3 const int TABLE_DEPTH = 5; // Max depth placed in map
4
5 int TicTacToe::chooseMove( Side s, int & bestRow, int & bestColumn,
6                            int alpha, int beta, int depth )
7 {
8     Side opp;                   // The other side
9     int reply;                  // Value of opponent's reply
10    int dc;                     // Placeholder
11    int simpleEval;             // Result of an immediate evaluation
12    Position thisPosition = board;
13    int value;
14
15    if( ( simpleEval = positionValue( ) ) != UNCLEAR )
16        return simpleEval;
17
18    if( depth == 0 )
19        transpositions = MapType( );    // makeEmpty
20    else if( depth >= 3 && depth <= TABLE_DEPTH )
21    {
22        MapItr itr = transpositions.find( thisPosition );
23        if( itr != transpositions.end( ) )
24            return (*itr).second;
25    }
26
27    if( s == COMPUTER )
28    {
29        opp = HUMAN; value = alpha;
30    }
31    else
32    {
33        opp = COMPUTER; value = beta;
34    }
```

Figure 11.16 The tic-tac-toe algorithm with alpha–beta pruning and transposition table (part 1)

from lines 54 onward. We consolidate the two return statements originally in the code into one by using a `goto`. (If you are one of those who cannot stand any use of a `goto`, it is easy enough to unconsolidate.) Immediately before the return, we store the value of the position in the transposition table.

The use of the transposition table in this tic-tac-toe algorithm removes about half the positions from consideration, with only a slight cost for the transposition table operations. The program's speed is almost doubled.

```
    for( int row = 0; row < 3; row++ )
        for( int column = 0; column < 3; column++ )
            if( squareIsEmpty( row, column ) )
            {
                place( row, column, s );
                reply = chooseMove( opp, dc, dc,
                                    alpha, beta, depth + 1 );
                place( row, column, EMPTY );

                if( s == COMPUTER && reply > value ||
                    s == HUMAN && reply < value )
                {
                    if( s == COMPUTER )
                        alpha = value = reply;
                    else
                        beta = value = reply;

                    bestRow = row; bestColumn = column;
                    if( alpha >= beta )
                        goto Done;   // Refutation
                }
            }
Done:
    if( depth <= TABLE_DEPTH )
        transpositions[ thisPosition ] = value;
    return value;
}
```

Figure 11.17 The tic-tac-toe algorithm with alpha–beta pruning and transposition table (part 2).

11.2.3 Computer Chess

Terminal positions cannot be searched in computer chess. In the best programs, considerable knowledge is built into the evaluation function.

In a complex game such as Chess or Go, it is infeasible to search all the way to the terminal nodes: Some estimates claim that there are roughly 10^{100} legal chess positions, and all the tricks in the world will not bring it down to a manageable level. In this case, we have to stop the search after a certain depth of recursion is reached. The nodes at which the recursion is stopped become terminal nodes. These terminal nodes are evaluated with a function that estimates the value of the position. For instance, in a chess program, the evaluation function measures such variables as the relative amount and strength of pieces and other positional factors.

The best computer chess programs play at grandmaster level.

Computers are especially adept at playing moves involving deep combinations that result in exchanges of material. The reason is that the strength of pieces is easily evaluated. However, extending the search depth merely one level requires an increase in processing speed by a factor of about 6 (because the number of positions increases by about a factor of 36). Each extra level of search greatly enhances the ability of the program, up to a certain limit (which appears to have been reached by the best programs). On the other hand, computers generally are not as good at playing quiet positional games in which more subtle evaluations and knowledge of the game is required. However, this shortcoming is apparent only when the computer is playing very strong opposition. The mass-marketed computer chess programs are better than all but a small fraction of today's players.

In 1997, the computer program *Deep Blue,* using an enormous amount of computational power (evaluating as many as 200 million moves per second) was able to defeat the reigning world chess champion in a six-game match. Its evaluation function, although top secret, is known to contain a large number of factors, was aided by several chess grandmasters, and was the result of years of experimentation. Writing the top computer chess program is certainly not a trivial task.

Summary

In this chapter we introduced an application of binary search and some algorithmic techniques that are commonly used in solving word search puzzles and in game-playing programs such as Chess, Checkers, and Othello. The top programs for these games are all world class. The game of Go, however, appears too complex for computer searching.

Objects of the Game

alpha–beta pruning A technique used to reduce the number of positions that are evaluated in a minimax search. Alpha is the value that the human player has to refute, and beta is the value that the computer has to refute. (p. 397)

minimax strategy A recursive strategy that allows the computer to select an optimal move in a game of Tic-Tac-Toe. (p. 395)

refutation A countermove that proves that a proposed move is not an improvement over moves previously considered. If we find a refutation, we do not have to examine any more moves and the recursive call can return. (p. 397)

terminal position A position in a game that can be evaluated immediately. (p. 395)

transposition table A map that stores previously evaluated positions. (p. 398)

word search puzzle A program that requires searching for words in a two-dimensional grid of letters. Words may be oriented in one of eight directions. (p. 389)

Common Errors

1. When using a transposition table, you should limit the number of stored positions to avoid running out of memory.
2. Verifying your assumptions is important. For instance, in the word search puzzle, be sure that the dictionary is sorted. A common error is to forget to check your assumptions.

On the Internet

Both the word search and the game Tic-Tac-Toe are completely coded, although the interface for the latter leaves a little to be desired.

WordSrch.cpp	Contains the word search puzzle algorithm.
TicTac.cpp	Contains the `TicTacToe` class, with a `main` function.

Exercises

In Short

11.1. What error checks are missing from Figure 11.6?

11.2. For the situation in Figure 11.18,

a. which of the responses to move C_2 is a refutation?
b. what is the value of the position?

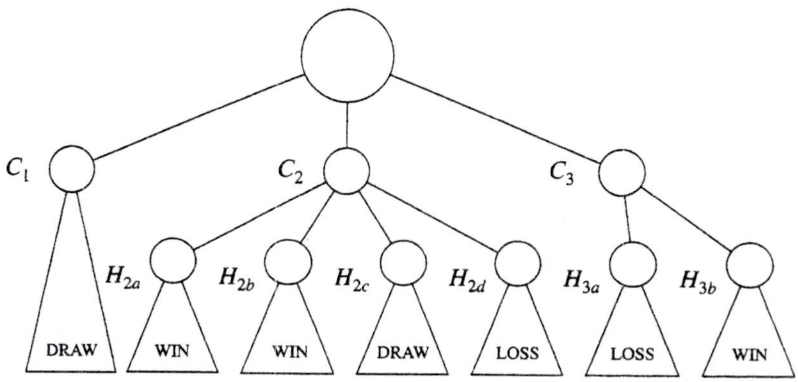

Figure 11.18 Alpha–beta pruning example for Exercise 11.2.

In Theory

11.3. Verify that, if `x` is a prefix of some word in the sorted array `a`, then `x` is a prefix of the word that `lower_bound` returns.

11.4. Explain how the running time of the word search algorithm changes when
a. the number of words doubles.
b. the number of rows and columns double (simultaneously).

In Practice

11.5. For the word search problem, replace the binary search with a sequential search. How does that change affect performance?

11.6. Compare the performance of the word search algorithm with and without the prefix search.

11.7. Write a more user-friendly interface for the tic-tac-toe program.

11.8. Even if the computer has a move that gives an immediate win, it may not make it if it detects another move that is also guaranteed to win. Some early chess programs had the problem that they would get into a repetition of position when a forced win was detected, allowing the opponent to claim a draw. In the tic-tac-toe program this outcome is not a problem because the program eventually will win. Modify the tic-tac-toe algorithm so that when a winning position is found, the move that leads to the shortest win is always taken. You can do so by adding `9-DEPTH` to `COMPUTER_WIN`, so that a quicker win gives the highest value.

11.9. Compare the performance of the tic-tac-toe program with and without alpha–beta pruning.

11.10. Implement the tic-tac-toe algorithm and measure the performance when various depths are allowed to be stored in the transposition table. Also measure the performance when no transposition table is used. How are the results affected by alpha–beta pruning?

Programming Projects

11.11. Write a program to play 5×5 tic-tac-toe, where 4 in a row wins. Can you search to terminal nodes?

11.12. The game of Boggle consists of a grid of letters and a word list. The object is to find words in the grid subject to the constraint that two adjacent letters must be adjacent in the grid (i.e., north, south, east, or west) of each other and each item in the grid can be used at most once per word. Write a program to play Boggle.

11.13. Write a program to play MAXIT. The board is represented as an $N \times N$ grid of numbers randomly placed at the start of the game. One position is designated as the initial current position. Two players alternate turns. At each turn, a player must select a grid element in the current row or column. The value of the selected position is added to the player's score, and that position becomes the current position and cannot be selected again. Players alternate until all grid elements in the current row and column have been selected, at which point the game ends and the player with the highest score wins.

11.14. Othello played on a 6×6 board is a forced win for black. Prove this assertion by writing a program. What is the final score if play on both sides is optimal?

References

If you are interested in computer games, a good starting point for information is the article cited in [1]. In this special issue of the journal, devoted exclusively to the subject, you will also find plenty of information and references to other works covering Chess, Checkers, and other computer games.

1. K. Lee and S. Mahajan, "The Development of a World Class Othello Program," *Artificial Intelligence* **43** (1990), 21–36.

Chapter 12

Stacks and Compilers

Stacks are used extensively in compilers. In this chapter we present two simple components of a compiler: a balanced symbol checker and a simple calculator. We do so to show simple algorithms that use stacks and to show how the STL classes described in Chapter 7 are used.

In this chapter, we show:

- how to use a stack to check for balanced symbols,
- how to use a *state machine* to parse symbols in a balanced symbol program, and
- how to use *operator precedence parsing* to evaluate infix expressions in a simple calculator program.

12.1 Balanced-Symbol Checker

As discussed in Section 7.2, compilers check your programs for syntax errors. Frequently, however, a lack of one symbol (such as a missing `*/` comment-ender or `}`) causes the compiler to produce numerous lines of diagnostics without identifying the real error. A useful tool to help debug compiler error messages is a program that checks whether symbols are balanced. In other words, every `{` must correspond to a `}`, every `[` to a `]`, and so on. However, simply counting the numbers of each symbol is insufficient. For example, the sequence `[()]` is legal, but the sequence `[(])` is wrong.

12.1.1 Basic Algorithm

A stack is useful here because we know that when a closing symbol such as `)` is seen, it matches the most recently seen unclosed `(`. Therefore, by placing an opening symbol on a stack, we can easily determine whether a closing symbol makes sense. Specifically, we have the following algorithm.

A stack can be used to detect mismatched symbols.

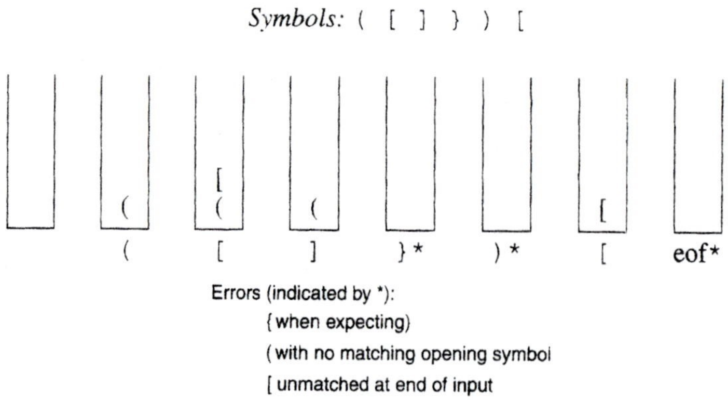

Figure 12.1 Stack operations in a balanced-symbol algorithm.

1. Make an empty stack.
2. Read symbols until the end of the file.
   a. If the symbol is an opening symbol, push it onto the stack.
   b. If it is a closing symbol do the following.
      i. If the stack is empty, report an error.
      ii. Otherwise, pop the stack. If the symbol popped is not the corresponding opening symbol, report an error.
3. At the end of the file, if the stack is not empty, report an error.

In this algorithm, illustrated in Figure 12.1, the fourth, fifth, and sixth symbols all generate errors. The } is an error because the symbol popped from the top of stack is a (, so a mismatch is detected. The) is an error because the stack is empty, so there is no corresponding (. The [is an error detected when the end of input is encountered and the stack is not empty.

Symbols in comments, string constants, and character constants need not be balanced.

To make this technique work for C++ programs, we need to consider all the contexts in which parentheses, braces, and brackets need not match. For example, we should not consider a parenthesis as a symbol if it occurs inside a comment, string constant, or character constant. We thus need routines to skip comments, string constants, and character constants. A character constant in C++ can be difficult to recognize because of the many escape sequences possible, so we need to simplify things. We want to design a program that works for the bulk of inputs likely to occur.

Line numbers are needed for meaningful error messages.

For the program to be useful, we must not only report mismatches but also attempt to identify where the mismatches occur. Consequently, we keep track of the line numbers where the symbols are seen. When an error is encountered, obtaining an accurate message is always difficult. If there is an extra }, does that mean that the } is extraneous? Or was a { missing earlier?

We keep the error handling as simple as possible, but once one error has been reported, the program may get confused and start flagging many errors. Thus only the first error can be considered meaningful. Even so, the program developed here is very useful.

12.1.2 Implementation

The program has two basic components. One part, called **tokenization,** is the process of scanning an input stream for opening and closing symbols (the tokens) and generating the sequence of tokens that need to be recognized. The second part is running the balanced symbol algorithm, based on the tokens. The two basic components are represented as separate classes.

Tokenization **is the process of generating the sequence of symbols (tokens) that need to be recognized.**

Figure 12.2 shows the `Tokenizer` class interface, and Figure 12.3 shows the `Balance` class interface. The `Tokenizer` class provides a constructor that requires an `istream` and then provides a set of accessors that can be used to get

- the next token (either an opening/closing symbol for the code in this chapter or an identifier for the code in Chapter 13),
- the current line number, and
- the number of errors (mismatched quotes and comments).

The `Tokenizer` class maintains most of this information in private data members. The `Balance` class also provides a similar constructor, but its only publicly visible routine is `checkBalance`, shown at line 24. Everything else is a supporting routine or a class data member.

We begin by describing the `Tokenizer` class. `inputStream` is a reference to an `istream` object and is initialized at construction. Because of the `ios` hierarchy (see Section 4.1), it may be initialized with an `ifstream` object. The current character being scanned is stored in `ch`, and the current line number is stored in `currentLine`. Finally, an integer that counts the number of errors is declared at line 37. The constructor, shown at lines 22 and 23, initializes the error count to 0 and the current line number to 1 and sets the `istream` reference.

We can now implement the class methods, which as we mentioned, are concerned with keeping track of the current line and attempting to differentiate symbols that represent opening and closing tokens from those that are inside comments, character constants, and string constants. This general process of recognizing tokens in a stream of symbols is called **lexical analysis.** Figure 12.4 shows a pair of routines, `nextChar` and `putBackChar`. The `nextChar` method reads the next character from `inputStream`, assigns it

Lexical analysis **is used to ignore comments and recognize symbols.**

```
#include <fstream>
#include <vector>
#include <stack>
#include <stdlib.h>
using namespace std;

// Tokenizer class.
// CONSTRUCTION: with an istream that is ready to be read.
//
// ******************PUBLIC OPERATIONS**********************
// char getNextOpenClose( ) --> Return next open/close symbol
// int getLineNumber( )      --> Return current line number
// int getErrorCount( )      --> Return number of parsing errors
// string getNextID( )       --> Return next C++ identifier
//                                (see Section 13.2)
// ******************ERRORS*********************************
// Mismatched ', ", and EOF reached in a comment are noted.

class Tokenizer
{
  public:
    Tokenizer( istream & input )
      : currentLine( 1 ), errors( 0 ), inputStream( input ) { }

      // The public routines.
    char getNextOpenClose( );
    string getNextID( );
    int getLineNumber( ) const;
    int getErrorCount( ) const;

  private:
    enum CommentType { SLASH_SLASH, SLASH_STAR };

    istream & inputStream;     // Reference to the input stream
    char ch;                   // Current character
    int currentLine;           // Current line
    int errors;                // Number of errors detected

      // A host of internal routines.
    bool nextChar( );
    void putBackChar( );
    void skipComment( CommentType start );
    void skipQuote( char quoteType );
    string getRemainingString( );
};
```

Figure 12.2 The `Tokenizer` class interface, used to retrieve tokens from an input stream.

```
#include "Tokenizer.h"
#include <iostream>
using namespace std;

// Symbol is the class that will be placed on the Stack.
struct Symbol
{
    char token;
    int  theLine;
};

// Balance class interface: check for balanced symbols.
//
// CONSTRUCTION: with an istream object.
// ******************PUBLIC OPERATIONS*******************
// int CheckBalance( )    --> Print mismatches
//                            return number of errors

class Balance
{
  public:
    Balance( istream & input ) : tok( input ), errors( 0 ) { }

    int checkBalance( );

  private:
    Tokenizer tok;        // Token source
    int errors;           // Mismatched open/close symbol errors

    void checkMatch( const Symbol & opSym, const Symbol & clSym );
};
```

Figure 12.3 Class interface for a balanced-symbol program.

to `ch`, and updates `currentLine` if a newline is encountered. It returns `false` only if the end of the file has been reached. The complementary procedure `putBackChar` puts the current character, `ch`, back onto the input stream, and decrements `currentLine` if the character is a newline. Clearly, `putBackChar` should be called at most once between calls to `nextChar`; as it is a private routine, we do not worry about abuse on the part of the class user. Putting characters back onto the input stream is a commonly used technique in parsing. In many instances we have read one too many characters, and undoing the read is useful. In our case this occurs after processing a `/`. We must determine whether the next character begins the comment start token; if it does not, we cannot simply disregard it because it could be an opening or closing symbol or a quote. Thus we pretend that it is never read.

```
// nextChar sets ch based on the next character in
// inputStream and adjusts currentLine if necessary.
// It returns the result of get.
// putBackChar puts the character back onto inputStream.
// Both routines adjust currentLine if necessary.
bool Tokenizer::nextChar( )
{
    if( !inputStream.get( ch ) )
        return false;
    if( ch == '\n' )
        currentLine++;
    return true;
}

void Tokenizer::putBackChar( )
{
    inputStream.putback( ch );
    if( ch == '\n' )
        currentLine--;
}
```

Figure 12.4 The `nextChar` routine for reading the next character, updating `currentLine` if necessary, and returning `true` if not at the end of file; and the `putBackChar` routine for putting back `ch` and updating `currentLine` if necessary.

Next is the routine `skipComment`, shown in Figure 12.5. Its purpose is to skip over the characters in the comment and position the input stream so that the next read is the first character after the comment ends. This technique is complicated by the fact that comments can either begin with `//`, in which case the line ends the comment, or `/*`, in which case `*/` ends the comment.[1] In the `//` case, we continually get the next character until either the end of file is reached (in which case the first half of the `&&` operator fails) or we get a newline. At that point we return. Note that the line number is updated automatically by `nextChar`. Otherwise, we have the `/*` case, which is processed starting at line 15.

The *state machine* is a common technique used to parse symbols; at any point, it is in some state, and each input character takes it to a new state. Eventually, the state machine reaches a state in which a symbol has been recognized.

The `skipComment` routine uses a simplified state machine. The **state machine** is a common technique used to parse symbols; at any point, it is in some state, and each input character takes it to a new state. Eventually, it reaches a state at which a symbol has been recognized.

In `skipComment`, at any point, it has matched 0, 1, or 2 characters of the `*/` terminator, corresponding to states 0, 1, and 2. If it matches two characters, it can return. Thus, inside the loop, it can be in only state 0 or 1 because, if it is in state 1 and sees a `/`, it returns immediately. Thus the state

1. We do not consider deviant cases involving `\`.

```
1 // Precondition: We are about to process a comment;
2 //                    have already seen comment start token.
3 // Postcondition: Stream will be set immediately after
4 //                    comment ending token.
5 void Tokenizer::skipComment( CommentType start )
6 {
7      if( start == SLASH_SLASH )
8      {
9          while( nextChar( ) && ( ch != '\n' ) )
10             ;
11         return;
12     }
13
14       // Look for */
15     bool state = false;    // Seen first char in comment ender.
16
17     while( nextChar( ) )
18     {
19         if( state && ch == '/' )
20             return;
21         state = ( ch == '*' );
22     }
23     errors++;
24     cout << "Unterminated comment at line "
25          << getLineNumber( ) << endl;
26 }
```

Figure 12.5 The `skipComment` routine for moving past an already started comment.

can be represented by a Boolean variable that is true if the state machine is in state 1. If it does not return, it either goes back to state 1 if it encounters a `*` or goes back to state 0 if it does not. This procedure is stated succinctly at line 21.

If we never find the comment-ending token, eventually `nextChar` returns `false` and the `while` loop terminates, resulting in an error message. The `skipQuote` method, shown in Figure 12.6, is similar. Here, the parameter is the opening quote character, which is either `"` or `'`. In either case, we need to see that character as the closing quote. However, we must be prepared to handle the `\` character; otherwise, our program will report errors when it is run on its own source. Thus we repeatedly digest characters. If the current character is a closing quote, we are done. If it is a newline, we have an unterminated character or string constant. And if it is a backslash, we digest an extra character without examining it.

Once we've written the skipping routine, writing `getNextOpenClose` is easier. If the current character is a `/`, we read a second character to see

```
// Precondition: We are about to process a quote;
//                    have already seen beginning quote.
// Postcondition: Stream will be set immediately after
//                    matching quote.
void Tokenizer::skipQuote( char quoteType )
{
    while( nextChar( ) )
    {
        if( ch == quoteType )
            return;
        if( ch == '\n' )
        {
            cout << "Missing closed quote at line " <<
                    ( getLineNumber( ) - 1 ) << endl;
            errors++;
            return;
        }
          // If a backslash, skip next character.
        else if( ch == '\\' )
            nextChar( );
    }
}
```

Figure 12.6 The `skipQuote` routine for moving past an already started character or string constant.

whether we have a comment. If so, we call `skipComment`; if not, we undo the second read. If we have a quote, we call `skipQuote`. If we have an opening or closing symbol, we can return. Otherwise, we keep reading until we eventually run out of input or find an opening or closing symbol. The entire routine is shown in Figure 12.7.

The `getLineNumber` and `getErrorCount` methods are one-liners that return the values of the corresponding data members and are not shown. We discuss the `getNextID` routine in Section 13.2.2 when it is needed.

In the `Balance` class, the balanced symbol algorithm requires that we place opening symbols on a stack. In order to print diagnostics, we store a line number with each symbol, as shown previously in the `Symbol struct` at lines 6 to 10 in Figure 12.3.

The `checkBalance` routine is implemented as shown in Figure 12.8. It follows the algorithm description almost verbatim. A stack that stores pending opening symbols is declared at line 7. Opening symbols are pushed onto the stack with the current line number. When a closing symbol is encountered and the stack is empty, the closing symbol is extraneous; otherwise, we remove the top item from the stack and verify that the opening symbol that was on the stack matches the closing symbol just read. To do so we use the

```
// Return the next opening or closing symbol or '\0' (if EOF).
// Skip past comments and character and string constants.
char Tokenizer::getNextOpenClose( )
{
    while( nextChar( ) )
    {
        if( ch == '/' )
        {
            if( nextChar( ) )
            {
                if( ch == '*' )
                    skipComment( SLASH_STAR );
                else if( ch == '/' )
                    skipComment( SLASH_SLASH );
                else if( ch != '\n' )
                    putBackChar( );
            }
        }
        else if( ch == '\'' || ch == '"' )
            skipQuote( ch );
        else if( ch == '(' || ch == '[' || ch == '{' ||
                 ch == ')' || ch == ']' || ch == '}' )
            return ch;
    }
    return '\0';          // End of file
}
```

Figure 12.7 The `getNextOpenClose` routine for skipping comments and quotes and returning the next opening or closing character.

`checkMatch` routine, which is shown in Figure 12.9. Once the end of input is encountered, any symbols on the stack are unmatched; they are repeatedly output in the `while` loop that begins at line 40. The total number of errors detected is then returned.

The `checkBalance` routine does all the algorithmic work.

Note that the current implementation allows multiple calls to `checkBalance`. However, if the input stream is not reset externally, all that happens is that the end of the file is immediately detected and we return immediately. We can add functionality to the `Tokenizer` class, allowing it to change the stream source, and then add functionality to the `Balance` class to change the input stream (passing on the change to the `Tokenizer` class). We leave this task for you to do as Exercise 12.9.

Figure 12.10 shows that we expect a `Balance` object to be created and then `checkBalance` to be invoked. In our example, if there are no command-line arguments, the associated `istream` is `cin`; otherwise, we repeatedly use `istreams` associated with the files given in the command-line argument list.

```
// Print error message for unbalanced symbols.
// Return number of errors detected.
int Balance::checkBalance( )
{
    char ch;
    Symbol lastSymbol, match;
    stack<Symbol, vector<Symbol> > pendingTokens;

    while( ( ch = tok.getNextOpenClose( ) ) != '\0' )
    {
        lastSymbol.token = ch;
        lastSymbol.theLine = tok.getLineNumber( );

        switch( ch )
        {
          case '(': case '[': case '{':
            pendingTokens.push( lastSymbol );
            break;

          case ')': case ']': case '}':
            if( pendingTokens.empty( ) )
            {
                cout << "Extraneous " << ch << " at line "
                     << tok.getLineNumber( ) << endl;
                errors++;
            }
            else
            {
                match = pendingTokens.top( );
                pendingTokens.pop( );
                checkMatch( match, lastSymbol );
            }
            break;

          default: // Can't happen
            break;
        }
    }

    while( !pendingTokens.empty( ) )
    {
        match = pendingTokens.top( );
        pendingTokens.pop( );
        cout << "Unmatched " << match.token << " at line "
             << match.theLine << endl;
        errors++;
    }

    return errors + tok.getErrorCount( );
}
```

Figure 12.8 The `checkBalance` algorithm.

```
// Print an error message if clSym does not match opSym.
// Update errors.
void Balance::checkMatch( const Symbol & opSym,
                          const Symbol & clSym )
{
    if( opSym.token == '(' && clSym.token != ')' ||
        opSym.token == '[' && clSym.token != ']' ||
        opSym.token == '{' && clSym.token != '}' )
    {
        cout << "Found " << clSym.token
             << " on line " << tok.getLineNumber( )
             << "; does not match " << opSym.token
             << " at line " << opSym.theLine << endl;
        errors++;
    }
}
```

Figure 12.9 The `checkMatch` routine for checking that the closing symbol matches the opening symbol.

```
// main routine for balanced symbol checker.
int main( int argc, char **argv )
{
    if( argc == 1 )
    {
        Balance p( cin );
        if( p.checkBalance( ) == 0 )
            cout << "No errors" << endl;
        return 0;
    }

    while( --argc )
    {
        ifstream ifp( *++argv );
        if( !ifp )
        {
            cerr << "Cannot open " << *argv << endl;
            continue;
        }
        cout << *argv << ":" << endl;
        Balance p( ifp );
        if( p.checkBalance( ) == 0 )
            cout << "No errors" << endl;
    }

    return 0;
}
```

Figure 12.10 The `main` routine with command-line arguments.

12.2 A Simple Calculator

Some of the techniques used to implement compilers can be used on a smaller scale in the implementation of a typical pocket calculator. Typically, calculators evaluate **infix expressions,** such as 1+2, which consist of a binary operator with arguments to its left and right. This format, although often fairly easy to evaluate, can be more complex. Consider the expression

```
1 + 2 * 3
```

In an *infix expression* a binary operator has arguments to its left and right.

Mathematically, this expression evaluates to 7 because the multiplication operator has higher precedence than addition. Some calculators give the answer 9, illustrating that a simple left-to-right evaluation is not sufficient; we cannot begin by evaluating 1+2. Now consider the expressions

```
10 - 4 - 3
2 ^ 3 ^ 3
```

When there are several operators, precedence and associativity determine how the operators are processed.

in which ^ is the exponentiation operator. Which subtraction and which exponentiation get evaluated first? On the one hand, subtractions are processed left-to-right, giving the result 3. On the other hand, exponentiation is generally processed right-to-left, thereby reflecting the mathematical 2^{3^3} rather than $(2^3)^3$. Thus subtraction associates left-to-right, whereas exponentiation associates from right-to-left. All of these possibilities suggest that evaluating an expression such as

```
1 - 2 - 4 ^ 5 * 3 * 6 / 7 ^ 2 ^ 2
```

would be quite challenging.

If the calculations are performed in integer math (i.e., rounding down on division), the answer is -8. To show this result, we insert parentheses to clarify ordering of the calculations:

```
( 1 - 2 ) - ( ( ( (4 ^ 5 ) * 3 ) * 6 ) / ( 7 ^ ( 2 ^ 2 ) ) )
```

Although the parentheses make the order of evaluations unambiguous, they do not necessarily make the mechanism for evaluation any clearer. A different expression form, called a **postfix expression,** which can be evaluated by a postfix machine without using any precedence rules, provides a direct mechanism for evaluation. In the next several sections we explain how it works. First, we examine the postfix expression form and show how expressions can be evaluated in a simple left-to-right scan. Next, we show algorithmically how the previous expressions, which are presented as infix expressions, can be converted to postfix. Finally, we give a C++ program that evaluates infix expressions containing additive, multiplicative, and exponentiation operators—as well as overriding parentheses. We use an algorithm called **operator precedence parsing** to convert an infix expression to a postfix expression in order to evaluate the infix expression.

12.2.1 Postfix Machines

A postfix expression is a series of operators and operands. A **postfix machine** is used to evaluate a postfix expression as follows. When an operand is seen, it is pushed onto a stack. When an operator is seen, the appropriate number of operands are popped from the stack, the operator is evaluated, and the result is pushed back onto the stack. For binary operators, which are the most common, two operands are popped. When the complete postfix expression is evaluated, the result should be a single item on the stack that represents the answer. The postfix form represents a natural way to evaluate expressions because precedence rules are not required.

A postfix expression can be evaluated as follows. Operands are pushed onto a single stack. An operator pops its operands and then pushes the result. At the end of the evaluation, the stack should contain only one element, which represents the result.

A simple example is the postfix expression

```
1 2 3 * +
```

The evaluation proceeds as follows: `1`, then `2`, and then `3` are each pushed onto the stack. To process `*`, we pop the top two items on the stack: `3` and then `2`. Note that the first item popped becomes the `rhs` parameter to the binary operator and that the second item popped is the `lhs` parameter; thus parameters are popped in reverse order. For multiplication, the order does not matter, but for subtraction and division, it does. The result of the multiplication is `6`, and that is pushed back onto the stack. At this point, the top of the stack is `6`; below it is `1`. To process the `+`, the `6` and `1` are popped, and their sum, `7`, is pushed. At this point, the expression has been read and the stack has only one item. Thus the final answer is `7`.

Every valid infix expression can be converted to postfix form. For example, the earlier long infix expression can be written in postfix notation as

```
1 2 - 4 5 ^ 3 * 6 * 7 2 2 ^ ^ / -
```

Figure 12.11 shows the steps used by the postfix machine to evaluate this expression. Each step involves a single push. Consequently, as there are 9 operands and 8 operators, there are 17 steps and 17 pushes. Clearly, the time required to evaluate a postfix expression is linear.

Evaluation of a postfix expression takes linear time.

The remaining task is to write an algorithm to convert from infix notation to postfix notation. Once we have it, we also have an algorithm that evaluates an infix expression.

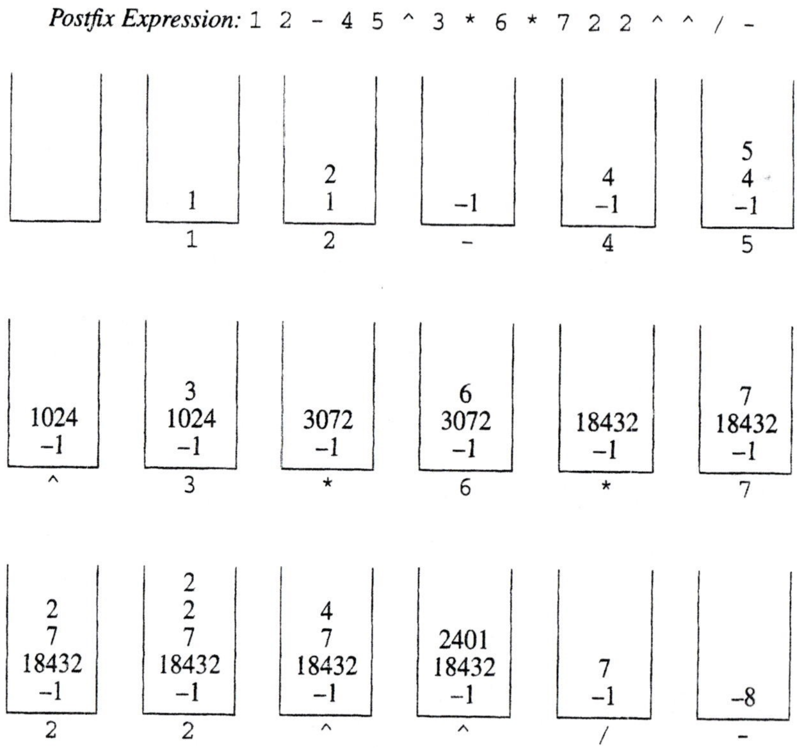

Figure 12.11 Steps in the evaluation of a postfix expression.

12.2.2 Infix to Postfix Conversion

The operator precedence parsing algorithm converts an infix expression to a postfix expression, so we can evaluate the infix expression.

The basic principle involved in the operator precedence parsing algorithm, which converts an infix expression to a postfix expression, is the following. When an operand is seen, we can immediately output it. However, when we see an operator, we can never output it because we must wait to see the second operand, so we must save it. In an expression such as

```
1 + 2 * 3 ^ 4
```

which in postfix form is

```
1 2 3 4 ^ * +
```

An operator stack is used to store operators that have been seen but not yet output.

a postfix expression in some cases has operators in the reverse order than they appear in an infix expression. Of course, this order can occur only if the precedence of the involved operators is increasing as we go from left to right. Even so, this condition suggests that a stack is appropriate for storing operators. Following this logic, then, when we read an operator it must somehow be placed on a stack. Consequently, at some point the operator must get off the stack. The rest of the algorithm involves deciding when operators go on and come off the stack.

In another simple infix expression

```
2 ^ 5 - 1
```

when we reach the - operator, 2 and 5 have been output and ^ is on the stack. Because - has lower precedence than ^, the ^ needs to be applied to 2 and 5. Thus we must pop the ^ and any other operands of higher precedence than - from the stack. After doing so, we push the -. The resulting postfix expression is

When an operator is seen on the input, operators of higher priority (or left associative operators of equal priority) are removed from the stack, signaling that they should be applied. The input operator is then placed on the stack.

```
2 5 ^ 1 -
```

In general, when we are processing an operator from input, we output those operators from the stack that the precedence (and associativity) rules tell us need to be processed.

A second example is the infix expression

```
3 * 2 ^ 5 - 1
```

When we reach the ^ operator, 3 and 2 have been output and * is on the stack. As ^ has higher precedence than *, nothing is popped and ^ goes on the stack. The 5 is output immediately. Then we encounter a - operator. Precedence rules tell us that ^ is popped, followed by the *. At this point, nothing is left to pop, we are done popping, and - goes onto the stack. We then output 1. When we reach the end of the infix expression, we can pop the remaining operators from the stack. The resulting postfix expression is

```
3 2 5 ^ * 1 -
```

Before the summarizing algorithm, we need to answer a few questions. First, if the current symbol is a + and the top of the stack is a +, should the + on the stack be popped or should it stay? The answer is determined by deciding whether the input + implies that the stack + has been completed. Because + associates from left to right, the answer is yes. However, if we are talking about the ^ operator, which associates from right to left, the answer is no. Therefore, when examining two operators of equal precedence, we look at the associativity to decide, as shown in Figure 12.12.

Infix Expression	Postfix Expression	Associativity
`2 + 3 + 4`	`2 3 + 4 +`	Left-associative: Input + is lower than stack +.
`2 ^ 3 ^ 4`	`2 3 4 ^ ^`	Right-associative: Input ^ is higher than stack ^.

Figure 12.12 Examples of using associativity to break ties in precedence.

A left parenthesis is treated as a high-precedence operator when it is an input symbol but as a low-precedence operator when it is on the stack. A left parenthesis is removed only by a right parenthesis.

What about parentheses? A left parenthesis can be considered a high-precedence operator when it is an input symbol but a low-precedence operator when it is on the stack. Consequently, the input left parenthesis is simply placed on the stack. When a right parenthesis appears on the input, we pop the operator stack until we come to a left parenthesis. The operators are written, but the parentheses are not.

The following is a summary of the various cases in the operator precedence parsing algorithm. With the exception of parentheses, everything popped from the stack is output.

- *Operands:* Immediately output.
- *Close parenthesis:* Pop stack symbols until an open parenthesis appears.
- *Operator:* Pop all stack symbols until a symbol of lower precedence or a right-associative symbol of equal precedence appears. Then push the operator.
- *End of input:* Pop all remaining stack symbols.

As an example, Figure 12.13 shows how the algorithm processes

```
1 - 2 ^ 3 ^ 3 - ( 4 + 5 * 6 ) * 7
```

Below each stack is the symbol read. To the right of each stack, in boldface, is any output.

12.2.3 Implementation

The `Evaluator` class will parse and evaluate infix expressions.

We now have the theoretical background required to implement a simple calculator. Our calculator supports addition, subtraction, multiplication, division, and exponentiation. We write a class template `Evaluator` that can be instantiated with the type in which the math is to be performed (presumably, `int` or `double` or perhaps a `HugeInt` class). We make a simplifying

Infix: `1 - 2 ^ 3 ^ 3 - ( 4 + 5 * 6 ) * 7`

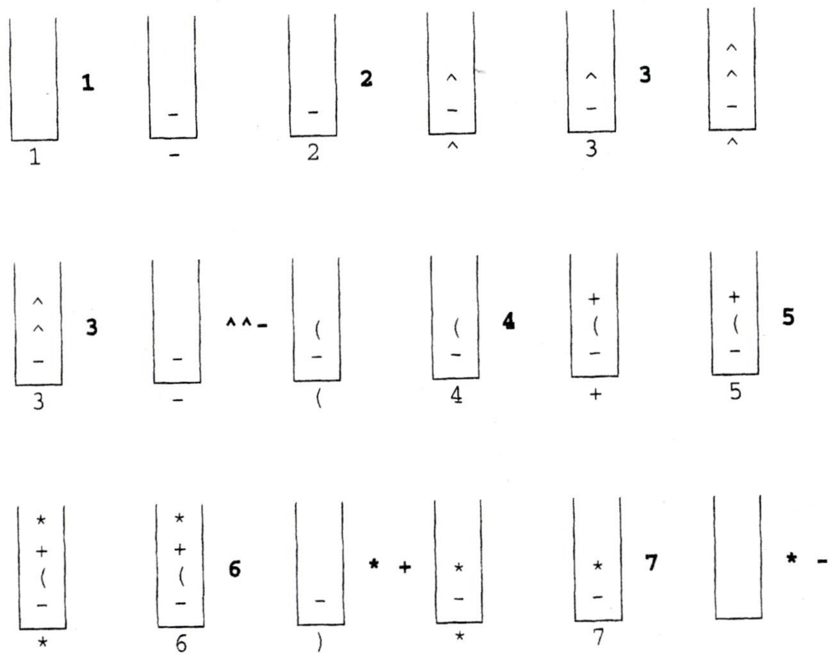

Postfix: `1 2 3 3 ^ ^ - 4 5 6 * + 7 * -`

Figure 12.13 Infix to postfix conversion.

assumption: Negative numbers are not allowed. Distinguishing between the binary minus operator and the unary minus requires extra work in the scanning routine and also complicates matters because it introduces a nonbinary operator. Incorporating unary operators is not difficult, but the extra code does not illustrate any unique concepts and thus we leave it for you to do as an exercise.

We need two stacks: an operator stack and a stack for the postfix machine.

Figure 12.14 shows the `Evaluator` class interface, which is used to process a single string of input. The basic evaluation algorithm requires two stacks. The first stack is used to evaluate the infix expression and generate the postfix expression. It is the stack of operators declared at line 33. An enumerated type, `TokenType`, is declared at line 20; note that the symbols are listed in order of precedence. Rather than explicitly outputting the postfix expression, we send each postfix symbol to the postfix machine as it is generated. Thus we also need a stack that stores operands. Consequently, the postfix machine stack, declared at line 34, is instantiated with `NumericType`. Note that, if we did not have templates, we would be in trouble because the two

```
// Evaluator class interface: evaluate infix expression.
// NumericType: Must have standard set of arithmetic operators
//
// CONSTRUCTION: with a string.
//
// *****************PUBLIC OPERATIONS*********************
// NumericType getValue( ) --> Return value of infix expression
// *****************ERRORS**********************************
// Some error checking is performed.

#include <stdlib.h>
#include <math.h>
#include <fstream>
#include <iostream>
#include <sstream>
#include <vector>
#include <string>
using namespace std;

enum TokenType { EOL, VALUE, OPAREN, CPAREN, EXP,
                 MULT, DIV, PLUS, MINUS };

template <class NumericType>
class Evaluator
{
  public:
    Evaluator( const string & s ) : str( s )
      { opStack.push_back( EOL ); }

    NumericType getValue( );          // Do the evaluation

  private:
    vector<TokenType> opStack; // Operator stack for conversion
    vector<NumericType> postFixStack; // Postfix machine stack

    istringstream str;                // The character stream

      // Internal routines
    NumericType getTop( );          // Get top of postfix stack
    void binaryOp( TokenType topOp ); // Process an operator
    void processToken( const Token<NumericType> & lastToken );
};
```

Figure 12.14 The `Evaluator` class interface.

```
template <class NumericType>
class Token
{
  public:
    Token( TokenType tt = EOL, const NumericType & nt = 0 )
      : theType( tt ), theValue( nt ) { }

    TokenType getType( ) const
      { return theType; }
    const NumericType & getValue( ) const
      { return theValue; }

  private:
    TokenType   theType;
    NumericType theValue;
};

template <class NumericType>
class Tokenizer
{
  public:
    Tokenizer( istream & is ) : in( is ) { }
    Token<NumericType> getToken( );

  private:
    istream & in;
};
```

Figure 12.15 The `Token` class and `Tokenizer` class interface.

stacks hold items of different types.[2] The remaining data member is an `istringstream` object used to step through the input line.[3]

As was the case with the balanced symbol checker, we can write a `Tokenizer` class that can be used to give us the token sequence. Although we could reuse code, there is in fact little commonality, so we write a `Tokenizer` class for this application only. Here, however, the tokens are a little more complex because, if we read an operand, the type of token is `VALUE`, but we must also know what the value is that has been read. Thus we define both a `Tokenizer` class and a `Token` class, shown in Figure 12.15. A `Token` stores both a `TokenType`, and if the token is a `VALUE`, its numeric value. Accessors can be used to obtain information about a token. (The

2. We use `vector` instead of the `stack` adapter, since it provides basic stack operations via `push_back`, `pop_back`, and `back`.
3. The `istringstream` function is not yet available on all compilers. The online code has a deprecated replacement for older compilers. See the online `README` file for details.

```
1 // Find the next token, skipping blanks, and return it.
2 // Print error message if input is unrecognized.
3 template <class NumericType>
4 Token<NumericType> Tokenizer<NumericType>::getToken( )
5 {
6     char ch;
7     NumericType theValue;
8
9       // Skip blanks
10    while( in.get( ch ) && ch == ' ' )
11        ;
12
13    if( in.good( ) && ch != '\n' && ch != '\0' )
14    {
15        switch( ch )
16        {
17          case '^': return EXP;
18          case '/': return DIV;
19          case '*': return MULT;
20          case '(': return OPAREN;
21          case ')': return CPAREN;
22          case '+': return PLUS;
23          case '-': return MINUS;
24
25          default:
26            in.putback( ch );
27            if( !( in >> theValue ) )
28            {
29                cerr << "Parse error" << endl;
30                return EOL;
31            }
32            return Token<NumericType>( VALUE, theValue );
33        }
34    }
35
36    return EOL;
37 }
```

Figure 12.16 The `getToken` routine for returning the next token in the input stream.

`getValue` function could be made more robust by signaling an error if `theType` is not `VALUE`.) The `Tokenizer` class has one member function.

Figure 12.16 shows the `getToken` routine. First we skip past any blanks, and when the loop at line 10 ends, we have gone past any blanks. If we have not reached the end of line, we check to see whether we match any of the one-character operators. If so, we return the appropriate token (a

```
// Public routine that performs the evaluation.
// Examines the postfix machine to see if a single result
// is left and if so, returns it; otherwise prints error.
template <class NumericType>
NumericType Evaluator<NumericType>::getValue( )
{
    Tokenizer<NumericType> tok( str );
    Token<NumericType> lastToken;

    do
    {
        lastToken = tok.getToken( );
        processToken( lastToken );
    } while( lastToken.getType( ) != EOL );

    if( postFixStack.empty( ) )
    {
        cerr << "Missing operand!" << endl;
        return 0;
    }

    NumericType theResult = postFixStack.back( );
    postFixStack.pop_back( );
    if( !postFixStack.empty( ) )
        cerr << "Warning: missing operators!" << endl;

    return theResult;
}
```

Figure 12.17 The `getValue` routine for reading and processing tokens and then returning the item at the top of the stack.

`Token` object is constructed by using an implicit type conversion by virtue of a one-parameter constructor). Otherwise, we reach the `default` case in the `switch` statement. We expect that what remains is an operand, so we unread `ch`, use `operator>>` to get the value, and then return a `Token` object by explicitly constructing a `Token` object based on the value read. Note that for the `putback` to work we must use `get`. That is why we do not simply use `operator>>` (in place of lines 10–13) to skip implicitly past the blanks.

C++ note: `get` must be used so that `putback` works.

We can now discuss the member functions of the `Evaluator` class. The only publicly visible member function is `getValue`. Shown in Figure 12.17, `getValue` repeatedly reads a token and processes it until the end of line is detected. At that point the item at the top of the stack is the answer.

```
// top and pop the postfix machine stack; return the result.
// If the stack is empty, print an error message.
template <class NumericType>
NumericType Evaluator<NumericType>::getTop( )
{
    if( postFixStack.empty( ) )
    {
        cerr << "Missing operand" << endl;
        return 0;
    }

    NumericType tmp = postFixStack.back( );
    postFixStack.pop_back( );
    return tmp;
}
```

Figure 12.18 The `getTop` routine for getting the top item in the postfix stack and removing it.

Figures 12.18 and 12.19 show the routines used to implement the postfix machine. The `getTop` routine returns and removes the top item in the postfix stack. The `binaryOp` routine applies `topOp` (which is expected to be the top item in the operator stack) to the top two items on the postfix stack and replaces them with the result. It also pops the operator stack (at line 33), signifying that processing for `topOp` is complete. The `pow` routine is presumed to exist for `NumericType` objects; we can either use the math library routine or adapt the one previously shown in Figure 8.14.

A *precedence table* is used to decide what is removed from the operator stack. Left-associative operators have the operator stack precedence set at 1 higher than the input symbol precedence. Right-associative operators go the other way.

Figure 12.20 declares a **precedence table,** which stores the operator precedences and is used to decide what is removed from the operator stack. The operators are listed in the same order as the enumeration type `TokenType`. Because enumeration types are assigned consecutive indices beginning with zero, they can be used to index an array. (The array initialization syntax used here was described in Section 1.2.6.)

We want to assign a number to each level of precedence. The higher the number, the higher is the precedence. We could assign the additive operators precedence 1, multiplicative operators precedence 3, exponentiation precedence 5, and parentheses precedence 99. However, we also need to take into account associativity. To do so, we assign each operator a number that represents its precedence when it is an input symbol and a second number that represents its precedence when it is on the operator stack. A left-associative operator has the operator stack precedence set at 1 higher than the input symbol precedence, and a right-associative operator goes the other way. Thus the precedence of the + operator on the stack is 2.

```
// Process an operator by taking two items off the postfix
// stack, applying the operator, and pushing the result.
// Print error if missing closing parenthesis or division by 0.
template <class NumericType>
void Evaluator<NumericType>::binaryOp( TokenType topOp )
{
    if( topOp == OPAREN )
    {
        cerr << "Unbalanced parentheses" << endl;
        opStack.pop_back( );
        return;
    }
    NumericType rhs = getTop( );
    NumericType lhs = getTop( );

    if( topOp == EXP )
        postFixStack.push_back( pow( lhs, rhs ) );
    else if( topOp == PLUS )
        postFixStack.push_back( lhs + rhs );
    else if( topOp == MINUS )
        postFixStack.push_back( lhs - rhs );
    else if( topOp == MULT )
        postFixStack.push_back( lhs * rhs );
    else if( topOp == DIV )
        if( rhs != 0 )
            postFixStack.push_back( lhs / rhs );
        else
        {
            cerr << "Division by zero" << endl;
            postFixStack.push_back( lhs );
        }

    opStack.pop_back( );
}
```

Figure 12.19 The `BinaryOp` routine for applying `topOp` to the postfix stack.

A consequence of this rule is that any two operators that have different precedences are still correctly ordered. However, if a + is on the operator stack and is also the input symbol, the operator on the top of the stack will appear to have higher precedence and thus will be popped. This is what we want for left-associative operators.

Similarly, if a ^ is on the operator stack and is also the input symbol, the operator on the top of the stack will appear to have lower precedence and thus it will not be popped. That is what we want for right-associative operators. The token `VALUE` never gets placed on the stack, so its precedence is meaningless. The end-of-line token is given lowest precedence because it is

```
  // PREC_TABLE matches order of TokenType enumeration.
struct Precedence
{
    int inputSymbol;
    int topOfStack;
} PREC_TABLE [ ] =
{
    { 0, -1 }, { 0, 0 },         // EOL, VALUE
    { 100, 0 }, { 0, 99 },       // OPAREN, CPAREN
    { 6, 5 },                    // EXP
    { 3, 4 }, { 3, 4 },          // MULT, DIV
    { 1, 2 }, { 1, 2 }           // PLUS, MINUS
};
```

Figure 12.20 Table of precedences used to evaluate an infix expression.

placed on the stack for use as a sentinel (which is done in the constructor). If we treat it as a right-associative operator, it is covered under the operator case.

The remaining method is `processToken`, which is shown in Figure 12.21. When we see an operand, we push it onto the postfix stack. When we see a closing parenthesis, we repeatedly pop and process the top operator on the operator stack until the opening parenthesis appears (lines 18–20). The opening parenthesis is then popped at line 22. (The test at line 21 is used to avoid popping the sentinel in the event of a missing opening parenthesis.) Otherwise, we have the general operator case, which is succinctly described by the code in lines 28–32.

A simple `main` routine is given in Figure 12.22. It repeatedly reads a line of input, instantiates an `Evaluator` object, and computes its value. As written, the program performs `int` math. We can change line 8 to use `double` math or perhaps a large-integer class.

12.2.4 Expression Trees

In an *expression tree,* the leaves contain operands and the other nodes contain operators.

Figure 12.23 shows an example of an **expression tree,** the leaves of which are operands (e.g., constants or variable names) and the other nodes contain operators. This particular tree happens to be binary because all the operations are binary. Although it is the simplest case, nodes can have more than two children. A node also may have only one child, as is the case with the unary minus operator.

We evaluate an expression tree *T* by applying the operator at the root to the values obtained by recursively evaluating the left and right subtrees. In this example, the left subtree evaluates to `(a+b)` and the right subtree evaluates to

```
// After token is read, use operator precedence parsing
// algorithm to process it; missing opening parentheses
// are detected here.
template <class NumericType>
void Evaluator<NumericType>::
processToken( const Token<NumericType> & lastToken )
{
    TokenType topOp;
    TokenType lastType = lastToken.getType( );

    switch( lastType )
    {
      case VALUE:
        postFixStack.push_back( lastToken.getValue( ) );
        return;

      case CPAREN:
        while( ( topOp = opStack.back( ) ) != OPAREN &&
                                        topOp != EOL )
            binaryOp( topOp );
        if( topOp == OPAREN )
            opStack.pop_back( ); // Get rid of opening parens
        else
            cerr << "Missing open parenthesis" << endl;
        break;

      default:    // General operator case
        while( PREC_TABLE[ lastType ].inputSymbol <=
                 PREC_TABLE[ topOp = opStack.back( ) ].topOfStack )
            binaryOp( topOp );
        if( lastToken != EOL )
            opStack.push_back( lastType );
        break;
    }
}
```

Figure 12.21 The `processToken` routine for processing `lastToken`, using the operator precedence parsing algorithm.

`(a-b)`. The entire tree therefore represents `((a+b)*(a-b))`. We can produce an (overly parenthesized) infix expression by recursively producing a parenthesized left expression, printing out the operator at the root, and recursively producing a parenthesized right expression. This general strategy (left, node, right) is called an *inorder traversal*. This type of traversal is easy to remember because of the type of expression it produces.

```
// A simple main to exercise Evaluator class.
int main( )
{
    string str;

    while( getline( cin, str ) )
    {
        Evaluator<int> e( str );
        cout << e.getValue( ) << endl;
    }

    return 0;
}
```

Figure 12.22 A simple `main` for evaluating expressions repeatedly.

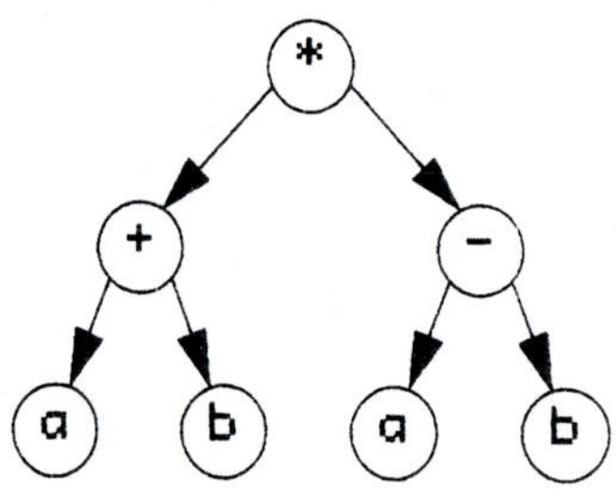

Figure 12.23 Expression tree for `(a+b)*(a-b)`.

Recursive printing of the expression tree can be used to obtain an infix, postfix, or prefix expression.

A second strategy is to print the left subtree recursively, then the right subtree, and then the operator (without parentheses). Doing so, we obtain the postfix expression, so this strategy is called a *postorder traversal of the tree*. A third strategy for evaluating a tree results in a prefix expression. We discuss all these strategies in Chapter 18. The expression tree (and its generalizations) are useful data structures in compiler design because they allow us to see an entire expression. This capability makes code generation easier and in some cases greatly enhances optimization efforts.

Expression trees can be constructed from a postfix expression similar to postfix evaluation.

Of interest is the construction of an expression tree given an infix expression. As we have already shown, we can always convert an infix expression to a postfix expression, so we merely need to show how to construct an expression tree from a postfix expression. Not surprisingly, this procedure is simple. We maintain a stack of (pointers to) trees. When we see an operand, we create a single-node tree and push a pointer to it onto our stack. When we see an operator, we pop and merge the top two trees on the stack. In the new tree, the node is the operator, the right child is the first tree popped from the stack, and the left child is the second tree popped. We then push a pointer to the result back onto the stack. This algorithm is essentially the same as that used in a postfix evaluation, with tree creation replacing the binary operator computation.

Summary

In this chapter we examined two uses of stacks in programming language and compiler design. We demonstrated that, even though the stack is a simple structure, it is very powerful. Stacks can be used to decide whether a sequence of symbols is well balanced. The resulting algorithm requires linear time and, equally important, consists of a single sequential scan of the input. Operator precedence parsing is a technique that can be used to parse infix expressions. It, too, requires linear time and a single sequential scan. Two stacks are used in the operator precedence parsing algorithm. Although the stacks store different types of objects, the generic mechanism (templates) allows the use of a single stack implementation for both types of objects.

Objects of the Game

expression tree A tree in which the leaves contain operands and the other nodes contain operators. (p. 432)

infix expression An expression in which a binary operator has arguments to its left and right. When there are several operators, precedence and associativity determine how the operators are processed. (p. 420)

lexical analysis The process of recognizing tokens in a stream of symbols. (p. 411)

operator precedence parsing An algorithm that converts an infix expression to a postfix expression in order to evaluate the infix expression. (p. 422)

postfix expression An expression that can be evaluated by a postfix machine without using any precedence rules. (p. 421)

postfix machine Machine used to evaluate a postfix expression. The algorithm it uses is as follows: Operands are pushed onto a stack and an operator pops its operands and then pushes the result. At the end of the evaluation, the stack should contain exactly one element, which represents the result. (p. 421)

precedence table A table used to decide what is removed from the operator stack. Left-associative operators have the operator stack precedence set at 1 higher than the input symbol precedence. Right-associative operators go the other way. (p. 430)

state machine A common technique used to parse symbols; at any point, the machine is in some state, and each input character takes it to a new state. Eventually, the state machine reaches a state at which a symbol has been recognized. (p. 414)

tokenization The process of generating the sequence of symbols (tokens) from an input stream. (p. 411)

Common Errors

1. In production code, input errors must be handled as carefully as possible. Being lax in this regard leads to programming errors.
2. For the balanced symbol routine, handling quotes incorrectly is a common error.
3. For the infix to postfix algorithm, the precedence table must reflect the correct precedence and associativity.

On the Internet

Both application programs are available. You should probably download the balancing program; it may help you debug other C++ programs.

Balance.cpp	Contains the balanced symbol program.
Tokenizer.h	Contains the `Tokenizer` class interface for checking C++ programs (Figure 12.2).
Tokenizer.cpp	Contains the `Tokenizer` class implementation for checking C++ programs.
Infix.cpp	Contains the expression evaluator, instantiated for `int`.

Exercises

In Short

12.1. Show the result of running the balanced symbol program on

a. `}.`

b. `( }.`

c. `[ [ [.`

d. `) (`.

e. `[ ) ]`.

12.2. Show the postfix expression for

a. `1 + 2 - 3 ^ 4`.

b. `1 ^ 2 - 3 * 4`.

c. `1 + 2 * 3 - 4 ^ 5 + 6`.

d. `( 1 + 2 ) * 3 - ( 4 ^ ( 5 - 6 ) )`.

12.3. For the infix expression `a + b ^ c * d ^ e ^ f - g - h / ( i + j )`, do the following.

a. Show how the operator precedence parsing algorithm generates the corresponding postfix expression.

b. Show how a postfix machine evaluates the resulting postfix expression.

c. Draw the resulting expression tree.

In Theory

12.4. For the balanced symbol program, explain how to print out an error message that is likely to reflect the probable cause.

12.5. In general terms, explain how unary operators are incorporated into expression evaluators. Assume that the unary operators precede their operands and have high precedence. Include a description of how they are recognized by the state machine.

In Practice

12.6. Use of the ^ operator for exponentiation is likely to confuse C++ programmers (because it is the bitwise exclusive-or operator). Rewrite the `Evaluator` class with `**` as the exponentiation operator.

12.7. The infix evaluator accepts illegal expressions in which the operators are misplaced.

a. What will `1 2 3 + *` be evaluated as?

b. How can we detect these illegalities?

c. Modify the `Evaluator` class to do so.

Programming Projects

12.8. Modify the expression evaluator to handle negative input numbers.

12.9. For the balanced symbol checker, modify the `Tokenizer` class by adding a public method that can change the input stream. Then add a public method to `Balance` that allows `Balance` to change the source of the input stream. (*Hint:* Have the `Tokenizer` class store a pointer to an `istream` instead of a reference to an `istream`.)

12.10. Implement a complete C++ expression evaluator. Handle all C++ operators that can accept constants and make arithmetic sense (e.g., do not implement `[]`).

12.11. Implement a C++ expression evaluator that includes variables. Assume that there are at most 26 variables—namely, `A` through `Z`—and that a variable can be assigned to by an `=` operator of low precedence.

12.12. Write a program that reads an infix expression and generates a postfix expression.

12.13. Write a program that reads a postfix expression and generates an infix expression.

References

The infix to postfix algorithm (*operator precedence parsing*) was first described in [3]. Two good books on compiler construction are [1] and [2].

1. A. V. Aho, R. Sethi, and J. D. Ullman, *Compiler Design: Principles, Techniques, and Tools,* Addison-Wesley, Reading, Mass., 1986.
2. C. N. Fischer and R. J. LeBlanc, *Crafting a Compiler with C,* Benjamin/Cummings, Redwood City, Calif., 1991.
3. R. W. Floyd, "Syntactic Analysis and Operator Precedence," *Journal of the ACM* **10:3** (1963), 316–333.

Chapter 13

Utilities

In this chapter we discuss two utility applications of data structures: data compression and cross-referencing. Data compression is an important technique in computer science. It can be used to reduce the size of files stored on disk (in effect increasing the capacity of the disk) and also to increase the effective rate of transmission by modems (by transmitting less data). Virtually all newer modems perform some type of compression. Cross-referencing is a scanning and sorting technique that is done, for example, to make an index for a book.

In this chapter, we show:

- an implementation of a file-compression algorithm called *Huffman's algorithm;* and
- an implementation of a cross-referencing program that lists, in sorted order, all identifiers in a program and gives the line numbers on which they occur.

13.1 File Compression

A standard encoding of C characters uses $\lceil \log C \rceil$ bits.

The ASCII character set consists of roughly 100 printable characters. To distinguish these characters, $\lceil \log 100 \rceil = 7$ bits are required. Seven bits allow the representation of 128 characters, so the ASCII character set adds some other "unprintable" characters. An eighth bit is added to allow parity checks. The important point, however, is that if the size of the character set is C, then $\lceil \log C \rceil$ bits are needed in a standard fixed-length encoding.

Suppose that you have a file that contains only the characters *a, e, i, s,* and *t,* blank spaces (*sp*), and newlines (*nl*). Suppose further that the file has 10 *a*'s, 15 *e*'s, 12 *i*'s, 3 *s*'s, 4 *t*'s, 13 blanks, and 1 newline. As Figure 13.1 shows, representing this file requires 174 bits because there are 58 characters and each character requires 3 bits.

In real life, files can be quite large. Many very large files are the output of some program, and there is usually a big disparity between the most frequently and least frequently used characters. For instance, many large data files have an inordinately large number of digits, blanks, and newlines but few q's and x's.

Reducing the number of bits required for data representation is called *compression*, which actually consists of two phases: the encoding phase (compressing) and the decoding phase (uncompressing).

In many situations reducing the size of a file is desirable. For instance, disk space is precious on virtually every machine, so decreasing the amount of space required for files increases the effective capacity of the disk. When data are being transmitted across phone lines by a modem, the effective rate of transmission is increased if the amount of data transmitted can be reduced. Reducing the number of bits required for data representation is called **compression,** which actually consists of two phases: the encoding phase (compression) and the decoding phase (uncompression). A simple strategy discussed in this chapter achieves 25 percent savings on some large files and as much as 50 or 60 percent savings on some large data files. Extensions provide somewhat better compression.

In a variable-length code, the most-frequent characters have the shortest representation.

The general strategy is to allow the code length to vary from character to character and to ensure that frequently occurring characters have short codes. If all characters occur with the same or very similar frequency, you cannot expect any savings.

13.1.1 Prefix Codes

In a *binary trie*, a left branch represents 0 and a right branch represents 1. The path to a node indicates its representation.

The binary code presented in Figure 13.1 can be represented by the binary tree shown in Figure 13.2. In this data structure, called a **binary trie** (pronounced "try"), characters are stored only in leaf nodes; the representation of each character is found by starting at the root and recording the path,

Character	Code	Frequency	Total Bits
a	000	10	30
e	001	15	45
i	010	12	36
s	011	3	9
t	100	4	12
sp	101	13	39
nl	110	1	3
Total			**174**

Figure 13.1 A standard coding scheme.

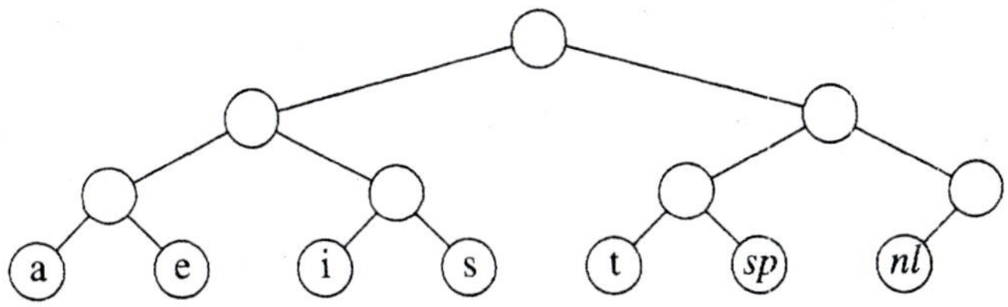

Figure 13.2 Representation of the original code by a tree.

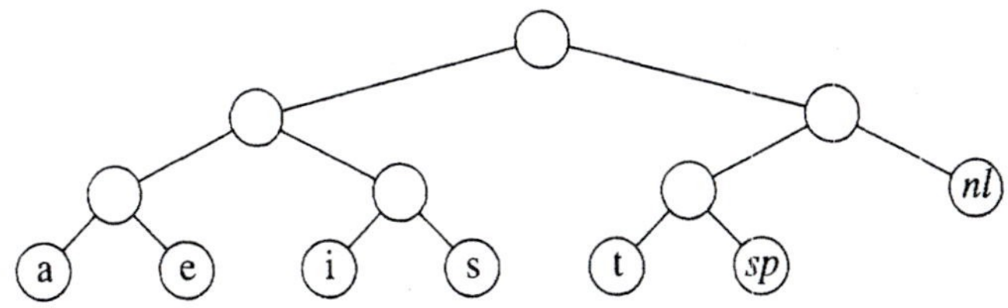

Figure 13.3 A slightly better tree.

using a 0 to indicate the left branch and a 1 to indicate the right branch. For instance, *s* is reached by going left, then right, and finally right. This is encoded as 011. If character c_i is at depth d_i and occurs f_i times, the *cost* of the code is $\sum d_i f_i$.

We can obtain a better code than the one given in Figure 13.2 by recognizing that *nl* is an only child. By placing it one level higher (replacing its parent), we obtain the new tree shown in Figure 13.3. This new tree has a cost of 173 but is still far from optimal.

Note that the tree in Figure 13.3 is a **full tree,** in which all nodes either are leaves or have two children. An optimal code always has this property; otherwise, as already shown, nodes with only one child could move up a level. If the characters are placed only at the leaves, any sequence of bits can always be decoded unambiguously.

In a *full tree*, all nodes either are leaves or have two children.

For instance, suppose that the encoded string is 0100111100010110001000111. Figure 13.3 shows that 0 and 01 are not character codes but that 010 represents *i*, so the first character is *i*. Then 011 follows, which is an *s*. Then 11 follows, which is a newline (*nl*). The remainder of the code is *a, sp, t, i, e,* and *nl.*

The character codes can be different lengths, so long as no character code is a prefix of another character code, an encoding called a **prefix code.** Conversely, if a character is contained in a nonleaf node, guaranteeing unambiguous decoding is no longer possible.

In a *prefix code*, no character code is a prefix of another character code. This is guaranteed if the characters are only in leaves. A prefix code can be decoded unambiguously.

Thus our basic problem is to find the full binary tree of minimum cost (as defined previously) in which all characters are contained in the leaves. The tree shown in Figure 13.4 is optimal for our sample alphabet. As shown

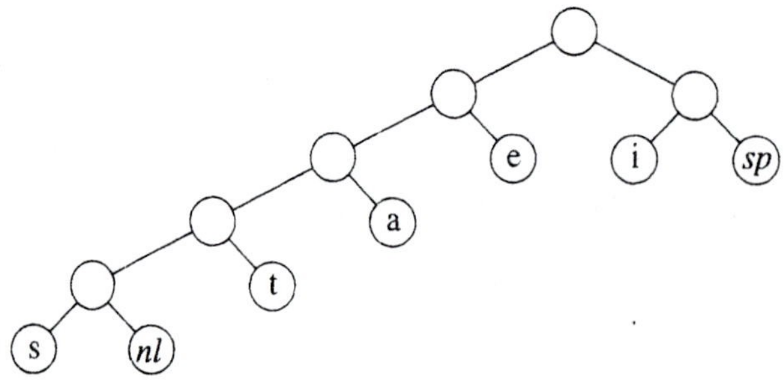

Figure 13.4 An optimal prefix code tree.

Character	Code	Frequency	Total Bits
a	001	10	30
e	01	15	30
i	10	12	24
s	00000	3	15
t	0001	4	16
sp	11	13	26
nl	00001	1	5
Total			**146**

Figure 13.5 Optimal prefix code.

in Figure 13.5, this code requires only 146 bits. There are many optimal codes, which can be obtained by swapping children in the encoding tree.

13.1.2 Huffman's Algorithm

***Huffman's algorithm* constructs an optimal prefix code. It works by repeatedly merging the two minimum weight trees.**

How is the coding tree constructed? The coding system algorithm was given by Huffman in 1952. Commonly called **Huffman's algorithm,** it constructs an optimal prefix code by repeatedly merging trees until the final tree is obtained.

Throughout this section, the number of characters is C. In Huffman's algorithm we maintain a forest of trees. The *weight* of a tree is the sum of the frequencies of its leaves. $C - 1$ times, two trees, T_1 and T_2, of smallest weight are selected, breaking ties arbitrarily, and a new tree is formed with subtrees T_1 and T_2. At the beginning of the algorithm, there are C single-node trees (one for each character). At the end of the algorithm, there is one tree, giving an optimal Huffman tree. In Exercise 13.4 you are asked to prove Huffman's algorithm gives an optimal tree.

Ties are broken arbitrarily.

An example helps make operation of the algorithm clear. Figure 13.6 shows the initial forest; the weight of each tree is shown in small type at the root. The two trees of lowest weight are merged, creating the forest shown in Figure 13.7. The new root is *T*1. We made *s* the left child arbitrarily; any tie-breaking procedure can be used. The total weight of the new tree is just the sum of the weights of the old trees and can thus be easily computed.

Now there are six trees, and we again select the two trees of smallest weight, *T*1 and *t*. They are merged into a new tree with root *T*2 and weight 8, as shown in Figure 13.8. The third step merges *T*2 and *a*, creating *T*3, with weight 10 + 8 = 18. Figure 13.9 shows the result of this operation.

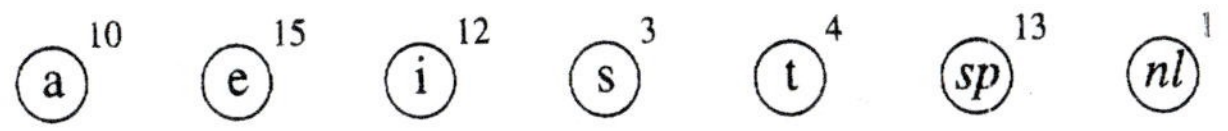

Figure 13.6 Initial stage of Huffman's algorithm.

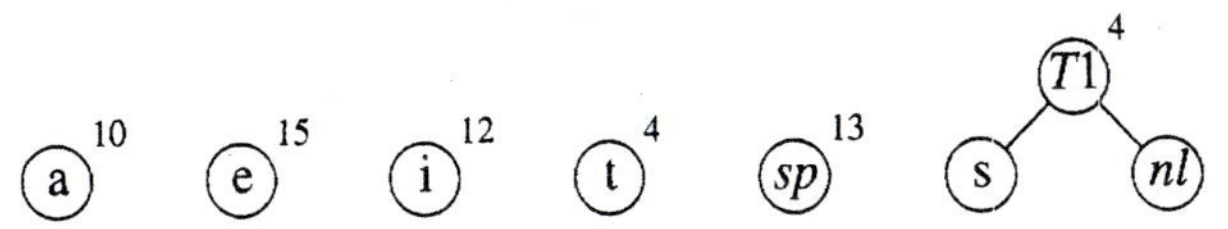

Figure 13.7 Huffman's algorithm after the first merge.

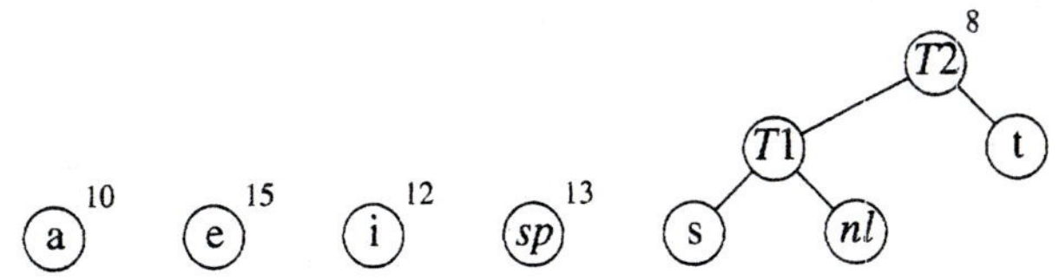

Figure 13.8 Huffman's algorithm after the second merge.

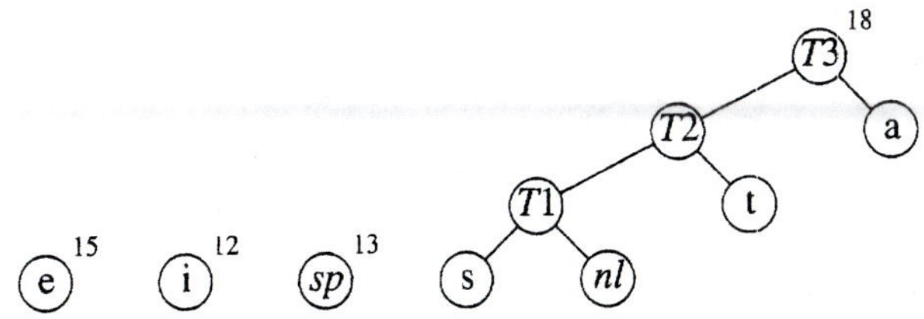

Figure 13.9 Huffman's algorithm after the third merge.

After completion of the third merge, the two trees of lowest weight are the single-node trees representing *i* and *sp*. Figure 13.10 shows how these trees are merged into the new tree with root *T*4. The fifth step is to merge the trees with roots *e* and *T*3 because these trees have the two smallest weights, giving the result shown in Figure 13.11.

Finally, an optimal tree, shown previously in Figure 13.4, is obtained by merging the two remaining trees. Figure 13.12 shows the optimal tree, with root *T*6.

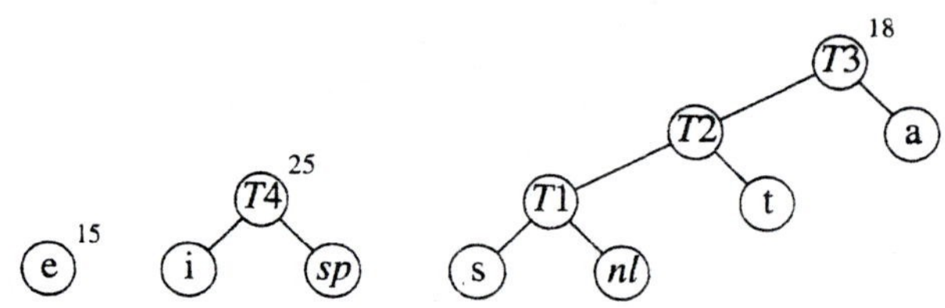

Figure 13.10 Huffman's algorithm after the fourth merge.

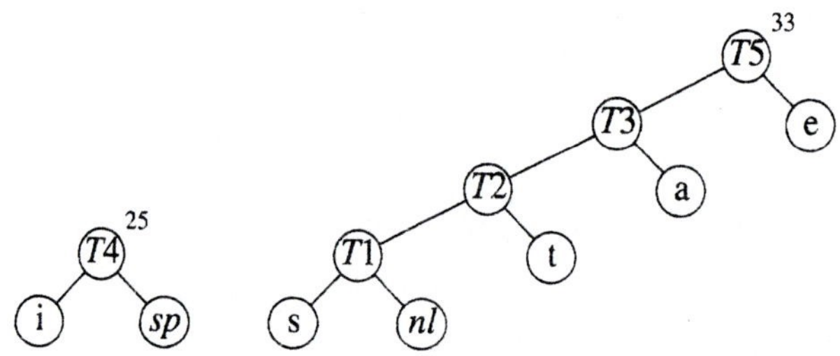

Figure 13.11 Huffman's algorithm after the fifth merge.

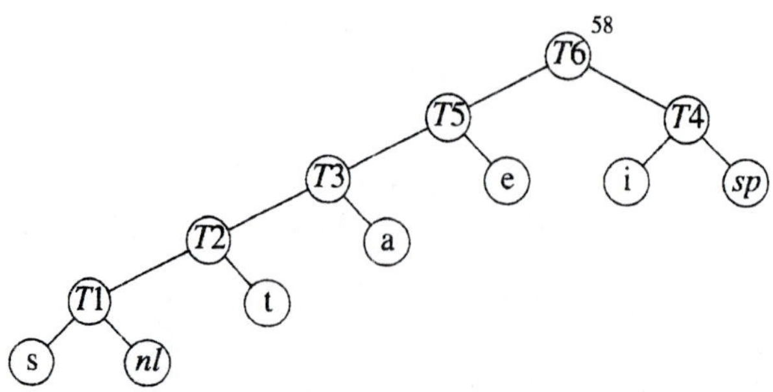

Figure 13.12 Huffman's algorithm after the final merge.

13.1.3 Implementation

We now provide an implementation of the Huffman coding algorithm, without attempting to perform any significant optimizations; we simply want a working program that illustrates the basic algorithmic issues. After discussing the implementation we comment on possible enhancements. Although significant error checking needs to be added to the program, we have not done so because we did not want to obscure the basic ideas.

Figure 13.13 illustrates some of the header files to be used. For simplicity we use maps and maintain a priority queue of (pointers to) tree nodes (recall that we are to select two trees of lowest weight). Thus we need <queue> and <functional> —and, as it turns out, Wrapper.h (because we need to wrap the pointer variables to make the comparison function meaningful). We also use <algorithm> because, in one of our routines, we use the reverse method.

In addition to the library classes, our program consists of several additional classes. Because we need to perform bit-at-a-time I/O, we write wrapper classes representing bit-input and bit-output streams. We write other classes to maintain character counts and create and return information about a Huffman coding tree. Finally, we write a class that contains the (static) compression and uncompression functions. To summarize, the classes that we write are:

ibstream	Wraps an istream and provides bit-at-a-time input.
obstream	Wraps an ostream and provides bit-at-a-time output.
CharCounter	Maintains character counts.
HuffmanTree	Manipulates Huffman coding trees.
Compressor	Contains compression and uncompression methods.

```
#include <iostream>
#include <fstream>
#include <map>
#include <vector>
#include <string>
#include <queue>
#include <functional>
#include <algorithm>
#include "Wrapper.h"
```

Figure 13.13 The include directives used in the compression program.

Bit-Input and Bit-Output Stream Classes

The class interfaces for `ibstream` and `obstream` are similar and are shown in Figures 13.14 and 13.15, respectively. Both work by wrapping a stream. A reference to the stream is stored as a private data member. Every eighth `readBit` of the `ibstream` (or `writeBit` of the `obstream`) causes a `char` to be read (or written) on the underlying stream. The `char` is stored in a buffer, appropriately named `buffer`, and `bufferPos` provides an indication of how much of the buffer is unused.

Implementation of `ibstream` is provided in Figure 13.16. The `getBit` and `setBit` methods are used to access an individual bit in an 8-bit character;[1] they work by using bit operations. (Appendix A.2.3 describes the bit operators in more detail.) In `readBit`, we check at line 26 to find out whether the bits in the buffer have already been used. If so, we get 8 more bits at line 28, and reset the position indicator at line 31. Then we can call `getBit` at line 33.

```
// ibstream class interface: Bit-input stream wrapper class.
//
// CONSTRUCTION: with an open istream.
//
// ******************PUBLIC OPERATIONS**********************
// int readBit( )                 --> Read one bit as a 0 or 1
// istream & getInputStream( )    --> Return underlying stream
// ******************ERRORS**********************************
// Error checking can be done on result of getInputStream( ).

class ibstream
{
  public:
    ibstream( istream & is );

    int readBit( );
    istream & getInputStream( ) const;

  private:
    istream & in;       // The underlying input stream
    char buffer;        // Buffer to store eight bits at a time
    int bufferPos;      // Position in buffer for next read
};
```

Figure 13.14 The `ibstream` class interface.

1. The Standard Library provides a `bitset` class, but not all compilers support it yet.

```
// obstream class interface: Bit-output stream wrapper class.
//
// CONSTRUCTION: with an open ostream.
//
// ******************PUBLIC OPERATIONS*********************
// void writeBit( val )          --> Write one bit (0 or 1)
// void writeBits( val )         --> Write a vector of bits
// void flush( )                 --> Flush buffered bits
// ostream & getOutputStream( ) --> Return underlying stream
// ******************ERRORS*********************************
// Error checking can be done on result of getOutputStream( ).

class obstream
{
  public:
    obstream( ostream & os );
    ~obstream( );

    void writeBit( int val );
    void writeBits( const vector<int> & val );
    void flush( );
    ostream & getOutputStream( ) const;

  private:
    ostream & out;     // The underlying output stream
    char buffer;       // Buffer to store eight bits at a time
    int bufferPos;     // Position in buffer for next write
};
```

Figure 13.15 The `obstream` class interface.

The `obstream` class, implemented in Figure 13.17, is similar to `ibstream`. One difference is that we provide a `flush` method because there may be bits left in the buffer at the end of a sequence of `writeBit` calls. The `flush` method is called when a call to `writeBit` fills the buffer and also is called by the destructor.

Neither class performs error checking, but we can get the underlying stream by use of an accessor function (`getInputStream` or `getOutputStream`), and then test the state of the streams. Thus full error checking is available.

The Character Counting Class

Figure 13.18 provides the `CharCounter` class, which is used to obtain the character counts in an input stream (typically a file). Alternatively, the character counts can be set manually and then obtained later.

```
static const int BITS_PER_CHAR = 8;
static const int DIFF_CHARS = 256;

// Return bit at position pos in a packed set of bits (pack).
int getBit( char pack, int pos )
{
    return ( pack & ( 1 << pos ) ) ? 1 : 0;
}

// Set bit at position pos in a packed set of bits (pack).
void setBit( char & pack, int pos, int val )
{
    if( val == 1 )
        pack |= ( val << pos );
}

// Construct the bit-input stream.
ibstream::ibstream( istream & is )
  : bufferPos( BITS_PER_CHAR ), in( is )
{
}

// Read one bit.
int ibstream::readBit( )
{
    if( bufferPos == BITS_PER_CHAR )
    {                           // No bits left in the buffer, so
        in.get( buffer );       // Get a new set of bits for buffer
        if( in.eof( ) )
            return EOF;
        bufferPos = 0;          // Reset bufferPos
    }
    return getBit( buffer, bufferPos++ );
}

// Return underlying input stream.
istream & ibstream::getInputStream( ) const
{
    return in;
}
```

Figure 13.16 Implementation of the `ibstream` class.

Our implementation uses a `map` (mapping characters to their counts), but a more efficient implementation could be obtained by simply using an array of 256 `int`s. Changing this implementation would not affect the rest of the program. In Exercise 13.11 you are asked to investigate whether making this change would affect performance.

```
// Construct the bit-output stream.
obstream::obstream( ostream & os )
  : bufferPos( 0 ), buffer( 0 ), out( os )
{
}

// Destructor (writes any bits left in the buffer).
obstream::~obstream( )
{
    flush( );
}

// If the buffer is non-empty, write one more char.
void obstream::flush( )
{
    if( bufferPos == 0 )      // If buffer is empty
        return;               // Nothing to do
    out.put( buffer );        // Write the buffer
    bufferPos = 0;            // Reset the position
    buffer = 0;               // Clear the buffer
}

// Write one bit.
void obstream::writeBit( int val )
{
    setBit( buffer, bufferPos++, val );
    if( bufferPos == BITS_PER_CHAR )
        flush( );
}

// Write a vector of bits.
void obstream::writeBits( const vector<int> & val )
{
    for( int i = 0; i < val.size( ); i++ )
        writeBit( val[ i ] );
}

// Return underlying output stream.
ostream & obstream::getOutputStream( ) const
{
    return out;
}
```

Figure 13.17 Implementation of the `obstream` class.

```
// CharCounter class interface: a character counting class.
//
// CONSTRUCTION: with no parameters or an open istream.
//
// ******************PUBLIC OPERATIONS**********************
// int getCount( ch )              --> Return # occurrences of ch
// void setCount( ch, count )      --> Set # occurrences of ch
// ******************ERRORS*********************************
// No error checks.

class CharCounter
{
  public:
    CharCounter( );
    CharCounter( istream & input );

    int getCount( char ch ) const;
    void setCount( char ch, int count );

  private:
    map<char,int,less<char> > theCounts;
};

// Constructor: All counts are zero.
CharCounter::CharCounter( ) : in( cin )
{
}

// Constructor: Get counts by reading from input stream.
CharCounter::CharCounter( istream & input )
{
    char ch;
    while( !input.get( ch ).eof( ) )
        theCounts[ ch ]++;
}

// Return the character count for ch.
int CharCounter::getCount( char ch ) const
{
    map<char,int,less<char> >::const_iterator itr;
    itr = theCounts.find( ch );
    return itr != theCounts.end( ) ? (*itr).second : 0;
}

// Set the character count for ch.
void CharCounter::setCount( char ch, int count )
{
    theCounts[ ch ] = count;
}
```

Figure 13.18 The `CharCounter` class.

The Huffman Tree Class

The tree is maintained as a collection of nodes. Each node has links to its left child, right child, and parent (in Chapter 18 we discuss the implementaton of trees in detail). The node declaration is shown in Figure 13.19.

The `HuffmanTree` class interface is provided in Figure 13.20. We can create a `HuffmanTree` object by providing a `CharCounter` object, in which case the tree is built immediately. Alternatively, it can be created without a `CharCounter` object. In that case, the character counts are read by a subsequent call to `readEncodingTable`, and at that point the tree is built.

The `HuffmanTree` class provides the `writeEncodingTable` member function to write the tree out to file (in a form suitable for a call to `readEncodingTable`). It also provides public methods to convert from a character to a code, and vice versa.[2] Codes are represented by a `vector<int>`, in which each vector element is either a 0 or 1.

Internally, `root` is a pointer to the root node of the tree, and `theCounts` is a `CharCounter` object that can be used to initialize the tree nodes. We also maintain a `map`, `theNodes`, which maps each character to (a pointer to) the tree node that contains it. As was the case with `CharCounter`, the `map` could be replaced with an array.

Figure 13.21 shows the constructors and the routine (public member function and private helper) to return the code for a given character. The constructors start with empty trees, and the one-parameter constructor initializes

```
// Basic node in a Huffman coding tree.
struct HuffNode
{
    int value;
    int weight;
    HuffNode *left;
    HuffNode *right;
    HuffNode *parent;

    HuffNode( int v, int w, HuffNode *lt,
                                HuffNode *rt, HuffNode *pt )
      : value( v ), weight( w ), left( lt ),
        right( rt ), parent( pt ) { }
};
```

Figure 13.19 Node declaration for the Huffman coding tree.

2. Technical alert: An `int` is used instead of `char` to allow all characters and the `EOF` symbol.

```
// Huffman tree class interface: manipulate Huffman coding tree.
//
// CONSTRUCTION: with no parameters or a CharCounter object.
//
// *****************PUBLIC OPERATIONS**********************
// vector getCode( ch )          --> Return code given character
// int getChar( code )           --> Return character given code
// void writeEncodingTable( out ) --> Write coding table to out
// void readEncodingTable( in ) --> Read encoding table from in
// *****************ERRORS*********************************
// Error check for illegal code.

class HuffmanTree
{
  public:
    HuffmanTree( );
    HuffmanTree( const CharCounter & cc );

    enum { ERROR = -3, INCOMPLETE_CODE = -2, END = -1 };

      // Here, vector<int> is usable by ibstream and obstreams.
    vector<int> getCode( int ch ) const;
    int getChar( const vector<int> & code ) const;

      // Write the encoding table using character counts.
    void writeEncodingTable( ostream & out );
    void readEncodingTable( istream & in );

  private:
    CharCounter theCounts;
    map<int,HuffNode *,less<int> > theNodes;
    HuffNode *root;

    void createTree( );
};
```

Figure 13.20 The `HuffmanTree` class interface.

the `CharCounter` object, and immediately calls the private routine `createTree`. The `CharCounter` object is initialized to be empty in the zero-parameter constructor.

For `getCode`, by consulting the map, we obtain a pointer to the tree node that stores the character whose code we are looking for. If the character is not in the map we signal an error by returning a zero-length vector. Otherwise we use a straightforward loop up the tree, following parent pointers, until we reach the root (which has no parent). Each step appends a 0 or 1 to

```
// Construct the tree given a CharCounter object.
// Tree will be usable.
HuffmanTree::HuffmanTree( const CharCounter & cc )
  : theCounts( cc )
{
    root = NULL;
    createTree( );
}

// Construct the tree in an unusable state.
// A call to readEncodingTable is expected to follow.
HuffmanTree::HuffmanTree( )
{
    root = NULL;
}

// Return the code corresponding to character ch.
// (The parameter is an int to accommodate EOF).
// If code is not found, return a vector of size 0.
vector<int> HuffmanTree::getCode( int ch ) const
{
    map<int,HuffNode *,less<int> >::const_iterator itr;
    itr = theNodes.find( ch );
    if( itr == theNodes.end( ) )
        return vector<int>( );
    HuffNode *current = (*itr).second;

    vector<int> v;
    HuffNode *par = current->parent;

    while( par != NULL )
    {
        if( par->left == current )
            v.push_back( 0 );  // current is a left child
        else
            v.push_back( 1 );  // current is a right child
        current = current->parent;
        par = current->parent;
    }

    reverse( v.begin( ), v.end( ) );
    return v;
}
```

Figure 13.21 Some of the Huffman tree methods, including constructors and the routine for returning a code for a given character.

```
// Get the character corresponding to code.
int HuffmanTree::getChar( const vector<int> & code ) const
{
    HuffNode *p = root;

    for( int i = 0; p != NULL && i < code.size( ); i++ )
        if( code[ i ] == 0 )
            p = p->left;
        else
            p = p->right;
    if( p == NULL )
        return ERROR;
    return p->value;
}
```

Figure 13.22 A routine for decoding (generating a character, given the code).

the end of the vector maintaining the code. These actions give the code in reverse order, so we use the `reverse` generic algorithm (provided as part of `<algorithm>`) to fix things.

The `getChar` method shown in Figure 13.22 is simpler: We start at the root, and branch left or right, as directed by the code. Reaching `NULL` prematurely generates an error. Otherwise, we return the value stored in the node (which for nonleaf nodes turns out to be the symbol `INCOMPLETE`).

In Figure 13.23 we have routines to read and write the encoding table. The format that we use is simple and is not necessarily the most space-efficient. For each character that has a code, we write it out (using one byte) and then write out its character count with formatted I/O. So the character count could take as little as 1 byte (if it occurs 9 times or less), or more than four bytes (if it occurs 10,000 or more times). After the character count, we write a newline. We signal the end of the table by writing out an extra entry containing a null terminator character `'\0'` with a count of zero. The count of zero is special.

The `readEncodingTable` method initializes all the character counts to zero and then reads the table, and updates the counts as they are read. It calls `createTree`, shown in Figure 13.24, to build the Huffman tree.

In that routine, we maintain a priority queue of pointers to tree nodes. To do so we must provide a comparison function for tree nodes. There are two important details. First, the Standard Library `priority_queue` function accesses the maximum item rather than the minimum. So we reverse the meaning of `operator<`, as shown on lines 3 to 6. Second, we cannot have a priority queue of pointers because the comparison function for pointers is meaningless (it compares memory locations). Thus we use the `Pointer`

```
// Write an encoding table to an output stream.
// Format is character, count (formatted), newline.
// A zero count terminates the encoding table.
void HuffmanTree::writeEncodingTable( ostream & out )
{
    for( int i = 0; i < DIFF_CHARS; i++ )
        if( theCounts.getCount( i ) > 0 )
            out << static_cast<char>( i )
                << theCounts.getCount( i ) << '\n';
    out << '\0' << 0 << '\n';    // The end-of-table sentinel
}

// Read the encoding table from an input stream in format
// given above and then construct the Huffman tree.
// Stream will then be positioned to read compressed data.
void HuffmanTree::readEncodingTable( istream & in )
{
    for( int i = 0; i < DIFF_CHARS; i++ )
        theCounts.setCount( i, 0 );

    char ch, nl;
    int num;

    for( ; ; )
    {
        in.get( ch );    // read the character
        in >> num;       // read the count
        in.get( nl );    // digest the newline
        if( num == 0 )
            break;       // sentinel reached
        theCounts.setCount( ch, num );
    }
    createTree( );       // build the tree
}
```

Figure 13.23 Routines for reading and writing encoding tables.

wrapper class that we wrote in Section 5.3.1. Its use results in the tortured declaration of the priority queue that spans lines 11–13.[3]

We then search for characters that have appeared at least once. When the test at line 16 succeeds, we have such a character. We create a new tree node at lines 18 and 19, add it to the map at line 20, and then add it to the priority queue at line 21 (note that we must wrap the pointer variable in a

3. The `Pointer` wrapper class, as written in Figure 5.7, requires `operator<`; thus we cannot use `operator>` and instantiate the `priority_queue` with a greater function template.

```
1 // Comparison function for HuffNode.
2 // Meaning is reversed so priority_queue will retrive the min.
3 bool operator< ( const HuffNode & lhs, const HuffNode & rhs )
4 {
5     return lhs.weight > rhs.weight;
6 }
7
8 // Construct the Huffman coding tree.
9 void HuffmanTree::createTree( )
10 {
11     priority_queue<Pointer<HuffNode>,
12                    vector<Pointer<HuffNode> >,
13                    less<Pointer<HuffNode> > > pq;
14
15     for( int i = 0; i < DIFF_CHARS; i++ )
16         if( theCounts.getCount( i ) > 0 )
17         {
18             HuffNode *newNode = new HuffNode( i,
19                    theCounts.getCount( i ), NULL, NULL, NULL );
20             theNodes[ i ] = newNode;
21             pq.push( Pointer<HuffNode>( newNode ) );
22         }
23
24     theNodes[ END ] = new HuffNode( END, 1, NULL, NULL, NULL );
25     pq.push( Pointer<HuffNode>( theNodes[ END ] ) );
26
27     while( pq.size( ) > 1 )
28     {
29         HuffNode *n1 = pq.top( ); pq.pop( );
30         HuffNode *n2 = pq.top( ); pq.pop( );
31         HuffNode *result = new HuffNode( INCOMPLETE_CODE,
32                        n1->weight + n2->weight, n1, n2, NULL );
33         n1->parent = n2->parent = result;
34         pq.push( Pointer<HuffNode>( result ) );
35     }
36     root = pq.top( );
37 }
```

Figure 13.24 A routine for constructing the Huffman coding tree.

`Pointer<HuffNode>` object in order to add it to the priority queue). At lines 24 and 25 we add the end-of-file symbol. The loop that extends from lines 27 to 35 is a line-for-line translation of the tree construction algorithm. While we have two or more trees, we extract two trees from the priority queue, merge the result, and put it back in the priority queue. At the end of the loop, only one tree is left in the priority queue, and we can extract it and set `root`.

The tree produced by `createTree` is dependent on how the priority queue breaks ties. Unfortunately, this means that if the program is compiled on two different machines, with two different STL `priority_queue` implementations, it is possible to compress a file on the first machine, and then be unable to obtain the original when attempting to uncompress on the second machine. Avoiding this problem requires some additional work.

Compressor Class

All that is left to do is to write a compression and uncompression routine and then a `main` that calls them. These functions could all be global, but instead, we make the compression and uncompression routines static member functions in a `Compressor` class. The main advantage of doing so is that we avoid polluting the global namespace. We repeat our earlier disclaimer about skimping on error checking so that we can illustrate the basic algorithmic ideas.

The `Compressor` class declaration is shown in Figure 13.25 along with the `compress` function. We need to read and write files that have non-ASCII characters, so we open the files in binary mode.

The `compress` routine opens the file for reading at line 21. It then constructs a `CharCounter` object at line 23 and a `HuffmanTree` object at line 24. At line 26 we open the output file, and at line 27 we write out the encoding table.

At this point we are ready to do the main encoding. We reset the input stream to the beginning of the file (line 29).[4] Then we create a bit-output stream object at line 30. The rest of the algorithm repeatedly reads a character (line 33) and writes its code (line 34). There is a tricky piece of code at line 34: The `int` passed to `getCode` may be confused with `EOF` if we simply use `ch` because the high bit can be interpreted as a sign bit. Thus we use a bit mask to treat the value as an unsigned quantity. When we exit the loop, we have reached the end of file, so we write out the end-of-file code at line 36. The `obstream` destructor flushes any remaining bits to the output file, so an explicit call to `flush` is not needed.

The `uncompress` routine is next, in Figure 13.26. Lines 10–19 form the name of the uncompressed file, and checks (somewhat lamely, as it uses only the name) whether the original is actually a compressed file. We then open the compressed file for reading and the target for writing at lines 21 and 22. We construct a `HuffmanTree` object by reading the encoding table (lines 24 and 25) from the compressed file. We then create a bit-input stream at line 27 and loop.

The `bits` object, declared at line 28, represents the (Huffman) code that we are currently examining. Each time we read a bit at line 33, we add the

4. Note that we must clear the `EOF` error state before going back to the beginning.

```
1  class Compressor
2  {
3    public:
4      static void compress( const string & inFile );
5      static void uncompress( const string & compressedFile );
6
7    private:
8      static const int READ_MODE;
9      static const int WRITE_MODE;
10 };
11
12 const int Compressor::READ_MODE = ios::in | ios::binary;
13 const int Compressor::WRITE_MODE = ios::out | ios::binary;
14
15 // Compress inFile; writes result to a file whose name is
16 // formed by appending ".huf".
17 // Very little error checking is performed.
18 void Compressor::compress( const string & inFile )
19 {
20     string compressedFile = inFile + ".huf";
21     ifstream in( inFile.c_str( ), READ_MODE );
22
23     CharCounter countObj( in );
24     HuffmanTree codeTree( countObj );
25
26     ofstream out( compressedFile.c_str( ), WRITE_MODE );
27     codeTree.writeEncodingTable( out );
28
29     in.clear( ); in.seekg( 0, ios::beg ); // Rewind the stream
30     obstream bout( out );
31
32     char ch;
33     while( in.get( ch ) )
34         bout.writeBits( codeTree.getCode( ch & 0xff ) );
35
36     bout.writeBits( codeTree.getCode( EOF ) );
37 }
```

Figure 13.25 The `Compressor` class, used to place compression and decompression routines outside global scope, and the compression routine.

bit to the end of the Huffman code (at line 34). We then look up the Huffman code at line 35. If it is incomplete, we continue the loop (lines 36 and 37). If there is an illegal Huffman code, we stop after printing an error message (lines 38 to 42). If we reach the end-of-file code, we break the loop (lines 43 and 44); otherwise, we have a match, so we output the character that matches the Huffman code (line 47) and then clear the current Huffman code prior to resuming (line 48).

```
// Uncompress a file. Write the result to a file whose name
// is formed by adding ".uc" (in reality we would simply
// form the new name by stripping off ".huf").
// Very little error checking is performed.
void Compressor::uncompress( const string & compressedFile )
{
    int i;
    string inFile, extension;

    for( i = 0; i < compressedFile.length( ) - 4; i++ )
        inFile += compressedFile[ i ];
    for( ; i < compressedFile.length( ); i++ )
        extension += compressedFile[ i ];
    if( extension != ".huf" )
    {
        cerr << "Not a compressed file" << endl;
        return;
    }
    inFile += ".uc"; // for debugging, to not clobber original

    ifstream in( compressedFile.c_str( ), READ_MODE );
    ofstream out( inFile.c_str( ), WRITE_MODE );

    HuffmanTree codeTree;
    codeTree.readEncodingTable( in );

    ibstream bin( in );
    vector<int> bits;
    int bit;
    int decode;
    for( ; ; )
    {
        bit = bin.readBit( );
        bits.push_back( bit );
        decode = codeTree.getChar( bits );
        if( decode == HuffmanTree::INCOMPLETE_CODE )
            continue;
        else if( decode == HuffmanTree::ERROR )
        {
            cerr << "Error decoding!" << endl;
            break;
        }
        else if( decode == HuffmanTree::END )
            break;
        else
        {
            out.put( static_cast<char>( decode ) );
            bits.resize( 0 );
        }
    }
}
```

Figure 13.26 A routine for performing uncompression.

```
// Simple main that performs compression and uncompression.
int main( int argc, char *argv[] )
{
    if( argc < 3 )
    {
        cerr << "Usage: " << argv[0] << " -[cu] files" << endl;
        return 1;
    }

    string option  = argv[ 1 ];
    for( int i = 2; i < argc; i++ )
    {
        string nextFile = argv[ i ];
        if( option == "-c" )
            Compressor::compress( nextFile );
        else if( option == "-u" )
            Compressor::uncompress( nextFile );
        else
        {
            cerr << "Illegal option; usage: " << argv[0]
                                 << " -[cu] files" << endl;
            return 1;
        }
    }

    return 0;
}
```

Figure 13.27 A simple `main` for file compression and uncompression.

The `main` Routine

Finally, `main` is shown in Figure 13.27. If invoked with the `-c` argument, it compresses; with the `-u` argument it uncompresses.

Improving the Program

The program, as written, serves its main purpose of illustrating the basics of the Huffman coding algorithm. It achieves some compression, even on moderately sized files. For instance, it obtains roughly 36 percent compression when run on its own source file, `hzip.cpp`. However, the program could be improved in several ways.

1. The error checking is extremely limited. A production program must verify that files open correctly and must check all reads and all writes. It must rigorously ensure that the file being decompressed is actually a compressed file. (One way to have it do so is to write extra information in the encoding table.) The internal routines should have more checks.

2. Little effort has been made to minimize the size of the encoding table. For large files this lack is of little consequence, but for smaller files a large encoding table can be unacceptable because the encoding table takes up space itself.
3. A robust program checks the size of the resulting compressed file and aborts if the size is larger than the original.
4. In many places we made little attempt to optimize for speed. During compression, input files are read twice, which can be slow on some systems. Further, memoization could be used to avoid repeated searching of the tree for codes, and maps could be replaced with a more efficient data structure when the key is simply a `char`. Often vectors are copied and returned, perhaps resulting in a performance hit.

Further improvements to the program are left as an exercise for you to do.

13.2 A Cross-Reference Generator

In this section, we design a program called a **cross-reference generator** that scans a C++ source file, sorts the identifiers, and outputs all the identifiers, along with the line numbers on which they occur. One compiler application is to list, for each function, the names of all other functions that it directly calls.

A *cross-reference generator* lists identifiers and their line numbers. It is a common application because it is similar to creating an index.

However, this is a general problem that occurs in many other contexts. For instance, it can be used to generalize the creation of an index for a book. Another use, spell checking, is described in Exercise 13.18. As a spelling checker detects misspelled words in a document, those words are gathered, along with the lines on which they occur. This process avoids repeatedly printing out the same misspelled word and indicates where the errors are.

13.2.1 Basic Ideas

Our main algorithmic idea is to use a map to store each identifier and the line numbers on which it occurs. In the map, the identifier is the key, and the list of line numbers is the value. After the source file has been read and the map built, we can iterate over the collection, outputting identifiers and their corresponding line numbers.

We use a map to store identifiers and their line numbers. We store the line numbers for each identifier in a list.

```
// Xref class interface: generate cross-reference.
//
// CONSTRUCTION: with an open istream.
//
// *****************PUBLIC OPERATIONS*********************
// void generateCrossReference( ) --> Name says it all ...
// *****************ERRORS**********************************
// Error checking on comments and quotes is performed.

#include <ctype.h>
#include <fstream>
#include <list>
#include <string>
#include <map>
#include <functional>
using namespace std;

class Xref
{
  public:
    Xref( istream & input ) : tok( input ) { }

    void generateCrossReference( );

  private:
    Tokenizer tok;        // Token source
};
```

Figure 13.28 The `Xref` class interface.

13.2.2 C++ Implementation

The `Xref` class interface is shown in Figure 13.28. It is similar to (but simpler than) the `Balance` class shown in Figure 12.3, which was part of a balanced symbol program. Like that class, it makes use of the `Tokenizer` class defined in Figure 12.2.

We can now discuss the implementation of the two remaining routines in the `Tokenizer` class: `getNextID` and `getRemainingString`. These new parsing routines deal with recognizing an identifier.

The parsing routines are straightforward, though as usual they require some effort.

A C++ identifier consists of alphanumeric characters and underscores, with the restriction that the first character may not be a digit. Consequently, the routine shown in Figure 13.29 tests whether a character is part of an identifier. In the `getRemainingString` routine shown in Figure 13.30 we assume that the first character of an identifier has already been read and is stored in the `Tokenizer` class data member `ch`. It repeatedly reads charac-

```
// Return indicates if ch can be part of a C++ identifier.
bool isIdChar( char ch )
{
    return ch == '_' || isalnum( ch );
}
```

Figure 13.29 A routine for testing whether a character could be part of an identifier.

```
1 // Return an identifier read from input stream.
2 // First character is already read into ch.
3 string Tokenizer::getRemainingString( )
4 {
5     string result;
6
7     for( result = ch; nextChar( ); result += ch )
8         if( !isIdChar( ch ) )
9         {
10            putBackChar( );
11            break;
12        }
13
14    return result;
15 }
```

Figure 13.30 A routine for returning a `string` from input.

ters until one that is not part of an identifier appears. At that point we put the character back (at line 10) and then return a `string`.

The `getNextID` routine shown in Figure 13.31 is similar to the routine shown in Figure 12.7. The difference is that here at line 22, if the first character of an identifier is encountered, we call `getRemainingString` to return the token. The fact that `getNextID` and `getNextOpenClose` are so similar suggests that it would have been worthwhile to write a private member function that performs their common tasks.

With all the supporting routines written, let us consider the only member function, `generateCrossReference`, shown in Figure 13.32. Line 7 declares the map. We read the input and build the map at lines 11 and 12. At each iteration, we have the `current` identifier. Let us see how the expression at line 12 works. There are two cases:

1. The `current` identifier is in the map. In this case, `xrefMap[current]` gives a reference to the `list` of line numbers, and the new line number is added to the end of the `list`.

```
// Return next identifier, skipping comments
// string constants, and character constants.
// Return "" if end of stream is reached.
string Tokenizer::getNextID( )
{
    while( nextChar( ) )
    {
        if( ch == '/' )
        {
            if( nextChar( ) )
            {
                if( ch == '*' )
                    skipComment( SLASH_STAR );
                else if( ch == '/' )
                    skipComment( SLASH_SLASH );
                else
                    putBackChar( );
            }
        }
        else if( ch == '\'' || ch == '"' )
            skipQuote( ch );
        else if( !isdigit( ch ) && isIdChar( ch ) )
            return getRemainingString( );
    }
    return "";        // End of file
}
```

Figure 13.31 A routine for returning the next identifier.

2. The `current` identifier is not in the map. In this case, `xrefMap[current]` adds `current` to the map with a default value. The default value is a `list`, constructed with its zero-parameter constructor. The `xrefMap[current]` returns a reference to the newly constructed `list`. Thus the call to `push_back` adds the new line number to the list, and as a result, the `list` contains the single line number, as desired.

The output is obtained by using a map traversal and an iterator class. A list iterator is used to get the line numbers.

Once we have built the map, we merely iterate through it by using an appropriate iterator. The iterator, which visits the map in sorted order, is declared at line 16, and line 17 is the standard iteration technique. Each time a map entry appears, we need to print out information for the identifier currently being examined by the map iterator.

Recall that a `map` iterator looks at `pairs`; in a `pair`, the key is the data member named `first`, and the value is the data member named `second`. Thus the list of line numbers is given by `(*itr).second`, as shown at

```
1 // Output the cross reference.
2 void Xref::generateCrossReference( )
3 {
4     typedef map<string,list<int>, less<string> > MapType;
5     typedef MapType::const_iterator MapIteratorType;
6
7     MapType xrefMap;
8     string current;
9
10        // Insert identifiers into the map.
11    while( ( current = tok.getNextID( ) ) != "" )
12        xrefMap[ current ].push_back( tok.getLineNumber( ) );
13
14        // Iterate through map and output
15        // identifiers and their line number.
16    MapIteratorType itr;
17    for( itr = xrefMap.begin( ); itr != xrefMap.end( ); ++itr )
18    {
19        const list<int> & theLines = (*itr).second;
20        list<int>::const_iterator lineItr = theLines.begin( );
21
22            // Print identifier and first line where it occurs.
23        cout << (*itr).first << ": " << *lineItr;
24
25            // Print all other lines on which it occurs.
26        for( ++lineItr; lineItr != theLines.end( ); ++lineItr )
27            cout << ", " << *lineItr;
28        cout << endl;
29    }
30 }
```

Figure 13.32 The main cross-reference algorithm.

line 19, and the identifier being scanned is given by `(*itr).first`, as shown at line 23. To access individual lines, we need a list iterator, `lineItr`, shown at 20.

We print the word and the first line number at line 23 (we are guaranteed that the list is not empty). Then, so long as we have not reached the end marker of the list, we repeatedly output line numbers in the loop that extends from line 26 to 27. We print out a newline at line 28. We do not provide a main program here because it is essentially the same as that shown in Figure 12.10.

Summary

In this chapter we presented implementations of two important utilities: text compression and cross-referencing. Text compression is an important technique that allows us to increase both effective disk capacity and effective modem speed. It is an area of active research. The simple method described here—namely, Huffman's algorithm—typically achieves compression of 25 percent on text files. Other algorithms and extensions of Huffman's algorithm perform better. Cross-referencing is a general approach that has many applications.

Objects of the Game

binary trie A data structure in which a left branch represents 0 and a right branch represents 1. The path to a node indicates its representation. (p. 440)

compression The act of reducing the number of bits required for data representation, which actually has two phases: the encoding phase (compression) and the decoding phase (uncompression). (p. 440)

cross-reference generator A program that lists identifiers and their line numbers. It is a common application because it is similar to creating an index. (p. 461)

full tree A tree whose nodes either are leaves or have two children. (p. 441)

Huffman's algorithm An algorithm that constructs an optimal prefix code by repeatedly merging the two minimum weight trees. (p. 442)

prefix code Code in which no character code is a prefix of another character code. This condition is guaranteed in a trie if the characters are only in leaves. A prefix code can be decoded unambiguously. (p. 441)

Common Errors

1. When working with character I/O, you often need to use an `int` to store the characters because of the additional `EOF` symbol. There are several other tricky coding issues. For instance, when reading an input stream a second time, you must clear the `EOF` error.

2. Using too much memory to store the compression table is a common mistake. Doing so limits the amount of compression that can be achieved.

On the Internet

The compression program and cross-reference generator is available.

hzip.cpp Contains the source for the Huffman coding compression and uncompression program.

Xref.cpp Contains the source for the cross-reference generator.

Exercises

In Short

13.1. Show the Huffman tree that results from the following distribution of punctuation characters and digits: colon (100), space (605), newline (100), comma (705), 0 (431), 1 (242), 2 (176), 3 (59), 4 (185), 5 (250), 6 (174), 7 (199), 8 (205), and 9 (217).

13.2. Most systems come with a compression program. Compress several types of files to determine the typical compression rate on your system. How large do the files have to be to make compression worthwhile? Compare their performance with the Huffman coding program (`hzip`) provided in the online source code.

13.3. What happens if a file compressed with Huffman's algorithm is used to transmit data over a phone line and a single bit is accidentally lost? What can be done in this situation?

In Theory

13.4. Prove the correctness of Huffman's algorithm by expanding the following steps.

a. Show that no node has only one child.
b. Show that the two least frequent characters must be the two deepest nodes in the tree.
c. Show that the characters in any two nodes at the same depth can be swapped without affecting optimality.
d. Use induction: As trees are merged, consider the new character set to be the characters in the tree roots.

13.5. Under what circumstances could a Huffman tree of ASCII characters generate a 2-bit code for some character? Under what circumstances could it generate a 20-bit code?

13.6. Show that, if the symbols have already been sorted by frequency, Huffman's algorithm can be implemented in linear time.

13.7. Huffman's algorithm occasionally generates compressed files that are larger than the original. Prove that all compression algorithms must have this property (i.e., no matter what compression algorithm you design, some input files must always exist for which the algorithm generates compressed files that are larger than the originals).

In Practice

13.8. In the cross-reference generator, store the line numbers in a `vector` instead of a `list` and compare performance.

13.9. If a word occurs twice on a line, the cross-reference generator will list it twice. Modify the algorithm so that duplicates are only listed once.

13.10. Modify the algorithm so that, if a word appears on consecutive lines, a range is indicated. For example,

```
if: 2, 4, 6-9, 11
```

Programming Projects

13.11. Modify the `CharCounter` class to use an array of `int`s instead of a map, and explain whether this modification is likely to affect the program's running time. Incorporate the change and measure the running time on a large data file for both compression and uncompression.

13.12. Storing the character counts in the encoding table gives the uncompression algorithm the ability to perform extra consistency checks. Add code that verifies that the result of the uncompression has the same character counts as the encoding table claimed.

13.13. Describe and implement a method of storing the encoding table that uses less space than the trivial method of storing character counts.

13.14. Add the robust error checks for the compression program suggested at the end of Section 13.1.3.

13.15. Analyze empirically the performance of the compression program and determine whether its speed can be significantly improved. If so, make the required changes.

13.16. Split the `Tokenizer` class into three classes: an abstract base class that handles the common functionality and two separate derived classes (one that handles the tokenization for the balanced symbol program, and another that handles the tokenization for the cross-reference generator).

13.17. Generate an index for a book. The input file consists of a set of index entries. Each line consists of the string `IX:`, followed by an index entry name enclosed in braces and then by a page number enclosed in braces. Each `!` in an index entry name represents a sublevel. A `|(` represents the start of a range and a `|)` represents the end of the range. Occasionally, this range will be the same page. In that case, output only a single page number. Otherwise, do not collapse or expand ranges on your own. As an example, Figure 13.33 shows sample input and Figure 13.34 shows the corresponding output.

```
IX: {Series|(}              {2}
IX: {Series!geometric|(}    {4}
IX: {Euler's constant}      {4}
IX: {Series!geometric|)}    {4}
IX: {Series!arithmetic|(}   {4}
IX: {Series!arithmetic|)}   {5}
IX: {Series!harmonic|(}     {5}
IX: {Euler's constant}      {5}
IX: {Series!harmonic|)}     {5}
IX: {Series|)}              {5}
```

Figure 13.33 Sample input for Exercise 13.17.

```
Euler's constant: 4, 5
Series: 2-5
   arithmetic: 4-5
   geometric: 4
   harmonic: 5
```

Figure 13.34 Sample output for Exercise 13.17.

13.18. Use a map to implement a spelling checker. Assume that the dictionary comes from two sources: one file containing an existing large dictionary and a second file containing a personal dictionary. Output all misspelled words and the line numbers on which they occur (note that keeping track of the misspelled words and their line numbers is identical to generating a cross-reference). Also, for each misspelled word, list any words in the dictionary that are obtainable by applying any of the following rules.

a. Add one character.
b. Remove one character.
c. Exchange adjacent characters.

References

The original paper on Huffman's algorithm is [3]. Variations on the algorithm are discussed in [2] and [4]. Another popular compression scheme is *Ziv-Lempel encoding,* described in [7] and [6]. It works by generating a series of fixed-length codes. Typically, we would generate 4096 12-bit codes that represent the most common substrings in the file. References [1] and [5] are good surveys of the common compression schemes.

1. T. Bell, I. H. Witten, and J. G. Cleary, "Modelling for Text Compression," *ACM Computing Surveys* **21** (1989), 557–591.
2. R. G. Gallager, "Variations on a Theme by Huffman," *IEEE Transactions on Information Theory* **IT-24** (1978), 668–674.
3. D. A. Huffman, "A Model for the Construction of Minimum Redundancy Codes," *Proceedings of the IRE* **40** (1952), 1098–1101.
4. D. E. Knuth, "Dynamic Huffman Coding," *Journal of Algorithms* **6** (1985), 163–180.
5. D. A. Lelewer and D. S. Hirschberg, "Data Compression," *ACM Computing Surveys* **19** (1987), 261–296.
6. T. A. Welch, "A Technique for High-Performance Data Compression," *Computer* **17** (1984), 8–19.
7. J. Ziv and A. Lempel, "Compression of Individual Sequences via Variable-Rate Coding," *IEEE Transactions on Information Theory* **IT-24** (1978), 530–536.

Chapter 14

Simulation

An important use of computers is for **simulation,** in which the computer is used to emulate the operation of a real system and gather statistics. For example, we might want to simulate the operation of a bank with k tellers to determine the minimum value of k that gives reasonable service time. Using a computer for this task has many advantages. First, the information would be gathered without involving real customers. Second, a simulation by computer can be faster than the actual implementation because of the speed of the computer. Third, the simulation could be easily replicated. In many cases, the proper choice of data structures can help us improve the efficiency of the simulation.

An important use of computers is *simulation,* in which the computer is used to emulate the operation of a real system and gather statistics.

In this chapter, we show:

- how to simulate a game modeled on the *Josephus problem,* and
- how to simulate the operation of a computer modem bank.

14.1 The Josephus Problem

The *Josephus problem* is the following game: N people, numbered 1 to N, are sitting in a circle; starting at person 1, a hot potato is passed; after M passes, the person holding the hot potato is eliminated, the circle closes ranks, and the game continues with the person who was sitting after the eliminated person picking up the hot potato; the last remaining person wins. A common assumption is that M is a constant, although a random number generator can be used to change M after each elimination.

In the *Josephus problem,* a hot potato is repeatedly passed; when passing terminates, the player holding the potato is eliminated; the game continues, and the last remaining player wins.

The Josephus problem arose in the first century A.D. in a cave on a mountain in Israel where Jewish zealots were being besieged by Roman soldiers. The historian Josephus was among them. To Josephus's consternation, the zealots voted to enter into a suicide pact rather than surrender to the Romans. He suggested the game that now bears his name. The hot potato

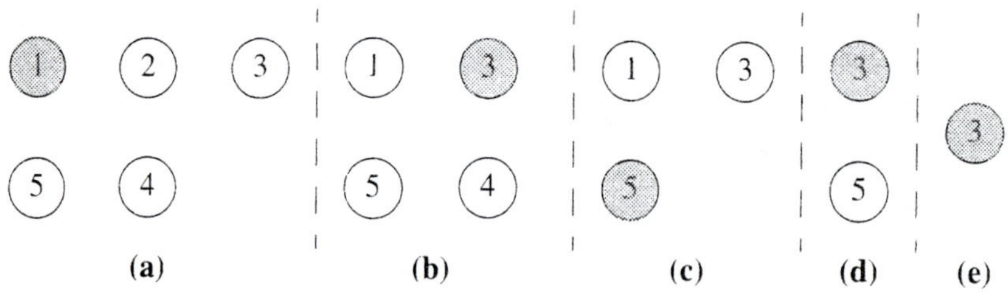

Figure 14.1 The Josephus problem: At each step, the darkest circle represents the initial holder and the lightly shaded circle represents the player who receives the hot potato (and is eliminated). Passes are made clockwise.

was the sentence of death to the person next to the one who got the potato. Josephus rigged the game to get the last lot and convinced the remaining intended victim that the two of them should surrender. That is how we know about this game; in effect, Josephus cheated.[1]

If $M = 0$, the players are eliminated in order, and the last player always wins. For other values of M, things are not so obvious. Figure 14.1 shows that if $N = 5$ and $M = 1$, the players are eliminated in the order 2, 4, 1, 5. In this case, player 3 wins. The steps are as follows.

1. At the start, the potato is at player 1. After one pass it is at player 2.
2. Player 2 is eliminated. Player 3 picks up the potato, and after one pass, it is at player 4.
3. Player 4 is eliminated. Player 5 picks up the potato and passes it to player 1.
4. Player 1 is eliminated. Player 3 picks up the potato and passes it to player 5.
5. Player 5 is eliminated, so player 3 wins.

First, we write a program that simulates, pass for pass, a game for any values of N and M. The running time of the simulation is $O(MN)$, which is acceptable if the number of passes is small. Each step takes $O(M)$ time because it performs M passes. We then show how to implement each step in $O(\log N)$ time, regardless of the number of passes performed. The running time of the simulation becomes $O(N \log N)$.

1. Thanks to David Teague for relaying this story. The version that we solve differs from the historical description. In Exercise 14.12 you are asked to solve the historical version.

14.1.1 The Simple Solution

The passing stage in the Josephus problem suggests that we represent the players in a linked list. We create a linked list in which the elements 1, 2, ..., *N* are inserted in order. We then set an iterator to the front element. Each pass of the potato corresponds to a ++ operation on the iterator. At the last player (currently remaining) in the list we implement the pass by resetting the iterator to the first element. This action mimics the circle. When we have finished passing, we remove the element on which the iterator has landed.

We can represent the players by a linked list and use the iterator to simulate the passing.

An implementation is shown in Figure 14.2 The linked list and iterator are declared at lines 8 and 9, respectively. We construct the initial list by using the loop at lines 14 and 15.

In Figure 14.2, the code at lines 20 to 33 plays one step of the algorithm by passing the potato (lines 20 to 25) and then eliminating a player (lines 30–33). This procedure is repeated until the test at line 18 tells us that only one player remains. At that point we return the player's number at line 36.

The running time of this routine is $O(MN)$ because that is exactly the number of passes that occur during the algorithm. For small *M*, this running time is acceptable, although we should mention that the case $M = 0$ does not yield a running time of $O(0)$; obviously the running time is $O(N)$. We do not merely multiply by zero when trying to interpret a Big-Oh expression.

14.1.2 A More Efficient Algorithm

A more efficient algorithm can be obtained if we use a data structure that supports accessing the *k*th smallest item (in logarithmic time). Doing so allows us to implement each round of passing in a single operation. Figure 14.1 shows why. Suppose that we have *N* players remaining and are currently at player *P* from the front. Initially *N* is the total number of players and *P* is 1. After *M* passes, a calculation tells us that we are at player $((P + M) \bmod N)$ from the front, except if that would give us player 0, in which case, we go to player *N*. The calculation is fairly tricky, but the concept is not.

If we implement each round of passing in a single logarithmic operation, the simulation will be faster.

Applying this calculation to Figure 14.1, we observe that *M* is 1, *N* is initially 5, and *P* is initially 1. So the new value of *P* is 2. After the deletion, *N* drops to 4, but we are still at position 2, as part (b) of the figure suggests. The next value of *P* is 3, also shown in part (b), so the third element in the list is deleted and *N* falls to 3. The next value of *P* is 4 mod 3, or 1, so we are back at the first player in the remaining list, as shown in part (c). This player is removed and *N* becomes 2. At this point, we add *M* to *P*, obtaining 2. Because 2 mod 2 is 0, we set *P* to player *N*, and thus the last player in the list is the one that is removed. This action agrees with part (d). After the removal, *N* is 1 and we are done.

The calculation is tricky because of the circle.

```
#include <list>
using namespace std;

// Return the winner in the Josephus problem.
// STL list implementation.
int josephus( int people, int passes )
{
    list<int> theList;
    list<int>::iterator itr;
    list<int>::iterator next;
    int i;

      // Construct the list.
    for( i = 1; i <= people; i++ )
        theList.push_back( i );

      // Play the game.
    for( itr = theList.begin( ); people-- != 1; itr = next )
    {
        for( i = 0; i < passes; i++ )
        {
            ++itr;                            // Advance
            if( itr == theList.end( ) )       // If past last player
                itr = theList.begin( );       // then go to first
        }

        next = itr;             // Maintain next node, for
        ++next;                 // player who is after removed player

        theList.erase( itr );                 // Remove player

        if( next == theList.end( ) )          // Set next
            next = theList.begin( );
    }

    return *itr;        // Return player's number
}
```

Figure 14.2 Linked list implementation of the Josephus problem.

`findKth` can be supported by a search tree.

All we need then is a data structure that efficiently supports the `findKth` operation. The `findKth` operation returns the *k*th (smallest) item, for any parameter `k`.[2] Unfortunately, no STL data structures support the `findKth`

2. The parameter `k` for `findKth` ranges from 1 to N, inclusive, where N is the number of items in the data structure.

operation. However, we can use one of the generic data structures that we implement in Part IV. Recall from the discussion in Section 7.7 that the data structures we implement in Chapter 19 follow a basic protocol that uses `insert`, `remove`, and `find`. We can then add `findKth` to the implementation.

There are several similar alternatives. All of them use the fact that, as discussed in Section 7.7, `set` could have supported the ranking operation in logarithmic time on average or logarithmic time in the worst case if we had used a sophisticated binary search tree. Consequently, we can expect an $O(N \log N)$ algorithm if we exercise care.

The simplest method is to insert the items sequentially into a worst-case efficient binary search tree such as a red–black tree, an AA-tree, or a splay tree (we discuss these trees in later chapters). We can then call `findKth` and `remove`, as appropriate. It turns out that a splay tree is an excellent choice for this application because the `findKth` and `insert` operations are unusually efficient and `remove` is not terribly difficult to code. We use an alternative here, however, because the implementations of these data structures that we provide in the later chapters leave implementing `findKth` for you to do as an exercise.

A balanced search tree will work, but it is not needed if we are careful and construct a simple binary search tree that is not unbalanced at the start. A class method can be used to construct a perfectly balanced tree in linear time.

We use the `BinarySearchTreeWithRank` class that supports the `findKth` operation and is completely implemented in Section 19.2. It is based on the simple binary search tree and thus does not have logarithmic worst-case performance but merely average-case performance. Consequently, we cannot merely insert the items sequentially; that would cause the search tree to exhibit its worst-case performance.

There are several options. One is to insert a random permutation of 1, ..., N into the search tree. The other is to build a perfectly balanced binary search tree with a class method. Because a class method would have access to the inner workings of the search tree, it could be done in linear time. This routine is left for you to do as Exercise 19.21 when search trees are discussed.

We construct the same tree by recursive insertions but use $O(N \log N)$ time.

The method we use is to write a recursive routine that inserts items in a balanced order. By inserting the middle item at the root and recursively building the two subtrees in the same manner, we obtain a balanced tree. The cost of our routine is an acceptable $O(N \log N)$. Although not as efficient as the linear-time class routine, it does not adversely affect the asymptotic running time of the overall algorithm. The `remove` operations are then guaranteed to be logarithmic. This routine is called `buildTree`; it and the `josephus` method are then coded as shown in Figure 14.3.

14.2 Event-Driven Simulation

Let us return to the bank simulation problem described in the introduction. Here, we have a system in which customers arrive and wait in line until one

```
#include "BinarySearchTree.h"

// Recursively construct a perfectly balanced binary search
// tree by repeated insertions in O( N log N ) time.
void buildTree( BinarySearchTreeWithRank<int> & t,
                int low, int high )
{
    int center = ( low + high ) / 2;

    if( low <= high )
    {
        t.insert( center );
        buildTree( t, low, center - 1 );
        buildTree( t, center + 1, high );
    }
}

// Return the winner in the Josephus problem.
// Search tree implementation.
int josephus( int people, int passes )
{
    BinarySearchTreeWithRank<int> t;

    buildTree( t, 1, people );

    int rank = 1;
    while( people > 1 )
    {
        if( ( rank = ( rank + passes ) % people ) == 0 )
            rank = people;

        t.remove( t.findKth( rank ).get( ) );
        people--;
    }

    return t.findKth( 1 ).get( );
}
```

Figure 14.3 An $O(N \log N)$ solution of the Josephus problem.

of k tellers is available. Customer arrival is governed by a probability distribution function, as is the service time (the amount of time to be served once a teller becomes available). We are interested in statistics such as how long on average a customer has to wait and what percentage of the time tellers are actually servicing requests. (If there are too many tellers, some will not do anything for long periods.)

With certain probability distributions and values of k, we can compute these answers exactly. However, as k gets larger the analysis becomes considerably more difficult and the use of a computer to simulate the operation of the bank is extremely helpful. In this way, bank officers can determine how many tellers are needed to ensure reasonably smooth service. Most simulations require a thorough knowledge of probability, statistics, and queueing theory.

14.2.1 Basic Ideas

A discrete event simulation consists of processing events. Here, the two events are (1) a customer arriving and (2) a customer departing, thus freeing up a teller.

We can use a probability function to generate an input stream consisting of ordered pairs of arrival and service time for each customer, sorted by arrival time.[3] We do not need to use the exact time of day. Rather, we can use a quantum unit, referred to as a **tick.**

The *tick* is the quantum unit of time in a simulation.

In a **discrete time-driven simulation** we might start a simulation clock at zero ticks and advance the clock one tick at a time, checking to see whether an event occurs. If so, we process the event(s) and compile statistics. When no customers are left in the input stream and all the tellers are free, the simulation is over.

A *discrete time-driven simulation* processes each unit of time consecutively. It is inappropriate if the interval between successive events is large.

The problem with this simulation strategy is that its running time does not depend on the number of customers or events (there are two events per customer in this case). Rather, it depends on the number of ticks, which is not really part of the input. To show why this condition is important, let us change the clock units to microticks and multiply all the times in the input by 1,000,000. The simulation would then take 1,000,000 times longer.

The key to avoiding this problem is to advance the clock to the next event time at each stage, called an **event-driven simulation,** which is conceptually easy to do. At any point, the next event that can occur is either the arrival of the next customer in the input stream or the departure of one of the customers from a teller's station. All the times at which the events will happen are available, so we just need to find the event that happens soonest and process that event (setting the current time to the time that the event occurs).

An *event-driven simulation* advances the current time to the next event.

If the event is a departure, processing includes gathering statistics for the departing customer and checking the line (queue) to determine whether another customer is waiting. If so, we add that customer, process whatever

3. The probability function generates interarrival times (times between arrivals), thus guaranteeing that arrivals are generated chronologically.

statistics are required, compute the time when the customer will leave, and add that departure to the set of events waiting to happen.

If the event is an arrival, we check for an available teller. If there is none, we place the arrival in the line (queue). Otherwise, we give the customer a teller, compute the customer's departure time, and add the departure to the set of events waiting to happen.

The event set (i.e., events waiting to happen) is organized as a priority queue.

The waiting line for customers can be implemented as a queue. Because we need to find the next soonest event, the set of events should be organized in a priority queue. The next event is thus an arrival or departure (whichever is sooner); both are easily available. An event-driven simulation is appropriate if the number of ticks between events is expected to be large.

14.2.2 Example: A Modem Bank Simulation

The main algorithmic item in a simulation is the organization of the events in a priority queue. To focus on this requirement, we write a simple simulation. The system we simulate is a *modem bank* at a university computing center.

A modem bank consists of a large collection of modems. For example, Florida International University (FIU) has 288 modems available for students. A modem is accessed by dialing one telephone number. If any of the 288 modems are available, the user is connected to one of them. If all the modems are in use, the phone will give a busy signal. Our simulation models the service provided by the modem bank. The variables are

- the number of modems in the bank,
- the probability distribution that governs dial-in attempts,
- the probability distribution that governs connect time, and
- the length of time the simulation is to be run.

The modem bank removes the waiting line from the simulation. Thus there is only one data structure.

The modem bank simulation is a simplified version of the bank teller simulation because there is no waiting line. Each dial-in is an arrival, and the total time spent once a connection has been established is the service time. By removing the waiting line, we remove the need to maintain a queue. Thus we have only one data structure, the priority queue. In Exercise 14.18 you are asked to incorporate a queue; as many as L calls will be queued if all the modems are busy.

We list each event as it happens; gathering statistics is a simple extension.

To simplify matters, we do not compute statistics. Instead, we list each event as it is processed. We also assume that attempts to connect occur at constant intervals; in an accurate simulation, we would model this interarrival time by a random process. Figure 14.4 shows the output of a simulation.

```
User 0 dials in at time 0 and connects for 1 minutes
User 0 hangs up at time 1
User 1 dials in at time 1 and connects for 5 minutes
User 2 dials in at time 2 and connects for 4 minutes
User 3 dials in at time 3 and connects for 11 minutes
User 4 dials in at time 4 but gets busy signal
User 5 dials in at time 5 but gets busy signal
User 6 dials in at time 6 but gets busy signal
User 1 hangs up at time 6
User 2 hangs up at time 6
User 7 dials in at time 7 and connects for 8 minutes
User 8 dials in at time 8 and connects for 6 minutes
User 9 dials in at time 9 but gets busy signal
User 10 dials in at time 10 but gets busy signal
User 11 dials in at time 11 but gets busy signal
User 12 dials in at time 12 but gets busy signal
User 13 dials in at time 13 but gets busy signal
User 3 hangs up at time 14
User 14 dials in at time 14 and connects for 6 minutes
User 8 hangs up at time 14
User 15 dials in at time 15 and connects for 3 minutes
User 7 hangs up at time 15
User 16 dials in at time 16 and connects for 5 minutes
User 17 dials in at time 17 but gets busy signal
User 15 hangs up at time 18
User 18 dials in at time 18 and connects for 7 minutes
```

Figure 14.4 Sample output for the modem bank simulation involving three modems: A dial-in is attempted every minute; the average connect time is 5 minutes; and the simulation is run for 18 minutes.

The simulation class requires another class to represent events. The `Event` class is shown in Figure 14.5. The data members consist of the customer number, the time that the event will occur, and an indication of what type of event (`DIAL_IN` or `HANG_UP`) it is. If this simulation were more complex, with several types of events, we would make `Event` an abstract base class and derive subclasses from it. We do not do that here because that would complicate things and obscure the basic workings of the simulation algorithm. The `Event` class contains a constructor and a comparison function used by the priority queue. The `Event` class grants friendship status to the modem simulation class so that `Event`'s internal members can be accessed by `ModemSim` methods.

The `Event` class represents events. In a complex simulation, it would derive all possible types of events as subclasses. Using inheritance for the `Event` class would complicate the code.

The modem simulation class, `ModemSim`, is shown in Figure 14.6. It consists of a lot of data members, a constructor, and two member functions. The data members include a random number object `r` shown at line 25. At

```
#include <limits.h>
#include <time.h>
#include <stdlib.h>
#include "Random.h"
#include <iostream>
#include <vector>
#include <queue>
#include <functional>
using namespace std;

class Event
{
    enum { DIAL_IN = 1, HANG_UP = 2 };
  public:
    Event( int name = 0, int tm = 0, int type = DIAL_IN )
      : time( tm ), who( name ), what( type ) { }

    bool operator> ( const Event & rhs ) const
      { return time > rhs.time; }

    friend class ModemSim;

  private:
    int who;          // the number of the user
    int time;         // when the event will occur
    int what;         // DIAL_IN or HANG_UP
};
```

Figure 14.5 The `Event` class used for modem simulation.

line 26 the `eventSet` is maintained as a priority queue of `Event` objects (`PQ` is a `typedef`, given at line 10, that hides a complicated `priority_queue` template instantiation). The remaining data members are `freeModems`, which is initially the number of modems in the simulation but changes as users connect and hang up, and `avgCallLen` and `freqOfCalls`, which are parameters of the simulation. Recall that a dial-in attempt will be made every `freqOfCalls` ticks. The constructor, declared at line 15, and implemented in Figure 14.7 initializes these members and places the first arrival in the `eventSet` priority queue.

The `nextCall` function adds a dial-in request to the event set.

The simulation class consists of only two member functions. First, `nextCall`, shown in Figure 14.8 adds a dial-in request to the event set. It maintains two static variables: the number of the next user who will attempt to dial in and when that event will occur. Again, we have made the simplifying assumption that calls are made at regular intervals. In practice, we would use a random number generator to model the arrival stream.

```
// ModemSim class interface: run a simulation.
//
// CONSTRUCTION: with three parameters: the number of
//     modems, the average connect time, and the
//     inter-arrival time.
//
// ******************PUBLIC OPERATIONS*********************
// void runSim( )        --> Run a simulation

typedef priority_queue<Event,vector<Event>,greater<Event> > PQ;

class ModemSim
{
  public:
    ModemSim( int modems, double avgLen, int callIntrvl );

      // Add a call to eventSet at the current time,
      // and schedule one for delta in the future.
    void nextCall( int delta );

      // Run the simulation.
    void runSim( int stoppingTime = INT_MAX );

  private:
    Random r;                          // A random source
    PQ eventSet;                       // Pending events

      // Basic parameters of the simulation.
    int freeModems;                    // Number of modems unused
    const double avgCallLen;           // Length of a call
    const int freqOfCalls;             // Interval between calls
};
```

Figure 14.6 The `ModemSim` class interface.

```
// Constructor for ModemSim.
ModemSim::ModemSim( int modems, double avgLen, int callIntrvl )
  : freeModems( modems ), avgCallLen( avgLen ),
    freqOfCalls( callIntrvl ), r( (int) time( 0 ) )
{
    nextCall( freqOfCalls );  // Schedule first call
}
```

Figure 14.7 The `ModemSim` constructor.

```
// Place a new DIAL_IN event into the event queue.
// Then advance the time when next DIAL_IN event will occur.
// In practice, we would use a random number to set the time.
void ModemSim::nextCall( int delta )
{
    static int nextCallTime = 0;
    static int userNum = 0;

    eventSet.push( Event( userNum++, nextCallTime ) );
    nextCallTime += delta;
}
```

Figure 14.8 The `nextCall` function places a new `DIAL_IN` event in the event queue and advances the time when the next `DIAL_IN` event will occur.

The `runSim` function runs the simulation.

The other member function is `runSim`, which is called to run the entire simulation. The `runSim` function does most of the work and is shown in Figure 14.9. It is called with a single parameter that indicates when the simulation should end. As long as the event set is not empty, we process events. Note that it should never be empty because at the time we arrive at line 10 there is exactly one dial-in request in the priority queue and one hang-up request for every currently connected modem. Whenever we remove an event at line 10 and it is confirmed to be a dial-in, we generate a replacement dial-in event at line 37. A hang-up event is also generated at line 32 if the dial-in succeeds. Thus the only way to finish the routine is if `nextCall` is set up not to generate an event eventually or (more likely) by executing the `break` statement at line 12.

A hang-up increases `freeModems`. A dial-in checks on whether a modem is available and if so decreases `freeModems`.

Let us summarize how the various events are processed. If the event is a hang-up, we increment `freeModems` at line 16 and print a message at line 17. If the event is a dial-in, we generate a partial line of output that records the attempt, and then, if any modems are available, we connect the user. To do so, we decrement `freeModems` at line 26, generate a connection time (using a Poisson distribution rather than a uniform distribution) at line 27, print the rest of the output at line 28, and add a hang-up to the event set (lines 30–32). Otherwise, no modems are available, and we give the busy signal message. Either way, an additional dial-in event is generated. Figure 14.10 shows the state of the priority queue after each `deleteMin` for the early stages of the sample output shown in Figure 14.4. The time at which each event occurs is shown in boldface, and the number of free modems (if any) are shown to the right of the priority queue. (Note that the call length is not actually stored in an `Event` object; we include it, when appropriate to make the figure more self-contained. A '?' for the call length signifies a dial-in event that eventually will result in a busy signal; however, that outcome is not known at the time the event is added to the priority queue.) The sequence of priority queue steps is as follows.

```
// Run the simulation until stopping time occurs.
// Print output as in Figure 14.4.
void ModemSim::runSim( int stoppingTime )
{
    static Event e;
    int howLong;

    while( !eventSet.empty( ) )
    {
        e = eventSet.top( ); eventSet.pop( );
        if( e.time > stoppingTime )
            break;

        if( e.what == Event::HANG_UP )    // HANG_UP
        {
            freeModems++;
            cout << "User " << e.who << " hangs up at time "
                 << e.time << endl;
        }
        else                              // DIAL_IN
        {
            cout << "User " << e.who << " dials in at time "
                 << e.time << " ";
            if( freeModems > 0 )
            {
                freeModems--;
                howLong = r.poisson( avgCallLen );
                cout << "and connects for "
                     << howLong << " minutes" << endl;
                e.time += howLong;
                e.what = Event::HANG_UP;
                eventSet.push( e );
            }
            else
                cout << "but gets busy signal" << endl;

            nextCall( freqOfCalls );
        }
    }
}
```

Figure 14.9 The basic simulation routine.

1. The first DIAL_IN request is inserted.
2. After DIAL_IN is removed, the request is connected, thereby resulting in a HANG_UP and a replacement DIAL_IN request.
3. A HANG_UP request is processed.
4. A DIAL_IN request is processed resulting in a connect. Thus both a HANG_UP event and a DIAL_IN event are added (three times).

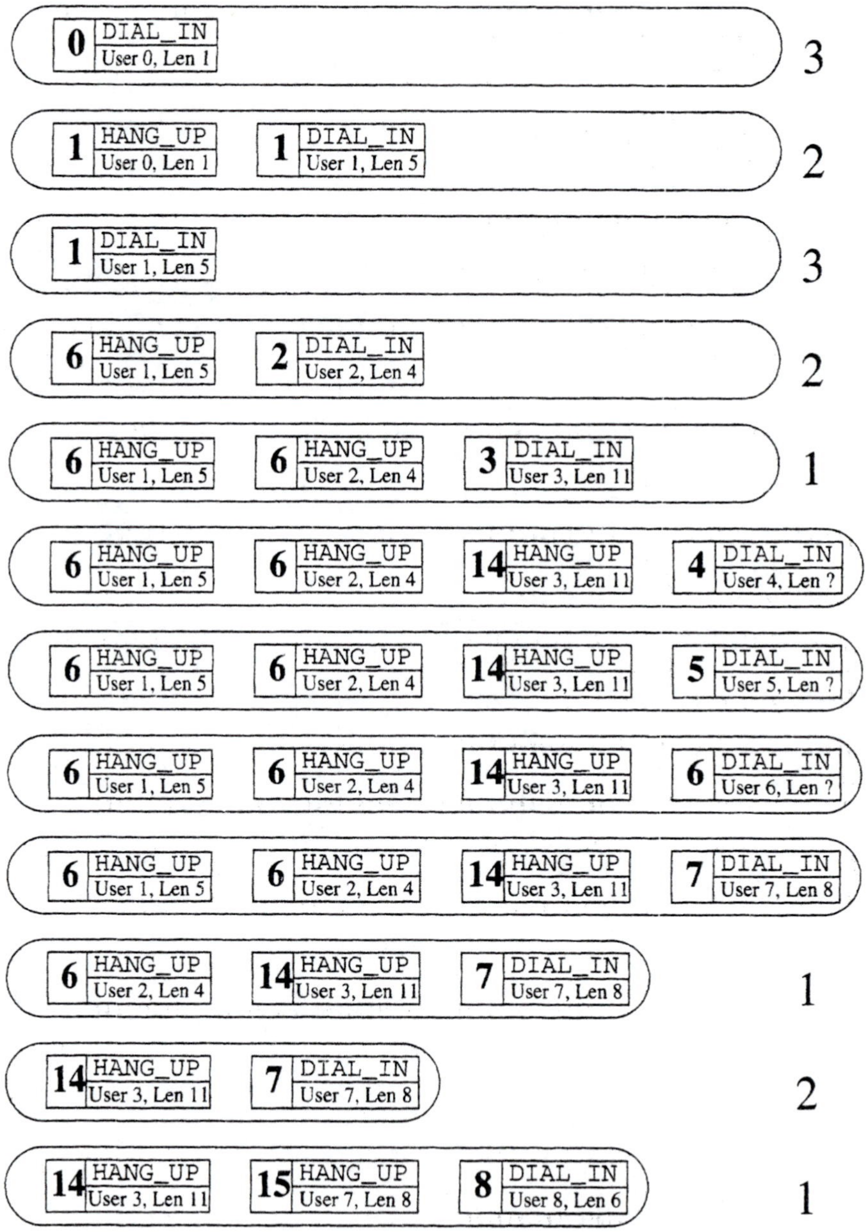

Figure 14.10 The priority queue for modem bank simulation after each step.

5. A `DIAL_IN` request fails; a replacement `DIAL_IN` is generated (three times).
6. A `HANG_UP` request is processed (twice).
7. A `DIAL_IN` request succeeds, and `HANG_UP` and `DIAL_IN` are added.

Again, if `Event` were an abstract base class, we would expect a procedure `doEvent` to be defined through the `Event` hierarchy; then we would not need long chains of `if/else` statements. However to access the priority queue, which is in the simulation class, we would need `Event` to store a pointer to the simulation `ModemSim` class as a data member. We would insert it at construction time.

A minimal `main` routine is shown for completeness in Figure 14.11. However, using a Poisson distribution to model connect time is not appropriate. A better choice would be to use a negative exponential distribution (but the reasons for doing so are beyond the scope of this text). Additionally, assuming a fixed time between dial-in attempts is also inaccurate. Again, a negative exponential distribution would be a better model. If we change the simulation to use these distributions, the clock would be represented as a `double`. In Exercise 14.14 you are asked to implement these changes.

The simulation uses a poor model. Negative exponential distributions would more accurately model the time between dial-in attempts and total connect time.

```
// Simple main to test ModemSim class.
int main( )
{
    int numModems;
    int totalTime;
    double avgConnectTime;
    int dialInFrequency;

    cout << "Enter: number of modems, length of simulation, "
         << " average connect time, how often calls occur: ";

    cin >> numModems >> totalTime >>
                     avgConnectTime >> dialInFrequency;

    ModemSim s( numModems, avgConnectTime, dialInFrequency );
    s.runSim( totalTime );

    return 0;
}
```

Figure 14.11 A simple `main` to test the simulation.

Summary

Simulation is an important area of computer science and involves many more complexities than we could discuss here. A simulation is only as good as the model of randomness, so a solid background in probability, statistics, and queueing theory is required in order for the modeler to know what types of probability distributions are reasonable to assume. Simulation is an important application area for object-oriented techniques.

Objects of the Game

discrete time-driven simulation A simulation in which each unit of time is processed consecutively. It is inappropriate if the interval between successive events is large. (p. 477)

event-driven simulation A simulation in which the current time is advanced to the next event. (p. 477)

Josephus problem A game in which a hot potato is repeatedly passed; when passing terminates, the player holding the potato is eliminated; the game then continues, and the last remaining player wins. (p. 471)

simulation An important use of computers, in which the computer is used to emulate the operation of a real system and gather statistics. (p. 471)

tick The quantum unit of time in a simulation. (p. 477)

Common Errors

1. The most common error in simulation is using a poor model. A simulation is only as good as the accuracy of its random input.

On the Internet

Both examples in this chapter are available online.

Josephus.cpp Contains both implementations of `josephus` and a `main` to test them.

Modems.cpp Contains the code for the modem bank simulation.

Exercises

In Short

14.1. If $M = 0$, who wins the Josephus game?

14.2. Show the operation of the Josephus algorithm in Figure 14.3 for the case of seven people with three passes. Include the computation of `rank` and a picture that contains the remaining elements after each iteration.

14.3. Are there any values of M for which player 1 wins a 30-person Josephus game?

14.4. Show the state of the priority queue after each of the first 10 lines of the simulation depicted in Figure 14.4.

In Theory

14.5. Let $N = 2^k$ for any integer k. Prove that if M is 1, then player 1 always wins the Josephus game.

14.6. Let $J(N)$ be the winner of an N-player Josephus game with $M = 1$. Show that

a. if N is even, then $J(N) = 2J(N/2) - 1$.
b. if N is odd and $J(\lceil N/2 \rceil) \neq 1$, then $J(N) = 2J(\lceil N/2 \rceil) - 3$.
c. if N is odd and $J(\lceil N/2 \rceil) = 1$, then $J(N) = N$.

14.7. Use the results in Exercise 14.6 to write an algorithm that returns the winner of an N-player Josephus game with $M = 1$. What is the running time of your algorithm?

14.8. Give a general formula for the winner of an N-player Josephus game with $M = 2$.

14.9. Using the algorithm for $N = 20$, determine the order of insertion into the `BinarySearchTreeWithRank`.

In Practice

14.10. Suppose that the Josephus algorithm shown in Figure 14.2 is implemented with a `vector` instead of a `list`.

a. If the change worked, what would be the running time?
b. The change has a subtle error. What is the problem and how can it be fixed?

14.11. In the Josephus algorithm shown in Figure 14.2, why can't we replace lines 27 and 28 with the single assignment `next=itr+1`?

14.12. Write a program that solves the historical version of the Josephus problem. Give both the linked list and search tree algorithms.

14.13. Implement the Josephus algorithm with a queue. Each pass of the potato is a `dequeue`, followed by an `enqueue`.

14.14. Rework the simulation so that the clock is represented as a double, the time between dial-in attempts is modeled with a negative exponential distribution, and the connect time is modeled with a negative exponential distribution.

14.15. Rework the modem bank simulation so that `Event` is an abstract base class and `DialInEvent` and `HangUpEvent` are derived classes. The `Event` class should store a pointer to a `ModemSim` object as an additional data member, which is initialized on construction. It should also provide an abstract method named `doEvent` that is implemented in the derived classes and that can be called from `runSim` to process the event.

Programming Projects

14.16. Implement the Josephus algorithm with splay trees (see Chapter 22) and sequential insertion. (The splay tree class is available online, but it will need a `findKth` method.) Compare the performance with that in the text and with an algorithm that uses a linear-time, balanced tree-building algorithm.

14.17. Rewrite the Josephus algorithm shown in Figure 14.3 to use a *median heap* (see Exercise 7.19). Use a simple implementation of the median heap; the elements are maintained in sorted order. Compare the running time of this algorithm with the time obtained by using the binary search tree.

14.18. Suppose that FIU has installed a system that queues phone calls when all modems are busy. Rewrite the simulation routine to allow for queues of various sizes. Make an allowance for an infinite queue.

14.19. Rewrite the modem bank simulation to gather statistics rather than output each event. Then compare the speed of the simulation, assuming several hundred modems and a very long simulation, with some other possible priority queues (some of which are available online)—namely, the following.

a. An asymptotically inefficient priority queue representation described in Exercise 7.14.
b. An asymptotically inefficient priority queue representation described in Exercise 7.15.
c. Splay trees (see Chapter 22).
d. Skew heaps (see Chapter 23).
e. Pairing heaps (see Chapter 23).

Chapter 15

Graphs and Paths

In this chapter we examine the *graph* and show how to solve a particular kind of problem—namely, calculation of shortest paths. The computation of shortest paths is a fundamental application in computer science because many interesting situations can be modeled by a graph. Finding the fastest routes for a mass transportation system, and routing electronic mail through a network of computers are but a few examples. We examine variations of the shortest path problems that depend on an interpretation of shortest and the graph's properties. Shortest-path problems are interesting because, although the algorithms are fairly simple, they are slow for large graphs unless careful attention is paid to the choice of data structures.

In this chapter, we show:

- formal definitions of a graph and its components,
- the data structures used to represent a graph, and
- algorithms for solving several variations of the shortest-path problem, with complete C++ implementations.

15.1 Definitions

A graph consists of a set of vertices and a set of edges that connect the vertices. That is, $G = (V, E)$, where V is the set of vertices and E is the set of edges. Each edge is a pair (v, w), where $v, w \in V$. Vertices are sometimes called *nodes*, and edges are sometimes called *arcs*. If the edge pair is ordered, the graph is called a **directed graph.** Directed graphs are sometimes called *digraphs*. In a digraph, vertex w is *adjacent* to vertex v if and only if $(v, w) \in E$. Sometimes an edge has a third component, called the **edge cost** (or **weight**) that measures the cost of traversing the edge. In this chapter, all graphs are directed.

A *graph* consists of a set of vertices and a set of edges that connect the vertices. If the edge pair is ordered, the graph is a *directed graph*.

Vertex *w* is *adjacent* to vertex *v* if there is an edge from *v* to *w*.

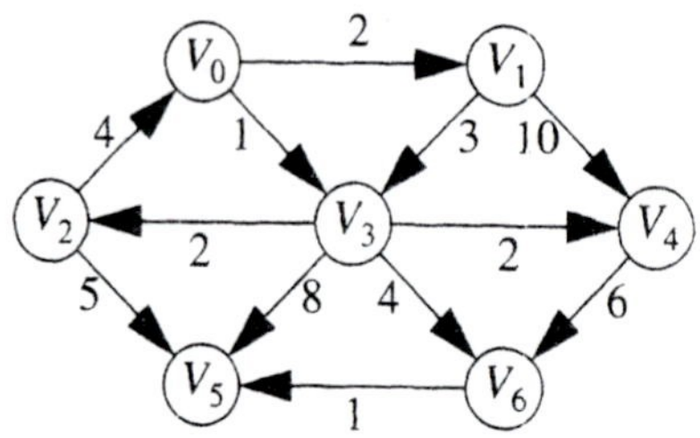

Figure 15.1 A directed graph.

The graph shown in Figure 15.1 has seven vertices,

$$V = \{V_0, V_1, V_2, V_3, V_4, V_5, V_6\},$$

and 12 edges,

$$E = \left\{ \begin{array}{l} (V_0, V_1, 2), (V_0, V_3, 1), (V_1, V_3, 3), (V_1, V_4, 10) \\ (V_3, V_4, 2), (V_3, V_6, 4), (V_3, V_5, 8), (V_3, V_2, 2) \\ (V_2, V_0, 4), (V_2, V_5, 5), (V_4, V_6, 6), (V_6, V_5, 1) \end{array} \right\}.$$

The following vertices are adjacent to V_3: V_2, V_4, V_5, and V_6. Note that V_0 and V_1 are not adjacent to V_3. For this graph, $|V| = 7$ and $|E| = 12$; here, $|S|$ represents the size of set S.

A *path* is a sequence of vertices connected by edges.

The *unweighted path length* measures the number of edges on a path.

The *weighted path length* is the sum of the edge costs on a path.

A **path** in a graph is a sequence of vertices connected by edges. In other words, $w_1, w_2, \ldots, w_N$ the sequence of vertices is such that $(w_i, w_{i+1}) \in E$ for $1 \le i < N$. The **path length** is the number of edges on the path—namely, $N - 1$—also called the **unweighted path length.** The **weighted path length** is the sum of the costs of the edges on the path. For example, V_0, V_3, V_5 is a path from vertex V_0 to V_5. The path length is two edges—the shortest path between V_0 and V_5, and the weighted path length is 9. However, if cost is important, the weighted shortest path between these vertices has cost 6 and is V_0, V_3, V_6, V_5. A path may exist from a vertex to itself. If this path contains no edges, the path length is 0, which is a convenient way to define an otherwise special case. A **simple path** is a path in which all vertices are distinct, except that the first and last vertices can be the same.

A *cycle* in a directed graph is a path that begins and ends at the same vertex and contains at least one edge.

A **cycle** in a directed graph is a path that begins and ends at the same vertex and contains at least one edge. That is, it has a length of at least 1 such that $w_1 = w_N$; this cycle is simple if the path is simple. A **directed acyclic graph (DAG)** is a type of directed graph having no cycles.

An example of a real-life situation that can be modeled by a graph is the airport system. Each airport is a vertex. If there is a nonstop flight between two airports, two vertices are connected by an edge. The edge could have a weight, representing time, distance, or the cost of the flight. In an undirected graph, an edge (v, w) would imply an edge (w, v). However, the costs of the edges might be different because flying in different directions might take longer (depending on prevailing winds) or cost more (depending on local taxes). Thus we use a directed graph with both edges listed, possibly with different weights. Naturally, we want to determine quickly the best flight between any two airports; *best* could mean the path with the fewest edges or one, or all, of the weight measures (distance, cost, and so on).

A *directed acyclic graph* has no cycles. Such graphs are an important class of graphs.

A second example of a real-life situation that can be modeled by a graph is the routing of electronic mail through computer networks. Vertices represent computers, the edges represent links between pairs of computers, and the edge costs represent communication costs (phone bill per megabyte), delay costs (seconds per megabyte), or combinations of these and other factors.

For most graphs, there is likely at most one edge from any vertex v to any other vertex w (allowing one edge in each direction between v and w). Consequently, $|E| \le |V|^2$. When most edges are present, we have $|E| = \Theta(|V|^2)$. Such a graph is considered to be a **dense graph**—that is, it has a large number of edges, generally quadratic.

A graph is *dense* if the number of edges is large (generally quadratic). Typical graphs are not dense. Instead, they are *sparse*.

In most applications, however, a **sparse graph** is the norm. For instance, in the airport model, we do not expect direct flights between every pair of airports. Instead, a few airports are very well connected and most others have relatively few flights. In a complex mass transportation system involving buses and trains, for any one station we have only a few other stations that are directly reachable and thus represented by an edge. Moreover, in a computer network most computers are attached to a few other local computers. So, in most cases, the graph is relatively sparse, where $|E| = \Theta(|V|)$ or perhaps slightly more (there is no standard definition of sparse). The algorithms that we develop, then, must be efficient for sparse graphs.

15.1.1 Representation

The first thing to consider is how to represent a graph internally. Assume that the vertices are sequentially numbered starting from 0, as the graph shown in Figure 15.1 suggests. One simple way to represent a graph is to use a two-dimensional array called an adjacency matrix. For each edge (v, w), we set `a[v][w]` equal to the edge cost; nonexistent edges can be initialized with a logical `INFINITY`. The initialization of the graph seems to require that the entire adjacency matrix be initialized to `INFINITY`. Then, as an edge is encountered, an appropriate entry is set. In this scenario, the initialization

An *adjacency matrix* represents a graph and uses quadratic space.

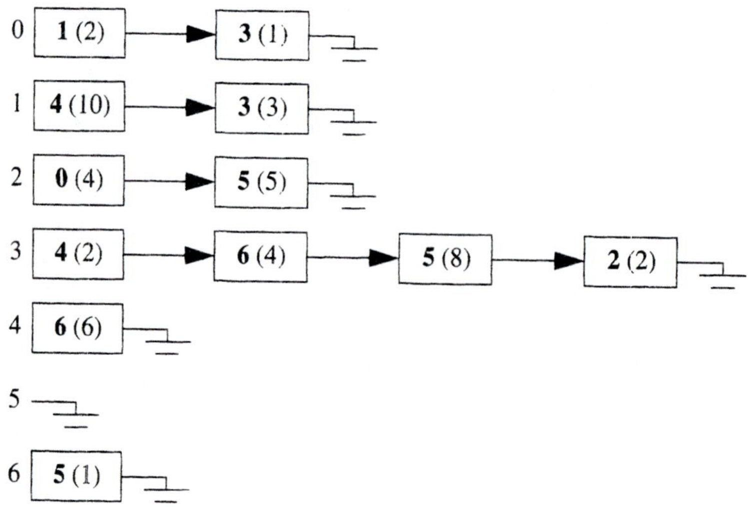

Figure 15.2 Adjacency list representation of the graph shown in Figure 15.1; the nodes in list *i* represent vertices adjacent to *i* and the cost of the connecting edge.

takes $O(|V|^2)$ time. Although the quadratic initialization cost can be avoided (see Exercise 15.6), the space cost is still $O(|V|^2)$, which is fine for dense graphs but completely unacceptable for sparse graphs.

An *adjacency list* represents a graph, using linear space.

For sparse graphs, a better solution is an **adjacency list,** which represents a graph by using linear space. For each vertex, we keep a list of all adjacent vertices. An adjacency list representation of the graph in Figure 15.1 using a linked list is shown in Figure 15.2. Because each edge appears in a list node, the number of list nodes equals the number of edges. Consequently, $O(|E|)$ space is used to store the list nodes. We have $|V|$ lists, so $O(|V|)$ additional space is also required. If we assume that every vertex is in some edge, the number of edges is at least $\lceil |V|/2 \rceil$. Hence we may disregard any $O(|V|)$ terms when an $O(|E|)$ term is present. Consequently, we say that the space requirement is $O(|E|)$, or linear in the size of the graph.

Adjacency lists can be constructed in linear time from a list of edges.

The adjacency list can be constructed in linear time from a list of edges. We begin by making all the lists empty. When we encounter an edge $(v, w, c_{v,w})$, we add an entry consisting of w and the cost $c_{v,w}$ to v's adjacency list. The insertion can be anywhere; inserting it at the front can be done in constant time. Each edge can be inserted in constant time, so the entire adjacency list structure can be constructed in linear time. Note that when inserting an edge, we do not check whether it is already present. That cannot be done in constant time (using a simple linked list), and doing the check would destroy the linear-time bound for construction. In most cases, ignoring this check is unimportant. If there are two or more edges of different cost connecting a pair of vertices, any shortest-path algorithm will choose the lower cost edge without resorting to any special processing. Note also that `vectors` can be used instead of linked lists, with the constant-time `push_back` operation replacing insertions at the front.

A map can be used to map vertex names to internal numbers.

In most real-life applications the vertices have names, which are unknown at compile time, instead of numbers. Consequently, we must provide a way to transform names to numbers. The easiest way to do so is to provide a *map* by which we map a vertex name to an internal number ranging from 0 to $|V| - 1$ (the number of vertices is determined as the program runs). The internal numbers are assigned as the graph is read. The first number assigned is 0. As each edge is input, we check whether each of the two vertices has been assigned a number, by looking in the map. If it has been assigned an internal number, we use it. Otherwise, we assign to the vertex the next available number and insert the vertex name and number in the map. With this transformation, all the graph algorithms use only the internal numbers. Eventually, we have to output the real vertex names, not the internal numbers, so for each internal number we must also record the corresponding vertex name. One way to do so is to keep a string for each vertex. We use this technique to implement a `Graph` class. The class and the shortest path algorithms require several data structures—namely, list, a queue, a map, and a priority queue. The `#include` directives for system headers are shown in Figure 15.3. The queue (implemented with a linked list) and priority queue are used in various shortest-path calculations. The adjacency list is represented with `vectors`. A `map` is also used to represent the graph.

When we write an actual C++ implementation, we do not need internal vertex numbers. Instead, each vertex is stored in a `Vertex` object, and instead of using a number, we can use the address of the `Vertex` object as its (uniquely identifying) number. As a result, the code makes frequent use

```
#include <limits.h>
#include <fstream>
#include <sstream>
#include <map>
#include <vector>
#include <string>
#include <queue>
#include <functional>
#include <list>
```

Figure 15.3 The `#include` directives for the `Graph` class.

of `Vertex*` variables. However, when describing the algorithms, assuming that vertices are numbered is often convenient, and we occasionally do so.

Before we show the `Graph` class interface, let us examine Figures 15.4 and 15.5, which show how our graph is to be represented. Figure 15.4 shows the representation in which we use internal numbers. Figure 15.5 replaces the internal numbers with `Vertex*` variables, as we do in our code. Although this simplifies the code, it greatly complicates the picture. Because the two figures represent identical inputs, Figure 15.4 can be used to follow the complications in Figure 15.5.

As indicated in the part labeled *Input,* we can expect the user to provide a list of edges, one per line. At the start of the algorithm, we do not know the names of any of the vertices, how many vertices there are, or how many edges there are. We use two basic data structures to represent the graph. As we mentioned in the preceding paragraph, for each vertex we maintain a `Vertex` object that stores some information. We describe the details of `Vertex` (in particular, how different `Vertex` objects interact with each other) last.

As mentioned earlier, the first major data structure is a map that allows us to find, for any vertex name, a pointer to the `Vertex` object that represents it. This map is shown in Figure 15.5 as `vertexMap` (Figure 15.4 maps the name to an `int` in the component labeled *Dictionary*).

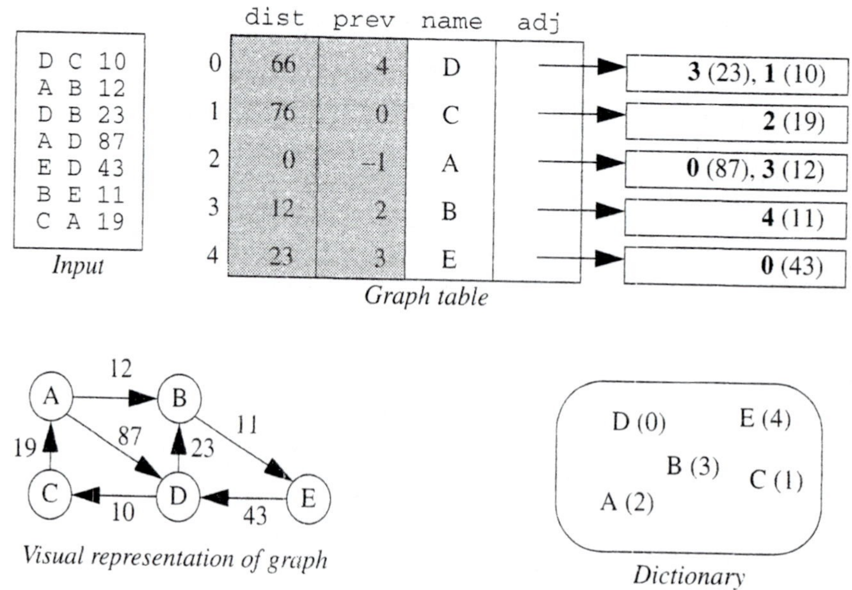

Figure 15.4 An abstract scenario of the data structures used in a shortest-path calculation, with an input graph taken from a file. The shortest weighted path from A to C is A to B to E to D to C (cost is 76).

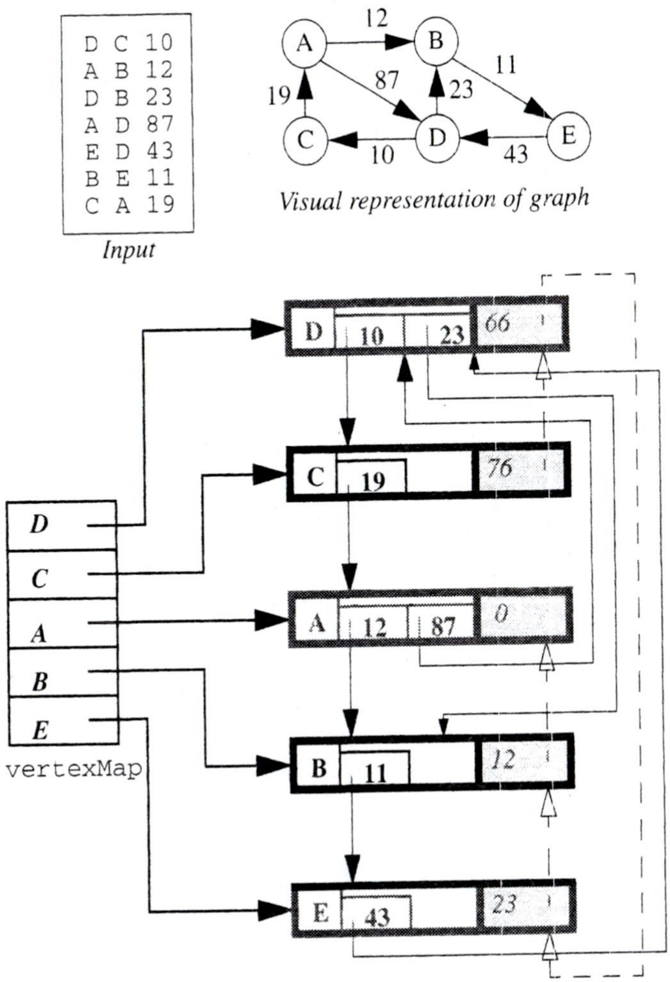

Legend: Dark-bordered boxes are `Vertex` objects. The unshaded portion in each box contains the name and adjacency list and does not change when shortest-path computation is performed. Each adjacency list entry contains an `Edge` that stores a pointer to another `Vertex` object and the edge cost. Shaded portion is `dist` and `prev`, filled in after shortest path computation runs.

Dark pointers emanate from `vertexMap`. Light pointers are adjacency list entries. Dashed-pointers are the `prev` data member that results from a shortest path computation.

Figure 15.5 Data structures used in a shortest-path calculation, with an input graph taken from a file; the shortest weighted path from `A` to `C` is: `A` to `B` to `E` to `D` to `C` (cost is 76).

The second major data structure is the `Vertex` object that stores information about all the vertices. Of particular interest is how it interacts with other `Vertex` objects. Figures 15.4 and 15.5 show that a `Vertex` object maintains four pieces of information for each vertex.

- `name`: The name corresponding to this vertex is established when the vertex is placed in map and never changes. None of the shortest-path algorithms examine this member. It is used only to print a final path.
- `adj`: This list of adjacent vertices is established when the graph is read. None of the shortest-path algorithms change the list. In the abstract, Figure 15.4 shows that it is a list of `Edge` objects that each contain an internal vertex number and edge cost. In reality, Figure 15.5 shows that each `Edge` object contains a `Vertex*` and edge cost and that the list is actually stored by using a `vector`.
- `dist`: The length of the shortest path (either weighted or unweighted, depending on the algorithm) from the starting vertex to this vertex is computed by the shortest-path algorithm.
- `prev`: The previous vertex on the shortest path to this vertex, which in the abstract (Figure 15.4) is an `int` but in reality (the code and Figure 15.5) is a `Vertex*`.

To be more specific, in Figures 15.4 and 15.5 the unshaded items are not altered by any of the shortest-path calculations. They represent the input graph and do not change unless the graph itself changes (perhaps by addition or deletion of edges at some later point). The shaded items are computed by the shortest-path algorithms. Prior to the calculation we can assume that they are uninitialized.[1]

The shortest-path algorithms are *single source algorithms* that compute the shortest paths from some starting point to all vertices.

The shortest-path algorithms are all **single-source algorithms,** which begin at some starting point and compute the shortest paths from it to all vertices. In this example the starting point is `A`, and by consulting the map we can find its `Vertex` object. Note that the shortest-path algorithm declares that the shortest path to `A` is `0`.

The `prev` member can be used to extract the actual path.

The `prev` data member allows us to print out the shortest path, not just its length. For instance, by consulting the `Vertex` object for `C`, we see that the shortest path from the starting vertex to `C` has a total cost of 76. Obviously, the last vertex on this path is `C`. The vertex before `C` on this path is `D`, before `D` is `E`, before `E` is `B`, and before `B` is `A`—the starting vertex. Thus, by tracing back through the `prev` data member, we can construct the shortest

1. The computed information (shaded) could be separated into a separate class, with `Vertex` maintaining a pointer to it, making the code more reusable but more complex.

path. Although this trace gives the path in reverse order, unreversing it is a simple matter. In the remainder of this section we describe how the unshaded parts of all the `Vertex` objects are constructed and give the function that prints out a shortest path, assuming that the `dist` and `prev` data members have been computed. We discuss individually the algorithms used to fill in the shortest path.

Figure 15.6 shows the `Edge` class that represents the basic item placed in the adjacency list. The `Edge` consists of a pointer to a `Vertex` and the edge cost. Note that we use an incomplete class declaration because the `Vertex` and `Edge` classes refer to each other. The `Vertex` class is shown in Figure 15.7. An additional member named `scratch` is provided and has different uses in the various algorithms. Everything else follows from our

The item in an adjacency list is a pointer to the `Vertex` object of the adjacent vertex and the edge cost.

```
struct Vertex;

// Basic item stored in adjacency list.
struct Edge
{
                            // First vertex in edge is implicit
    Vertex  *dest;          // Second vertex in edge
    double   cost;          // Edge cost

    Edge( Vertex *d = 0, double c = 0.0 )
      : dest( d ), cost( c ) { }
};
```

Figure 15.6 The basic item stored in an adjacency list.

```
// Basic info for each vertex.
struct Vertex
{
    string          name;     // Vertex name
    vector<Edge>    adj;      // Adjacent vertices (and costs)
    double          dist;     // Cost
    Vertex         *prev;     // Previous vertex on shortest path
    int             scratch;  // Extra variable used in algorithm

    Vertex( const string & nm ) : name( nm )
      { reset( ); }

    void reset( )
      { dist = INFINITY; prev = NULL; scratch = 0; }
};
```

Figure 15.7 The `Vertex` class stores information for each vertex.

preceding description. The `reset` function is used to initialize the (shaded) data members that are computed by the shortest-path algorithms; it is called when a shortest-path computation is restarted.

We are now ready to examine the `Graph` class interface, which is shown in Figure 15.8. `vertexMap` stores the map. The rest of the class provides member functions that perform initialization, add vertices and edges, print the shortest path, and perform various shortest-path calculations. We discuss each routine when we examine its implementation.

First, we consider the constructor. The default creates an empty map; that works, so we accept it. Figure 15.9 shows the destructor that destroys all the dynamically allocated `Vertex` objects. It does so at lines 4 to 6. We know from Section 2.2.4 that, if a destructor is written, the defaults for the copy constructor and `operator=` generally will not work, which is the case here. The default copy would have two maps sharing pointers to `Vertex` objects, with both `Graph` objects claiming responsibility for their destruction. To avoid such problems, we simply disable copying.

Edges are added by insertions in the appropriate adjacency list.

We can now look at the main methods. The `getVertex` method is shown in Figure 15.10. We consult the map to get the `Vertex` entry. If the `Vertex` does not exist, we create a new `Vertex` and update the map. The `addEdge` function, shown in Figure 15.11 is short. We get the corresponding `Vertex` entries and then update an adjacency list.

The `clearAll` routine clears out the data members so that the shortest path algorithms can begin.

The `printPath` routine prints the shortest path after the algorithm has run.

The members that are eventually computed by the shortest-path algorithm are initialized by the routine `clearAll`, shown in Figure 15.12. The next routine prints a shortest path after the computation has been performed. As we mentioned earlier, we can use the `prev` member to trace back the path, but doing so gives the path in reverse order. This order is not a problem if we use recursion: The vertices on the path to `dest` are the same as those on the path to `dest`'s previous vertex (on the path), followed by `dest`. This strategy translates directly into the short recursive routine shown in Figure 15.13, assuming of course that a path actually exists. The `printPath` routine, shown in Figure 15.14, performs this check first and then prints a message if the path does not exist. Otherwise, it calls the recursive routine and outputs the cost of the path.

The `Graph` class is easy to use.

We provide a simple test program that reads a graph from an input file, prompts for a start vertex and a destination vertex and then runs one of the shortest-path algorithms. Figure 15.15 illustrates that to construct the `Graph` object, we repeatedly read one line of input, assign the line to an `istringstream` object, parse that line, and call `addEdge`. Using an `istringstream` allows us to verify that every line has at least the three pieces corresponding to an edge. We could do more work, adding code to ensure that there are exactly three pieces of data per line, but we prefer to avoid the additional complexity involved in doing so.

```
// Graph class interface: evaluate shortest paths.
//
// CONSTRUCTION: with no parameters.
//
// ******************PUBLIC OPERATIONS*********************
// void addEdge( string v, string w, double cvw )
//                              --> Add additional edge
// void printPath( string w )   --> Print path after alg is run
// void unweighted( string s )  --> Single-source unweighted
// void dijkstra( string s )    --> Single-source weighted
// void negative( string s )    --> Single-source negative
// void acyclic( string s )     --> Single-source acyclic
// ******************ERRORS*********************************
// Some error checking is performed to make sure graph is ok,
// and to make sure graph satisfies properties needed by each
// algorithm. GraphException is thrown if error is detected.

class Graph
{
  public:
    Graph( ) { }
    ~Graph( );

    void addEdge( const string & sourceName,
                  const string & destName, double cost );
    void printPath( const string & destName ) const;
    void unweighted( const string & startName );
    void dijkstra( const string & startName );
    void negative( const string & startName );
    void acyclic( const string & startName );

  private:
    Vertex * getVertex( const string & vertexName );
    void printPath( const Vertex & dest ) const;
    void clearAll( );

    typedef map<string,Vertex *,less<string> > vmap;

      // Copy semantics are disabled; these make no sense.
    Graph( const Graph & rhs ) { }
    const Graph & operator= ( const Graph & rhs )
      { return *this; }

    vmap vertexMap;
};
```

Figure 15.8 The Graph class interface.

```
// Destructor: clean up the Vertex objects.
Graph::~Graph( )
{
    for( vmap::iterator itr = vertexMap.begin( );
                        itr != vertexMap.end( ); ++itr )
        delete (*itr).second;
}
```

Figure 15.9 The `Graph` class destructor.

```
// If vertexName is not present, add it to vertexMap.
// In either case, return (a pointer to) the Vertex.
Vertex * Graph::getVertex( const string & vertexName )
{
    vmap::iterator itr = vertexMap.find( vertexName );

    if( itr == vertexMap.end( ) )
    {
        Vertex *newv = new Vertex( vertexName );
        vertexMap[ vertexName ] = newv;
        return newv;
    }
    return (*itr).second;
}
```

Figure 15.10 The `getVertex` routine returns a pointer to the `Vertex` object that represents `vertexName`, creating the object if it needs to do so.

```
// Add a new edge to the graph.
void Graph::addEdge( const string & sourceName,
                     const string & destName, double cost )
{
    Vertex * v = getVertex( sourceName );
    Vertex * w = getVertex( destName );
    v->adj.push_back( Edge( w, cost ) );
}
```

Figure 15.11 Add an edge to the graph.

```
// Initialize the vertex output info prior to running
// any shortest path algorithm.
void Graph::clearAll( )
{
    for( vmap::iterator itr = vertexMap.begin( );
                        itr != vertexMap.end( ); ++itr )
        (*itr).second->reset( );
}
```

Figure 15.12 Private routine for initializing the output members for use by the shortest-path algorithms.

```
// Recursive routine to print shortest path to dest
// after running shortest path algorithm. The path
// is known to exist.
void Graph::printPath( const Vertex & dest ) const
{
    if( dest.prev != NULL )
    {
        printPath( *dest.prev );
        cout << " to ";
    }
    cout << dest.name;
}
```

Figure 15.13 A recursive routine for printing the shortest path.

```
// Driver routine to handle unreachables and print total cost.
// It calls recursive routine to print shortest path to
// destNode after a shortest path algorithm has run.
void Graph::printPath( const string & destName ) const
{
    vmap::const_iterator itr = vertexMap.find( destName );
    if( itr == vertexMap.end( ) )
        throw GraphException( "Destination vertex not found" );

    const Vertex & w = *(*itr).second;
    if( w.dist == INFINITY )
        cout << destName << " is unreachable";
    else
    {
        cout << "(Cost is: " << w.dist << ") ";
        printPath( w );
    }
    cout << endl;
}
```

Figure 15.14 A routine for printing the shortest path by consulting the graph table (see Figure 15.5).

```
// A simple main that reads the file given by argv[1]
// and then calls processRequest to compute shortest paths.
// Skimpy error checking in order to concentrate on the basics.
int main( int argc, char *argv[ ] )
{
    if( argc != 2 )
    {
        cerr << "Usage: " << argv[ 0 ] << " graphfile" << endl;
        return 1;
    }

    ifstream inFile( argv[ 1 ] );
    if( !inFile )
    {
        cerr << "Cannot open " << argv[ 1 ] << endl;
        return 1;
    }

    cout << "Reading file... " << endl;
    string oneLine;

      // Read the edges; add them to g
    Graph g;
    while( !getline( inFile, oneLine ).eof( ) )
    {
        string source, dest;
        double cost;
        istringstream st( oneLine );

        st >> source; st >> dest; st >> cost;
        if( st.fail( ) )
            cerr << "Bad line: " << oneLine << endl;
        else
            g.addEdge( source, dest, cost );
    }
    cout << "File read" << endl << endl;

    while( processRequest( cin, g ) )
        ;

    return 0;
}
```

Figure 15.15 A simple main.

```
// Process a request; return false if end of file.
bool processRequest( istream & in, Graph & g )
{
    string startName, destName;

    cout << "Enter start node: ";
    if( !( in >> startName ) )
        return false;
    cout << "Enter destination node: ";
    if( !( in >> destName ) )
        return false;

    try
    {
        g.negative( startName );
        g.printPath( destName );
    }
    catch( const GraphException & e )
    {
        cerr << e.toString( ) << endl;
    }
    return true;
}
```

Figure 15.16 For testing purposes, `processRequest` calls one of the shortest-path algorithms.

Once the graph has been read, we repeatedly call `processRequest`, shown in Figure 15.16. This version (which is simplified slightly from the online code) prompts for a starting and ending vertex and then calls one of the shortest-path algorithms. This algorithm throws a `GraphException` if, for instance, it is asked for a path between vertices that are not in the graph. Thus `processRequest` catches any `GraphException` that might be generated and prints an appropriate error message.

15.2 Unweighted Shortest-Path Problem

Recall that the unweighted path length measures the number of edges. In this section we consider the problem of finding the shortest unweighted path length between specified vertices.

The *unweighted path length* measures the number of edges on a path.

UNWEIGHTED SINGLE-SOURCE, SHORTEST-PATH PROBLEM

FIND THE SHORTEST PATH (MEASURED BY NUMBER OF EDGES) FROM A DESIGNATED VERTEX S TO EVERY VERTEX.

The unweighted shortest-path problem is a special case of the weighted shortest-path problem (in which all weights are 1). Hence it should have a more efficient solution than the weighted shortest-path problem. That turns out to be true, although the algorithms for all the path problems are similar.

15.2.1 Theory

All variations of the shortest-path problem have similar solutions.

To solve the unweighted shortest-path problem, we use the graph previously shown in Figure 15.1, with V_2 as the starting vertex S. For now, we are concerned with finding the length of all shortest paths. Later, we maintain the corresponding paths.

We can see immediately that the shortest path from S to V_2 is a path of length 0. This information yields the graph shown in Figure 15.17. Now we can start looking for all vertices that are distance 1 from S. We can find them by looking at the vertices adjacent to S. If we do so, we see that V_0 and V_5 are one edge away from S, as shown in Figure 15.18.

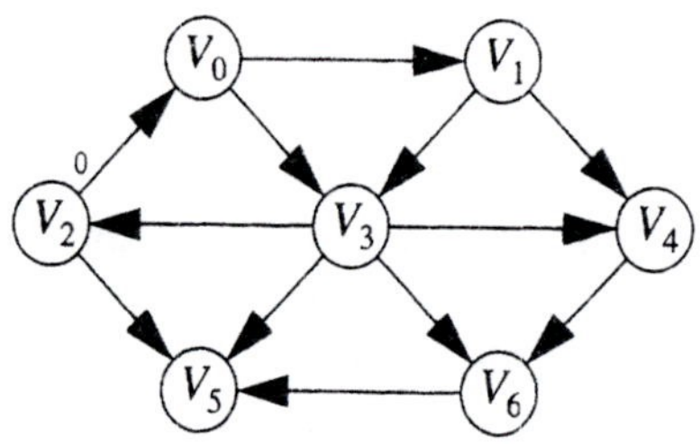

Figure 15.17 The graph, after the starting vertex has been marked as reachable in zero edges.

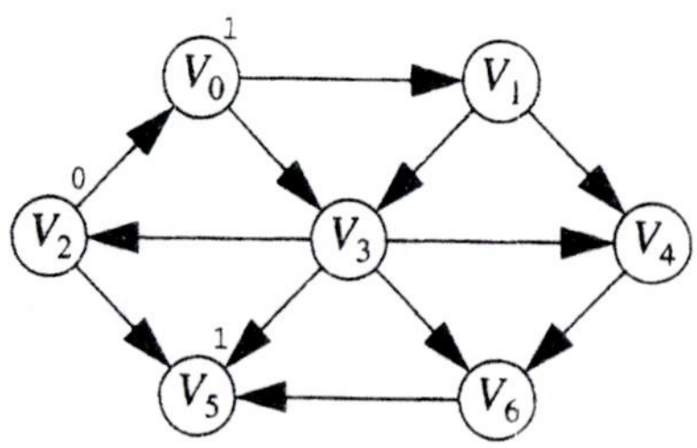

Figure 15.18 The graph, after all the vertices whose path length from the starting vertex is 1 have been found.

Next, we find each vertex whose shortest path from S is exactly 2. We do so by finding all the vertices adjacent to V_0 or V_5 (the vertices at distance 1) whose shortest paths are not already known. This search tells us that the shortest path to V_1 and V_3 is 2. Figure 15.19 shows our progress so far.

Finally, by examining the vertices adjacent to the recently evaluated V_1 and V_3, we find that V_4 and V_6 have a shortest path of 3 edges. All vertices have now been calculated. Figure 15.20 shows the final result of the algorithm.

Breadth-first search processes vertices in layers: Those closest to the start are evaluated first.

This strategy for searching a graph is called **breadth-first search,** which operates by processing vertices in layers: Those closest to the start are evaluated first, and those most distant are evaluated last.

Figure 15.21 illustrates a fundamental principle: If a path to vertex v has cost D_v and w is adjacent to v, then there exists a path to w of cost $D_w = D_v + 1$. All the shortest-path algorithms work by starting with $D_w = \infty$ and reducing its value when an appropriate v is scanned. To do this task efficiently, we must scan vertices v systematically. When a given v is scanned, we update the vertices w adjacent to v by scanning through v's adjacency list.

The roving eyeball moves from vertex to vertex and updates distances for adjacent vertices.

From the preceding discussion, we conclude that an algorithm for solving the unweighted shortest-path problem is as follows. Let D_i be the length of the shortest path from S to i. We know that $D_S = 0$ and initially that $D_i = \infty$ for all $i \neq S$. We maintain a *roving eyeball* that hops from vertex

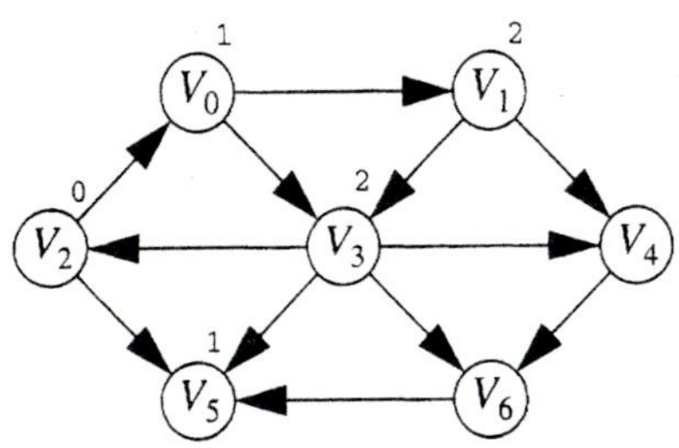

Figure 15.19 The graph, after all the vertices whose shortest path from the starting vertex is 2 have been found.

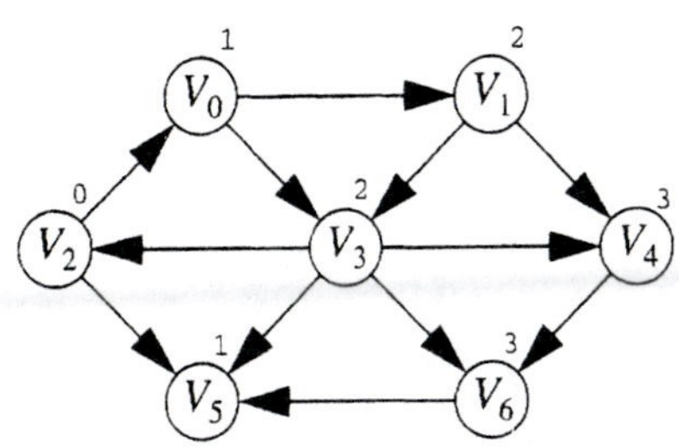

Figure 15.20 The final shortest paths.

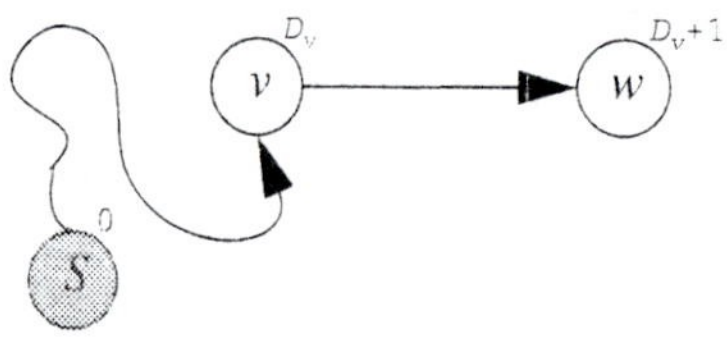

Figure 15.21 If w is adjacent to v and there is a path to v, there also is a path to w.

to vertex and is initially at S. If v is the vertex that the eyeball is currently on, then, for all w that are adjacent to v, we set $D_w = D_v + 1$ if $D_w = \infty$. This reflects the fact that we can get to w by following a path to v and extending the path by the edge (v, w)—again, illustrated in Figure 15.21. So we update vertices w as they are seen from the vantage point of the eyeball. Because the eyeball processes each vertex in order of its distance from the starting vertex and the edge adds exactly 1 to the length of the path to w, we are guaranteed that the first time D_w is lowered from ∞, it is lowered to the value of the length of the shortest path to w. These actions also tell us that the next-to-last vertex on the path to w is v, so one extra line of code allows us to store the actual path.

After we have processed all of v's adjacent vertices, we move the eyeball to another vertex u (that has not been visited by the eyeball) such that $D_u \equiv D_v$. If that is not possible, we move to a u that satisfies $D_u = D_v + 1$. If that is not possible, we are done. Figure 15.22 shows how the eyeball visits vertices and updates distances. The lightly shaded node at each stage represents the position of the eyeball. In this picture and those that follow, the stages are shown top to bottom, left-to-right.

All vertices adjacent to v are found by scanning v's adjacency list.

The remaining detail is the data structure, and there are two basic actions to take. First, we repeatedly have to find the vertex at which to place the eyeball. Second, we need to check all w's adjacent to v (the current vertex) throughout the algorithm. The second action is easily implemented by iterating through v's adjacency list. Indeed, as each edge is processed only once, the total cost of all the iterations is $O(|E|)$. The first action is more challenging: We cannot simply scan through the graph table (see Figure 15.4) looking for an appropriate vertex because each scan could take $O(|V|)$ time and we need to perform it $|V|$ times. Thus the total cost would be $O(|V|^2)$, which is unacceptable for sparse graphs. Fortunately, this technique is not needed.

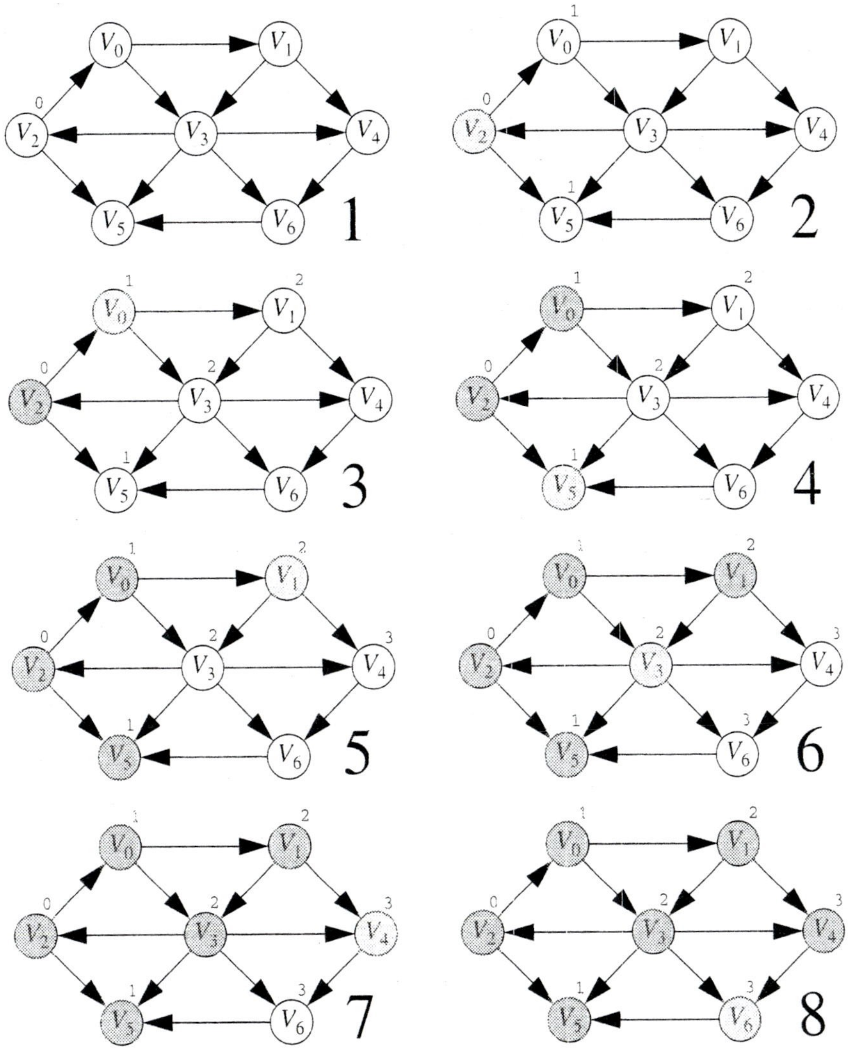

Figure 15.22 Searching the graph in the unweighted shortest-path computation. The darkest-shaded vertices have already been completely processed, the lightest-shaded vertices have not yet been used as *v*, and the medium-shaded vertex is the current vertex, *v*. The stages proceed left to right, top to bottom, as numbered.

When a vertex has its distance lowered (which can happen only once), it is placed on the queue so that the eyeball can visit it in the future. The starting vertex is placed on the queue when its distance is initialized to zero.

When a vertex w has its D_w lowered from ∞, it becomes a candidate for an eyeball visitation at some point in the future. That is, after the eyeball visits its vertices in the current distance group D_v, it visits the next distance group $D_v + 1$, which is the group containing w. Thus w just needs to wait in line for its turn. Also, as it clearly does not need to go before any other vertices that have already had their distances lowered, w needs to be placed at the end of a queue of vertices waiting for an eyeball visitation.

To select a vertex v for the eyeball, we merely choose the front vertex from the queue. We start with an empty queue and then we enqueue the starting vertex S. A vertex is enqueued and dequeued at most once per shortest-path calculation and queue operations are constant time, so the cost of choosing the vertex to select is only $O(|V|)$ *for the entire algorithm*. Thus the cost of the breadth-first search is dominated by the scans of the adjacency list and is $O(|E|)$, or linear, in the size of the graph.

```
// Single-source unweighted shortest-path algorithm.
void Graph::unweighted( const string & startName )
{

    vmap::iterator itr = vertexMap.find( startName );
    if( itr == vertexMap.end( ) )
        throw GraphException( startName + " is not a vertex" );

    clearAll( );
    Vertex *start = (*itr).second;
    list<Vertex *> q;
    q.push_back( start ); start->dist = 0;

    while( !q.empty( ) )
    {
        Vertex *v = q.front( );
        q.pop_front( );

        for( int i = 0; i < v->adj.size( ); i++ )
        {
            Edge e = v->adj[ i ];
            Vertex *w = e.dest;
            if( w->dist == INFINITY )
            {
                w->dist = v->dist + 1;
                w->prev = v;
                q.push_back( w );
            }
        }
    }
}
```

Figure 15.23 The unweighted shortest-path algorithm, using breadth-first search.

15.2.2 C++ Implementation

The unweighted shortest-path algorithm is implemented by the method `unweighted`, as shown in Figure 15.23. The code is a line-for-line translation of the algorithm described previously. The initialization at lines 9–12 makes all the distances infinity, sets D_S to 0, and then enqueues the start vertex. The queue is declared at line 11 as a `list<Vertex *>`.While the queue is not empty, there are vertices to visit. Thus at line 16 we move to the vertex v that is at the front of the queue. Line 19 iterates over the adjacency list and produces all the w's that are adjacent to v. The test $D_w = \infty$ is performed at line 23. If it returns `true`, the update $D_w = D_v + 1$ is performed at line 25 along with the update of w's `prev` data member and enqueueing of w at lines 26 and 27, respectively.

Implementation is much simpler than it sounds. It follows the algorithm description verbatim.

15.3 Positive-Weighted, Shortest-Path Problem

Recall that the weighted path length of a path is the sum of the edge costs on the path. In this section we consider the problem of finding the weighted shortest path, in a graph whose edges have nonnegative cost. We want to find the shortest weighted path from some starting vertex to all vertices. As we show shortly, the assumption that edge costs are nonnegative is important because it allows a relatively efficient algorithm. The method used to solve the positive-weighted, shortest-path problem is known as **Dijkstra's algorithm.** In the next section we examine a slower algorithm that works even if there are negative edge costs.

The *weighted path length* is the sum of the edge costs on a path.

POSITIVE-WEIGHTED, SINGLE-SOURCE, SHORTEST-PATH PROBLEM

FIND THE SHORTEST PATH (MEASURED BY TOTAL COST) FROM A DESIGNATED VERTEX S TO EVERY VERTEX. ALL EDGE COSTS ARE NONNEGATIVE.

15.3.1 Theory: Dijkstra's Algorithm

The positive-weighted, shortest-path problem is solved in much the same way as the unweighted problem. However, because of the edge costs, a few things change. The following issues must be examined:

Dijkstra's *algorithm* is used to solve the positive-weighted shortest-path problem.

1. How do we adjust D_w?
2. How do we find the vertex v for the eyeball to visit?

We use $D_v + c_{v,w}$ as the new distance and to decide whether the distance should be updated.

We begin by examining how to alter D_w. In solving the unweighted shortest-path problem, if $D_w = \infty$, we set $D_w = D_v + 1$ because we lower the value of D_w if vertex v offers a shorter path to w. The dynamics of the algorithm ensure that we need alter D_w only once. We add 1 to D_v because the length of the path to w is 1 more than the length of the path to v. If we apply this logic to the weighted case, we should set $D_w = D_v + c_{v,w}$ if this new value of D_w is better than the original value. However, we are no longer guaranteed that D_w is altered only once. Consequently, D_w should be altered if its current value is larger than $D_v + c_{v,w}$ (rather than merely testing against ∞). Put simply, the algorithm decides whether v should be used on the path to w. The original cost D_w is the cost without using v; the cost $D_v + c_{v,w}$ is the cheapest path using v (so far).

A queue is no longer appropriate for storing vertices awaiting an eyeball visit.

Figure 15.24 shows a typical situation. Earlier in the algorithm, w had its distance lowered to 8 when the eyeball visited vertex u. However, when the eyeball visits vertex v, vertex w needs to have its distance lowered to 6 because we have a new shortest path. This result never occurs in the unweighted algorithm because all edges add 1 to the path length, so $D_u \le D_v$ implies $D_u + 1 \le D_v + 1$ and thus $D_w \le D_v + 1$. Here, even though $D_u \le D_v$, we can still improve the path to w by considering v.

The distance for unvisited vertices represents a path with only visited vertices as intermediate nodes.

Figure 15.24 illustrates another important point. When w has its distance lowered, it does so only because it is adjacent to some vertex that has been visited by the eyeball. For instance, after the eyeball visits v and processing has been completed, the value of D_w is 6 and the last vertex on the path is a vertex that has been visited by the eyeball. Similarly, the vertex prior to v must also have been visited by the eyeball, and so on. Thus at any point the value of D_w represents *a path from S to w using only vertices that have been visited by the eyeball as intermediate nodes.* This crucial fact gives us Theorem 15.1.

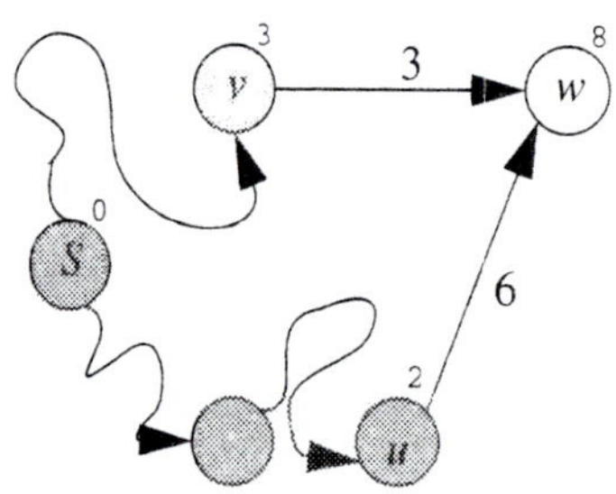

Figure 15.24 The eyeball is at v and w is adjacent, so D_w should be lowered to 6.

Theorem 15.1

If we move the eyeball to the unseen vertex with minimum D_i, the algorithm correctly produces the shortest paths if there are no negative edge costs.

Proof

Call each eyeball visit a "stage." We prove by induction that, after any stage, the values of D_i for vertices visited by the eyeball form the shortest path and that the values of D_i for the other vertices form the shortest path using only vertices visited by the eyeball as intermediates. Because the first vertex visited is the starting vertex, this statement is correct through the first stage. Assume that it is correct for the first k stages. Let v be the vertex chosen by the eyeball in stage $k + 1$. Suppose, for the purpose of showing a contradiction, that there is a path from S to v of length less than D_v.

This path must go through an intermediate vertex that has not yet been visited by the eyeball. Call the first intermediate vertex on the path not visited by the eyeball u. This situation is shown in Figure 15.25. The path to u uses only vertices visited by the eyeball as intermediates, so by induction D_u represents the optimal distance to u. Moreover, $D_u < D_v$ because u is on the supposed shorter path to v. This inequality is a contradiction because then we would have moved the eyeball to u instead of v. The proof is completed by showing that all the D_i values remain correct for nonvisited nodes, which is clear by the update rule.

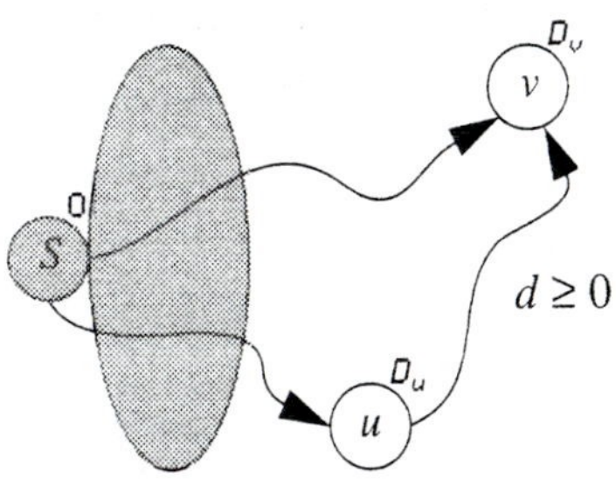

Figure 15.25 If D_v is minimal among all unseen vertices and if all edge costs are nonnegative, D_v represents the shortest path.

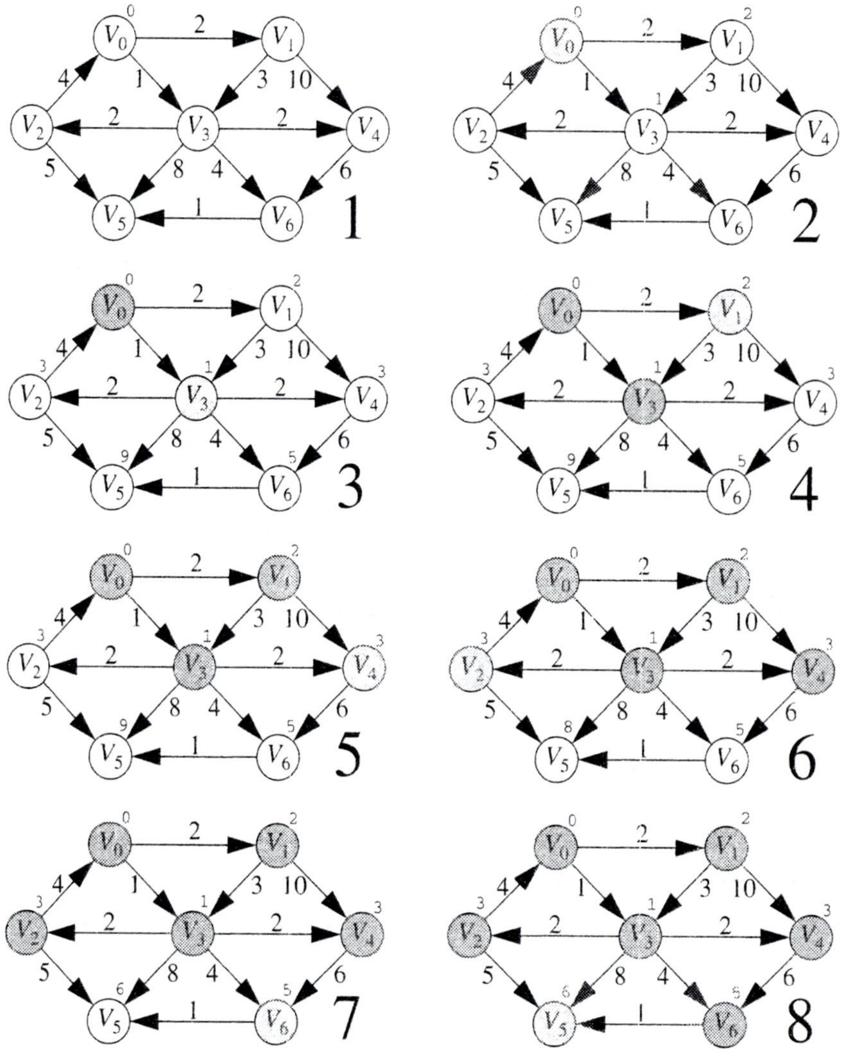

Figure 15.26 Stages of Dijkstra's algorithm. The conventions are the same as those in Figure 15.22.

Figure 15.26 shows the stages of Dijkstra's algorithm. The remaining issue is the selection of an appropriate data structure. For dense graphs, we can scan down the graph table looking for the appropriate vertex. As with the unweighted shortest-path algorithm, this scan will take $O(|V|^2)$ time, which is optimal for a dense graph. For a sparse graph, we want to do better.

Certainly, a queue does not work. The fact that we need to find the vertex v with minimum D_v suggests that a priority queue is the method of choice. There are two ways to use the priority queue. One is to store each vertex in the priority queue and use the distance (obtained by consulting the graph table) as the ordering function. When we alter any D_w, we must update the priority queue by reestablishing the ordering property. This action amounts to a `decreaseKey` operation. To take it we need to be able to find the location of w in the priority queue. Many implementations of the priority queue, including the STL priority queue, do not support `decreaseKey`. One that does is the *pairing heap;* we discuss use of the pairing heap for this application in Chapter 23.

The priority queue is an appropriate data structure. The easiest method is to add a new entry, consisting of a vertex and a distance, to the priority queue every time a vertex has its distance lowered. We can find the new vertex to move to by repeatedly removing the minimum distance vertex from the priority queue until an unvisited vertex emerges.

Rather than use a fancy priority queue, we use a method that works with the STL priority queue. Our method involves inserting an object consisting of w and D_w in the priority queue whenever we lower D_w. To select a new vertex v for visitation, we repeatedly remove the minimum item (based on distance) from the priority queue until an unvisited vertex emerges. Because the size of the priority queue could be as large as $|E|$ and there are at most $|E|$ priority queue insertions and deletions, the running time is $O(|E|\log|E|)$. Because $|E| \le |V|^2$ implies $\log|E| \le 2\log|V|$, we have the same $O(|E|\log|V|)$ algorithm that we would have if we used the first method (in which the priority queue size is at most $|V|$).

15.3.2 C++ Implementation

The object placed on the priority queue is shown in Figure 15.27. It consists of w and D_w and a comparison function defined on the basis of D_w. Figure 15.28 shows the routine `dijkstra` that calculates the shortest paths.

Again, the implementation follows the description fairly closely.

Line 4 declares the priority queue `pq`. We declare `vrec` at line 5 to store the result of each `deleteMin`. As with the unweighted shortest-path algorithm, we begin by setting all distances to infinity, setting $D_S = 0$, and placing the starting vertex in our data structure.

Each iteration of the outermost `for` loop that begins at line 16 puts the eyeball at a vertex v and processes it by examining adjacent vertices w. v is chosen by repeatedly removing entries from the priority queue (at line 22) until we encounter a vertex that has not been processed. We use the `scratch` variable to record it. Initially, `scratch` is 0. Thus, if the vertex is unprocessed, the `while` test fails at line 23. Then, when the vertex is processed, `scratch` is set to 1 (at line 26). The priority queue might be empty, if, for instance, some of the vertices are unreachable. In that case, we can return immediately. The loop at lines 28–43 is much like the loop in the unweighted algorithm. The difference is that at line 32, we must extract `cvw` from the adjacency list entry, ensure that the edge is nonnegative (otherwise,

```
// Structure stored in priority queue for Dijkstra's algorithm.
struct Path
{
    Vertex *dest;   // w
    double  cost;   // d(w)

    Path( Vertex *d = 0, double c = 0.0 )
      : dest( d ), cost( c ) { }

    bool operator> ( const Path & rhs ) const
      { return cost > rhs.cost; }
    bool operator< ( const Path & rhs ) const
      { return cost < rhs.cost; }
};
```

Figure 15.27 Basic item stored in the priority queue.

our algorithm could produce incorrect answers), add `cvw` instead of `1` at lines 37 and 39, and `insert` rather than `enqueue` at line 41.[2]

15.4 Negative-Weighted, Shortest-Path Problem

Negative edges cause Dijkstra's algorithm not to work. An alternative algorithm is needed.

Dijkstra's algorithm requires that edge costs be nonnegative. This requirement is reasonable for most graph applications, but sometimes it is too restrictive. In this section we briefly discuss the most general case: the negative-weighted, shortest-path algorithm.

NEGATIVE-WEIGHTED, SINGLE-SOURCE, SHORTEST-PATH PROBLEM

FIND THE SHORTEST PATH (MEASURED BY TOTAL COST) FROM A DESIGNATED VERTEX S TO EVERY VERTEX. EDGE COSTS MAY BE NEGATIVE.

15.4.1 Theory

The proof of Dijkstra's algorithm required the condition that edge costs, and thus paths, be nonnegative. Indeed, if the graph has negative edge costs, Dijkstra's algorithm does not work. The problem is that, once a vertex v has been processed, there may be, from some other unprocessed vertex u, a negative

2. Note that the method name is `push`, which is the advantage of using the same names for the various methods in the STL data structures. The disadvantage, however, is that reading the code may be harder because the declaration that gives the type of the container is far removed from the point of its use.

```
// Single-source weighted shortest-path algorithm.
void Graph::dijkstra( const string & startName )
{
    priority_queue<Path, vector<Path>, greater<Path> > pq;
    Path vrec;     // Stores the result of a deleteMin

    vmap::iterator itr = vertexMap.find( startName );
    if( itr == vertexMap.end( ) )
        throw GraphException( startName + " is not a vertex" );

    clearAll( );
    Vertex *start = (*itr).second;
    pq.push( Path( start, 0 ) ); start->dist = 0;

    int nodesSeen = 0;
    for( ; nodesSeen < vertexMap.size( ); nodesSeen++ )
    {
        do    // Find an unvisited vertex
        {
            if( pq.empty( ) )
                return;
            vrec = pq.top( ); pq.pop( );
        } while( vrec.dest->scratch != 0 );

        Vertex *v = vrec.dest;
        v->scratch = 1;

        for( int i = 0; i < v->adj.size( ); i++ )
        {
            Edge e = v->adj[ i ];
            Vertex *w = e.dest;
            double cvw = e.cost;

            if( cvw < 0 )
                throw GraphException( "Negative edge seen" );

            if( w->dist > v->dist + cvw )
            {
                w->dist = v->dist + cvw;
                w->prev = v;
                pq.push( Path( w, w->dist ) );
            }
        }
}
```

Figure 15.28 A positive-weighted, shortest-path algorithm: Dijkstra's algorithm.

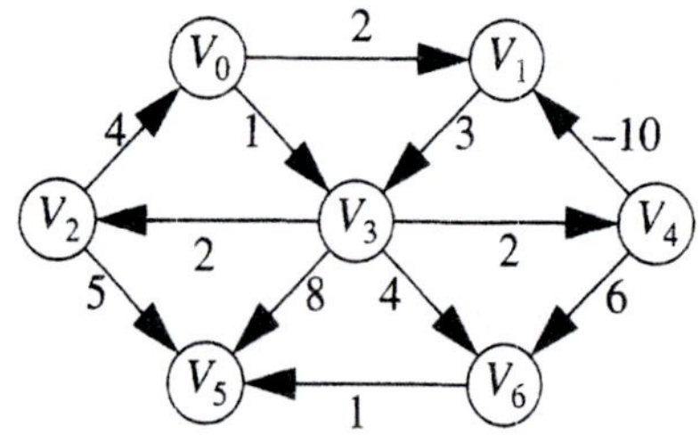

Figure 15.29 A graph with a negative cost cycle.

path back to v. In such a case, taking a path from S to u to v is better than going from S to v without using u. If the latter were to happen, we would be in trouble. Not only would the path to v be wrong, but we also would have to revisit v because the distances of vertices reachable from v may be affected. (In Exercise 15.10 you are asked to construct an explicit example; three vertices suffice.)

A *negative-cost cycle* makes most, if not all, paths undefined because we can stay in the cycle arbitrarily long and obtain an arbitrarily small weighted path length.

We have an additional problem to worry about. Consider the graph shown in Figure 15.29. The path from V_3 to V_4 has a cost of 2. However, a shorter path exists by following the loop V_3, V_4, V_1, V_3, V_4, which has a cost of –3. This path is still not the shortest because we could stay in the loop arbitrarily long. Thus the shortest path between these two points is undefined.

This problem is not restricted to nodes in the cycle. The shortest path from V_2 to V_5 is also undefined because there is a way to get into and out of the loop. This loop is called a **negative-cost cycle,** which when present in a graph makes most, if not all, the shortest paths undefined. Negative-cost edges by themselves are not necessarily bad; it is the cycles that are. Our algorithm either finds the shortest paths or reports the existence of a negative-cost cycle.

Whenever a vertex has its distance lowered, it must be placed on a queue. This may happen repeatedly for each vertex.

A combination of the weighted and unweighted algorithms will solve the problem, but at the cost of a potentially drastic increase in running time. As suggested previously, when D_w is altered, we must revisit it at some point in the future. Consequently, we use the queue as in the unweighted algorithm, but we use $D_v + c_{v,w}$ as the distance measure (as in Dijkstra's algorithm). The algorithm that is used to solve the negative-weighted, shortest-path problem is known as the **Bellman–Ford algorithm.**

The running time can be large, especially if there is a negative-cost cycle.

When the eyeball visits vertex v for the ith time, the value of D_v is the length of the shortest weighted path consisting of i or fewer edges. We leave the proof for you to do as Exercise 15.12. Consequently, if there are no negative-cost cycles, a vertex can dequeue at most $|V|$ times and the algorithm takes at most $O(|E||V|)$ time. Further, if a vertex dequeues more than $|V|$ times, we have detected a negative-cost cycle.

15.4.2 C++ Implementation

Implementation of the negative-weighted, shortest-path algorithm is given in Figure 15.30. We make one small change to the algorithm description—namely, we do not enqueue a vertex if it is already on the queue. This change involves use of the `scratch` data member. When a vertex is enqueued, we increment `scratch` (at line 30). When it is dequeued, we increment it again (at line 16). Thus `scratch` is odd if the vertex is on the queue, and `scratch/2` tells us how many times it has left the queue (which explains the test at line 16). When some w has its distance changed, but it is already on the queue (because `scratch` is odd), we do not enqueue it. However, we add 2 to it to indicate that it logically could have gone on (and off) the queue (which may speed the algorithm somewhat in the event of a negative cycle) at lines 30 and 33. The rest of the algorithm uses code that has already been introduced in both the unweighted shortest-path algorithm (Figure 15.23) and Dijkstra's algorithm (Figure 15.28).

The tricky part of the implementation is the manipulation of the `scratch` variable. We attempt to avoid having any vertex appear on the queue twice at any instant.

15.5 Path Problems in Acyclic Graphs

Recall that a directed acyclic graph has no cycles. This important class of graphs simplifies the solution to the shortest-path problem. For instance, we do not have to worry about negative-cost cycles because there are no cycles. Thus we consider the following problem.

WEIGHTED SINGLE-SOURCE, SHORTEST-PATH PROBLEM FOR ACYCLIC GRAPHS

FIND THE SHORTEST PATH (MEASURED BY TOTAL COST) FROM A DESIGNATED VERTEX S TO EVERY VERTEX IN AN ACYCLIC GRAPH. EDGE COSTS ARE UNRESTRICTED.

15.5.1 Topological Sorting

Before considering the shortest-path problem, let us examine a related problem: a topological sort. A **topological sort** orders vertices in a directed acyclic graph such that if there is a path from u to v, then v appears after u in the ordering. For instance, a graph is typically used to represent the prerequisite requirement for courses at universities. An edge (v, w) indicates that course v must be completed before course w may be attempted. A topological order of the courses is any sequence that does not violate the prerequisite requirements.

A *topological sort* orders vertices in a directed acyclic graph such that if there is a path from u to v, then v appears *after* u in the ordering. A graph that has a cycle cannot have a topological order.

```
// Single-source negative-weighted shortest-path algorithm.
void Graph::negative( const string & startName )
{
    vmap::iterator itr = vertexMap.find( startName );
    if( itr == vertexMap.end( ) )
        throw GraphException( startName + " is not a vertex" );

    clearAll( );
    Vertex *start = (*itr).second;
    list<Vertex *> q;
    q.push_back( start ); start->dist = 0; start->scratch++;

    while( !q.empty( ) )
    {
        Vertex *v = q.front( ); q.pop_front( );
        if( v->scratch++ > 2 * vertexMap.size( ) )
            throw GraphException( "Negative cycle detected" );

        for( int i = 0; i < v->adj.size( ); i++ )
        {
            Edge e = v->adj[ i ];
            Vertex *w = e.dest;
            double cvw = e.cost;

            if( w->dist > v->dist + cvw )
            {
                w->dist = v->dist + cvw;
                w->prev = v;
                  // Enqueue only if not already on the queue
                if( w->scratch++ % 2 == 0 )
                    q.push_back( w );
                else
                    w->scratch++;    // In effect, adds 2
            }
        }
    }
}
```

Figure 15.30 A negative-weighted, shortest-path algorithm: Negative edges are allowed.

Clearly, a topological sort is not possible if a graph has a cycle because, for two vertices *v* and *w* on the cycle, there is a path from *v* to *w* and *w* to *v*. Thus any ordering of *v* and *w* would contradict one of the two paths. A graph may have several topological orders, and in most cases, any legal ordering will do.

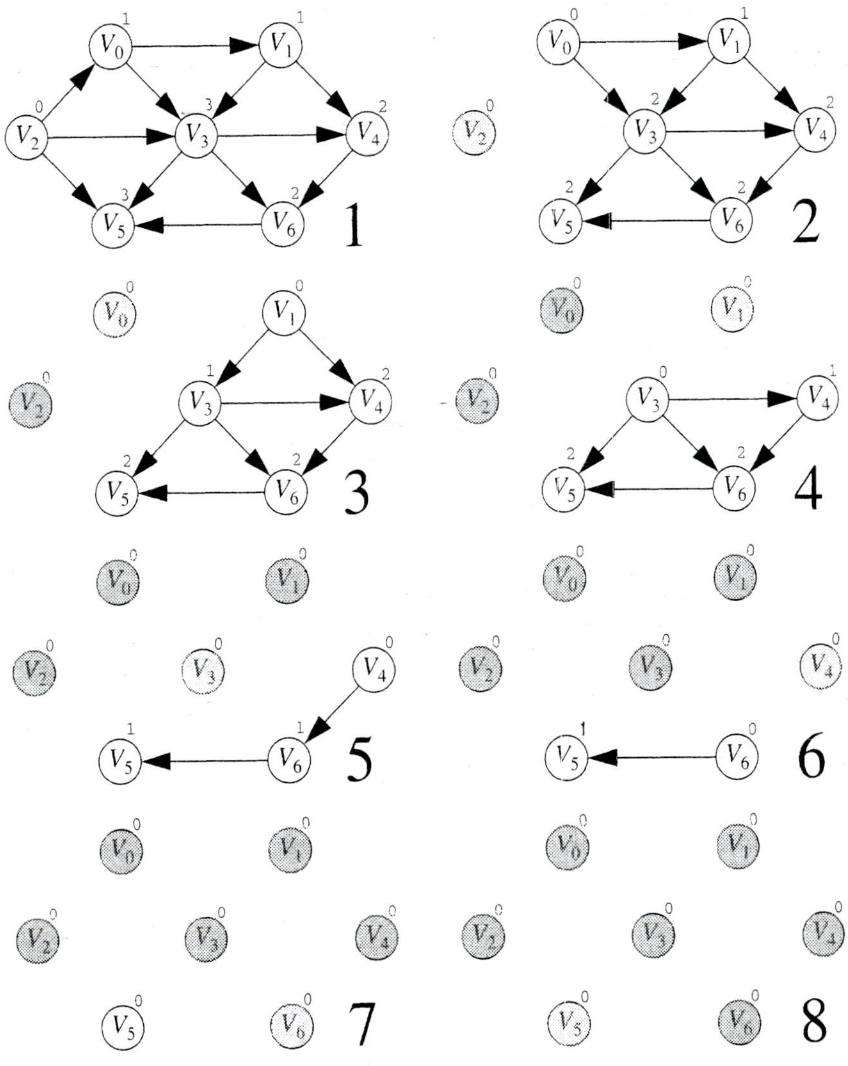

Figure 15.31 A topological sort. The conventions are the same as those in Figure 15.22.

In a simple algorithm for performing a topological sort we first find any vertex v that has no incoming edges. Then we print the vertex and logically remove it, along with its edges, from the graph. Finally, we apply the same strategy to the rest of the graph. More formally, we say that the **indegree** of a vertex v is the number of incoming edges (u, v).

The *indegree* of a vertex is the number of incoming edges. A topological sort can be performed in linear time by repeatedly and logically removing vertices that have no incoming edges.

We compute the indegrees of all vertices in the graph. In practice, *logically remove* means that we lower the count of incoming edges for each vertex adjacent to v. Figure 15.31 shows the algorithm applied to an acyclic graph. The indegree is computed for each vertex. Vertex V_2 has indegree 0, so it is first in the topological order. If there were several vertices of indegree 0, we could choose any one of them. When V_2 and its edges are removed from the graph, the indegrees of V_0, V_3, and V_5 are all decremented by 1. Now V_0 has indegree 0, so it is next in the topological order, and V_1 and V_3 have their indegrees lowered. The algorithm continues, and the remaining vertices are examined in the order V_1, V_3, V_4, V_6, and V_5. To reiterate, we do not physically delete edges from the graph; removing edges just makes it easier to see how the indegree count is lowered.

The algorithm produces the correct answer and detects cycles if the graph is not acyclic.

Two important issues to consider are *correctness* and *efficiency*. Clearly, any ordering produced by the algorithm is a topological order. The question is whether every acyclic graph has a topological order, and if so, whether our algorithm is guaranteed to find one. The answer is yes to both questions.

If at any point there are unseen vertices but none of them have an indegree of 0, we are guaranteed that a cycle exists. To illustrate we can pick any vertex A_0. Because A_0 has an incoming edge, let A_1 be the vertex connected to it. And as A_1 has an incoming edge, let A_2 be the vertex connected to it. We repeat this process N times, where N is the number of unprocessed vertices left in the graph. Among $A_0, A_1, \ldots, A_N$, there must be two identical vertices (because there are N vertices but $N + 1$ A_i's). Tracing backward between those identical A_i and A_j exhibits a cycle.

The running time is linear if a queue is used.

We can implement the algorithm in linear time by placing all unprocessed indegree 0 vertices on a queue. Initially, all vertices of indegree 0 are placed on the queue. To find the next vertex in the topological order, we merely get and remove the front item from the queue. When a vertex has its indegree lowered to 0, it is placed on the queue. If the queue empties before all the vertices have been topologically sorted, the graph has a cycle. The running time is clearly linear, by the same reasoning used in the unweighted shortest-path algorithm.

15.5.2 Theory of the Acyclic Shortest-Path Algorithm

In an acyclic graph, the eyeball merely visits vertices in topological order.

An important application of topological sorting is its use in solving the shortest-path problem for acyclic graphs. The idea is to have the eyeball visit vertices in topological order.

This idea works because, when the eyeball visits vertex v, we are guaranteed that D_v can no longer be lowered; by the topological ordering rule, it has no incoming edges emanating from unvisited nodes. Figure 15.32 shows the stages of the shortest-path algorithm, using topological ordering to guide the vertex visitations. Note that the sequence of vertices visited is not the

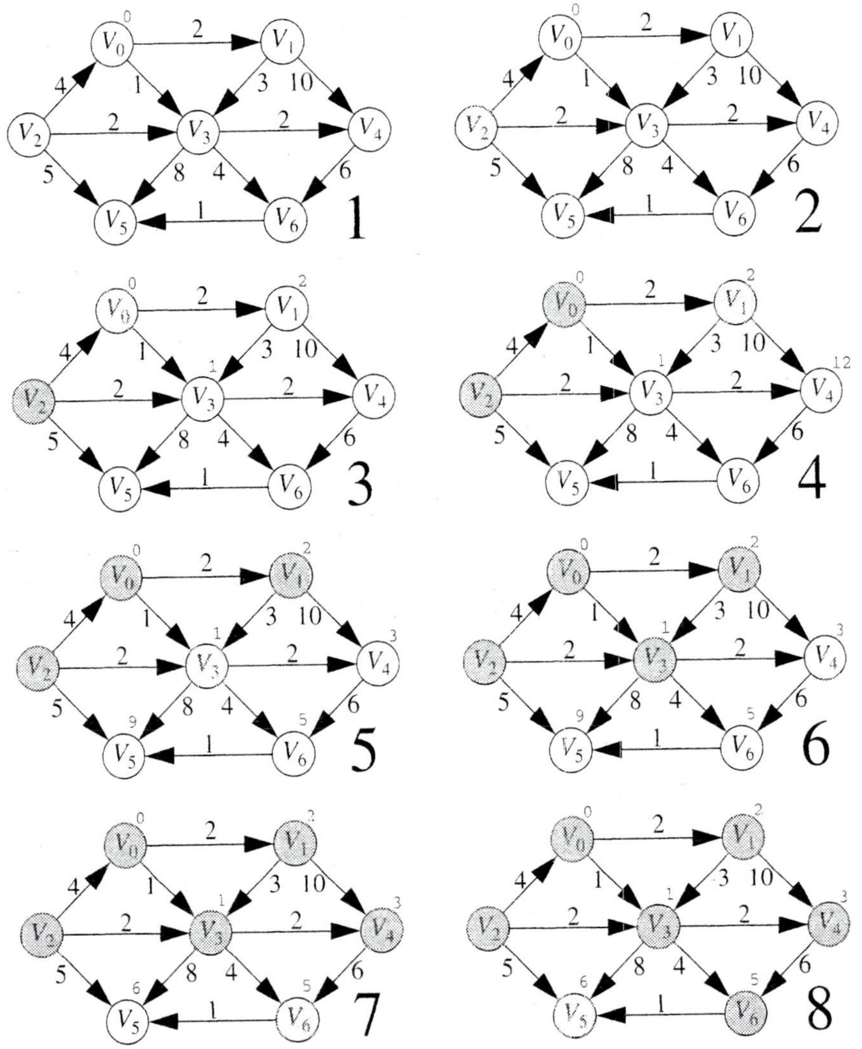
Figure 15.32 The stages of acyclic graph algorithm. The conventions are the same as those in Figure 15.22.

same as in Dijkstra's algorithm. Also note that vertices visited by the eyeball prior to its reaching the starting vertex are unreachable from the starting vertex and have no influence on the distances of any vertex.

We do not need a priority queue. Instead, we need only to incorporate the topological sort into the shortest-path computation. Thus we find that the algorithm runs in linear time and works even with negative edge weights.

The result is a linear time algorithm even with negative edge weights.

15.5.3 C++ Implementation

The implementation combines a topological sort calculation and a shortest-path calculation. The indegree information is stored in the `scratch` data member.

The implementation of the shortest-path algorithm for acyclic graphs is shown in Figure 15.33. We use a queue to perform the topological sort and maintain the indegree information in the `scratch` data member. Lines 13–18 compute the indegrees, and at lines 20–25 we place any indegree 0 vertices on the queue.

We then repeatedly remove a vertex from the queue at line 30. Note that, if the queue is empty, the `for` loop is terminated by the test at line 28. If the loop terminates because of a cycle, this fact is reported at line 50. Otherwise, the loop at line 31 steps through the adjacency list and a value of *w* is obtained at line 34. Immediately we lower *w*'s indegree at line 36 and, if it has fallen to 0, we place it on the queue at line 37.

Vertices that appear before *S* in the topological order are unreachable.

Recall that if the current vertex *v* appears prior to *S* in topological order, *v* must be unreachable from *S*. Consequently, it still has $D_v \equiv \infty$ and thus cannot hope to provide a path to any adjacent vertex *w*. We perform a test at line 38, and if a path cannot be provided, we do not attempt any distance calculations. Otherwise, at lines 41 to 46, we use the same calculations as in Dijkstra's algorithm to update D_w if necessary.

15.5.4 An Application: Critical-Path Analysis

***Critical-path analysis* is used to schedule tasks associated with a project.**

An important use of acyclic graphs is **critical-path analysis,** a form of analysis used to schedule tasks associated with a project. The graph shown in Figure 15.34 provides an example. Each vertex represents an activity that must be completed, along with the time needed to complete it. The graph is thus called an **activity-node graph,** in which vertices represent activities and edges represent precedence relationships. An edge (*v, w*) indicates that activity *v* must be completed before activity *w* may begin, which implies that the graph must be acyclic. We assume that any activities that do not depend (either directly or indirectly) on each other can be performed in parallel by different servers.

An *activity-node graph* represents activities as vertices and precedence relationships as edges.

This type of graph could be (and frequently is) used to model construction projects. Two important questions must be answered. First, what is the earliest completion time for the project? The answer, as the graph shows, is 10 time units—required along path *A, C, F, H*. Second, which activities can be delayed, and by how long, without affecting the minimum completion time? For instance, delaying any of *A, C, F,* or *H* would push the completion time past 10 time units. However, activity *B* is less critical and can be delayed up to 2 time units without affecting the final completion time.

```
void Graph::acyclic( const string & startName )
{
    vmap::iterator itr = vertexMap.find( startName );
    if( itr == vertexMap.end( ) )
        throw GraphException( startName + " is not a vertex" );

    clearAll( );
    Vertex *start = (*itr).second;
    start->dist = 0;
    list<Vertex *> q;

      // Compute the indegrees.
    for( itr = vertexMap.begin( ); itr != vertexMap.end( ); ++itr )
    {
        Vertex *v = (*itr).second;
        for( int i = 0; i < v->adj.size( ); i++ )
            v->adj[ i ].dest->scratch++;
    }
      // Enqueue vertices of indegree zero.
    for( itr = vertexMap.begin( ); itr != vertexMap.end( ); ++itr )
    {
        Vertex *v = (*itr).second;
        if( v->scratch == 0 )
            q.push_back( v );
    }

    int iterations;
    for( iterations = 0; !q.empty( ); iterations++ )
    {
        Vertex *v = q.front( ); q.pop_front( );
        for( int i = 0; i < v->adj.size( ); i++ )
        {
            Edge e = v->adj[ i ];
            Vertex *w = e.dest;

            if( --w->scratch == 0 )
                q.push_back( w );
            if( v->dist == INFINITY )
                continue;

            double cvw = e.cost;
            if( w->dist > v->dist + cvw )
            {
                w->dist = v->dist + cvw;
                w->prev = v;
            }
        }
    }
    if( iterations != vertexMap.size( ) )
        throw GraphException( "Graph has a cycle!" );
}
```

Figure 15.33 A shortest-path algorithm for acyclic graphs.

The *event-node graph* consists of event vertices that correspond to the completion of an activity and all its dependent activities.

To perform these calculations, we convert the activity-node graph to an **event-node graph,** in which each event corresponds to the completion of an activity and all its dependent activities. Events reachable from a node v in the event-node graph may not commence until after the event v is completed. This graph can be constructed automatically or by hand (from the activity-node graph). Dummy edges and vertices may need to be inserted to avoid introducing false dependencies (or false lack of dependencies). The event-node graph corresponding to the activity-node graph in Figure 15.34 is shown in Figure 15.35.

Edges show which activity must be completed to advance from one vertex to the next. The earliest completion time is the longest path.

To find the earliest completion time of the project, we merely need to find the length of the *longest* path from the first event to the last event. For general graphs, the longest-path problem generally does not make sense because of the possibility of a **positive-cost cycle,** which is equivalent to a negative-cost cycle in shortest-path problems. If any positive-cost cycles are present, we could ask for the longest simple path. However, no satisfactory solution is known for this problem. Fortunately, the event-node graph is acyclic; thus we need not worry about cycles. We can easily adapt the shortest-path algorithm to compute the earliest completion time for all nodes in the graph. If EC_i is the earliest completion time for node i, the applicable rules are

$$EC_1 = 0 \quad \text{and} \quad EC_w = \text{Max}_{(v,\,w) \in E}(EC_v + c_{v,\,w}).$$

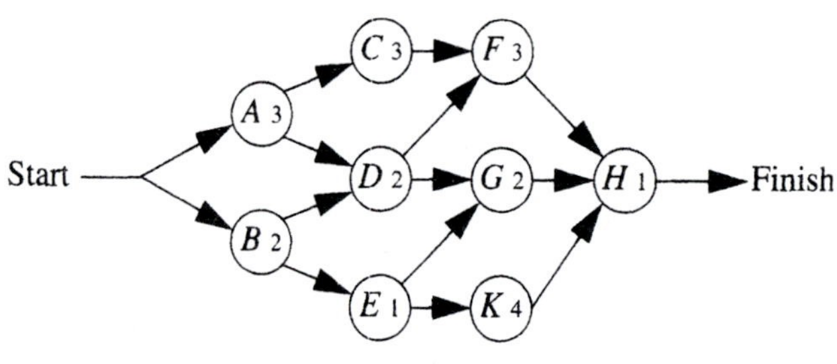

Figure 15.34 An activity-node graph.

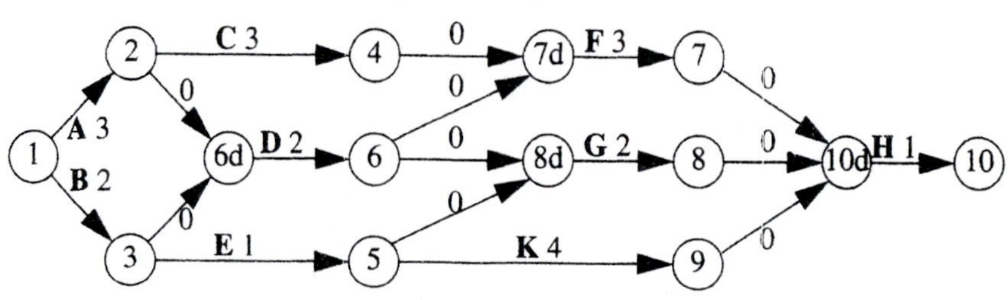

Figure 15.35 An event-node graph.

Figure 15.36 shows the earliest completion time for each event in our example event-node graph. We can also compute the latest time, LC_i, that each event can finish without affecting final completion time. The formulas to do this are

The latest time an event can finish without delaying the project is also easily computable.

$$LC_N = EC_N \quad \text{and} \quad LC_v = \text{Min}_{(v,\, w) \in E}(LC_w - c_{v,\, w}).$$

These values can be computed in linear time by maintaining for each vertex a list of all adjacent and preceding vertices. The earliest completion times are computed for vertices by their topological order, and the latest completion times are computed by reverse topological order. The latest completion times are shown in Figure 15.37.

The **slack time** for each edge in the event-node graph is the amount of time that the completion of the corresponding activity can be delayed without delaying the overall completion, or

Slack time **is the amount of time that an activity can be delayed without delaying overall completion.**

$$\text{Slack}_{(v,\, w)} = LC_w - EC_v - c_{v,\, w}.$$

Figure 15.38 shows the slack (as the third entry) for each activity in the event-node graph. For each node, the top number is the earliest completion time and the bottom number is the latest completion time.

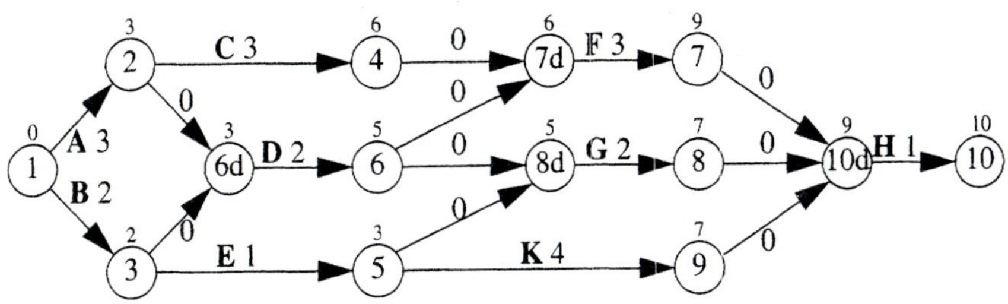

Figure 15.36 Earliest completion times.

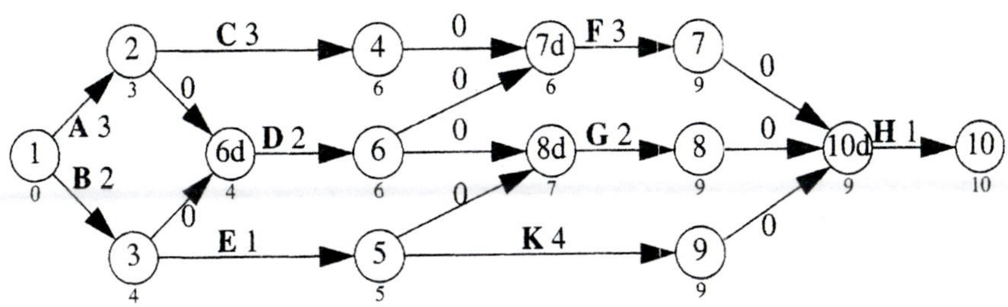

Figure 15.37 Latest completion times.

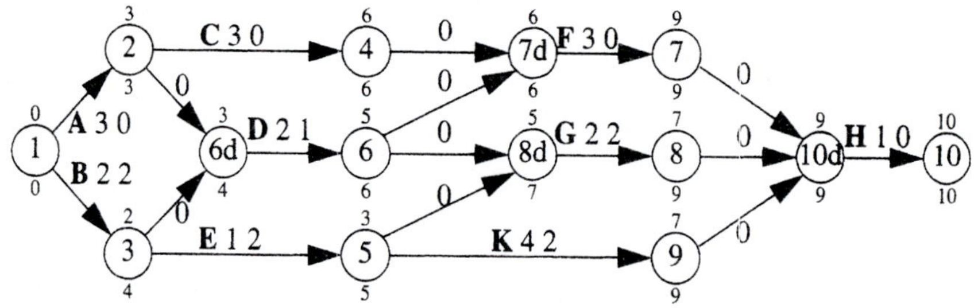

Figure 15.38 Earliest completion time, latest completion time, and slack (additional edge item).

Zero-slack activities are critical and cannot be delayed. A path of zero-slack edges is a critical path.

Some activities have zero slack. These are critical activities that must be finished on schedule. A path consisting entirely of zero-slack edges is a **critical path.**

Summary

In this chapter we showed how graphs can be used to model many real-life problems and in particular how to calculate the shortest path under a wide variety of circumstances. Many of the graphs that occur are typically very sparse, so choosing appropriate data structures to implement them is important.

For unweighted graphs, the shortest path can be computed in linear time, using breadth-first search. For positive-weighted graphs, slightly more time is needed, using Dijkstra's algorithm and an efficient priority queue. For negative-weighted graphs, the problem becomes more difficult. Finally, for acyclic graphs, the running time reverts to linear time with the aid of a topological sort.

Figure 15.39 summarizes those characteristics for these algorithms.

Type of Graph Problem	Running Time	Comments
Unweighted	$O(\lvert E\rvert)$	Breadth-first search
Weighted, no negative edges	$O(\lvert E\rvert \log \lvert V\rvert)$	Dijkstra's algorithm
Weighted, negative edges	$O(\lvert E\rvert \cdot \lvert V\rvert)$	Bellman–Ford algorithm
Weighted, acyclic	$O(\lvert E\rvert)$	Uses topological sort

Figure 15.39 Worst-case running times of various graph algorithms.

Objects of the Game

activity-node graph A graph of vertices as activities and edges as precedence relationships. (p. 522)

adjacency lists An array of lists used to represent a graph, using linear space. (p. 492)

adjacency matrix A matrix representation of a graph that uses quadratic space. (p. 491)

adjacent vertices Vertex *w* is adjacent to vertex *v* if there is an edge from *v* to *w*. (p. 489)

Bellman–Ford algorithm An algorithm that is used to solve the negative-weighted, shortest-path problem. (p. 516)

breadth-first search A search procedure that processes vertices in layers: Those closest to the start are evaluated first, and those most distant are evaluated last. (p. 505)

critical-path analysis A form of analysis used to schedule tasks associated with a project. (p. 522)

cycle In a directed graph, a path that begins and ends at the same vertex and contains at least one edge. (p. 490)

dense and sparse graphs A dense graph has a large number of edges (generally quadratic). Typical graphs are not dense but are sparse. (p. 491)

Dijkstra's algorithm An algorithm that is used to solve the positive-weighted, shortest-path problem. (p. 509)

directed acyclic graph (DAG) A type of directed graph having no cycles. (p. 490)

directed graph A graph in which edges are ordered pairs of vertices. (p. 489)

edge cost (weight) The third component of an edge that measures the cost of traversing the edge. (p. 489)

event-node graph A graph that consists of event vertices that correspond to the completion of an activity and all its dependent activities. Edges show what activity must be completed to advance from one vertex to the next. The earliest completion time is the longest path. (p. 522)

graph A set of vertices and a set of edges that connect the vertices. (p. 489)

indegree The number of incoming edges of a vertex. (p. 519)

negative-cost cycle A cycle whose cost is less than zero and makes most, if not all, paths undefined because we can loop around the cycle arbitrarily many times and obtain an arbitrarily small weighted path length. (p. 516)

path A sequence of vertices connected by edges. (p. 490)

path length The number of edges on a path. (p. 490)

positive-cost cycle In a longest-path problem, the equivalent of a negative-cost cycle in a shortest-path problem. (p. 524)

simple path A path in which all vertices are distinct, except that the first and last vertices can be the same. (p. 490)

single-source algorithms Algorithms that compute the shortest paths from some starting point to all vertices in a graph. (p. 496)

slack time The amount of time that an activity can be delayed without delaying overall completion. (p. 525)

topological sort A process that orders vertices in a directed acyclic graph such that if there is a path from *u* to *v*, then *v* appears after *u* in the ordering. A graph that has a cycle cannot have a topological order. (p. 517)

unweighted path length The number of edges on a path. (p. 503)

weighted path length The sum of the edge costs on a path. (p. 509)

Common Errors

1. A common error is failing to ensure that the input graph satisfies the requisite conditions for the algorithm being used (i.e., acyclic or positive weighted).
2. For `Path`, the comparison function compares the `cost` data member only. If the `dest` data member is used to drive the comparison function, the algorithm may appear to work for small graphs, but for larger graphs, it is incorrect and gives slightly suboptimal answers. It never produces a path that does not exist, however. Thus this error is difficult to track down.
3. The shortest-path algorithm for negative-weighted graphs must have a test for negative cycles; otherwise, it runs forever.

On the Internet

All the algorithms in this chapter are online in one file. The `Vertex` class has an additional data member that is used in the alternative implementation of Dijkstra's algorithm shown in Section 23.2.3.

Paths.cpp Contains everything in one file with the simple `main` shown in Figure 15.15.

Exercises

In Short

15.1. Find the shortest unweighted path from V_3 to all others in the graph shown in Figure 15.1.

15.2. Find the shortest weighted path from V_2 to all others in the graph shown in Figure 15.1.

15.3. Which algorithms in this chapter can be used to solve Exercise 15.2?

15.4. In Figure 15.5, reverse the direction of edges (D, C) and (E, D). Show the changes that result in the figure and the result of running the topological sorting algorithm.

15.5. Suppose that edges (C, B) with a cost of 11 and (B, F) with a cost of 10 are added to the end of the input in Figure 15.5. Show the changes that result in the figure and recompute the shortest path emanating from vertex A.

In Theory

15.6. Show how to avoid quadratic initialization inherent in adjacency matrices while maintaining constant-time access of any edge.

15.7. Explain how to modify the unweighted shortest-path algorithm so that, if there is more than one minimum path (in terms of number of edges), the tie is broken in favor of the smallest total weight.

15.8. Explain how to modify Dijkstra's algorithm to produce a count of the number of different minimum paths from v to w.

15.9. Explain how to modify Dijkstra's algorithm so that, if there is more than one minimum path from v to w, a path with the fewest edges is chosen.

15.10. Give an example of when Dijkstra's algorithm gives the wrong answer in the presence of a negative edge but no negative-cost cycle.

15.11. Consider the following algorithm to solve the negative-weighted, shortest-path problem: Add a constant c to each edge cost, thus removing negative edges; calculate the shortest path on the new graph; and then use that result on the original. What is wrong with this algorithm?

15.12. Prove the correctness of the negative-weighted, shortest-path algorithm. To do so, show that when the eyeball visits vertex v for the ith time, the value of D_v is the length of the shortest weighted path consisting of i or fewer edges.

15.13. Give a linear-time algorithm to find the longest weighted path in an acyclic graph. Does your algorithm extend to graphs that have cycles?

15.14. Show that if edge weights are 0 or 1, exclusively, Dijkstra's algorithm can be implemented in linear time by using a *deque* (Section 16.5).

15.15. For any path in a graph, the *bottleneck cost* is given by the weight of the shortest edge on the path. For example, in Figure 15.4, the bottleneck cost of the path E, D, B is 23 and the bottleneck cost of the path E, D, C, A, B is 10. The *maximum bottleneck problem* is to find the path between two specified vertices with the maximum bottleneck cost. Thus the maximum bottleneck path between E and B is the path E, D, B. Give an efficient algorithm to solve the maximum bottleneck problem.

15.16. Let G be a (directed) graph and u and v be any two distinct vertices in G. Prove or disprove each of the following.

a. If G is acyclic, at least one of (u, v) or (v, u) can be added to the graph without creating a cycle.
b. If adding one of either (u, v) or (v, u) to G without creating a cycle is impossible, then G already has a cycle.

In Practice

15.17. In this chapter we claim that, for the implementation of graph algorithms that run on large input, data structures are crucial to ensure reasonable performance. For each of the following instances in which a poor data structure or algorithm is used, provide a Big-Oh analysis of the result and compare the actual performance with the algorithms and data structures presented in the text. Implement only one change at a time. You should run your tests on a reasonably large and somewhat sparse random graph. Then do the following.

a. When an edge is read, determine whether it is already in the graph.
b. Implement the "dictionary" by using a sequential scan of the vertex table.
c. Implement the queue by using the algorithm in Exercise 7.12 (which should affect the unweighted shortest-path algorithm).
d. In the unweighted shortest-path algorithm, implement the search for the minimum-cost vertex as a sequential scan of the vertex table.
e. Implement the priority queue by using the algorithm in Exercise 7.14 (which should affect the weighted shortest-path algorithm).
f. Implement the priority queue by using the algorithm in Exercise 7.15 (which should affect the weighted shortest-path algorithm).
g. In the weighted shortest-path algorithm, implement the search for the minimum-cost vertex as a sequential scan of the vertex table.
h. In the acyclic shortest-path algorithm, implement the search for a vertex with indegree 0 as a sequential scan of the vertex table.
i. Implement any of the graph algorithms by using an adjacency matrix instead of adjacency lists.

Programming Projects

15.18. A directed graph is strongly connected if there is a path from every vertex to every other vertex. Do the following.

a. Pick any vertex *S*. Show that, if the graph is strongly connected, a shortest-path algorithm will declare that all nodes are reachable from *S*.
b. Show that, if the graph is strongly connected and then the directions of all edges are reversed and a shortest-path algorithm is run from *S*, all nodes will be reachable from *S*.
c. Show that the tests in parts (a) and (b) are sufficient to decide whether a graph is strongly connected (i.e., a graph that passes both tests must be strongly connected).
d. Write a program that checks whether a graph is strongly connected. What is the running time of your algorithm?

Explain how each of the following problems can be solved by applying a shortest-path algorithm. Then design a mechanism for representing an input and write a program that solves the problem.

15.19. The input is a list of league game scores (and there are no ties). If all teams have at least one win and a loss, we can generally "prove," by a silly transitivity argument, that any team is better than any other. For instance, in the six-team league where everyone plays three games, suppose that we have the following results: *A* beat *B* and *C*; *B* beat *C* and *F*; *C* beat *D*; *D* beat *E*; *E* beat *A*; and *F* beat *D* and *E*. Then we can prove that *A* is better than *F* because *A* beat *B* who in turn beat *F*. Similarly, we can prove that *F* is better than *A* because *F* beat *E* and *E* beat *A*. Given a list of game scores and two teams *X* and *Y*, either find a proof (if one exists) that *X* is better than *Y* or indicate that no proof of this form can be found.

15.20. A word can be changed to another word by a one-character substitution. Assume that a dictionary of five-letter words exists. Give an algorithm to determine whether a word *A* can be transformed to a word *B* by a series of one-character substitutions, and if so, outputs the corresponding sequence of words. For example, `bleed` converts to `blood` by the sequence `bleed`, `blend`, `blond`, `blood`.

15.21. The input is a collection of currencies and their exchange rates. Is there a sequence of exchanges that makes money instantly? For instance, if the currencies are *X*, *Y*, and *Z* and the exchange rate is 1 *X* equals 2 *Y*s, 1 *Y* equals 2 *Z*s, and 1 *X* equals 3 *Z*s, then 300 *Z*s will buy 100 *X*s, which in turn will buy 200 *Y*s, which in turn will buy 400 *Z*s. We have thus made a profit of 33 percent.

15.22. A student needs to take a certain number of courses to graduate, and these courses have prerequisites that must be followed. Assume that all courses are offered every semester and that the student can take an unlimited number of courses. Given a list of courses and their prerequisites, compute a schedule that requires the minimum number of semesters.

15.23. The object of the *Kevin Bacon Game* is to link a movie actor to Kevin Bacon via shared movie roles. The minimum number of links is an actor's *Bacon number*. For instance, Tom Hanks has a Bacon number of 1. He was in *Apollo 13* with Kevin Bacon. Sally Field has a Bacon number of 2 because she was in *Forest Gump* with Tom

Hanks, who was in *Apollo 13* with Kevin Bacon. Almost all well-known actors have a Bacon number of 1 or 2. Assume that you have a comprehensive list of actors, with roles, and do the following.

a. Explain how to find an actor's Bacon number.
b. Explain how to find the actor with the highest Bacon number.
c. Explain how to find the minimum number of links between two arbitrary actors.

References

The use of adjacency lists to represent graphs was first advocated in [3]. Dijkstra's shortest-path algorithm was originally described in [2]. The algorithm for negative edge costs is taken from [1]. A more efficient test for termination is described in [6], which also shows how data structures play an important role in a wide range of graph theory algorithms. The topological sorting algorithm is from [4]. Many real-life applications of graph algorithms are presented in [5], along with references for further reading.

1. R. E. Bellman, "On a Routing Problem," *Quarterly of Applied Mathematics* **16** (1958), 87–90.
2. E. W. Dijkstra, "A Note on Two Problems in Connexion with Graphs," *Numerische Mathematik* **1** (1959), 269–271.
3. J. E. Hopcroft and R. E. Tarjan, "Algorithm 447: Efficient Algorithms for Graph Manipulation," *Communications of the ACM* **16** (1973), 372–378.
4. A. B. Kahn, "Topological Sorting of Large Networks," *Communications of the ACM* **5** (1962), 558–562.
5. D. E. Knuth, *The Stanford GraphBase*, Addison-Wesley, Reading, Mass., 1993.
6. R. E. Tarjan, *Data Structures and Network Algorithms*, Society for Industrial and Applied Mathematics, Philadelphia, 1985.

Part IV

Implementations

Chapter 16

Stacks and Queues

In this chapter we discuss implementation of the stack and queue data structures. Recall from Chapter 7 that the basic operations are expected to take constant time. For both the stack and queue, there are two basic ways to arrange for constant-time operations. The first is to store the items contiguously in an array, and the second is to store items noncontiguously in a linked list. We present implementations for both data structures, using both methods, in this chapter. The code follows the protocols given previously in Figures 7.3 and 7.5.

In this chapter, we show:

- an array-based implementation of the stack and queue,
- a linked list–based implementation of the stack and queue,
- a brief comparison of the two methods,
- an illustration of STL stack implementation, and
- inheritance used to derive a new data structure, called the *double-ended queue.*

16.1 Dynamic Array Implementations

In this section we use a simple array to implement the stack and queue. The resulting algorithms are extremely efficient and also are simple to code. Recall that we have been using `vector` to implement arrays. Applying `push_back`, `pop_back`, and `back`, we have already used a `vector` to support stack operations. However, because we are interested in a general discussion of the algorithms, we pretend that these operations do not exist in the `vector` class for our `vector` implementation.

16.1.1 Stacks

A stack can be implemented with an array and an integer that indicates the index of the top element.

As Figure 16.1 shows, a stack can be implemented with an array and an integer. The integer `tos` (*top of stack*) provides the array index of the top element of the stack. Thus when `tos` is –1, the stack is empty. To `push`, we increment `tos` and place the new element in the array position `tos`. Accessing the top element is thus trivial, and we can perform the `pop` by decrementing `tos`. In Figure 16.1, we begin with an empty stack. Then we show the stack after three operations: `push(a)`, `push(b)`, and `pop`.

Figure 16.2 shows the interface for the array-based `Stack` class. It specifies two data members: `theArray`, which is expanded as needed, stores the items in the stack; and `topOfStack` gives the index of the current top of the stack. For an empty stack, this index is –1. The constructor is shown in Figure 16.3. Because the data members are first-class objects, the Big-Three is automatically defined correctly. Thus we do not need to provide a destructor, copy constructor, or copy assignment operator.

Most of the stack routines are applications of previously discussed ideas.

The public methods are listed in lines 21–27 of the interface. Most of these routines have simple implementations. The `isEmpty` and `makeEmpty` routines are one-liners, as shown in Figure 16.4. The `push` method is shown in Figure 16.5. If it were not for the array doubling, the `push` routine would be only the single line of code shown at line 7. Recall that the use of the prefix `++` operator means that `topOfStack` is incremented and that its new value is used to index `theArray`. The remaining routines are equally short, as shown in Figures 16.6 and 16.7. The postfix `--` operator used in Figure 16.7 indicates that, although `topOfStack` is decremented, its prior value is used to index `theArray`.

Recall that array doubling does not affect performance in the long run.

If there is no array doubling, every operation takes constant time. A `push` that involves array doubling will take $O(N)$ time. If this were a frequent occurrence, we would need to worry. However, it is infrequent because an array doubling that involves N elements must be preceded by at least $N/2$ `push`es that do not involve an array doubling. Consequently, we

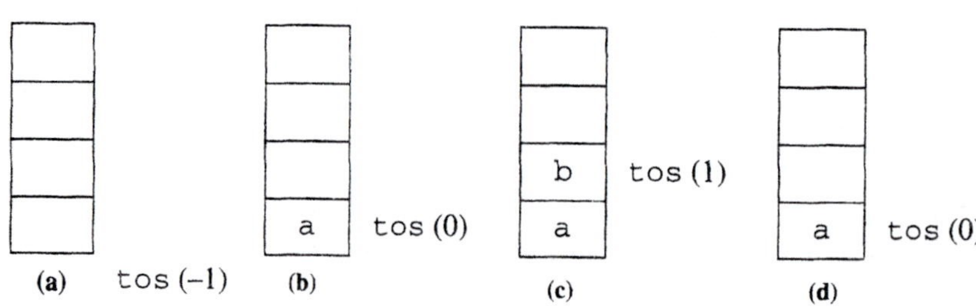

Figure 16.1 How the stack routines work: (a) empty stack: (b) `push(a)`; (c) `push(b)`; and (d) `pop`.

```
// Stack class -- array implementation.
//
// CONSTRUCTION: with no parameters.
//
// ******************PUBLIC OPERATIONS*********************
// void push( x )          --> Insert x
// void pop( )             --> Remove most recently inserted item
// Object top( )           --> Return most recently inserted item
// Object topAndPop( )     --> Return and remove most recent item
// bool isEmpty( )         --> Return true if empty; else false
// void makeEmpty( )       --> Remove all items
// ******************ERRORS********************************
// UnderflowException thrown as needed.

template <class Object>
class Stack
{
  public:
    Stack( );

    bool isEmpty( ) const;
    const Object & top( ) const;

    void makeEmpty( );
    void pop( );
    void push( const Object & x );
    Object topAndPop( );

  private:
    vector<Object> theArray;
    int            topOfStack;
};
```

Figure 16.2 Interface for the array-based `Stack` class.

```
// Construct the stack.
template <class Object>
Stack<Object>::Stack( ) : theArray( 1 )
{
    topOfStack = -1;
}
```

Figure 16.3 The zero-parameter constructor for the array-based `Stack` class.

```
// Test if the stack is logically empty.
// Return true if empty, false, otherwise.
template <class Object>
bool Stack<Object>::isEmpty( ) const
{
    return topOfStack == -1;
}

// Make the stack logically empty.
template <class Object>
void Stack<Object>::makeEmpty( )
{
    topOfStack = -1;
}
```

Figure 16.4 The `isEmpty` and `makeEmpty` routines for the array-based `Stack` class.

```
// Insert x into the stack.
template <class Object>
void Stack<Object>::push( const Object & x )
{
    if( topOfStack == theArray.size( ) - 1 )
        theArray.resize( theArray.size( ) * 2 + 1 );
    theArray[ ++topOfStack ] = x;
}
```

Figure 16.5 The `push` method for the array-based `Stack` class.

can charge the $O(N)$ cost of the doubling over these $N/2$ easy `push`es, thereby effectively raising the cost of each `push` by only a small constant. This technique is known as *amortization*.

A real-life example of amortization is payment of income taxes. Rather than pay your entire bill on April 15, the government requires that you pay most of your taxes through withholding. The total tax bill is always the same; it is *when* the tax is paid that varies. The same is true for the time spent in the `push` operations. We can charge for the array doubling at the time it occurs, or we can bill each `push` operation equally. An amortized bound requires that we bill each operation in a sequence for its fair share of the total cost. In our example, the cost of array doubling therefore is not excessive.

```
// Return the most recently inserted item in the stack.
// Does not alter the stack.
// Throws UnderflowException if stack is already empty.
template <class Object>
const Object & Stack<Object>::top( ) const
{
    if( isEmpty( ) )
        throw UnderflowException( );
    return theArray[ topOfStack ];
}

// Remove the most recently inserted item from the stack.
// Throw UnderflowException if stack is already empty.
template <class Object>
void Stack<Object>::pop( )
{
    if( isEmpty( ) )
        throw UnderflowException( );
    topOfStack--;
}
```

Figure 16.6 The `top` and `pop` methods for the array-based `Stack` class.

```
// Return and remove most recently inserted item from the stack.
// Throws UnderflowException if stack is already empty.
template <class Object>
Object Stack<Object>::topAndPop( )
{
    if( isEmpty( ) )
        throw UnderflowException( );
    return theArray[ topOfStack-- ];
}
```

Figure 16.7 The `topAndPop` method for the array-based `Stack` class.

16.1.2 Queues

Storing the queue items beginning at the start of any array makes dequeueing expensive.

The easiest way to implement the queue is to store the items in an array with the front item in the front position (i.e., array index 0). If `back` represents the position of the last item in the queue, then to `enqueue` we merely increment `back` and place the item there. The problem is that the `dequeue` operation is very expensive. The reason is that, by requiring that the items be placed at the start of the array, we force the `dequeue` to shift all the items one position after we remove the front item.

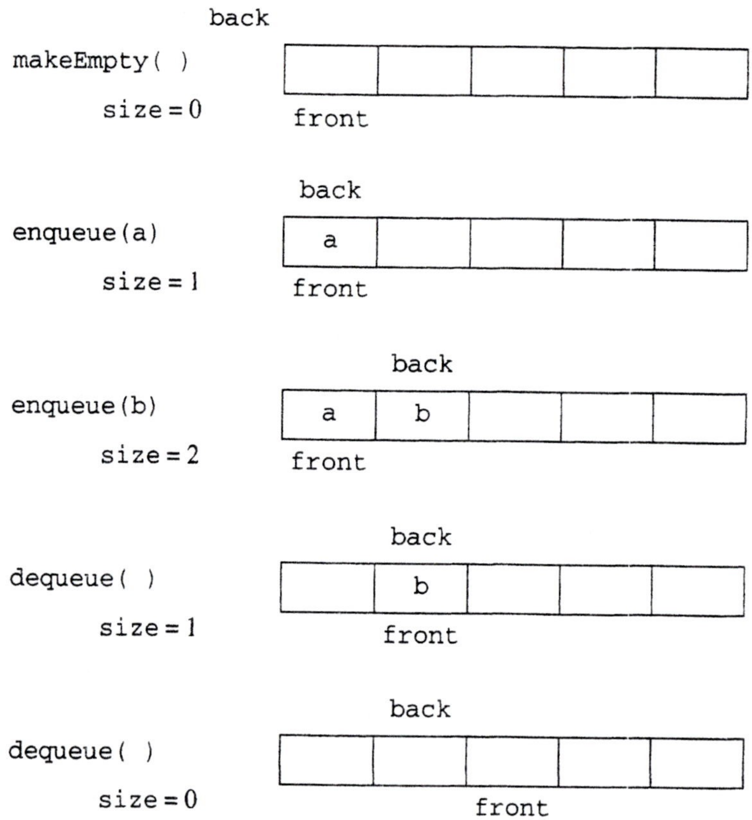

Figure 16.8 Basic array implementation of the queue.

A dequeue is implemented by incrementing the front position.

Figure 16.8 shows that we can overcome this problem when performing a dequeue by incrementing front rather than shifting all the elements. When the queue has one element, both front and back represent the array index of that element. Thus, for an empty queue, back must be initialized to front-1.

This implementation ensures that both enqueue and dequeue can be performed in constant time. The fundamental problem with this approach is shown in the first line of Figure 16.9. After three more enqueue operations, we cannot add any more items, even though the queue is not really full. Array doubling does not solve the problem because, even if the size of the array is 1000, after 1000 enqueue operations there is no room in the queue, regardless of its actual size. Even if 1000 dequeue operations have been performed, thus abstractly making the queue empty, we cannot add to it.

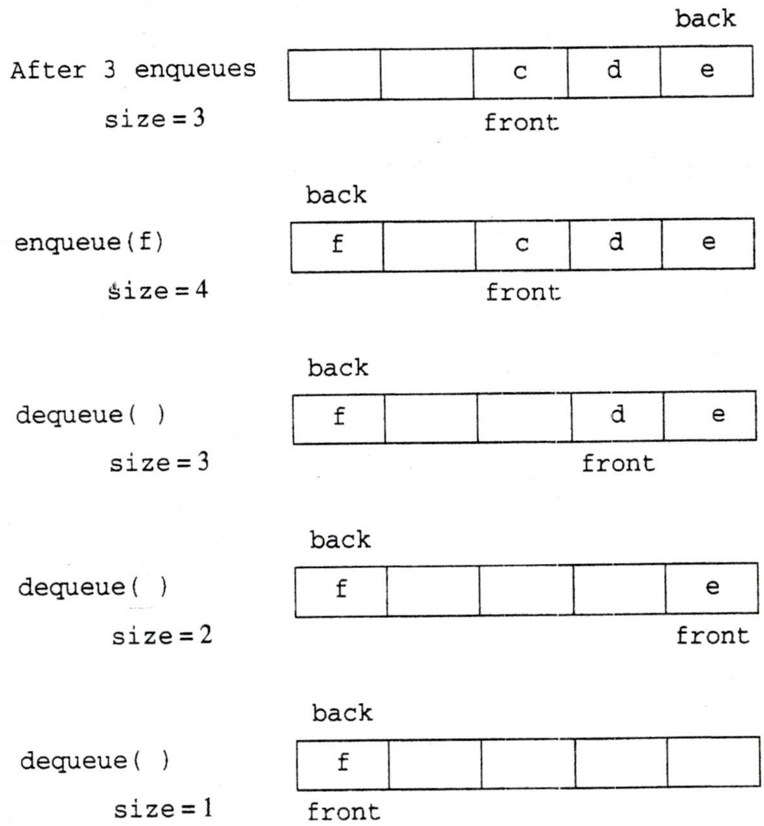

Figure 16.9 Array implementation of the queue with wraparound.

As Figure 16.9 shows, however, there is plenty of extra space: All the positions before `front` are unused and can thus be recycled. Hence we use **wraparound;** that is, when either `back` or `front` reaches the end of the array, we reset it to the beginning. This operation implementing a queue is called a **circular array implementation.** We need to double the array only when the number of elements in the queue equals the number of array positions. To `enqueue(f)`, we therefore reset `back` to the start of the array and place `f` there. After three `dequeue` operations, `front` is also reset to the start of the array.

The interface for the generic `Queue` class is shown in Figure 16.10. The `Queue` class has four data members: a dynamically expanding array, the number of items currently in the queue, the array index of the front item and the array index of the back item.

Wraparound **returns `front` or `back` to the beginning of the array when either reaches the end. Using wraparound to implement the queue is called a *circular array implementation.***

```
// Queue class -- array implementation.
//
// CONSTRUCTION: with no parameters.
//
// *****************PUBLIC OPERATIONS*********************
// void enqueue( x )     --> Insert x
// void dequeue( )       --> Return and remove least recent item
// Object getFront( )    --> Return least recently inserted item
// bool isEmpty( )       --> Return true if empty; else false
// void makeEmpty( )     --> Remove all items
// *****************ERRORS********************************
// UnderflowException thrown as needed.
template <class Object>
class Queue
{
  public:
    Queue( );

    bool isEmpty( ) const;
    const Object & getFront( ) const;

    void makeEmpty( );
    Object dequeue( );
    void enqueue( const Object & x );

  private:
    vector<Object> theArray;
    int            currentSize;
    int            front;
    int            back;

    void increment( int & x ) const;
    void doubleQueue( );
};
```

Figure 16.10 Interface for the array-based `Queue` class.

If the queue is full, we must implement array doubling carefully.

We declare two methods in the private section. These methods are used internally by the `Queue` methods but are not made available to the user of the class. One of these methods is the `increment` routine, which adds 1 to its parameter and returns the new value. Because this method implements wraparound, if the result would equal the array size it is wrapped around to zero. This routine is shown in Figure 16.11. The other routine is `doubleQueue`, which is called if an `enqueue` requires a doubling of the array. It is slightly more complex than a simple call to the

```
// Internal method to increment x with wraparound.
template <class Object>
void Queue<Object>::increment( int & x ) const
{
    if( ++x == theArray.size( ) )
        x = 0;
}
```

Figure 16.11 The wraparound routine.

```
// Construct the queue.
template <class Object>
Queue<Object>::Queue( ) : theArray( 1 )
{
    makeEmpty( );
}
```

Figure 16.12 The constructor for the array-based `Queue` class.

```
// Test if the queue is logically empty.
// Return true if empty, false, otherwise.
template <class Object>
bool Queue<Object>::isEmpty( ) const
{
    return currentSize == 0;
}
```

Figure 16.13 The `isEmpty` routine for the array-based `Queue` class.

`vector`'s `resize` method because the queue items are not necessarily stored in an array starting at location 0. Thus items must be copied carefully. We discuss `doubleQueue` along with `enqueue`.

Many of the public methods resemble their stack counterparts, including the constructor shown in Figure 16.12 and `isEmpty`, shown in Figure 16.13. This constructor is not particularly special, except that we must be sure that we have the correct initial values for both `front` and `back`. This is done by calling `makeEmpty`.

When we double the queue array, we cannot simply copy the entire array directly.

The `enqueue` routine is shown in Figure 16.14. The basic strategy is simple enough, as illustrated by lines 7–9 in the `enqueue` routine. The `doubleQueue` routine, shown in Figure 16.15, begins by resizing the array. However, if `front` is not 0, we must move items because the implied wraparound of the original is no longer wrapped around once the array has become larger. The simplest solution is to take the wrapped-around portion (those items in positions 0 to `back`) and move them to the new part of the array.

```
// Insert x into the queue.
template <class Object>
void Queue<Object>::enqueue( const Object & x )
{
    if( currentSize == theArray.size( ) )
        doubleQueue( );
    increment( back );
    theArray[ back ] = x;
    currentSize++;
}
```

Figure 16.14 The enqueue routine for the array-based Queue class.

```
1 // Internal method to double capacity.
2 template <class Object>
3 void Queue<Object>::doubleQueue( )
4 {
5     theArray.resize( theArray.size( ) * 2 + 1 );
6     if( front != 0 )
7     {
8         for( int i = 0; i < front; i++ )
9             theArray[ i + currentSize ] = theArray[ i ];
10        back += currentSize;
11    }
12 }
```

Figure 16.15 Dynamic expansion for the array-based Queue class.

Thus doubleQueue steps through the old array and copies each item to the new part of the array at lines 8–9. Then we reset back at line 10. The dequeue and getFront routines are shown in Figure 16.16; both are short. Finally, the makeEmpty routine is shown in Figure 16.17. The queue routines clearly are constant-time operations, so the cost of array doubling can be amortized over the sequence of enqueue operations, as for the stack.

The circular array implementation of the queue can easily be done incorrectly when attempts to shorten the code are made. For instance, if you attempt to avoid using the size member by using front and back to infer the size, the array must be resized when the number of items in the queue is 1 less than the array's size.

```
// Return and remove least recently inserted item from the queue.
// Throws UnderflowException if queue is already empty.
template <class Object>
Object Queue<Object>::dequeue( )
{
    if( isEmpty( ) )
        throw UnderflowException( );
    currentSize--;

    Object frontItem = theArray[ front ];
    increment( front );
    return frontItem;
}

// Return the least recently inserted item in the queue
// or throw UnderflowException if empty.
template <class Object>
const Object & Queue<Object>::getFront( ) const
{
    if( isEmpty( ) )
        throw UnderflowException( );
    return theArray[ front ];
}
```

Figure 16.16 The `dequeue` and `getFront` routines for the array-based `Queue` class.

```
// Make the queue logically empty.
template <class Object>
void Queue<Object>::makeEmpty( )
{
    currentSize = 0;
    front = 0;
    back = theArray.size( ) - 1;
}
```

Figure 16.17 The `makeEmpty` routine for the array-based `Queue` class.

16.2 Linked List Implementations

The advantage of a linked list implementation is that the excess memory is only one pointer per item. The disadvantage is that the memory management could be time consuming.

An alternative to the contiguous array implementation is a linked list. Recall from Section 1.6 that in a linked list, we store each item in a separate object that also contains a pointer to the next object in the list.

The advantage of the linked list is that the excess memory is only one pointer per item. In contrast, a contiguous array implementation uses excess space equal to the number of vacant array items (plus some additional memory during the doubling phase). The linked list advantage can be significant if the vacant array items store uninitialized instances of objects that consume significant space. If first-class strings and vectors are used, the advantage isn't all that huge because uninitialized first-class strings and vectors use little space. Even so, we discuss the linked list implementations for three reasons.

1. An understanding of implementations that might be useful in other languages is important.
2. Implementations that use linked lists can be shorter for the queue than the comparable array versions.
3. These implementations illustrate the principles behind the more general linked list operations given in Chapter 17.

For the implementation to be competitive with contiguous array implementations, we must be able to perform the basic linked list operations in constant time. Doing so is easy because the changes in the linked list are restricted to the elements at the two ends (front and back) of the list.

16.2.1 Stacks

In implementing the `Stack` class, the top of the stack is represented by the first item in a linked list.

The `Stack` class can be implemented as a linked list in which the top of the stack is represented by the first item in the list, as shown in Figure 16.18. To implement a `push`, we create a new node in the list and attach it as the new first element. This node can be allocated by a call to `new`. To implement a `pop`, we merely advance the top of the stack to the second item in the list (if there is one). We should call `delete` on the old first node to avoid memory leaks. An empty stack is represented by an empty linked list. Clearly, each operation is performed in constant time because, by restricting operations to the first node, we have made all calculations independent of the size of the list. All that remains is the C++ implementation.

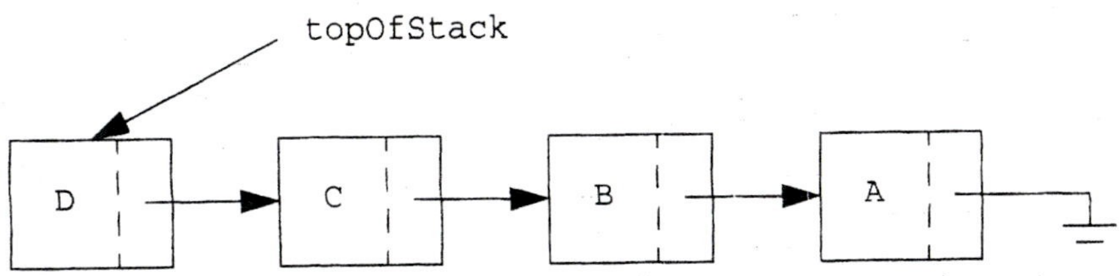

Figure 16.18 Linked list implementation of the `Stack` class.

Figure 16.19 provides the class interface. Lines 34 to 42 give the type declaration for the nodes in the list. A `ListNode` consists of two data members: `element` stores the item and `next` stores a pointer to the next `ListNode` in the linked list. We provide a constructor for `ListNode` that can be used to execute both

```
ListNode *ptr1 = new ListNode( x );
```

and

```
ListNode *ptr2 = new ListNode( x, ptr2 );
```

The `ListNode` declaration is nested in the private section of the `Stack` class, so it is not visible by users of the `Stack` class.

Note that the new type `ListNode` is nested in the `Stack` class. Thus it is not a type in the normal global scope, which is a good thing because it enforces information hiding: The `ListNode` declaration is certainly an internal detail of the `Stack` class. Moreover, by virtue of the private declaration, it is invisible to the `Stack` class users. Not all compilers implement nested class declarations in conjunction with templates, so you may need to rework the code by removing the `ListNode` declaration from the `Stack` class. This alternative is clearly less desirable because it weakens the hiding of information. The `Stack` itself is represented by a single data member, `topOfStack`, which is a pointer to the first `ListNode` in the linked list.

We use the constructor at line 19 to create an empty stack by setting `topOfStack` to `NULL`. The destructor declared at line 21 calls the member function `makeEmpty` to deallocate all the dynamically allocated nodes in the stack. `makeEmpty` works by popping the stack until it is empty.

A deep copy of `operator=` requires that we step through the second stack and allocate new nodes to be placed in the first stack.

The copy assignment operator is shown in Figure 16.20. At line 6 we check for aliasing and return immediately if it is detected. Otherwise, we can safely make the current object empty. The stack is now empty, so if the stack on the right-hand side is empty, we can return immediately. This option is checked at line 9. Otherwise, we have at least one item to copy. We have `ptr` point at a newly allocated node that is a copy of the first item in the `rhs` list at line 13. This item will be at the top of the new stack (line 14).

```
// Stack class -- linked list implementation.
//
// CONSTRUCTION: with no parameters.
//
// ******************PUBLIC OPERATIONS*********************
// void push( x )           --> Insert x
// void pop( )              --> Remove most recently inserted item
// Object top( )            --> Return most recently inserted item
// Object topAndPop( )      --> Return and remove most recent item
// bool isEmpty( )          --> Return true if empty; else false
// void makeEmpty( )        --> Remove all items
// ******************ERRORS********************************
// UnderflowException thrown as needed.

template <class Object>
class Stack
{
  public:
    Stack( ) : topOfStack( NULL ) { }
    Stack( const Stack & rhs );
    ~Stack( ) { makeEmpty( ); }

    bool isEmpty( ) const;
    const Object & top( ) const;

    void makeEmpty( );
    void pop( );
    void push( const Object & x );
    Object topAndPop( );

    const Stack & operator=( const Stack & rhs );

  private:
    struct ListNode
    {
        Object    element;
        ListNode *next;

        ListNode( const Object & theElement,
                  ListNode * n = NULL )
          : element( theElement ), next( n ) { }
    };

    ListNode *topOfStack;
};
```

Figure 16.19 Interface for linked list–based `Stack` class.

```
1 // Deep copy.
2 template <class Object>
3 const Stack<Object> &
4 Stack<Object>::operator=( const Stack<Object> & rhs )
5 {
6     if( this != &rhs )
7     {
8         makeEmpty( );
9         if( rhs.isEmpty( ) )
10            return *this;
11
12        ListNode *rptr = rhs.topOfStack;
13        ListNode *ptr  = new ListNode( rptr->element );
14        topOfStack = ptr;
15
16        for( rptr = rptr->next; rptr != NULL; rptr = rptr->next )
17            ptr = ptr->next = new ListNode( rptr->element );
18    }
19    return *this;
20 }
21
22 // Copy constructor.
23 template <class Object>
24 Stack<Object>::Stack( const Stack<Object> & rhs )
25 {
26     topOfStack = NULL;
27     *this = rhs;
28 }
```

Figure 16.20 Copy assignment operator and copy constructor for the linked list–based `Stack` class.

Note that the `next` pointer of the last node is `NULL` by virtue of the `ListNode` constructor.

We have `rptr` point at the second item in the `rhs` list in the `for` loop initialization at line 16. We then loop: `rptr` points at a cell containing the next item in the `rhs` list, and `ptr` points at the last cell in the newly created stack list. At line 16 we direct the loop to continue until the `rhs` list is exhausted. While it is not, we create a new node by using an item in the `rhs` list and then attach that new node at the end of the new list. The attachment is performed by the assignment to `ptr->next` at line 17. We must now update `ptr` (also done at line 17) so that `ptr` points to the last node in the new list. We then advance to the next node in the `rhs` list in the adjustment

```
1 // Insert x into the stack.
2 template <class Object>
3 void Stack<Object>::push( const Object & x )
4 {
5     topOfStack = new ListNode( x, topOfStack );
6 }
7
8 // Remove the most recently inserted item from the stack.
9 // Throws UnderflowException if the stack is empty.
10 template <class Object>
11 void Stack<Object>::pop( )
12 {
13     if( isEmpty( ) )
14         throw UnderflowException( );
15     ListNode *oldTop = topOfStack;
16     topOfStack = topOfStack->next;
17     delete oldTop;
18 }
```

Figure 16.21 The `push` and `pop` routines for the linked list–based `Stack` class.

part of the `for` loop. When we are done with the loop, everything has been copied over, and we can return. Note that the `next` pointer for the last node in the list is automatically `NULL` by virtue of the constructor.

Figure 16.20 also contains an implementation of the copy constructor. We used the standard idiom of constructing the object in a neutral state and then applied `operator=`.

The stack routines are essentially one-liners.

Two more routines are shown in Figure 16.21. The `push` operation is essentially one line of code, in which we allocate a new `ListNode` whose data member contains the item `x` to be pushed. The `next` pointer for this new node is the original `topOfStack`. This node then becomes the new `topOfStack`. We do all this at line 5.

The `pop` operation also is conceptually simple. After the obligatory test for emptiness, we save a pointer to the node at the top of the stack. We then reset `topOfStack` to the second node in the list and call `delete` to remove the popped node.

Finally, `top` and `makeEmpty` are straightforward routines and are implemented as shown in Figure 16.22. The `topAndPop` routine simply calls `top` and then `pop` and is not shown. `makeEmpty` pops the stack until it is empty.

```
// Return the most recently inserted item in the stack
// or throw an UnderflowException if empty.
template <class Object>
const Object & Stack<Object>::top( ) const
{
    if( isEmpty( ) )
        throw UnderflowException( );
    return topOfStack->element;
}

// Make the stack logically empty.
template <class Object>
void Stack<Object>::makeEmpty( )
{
    while( !isEmpty( ) )
        pop( );
}
```

Figure 16.22 The `top` and `makeEmpty` routines for the linked list–based `Stack` class.

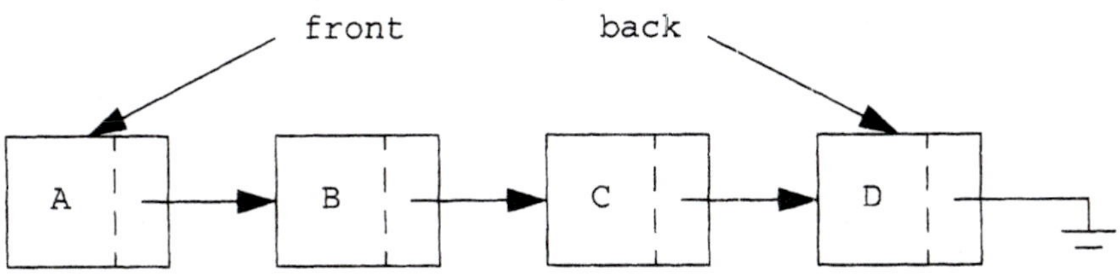

Figure 16.23 Linked list implementation of the `Queue` class.

16.2.2 Queues

A linked list in which we maintain a pointer to the first and last item can be used to implement the queue in constant time per operation.

The queue can be implemented by a linked list, provided we keep pointers to both the `front` and `back` of the list. Figure 16.23 shows the general idea.

The `Queue` class is similar to the `Stack` class. It is so similar, in fact, that we could derive the `Queue` class from the `Stack` class by using private inheritance. However, we give an independent implementation to make the ideas clearer and leave the possibility of using inheritance as Exercise 16.11. We present an easier to follow example of inheritance in Section 16.5, where we show how to use the `Queue` class to derive an extended set of operations.

The `Queue` class interface is given in Figure 16.24. The only new thing here is that we maintain two pointers instead of one. Figure 16.25 shows the constructors for the `Queue` class, and Figure 16.26 shows the `operator=`.

```
// Queue class -- linked list implementation.
//
// CONSTRUCTION: with no parameters.
//
// *****************PUBLIC OPERATIONS********************
// void enqueue( x )   --> Insert x
// void dequeue( )     --> Return and remove least recent item
// Object getFront( ) --> Return least recently inserted item
// bool isEmpty( )     --> Return true if empty; else false
// void makeEmpty( )   --> Remove all items
// *****************ERRORS*******************************
// UnderflowException thrown as needed.

template <class Object>
class Queue
{
  public:
    Queue( );
    Queue( const Queue & rhs );
    ~Queue( );
    const Queue & operator= ( const Queue & rhs );

    bool isEmpty( ) const;
    const Object & getFront( ) const;

    void makeEmpty( );
    Object dequeue( );
    void enqueue( const Object & x );

  private:
    struct ListNode
    {
        Object    element;
        ListNode *next;

        ListNode( const Object & theElement,
                  ListNode * n = NULL )
          : element( theElement ), next( n ) { }
    };

    ListNode *front;
    ListNode *back;
};
```

Figure 16.24 Interface for the linked list–based `Queue` class.

```
// Construct the queue.
template <class Object>
Queue<Object>::Queue( )
{
    front = back = NULL;
}

// Copy constructor.
template <class Object>
Queue<Object>::Queue( const Queue<Object> & rhs )
{
    front = back = NULL;
    *this = rhs;
}
```

Figure 16.25 Constructors for the linked list–based `Queue` class.

```
// Deep copy.
template <class Object>
const Queue<Object> &
Queue<Object>::operator=( const Queue<Object> & rhs )
{
    if( this != &rhs )
    {
        makeEmpty( );
        ListNode *rptr;
        for( rptr = rhs.front; rptr != NULL; rptr = rptr->next )
            enqueue( rptr->element );
    }
    return *this;
}
```

Figure 16.26 Copy assignment operator for the linked list–based `Queue` class.

This operator is simpler than the stack `operator=` because we can step through `rhs`, enqueueing items as we see them.

Figure 16.27 implements both `enqueue` and `dequeue`. The `dequeue` routine is logically identical to a stack `pop` (actually `popAndTop`). The `enqueue` routine has two cases. If the queue is empty, we create a one-element queue by calling `new` and having both `front` and `back` point at the single node. Otherwise, we create a new node with data value `x`, attach it at the end of the list, and then reset the end of the list to this new node, as illustrated in Figure 16.28. Note that enqueueing the first element is a special case because there is no `next` pointer to which a new node can be attached. We do all this at line 8 in Figure 16.27.

Enqueueing the first element is a special case because there is no `next` pointer to which a new node can be attached.

```
// Insert x into the queue.
template <class Object>
void Queue<Object>::enqueue( const Object & x )
{
    if( isEmpty( ) )
        back = front = new ListNode( x );
    else
        back = back->next = new ListNode( x );
}

// Return and remove the least recently inserted item from
// the queue. Throws UnderflowException if empty.
template <class Object>
Object Queue<Object>::dequeue( )
{
    Object frontItem = getFront( );

    ListNode *old = front;
    front = front->next;
    delete old;
    return frontItem;
}
```

Figure 16.27 The `enqueue` and `dequeue` routines for the linked list–based `Queue` class.

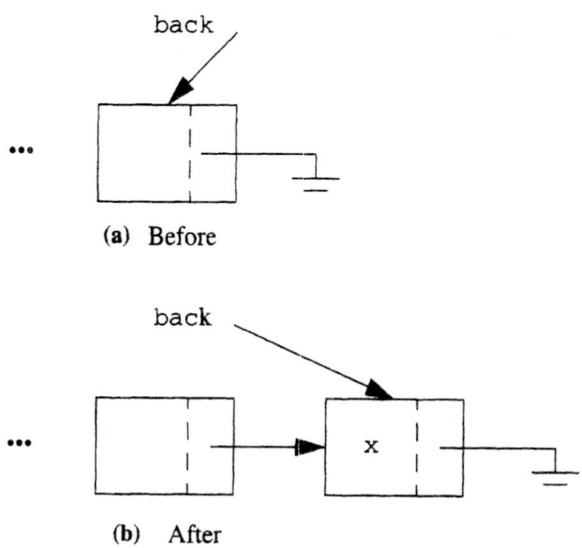

Figure 16.28 The `enqueue` operation for the linked list–based implementation.

```
// Return the least recently inserted item in the queue
// or throw UnderflowException if empty.
template <class Object>
const Object & Queue<Object>::getFront( ) const
{
    if( isEmpty( ) )
        throw UnderflowException( );
    return front->element;
}

// Make the queue logically empty.
template <class Object>
void Queue<Object>::makeEmpty( )
{
    while( !isEmpty( ) )
        dequeue( );
}
```

Figure 16.29 Supporting routines for the linked list–based `Queue` class.

The remaining member functions for the `Queue` class are identical to the corresponding `Stack` routines. They are shown in Figure 16.29.

16.3 Comparison of the Two Methods

The array versus linked list implementations represent a classic time-space trade-off.

Both the array and linked list versions run in constant time per operation. Thus they are so fast that they are unlikely to be the bottleneck of any algorithm and, in that regard, which version is used rarely matters.

The array versions of these data structures are likely to be faster than their linked list counterparts, especially if an accurate estimation of capacity is available. If an additional constructor is provided to specify the initial capacity (see Exercise 16.3) and the estimate is correct, no doubling is performed. Also, the sequential access provided by an array is typically faster than the potential nonsequential access offered by dynamic memory allocation.

The array implementation does have two drawbacks, however. First, for queues, the array implementation is arguably more complex than the linked list implementation, owing to the combined code for wraparound and array doubling. Our implementation of array doubling was not as efficient as possible (see Exercise 16.10), thus a faster implementation of the queue would require a few additional lines of code. Even the array implementation of the stack uses a few more lines of code than its linked list counterpart.

The second drawback is that, when doubling, we temporarily require three times as much space as the number of data items suggests. The reason is that, when the array is doubled, we need to have memory to store both the old and the new (double-sized) array. Further, at the queue's peak size, the array is between 50 percent and 100 percent full; on average it is 75 percent full, so for every three items in the array, one spot is empty. The wasted space is thus 33 percent on average and 100 percent when the table is only half full. As discussed earlier, the wasted space could be significant when compared to the linked list–based version that uses only an extra pointer per item.

In short, the array implementation is often preferable for small objects. The linked list implementation is preferable for large objects if space is scarce or if `Object` copies are so expensive that the cost of array doubling becomes significant. However, as stack and queue operations are performed in constant time, which implementation is used probably does not matter either.

16.4 The STL Stack and Queue Adapters

The STL provides `stack` and `queue` classes. These classes are adapters of the basic containers. That is, they use private inheritance to create a new class with a slightly different interface than the standard `list` container. These adapters are templates that require specification of both the type of object being stored in the container and the type of the container. (More details were presented in Section 7.6.2.)

In this section, we provide a simplified version, showing how the `stack` class template can be written from a `list` class template. The code is short and is shown in Figure 16.30.

16.5 Double-Ended Queues

A *double-ended queue (deque)* allows access at both ends. Much of its functionality can be derived from the Queue class.

We close this chapter with a discussion of the use of inheritance to derive a new data structure. A **double-ended queue (deque)** is like a queue, except that access is allowed at both ends. Exercise 15.14 describes an application of the deque. Rather than the terms `enqueue` and `dequeue`, the terms used are `addFront`, `addRear`, `removeFront`, and `removeRear`. Figure 16.31 shows the derived class `Deque`. We must derive it from the array-based version of `Queue` because deletion from the back of the list is not efficiently supported.

First, we automatically get sensible semantics for default construction and the Big Three. So we don't have to do anything there.

```
template <class Object>
class stack : private list<Object>      // Private inheritance
{
  public:
    int size( ) const
      { return list<Object>::size( ); }
    bool empty( ) const
      { return list<Object>::empty( ); }

    Object & top( )
      { return list<Object>::back( ); }
    const Object & top( ) const
      { return list<Object>::back( ); }
    void push( const Object & x )
      { push_back( x ); }
    void pop( )
      { pop_back( ); }
};
```

Figure 16.30 A simplified STL-style `stack` class, based on the STL `list` class.

Implementation of the deque is relatively simple with private inheritance.

The `enqueue` and `dequeue` routines become disabled for the `Deque` class by virtue of private inheritance. Methods such as `isEmpty`, `makeEmpty`, and `getFront` are written by partial overriding. The `addBack` and `removeFront` methods call the existing `enqueue` and `dequeue` routines. The only routines that need to be written are `addFront`, `removeBack`, and `getBack`. We leave this for you to do as Exercise 16.6.

The STL provides a `deque` class, but this class does not use private inheritance to extend the `queue` class. Instead, it is written as a class equivalent to `vector` (or `list`). Recall that the STL `stack` and `queue` adapters are templates that require specification of both the type of object being stored in the container and the type of the container. The STL `deque` can be used as the container type to instantiate `stack` and `queue`.

Summary

In this chapter we described implementation of the `Stack` and `Queue` classes. Both the `Stack` and `Queue` classes can be implemented by using a contiguous array or a linked list. In each case, all operations use constant time; thus all operations are fast.

```
// Double ended queue (Deque) class.
//
// CONSTRUCTION: with no parameters.
//
// ******************PUBLIC OPERATIONS*********************
// void addFront( Object x )--> Insert x at front
// void addBack( Object x ) --> Insert x at back
// void removeFront( )       --> Remove front item
// void removeBack( )        --> Remove back item
// Object getFront( )        --> Return front item
// Object getBack( )         --> Return back item
// bool isEmpty( )           --> Return true if empty
// void makeEmpty( )         --> Remove all items
// ******************ERRORS********************************
// UnderflowException thrown as needed.

template <class Object>
class Deque : private Queue<Object>
{
  public:
    void addFront( const Object & x );

    void addBack( const Object & x )
      { enqueue( x ); }

    void removeFront( )
      { dequeue( ); }

    void removeBack( );

    const Object & getBack( ) const;

    const Object & getFront( ) const
      { return Queue<Object>::getFront( ); }

    bool isEmpty( ) const
      { return Queue<Object>::isEmpty( ); }
    void makeEmpty( )
      { Queue<Object>::makeEmpty( ); }
};
```

Figure 16.31 Double-ended queue class `Deque` derived from the array-based `Queue` class.

Objects of the Game

circular array implementation The use of wraparound to implement a queue. (p. 543)

double-ended queue (deque) A queue that allows access at both ends. Much of its functionality can be derived from the queue class. (p. 558)

wraparound Occurs when `front` or `back` returns to the beginning of the array when it reaches the end. (p. 543)

Common Errors

1. Using an implementation that does not provide constant time access is a bad error. There is no justification for this inefficiency.
2. In the linked list implementation of the `Stack` class we must save a pointer to the front node prior to adjusting the top of the stack; otherwise, the `delete` does not work. A common error is to `delete` the top node directly and then adjust the top of the stack. This generally appears to work because the deleted node's contents are not immediately overwritten (so the `next` member still points at the new top of stack), but it is unsafe programming.
3. For all these routines, memory leaks are common programming errors.
4. Shallow copies can result in errors.
5. Not all compilers support nested class templates. You may need to rewrite the linked list–based `Stack` and `Queue` classes without nested classes to avoid this limitation.

On the Internet

The files listed are available.

StackAr.h	Contains the interface for an array-based stack.
StackAr.cpp	Contains the implementation of an array-based stack.
TestStackAr.cpp	Contains a test program for an array-based stack.
StackLi.h	Contains the interface for a linked list–based stack.
StackLi.cpp	Contains the implementation of a linked list–based stack.
TestStackLi.cpp	Contains a test program for a linked list–based stack.

QueueAr.h	Contains the interface for an array-based queue.
QueueAr.cpp	Contains the implementation of an array-based queue.
TestQueueAr.cpp	Contains a test program for an array-based queue.
QueueLi.h	Contains the interface for a linked list–based queue.
QueueLi.cpp	Contains the implementation of a linked list–based queue.
TestQueueLi.cpp	Contains a test program for a linked list–based queue.
stack.h	Contains the implementation of an STL-like stack.

Exercises

In Short

16.1. In each of the four implementations, what happens if the alias test in `operator=` is omitted?

16.2. Draw the stack and queue data structures (for both the array and linked list implementations) for each step in the following sequence: *add*(1), *add*(2), *remove*, *add*(3), *add*(4), *remove*, *remove*, *add*(5). Assume an initial size of 3 for the array implementation.

In Practice

16.3. Add constructors to the array-based `Stack` and `Queue` classes that allow the user to specify an initial capacity.

16.4. Compare the running times for the array and linked list versions of the `Stack` class. Use `int` objects.

16.5. Write a `main` that declares and uses a stack of `int` and a stack of `double` simultaneously.

16.6. Complete the implementation of the `Deque` class.

16.7. Implement `operator=` for the array-based queue to copy the elements in `rhs` to the same array positions. Do not do more copies than are necessary.

16.8. Implement the array-based `Stack` class with a primitive array. What are the advantages and disadvantages of this approach?

16.9. Implement the array-based `Queue` class with a primitive array. What are the advantages and disadvantages of this approach?

16.10. For the queue implementation presented in Section 16.1.2, show how to rearrange the queue elements in the `doubleQueue` operation so that at most half the elements move.

Programming Projects

16.11. Implement the linked list–based `Queue` class by private inheritance from the linked list–based `Stack` class. Make appropriate choices of members to be made protected.

16.12. An output-restricted double-ended queue supports insertions from both ends but accesses and deletions only from the front.

a. Use inheritance to derive this new class from the `Queue` class.
b. Use inheritance to derive this new class from the `Deque` class.

16.13. Suppose that you want to add the `findMin` (but not `deleteMin`) operation to the `Stack` repertoire.

a. Use inheritance to derive the new class and implement `findMin` as a sequential scan of the stack items.
b. Do not use inheritance but instead implement the new class as two stacks, as described in Exercise 7.5.

16.14. Suppose that you want to add the `findMin` (but not `deleteMin`) operation to the `Deque` repertoire.

a. Use inheritance to derive the new class and implement `findMin` as a sequential scan of the `Deque` items. As in Exercise 16.11, make appropriate choices of members to be made protected.
b. Do not use inheritance but instead implement the new class as four stacks. If a deletion empties a stack, you will need to reorganize the remaining items evenly.

Chapter 17

Linked Lists

In Chapter 16 we demonstrated that linked lists can be used to store items noncontiguously. The linked lists used in that chapter were simplified, with all the accesses performed at one of the list's two ends.

In this chapter, we show:

- how to allow access to any item by using a general linked list,
- the general algorithms for the linked list operations,
- how the iterator class provides a safe mechanism for traversing and accessing linked lists,
- list variations, such as doubly linked lists and circularly linked lists,
- how to use inheritance to derive a sorted linked list class, and
- how to implement the STL `list` class.

17.1 Basic Ideas

In this chapter we implement the linked list and allow general access (arbitrary insertion, deletion, and find operations) through the list. The basic linked list consists of a collection of connected, dynamically allocated nodes. In a **singly linked list,** each node consists of the data element and a pointer to the next node in the list. The last node in the list has a `NULL next` pointer. In this section we assume that the node is given by the following type declaration:

```
struct Node
{
    Object element;
    Node   *next;
};
```

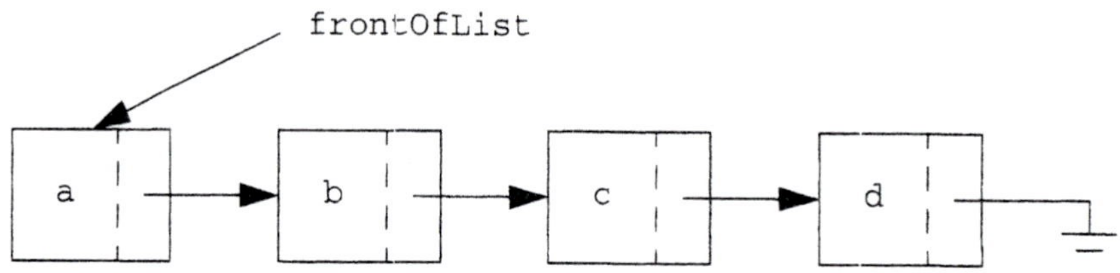

Figure 17.1 Basic linked list.

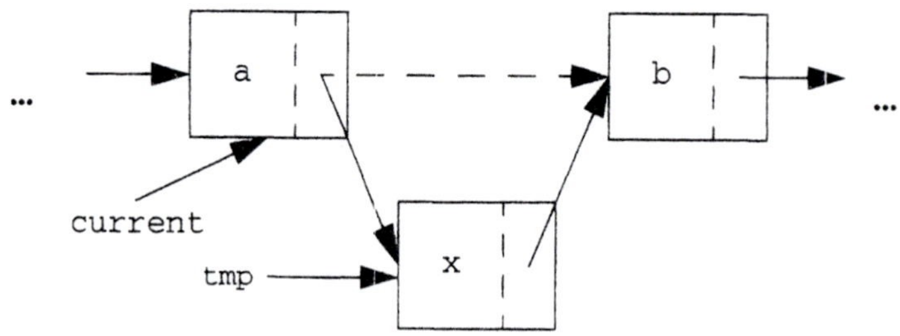

Figure 17.2 Insertion in a linked list: Create new node (`tmp`), copy in `x`, set `tmp`'s next pointer, and set `current`'s next pointer.

When we write code later in the chapter, `Node` has a different name and is a template.

The first node in the linked list is accessible by a pointer, as shown in Figure 17.1. We can print or search in the linked list by starting at the first item and following the chain of `next` pointers. The two basic operations that must be performed are insertion and deletion of an arbitrary item `x`.

Insertion consists of splicing a node into the list and can be accomplished with one statement.

For insertion we must define where the insertion is to take place. If we have a pointer to some node in the list, the easiest place to insert is immediately after that item.[1] As an example, Figure 17.2 shows how we insert `x` after item `a` in a linked list. We must perform the following steps:

```
tmp = new Node;                // Get a new node from the system
tmp->element = x;              // Place x in the element member
tmp->next = current->next;  // x's next node is b
current->next = tmp;           // a's next node is x
```

As a result of these statements, the old list ... `a`, `b`, ... now appears as ... `a`, `x`, `b`, ... We can simplify the code if the `Node` has a constructor that initializes the data members directly. In that case, we obtain

1. This is not what the STL does. In the STL, `insert` comes before a specified point in the list.

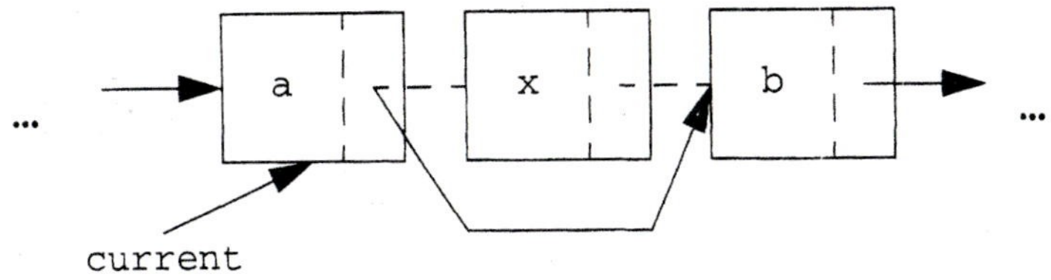

Figure 17.3 Deletion from a linked list.

```
tmp = new Node( x, current->next ); // Get new node
current->next = tmp;                // a's next node is x
```

We now see that `tmp` is no longer necessary. Thus we have the one-liner

```
current->next = new Node( x, current->next );
```

Removal can be accomplished by bypassing the node. We need a pointer to the node prior to the one we want to remove.

The remove command can be executed in one pointer move. Figure 17.3 shows that to remove item `x` from the linked list, we set `current` to be the node prior to `x` and then have `current`'s `next` pointer bypass `x`. This operation is expressed by the statement

```
current->next = current->next->next;
```

The list ... `a, x, b,` ... now appears as ... `a, b,` ... .

To avoid leaking, we save a pointer to the node before bypassing it; then we call `delete`.

A problem with this implementation is that it leaks memory: The node storing `x` is still allocated but is now unreferenced. By saving a pointer to it first and then calling `delete` after the bypass, we can reclaim the memory:

```
Node *deletedNode = current->next;      // Save pointer
current->next = current->next->next;    // Bypass the node
delete deletedNode;                     // Free the memory
```

Linked list operations use only a constant number of data movements.

The preceding discussion summarizes the basics of inserting and removing items at arbitrary places in a linked list. The fundamental property of a linked list is that changes to it can be made by using only a constant number of data movements, which is a great improvement over an array implementation. Maintaining contiguousness in an array means that whenever an item is added or deleted, all items that follow it in the list must move.

17.1.1 Header Nodes

There is one problem with the basic description: It assumes that whenever an item `x` is removed, some previous item is always present to allow a bypass. Consequently, removal of the first item in the linked list becomes a special

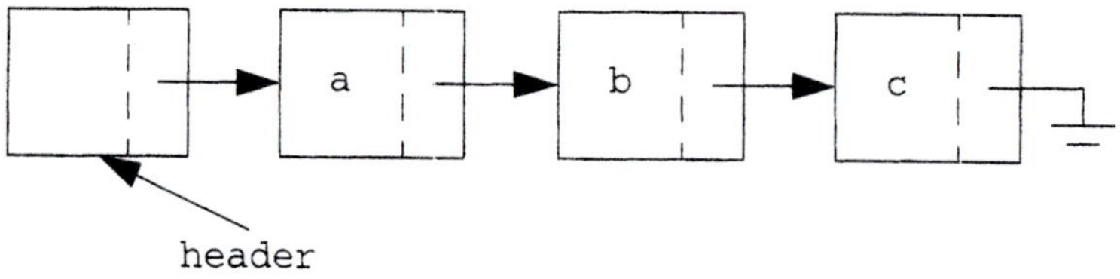

Figure 17.4 Using a header node for the linked list.

case. Similarly, the insert routine does not allow us to insert an item to be the new first element in the list. The reason is that insertions must follow some existing item. So, although the basic algorithm works fine, some annoying special cases must be dealt with.

Special cases are always problematic in algorithm design and frequently lead to bugs in the code. Consequently, writing code that avoids special cases is generally preferable. One way to do that is to introduce a header node.

A *header node* holds no data but serves to satisfy the requirement that every node have a previous node. A header node allows us to avoid special cases such as insertion of a new first element and removal of the first element.

A **header node** is an extra node in a linked list that holds no data but serves to satisfy the requirement that every node containing an item have a previous node in the list. The header node for the list `a`, `b`, `c` is shown in Figure 17.4. Note that `a` is no longer a special case. It can be deleted just like any other node by having `current` point at the node before it. We can also add a new first element to the list by setting `current` equal to the header node and calling the insertion routine. By using the header node, we greatly simplify the code—with a negligible space penalty. In more complex applications, header nodes not only simplify the code but also improve speed because, after all, fewer tests mean less time.

The use of a header node is somewhat controversial. Some argue that avoiding special cases is not sufficient justification for adding fictitious cells; they view the use of header nodes as little more than old-style hacking. Even so, we use them here precisely because they allow us to demonstrate the basic pointer manipulations without obscuring the code with special cases. Whether a header should be used is a matter of personal preference. Furthermore, in a class implementation, its use would be completely transparent to the user. However, we must be careful: The printing routine must skip over the header node, as must all searching routines. Moving to the front now means setting the current position to `header->next`, and so on. Furthermore, as Figure 17.5 shows, with a dummy header node, a list is empty if `header->next` is `NULL`.

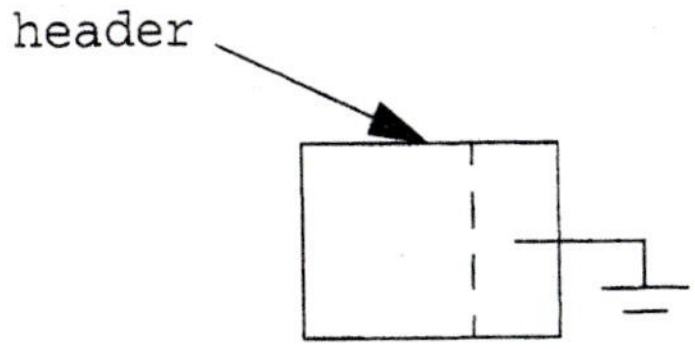

Figure 17.5 Empty list when a header node is used.

17.1.2 Iterator Classes

By storing a current pointer in a list class, we ensure that access is controlled.

The typical primitive strategy identifies a linked list by a pointer to the header node. Each individual item in the list can then be accessed by providing a pointer to the node that stores it. The problem with that strategy is that checking for errors is difficult. For example, a user could pass a pointer to something that is a node in a different list. One way to guarantee that this cannot happen is to store a current position as part of a list class. To do so, we add a second data member, `current`. Then, as all access to the list goes through the class member functions, we can be certain that `current` always represents a pointer to a node in the list, a pointer to the header node, or `NULL`.

An *iterator class* maintains a current position and typically is a friend of a list (or other container) class.

This scheme has a problem: With only one position, the case of two iterators needing to access the list independently is left unsupported. One way to avoid this problem is to define a separate **iterator class,** which maintains a notion of its current position. A list class would then not maintain any notion of a current position and would only have member functions that treat the list as a unit, such as `isEmpty`, `makeEmpty`, and `operator=`, or that accept an iterator as a parameter, such as `insert`. Routines that depend only on an iterator itself, such as the `advance` routine that advances the iterator to the next position, would reside in the iterator class. Access to the list is granted by making the iterator class a friend of the list class. We can view each instance of an iterator class as one in which only legal list operations, such as advancing in the list, are allowed.

In Section 17.2 we define a list class `LList` and an iterator class `LListItr`. To show how this works, let us look at a nonmember function that returns the size of a linked list, as shown in Figure 17.6. We declare `itr` as an iterator that can access the linked list `theList`.

We initialize `itr` to the first element in `theList` (skipping over the header, of course) by copying the iterator given by `theList.first()`.

The test `itr.isValid()` attempts to mimic the test `p!=NULL` that would be conducted if `p` were a normal pointer. Finally, the expression `itr.advance()` mimics the conventional idiom `p=p->next`.

```
// In this routine, LList and LListItr are the
// list and iterator class written in Section 17.2.
template <class Object>
int listSize( const LList<Object> & theList )
{
    LListItr<Object> itr;

    int size = 0;
    for( itr = theList.first( ); itr.isValid( ); itr.advance( ) )
        size++;
    return size;
}
```

Figure 17.6 A nonmember function that returns the size of a list.

Thus, so long as the iterator class defines a few simple operations, we can iterate over the list naturally. In Section 17.2 we provide its implementation in C++. The routines are surprisingly simple, although the templated syntax can be tedious in places.

There is a natural parallel between the methods defined in the `LList` and `LListItr` classes and those in the STL `list` class. For instance, the `LListItr advance` method is roughly equivalent to `operator++` in the STL `list` class's iterators. The list class in Section 17.2 is simpler than the STL `list` class; as such it illustrates many basic points and is worth examining. In Section 17.5 we implement most of the STL `list` class.

17.2 C++ Implementation

As suggested in the preceding description, a list is implemented as three separate classes: one class is the list itself (`LList`), another represents the node (`LListNode`), and the third represents the position (`LListItr`).

Figure 17.7 contains the code for the node class, `LListNode`, which consists of two data members: the stored element and the link to the next node. The only methods are the constructors. Note that the data members of `LListNode` are private. However, `LList` and `LListItr` need access to these data members. To allow that, `LListNode` declares that the `LList` and `LListItr` classes are *friends*. Recall from Section 2.3.4 that a friend of a class is granted access to the class's private section. Here we make entire classes friends of other classes. This access is one-way: `LList` and `LListItr` can see internal `LListNode` details but not vice versa. Note that template instantiations are required.

```
template <class Object>
class LList;       // Incomplete declaration.

template <class Object>
class LListItr;   // Incomplete declaration.

template <class Object>
class LListNode
{
      LListNode( const Object & theElement = Object( ),
                 LListNode * n = NULL )
        : element( theElement ), next( n ) { }

      Object     element;
      LListNode *next;

      friend class LList<Object>;
      friend class LListItr<Object>;
};
```

Figure 17.7 Type declaration of the linked list node `LListNode`.

An *incomplete class declaration* is used to inform the compiler of the existence of another class.

The `friend` declaration requires additional syntax baggage. The `LList` and `LListItr` class templates have not been declared yet, so the compiler is likely to be confused by the template expansions `LList<Object>` and `LListItr<Object>`. To circumvent this problem, we provide an **incomplete class declaration** prior to the `LListNode` definition, telling the compiler that the class templates exist and that details will be provided later. That is enough for the compiler to understand what the `friend` declarations mean.

Next, Figure 17.8 presents the class that implements the concept of position—namely, `LListItr`. The class stores a pointer to a `LListNode`, representing the current position of the iterator. The `isValid` function returns `true` if the position is not past the end of the list, `retrieve` returns the element stored in the current position, and `advance` advances the current position to the next position. The constructor for `LListItr` requires a pointer to a node that is to be the current node. Note that this constructor is private and thus cannot be used by client methods. Instead, the general idea is that the `LList` class returns preconstructed `LListItr` objects, as appropriate; `LList` is a friend of the class, so the privacy of the `LListItr` constructor is not applicable to `LList`.

The existence of one constructor removes the default zero-parameter constructor. This makes it impossible to have a vector of iterators, and introduces a complication for classes that would store an iterator as a data member. Thus we also provide a zero-parameter constructor for `LListItr`, but

```
// LListItr class; maintains "current position".
//
// CONSTRUCTION: With no parameters. The LList class may
//      construct a LListItr with a pointer to a LListNode.
//
// ******************PUBLIC OPERATIONS*********************
// bool isValid( )         --> True if not NULL
// void advance( )         --> Advance (if not already NULL)
// Object retrieve( )      --> Return item in current position
// ******************ERRORS********************************
// Throws BadIterator for illegal retrieve.

template <class Object>
class LListItr
{
  public:
    LListItr( ) : current( NULL ) { }

    bool isValid( ) const
      { return current != NULL; }

    void advance( )
      { if( isValid( ) ) current = current->next; }

    const Object & retrieve( ) const
      { if( !isValid( ) ) throw BadIterator( );
        return current->element; }

  private:
    LListNode<Object> *current;   // Current position

    LListItr( LListNode<Object> *theNode )
      : current( theNode ) { }

    friend class LList<Object>;   // Grant access to constructor
};
```

Figure 17.8 The `LListItr` class.

its use is generally a matter of convenience. Because all the methods of the `LListItr` class are basically trivial, we take the unusual step of implementing them inline.

The `LList` class interface is shown in Figure 17.9. The single data member is a pointer to the header node allocated by the constructor. `isEmpty` is an easily implemented short one-liner. The methods `zeroth` and `first` return iterators corresponding to the header and first element, respectively, as shown in Figure 17.10. Other routines either search the list for some item or change the list via insertion or deletion, and are shown later.

```
// LList class.
//
// CONSTRUCTION: with no initializer.
// Access is via LListItr class.
//
// ******************PUBLIC OPERATIONS*********************
// bool isEmpty( )          --> Return true if empty; else false
// void makeEmpty( )        --> Remove all items
// LListItr zeroth( )       --> Return position to prior to first
// LListItr first( )        --> Return first position
// void insert( x, p )      --> Insert x after position p
// void remove( x )         --> Remove x
// LListItr find( x )       --> Return position that views x
// LListItr findPrevious( x )
//                          --> Return position prior to x
// ******************ERRORS********************************
// No special errors.

template <class Object>
class LList
{
  public:
    LList( );
    LList( const LList & rhs );
    ~LList( );

    bool isEmpty( ) const;
    void makeEmpty( );
    LListItr<Object> zeroth( ) const;
    LListItr<Object> first( ) const;
    void insert( const Object & x, const LListItr<Object> & p );
    LListItr<Object> find( const Object & x ) const;
    LListItr<Object> findPrevious( const Object & x ) const;
    void remove( const Object & x );

    const LList & operator=( const LList & rhs );

  private:
    LListNode<Object> *header;
};
```

Figure 17.9 The `LList` class interface.

Figure 17.11 illustrates how the `LList` and `LListItr` classes interact. The `printList` method outputs the contents of a list. This function uses only public methods and a typical iteration sequence of obtaining a starting point (via `first`), testing that it has not gone past the ending point (via `isValid`), and advancing in each iteration (via `advance`).

```
// Construct the list.
template <class Object>
LList<Object>::LList( )
{
    header = new LListNode<Object>;
}

// Test if the list is logically empty.
// Return true if empty, false, otherwise.
template <class Object>
bool LList<Object>::isEmpty( ) const
{
    return header->next == NULL;
}

// Return an iterator representing the header node.
template <class Object>
LListItr<Object> LList<Object>::zeroth( ) const
{
    return LListItr<Object>( header );
}

// Return an iterator representing the first node in the list.
// This operation is valid for empty lists.
template <class Object>
LListItr<Object> LList<Object>::first( ) const
{
    return LListItr<Object>( header->next );
}
```

Figure 17.10 Some `LList` class one-liners.

Let us revisit the issue of whether all three classes are necessary. For instance, couldn't we just have the `LList` class maintain a notion of a current position? Although this option is feasible and works for many applications, using a separate iterator class expresses the abstraction that the position and list actually are separate objects. Moreover, it allows for a list to be accessed in several places simultaneously. For instance to remove a sublist from a list, we can easily add a `remove` operation to the list class that uses two iterators to specify the starting and ending points of the sublist to be removed. Without the iterator class this action would be more difficult to express.

Short-circuiting is used in the `find` routine at line 8 and in the similar part of the `remove` routine.

We can now implement the remaining `LList` methods. First is `find`, shown in Figure 17.12, which returns the position in the list of some element. Line 8 takes advantage of the fact that the *and* (`&&`) operation is short-circuited: If the first half of the *and* is false, the result is automatically false and the second half is not evaluated.

```
// Simple print function.
template <class Object>
void printList( const LList<Object> & theList )
{
    if( theList.isEmpty( ) )
        cout << "Empty list" << endl;
    else
    {
        LListItr<Object> itr = theList.first( );
        for( ; itr.isValid( ); itr.advance( ) )
            cout << itr.retrieve( ) << " ";
    }
    cout << endl;
}
```

Figure 17.11 The function for printing the contents of a `LList`.

```
// Return iterator corresponding to the first node matching x.
// Iterator is not valid if item is not found.
template <class Object>
LListItr<Object> LList<Object>::find( const Object & x ) const
{
    LListNode<Object> *p = header->next;

    while( p != NULL && p->element != x )
        p = p->next;

    return LListItr<Object>( p );
}
```

Figure 17.12 The `find` routine for the `LList` class.

This code is not foolproof: There may be two iterators, and one can be left dangling if the other removes a node.

Our next routine removes some element x from the list. We need to decide what to do if x occurs more than once or not at all. Our routine removes the first occurrence of x and does nothing if x is not in the list. To make that happen, we find p, which is the cell prior to the one containing x, via a call to `findPrevious`. The code for implementing the `remove` routine is shown in Figure 17.13. This code is not foolproof: There may be two iterators, and one can be left dangling if the other removes a node. The `findPrevious` routine is similar to the `find` routine and is shown in Figure 17.14.

The `insert` routine takes constant time.

The last routine we write here is an insertion routine. We pass an element to be inserted and a position p. This particular insertion routine inserts an element after position p, as shown in Figure 17.15. Note that the `insert` routine makes no use of the list it is in; it depends only on p. The STL `list`

```
// Remove the first occurrence of an item x.
template <class Object>
void LList<Object>::remove( const Object & x )
{
    LListNode<Object> *p = findPrevious( x ).current;

    if( p->next != NULL )
    {
        LListNode<Object> *oldNode = p->next;
        p->next = p->next->next; // Bypass
        delete oldNode;
    }
}
```

Figure 17.13 The `remove` routine for the `LList` class.

```
// Return iterator prior to the first node containing item x.
template <class Object>
LListItr<Object>
LList<Object>::findPrevious( const Object & x ) const
{
    LListNode<Object> *p = header;

    while( p->next != NULL && p->next->element != x )
        p = p->next;

    return LListItr<Object>( p );
}
```

Figure 17.14 The `findPrevious` routine—similar to the `find` routine—for use with `remove`.

```
// Insert item x after p.
template <class Object>
void LList<Object>::
insert( const Object & x, const LListItr<Object> & p )
{
    if( p.current != NULL )
        p.current->next = new LListNode<Object>( x,
                                                 p.current->next );
}
```

Figure 17.15 The insertion routine for the `LList` class.

class also makes no use of the list it is in. However, in the `list` class that we write in Section 17.5 we add tests to ensure that the iterator corresponds to the list. We do so by logically adding a reference to the list as an extra data member for the list iterator.

With the exception of the `find` and `findPrevious` routines (and `remove`, which calls `findPrevious`), all the operations that we have coded so far take $O(1)$ time. The `find` and `findPrevious` routines take $O(N)$ time in the worst case because the entire list might need to be traversed if the element either is not found or is last in the list. On average the running time is $O(N)$ because on average half the list must be traversed.

The `find` and `findPrevious` routines take $O(N)$ time.

Because the insertion routines consistently allocate `LListNode` objects, via calls to `new`, these objects must be reclaimed when they are no longer referenced; otherwise, we have a memory leak. We reclaim them by calling `delete`. We must do so in several places: in the `remove` method (which removes 1 node), the `makeEmpty` method (which removes N nodes), and the destructor (which removes $N + 1$ nodes, including the header node).

Figure 17.13 illustrates the general mechanism. We save a pointer to the node that is about to be unreferenced. After the pointer manipulations bypass the node, we can then call `delete`. The order is important: Once a node has been subjected to a `delete`, its contents are *unstable*, which means that the node may be used to satisfy a future `new` request. In the code shown in Figure 17.13, moving the `delete` statement up one line will probably not have any adverse affects, depending on how the compiler chooses to do things—nonetheless, it is incorrect. In fact, this action leads to the worst kind of bug: one that might only occasionally give incorrect behavior.

After the pointer manipulations bypass the node, we can then call `delete`. The order is important because once a node has been subjected to a `delete`, its contents are unstable, meaning that the node may be used to satisfy a future `new` request.

The `makeEmpty` routine, which must remove N nodes, and the destructor, which must remove $N + 1$ nodes seem to be more complicated. However, as memory reclamation is often tricky (and tends to lead to a large percentage of errors), you should avoid using `delete` as much as possible. For `makeEmpty`, we can do so by repeatedly calling `remove` on the first element (until the list is empty). Thus `remove` automatically handles memory reclamation. For the destructor, we can call `makeEmpty` and then call `delete` for the header node. Both routines are shown in Figure 17.16.

In Section 2.2.4, we stated that, if the default destructor is unacceptable, the copy assignment operator (`operator=`) and copy constructor are likely to be unacceptable. For `operator=`, we can give a simple implementation in terms of public list methods, as shown in Figure 17.17. This code contains the usual aliasing test and return of `*this`. Prior to copying, we make the current list empty to avoid leaking memory previously allocated for the list. With an empty list, we create the first node and then go down the `rhs` list, appending new `LListNodes` to the end of the target list.

The copy assignment operator for a linked list can be implemented by using two iterators.

```
// Make the list logically empty.
template <class Object>
void LList<Object>::makeEmpty( )
{
    while( !isEmpty( ) )
        remove( first( ).retrieve( ) );
}

// Destructor.
template <class Object>
LList<Object>::~LList( )
{
    makeEmpty( );
    delete header;
}
```

Figure 17.16 The `makeEmpty` method and the `LList` destructor.

```
// Copy constructor.
template <class Object>
LList<Object>::LList( const LList<Object> & rhs )
{
    header = new LListNode<Object>;
    *this = rhs;
}

// Deep copy of linked lists.
template <class Object>
const LList<Object> &
LList<Object>::operator=( const LList<Object> & rhs )
{
    if( this != &rhs )
    {
        makeEmpty( );

        LListItr<Object> ritr = rhs.first( );
        LListItr<Object> itr = zeroth( );
        for( ; ritr.isValid( ); ritr.advance( ), itr.advance( ) )
            insert( ritr.retrieve( ), itr );
    }
    return *this;
}
```

Figure 17.17 Two `LList` copy routines: `operator=` and copy constructor.

For the copy constructor, we can create an empty list by calling `new` to allocate a header node and then using `operator=` to copy `rhs`, as shown in Figure 17.17. A commonly used technique is to make the copy constructor private, with the intention of having the compiler generate an error message when a `LList` is passed by using call by value (instead of a constant reference).

We certainly could have added more operations, but this basic set is quite powerful. Some operations, such as `retreat`, are not efficiently supported by this version of the linked list; variations on the linked list that allow constant-time implementation of that and other operators are discussed later in this chapter.

The `retreat` method is not efficiently supported. A doubly linked list is used if that is a liability.

17.3 Doubly Linked Lists and Circularly Linked Lists

As we mentioned in Section 17.2, the singly linked list does not efficiently support some important operations. For instance, although it is easy to go to the front of the list, it is time consuming to go to the end. Although we can easily advance via `advance`, implementing `retreat` cannot be done efficiently with only a `next` pointer. In some applications that might be crucial. For instance, when designing a text editor, we can maintain the internal image of the file as a linked list of lines. We want to be able to move up just as easily as down in the list, to insert both before and after a line rather than just after, and to be able to get to the last line quickly. A moment's thought suggests that to implement this procedure efficiently we should have each node maintain two pointers: one to the next node in the list and one to the previous node. Then, to make everything symmetric, we should have not only a header but also a tail. A linked list that allows bidirectional traversal by storing two pointers per node is called a **doubly linked list.** Figure 17.18 shows the doubly linked list representing `a` and `b`. Each node now has two pointers (`next` and `prev`), and searching and moving can easily be performed in both directions. Obviously, there are some important changes from the singly linked list.

A *doubly linked list* allows bidirectional traversal by storing two pointers per node.

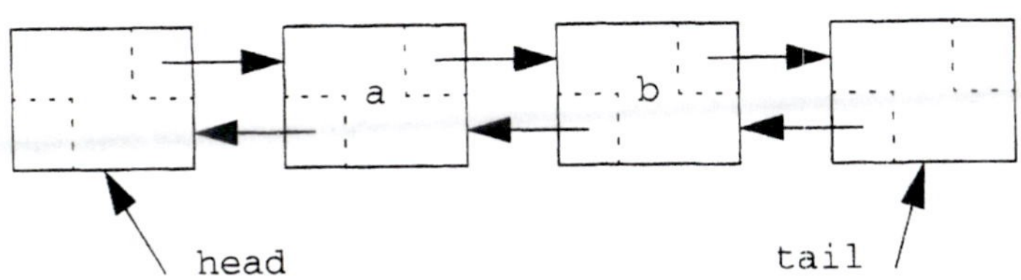

Figure 17.18 A doubly linked list.

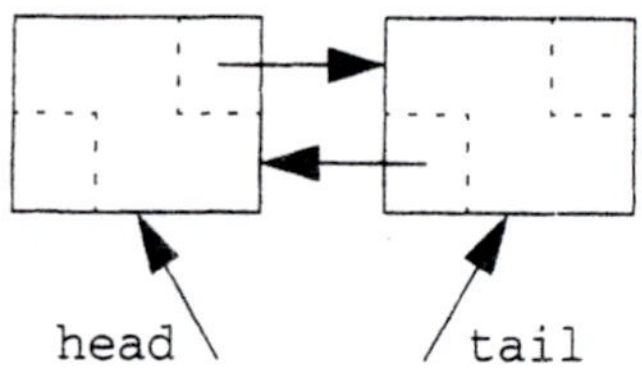

Figure 17.19 An empty doubly linked list.

Symmetry demands that we use both a `head` and a `tail` and that we support roughly twice as many operations.

First, an empty list now consists of a `head` and `tail`, connected as shown in Figure 17.19. Note that `head->prev` and `tail->next` are not needed in the algorithms and are not even initialized. The test for emptiness is now

```
head->next == tail
```

or

```
tail->prev == head
```

When we advance past the end of the list, we now hit the `tail` node instead of `NULL`.

We no longer use `NULL` to decide whether an advance has taken us past the end of the list. Instead, we have gone past the end if `current` is either `head` or `tail` (recall that we can go in either direction). The `retreat` operation can be implemented by

```
current = current->prev;
```

Insertion and removal involve twice as many pointer changes as for a singly linked list.

Before describing some of the additional operations that are available, let us consider how the insertion and removal operations change. Naturally, we can now do both `insertBefore` and `insertAfter`. Twice as many pointer moves are involved for `insertAfter` with doubly linked lists as with singly linked lists. If we write each statement explicitly, we obtain

```
newNode = new Node( x );
newNode->prev = current;               // Set x's prev pointer
newNode->next = current->next;         // Set x's next pointer
newNode->prev->next = newNode;         // Set a's next pointer
newNode->next->prev = newNode;         // Set b's prev pointer
current = newNode;
```

As we showed earlier, the first two pointer moves can be collapsed into the `Node` construction that is done by `new`. The changes (in order *1*, *2*, *3*, *4*) are illustrated in Figure 17.20.

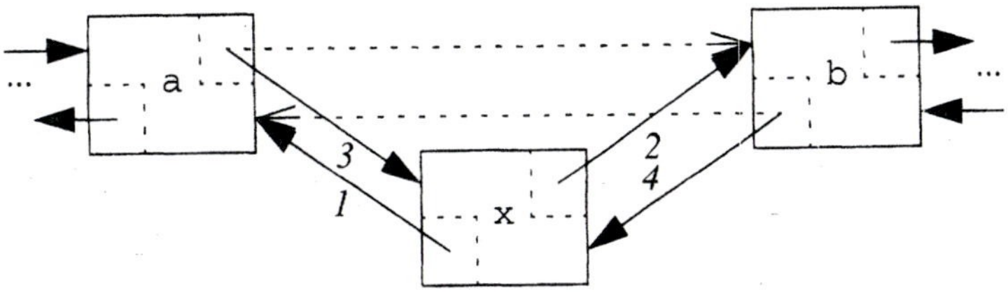

Figure 17.20 Insertion in a doubly linked list by getting new node and then changing pointers in the order indicated.

The `remove` operation can proceed from the current node because we can obtain the previous node instantly.

Figure 17.20 can also be used as a guide in the removal algorithm. Unlike the singly linked list, we can remove the current node because the previous node is available to us automatically. Thus to `remove x` we have to change `a`'s `next` pointer and `b`'s `prev` pointer. The basic moves are

```
oldNode = current;
oldNode->prev->next = oldNode->next;// Set a's next pointer
oldNode->next->prev = oldNode->prev;// Set b's prev pointer
delete oldNode;
current = head;                     // So current is not stale
```

To do a complete doubly linked list implementation, we need to decide which operations to support. We can reasonably expect twice as many operations as in the singly linked list. Each individual procedure is similar to the linked list routines; only the dynamic operations involve additional pointer moves. Moreover, for many of the routines, the code is dominated by error checks. Although some of the checks will change (e.g., we do not test against `NULL`), they certainly do not become any more complex. In Section 17.5, we use a doubly linked list to implement the STL list class, along with its associated iterators. There are lots of routines, but most are short.

In a *circularly linked list*, the last cell's `next` pointer points to `first`. This action is useful when wraparound matters.

A popular convention is to create a **circularly linked list,** in which the last cell's `next` pointer points back to `first`, which can be done with or without a header. Typically, it is done without a header because the header's main purpose is to ensure that every node has a previous node, which is already true for a nonempty circularly linked list. Without a header, we have only the empty list as a special case. We maintain a pointer to the first node, but that is not the same as a header node. We can use circularly linked lists and doubly linked lists simultaneously, as shown in Figure 17.21. The circular list is useful when we want searching to allow wraparound, as is the case for some text editors. In Exercise 17.20 you are asked to implement a circularly and doubly linked list.

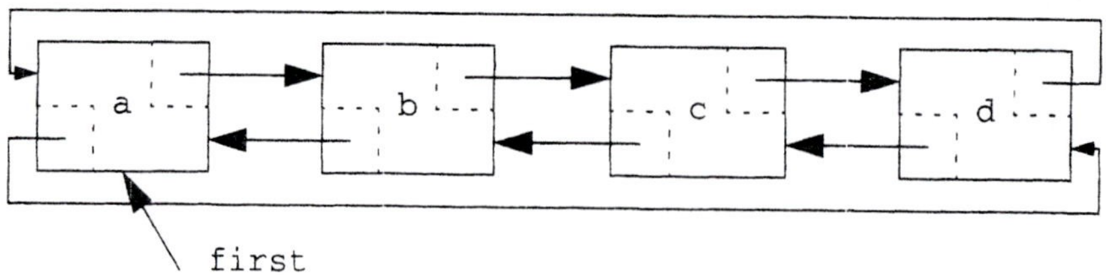

Figure 17.21 A circularly and doubly linked list.

17.4 Sorted Linked Lists

We can maintain items in sorted order by deriving a `SortedLList` class from `LList`.

Sometimes we want to keep the items in a linked list in sorted order, which we can do with a **sorted linked list.** The fundamental difference between a sorted linked list and an unsorted linked list is the insertion routine. Indeed, we can obtain a sorted list class by simply altering the insertion routine from our already written list class. Because the `insert` routine is part of the `LList` class, we should be able to base a new derived class, `SortedLList`, on `LList`. We can, and it is shown in Figure 17.22.

The new class has two versions of `insert`. One version takes a position and then ignores it; the insertion point is determined solely by the sorted order. The other version of `insert` requires more code.

The one-parameter `insert` uses two `LListItr` objects to traverse down the corresponding list until the correct insertion point is found. At that point we can apply the base class `insert` routine.

The `insert` method should be declared virtual in the base class.

For this approach to work correctly in all instances, the base class `insert` method should be declared `virtual`, so that if we access a `SortedLList` object through a `LList` pointer, we get the correct `insert`. Without the `virtual` declaration, we do not. The online code makes `insert virtual`.

17.5 Implementing the STL `list` Class

In this section we implement the STL `list` class discussed in Section 7.6. Although we present lots of code, we described most of the techniques earlier in this chapter.

Our code already takes up many pages, so to save some space we do not show all the include directives and we occasionally skimp on the commenting.

As we indicated previously, we need a class to store the basic list node, a class for the iterator, and a class for the list itself. The STL provides two types of iterators: the `const_iterator` and `iterator`, so we will have two iterator classes and a grand total of four classes. As we will see, `const_iterator` and `iterator` are `typedefs` representing the two iterator class templates.

```
// SortedLList class.
//
// CONSTRUCTION: with no initializer.
// Access is via LListItr class.
//
// ******************PUBLIC OPERATIONS*********************
// void insert( x )         --> Insert x in sorted order
// void insert( x, p )      --> Insert x in sorted order; ignore p
// All other LList operations
// ******************ERRORS*********************************
// No special errors.

template <class Object>
class SortedLList : public LList<Object>
{
  public:
    void insert( const Object & x );
    void insert( const Object & x, const LListItr<Object> & p )
      { insert( x ); }
};

// Insert item x into the list.
template <class Object>
void SortedLList<Object>::insert( const Object & x )
{
    LListItr<Object> prev = zeroth( );
    LListItr<Object> curr = first( );
    while( curr.isValid( ) && curr.retrieve( ) < x )
    {
        prev.advance( );
        curr.advance( );
    }
    LList<Object>::insert( x, prev );
}
```

Figure 17.22 The `SortedLList` class, in which insertions are restricted to sorted order.

We used the same technique in the `vector` implementation shown in Figure 7.10. Because the iterators are bidirectional, we need a doubly linked list. Finally, our implementation is safer than the STL's in that the use of bad iterators (e.g., advancing past the endmarker) causes an exception to be thrown.

The four classes are `list`, `ListItr`, `ConstListItr`, and `ListNode`. We begin by discussing `ListNode`, then look at `list`, and finally look at the two iterator classes.

```
// Incomplete class declarations for
// the const_iterator, iterator, and list,
// because all these classes refer to each other.
template <class Object>
class ConstListItr;

template <class Object>
class ListItr;

template <class Object>
class list;

// The basic doubly linked list node.
// Everything is private, and is accessible
// only by the iterators and list classes.
template <class Object>
class ListNode
{
    Object    data;
    ListNode *prev;
    ListNode *next;

    ListNode( const Object & d = Object( ),
              ListNode * p = NULL, ListNode * n = NULL )
      : data( d ), prev( p ), next( n ) { }

    friend class ConstListItr<Object>;
    friend class ListItr<Object>;
    friend class list<Object>;
};
```

Figure 17.23 The `ListNode` class and declarations for other classes.

Figure 17.23 shows the `ListNode` class, which is similar to the `LListNode` class (see Figure 17.7). The main difference is that, because we use a doubly linked list, we have both `prev` and `next` pointers. As we showed before, we make all the members private and then make the three remaining classes friends. Thus we also illustrate the technique of using an incomplete class declaration.

Next we consider the `list` class interface shown in Figure 17.24. As mentioned earlier, lines 5 and 6 are `typedefs` for the `iterator` and `const_iterator`. At line 42, we use another `typedef`—simply for convenience. When writing member functions, we can now use `node` instead of using `ListNode<Object>`. We do so immediately in the declarations of `head` and `tail` at lines 45 and 46. Note also that the list class keeps track of

```
template <class Object>
class list
{
  public:
    typedef ListItr<Object>      iterator;
    typedef ConstListItr<Object> const_iterator;

    list( );
    ~list( );

    list( const list & rhs );
    const list & operator= ( const list & rhs );

    iterator begin( );
    const_iterator begin( ) const;

    iterator end( );
    const_iterator end( ) const;

    int size( ) const;
    bool empty( ) const;

    Object & front( );
    const Object & front( ) const;

    Object & back( );
    const Object & back( ) const;

    void push_front( const Object & x );
    void push_back( const Object & x );
    void pop_front( );
    void pop_back( );

    iterator insert( iterator itr, const Object & x );
    iterator erase( iterator itr );
    iterator erase( iterator start, iterator end );

    friend class ConstListItr<Object>;
    friend class ListItr<Object>;

  private:
    typedef ListNode<Object> node;

    int   theSize;
    node *head;
    node *tail;

    void init( );
    void makeEmpty( );
};
```

Figure 17.24 The `list` class interface.

its size in a data member declared at line 44. We use this approach so that the `size` method can be performed in constant time.

Almost all the member functions use signatures that we've shown before. So, for instance, there are two versions of `begin` and `end`, as in the `vector` class shown in Figure 7.10.

Some unusual lines of code occur at lines 34–39. The three member functions (`insert` and both `erase` methods) pass an iterator using call by value instead of by the normal (for nonprimitive objects) constant reference. This procedure is safe because the iterator is a small object. Also unusual is that the friend declarations do not use `const_iterator` and `iterator` directly. One of our compilers didn't like it, so we played it safe. This rejection illustrates the typical C++ problem of combining too many features at the same time: Often we run into compiler bugs by doing so.

The implementation of `list` begins in Figure 17.25, where we have a constructor and the Big Three. The `makeEmpty` and `init` methods are private helpers. `init` contains the basic functionality of the zero-parameter constructor. However, it is a separate function so that the copy constructor can be implemented by logically using a zero-parameter constructor and `operator=`. All in all, little is new here; we combined a lot of the `LList` code with the concepts presented in Section 17.3.

Figure 17.26 contains the `begin`, `end`, `size`, and `empty` methods. The `begin` method looks much like the `zeroth` method of the `LList` class (see Figure 17.10), except that the iterators are constructed by passing not only a pointer to a node, but also a reference to the list that contains the node. This procedure allows additional error checking for the `insert` and `erase` methods. However, `zeroth` returns the header, but we want the first node. Hence we advance the iterator with `operator++`, and use its new value as the return value. The `end`, `size`, and `empty` methods are one-liners.

Figure 17.27 contains the double-ended queue operations. All are one-liners that combine calls to `begin`, `end`, `operator*`, `operator--`, `insert`, and `erase`. Recall that the `insert` method inserts prior to a position, so `push_back` inserts prior to the endmarker, as required. In `pop_back`, note that `erase(--end())` creates a temporary iterator corresponding to the endmarker, retreats the temporary iterator, and uses that iterator to `erase`. Similar behavior occurs in `back`.

The `insert` and `erase` methods are shown in Figure 17.28. The `assertIsValid` routine, called at line 6, throws an exception if `itr` is not at an insertable location, which could occur if it was never initialized. At line 7 we test whether `itr` belongs to this list, and at line 8 we throw an exception if it does not. The rest of the code is the usual splicing already discussed for a doubly linked list. At line 14, an iterator representing the newly inserted item is returned.

```
template <class Object>
list<Object>::list( )
{
    init( );
}

template <class Object>
void list<Object>::init( )
{
    theSize = 0;
    head = new node;
    tail = new node;
    head->next = tail;
    tail->prev = head;
}

template <class Object>
list<Object>::~list( )
{
    makeEmpty( );
    delete head;
    delete tail;
}

template <class Object>
void list<Object>::makeEmpty( )
{
    while( !empty( ) )
        pop_front( );
}

template <class Object>
list<Object>::list( const list<Object> & rhs )
{
    init( );
    *this = rhs;
}

template <class Object>
const list<Object> &
list<Object>::operator= ( const list & rhs )
{
    if( this == &rhs )
        return *this;

    makeEmpty( );
    const_iterator itr = rhs.begin( );
    while( itr != rhs.end( ) )
        push_back( *itr++ );
    return *this;
}
```

Figure 17.25 Constructor and Big Three for the STL `list` class.

```
// Return iterator representing beginning of list.
// Mutator version is first, then accessor version.
template <class Object>
list<Object>::iterator list<Object>::begin( )
{
    iterator itr( *this, head );
    return ++itr;
}

template <class Object>
list<Object>::const_iterator list<Object>::begin( ) const
{
    const_iterator itr( *this, head );
    return ++itr;
}

// Return iterator representing endmarker of list.
// Mutator version is first, then accessor version.
template <class Object>
list<Object>::iterator list<Object>::end( )
{
    return iterator( *this, tail );
}

template <class Object>
list<Object>::const_iterator list<Object>::end( ) const
{
    return const_iterator( *this, tail );
}

// Return number of elements currently in the list.
template <class Object>
int list<Object>::size( ) const
{
    return theSize;
}

// Return true if the list is empty, false otherwise.
template <class Object>
bool list<Object>::empty( ) const
{
    return size( ) == 0;
}
```

Figure 17.26 The `begin`, `end`, `size`, and `empty` methods for the STL `list` class.

```
// front, back, push_front, push_back, pop_front, and pop_back
// are the basic double-ended queue operations.
template <class Object>
Object & list<Object>::front( )
{
    return *begin( );
}

template <class Object>
const Object & list<Object>::front( ) const
{
    return *begin( );
}

template <class Object>
Object & list<Object>::back( )
{
    return *--end( );
}

template <class Object>
const Object & list<Object>::back( ) const
{
    return *--end( );
}

template <class Object>
void list<Object>::push_front( const Object & x )
{
    insert( begin( ), x );
}

template <class Object>
void list<Object>::push_back( const Object & x )
{
    insert( end( ), x );
}

template <class Object>
void list<Object>::pop_front( )
{
    erase( begin( ) );
}

template <class Object>
void list<Object>::pop_back( )
{
    erase( --end( ) );
}
```

Figure 17.27 Double-ended queue STL `list` class operations.

```
// Insert x before itr.
template <class Object>
list<Object>::iterator
list<Object>::insert( iterator itr, const Object & x )
{
    itr.assertIsValid( );
    if( itr.head != head )  // itr is not in this list
        throw IteratorMismatchException( );

    node *p = itr.current;
    p->prev->next = new node( x, p->prev, p );
    p->prev = p->prev->next;
    theSize++;
    return iterator( *this, p->prev );
}

// Erase item at itr.
template <class Object>
list<Object>::iterator list<Object>::erase( iterator itr )
{
    itr.assertIsValid( );
    if( itr == end( ) )      // can't erase endmarker
        throw IteratorOutOfBoundsException( );
    if( itr.head != head )  // itr is not in this list
        throw IteratorMismatchException( );

    node *p = itr.current;
    iterator retVal( *this, p->next );
    p->prev->next = p->next;
    p->next->prev = p->prev;
    delete p;
    theSize--;
    return retVal;
}

// Erase items in the range [from,to).
template <class Object>
list<Object>::iterator
list<Object>::erase( iterator from, iterator to )
{
    for( iterator itr = from; itr != to; )
        itr = erase( itr );
    return to;
}
```

Figure 17.28 Methods for insertion and removal from the STL `list` class.

The first version of erase contains an additional error check. Afterward, we perform the standard deletion in a doubly linked list; we return an iterator representing the item after the deleted element. Like insert, erase must update theSize. The second version of erase simply uses an iterator to call the first version of erase. Note that we cannot simply use itr++ in the for loop at line 41 and ignore the return value of erase at line 42. The value of itr is stale immediately after the call to erase, which is why erase returns an iterator.

The value of itr is stale immediately after the call to erase, which is why erase returns an iterator.

Figure 17.29 shows the class interfaces for ConstListItr and ListItr. The iterators store the current position and a pointer to the header. Of most interest is the use of inheritance. We want to be able to send an iterator to any method that accepts a const_iterator, but not vice versa. So an iterator IS-A const_iterator. As a result, the private assert methods need to be written only once for the two classes. At line 6, the base class destructor is declared virtual, as is normal for base classes. operator* is also declared virtual.

However, operator++ and operator-- are not virtual, mostly because their return types change. The versions that do not return references cannot be virtual, whereas those that return references can be virtual because they have compatible return types (the return type changes from a reference to a base class to a reference to a derived class; see Section 4.4.4). However, our compilers did not agree with the newer rules.

The iterator classes each declare operator++ and operator-- to mirror advance and retreat (see Section 2.3.3 for a discussion of operator overloading). The public comparison operators and the private helper retrieve are declared in const_iterator and are inherited unchanged.

The iterator constructors are shown in Figure 17.30 and are straightforward. As we mentioned earlier, the zero-parameter constructor is public, whereas the two-parameter constructor that sets the current position and the header position, is private. Various assertion methods are shown in Figure 17.31. All test the validity of an iterator and throw an exception if the iterator is determined to be invalid. Otherwise, these methods return safely.

In Figure 17.32, we present three versions of operator*, which is used to get the Object stored at the current position. Recall that we have an accessor method that returns a constant reference and a mutator method that returns a reference (through which the Object can be changed). The mutator method cannot be made available for const_iterator, so we have only three methods. Except for the return type, they are identical and simply call the retrieve method.

Various implementations of operator++ are shown in Figure 17.33. The postfix version (itr++) is implemented in terms of the prefix version (++itr), the derived class versions are identical to the base class versions

```
template <class Object>
class ConstListItr
{
  public:
    ConstListItr( );
    virtual ~ConstListItr( ) { }

    virtual const Object & operator* ( ) const;
    ConstListItr & operator++ ( );
    ConstListItr operator++ ( int );
    ConstListItr & operator-- ( );
    ConstListItr operator-- ( int );

    bool operator== ( const ConstListItr & rhs ) const;
    bool operator!= ( const ConstListItr & rhs ) const;

  protected:
    typedef ListNode<Object> node;
    node *head;
    node *current;

    friend class list<Object>;
    void assertIsInitialized( ) const;
    void assertIsValid( ) const;
    void assertCanAdvance( ) const;
    void assertCanRetreat( ) const;
    Object & retrieve( ) const;

    ConstListItr( const list<Object> & source, node *p );
};

template <class Object>
class ListItr : public ConstListItr<Object>
{
  public:
    ListItr( );

    Object & operator* ( );
    const Object & operator* ( ) const;
    ListItr & operator++ ( );
    ListItr operator++ ( int );
    ListItr & operator-- ( );
    ListItr operator-- ( int );

  protected:
    typedef ListNode<Object> node;
    friend class list<Object>;

    ListItr( const list<Object> & source, node *p );
};
```

Figure 17.29 Interface for two STL `list` class iterators.

```
// Public constructor for const_iterator.
template <class Object>
ConstListItr<Object>::ConstListItr( )
  : head( NULL ), current( NULL )
{
}

// Protected constructor for const_iterator.
// Expects the list that owns the iterator and a
// pointer that represents the current position.
template <class Object>
ConstListItr<Object>::
ConstListItr( const list<Object> & source, node *p )
  : head( source.head ), current( p )
{
}

// Public constructor for iterator.
// Calls the base-class constructor.
// Must be provided because the private constructor
// is written; otherwise zero-parameter constructor
// would be disabled.
template <class Object>
ListItr<Object>::ListItr( )
{
}

// Protected constructor for iterator.
// Expects the list that owns the iterator and a
// pointer that represents the current position.
template <class Object>
ListItr<Object>::
ListItr( const list<Object> & source, node *p )
  : ConstListItr<Object>( source, p )
{
}
```

Figure 17.30 Constructors for the STL `list` class iterators.

(except for class name), and `operator--` uses the same logic as `operator++`. Consequently, we omit two versions of `operator--`. Finally, Figure 17.34 shows an implementation of the equality operators.

All in all, there is a large amount of code, but it simply embellishes the basics presented in the original implementation of the `LList` class in Section 17.2.

```
// Throws an exception if this iterator is obviously
// uninitialized. Otherwise, returns safely.
template <class Object>
void ConstListItr<Object>::assertIsInitialized( ) const
{
    if( head == NULL || current == NULL )
        throw IteratorUninitializedException( );
}

// Throws an exception if the current position is
// not somewhere in the range from begin to end, inclusive.
// Otherwise, returns safely.
template <class Object>
void ConstListItr<Object>::assertIsValid( ) const
{
    assertIsInitialized( );
    if( current == head )
        throw IteratorOutOfBoundsException( );
}

// Throws an exception if operator++ cannot be safely applied
// to the current position. Otherwise, returns safely.
template <class Object>
void ConstListItr<Object>::assertCanAdvance( ) const
{
    assertIsInitialized( );
    if( current->next == NULL )
        throw IteratorOutOfBoundsException( );
}

// Throws an exception if operator-- cannot be safely applied
// to the current position. Otherwise, returns safely.
template <class Object>
void ConstListItr<Object>::assertCanRetreat( ) const
{
    assertIsValid( );
    if( current->prev == head )
        throw IteratorOutOfBoundsException( );
}
```

Figure 17.31 Various assertions that throw exceptions if the assertion fails.

```
// Return the object stored at the current position.
// For const_iterator, this is an accessor with a
// const reference return type.
template <class Object>
const Object & ConstListItr<Object>::operator* ( ) const
{
    return retrieve( );
}

// Return the object stored at the current position.
// For iterator, there is an accessor with a
// const reference return type and a mutator with
// a reference return type. The accessor is shown first.
template <class Object>
const Object & ListItr<Object>::operator* ( ) const
{
    return ConstListItr<Object>::operator*( );
}

template <class Object>
Object & ListItr<Object>::operator* ( )
{
    return retrieve( );
}

// Protected helper in const_iterator that returns the object
// stored at the current position. Can be called by all
// three versions of operator* without any type conversions.
template <class Object>
Object & ConstListItr<Object>::retrieve( ) const
{
    assertIsValid( );
    if( current->next == NULL )
        throw IteratorOutOfBoundsException( );

    return current->data;
}
```

Figure 17.32 Various operator* implementations.

```
template <class Object>    // prefix
ConstListItr<Object> & ConstListItr<Object>::operator++ ( )
{
    assertCanAdvance( );
    current = current->next;
    return *this;
}

template <class Object>    // postfix
ConstListItr<Object> ConstListItr<Object>::operator++ ( int )
{
    ConstListItr<Object> old = *this;
    ++( *this );
    return old;
}

template <class Object>    // prefix
ListItr<Object> & ListItr<Object>::operator++ ( )
{
    assertCanAdvance( );
    current = current->next;
    return *this;
}

template <class Object>    // postfix
ListItr<Object> ListItr<Object>::operator++ ( int )
{
    ListItr<Object> old = *this;
    ++( *this );
    return old;
}

template <class Object>    // prefix
ConstListItr<Object> & ConstListItr<Object>::operator-- ( )
{
    assertCanRetreat( );
    current = current->prev;
    return *this;
}

template <class Object>    // postfix
ConstListItr<Object> ConstListItr<Object>::operator-- ( int )
{
    ConstListItr<Object> old = *this;
    --( *this );
    return old;
}
```

Figure 17.33 Four versions of `operator++` (two for each iterator) and two versions of `operator--` (for `ConstListItr`); two additional versions of `operator--` are similar and not shown.

```
template <class Object>
bool ConstListItr<Object>::
operator== ( const ConstListItr & rhs ) const
{
    return current == rhs.current;
}

template <class Object>
bool ConstListItr<Object>::
operator!= ( const ConstListItr & rhs ) const
{
    return !( *this == rhs );
}
```

Figure 17.34 Equality operators for list iterators, which are inherited unchanged by `ListItr`.

Summary

In this chapter we described why and how linked lists are implemented, illustrating the interactions among the list, iterator, and node classes. We examined variations of the linked list including doubly linked lists. The doubly linked list allows bidirectional traversal of the list. We also showed how a sorted linked list class can easily be derived from the basic linked list class. Finally, we provided an implementation of most of the STL `list` class.

Objects of the Game

circularly linked list A linked list in which the last cell's `next` pointer points to `first`. This action is useful when wraparound matters. (p. 581)

doubly linked list A linked list that allows bidirectional traversal by storing two pointers per node. (p. 579)

header node An extra node in a linked list that holds no data but serves to satisfy the requirement that every node have a previous node. A header node allow us to avoid special cases such as the insertion of a new first element and the removal of the first element. (p. 567)

incomplete class declaration Code used to inform the compiler of the existence of a class. Incomplete class declarations are necessary when two or more classes refer to each circularly. (p. 571)

iterator class A class that maintains a current position in a container, such as a list. An iterator class is usually a friend of a list class. (p. 569)

sorted linked list A list in which items are in sorted order. A sorted linked list class can be derived from a list class. (p. 582)

Common Errors

1. The most common linked list error is splicing in nodes incorrectly when performing an insertion. This procedure is especially tricky with doubly linked lists.
2. When a header node is used, the list header must be deleted in the destructor.
3. Member functions should not be allowed to dereference a `NULL` pointer. We perform error checks to catch this mistake and throw exceptions as warranted.
4. When several iterators access a list simultaneously, problems can result. For instance, what if one iterator deletes the node that the other iterator is about to access? Solving these types of problems requires additional work, such as the use of an observer pattern (Section 5.6).
5. Forgetting the incomplete class declaration can lead to compilation errors.
6. A common error is calling `delete` at the wrong time during execution of `remove` or `makeEmpty`.

On the Internet

The singly linked list class, including the sorted linked list is available, as is our STL list implementation.

LinkedList.h	Contains the interface for `LList` and associated friends.
LinkedList.cpp	Contains the implementation for `LList` and associated friends.
SortLinkedList.h	Contains the interface for `SortedLList`.
SortLinkedList.cpp	Contains the implementation for `SortedLList`.
TestSortList.cpp	Contains a program that tests the `LList` and `SortedLList` implementations.

list.h	Contains the interface of the STL `list` and associated friends.
list.cpp	Contains the implementation of the STL `list` and associated friends.
TestList.cpp	Contains a program that tests the STL `list` implementation.

Exercises

In Short

17.1. Draw an empty linked list with header implementation.

17.2. Draw an empty doubly linked list that uses both a header and a tail.

In Theory

17.3. Write an algorithm for printing a singly linked list in reverse, using only constant extra space. This instruction implies that you cannot use recursion but you may assume that your algorithm is a list member function. Can such an algorithm be written if the routine is a constant member function?

17.4. A linked list contains a cycle if, starting from some node p, following a sufficient number of `next` links brings us back to node p. Node p does not have to be the first node in the list. Assume that you have a linked list that contains N nodes. However, the value of N is unknown.

a. Design an $O(N)$ algorithm to determine whether the list contains a cycle. You may use $O(N)$ extra space.

b. Repeat part (a), but use only $O(1)$ extra space. (*Hint:* Use two iterators that are initially at the start of the list, but advance at different speeds.)

17.5. When a `remove` function is applied to a `LList`, it invalidates any `LListItr` that is referencing the removed node. Recall that such an iterator is called *stale*. Describe an efficient algorithm that guarantees that any operation on a stale iterator acts as though the iterator's `current` is `NULL`. Note that there may be many stale iterators. You must explain which classes need to be rewritten in order to implement your algorithm.

17.6. One way to implement a queue is to use a circularly linked list. Assume that the list does not contain a header and that you can maintain one iterator for the list. For which of the following representations can all basic queue operations be performed in constant worst-case time? Justify your answers.

a. Maintain an iterator that corresponds to the first item in the list.
b. Maintain an iterator that corresponds to the last item in the list.

17.7. Suppose that you have a pointer to a node in a singly linked list that is guaranteed *not to be the last node* in the list. You do not have pointers to any other nodes (except by following links). Describe an $O(1)$ algorithm that logically removes the value stored in such a node from the linked list, maintaining the integrity of the linked list. (*Hint:* Involve the next node.)

17.8. Suppose that a singly linked list is implemented with both a header and a tail node. Using the ideas discussed in Exercise 17.7, describe constant-time algorithms to

a. insert item `x` before position `p`.
b. remove the item stored at position `p`.

In Practice

17.9. Modify the `find` routine in the `LList` class to return the last occurrence of item `x`.

17.10. Modify `remove` in the `LList` class to remove all occurrences of `x`.

17.11. An alternative to `isValid` (that tests whether the current position is within the list) is to write a type conversion operator:

```
operator bool( ) const;
```

Discuss the benefits and liabilities of this approach and provide an implementation.

17.12. At times you may want to update an entry that is already in the linked list. One way to do so in the `LList` class is to have `retrieve` return a nonconstant reference.

a. Discuss the advantages and disadvantages of this approach.
b. Implement a constant reference return `retrieve` and a nonconstant reference return `retrieve` simultaneously, by making one a constant member function and the other a nonconstant member.

17.13. Suppose that you want to splice part of one linked list into another (a so-called *cut and paste* operation). Assume that three `LListItr` parameters represent the starting point of the *cut*, the ending point of the *cut*, and the point at which the *paste* is to be attached. Assume that all iterators are valid and that the number of items cut is not zero.

a. Write a function to cut and paste that is not a friend of the `LList` classes. What is the running time of the algorithm?
b. Write a function in the `LList` class to do the cut and paste. What is the running time of the algorithm?

17.14. The `SortedLList insert` method uses only public iterator methods. Can it access private members of the iterator?

17.15. Implement an efficient `Stack` class by using a `LList` as a data member. You need to use a `LListItr`, but it can be either a data member or a local variable for any routine that needs it.

17.16. Implement an efficient `Queue` class by using (as in Exercise 17.15) a singly linked list and appropriate iterators. How many of these iterators must be data members in order to achieve an efficient implementation?

17.17. Implement `retreat` for singly linked lists. Note that it will take linear time.

17.18. Implement the `LList` class without the header node.

17.19. Looking ahead in an STL `iterator` object requires an application of `operator++`, which in turn advances in the list. In some cases looking at the next item in the list, without advancing to it, may be preferable. Write the member function with the declaration

```
const_iterator operator+( int k ) const;
```

to facilitate this in a general case. The binary `operator+` returns an iterator that corresponds to `k` positions ahead of `current`. Do any exceptions need to be thrown?

Programming Projects

17.20. Implement a circularly and doubly linked list.

17.21. If the order that items in a list are stored is not important, you can frequently speed searching with the heuristic known as *move to front:* Whenever an item is accessed, move it to the front of the list. This action usually results in an improvement because frequently accessed items tend to migrate toward the front of the list, whereas less frequently accessed items tend to migrate toward the end of the list. Consequently, the most frequently accessed items tend to require the least searching. Implement the move-to-front heuristic for linked lists.

17.22. Modify the `vector` class presented in Figure 7.10 with bounds-checked iterators. In other words, `const_iterator` and `iterator` should be `typedef`s representing classes instead of pointers.

17.23. Add reverse iterators to the STL `list` class implementation. Define `reverse_iterator` and `const_reverse_iterator`. Add the methods `rbegin` and `rend` to return appropriate reverse iterators representing the position prior to the endmarker and the position that is the header node. Reverse iterators internally reverse the meaning of the `++` and `--` operators. You should be able to print a list `L` in reverse by using the code

```
list<Object>::reverse_iterator itr = L.rbegin( );
while( itr != L.rend( ) )
    cout << *itr++ << endl;
```

17.24. Write routines `makeUnion` and `intersect` that return the union and intersection of two sorted linked lists.

17.25. Write a line-based text editor. The command syntax is similar to the Unix line editor *ed*. The internal copy of the file is maintained as a linked list of lines. To be able to go up and down in the file, you have to maintain a doubly linked list. Most commands are represented by a one-character string. Some are two characters and require an argument (or two). Support the commands lines shown in Figure 17.35.

Command	Function
`1`	Go to the top.
`a`	Add text after current line until `.` on its own line appears.
`d`	Delete current line.
`dr num num`	Delete several lines.
`f name`	Change name of the current file (for next write).
`g num`	Go to a numbered line.
`h`	Get help.
`i`	Like append, but add lines before current line.
`m num`	Move current line after some other line.
`mr num num num`	Move several lines as a unit after some other line.
`n`	Toggle whether line numbers are displayed.
`p`	Print current line.
`pr num num`	Print several lines.
`q!`	Abort without write.
`r name`	Read and paste another file into the current file.
`s text text`	Substitute text with other text.
`t num`	Copy current line to after some other line.
`tr num num num`	Copy several lines to after some other line.
`w`	Write file to disk.
`x!`	Exit with write.
`$`	Go to the last line.
`-`	Go up one line.
`+`	Go down one line.
`=`	Print current line number.
`/ text`	Search forward for a pattern.
`? text`	Search backward for a pattern.
`#`	Print number of lines and characters in file.

Figure 17.35 Commands for editor in Exercise 17.25.

Chapter 18

Trees

The *tree* is a fundamental structure in computer science. Almost all operating systems store files in trees or treelike structures. Trees are also used in compiler design, text processing, and searching algorithms. We discuss the latter application in Chapter 19.

In this chapter, we show:

- a definition of a general tree and discuss how it is used in a file system,
- an examination of the binary tree,
- implementation of tree operations, using recursion, and
- nonrecursive traversal of a tree.

18.1 General Trees

Trees can be defined in two ways: nonrecursively and recursively. The nonrecursive definition is the more direct technique, so we begin with it. The recursive formulation allows us to write simple algorithms to manipulate trees.

18.1.1 Definitions

Nonrecursively, a **tree** consists of a set of nodes and a set of directed edges that connect pairs of nodes. Throughout this text we consider only rooted trees. A rooted tree has the following properties.

A *tree* can be defined nonrecursively as a set of nodes and a set of directed edges that connect them.

- One node is distinguished as the root.
- Every node c, except the root, is connected by an edge from exactly one other node p. Node p is c's *parent*, and c is one of p's *children*.
- A unique path traverses from the root to each node. The number of edges that must be followed is the *path length*.

Parents and children are naturally defined. A directed edge connects the *parent* to the *child*.

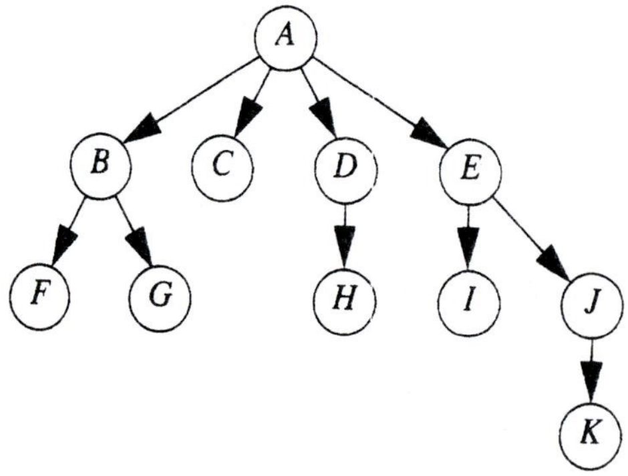

Node	Height	Depth
A	3	0
B	1	1
C	0	1
D	1	1
E	2	1
F	0	2
G	0	2
H	0	2
I	0	2
J	1	2
K	0	3

Figure 18.1 A tree, with height and depth information.

Parents and children are naturally defined. A directed edge connects the **parent** to the **child.**

A *leaf* has no children.

Figure 18.1 illustrates a tree. The root node is *A*; *A*'s children are *B*, *C*, *D*, and *E*. Because *A* is the root, it has no parent; all other nodes have parents. For instance, *B*'s parent is *A*. A node that has no children is called a **leaf.** The leaves in this tree are *C*, *F*, *G*, *H*, *I*, and *K*. The length of the path from *A* to *K* is 3 (edges); the length of the path from *A* to *A* is 0 (edges).

The *depth of a node* is the length of the path from the root to the node. The *height of a node* is the length of the path from the node to the deepest leaf.

A tree with *N* nodes must have $N - 1$ edges because every node except the parent has an incoming edge. The **depth of a node** in a tree is the length of the path from the root to the node. Thus the depth of the root is always 0, and the depth of any node is 1 more than the depth of its parent. The **height of a node** in a tree is the length of the path from the node to the deepest leaf. Thus the height of *E* is 2. The height of any node is 1 more than the height of its maximum-height child. Thus the height of a tree is the height of the root.

The *size of a node* is the number of descendants the node has (including the node itself).

Nodes with the same parent are called **siblings;** thus *B*, *C*, *D*, and *E* are all siblings. If there is a path from node *u* to node *v*, then *u* is an **ancestor** of *v* and *v* is a **descendant** of *u*. If $u \neq v$, then *u* is a **proper ancestor** of *v* and *v* is a **proper descendant** of *u*. The **size of a node** is the number of descendants the node has (including the node itself). Thus the size of *B* is 3, and the size of *C* is 1. The size of a tree is the size of the root. Thus the size of the tree shown in Figure 18.1 is the size of its root *A*, or 11.

An alternative definition of the tree is recursive: Either a tree is empty or it consists of a root and zero or more nonempty subtrees $T_1, T_2, \ldots, T_k$, each of whose roots are connected by an edge from the root, as illustrated in Figure 18.2. In certain instances (most notably, the *binary trees* discussed later in the chapter), we may allow some of the subtrees to be empty.

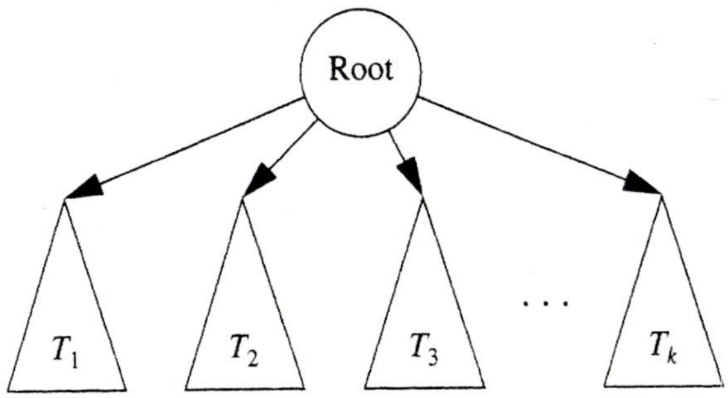

Figure 18.2 A tree viewed recursively.

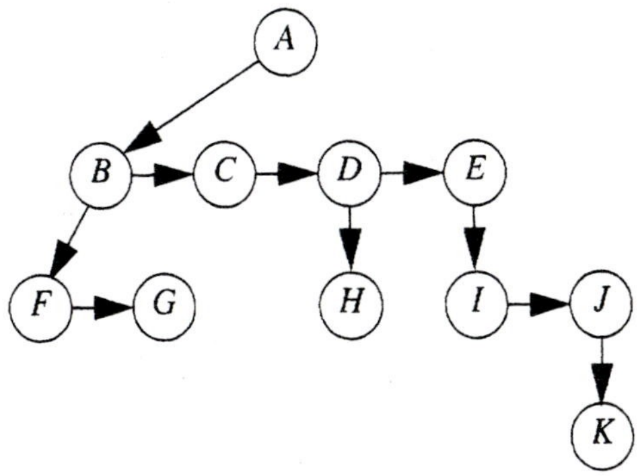

Figure 18.3 First child/next sibling representation of the tree shown in Figure 18.1.

18.1.2 Implementation

General trees can be implemented by using the *first child/next sibling method*, which requires two pointers per item.

One way to implement a tree would be to have in each node a pointer to each child of the node in addition to its data. However, as the number of children per node can vary greatly and is not known in advance, making the children direct links in the data structure might not be feasible—there would be too much wasted space. The solution—called the **first child/next sibling method**—is simple: Keep the children of each node in a linked list of tree nodes, with each node keeping two pointers, one to its leftmost child (if it is not a leaf) and one to its right sibling (if it is not the rightmost sibling). This type of implementation is illustrated in Figure 18.3. Arrows that point downward are `firstChild` pointers, and arrows that point left to right are `nextSibling` pointers. We did not draw `NULL` pointers because there are too many of them. In this tree, node *B* has both a pointer to a sibling (*C*) and a pointer to a leftmost child (*F*); some nodes have only one of these pointers and some have neither. Given this representation, implementing a tree class is straightforward.

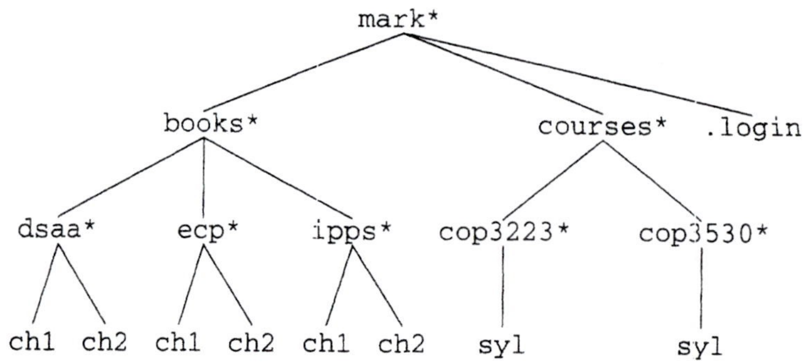

Figure 18.4 A Unix directory.

18.1.3 An Application: File Systems

File systems use treelike structures.

Trees have many applications. One of their popular uses is the directory structure in many operating systems, including Unix, VAX/VMS, and Windows/DOS. Figure 18.4 shows a typical directory in the Unix file system. The root of this directory is `mark`. (The asterisk next to the name indicates that `mark` is itself a directory.) Note that `mark` has three children: `books`, `courses`, and `.login`, two of which are themselves directories. Thus `mark` contains two directories and one regular file. The filename `mark/books/dsaa/ch1` is obtained by following the leftmost child three times. Each `/` after the first name indicates an edge; the result is a pathname. If the path begins at the root of the entire file system, rather than at an arbitrary directory inside the file system, it is a full pathname; otherwise, it is a relative pathname (to the current directory).

This hierarchical file system is popular because it allows users to organize their data logically. Furthermore, two files in different directories can share the same name because they have different paths from the root and thus have different full pathnames. A directory in the Unix file system is just a file with a list of all its children,[1] so the directories can be traversed with an iteration scheme; that is, we can sequentially iterate over each child. Indeed, on some systems, if the normal command to print a file is applied to a directory, the filenames in the directory appear in the output (along with other non-ASCII information).

1. Each directory in the Unix file system also has one entry (`.`) that points to itself and another entry (`..`) that points to the parent of the directory, which introduces a cycle. Thus, technically, the Unix file system is not a tree but is treelike. The same is true for Windows/DOS.

```
void FileSystem::listAll( int depth = 0 ) const
{
    printName( depth );        // Print the name of the object
    if( isDirectory( ) )
        for each file c in this directory (for each child)
            c.listAll( depth + 1 );
}
```

Figure 18.5 A routine for listing a directory and its subdirectories in a hierarchical file system.

```
mark
        books
                dsaa
                        ch1
                        ch2
                ecp
                        ch1
                        ch2
                ipps
                        ch1
                        ch2
        courses
                cop3223
                        syl
                cop3530
                        syl
        .login
```

Figure 18.6 The directory listing for the tree shown in Figure 18.4.

The directory structure is most easily traversed by using recursion.

Suppose that we want to list the names of all the files in a directory (including its subdirectories) and in our output format files of depth d have their names indented by d tab characters. A short algorithm to do this task is given in Figure 18.5. Output for the directory presented in Figure 18.4 is shown in Figure 18.6.

We assume the existence of the class `FileSystem` and two member functions, `printName` and `isDirectory`. The function `printName` outputs the current `FileSystem` object indented by `depth` tab stops; the function `isDirectory` tests whether the current `FileSystem` object is a directory, returning `true` if it is. Then we can write the recursive routine `listAll`. We need to pass it the parameter `depth`, indicating the current level in the directory relative to the root. The `listAll` routine is started with `depth` 0 to signify no indenting for the root. This depth is an internal bookkeeping variable and is hardly a parameter about which a calling routine should be expected to know. Thus the default value of 0 is provided for `depth`.

The logic of the algorithm is simple to follow. The current object is printed out, with appropriate indentation. If the entry is a directory, we process all the children recursively, one by one. These children are one level deeper in the tree and thus must be indented an extra tab stop. We make the recursive call with `depth+1`. It is hard to imagine a shorter piece of code that performs what appears to be a very difficult task.

In a *preorder tree traversal*, work at a node is performed before its children are processed. The traversal takes constant time per node.

In this algorithmic technique, known as a **preorder tree traversal,** work at a node is performed before (*pre*) its children are processed. In addition to being a compact algorithm, the preorder traversal is efficient because it takes constant time per node. We discuss why later in this chapter.

In a *postorder tree traversal*, work at a node is performed after its children are evaluated. The traversal takes constant time per node.

Another common method of traversing a tree is the **postorder tree traversal,** in which the work at a node is performed after (*post*) its children are evaluated. It also takes constant time per node. As an example, Figure 18.7 represents the same directory structure as that shown in Figure 18.4. The numbers in parentheses represent the number of disk blocks taken up by each file. The directories themselves are files, so they also use disk blocks (to store the names and information about their children).

Suppose that we want to compute the total number of blocks used by all files in our example tree. The most natural way to do so is to find the total number of blocks contained in all the children (which may be directories that must be evaluated recursively): `books` (41), `courses` (8), and `.login` (2). The total number of blocks is then the total in all the children plus the blocks used at the root (1), or 52. The `size` routine shown in Figure 18.8 implements this strategy. If the current `FileSystem` object is not a directory, `size` merely returns the number of blocks it uses. Otherwise, the number of

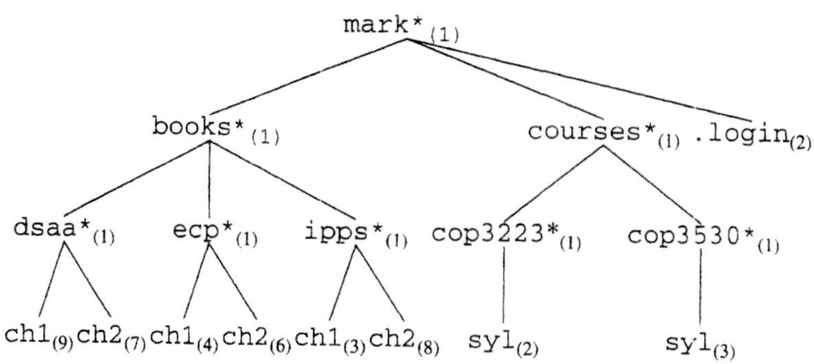

Figure 18.7 The Unix directory with file sizes.

```
int FileSystem::size( ) const
{
    int totalSize = sizeOfThisFile( );

    if( isDirectory( ) )
        for each file c in this directory (for each child)
            totalSize += c.size( );

    return totalSize;
}
```

Figure 18.8 A routine for calculating the total size of all files in a directory.

```
                        ch1            9
                        ch2            7
                dsaa                  17
                        ch1            4
                        ch2            6
                ecp                   11
                        ch1            3
                        ch2            8
                ipps                  12
        books                         41
                        syl            2
                cop3223                3
                        syl            3
                cop3530                4
        courses                        8
        .login                         2
mark                                  52
```

Figure 18.9 A trace of the `size` function.

blocks in the current directory is added to the number of blocks (recursively) found in all the children. To illustrate the difference between postorder traversal and preorder traversal, in Figure 18.9 we show how the size of each directory (or file) is produced by the algorithm. We get a classic postorder signature because the total size of an entry is not computable until the information for its children has been computed. As indicated previously, the running time is linear. We have much more to say about tree traversals in Section 18.4.

18.2 Binary Trees

A ***binary tree*** has no node with more than two children.

A **binary tree** is a tree in which no node can have more than two children. Because there are only two children, we can name them `left` and `right`.

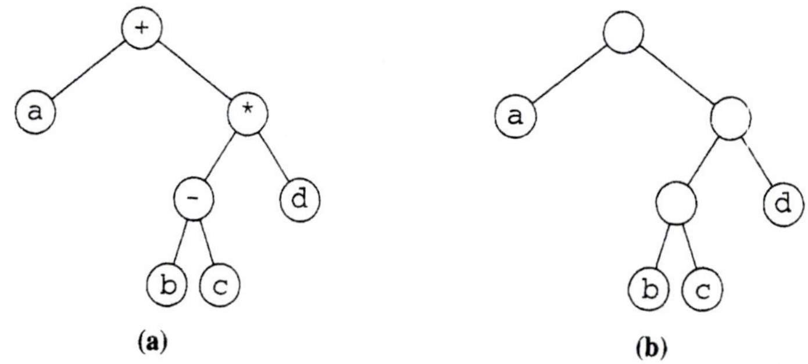

Figure 18.10 Uses of binary trees: (a) an expression tree and (b) a Huffman coding tree.

Recursively, a binary tree is either empty or consists of a root, a left tree, and a right tree. The left and right trees may themselves be empty; thus a node with one child could have either a left or right child. We use the recursive definition several times in the design of binary tree algorithms. Binary trees have many important uses, two of which are illustrated in Figure 18.10.

An expression tree is one example of the use of binary trees. Such trees are central data structures in compiler design.

One use of the binary tree is in the *expression tree,* which is a central data structure in compiler design. The leaves of an expression tree are operands, such as constants or variable names; the other nodes contain operators. This particular tree is binary because all the operations are binary. Although this case is the simplest, nodes can have more than two children (and in the case of unary operators, only one child). We can evaluate an expression tree *T* by applying the operator at the root to the values obtained by recursively evaluating the left and right subtrees. Doing so yields the expression `(a+((b-c)*d))`. (See Section 12.2 for a discussion of the construction of expression trees and their evaluation.)

A second use of the binary tree is the *Huffman coding tree,* which is used to implement a simple but relatively effective data compression algorithm. Each symbol in the alphabet is stored at a leaf. Its code is obtained by following the path to it from the root. A left link corresponds to a 0 and a right link to a 1. Thus `b` is coded as 100. (See Section 13.1 for a discussion of the construction of the optimal tree, that is, the best code.)

An important use of binary trees is in other data structures, notably the binary search tree and the priority queue.

Other uses of the binary tree are in binary search trees (discussed in Chapter 19), which allow logarithmic time insertions and accessing of items, and priority queues, which support the access and deletion of the minimum in a collection of items. Several efficient implementations of priority queues use trees (discussed in Chapters 21–23).

```
1 // BinaryNode class; stores a node in a tree.
2 //
3 // CONSTRUCTION: with (a) no parameters, or (b) an Object,
4 //     or (c) an Object, left pointer, and right pointer.
5 //
6 // ******************PUBLIC OPERATIONS*********************
7 // int size( )              --> Return size of subtree at node
8 // int height( )            --> Return height of subtree at node
9 // void printPostOrder( ) --> Print a postorder tree traversal
10 // void printInOrder( )    --> Print an inorder tree traversal
11 // void printPreOrder( )   --> Print a preorder tree traversal
12 // BinaryNode * duplicate( )    --> Return a duplicate tree
13 // ******************ERRORS********************************
14 // None.
15
16 template <class Object>
17 class BinaryNode
18 {
19   public:
20     BinaryNode( const Object & theElement = Object( ),
21                 BinaryNode *lt = NULL, BinaryNode *rt = NULL );
22
23     static int size( BinaryNode *t );          // See Figure 18.20
24     static int height( BinaryNode *t );        // See Figure 18.22
25
26     void printPostOrder( ) const;              // See Figure 18.23
27     void printInOrder( ) const;                // See Figure 18.23
28     void printPreOrder( ) const;               // See Figure 18.23
29
30     BinaryNode *duplicate( ) const;            // See Figure 18.17
31
32   public:    // To keep things simple
33     Object      element;
34     BinaryNode *left;
35     BinaryNode *right;
36 };
```

Figure 18.11 The `BinaryNode` class interface.

Figure 18.11 gives the skeleton for the `BinaryNode` class. Lines 33–35 indicate that each node consists of a data item plus two pointers. The constructor, shown at line 20, initializes all the data members of the `BinaryNode` class. For convenience, everything in `BinaryNode` is public, which simplifies the coding and allows us to concentrate on algorithmic details.

Many of the `BinaryNode` routines are recursive. The `BinaryTree` methods use the `BinaryNode` routines on the `root`.

The `duplicate` method, declared at line 30, is used to replicate a copy of the tree rooted at the current node. The routines `size` and `height`, declared at lines 23 and 24, compute the named properties for the node pointed at by parameter `t`. We implement these routines in Section 18.3. (Recall that static member functions do not require a controlling object.) We also provide, at lines 26–28, routines that print out the contents of a tree rooted at the current node, using various recursive traversal strategies. We discuss tree traversals in Section 18.4. Why do we pass a parameter for `size` and `height` and make them `static` but use the current object for the traversals and `duplicate`? There is no particular reason; it is a matter of style, and we show both styles here. The implementations show that the difference between them occurs when the required test for an empty tree (given by a `NULL` pointer) is performed.[2]

The `BinaryNode` class is implemented separately from the `BinaryTree` class. The only data member in the `BinaryTree` class is a pointer to the root node.

In this section we describe implementation of the `BinaryTree` class. The `BinaryNode` class is implemented separately, instead of as a nested class, to simplify some of the recursive routines used. The `BinaryTree` class interface is shown in Figure 18.12. For the most part, the routines are short because they call `BinaryNode` methods. Line 46 declares the only data member—a pointer to the `root` node. The internal private method `makeEmpty` is used to make the tree empty while reclaiming the dynamically allocated nodes. It is called from a public `makeEmpty`, which in turn is called by the destructor.

Two basic constructors are provided. The one at line 18 creates an empty tree, and the one at line 19 creates a one-node tree. Routines to traverse the tree are declared at lines 28–33. They apply a `BinaryNode` method to the `root`, after verifying that the tree is not empty. An alternative traversal strategy that can be implemented is level-order traversal. We discuss these traversal routines in Section 18.4 (at which point line 48 is used). Routines to make an empty tree and test for emptiness are given, with their inline implementations, at lines 34 and 36, respectively, as are routines to compute the tree's size and height. Note that, as `size` and `height` are static methods in `BinaryNode`, we can call them by simply using the `BinaryNode` scope; we do not need a controlling `BinaryNode` object. (The `typedef` uses `Node` as a shorthand for `BinaryNode<Object>`.)

2. Some compilers do not handle static member functions in class templates. You may need to slightly modify this code if your compiler is old. To do so, remove `static` from lines 23 and 24 in Figure 18.11 and make the methods constant member functions. Then change `Node::` to `root->` at lines 39 and 41 in Figure 18.12. Prior to the calls at lines 39 and 41, you will need to handle the special case of an empty tree.

```
// BinaryTree class; stores a binary tree.
//
// CONSTRUCTION: with (a) no parameters or (b) an object to
//     be placed in the root of a one-element tree.
//
// *******************PUBLIC OPERATIONS*********************
// Various tree traversals, size, height, isEmpty, makeEmpty.
// Also, the following tricky method:
// void merge( Object root, BinaryTree t1, BinaryTree t2 )
//                           --> Construct a new tree
// ******************ERRORS*********************************
// Error message printed for illegal merges.

template <class Object>
class BinaryTree
{
  public:
    BinaryTree( ) : root( NULL ) { }
    BinaryTree( const Object & rootItem )
      : root( new Node( rootItem ) ) { }

    BinaryTree( const BinaryTree & rhs )
      : root( NULL ) { *this = rhs; }
    ~BinaryTree( )
      { makeEmpty( ); }
    const BinaryTree & operator= ( const BinaryTree & rhs );

    void printPreOrder( ) const
      { if( root != NULL ) root->printPreOrder( ); }
    void printInOrder( ) const
      { if( root != NULL ) root->printInOrder( ); }
    void printPostOrder( ) const
      { if( root != NULL ) root->printPostOrder( ); }
    void makeEmpty( )
      { makeEmpty( root ); }
    bool isEmpty( ) const
      { return root == NULL; }
    int size( ) const
      { return Node::size( root ); }
    int height( ) const
      { return Node::height( root ); }
    void merge( const Object & rootItem, BinaryTree & t1,
                                         BinaryTree & t2 );
  private:
    typedef BinaryNode<Object> Node;
    Node *root;

    friend class TreeIterator<Object>;  // Used in Section 18.4
    void makeEmpty( Node * & t );
};
```

Figure 18.12 The `BinaryTree` class interface.

```
1  template <class Object>
2  const BinaryTree<Object> &
3  BinaryTree<Object>::operator=( const BinaryTree<Object> & rhs )
4  {
5      if( this != &rhs )
6      {
7          makeEmpty( );
8          if( rhs.root != NULL )
9              root = rhs.root->duplicate( );
10     }
11
12     return *this;
13 }
```

Figure 18.13 The copy assignment operator for the `BinaryTree` class.

Before we can apply the `BinaryNode` member to the node pointed at by the `root`, we must verify that the `root` is not `NULL`.

The copy assignment operator is declared at line 26 and is implemented in Figure 18.13. After testing for aliasing at line 5, we call `makeEmpty` at line 7 to reclaim the memory. At line 9 we call the `duplicate` member function to get a copy of the `rhs`'s tree. Then we assign the result as the root of the tree. Note the test at line 8. Before we can apply the `BinaryNode` method to the node pointed at by the `rhs.root`, we must verify that `rhs.root` is not `NULL`. As usual, `operator=` returns a constant reference to the current object, at line 12. The copy constructor, shown in the class interface at line 22, simply initializes the `root` to `NULL` and then calls `operator=`.

The `merge` routine is a one-liner in principle. However, we must also handle aliasing, avoid memory leaks, ensure that a node is not in two trees, and check for errors.

The last method in the class is the `merge` routine, which uses two trees—`t1` and `t2`—and an element to create a new tree, with the element at the root and the two existing trees as left and right subtrees. In principle, it is a one-liner:

```
root = new BinaryNode<Object>( rootItem, t1.root, t2.root );
```

If things were always this simple, programmers would be unemployed. Fortunately for our careers, there are a host of complications. Figure 18.14 shows the result of the simple one-line `merge`. Two problems become apparent.

- The nodes that `root` used to point at are now unreferenced, and thus we have a memory leak.
- Nodes in `t1` and `t2`'s trees are now in two trees (their original trees and the merged result). This sharing is a problem because, when the destructor for `t1` is called, it `delete`s nodes in the merged tree too, possibly resulting in erroneous behavior; furthermore, when the merged tree's

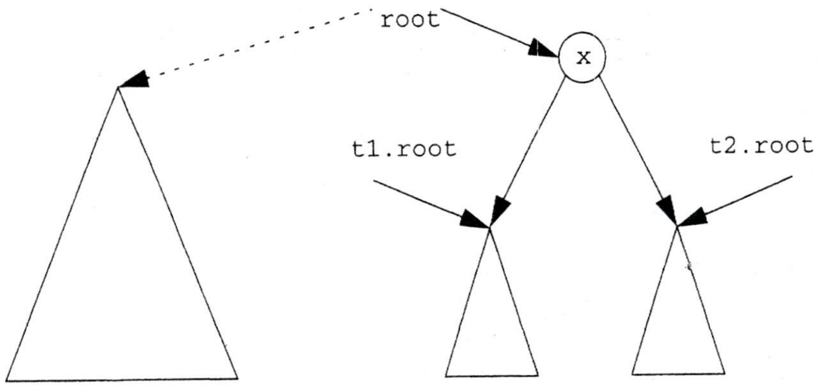

Figure 18.14 Result of a naive `merge` operation: Subtrees are shared.

destructor is called, it will attempt to `delete` nodes that are already deleted, almost certainly resulting in a disaster.

The solution to these problems is simple in principle. We can avoid the memory leak by calling `makeEmpty` on the original tree. All we need to do is save a pointer to the `root` before calling `new`. We can ensure that nodes do not appear in two trees by setting `t1.root` and `t2.root` to `NULL` after the `merge`.

Memory leaks are avoided by calling `makeEmpty` on the original tree. We set the original trees' `root` to `NULL` so that each node is in one tree.

Complications ensue when we consider some possible calls that contain aliasing:

If the two input trees are aliases, we should disallow the operation unless the trees are empty.

```
t1.merge( x, t1, t2 );
t2.merge( x, t1, t2 );
t1.merge( x, t3, t3 );
```

The first two cases are similar, so we consider only the first one. A diagram of the situation is shown in Figure 18.15. If we call `makeEmpty` for the original tree, we destroy part of the merged tree. Thus, when we detect an aliasing condition, we do not call `makeEmpty`. A second problem is harder to spot unless we draw the diagram carefully. Because `t1` is an alias for the current object, `t1.root` and `root` are aliases. Thus, after the call to `new`, if we execute `t1.root=NULL`, we change `root` to the `NULL` pointer, too. Consequently, we need to be very careful with the aliases for these cases.

If an input tree is aliased to the output tree, we must avoid having the resultant `root` point to `NULL`.

The third case must be disallowed because it would place all the nodes that are in tree `t3` in two places in `t1`. However, if `t3` represents an empty tree, the third case should be allowed. All in all, we got a lot more than we bargained for. The resulting code is shown in Figure 18.16. What used to be a one-line routine has gotten quite large.

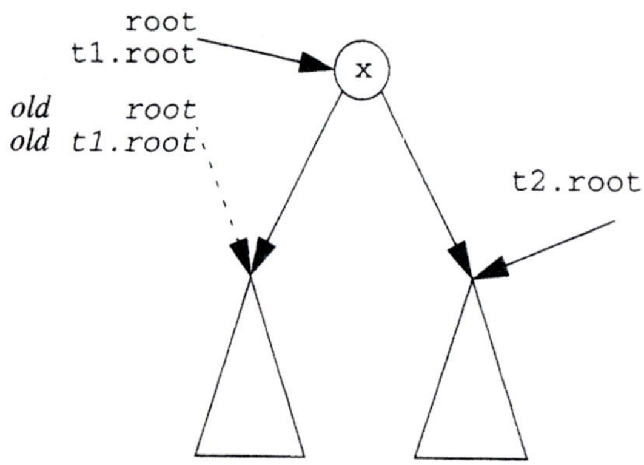

Figure 18.15 Aliasing problems in the `merge` operation; `t1` is also the current object

```
// Merge routine for BinaryTree class.
// Forms a new tree from rootItem, t1 and t2.
// Does not allow t1 and t2 to be the same.
// Correctly handles other aliasing conditions.
template <class Object>
void BinaryTree<Object>::merge( const Object & rootItem,
                BinaryTree<Object> & t1, BinaryTree<Object> & t2 )
{
    if( t1.root == t2.root && t1.root != NULL )
    {
        cerr << "Cannot merge a tree with itself" << endl;
        return;
    }

    Node *oldRoot = root;    // Save old root

      // Allocate new node
    root = new Node( rootItem, t1.root, t2.root );

      // Deallocate nodes in the original tree
    if( this != &t1 && this != &t2 )
        makeEmpty( oldRoot );

      // Ensure that every node is in one tree
    if( this != &t1 )
        t1.root = NULL;
    if( this != &t2 )
        t2.root = NULL;
}
```

Figure 18.16 The `merge` routine for the `BinaryTree` class.

18.3 Recursion and Trees

Recursive routines are used for `size`, `makeEmpty`, and `duplicate`.

Because trees can be defined recursively, many tree routines, not surprisingly, are most easily implemented by using recursion. Recursive implementations for almost all the remaining `BinaryNode` and `BinaryTree` methods are provided here. The resulting routines are amazingly compact.

Because `duplicate` is a `BinaryNode` method, we make recursive calls only after verifying that the subtrees are not `NULL`.

We begin with the `duplicate` method of the `BinaryNode` class. Because it is a `BinaryNode` method, we are assured that the tree we are duplicating is not empty. The recursive algorithm is then simple. First, we create a new node with the same data field as the current root. Then we attach a left tree by calling `duplicate` recursively and attach a right tree by calling `duplicate` recursively. In both cases, we make the recursive call after verifying that there is a tree to copy. This description is coded verbatim in Figure 18.17.

As `makeEmpty` is not a `BinaryNode` member, the parameter `t` might be `NULL`. We thus test for it at the start of the routine and do not test prior to a recursive call.

Next we code `makeEmpty`. There is a slight difference between `makeEmpty` and `duplicate` because `makeEmpty` is a member of the `BinaryTree` class and receives a pointer to the root of the tree. However, this pointer might be `NULL`. Consequently, we must test for `NULL` first. Doing so, however, makes testing against `NULL` prior to making the recursive call unnecessary (although, arguably, it would be more efficient to do so, as shown in Exercise 18.10). To `delete` all the nodes in a tree, we `delete` (recursively) all the nodes in the left subtree, then the nodes in the right subtree (again, recursively), and finally the root, as shown in Figure 18.18. Note that the `delete` of `t` must be done last but that the order of the two recursive calls is not important. Note also that `t` is passed by reference, so after the call returns, the actual parameter now points at `NULL`.

```
// Return a pointer to a node that is the root of a
// duplicate of the tree rooted at the current node.
template <class Object>
BinaryNode<Object> * BinaryNode<Object>::duplicate( ) const
{
    BinaryNode<Object> *root =
                        new BinaryNode<Object>( element );

    if( left != NULL )              // If there's a left subtree
        root->left = left->duplicate( );   // Duplicate; attach
    if( right != NULL )             // If there's a right subtree
        root->right = right->duplicate( ); // Duplicate; attach
    return root;                           // Return resulting tree
}
```

Figure 18.17 A routine for returning a copy of the tree rooted at the current node.

```
// Make tree rooted at t empty, freeing nodes,
// and setting t to NULL.
template <class Object>
void BinaryTree<Object>::makeEmpty( BinaryNode<Object> * & t )
{
    if( t != NULL )
    {
        makeEmpty( t->left );
        makeEmpty( t->right );
        delete t;
        t = NULL;
    }
}
```

Figure 18.18 A routine to `delete` all nodes in a tree rooted at `t`.

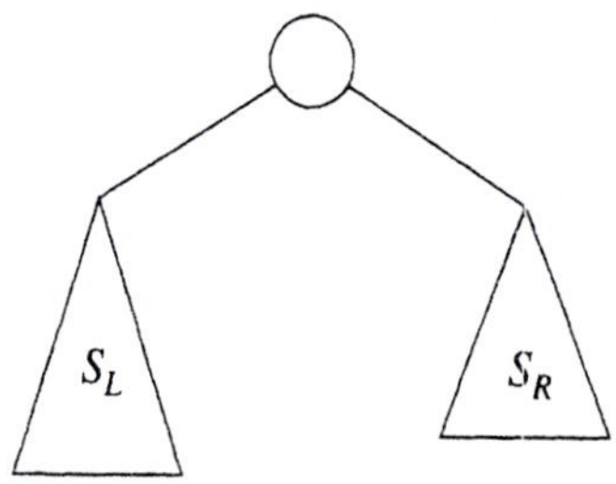

Figure 18.19 Recursive view used to calculate the size of a tree: $S_T = S_L + S_R + 1$.

The `size` routine is easily implemented recursively after a drawing is made.

The next method we write is the `size` routine in the `BinaryNode` class. It returns the size of the tree rooted at a node pointed at by `t`, which is passed as a parameter. If we draw the tree recursively, as shown in Figure 18.19, we see that the size of a tree is the size of the left subtree plus the size of the right subtree plus 1 (because the root counts as a node). A recursive routine requires a base case that can be solved without recursion. The smallest tree that `size` might have to handle is the empty tree (if `t` is `NULL`), and the size of an empty tree is clearly 0. We should verify that the recursion produces the correct answer for a tree of size 1. Doing so is easy, and the recursive routine is implemented as shown in Figure 18.20.

The `height` routine is also easily implemented recursively. The height of an empty tree is –1.

The final recursive routine presented in this section calculates the height of a node. Implementing this routine is difficult to do nonrecursively but is trivial recursively, once we have made a drawing. Figure 18.21 shows a tree viewed recursively. Suppose that the left subtree has height H_L and the right subtree has height H_R. Any node that is d levels deep with respect to the root

```
// Return size of tree rooted at t.
template <class Object>
int BinaryNode<Object>::size( BinaryNode<Object> * t )
{
    if( t == NULL )
        return 0;
    else
        return 1 + size( t->left ) + size( t->right );
}
```

Figure 18.20 A routine for computing the size of a node.

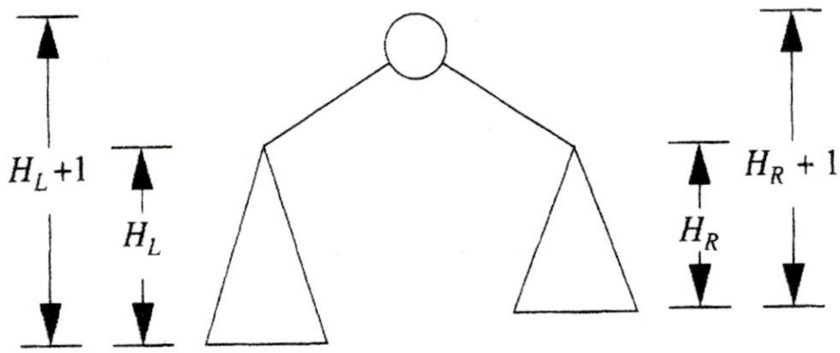

Figure 18.21 Recursive view of the node height calculation: $H_T = \text{Max}\ (H_L + 1, H_R + 1)$.

```
// Return height of tree rooted at t.
template <class Object>
int BinaryNode<Object>::height( BinaryNode<Object> * t )
{
    if( t == NULL )
        return -1;
    else
        return 1 + max( height( t->left ),height( t->right ) );
}
```

Figure 18.22 A routine for computing the height of a node.

of the left subtree is $d + 1$ levels deep with respect to the root of the entire tree. The same holds for the right subtree. Thus the path length of the deepest node in the original tree is 1 more than its path length with respect to the root of its subtree. If we compute this value for both subtrees, the maximum of these two values plus 1 is the answer we want. The code for doing so is shown in Figure 18.22.

18.4 Tree Traversal: Iterator Classes

In this chapter we have shown how recursion can be used to implement the binary tree methods. When recursion is applied, we compute information about not only a node but also about all its descendants. We say then that we are *traversing the tree*. Two popular traversals that we have already mentioned are the preorder and postorder traversals.

In a preorder traversal, the node is processed and then its children are processed recursively. The `duplicate` routine is an example of a preorder traversal because the root is created first. Then a left subtree is copied recursively, followed by copying the right subtree.

In a postorder traversal, the node is processed after both children are processed recursively. Three examples are the methods `size`, `height`, and `makeEmpty`. In every case, information about a node (e.g., its size or height) can be obtained only after the corresponding information is known for its children. In `makeEmpty`, a node is deleted only after its children are recursively deleted.

In an *inorder traversal*, the current node is processed between recursive calls.

A third common recursive traversal is the **inorder traversal,** in which the left child is recursively processed, the current node is processed, and the right child is recursively processed. This mechanism is used to generate an algebraic expression corresponding to an expression tree. For example, in Figure 18.10 the inorder traversal yields `(a+((b-c)*d))`.

Simple traversal using any of these strategies takes linear time.

Figure 18.23 illustrates routines that print the nodes in a binary tree using each of the three recursive tree traversal algorithms. Figure 18.24 shows the order in which nodes are visited for each of the three strategies. The running time of each algorithm is linear. In every case, each node is output only once. Consequently, the total cost of an output statement over any traversal is $O(N)$. As a result, each `if` statement is also executed at most once per node, for a total cost of $O(N)$. The total number of method calls made (which involves the constant work of the internal run-time stack pushes and pops) is likewise once per node, or $O(N)$. Thus the total running time is $O(N)$.

We can traverse nonrecursively by maintaining the stack ourselves.

Must we use recursion to implement the traversals? The answer is clearly no because, as discussed in Section 8.3, recursion is implemented by using a stack. Thus we could keep our own stack.[3] We might expect that a somewhat faster program could result because we can place only the essentials on the stack rather than have the compiler place an entire activation record on the stack. The difference in speed between a recursive and nonrecursive algorithm

3. We can also add parent pointers to each tree node to avoid both recursion and stacks. In this chapter we demonstrate the relation between recursion and stacks, so we do not use parent pointers.

```
// Print tree rooted at current node using preorder traversal.
template <class Object>
void BinaryNode<Object>::printPreOrder( ) const
{
    cout << element << endl;                        // Node
    if( left != NULL )
        left->printPreOrder( );                     // Left
    if( right != NULL )
        right->printPreOrder( );                    // Right
}

// Print tree rooted at current node using postorder traversal.
template <class Object>
void BinaryNode<Object>::printPostOrder( ) const
{
    if( left != NULL )                              // Left
        left->printPostOrder( );
    if( right != NULL )                             // Right
        right->printPostOrder( );
    cout << element << endl;                        // Node
}

// Print tree rooted at current node using inorder traversal.
template <class Object>
void BinaryNode<Object>::printInOrder( ) const
{
    if( left != NULL )                              // Left
        left->printInOrder( );
    cout << element << endl;                        // Node
    if( right != NULL )
        right->printInOrder( );                     // Right
}
```

Figure 18.23 Routines for printing nodes in preorder, postorder, and inorder.

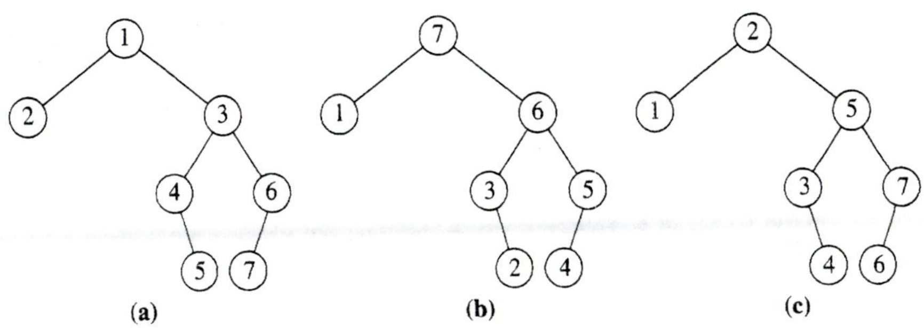

Figure 18.24 (a) Preorder, (b) postorder, and (c) inorder visitation routes.

is very dependent on the platform, and on modern computers may well be negligible. Thus in many cases, the speed improvement does not justify the effort involved in removing recursion. Even so, knowing how to do so is worthwhile, in case your platform is one that would benefit from recursion removal and also because seeing how a program is implemented nonrecursively can sometimes make the recursion clearer.

An iterator class allows step-by-step traversal.

We write three iterator classes, each in the spirit of the linked list. Each allows us to go to the first node, advance to the next node, test whether we have gone past the last node, and access the current node. The order in which nodes are accessed is determined by the type of traversal. We also implement a level-order traversal, which is inherently nonrecursive and in fact uses a queue instead of a stack and is similar to the preorder traversal.

The abstract tree iterator class has methods similar to those of the linked-list iterator. Each type of traversal is represented by a derived class.

Figure 18.25 provides an abstract class for tree iteration. Each iterator stores a pointer to the tree root and an indication of the current node.[4] These are declared at lines 28 and 29, respectively, and initialized in the constructor. They are `protected` to allow the derived classes to access them. Note also that the root of `theTree` is accessible only because `TreeIterator` is a friend of `BinaryTree` (see Figure 18.12, line 48). Four methods are declared at lines 22–25. The `isValid` and `retrieve` methods are invariant over the hierarchy, so an implementation is provided and they are not declared virtual. The abstract methods `first` and `advance` must be provided by each type of iterator. As usual, the destructor is virtual, even though we use shallow pointer semantics, and thus it appears that there is nothing to do. In the derived classes, additional data members are added, and they do need nontrivial destructors. This iterator is similar to the linked list iterator (`LListItr`, in Section 17.2), except that here the `first` method is part of the tree iterator, whereas in the linked list the `first` method was part of the list class itself.

18.4.1 Postorder Traversal

Postorder traversal maintains a stack that stores nodes that have been visited but whose recursive calls are not yet complete.

The postorder traversal is implemented by using a stack to store the current state. The top of the stack will represent the node that we are visiting at some instant in the postorder traversal. However, we may be at one of three places in the algorithm:

1. about to make a recursive call to the left subtree,
2. about to make a recursive call to the right subtree, or
3. about to process the current node.

---

4. In these implementations, once the iterators have been constructed, structurally modifying the tree during an iteration is unsafe because pointers may become stale.

```
// TreeIterator class interface; maintains "current position".
//
// CONSTRUCTION: with a tree to which the iterator is bound.
//
// ******************PUBLIC OPERATIONS*********************
//     First two are not virtual, last two are pure virtual
// bool isValid( )       --> True if at valid position in tree
// Object retrieve( )    --> Return item in current position
// void first( )         --> Set current position to first
// void advance( )       --> Advance
// ******************ERRORS********************************
// BadIterator is thrown for illegal access or advance.

template <class Object>
class TreeIterator
{
  public:
    TreeIterator( const BinaryTree<Object> & theTree )
      : root( theTree.root ), current( NULL ) { }
    virtual ~TreeIterator( ) { }

    virtual void first( ) = 0;
    bool isValid( ) const { return current != NULL; }
    const Object & retrieve( ) const;
    virtual void advance( ) = 0;

  protected:
    const BinaryNode<Object> *root;
    const BinaryNode<Object> *current;
};

// Return the item stored in the current position.
// Throw BadIterator exception if current position is invalid.
template <class Object>
const Object & TreeIterator<Object>::retrieve( ) const
{
    if( !isValid( ) )
        throw BadIterator( "Illegal retrieve" );
    return current->element;
}
```

Figure 18.25 The tree iterator abstract base class.

Consequently, each node is placed on the stack three times during the course of the traversal. If a node is popped from the stack a third time, we can mark it as the current node to be visited.

Each node is placed on the stack three times. The third time off, the node is declared visited. The other times, we simulate a recursive call.

Otherwise, the node is being popped for either the first time or the second time. In this case, it is not yet ready to be visited, so we push it back onto the stack and simulate a recursive call. If the node was popped for a first time, we need to push the left child (if it exists) onto the stack. Otherwise, the node was popped for a second time, and we push the right child (if it exists) onto the stack. In any event, we then pop the stack, applying the same test. Note that, when we pop the stack, we are simulating the recursive call to the appropriate child. If the child does not exist and thus was never pushed onto the stack, when we pop the stack we pop the original node again.

When the stack is empty, every node has been visited.

Eventually, either the process pops a node for the third time or the stack empties. In the latter case, we have iterated over the entire tree. We initialize the algorithm by pushing a pointer to the root onto the stack. An example of how the stack is manipulated is shown in Figure 18.26.

A quick summary: The stack contains nodes that we have traversed but not yet completed. When a node is pushed onto the stack, the counter is 1, 2, or 3 as follows:

1: If we are about to process the node's left subtree,

2: if we are about to process the node's right subtree, or

3: if we are about to process the node itself.

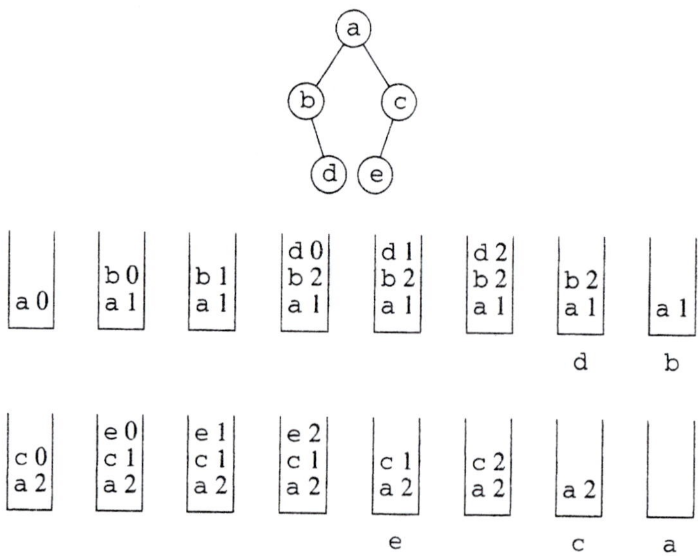

Figure 18.26 Stack states during postorder traversal.

Let us trace through the postorder traversal. We initialize the traversal by pushing root a onto the stack. The first pop visits a. This is a's first pop, so it is placed back on the stack, and we push its left child, b, onto the stack. Next b is popped. It is b's first pop, so it is placed back on the stack. Normally, b's left child would then be pushed, but b has no left child, so nothing is pushed. Thus the next pop reveals b for the second time, b is placed back on the stack, and its right child, d, is pushed onto the stack. The next pop produces d for the first time, and d is pushed back onto the stack. No other push is performed because d has no left child. Thus d is popped for the second time and is pushed back, but as it has no right child, nothing else is pushed. Therefore the next pop yields d for the third time, and d is marked as a visited node. The next node popped is b, and as this pop is b's third, it is marked visited.

Then a is popped for the second time, and it is pushed back onto the stack along with its right child, c. Next, c is popped for the first time, so it is pushed back, along with its left child, e. Now e is popped, pushed, popped, pushed, and finally popped for the third time (typical for leaf nodes). Thus e is marked as a visited node. Next, c is popped for the second time and is pushed back onto the stack. However, it has no right child, so it is immediately popped for the third time and marked as visited. Finally, a is popped for the third time and marked as visited. At this point, the stack is empty and the postorder traversal terminates.

An `StNode` stores a pointer to a node and a count that tells how many times it has already been popped.

The `PostOrder` class is implemented directly from the algorithm described previously and is shown in Figure 18.27. The `StNode` class represents the objects placed on the stack. It contains a pointer to a node and an integer that stores the number of times the item has been popped from the stack. An `StNode` object is always initialized to reflect the fact that it has not yet been popped from the stack. (We use a `Stack` class from Chapter 16.)

The `PostOrder` class is derived from `TreeIterator` and adds an internal stack to the inherited data members. The `PostOrder` class is initialized by initializing the `TreeIterator` data members and then pushing the root onto the stack. This process is illustrated in the constructor at lines 34 to 39. Then `first` is implemented by clearing the stack, pushing the root, and calling `advance`.

The `advance` routine is complicated. Its code follows the earlier description almost verbatim.

Figure 18.28 implements `advance`. It follows the outline almost verbatim. Line 7 tests for an empty stack. If the stack is empty, we have completed the iteration and can set `current` to `NULL` and return. (If `current` is already `NULL`, we have advanced past the end, and an exception is thrown.) Otherwise, we repeatedly perform stack pushes and pops until an item emerges from the stack for a third time. When this happens, the test at line 19 is successful and we can return. Otherwise, at line 25 we push the node back onto the stack (note that the `timesPopped` component has already been incremented at line 19). We then implement the recursive call. If the

```
// PostOrder class interface; maintains "current position".
//
// CONSTRUCTION: with a tree to which the iterator is bound.
//
// ******************PUBLIC OPERATIONS*********************
// bool isValid( )       --> True if at valid position in tree
// Object retrieve( )    --> Return item in current position
// void first( )         --> Set current position to first
// void advance( )       --> Advance
// ******************ERRORS********************************
// BadIterator is thrown for illegal access or advance.

template <class Object>
struct StNode
{
    const BinaryNode<Object> *node;
    int timesPopped;
    StNode( const BinaryNode<Object> *n = 0 )
      : node( n ), timesPopped( 0 ) { }
};

template <class Object>
class PostOrder : public TreeIterator<Object>
{
  public:
    PostOrder( const BinaryTree<Object> & theTree );
    ~PostOrder( ) { }
    void first( );
    void advance( );
  protected:
    Stack< StNode<Object> > s;
};

template <class Object>
PostOrder<Object>::PostOrder( const BinaryTree<Object> &
                       theTree ) : TreeIterator<Object>( theTree )
{
    s.push( StNode<Object>( root ) );
}

template <class Object>
void PostOrder<Object>::first( )
{
    s.makeEmpty( );
    if( root != NULL )
    {
        s.push( StNode<Object>( root ) );
        advance( );
    }
}
```

Figure 18.27 The `PostOrder` class (complete class except for `advance`).

```
// Advance to the next position.
// Throw BadIterator exception if the iteration has been
// exhausted prior to the call.
template <class Object>
void PostOrder<Object>::advance( )
{
    if( s.isEmpty( ) )
    {
        if( current == NULL )
            throw BadIterator( "Advance past end" );
        current = NULL;
        return;
    }
    StNode <Object> cnode;
    for( ; ; )
    {
        cnode = s.topAndPop( );

        if( ++cnode.timesPopped == 3 )
        {
            current = cnode.node;
            return;
        }

        s.push( cnode );
        if( cnode.timesPopped == 1 )
        {
            if( cnode.node->left != NULL )
                s.push( StNode<Object>( cnode.node->left ) );
        }
        else   // cnode.timesPopped == 2
        {
            if( cnode.node->right != NULL )
                s.push( StNode<Object>( cnode.node->right ) );
        }
    }
}
```

Figure 18.28 The `advance` routine for the `PostOrder` iterator class.

node was popped for the first time and it has a left child, its left child is pushed onto the stack. Likewise, if the node was popped for a second time and it has a right child, its right child is pushed onto the stack. Note that, in either case, the construction of the `StNode` object implies that the pushed node goes on the stack with zero pops.

Eventually, the `for` loop terminates because some node will be popped for the third time. Over the entire iteration sequence, there can be at most $3N$ stack pushes and pops, which is another way of establishing the linearity of a postorder traversal

18.4.2 Inorder Traversal

Inorder traversal is similar to postorder, except that a node is declared visited when it is popped for the second time.

The inorder traversal is the same as the postorder traversal, except that a node is declared visited after it is popped a second time. Prior to returning, the iterator pushes the right child (if it exists) onto the stack so that the next call to `advance` can continue by traversing the right child. Because this action is so similar to a postorder traversal, we derive the `InOrder` class from the `PostOrder` class (even though an IS-A relationship does not exist). The only change is the minor alteration to `advance`. The new class is shown in Figure 18.29.

18.4.3 Preorder Traversal

Preorder is the same as postorder, except that a node is declared visited the first time it is popped. The right and then left children are pushed prior to the return.

The preorder traversal is the same as the inorder traversal, except that a node is declared visited after it has been popped the first time. Prior to returning, the iterator pushes the right child onto the stack and then pushes the left child. Note the order: We want the left child to be processed before the right child, so we must push the right child first and the left child second.

We could derive the `PreOrder` class from the `InOrder` or `PostOrder` class, but doing so would be wasteful because the stack no longer needs to maintain a count of the number of times an object has been popped. Consequently, the `PreOrder` class is derived directly from `TreeIterator`. The resulting class interface with the constructor and `first` method is shown in Figure 18.30.

Popping only once allows some simplification.

At line 23, we added a stack of pointers to tree nodes to the `TreeIterator` data fields. The constructor and `first` methods are similar to those already presented. As illustrated by Figure 18.31, `advance` is simpler: We no longer need a `for` loop. As soon as a node is popped at line 15, it becomes the current node. We then push the right child and the left child, if they exist.

18.4.4 Level-Order Traversals

In a *level-order traversal*, nodes are visited top to bottom, left to right. Level-order traversal is implemented via a queue. The traversal is a breadth-first search.

We close by implementing a **level-order traversal,** which processes nodes starting at the root and going from top to bottom, left to right. The name is derived from the fact that we output level 0 nodes (the root), level 1 nodes (root's children), level 2 nodes (grandchildren of the root), and so on. A level-order traversal is implemented by using a queue instead of a stack. The queue stores nodes that are yet to be visited. When a node is visited, its children are placed at the end of the queue where they are visited after the nodes that are already in the queue have been visited. This procedure guarantees that nodes are visited in level order. The `LevelOrder` class shown in Figures 18.32 and

```
// InOrder class interface; maintains "current position".
//
// CONSTRUCTION: with a tree to which the iterator is bound.
//
// ******************PUBLIC OPERATIONS*********************
// Same as TreeIterator
// ******************ERRORS********************************
// BadIterator is thrown for illegal access or advance.

template <class Object>
class InOrder : public PostOrder<Object>
{
    // Accept PostOrder construction and default destruction.
  public:
    InOrder( const BinaryTree<Object> & theTree )
      : PostOrder<Object>( theTree ) { }
    void advance( );
};

// Advance to the next position. Throw BadIterator exception
// if the iteration has been exhausted prior to the call.
template <class Object>
void InOrder<Object>::advance( )
{
    if( s.isEmpty( ) )
    {
        if( current == NULL )
            throw BadIterator( "Advance past end" );
        current = NULL;
        return;
    }
    StNode<Object> cnode;
    for( ; ; )
    {
        cnode = s.topAndPop( );

        if( ++cnode.timesPopped == 2 )
        {
            current = cnode.node;
            if( cnode.node->right != NULL )
                s.push( StNode<Object>( cnode.node->right ) );
            return;
        }
          // First time through
        s.push( cnode );
        if( cnode.node->left != NULL )
            s.push( StNode<Object>( cnode.node->left ) );
    }
}
```

Figure 18.29 The complete `InOrder` iterator class.

```
// PreOrder class interface; maintains "current position".
//
// CONSTRUCTION: with a tree to which the iterator is bound.
//
// ******************PUBLIC OPERATIONS*********************
// bool isValid( )      --> True if at valid position in tree
// Object retrieve( )   --> Return item in current position
// void first( )        --> Set current position to first
// void advance( )      --> Advance
// ******************ERRORS********************************
// BadIterator is thrown for illegal access or advance.

template <class Object>
class PreOrder: public TreeIterator<Object>
{
  public:
    PreOrder( const BinaryTree<Object> & theTree );
    ~PreOrder( ) { }
    void first( );
    void advance( );

  protected:
    Stack< const BinaryNode<Object> * > s;
};

template <class Object>
PreOrder<Object>::PreOrder( const BinaryTree<Object> & theTree)
  : TreeIterator<Object>( theTree )
{
    s.push( root );
}

template <class Object>
void PreOrder<Object>::first( )
{
    s.makeEmpty( );
    if( root != NULL )
    {
        s.push( root );
        advance( );
    }
}
```

Figure 18.30 The `PreOrder` class interface and all members except `advance`.

```
// Advance to the next position.
// Throw BadIterator exception if the iteration has been
// exhausted prior to the call.
template <class Object>
void PreOrder<Object>::advance( )
{
    if( s.isEmpty( ) )
    {
        if( current == NULL )
            throw BadIterator( "Advance past end" );
        current = NULL;
        return;
    }

    current = s.topAndPop( );
    if( current->right != NULL )
        s.push( current->right );
    if( current->left != NULL )
        s.push( current->left );
}
```

Figure 18.31 The `PreOrder` iterator class `advance` routine.

18.33 looks very much like the `PreOrder` class. The only differences are that we use a queue instead of a stack and that we enqueue the left child and then the right child, rather than vice versa. Note that the queue can get very large. In the worst case, all the nodes on the last level (possibly $N/2$) could be in the queue simultaneously.

The level-order traversal implements a more general technique known as *breadth-first search*. We illustrated an example of this in a more general setting in Section 15.2.

Summary

In this chapter we discussed the tree and in particular, the binary tree. We demonstrated the use of trees to implement file systems on many computers and also some other applications, such as expression trees and coding, that we more fully explored in Part III. Algorithms that work on trees make heavy use of recursion. We examined three recursive traversal algorithms—preorder, postorder, and inorder—and showed how they can be implemented nonrecursively. We also examined the level-order traversal, which forms the basis for an important searching technique known as breadth-first search. In Chapter 19 we examine another fundamental type of tree—the *binary search tree*.

```
// LevelOrder class interface; maintains "current position".
//
// CONSTRUCTION: with a tree to which the iterator is bound.
//
// ******************PUBLIC OPERATIONS*********************
// bool isValid( )       --> True if at valid position in tree
// Object retrieve( )    --> Return item in current position
// void first( )         --> Set current position to first
// void advance( )       --> Advance
// ******************ERRORS********************************
// BadIterator is thrown for illegal access or advance.

template <class Object>
class LevelOrder : public TreeIterator<Object>
{
  public:
    LevelOrder( const BinaryTree<Object> & theTree );
    ~LevelOrder( ) { }

    void first( );
    void advance( );

  private:
    Queue< const BinaryNode<Object> * > q;
};

template <class Object>
LevelOrder<Object>::LevelOrder( const BinaryTree<Object> &
                    theTree ) : TreeIterator<Object>( theTree )
{
    q.enqueue( root );
}
```

Figure 18.32 The `LevelOrder` iterator class interface and constructor.

```
// Set the current position to the first.
template <class Object>
void LevelOrder<Object>::first( )
{
    q.makeEmpty( );
    if( root != NULL )
    {
        q.enqueue( root );
        advance( );
    }
}

// Advance to the next position.
// Throw BadIterator exception if the iteration has been
// exhausted prior to the call.
template <class Object>
void LevelOrder<Object>::advance( )
{
    if( q.isEmpty( ) )
    {
        if( current == NULL )
            throw BadIterator( "Advance past end" );
        current = NULL;
        return;
    }
    current = q.getFront( );
    q.dequeue( );

    if( current->left != NULL )
        q.enqueue( current->left );
    if( current->right != NULL )
        q.enqueue( current->right );
}
```

Figure 18.33 The `first` and `advance` routines for the `LevelOrder` iterator class.

Objects of the Game

ancestor and **descendant** If there is a path from node u to node v, then u is an ancestor of v and v is a descendant of u. (p. 606)

binary tree A tree in which no node can have more than two children. A convenient definition is recursive. (p. 611)

depth of a node The length of the path from the root to a node in a tree. (p. 606)

first child/next sibling method A general tree implementation in which each node keeps two pointers per item: one to the leftmost child (if it is not a leaf) and one to its right sibling (if it is not the rightmost sibling). (p. 607)

height of a node The length of the path from a node to the deepest leaf in a tree. (p. 606)

inorder traversal The current node is processed between recursive calls. (p. 622)

leaf A tree node that has no children. (p. 606)

level-order traversal Nodes are visited top to bottom, left to right. Level-order traversal is implemented by using a queue. The traversal is breadth first. (p. 630)

parent and **child** Parents and children are naturally defined. A directed edge connects the parent to the child. (p. 605)

postorder tree traversal Work at a node is performed after its children are evaluated. The traversal takes constant time per node. (p. 610)

preorder tree traversal Work at a node is performed before its children are processed. The traversal takes constant time per node. (p. 610)

proper ancestor and **proper descendant** On a path from node u to node v, if $u \neq v$, then u is a proper ancestor of v and v is a proper descendant of u. (p. 606)

siblings Nodes with the same parents. (p. 606)

size of a node The number of descendants a node has (including the node itself). (p. 606)

tree Defined nonrecursively, a set of nodes and the directed edges that connect them. Defined recursively, a tree is either empty or consists of a root and zero or more subtrees. (p. 605)

Common Errors

1. Allowing a node to be in two trees simultaneously is generally a bad idea because changes to a subtree may inadvertently cause changes in multiple subtrees.
2. Failing to check for empty trees is a common error. If this failure is part of a recursive algorithm, the program will likely crash.
3. A common error when working with trees is thinking iteratively instead of recursively. Design algorithms recursively first. Then convert them to iterative algorithms, if appropriate.

On the Internet

Many of the examples discussed in this chapter are explored in Chapter 19, where we discuss binary search trees. Consequently, the only code available is for the iterator classes.

BinaryTree.h	Contains the interfaces for `BinaryNode` and `BinaryTree`.
BinaryTree.cpp	Contains the implementation of `BinaryNode` and `BinaryTree`.
Iterate.h	Contains the interfaces for the entire `TreeIterator` hierarchy.
Iterate.cpp	Contains the implementation of the `TreeIterator` hierarchy.
TestBinaryTree.cpp	Contains tests for the `BinaryTree` methods and `TreeIterator` hierarchy.

Exercises

In Short

18.1. For the tree shown in Figure 18.34, determine
   a. which node is the root.
   b. which nodes are leaves.
   c. the tree's depth.
   d. the result of preorder, postorder, inorder, and level-order traversals.

18.2. For each node in the tree shown in Figure 18.34,
   a. name the parent node.
   b. list the children.
   c. list the siblings.

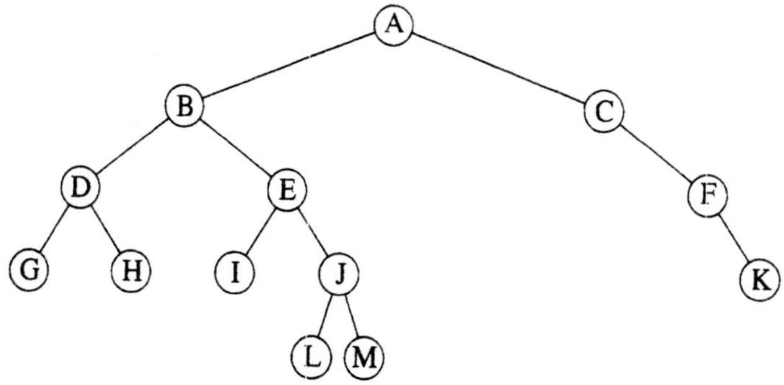

Figure 18.34 Tree for Exercises 18.1 and 18.2.

d. compute the height.
e. compute the depth.
f. compute the size.

18.3. What is output of the function presented in Figure 18.35 for the tree shown in Figure 18.26?

18.4. Show the stack operations when an inorder and preorder traversal is applied to the tree shown in Figure 18.26.

In Theory

18.5. Show that the maximum number of nodes in a binary tree of height H is $2^{H+1} - 1$.

```
void mysteryPrint( BinaryNode<char> * t )
{
    if( t != NULL )
    {
        cout << t->element << endl;
        mysteryPrint( t->left );
        cout << t->element << endl;
        mysteryPrint( t->right );
        cout << t->element << endl;
    }
}
```

Figure 18.35 Mystery program for Exercise 18.3.

18.6. A *full node* is a node with two children. Prove that in a binary tree the number of full nodes plus 1 equals the number of leaves.

18.7. How many NULL children are there in a binary tree of N nodes? How many are in an M-ary tree of N nodes?

18.8. Suppose that a binary tree has leaves $l_1, l_2, \ldots, l_M$ at depths $d_1, d_2, \ldots, d_M$, respectively. Prove that $\sum_{i=1}^{M} 2^{-d_i} \le 1$ and determine when equality is true (known as Kraft's inequality).

In Practice

18.9. Write efficient functions (and give their Big-Oh running times) that take a pointer to a binary tree root T and compute

a. the number of leaves in T.
b. the number of nodes in T that contain one non-NULL child.
c. the number of nodes in T that contain two non-NULL children.

18.10. Implement some of the recursive routines with tests that ensure that a recursive call is not made on a NULL subtree. Compare the running time with identical routines that defer the test until the first line of the recursive function.

18.11. Rewrite the iterator class to throw an exception when `first` is applied to an empty tree. Why might this be a bad idea?

Programming Projects

18.12. A binary tree can be generated automatically for desktop publishing by a program. You can write this program by assigning an x-y coordinate to each tree node, drawing a circle around each coordinate, and connecting each nonroot node to its parent. Assume that you have a binary tree stored in memory and that each node has two extra data members for storing the coordinates. Assume that (0, 0) is the top-left corner. Do the following.

a. The x-coordinate can be computed by assigning the inorder traversal number. Write a routine to do so for each node in the tree.
b. The y-coordinate can be computed by using the negative of the depth of the node. Write a routine to do so for each node in the tree.
c. In terms of some imaginary unit, what will be the dimensions of the picture? Also determine how can you adjust the units so that the tree is always roughly two-thirds as high as it is wide.

d. Prove that when this system is used, no lines cross and that for any node *X*, all elements in *X*'s left subtree appear to the left of *X*, and all elements in *X*'s right subtree appear to the right of *X*.

e. Determine whether both coordinates can be computed in one recursive function.

f. Write a general-purpose tree-drawing program to convert a tree into the following graph-assembler instructions (circles are numbered in the order in which they are drawn):

```
circle( x, y );    // Draw circle with center (x, y)
drawLine( i, j ); // Connect circle i to circle j
```

g. Write a program that reads graph-assembler instructions and outputs the tree to your favorite device.

18.13. If you are running on a Unix system, implement the *du* command.

Chapter 19

Binary Search Trees

For large amounts of input, the linear access time of linked lists is prohibitive. In this chapter we look at an alternative to the linked list: the *binary search tree,* a simple data structure that can be viewed as extending the binary search algorithm to allow insertions and deletions. The running time for most operations is $O(\log N)$ on average. Unfortunately, the worst-case time is $O(N)$ per operation.

In this chapter, we show:

- the basic binary search tree,
- a method for adding order statistics (i.e., the `findKth` operation),
- three different ways to eliminate the $O(N)$ worst case (namely, the *AVL tree, red-black tree,* and *AA-tree*),
- implementation of the STL `set` and `map`, and
- use of the *B-tree* to search a large database quickly.

19.1 Basic Ideas

In the general case, we search for an item (or element) by using its *key.* For instance, a student transcript could be searched on the basis of a student ID number. In this case, the ID number is referred to as the item's key.

For any node in the *binary search tree,* all smaller keyed nodes are in the left subtree and all larger keyed nodes are in the right subtree. Duplicates are not allowed.

The **binary search tree** satisfies the search order property; that is, for every node X in the tree, the values of all the keys in the left subtree are smaller than the key in X and the values of all the keys in the right subtree are larger than the key in X. The tree shown in Figure 19.1(a) is a binary search tree, but the tree shown in Figure 19.1(b) is not because key 8 does not belong in the left subtree of key 7. The binary search tree property implies that all the items in the tree can be ordered consistently (indeed, an inorder traversal yields the items in sorted order). This property also does

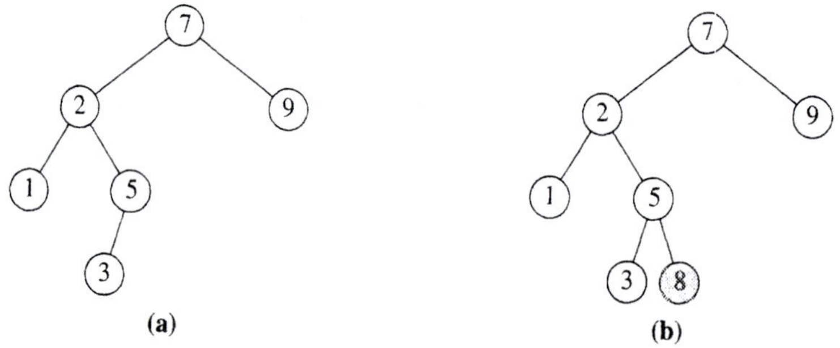

Figure 19.1 Two binary trees: (a) a search tree; (b) not a search tree.

not allow duplicate items. We could easily allow duplicate keys, storing different items having identical keys in a secondary structure is generally better. If these items are exact duplicates, having one item and keeping a count of the number of duplicates is best.

BINARY SEARCH TREE ORDER PROPERTY

In a binary search tree, for every node X, all keys in X's left subtree have smaller values than the key in X, and all keys in X's right subtree have larger values than the key in X.

19.1.1 The Operations

A `find` operation is performed by repeatedly branching either left or right, depending on the result of a comparison.

For the most part, the operations on a binary search tree are simple to visualize. We can perform a `find` operation by starting at the root and then repeatedly branching either left or right, depending on the result of a comparison. For instance, to find 5 in the binary search tree shown in Figure 19.1(a), we start at 7 and go left. This takes us to 2, so we go right, which takes us to 5. To look for 6, we follow the same path. At 5, we would go right and encounter a `NULL` pointer and thus not find 6, as shown in Figure 19.2(a). Figure 19.2(b) shows that 6 can be inserted at the point at which the unsuccessful search terminated.

The `findMin` operation is performed by following left nodes as long as there is a left child. The `findMax` operation is similar.

The binary search tree efficiently supports the `findMin` and `findMax` operations. To perform a `findMin`, we start at the root and repeatedly branch left as long as there is a left child. The stopping point is the smallest element. The `findMax` operation is similar, except that branching is to the right. Note that the cost of all the operations is proportional to the number of nodes on the search path. The cost tends to be logarithmic, but it can be linear in the worst case. We establish this result later in the chapter.

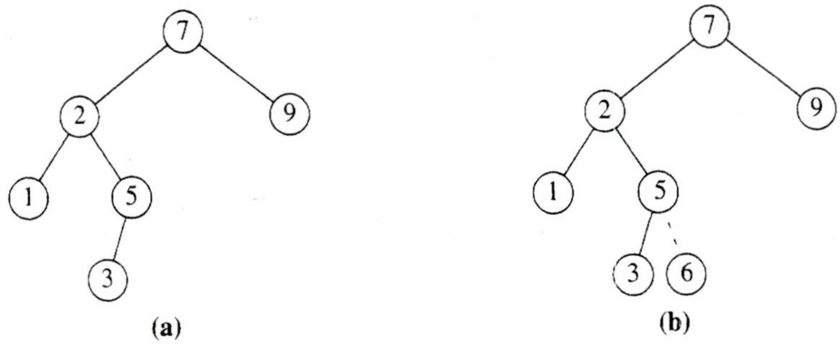

Figure 19.2 Binary search trees (a) before and (b) after the insertion of 6.

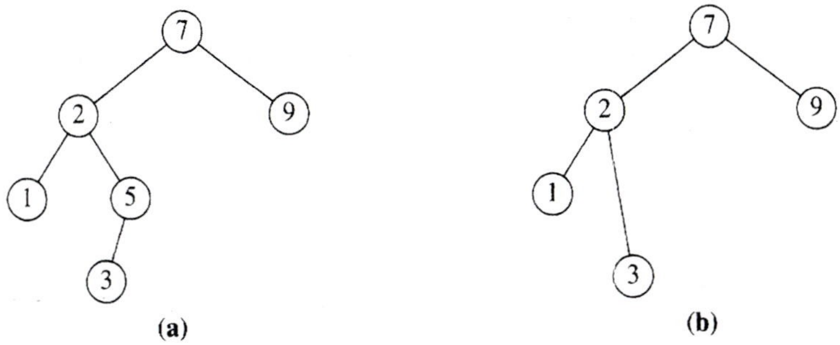

Figure 19.3 Deletion of node 5 with one child: (a) before and (b) after.

The hardest operation is `remove`. Once we have found the node to be removed, we need to consider several possibilities. The problem is that the removal of a node may disconnect parts of the tree. If that happens, we must carefully reattach the tree and maintain the binary search tree property. We also want to avoid making the tree unnecessarily deep because the depth of the tree affects the running time of the tree algorithms.

The `remove` operation is difficult because nonleaf nodes hold the tree together and we do not want to disconnect the tree.

When we are designing a complex algorithm, solving the simplest case first is often easiest, leaving the most complicated case until last. Thus, in examining the various cases, we start with the easiest. If the node is a leaf, its removal does not disconnect the tree, so we can delete it immediatley. If the node has only one child, we can remove the node after adjusting its parent's child link to bypass the node. This is illustrated in Figure 19.3, with the removal of node 5. Note that `removeMin` and `removeMax` are not complex because the affected nodes are either leaves or have only one child. Note also that the root is a special case because it does not have a parent. However, when the `remove` method is implemented, the special case is handled automatically.

If a node has one child, it can be removed by having its parent bypass it. The root is a special case because it does not have a parent.

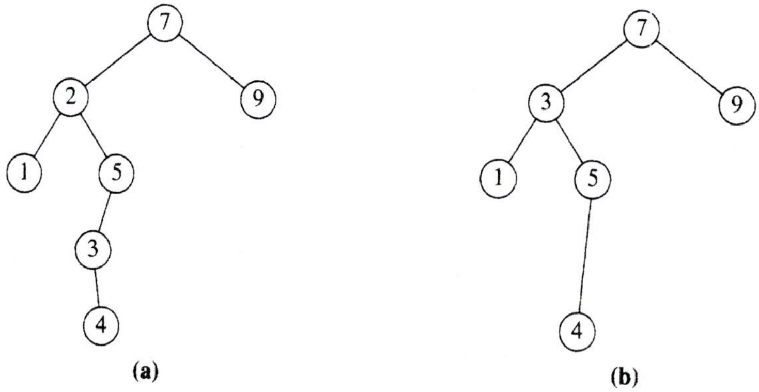

Figure 19.4 Deletion of node 2 with two children: (a) before and (b) after.

A node with two children is replaced by using the smallest item in the right subtree. Then another node is removed.

The complicated case deals with a node having two children. The general strategy is to replace the item in this node with the smallest item in the right subtree (which is easily found, as mentioned earlier) and then remove that node (which is now logically empty). The second `remove` is easy to do because, as just indicated, the minimum node in a tree does not have a left child. Figure 19.4 shows an initial tree and the result of removing node 2. We replace the node with the smallest node (3) in its right subtree and then remove 3 from the right subtree. Note that in all cases removing a node does not make the tree deeper.[1] Many alternatives do make the tree deeper; thus these alternatives are poor options.

19.1.2 C++ Implementation

In principle, the binary search tree is easy to implement. To keep the C++ features from clogging up the code, we introduce a few simplifications. First, Figure 19.5 shows the `BinaryNode` class. We could try to inherit the class from Section 18.2, but things start to get messy because of privacy considerations. Reuse is nice, but at some point practicality must take over. In the new `BinaryNode` class, we make everything private but then use a friend declaration to grant visibility to all the classes involved in the binary search tree implementation. Because we want to be able to use the same declarations for a more advanced binary search tree (discussed in Section 19.2), we include an additional class member at line 7 that is not used in the implementation in this section. The `BinaryNode` class contains the usual list of

1. The deletion can, however, increase the average node depth if a shallow node is removed.

```
template <class Comparable>
class BinaryNode
{
    Comparable  element;
    BinaryNode *left;
    BinaryNode *right;
    int         size;

    BinaryNode( const Comparable & theElement, BinaryNode *lt,
                BinaryNode *rt, int sz = 1 )
      : element( theElement ), left( lt ),
                             right( rt ), size( sz ) { }

    friend class BinarySearchTree<Comparable>;
};
```

Figure 19.5 The `BinaryNode` class for the binary search tree.

data members (the item and two pointers), the additional `size` data member used later, a constructor, and a friend declaration.

The `root` pointer points at the root of the tree, which is `NULL` if the tree is empty.

The `BinarySearchTree` class interface is shown in Figure 19.6. The only data member is the pointer to the root of the tree, `root`. If the tree is empty, `root` is NULL.

Next in the interface are the copy constructor and copy assignment operator. `operator=` is easily implemented, as we showed previously in Figure 18.13 (and as shown in the online code). The destructor at line 24 calls `makeEmpty` (which has the same implementation as the routine in Figure 18.18).

The public class functions call hidden private routines.

The rest of the public `BinarySearchTree` class interface is a straightforward listing of the member functions with implementations that call the hidden functions. The constructor, declared at line 19, merely sets `root` to NULL. The publicly visible members are listed at lines 26–34. Some of the public member functions return a `Cref` object.

A `Cref` object is returned so that we can distinguish between successful and unsuccessful searches.

Recall that the `Cref` class template (see Section 5.3.2) wraps a constant reference variable. However, its advantage is that it can also store a null reference. Recall further that we can use `isNull` to test whether a null reference is being stored and that we can get the constant reference variable that is being wrapped by calling `get`.

Next, we have several functions that operate on a node passed as a parameter, a general technique that we used in Chapter 18. The idea is that the publicly visible class routines call these hidden routines and pass `root` as a parameter. These hidden routines do all the work. Two details are important: First, at line 38, we use `protected` rather than `private` because we

```
// BinarySearchTree class.
//
// CONSTRUCTION: with no parameters or another BinarySearchTree.
//
// ******************PUBLIC OPERATIONS*********************
// void insert( x )          --> Insert x
// void remove( x )          --> Remove x
// void removeMin( )         --> Remove smallest item
// Comparable find( x )      --> Return item that matches x
// Comparable findMin( )     --> Return smallest item
// Comparable findMax( )     --> Return largest item
// bool isEmpty( )           --> Return true if empty; else false
// void makeEmpty( )         --> Remove all items

template <class Comparable>
class BinarySearchTree
{
  public:
    BinarySearchTree( );
    BinarySearchTree( const BinarySearchTree & rhs );
    const BinarySearchTree & operator=(
                                 const BinarySearchTree & rhs );

    virtual ~BinarySearchTree( );

    Cref<Comparable> findMin( ) const;
    Cref<Comparable> findMax( ) const;
    Cref<Comparable> find( const Comparable & x ) const;
    bool isEmpty( ) const;

    void makeEmpty( );
    void insert( const Comparable & x );
    void remove( const Comparable & x );
    void removeMin( );

    typedef BinaryNode<Comparable> Node;

  protected:
    Node *root;

    Cref<Comparable> elementAt( Node *t ) const;
    virtual void insert( const Comparable & x, Node * & t ) const;
    virtual void remove( const Comparable & x, Node * & t ) const;
    virtual void removeMin( Node * & t ) const;
    Node * findMin( Node *t ) const;
    Node * findMax( Node *t ) const;
    Node * find( const Comparable & x, Node *t ) const;
    void makeEmpty( Node * & t ) const;
    Node * clone( Node *t ) const;
};
```

Figure 19.6 The `BinarySearchTree` class interface.

```
// Find item x in the tree.
// Return the matching item wrapped in a Cref object.
template <class Comparable>
Cref<Comparable> BinarySearchTree<Comparable>::
find( const Comparable & x ) const
{
    return elementAt( find( x, root ) );
}

// Internal method to wrap the element field in node t
// inside a Cref object.
template <class Comparable>
Cref<Comparable> BinarySearchTree<Comparable>::
elementAt( Node *t ) const
{
    return t == NULL ? Cref<Comparable>( ) :
                       Cref<Comparable>( t->element );
}
```

Figure 19.7 The `find` public member function that calls a hidden routine and the `elementAt` member function.

derive another class from `BinarySearchTree` in Section 19.2. Second, some of the routines must be declared virtual because they are overridden with new definitions in a derived class.

The `insert` function adds `x` to the current tree by calling the hidden `insert` with `root` as an additional parameter. This action fails if `x` is already in the tree; in that case, a `DuplicateItemException` would be thrown. The `findMin`, `findMax`, and `find` operations return the minimum, maximum, or named item (respectively) from the tree. If the item is not found because the tree is empty or the named item is not present, then applying `isNull` to the returned `Cref` object will produce `true`. Figure 19.7 shows this technique of a public member function calling a private function, as applied to the `find` method.

The `removeMin` operation removes the minimum item from the tree; it throws an exception if the tree is empty. The `remove` operation removes a named item `x` from the tree; it throws an exception if warranted. The `makeEmpty` and `isEmpty` methods are the usual fare.

As is typical of most data structures, the `find` operation is easier than `insert`, and `insert` is easier than `remove`. Figure 19.8 illustrates the `find` routine. So long as a `NULL` pointer has not been reached, we either have a match or need to branch left or right. The code implements this algorithm quite succinctly. Note the order of the tests. The test against `NULL` must be performed first; otherwise, the access `t->element` would

```
// Internal method to find an item in a subtree.
// x is item to search for.
// t is the node that roots the tree.
// Return node containing the matched item.
template <class Comparable>
BinaryNode<Comparable> * BinarySearchTree<Comparable>::
find( const Comparable & x, Node *t ) const
{
    while( t != NULL )
        if( x < t->element )
            t = t->left;
        else if( t->element < x )
            t = t->right;
        else
            return t;     // Match

    return NULL;          // Not found
}
```

Figure 19.8 The `find` operation for binary search trees.

be illegal. The remaining tests are arranged with the least likely case last. A recursive implementaion is possible, but we use a loop instead; we use recursion in the `insert` and `remove` functions. In Exercise 19.17 you are asked to write the searching algorithms recursively.

Because of call by value, the actual argument (`root`) is not changed.

At first glance statements such as `t=t->left` may seem to change the root of the tree. That is not the case, however, because `t` is passed by value. This has nothing to do with the `const` in the function declaration. It is the call by value mechanism that matters here. In the initial call, `t` is simply a *copy* of `root`. Although `t` changes, `root` does not. The calls to `findMin` and `findMax` are even simpler because branching is unconditionally in one direction. These routines are shown in Figure 19.9. Note how the case of an empty tree is handled.

For `insert`, we must pass the tree `t` by reference to effect a change.

The `insert` routine is shown in Figure 19.10. Here we use recursion to simplify the code. A nonrecursive implementation is also possible; we apply this technique when we discuss red–black trees later in this chapter. The basic algorithm is simple. If the tree is empty, we can create a one-node tree. The test is performed at line 10, and the new node is allocated at line 11. In this case `t` is passed by reference (at line 8). Thus, if the actual argument is `root`, then at line 11, when `t` is changed to point at the newly allocated node, the change applies to `root`, and `root` will also point at the newly allocated node.

If the tree is not already empty, we have three possibilities. First, if the item to be inserted is smaller than the item in node `t`, we call `insert`

```
// Internal method to find the smallest item in a subtree t.
// Return node containing the smallest item.
template <class Comparable>
BinaryNode<Comparable> * BinarySearchTree<Comparable>::
findMin( Node *t ) const
{
    if( t != NULL )
        while( t->left != NULL )
            t = t->left;

    return t;
}

// Internal method to find the largest item in a subtree t.
// Return node containing the largest item.
template <class Comparable>
BinaryNode<Comparable> * BinarySearchTree<Comparable>::
findMax( Node *t ) const
{
    if( t != NULL )
        while( t->right != NULL )
            t = t->right;

    return t;
}
```

Figure 19.9 The `findMin` and `findMax` methods for binary search trees.

recursively on the left subtree. Second, if the item is larger than the item in node `t`, we call `insert` recursively on the right subtree (these two cases are coded at lines 12 to 15). Third, if the item to insert matches the item in `t`, we throw an exception.

Because `t` is passed by reference, the subtree is automatically connected.

An important question to answer is, If the recursive insertion at line 13 changes the root of the left subtree, how can we be sure that the subtree will not be disconnected? The answer is that, as the tree is passed by reference, any changes to the root of the left subtree will be reflected in the object `t->left`, thus guaranteeing that the tree stays connected. The only time that this happens is when `t->left` is `NULL` and we add a node in the left subtree. But even if the changes were more general, we would still be safe. The key here is that `t->left` at line 13 and `t->right` at line 15 are passed by reference. If we wrote the routine nonrecursively, we would have to maintain a pointer to the parent node as we descend the tree.

The remaining routines concern deletion. As described earlier, the `removeMin` operation is simple because the minimum node has no left child. Thus the removed node merely needs to be bypassed, which appears

```
// Internal method to insert into a subtree.
// x is the item to insert.
// t is the node that roots the tree.
// Set the new root.
// Throw DuplicateItemException if x is already in t.
template <class Comparable>
void BinarySearchTree<Comparable>::
insert( const Comparable & x, Node * & t ) const
{
    if( t == NULL )
        t = new Node( x, NULL, NULL );
    else if( x < t->element )
        insert( x, t->left );
    else if( t->element < x )
        insert( x, t->right );
    else
        throw DuplicateItemException( );
}
```

Figure 19.10 The recursive `insert` for the `BinarySearchTree` class.

to require us to keep track of the parent of the current node as we descend the tree. But, again, we can avoid the explicit use of a parent pointer by using recursion. The code is shown in Figure 19.11.

Passing `t` by reference also works in the `remove` routines. In effect we maintain the parent in the recursion stack.

If the tree `t` is empty, `removeMin` fails. Otherwise, if `t` has a left child, we recursively remove the minimum item in the left subtree via the recursive call at line 12. If we reach line 15, we know that we are currently at the minimum node, and thus `t` is the root of a subtree that has no left child. If we set `t` to `t->right` and then `delete` the node that `t` used to point at, `t` is now the root of a subtree that is missing its former minimum element. That is what we do at lines 15–17. But doesn't that disconnect the tree? The answer again is no. If `t` was `root`, then, as `t` is passed by reference, `root` is changed to point at the new tree. If `t` was not `root`, it is `p->left`, where `p` is `t`'s parent at the time of the recursive call. The change to `t`, being by reference, also changes `p->left`. Thus the parent's `left` pointer points at `t`, and the tree is connected. All in all, it is a nifty maneuver—we have maintained the parent in the recursion stack rather than explicitly kept track of it in an iterative loop.

Having used this trick for the simple case, we can then adapt it for the general `remove` routine shown in Figure 19.12. If the tree is empty, the `remove` is unsuccessful and we can throw an exception at line 10. If we do not have a match, we can recursively call `remove` for either the left or right subtree, as appropriate. Otherwise, we reach line 15, indicating that we have found the node that needs to be removed.

```
// Internal method to remove minimum item from a subtree.
// t is the node that roots the tree.
// Set the new root.
// Throws UnderflowException if t is empty.
template <class Comparable>
void BinarySearchTree<Comparable>::
removeMin( Node * & t ) const
{
    if( t == NULL )
        throw UnderflowException( );
    else if( t->left != NULL )
        removeMin( t->left );
    else
    {
        Node *tmp = t;
        t = t->right;
        delete tmp;
    }
}
```

Figure 19.11 The `removeMin` method for the `BinarySearchTree` class.

```
// Internal method to remove from a subtree.
// x is the item to remove, t is the node that roots the tree.
// Set the new root.
// Throw ItemNotFoundException is x is not in t.
template <class Comparable>
void BinarySearchTree<Comparable>::
remove( const Comparable & x, Node * & t ) const
{
    if( t == NULL )
        throw ItemNotFoundException( );
    if( x < t->element )
        remove( x, t->left );
    else if( t->element < x )
        remove( x, t->right );
    else if( t->left != NULL && t->right != NULL )// 2 children
    {
        t->element = findMin( t->right )->element;
        removeMin( t->right );                    // Remove minimum
    }
    else // One or zero children
    {
        BinaryNode<Comparable> *oldNode = t;
        t = ( t->left != NULL ) ? t->left : t->right; // Reroot
        delete oldNode;                          // delete old root
    }
}
```

Figure 19.12 The `remove` member routine for the `BinarySearchTree` class.

The `remove` routine involves tricky coding but is not too bad if recursion is used. The case for one child, root with one child, and zero children are all handled together at lines 22–24.

Recall (as illustrated in Figure 19.4) that, if there are two children, we replace the node with the minimum element in the right subtree and then remove the right subtree's minimum (coded at lines 17–18). Otherwise, we have either one or zero children. We save a pointer to the current node at line 22 so that we can `delete` it at line 24. If there is a left child, we set `t` equal to its left child, as we would do in `removeMax`. Otherwise, we know that there is no left child and that we can set `t` equal to its right child. This procedure is succinctly coded in line 23, which also covers the leaf case.

Two points need to be made about this implementation. First, during the basic `insert`, `find`, or `remove` operation, we perform two comparisons per node accessed to distinguish among the cases <, =, and >. Actually, however, we can get by with only one comparison per node. The strategy is similar to what we did in the binary search algorithm in Section 6.6. We discuss the technique for binary search trees in Section 19.6.2 when we illustrate the deletion algorithm for AA-trees.

Second, we do not have to use recursion to perform the insertion. In fact, a recursive implementation is probably slower than a nonrecursive implementation. We discuss an iterative implementation of `insert` in Section 19.5.3 in the context of red–black trees.

19.2 Order Statistics

The binary search tree allows us to find either the minimum or maximum item in time that is equivalent to an arbitrarily named `find`. Sometimes, we also have to be able to access the Kth smallest element, for an arbitrary K provided as a parameter. We can do so if we keep track of the size of each node in the tree.

We can implement `findKth` by maintaining the size of each node as we update the tree.

Recall from Section 18.1 that the size of a node is the number of its descendants (including itself). Suppose that we want to find the Kth smallest element and that K is at least 1 and at most the number of nodes in the tree. Figure 19.13 shows three possible cases, depending on the relation of K and the size of the left subtree, denoted S_L. If K equals $S_L + 1$, the root is the Kth smallest element and we can stop. If K is smaller than $S_L + 1$ (i.e., smaller than or equal to S_L), the Kth smallest element must be in the left subtree and we can find it recursively. (The recursion can be avoided; we use it to simplify the algorithm description.) Otherwise, the Kth smallest element is the $(K - S_L - 1)$th smallest element in the right subtree and can be found recursively.

The main effort is maintaining the node sizes during tree changes. These changes occur in the `insert`, `remove`, and `removeMin` operations.

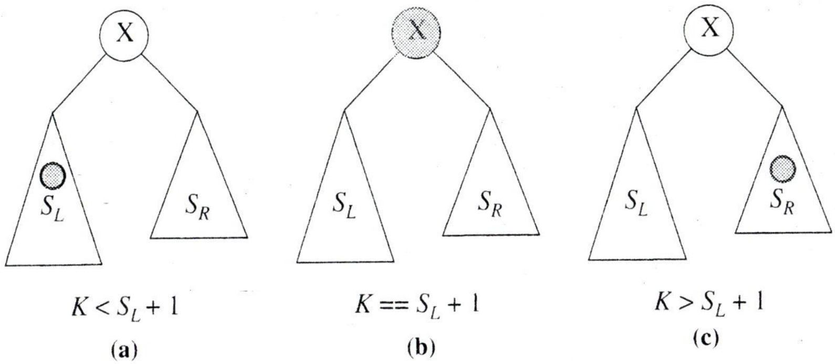

Figure 19.13 Using the `size` data member to implement `findKth`.

In principle, this maintenance is simple enough. During an `insert`, each node on the path to the insertion point gains one node in its subtree. Thus the size of each node increases by 1, and the inserted node has size 1. In `removeMin`, each node on the path to the minimum loses one node in its subtree; thus the size of each node decreases by 1. During a `remove`, all nodes on the path to the node that is physically removed also lose one node in their subtrees. Consequently, we can maintain the sizes at the cost of only a slight amount of overhead.

19.2.1 C++ Implementation

We derive a new class that supports the order statistic.

Logically, the only changes required are the adding of `findKth` and the maintenance of the `size` data members in `insert`, `remove`, and `removeMin`. We derive a new class from `BinarySearchTree`, the interface for which is shown in Figure 19.14. We need to make the new class a friend of `BinaryNode`.

Let us first examine the new public member functions. Because constructors and a destructor are not explicitly provided, the defaults are used. For the constructor, the inherited data member is initialized by the `BinarySearchTree` constructor. For the destructor, the base class destructor is eventually called to clean up the memory.

We must redefine both the hidden and public update functions.

The publicly visible member functions `findKth`, `insert`, `remove`, and `removeMin`, declared at lines 15, 17, 19, and 21, respectively, logically call a corresponding hidden member function. We might expect that a routine such as `insert` at line 17 does not need to be redefined, as its body is simply a call to the `BinarySearchTree` `insert`. However, because we are rewriting the hidden recursive versions of `insert`, `remove`, and `removeMin`,

```
1  // BinarySearchTreeWithRank class.
2  //
3  // CONSTRUCTION: with no parameters or
4  //               another BinarySearchTreeWithRank.
5
6  // *****************PUBLIC OPERATIONS*********************
7  // Comparable findKth( k )--> Return kth smallest item
8  // All other operations are in effect inherited.
9
10 template <class Comparable>
11 class BinarySearchTreeWithRank :
12                        public BinarySearchTree<Comparable>
13 {
14   public:
15     Cref<Comparable> findKth( int k ) const
16       { return elementAt( findKth( k, root ); }
17     void insert( const Comparable & x )
18       { BinarySearchTree<Comparable>::insert( x ); }
19     void remove( const Comparable & x )
20       { BinarySearchTree<Comparable>::remove( x ); }
21     void removeMin( )
22       { BinarySearchTree<Comparable>::removeMin( ); }
23
24     typedef BinaryNode<Comparable> Node;
25
26   private:
27     void insert( const Comparable & x, Node * & t ) const;
28     void remove( const Comparable & x, Node * & t ) const;
29     void removeMin( Node * & t ) const;
30     Node *findKth( int k, Node *t ) const;
31
32     int treeSize( Node *t ) const
33       { return t == NULL ? 0 : t->size; }
34 };
```

Figure 19.14 The `BinarySearchTree` class interface.

these versions *hide* the public members with the same name (see Section 4.4.3). Thus for this technical reason, we rewrite the public member functions and have them simply call the corresponding base class member functions. This is C++ ugliness because, if the private member functions in the `BinarySearchTree` base class simply would have had different *names* than their public counterparts, we would have been able to completely remove lines 17–22 in Figure 19.14 and only had to override the private member functions. (In Exercise 19.19 you are asked to rewrite both classes to verify that this assertion is true.)

```
1 // Internal method to find kth item in a subtree.
2 // k is the desired rank.
3 // t is the node that roots the tree.
4 template <class Comparable>
5 BinaryNode<Comparable> * BinarySearchTreeWithRank<Comparable>::
6 findKth( int k, Node * t ) const
7 {
8     if( t == NULL )
9         return NULL;
10
11     int leftSize = treeSize( t->left );
12
13     if( k <= leftSize )
14         return findKth( k, t->left );
15     else if( k == leftSize + 1 )
16         return t;
17     else
18         return findKth( k - leftSize - 1, t->right );
19 }
```

Figure 19.15 The `findKth` operation for a search tree with order statistics.

The `findKth` operation is easily implemented once the size members are known.

The `findKth` operation shown in Figure 19.15 is written recursively, although clearly it need not be. It follows the algorithmic description line for line. The test against `NULL` at line 8 is necessary because `k` could be invalid. At line 11 we compute the size of the left subtree. If the left subtree exists, accessing its `size` member gives the required answer. If the left subtree does not exist, its size can be taken to be 0 (see the definition of `treeSize` at lines 32 and 33 in the class interface). Note that this test is performed after we are sure that `t` is not `NULL`.

The `insert` and `remove` operations are potentially tricky because we do not update the size information if the operation is unsuccessful.

The `insert` operation is shown in Figure 19.16. The potentially tricky part is that, if the insertion call succeeds, we want to increment `t`'s `size` member. If the recursive call fails, `t`'s `size` member is unchanged and an exception should be thrown. In an unsuccessful insertion can some sizes change? The answer is no; `size` is updated only if the recursive call succeeds without an exception. Note that when a new node is allocated by a call to `new`, the `size` member is set to 0 by the `BinaryNode` constructor, and then incremented at line 18.

Figure 19.17 shows that the same trick can be used for `removeMin`. If the recursive call succeeds, the `size` member is decremented; if the recursive call fails, `size` is unchanged. The `remove` operation is similar and is shown in Figure 19.18.

```
// Internal method to insert into a subtree.
// x is the item to insert.
// t is the node that roots the tree.
// Set the new root.
// Throw DuplicateItemException if x is already in t.
template <class Comparable>
void BinarySearchTreeWithRank<Comparable>::
insert( const Comparable & x, Node * & t ) const
{
    if( t == NULL )
        t = new Node( x, NULL, NULL, 0 );
    else if( x < t->element )
        insert( x, t->left );
    else if( t->element < x )
        insert( x, t->right );
    else
        throw DuplicateItemException( );
    t->size++;
}
```

Figure 19.16 The `insert` operation for a search tree with order statistics.

```
// Internal method to remove minimum item from a subtree.
// t is the node that roots the tree.
// Set the new root.
// Throw UnderflowException if t is empty.
template <class Comparable>
void BinarySearchTreeWithRank<Comparable>::
removeMin( Node * & t ) const
{
    if( t == NULL )
        throw UnderflowException( );
    else if( t->left != NULL )
        removeMin( t->left );
    else
    {
        Node *tmp = t;
        t = t->right;
        delete tmp;
        return;
    }
    t->size--;
}
```

Figure 19.17 The `removeMin` operation for a search tree with order statistics.

```
// Internal method to remove from a subtree.
// x is the item to remove.
// t is the node that roots the tree.
// Set the new root.
// Throw ItemNotFoundException is x is not in t.
template <class Comparable>
void BinarySearchTreeWithRank<Comparable>::
remove( const Comparable & x, Node * & t ) const
{
    if( t == NULL )
        throw ItemNotFoundException( );
    if( x < t->element )
        remove( x, t->left );
    else if( t->element < x )
        remove( x, t->right );
    else if( t->left != NULL && t->right != NULL )// 2 children
    {
        t->element = findMin( t->right )->element;
        removeMin( t->right );                  // Remove minimum
    }
    else
    {
        BinaryNode<Comparable> *oldNode = t;
        t = ( t->left != NULL ) ? t->left : t->right; // Reroot
        delete oldNode;                         // delete old root
        return;
    }
    t->size--;
}
```

Figure 19.18 The `remove` operation for a search tree with order statistics.

19.3 Analysis of Binary Search Tree Operations

The cost of each binary search tree operation (`insert`, `find`, and `remove`) is proportional to the number of nodes accessed during the operation. We can thus charge the access of any node in the tree a cost of 1 plus its depth (recall that the depth measures the number of edges on a path rather than the number of nodes), which gives the cost of a successful search.

The cost of an operation is proportional to the depth of the last accessed node. The cost is logarithmic for a well-balanced tree, but it could be as bad as linear for a degenerate tree.

Figure 19.19 shows two trees. Exercise 19.19(a) shows a balanced tree of 15 nodes. The cost to access any node is at most 4 units, and some nodes require fewer accesses. This situation is analogous to the one that occurs in the binary search algorithm. If the tree is perfectly balanced, the access cost is logarithmic.

Unfortunately, we have no guarantee that the tree is perfectly balanced. The tree shown in Figure 19.19(b) is the classic example of an unbalanced

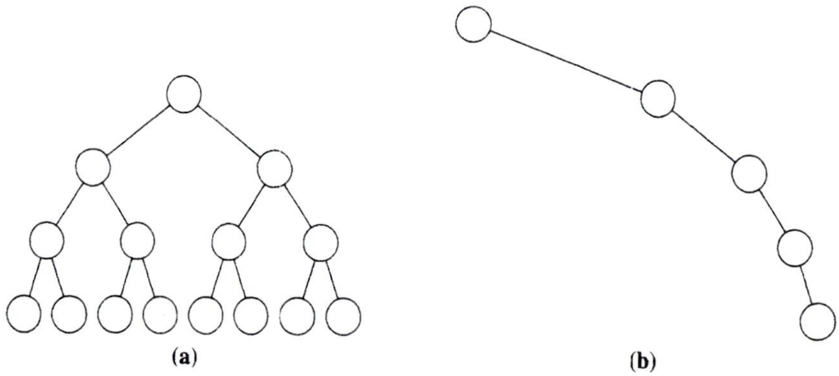

Figure 19.19 (a) The balanced tree has a depth of $\lfloor \log N \rfloor$; (b) the unbalanced tree has a depth of $N - 1$.

tree. Here, all N nodes are on the path to the deepest node, so the worst-case search time is $O(N)$. Because the search tree has degenerated to a linked list, the average time required to search in *this particular instance* is half the cost of the worst case and is also $O(N)$. So we have two extremes: In the best case, we have logarithmic access cost, and in the worst case we have linear access cost. What, then, is the average? Do most binary search trees tend toward the balanced or unbalanced case, or is there some middle ground, such as $\sqrt{N}$? The answer is identical to that for quicksort: The average is 38 percent worse than the best case.

On average the depth is 38 percent worse than the best case. This result is identical to that obtained using quicksort.

We prove in this section that the average depth over all nodes in a binary search tree is logarithmic, under the assumption that each tree is created as a result of random insertion sequences (with no `remove` operations). To see what that means, consider the result of inserting three items in an empty binary search tree. Only their relative ordering is important, so we can assume without loss of generality that the three items are 1, 2, and 3. Then there are six possible insertion orders: (1, 2, 3), (1, 3, 2), (2, 1, 3), (2, 3, 1), (3, 1, 2), and (3, 2, 1). We assume in our proof that each insertion order is equally likely. The binary search trees that can result from these insertions are shown in Figure 19.20. Note that the tree with root 2, shown in Figure 19.20(c), is formed from either the insertion sequence (2, 3, 1) or the sequence (2, 1, 3). Thus some trees are more likely to result than others, and as we show, balanced trees are more likely to occur than unbalanced trees (although this result is not evident from the three-element case).

We begin with the following definition.

DEFINITION: The **internal path length** of a binary tree is the sum of the depths of its nodes.

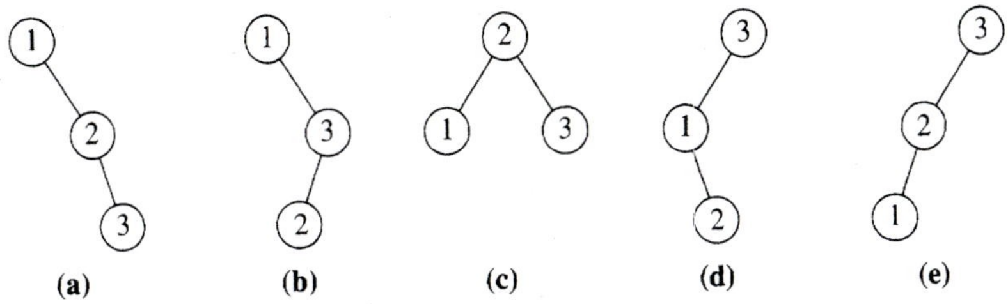

Figure 19.20 Binary search trees that can result from inserting a permutation 1, 2, and 3; the balanced tree shown in part (c) is twice as likely to result as any of the others.

When we divide the internal path length of a tree by the number of nodes in the tree, we obtain the average node depth. Adding 1 to this average gives the average cost of a successful search in the tree. Thus we want to compute the average internal path length for a binary search tree, where the average is taken over all (equally probable) input permutations. We can easily do so by viewing the tree recursively and by using techniques from the analysis of quicksort given in Section 9.6. The average internal path length is established in Theorem 19.1.

The *internal path length* is used to measure the cost of a successful search.

Theorem 19.1

The internal path length of a binary search tree is approximately $1.38\,N \log N$ *on average, under the assumption that all permutations are equally likely.*

Proof

Let $D(N)$ *be the average internal path length for trees of* N *nodes, so* $D(1) = 0$. *An* N*-node tree* T *consists of an* i*-node left subtree and an* $(N - i - 1)$*-node right subtree, plus a root at depth 0 for* $0 \le i < N$. *By assumption, each value of* i *is equally likely. For a given* i, $D(i)$ *is the average internal path length of the left subtree with respect to its root. In* T, *all these nodes are one level deeper. Thus the average contribution of the nodes in the left subtree to the internal path length of* T *is* $(1/N)\sum_{i=0}^{N-1} D(i)$, *plus 1 for each node in the left subtree. The same holds for the right subtree. We thus obtain the recurrence formula* $D(N) = (2/N)(\sum_{i=0}^{N-1} D(i)) + N - 1$, *which is identical to the quicksort recurrence solved in Section 9.6. The result is an average internal path length of* $O(N \log N)$.

The *external path length* is used to measure the cost of an unsuccessful search.

The insertion algorithm implies that the cost of an insert equals the cost of an unsuccessful search, which is measured by using the external path length. In an insertion or unsuccessful search, we eventually reach the test `t==NULL`. Recall that in a tree of N nodes there are $N + 1$ `NULL` pointers. The external path length measures the total number of nodes that are accessed, including the `NULL` node for each of these $N + 1$ `NULL` pointers. The `NULL` node is sometimes called an **external tree node,** which explains the term *external path length*. As we show later in the chapter, replacing the `NULL` node with a sentinel may be convenient.

DEFINITION: The **external path length** of a binary search tree is the sum of the depths of the $N + 1$ `NULL` pointers. The terminating `NULL` node is considered a node for these purposes.

One plus the result of dividing the average external path length by $N + 1$ yields the average cost of an unsuccessful search or insertion. As with the binary search algorithm, the average cost of an unsuccessful search is only slightly more than the cost of a successful search, which follows from Theorem 19.2.

Theorem 19.2

For any tree T, let IPL(T) be the internal path length of T and let EPL(T) be its external path length. Then, if T has N nodes, $EPL(T) = IPL(T) + 2N$.

Proof

This theorem is proved by induction and is left as Exercise 19.9.

Random `remove` operations do not preserve the randomness of a tree. The effects are not completely understood theoretically, but they apparently are negligible in practice.

It is tempting to say immediately that these results imply that the average running time of all operations is $O(\log N)$. This implication is true in practice, but it has not been established analytically because the assumption used to prove the previous results do not take into account the deletion algorithm. In fact, close examination suggests that we might be in trouble with our deletion algorithm because the `remove` operation always replaces a two-child deleted node with a node from the right subtree. This result would seem to have the effect of eventually unbalancing the tree and tending to make it left-heavy. It has been shown that if we build a random binary search tree and then perform roughly N^2 pairs of random `insert`/`remove` combinations, the binary search trees will have an expected depth of $O(\sqrt{N})$. However, a reasonable number of random `insert` and `remove` operations (in which the order of `insert` and `remove` is also random) does not unbalance the tree in any observable way. In fact, for small search trees, the `remove` algorithm seems to balance the tree. Consequently, we can reasonably assume that for random input all operations behave in logarithmic average time, although this result has not been proved mathematically. In Exercise 19.28 we describe some alternative deletion strategies.

The most important problem is not the potential imbalance caused by the `remove` algorithm. Rather, it is that, if the input sequence is sorted, the worst-case tree occurs. When that happens, we are in deep trouble: We have linear time per operation (for a series of N operations) rather than logarithmic cost per operation. This case is analogous to passing items to quicksort but having an insertion sort executed instead. The resulting running time is completely unacceptable. Moreover, it is not just sorted input that is problematic, but also any input that contains long sequences of nonrandomness. One solution to this problem is to insist on an extra structural condition called *balance:* No node is allowed to get too deep.

Any of several algorithms can be used to implement a **balanced binary search tree,** which has an added structure property that guarantees logarithmic depth in the worst case. Most of these algorithms are much more complicated than those for the standard binary search trees, and all take longer on average for insertion and deletion. They do, however, provide protection against the embarrassingly simple cases that lead to poor performance for (unbalanced) binary search trees. Also, because they are balanced, they tend to give faster access time than those for the standard tres. Typically, their internal path lengths are very close to the optimal $N \log N$ rather than $1.38N \log N$, so searching time is roughly 25 percent faster.

A *balanced binary search tree* has an added structure property to guarantee logarithmic depth in the worst case. Updates are slower, but accesses are faster.

19.4 AVL Trees

The first balanced binary search tree was the *AVL tree* (named after its discoverers, Adelson-Velskii and Landis), which illustrates the ideas that are thematic for a wide class of balanced binary search trees. It is a binary search tree that has an additional balance condition. Any balance condition must be easy to maintain and ensures that the depth of the tree is $O(\log N)$. The simplest idea is to require that the left and right subtrees have the same height. Recursion dictates that this idea apply to all nodes in the tree because each node is itself a root of some subtree. This balance condition ensures that the depth of the tree is logarithmic. However, it is too restrictive because inserting new items while maintaining balance is too difficult. Thus the definition of an AVL tree uses a notion of balance that is somewhat weaker but still strong enough to guarantee logarithmic depth.

The *AVL tree* was the first balanced binary search tree. It has historical significance and also illustrates most of the ideas that are used in other schemes.

> **DEFINITION:** An **AVL tree** is a binary search tree with the additional balance property that, for any node in the tree, the height of the left and right subtrees can differ by at most 1. As usual, the height of an empty subtree is -1.

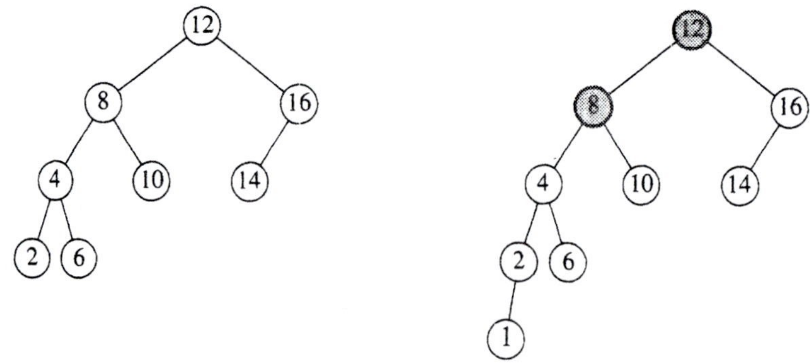

Figure 19.21 Two binary search trees: (a) an AVL tree; (b) not an AVL tree (unbalanced nodes are darkened).

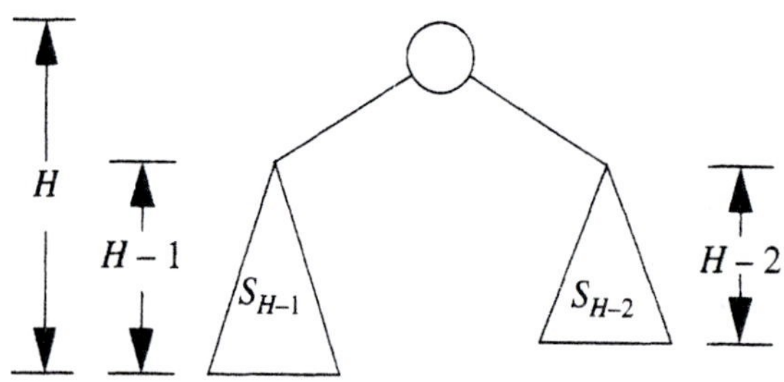

Figure 19.22 Minimum tree of height *H*.

19.4.1 Properties

Every node in an AVL tree has subtrees whose heights differ by at most 1. An empty subtree has height −1.

Figure 19.21 shows two binary search trees. The tree shown in Figure 19.21(a) satisfies the AVL balance condition and is thus an AVL tree. The tree shown in Figure 19.21(b), which results from inserting 1, using the usual algorithm, is not an AVL tree because the darkened nodes have left subtrees whose heights are 2 larger than their right subtrees. If 13 were inserted, using the usual binary search tree insertion algorithm, node 16 would also be in violation. The reason is that the left subtree would have height 1, while the right subtree would have height −1.

The AVL tree has height at most roughly 44 percent greater than the minimum.

The AVL balance condition implies that the tree has only logarithmic depth. To prove this assertion we need to show that a tree of height H must have at least C^H nodes for some constant $C > 1$. In other words, the minimum number of nodes in a tree is exponential in its height. Then the maximum depth of an N-item tree is given by $\log_C N$. Theorem 19.3 shows that every AVL tree of height H has many nodes.

Theorem 19.3

An AVL tree of height H has at least $F_{H+3} - 1$ nodes, where F_i is the ith Fibonacci number (see Section 8.3.4).

Proof

Let S_H be the size of the smallest AVL tree of height H. Clearly, $S_0 = 1$ and $S_1 = 2$. Figure 19.22 shows that the smallest AVL tree of height H must have subtrees of height H – 1 and H – 2. The reason is that at least one subtree has height H – 1 and the balance condition implies that subtree heights can differ by at most 1. These subtrees must themselves have the fewest number of nodes for their heights, so $S_H = S_{H-1} + S_{H-2} + 1$. The proof can be completed by using an induction argument.

From Exercise 8.8, $F_i \approx \phi^i/\sqrt{5}$, where $\phi = (1+\sqrt{5})/2 \approx 1.618$. Consequently, an AVL tree of height H has at least (roughly) $\phi^{H+3}/\sqrt{5}$ nodes. Hence its depth is at most logarithmic. The height of an AVL tree satisfies

$$H < 1.44 \log (N+2) - 1.328, \qquad \textbf{(19.1)}$$

so the worst-case height is at most roughly 44 percent more than the minimum possible for binary trees.

The depth of a typical node in an AVL tree is very close to the optimal log *N*.

The depth of an average node in a randomly constructed AVL tree tends to be very close to log N. The exact answer has not yet been established analytically. We do not even known whether the form is log $N + C$ or $(1+\varepsilon)\log N + C$, for some ε that would be approximately 0.01. Simulations have been unable to demonstrate convincingly that one form is more plausible than the other.

An update in an AVL tree could destroy the balance. It must then be rebalanced before the operation can be considered complete.

A consequence of these arguments is that all searching operations in an AVL tree have logarithmic worst-case bounds. The difficulty is that operations that change the tree, such as `insert` and `remove`, are not quite as simple as before. The reason is that an insertion (or deletion) can destroy the balance of several nodes in the tree, as shown in Figure 19.21. The balance must then be restored before the operation can be considered complete. The insertion algorithm is described here, and the deletion algorithm is left for Exercise 19.11.

Only nodes on the path from the root to the insertion point can have their balances altered.

A key observation is that after an insertion, only nodes that are on the path from the insertion point to the root might have their balances altered because only those nodes have their subtrees altered. This result applies to almost all the balanced search tree algorithms. As we follow the path up to the root and update the balancing information, we may find a node whose new balance violates the AVL condition. In this section we show how to rebalance the tree at the first (i.e., the deepest) such node and prove that this rebalancing guarantees that the entire tree satisfies the AVL property.

If we fix the balance at the deepest unbalanced node, we rebalance the entire tree. There are four cases that we might have to fix; two are mirror images of the other two.

The node to be rebalanced is X. Because any node has at most two children and a height imbalance requires that the heights of X's two subtrees differ by 2, a violation might occur in

1. an insertion in the left subtree of the left child of X,
2. an insertion in the right subtree of the left child of X,
3. an insertion in the left subtree of the right child of X, or
4. an insertion in the right subtree of the right child of X.

Cases 1 and 4 are mirror-image symmetries with respect to X, as are cases 2 and 3. Consequently, there theoretically are two basic cases. From a programming perspective, of course, there are still four cases and numerous special cases.

Balance is restored by tree rotations. A *single rotation* switches the roles of the parent and child while maintaining the search order.

The first case, in which the insertion occurs on the *outside* (i.e., left–left or right–right), is fixed by a single rotation of the tree. A **single rotation** switches the roles of the parent and child while maintaining search order. The second case, in which the insertion occurs on the *inside* (i.e., left–right or right–left), is handled by the slightly more complex **double rotation.** These fundamental operations on the tree are used several times in balanced tree algorithms. In the remainder of this section we describe these rotations and prove that they suffice to maintain the balance condition.

19.4.2 Single Rotation

A single rotation handles the outside cases (1 and 4). We rotate between a node and its child. The result is a binary search tree that satisfies the AVL property.

Figure 19.23 shows the single rotation that fixes case 1. In Figure 19.23(a), node k_2 violates the AVL balance property because its left subtree is two levels deeper than its right subtree (the dashed lines mark the levels in this section). The situation depicted is the only possible case 1 scenario that allows k_2 to satisfy the AVL property before the insertion but violate it afterward. Subtree A has grown to an extra level, causing it to be two levels deeper than C. Subtree B cannot be at the same level as the new A because then k_2 would have been out of balance *before* the insertion. Subtree B cannot be at the same level as C because then k_1 would have been the first node on the path that was in violation of the AVL balancing condition (and we are claiming that k_2 is).

Ideally, to rebalance the tree, we want to move A up one level and C down one level. Note that these actions are more than the AVL property require. To do so we rearrange nodes into an equivalent search tree, as

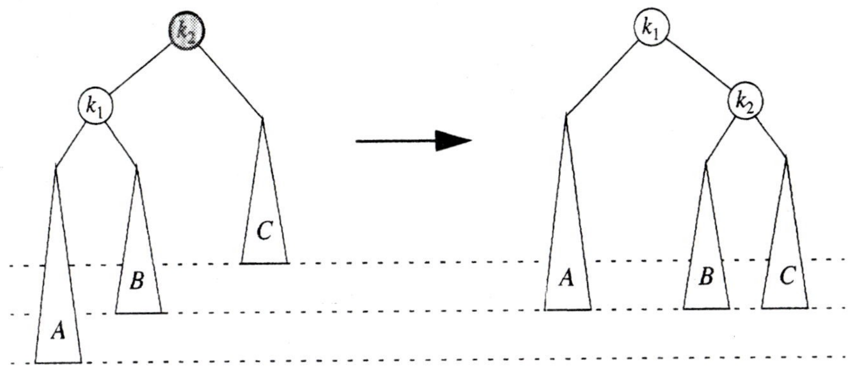

(a) Before rotation **(b) After rotation**

Figure 19.23 Single rotation to fix case 1.

```
// Rotate binary tree node with left child.
template <class Comparable>
void BST<Comparable>::rotateWithLeftChild( Node * & k2 ) const
{
    Node *k1 = k2->left;
    k2->left = k1->right;
    k1->right = k2;
    k2 = k1;
}
```

Figure 19.24 Pseudocode for a single rotation (case 1).

shown in Figure 19.23(b). Here is an abstract scenario: Visualize the tree as being flexible, grab the child node k_1, close your eyes, and shake the tree, letting gravity take hold. The result is that k_1 will be the new root. The binary search tree property tells us that in the original tree, $k_2 > k_1$, so k_2 becomes the right child of k_1 in the new tree. Subtrees A and C remain as the left child of k_1 and the right child of k_2, respectively. Subtree B, which holds items between k_1 and k_2 in the original tree, can be placed as k_2's left child in the new tree and satisfy all the ordering requirements.

One rotation suffices to fix cases 1 and 4 in an AVL tree.

This work requires only the few child pointer changes shown as pseudocode in Figure 19.24 and results in another binary tree that is an AVL tree. This outcome occurs because A moves up one level, B stays at the same level, and C moves down one level. Thus k_1 and k_2 not only satisfy the AVL requirements, but they also have subtrees that are the same height. Furthermore, the new height of the entire subtree is *exactly the same* as the height of the original subtree before the insertion that caused A to grow. Thus no further updating of the heights on the path to the root is needed, and consequently, *no*

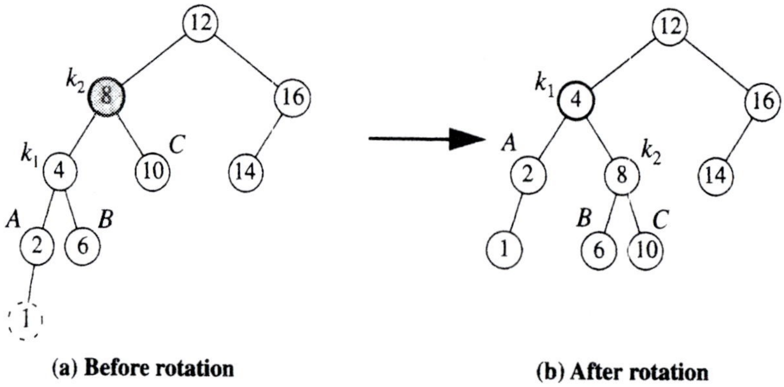

Figure 19.25 Single rotation fixes an AVL tree after insertion of 1.

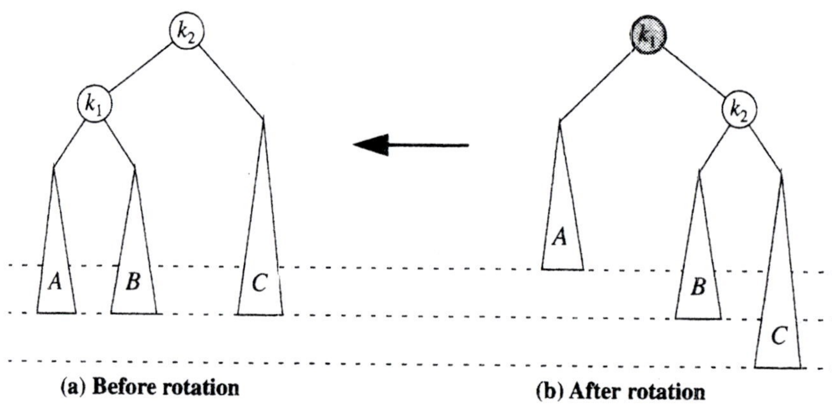

Figure 19.26 Symmetric single rotation to fix case 4.

further rotations are needed. We use this single rotation often in other balanced tree algorithms in this chapter.

Figure 19.25(a) shows that after the insertion of 1 into an AVL tree, node 8 becomes unbalanced. This is clearly a case 1 problem because 1 is in 8's left–left subtree. Thus we do a single rotation between 8 and 4, thereby obtaining the tree shown in Figure 19.25(b). As mentioned earlier in this section, case 4 represents a symmetric case. The required rotation is shown in Figure 19.26, and the pseudocode that implements it is shown in Figure 19.27. This routine, along with other rotations in this section, is replicated in various balanced search trees later in this text. These rotation routines appear in the online code for several balanced search tree implementations.

```
// Rotate binary tree node with right child.
template <class Comparable>
void BST<Comparable>::rotateWithRightChild( Node * & k1 ) const
{
    Node *k2 = k1->right;
    k1->right = k2->left;
    k2->left = k1;
    k1 = k2;
}
```

Figure 19.27 Pseudocode for a single rotation (case 4).

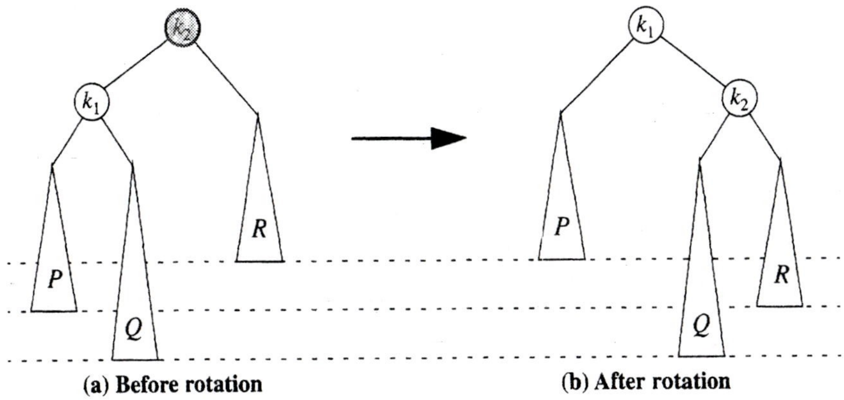

Figure 19.28 Single rotation does not fix case 2.

19.4.3 Double Rotation

The single rotation has a problem: As Figure 19.28 shows, it does not work for case 2 (or, by symmetry, for case 3). The problem is that subtree Q is too deep, and a single rotation does not make it any less deep. The double rotation that solves the problem is shown in Figure 19.29.

The single rotation does not fix the inside cases (2 and 3). These cases require a double rotation, involving three nodes and four subtrees.

The fact that subtree Q in Figure 19.28 has had an item inserted into it guarantees that it is not empty. We may assume that it has a root and two (possibly empty) subtrees, so we may view the tree as four subtrees connected by three nodes. We therefore rename the four trees A, B, C, and D. As Figure 19.29 suggests, either subtree B or subtree C is two levels deeper than subtree D, but we cannot be sure which one. Actually it does not matter; here, both B and C are drawn at 1.5 levels below D.

To rebalance, we cannot leave k_3 as the root. In Figure 19.28 we showed that a rotation between k_3 and k_1 does not work, so the only alternative is to place k_2 as the new root. Doing so forces k_1 to be k_2's left child and k_3 to be

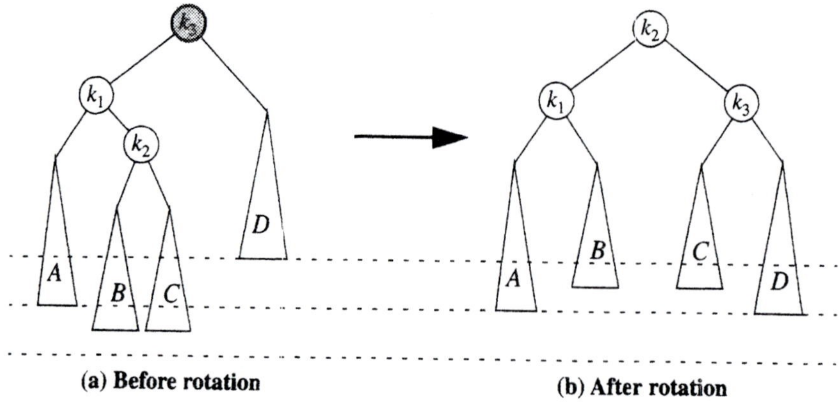

Figure 19.29 Left–right double rotation to fix case 2.

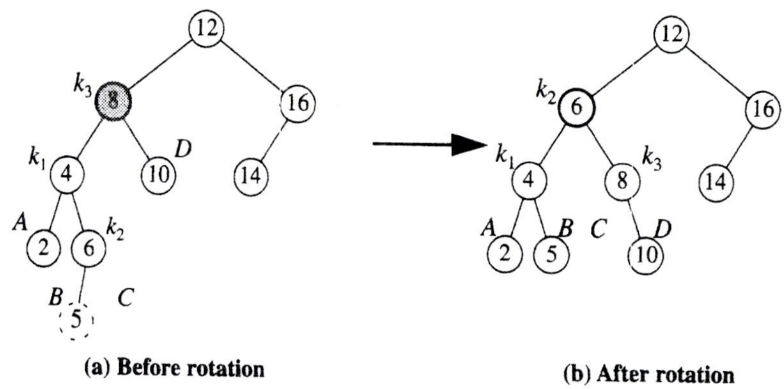

Figure 19.30 Double rotation fixes AVL tree after the insertion of 5.

k_2's right child. It also determines the resulting locations of the four subtrees, and the resulting tree satisfies the AVL property. Also, as was the case with the single rotation, it restores the height to the height before the insertion, thus guaranteeing that all rebalancing and height updating are complete.

As an example, Figure 19.30(a) shows the result of inserting 5 into an AVL tree. A height imbalance is caused at node 8, resulting in a case 2 problem. We perform a double rotation at that node, thereby producing the tree shown in Figure 19.30(b).

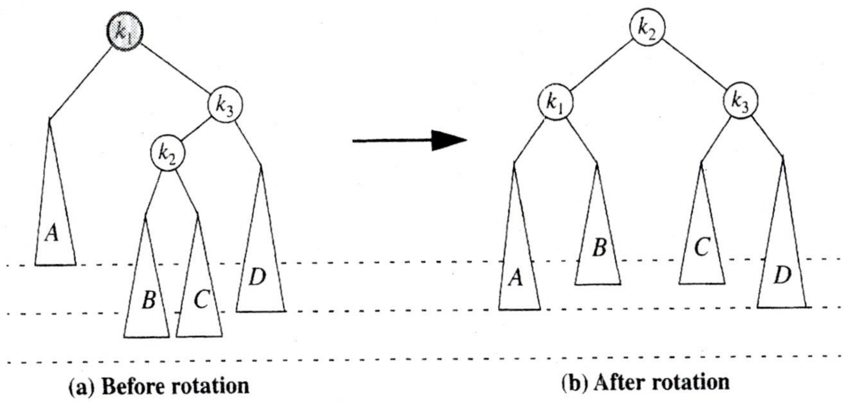

Figure 19.31 Left–right double rotation to fix case 3.

```
// Double rotate binary tree node: first left child
// with its right child; then node k3 with new left child.
// For AVL trees, this is a double rotation for case 2.
template <class Comparable>
void BST<Comparable>::
doubleRotateWithLeftChild( Node * & k3 ) const
{
    rotateWithRightChild( k3->left );
    rotateWithLeftChild( k3 );
}
```

Figure 19.32 Pseudocode for a double rotation (case 2).

A *double rotation* is equivalent to two single rotations.

Figure 19.31 shows that the symmetric case 3 can also be fixed by a double rotation. Finally, note that, although a double rotation appears complex, it turns out to be equivalent to

- a rotation between *X*'s child and grandchild, and
- a rotation between *X* and its new child.

The pseudocode to implement the case 2 double rotation is compact and is shown in Figure 19.32. The mirror-image pseudocode for case 3 is shown in Figure 19.33.

```
// Double rotate binary tree node: first right child
// with its left child; then node k1 with new right child.
// For AVL trees, this is a double rotation for case 3.
template <class Comparable>
void BST<Comparable>::
doubleRotateWithRightChild( Node * & k1 ) const
{
    rotateWithLeftChild( k1->right );
    rotateWithRightChild( k1 );
}
```

Figure 19.33 Pseudocode for a double rotation (case 3).

19.4.4 Summary of AVL Insertion

A casual AVL implementation is not excessively complex, but it is not efficient. Better balanced search trees have since been discovered, so implementing an AVL tree is not worthwhile.

Here is a brief summary how an AVL insertion is implemented. A recursive algorithm turns out to be the simplest method of implementing an AVL insertion. To insert a new node with key X in an AVL tree T, we recursively insert it in the appropriate subtree of T (denoted T_{LR}). If the height of T_{LR} does not change, we are done. Otherwise, if a height imbalance appears in T, we do the appropriate single or double rotation (rooted at T), depending on X and the keys in T and T_{LR}, and then we are done (because the old height is the same as the postrotation height). This recursive description is best described as a *casual implementation.* For instance, at each node we compare the subtree's heights. In general, storing the result of the comparison in the node is more efficient than maintaining the height information. This approach avoids the repetitive calculation of balance factors. Furthermore, recursion incurs substantially more overhead than does an iterative version. The reason is that, in effect, we go down the tree and completely back up instead of stopping as soon as a rotation has been performed. Consequently, in practice, other balanced search tree schemes are used.

19.5 Red–Black Trees

A *red–black tree* is a good alternative to the AVL tree. The coding details tend to give a faster implementation because a single top–down pass can be used during the insertion and deletion routines.

A historically popular alternative to the AVL tree is the **red–black tree,** in which a single top–down pass can be used during the insertion and deletion routines. This approach contrasts with an AVL tree, in which a pass down the tree is used to establish the insertion point and a second pass up the tree is used to update heights and possibly rebalance. As a result, a careful nonrecursive implementation of the red–black tree is simpler and faster than an AVL tree implementation. As on AVL trees, operations on red–black trees take logarithmic worst-case time.

A red–black tree is a binary search tree having the following ordering properties:

Consecutive red nodes are disallowed, and all paths have the same number of black nodes.

1. Every node is colored either red or black.
2. The root is black.
3. If a node is red, its children must be black.
4. Every path from a node to a NULL pointer must contain the same number of black nodes.

In this discussion of red–black trees, shaded nodes represent red nodes. Figure 19.34 shows a red–black tree. Every path from the root to a NULL node contains three black nodes.

Shaded nodes are red throughout this discussion.

We can show by induction that, if every path from the root to a NULL node contains B black nodes, the tree must contain at least $2^B - 1$ black nodes. Furthermore, as the root is black and there cannot be two consecutive red nodes on a path, the height of a red–black tree is at most $2 \log (N + 1)$. Consequently, searching is guaranteed to be a logarithmic operation.

The depth of a red–black tree is guaranteed to be logarithmic. Typically, the depth is the same as for an AVL tree.

The difficulty, as usual, is that operations can change the tree and possibly destroy the coloring properties. This possibility makes insertion difficult and removal especially so. First, we implement the insertion, and then we examine the deletion algorithm.

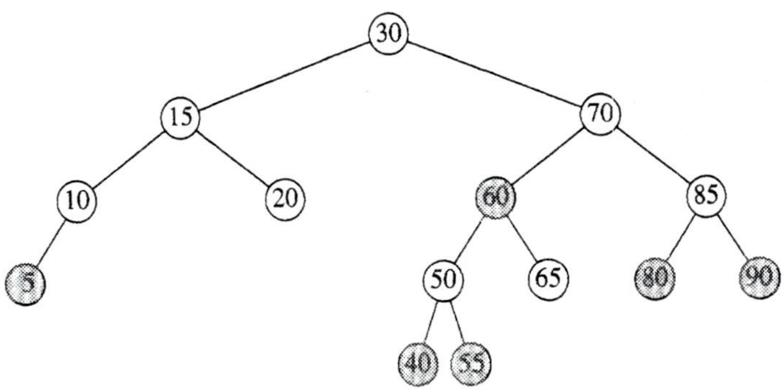

Figure 19.34 A red–black tree: The insertion sequence is 10, 85, 15, 70, 20, 60, 30, 50, 65, 80, 90, 40, 5, and 55 (shaded nodes are red).

19.5.1 Bottom–Up Insertion

New items must be colored red. If the parent is already red, we must recolor and/or rotate to remove consecutive red nodes.

Recall that a new item is always inserted as a leaf in the tree. If we color a new item black, we violate property 4 because we create a longer path of black nodes. Thus a new item must be colored red. If the parent is black, we are done; thus the insertion of 25 into the tree shown in Figure 19.34 is trivial. If the parent is already red, we violate property 3 by having consecutive red nodes. In this case, we have to adjust the tree to ensure that property 3 is enforced and do so without introducing a violation of property 4. The basic operations used are color changes and tree rotations.

If the parent's sibling is black, a single or double rotation fixes things, as in an AVL tree.

We have to consider several cases (each with mirror-image symmetry) if the parent is red. First, suppose that the sibling of the parent is black (we adopt the convention that NULL nodes are black), which would apply for the insertions of 3 or 8 but not for the insertion of 99. Let *X* be the newly added leaf, *P* be its parent, *S* be the sibling of the parent (if it exists), and *G* be the grandparent. Only *X* and *P* are red in this case; *G* is black because otherwise there would be two consecutive red nodes *prior* to the insertion—a violation of property 3. Adopting the AVL tree terminology, we say that relative to *G*, *X* can be either an outside or inside node.[2] If *X* is an outside grandchild, a single rotation of its parent and grandparent along with some color changes will restore property 3. If *X* is an inside grandchild, a double rotation along with some color changes are needed. The single rotation is shown in Figure 19.35, and the double rotation is shown in Figure 19.36. Even though *X* is a leaf, we have drawn a more general case that allows *X* to be in the middle of the tree. We use this more general rotation later in the algorithm.

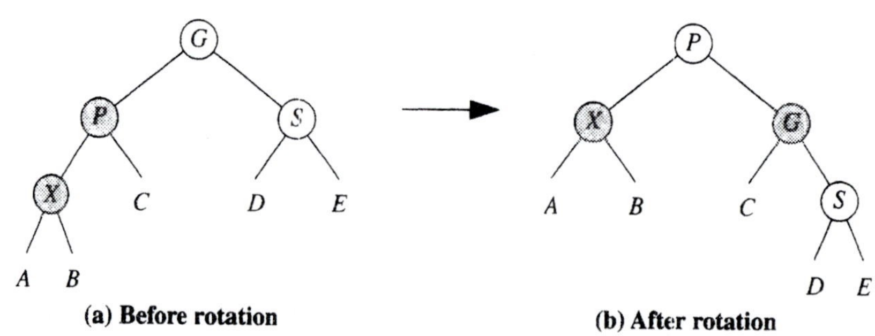

Figure 19.35 If *S* is black, a single rotation between parent and grandparent, with appropriate color changes, restores property 3 if *X* is an outside grandchild.

2. See Section 19.4.1, page 664.

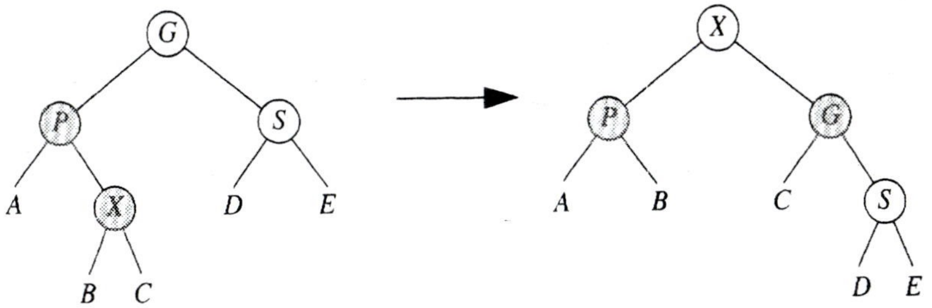

(a) Before rotation (b) After rotation

Figure 19.36 If S is black, a double rotation involving X, the parent, and the grandparent, with appropriate color changes, restores property 3 if X is an inside grandchild.

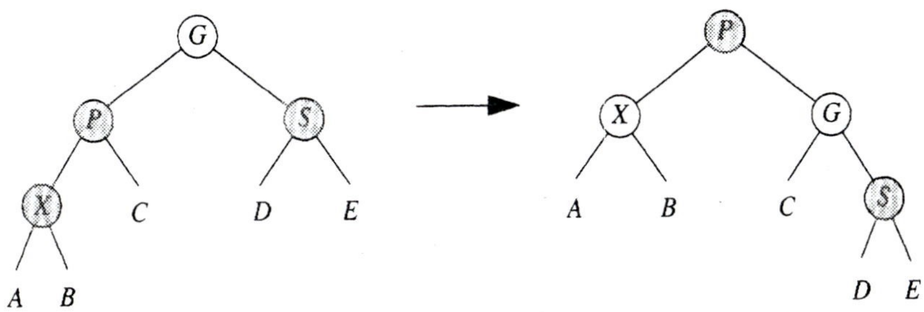

(a) Before rotation (b) After rotation

Figure 19.37 If S is red, a single rotation between parent and grandparent, with appropriate color changes, restores property 3 between X and P.

Before continuing, consider why these rotations are correct. We need to be sure that there are never two consecutive red nodes. As shown in Figure 19.36, for instance, the only possible instances of consecutive red nodes would be between P and one of its children or between G and C. But the roots of A, B, and C must be black; otherwise, there would have been additional property 3 violations in the original tree. In the original tree, there is one black node on the path from the subtree root to A, B, and C and two black nodes on the paths to D and E. We can verify that this pattern holds after rotation and recoloring.

So far so good. But what happens if S is red, as when we attempt to insert 79 in the tree shown in Figure 19.34? Then neither the single nor the double rotation works because both result in consecutive red nodes. In fact, in this case three nodes must be on the path to D and E and only one can be black. Hence both S and the subtree's new root must be colored red. For instance, the single rotation case that occurs when X is an outside grandchild is shown in Figure 19.37. Although this rotation seems to work, there is a

If the parent's sibling is red, then after we fix things, we induce consecutive red nodes at a higher level. We need to iterate up the tree to fix things.

problem: What happens if the parent of the subtree root (i.e., *X*'s original great grandparent) is also red? We could percolate this procedure up toward the root until we no longer have two consecutive red nodes or we reach the root (which would be recolored black). But then we would be back to making a pass up the tree, as in the AVL tree.

19.5.2 Top–Down Red–Black Trees

To avoid iterating back up the tree, we ensure as we descend the tree that the sibling's parent is not red. We can do so with color flips and/or rotations.

To avoid the possibility of having to rotate up the tree, we apply a top–down procedure as we are searching for the insertion point. Specifically, we guarantee that, when we arrive at a leaf and insert a node, *S* is not red. Then we can just add a red leaf and if necessary use one rotation (either single or double). The procedure is conceptually easy.

On the way down, when we see a node *X* that has two red children, we make *X* red and its two children black. Figure 19.38 shows this color flip. The number of black nodes on paths below *X* remains unchanged. However, if *X*'s parent is red, we would introduce two consecutive red nodes. But in this case, we can apply either the single rotation in Figure 19.35 or the double rotation in Figure 19.36. But what if *X*'s parent's sibling is also red? *This situation cannot happen.* If on the way down the tree, we see a node *Y* that has two red children, we know that *Y*'s grandchildren must be black. And as *Y*'s children are also made black via the color flip—even after the rotation that may occur—we would not see another red node for two levels. Thus when we see *X*, if *X*'s parent is red, *X*'s parent's sibling cannot also be red.

For example, suppose that we want to insert 45 in the tree shown in Figure 19.34. On the way down the tree we see node 50, which has two red children. Thus we perform a color flip, making 50 red and 40 and 55 black. The result is shown in Figure 19.39. However, now 50 and 60 are both red. We perform a single rotation (because 50 is an outside node) between 60 and 70, thus making 60 the black root of 30's right subtree and making 70 red, as shown in Figure 19.40. We then continue, performing an identical action if we see other nodes on the path that contain two red children. It happens that there are none.

Figure 19.38 Color flip: Only if *X*'s parent is red do we continue with a rotation.

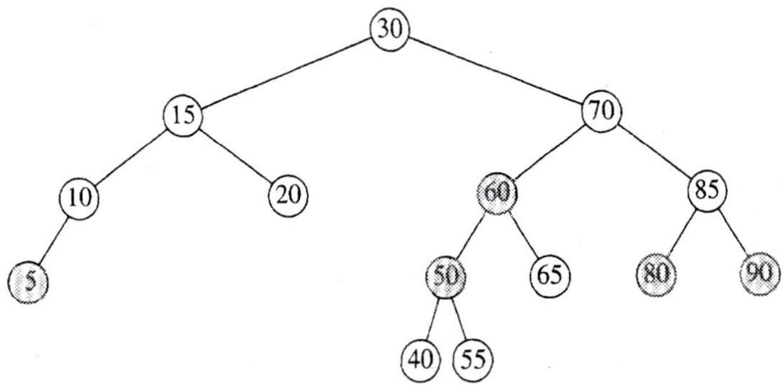

Figure 19.39 A color flip at 50 induces a violation; because the violation is outside, a single rotation fixes it.

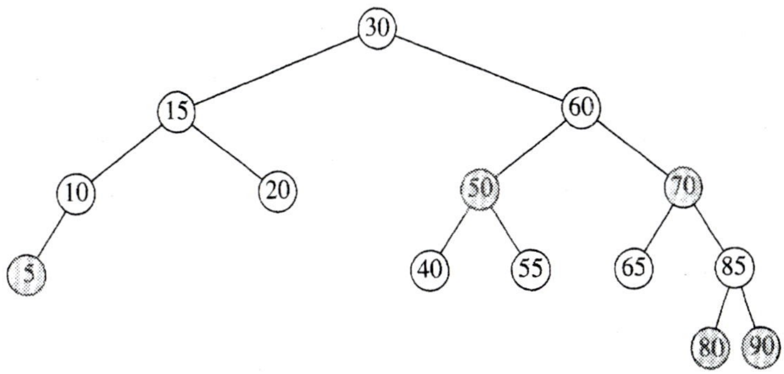

Figure 19.40 Result of single rotation that fixes the violation at node 50.

When we get to the leaf, we insert 45 as a red node, and as the parent is black, we are done. The resulting tree is shown in Figure 19.41. Had the parent been red, we would have needed to perform one rotation.

As Figure 19.41 shows, the red–black tree that results is frequently well balanced. Experiments suggest that the number of nodes traversed during an average red–black tree search is almost identical to the average for AVL trees, even though the red–black tree's balancing properties are slightly weaker. The advantage of a red–black tree is the relatively low overhead required to perform insertion and the fact that, in practice, rotations occur relatively infrequently.

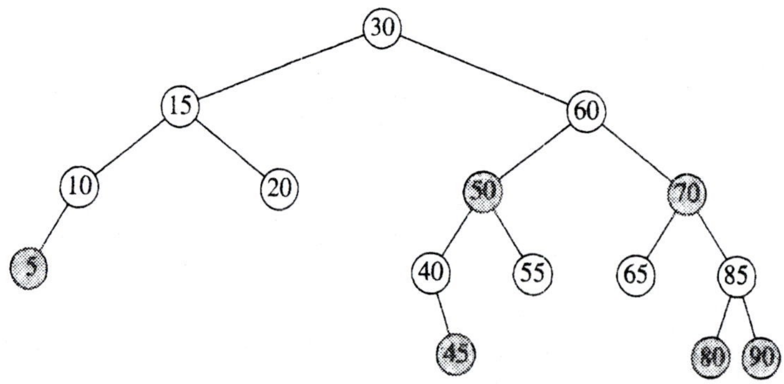

Figure 19.41 Insertion of 45 as a red node.

19.5.3 C++ Implementation

We remove special cases by using a sentinel for the NULL pointer and a pseudoroot. Doing so requires minor modifications of almost every routine.

An actual implementation is complicated, not only by many possible rotations, but also by the possibility that some subtrees (such as the right subtree of the node containing 10 in Figure 19.41) might be empty and by the special case of dealing with the root (which among other things, has no parent). To remove special cases, we use two sentinels.

- We use `nullNode` in place of a `NULL` pointer; `nullNode` will always be colored black.
- We use `header` as a pseudoroot; it has a key value of $-\infty$ and a right pointer to the real root.

On the way down, we maintain pointers to the current, parent, grandparent, and great-grandparent nodes.

Therefore even basic routines such as `isEmpty` need to be altered. Consequently, inheriting from `BinarySearchTree` does not make sense, and we write the class from scrat-h. The `RedBlackNode` class is shown in Figure 19.42 and is straightforward. The `RedBlackTree` class interface is shown in Figure 19.43. Lines 32 and 33 declare the sentinels that we discussed previously. Four pointers—`current`, `parent`, `grand`, and `great`—are used in the `insert` routine. Their placement in the interface (at lines 36–39) indicates that they are essentially global variables. The reason is that, as we show shortly, having them shared by `insert` and the `handleReorient` routine is convenient. The `remove` operator is unimplemented.

The remaining routines are similar to their `BinarySearchTree` counterparts, except that they have different implementations because of the sentinel nodes. The constructor must be provided with the value of $-\infty$, and the destructor must `delete` the `nullNode` sentinel and `header`. A constructor and destructor are shown in Figure 19.44. The constructor allocates the two sentinels and sets all their `left` and `right` pointers to `nullNode`.

```
template <class Comparable>
class RedBlackTree;

template <class Comparable>
class RedBlackNode
{
    Comparable    element;
    RedBlackNode *left;
    RedBlackNode *right;
    int           color;

    RedBlackNode( const Comparable & theElement = Comparable( ),
                  RedBlackNode *lt = NULL,
                  RedBlackNode *rt = NULL,
                  int c = RedBlackTree<Comparable>::BLACK )
      : element( theElement ), left( lt ), right( rt ),
        color( c ) { }

    friend class RedBlackTree<Comparable>;
};
```

Figure 19.42 The `RedBlackNode` class.

Figure 19.45 shows the simplest change that results from the use of the sentinels. The test against `NULL` needs to be replaced with a test against `nullNode`. Instead, we use the fact that for `nullNode`, `t->left` equals `t`. This test is simpler for other internal routines in which `t` might belong to a different tree (e.g., the `clone` method) because each tree has a unique `nullNode`.

Tests against `NULL` are replaced by tests against `nullNode`.

For the `find` routine shown in Figure 19.46 we use a common trick. Before we begin the search, we place `x` in the `nullNode` sentinel. Thus we are guaranteed to match `x` eventually, even if `x` is not found. If the match occurs at `nullNode`, we can tell that the item was not found. We use this trick in the `insert` procedure. Of course, if copying is expensive, use of the trick may not be wise. However, the cost of a single copy rarely has much impact on performance.

When performing a `find` operation, we copy `x` into the `nullNode` sentinel to avoid extra tests.

The `insert` method follows directly from our description and is shown in Figure 19.47. The `while` loop encompassing lines 9 to 19 descends the tree and fixes nodes that have two red children by calling `handleReorient`, as shown in Figure 19.48. To do so, it keeps track of not only the current node but also the parent, grandparent, and great-grandparent. Note that after a rotation the values stored in the grandparent and great-grandparent are no longer correct. However, they will be restored by the time they are next needed. When the loop ends, either `x` is found (as indicated by `current !=nullNode`) or `x` is not found (as indicated by `current==nullNode`). If

The code is relatively compact for the number of cases involved and the fact that the implementation is nonrecursive. For these reasons the red–black tree performs well.

```
// Red-black tree class.
//
// CONSTRUCTION: with negative infinity object.
//
// ******************PUBLIC OPERATIONS*********************
// void insert( x )       --> Insert x
// void remove( x )       --> Remove x (unimplemented)
// Comparable find( x )   --> Return item that matches x
// bool isEmpty( )        --> Return true if empty; else false
// void makeEmpty( )      --> Remove all items

template <class Comparable>
class RedBlackTree
{
  public:
    RedBlackTree( const Comparable & negInf );
    RedBlackTree( const RedBlackTree & rhs );
    ~RedBlackTree( );

    Cref<Comparable> find( const Comparable & x ) const;
    bool isEmpty( ) const;
    void makeEmpty( );
    void insert( const Comparable & x );
    void remove( const Comparable & x );

    enum { RED, BLACK };
    const RedBlackTree & operator=( const RedBlackTree & rhs );

    typedef RedBlackNode<Comparable> Node;

  private:
    Node *header;   // The tree header
    Node *nullNode;

      // Used in insert routine and its helpers
    Node *current;
    Node *parent;
    Node *grand;
    Node *great;

      // Usual recursive stuff
    void reclaimMemory( Node *t ) const;
    RedBlackNode<Comparable> * clone( Node * t ) const;

      // Red-black tree manipulations
    void handleReorient( const Comparable & item );
    RedBlackNode<Comparable> * rotate( const Comparable & item,
                                        Node *parent ) const;
    void rotateWithLeftChild( Node * & k2 ) const;
    void rotateWithRightChild( Node * & k1 ) const;
};
```

Figure 19.43 The `RedBlackTree` class interface.

```
// Construct the tree.
// negInf is a value less than or equal to all others.
template <class Comparable>
RedBlackTree<Comparable>::
RedBlackTree( const Comparable & negInf )
{
    nullNode    = new Node;
    nullNode->left = nullNode->right = nullNode;
    header      = new Node( negInf );
    header->left = header->right = nullNode;
}

// Destroy the tree.
template <class Comparable>
RedBlackTree<Comparable>::~RedBlackTree( )
{
    makeEmpty( );
    delete nullNode;
    delete header;
}
```

Figure 19.44 The `RedBlackTree` constructor and destructor.

```
// Internal method to reclaim internal nodes in subtree t.
template <class Comparable>
void RedBlackTree<Comparable>::reclaimMemory( Node *t ) const
{
    if( t != t->left )
    {
        reclaimMemory( t->left );
        reclaimMemory( t->right );
        delete t;
    }
}
```

Figure 19.45 The `reclaimMemory` method for the `RedBlackTree` class.

`x` is found, we throw an exception at line 23. Otherwise, `x` is not already in the tree, and it needs to be made a child of `parent`. We allocate a new node (as the new `current` node), attach it to the parent, and call `handleReorient` at lines 24–31.

```
// Find item x in the tree.
// Return the matching item wrapped in a Cref object.
template <class Comparable>
Cref<Comparable> RedBlackTree<Comparable>::
find( const Comparable & x ) const
{
    nullNode->element = x;
    Node *curr = header->right;

    for( ; ; )
    {
        if( x < curr->element )
            curr = curr->left;
        else if( curr->element < x )
            curr = curr->right;
        else if( curr != nullNode )
            return Cref<Comparable>( curr->element );
        else
            return Cref<Comparable>( );
    }
}
```

Figure 19.46 The `RedBlackTree` `find` routine. Note the use of `header` and `nullNode`.

The `rotate` function has four possibilities. The `?:` operator collapses the code but is logically equivalent to an `if/else` test.

The code used to perform a single rotation is shown in the `rotate` function in Figure 19.49. Because the resultant tree must be attached to a parent, `rotate` takes the parent node as a parameter. Rather than keep track of the type of rotation (left or right) as we descend the tree, we pass `x` as a parameter. We expect very few rotations during the insertion, so doing it this way is not only simple but is actually faster.

The `handleReorient` routine calls `rotate` as necessary to perform either single or double rotation. As a double rotation is just two single rotations, we can test whether we have an inside case, and if so, do an extra rotation between the current node and its parent (by passing the grandparent to `rotate`). In either case we rotate between the parent and grandparent (by passing the great-grandparent to `rotate`). This action is succinctly coded in lines 16–18 of Figure 19.48.

19.5.4 Top–Down Deletion

Deletion in red–black trees can also be performed top–down. Needless to say, an actual implementation is fairly complicated because the `remove` algorithm for unbalanced search trees is nontrivial in the first place. The normal

```
// Insert item x into the tree.
// Throws DuplicateItemException if x is already present.
template <class Comparable>
void RedBlackTree<Comparable>::insert( const Comparable & x )
{
    current = parent = grand = header;
    nullNode->element = x;

    while( current->element != x )
    {
        great = grand; grand = parent; parent = current;
        current = x < current->element ?
                        current->left : current->right;

          // Check if two red children; fix if so
        if( current->left->color == RED &&
                              current->right->color == RED )
            handleReorient( x );
    }

      // Insertion fails if already present
    if( current != nullNode )
        throw DuplicateItemException( );
    current = new Node( x, nullNode, nullNode );

      // Attach to parent
    if( x < parent->element )
        parent->left = current;
    else
        parent->right = current;
    handleReorient( x );
}
```

Figure 19.47 The `insert` routine for the `RedBlackTree` class.

binary search tree deletion algorithm removes nodes that are leaves or have one child. Recall that nodes with two children are never removed; their contents are simply replaced.

If the node to be deleted is red, there is no problem. However, if the node to be deleted is black, its removal will violate property 4. The solution to the problem is to ensure that any node we are about to delete is red.

Deletion is fairly complex. The basic idea is to ensure that the deleted node is red.

Throughout this discussion, we let *X* be the current node, *T* be its sibling, and *P* be their parent. We begin by coloring the sentinel root red. As we traverse down the tree, we attempt to ensure that *X* is red. When we arrive at a new node, we are certain that *P* is red (inductively, by the invariant that we

```
// Internal routine that is called during an insertion
// if a node has two red children. Performs flip and rotations.
// item is the item being inserted.
template <class Comparable>
void RedBlackTree<Comparable>::
handleReorient( const Comparable & item )
{
        // Do the color flip
    current->color = RED;
    current->left->color = BLACK;
    current->right->color = BLACK;

    if( parent->color == RED )      // Have to rotate
    {
        grand->color = RED;
        if( item < grand->element != item < parent->element )
            parent = rotate( item, grand ); // Start dbl rotate
        current = rotate( item, great );
        current->color = BLACK;
    }
    header->right->color = BLACK;  // Make root black
}
```

Figure 19.48 The `handleReorient` routine, which is called if a node has two red children or when a new node is inserted.

are trying to maintain) and that *X* and *T* are black (because we cannot have two consecutive red nodes). There are two main cases, along with the usual symmetric variants (which are omitted).

First, suppose that *X* has two black children. There are three subcases, which depend on *T*'s children.

1. *T* has two black children: Flip colors (Figure 19.50).
2. *T* has an outer red child: Perform a single rotation (Figure 19.51).
3. *T* has an inner red child: Perform a double rotation (Figure 19.52).

Examination of the rotations shows that if *T* has two red children, either a single rotation or double rotation will work (so it makes sense to do the single rotation). Note that, if *X* is a leaf, its two children are black, so we can always apply one of these three mechanisms to make *X* red.

Second, suppose that one of *X*'s children is red. Because the rotations in the first main case always color *X* red, if *X* has a red child, consecutive red nodes would be introduced. Thus we need an alternative solution. In this case, we fall through to the next level, obtaining a new *X*, *T*, and *P*. If we are

```
// Internal routine that performs a single or double rotation.
// Because the result is attached to the parent, there are
// four cases. Called by handleReorient.
// item is the item in handleReorient.
// parent is the parent of the root of the rotated subtree.
// Return the root of the rotated subtree.
template <class Comparable>
RedBlackNode<Comparable> * RedBlackTree<Comparable>::
rotate( const Comparable & item, Node *theParent ) const
{
    if( item < theParent->element )
    {
        item < theParent->left->element ?
            rotateWithLeftChild( theParent->left )  :   // LL
            rotateWithRightChild( theParent->left ) ;   // LR
        return theParent->left;
    }
    else
    {
        item < theParent->right->element ?
            rotateWithLeftChild( theParent->right ) :   // RL
            rotateWithRightChild( theParent->right );   // RR
        return theParent->right;
    }
}
```

Figure 19.49 A routine for performing an appropriate rotation.

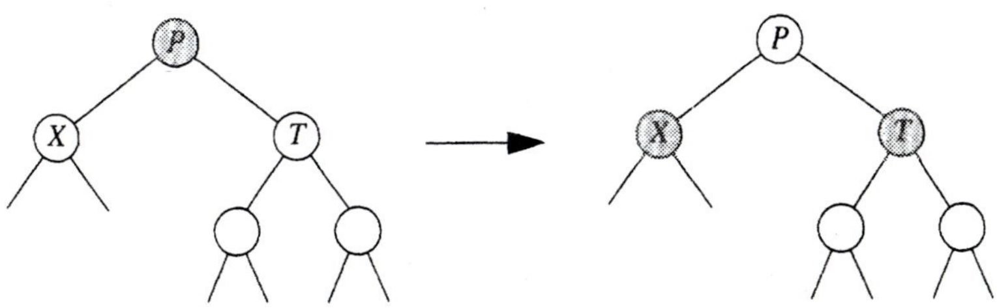

Figure 19.50 *X* has two black children, and both of its sibling's children are black; do a color flip.

lucky, we will fall onto a red node (we have at least a 50 percent chance that this will happen), thereby making the new current node red. Otherwise, we have the situation shown in Figure 19.53. That is, the current *X* is black, the current *T* is red, and the current *P* is black. We can then rotate *T* and *P*, thereby making *X*'s new parent red; *X* and its new grandparent are black. Now *X* is not yet red, but we are back to the starting point (although one

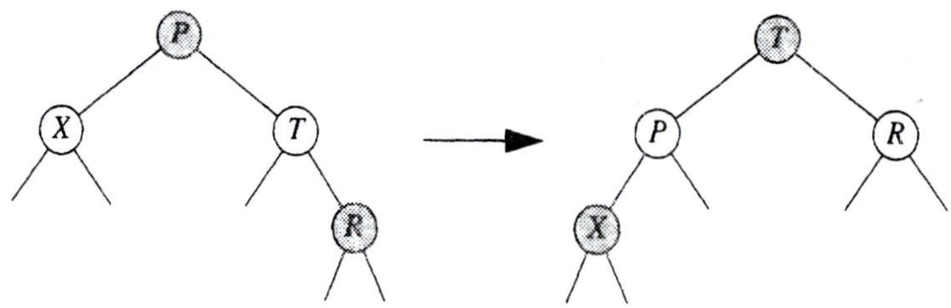

Figure 19.51 *X* has two black children, and the outer child of its sibling is red; do a single rotation.

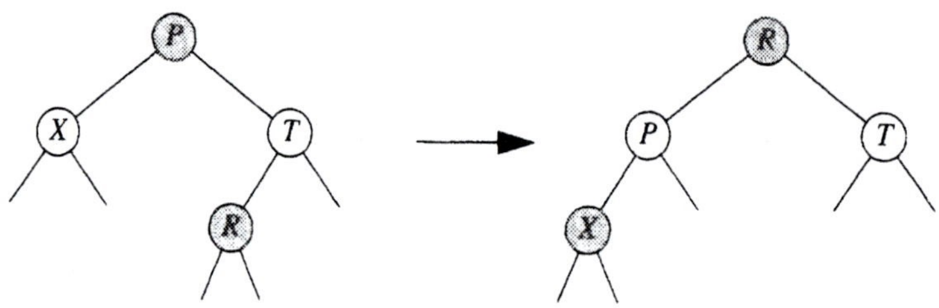

Figure 19.52 *X* has two black children, and the inner child of its sibling is red; do a double rotation.

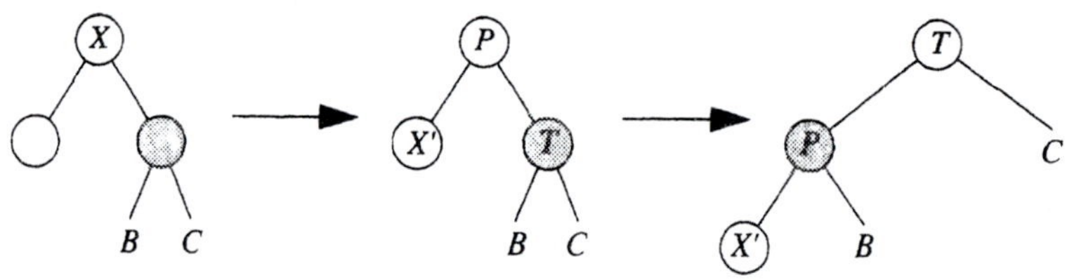

Figure 19.53 *X* is black, and at least one child is red; if we fall through to the next level and land on a red child, fine; if not, we rotate a sibling and parent.

level deeper). This outcome is good enough because it shows that we can iteratively descend the tree. Thus, so long as we eventually either reach a node that has two black children or land on a red node, we are okay. This result is guaranteed for the deletion algorithm because the two eventual states are

- *X* is a leaf, which is always handled by the main case since *X* has two black children; and
- *X* has only one child, for which the main case applies if the child is black, and if it is red, we can delete *X*, if necessary, and make the child black.

Lazy deletion, in which items are marked as deleted but not actually deleted, is sometimes used. However, lazy deletion wastes space and complicates other routines (see Exercise 19.26).

Lazy deletion **is the marking of items as deleted.**

19.6 AA-Trees

Because of many possible rotations, the red–black tree is fairly tricky to code. In particular, the `remove` operation is quite challenging. In this section we describe a simple but competitive balanced search tree known as an *AA-tree.* The **AA-tree** is the method of choice when a balanced tree is needed, a casual implementation is acceptable, and deletions are needed. The AA-tree adds one extra condition to the red–black tree: Left children may not be red.

The *AA-tree* is the method of choice when a balanced tree is needed, a casual implementation is acceptable, and deletions are needed.

This simple restriction greatly simplifies the red–black tree algorithms for two reasons: First, it eliminates about half of the restructuring cases; second, it simplifies the `remove` algorithm by removing an annoying case. That is, if an internal node has only one child, the child must be a red right child because red left children are now illegal, whereas a single black child would violate property 4 for red–black trees. Thus we can always replace an internal node with the smallest node in its right subtree. That smallest node is either a leaf or has a red child and can be easily bypassed and removed.

To simplify the implementation further, we represent balance information in a more direct way. Instead of storing a color with each node, we store the node's level. The **level of a node** represents the number of left links on the path to the `nullNode` sentinel and is

The *level of a node* in an AA-tree represents the number of left links on the path to the `nullNode` sentinel.

- level 1, if the node is a leaf;
- the level of its parent, if the node is red; and
- one less than the level of its parent, if the node is black.

The result is an AA-tree. If we translate the structure requirement from colors to levels, we know that the left child must be one level lower than its parent and that the right child may be zero or one level lower than its parent (but not more). A **horizontal link** is a connection between a node and a child of equal levels. The coloring properties imply that

A *horizontal link* in an AA-tree is a connection between a node and a child of equal levels. A horizontal link should go only to the right, and there should not be two consecutive horizontal links.

1. horizontal links are right links (because only right children may be red),
2. there may not be two consecutive horizontal links (because there cannot be consecutive red nodes),
3. nodes at level 2 or higher must have two children, and
4. if a node does not have a right horizontal link, its two children are at the same level.

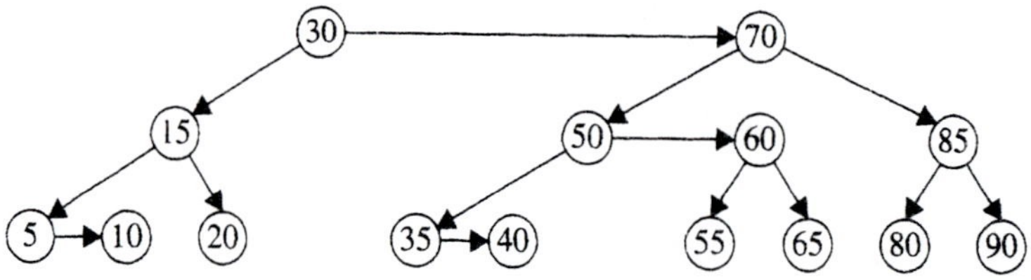

Figure 19.54 AA-tree resulting from the insertion of 10, 85, 15, 70, 20, 60, 30, 50, 65, 80, 90, 40, 5, 55, and 35.

Figure 19.54 shows a sample AA-tree. The root of this tree is the node with key 30. Searching is done with the usual algorithm. And as usual, `insert` and `remove` are more difficult because the natural binary search tree algorithms may induce a violation of the horizontal link properties. Not surprisingly, tree rotations can fix all the problems encountered.

19.6.1 Insertion

Insertion is done by using the usual recursive algorithm and two method calls.

Insertion of a new item is always done at the bottom level. As usual, that may create problems. In the tree shown in Figure 19.54, insertion of 2 would create a horizontal left link, whereas insertion of 45 would generate consecutive right links. Consequently, after a node has been added at the bottom level, we may need to perform some rotations to restore the horizontal link properties.

Left horizontal links are removed by a `skew` (rotation between a node and its left child). Consecutive right horizontal links are fixed by a `split` (rotation between a node and its right child). A `skew` precedes a `split`.

In both cases, a single rotation fixes the problem. We remove left horizontal links by rotating between the node and its left child, a procedure called `skew`. We fix consecutive right horizontal links by rotating between the first and second (of the three) nodes joined by the two links, a procedure called `split`.

The `skew` procedure is illustrated in Figure 19.55, and the `split` procedure is illustrated in Figure 19.56. Although a `skew` removes a left horizontal link, it might create consecutive right horizontal links because *X*'s right child might also be horizontal. Thus we would process a `skew` first and then a `split`. After a `split`, the middle node increases in level. That may cause problems for the original parent of *X* by creating either a left horizontal link or consecutive right horizontal links: Both problems can be fixed by applying the `skew`/`split` strategy on the path up toward the root. It can be done automatically if we use recursion, and a recursive implementation of `insert` is only two method calls longer than the corresponding unbalanced search tree routine.

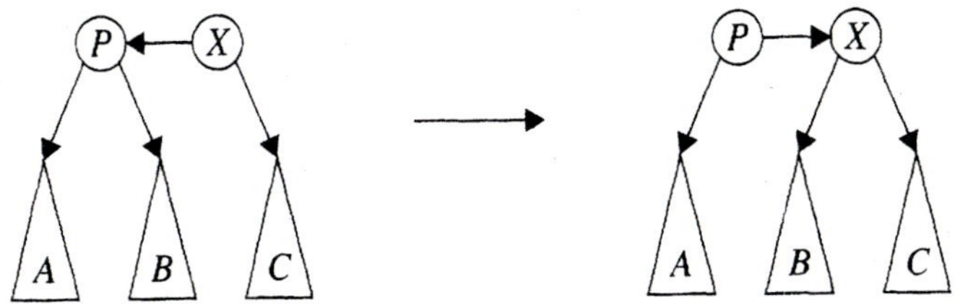

Figure 19.55 The `skew` procedure is a simple rotation between *X* and *P*.

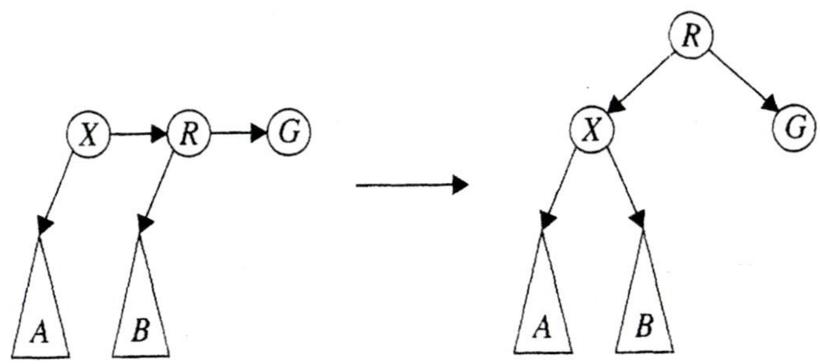

Figure 19.56 The `split` procedure is a simple rotation between *X* and *R*; note that *R*'s level increases.

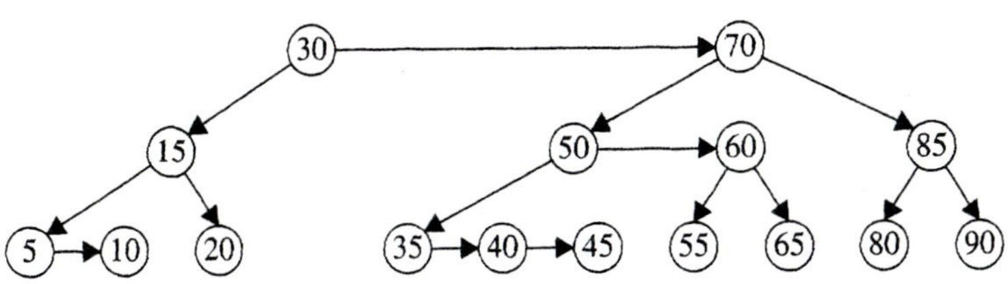

Figure 19.57 After insertion of 45 in the sample tree; consecutive horizontal links are introduced, starting at 35.

This is a rare algorithm in that it is harder to simulate on paper than implement on a computer.

To show the algorithm in action, we insert 45 in the AA-tree shown in Figure 19.54. In Figure 19.57 when 45 is added at the bottom level, consecutive horizontal links form. Then `skew`/`split` pairs are applied as necessary from the bottom up toward the root. Thus, at node 35 a `split` is needed because of the consecutive horizontal right links. The result of the `split` is shown in Figure 19.58. When the recursion backs up to node 50, we encounter a horizontal left link. Thus we perform a `skew` at 50 to remove the horizontal left link (the result is shown in Figure 19.59) and then a `split` at 40 to remove the consecutive horizontal right links. The result after the `split` is shown in Figure 19.60. The result of the `split` is that 50 is on level 3 and is a left horizontal child of

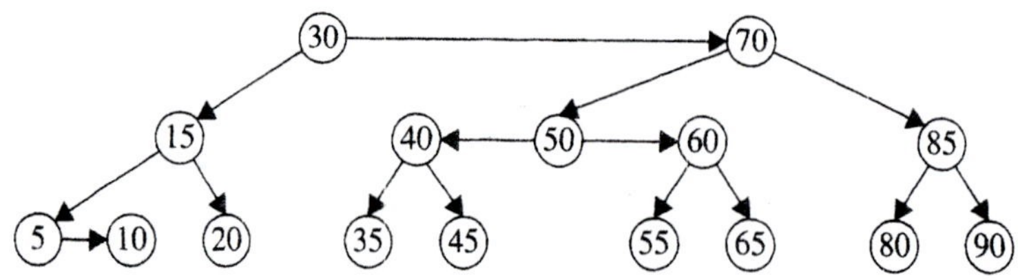

Figure 19.58 After split at 35; a left horizontal link at 50 is introduced.

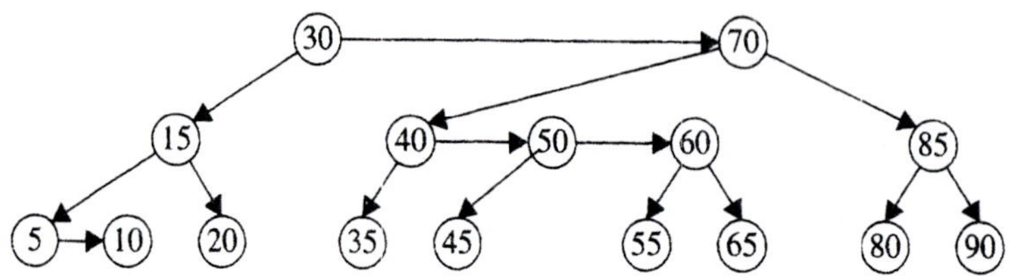

Figure 19.59 After skew at 50; consecutive horizontal nodes are introduced starting at 40.

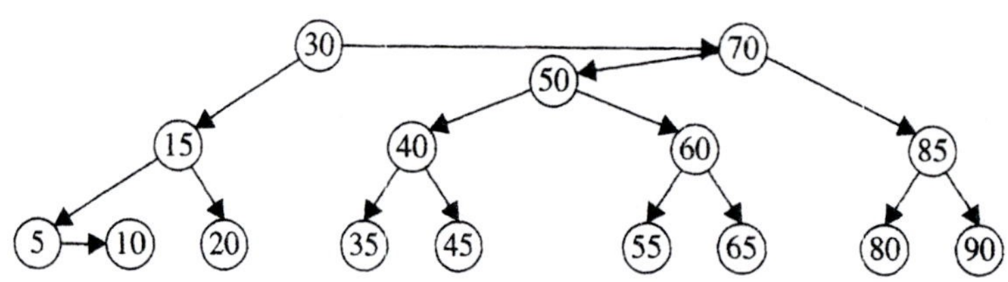

Figure 19.60 After split at 40; 50 is now on the same level as 70, inducing an illegal left horizontal link.

70. Therefore we need to perform another skew/split pair. The skew at 70 removes the left horizontal link at the top level but creates consecutive right horizontal nodes, as shown in Figure 19.61. When the final split is applied, the consecutive horizontal nodes are removed and 50 becomes the new root of the tree. The result is shown in Figure 19.62.

19.6.2 Deletion

Deletion is made easier because the one-child case can occur only at level 1 and we are willing to use recursion.

For general binary search trees, the remove algorithm is broken into three cases: The item to be removed is a leaf, has one child, or has two children. For AA-trees, we treat the one-child case the same way as the two-child case because the one-child case can occur only at level 1. Moreover, the two-child case is also easy because the node used as the replacement value is

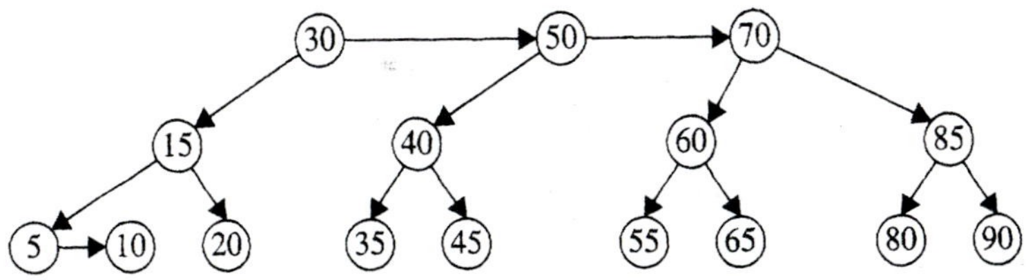

Figure 19.61 After `skew` at 70; consecutive horizontal links are introduced, starting at 30.

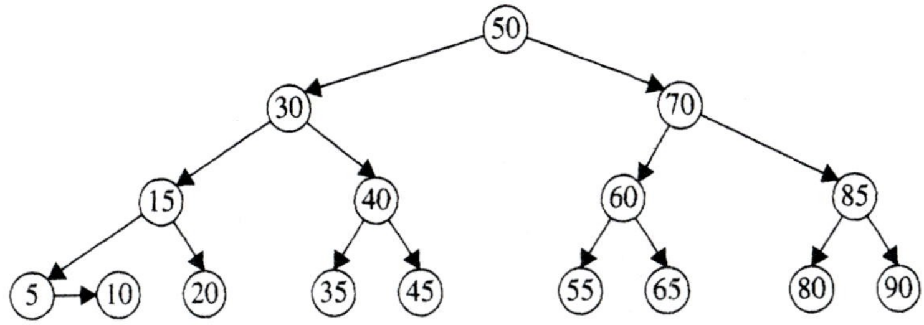

Figure 19.62 After `split` at 30; the insertion is complete.

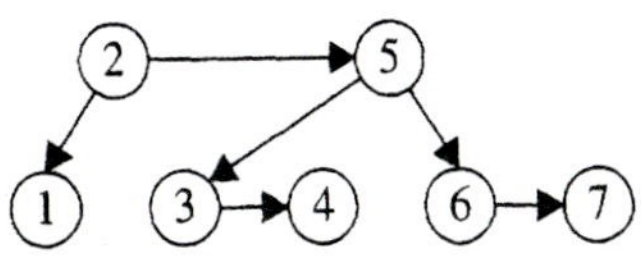

Figure 19.63 When 1 is deleted, all nodes become level 1, thereby introducing horizontal left links.

guaranteed to be at level 1 and at worst has only a right horizontal link. Thus everything boils down to being able to `remove` a level-1 node. Clearly, this action might affect the balance (consider, for instance, the removal of 20 in Figure 19.62).

We let *T* be the current node and use recursion. If the deletion has altered one of *T*'s children to two less than *T*'s level, *T*'s level needs to be lowered also (only the child entered by the recursive call could actually be affected, but for simplicity we do not keep track of it). Furthermore, if *T* has a horizontal right link, its right child's level must also be lowered. At this point, we could have six nodes on the same level: *T*, *T*'s horizontal right child *R*, *R*'s two children, and those children's horizontal right children. Figure 19.63 shows the simplest possible scenario.

After a recursive removal, three skews and two splits guarantee rebalancing.

After node 1 has been removed, node 2 and thus node 5 become level-1 nodes. First, we must fix the left horizontal link that is now introduced between nodes 5 and 3. Doing so essentially requires two rotations: one between nodes 5 and 3 and then one between nodes 5 and 4. In this case, the current node *T* is not involved. However, if a deletion came from the right side, *T*'s left node could suddenly become horizontal; that would require a similar double rotation (starting at *T*). To avoid testing all these cases, we merely call `skew` three times. Once we have done that, two calls to `split` suffice to rearrange the horizontal edges.

19.6.3 C++ Implementation

The interface and routines are relatively simple (compared to those of the red–black tree).

The node class for the AA-tree is shown in Figure 19.64, followed by the class interface for the AA-tree in Figure 19.65. Much of it duplicates previous tree interfaces. Again, we use a `nullNode` sentinel; however, we do not need a pseudoroot. The constructor, which is not shown, allocates `nullNode`, as for red–black trees, and has `root` point at it. The `nullNode` is at level 0. The routines use private helpers.

The `insert` method is shown in Figure 19.66. As mentioned earlier this section, it is nearly identical to the recursive binary search tree `insert`. The only difference is that it adds a call to `skew` followed by a call to `split`. In

```
template <class Comparable>
class AATree;

template <class Comparable>
class AANode
{
    Comparable element;
    AANode    *left;
    AANode    *right;
    int        level;

    AANode( ) : left( NULL ), right( NULL ), level( 1 ) { }
    AANode( const Comparable & e, AANode *lt, AANode *rt,
            int lv = 1 )
      : element( e ), left( lt ), right( rt ), level( lv ) { }

    friend class AATree<Comparable>;
};
```

Figure 19.64 The node declaration for AA-trees.

```
// AATree class.
//
// CONSTRUCTION: with no parameter or another AA-tree.
//
// ******************PUBLIC OPERATIONS*********************
// void insert( x )       --> Insert x
// void remove( x )       --> Remove x
// Comparable find( x )   --> Return item that matches x
// bool isEmpty( )        --> Return true if empty; else false
// void makeEmpty( )      --> Remove all items
// ******************ERRORS*******************************
// Throws exceptions as warranted.

template <class Comparable>
class AATree
{
  public:
    AATree( );
    AATree( const AATree & rhs );
    ~AATree( );

    Cref<Comparable> find( const Comparable & x ) const;
    bool isEmpty( ) const;

    void makeEmpty( );
    void insert( const Comparable & x );
    void remove( const Comparable & x );

    const AATree & operator=( const AATree & rhs );

    typedef AANode<Comparable> Node;

  private:
    Node *root;
    Node *nullNode;
    Cref<Comparable> elementAt( Node *t ) const;

      // Recursive routines
    void insert( const Comparable & x, Node * & t );
    void remove( const Comparable & x, Node * & t );
    void makeEmpty( Node * & t );

      // Rotations
    void skew( Node * & t ) const;
    void split( Node * & t ) const;
    void rotateWithLeftChild( Node * & t ) const;
    void rotateWithRightChild( Node * & t ) const;

    AANode<Comparable> * clone( Node * t ) const;
};
```

Figure 19.65 The class interface for AA-trees.

```
// Internal method to insert into a subtree.
// x is the item to insert.
// t is the node that roots the tree.
// Set the new root.
// Throw DuplicateItemException if x is already in t.
template <class Comparable>
void AATree<Comparable>::
insert( const Comparable & x, Node * & t )
{
    if( t == nullNode )
        t = new Node( x, nullNode, nullNode );
    else if( x < t->element )
        insert( x, t->left );
    else if( t->element < x )
        insert( x, t->right );
    else
        throw DuplicateItemException( );
    skew( t );
    split( t );
}
```

Figure 19.66 The `insert` routine for the `AATree` class.

Figure 19.67 `skew` and `split` are easily implemented, using the already existing tree rotations. Finally, `remove` is shown in Figure 19.68.

The `deletedNode` variable points at the node containing `x` (if `x` is found) or `nullNode` if `x` is not found. The `lastNode` variable points at the replacement node. We use two-way comparisons instead of three-way comparisons.

To help us out, we keep two variables, `deletedNode` and `lastNode`, that have lifetime scope by virtue of their `static` declaration. When we traverse a right child, we adjust `deletedNode`. Because we call `remove` recursively until we reach the bottom (we do not test for equality on the way down), we are guaranteed that, if the item to be removed is in the tree, `deletedNode` will point at the node that contains it. Note that this technique can be used in the `find` procedure to replace the three-way comparisons done at each node with two-way comparisons at each node plus one extra equality test at the bottom. `lastNode` points at the level-1 node at which this search terminates. Because we do not stop until we reach the bottom, if the item is in the tree, `lastNode` will point at the level-1 node that contains the replacement value and must be removed from the tree.

After a given recursive call terminates, we are either at level 1 or we are not. If we are at level 1, we can copy the node's value into the internal node that is to be replaced; we can then call `delete`. Otherwise, we are at a higher level, and we need to determine whether the balance condition has been violated. If so, we restore the balance and then make three calls to `skew` and two calls to `split`. As discussed previously, these actions guarantee that the AA-tree properties will be restored.

```
// Skew primitive for AA-trees.
// t is the node that roots the tree.
template <class Comparable>
void AATree<Comparable>::skew( Node * & t ) const
{
    if( t->left->level == t->level )
        rotateWithLeftChild( t );
}

// Split primitive for AA-trees.
// t is the node that roots the tree.
template <class Comparable>
void AATree<Comparable>::split( Node * & t ) const
{
    if( t->right->right->level == t->level )
    {
        rotateWithRightChild( t );
        t->level++;
    }
}
```

Figure 19.67 The `skew` and `split` procedures for the `AATree` class.

19.7 Implementing the STL `set` and `map` Classes

In this section we provide a reasonably efficient implementation of the STL `set` and `map` classes, with additional error checking that is not provided in the STL. The code is a blend of the STL list implementation presented in Section 17.5 and the AA-tree implementation in Section 19.6. The AA-tree details are, for the most part, not reproduced here because the core private routines such as the tree rotations, recursive insertion and removal, and `makeEmpty` and `clone` are essentially unchanged. Those routines are contained in the online code. Additionally, owing to space constraints, this code is poorly commented and relies on the accompanying text for explanation of any tricky details. The online code has the appropriate comments.

The basic implementation resembles that of the `list` class with its node, set, and iterator classes. However, there are three main differences between the classes.

1. The `set` class has two template parameters. The second template parameter is a comparison function that assigns a meaning to `lessThan`.

```
// Internal method to remove from a subtree.
// x is the item to remove.
// t is the node that roots the tree.
// Set the new root.
// Throw ItemNotFoundException is x is not in t.
template <class Comparable>
void AATree<Comparable>::
remove( const Comparable & x, Node * & t )
{
    static Node *lastNode, *deletedNode = nullNode;

    if( t != nullNode )
    {
          // Step 1: Search down the tree and
          //         set lastNode and deletedNode
        lastNode = t;
        if( x < t->element )
            remove( x, t->left );
        else
        {
            deletedNode = t;
            remove( x, t->right );
        }
          // Step 2: If at the bottom of the tree and
          //         x is present, we remove it
        if( t == lastNode )
        {
            if( deletedNode == nullNode ||
                                    x != deletedNode->element )
                throw ItemNotFoundException( );
            deletedNode->element = t->element;
            deletedNode = nullNode;
            t = t->right;
            delete lastNode;
        }
          // Step 3: Otherwise, not at the bottom; rebalance
        else
            if( t->left->level < t->level - 1 ||
                t->right->level < t->level - 1 )
            {
                if( t->right->level > --t->level )
                    t->right->level = t->level;
                skew( t );
                skew( t->right );
                skew( t->right->right );
                split( t );
                split( t->right );
            }
    }
}
```

Figure 19.68 The `remove` method for AA-trees.

2. Generally speaking, the `set` class has more methods than does the `list` class.
3. The `set` iteration routines are more complex than those of the `list` class.

For simplicity, our implementation provides only forward iteration. We must decide how to perform the traversal. Several alternatives are available:

1. use parent pointers;
2. have the iterator maintain a stack that represents the nodes on the path to the current position; and
3. have each node maintain a pointer to its inorder successor, a technique known as a *threaded tree*.

To make the code look as much as possible like the AA-tree code in Section 19.6, we use the option of having the iterator maintain a stack. However, this approach has the significant disadvantage of potentially making iterator objects expensive to copy. We leave using parent pointers for you to do as Exercise 19.31.

Figure 19.69 shows the basic node class, along with the typical set of incomplete class declarations. The `set` class interface is shown next, in Figure 19.70. At line 35 is the data member that stores the comparison function object. The routines in lines 41–50 are essentially identical to their AA-tree counterparts. For instance, the only difference between the `insert` method at line 42 and the one in the `AATree` class is that the `AAtree` version throws an exception if a duplicate is inserted, whereas this `insert` returns `false`. The public methods simply follow the specifications described in Section 7.7.

Figure 19.71 contains the interface for the `ConstSetItr` class. Much of it is similar to that in the `list` class. Line 21 declares `path`, which is a stack that keeps track of the path to the current node. Various assertions are declared at lines 24–27. We also provide some hidden methods that can be used to traverse the tree (`goLeft`, for example, moves left, and updates `path`) at lines 31–36. There is no nonconstant iterator class. The reason is that if we allow `*itr` to change a value in the `set`, it is possible to destroy the order in the `set`. Thus `iterator` and `const_iterator` represent the same type in our implementation.

The constructors and Big Three for the `set` class are shown in Figure 19.72. The private helpers, `init` and `makeEmpty`, are also shown (but the recursive `makeEmpty` is not). Figure 19.73 shows `begin`, `end`, `size`, and `empty`. The `begin` algorithm is to simply go left repeatedly. For `end`, recall that the `end` iterator represents a position that is one past the last item (the *endmarker*). We use the one-parameter (private) iterator constructor to create an iterator representing this position. The `size` and `empty` methods are trivial functions.

The `find` routine is shown in Figure 19.74. The endmarker is returned if needed at lines 6 and 18. Otherwise, the routine is similar to the corresponding code written in Figure 19.8. Public versions of `insert` and `erase` are shown next in Figure 19.75. Recall that `insert` returns a `pair`. For the most part, these are short routines. The private routines that they call are not shown but are similar to the AA-tree routines described in Section 19.6.

The `lower_bound` and `upper_bound` routines are shown in Figure 19.76. Like the version described in Section 7.4.2, `lower_bound` returns an iterator representing the earliest position that is larger than or equal to `x`. `upper_bound` returns an iterator representing the earliest position that is larger than `x`. The difference between the two occurs if `x` is in the set. In that case, `lower_bound`'s iterator refers to `x`, and `upper_bound`'s iterator refers to the position after `x`. Clearly there is commonality, which is encapsulated in the private `bound` routine.

```
#include "list.h"
#include "pair.h"

template <class Object, class Compare>
class ConstSetItr;

template <class Object, class Compare>
class set;

template <class Object, class Compare>
class TreeNode
{
    Object    data;
    int       level;
    TreeNode *left;
    TreeNode *right;

    TreeNode( const Object & d = Object( ), TreeNode * lt =
              NULL, TreeNode * rt = NULL, int lv = 1 )
      : data( d ), left( lt ), right( rt ), level( lv ) { }

    friend class ConstSetItr<Object,Compare>;
    friend class set<Object, Compare>;
};
```

Figure 19.69 The basic node class, along with the typical set of incomplete class declarations for the `set`.

```
template <class Object, class Compare>
class set
{
  public:
    typedef ConstSetItr<Object,Compare> iterator;
    typedef ConstSetItr<Object,Compare> const_iterator;
    typedef pair<iterator,bool>         returnPair;

    set( );
    ~set( );
    set( const set & rhs );
    const set & operator= ( const set & rhs );

    iterator begin( );
    const_iterator begin( ) const;
    iterator end( );
    const_iterator end( ) const;
    int size( ) const;
    bool empty( ) const;

    iterator lower_bound( const Object & x ) const;
    iterator upper_bound( const Object & x ) const;
    iterator find( const Object & x ) const;
    returnPair insert( const Object & x );
    int erase( const iterator & itr );
    int erase( const Object & x );

    friend class ConstSetItr<Object,Compare>;
    typedef TreeNode<Object,Compare> node;

  private:
    int      theSize;
    node    *root;
    node    *nullNode;
    Compare lessThan;

    void init( );
    void makeEmpty( );
    iterator bound( const Object & x, bool lower ) const;

      // Recursive routines
    bool insert( const Object & x, node * & t );
    void remove( const Object & x, node * & t );
    void makeEmpty( node * & t );
      // Rotations
    void skew( node * & t ) const;
    void split( node * & t ) const;
    void rotateWithLeftChild( node * & t ) const;
    void rotateWithRightChild( node * & t ) const;
    node * clone( node * t ) const;
};
```

Figure 19.70 The `set` class interface.

```
template <class Object, class Compare>
class ConstSetItr
{
  public:
    ConstSetItr( );
    const Object & operator* ( ) const;

    ConstSetItr & operator++ ( );
    ConstSetItr operator++ ( int );

    bool operator== ( const ConstSetItr & rhs ) const;
    bool operator!= ( const ConstSetItr & rhs ) const;

  protected:
    typedef TreeNode<Object,Compare> node;
    ConstSetItr( const set<Object,Compare> & source );

    node *root;
    node *current;

    list<node *> path;
    friend class set<Object,Compare>;

    void assertIsInitialized( ) const;
    void assertIsValid( ) const;
    void assertCanAdvance( ) const;
    void assertCanRetreat( ) const;

    Object & retrieve( ) const;

    void goLeft( );
    void goRight( );
    void goRoot( );

    bool hasLeft( ) const;
    bool hasRight( ) const;

    void advance( );
};
```

Figure 19.71 The `set::const_iterator` class interface.

```
template <class Object, class Compare>
set<Object,Compare>::set( )
{
    init( );
}

template <class Object, class Compare>
void set<Object,Compare>::init( )
{
    theSize = 0;
    nullNode = new node;
    nullNode->left = nullNode->right = nullNode;
    nullNode->level = 0;
    root = nullNode;
}

template <class Object, class Compare>
set<Object,Compare>::~set( )
{
    makeEmpty( );
    delete nullNode;
}

template <class Object, class Compare>
void set<Object,Compare>::makeEmpty( )
{
    makeEmpty( root );
    theSize = 0;
}

template <class Object, class Compare>
set<Object,Compare>::set( const set<Object,Compare> & rhs )
{
    init( );
    *this = rhs;
}

template <class Object, class Compare>
const set<Object,Compare> & set<Object,Compare>::
operator= ( const set<Object,Compare> & rhs )
{
    if( this == &rhs )
        return *this;

    makeEmpty( );
    root = clone( rhs.root );
    theSize = rhs.theSize;

    return *this;
}
```

Figure 19.72 Constructors, destructor, and copies for the `set` class.

```
template <class Object, class Compare>
set<Object,Compare>::iterator set<Object,Compare>::begin( )
{
    if( empty( ) )
        return end( );

    iterator itr( *this );
    itr.goRoot( );
    while( itr.hasLeft( ) )
        itr.goLeft( );
    return itr;
}

template <class Object, class Compare>
set<Object,Compare>::const_iterator
set<Object,Compare>::begin( ) const
{
    if( empty( ) )
        return end( );

    const_iterator itr( *this );
    itr.goRoot( );
    while( itr.hasLeft( ) )
        itr.goLeft( );
    return itr;
}

template <class Object, class Compare>
set<Object,Compare>::iterator set<Object,Compare>::end( )
{
    return iterator( *this );
}

template <class Object, class Compare>
set<Object,Compare>::const_iterator
set<Object,Compare>::end( ) const
{
    return const_iterator( *this );
}

template <class Object, class Compare>
int set<Object,Compare>::size( ) const
{
    return theSize;
}

template <class Object, class Compare>
bool set<Object,Compare>::empty( ) const
{
    return size( ) == 0;
}
```

Figure 19.73 The `begin`, `end`, `size`, and `empty` methods for the `set` class.

```
template <class Object, class Compare>
set<Object,Compare>::iterator
set<Object,Compare>::find( const Object & x ) const
{
    if( empty( ) )
        return end( );

    iterator itr( *this );
    itr.goRoot( );
    while( itr.current != nullNode )
        if( lessThan( x, *itr ) )
            itr.goLeft( );
        else if( lessThan( *itr, x ) )
            itr.goRight( );
        else
            return itr;

    return end( );
}
```

Figure 19.74 The `find` method for the `set` class.

```
template <class Object, class Compare>
set<Object,Compare>::returnPair
set<Object,Compare>::insert( const Object & x )
{
    bool result = insert( x, root );
    if( result )
        theSize++;
    return returnPair( find( x ), result );
}

template <class Object, class Compare>
int set<Object,Compare>::erase( const iterator & itr )
{
    return erase( *itr );
}

template <class Object, class Compare>
int set<Object,Compare>::erase( const Object & x )
{
    if( find( x ) == end( ) )
        return 0;

    remove( x, root );
    theSize--;
    return 1;
}
```

Figure 19.75 The public `insert` and `erase` routines for the `set` class.

```
template <class Object, class Compare>
set<Object,Compare>::iterator set<Object,Compare>::
bound( const Object & x, bool lower ) const
{
    if( empty( ) )
        return iterator( *this );

    iterator itr( *this );
    itr.goRoot( );
    node *lastLeft = NULL;

    while( itr.current != nullNode )
        if( lessThan( x, *itr ) )
        {
            lastLeft = itr.current;
            itr.goLeft( );
        }
        else if( lower && !lessThan( *itr, x ) )
            return itr;
        else
            itr.goRight( );

    if( lastLeft == NULL )
        return iterator( *this );

    while( itr.path.back( ) != lastLeft )
        itr.path.pop_back( );

    itr.path.pop_back( );
    itr.current = lastLeft;
    return itr;
}

template <class Object, class Compare>
set<Object,Compare>::iterator
set<Object,Compare>::lower_bound( const Object & x ) const
{
    return bound( x, true );
}

template <class Object, class Compare>
set<Object,Compare>::iterator
set<Object,Compare>::upper_bound( const Object & x ) const
{
    return bound( x, false );
}
```

Figure 19.76 The `lower_bound` and `upper_bound` routines and the private helper for the `set` class.

In bound, we traverse the tree. If we are performing a logical lower_bound and find a match, we can return an iterator immediately. Otherwise, lastLeft represents the last node at which we made a left turn. That is the node that we want. If we never made a left turn, we need to return the endmarker.

Various short routines are shown in Figure 19.77, and basic forward iteration is shown in Figure 19.78. The core routine is the private method advance. If the current node has a right child, we go right once and then left as far as possible. Otherwise, we need to go back up the path toward the root, until we find the node from which we turned left. That node is the next node in the iteration. If no such node exists, we set the iterator's state to be the endmarker.

Many of the one-line support routines are shown in Figure 19.79, along with the equality operators for the const_iterator.

We finish by providing an implementation of the map class. A map is simply a set in which we store key/value pairs. We can use either composition or private inheritance to implement the map class. We chose composition. Using private inheritance is left for you in Exercise 19.35.

A function object that can be used to instantiate the underlying set is shown in Figure 19.80. The map class interface is shown in Figure 19.81. The data member at line 45 stores the underlying set. Note how each method simply makes a call to this underlying set's method. The only new method is the mutator operator[]. The accessor version is not available for the map.

For the mutator, we use the code presented in Figure 19.82. The code constructs a pair and calls find on the underlying set. The result of find is an iterator; applying operator* (at line 11) gives a pair, and the value is obtained by accessing second. If the find returns the endmarker, we insert the key with a default value (the pair created at line 5), and return a reference to the newly inserted default value. The technical complication is that since *itr yields a *constant* pair, (*itr).second is a constant ValueType, and we cannot return a reference to it. Instead, we must first cast away the constness. The preferred method is to use const_cast, but this does not work on older compilers. Our alternative does: it obtains a pointer to a constant ValueType, typecasts to a pointer to non-constant ValueType, and then dereferences the pointer to obtain a non-constant ValueType.

```
template <class Object, class Compare>
ConstSetItr<Object,Compare>::ConstSetItr( )
  : root( NULL ), current( NULL )
{ }

template <class Object, class Compare>
void ConstSetItr<Object,Compare>::assertIsInitialized( ) const
{
    if( root == NULL )
        throw IteratorUninitializedException( );
}

template <class Object, class Compare>
void ConstSetItr<Object,Compare>::assertIsValid( ) const
{
    assertIsInitialized( );
}

template <class Object, class Compare>
void ConstSetItr<Object,Compare>::assertCanAdvance( ) const
{
    assertIsInitialized( );
    if( current == NULL )
        throw IteratorOutOfBoundsException( );
}

template <class Object, class Compare>
Object & ConstSetItr<Object,Compare>::retrieve( ) const
{
    assertIsValid( );
    if( current == NULL )
        throw IteratorOutOfBoundsException( );
    return current->data;
}

template <class Object, class Compare>
const Object & ConstSetItr<Object,Compare>::operator* ( ) const
{
    return retrieve( );
}
```

Figure 19.77 Various private routines and `operator*` for the `set` class.

```
template <class Object, class Compare>
void ConstSetItr<Object,Compare>::advance( )
{
    if( hasRight( ) )
    {
        goRight( );
        while( hasLeft( ) )
            goLeft( );
        return;
    }

    node *parent;
    for( ; !path.empty( ); current = parent )
    {
        parent = path.back( ); path.pop_back( );
        if( parent->left == current )
        {
            current = parent;
            return;
        }
    }

    current = NULL;
}

template <class Object, class Compare>
ConstSetItr<Object,Compare> &
ConstSetItr<Object,Compare>::operator++ ( )
{
    assertCanAdvance( );
    advance( );
    return *this;
}

template <class Object, class Compare>
ConstSetItr<Object,Compare>
ConstSetItr<Object,Compare>::operator++ ( int )
{
    ConstSetItr<Object,Compare> old = *this;
    ++( *this );
    return old;
}
```

Figure 19.78 Advancing for the set class.

```
template <class Object, class Compare>
bool ConstSetItr<Object,Compare>::
operator== ( const ConstSetItr & rhs ) const
{
    return root == rhs.root && current == rhs.current;
}

template <class Object, class Compare>
bool ConstSetItr<Object,Compare>::
operator!= ( const ConstSetItr & rhs ) const
{
    return !( *this == rhs );
}

template <class Object, class Compare>
ConstSetItr<Object,Compare>::
ConstSetItr( const set<Object,Compare> & source )
  : root( source.root ), current( NULL ) { }

template <class Object, class Compare>
void ConstSetItr<Object,Compare>::goLeft( )
{
    path.push_back( current );
    current = current->left;
}

template <class Object, class Compare>
void ConstSetItr<Object,Compare>::goRight( )
{
    path.push_back( current );
    current = current->right;
}

template <class Object, class Compare>
void ConstSetItr<Object,Compare>::goRoot( )
{
    current = root;
    while( !path.empty( ) )
        path.pop_back( );
}

template <class Object, class Compare>
bool ConstSetItr<Object,Compare>::hasLeft( ) const
{
    return current->left != current->left->left;
}

template <class Object, class Compare>
bool ConstSetItr<Object,Compare>::hasRight( ) const
{
   return current->right != current->right->right;
}
```

Figure 19.79 Various one-line routines for the `set` class.

```
template <class kvpair, class Compare>
class lessKV
{
  public:
    bool operator( ) ( const kvpair & lhs,
                       const kvpair & rhs ) const
      { return less( lhs.first, rhs.first ); }
    Compare less;
};
```

Figure 19.80 A function object for the map class that uses the key to compare.

19.8 B-Trees

So far, we have assumed that we can store an entire data structure in the main memory of a computer. Suppose, however, that we have more data than can fit in main memory, and, as a result, we must have the data structure reside on disk. When that happens, the rules of the game change, because the Big-Oh model is no longer meaningful.

The problem is that a Big-Oh analysis assumes that all operations are equal. However, that is not true, especially when disk I/O is involved. On the one hand, a 500-MIPS machine supposedly executes 500 million instructions per second. That is fairly fast, mainly because the speed depends largely on electrical properties. On the other hand, a disk is mechanical. Its speed depends largely on the time required to spin the disk and move a disk head. Many disks spin at 7200 RPM. Thus in 1 minute, it makes 7200 revolutions; hence one revolution occurs in 1/120 of a second, or 8.3 ms. On average we might expect that we have to spin a disk halfway to find what we are looking for, but this is compensated by the time to move the disk head, so we get an access time of 8.3 ms. (This estimate is very charitable; 9 to 11 ms. access times are more common.) Consequently, we can do approximately 120 disk accesses per second. This number of accesses sounds good, until we compare it with the processor speed: We have 500 million instructions versus 120 disk accesses. Put another way, one disk access is worth about 4,000,000 instructions. Of course, everything here is a rough calculation, but the relative speeds are rather clear: Disk accesses are incredibly expensive. Furthermore, processor speeds are increasing at a much faster rate than disk speeds (it is disk *sizes* that are increasing quite quickly). Thus, we are willing to do lots of calculations just to save a disk access. In almost all cases, the number of disk accesses dominates the running time. By halving the number of disk accesses, we can halve the running time.

When data are too large to fit in memory, the number of disk accesses becomes important. A disk access is unbelievably expensive compared to a typical computer instruction.

```
template <class KeyType, class ValueType, class Compare>
class map
{
  public:
    typedef pair<KeyType,ValueType>                kvpair;
    typedef set<kvpair,lessKV<kvpair,Compare> > setType;
    typedef setType::iterator iterator;
    typedef setType::const_iterator const_iterator;

    iterator begin( )
      { return theSet.begin( ); }
    const_iterator begin( ) const
      { return theSet.begin( ); }
    iterator end( )
      { return theSet.end( ); }
    const_iterator end( ) const
      { return theSet.end( ); }
    int size( ) const
      { return theSet.size( ); }
    bool empty( ) const
      { return theSet.empty( ); }

    ValueType & operator[] ( const KeyType & key );

    iterator lower_bound( const KeyType & key )
      { return theSet.lower_bound( kvpair( key ) ); }
    const_iterator lower_bound( const KeyType & key ) const
      { return theSet.lower_bound( kvpair( key ) ); }
    iterator upper_bound( const KeyType & key )
      { return theSet.upper_bound( kvpair( key ) ); }
    const_iterator upper_bound( const KeyType & key ) const
      { return theSet.upper_bound( kvpair( key ) ); }
    iterator find( const KeyType & key )
      { return theSet.find( kvpair( key ) ); }
    const_iterator find( const KeyType & key ) const
      { return theSet.find( kvpair( key ) ); }
    pair<iterator,bool> insert( const kvpair & x )
      { return theSet.insert( x ); }
    int erase( const iterator & itr )
      { return theSet.erase( itr ); }
    int erase( const KeyType & key )
      { return theSet.erase( kvpair( key ) ); }

  private:
    setType theSet;
};
```

Figure 19.81 The map class interface.

```
template <class KeyType, class ValueType, class Compare>
ValueType & map<KeyType,ValueType,Compare>::
operator[] ( const KeyType & key )
{
    kvpair x( key );

    iterator itr = theSet.find( x );
    if( itr == theSet.end( ) )
        itr = theSet.insert( x ).first;

    return *(ValueType *)&(*itr).second;
}
```

Figure 19.82 Implementation of the map class `operator[]`.

Here is how the typical search tree performs on disk. Suppose that we want to access the driving records for citizens in the State of Florida. We assume that we have 10,000,000 items, that each key is 32 bytes (representing a name), and that a record is 256 bytes. We assume that this data set does not fit in main memory and that we are 1 of 20 users on a system (so we have 1/20 of the resources). Thus in 1 sec. we can execute 25 million instructions or perform six disk accesses.

Even logarithmic performance is unacceptable. We need to perform searches in three or four accesses. Updates can take slightly longer.

The unbalanced binary search tree is a disaster. In the worst case, it has linear depth and thus could require 10,000,000 disk accesses. On average a successful search would require 1.38 log N disk accesses, and as log 10,000,000 ≈ 24, an average search would require 32 disk accesses, or 5 sec. In a typical randomly constructed tree, we would expect that a few nodes are three times deeper; they would require about 100 disk accesses, or 16 sec. A red–black tree is somewhat better: the worst case of 1.44 log N is unlikely to occur, and the typical case is very close to log N. Thus a red–black tree would use about 25 disk accesses on average, requiring 4 sec.

An *M*-ary search tree allows *M*-way branching. As branching increases, the depth decreases.

We want to reduce disk accesses to a very small constant number, such as three or four. We are willing to write complicated code to do so because machine instructions are essentially free, so long as we are not ridiculously unreasonable. A binary search tree does not work because the typical red–black tree is close to optimal height, and we cannot go below log N with a binary search tree. The solution is intuitively simple: If we have more branching, we have less height. Thus, whereas a perfect binary tree of 31 nodes has five levels, a 5-ary tree of 31 nodes has only three levels, as shown in Figure 19.83. An ***M*-ary search tree** allows M-way branching, and as branching increases, the depth decreases. Whereas a complete binary tree has height that is roughly $\log_2 N$, a complete M-ary tree has height that is roughly $\log_M N$.

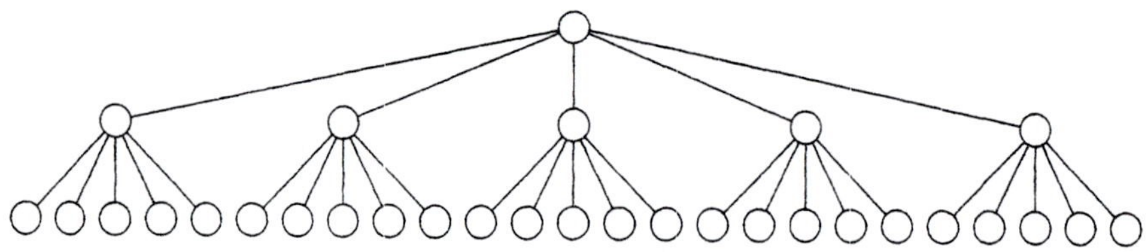

Figure 19.83 A 5-ary tree of 31 nodes has only three levels.

We can create an M-ary search tree in much the same way we created a binary search tree. In a binary search tree, we need one key to decide which of two branches to take. In an M-ary search tree, we need $M - 1$ keys to decide which branch to take. To make this scheme efficient in the worst case, we need to ensure that the M-ary search tree is balanced in some way. Otherwise, like a binary search tree, it could degenerate into a linked list. Actually, we want an even more restrictive balancing condition. That is, we do not want an M-ary search tree to degenerate to even a binary search tree because then we would be stuck with $\log N$ accesses.

The *B-tree* is the most popular data structure for disk-bound searching.

One way to implement this is to use a **B-tree,** which is the most popular data structure for disk-bound searching. Here, we describe the basic B-tree;[3] many variations and improvements exist, and an implementation is somewhat complex because quite a few cases must be addressed. However, in principle this technique guarantees only a few disk accesses.

The B-tree has a host of structure properties.

A B-tree of order M is an M-ary tree with the following properties.[4]

1. The data items are stored at leaves.
2. The nonleaf nodes store as many as $M - 1$ keys to guide the searching; key i represents the smallest key in subtree $i + 1$.
3. The root is either a leaf or has between 2 and M children.
4. All nonleaf nodes (except the root) have between $\lceil M/2 \rceil$ and M children.
5. All leaves are at the same depth and have between $\lceil L/2 \rceil$ and L data items, for some L (the determination of L is described shortly).

Nodes must be half full to guarantee that the tree does not degenerate into a simple binary tree.

An example of a B-tree of order 5 is shown in Figure 19.84. Note that all nonleaf nodes have between three and five children (and thus between two and four keys); the root could possibly have only two children. Here, $L = 5$, which means that L and M are the same in this example, but this condition is

3. What we describe is popularly known as a B^+ tree.

4. Properties 3 and 5 must be relaxed for the first L insertions. (L is a parameter used in property 5.)

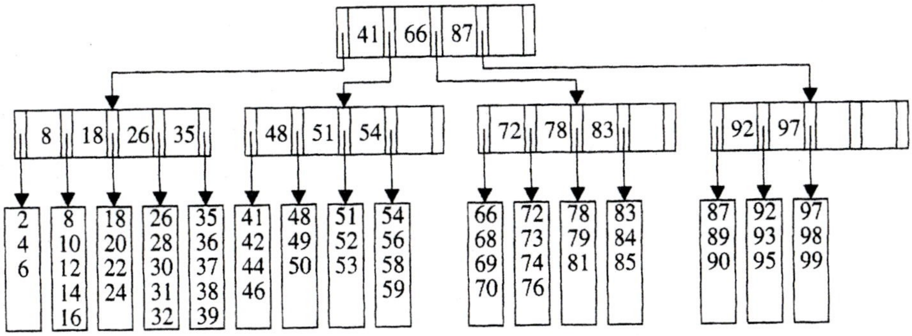

Figure 19.84 A B-tree of order 5.

not necessary. Because L is 5, each leaf has between three and five data items. Requiring nodes to be half full guarantees that the B-tree does not degenerate into a simple binary tree. Various definitions of B-trees change this structure, mostly in minor ways, but the definition presented here is one of the most commonly used.

We choose the maximum *M* and *L* that allow a node to fit in one disk block.

Each node represents a disk block, so we choose M and L on the basis of the size of the items being stored. Suppose that one block holds 8192 bytes. In our Florida example, each key uses 32 bytes, so in a B-tree of order M, we would have $M - 1$ keys, for a total of $32M - 32$ bytes plus M branches. Because each branch is essentially a number of another disk block, we can assume that a branch is 4 bytes. Thus the branches use $4M$ bytes, and the total memory requirement for a nonleaf node is $36M - 32$. The largest value of M for which $36M - 32$ is no more than 8192 is 228, so we would choose $M = 228$. As each data record is 256 bytes, we would be able to fit 32 records in a block. Thus we would choose $L = 32$. Each leaf has between 16 and 32 data records, and each internal node (except the root) branches in at least 114 ways. For the 10,000,000 records, there are at most 625,500 leaves. Consequently, in the worst case, leaves would be on level 4. In more concrete terms, the worst-case number of accesses is given by approximately $\log_{M/2} N$, give or take 1.

The remaining issue is how to add and remove items from the B-tree. In the ideas sketched note that many themes presented earlier recur.

If the leaf contains room for a new item, we insert it and are done.

We begin by examining insertion. Suppose that we want to insert 57 into the B-tree shown previously in Figure 19.84. A search down the tree reveals that it is not already in the tree. We can add it to the leaf as a fifth child, but we may have to reorganize all the data in the leaf to do so. However, the cost is negligible compared to that of the disk access, which in this case also includes a disk write.

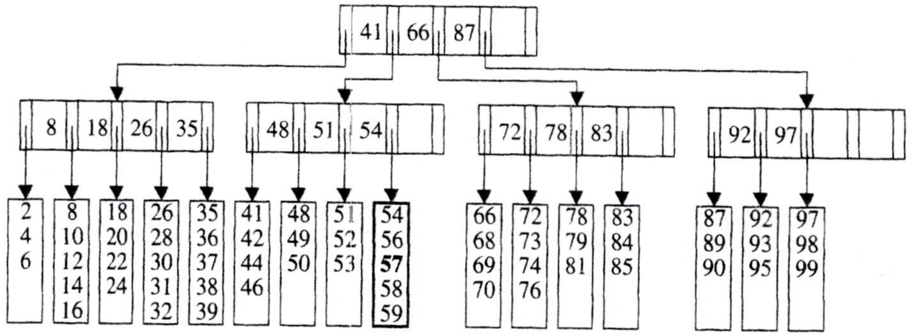

Figure 19.85 The B-tree after insertion of 57 in the tree shown in Figure 19.84.

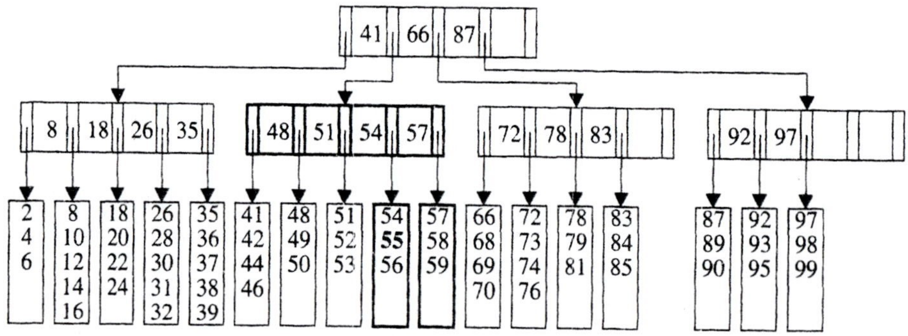

Figure 19.86 Insertion of 55 in the B-tree shown in Figure 19.85 causes a split into two leaves.

If the leaf is full, we can insert a new item by splitting the leaf and forming two half-empty nodes.

That procedure was relatively painless because the leaf was not already full. Suppose that we now want to insert 55. Figure 19.85 shows a problem: The leaf where 55 should go is already full. The solution is simple: We now have $L + 1$ items, so we split them into two leaves, both guaranteed to have the minimum number of data records needed. Hence we form two leaves with three items each. Two disk accesses are required to write these leaves and a third disk access is required to update the parent. Note that in the parent, both keys and branches change, but they do so in a controlled way that can easily be calculated. The resulting B-tree is shown in Figure 19.86. Although splitting nodes is time consuming because it requires at least two additional disk writes, it is a relatively rare occurrence. If L is 32, for example, when a node is split two leaves with 16 and 17 items, respectively, are created. For the leaf with 17 items, we can perform 15 more insertions without another split. Put another way, for every split, there are roughly $L/2$ nonsplits.

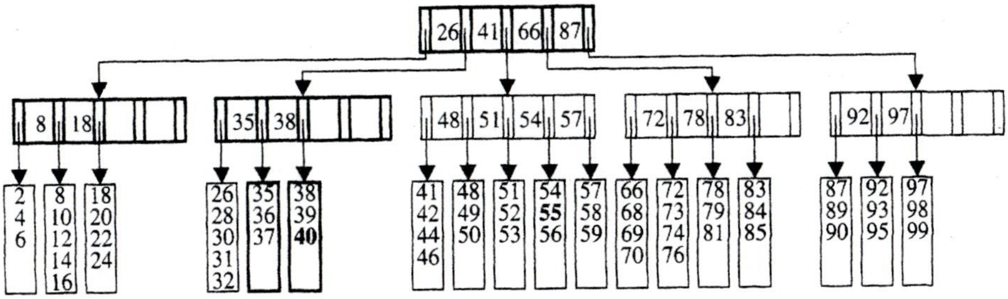

Figure 19.87 Insertion of 40 in the B-tree shown in Figure 19.86 causes a split into two leaves and then a split of the parent node.

Node splitting creates an extra child for the leaf's parent. If the parent already has a full number of children, we split the parent.

The node splitting in the preceding example worked because the parent did not have its full complement of children. But what would happen if it did? Suppose that we insert 40 into the B-tree shown in Figure 19.86. We must split the leaf containing the keys 35 through 39 and now 40 into two leaves. But doing so would give the parent six children, and it is allowed only five. The solution is to split the parent, the result of which is shown in Figure 19.87. When the parent is split, we must update the values of the keys and also the parent's parent, incurring an additional two disk writes (so this insertion costs five disk writes). Again, however, the keys change in a very controlled manner, although the code is certainly not simple because of the number of cases involved.

We may have to continue splitting all the way up the tree (though this possibility is unlikely). In the worst case, we split the root, creating a new root with two children.

When a nonleaf node is split, as here, its parent gains a child. What if the parent already has reached its limit of children? Then we continue splitting nodes up the tree until we find a parent that does not need to be split or we reach the root. Note that we introduced this idea in bottom–up red–black trees and AA-trees. If we split the root, we have two roots, but obviously, this outcome is unacceptable. However, we can create a new root that has the split roots as its two children, which is why the root is granted the special two-child minimum exemption. It is also the only way that a B-tree gains height. Needless to say, splitting all the way up to the root is an exceptionally rare event because a tree with four levels indicates that the root has been split two times throughout the entire sequence of insertions (assuming that no deletions have occurred). In fact, splitting of any nonleaf node is also quite rare.

There are other ways to handle the overflowing of children. One technique is to put a child up for adoption should a neighbor have room. To insert 29 in the B-tree shown in Figure 19.87, for example, we could make room by moving 32 to the next leaf. This technique requires a modification of the parent because the keys are affected. However, it tends to keep nodes fuller and saves space in the long run.

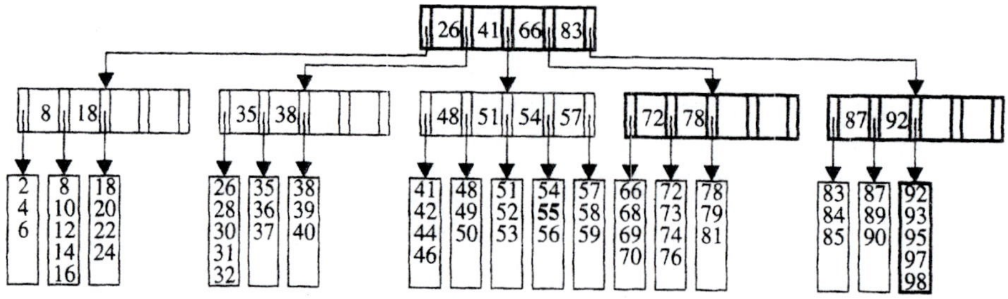

Figure 19.88 The B-tree after deletion of 99 from the tree shown in Figure 19.87.

Deletion works in reverse: If a leaf loses a child, it may need to combine with another leaf. Combining of nodes may continue all the way up the tree, though this possibility is unlikely. In the worst case, the root loses one of its two children. Then we delete the root and use the other child as the new root.

We can perform deletion by finding the item that needs to be removed and removing it. The problem is that, if the leaf it was in had the minimum number of data items, it is now below the minimum. We can rectify the situation by adopting a neighboring item, if the neighbor is not itself at its minimum. If it is, we can combine with the neighbor to form a full leaf. Unfortunately, in this case the parent has lost a child. If that causes the parent to fall below its minimum, we follow the same strategy. This process could percolate up all the way up to the root. The root cannot have just one child (and even if it were allowed, it would be silly). If a root is left with one child as a result of the adoption process, we remove the root, making its child the new root of the tree—the only way for a B-tree to lose height. Suppose that we want to remove 99 from the B-tree shown in Figure 19.87. The leaf has only two items and its neighbor is already at its minimum of three, so we combine the items into a new leaf of five items. As a result, the parent has only two children. However, it can adopt from a neighbor because the neighbor has four children. As a result of the adoption, both end up with three children, as shown in Figure 19.88.

Summary

Binary search trees support almost all of the useful operations in algorithm design, and the logarithmic average cost is very small. Nonrecursive implementations of search trees are somewhat faster than recursive versions, but the latter are sleeker, more elegant, and easier to understand and debug. The problem with search trees is that their performance depends heavily on the input's being random. If it is not, running time increases significantly, even to the point where search trees become expensive linked lists.

Ways of dealing with this problem all involve restructuring the tree to ensure some sort of balance at each node. Restructuring is achieved through tree rotations that preserve the binary search tree property. The cost of a search is typically less than for an unbalanced binary search tree because the average node tends to be closer to the root. Insertion and deletion costs, however, are usually higher. The balanced variations differ in the amount of coding effort involved in implementing operations that change the tree.

The classic scheme is the AVL tree in which, for every node, the heights of its left and right subtrees can differ by at most 1. The practical problem with AVL trees is that they involve large numbers of different cases, making the overhead of each insertion and deletion relatively high. We examined two alternatives in the chapter. The first was the top–down red–black tree. Its primary advantage is that rebalancing can be implemented in a single pass down the tree, rather than the traditional pass down and back up. This technique leads to simpler code and faster performance than the AVL tree allows. The second is the AA-tree, which is similar to the bottom–up red–black tree. Its primary advantage is a relatively simple recursive implementation of both insertion and deletion. Both structures use sentinel nodes to eliminate annoying special cases.

You should use an unbalanced binary search tree only if you are sure that the data are reasonably random or that the amount of data is relatively small. Use the red–black tree if you are concerned about speed (and are not too concerned about deletion). Use the AA-tree if you want an easy implementation that has more than acceptable performance. Use the B-tree when the amount of data is too large to store in main memory.

In Chapter 22 we examine another alternative: the splay tree. It is an interesting alternative to the balanced search tree, is simple to code, and is competitive in practice. In Chapter 20 we examine the hash table, a completely different method used to implement searching operations.

Objects of the Game

AA-tree A balanced search tree that is the tree of choice when an $O(\log N)$ worst case is needed, a casual implementation is acceptable, and deletions are needed. (p. 685)

AVL tree A binary search tree with the additional balance property that, for any node in the tree, the height of the left and right subtrees can differ by at most 1. As the first balanced search tree, it has historical significance. It also illustrates most of the ideas that are used in other search tree schemes. (p. 661)

balanced binary search tree A tree that has an added structure property to guarantee logarithmic depth in the worst case. Updates are slower than with the binary search tree, but accesses are faster. (p. 661)

binary search tree A data structure that supports insertion, searching, and deletion in $O(\log N)$ average time. For any node in the binary search tree, all smaller keyed nodes are in the left subtree and all larger keyed nodes are in the right subtree. Duplicates are not allowed. (p. 641)

B-tree The most popular data structure for disk-bound searching. There are many variations of the same idea. (p. 710)

double rotation Equivalent to two single rotations. (p. 667)

external path length The sum of the cost of accessing all external tree nodes in a binary tree, which measures the cost of an unsuccessful search. (p. 660)

external tree node The `NULL` node. (p. 660)

horizontal link In an AA-tree, a connection between a node and a child of equal levels. A horizontal link should go only to the right, and there should not be two consecutive horizontal links. (p. 685)

internal path length The sum of the depths of the nodes in a binary tree, which measures the cost of a successful search. (p. 659)

lazy deletion A method that marks items as deleted but does not actually delete them. (p. 685)

level of a node In an AA-tree, the number of left links on the path to the `nullNode` sentinel. (p. 685)

***M*-ary tree** A tree that allows M-way branching, and as branching increases, the depth decreases. (p. 709)

red–black tree A balanced search tree that is a good alternative to the AVL tree because a single top–down pass can be used during the insertion and deletion routines. Nodes are colored red and black in a restricted way that guarantees logarithmic depth. The coding details tend to give a faster implementation. (p. 670)

single rotation Switches the roles of the parent and child while maintaining search order. Balance is restored by tree rotations. (p. 664)

`skew` Removal of left horizontal links by performing a rotation between a node and its left child. (p. 686)

`split` Fixing consecutive right horizontal links by performing a rotation between a node and its right child. (p. 686)

Common Errors

1. Using an unbalanced search tree when the input sequence is not random will give poor performance.
2. The `remove` operation is very tricky to code correctly, especially for a balanced search tree.
3. Lazy deletion is a good alternative to the standard `remove`, but you must then change other routines, such as `findMin`.
4. Code for balanced search trees is almost always error-prone.
5. Passing a pointer to a tree by value is wrong for `insert` and `remove`. The pointer must be passed by reference.
6. Using sentinels and then writing code that forgets about the sentinels can lead to infinite loops. A common case is testing against `NULL` when a `nullNode` sentinel is used.

On the Internet

All of the code in this chapter is available online.

BinarySearchTree.h	Contains the class interface for both the `BinarySearchTreeWithRank` and `BinarySearchTree` classes.
BinarySearchTree.cpp	Contains the implementation of both the `BinarySearchTreeWithRank` and `BinarySearchTree` classes.
TestBinarySearchTree.cpp	Contains a test program for both the `BinarySearchTreeWithRank` and `BinarySearchTree` classes.
RedBlackTree.h	Contains the interface for the `RedBlackTree` class.
RedBlackTree.cpp	Contains the implementation of the `RedBlackTree` class.
TestRedBlackTree.cpp	Contains a test program for the `RedBlackTree` class.
AATree.h	Contains the interface for the `AATree` class.
AATree.cpp	Contains the implementation of the `AATree` class
TestAATree.cpp	Contains a test program for the `AATree` class.

set.h	Contains the interface for the `set` class.
set.cpp	Contains the implementation of the `set` class.
TestSet.cpp	Contains a test program for the `set` class.
map.h	Contains the interface for the `map` class.
map.cpp	Contains the implementation of the `map` class.
TestMap.cpp	Contains a test program for the `map` class.

Exercises

In Short

19.1. Show the result of inserting 3, 1, 4, 6, 9, 2, 5, and 7 in an initially empty binary search tree. Then show the result of deleting the root.

19.2. Draw all binary search trees that can result from inserting permutations of 1, 2, 3, and 4. How many trees are there? What are the probabilities of each tree's occurring if all permutations are equally likely?

19.3. What happens if, in Figure 19.9, the first parameter is `Node * & t` (that is, `t` is passed by reference)? Be specific.

19.4. What happens if, in Figure 19.10, the second parameter is merely `Node * t` (i.e., `t` is not passed by reference)? Be specific.

19.5. Draw all AVL trees that can result from inserting permutations of 1, 2, and 3. How many trees are there? What are the probabilities of each tree's occurring if all permutations are equally likely?

19.6. Repeat Exercise 19.5 for four elements.

19.7. Show the result of inserting 2, 1, 4, 5, 9, 3, 6, and 7 into an initially empty AVL tree. Then show the result for a top–down red–black tree.

19.8. Repeat Exercises 19.5 and 19.6 for a red–black tree.

In Theory

19.9. Prove Theorem 19.2.

19.10. Show the result of inserting items 1 through 15 in order in an initially empty AVL tree. Generalize this result (with proof) to show what happens when items 1 through $2^k - 1$ are inserted into an initially empty AVL tree.

19.11. Give an algorithm to perform `remove` in an AVL tree.

19.12. Prove that the height of a red–black tree is at most approximately $2 \log N$ and give an insertion sequence that achieves this bound.

19.13. Show that every AVL tree can be colored as a red–black tree. Do all red–black trees satisfy the AVL tree property?

19.14. Prove that the algorithm for deletion in an AA-tree is correct.

19.15. Suppose that the `level` data member in an AA-tree is represented by an 8-bit `char`. What is the smallest AA-tree that would overflow the `level` data member at the root?

19.16. A B*-tree of order M is a B-tree in which each interior node has between $2M/3$ and M children. Leaves are similarly filled. Describe a method that can be used to perform insertion in a B*-tree.

In Practice

19.17. Implement `find`, `findMin`, and `findMax` recursively.

19.18. Implement `findKth` nonrecursively, using the same technique used for a nonrecursive `find`.

19.19. Verify that if the private functions `insert`, `remove`, and `removeMin`, of `BinarySearchTree` are renamed, then in Figure 19.14, lines 17–22 can be removed from the `BinarySearchTreeWithRank` class interface and only the private functions need to be overridden.

19.20. An alternative representation that allows the `findKth` operation is to store in each node the value of 1 plus the size of the left subtree. Why might this approach be advantageous? Rewrite the search tree class to use this representation.

19.21. Write a binary search tree method that takes two keys, `low` and `high`, and prints all elements X that are in the range specified by `low` and `high`. Your program should run in $O(K + \log N)$ average time, where K is the number of keys printed. Thus if K is small, you should be examining only a small part of the tree. Use a hidden recursive method and do not use an inorder iterator. Bound the running time of your algorithm.

19.22. Write a binary search tree method that takes two integers, `low` and `high`, and constructs an optimally balanced `BinarySearchTreeWithRank` that contains all the integers between `low` and `high`, inclusive. All leaves should be at the same level (if the tree size is 1 less than a power of 2) or on two consecutive levels. *Your routine should take linear time.* Test your routine by using it to solve the Josephus problem presented in Section 14.1.

19.23. The routines for performing double rotations are inefficient because they perform unnecessary changes to children pointers. Rewrite them to avoid calls to the single rotation routine.

19.24. Give a nonrecursive top–down implementation of an AA-tree. Compare the implementation with the text's for simplicity and efficiency.

19.25. Write the `skew` and `split` procedures recursively so that only one call of each is needed for `remove`.

Programming Projects

19.26. Redo the `BinarySearchTree` class to implement lazy deletion. Note that doing so affects all the routines. Especially challenging are `findMin` and `findMax`, which must now be done recursively.

19.27. Implement the binary search tree to use only one comparison per level for `find`, `insert`, and `remove`.

19.28. Write a program to evaluate empirically the following strategies for removing nodes with two children. Recall that a strategy involves replacing the value in a deleted node with some other value. Which strategy gives the best balance? Which takes the least CPU time to process an entire sequence of operations?

a. Replace with the value in the largest node, X, in T_L and recursively remove X.

b. Alternatively replace with the value in the largest node in T_L or the value in the smallest node in T_R and recursively remove the appropriate node.

c. Replace with the value in the largest node in T_L or the value in the smallest node in T_R (recursively remove the appropriate node), making the choice randomly.

19.29. Write the `remove` method for red–black trees.

19.30. Implement the search tree operations with order statistics for the balanced search tree of your choice.

19.31. Reimplement the `set` class by using parent pointers.

19.32. Modify the `set` and `map` classes so that their iterators are bidirectional.

19.33. Add reverse iterators to the `set` and `map` classes. (Reverse iterators are described in Exercise 17.3.)

19.34. A `multiset` is a `set` in which duplicates are allowed. All operations are the same except for `insert` (duplicates are allowed), `find` (if `x` is present, an iterator representing any occurrence of `x` may be returned), and `erase` (which may return a value larger than 1). Implement a `multiset`.

19.35. Implement the `map` class by using private inheritance.

19.36. Implement a B-tree that works in main memory.

19.37. Implement a B-tree that works for disk files.

References

More information on binary search trees, and in particular the mathematical properties of trees, is available in [18 and 19].

Several papers deal with the theoretical lack of balance caused by biased deletion algorithms in binary search trees. Hibbard [16] proposed the original deletion algorithm and established that one deletion preserves the randomness of the trees. A complete analysis has been performed only for trees with three nodes [17] and four nodes [3]. Eppinger [10] provided early empirical evidence of nonrandomness, and Culberson and Munro [7 and 8] provide some analytical evidence (but not a complete proof for the general case of intermixed insertions and deletions). The claim that the deepest node in a random binary search tree is three times deeper than the average node is proved in [11]; the result is by no means simple.

AVL trees were proposed by Adelson-Velskii and Landis [2]. A deletion algorithm is presented in [19]. Analysis of the average costs of searching an AVL tree is incomplete, but some results are contained in [20]. The top–down red–black tree algorithm is from [15]; a more accessible description is presented in [21]. An implementation of top–down red–black trees without sentinel nodes is given in [12]; it provides a convincing demonstration of the usefulness of `nullNode`. The AA-tree is based on the symmetric binary B-tree discussed in [4]. The implementation shown in the text is adapted from the description in [1]. Many other balanced search trees are described in [13].

B-trees first appeared in [5]. The implementation described in the original paper allows data to be stored in internal nodes as well as in leaves. The data structure described here is sometimes called a B^+-tree. Information on the B*-tree, described in Exercise 19.16, is available in [9]. A survey of the different types of B-trees is presented in [6]. Empirical results of the various schemes are reported in [14]. A C++ implementation is contained in [12].

1. A. Andersson, "Balanced Search Trees Made Simple," *Proceedings of the Third Workshop on Algorithms and Data Structures* (1993), 61–71.
2. G. M. Adelson-Velskii and E. M. Landis, "An Algorithm for the Organization of Information," *Soviet Math. Doklady* **3** (1962), 1259–1263.
3. R. A. Baeza-Yates, "A Trivial Algorithm Whose Analysis Isn't: A Continuation," *BIT* **29** (1989), 88–113.
4. R. Bayer, "Symmetric Binary B-Trees: Data Structure and Maintenance Algorithms," *Acta Informatica* **1** (1972), 290–306.
5. R. Bayer and E. M. McCreight, "Organization and Maintenance of Large Ordered Indices," *Acta Informatica* **1** (1972), 173–189.
6. D. Comer, "The Ubiquitous B-tree," *Computing Surveys* **11** (1979), 121–137.
7. J. Culberson and J. I. Munro, "Explaining the Behavior of Binary Search Trees Under Prolonged Updates: A Model and Simulations," *Computer Journal* **32** (1989), 68–75.
8. J. Culberson and J. I. Munro, "Analysis of the Standard Deletion Algorithm in Exact Fit Domain Binary Search Trees," *Algorithmica* **5** (1990), 295–311.
9. K. Culik, T. Ottman, and D. Wood, "Dense Multiway Trees," *ACM Transactions on Database Systems* **6** (1981), 486–512.
10. J. L. Eppinger, "An Empirical Study of Insertion and Deletion in Binary Search Trees," *Communications of the ACM* **26** (1983), 663–669.
11. P. Flajolet and A. Odlyzko, "The Average Height of Binary Search Trees and Other Simple Trees," *Journal of Computer and System Sciences* **25** (1982), 171–213.

12. B. Flamig, *Practical Data Structures in C++*, John Wiley & Sons, New York, New York, 1994.

13. G. H. Gonnet and R. Baeza-Yates, *Handbook of Algorithms and Data Structures*, 2d ed., Addison-Wesley, Reading, Mass., 1991.

14. E. Gudes and S. Tsur, "Experiments with B-tree Reorganization," *Proceedings of ACM SIGMOD Symposium on Management of Data* (1980), 200–206.

15. L. J. Guibas and R. Sedgewick, "A Dichromatic Framework for Balanced Trees," *Proceedings of the Nineteenth Annual IEEE Symposium on Foundations of Computer Science* (1978), 8–21.

16. T. H. Hibbard, "Some Combinatorial Properties of Certain Trees with Applications to Searching and Sorting," *Journal of the ACM* **9** (1962), 13–28.

17. A. T. Jonassen and D. E. Knuth, "A Trivial Algorithm Whose Analysis Isn't," *Journal of Computer and System Sciences* **16** (1978), 301–322.

18. D. E. Knuth, *The Art of Computer Programming: Volume 1: Fundamental Algorithms*, 3d ed., Addison-Wesley, Reading, Mass., 1997.

19. D. E. Knuth, *The Art of Computer Programming: Volume 3: Sorting and Searching*, 2d ed., Addison-Wesley, Reading, Mass., 1998.

20. K. Melhorn, "A Partial Analysis of Height-Balanced Trees Under Random Insertions and Deletions," *SIAM Journal on Computing* **11** (1982), 748–760.

21. R. Sedgewick, *Algorithms in C++*, Addison-Wesley, Reading, Mass., 1992.

Chapter 20

Hash Tables

In Chapter 19 we discussed the binary search tree, which allows various operations on a set of elements. In this chapter we discuss the hash table, which supports only a subset of the operations allowed by binary search trees. The implementation of hash tables is frequently called **hashing,** which performs insertions, deletions, and finds in constant average time.

Unlike with the binary search tree, the average-case running time of hash table operations is based on statistical properties rather than the expectation of random-looking input. This improvement is obtained at the expense of a loss of ordering information among the elements: Operations such as `findMin` and `findMax` and the printing of an entire table in sorted order in linear time are not supported. Consequently, the hash table and binary search tree have somewhat different uses and performance properties.

In this chapter, we show:

- several methods of implementing the hash table,
- analytical comparisons of these methods,
- some applications of hashing, and
- comparisons of hash tables and binary search trees.

20.1 Basic Ideas

The *hash table* is used to implement a set in constant time per operation.

The **hash table** supports the retrieval or deletion of any named item. We want to be able to support the basic operations in constant time, as for the stack and queue. Because the accesses are much less restricted, this support seems like an impossible goal. That is, surely when the size of the set increases, searches in the set should take longer. However, that is not necessarily the case.

Suppose that all the items we are dealing with are small nonnegative integers, ranging from 0 to 65,535. We can use a simple array to implement each operation as follows. First, we initialize an array `a` that is indexed from 0 to 65,535 with all 0s. To perform `insert(i)`, we execute `a[i]++`. Note that `a[i]` represents the number of times that `i` has been inserted. To perform `find(i)`, we verify that `a[i]` is not 0. To perform `remove(i)`, we make sure that `a[i]` is positive and then execute `a[i]--`. The time for each operation is clearly constant; even the overhead of the array initialization is a constant amount of work (65,536 assignments).

There are two problems with this solution. First, suppose that we have 32-bit integers instead of 16-bit integers. Then the array `a` must hold 4 billion items, which is impractical. Second, if the items are not integers but instead are strings (or something even more generic), they cannot be used to index an array.

The second problem is not really a problem at all. Just as a number `1234` is a collection of digits `1`, `2`, `3`, and `4`, the string `"junk"` is a collection of characters `'j'`, `'u'`, `'n'`, and `'k'`. Note that the number `1234` is just $1 \cdot 10^3 + 2 \cdot 10^2 + 3 \cdot 10^1 + 4 \cdot 10^0$. Recall from Figure 13.1 that a character can typically be represented in 7 bits as a number between 0 and 127. Because a character is basically a small integer, we can interpret a string as an integer. One possible representation is `'j'` $\cdot 128^3 +$ `'u'` $\cdot 128^2 +$ `'n'` $\cdot 128^1 +$ `'k'` $\cdot 128^0$. This approach allows the simple array implementation discussed previously.

The problem with this strategy is that the integer representation described generates huge integers: The representation for `"junk"` yields 224,229,227, and longer strings generate much larger representations. This result brings us back to the first problem: How do we avoid using an absurdly large array?

A *hash function* converts the item into an integer suitable to index an array where the item is stored. If the hash function were one to one, we could access the item by its array index.

We do so by using a function that maps large numbers (or strings interpreted as numbers) into smaller, more manageable numbers. A function that maps an item into a small index is known as a **hash function.** If `x` is an arbitrary (nonnegative) integer, then `x%tableSize` generates a number between `0` and `tableSize-1` suitable for indexing into an array of size `tableSize`. If `s` is a string, we can convert `s` to a large integer `x` by using the method suggested previously and then apply the mod operator (`%`) to get a suitable index. Thus, if `tableSize` is 10,000, `"junk"` would be indexed to 9,227. In Section 20.2 we discuss implementation of the hash function for strings in detail.

The use of the hash function introduces a complication: Two or more different items can hash out to the same position, causing a **collision.** This situation can never be avoided because there are many more items than positions. However, many methods are available for quickly resolving a collision. We investigate three of the simplest: linear probing, quadratic probing, and separate chaining. Each method is simple to implement, but each yields a different performance, depending on how full the array is.

Because the hash function is not one to one, several items collide at the same index and cause a *collision*.

20.2 Hash Function

Computing the hash function for strings has a subtle complication: The conversion of the `string` `s` to `x` generates an integer that is almost certainly larger than the machine can store conveniently—because $128^4 = 2^{28}$. This integer size is only a factor of 8 from the largest integer on a 32-bit machine. Consequently, we cannot expect to compute the hash function by directly computing powers of 128. Instead, we use the following observation. A general polynomial

$$A_3X^3 + A_2X^2 + A_1X^1 + A_0X^0 \tag{20.1}$$

can be evaluated as

$$(((A_3)X + A_2)X + A_1)X + A_0. \tag{20.2}$$

Note that in Equation 20.2, we avoid computation of X directly, which is good for three reasons. First, it avoids a large intermediate result, which, as we have shown, overflows. Second, the calculation in the equation involves only three multiplications and three additions; an N-degree polynomial is computed in N multiplications and additions. These operations compare favorably with the computation in Equation 20.1. Third, the calculation proceeds left to right (A_3 corresponds to `'j'`, A_2 to `'u'`, and so on, and X is 128).

By using a trick, we can evaluate the hash function efficiently and without overflow.

However, an overflow problem persists: The result of the calculation is still the same and is likely to be too large. But, we need only the result taken mod `tableSize`. By applying the `%` operator after each multiplication (or addition), we can ensure that the intermediate results remain small.[1] The resulting hash function is shown in Figure 20.1. An annoying feature of this hash function is that the mod computation is expensive. Because overflow is allowed (and its results are consistent on a given platform), we can make the hash function somewhat faster by performing a single mod operation immediately prior to the return. Unfortunately, the repeated multiplication by 128

1. Section 8.4 contains the properties of the mod operation.

```
// Acceptable hash function.
unsigned int hash( const string & key, int tableSize )
{
    unsigned int hashVal = 0;

    for( int i = 0; i < key.length( ); i++ )
        hashVal = ( hashVal * 128 + key[ i ] ) % tableSize;

    return hashVal;
}
```

Figure 20.1 A first attempt at a hash function implementation.

```
// A hash routine for string objects.
// key is the string to hash.
// tableSize is the size of the hash table.
unsigned int hash( const string & key, int tableSize )
{
    unsigned int hashVal = 0;

    for( int i = 0; i < key.length( ); i++ )
        hashVal = 37 * hashVal + key[ i ];

    return hashVal % tableSize;
}
```

Figure 20.2 A faster hash function that takes advantage of overflow.

would tend to shift the early characters to the left—out of the answer. To alleviate this situation, we multiply by 37 instead of 128, which slows the shifting of early characters.

The result is shown in Figure 20.2. It is not necessarily the best function possible. Also, in some applications (e.g., if long strings are involved), we may want to tinker with it. Generally speaking, however, the function is quite good. Note that the result obtained by allowing overflow and doing a final mod is not the same as performing the mod after every step. Thus we have slightly altered the hash function—which is not a problem.

The hash function must be simple to compute but also distribute the keys equitably. If there are too many collisions, the performance of the hash table will suffer dramatically.

Although speed is an important consideration in designing a hash function, we also want to be sure that it distributes the keys equitably. Consequently, we must not take our optimizations too far. An example is the hash function shown in Figure 20.3. It simply adds the characters in the keys and returns the result mod `tableSize`. What could be simpler? The answer is that little could be simpler. The function is easy to implement and computes a hash value very quickly. However, if `tableSize` is large, the function

```
// A poor hash function when tableSize is large.
unsigned int hash( const string & key, int tableSize )
{
    unsigned int hashVal = 0;

    for( int i = 0; i < key.length( ); i++ )
        hashVal += key.charAt( i );

    return hashVal % tableSize;
}
```

Figure 20.3 A bad hash function if `tableSize` is large.

does not distribute the keys well. For instance, suppose that `tableSize` is 10,000. Also suppose that all keys are 8 or fewer characters long. Because an ASCII `char` is an integer between 0 and 127, the hash function can assume values only between 0 and 1016 (127 × 8). This restriction certainly does not permit an equitable distribution. Any speed gained by the quickness of the hash function calculation is more than offset by the effort taken to resolve a larger than expected number of collisions. However, a reasonable alternative is described in Exercise 20.15.

The table runs from 0 to `tableSize-1`.

Finally, note that 0 is a possible result of the hash function, so hash tables are indexed starting at 0.

20.3 Linear Probing

In *linear probing*, collisions are resolved by sequentially scanning an array (with wraparound) until an empty cell is found.

Now that we have a hash function, we need to decide what to do when a collision occurs. Specifically, if X hashes out to a position that is already occupied, where do we place it? The simplest possible strategy is **linear probing,** or searching sequentially in the array until we find an empty cell. The search wraps around from the last position to the first, if necessary. Figure 20.4 shows the result of inserting the keys 89, 18, 49, 58, and 9 in a hash table when linear probing is used. We assume a hash function that returns the key X mod the size of the table. Figure 20.4 includes the result of the hash function.

The first collision occurs when 49 is inserted; the 49 is put in the next available spot—namely, spot 0, which is open. Then 58 collides with 18, 89, and 49 before an empty spot is found three slots away in position 1. The collision for element 9 is resolved similarly. So long as the table is large enough, a free cell can always be found. However, the time needed to find a free cell can get to be quite long. For example, if there is only one free cell left in the table, we may have to search the entire table to find it. On average we would expect to have to search half the table to find it, which is far from

```
hash( 89, 10 ) = 9
hash( 18, 10 ) = 8
hash( 49, 10 ) = 9
hash( 58, 10 ) = 8
hash(  9, 10 ) = 9
```

	After insert 89	*After insert 18*	*After insert 49*	*After insert 58*	*After insert 9*
0			49	49	49
1				58	58
2					9
3					
4					
5					
6					
7					
8		18	18	18	18
9	89	89	89	89	89

Figure 20.4 Linear probing hash table after each insertion.

the constant time per access that we are hoping for. But, if the table is kept relatively empty, insertions should not be so costly. We discuss this approach shortly.

The `find` algorithm follows the same probe sequence as the `insert` algorithm.

The `find` algorithm merely follows the same path as the `insert` algorithm. If it reaches an empty slot, the item we are searching for is not found; otherwise, it finds the match eventually. For example, to find 58, we start at slot 8 (as indicated by the hash function). We see an item, but it is the wrong one, so we try slot 9. Again, we have an item, but it is the wrong one, so we try slot 0 and then slot 1 until we find a match. A `find` for 19 would involve trying slots 9, 0, 1, and 2 before finding the empty cell in slot 3. Thus 19 is not found.

We must use *lazy deletion.*

Standard deletion cannot be performed because, as with a binary search tree, an item in the hash table not only represents itself, but it also connects other items by serving as a placeholder during collision resolution. Thus, if we removed 89 from the hash table, virtually all the remaining `find` operations would fail. Consequently, we implement **lazy deletion,** or marking items as deleted rather than physically removing them from the table. This information is recorded in an extra data member. Each item is either *active* or *deleted*.

20.3.1 Naive Analysis of Linear Probing

To estimate the performance of linear probing, we make two assumptions:

1. the hash table is large, and
2. each probe in the hash table is independent of the previous probe.

The simplistic analysis of linear probing is based on the assumption that successive probes are independent. This assumption is not true and thus the analysis underestimates the costs of searching and insertion.

Assumption 1 is reasonable; otherwise, we would not be bothering with a hash table. Assumption 2 says that, if the fraction of the table that is full is λ, each time we examine a cell the probability that it is occupied is also λ, independent of any previous probes. Independence is an important statistical property that greatly simplifies the analysis of random events. Unfortunately, as discussed in Section 20.3.2, the assumption of independence is not only unjustified, but it also is erroneous. Thus the naive analysis that we perform is incorrect. Even so, it is helpful because it tells us what we can hope to achieve if we are more careful about how collisions are resolved. As mentioned earlier in the chapter, the performance of the hash table depends on how full the table is. Its fullness is given by the load factor.

DEFINITION: The **load factor,** λ, of a probing hash table is the fraction of the table that is full. The load factor ranges from 0 (empty) to 1 (completely full).

The *load factor* of a probing hash table is the fraction of the table that is full. It ranges from 0 (empty) to 1 (full).

We can now give a simple but incorrect analysis of linear probing in Theorem 20.1.

Theorem 20.1

If independence of probes is assumed, the average number of cells examined in an insertion using linear probing is $1/(1 - \lambda)$.

Proof

For a table with a load factor of λ*, the probability of any cell's being empty is* $1 - \lambda$*. Consequently, the expected number of independent trials required to find an empty cell is* $1/(1 - \lambda)$.

In the proof of Theorem 20.1 we use the fact that, if the probability of some event's occurring is p, then on average $1/p$ trials are required until the event occurs, provided that the trials are independent. For example, the expected number of coin flips until a heads occurs is two, and the expected number of rolls of a single six-sided die until a 4 occurs is six, assuming independence.

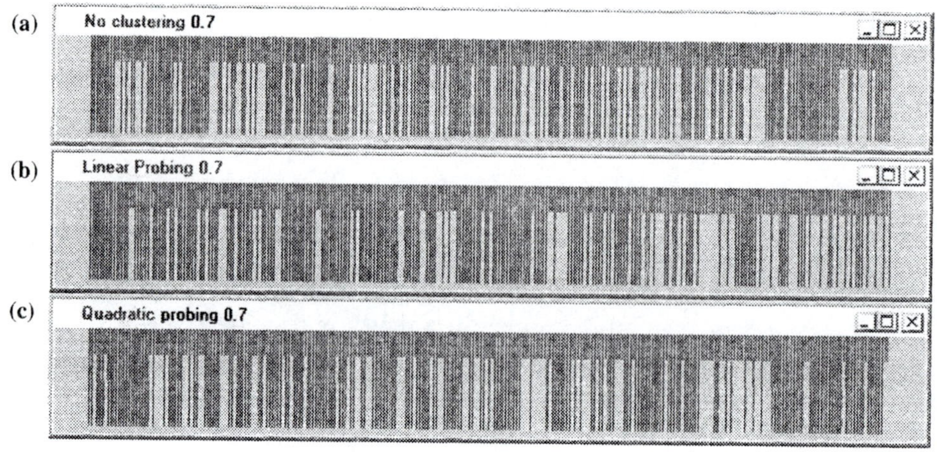

Figure 20.5 Illustration of primary clustering in linear probing (b) versus no clustering (a) and the less significant secondary clustering in quadratic probing (c). Long lines represent occupied cells, and the load factor is 0.7.

20.3.2 What Really Happens: Primary Clustering

The effect of *primary clustering* is the formation of large clusters of occupied cells, making insertions into the cluster expensive (and then the insertion makes the cluster even larger).

Unfortunately, independence does not hold, as shown in Figure 20.5. Part (a) shows the result of filling a hash table to 70 percent capacity, if all successive probes are independent. Part (b) shows the result of linear probing. Note the group of clusters: the phenomenon known as *primary clustering*.

In **primary clustering,** large blocks of occupied cells are formed. Any key that hashes into this cluster requires excessive attempts to resolve the collision, and then it adds to the size of the cluster. Not only do items that collide because of identical hash functions cause degenerate performance, but also an item that collides with an alternative location for another item causes poor performance. The mathematical analysis required to take this phenomenon into account is complex but has been solved, yielding Theorem 20.2.

Theorem 20.2 *The average number of cells examined in an insertion using linear probing is roughly* $(1 + 1/(1 - \lambda)^2)/2$.

Proof *The proof is beyond the scope of this text. See reference [6].*

For a half-full table, we obtain 2.5 as the average number of cells examined during an insertion. This outcome is almost the same as what the naive analysis indicated. The main difference occurs as λ gets close to 1. For instance, if the table is 90 percent full, $\lambda = 0.9$. The naive analysis suggests that 10 cells would have to be examined—a lot but not completely out of the question. However, by Theorem 20.2, the real answer is that some 50 cells need to be examined. That is excessive (especially as this number is only an average and thus some insertions must be worse).

Primary clustering is a problem at high load factors. For half-empty tables, the effect is not disastrous.

20.3.3 Analysis of the `find` Operation

The cost of an insertion can be used to bound the cost of a `find`. There are two types of `find` operations: unsuccessful and successful. An unsuccessful `find` is easy to analyze. The sequence of slots examined for an unsuccessful search of X is the same as the sequence examined to `insert` X. Thus we have an immediate answer for the cost of an unsuccessful `find`.

An unsuccessful `find` costs the same as an insertion.

For successful `find`s, things are slightly more complicated. Figure 20.4 shows a table with $\lambda = 0.5$. Thus the average cost of an insertion is 2.5. The average cost to `find` the newly inserted item would then be 2.5, no matter how many insertions follow. The average cost to find the first item inserted in the table is always 1.0 probe. Thus, in a table with $\lambda = 0.5$, some searches are easy and some are hard. In particular, the cost of a successful search of X is equal to the cost of inserting *X at the time X was inserted.* To find the average time to perform a successful search in a table with load factor λ, we must compute the average insertion cost by averaging over all the load factors leading to λ. With this groundwork, we can compute the average search times for linear probing, as asserted and proved in Theorem 20.3.

The cost of a successful `find` is an average of the insertion costs over all smaller load factors.

Theorem 20.3

The average number of cells examined in an unsuccessful search using linear probing is roughly $(1 + 1/(1 - \lambda)^2)/2$. The average number of cells examined in a successful search is approximately $(1 + 1/(1 - \lambda))/2$.

Proof

The cost of an unsuccessful search is the same as the cost of an insertion. For a successful search, we compute the average insertion cost over the sequence of insertions. Because the table is large, we can compute this average by evaluating $S(\lambda) = \frac{1}{\lambda}\int_{x=0}^{\lambda} I(x)dx$. In other words, the average cost of a successful search for a table with a load factor of λ

Proof (continued) *equals the cost of an insertion in a table of load factor x, averaged from load factors 0 through λ. From Theorem 20.2, we can derive the following equation:*

$$
\begin{aligned}
S(\lambda) &= \frac{1}{\lambda}\int_{x=0}^{\lambda} \frac{1}{2}\left(1 + \frac{1}{(1-x)^2}\right) dx \\
&= \frac{1}{2\lambda}\left(x + \frac{1}{(1-x)}\right)\Bigg|_{x=0}^{\lambda} \\
&= \frac{1}{2\lambda}\left(\left(\lambda + \frac{1}{(1-\lambda)}\right) - 1\right) \\
&= \frac{1}{2}\left(\frac{2-\lambda}{1-\lambda}\right) \\
&= \frac{1}{2}\left(1 + \frac{1}{(1-\lambda)}\right).
\end{aligned}
$$

We can apply the same technique to obtain the cost of a successful `find` under the assumption of independence (by using $I(x) = 1/(1-x)$ in Theorem 20.3). If there is no clustering, the average cost of a successful `find` for linear probing is $-\ln(1-\lambda)/\lambda$. If the load factor is 0.5, the average number of probes for a successful search using linear probing is 1.5, whereas the nonclustering analysis suggests 1.4 probes. Note that this average does not depend on any ordering of the input keys; it depends only on the fairness of the hash function. Note also that, even when we have good hash functions, both longer and shorter probe sequences are bound to contribute to the average. For instance, there are certain to be some sequences of length 4, 5, and 6, even in a hash table that is half empty. Determining the expected longest probe sequence is a challenging calculation. Primary clustering not only makes the average probe sequence longer, but it also makes a long probe sequence more likely. The main problem with primary clustering therefore is that performance degrades severely for insertion at high load factors. Also, some of the longer probe sequences typically encountered (those at the high end of the average) are made more likely to occur.

To reduce the number of probes, we need a collision resolution scheme that avoids primary clustering. Note, however, that, if the table is half empty, removing the effects of primary clustering would save only half a probe on average for an insertion or unsuccessful search and one-tenth a probe on average for a successful search. Even though we might expect to reduce the probability of getting a somewhat lengthier probe sequence, *linear probing is not a terrible strategy.* Because it is so easy to implement, any method we use to remove primary clustering must be of comparable complexity. Otherwise, we expend too much time in saving only a fraction of a probe. One such method is *quadratic probing*.

20.4 Quadratic Probing

Quadratic probing is a collision resolution method that eliminates the primary clustering problem of linear probing by examining certain cells away from the original probe point. Its name is derived from the use of the formula $F(i) = i^2$ to resolve collisions. Specifically, if the hash function evaluates to H and a search in cell H is inconclusive, we try cells $H + 1^2$, $H + 2^2$, $H + 3^2$, ..., $H + i^2$ (employing wraparound) in sequence. This strategy differs from the linear probing strategy of searching $H + 1$, $H + 2$, $H + 3$, ..., $H + i$.

***Quadratic probing* examines cells 1, 4, 9, and so on, away from the original probe point.**

Figure 20.6 shows the table that results when quadratic probing is used instead of linear probing for the insertion sequence shown in Figure 20.4. When 49 collides with 89, the first alternative attempted is one cell away. This cell is empty, so 49 is placed there. Next, 58 collides at position 8. The cell at position 9 (which is one away) is tried, but another collision occurs. A vacant

Remember that subsequent probe points are a quadratic number of positions from the *original probe point.*

```
hash( 89, 10 ) = 9
hash( 18, 10 ) = 8
hash( 49, 10 ) = 9
hash( 58, 10 ) = 8
hash(  9, 10 ) = 9
```

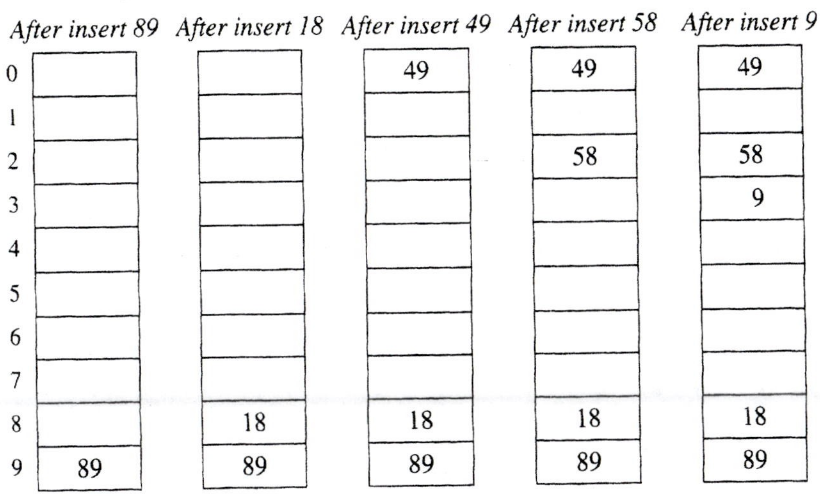

Figure 20.6 A quadratic probing hash table after each insertion (note that the table size was poorly chosen because it is not a prime number).

cell is found at the next cell tried, which is $2^2 = 4$ positions away *from the original hash position*. Thus 58 is placed in cell 2. The same thing happens for 9. Note that the alternative locations for items that hash to position 8 and the alternative locations for the items that hash to position 9 are not the same. The long probe sequence to insert 58 did not affect the subsequent insertion of 9, which contrasts with what happened with linear probing.

We need to consider a few details before we write code.

- In linear probing, each probe tries a different cell. Does quadratic probing guarantee that, when a cell is tried, we have not already tried it during the course of the current access? Does quadratic probing guarantee that when we are inserting X and the table is not full, X will be inserted?
- Linear probing is easily implemented. Quadratic probing appears to require multiplication and mod operations. Does this apparent added complexity make quadratic probing impractical?
- What happens (in both linear probing and quadratic probing) if the load factor gets too high? Can we dynamically expand the table, as is typically done with other array-based data structures?

If the table size is prime and the load factor is no larger than 0.5, all probes will be to different locations and an item can always be inserted.

Fortunately, the news is relatively good on all cases. If the table size is prime and the load factor never exceeds 0.5, we can always place a new item X and no cell is probed twice during an access. However, for these guarantees to hold, we need to ensure that the table size is a prime number. We prove this case in Theorem 20.4. For completeness, Figure 20.7 shows a routine that generates prime numbers, using the algorithm shown in Figure 10.8 (a more complex algorithm is not warranted).

Theorem 20.4

If quadratic probing is used and the table size is prime, then a new element can always be inserted if the table is at least half empty. Furthermore, in the course of the insertion, no cell is probed twice.

Proof

Let M be the size of the table. Assume that M is an odd prime greater than 3. We show that the first $\lceil M/2 \rceil$ alternative locations (including the original) are distinct. Two of these locations are $H + i^2 \pmod M$ and $H + j^2 \pmod M$, where $0 \le i,\ j \le \lfloor M/2 \rfloor$. Suppose, for the sake of contradiction, that these two locations are the same but that $i \ne j$. Then

Proof (continued)

$$H + i^2 \equiv H + j^2 (\text{mod } M);$$
$$i^2 \equiv j^2 (\text{mod } M);$$
$$i^2 - j^2 \equiv 0 (\text{mod } M);$$
$$(i - j)(i + j) \equiv 0 (\text{mod } M).$$

Because M is prime, it follows that either $i - j$ or $i + j$ is divisible by M. As i and j are distinct and their sum is smaller than M, neither of these possibilities can occur. Thus we obtain a contradiction. It follows that the first $\lceil M/2 \rceil$ alternatives (including the original location) are all distinct and guarantee that an insertion must succeed if the table is at least half empty.

If the table is even 1 more than half full, the insertion could fail (although failure is extremely unlikely). If we keep the table size prime and the load factor below 0.5, we have a guarantee of success for the insertion. If the table size is not prime, the number of alternative locations can be severely reduced. For example, if the table size was 16, the only alternative locations would be at distances 1, 4, or 9 from the original probe point. Again, size is not really an issue: Although we would not have a guarantee of $\lfloor M/2 \rfloor$ alternatives, we would usually have more than we need. However, it is best to play it safe and use the theory to guide us in selecting parameters. Furthermore, it has been shown empirically that prime numbers tend to be best for hash tables because they tend to remove some of the nonrandomness that is occasionally introduced by the hash function.

```
// Internal method to return a prime number at least as
// large as n. See Figure 10.8 for usable isPrime.
int nextPrime( int n )
{
    if( n % 2 == 0 )
        n++;

    for( ; !isPrime( n ); n += 2 )
        ;

    return n;
}
```

Figure 20.7 A routine used in quadratic probing to find a prime greater than or equal to *N*.

Quadratic probing can be implemented without multiplications and mod operations. Because it does not suffer from primary clustering, it outperforms linear probing in practice.

The second important consideration is efficiency. Recall that, for a load factor of 0.5, removing primary clustering saves only 0.5 probe for an average insertion and 0.1 probe for an average successful search. We do get some additional benefits: Encountering a long probe sequence is significantly less likely. However, if performing a probe using quadratic probing takes twice as long, doing so is hardly worth the effort. Linear probing is implemented with a simple addition (by 1), a test to determine whether wraparound is needed, and a very rare subtraction (if we need to do the wraparound). The formula for quadratic probing suggests that we need to do an addition by 1 (to go from $i-1$ to i), a multiplication (to compute i^2), another addition, and then a mod operation. Certainly this calculation appears to be much too expensive to be practical. However, we can use the following trick, as explained in Theorem 20.5.

Theorem 20.5 *Quadratic probing can be implemented without expensive multiplications and divisions.*

Proof *Let H_{i-1} be the most recently computed probe (H_0 is the original hash position) and H_i be the probe we are trying to compute. Then we have*

$$\begin{aligned} H_i &= H_0 + i^2 (\text{mod } M); \\ H_{i-1} &= H_0 + (i-1)^2 (\text{mod } M). \end{aligned} \tag{20.3}$$

If we subtract these two equations, we obtain

$$H_i = H_{i-1} + 2i - 1 (\text{mod } M). \tag{20.4}$$

Equation 20.4 tells us that we compute the new value H_i from the previous value H_{i-1} without squaring i. Although we still have a multiplication, the multiplication is by 2, which is a trivially implemented bit shift on most computers. What about the mod operation? That, too, is not really needed because the expression $2i-1$ must be smaller than M. Therefore, if we add it to H_{i-1}, the result will be either still smaller than M (in which case we do not need the mod) or just a little larger than M (in which case, we can compute the mod equivalent by subtracting M).

Theorem 20.5 shows that we can compute the next position to probe by using an addition (to increment i), a bit shift (to evaluate $2i$), a subtraction by 1 (to evaluate $2i-1$), another addition (to increment the old position by $2i-1$), a test to determine whether wraparound is needed, and a very rare subtraction to implement the mod operation. The difference is thus a bit shift, a subtraction by 1, and an addition per probe. The cost of this operation is likely to be less than the cost of doing an extra probe if complex keys (such as strings) are involved.

The final detail to consider is dynamic expansion. If the load factor exceeds 0.5, we want to double the size of the hash table. This approach raises a few issues. First, how hard will it be to find another prime number? The answer is that prime numbers are easy to find. We expect to have to test only $O(\log N)$ numbers until we find a number that is prime. Consequently, the routine shown in Figure 20.7 is very fast. The primality test takes at most $O(N^{1/2})$ time, so the search for a prime number takes at most $O(N^{1/2} \log N)$ time.[2] This cost is much less than the $O(N)$ cost of transferring the contents of the old table to the new.

Expand the table as soon as the load factor reaches 0.5, which is called rehashing. Always double to a prime number. Prime numbers are easy to find.

Once we have allocated a larger array, do we just copy everything over? The answer is most definitely no. The new array implies a new hash function, so we cannot use the old array positions. Thus we have to examine each element in the old table, compute its new hash value, and insert it in the new hash table. This process is called *rehashing*. Rehashing is easily implemented in C++.

When expanding a hash table, reinsert in the new table by using the new hash function.

20.4.1 C++ Implementation

We are now ready to give a complete C++ implementation of a quadratic probing hash table. We use a class template and assume that the user has provided an appropriate hash function of the form

The user must provide an appropriate hash function and inequality operator for the instantiated `Object`.

```
unsigned int hash( const Object & x );
```

for each instantiated type. Note that there is no `tableSize` parameter; the quadratic probing algorithms perform a final mod operation internally after using the user-supplied hash function. A version for `string` is provided in the class, with its declaration at line 48. (A default is also supplied later in the form of a function template, but it is unlikely to make sense for complicated objects.) Finally, we assume that `operator!=` is defined for `Object`. The class interface is shown in Figure 20.8. For the algorithms to work correctly, `operator!=` and `hash` must be consistent. That is, if two objects are equal, their hash values must be equal.

The hash table consists of an array of structures. Each structure stores an item and a data member that tells us that the entry is empty, active, or deleted. We use the enumerated type `EntryType`, declared at line 27, for

2. This routine is also required if we add a constructor that allows the user to specify an approximate initial size for the hash table. The hash table implementation must ensure that a prime number is used.

```
// QuadraticProbing Hash table class.
//
// Object must have operator!= and global function
//     unsigned int hash( const Object & key );
// CONSTRUCTION: with no parameters or another hash table.
//
// ******************PUBLIC OPERATIONS*********************
// void insert( x )        --> Insert x
// void remove( x )        --> Remove x
// Object find( x )        --> Return item that matches x
// void makeEmpty( )       --> Remove all items
// ******************ERRORS*********************************
// Throws exceptions as warranted.

template <class Object>
class HashTable
{
  public:
    HashTable( );

    void makeEmpty( );

    Cref<Object> find( const Object & x ) const;
    void insert( const Object & x );
    void remove( const Object & x );

    enum EntryType { ACTIVE, EMPTY, DELETED };

  private:
    struct HashEntry
    {
        Object    element;
        EntryType info;

        HashEntry( const Object & e = Object( ),
                   EntryType i = EMPTY )
          : element( e ), info( i ) { }
    };

    vector<HashEntry> array;
    int occupied;

    bool isActive( int currentPos ) const;
    int findPos( const Object & x ) const;
    void rehash( );
};

unsigned int hash( const string & key );
```

Figure 20.8 The class interface for a quadratic probing hash table.

that purpose. It is placed in the public section because at least one compiler complains at line 36 if it is private. The array is declared at line 40. We need to keep track of the number of items in the hash table (including elements marked as deleted); this value is stored in `occupied`, which is declared at line 41.

The general layout is similar to that for the binary search tree routines.

The rest of the class interface contains declarations for the hash table routines. Because the data members are all first-class objects, the Big Three defaults are acceptable. The only interesting public method is `find`, which returns the element found in the search for `x` wrapped in a `Cref` object.

Recall that the `Cref` class template (defined in Section 5.3.2) wraps a constant reference variable. However, its advantage is that it can also store a null reference. As discussed in Section 5.3.2, we can use `isNull` to test whether a null reference is being stored, and we can get the constant reference variable that is being wrapped by calling `get`.

Three private methods are declared; we describe them when they are used in the class implementation. We can now discuss the implementation of the `HashTable` class.

Most routines are just a few lines of code because they call `findPos` to perform quadratic probing.

The hash table constructor and `makeEmpty` are shown in Figure 20.9; nothing special is going on here. The searching routine is shown in Figure 20.10. It uses the private member function `isActive`, shown in Figure 20.11. It also calls `findPos`, shown later, to implement quadratic probing. The `findPos` method is the only place in the entire code that depends on quadratic probing. Then `find` is easy to implement: An element is found if the result of `findPos` is an active cell (if `findPos` stops on an active cell,

```
// Construct the hash table.
template <class Object>
HashTable<Object>::HashTable( )
  : array( nextPrime( 101 ) )
{
    makeEmpty( );
}

// Make the hash table logically empty.
template <class Object>
void HashTable<Object>::makeEmpty( )
{
    occupied = 0;
    for( int i = 0; i < array.size( ); i++ )
        array[ i ].info = EMPTY;
}
```

Figure 20.9 Hash table initialization and the `makeEmpty` method.

```
// Find item x in the hash table.
// Return the matching item, wrapped in a Cref object.
template <class Object>
Cref<Object> HashTable<Object>::find( const Object & x ) const
{
    int currentPos = findPos( x );

    if( isActive( currentPos ) )
        return Cref<Object>( array[ currentPos ].element );
    else
        return Cref<Object>( );
}
```

Figure 20.10 The `find` routine for a quadratic probing hash table.

```
// Return true if currentPos exists and is active.
template <class Object>
bool HashTable<Object>::isActive( int currentPos ) const
{
    return array[ currentPos ].info == ACTIVE;
}
```

Figure 20.11 The `isActive` method for a quadratic probing hash table.

```
// Remove item x from the hash table.
// Throw ItemNotFoundException if x is not present.
template <class Object>
void HashTable<Object>::remove( const Object & x )
{
    int currentPos = findPos( x );
    if( isActive( currentPos ) )
        array[ currentPos ].info = DELETED;
    else
        throw ItemNotFoundException( );
}
```

Figure 20.12 The `remove` routine for a quadratic probing hash table.

there must be a match). Similarly, the `remove` routine shown in Figure 20.12 is short. We check whether `findPos` takes us to an active cell; if so, the cell is marked deleted. Otherwise, an exception is thrown.

The `insert` routine performs rehashing if the table is (half) full.

The `insert` routine is shown in Figure 20.13. At line 7 we call `findPos`. If `x` is found, we throw an exception at line 9; otherwise, `findPos` gives the place to insert `x`. The insertion is performed at line 10. We adjust `occupied`

```
1 // Insert item x into the hash table. If the item is
2 // already present, then throw DuplicateItemException.
3 template <class Object>
4 void HashTable<Object>::insert( const Object & x )
5 {
6         // Insert x as active
7     int currentPos = findPos( x );
8     if( isActive( currentPos ) )
9         throw DuplicateItemException( );
10    array[ currentPos ] = HashEntry( x, ACTIVE );
11
12    if( ++occupied > array.size( ) / 2 )
13        rehash( );
14 }
```

Figure 20.13 The `insert` routine for a quadratic probing hash table.

```
1 // Expand the hash table.
2 template <class Object>
3 void HashTable<Object>::rehash( )
4 {
5     vector<HashEntry> oldArray = array;
6
7         // Create new double-sized, empty table
8     array.resize( nextPrime( 2 * oldArray.size( ) ) );
9     for( int j = 0; j < array.size( ); j++ )
10        array[ j ].info = EMPTY;
11
12        // Copy table over
13    makeEmpty( );
14    for( int i = 0; i < oldArray.size( ); i++ )
15        if( oldArray[ i ].info == ACTIVE )
16            insert( oldArray[ i ].element );
17 }
```

Figure 20.14 The `rehash` method for a quadratic probing hash table.

at line 12 and return unless a rehash is in order; otherwise, we call the private method `rehash`.

The code that implements rehashing is shown in Figure 20.14. Line 5 makes a copy of the original table. We create a new, double-sized, empty hash table at line 13. Then we scan through the original array and `insert` any active elements in the new table. The `insert` routine uses the new hash function (as it is based on the size of `array`, which is now larger) and automatically resolves all collisions. We can be sure that the recursive call to `insert`

```
1 // Method that performs quadratic probing resolution.
2 // Return the position where the search for x terminates.
3 template <class Object>
4 int HashTable<Object>::findPos( const Object & x ) const
5 {
6     int i = 0;
7     int currentPos = hash( x ) % array.size( );
8
9     while( array[ currentPos ].info != EMPTY &&
10            array[ currentPos ].element != x )
11     {
12         currentPos += 2 * ++i - 1;  // Compute ith probe
13         if( currentPos >= array.size( ) )
14             currentPos -= array.size( );
15     }
16     return currentPos;
17 }
```

Figure 20.15 The routine that finally deals with quadratic probing.

(at line 16) does not force another rehash. Alternatively, we could replace line 16 with two lines of code surrounded by braces (see Exercise 20.14).

Quadratic probing is implemented in `findPos`. It uses the previously described trick to avoid multiplications and mods.

So far, nothing that we have done depends on quadratic probing. Figure 20.15 implements `findPos`, which finally deals with the quadratic probing algorithm. We keep searching the table until we find an empty cell or a match. Lines 12–14 directly implement the methodology described in Theorem 20.5.

Finally, Figure 20.16 gives a generic hash function. By performing the type conversion at line 7, it works by treating the byte pattern of `key` as a primitive string (but one that might not have a null terminator) and then using the same hash function as for strings. This hash function works for primitive types, but it is unlikely to be suitable for complicated objects because it might not satisfy the requirement that two objects that are declared equal always have equal hash values. This hash function is more discriminating because the only guarantee is that two objects with equal bit patterns will have equal hash values.

```
// Generic hash function -- used if no other matches.
template <class Object>
unsigned int hash( const Object & key )
{
    unsigned int hashVal = 0;

    const char *keyp = reinterpret_cast<const char *>( &key );
    for( size_t i = 0; i < sizeof( Object ); i++ )
        hashVal = 37 * hashVal + keyp[ i ];

    return hashVal;
}
```

Figure 20.16 A generic hash function.

20.4.2 Analysis of Quadratic Probing

Quadratic probing has not yet been mathematically analyzed, although we know that it eliminates primary clustering. In quadratic probing, elements that hash to the same position probe the same alternative cells, which is known as **secondary clustering.** Again, the independence of successive probes cannot be assumed. Secondary clustering is a slight theoretical blemish. Simulation results suggest that it generally causes less than an extra one-half probe per search and that this increase is true only for high load factors. Figure 20.5 illustrates the difference between linear probing and quadratic probing and shows that quadratic probing does not suffer from as much clustering as does linear probing.

In *secondary clustering,* elements that hash to the same position probe the same alternative cells. Secondary clustering is a minor theoretical blemish.

Techniques that eliminate secondary clustering are available. The most popular is **double hashing,** in which a second hash function is used to drive the collision resolution. Specifically, we probe at a distance $Hash_2(X)$, $2Hash_2(X)$, and so on. The second hash function must be carefully chosen (e.g., it should *never* evaluate to 0), and all cells must be capable of being probed. A function such as $Hash_2(X) = R - (X \bmod R)$, with R a prime smaller than M, generally works well. Double hashing is theoretically interesting because it can be shown to use essentially the same number of probes as the purely random analysis of linear probing would imply. However, it is somewhat more complicated than quadratic probing to implement and requires careful attention to some details.

***Double hashing* is a hashing technique that does not suffer from secondary clustering. A second hash function is used to drive the collision resolution.**

There seems to be no good reason not to use a quadratic probing strategy, unless the overhead of maintaining a half-empty table is burdensome. That would be the case in other programming languages if the items being stored were very large.

20.5 Separate Chaining Hashing

***Separate chaining hashing* is a space-efficient alternative to quadratic probing in which an array of linked lists is maintained. It is less sensitive to high load factors.**

A popular and space-efficient alternative to quadratic probing is **separate chaining hashing** in which an array of linked lists is maintained. For an array of linked lists, L_0, L_1, ..., L_{M-1}, the hash function tells us in which list to insert an item X and then, during a `find`, which list contains X. The idea is that, although searching a linked list is a linear operation, if the lists are sufficiently short, the search time will be very fast. In particular, suppose that the load factor, N/M, is λ, which is not bounded by 1.0. Thus the average list has length λ, making the expected number of probes for an insertion or unsuccessful search λ and the expected number of probes for a successful search $1 + \lambda/2$. The reason is that a successful search must occur in a non-empty list, and in such a list we expect to have to traverse halfway down the list. The relative cost of a successful search versus an unsuccessful search is unusual in that, if $\lambda < 2$, the successful search is more expensive than the unsuccessful search. This condition makes sense, however, because many unsuccessful searches encounter an empty linked list.

For separate chaining hashing, a reasonable load factor is 1.0. A lower load factor does not significantly improve performance; a moderately higher load factor is acceptable and can save space.

A typical load factor is 1.0; a lower load factor does not significantly enhance performance, but it costs extra space. The appeal of separate chaining hashing is that performance is not affected by a moderately increasing load factor; thus rehashing can be avoided. For languages that do not allow dynamic array expansion, this consideration is significant. Furthermore, the expected number of probes for a search is less than in quadratic probing, particularly for unsuccessful searches.

We can implement separate chaining hashing by using our existing linked list classes. However, because the header node adds space overhead and is not really needed, if space were at a premium we could elect not to reuse components and instead implement a simple stacklike list. The coding effort turns out to be remarkably light. Also, the space overhead is essentially one pointer per node, plus an additional pointer per list; for example, when the load factor is 1.0, it is two pointers per item. This feature could be important if the size of an item is large. In that case, we have the same trade-offs as with the array and linked list implementations of stacks.

20.6 Hash Tables Versus Binary Search Trees

Use a hash table instead of a binary search tree if you do not need order statistics and are worried about nonrandom inputs.

We can also use binary search trees to implement `insert` and `find` operations. Although the resulting average time bounds are $O(\log N)$, binary search trees also support routines that require order and thus are more powerful. Using a hash table, we cannot efficiently find the minimum element or extend the table to allow computation of an order statistic. We cannot search efficiently for a string unless the exact string is known. A binary search tree could quickly find all items in a certain range, but this capability is not supported by a hash table. Furthermore, the $O(\log N)$ bound is not necessarily that much more than $O(1)$, especially since no multiplications or divisions are required by search trees.

The worst case for hashing generally results from an implementation error, whereas sorted input can make binary search trees perform poorly. Balanced search trees are quite expensive to implement. Hence, if no ordering information is required and there is any suspicion that the input might be sorted, hashing is the data structure of choice.

20.7 Hashing Applications

Hashing applications are abundant.

Hashing applications are abundant. Compilers use hash tables to keep track of declared variables in source code. The data structure is called a *symbol table*. Hash tables are the ideal application for this problem because only `insert` and `find` operations are performed. Identifiers are typically short, so the hash function can be computed quickly. In this application, most searches are successful.

Another common use of hash tables is in game programs. As the program searches through different lines of play, it keeps track of positions that it has encountered by computing a hash function based on the position (and storing its move for that position). If the same position recurs, usually by a simple transposition of moves, the program can avoid expensive recomputation. This general feature of all game-playing programs is called the *transposition table*. We discussed this feature in Section 11.2, where we implemented the tic-tac-toe algorithm.

A third use of hashing is in online spelling checkers. If misspelling detection (as opposed to correction) is important, an entire dictionary can be prehashed and words can be checked in constant time. Hash tables are well suited for this purpose because the words do not have to be alphabetized. Printing out misspellings in the order they occurred in the document is acceptable.

Summary

Hash tables can be used to implement the `insert` and `find` operations in constant average time. Paying attention to details such as load factor is especially important in the use of hash tables; otherwise, the constant time bounds are not meaningful. Choosing the hash function carefully is also important when the key is not a short string or integer. You should pick an easily computable function that distributes well.

For separate chaining hashing, the load factor is typically close to 1, although performance does not significantly degrade unless the load factor becomes very large. For quadratic probing, the table size should be prime and the load factor should not exceed 0.5. Rehashing should be used for quadratic probing to allow the table to grow and maintain the correct load factor. This approach is important if space is tight and it is not possible just to declare a huge hash table.

This completes the discussion of basic searching algorithms. In Chapter 21 we examine the binary heap, which implements the priority queue and thus supports efficient access of the minimum item in a collection of items.

Objects of the Game

collision The result when two or more items in a hash table hash out to the same position. This problem is unavoidable because there are more items than positions. (p. 727)

double hashing A hashing technique that does not suffer from secondary clustering. A second hash function is used to drive the collision resolution. (p. 745)

hashing The implementation of hash tables to perform insertions, deletions, and finds. (p. 725)

hash function A function that converts the item into an integer suitable to index an array where the item is stored. If the hash function were one to one, we could access the item by its array index. Since the hash function is not one to one, several items will collide at the same index. (p. 726)

hash table A table used to implement a dictionary in constant time per operation. (p. 725)

linear probing A way to avoid collisions by sequentially scanning an array until an empty cell is found. (p. 729)

load factor The number of elements in a hash table divided by the size of the hash table array, or the fraction of the table that is full. In a probing hash table, the load factor ranges from 0 (empty) to 1 (full). In separate chaining hashing, it can be greater than 1. (p. 731)

lazy deletion The technique of marking elements as deleted instead of physically removing them from a hash tabale. It is required in probing hash tables. (p. 730)

primary clustering Large clusters of occupied cells form during linear probing, making insertions in the cluster expensive (and then the insertion makes the cluster even larger) and affecting performance. (p. 732)

quadratic probing A collision resolution method that examines cells 1, 4, 9, and so on, away from the original probe point. (p. 735)

secondary clustering Clustering that occurs when elements that hash to the same position probe the same alternative cells. It is a minor theoretical blemish. (p. 745)

separate chaining A space-efficient alternative to quadratic probing in which an array of linked lists is maintained. It is less sensitive to high load factors and exhibits some of the trade-offs considered in the array versus linked list stack implementations. (p. 746)

Common Errors

1. The hash function returns an `unsigned int`. Because intermediate calculations allow overflow, the local variable should also be `unsigned` to avoid risking an out-of-bounds return value.
2. The performance of a probing table degrades severely as the load factor approaches 1.0. Do not let this happen. Rehash when the load factor reaches 0.5.
3. The performance of all hashing methods depends on using a good hash function. A common error is providing a poor function.

On the Internet

The quadratic probing hash table is available for your perusal.

QuadraticProbing.h	Contains the `HashTable` class interface.
QuadraticProbing.cpp	Contains the implementation of the `HashTable` class.
TestQuadraticProbing.cpp	Contains a test program for the `HashTable` class.

Exercises

In Short

20.1. What are the array indices for a hash table of size 11?

20.2. What is the appropriate probing table size if the number of items in the hash table is 10?

20.3. Explain how deletion is performed in both probing and separate chaining hash tables.

20.4. What is the expected number of probes for both successful and unsuccessful searches in a linear probing table with load factor 0.25?

20.5. Given the input {4371, 1323, 6173, 4199, 4344, 9679, 1989}, a fixed table size of 10, and a hash function $H(X) = X \bmod 10$, show the resulting

a. linear probing hash table.
b. quadratic probing hash table.
c. separate chaining hash table.

20.6. Show the result of rehashing the probing tables in Exercise 20.5. Rehash to a prime table size.

20.7. The `isEmpty` routine has not been written. Can you implement it by returning the expression `occupied==0`? Explain.

In Theory

20.8. An alternative collision resolution strategy is to define a sequence, $F(i) = R_i$, where $R_0 = 0$ and $R_1, R_2, \ldots, R_{M-1}$ is a random permutation of the first $M - 1$ integers (recall that the table size is M).

a. Prove that under this strategy, if the table is not full, the collision can always be resolved.
b. Would this strategy be expected to eliminate primary clustering?
c. Would this strategy be expected to eliminate secondary clustering?
d. If the load factor of the table is λ, what is the expected time to perform an insertion?
e. Generating a random permutation using the algorithm in Section 10.4 involves a large number of (expensive) calls to a random number generator. Give an efficient algorithm to generate a random-looking permutation that avoids calling a random number generator.

20.9. If rehashing is implemented as soon as the load factor reaches 0.5, when the last element is inserted the load factor is at least 0.25 and at most 0.5. What is the expected load factor? In other words, is it true or false that the load factor is 0.375 on average?

20.10. When the rehashing step is implemented, you must use $O(N)$ probes to reinsert the N elements. Give an estimate for the number of probes (i.e., N or $2N$ or something else). (*Hint:* Compute the average cost of inserting in the new table. These insertions vary from load factor 0 to load factor 0.25.)

20.11. Under certain assumptions, the expected cost of an insertion in a hash table with secondary clustering is given by $1/(1 - \lambda) - \lambda - \ln(1 - \lambda)$. Unfortunately, this formula is not accurate for quadratic probing. However, assuming that it is,

a. what is the expected cost of an unsuccessful search?
b. what is the expected cost of a successful search?

20.12. A quadratic probing hash table is used to store 10,000 `string` objects (using the `string` class implemented in Section 2.6). Assume that the load factor is 0.4 and that the average string length is 8. Determine

a. the hash table size.
b. the amount of memory used to store the 10,000 `string` objects.
c. the amount of memory used to store the remaining (uninitialized) `string` objects.
d. the amount of additional memory used by the hash table.
e. the total memory used by the hash table.
f. the space overhead.

In Practice

20.13. Implement linear probing.

20.14. For the probing hash table, implement the rehashing code without making a recursive call to `insert`.

20.15. Experiment with the following alternative for line 9 in Figure 20.2:

```
hashVal = ( hashVal << 5 ) ^ hashVal ^ key[ i ];
```

20.16. Experiment with a hash function that examines every other character in a string. Is this a better choice than the one in the text? Explain.

20.17. Modify the `HashTable` class so that the `isEmpty` operation can be supported in constant time.

20.18. Modify the deletion algorithm so that, if the load factor goes below 1/8, a rehash is performed to yield a table half as large.

Programming Problems

20.19. Implement an STL-style `map` class using a hash table. The class is instantiated with the types of the objects being stored, a not-equals function object, and a hash function object.

20.20. Find yourself a large online dictionary. Choose a table size that is twice as large as the dictionary. Apply the hash function described in the text to each word, and store a count of the number of times each position is hashed to. You will get a distribution: Some percentage of the positions will not be hashed to, some will be hashed to once, some twice, and so on. Compare this distribution with what would occur for theoretical random numbers (discussed in Section 10.3).

20.21. Perform simulations to compare the observed performance of hashing with the theoretical results. Declare a probing hash table, insert 10,000 randomly generated integers into the table, and count the average number of probes used. This number is the average cost of a successful search. Repeat the test several times for a good average. Run it for both linear probing and quadratic probing, and do it for final load factors 0.1, 0.2, ..., 0.9. Always declare the table so that no rehashing is needed. Thus the test for load factor 0.4 would declare a table of size approximately 25,000 (adjusted to be prime).

20.22. Compare the time required to perform successful searches and insertions in a separate chaining table with load factor 1 and a quadratic probing table with load factor 0.5. Run it for simple integers, strings, and complex records in which the search key is a string.

20.23. A BASIC program consists of a series of statements, each of which is numbered in ascending order. Control is passed by use of a *goto* or *gosub* and a statement number. Write a program that reads a legal basic program and renumbers the statements so that the first starts at number F and each statement has a number D higher than the previous statement. The statement numbers in the input might be as large as a 32-bit integer, and you may assume that the renumbered statement numbers fit in a 32-bit integer. Your program must run in linear time.

References

Despite the apparent simplicity of hashing, much of the analysis is quite difficult and many questions remain unresolved. Also there are many interesting ideas that generally attempt to make it unlikely that worst-case possibilities of hashing arise.

An early paper on hashing is [11]. A wealth of information on the subject, including an analysis of hashing with linear probing, is presented in [6]. Double hashing is analyzed in [5] and [7]. Yet another collision resolution scheme, *coalesced hashing,* is described in [12]. An excellent survey on the subject is [8], and [9] contains suggestions for and pitfalls in choosing hash functions. Precise analytic and simulation results for all the methods described in this chapter are available in [4]. Uniform hashing, in which no clustering exists, is optimal with respect to the cost of a successful search [13].

If the input keys are known in advance, perfect hash functions, which do not allow collisions, exist [1]. Some more complicated hashing schemes, for which the worst case depends not on the particular input but on random numbers chosen by the algorithm, appear in [2] and [3]. These schemes guarantee that only a constant number of collisions occur in the worst case (although construction of a hash function can take a long time in the unlikely case of bad random numbers). They are useful for implementing tables in hardware.

One method of implementing Exercise 20.8 is described in [10].

1. J. L. Carter and M. N. Wegman, "Universal Classes of Hash Functions," *Journal of Computer and System Sciences* **18** (1979), 143–154.
2. M. Dietzfelbinger, A. R. Karlin, K. Melhorn, F. Meyer auf def Heide, H. Rohnert, and R. E. Tarjan, "Dynamic Perfect Hashing: Upper and Lower Bounds," *SIAM Journal on Computing* **23** (1994), 738–761.
3. R. J. Enbody and H. C. Du, "Dynamic Hashing Schemes," *Computing Surveys* **20** (1988), 85–113.
4. G. H. Gonnet and R. Baeza-Yates, *Handbook of Algorithms and Data Structures,* 2d ed., Addison-Wesley, Reading, Mass., 1991.
5. L. J. Guibas and E. Szemeredi, "The Analysis of Double Hashing," *Journal of Computer and System Sciences* **16** (1978), 226–274.
6. D. E. Knuth, *The Art of Computer Programming, Vol 3: Sorting and Searching,* 2d ed., Addison-Wesley, Reading, Mass., 1998.
7. G. Lueker and M. Molodowitch, "More Analysis of Double Hashing," *Combinatorica* **13** (1993), 83–96.
8. W. D. Maurer and T. G. Lewis, "Hash Table Methods," *Computing Surveys* **7** (1975), 5–20.
9. B. J. McKenzie, R. Harries, and T. Bell, "Selecting a Hashing Algorithm," *Software-Practice and Experience* **20** (1990), 209–224.

10. R. Morris, "Scatter Storage Techniques," *Communications of the ACM* **11** (1968), 38–44.
11. W. W. Peterson, "Addressing for Random Access Storage," *IBM Journal of Research and Development* **1** (1957), 130–146.
12. J. S. Vitter, "Implementations for Coalesced Hashing," *Information Processing Letters* **11** (1980), 84–86.
13. A. C. Yao, "Uniform Hashing Is Optimal," *Journal of the ACM* **32** (1985), 687–693.

Chapter 21

A Priority Queue: The Binary Heap

The priority queue is a fundamental data structure that allows access only to the minimum item. In this chapter we discuss one implementation of the priority queue data structure, the elegant *binary heap*. The binary heap supports the insertion of new items and the deletion of the minimum item in logarithmic worst-case time. It uses only an array and is easy to implement.

In this chapter, we show:

- the basic properties of the binary heap,
- how the `insert` and `deleteMin` operations can be performed in logarithmic time,
- a linear-time heap construction algorithm,
- a C++ implementation, using both the generic and STL protocols in Section 7.9,
- an easily implemented sorting algorithm, *heapsort,* that runs in $O(N \log N)$ time but uses no extra memory, and
- the use of heaps to implement external sorting.

21.1 Basic Ideas

A linked list or array requires that some operation use linear time.

As discussed in Section 7.9, the priority queue supports the access and deletion of the minimum item with `findMin` and `deleteMin`, respectively. We could use a simple linked list, performing insertions at the front in constant time, but then finding and/or deleting the minimum would require a linear scan of the list. Alternatively, we could insist that the list always be kept sorted. This condition makes the access and deletion of the minimum cheap, but then insertions would be linear.

An unbalanced binary search tree does not have a good worst case. A balanced search tree requires lots of work.

Another way of implementing priority queues is to use a binary search tree, which gives an $O(\log N)$ average running time for both operations. However, a binary search tree is a poor choice because the input is typically not sufficiently random. We could use a balanced search tree, but the structures shown in Chapter 19 are cumbersome to implement and lead to sluggish performance in practice. (In Chapter 22, however, we cover a data structure, the *splay tree,* that has been shown empirically to be a good alternative in some situations.)

The priority queue has properties that are a compromise between a queue and a binary search tree.

On the one hand, because the priority queue supports only some of the search tree operations, it should not be more expensive to implement than a search tree. On the other hand, the priority queue is more powerful than a simple queue because we can use a priority queue to implement a queue as follows. First, we insert each item with an indication of its insertion time. Then, a `deleteMin` on the basis of minimum insertion time implements a `dequeue`. Consequently, we can expect to obtain an implementation with properties that are a compromise between a queue and a search tree. This compromise is realized by the binary heap, which

- can be implemented by using a simple array (like the queue),
- supports `insert` and `deleteMin` in $O(\log N)$ worst-case time (a compromise between the binary search tree and the queue), and
- supports `insert` in constant average time and `findMin` in constant worst-case time (like the queue).

The *binary heap* is the classic method used to implement priority queues.

The **binary heap** is the classic method used to implement priority queues and—like the balanced search tree structures in Chapter 19—has two properties: a structure property and an ordering property. And as with balanced search trees, an operation on a binary heap can destroy one of the properties, so a binary heap operation must not terminate until both properties are in order. This outcome is simple to achieve. (In this chapter, we use the word *heap* to refer to the binary heap.)

21.1.1 Structure Property

The heap is a *complete binary tree,* allowing representation by a simple array and guaranteeing logarithmic depth.

The only structure that gives dynamic logarithmic time bounds is the tree, so it seems natural to organize the heap's data as a tree. Because we want the logarithmic bound to be a worst-case guarantee, the tree should be balanced.

A **complete binary tree** is a tree that is completely filled, with the possible exception of the bottom level, which is filled from left to right and has no missing nodes. An example of a complete binary tree of 10 items is

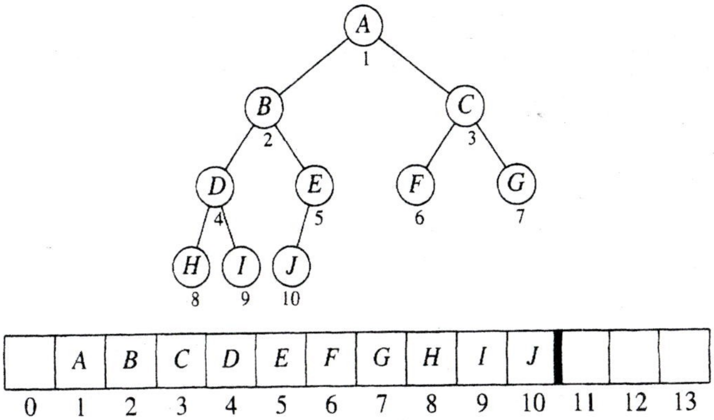

Figure 21.1 A complete binary tree and its array representation.

shown in Figure 21.1. Had the node *J* been a right child of *E*, the tree would not be complete because a node would be missing.

The complete tree has a number of useful properties. First, the height (longest path length) of a complete binary tree of *N* nodes is at most $\lfloor \log N \rfloor$. The reason is that a complete tree of height *H* has between 2^H and $2^{H+1} - 1$ nodes. This characteristic implies that we can expect logarithmic worst-case behavior if we restrict changes in the structure to one path from the root to a leaf.

The parent is in position $\lfloor i/2 \rfloor$, the left child is in position $2i$, and the right child is in position $2i + 1$.

Second and equally important, in a complete binary tree, `left` and `right` pointers are not needed. As shown in Figure 21.1, we can represent a complete binary tree by storing its level-order traversal in an array. We place the root in position 1 (position 0 is often left vacant, for a reason discussed shortly). We also need to maintain an integer that tells us the number of nodes currently in the tree. Then for any element in array position *i*, its left child can be found in position $2i$. If this position extends past the number of nodes in the tree, we know that the left child does not exist. Similarly, the right child is located immediately after the left child; thus it resides in position $2i + 1$. We again test against the actual tree size to be sure that the child exists. Finally, the parent is in position $\lfloor i/2 \rfloor$.

Note that every node except the root has a parent. If the root were to have a parent, the calculation would place it in position 0. Thus we reserve position 0 for a dummy item that can serve as the root's parent. Doing so can simplify one of the operations. If instead we choose to place the root in position 0, the locations of the children and parent of the node in position *i* change slightly (in Exercise 21.15 you are asked to determine the new locations).

Using an array to store a tree is called *implicit representation.*

Using an array to store a tree is called **implicit representation.** As a result of this representation, not only are child pointers not required, but also the operations required to traverse the tree are extremely simple and likely to be very fast on most computers. The heap entity consists of an array of objects and an integer representing the current heap size.

In this chapter, heaps are drawn as trees to make the algorithms easier to visualize. In the implementation of these trees we use an array. We do not use the implicit representation for all search trees. Some of the problems with doing so are covered in Exercise 21.8.

21.1.2 Heap-Order Property

The *heap-order property* states that, in a heap, the item in the parent is never larger than the item in a node.

The property that allows operations to be performed quickly is the **heap-order property.** We want to be able to find the minimum quickly, so it makes sense that the smallest element should be at the root. If we consider that any subtree should also (recursively) be a heap, any node should be smaller than all of its descendants. Applying this logic, we arrive at the heap-order property.

HEAP-ORDER PROPERTY

IN A HEAP, FOR EVERY NODE X WITH PARENT P, THE KEY IN P IS SMALLER THAN OR EQUAL TO THE KEY IN X.

The root's parent can be stored in position 0 and given a value of negative infinity.

The heap-order property is illustrated in Figure 21.2. In Figure 21.3(a), the tree is a heap, but in Figure 21.3(b), the tree is not (the dashed line shows the violation of heap order). Note that the root does not have a parent. In the implicit representation, we could place the value $-\infty$ in position 0 to remove this special case when we implement the heap.[1] By the heap-order property, we see that the minimum element can always be found at the root. Thus

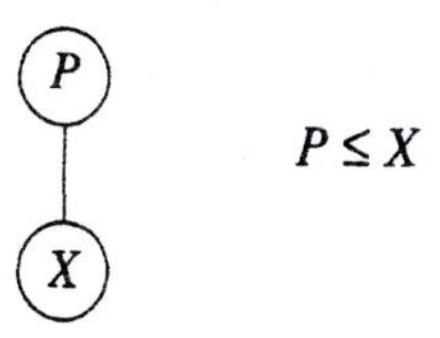

Figure 21.2 Heap-order property.

1. However, we do not do so because specifying negative infinity makes the template code a little more complicated. The technique of using a sentinel was popular in older programming languages that did not have templates (or their equivalent). Instead, as we will see later, we use a different trick.

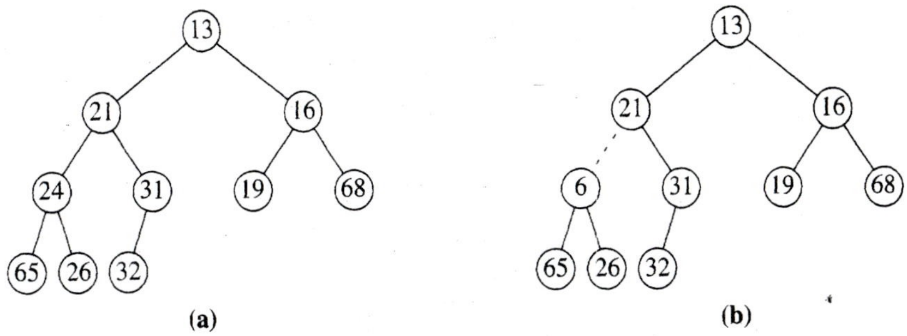

Figure 21.3 Two complete trees: (a) a heap; (b) not a heap.

`findMin` is a constant time operation. A **max heap** supports access of the maximum *instead* of the minimum. Minor changes can be used to implement max heaps.

21.1.3 Allowed Operations

Now that we have settled on the representation, we can start writing code. We already know that our heap supports the basic `insert`, `findMin`, and `deleteMin` operations and the usual `isEmpty` and `makeEmpty` routines. Figure 21.4 shows the class interface.

We begin by examining the public member functions. A pair of constructors are declared at lines 19 and 20. The second constructor accepts a `vector` that contains a set of items that should initially be in the priority queue. Why not just insert the items one at a time?

We provide a constructor that accepts a `vector` containing an initial set of items and calls `buildHeap`.

The reason is that in numerous applications we can add many items before the next `deleteMin` occurs. In those cases, we do not need to have heap order in effect until the `deleteMin` occurs. The `buildHeap` operation, declared at line 34, reinstates the heap order—no matter how messed up the heap is—and it works in linear time. Thus, if we need to place N items in the heap before the first `deleteMin`, placing them in the array sloppily and then doing one `buildHeap` is more efficient than doing N `insert` operations.

The `insert` function is declared at line 25. It adds a new item `x` into the heap, performing the necessary operations to maintain the heap-order property.

The remaining operations are as expected. The `findMin` routine is declared at line 23 and returns the minimum item in the heap. We provide two forms of `deleteMin`: The one at line 27 passes the minimum item

```
1 // BinaryHeap class.
2 //
3 // CONSTRUCTION: with no parameters or vector containing items.
4 //
5 // ******************PUBLIC OPERATIONS*********************
6 // void insert( x )       --> Insert x
7 // void deleteMin( )      --> Remove smallest item
8 // void deleteMin( min ) --> Remove and send back smallest item
9 // Comparable findMin( ) --> Return smallest item
10 // bool isEmpty( )       --> Return true if empty; else false
11 // void makeEmpty( )     --> Remove all items
12 // ******************ERRORS********************************
13 // Throws UnderflowException as warranted.
14
15 template <class Comparable>
16 class BinaryHeap
17 {
18   public:
19     BinaryHeap( );
20     BinaryHeap( const vector<Comparable> & v );
21
22     bool isEmpty( ) const;
23     const Comparable & findMin( ) const;
24
25     void insert( const Comparable & x );
26     void deleteMin( );
27     void deleteMin( Comparable & minItem );
28     void makeEmpty( );
29
30   private:
31     int                theSize;  // Number of elements in heap
32     vector<Comparable> array;    // The heap array
33
34     void buildHeap( );
35     void percolateDown( int hole );
36 };
```

Figure 21.4 The `BinaryHeap` class interface.

back by reference, and the other form does not. The usual `isEmpty` and `makeEmpty` routines are declared at lines 22 and 28.

The two constructors are shown in Figure 21.5. Both initialize the array and its size; the one-parameter constructor additionally copies in the array passed as a parameter and then calls `buildHeap`. Figure 21.6 shows `findMin`. The `isEmpty` and `makeEmpty` routines are trivial one-liners and thus are not shown.

```
// Construct the binary heap.
template <class Comparable>
BinaryHeap<Comparable>::BinaryHeap( )
  : array( 11 ), theSize( 0 )
{
}

// Construct the binary heap.
// v is a vector containing the initial items.
template <class Comparable>
BinaryHeap<Comparable>::
BinaryHeap( const vector<Comparable> & v )
  : array( v.size( ) + 1 ), theSize( v.size( ) + 1 )
{
    for( int i = 0; i < v.size( ); i++ )
        array[ i + 1 ] = v[ i ];
    buildHeap( );
}
```

Figure 21.5 Constructors for the `BinaryHeap` class.

```
// Find the smallest item in the priority queue.
// Return the smallest item, or throw an exception if empty.
template <class Comparable>
const Comparable & BinaryHeap<Comparable>::findMin( ) const
{
    if( isEmpty( ) )
        throw UnderflowException( );
    return array[ 1 ];
}
```

Figure 21.6 The `findMin` routine.

21.2 Implementation of the Basic Operations

The heap-order property looks promising so far because easy access to the minimum is provided. We must now show that we can efficiently support `insert` and `deleteMin` in logarithmic time. Performing the two required operations is easy (both conceptually and practically): The work merely involves ensuring that the heap-order property is maintained.

21.2.1 The `insert` Operation

Insertion is implemented by creating a hole at the next available location and then *percolating* it up until the new item can be placed in it without introducing a heap-order violation with the hole's parent.

To insert an element *X* in the heap, we must first add a node to the tree. The only option is to create a hole in the next available location; otherwise, the tree is not complete and we would violate the structure property. If *X* can be placed in the hole without violating heap order, we do so and are done. Otherwise, we slide the element that is in the hole's parent node into the node, bubbling the hole up toward the root. We continue this process until *X* can be placed in the hole. Figure 21.7 shows that to insert 14, we create a hole in the next available heap location. Inserting 14 into the hole would violate the heap-order property, so 31 is slid down into the hole. This strategy is continued in Figure 21.8 until the correct location for 14 is found.

This general strategy is called **percolate up,** in which insertion is implemented by creating a hole at the next available location and bubbling it up the heap until the correct location is found. Figure 21.9 shows the `insert` method, which implements the percolate up strategy by using a very tight loop. At line 6, we place `x` as the $-\infty$ sentinel in position 0. The statement at line 11 increments the current size and sets the hole to the newly added node. We iterate the loop at line 12 so long as the item in the parent node is larger than `x`. Line 13 moves the item in the parent down into the hole, and

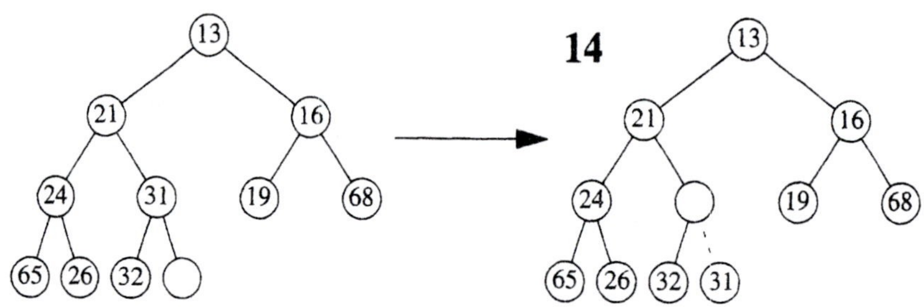

Figure 21.7 Attempt to insert 14, creating the hole and bubbling the hole up.

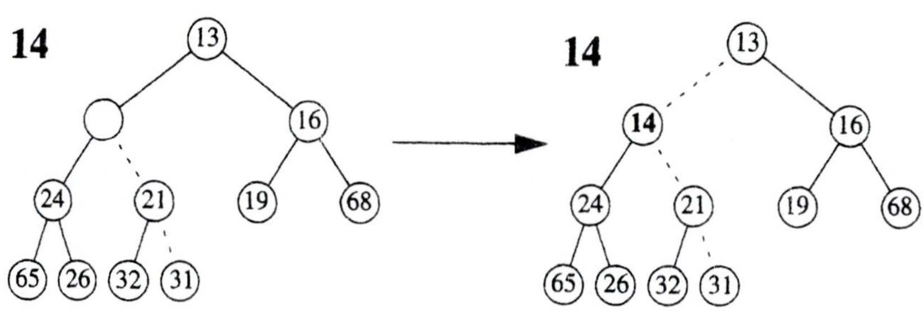

Figure 21.8 The remaining two steps required to insert 14 in the original heap shown in Figure 21.7.

```
1 // Insert item x into the priority queue, with heap order.
2 // Duplicates are allowed.
3 template <class Comparable>
4 void BinaryHeap<Comparable>::insert( const Comparable & x )
5 {
6     array[ 0 ] = x;    // initialize sentinel
7     if( theSize + 1 == array.size( ) )
8         array.resize( array.size( ) * 2 + 1 );
9
10      // Percolate up
11     int hole = ++theSize;
12     for( ; x < array[ hole / 2 ]; hole /= 2 )
13         array[ hole ] = array[ hole / 2 ];
14     array[ hole ] = x;
15 }
```

Figure 21.9 The `insert` member function.

then the third expression in the `for` loop moves the hole up to the parent. When the loop terminates, line 14 places x in the hole.

The time required to do the insertion could be as much as $O(\log N)$ if the element to be inserted is the new minimum. The reason is that it will be percolated up all the way to the root. On average the percolation terminates early: It has been shown that 2.6 comparisons are required on average to perform the `insert`, so the average `insert` moves an element up 1.6 levels.

Insertion takes constant time on average but logarithmic time in the worst case.

21.2.2 The `deleteMin` Operation

The `deleteMin` operation is handled in a similar manner to the `insert` operation. As shown already, finding the minimum is easy; the hard part is removing it. When the minimum is removed, a hole is created at the root. The heap now becomes one size smaller, and the structure property tells us that the last node must be eliminated. Figure 21.10 shows the situation: The minimum item is 13, the root has a hole, and the former last item needs to be placed in the heap somewhere.

Deletion of the minimum involves placing the former last item in a hole that is created at the root. The hole is *percolated down* the tree through minimum children until the item can be placed without violating the heap-order property.

If the last item could be placed in the hole, we would be done. That is impossible, however, unless the size of the heap is two or three, because elements at the bottom are expected to be larger than elements on the second level. We must play the same game as for insertion: We put some item in the hole and then move the hole. The only difference is that for the `deleteMin` we move down the tree. To do so, we find the smaller child of the hole, and if that child is smaller than the item that we are trying to place, we move the child into the hole, pushing the hole down one level and repeating these

The `deleteMin` operation is logarithmic in both the worst and average cases.

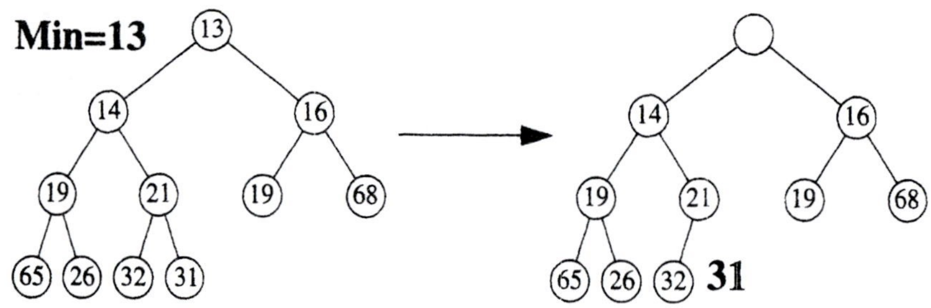

Figure 21.10 Creation of the hole at the root.

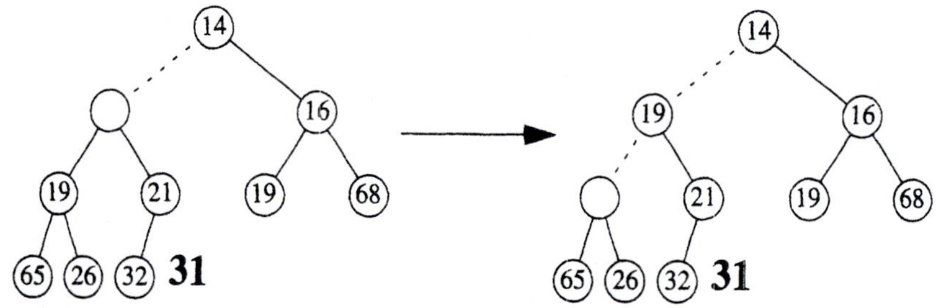

Figure 21.11 The next two steps in the `deleteMin` operation.

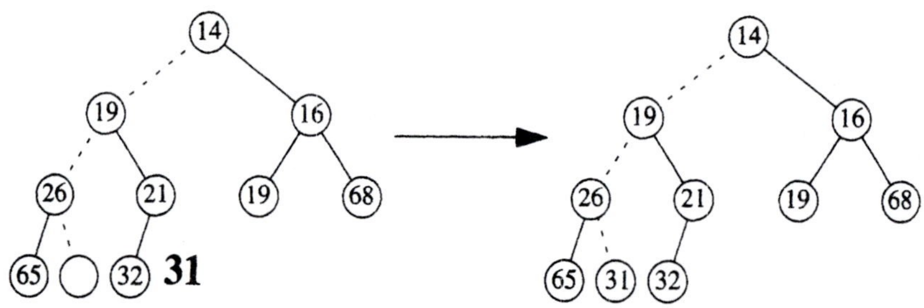

Figure 21.12 The Last two steps in the `deleteMin` operation.

actions until the item can be correctly placed—a process called **percolate down.** In Figure 21.11, we place the smaller child (14) in the hole, sliding the hole down one level. We repeat this action, placing 19 in the hole and creating a new hole one level deeper. We then place 26 in the hole and create a new hole on the bottom level. Finally, we are able to place 31 in the hole, as shown in Figure 21.12. Because the tree has logarithmic depth,

```
1 // Remove the smallest item from the priority queue.
2 // Throw UnderflowException if empty.
3 template <class Comparable>
4 void BinaryHeap<Comparable>::deleteMin( )
5 {
6     if( isEmpty( ) )
7         throw UnderflowException( );
8     array[ 1 ] = array[ theSize-- ];
9     percolateDown( 1 );
10 }
11
12 // Remove the smallest item from the priority queue
13 // and place it in minItem. Throw UnderflowException if empty.
14 template <class Comparable>
15 void BinaryHeap<Comparable>::deleteMin( Comparable & minItem )
16 {
17     minItem = findMin( );
18     array[ 1 ] = array[ theSize-- ];
19     percolateDown( 1 );
20 }
```

Figure 21.13 The `deleteMin` methods.

`deleteMin` is a logarithmic operation in the worst case. Not surprisingly, percolation rarely terminates more than one or two levels early, so `deleteMin` is logarithmic on average, too.

Figure 21.13 shows the `deleteMin` methods. The test for emptiness in the one-parameter `deleteMin` is automatically done by the call to `findMin` at line 17. The real work is done in `percolateDown`, shown in Figure 21.14. The code shown there is similar in spirit to the percolation up code in the `insert` routine. However, because there are two children rather than one parent, the code is a bit more complicated. The `percolateDown` method takes a single parameter that indicates where the hole is to be placed. The item in the hole is then moved out, and the percolation begins. For `deleteMin`, `hole` will be position 1. The `for` loop at line 9 terminates when there is no left child. The third expression moves the hole to the child. The smaller child is found at lines 12–13. We have to be careful because the last node in an even-sized heap is an only child; we cannot always assume that there are two children, which is why we have the first test at line 12.

```
// Internal method to percolate down in the heap.
// hole is the index at which the percolate begins.
template <class Comparable>
void BinaryHeap<Comparable>::percolateDown( int hole )
{
    int child;
    Comparable tmp = array[ hole ];

    for( ; hole * 2 <= theSize; hole = child )
    {
        child = hole * 2;
        if( child != theSize && array[child+1] < array[child] )
            child++;
        if( array[ child ] < tmp )
            array[ hole ] = array[ child ];
        else
            break;
    }
    array[ hole ] = tmp;
}
```

Figure 21.14 The `percolateDown` method used for `deleteMin` and `buildHeap`.

21.3 The `buildHeap` Operation: Linear-Time Heap Construction

The `buildHeap` operation can be done in linear time by applying a percolate down routine to nodes in reverse level order.

The **`buildHeap` operation** takes a complete tree that does not have heap order and reinstates it. We want it to be a linear-time operation, since N insertions could be done in $O(N \log N)$ time. We expect that $O(N)$ is attainable because N successive insertions take a total of $O(N)$ time on average, based on the result stated at the end of Section 21.2.1. The N successive insertions do more work than we require because they maintain heap order after every insertion and we need heap order only at one instant.

The easiest abstract solution is obtained by viewing the heap as a recursively defined structure, as shown in Figure 21.15: We recursively call `buildHeap` on the left and right subheaps. At that point, we are guaranteed that heap order has been established everywhere except at the root. We can establish heap order everywhere by calling `percolateDown` for the root. The recursive routine works by guaranteeing that when we apply `percolateDown(i)`, all descendants of `i` have been processed recursively by their own calls to `percolateDown`. The recursion, however, is not necessary, for the following reason. If we call `percolateDown` on nodes in reverse level order, then at the point `percolateDown(i)` is processed, all descendants of node `i` will have been processed by a prior call to

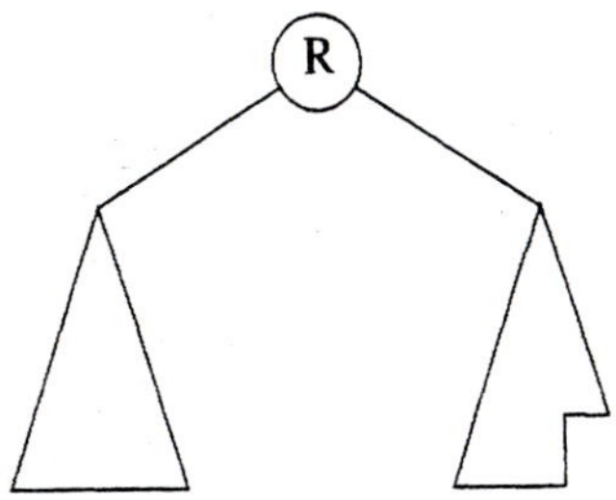

Figure 21.15 Recursive view of the heap.

```
// Establish heap-order property from an arbitrary
// arrangement of items. Runs in linear time.
template <class Comparable>
void BinaryHeap<Comparable>::buildHeap( )
{
    for( int i = theSize / 2; i > 0; i-- )
        percolateDown( i );
}
```

Figure 21.16 Implementation of the linear-time `buildHeap` method.

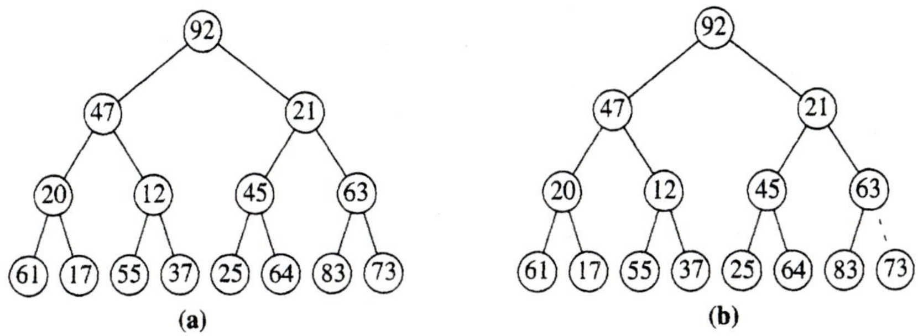

Figure 21.17 (a) Initial heap; (b) after `percolateDown(7)`.

`percolateDown`. This process leads to an incredibly simple algorithm for `buildHeap`, which is shown in Figure 21.16. Note that `percolateDown` need not be performed on a leaf. Thus we start at the highest numbered non-leaf node.

The tree in Figure 21.17(a) is the unordered tree. The seven remaining trees in Figures 21.17(b) through 21.20 show the result of each of the seven `percolateDown` operations. Each dashed line corresponds to two comparisons: one to find the smaller child and one to compare the smaller child with the node. Notice that the ten dashed lines in the algorithm correspond to 20 comparisons. (There could have been an eleventh line.)

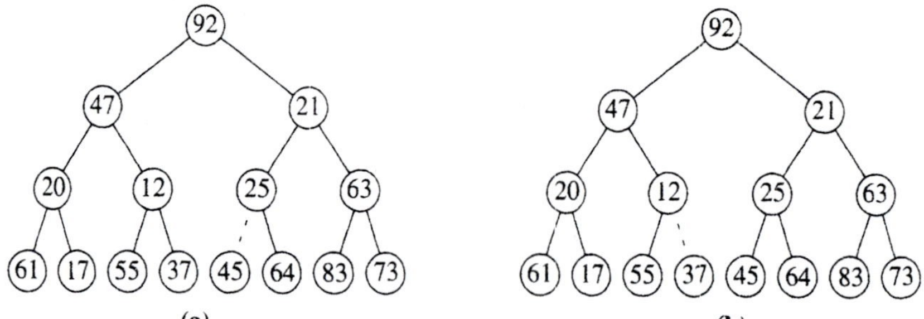

(a) (b)

Figure 21.18 (a) After `percolateDown(6)`; (b) after `percolateDown(5)`.

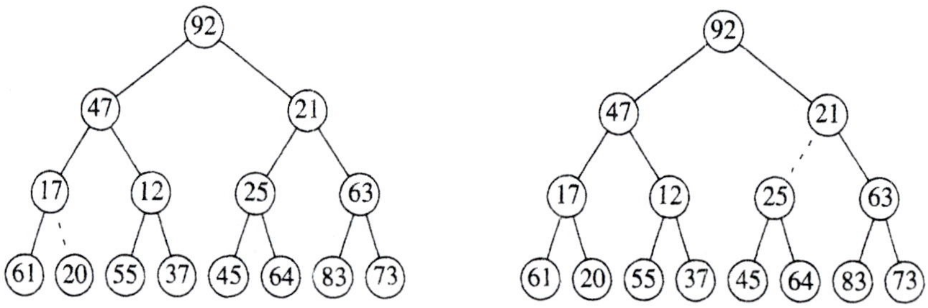

(a) (b)

Figure 21.19 (a) After `percolateDown(4)`; (b) after `percolateDown(3)`.

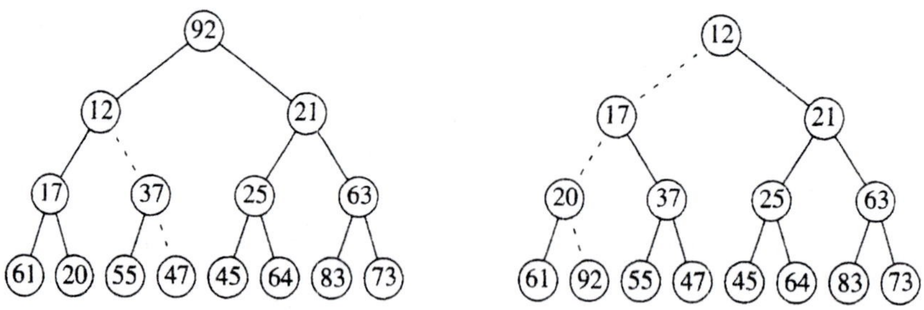

(a) (b)

Figure 21.20 (a) After `percolateDown(2)`; (b) after `percolateDown(1)` and `buildHeap` terminates.

To bound the running time of `buildHeap`, we must bound the number of dashed lines. We can do so by computing the sum of the heights of all the nodes in the heap, which is the maximum number of dashed lines. We expect a small number because half the nodes are leaves and have height 0 and a quarter of the nodes have height 1. Thus only a quarter of the nodes (those not already counted in the first two cases) can contribute more than 1 unit of height. In particular, only one node contributes the maximum height of $\lfloor \log N \rfloor$.

The linear time bound can be shown by computing the sum of the heights of all the nodes in the heap.

To obtain a linear time bound for `buildHeap`, we need to establish that the sum of the heights of the nodes of a complete binary tree is $O(N)$. We do so in Theorem 21.1, proving the bound for perfect trees by using a marking argument.

We prove the bound for perfect trees by using a marking argument.

Theorem 21.1

For the perfect binary tree of height H containing $N = 2^{H+1} - 1$ nodes, the sum of the heights of the nodes is $N - H - 1$.

Proof

We use a tree marking argument. (A more direct brute force calculation could also be done, as in Exercise 21.10.) For any node in the tree that has some height h, we darken h tree edges as follows. We go down the tree by traversing the left edge and then only right edges. Each edge traversed is darkened. An example is a perfect tree of height 4. Nodes that have height 1 have their left edge darkened, as shown in Figure 21.21. Next, nodes of height 2 have a left edge and then a right edge darkened on the path from the node to the bottom, as shown in Figure 21.22. In Figure 21.23, three edges are darkened for each node of height 3: the first left edge leading out of the node and then the two right edges on the path to the bottom. Finally, in Figure 21.24 four edges are darkened: the left edge leading out of the root and the three right edges on the path to the bottom. Note that no edge is ever darkened twice and that every edge except those on the right path is darkened. As there are $(N - 1)$ tree edges (every node has an edge coming into it except the root) and H edges on the right path, the number of darkened edges is $N - 1 - H$. This proves the theorem.

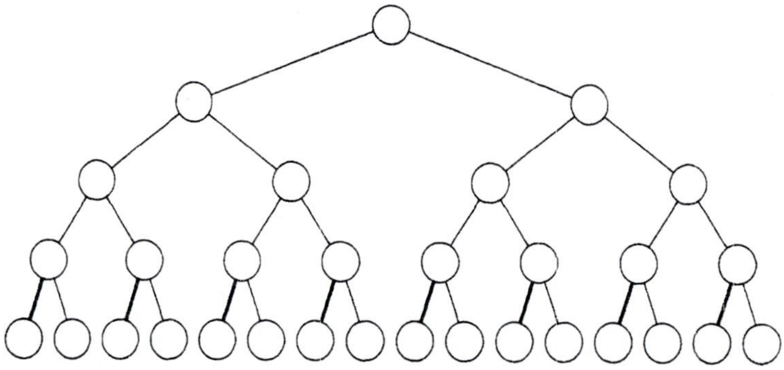

Figure 21.21 Marking the left edges for height 1 nodes.

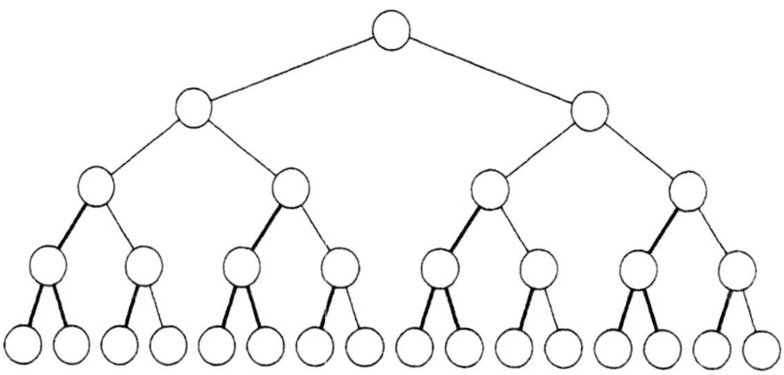

Figure 21.22 Marking the first left edge and the subsequent right edge for height 2 nodes.

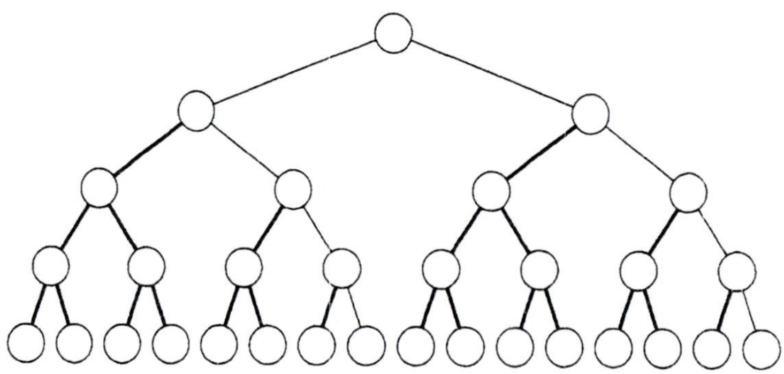

Figure 21.23 Marking the first left edge and the subsequent two right edges for height 3 nodes.

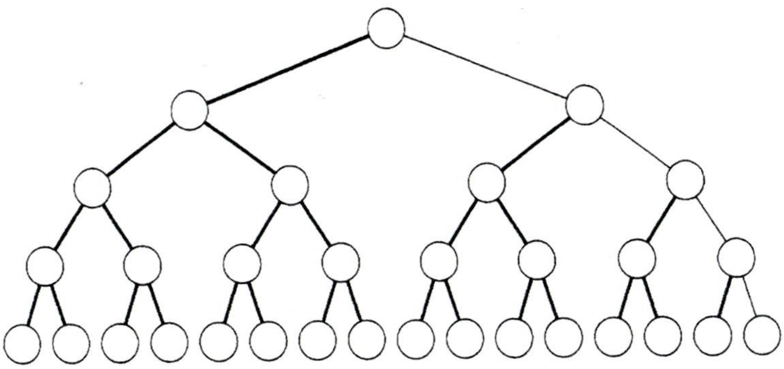

Figure 21.24 Marking the first left edge and the subsequent two right edges for the height 4 node.

A complete binary tree is not a perfect binary tree, but the result we have obtained is an upper bound on the sum of the heights of the nodes in a complete binary tree. A complete binary tree has between 2^H and $2^{H+1} - 1$ nodes, so this theorem implies that the sum is $O(N)$. A more careful argument establishes that the sum of the heights is $N - \nu(N)$, where $\nu(N)$ is the number of 1s in the binary representation of N. A proof of this is left for you to do as Exercise 21.12.

21.4 STL `priority_queue` Implementation

The binary heap can be used to implement the STL `priority_queue` class. Recall that `priority_queue` is a class template that requires template parameters representing the type of objects being stored, the type of the container that stores them, and a comparison function that implements the less-than function. Recall also that the STL priority queue is a max-heap and keeps the maximum, rather than the minimum, item at the root.

Figure 21.25 shows the `priority_queue` class interface. The comparison function is stored in the `lessThan` object, which is initialized in the constructor. `theItems` stores the array (if `theItems` is not indexible, the template does not expand); the size is maintained automatically as an invariant of `theItems`.

Figure 21.26 shows the constructors and accessors for `priority_queue`. We leave array position 0 empty, as in Section 21.2. Hence an empty priority queue consists of a vector of length 1, and the maximum item (as this is a max heap) is stored in position 1.

```
template <class Object, class Container, class Compare>
class priority_queue
{
  public:
    priority_queue( );

    int size( ) const;
    bool empty( ) const;

    const Object & top( ) const;
    void push( const Object & x );
    void pop( );

  private:
    Container theItems;
    Compare   lessThan;
};
```

Figure 21.25 The `priority_queue` class interface.

```
template <class Object, class Container, class Compare>
priority_queue<Object,Container,Compare>::priority_queue( )
  : theItems( 1 ), lessThan( Compare( ) )
{
}

template <class Object, class Container, class Compare>
int priority_queue<Object,Container,Compare>::size( ) const
{
    return theItems.size( ) - 1;
}

template <class Object, class Container, class Compare>
bool priority_queue<Object,Container,Compare>::empty( ) const
{
    return size( ) == 0;
}

template <class Object, class Container, class Compare>
const Object & priority_queue<Object,Container,Compare>::
top( ) const
{
    if( empty( ) )
        throw UnderflowException( );
    return theItems[ 1 ];
}
```

Figure 21.26 Constant-time methods in `priority_queue`.

The mutators (logically, `insert` and `deleteMax`) are shown in Figure 21.27. The code is basically the same as that in Section 21.2, except that the `lessThan` function object is used instead of `operator<`, and the logic is reversed in order to implement a max heap. In `push`, we use `push_back` on the underlying container, automatically expanding as needed and maintaining the container size at 1 more than the size of the priority queue (because position 0 stores the sentinel). In `pop`, we use `back` to get the last item and then use `pop_back` to reinstate our invariant. At line 38 we test to be sure the priority queue is not empty prior to putting `tmp` back in `theItems` at line 39. Otherwise, `hole` is 1, but `theItems.size()` is also 1, so we would be out of bounds.

21.5 Advanced Operations: `decreaseKey` and `merge`

In Chapter 23 we examine priority queues that support two additional operations. The `decreaseKey` operation lowers the value of an item in the priority queue. The item's position is presumed known. In a binary heap this operation is easily implemented by percolating up until heap order is reestablished. However, we must be careful because by assumption each item's position is being stored separately, and all items involved in the percolation have their positions altered. The `decreaseKey` operation is useful in implementing graph algorithms (e.g., Dijkstra's algorithm presented in Section 15.3).

The `merge` routine combines two priority queues. Because the heap is array-based, the best we can hope to achieve with a merge is to copy the items from the smaller heap to the larger heap and do some rearranging. Doing so takes at least linear time per operation. If we use general trees with nodes connected by pointers, we can reduce the bound to logarithmic cost per operation. Merging has uses in advanced algorithm design.

21.6 Internal Sorting: Heapsort

A priority queue can be used to sort in $O(N \log N)$ time. An algorithm based on this idea is *heapsort*.

The priority queue can be used to sort N items by

1. inserting every item into a binary heap and
2. extracting every item by calling `deleteMin` N times, thus sorting the result.

```
template <class Object, class Container, class Compare>
void priority_queue<Object,Container,Compare>::
push( const Object & x )
{
    theItems.push_back( x );
    theItems[ 0 ] = x;  // initialize sentinel

      // Percolate up
    int hole = size( );
    for( ; lessThan( theItems[ hole / 2 ], x ); hole / = 2 )
        theItems[ hole ] = theItems[ hole / 2 ];
    theItems[ hole ] = x;
}

template <class Object, class Container, class Compare>
void priority_queue<Object,Container,Compare>::pop( )
{
    if( empty( ) )
        throw UnderflowException( );

    int hole = 1;
    int child;

    Object tmp = theItems.back( ); theItems.pop_back( );
    int theSize = size( );

    for( ; hole * 2 <= theSize; hole = child )
    {
        child = hole * 2;
        if( child != theSize &&
                lessThan( theItems[child], theItems[child+1] ) )
            child++;
        if( lessThan( tmp, theItems[ child ] ) )
            theItems[ hole ] = theItems[ child ];
        else
            break;
    }
    if( !empty( ) )
        theItems[ hole ] = tmp;
}
```

Figure 21.27 The `priority_queue` class mutators `push` and `pop`, which are the equivalent of `insert` and `deleteMax`.

Using the observation in Section 21.5, we can more efficiently implement this procedure by

1. `tossing` each item into a binary heap,
2. applying `buildHeap`, and
3. calling `deleteMin` N times, with the items exiting the heap in sorted order.

Step 1 takes linear time total, and step 2 takes linear time. In step 3, each call to `deleteMin` takes logarithmic time, so N calls take $O(N \log N)$ time. Consequently, we have an $O(N \log N)$ worst-case sorting algorithm, called **heapsort,** which is as good as can be achieved by a comparison-based algorithm (see Section 9.8). One problem with the algorithm as it stands now is that sorting an array requires the use of the binary heap data structure, which itself carries the overhead of an array. Emulating the heap data structure on the array that is input—rather than going through the heap class apparatus—would be preferable. We assume for the rest of this discussion that this is done.

Even though we do not use the heap class directly, we still seem to need a second array. The reason is that we have to record the order in which items exit the heap equivalent in a second array and then copy that ordering back into the original array. The memory requirement is doubled, which could be crucial in some applications. Note that the extra time spent copying the second array back to the first is only $O(N)$, so, unlike mergesort, the extra array does not affect the running *time* significantly. The problem is *space.*

By using empty parts of the array, we can perform the sort in place.

A clever way to avoid using a second array makes use of the fact that, after each `deleteMin`, the heap shrinks by 1. Thus the cell that was last in the heap can be used to store the element just deleted. As an example, suppose that we have a heap with six elements. The first `deleteMin` produces A_1. Now the heap has only five elements, so we can place A_1 in position 6. The next `deleteMin` produces A_2. As the heap now has only four elements, we can place A_2 in position 5.

If we use a max heap, we obtain items in increasing order.

When we use this strategy, after the last `deleteMin` the array will contain the elements in *decreasing* sorted order. If we want the array to be in the more typical *increasing* sorted order, we can change the ordering property so that the parent has a larger key than the child does. Thus we have a max heap. For example, let us say that we want to sort the input sequence 59, 36, 58, 21, 41, 97, 31, 16, 26, and 53. After tossing the items into the max heap and applying `buildHeap`, we obtain the arrangement shown in Figure 21.28. (Note that there is no sentinel; we presume the data starts in position 0, as is typical for the other sorts described in Chapter 9.)

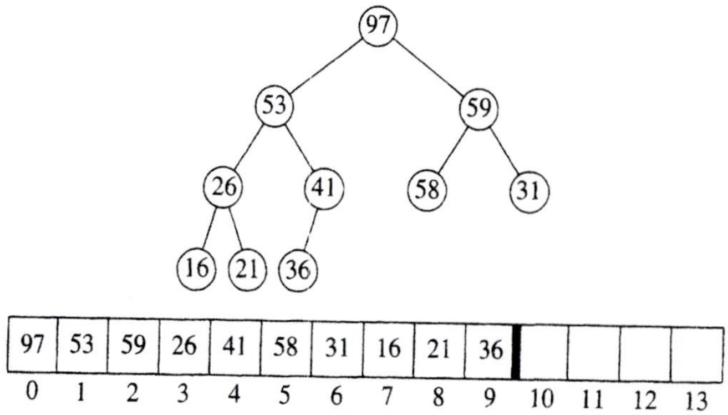

Figure 21.28 Max heap after the `buildHeap` phase.

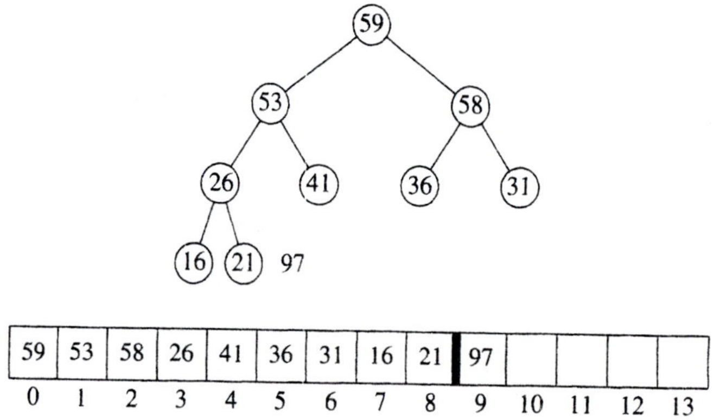

Figure 21.29 Heap after the first `deleteMax` operation.

Figure 21.29 shows the heap that results after the first `deleteMax`. The last element in the heap is 21; 97 has been placed in a part of the heap array that is technically no longer part of the heap.

Figure 21.30 shows that after a second `deleteMax`, 16 becomes the last element. Now only eight items remain in the heap. The maximum element removed, 59, is placed in the dead spot of the array. After seven more `deleteMax` operations, the heap represents only one element, but the elements left in the array will be sorted in increasing order.

Minor changes are required for heapsort because the root is stored in position 0.

Implementation of the heapsort operation is simple because it basically follows the heap operation. There are three minor differences between the two operations. First, because we are using a max heap, we need to reverse the logic of the comparisons from > to <. Second, we can no longer assume that there is a sentinel position 0. The reason is that all our other sorting

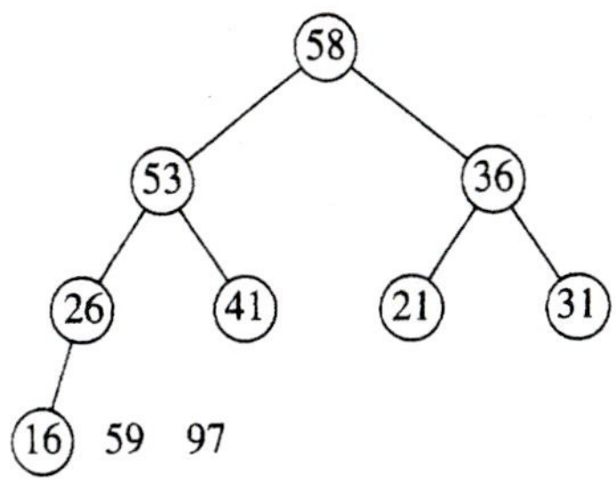

58	53	36	26	41	21	31	16	59	97				
0	1	2	3	4	5	6	7	8	9	10	11	12	13

Figure 21.30 Heap after the second `deleteMax` operation.

```
// Standard heapsort.
void heapsort( vector<Comparable> & a )
{
    for( int i = a.size( ) / 2; i >= 0; i-- ) // Build heap
        percDown( a, i, a.length( ) );
    for( int j = a.size( ) - 1; j > 0; j-- )
    {
        swap( a[ 0 ], a[ j ] );                // deleteMax
        percDown( a, 0, j );
    }
}
```

Figure 21.31 The `heapSort` routine.

algorithms store data at position 0, and we must assume that `heapSort` is no different. Although the sentinel is not needed anyway (there are no percolate up operations), its absence affects calculations of the child and parent. That is, for a node in position *i*, the parent is in position $(i-1)/2$, the left child is in position $2i+1$, and the right child is next to the left child. Third, `percDown` needs to be informed of the current heap size (which is lowered by 1 in each iteration of `deleteMax`). The implementation of `percDown` is left for you to do as Exercise 21.23. Assuming that we have written `percDown`, we can easily express `heapSort` as shown in Figure 21.31.

Although heapsort is not as fast as quicksort, it can still be useful. As discussed in Section 9.6 (and detailed in Exercise 9.19), in quicksort we can keep track of each recursive call's depth, and switch to an $O(N \log N)$ worst-case sort for any recursive call that is too deep (roughly $2 \log N$ nested calls). Exercise 9.19 suggested mergesort, but actually heapsort is the better candidate.

21.7 External Sorting

***External sorting* is used when the amount of data is too large to fit in main memory.**

So far, all the sorting algorithms examined require that the input fit in main memory. However, the input for some applications is much too large to fit in main memory. In this section we discuss **external sorting,** which is used to handle such very large inputs. Some of the external sorting algorithms involve the use of heaps.

21.7.1 Why We Need New Algorithms

Most of the internal sorting algorithms take advantage of the fact that memory is directly accessible. Shellsort compares elements `a[i]` and `a[i-gap]` in one time unit. Heapsort compares `a[i]` and `a[child=i*2]` in one time unit. Quicksort, with median-of-three pivoting, requires comparing `a[first]`, `a[center]`, and `a[last]` in a constant number of time units. If the input is on a tape, all these operations lose their efficiency because elements on a tape can be accessed only sequentially. Even if the data are on a disk, efficiency still suffers because of the delay required to spin the disk and move the disk head.

To demonstrate how slow external accesses really are, we could create a random file that is large but not too big to fit in main memory. When we read in the file and sort it by using an efficient algorithm, the time needed to read the input is likely to be significant compared to the time required to sort the input, even though sorting is an $O(N \log N)$ operation (or worse for Shellsort) and reading the input is only $O(N)$.

21.7.2 Model for External Sorting

We assume that sorts are performed on tape. Only sequential access of the input is allowed.

The wide variety of mass storage devices makes external sorting much more device-dependent than internal sorting does. The algorithms considered here work on tapes, which are probably the most restrictive storage medium. Access to an element on tape is gained by winding the tape to the correct location, so tapes can be efficiently accessed only in sequential order (in either direction).

Let us assume that we have at least three tape drives for performing the sort. We need two drives to do an efficient sort; the third drive simplifies matters. If only one tape drive is present, we are in trouble: Any algorithm will require $\Omega(N^2)$ tape accesses.

21.7.3 The Simple Algorithm

The basic external sorting algorithm involves the use of the merge routine from mergesort. Suppose that we have four tapes A1, A2, B1, and B2, which are two input and two output tapes. Depending on the point in the algorithm, the A tapes are used for input and the B tapes for output, or vice versa. Suppose further that the data are initially on A1 and that the internal memory can hold (and sort) M records at a time. The natural first step is to read M records at a time from the input tape, sort the records internally, and then write the sorted records alternately to B1 and B2. Each group of sorted records is called a **run.** When done, we rewind all the tapes. If we have the same input as in our example for Shellsort, the initial configuration is as shown in Figure 21.32. If $M = 3$, after the runs have been constructed, the tapes contain the data, as shown in Figure 21.33.

The basic external sort uses repeated two-way merging. Each group of sorted records is a *run*. As a result of a pass, the length of the runs doubles and eventually only a single run remains.

Now B1 and B2 contain a group of runs. We take the first runs from each tape, merge them, and write the result—which is a run twice as long—to A1. Then we take the next runs from each tape, merge them, and write the result to A2. We continue this process, alternating output to A1 and A2 until either B1 or B2 is empty. At this point, either both are empty or one (possibly short) run is left. In the latter case, we copy this run to the appropriate tape. We rewind all four tapes and repeat the same steps, this time using the A tapes as input and the B tapes as output. This process gives runs of length $4M$. We continue this process until we get one run of length N, at which

A1	81	94	11	96	12	35	17	99	28	58	41	75	15
A2													
B1													
B2													

Figure 21.32 Initial tape configuration.

A1							
A2							
B1	11	81	94	17	28	99	15
B2	12	35	96	41	58	75	

Figure 21.33 Distribution of length 3 runs to two tapes.

point the run represents the sorted arrangement of the input. Figures 21.34–21.36 show how this process works for our sample input.

We need $\lceil \log(N/M) \rceil$ passes over the input before we have one giant run.

The algorithm will require $\lceil \log(N/M) \rceil$ passes, plus the initial run-constructing pass. For instance, if we have 10,000,000 records of 6400 bytes each and 200 MB of internal memory, the first pass creates 320 runs. We would then need nine more passes to complete the sort. This formula also correctly tells us that our example in Figure 21.33 requires $\lceil \log(13/3) \rceil$, or three more passes.

A1	11	12	35	81	94	96	15
A2	17	28	41	58	75	99	
B1							
B2							

Figure 21.34 Tapes after the first round of merging (run length = 6).

A1												
A2												
B1	11	12	17	28	35	41	58	75	81	94	96	99
B2	15											

Figure 21.35 Tapes after the second round of merging (run length = 12).

A1	11	12	15	17	28	35	41	58	75	81	94	96	99
A2													
B1													
B2													

Figure 21.36 Tapes after the third round of merging.

21.7.4 Multiway Merge

_K_-way merging reduces the number of passes. The obvious implementation uses 2_K_ tapes.

If we have extra tapes, we can reduce the number of passes required to sort our input with a **multiway** (or K-way) **merge**. We do so by extending the basic (two-way) merge to a K-way merge and use $2K$ tapes.

Merging two runs is done by winding each input tape to the beginning of each run. Then the smaller element is found and placed on an output tape, and the appropriate input tape is advanced. If there are K input tapes, this strategy works in the same way; the only difference is that finding the smallest of the K elements is slightly more complicated. We can do so by using a priority queue. To obtain the next element to write on the output tape, we perform a `deleteMin` operation. The appropriate input tape is advanced, and if the run on that input tape has not yet been completed, we `insert` the new element in the priority queue. Figure 21.37 shows how the input from the previous example is distributed onto three tapes. Figures 21.38 and 21.39 show the two passes of three-way merging that complete the sort.

A1						
A2						
A3						
B1	11	81	94	41	58	75
B2	12	35	96	15		
B3	17	28	99			

Figure 21.37 Initial distribution of length 3 runs to three tapes.

A1	11	12	17	28	35	81	94	96	99
A2	15	41	58	75					
A3									
B1									
B2									
B3									

Figure 21.38 After one round of three-way merging (run length = 9).

A1													
A2													
A3													
B1	11	12	15	17	28	35	41	58	75	81	94	96	99
B2													
B3													

Figure 21.39 After two rounds of three-way merging.

After the initial run-construction phase, the number of passes required using K-way merging is $\lceil \log_K(N/M) \rceil$ because the length of the runs gets K times larger in each pass. For our example, the formula is verified because $\lceil \log_3 13/3 \rceil = 2$. If we have 10 tapes, $K = 5$. For the large example in Section 21.7.3, 320 runs would require $\log_5 320 = 4$ passes.

21.7.5 Polyphase Merge

The *polyphase merge* implements a *K*-way merge with *K* + 1 tapes.

The K-way merging strategy requires the use of $2K$ tapes, which could be prohibitive for some applications. We can get by with only $K + 1$ tapes, called a **polyphase merge.** An example is performing two-way merging with only three tapes.

Suppose that we have three tapes—T1, T2, and T3—and an input file on T1 that can produce 34 runs. One option is to put 17 runs each on T2 and T3. We could then merge this result onto T1, thereby obtaining one tape with 17 runs. The problem is that, as all the runs are on one tape, we must now put some of these runs on T2 to perform another merge. The logical way to do that is to copy the first eight runs from T1 to T2 and then perform the merge. This approach adds an extra half pass for every pass that we make. The question is, can we do better?

The distribution of runs affects performance. The best distribution is related to the Fibonacci numbers.

An alternative method is to split the original 34 runs unevenly. If we put 21 runs on T2 and 13 runs on T3, we could merge 13 runs on T1 before T3 was empty. We could then rewind T1 and T3 and merge T1, with 13 runs, and T2, with 8 runs, on T3. Next, we could merge 8 runs until T2 was empty, leaving 5 runs on T1 and 8 runs on T3. We could then merge T1 and T3, and so on. Figure 21.40 shows the number of runs on each tape after each pass.

The original distribution of runs makes a great deal of difference. For instance, if 22 runs are placed on T2, with 12 on T3, after the first merge we obtain 12 runs on T1 and 10 runs on T2. After another merge, there are 10 runs

	Run Const.	After						
		T3 + T2	T1 + T2	T1 + T3	T2 + T3	T1 + T2	T1 + T3	T2 + T3
T1	0	13	5	0	3	1	0	1
T2	21	8	0	5	2	0	1	0
T3	13	0	8	3	0	2	1	0

Figure 21.40 The number of runs for a polyphase merge.

on T1 and 2 runs on T3. At this point, the going gets slow because we can merge only two sets of runs before T3 is exhausted. Then T1 has 8 runs and T2 has 2 runs. Again we can merge only two sets of runs, obtaining T1 with 6 runs and T3 with 2 runs. After three more passes, T2 has 2 runs and the other tapes are empty. We must copy 1 run to another tape. Then we can finish the merge.

Our first distribution turns out to be optimal. If the number of runs is a Fibonacci number, F_N, the best way to distribute them is to split them into two Fibonacci numbers, F_{N-1} and F_{N-2}. Otherwise, the tape must be padded with dummy runs in order to increase the number of runs to a Fibonacci number. We leave the details of how to place the initial set of runs on the tapes for you to handle as Exercise 21.22. We can extend this technique to a K-way merge, in which we need Kth-order Fibonacci numbers for the distribution. The Kth-order Fibonacci number is defined as the sum of the K previous Kth-order Fibonacci numbers:

$$F^{(K)}N = F^{(K)}(N-1) + F^{(K)}(N-2) + \cdots + F^{(K)}(N-K);$$

$$F^{(K)}(0 \le N \le K-2) = 0;$$

$$F^{(K)}(K-1) = 1.$$

21.7.6 Replacement Selection

The last topic we consider in this chapter is construction of the runs. The strategy used so far is the simplest: We read as many elements as possible and sort them, writing the result to a tape. This seems like the best approach possible, until we realize that as soon as the first element is written to the output tape, the memory it used becomes available for another element. If the next element on the input tape is larger than the element just output, it can be included in the run.

	Three Elements in Heap Array				
	`array[1]`	`array[2]`	`array[3]`	Output	Next Item Read
Run 1	11	94	81	11	96
	81	94	96	81	12
	94	96	12	94	35
	96	35	12	96	17
	17	35	12	End of Run	Rebuild
Run 2	12	35	17	12	99
	17	35	99	17	28
	28	99	35	28	58
	35	99	58	35	41
	41	99	58	41	75
	58	99	75	58	15
	75	99	15	75	End of
	99		15	99	
			15	End of Run	Rebuild
Run 3	15			15	

Figure 21.41 Example of run construction.

If we are clever, we can make the length of the runs that we initially construct larger than the amount of available main memory. This technique is called *replacement selection.*

Using this observation, we can write an algorithm for producing runs, commonly called **replacement selection.** Initially, M elements are read into memory and placed in a priority queue efficiently with a single `buildHeap`. We perform a `deleteMin`, writing the smallest element to the output tape. We read the next element from the input tape. If it is larger than the element just written, we can add it to the priority queue with an `insert`; otherwise, it cannot go into the current run. Because the priority queue is smaller by one element, this element is stored in the dead space of the priority queue until the run has been completed and is then used for the next run. Storing an element in the dead space is exactly what is done in heapsort. We continue doing this process until the size of the priority queue is 0, at which point the run is over. We start a new run by rebuilding a new priority queue with a `buildHeap` operation, in the process using all of the elements in the dead space.

Figure 21.41 shows the run construction for the small example we have been using, with $M = 3$. Elements that are reserved for the next run are shaded. Elements 11, 94, and 81 are placed with `buildHeap`. Element 11 is output, and then 96 is placed in the heap by an insertion because it is larger than 11. Element 81 is output next, and then 12 is read. As 12 is smaller than the 81 just output, it cannot be included in the current run. Thus it is placed in the heap dead space. The heap now logically contains only 94 and 96. After they are output, we have only dead space elements, so we construct a heap and begin run 2.

In this example, replacement selection produces only 3 runs, compared to the 5 runs obtained by sorting. As a result, a three-way merge finishes in one pass instead of two. If the input is randomly distributed, replacement selection produces runs of average length $2M$. For our large example, we would expect 160 runs instead of 320 runs, so a five-way merge would still require four passes. In this case, we have not saved a pass, although we might if we get lucky and have 125 runs or fewer. Because external sorts take so long, every pass saved can make a significant difference in the running time.

As we have shown, replacement selection may do no better than the standard algorithm. However, the input is frequently nearly sorted to start with, in which case replacement selection produces only a few abnormally long runs. This kind of input is common for external sorts and makes replacement selection extremely valuable.

Summary

In this chapter we showed an elegant implementation of the priority queue. The binary heap uses only an array, yet it supports the basic operations in logarithmic worst-case time. The heap leads to a popular sorting algorithm, heapsort. In Exercises 21.26 and 21.27 you are asked to compare the performance of heapsort with that of quicksort. Generally speaking, heapsort is slower than quicksort but it is certainly easier to implement. Finally, we showed that priority queues are important data structures for external sorting.

This completes implementation of the fundamental and classic data structures. In Part V we examine more sophisticated data structures, beginning with the splay tree, a binary search tree that has some remarkable properties.

Objects of the Game

binary heap The classic method used to implement priority queues. The binary heap has two properties: structure and ordering. (p. 756)

`buildHeap` operation The process of reinstating heap order in a complete tree, which can be done in linear time by applying a percolate down routine to nodes in reverse level order. (p. 766)

complete binary tree A tree that is completely filled and has no missing nodes. The heap is a complete binary tree, which allows representation by a simple array and guarantees logarithmic depth. (p. 756)

external sorting A form of sorting used when the amount of data is too large to fit in main memory. (p. 778)

heap-order property States that in a (min) heap, the item in the parent is never larger than the item in a node. (p. 758)

heapsort An algorithm based on the idea that a priority queue can be used to sort in $O(N \log N)$ time. (p. 773)

implicit representation Using an array to store a tree. (p. 758)

max heap Supports access of the maximum instead of the minimum. (p. 759)

multiway merge K-way merging that reduces the number of passes. The obvious implementation uses $2K$ tapes. (p. 781)

percolate down Deletion of the minimum involves placing the former last item in a hole that is created at the root. The hole is pushed down the tree through minimum children until the item can be placed without violating the heap-order property. (p. 763)

percolate up Implements insertion by creating a hole at the next available location and then bubbling it up until the new item can be placed in it without introducing a heap-order violation with the hole's parent. (p. 762)

polyphase merge Implements a K-way merge with $K + 1$ tapes. (p. 782)

replacement selection The length of the runs initially constructed can be larger than the amount of available main memory. If we can store M objects in main memory, then we can expect runs of length $2M$. (p. 784)

run A sorted group in the external sort. At the end of the sort, a single run remains. (p. 779)

Common Errors

1. The trickiest part of the binary heap is the percolate down case in which only one child is present. This case occurs rarely, so spotting an incorrect implementation is difficult.
2. For heapsort, the data begins in position 0, so the children of node i are in positions $2i + 1$ and $2i + 2$.
3. The STL priority queue is a max heap, not a min heap.

On the Internet

The code to implement the `BinaryHeap` is available in two files.

BinaryHeap.h Contains the interface for the `BinaryHeap` class.

BinaryHeap.cpp Contains the implementation of the `BinaryHeap` class.

TestBinaryHeap.cpp Contains a test program for the `BinaryHeap` class.

queue.h Contains the interface for the `priority_queue` class.

queue.cpp Contains the implementation of the `priority_queue` class.

TestQueue.cpp Contains a test program for the `priority_queue` class.

Exercises

In Short

21.1. Describe the structure and ordering properties of the binary heap.

21.2. In a binary heap, for an item in position i where are the parent, left child, and right child located?

21.3. Show the result of inserting 10, 12, 1, 14, 6, 5, 8, 15, 3, 9, 7, 4, 11, 13, and 2, one at a time, in an initially empty heap. Then show the result of using the linear-time `buildHeap` algorithm instead.

21.4. Where could the 11th dashed line in Figures 21.17–21.20 have been?

21.5. A max heap supports `insert`, `deleteMax`, and `findMax` (but not `deleteMin` or `findMin`). Describe in detail how max heaps can be implemented.

21.6. Show the result of the heapsort algorithm after the initial construction and then two `deleteMax` operations on the input in Exercise 21.3.

21.7. Is heapsort a stable sort (i.e., if there are duplicates, do the duplicate items retain their initial ordering among themselves)?

In Theory

21.8. A complete binary tree of N elements uses array positions 1 through N. Determine how large the array must be for
  a. a binary tree that has two extra levels (i.e., is slightly unbalanced).
  b. a binary tree that has a deepest node at depth $2 \log N$.
  c. a binary tree that has a deepest node at depth $4.1 \log N$.
  d. the worst-case binary tree.

21.9. Show the following regarding the maximum item in the heap.
  a. It must be at one of the leaves.
  b. There are exactly $\lceil N/2 \rceil$ leaves.
  c. Every leaf must be examined to find it.

21.10. Prove Theorem 21.1 by using a direct summation. Do the following.
  a. Show that there are 2^i nodes of height $H - i$.
  b. Write the equation for the sum of the heights using part (a).
  c. Evaluate the sum in part (b).

21.11. Verify that the sum of the heights of all the nodes in a perfect binary tree satisfies $N - \nu(N)$, where $\nu(N)$ is the number of 1s in N's binary representation.

21.12. Prove the bound in Exercise 21.11 by using an induction argument.

21.13. For heapsort, $O(N \log N)$ comparisons are used in the worst case. Derive the leading term (i.e., decide whether it is $N \log N$, $2N \log N$, $3N \log N$, and so on).

21.14. Show that there are inputs that force every `percDown` in heapsort to go all the way to a leaf. (*Hint:* Work backward.)

21.15. Suppose that the binary heap is stored with the root at position r. Give formulas for the locations of the children and parent of the node in position i.

21.16. Suppose that binary heaps are represented by explicit links. Give a simple algorithm to find the tree node that is at implicit position i.

21.17. Suppose that binary heaps are represented by explicit links. Consider the problem of merging binary heap `lhs` with `rhs`. Assume that both heaps are full complete binary trees, containing $2^l - 1$ and $2^r - 1$ nodes, respectively.
  a. Give an $O(\log N)$ algorithm to merge the two heaps if $l = r$.

b. Give an $O(\log N)$ algorithm to merge the two heaps if $|l - r| = 1$.
c. Give an $O(\log^2 N)$ algorithm to merge the two heaps regardless of l and r.

21.18. A *d-heap* is an implicit data structure that is like a binary heap, except that nodes have d children. A d-heap is thus shallower than a binary heap, but finding the minimum child requires examining d children instead of two children. Determine the running time (in terms of d and N) of the `insert` and `deleteMin` operations for a d-heap.

21.19. A *min–max heap* is a data structure that supports both `deleteMin` and `deleteMax` at logarithmic cost. The structure is identical to the binary heap. The min–max heap-order property is that for any node X at even depth, the key stored at X is the smallest in its subtree, whereas for any node X at odd depth, the key stored at X is the largest in its subtree. The root is at even depth. Do the following.
a. Draw a possible min–max heap for the items 1, 2, 3, 4, 5, 6, 7, 8, 9, and 10. Note that there are many possible heaps.
b. Determine how to find the minimum and maximum elements.
c. Give an algorithm to insert a new node into the min–max heap.
d. Give an algorithm to perform `deleteMin` and `deleteMax`.
e. Give an algorithm to perform `buildHeap` in linear time.

21.20. The *2-D heap* is a data structure that allows each item to have two individual keys. The `deleteMin` operation can be performed with respect to either of these keys. The 2-D heap-order property is that for any node X at even depth, the item stored at X has the smallest key #1 in its subtree, and for any node X at odd depth, the item stored at X has the smallest key #2 in its subtree. Do the following.
a. Draw a possible 2-D heap for the items (1, 10), (2, 9), (3, 8), (4, 7), and (5, 6).
b. Explain how to find the item with minimum key #1.
c. Explain how to find the item with minimum key #2.
d. Give an algorithm to insert a new item in the 2-D heap.
e. Give an algorithm to perform `deleteMin` with respect to either key.
f. Give an algorithm to perform `buildHeap` in linear time.

21.21. A *treap* is a binary search tree in which each node stores an item, two children, and a randomly assigned priority generated when the node is constructed. The nodes in the tree obey the usual binary search tree order, but they must also maintain heap order with respect to the priorities. The treap is a good alternative to the balanced search tree because balance is based on the random priorities, rather than on the items. Thus the average case results for binary search trees apply. Do the following.

a. Prove that a collection of distinct items, each of which has a distinct priority, can be represented by only one treap.
b. Show how to perform insertion in a treap by using a bottom–up algorithm.
c. Show how to perform insertion in a treap by using a top–down algorithm.
d. Show how to perform deletion from a treap.

21.22. Explain how to place the initial set of runs on two tapes when the number of runs is not a Fibonacci number.

In Practice

21.23. Write the `percDown` routine with the declaration

```
void percDown( vector<Comparable> & a, int index, int size );
```

Recall that the max heap starts at position 0, not position 1.

Programming Projects

21.24. Write a program to compare the running time of using the `BinaryHeap`'s one-parameter constructor to initialize the heap with N items versus starting with an empty `BinaryHeap` and performing N separate `inserts`. Run your program for sorted, reverse sorted, and random inputs.

21.25. Suppose that you have a number of boxes, each of which can hold total weight 1.0 and items $i_1, i_2, i_3, \ldots, i_N$, which weigh $w_1, w_2, w_3, \ldots, w_N$, respectively. The object is to pack all the items, using as few boxes as possible, without placing more weight in any box than its capacity. For instance, if the items have weights 0.4, 0.4, 0.6 and 0.6, you can solve the problem with two boxes. This problem is difficult, and no efficient alogrithm is known. Several strategies give good, but not optimal, packings. Write programs to implement efficiently the following approximation strategies.

a. Scan the items in the order given; place each new item in the most-filled box that can accept it without overflowing. Use a priority queue to determine the box that an item goes in.
b. Sort the items, placing the heaviest item first; then use the strategy in part (a).

21.26. Implement both heapsort and quicksort and compare their performances on both sorted inputs and random inputs. Use different types of data for the tests.

21.27. Suppose that you have a hole at node *X*. The normal `percDown` routine is to compare *X*'s children and then move the child up to *X* if it is larger (in the case of a max heap) than the element to be placed, thereby pushing the hole down. Stop when placing the new element in the hole is safe. Consider the following alternative strategy for `percDown`. Move elements up and the hole down as far as possible without testing whether the new cell can be inserted. These actions would place the new cell in a leaf and probably violate heap order. To fix the heap order, percolate the new cell up in the normal manner. The expectation is that the percolation up will be only one or two levels on average. Write a routine to include this idea. Compare the running time with that of a standard implementation of heapsort.

21.28. Redo Exercise 9.19, using heapsort instead of mergesort.

21.29. Implement an external sort.

References

The binary heap was first described in the context of heapsort in [8]. The linear-time `buildHeap` algorithm is from [4]. Precise results on the number of comparisons and data movements used by heapsort in the best, worst, and average case are given in [7]. External sorting is discussed in detail in [6]. Exercise 21.18 is solved in [5]. Exercise 21.19 is solved in [2]. Exercise 21.20 is solved in [3]. Treaps are described in [1].

1. C. Aragon and R. Seidel, "Randomized Search Trees," *Algorithmica* **16** (1996), 464–497.
2. M. D. Atkinson, J. R. Sack, N. Santoro, and T. Strothotte, "Min-Max Heaps and Generalized Priority Queues," *Communications of the ACM* **29** (1986), 996–1000.

3. Y. Ding and M. A. Weiss, "The k-d Heap: An Efficient Multi-dimensional Priority Queue," *Proceedings of the Third Workshop on Algorithms and Data Structures* (1993), 302–313.
4. R. W. Floyd, "Algorithm 245: Treesort 3," *Communications of the ACM* **7** (1964), 701.
5. D. B. Johnson, "Priority Queues with Update and Finding Minimum Spanning Trees," *Information Processing Letters* **4** (1975), 53–57.
6. D. E. Knuth, *The Art of Computer Programming. Volume 3: Sorting and Searching*, 2d ed., Addison-Wesley, Reading, Mass., 1998.
7. R. Schaffer and R. Sedgewick, "The Analysis of Heapsort," *Journal of Algorithms* **14** (1993), 76–100.
8. J. W. J. Williams, "Algorithm 232: Heapsort," *Communications of the ACM* **7** (1964), 347–348.

Part V

Advanced Data Structures

Chapter 22

Splay Trees

In this chapter we describe a remarkable data structure called the *splay tree,* which supports all the binary search tree operations but does not guarantee $O(\log N)$ worst-case performance. Instead, its bounds are *amortized,* meaning that, although individual operations can be expensive, any sequence of operations is guaranteed to behave as though each operation in the sequence exhibited logarithmic behavior. Because this guarantee is weaker than that provided by balanced search trees, only the data and two pointers per node are required for each item and the operations are somewhat simpler to code. The splay tree has some other interesting properties, which we reveal in this chapter.

In this chapter, we show:

- the concepts of amortization and self-adjustment,
- the basic bottom–up splay tree algorithm and a proof that it has logarithmic amortized cost per operation,
- implementation of splay trees with a top–down algorithm, using a complete splay tree implementation (including a deletion algorithm), and
- comparisons of splay trees with other data structures.

22.1 Self-Adjustment and Amortized Analysis

Although balanced search trees provide logarithmic worst-case running time per operation, they have several limitations.

- They require storing an extra piece of balancing information per node.

- They are complicated to implement. As a result, insertions and deletions are expensive and potentially error-prone.
- They do not provide a win when easy inputs occur.

The real problem is that the extra data members add complications.

Let us examine the consequences of each of these deficiencies. First, balanced search trees require an extra data member. Although in theory this member can be as small as a single bit (as in a red–black tree), in practice the extra data member uses an entire integer for storage in order to satisfy hardware restrictions. Because computer memories are becoming huge, we must ask whether worrying about memory is a large issue. The answer in most cases is probably not, except that maintaining the extra data members requires more complex code and tends to lead to longer running times and more errors. Indeed, identifying whether the balancing information for a search tree is correct is difficult because errors lead only to an unbalanced tree. If one case is slightly wrong, spotting the errors might be difficult. Thus, as a practical matter, algorithms that allow us to remove some complications without sacrificing performance deserve serious consideration.

The *90-10 rule* states that 90 percent of the accesses are to 10 percent of the data items. However, balanced search trees do not take advantage of this rule.

Second, the worst-case, average-case, and best-case performances of a balanced search are essentially identical. An example is a `find` operation for some item *X*. We could reasonably expect that, not only the cost of the `find` will be logarithmic, but also that if we perform an immediate second `find` for *X*, the second access will be cheaper than the first. However, in a red–black tree, this condition is not true. We would also expect that, if we perform an access of *X*, *Y*, and *Z* in that order, a second set of accesses for the same sequence would be easy. This assumption is important because of the 90–10 rule. As suggested by empirical studies, the **90–10 rule** states that in practice 90 percent of the accesses are to 10 percent of the data items. Thus we want easy wins for the 90 percent case, but balanced search trees do not take advantage of this rule.

The 90–10 rule has been used for many years in disk I/O systems. A *cache* stores in main memory the contents of some of the disk blocks. The hope is that when a disk access is requested, the block can be found in the main memory cache and thus save the cost of an expensive disk access. Of course, only relatively few disk blocks can be stored in memory. Even so, storing the most recently accessed disk blocks in the cache enables large improvements in performance because many of the same disk blocks are accessed repeatedly. Browsers make use of the same idea: A cache stores locally the previously visited Web pages.

22.1.1 Amortized Time Bounds

We are asking for a lot: We want to avoid balancing information and, at the same time, we want to take advantage of the 90–10 rule. Naturally, we should expect to have to give up some feature of the balanced search tree.

We choose to sacrifice the logarithmic worst-case performance. We are hoping that we do not have to maintain balance information, so this sacrifice seems inevitable. However, we cannot accept the typical performance of an unbalanced binary search tree. But there is a reasonable compromise: $O(N)$ time for a single access may be acceptable so long as it does not happen too often. In particular, if any M operations (starting with the first operation) take a total of $O(M \log N)$ worst-case time, the fact that some operations are expensive might be inconsequential. When we can show that a worst-case bound for a sequence of operations is better than the corresponding bound obtained by considering each operation separately and can be spread evenly to each operation in the sequence, we have performed an **amortized analysis** and the running time is said to be *amortized*. In the preceding example, we have logarithmic amortized cost. That is, some single operations may take more than logarithmic time, but we are guaranteed compensation by some cheaper operations that occur earlier in the sequence.

***Amortized analysis* bounds the cost of a sequence of operations and distributes this cost evenly to each operation in the sequence.**

However, amortized bounds are not always acceptable. Specifically, if a single bad operation is too time consuming, we really do need worst-case bounds rather than amortized bounds. Even so, in many cases a data structure is used as part of an algorithm and only the total amount of time used by the data structure in the course of running an algorithm is important.

We have already presented one example of an amortized bound. When we implement array doubling in a stack or queue, the cost of a single operation can be either constant, if no doubling is needed, or $O(N)$, if doubling is needed. However, for any sequence of M stack or queue operations, the total cost is guaranteed to be $O(M)$, yielding constant amortized cost per operation. The fact that the array doubling step is expensive is inconsequential because its cost can be distributed to many earlier inexpensive operations.

22.1.2 A Simple Self-Adjusting Strategy (That Does Not Work)

In a binary search tree, we cannot expect to store the frequently accessed items in a simple table. The reason is that the caching technique benefits from the great discrepancy between main memory and disk access times. Recall that the cost of an access in a binary search tree is proportional to the depth of the accessed node. Thus we can attempt to restructure the tree by moving frequently accessed items toward the root. Although this process costs extra time during the first `find` operation, it could be worthwhile in the long run.

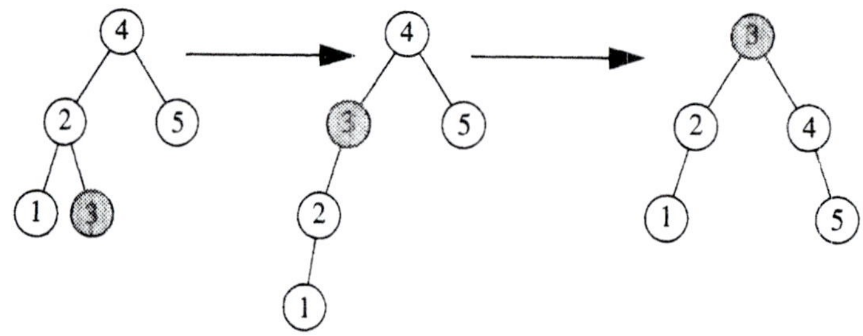

Figure 22.1 Rotate-to-root strategy applied when node 3 is accessed.

The *rotate-to-root strategy* rearranges a binary search tree after each access so as to move frequently accessed items closer to the root.

The rotate-to-root strategy is good if the 90–10 rule applies. It can be a bad strategy when the rule does not apply.

The easiest way to move a frequently accessed item toward the root is to rotate it continually with its parent, moving the item closer to the root, a process called the **rotate-to-root strategy.** Then, if the item is accessed a second time, the second access is cheap, and so on. Even if a few other operations intervene before the item is reaccessed, that item will remain close to the root and thus will be quickly found. An application of the rotate-to-root strategy to node 3 is shown in Figure 22.1[1]

As a result of the rotation, future accesses of node 3 are cheap (for a while). Unfortunately, in the process of moving node 3 up two levels, nodes 4 and 5 each move down a level. Thus, if access patterns do not follow the 90–10 rule, a long sequence of bad accesses can occur. As a result, the rotate-to-root rule does not exhibit logarithmic amortized behavior, which is likely unacceptable. A bad case is illustrated in Theorem 22.1.

Theorem 22.1 *There are arbitrarily long sequences for which M rotate-to-root accesses use $\Theta(MN)$ time.*

Proof *Consider the tree formed by the insertion of keys 1, 2, 3, ..., N in an initially empty tree. The result is a tree consisting of only left children. This outcome is not bad, as the time to construct the tree is only O(N) total. As illustrated in Figure 22.2, each newly added item is made a child of the root. Then, only one rotation is needed to place the new item at the root. The bad part, as shown in Figure 22.3, is that accessing the node with key 1 takes N units of time. After the rotations have been completed, access of the node*

1. An insertion counts as an access. Thus an item would always be inserted as a leaf and then immediately rotated to the root. An unsuccessful search counts as an access on the leaf at which the search terminates.

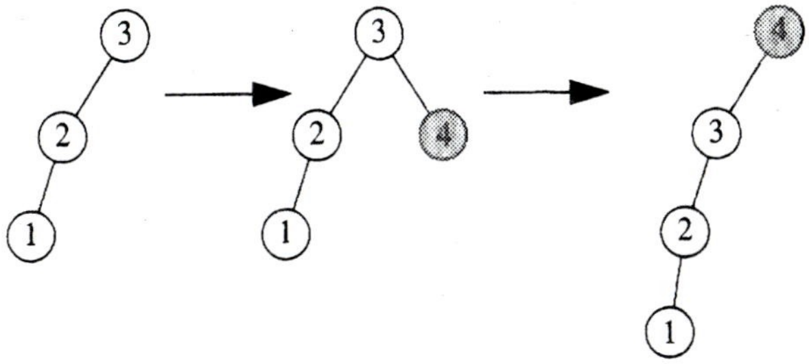

Figure 22.2 Insertion of 4 using the rotate-to-root strategy.

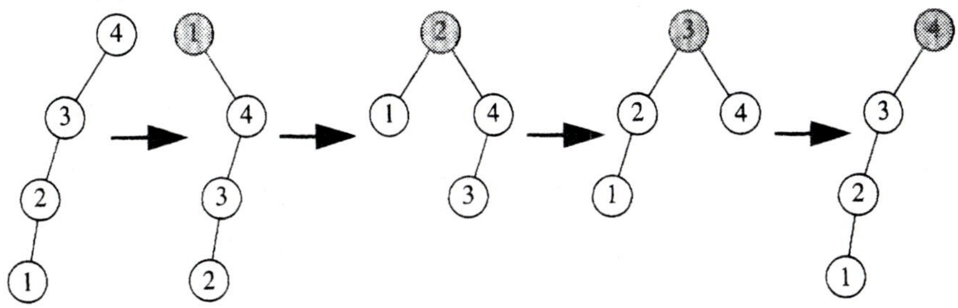

Figure 22.3 Sequential access of items takes quadratic time.

Proof (continued)

with key 2 takes N units of time and access of key 3 takes $N - 1$ *units of time. The total for accessing the N keys in order is* $N + \sum_{i=2}^{N} i = \Theta(N^2)$. *After they have been accessed, the tree reverts to its original state and we can repeat the sequence. Thus we have an amortized bound of only* $\Theta(N)$.

22.2 The Basic Bottom–Up Splay Tree

In a basic *bottom-up splay tree,* items are rotated to the root by using a slightly more complicated method than that used for a simple rotate-to-root strategy.

Achieving logarithmic amortized cost seems impossible because, when we move an item to the root via rotations, other items are pushed deeper. Seemingly, that would always result in some very deep nodes if no balancing information is maintained. Amazingly, we can apply a simple fix to the rotate-to-root strategy that allows the logarithmic amortized bound to be obtained. Implementation of this slightly more complicated rotate-to-root method called **splaying** leads to the basic **bottom–up splay tree.**

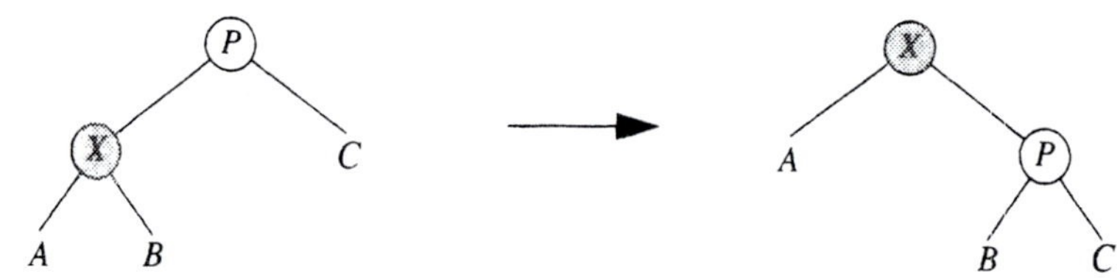

Figure 22.4 The zig case (normal single rotation).

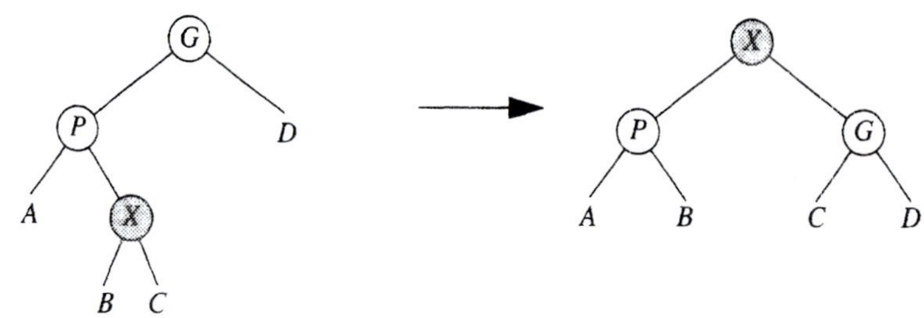

Figure 22.5 The zig-zag case (same as a double rotation); the symmetric case has been omitted.

The splaying strategy is similar to the simple rotate-to-root strategy, but it has one subtle difference. We still rotate from the bottom up along the access path (later in the chapter we describe a top–down strategy). If X is a nonroot node on the access path on which we are rotating and the parent of X is the root of the tree, we merely rotate X and the root, as shown in Figure 22.4. This rotation is the last along the access path, and it places X at the root. Note that this action is exactly the same as that in the rotate-to-root algorithm and is referred to as the **zig** case.

The *zig* and *zig-zag* cases are identical to rotate-to-root.

Otherwise, X has both a parent P and a grandparent G, and we must consider two cases and symmetries. The first case is the so called **zig-zag** case, which corresponds to the inside case for AVL trees. Here X is a right child and P is a left child (or vice versa). We perform a double rotation exactly like an AVL double rotation, as shown in Figure 22.5. Note that, as a double rotation is the same as two bottom–up single rotations, this case is no different than the rotate-to-root strategy. In Figure 22.1, the splay at node 3 is a single zig-zag rotation.

The *zig-zig* case is unique to the splay tree.

The final case, the **zig-zig** case, is unique to the splay tree and is the outside case for AVL trees. Here, X and P are either both left children or both right children. In this case, we transform the left-hand tree of Figure 22.6 to the right-hand tree. Note that this method differs from the rotate-to-root strategy. The zig-zig splay rotates between P and G and then X and P, whereas the rotate-to-root strategy rotates between X and P and then between X and G.

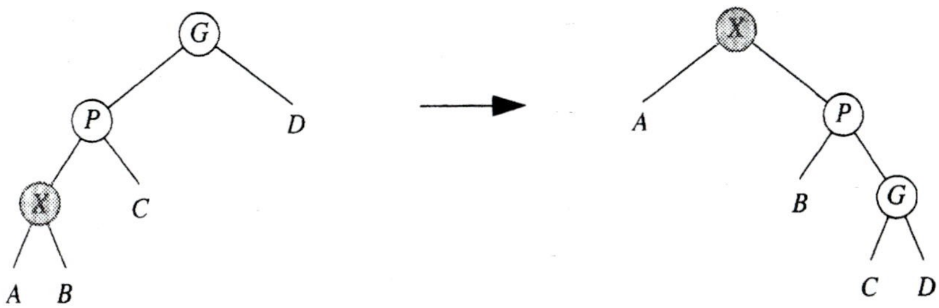

Figure 22.6 Zig-zig case (unique to the splay tree); the symmetric case has been omitted.

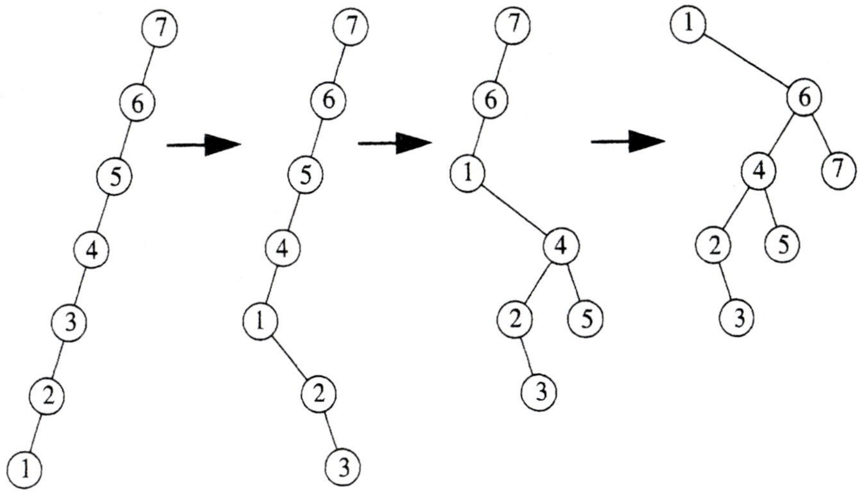

Figure 22.7 Result of splaying at node 1 (three zig-zigs and a zig).

Splaying has the effect of roughly halving the depth of most nodes on the access path and increasing by at most two levels the depth of a few other nodes.

The difference seems quite minor, and the fact that it matters is somewhat surprising. To see this difference consider the sequence that gave the poor results in Theorem 22.1. Again, we insert keys 1, 2, 3, ..., N in an initially empty tree in linear total time and obtain an unbalanced left-child-only tree. However, the result of a splay is somewhat better, as shown in Figure 22.7. After the splay at node 1, which takes N node accesses, a splay at node 2 takes only roughly $N/2$ accesses, rather than $N - 1$ accesses. Splaying not only moves the accessed node to the root, but it also roughly halves the depth of most nodes on the access path (some shallow nodes are pushed down at most two levels). A subsequent splay at node 2 brings nodes to within $N/4$ of the root. Splaying is repeated until the depth becomes roughly log N. In fact, a complicated analysis shows that what used to be a bad case for the rotate-to-root algorithm is a good case for splaying: Sequential access of the N items in the splay tree takes a total of only $O(N)$ time. Thus we win on easy input. In Section 22.4 we show, by subtle accounting, that there are no bad access sequences.

22.3 Basic Splay Tree Operations

After an item has been inserted as a leaf, it is splayed to the root.

As mentioned earlier, a splay operation is performed after each access. When an insertion is performed, we perform a splay. As a result, the newly inserted item becomes the root of the tree. Otherwise, we could spend quadratic time constructing an N item tree.

All searching operations incorporate a splay.

For the `find`, we splay at the last node accessed during the search. If the search is successful, the node found is splayed and becomes the new root. If the search is unsuccessful, the last node accessed prior to reaching the `NULL` pointer is splayed and becomes the new root. This behavior is necessary because, otherwise, we could repeatedly perform a `find` for 0 in the initial tree in Figure 22.7 and use linear time per operation. Likewise, operations such as `findMin` and `findMax` perform a splay after the access.

The interesting operations are the deletions. Recall that the `deleteMin` and `deleteMax` are important priority queue operations. With splay trees, these operations become simple. We can implement `deleteMin` as follows. First, we perform a `findMin`. This brings the minimum item to the root, and by the binary search tree property, there is no left child. We can use the right child as the new root. Similarly, `deleteMax` can be implemented by calling `findMax` and setting the root to the post–splay root's left child.

Deletion operations are much simpler than usual. They also contain a splaying step (sometimes two).

Even the `remove` operation is simple. To perform deletion, we access the node to be deleted, which puts the node at the root. If it is deleted, we get two subtrees, L and R (left and right). If we find the largest element in L, using a `findMax` operation, its largest element is rotated to L's root and L's root has no right child. We finish the `remove` operation by making R the right child of L's root. An example of the `remove` operation is shown in Figure 22.8.

The cost of the `remove` operation is two splays. All other operations cost one splay. Thus we need to analyze the cost of a series of splay steps. The next section shows that the amortized cost of a splay is at most $3 \log N + 1$ single rotations. Among other things, this means we do not have to worry that the remove algorithm described previously is biased. The splay tree's amortized bound guarantees that any sequence of M splays will use at most $3M \log N + M$ tree rotations. Consequently, any sequence of M operations starting from an empty tree will take a total of at most $O(M \log N)$ time.

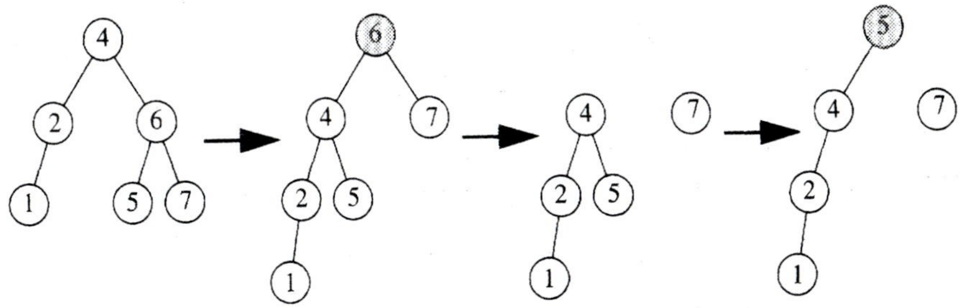

Figure 22.8 The `remove` operation applied to node 6: First, 6 is splayed to the root, leaving two subtrees; a `findMax` is performed on the left subtree, raising 5 to the root of the left subtree; then the right subtree can be attached (not shown).

22.4 Analysis of Bottom–Up Splaying

The analysis of the splay tree algorithm is complicated because each splay can vary from a few rotations to $O(N)$ rotations. Each splay can drastically change the structure of the tree. In this section we prove that the amortized cost of a splay is at most $3\log N + 1$ single rotations. The splay tree's amortized bound guarantees that any sequence of M splays use at most $3M\log N + M$ tree rotations, and consequently any sequence of M operations starting from an empty tree take a total of at most $O(M \log N)$ time.

The analysis of the splay tree is complicated and is part of a much larger theory of amortized analysis.

To prove this bound, we introduce an accounting function called the *potential function*. Not maintained by the algorithm, the **potential function** is merely an accounting device used to establish the required time bound. Its choice is not obvious and is the result of a large amount of trial and error.

The *potential function* is an accounting device used to establish the required time bound.

For any node i in the splay tree, let $S(i)$ be the number of descendants of i (including i itself). The potential function is the sum, over all nodes i in the tree T, of the logarithm of $S(i)$. Specifically,

$$\Phi(T) = \sum_{i \in T} \log S(i).$$

To simplify the notation, we let $R(i) = \log S(i)$, which gives

$$\Phi(T) = \sum R(i).$$

The *rank* of a node is the logarithm of its size. Ranks and sizes are not maintained but are merely accounting tools for the proof. Only nodes on the splay path have their ranks changed.

The term $R(i)$ represents the **rank** of node i, or the logarithm of its size. Note that the rank of the root is $\log N$. Recall that neither ranks nor sizes are maintained by splay tree algorithms (unless, of course, order statistics are needed). When a zig rotation is performed, only the ranks of the two nodes involved in the rotation change. When a zig-zig or a zig-zag rotation is performed, only the ranks of the three nodes involved in the rotation change. And finally, a single splay consists of some number of zig-zig or zig-zag rotations followed by perhaps one zig rotation. Each zig-zig or zig-zag rotation can be counted as two single rotations.

For Theorem 22.2 we let Φ_i be the potential function of the tree immediately after the ith splay and Φ_0 be the potential prior to the zeroth splay.

Theorem 22.2 *If the* i*th splay operation uses* r_i *rotations,* $\Phi_i - \Phi_{i-1} + r_i \le 3 \log N + 1$.

In all the proofs in this section we use the concept of telescoping sums.

Before proving Theorem 22.2, let us determine what it means. The cost of M splays can be taken as $\sum_{i=1}^{M} r_i$ rotations. If the M splays are consecutive (i.e., no insertions or deletions intervene), the potential of the tree after the ith splay is the same as prior to the $(i+1)$th splay. Thus we can use Theorem 22.2 M times to obtain the following sequence of equations:

$$\begin{aligned}
\Phi_1 - \Phi_0 + r_1 &\le 3 \log N + 1; \\
\Phi_2 - \Phi_1 + r_2 &\le 3 \log N + 1; \\
\Phi_3 - \Phi_2 + r_3 &\le 3 \log N + 1; \\
&\cdots \\
\Phi_M - \Phi_{M-1} + r_M &\le 3 \log N + 1.
\end{aligned} \tag{22.1}$$

These equations telescope, so if we add them, we obtain

$$\Phi_M - \Phi_0 + \sum_{i=1}^{M} r_i \le (3 \log N + 1)M, \tag{22.2}$$

which bounds the total number of rotations as

$$\sum_{i=1}^{M} r_i \le (3 \log N + 1)M - (\Phi_M - \Phi_0).$$

Now consider what happens when insertions are intermingled with find operations. The potential of an empty tree is 0, so when a node is inserted in the tree as a leaf, prior to the splay the potential of the tree increases by at most $\log N$ (which we prove shortly). Suppose that r_i rotations are used for an insertion and that the potential prior to the insertion is Φ_{i-1}. After the insertion, the potential is at most $\Phi_{i-1} + \log N$. After the splay that moves the inserted node to the root, the new potential will satisfy

$$\begin{aligned} \Phi_i - (\Phi_{i-1} + \log N) + r_i &\le 3 \log N + 1; \\ \Phi_i - \Phi_{i-1} + r_i &\le 4 \log N + 1. \end{aligned} \qquad \textbf{(22.3)}$$

Suppose further that there are F finds and I insertions and that Φ_i represents the potential after the ith operation. Then, because each find is governed by Theorem 22.2 and each insertion is governed by Equation 22.3, the telescoping logic indicates that

$$\sum_{i=1}^{M} r_i \le (3 \log N + 1)F + (4 \log N + 1)I - (\Phi_M - \Phi_0). \qquad \textbf{(22.4)}$$

Moreover, before the first operation the potential is 0, and since it can never be negative, $\Phi_M - \Phi_0 \ge 0$. Consequently, we obtain

$$\sum_{i=1}^{M} r_i \le (3 \log N + 1)F + (4 \log N + 1)I, \qquad \textbf{(22.5)}$$

showing that the cost of any sequence of finds and insertions is at most logarithmic per operation. A deletion is equivalent to two splays, so it too is logarithmic. Thus we must prove the two dangling claims—namely, Theorem 22.2 and the fact that an insertion of a node adds at most $\log N$ to the potential. We prove both theorems by using telescoping arguments. We take care of the insertion claim first, as Theorem 22.3.

Theorem 22.3

Insertion of the Nth node in a tree as a leaf adds at most $\log N$ *to the potential of the tree.*

Proof

The only nodes whose ranks are affected are those on the path from the inserted leaf to the root. Let $S_1, S_2, \ldots, S_k$ *be their sizes prior to the insertion and note that* $S_k = N - 1$ *and* $S_1 < S_2 < \cdots < S_k$. *Let* $S'_1, S'_2, \ldots, S'_k$ *be the sizes after the insertion. Clearly,* $S'_i \le S_{i+1}$ *for* $i < k$, *since* $S'_i = S_i + 1$. *Consequently,* $R'_i \le R_{i+1}$. *The change in potential is thus*

$$\sum_{i=1}^{k} (R'_i - R_i) \le R'_k - R_k + \sum_{i=1}^{k-1} (R_{i+1} - R_i) \le \log N - R_1 \le \log N.$$

To prove Theorem 22.2, we break each splay step into its constituent zig, zig-zag, and zig-zig parts and establish a bound for the cost of each type of rotation. By telescoping these bounds, we obtain a bound for the splay. Before continuing, we need a technical theorem, Theorem 22.4.

Theorem 22.4 *If $a + b \le c$ and a and b are both positive integers, then $\log a + \log b \le 2 \log c - 2$.*

Proof *By the arithmetic–geometric mean inequality, $\sqrt{ab} \le (a+b)/2$. Thus $\sqrt{ab} \le c/2$. Squaring both sides gives $ab \le c^2/4$. Then taking logarithms of both sides proves the theorem.*

We are now ready to prove Theorem 22.2.

22.4.1 Proof of the Splaying Bound

First, if the node to splay is already at the root, there are no rotations and no potential change. Thus the theorem is trivially true, and we may assume at least one rotation. We let X be the node involved in the splay. We need to show that, if r rotations are performed (a zig-zig or zig-zag counts as two rotations), r plus the change in potential is at most $3 \log N + 1$. Next, we let Δ be the change in potential caused by any of the splay steps zig, zig-zag, or zig-zig. Finally, we let $R_i(X)$ and $S_i(X)$ be the rank and size of any node X immediately before a splay step and $R_f(X)$ and $S_f(X)$ be the rank and size of any node X immediately after a splay step. Following are the bounds that are to be proven.

For a zig step that promotes node X, $\Delta \le 3(R_f(X) - R_i(X))$; for the other two steps, $\Delta \le 3(R_f(X) - R_i(X)) - 2$. When we add these bounds over all the steps that comprise a splay, the sum telescopes to the desired bound. We prove each bound separately in Theorems 22.5–22.7. Then we can complete the proof of Theorem 22.2 by applying a telescoping sum.

Theorem 22.5 *For a zig step, $\Delta \le 3(R_f(X) - R_i(X))$.*

Proof *As mentioned earlier in this section, the only nodes whose ranks change in a zig step are X and P. Consequently, the potential change is $R_f(X) - R_i(X) + R_f(P) - R_i(P)$. From Figure 22.4, $S_f(P) < S_i(P)$; thus it follows that $R_f(P) - R_i(P) < 0$. Consequently, the potential change satisfies $\Delta \le R_f(X) - R_i(X)$. As $S_f(X) > S_i(X)$, it follows that $R_f(X) - R_i(X) > 0$; hence $\Delta \le 3(R_f(X) - R_i(X))$.*

The zig-zag and zig-zig steps are more complicated because the ranks of three nodes are affected. First, we prove the zig-zag case.

Theorem 22.6

For a zig-zag step, $\Delta \le 3(R_f(X) - R_i(X)) - 2$.

Proof

As before, we have three changes, so the potential change is given by

$$\Delta = R_f(X) - R_i(X) + R_f(P) - R_i(P) + R_f(G) - R_i(G).$$

From Figure 22.5, $S_f(X) = S_i(G)$, so their ranks must be equal. Thus we obtain

$$\Delta = -R_i(X) + R_f(P) - R_i(P) + R_f(G).$$

Also, $S_i(P) \ge S_i(X)$. Consequently, $R_i(P) \ge R_i(X)$. Making this substitution and rearranging terms gives

$$\Delta \le R_f(P) + R_f(G) - 2R_i(X). \qquad \textbf{(22.6)}$$

From Figure 22.5, $S_f(P) + S_f(G) \le S_f(X)$. Applying Theorem 22.4, we obtain $\log S_f(P) + \log S_f(G) \le 2 \log S_f(X) - 2$, *which by the definition of rank, becomes*

$$R_f(P) + R_f(G) \le 2R_f(X) - 2. \qquad \textbf{(22.7)}$$

Substituting Equation 22.7 into Equation 22.6 yields

$$\Delta \le 2R_f(X) - 2R_i(X) - 2. \qquad \textbf{(22.8)}$$

As for the zig rotation, $R_f(X) - R_i(X) > 0$, so we can add it to the right side of Equation 22.8, factor, and obtain the desired

$$\Delta \le 3(R_f(X) - R_i(X)) - 2.$$

Finally, we prove the bound for the zig-zig case.

Theorem 22.7 *For a zig-zig step,* $\Delta \le 3(R_f(X) - R_i(X)) - 2$.

Proof *As before, we have three changes, so the potential change is given by*

$$\Delta = R_f(X) - R_i(X) + R_f(P) - R_i(P) + R_f(G) - R_i(G).$$

From Figure 22.6, $S_f(X) = S_i(G)$; *their ranks must be equal, so we obtain*

$$\Delta = -R_i(X) + R_f(P) - R_i(P) + R_f(G).$$

We also can obtain $R_i(P) > R_i(X)$ *and* $R_f(P) < R_f(X)$. *Making this substitution and rearranging gives*

$$\Delta < R_f(X) + R_f(G) - 2R_i(X). \qquad \textbf{(22.9)}$$

From Figure 22.6, $S_i(X) + S_f(G) \le S_f(X)$, *so applying Theorem 22.4 yields*

$$R_i(X) + R_f(G) \le 2R_f(X) - 2. \qquad \textbf{(22.10)}$$

Rearranging Equation 22.10, we obtain

$$R_f(G) \le 2R_f(X) - R_i(X) - 2. \qquad \textbf{(22.11)}$$

When we substitute Equation 22.11 into Equation 22.9, we get

$$\Delta \le 3(R_f(X) - R_i(X)) - 2.$$

Now that we have established bounds for each splaying step, we can finally complete the proof of Theorem 22.2.

Proof of Theorem 22.2 *Let* $R_0(X)$ *be the rank of X prior to the splay. Let* $R_i(X)$ *be X's rank after the ith splaying step. Prior to the last splaying step, all splaying steps must be zig-zags or zig-zigs. Suppose that there are k such steps. Then the total number of rotations performed at that point is 2k. The total potential change is* $\sum_{i=1}^{k} (3(R_i(X) - R_{i-1}(X)) - 2$. *This sum telescopes to* $3(R_k(X) - R_0(X)) - 2k$. *At this point, the total number of rotations plus the total potential change is bounded by* $3R_k(X)$ *because the 2k term* *cancels and the initial rank of X is not negative. If the last rotation is a zig-zig or a zig-zag, then a continuation of the telescoping sum gives a total of* $3R(root)$. *Note that here, on the one hand, the –2 in the potential increase cancels the cost of two rotations. On the other hand, this cancellation does not happen in the zig, so we would get a total of* $3R(root)+1$. *The rank of the root is* $\log N$, *so then—in the worst case—the total number of rotations plus the change in potential during a splay is at most* $3 \log N + 1$.

Proof of Theorem 22.2 (continued)

Although it is complex, the proof of the splay tree bound illustrates several interesting points. First, the zig-zig case is apparently the most expensive: It contributes a leading constant of 3, whereas the zig-zag contributes 2. The proof would fall apart if we tried to adapt it to the rotate-to-root algorithm because, in the zig case, the number of rotations plus the potential change is $R_f(X) - R_i(X) + 1$. The 1 at the end does not telescope out, so we would not be able to show a logarithmic bound. This is fortunate because we already know that a logarithmic bound would be incorrect.

The technique of amortized analysis is very interesting, and some general principles have been developed to formalize the framework. Check the references for more details.

22.5 Top–Down Splay Trees

A direct implementation of the bottom–up splay strategy requires a pass down the tree to perform an access and then a second pass back up the tree. These passes can be made by maintaining parent pointers, by storing the access path on a stack, or by using a clever trick to store the path (using the available pointers in the accessed nodes). Unfortunately, all these methods require expending a substantial amount of overhead and handling many special cases. Recall from Section 19.5 that implementing search tree algorithms with a single top–down pass is a better approach and we can use dummy nodes to avoid special cases. In this section we describe a **top–down splay tree** that maintains the logarithmic amortized bound, is faster in practice, and uses only constant extra space. It is the method recommended by the inventors of the splay tree.

As for red–black trees, *top–down splay trees* are more efficient in practice than their bottom–up counterparts.

The basic idea behind the top–down splay tree is that, as we descend the tree searching for some node X, we must take the nodes that are on the access path and move them and their subtrees out of the way. We must also perform some tree rotations to guarantee the amortized time bound.

We maintain three trees during the top–down pass.

At any point in the middle of the splay, a current node *X* is the root of its subtree; it is represented in the diagrams as the middle tree. Tree *L* stores nodes that are less than *X;* similarly, tree *R* stores nodes that are larger than *X*. Initially, *X* is the root of *T,* and *L* and *R* are empty. Descending the tree two levels at a time, we encounter a pair of nodes. Depending on whether these nodes are smaller or larger than *X,* we place them in *L* or *R,* along with subtrees that are not on the access path to *X*. Thus the current node on the search path is *always* the root of the middle tree. When we finally reach *X,* we can then attach *L* and *R* to the bottom of the middle tree. As a result, *X* has been moved to the root. The remaining tasks then are to place nodes in *L* and *R* and to perform the reattachment at the end, as illustrated in the trees shown in Figure 22.9. As is customary, three symmetric cases are omitted.

In all the diagrams, *X* is the current node, *Y* is its child, and *Z* is a grandchild (should an applicable node exist. The precise meaning of the term *applicable* is made clear during the discussion of the zig case.)

If the rotation should be a zig, the tree rooted at *Y* becomes the new root of the middle tree. Node *X* and subtree *B* are attached as a left child of the smallest item in *R;* *X*'s left child is logically made NULL.[2] As a result, *X* is the new smallest element in *R,* making future attachments easy.

Note that *Y* does not have to be a leaf for the zig case to apply. If the item sought is found in *Y,* a zig case will apply even if *Y* has children. A zig case also applies if the item sought is smaller than *Y* and *Y* has no left child, even if *Y* has a right child, and also for the symmetric case.

A similar dissection applies to the zig-zig case. The crucial point is that a rotation between *X* and *Y* is performed. The zig-zag case brings the bottom node *Z* to the top of the middle tree and attaches subtrees *X* and *Y* to *R* and *L,* respectively. Note that *Y* is attached to, and then becomes, the largest item in *L*.

The zig-zag step can be simplified somewhat because no rotations are performed. Instead of making *Z* the root of the middle tree, we make *Y* the root, as shown in Figure 22.10. This action simplifies the coding because the action for the zig-zag case becomes identical to the zig case and would seem advantageous, as testing for a host of cases is time-consuming. The disadvantage is that a descent of only one level results in more iterations in the splaying procedure.

Eventually, the three trees are reassembled into one.

Once we have performed the final splaying step, *L, R,* and the middle tree are arranged to form a single tree, as shown in Figure 22.11. Note that the result is different from that obtained with bottom–up splaying. The crucial fact is that the $O(\log N)$ amortized bound is preserved (see Exercise 22.3).

---

2. In the code written here, the smallest node in *R* does not have a NULL left pointer because it is not needed.

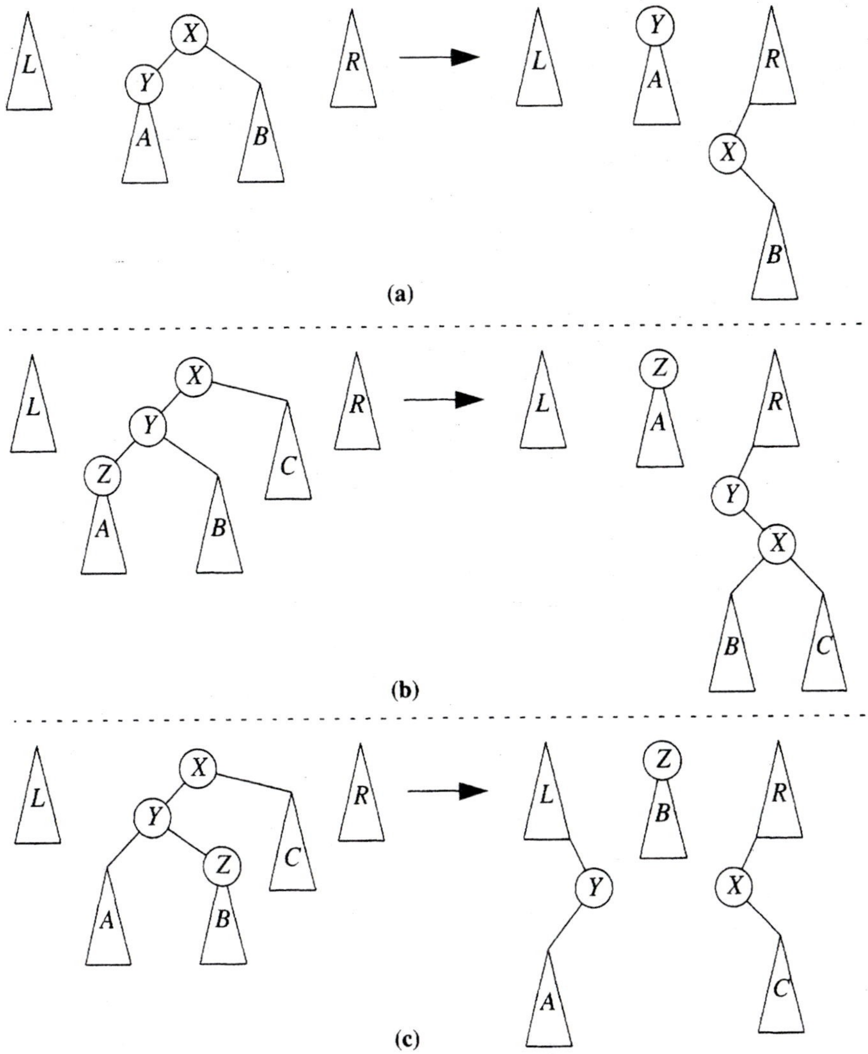

Figure 22.9 Top-down splay rotations: (a) zig, (b) zig-zig, and (c) zig-zag.

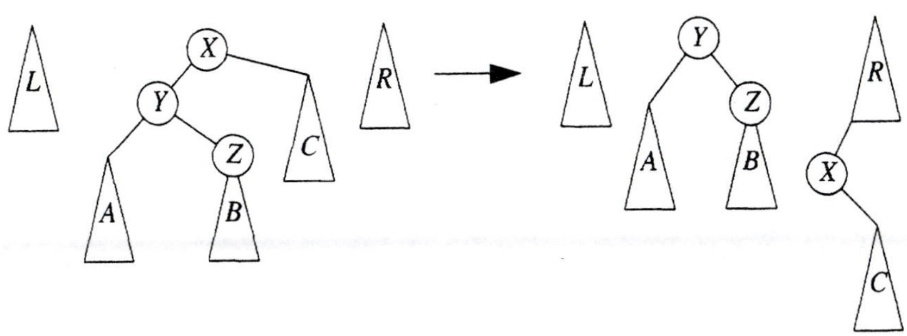

Figure 22.10 Simplified top–down zig-zag.

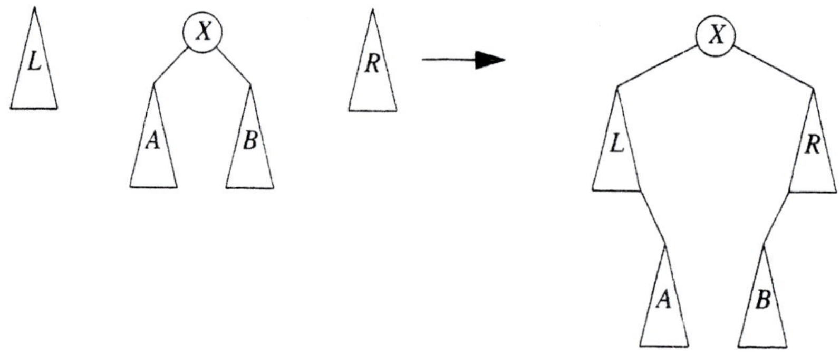

Figure 22.11 Final arrangement for top–down splaying.

An example of the simplified top–down splaying algorithm is shown in Figure 22.12. When we attempt to access 19, the first step is a zig-zag. In accordance with a symmetric version of Figure 22.10, we bring the subtree rooted at 25 to the root of the middle tree and attach 12 and its left subtree to *L*.

Next, we have a zig-zig: 15 is elevated to the root of the middle tree, and a rotation between 20 and 25 is performed, with the resulting subtree being attached to *R*. The search for 19 then results in a terminal zig. The middle's new root is 18, and 15 and its left subtree are attached as a right child of *L*'s largest node. The reassembly, in accordance with Figure 22.11, terminates the splay step.

22.6 Implementation of Top–Down Splay Trees

The splay tree class interface is shown in Figure 22.13. We have the usual methods, except that `find` is a mutator rather than an accessor. The `BinaryNode` class is our standard node class that contains data and two pointers and declares that `SplayTree` is a friend, but it is not shown. To eliminate annoying special cases, we maintain a `nullNode` sentinel. We allocate and initialize the sentinel in the constructor, as shown in Figure 22.14. Implementing the copy assignment operator and destructor turns out to be tricky, so we discuss this problem last.

Figure 22.15 shows the member function for insertion of an item `x`. A new node (`newNode`) is allocated, and if the tree is empty, a one-node tree is created. Otherwise, we splay around `x`. If the data in the tree's new root equal `x`, we have a duplicate. In this case, we do not want to insert `x`; we throw an exception instead. Before throwing the exception at line 36, we would normally call `delete` to avoid a memory leak. However, rather than calling `delete` for the newly allocated node, we use a `static` local variable so that the next call to `insert` can avoid calling `new`.

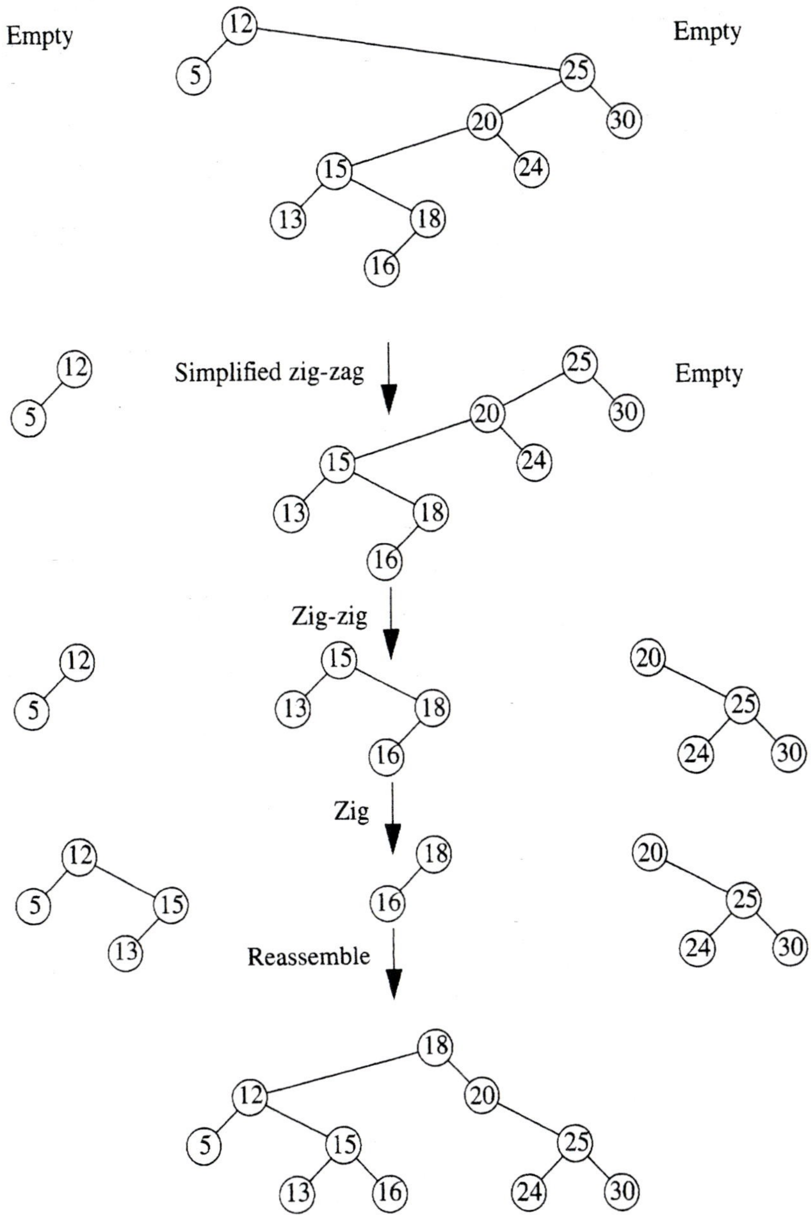

Figure 22.12 Steps in a top–down splay (accessing 19 in the top tree).

```
// SplayTree class.
//
// CONSTRUCTION: with no parameters or another SplayTree.
//
// ******************PUBLIC OPERATIONS*********************
// void insert( x )        --> Insert x
// void remove( x )        --> Remove x
// Comparable find( x )    --> Return item that matches x
// bool isEmpty( )         --> Return true if empty; else false
// void makeEmpty( )       --> Remove all items
// ******************ERRORS********************************
// Throws exceptions as warranted.

template <class Comparable>
class SplayTree
{
  public:
    SplayTree( );
    SplayTree( const SplayTree & rhs );
    ~SplayTree( );

    bool isEmpty( ) const;
    void makeEmpty( );

    Cref<Comparable> find( const Comparable & x );
    void insert( const Comparable & x );
    void remove( const Comparable & x );
    const SplayTree & operator=( const SplayTree & rhs );

  private:
    BinaryNode<Comparable> *root;
    BinaryNode<Comparable> *nullNode;

    typedef BinaryNode<Comparable> Node;
    Cref<Comparable> elementAt( Node *t ) const;
    Node * clone( Node *t ) const;

        // Tree manipulations
    void rotateWithLeftChild( Node * & k2 ) const;
    void rotateWithRightChild( Node * & k1 ) const;
    void splay( const Comparable & x, Node * & t ) const;
};
```

Figure 22.13 The top–down `SplayTree` class interface.

```
template <class Comparable>
SplayTree<Comparable>::SplayTree( )
{
    nullNode = new BinaryNode<Comparable>;
    nullNode->left = nullNode->right = nullNode;
    root = nullNode;
}
```

Figure 22.14 The `SplayTree` class constructor.

```
// Insert x into the tree.
// Throws DuplicateItemException if x is already there.
template <class Comparable>
void SplayTree<Comparable>::insert( const Comparable & x )
{
    static BinaryNode<Comparable> *newNode = NULL;

    if( newNode == NULL )
        newNode = new BinaryNode<Comparable>;

    newNode->element = x;
    if( root == nullNode )
    {
        newNode->left = newNode->right = nullNode;
        root = newNode;
    }
    else
    {
        splay( x, root );
        if( x < root->element )
        {
            newNode->left = root->left;
            newNode->right = root;
            root->left = nullNode;
            root = newNode;
        }
        else
        if( root->element < x )
        {
            newNode->right = root->right;
            newNode->left = root;
            root->right = nullNode;
            root = newNode;
        }
        else
            throw DuplicateItemException( );
    }
    newNode = NULL;    // So next insert will call new
}
```

Figure 22.15 The top–down `SplayTree` class insertion routine.

```
// Remove x from the tree.
// Throws ItemNotFoundException if x is not in the tree.
template <class Comparable>
void SplayTree<Comparable>::remove( const Comparable & x )
{
    BinaryNode<Comparable> *newTree;

      // If x is found, it will be at the root
    splay( x, root );
    if( root->element != x )
        throw ItemNotFoundException( );

    if( root->left == nullNode )
        newTree = root->right;
    else
    {
          // Find the maximum in the left subtree
          // Splay it to the root; and then attach right child
        newTree = root->left;
        splay( x, newTree );
        newTree->right = root->right;
    }
    delete root;
    root = newTree;
}
```

Figure 22.16 The top–down `SplayTree` class deletion routine.

If the new root contains a value larger than x, the new root and its right subtree become a right subtree of `newNode`, and the root's left subtree becomes a left subtree of `newNode`. Similar logic applies if the new root contains a value smaller than x. In either case, `newNode` is assigned to `root` to indicate that it is the new root. Then we make `newNode` `NULL` at line 38 so that the next call to `insert` will call `new`.

Figure 22.16 shows the deletion routine for splay trees. A deletion procedure rarely is shorter than the corresponding insertion procedure. Next, is the top–down splaying routine.

Our implementation, shown in Figure 22.17, uses a header with left and right pointers to contain eventually the roots of the left and right trees. These trees are initially empty, a header is used to correspond to the min or max node of the right or left tree, respectively, in this initial state. In this way we can avoid checking for empty trees. The first time the left tree becomes non-empty, the header's right pointer is initialized and does not change in the future. Thus it contains the root of the left tree at the end of the top–down search. Similarly, the header's left pointer eventually contains the root of the

```
// Internal method to perform a top-down splay.
// The last accessed node becomes the new root.
// x is the target item to splay around.
// t is the root of the subtree to splay.
template <class Comparable>
void SplayTree<Comparable>::splay( const Comparable & x,
                              BinaryNode<Comparable> * & t ) const
{
    BinaryNode<Comparable> *leftTreeMax, *rightTreeMin;
    static BinaryNode<Comparable> header;

    header.left = header.right = nullNode;
    leftTreeMax = rightTreeMin = &header;
    nullNode->element = x;   // Guarantee a match

    for( ; ; )
        if( x < t->element )
        {
            if( x < t->left->element )
                rotateWithLeftChild( t );
            if( t->left == nullNode )
                break;
              // Link Right
            rightTreeMin->left = t;
            rightTreeMin = t;
            t = t->left;
        }
        else if( t->element < x )
        {
            if( t->right->element < x )
                rotateWithRightChild( t );
            if( t->right == nullNode )
                break;
              // Link Left
            leftTreeMax->right = t;
            leftTreeMax = t;
            t = t->right;
        }
        else
            break;

    leftTreeMax->right = t->left;
    rightTreeMin->left = t->right;
    t->left = header.right;
    t->right = header.left;
}
```

Figure 22.17 A top–down splay algorithm.

```
// Make the tree logically empty.
template <class Comparable>
void SplayTree<Comparable>::makeEmpty( )
{
    findMax( );          // Splay max item to root
    while( !isEmpty( ) )
        remove( root->element );
}
```

Figure 22.18 The `makeEmpty` routine, which runs in linear time without extra space.

right tree. The `header` variable is declared as `static` because we want to allocate it only once over the entire sequence of splays.

Before the reassembly at the end of the splay, `header.left` and `header.right` point at *R* and *L*, respectively (this is not a typo—follow the links). Note that we are using the simplified top–down splay.

The destructor is implemented by calling the public `makeEmpty` routine. We would expect that, as in Chapter 19, `makeEmpty` would then call a private recursive routine and perform a postorder deletion of all tree nodes. However, that does not always work. The problem is that splay trees can be very unbalanced, even while giving good performance, and the recursion could run out of stack space. Figure 22.18 gives a simple alternative that is still $O(N)$ (though that is far from obvious). It is based on a theorem—which is very difficult to prove—that, if the items of a splay tree are accessed in sequential order, the total cost in linear. Similar considerations are required for `operator=` and any other function that would normally have a recursive implementation. However, only `makeEmpty` (which is called by the destructor) cannot be considered an optional method, and must be implemented.

22.7 Comparison of the Splay Tree with Other Search Trees

The implementation just presented suggests that splay trees are not as complicated as red–black trees and almost as simple as AA-trees. Are they worth using? The answer has yet to be resolved completely, but if the access patterns are nonrandom, splay trees seem to perform well in practice. Some properties relating to their performances also can be proved analytically. Nonrandom accesses include those that follow the 90–10 rule, as well as several special cases such as sequential access, double-ended access, and apparently access patterns that are typical of priority queues during some types of event simulations. In the exercises you are asked to examine this question in more detail.

Splay trees are not perfect. One problem with them is that the `find` operation is expensive because of the splay. Hence when access sequences are random and uniform, splay trees do not perform as well as other balanced trees.

Summary

In this chapter we described the splay tree, which is a recent alternative to the balanced search tree. Splay trees have several remarkable properties that can be proved, including their logarithmic cost per operation. Other properties are suggested in the exercises. Some studies have suggested that splay trees can be used for a wide range of applications because of their apparent ability to adapt to easy access sequences.

In Chapter 23 we describe two priority queues that, like the splay tree, have poor worst-case performance but good amortized performance. One of these, the pairing heap, seems to be an excellent choice for some applications.

Objects of the Game

90–10 rule States 90 percent of the accesses are to 10 percent of the data items. However, balanced search trees do not take advantage of this rule. (p. 796)

amortized analysis Bounds the cost of a sequence of operations and distributes the cost evenly to each operation in the sequence. (p. 797)

bottom–up splay tree A tree in which items are rotated to the root by using a slightly more complicated method than that used for a simple rotate-to-root strategy. (p. 799)

potential function An accounting device used to establish an amortized time bound. (p. 803)

rank In the splay tree analysis, the logarithm of a node's size. (p. 804)

rotate-to-root strategy Rearranges a binary search tree after each access so as to move frequently accessed items closer to the root. (p. 798)

splaying A rotate-to-root strategy that allows the logarithmic amortized bound to be obtained. (p. 800)

top–down splay tree A type of splay tree that is more efficient in practice than its bottom–up counterpart, as was the case for red–black trees. (p. 809)

zig and **zig-zag** Cases that are identical to the rotate-to-root cases. Zig is used when X is a child of the root, and zig-zag is used when X is an inside node. (p. 800)

zig-zig A case unique to the splay tree, which is used when X is an outside node. (p. 800)

Common Errors

1. A splay must be performed after every access, even an unsuccessful one, or the performance bounds are not valid.
2. The code is still tricky.
3. The `find` operation adjusts the data structure and is thus not an accessor. As a result the splay tree might not be compatible with some other search trees without code modifications.
4. Recursive private methods cannot be used safely in the `SplayTree` class because the tree depth may be large, even while performance is otherwise acceptable.

On the Internet

The `SplayTree` class is available online. The code includes versions of `findMin` and `findMax` that are efficient in an amortized sense, but not completely optimized. It also contains an `operator=` that calls a recursive `clone` method. As we stated at the end of Section 22.6, using recursion is not acceptable. Fixing this is left for you to do as Exercise 22.10.

SplayTree.h Contains the interface for the `SplayTree` class.

SplayTree.cpp Contains the implementation for the `SplayTree` class.

TestSplayTree.cpp Contains a test program for the `SplayTree` class.

Exercises

In Short

22.1. Show the result of inserting 3, 1, 4, 5, 2, 9, 6, and 8 into a

a. bottom–up splay tree.
b. top–down splay tree.

22.2. Show the result of deleting 3 from the splay tree shown in Exercise 22.1 for both the bottom–up and top–down versions.

In Theory

22.3. Prove that the amortized cost of a top–down splay is $O(\log N)$.

22.4. Prove that if all nodes in a splay tree are accessed in sequential order, the resulting tree consists of a chain of left children.

22.5. Suppose that, in an attempt to save time, we splay on every second tree operation. Does the amortized cost remain logarithmic?

22.6. Nodes 1 through $N = 1024$ form a splay tree of left children.

a. What is the internal path length of the tree (exactly)?

b. Calculate the internal path length after each of `find(1)`, `find(2)`, and `find(3)` when a bottom–up splay is performed.

22.7. By changing the potential function, you can prove different bounds for splaying. Let the weight function $W(i)$ be some function assigned to each node in the tree and $S(i)$ be the sum of the weights of all nodes in the subtree rooted at i, including i itself. The special case $W(i) = 1$ for all nodes corresponds to the function used in the proof of the splaying bound. Let N be the number of nodes in the tree and M be the number of accesses. Prove the following two theorems.

a. The total access time is $O(M + (M + N) \log N)$.

b. If q_i is the total number of times that item i is accessed and $q_i > 0$ for all i, then the total access time is $O(M + \sum_{i=1}^{N} q_i \log(M/q_i))$.

In Practice

22.8. Use the splay tree to implement a priority queue class.

22.9. Modify the splay tree to support order statistics.

22.10. Implement the `SplayTree operator=` and copy constructor correctly. If necessary, you may change the `rhs` parameter to be a nonconstant reference (such a change is allowed by the Standard).

Programming Projects

22.11. Compare empirically the simplified top–down splay implemented in Section 22.6 with the original top–down splay discussed in Section 22.5.

22.12. Unlike balanced search trees, splay trees incur overhead during a `find` operation that can be undesirable if the access sequence is sufficiently random. Experiment with a strategy that splays on a `find` operation only after a certain depth *d* is traversed in the top–down search. The splay does not move the accessed item all the way to the root, but rather to the point at depth *d* where the splaying is started.

22.13. Compare empirically a top–down splay tree priority queue implementation with a binary heap by using

a. random `insert` and `deleteMin` operations.

b. `insert` and `deleteMin` operations corresponding to an event-driven simulation.

c. `insert` and `deleteMin` operations corresponding to Dijkstra's algorithm.

References

The splay tree is described in the paper [3]. The concept of amortized analysis is discussed in the survey paper [4] and also in greater detail in [5]. A comparison of splay trees and AVL trees is given in [1], and [2] shows that splay trees perform well in some types of event-driven simulations.

1. J. Bell and G. Gupta, "An Evaluation of Self-Adjusting Binary Search Tree Techniques," *Software-Practice and Experience* **23** (1993), 369–382.
2. D. W. Jones, "An Empirical Comparison of Priority-Queue and Event-Set Implementations," *Communications of the ACM* **29** (1986), 300–311.
3. D. D. Sleator and R. E. Tarjan, "Self-adjusting Binary Search Trees," *Journal of the ACM* **32** (1985), 652–686.
4. R. E. Tarjan, "Amortized Computational Complexity," *SIAM Journal on Algebraic and Discrete Methods* **6** (1985), 306–318.
5. M. A. Weiss, *Data Structures and Algorithm Analysis in C++*, 2d ed., Addison-Wesley, Reading, Mass., 1999.

Chapter 23

Merging Priority Queues

In this chapter we examine priority queues that support an additional operation: The `merge` operation, which is important in advanced algorithm design, combines two priority queues into one (and logically destroys the originals). We represent the priority queues as general trees, which simplifies somewhat the `decreaseKey` operation and is important in some applications.

In this chapter, we show:

- how the *skew heap*—a mergeable priority queue implemented with binary trees—works.
- how the *pairing heap*—a mergeable priority queue based on the *M*-ary tree—works. The pairing heap appears to be a practical alternative to the binary heap even if the `merge` operation is not needed.

23.1 The Skew Heap

The **skew heap** is a heap-ordered binary tree without a balancing condition. Without this structural constraint on the tree—unlike with the heap or the balanced binary search trees—there is no guarantee that the depth of the tree is logarithmic. However, it supports all operations in logarithmic amortized time. The skew heap is thus somewhat similar to the splay tree.

The *skew heap* is a heap-ordered binary tree without a balancing condition and supports all operations in logarithmic amortized time.

23.1.1 Merging Is Fundamental

If a heap-ordered, structurally unconstrained binary tree is used to represent a priority queue, merging becomes the fundamental operation. This is because we can perform other operations as follows:

- `h.insert( x )`: Create a one-node tree containing `x` and merge that tree into the priority queue.
- `h.findMin( )`: Return the item at the root.

- `h.deleteMin( )`: Delete the root and merge its left and right subtrees.

The `decreaseKey` operation is implemented by detaching a subtree from its parent and then using `merge`.

- `h.decreaseKey( p, newVal )`: Assuming that `p` is a pointer to a node in the priority queue, we can lower `p`'s key value appropriately and then detach `p` from its parent. Doing so yields two priority queues that can be merged. Note that `p` (meaning the position) does not change as a result of this operation (in contrast to the equivalent operation in a binary heap).

We need only show how to implement merging; the other operations become trivial. The `decreaseKey` operation is important in some advanced applications. We presented one illustration in Section 15.3—Dijkstra's algorithm for shortest paths in a graph. We did not use the `decreaseKey` operation in our implementation because of the complications of maintaining the position of each item in the binary heap. In a merging heap, the position can be maintained as a pointer to the tree node, and unlike in the binary heap, the position never changes.

In this section we discuss one implementation of a mergeable priority queue that uses a binary tree: the skew heap. First, we show that, if we are not concerned with efficiency, merging two heap-ordered trees is easy. Next, we cover a simple modification (the skew heap) that avoids the obvious inefficiencies in the original algorithm. Finally, we give a proof that the `merge` operation for skew heaps is logarithmic in an amortized sense and comment on the practical significance of this result.

23.1.2 Simplistic Merging of Heap-Ordered Trees

Two trees are easily merged recursively.

Let us assume that we have two heap-ordered trees, H_1 and H_2, that need to be merged. Clearly, if either of the two trees is empty, the other tree is the result of the merge. Otherwise, to merge the two trees, we compare their roots. We recursively merge the tree with the larger root into the right subtree of the tree with the smaller root.[1]

The result is that right paths are merged. We must be careful not to create unduly long right paths.

Figure 23.1 shows the effect of this recursive strategy: The right paths of the two priority queues are merged to form the new priority queue. Each node on the right path retains its original left subtree, and only the nodes on the right path are touched. The outcome shown in Figure 23.1 is unattainable by using only insertions and merges because, as just mentioned, left children cannot be added by a merge. The practical effect is that what seems to be a heap-ordered binary tree is in fact an ordered arrangement consisting only of a single right path. Thus all operations take linear time. Fortunately, a simple modification ensures that the right path is not always long.

---

1. Clearly, either subtree could be used. We arbitrarily use the right subtree.

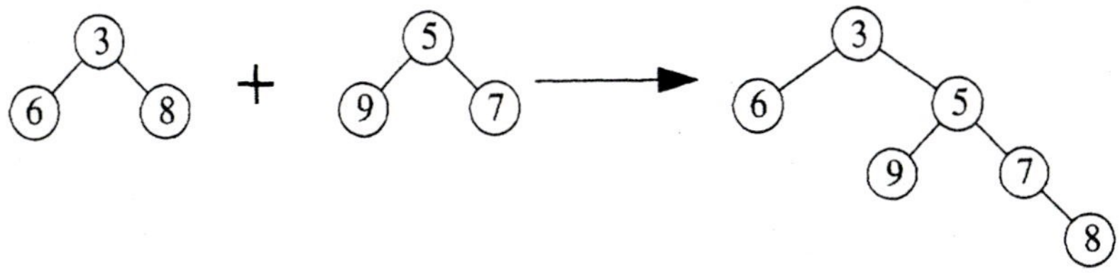

Figure 23.1 Simplistic merging of heap-ordered trees: Right paths are merged.

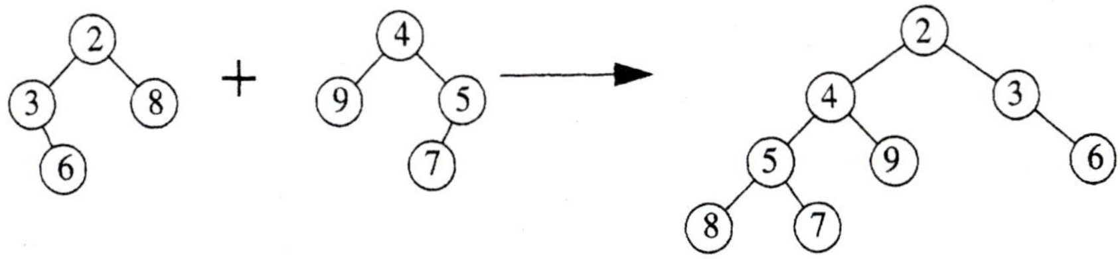

Figure 23.2 Merging of skew heap; right paths are merged, and the result is made a left path.

23.1.3 The Skew Heap: A Simple Modification

The merge shown in Figure 23.1 creates a temporary merged tree. We can make a simple modification in the operation as follows. Prior to the completion of a merge, we swap the left and right children for every node in the resulting right path of the temporary tree. Again, only those nodes on the original right paths are on the right path in the temporary tree. As a result of the swap, shown in Figure 23.2, these nodes then form the left path of the resulting tree. When a merge is performed in this way, the heap-ordered tree is also called a **skew heap.**

To avoid the problem of unduly long right paths, we make the resulting right path after a `merge` a left path. Such a merge results in a *skew heap*.

A recursive viewpoint is as follows. If we let L be the tree with the smaller root and R be the other tree, the following is true.

1. If one tree is empty, the other can be used as the merged result.
2. Otherwise, let *Temp* be the right subtree of L.
3. Make L's left subtree its new right subtree.
4. Make the result of the recursive merge of *Temp* and R the new left subtree of L.

A long right path is still possible. However, it rarely occurs and must be preceded by many merges involving short right paths.

We expect the result of the child swapping to be that the length of the right path will not be unduly large all the time. For instance, if we merge a pair of long right-path trees, the nodes involved in the path do not reappear on a right path for quite some time in the future. Obtaining trees that have the property that every node appears on a right path is still possible, but that can be done only as a result of a large number of relatively inexpensive merges. In Section 23.1.4, we prove this assertion rigorously by establishing that the amortized cost of a merge operation is only logarithmic.

23.1.4 Analysis of the Skew Heap

The actual cost of a merge is the number of nodes on the right paths of the two trees that are merged.

Suppose that we have two heaps, H_1 and H_2 and that there are r_1 and r_2 nodes on their respective right paths. Then the time required to perform the merge is proportional to $r_1 + r_2$. When we charge 1 unit for each node on the right paths, the cost of the merge is proportional to the number of charges. Because the trees have no structure, all the nodes in both trees may lie on the right path. This condition would give a $\Theta(N)$ worst-case bound for merging the trees (in Exercise 23.4 you are asked to construct such a tree). As we demonstrate shortly, the amortized time needed to merge two skew heaps is $O(\log N)$.

As with the splay tree, we introduce a potential function that cancels the varying costs of skew heap operations. We want the potential function to increase by a total of $O(\log N) - (r_1 + r_2)$ so that the total of the merge cost and potential change is only $O(\log N)$. If the potential is minimal prior to the first operation, applying the telescoping sum guarantees that the total spent for any M operations is $O(M \log N)$, as with the splay tree.

What we need is some potential function that captures the effect of skew heap operations. Finding such a function is quite challenging. Once we have found one, however, the proof is relatively short.

> **DEFINITION:** A node is a **heavy node** if the size of its right subtree is larger than the size of its left subtree. Otherwise, it is a **light node;** a node is light if its subtrees are of equal size.

The potential function is the number of heavy nodes. Only nodes on the merged path have their heavy or light status changed. The number of light nodes on a right path is logarithmic.

In Figure 23.3, prior to the merge, nodes 3 and 4 are heavy. After the merge, only node 3 is heavy. Three facts are easily shown. First, as a result of a merge, only nodes on the right path can have their heavy or light status changed because no other nodes have their subtrees altered. Second, a leaf is light. Third, the number of light nodes on the right path of an N node tree is at most $\lfloor \log N \rfloor + 1$. The reason is that the right child of a light node is less than half the size of the light node itself, and the halving principle applies. The additional +1 is a result of the leaf's being light. With these preliminaries, we can now state and prove Theorems 23.1 and 23.2.

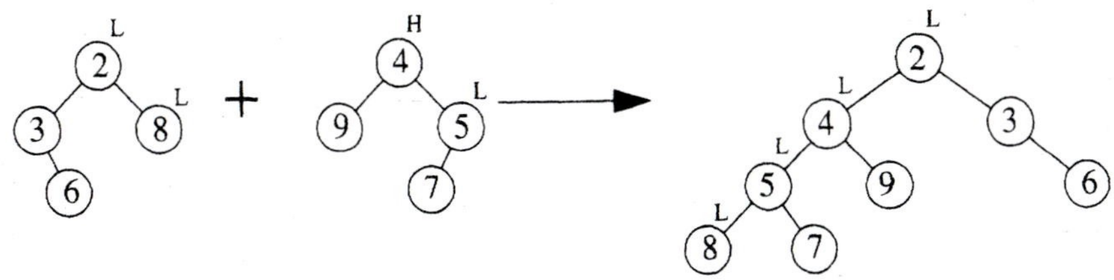

Figure 23.3 Change in the heavy or light status of nodes after a merge.

Theorem 23.1

Let H_1 and H_2 be two skew heaps with N_1 and N_2 nodes, respectively, and let N be their combined size (that is, $N_1 + N_2$). Suppose that the right path of H_1 has l_1 light nodes and h_1 heavy nodes, for a total of $l_1 + h_1$, whereas the right path of H_2 has l_2 light nodes and h_2 heavy nodes, for a total of $l_2 + h_2$. If the potential is defined as the total number of heavy nodes in the collection of skew heaps, then the merge costs at most $2 \log N + (h_1 + h_2)$, but the change in potential is at most $2 \log N - (h_1 + h_2)$.

Proof

The cost of the merge is merely the total number of nodes on the right paths, $l_1 + l_2 + h_1 + h_2$. The number of light nodes is logarithmic, so $l_1 \le \lfloor \log N_1 \rfloor + 1$ and $l_2 \le \lfloor \log N_2 \rfloor + 1$. Thus $l_1 + l_2 \le \log N_1 + \log N_2 + 2 \le 2 \log N$, where the last inequality follows from Theorem 22.4. The merge cost is thus at most $2 \log N + (h_1 + h_2)$. The bound on the potential change follows from the fact that only the nodes involved in the merge can have their heavy/light status changed and from the fact that any heavy node on the path must become light because its children are swapped. Even if all the light nodes became heavy, the potential change would still be limited to $l_1 + l_2 - (h_1 + h_2)$. Based on the same argument as before, that is at most $2 \log N - (h_1 + h_2)$.

Theorem 23.2

The amortized cost of the skew heap is at most $4 \log N$ for the `merge`, `insert`, *and* `deleteMin` *operations.*

Proof

Let Φ_i be the potential in the collection of skew heaps immediately following the ith operation. Note that $\Phi_0 = 0$ and $\Phi_i \ge 0$. An insertion creates a single node tree whose root is by definition light and thus does

Proof (continued)

not alter the potential prior to the resulting merge. A `deleteMin` *operation discards the root prior to the merge, so it cannot raise the potential (it may, in fact, lower it). We need to consider only the merging costs. Let* c_i *be the cost of the merge that occurs as a result of the ith operation. Then* $c_i + \Phi_i - \Phi_{i-1} \le 4 \log N$*. Telescoping over any M operations yields* $\sum_{i=1}^{M} c_i \le 4M \log N$ *because* $\Phi_M - \Phi_0$ *is not negative.*

Finding a useful potential function is the most difficult part of the analysis.

The skew heap is a remarkable example of a simple algorithm with an analysis that is not obvious. The analysis, however, is easy to perform once we have identified the appropriate potential function. Unfortunately, there is still no general theory that allows us to decide on a potential function. Typically, many different functions have to be tried before a usable one is found.

A nonrecursive algorithm should be used because of the possibility that we could run out of stack space.

One comment is in order: Although the initial description of the algorithm uses recursion and recursion provides the simplest code, it cannot be used in practice. The reason is that the linear worst-case time for an operation could cause an overflow of the procedure stack when the recursion is implemented. Consequently, a nonrecursive algorithm must be used. Rather than explore those possibilities, we discuss an alternative data structure that is slightly more complicated: the pairing heap. This data structure has not been completely analyzed, but it seems to perform well in practice.

23.2 The Pairing Heap

The *pairing heap* is a heap-ordered *M*-ary tree with no structural constraints. Its analysis is incomplete, but it appears to perform well in practice.

The **pairing heap** is a structurally unconstrained heap-ordered M-ary tree for which all operations except deletion take constant worst-case time. Although `deleteMin` could take linear worst-case time, any *sequence* of pairing heap operations has logarithmic amortized performance. It has been conjectured—but not proved—that even better performance is guaranteed. However, the best possible scenario—namely, that all operations except for `deleteMin` have constant amortized cost, while `deleteMin` has logarithmic amortized cost—has recently been shown to be untrue.

The pairing heap is stored by using a left child/right sibling representation. A third pointer is used for `decreaseKey`.

Figure 23.4 shows an abstract pairing heap. The actual implementation uses a left child/right sibling representation (see Chapter 18). The `decreaseKey` method, as we discuss shortly, requires that each node contain an additional pointer. A node that is a leftmost child contains a pointer to its parent; otherwise, the node is a right sibling and contains a pointer to its left sibling. This representation is shown in Figure 23.5, where the darkened line indicates that two pointers (one in each direction) connect pairs of nodes.

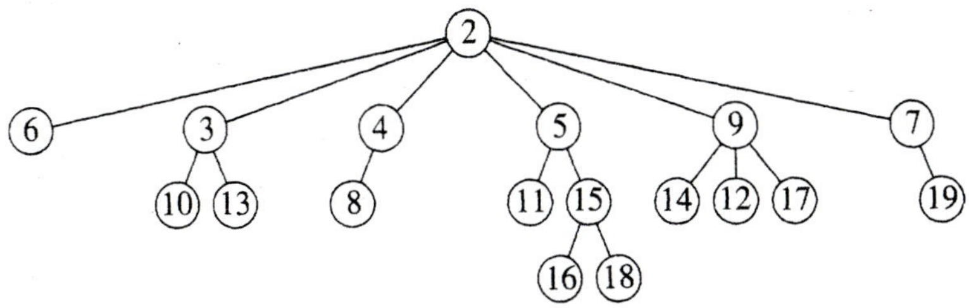

Figure 23.4 Abstract representation of a sample pairing heap.

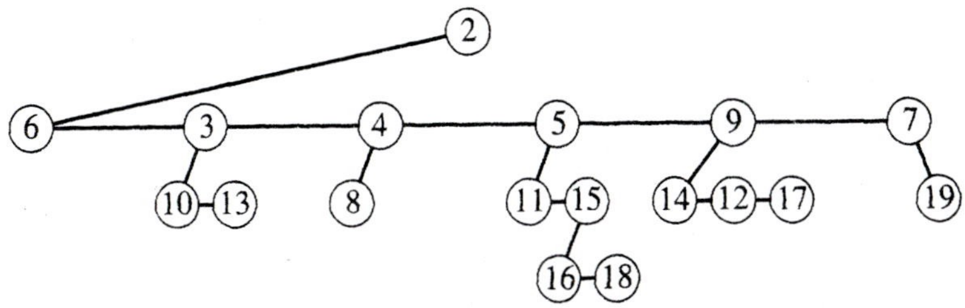

Figure 23.5 Actual representation of the pairing heap shown in Figure 23.4; the dark line represents a pair of pointers that connect nodes in both directions.

23.2.1 Pairing Heap Operations

Merging is simple: Attach the larger root tree as a left child of the smaller root tree. Insertion and decreasing are also simple.

In principle, the basic pairing heap operations are simple, which is why the pairing heap performs well in practice. To merge two pairing heaps, we make the heap with the larger root the new first child of the heap with the smaller root. Insertion is a special case of merging. To perform a `decreaseKey` operation, we lower the value of the requested node. Because we are not maintaining parent pointers for all nodes, we do not know if this action violates the heap order. Thus we detach the adjusted node from its parent and complete `decreaseKey` by merging the two pairing heaps that result. Figure 23.5 shows that detaching a node from its parent means removing it from what is essentially a linked list of children. So far we are in great shape: Every operation described takes constant time. However, we are not so lucky with the `deleteMin` operation.

The `deleteMin` operation is expensive because the new root could be any of the *c* children of the old root. We need *c* − 1 merges.

To perform a `deleteMin`, we must remove the root of the tree, creating a collection of heaps. If there are c children of the root, combining these heaps into one heap requires $c - 1$ merges. Hence, if there are lots of children of the root, the `deleteMin` operation costs lots of time. If the insertion sequence is 1, 2, ..., N, then 1 is at the root and all the other items are in nodes that are children of the root. Consequently, `deleteMin` is $O(N)$ time. The best that we can hope to do is to arrange the merges so that we do not have repeatedly expensive `deleteMin` operations.

The order in which pairing heap subtrees are merged is important. The simplest algorithm is *two-pass merging*.

The order in which pairing heap subtrees are merged is important. The simplest and most practical of the many variants of doing so that have been proposed is **two-pass merging,** in which a first scan merges pairs of children from left to right[2] and then a second scan, right to left, is performed to complete the merging. After the first scan, we have half as many trees to merge. In the second scan, at each step, we merge the rightmost tree that remains from the first scan with the current merged result. For example, if we have children c_1 through c_8, the first scan performs the merges c_1 and c_2, c_3 and c_4, c_5 and c_6, and c_7 and c_8. The result is d_1, d_2, d_3, and d_4. We perform the second pass by merging d_3 and d_4; d_2 is then merged with that result, and d_1 is then merged with the result of that merge, completing the `deleteMin` operation. Figure 23.6 shows the result of using `deleteMin` on the pairing heap shown in Figure 23.5.

Several alternatives have been proposed. Most are indistinguishable, but using a single left-to-right pass is a bad idea.

Other merging strategies are possible. For instance, we can place each subtree (corresponding to a child) on a queue, repeatedly dequeue two trees, and then enqueue the result of merging them. After $c - 1$ merges, only one tree remains on the queue, which is the result of the `deleteMin`. However, using a stack instead of a queue is a disaster because the root of the resulting tree may possibly have $c - 1$ children. If that occurs in a sequence, the `deleteMin` operation will have linear, rather than logarithmic, amortized cost per operation. In Exercise 23.12 you are asked to construct such a sequence.

23.2.2 Implementation of the Pairing Heap

The `prev` data member points to either a left sibling or a parent.

The `PairingHeap` class interface is shown in Figure 23.7. The nested typedef `Position`, declared at line 28, is declared as equivalent to a pointer to a `PairNode<Comparable>`. The standard priority queue operations are provided, with three main differences.

The `insert` routine returns a pointer to the new node for use by `decreaseKey`.

First, `insert` returns a `Position`. Second, we add the `decreaseKey` method, which requires a `Position` as a parameter. Third, the Big Three cannot safely be implemented with the normal recursive algorithm because the depth of the recursion may be too large. The online code has an unsafe implementation, and in Exercise 23.12 you are asked to improve it.

The basic node of a pairing heap, `PairNode`, is shown in Figure 23.8 and consists of an item and three pointers. Two of these pointers are the left

---

2. Care must be exercised if there are an odd number of children. When that happens, we merge the last child with the result of the rightmost merge to complete the first scan.

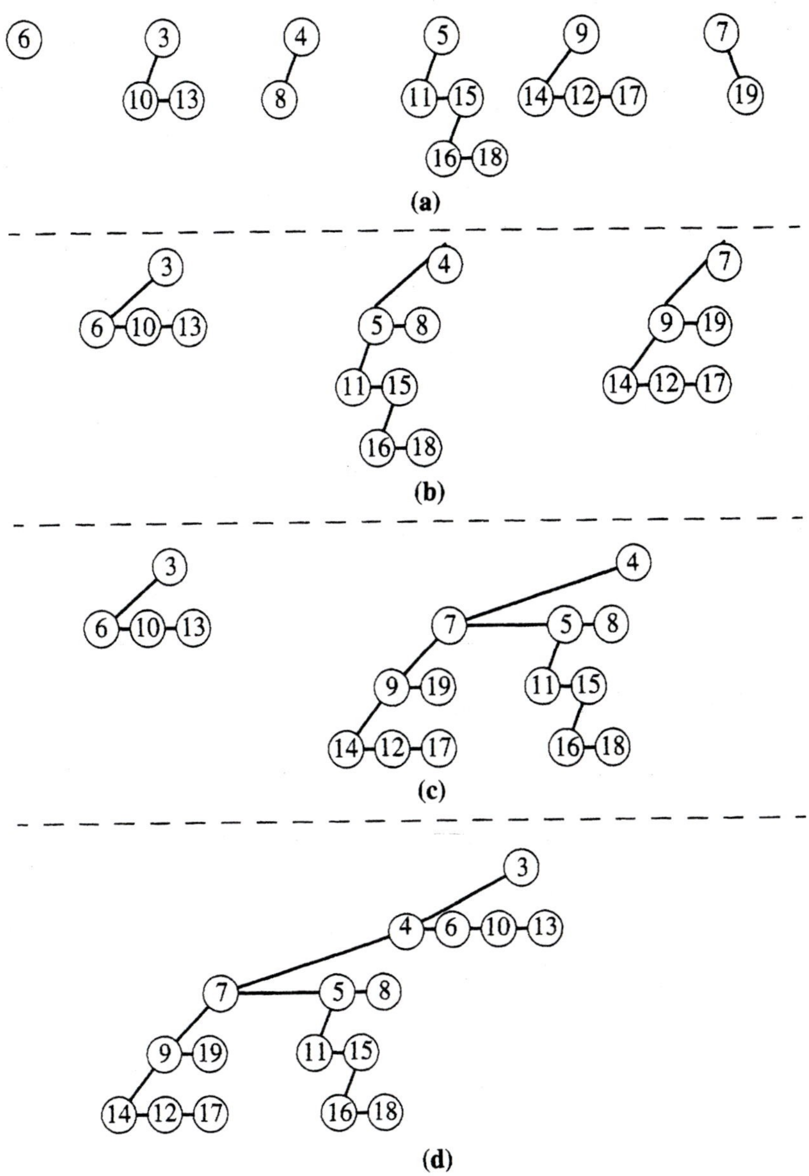

Figure 23.6 Recombination of siblings after a `deleteMin`. In each merge, the larger root tree is made the left child of the smaller root tree: (a) the resulting trees; (b) after the first pass; (c) after the first merge of the second pass; (d) after the second merge of the second pass.

```
template <class Comparable>
class PairNode;

// Pairing heap class.
//
// CONSTRUCTION: with no parameters.
//
// *****************PUBLIC OPERATIONS*********************
// Position insert( x )    --> Insert x
// void deleteMin( min )   --> Remove smallest item
// Comparable findMin( )   --> Return smallest item
// bool isEmpty( )         --> Return true if empty; else false
// void makeEmpty( )       --> Remove all items
// void decreaseKey( Position p, newVal )
//                         --> Decrease value in position p
// *****************ERRORS*******************************
// Throws exceptions as warranted.

template <class Comparable>
class PairingHeap
{
  public:
    PairingHeap( );
    PairingHeap( const PairingHeap & rhs );
    ~PairingHeap( );

    typedef PairNode<Comparable> Node;
    typedef Node * Position;

    bool isEmpty( ) const;
    const Comparable & findMin( ) const;

    Position insert( const Comparable & x );
    void deleteMin( );
    void deleteMin( Comparable & minItem );
    void makeEmpty( );
    void decreaseKey( Position p, const Comparable & newVal );

    const PairingHeap & operator=( const PairingHeap & rhs );

  private:
    PairNode<Comparable> *root;

    void reclaimMemory( Node *t ) const;
    void compareAndLink( Node * & first, Node *second ) const;
    PairNode<Comparable> *combineSiblings(
                                Node *firstSibling ) const;
    PairNode<Comparable> *clone( Node *t ) const;
};
```

Figure 23.7 The `PairingHeap` class interface.

```
template <class Comparable>
class PairNode
{
    Comparable   element;
    PairNode    *leftChild;
    PairNode    *nextSibling;
    PairNode    *prev;

    PairNode( const Comparable & theElement )
      : element( theElement ), leftChild( NULL ),
        nextSibling( NULL ), prev( NULL ) { }
    friend class PairingHeap<Comparable>;
};
```

Figure 23.8 The `PairNode` class.

```
// Find the smallest item in the priority queue.
// Return the smallest item, or throw UnderflowException if empty.
template <class Comparable>
const Comparable & PairingHeap<Comparable>::findMin( ) const
{
    if( isEmpty( ) )
        throw UnderflowException( );
    return root->element;
}
```

Figure 23.9 The `findMin` member for the `PairingHeap` class.

child and the next sibling. The third pointer is `prev`, which points to the parent if the node is a first child or to a left sibling otherwise.

The `findMin` routine is coded in Figure 23.9. The minimum is at the root, so this routine is easily implemented. The `insert` routine, shown in Figure 23.10, creates a one-node tree and merges it with the `root` to obtain a new tree. As mentioned earlier in the section, `insert` returns a pointer to the newly allocated node. Note that we must handle the special case of an insertion in an empty tree.

Figure 23.11 implements the two `deleteMin` routines. If the pairing heap is empty, we have an error. Otherwise, at line 9 we save a pointer to the root (so that it can be deleted at line 16). After saving the value in the root, we make a call to `combineSiblings` at line 14 to merge the root's subtrees and set the result to the new root. If there are no subtrees, we merely set `root` to `NULL` at line 12.

The `deleteMin` operation is implemented as a call to `combineSiblings`.

The `decreaseKey` method is implemented in Figure 23.12. If the new value is larger than the original, we might destroy the heap order. We have no way of knowing that without examining all the children. Because many

```
// Insert item x into the priority queue.
// Return a pointer to the node containing the new item.
template <class Comparable>
PairingHeap<Comparable>::Position
PairingHeap<Comparable>::insert( const Comparable & x )
{
    Node *newNode = new Node( x );

    if( root == NULL )
        root = newNode;
    else
        compareAndLink( root, newNode );
    return newNode;
}
```

Figure 23.10 The `insert` routine for the `PairingHeap` class.

```
// Remove the smallest item from the priority queue.
// Throws UnderflowException if empty.
template <class Comparable>
void PairingHeap<Comparable>::deleteMin( )
{
    if( isEmpty( ) )
        throw UnderflowException( );

    Node *oldRoot = root;

    if( root->leftChild == NULL )
        root = NULL;
    else
        root = combineSiblings( root->leftChild );

    delete oldRoot;
}

// Remove the smallest item from the priority queue.
// Pass back the smallest item, or throw UnderflowException if empty.
template <class Comparable>
void PairingHeap<Comparable>::deleteMin( Comparable & minItem )
{
    minItem = findMin( );
    deleteMin( );
}
```

Figure 23.11 The `deleteMin` members for the `PairingHeap` class.

```
1 // Change the value of the item stored in the pairing heap.
2 // p is a position returned by insert.
3 // newVal is the new value, which must be smaller
4 //    than the currently stored value.
5 // Throws BadArgumentException if newVal is not small enough.
6 template <class Comparable>
7 void PairingHeap<Comparable>::
8 decreaseKey( Position p, const Comparable & newVal )
9 {
10     if( p->element < newVal )
11         throw BadArgumentException( );
12
13     p->element = newVal;
14     if( p != root )
15     {
16         if( p->nextSibling != NULL )
17             p->nextSibling->prev = p->prev;
18         if( p->prev->leftChild == p )
19             p->prev->leftChild = p->nextSibling;
20         else
21             p->prev->nextSibling = p->nextSibling;
22
23         p->nextSibling = NULL;
24         compareAndLink( root, p );
25     }
26 }
```

Figure 23.12 The `decreaseKey` method for the `PairingHeap` class.

children may exist, doing so would be inefficient. Thus we assume that it is always an error to attempt to increase the key by using the `decreaseKey`. (In Exercise 23.9 you are asked to describe an algorithm for `increaseKey`.) After performing this test, we lower the value in the node. If the node is the root, we are done. Otherwise, we splice the node out of the list of children that it is in, using the code in lines 16 to 23. After doing that, we merely merge the resulting tree with the root.

The two remaining routines are `compareAndLink`, which combines two trees, and `combineSiblings`, which combines all the siblings, when given the first sibling. Figure 23.13 shows how two subheaps are combined. The procedure is generalized to allow the second subheap to have siblings (which is needed for the second pass in the two-pass merge). As mentioned earlier in the chapter, the subheap with the larger root is made a leftmost child of the other subheap, the code for which is shown in Figure 23.14. Note that in several instances a pointer is tested against `NULL` before it accesses its `prev` data member. This action suggests that having a `nullNode` sentinel—as was customary in the advanced search tree implementations—might be useful. This possibility is left for you to explore as Exercise 23.14.

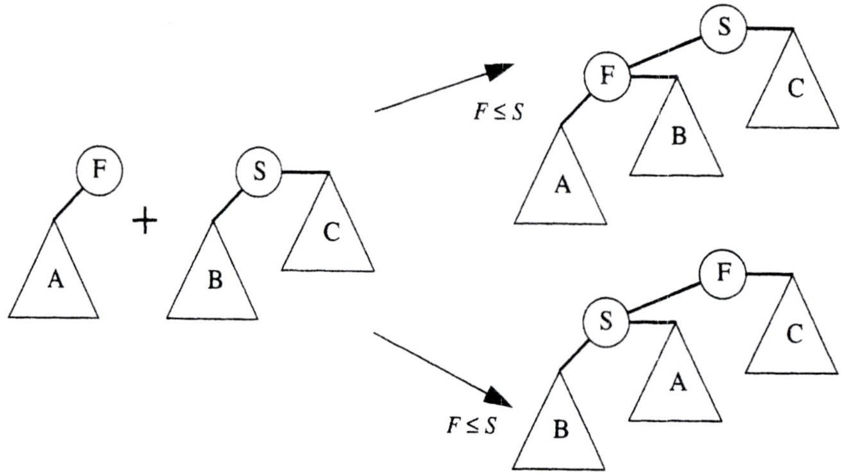

Figure 23.13 The `compareAndLink` method merges two trees.

Finally, Figure 23.15 implements `combineSiblings`. We use the `vector treeArray` to store the subtrees. We begin by separating the subtrees and storing them in `treeArray`, using the loop at lines 15 to 20. Assuming that we have more than one sibling to merge, we make a left-to-right pass at lines 26 and 27. The special case of an odd number of trees is handled at lines 31–33. We finish the merging with a right-to-left pass at lines 37 and 38. Once we have finished, the result appears in array position 0 and can be returned.

As a practical matter, dynamically allocating and deallocating the `vector` can be unduly expensive and is probably not always needed. We may be better off using a static `vector` object that can be resized as needed and build the entries without using `push_back`.

23.2.3 Application: Dijkstra's Shortest Weighted Path Algorithm

The `decreaseKey` operation is an improvement for Dijkstra's algorithm in instances for which there are many calls to it.

As an example of how the `decreaseKey` operation is used, we rewrite Dijkstra's algorithm (see Section 15.3). Recall that at any point we are maintaining a priority queue of `Path` objects, ordered by the `dist` data member. For each vertex in the graph, we needed only one `Path` object in the priority queue at any instant, but for convenience we had many. In this section, we rework the code so that if a vertex w's distance is lowered, its position in the priority queue is found, and a `decreaseKey` operation is performed for its corresponding `Path` object.

```
// Internal method that is the basic operation to
// maintain order.
// Links first and second together to satisfy heap order.
// first is root of tree 1, which may not be NULL.
//    first->nextSibling MUST be NULL on entry.
// second is root of tree 2, which may be NULL.
// first becomes the result of the tree merge.
template <class Comparable>
void PairingHeap<Comparable>::
compareAndLink( Node * & first, Node *second ) const
{
    if( second == NULL )
        return;

    if( second->element < first->element )
    {
          // Attach first as leftmost child of second
        second->prev = first->prev;
        first->prev = second;
        first->nextSibling = second->leftChild;
        if( first->nextSibling != NULL )
            first->nextSibling->prev = first;
        second->leftChild = first;
        first = second;
    }
    else
    {
          // Attach second as leftmost child of first
        second->prev = first;
        first->nextSibling = second->nextSibling;
        if( first->nextSibling != NULL )
            first->nextSibling->prev = first;
        second->nextSibling = first->leftChild;
        if( second->nextSibling != NULL )
            second->nextSibling->prev = second;
        first->leftChild = second;
    }
}
```

Figure 23.14 The `compareAndLink` routine.

The new code is shown in Figure 23.16, and all the changes are relatively minor. First, at line 4 we declare that `pq` is a pairing heap rather than a binary heap. Note that the `Vertex` object has an additional data member `pos` that represents its position in the priority queue (and is `NULL` if the `Vertex` is not in the priority queue). Initially, all the positions are `NULL` (which is done in `clearAll`). Whenever a vertex is inserted in the pairing

```
// Internal method that implements two-pass merging.
// firstSibling is the root of the conglomerate and
// is assumed not NULL.
template <class Comparable>
PairNode<Comparable> *
PairingHeap<Comparable>::
combineSiblings( Node *firstSibling ) const
{
    if( firstSibling->nextSibling == NULL )
        return firstSibling;

    vector<Node *> treeArray;

      // Store the subtrees in an array
    while( firstSibling != NULL )
    {
        treeArray.push_back( firstSibling );
        firstSibling->prev->nextSibling = NULL;  // break links
        firstSibling = firstSibling->nextSibling;
    }

    int numSiblings = treeArray.size( );

      // Combine subtrees two at a time, going left to right
    int i = 0;
    for( ; i + 1 < numSiblings; i += 2 )
        compareAndLink( treeArray[ i ], treeArray[ i + 1 ] );

      // j has the result of last compareAndLink.
      // If an odd number of trees, get the last one.
    int j = i - 2;
    if( j == numSiblings - 3 )
        compareAndLink( treeArray[ j ], treeArray[ j + 2 ] );

      // Now go right to left, merging last tree with
      // next to last. The result becomes the new last.
    for( ; j >= 2; j -= 2 )
        compareAndLink( treeArray[ j - 2 ], treeArray[ j ] );

    return treeArray[ 0 ];
}
```

Figure 23.15 The heart of the pairing heap algorithm: implementing a two-pass merge to combine all the siblings, given the first sibling.

```
// Single-source weighted shortest-path algorithm.
void Graph::dijkstra( const string & startName )
{
    PairingHeap<Path> pq;
    Path vrec;     // Stores the result of a deleteMin

    vmap::iterator itr = vertexMap.find( startName );
    if( itr == vertexMap.end( ) )
        throw GraphException( startName + " not in graph" );

    clearAll( );
    Vertex *start = (*itr).second;
    start->dist = 0;
    start->pos = pq.insert( Path( start, 0 ) );

    while( !pq.isEmpty( ) )
    {
        pq.deleteMin( vrec );
        Vertex *v = vrec.dest;

        for( int i = 0; i < v->adj.size( ); i++ )
        {
            Edge e = v->adj[ i ];
            Vertex *w = e.dest;
            double cvw = e.cost;

            if( cvw < 0 )
                throw GraphException( "Negative edges" );

            if( w->dist > v->dist + cvw )
            {
                w->dist = v->dist + cvw;
                w->path = v;
                Path newVal( w, w->dist );

                if( w->pos == NULL )
                    w->pos = pq.insert( newVal );
                else
                    pq.decreaseKey( w->pos, newVal );
            }
        }
    }
}
```

Figure 23.16 Dijkstra's algorithm, using the pairing heap and the `decreaseKey` operation.

heap, we adjust its `pos` data member—at lines 14 and 37. The algorithm itself is simplified. Now, we merely call `deleteMin` so long as the pairing heap is not empty, rather than repeatedly calling `deleteMin` until an unseen vertex emerges. Consequently, we no longer need the `scratch` data member. Compare lines 16–19 to the corresponding code presented in Figure 15.28. All that remains to be done are the updates after line 30 that indicate a change is in order. If the vertex has never been placed in the priority queue, we insert it for the first time, updating its `pos` data member. Otherwise, we merely call `decreaseKey` at line 39.

Whether the binary heap implementation of Dijkstra's algorithm is faster than the pairing heap implementation depends on several factors. One study (see the Reference section), suggests that the pairing heap is slightly better than the binary heap when both are carefully implemented. The results depend heavily on the coding details and the frequency of the `decreaseKey` operations. More study is needed to decide when the pairing heap is suitable in practice.

Summary

In this chapter we described two data structures that support merging and that are efficient in the amortized sense: the skew heap and the pairing heap. Both are easy to implement because they lack a rigid structure property. The pairing heap seems to have practical utility, but its complete analysis remains an intriguing open problem.

In Chapter 24, which is the last chapter, we describe a data structure that is used to maintain disjoint sets and that also has a remarkable amortized analysis.

Objects of the Game

pairing heap A structurally unconstrained heap-ordered M-ary tree for which all operations except deletion take constant worst-case time. Its analysis is not complete, but it appears to perform well in practice. (p. 828)

skew heap A heap-ordered binary tree without a balancing condition that supports all operations in logarithmic amortized time. (p. 823)

two-pass merging The order in which the pairing heap subtrees are merged is important. The simplest algorithm is two-pass merging, in which subtrees are merged in pairs in a left-to-right scan and then a right-to-left scan is performed to finish the merging. (p. 832)

Common Errors

1. A recursive implementation of the skew heap cannot be used in practice because the depth of the recursion could be linear.
2. Be careful not to lose track of the `prev` pointers in the skew heap.
3. Tests to ensure that references are not `NULL` must be made throughout the pairing heap code.
4. When a merge is performed, a node should not reside in two pairing heaps.

On the Internet

The pairing heap class is available, with a test program. It does not carefully implement the Big Three. Figure 23.16 is part of the `Graph` class shown in Chapter 15 (**Paths.cpp**).

PairingHeap.h	Contains the `PairingHeap` class interface.
PairingHeap.cpp	Contains the implementation for the `PairingHeap` class.
TestPairingHeap.cpp	Contains a test program for the `PairingHeap` class.

Exercises

In Short

23.1. Show the result of a skew heap built from the insertion sequence
  a. 1, 2, 3, 4, 5, 6, 7.
  b. 4, 3, 5, 2, 6, 7, 1.

23.2. Show the result of a pairing heap built from the insertion sequence
  a. 1, 2, 3, 4, 5, 6, 7.
  b. 4, 3, 5, 2, 6, 7, 1.

23.3. For each heap in Exercises 23.1 and 23.2, show the result of two `deleteMin` operations.

In Theory

23.4. Show that the logarithmic amortized bound for skew heap operations is not a worst-case bound by giving a sequence of operations that lead to a `merge` that requires linear time.

23.5. Show that both the `decreaseKey` and `increaseKey` operations can be supported by skew heaps in logarithmic amortized time.

23.6. Describe a linear-time `buildHeap` algorithm for the skew heap.

23.7. Show that storing the length of the right path for each node in the tree enables you to impose a balancing condition that yields logarithmic worst-case time per operation. Such a structure is called a *leftist heap*.

23.8. Show that using a stack to implement the `combineSiblings` operation for pairing heaps is bad. Do so by constructing a sequence that has linear amortized cost per operation.

23.9. Describe how to implement `increaseKey` for pairing heaps.

23.10. Give a simple algorithm to remove all the nodes from a skew heap. Keep in mind that the depth may be $O(N)$.

In Practice

23.11. Add the public `merge` member function to the `PairingHeap` class. Be sure that a node appears in only one tree.

Programming Problems

23.12. Implement the Big Three for the pairing heap.

23.13. Implement a nonrecursive version of the skew heap algorithm.

23.14. Implement the pairing heap algorithm with a `nullNode` sentinel.

23.15. Implement the queue algorithm for `combineSiblings` and compare its performance with the two-pass algorithm code shown in Figure 23.15.

23.16. If the `decreaseKey` operation is not supported, parent pointers are not necessary. Implement the pairing heap algorithm without parent pointers and compare its performance with the binary heap and/or skew heap and/or splay tree algorithm.

References

The *leftist heap* [1] was the first efficient mergeable priority queue. It is the worst-case variant of the skew heap suggested in Exercise 23.7. Skew heaps are described in [6], which also contains solutions to Exercises 23.4 and 23.5.

[3] describes the pairing heap and proves that, when two-pass merging is used, the amortized cost of all operations is logarithmic. It was long conjectured that the amortized cost of all operations except `deleteMin` is actually constant and that the amortized cost of the `deleteMin` is logarithmic, so that any sequence of D `deleteMin` and I other operations takes $O(I + D \log N)$ time. However, this conjecture was recently shown to be false [2]. A data structure that does achieve this bound, but is too complicated to be practical, is the *Fibonacci heap* [4]. The hope is that the pairing heap is a practical alternative to the theoretically interesting Fibonacci heap, even though its worst-case is slightly worse. Leftist heaps and Fibonacci heaps are discussed in [7].

In [5] is a comparison of various priority queues in the setting of solving the minimum spanning tree problem (discussed in Section 24.2.2) using a method very similar to Dijkstra's algorithm.

1. C. A. Crane, "Linear Lists and Priority Queues as Balanced Binary Trees," *Technical Report STAN-CS-72-259,* Computer Science Department, Stanford University, Palo Alto, Calif., 1972.
2. M. L. Fredman, "On the Efficiency of Pairing Heaps and Related Data Structures," *Journal of the ACM,* to appear.
3. M. L. Fredman, R. Sedgewick, D. D. Sleator, and R. E. Tarjan, "The Pairing Heap: A New Form of Self-adjusting Heap," *Algorithmica* **1** (1986), 111–129.
4. M. L. Fredman and R. E. Tarjan, "Fibonacci Heaps and Their Uses in Improved Network Optimization Algorithms," *Journal of the ACM* **34** (1987), 596–615.
5. B. M. E. Moret and H. D. Shapiro, "An Empirical Analysis of Algorithms for Constructing a Minimum Spanning Tree," *Proceedings of the Second Workshop on Algorithms and Data Structures* (1991), 400–411.
6. D. D. Sleator and R. E. Tarjan, "Self-adjusting Heaps," *SIAM Journal on Computing* **15** (1986), 52–69.
7. M. A. Weiss, *Data Structures and Algorithm Analysis in C++*, 2d ed., Addison-Wesley, Reading, Mass., 1999.

Chapter 24

The Disjoint Set Class

In this chapter we describe an efficient data structure for solving the equivalence problem: the disjoint set class. This data structure is simple to implement, with each routine requiring only a few lines of code. Its implementation is also extremely fast, requiring constant average time per operation. This data structure is also very interesting from a theoretical point of view because its analysis is extremely difficult; the functional form of the worst case is unlike any discussed so far in this text.

In this chapter, we show:

- three simple applications of the disjoint set class,
- a way to implement the disjoint set class with minimal coding effort,
- a method for increasing the speed of the disjoint set class, using two simple observations, and
- an analysis of the running time of a fast implementation of the disjoint set class.

24.1 Equivalence Relations

A **relation** R is defined on a set S if for every pair of elements (a, b), $a, b \in S$, $a\ R\ b$ is either true or false. If $a\ R\ b$ is true, we say that a is related to b.

A *relation* is defined on a set if every pair of elements either is related or is not. An *equivalence relation* is reflexive, symmetric, and transitive.

An **equivalence relation** is a relation R that satisfies three properties.

1. *Reflexive:* $a\ R\ a$ is true for all $a \in S$.
2. *Symmetric:* $a\ R\ b$ if and only if $b\ R\ a$.
3. *Transitive:* $a\ R\ b$ and $b\ R\ c$ implies that $a\ R\ c$.

Electrical connectivity, where all connections are by metal wires, is an equivalence relation. The relation is clearly reflexive, as any component is connected to itself. If a is electrically connected to b, then b must be electrically connected to a, so the relation is symmetric. Finally, if a is connected to b and b is connected to c, then a is connected to c.

Likewise, connectivity through a bidirectional network forms equivalence classes of connected components. However, if the connections in the network are directed (i.e., a connection from v to w does not imply one from w to v), we do not have an equivalence relation because the symmetric property does not hold. An example is a relation in which town a is related to town b if traveling from a to b by road is possible. This relationship is an equivalence relation if the roads are two-way.

24.2 Dynamic Equivalence and Two Applications

For any equivalence relation, denoted ~, the natural problem is to decide for any a and b whether $a \sim b$. If the relation is stored as a two-dimensional array of Boolean variables, equivalence can be tested in constant time. The problem is that the relation is usually implicitly, rather than explicitly, defined.

For example, an equivalence relation is defined over the five-element set $\{a_1, a_2, a_3, a_4, a_5\}$. This set yields 25 pairs of elements, each of which either is or is not related. However, the information that $a_1 \sim a_2$, $a_3 \sim a_4$, $a_1 \sim a_5$, and $a_4 \sim a_2$ are all related implies that all pairs are related. We want to be able to infer this condition quickly.

The *equivalence class* of an element *x* in set *S* is the subset of *S* that contains all the elements related to *x*. The equivalence classes form *disjoint sets*.

The **equivalence class** of an element $x \in S$ is the subset of S that contains all the elements related to x. Note that the equivalence classes form a partition of S: Every member of S appears in exactly one equivalence class. To decide whether $a \sim b$, we need only check whether a and b are in the same equivalence class. This information provides the strategy to solve the equivalence problem.

The input is initially a collection of N sets, each with one element. In this initial representation all relations (except reflexive relations) are false. Each set has a different element, so $S_i \cap S_j = \varnothing$ and such sets (in which any two sets contain no common elements) are called **disjoint sets.**

The two basic disjoint set class operations are `union` and `find`.

The two basic **disjoint set class** operations are `find`, which returns the name of the set (i.e., the equivalence class) containing a given element, and the `union`, which adds relations. If we want to add the pair (a, b) to the list of relations, we first determine whether a and b are already related. We do so by performing `find` operations on both a and b and finding out whether they are in the same equivalence class; if they are not, we apply `union`.[1] This operation merges the two equivalence classes containing a and b into a new equivalence class. In terms of sets the result is a new set $S_k = S_i \cup S_j$, which we create by simultaneously destroying the originals and preserving the disjointedness of all the sets. The data structure to do this is often called the disjoint set **union/find data structure.** The **union/find algorithm** is executed by processing union/find requests within the disjoint set data structure.

The algorithm is *dynamic* because, during the course of algorithm execution, the sets can change via the `union` operation. The algorithm must also operate as an **online algorithm** so that, when a `find` is performed, an answer must be given before the next query can be viewed. Another possibility is an **offline algorithm** in which the entire sequence of `union` and `find` requests are made visible. The answer it provides for each `find` must still be consistent with all the `union`s performed before the `find`. However, the algorithm can give all its answers after it has dealt with *all* the questions. This distinction is similar to the difference between taking a written exam (which is generally offline because you only have to give the answers before time expires) and taking an oral exam (which is online because you must answer the current question before proceeding to the next question).

In an *online algorithm*, an answer must be provided for each query before the next query can be viewed.

Note that we do not perform any operations to compare the relative values of elements but merely require knowledge of their location. For this reason, we can assume that all elements have been numbered sequentially, starting from 0, and that the numbering can be determined easily by some hashing scheme.

The set elements are numbered sequentially, starting from 0.

Before describing how to implement the `union` and `find` operations, we provide three applications of the data structure.

24.2.1 Application: Generating Mazes

An example of the use of the union/find data structure is to generate mazes, such as the one shown in Figure 24.1. The starting point is the top-left corner, and the ending point is the bottom-right corner. We can view the maze as a 50×88 rectangle of cells in which the top-left cell is connected to the bottom-right cell, and cells are separated from their neighboring cells via walls.

A simple algorithm to generate the maze is to start with walls everywhere (except for the entrance and exit). We then continually choose a wall randomly, and knock it down if the cells that the wall separates are not already connected to each other. If we repeat this process until the starting and ending cells are connected, we have a maze. Continuing to knock down

1. Unfortunately, `union` is a (little-used) keyword in C++. We use `union` throughout this section, but when we write code, we use `unionSets` as the function name.

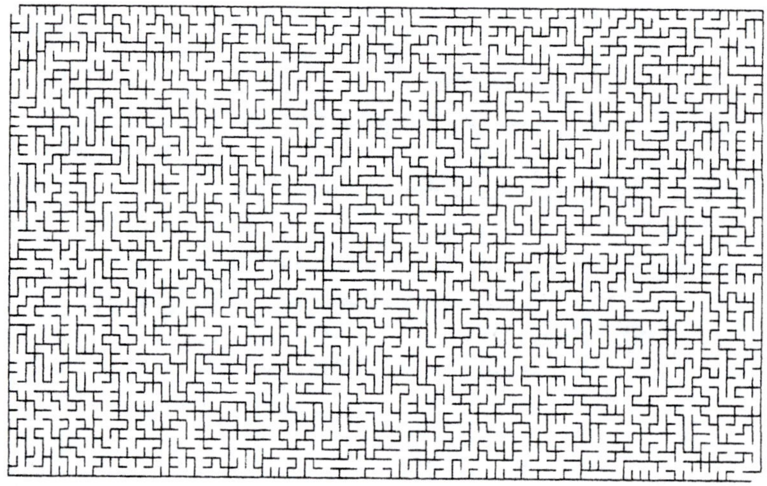

Figure 24.1 A 50 × 88 maze.

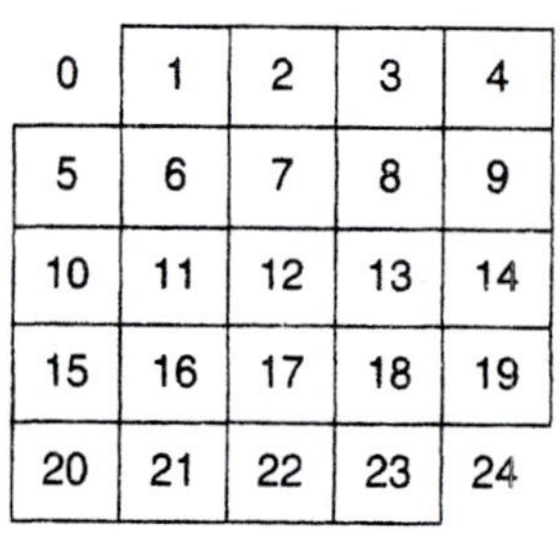

{0} {1} {2} {3} {4} {5} {6} {7} {8} {9} {10} {11} {12} {13} {14}
{15} {16} {17} {18} {19} {20} {21} {22} {23} {24}

Figure 24.2 Initial state: All walls are up, and all cells are in their own sets.

walls until every cell is reachable from every other cell is actually better because doing so generates more false leads in the maze.

We illustrate the algorithm with a 5 × 5 maze, and Figure 24.2 shows the initial configuration. We use the union/find data structure to represent sets of cells that are connected to each other. Initially, walls are everywhere, and each cell is in its own equivalence class.

Figure 24.3 shows a later stage of the algorithm, after a few walls have been knocked down. Suppose, at this stage, that we randomly target the wall that connects cells 8 and 13. Because 8 and 13 are already connected (they are in the same set), we would not remove the wall because to do so would simply

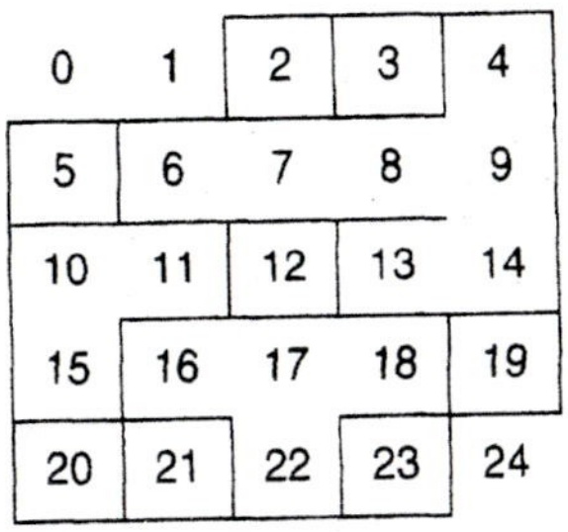

{0, 1} {2} {3} {4, 6, 7, 8, 9, 13, 14} {5} {10, 11, 15} {12}
{16, 17, 18, 22} {19} {20} {21} {23} {24}

Figure 24.3 At some point in the algorithm, several walls have been knocked down and sets have been merged. At this point, if we randomly select the wall between 8 and 13, this wall is not knocked down because 8 and 13 are already connected.

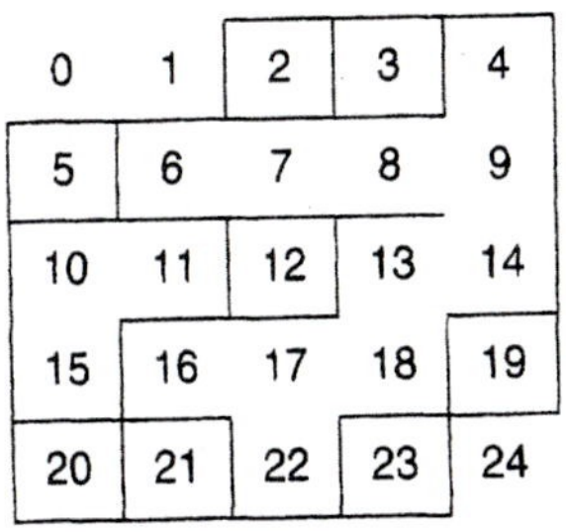

{0, 1} {2} {3} {5} {10, 11, 15} {12}
{4, 6, 7, 8, 9, 13, 14, 16, 17, 18, 22} {19} {20} {21} {23} {24}

Figure 24.4 We randomly select the wall between squares 18 and 13 in Figure 24.3; this wall has been knocked down because 18 and 13 were not already connected, and their sets have been merged.

trivialize the maze. Suppose that we randomly target cells 18 and 13 next. By performing two `find` operations, we determine that these cells are in different sets; thus 18 and 13 are not already connected. Therefore we knock down the wall that separates them, as shown in Figure 24.4. As a result of this operation, the sets containing cells 18 and 13 are combined by a `union` operation. The reason is that all the cells previously connected to 18 are now connected to all the cells previously connected to 13. At the end of the algorithm, as depicted in Figure 24.5, all the cells are connected, and we are done.

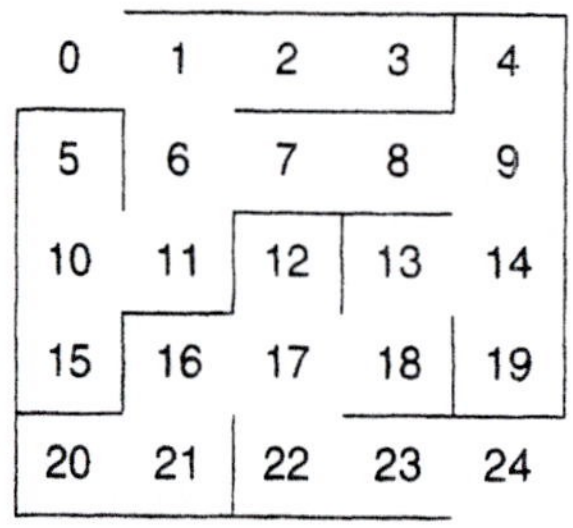

{0, 1, 2, 3, 4, 5, 6, 7, 8, 9, 10, 11, 12, 13, 14, 15, 16, 17, 18, 19, 20, 21, 22, 23, 24}

Figure 24.5 Eventually, 24 walls have been knocked down, and all the elements are in the same set.

The running time of the algorithm is dominated by the union/find costs. The size of the union/find universe is the number of cells. The number of `find` operations is proportional to the number of cells because the number of removed walls is 1 less than the number of cells. If we look carefully, however, we can see that there are only about twice as many walls as cells in the first place. Thus, if N is the number of cells and as there are two `find`s per randomly targeted wall, we get an estimate of between (roughly) $2N$ and $4N$ `find` operations throughout the algorithm. Therefore the algorithm's running time depends on the cost of $O(N)$ `union` and $O(N)$ `find` operations.

24.2.2 Application: Minimum Spanning Trees

The *minimum spanning tree* is a connected subgraph of *G* that spans all vertices at minimum total cost.

A **spanning tree** of an undirected graph is a tree formed by graph edges that connect all the vertices of the graph. Unlike the graphs in Chapter 15, an edge (u, v) in a graph G is identical to an edge (v, u). The cost of a spanning tree is the sum of the costs of the edges in the tree. The **minimum spanning tree** is a connected subgraph of G that spans all vertices at minimum cost. A minimum spanning tree exists only if the subgraph of G is connected. As we show shortly, testing a graph's connectivity can be done as part of the minimum spanning tree computation.

In Figure 24.6(b), the graph is a minimum spanning tree of the graph in Figure 24.6(a) (it happens to be unique, which is unusual if the graph has many edges of equal cost). Note that the number of edges in the minimum spanning tree is $|V| - 1$. The minimum spanning tree is a *tree* because it is acyclic, it is *spanning* because it covers every vertex, and it is *minimum* for the obvious reason. Suppose that we need to connect several towns with roads, minimizing the total construction cost, with the provision that we can

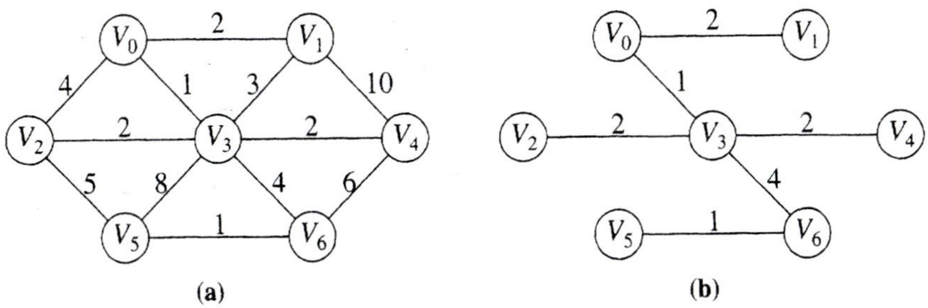

Figure 24.6 (a) A graph G and (b) its minimum spanning tree.

transfer to another road only at a town (in other words, no extra junctions are allowed). Then we need to solve a minimum spanning tree problem, where each vertex is a town, and each edge is the cost of building a road between the two cities it connects.

A related problem is the *minimum Steiner tree problem*, which is like the minimum spanning tree problem, except that junctions can be created as part of the solution. The minimum Steiner tree problem is much more difficult to solve. However, it can be shown that if the cost of a connection is proportional to the Euclidean distance, the minimum spanning tree is at most 15 percent more expensive than the minimum Steiner tree. Thus a minimum spanning tree, which is easy to compute, provides a good approximation for the minimum Steiner tree, which is hard to compute.

Kruskal's algorithm **is used to select edges in order of increasing cost and adds an edge to the tree if it does not create a cycle.**

A simple algorithm, commonly called **Kruskal's algorithm,** is used to select edges continually in order of smallest weight and to add an edge to the tree if it does not cause a cycle. Formally, Kruskal's algorithm maintains a forest—a collection of trees. Initially, there are $|V|$ single-node trees. Adding an edge merges two trees into one. When the algorithm terminates, there is only one tree, which is the minimum spanning tree.[2] By counting the number of accepted edges, we can determine when the algorithm should terminate.

Figure 24.7 shows the action of Kruskal's algorithm on the graph shown in Figure 24.6. The first five edges are all accepted because they do not create cycles. The next two edges, (v_1, v_3) (of cost 3) and then (v_0, v_2) (of cost 4), are rejected because each would create a cycle in the tree. The next edge considered is accepted, and because it is the sixth edge in a seven-vertex graph, we can terminate the algorithm.

2. If the graph is not connected, the algorithm will terminate with more than one tree. Each tree then represents a minimum spanning tree for each connected component of the graph.

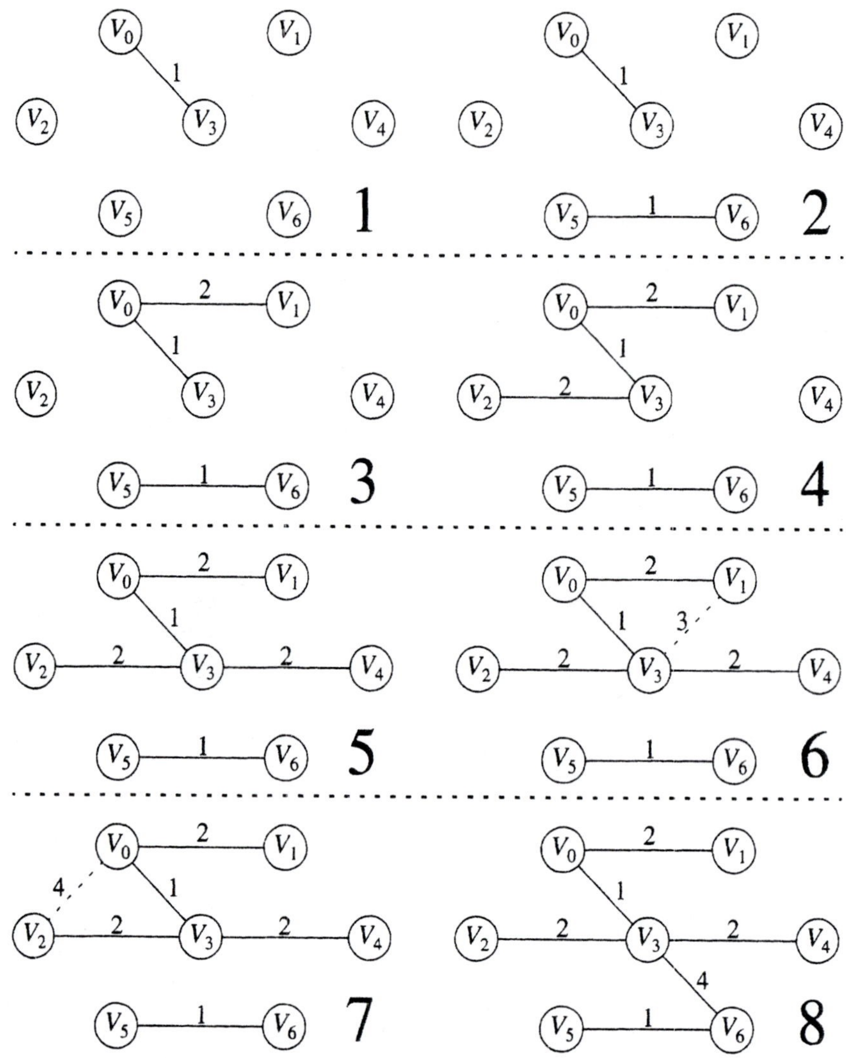

Figure 24.7 Kruskal's algorithm after each edge has been considered. The stages proceed left-to-right, top-to-bottom, as numbered.

The edges can be sorted, or a priority queue can be used.

Ordering the edges for testing is simple enough to do. We can sort them at a cost of $|E|\log|E|$ and then step through the ordered array of edges. Alternatively, we can construct a priority queue of $|E|$ edges and repeatedly obtain edges by calling `deleteMin`. Although the worst-case bound is unchanged, using a priority queue is sometimes better because Kruskal's algorithm tends to test only a small fraction of the edges on random graphs. Of course, in the worst case, all the edges may have to be tried. For instance, if there were an extra vertex v_8 and edge (v_5, v_8) of cost 100, all the edges would have to be examined. In this case, a quicksort at the start would be faster. In effect, the choice between a priority queue and an initial sort is a gamble on how many edges are likely to have to be examined.

More interesting is the issue of how we decide whether an edge (u, v) should be accepted or rejected. Clearly, adding the edge (u, v) causes a cycle if (and only if) u and v are already connected in the current spanning **forest,** which is a collection of trees. Thus we merely maintain each connected component in the spanning forest as a disjoint set. Initially, each vertex is in its own disjoint set. If u and v are in the same disjoint set, as determined by two `find` operations, the edge is rejected because u and v are already connected. Otherwise, the edge is accepted and a `union` operation is performed on the two disjoint sets containing u and v, in effect, combining the connected components. This result is what we want because once edge (u, v) has been added to the spanning forest, if w was connected to u and x was connected to v, x and w must be connected and thus belong in the same set.

The test for cycles is done by using a union/find data structure.

24.2.3 Application: The Nearest Common Ancestor Problem

Another illustration of the union/find data structure is the offline **nearest common ancestor** (NCA) **problem.**

OFFLINE NEAREST COMMON ANCESTOR PROBLEM

GIVEN A TREE AND A LIST OF PAIRS OF NODES IN THE TREE, FIND THE NEAREST COMMON ANCESTOR FOR EACH PAIR OF NODES.

As an example, Figure 24.8 shows a tree with a pair list containing five requests. For the pair of nodes u and z, node C is the nearest ancestor of both. (A and B are also ancestors, but they are not the closest.) The problem is offline because we can see the entire request sequence prior to providing the first answer. Solution of this problem is important in graph theory applications and computational biology (where the tree represents evolution) applications.

Solutions of the NCA is important in graph algorithm and computational biology applications.

The algorithm works by performing a postorder tree traversal. When we are about to return from processing a node, we examine the pair list to determine whether any ancestor calculations are to be performed. If u is the current node, (u, v) is in the pair list and we have already finished the recursive call to v, we have enough information to determine NCA(u, v).

A postorder traversal can be used to solve the problem.

Figure 24.9 helps in understanding how this algorithm works. Here, we are about to finish the recursive call to D. All shaded nodes have been visited by a recursive call, and except for the nodes on the path to D, all the recursive calls have already finished. We mark a node after its recursive call has been completed. If v is marked, then NCA(D, v) is some node on the path to D. The **anchor** of a visited (but not necessarily marked) node v is the node

The *anchor* of a visited (but not necessarily marked) node v is the node on the current access path that is closest to v.

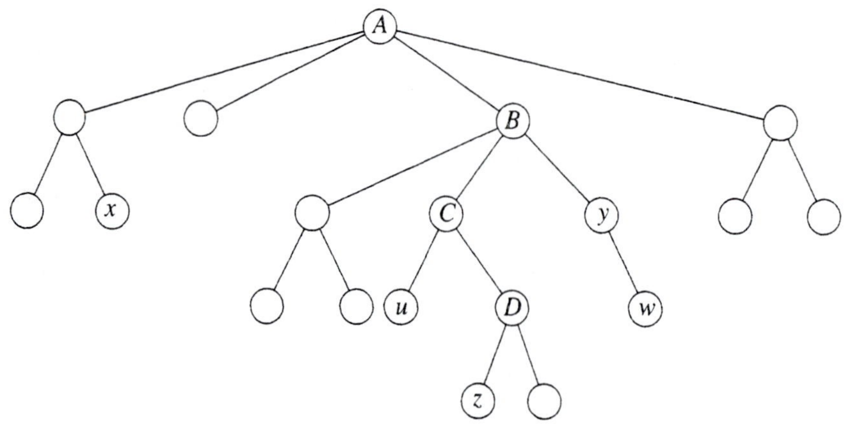

Figure 24.8 The nearest common ancestor for each request in the pair sequence (x, y), (u, z), (w, x), (z, w), and (w, y), is A, C, A, B, and y, respectively.

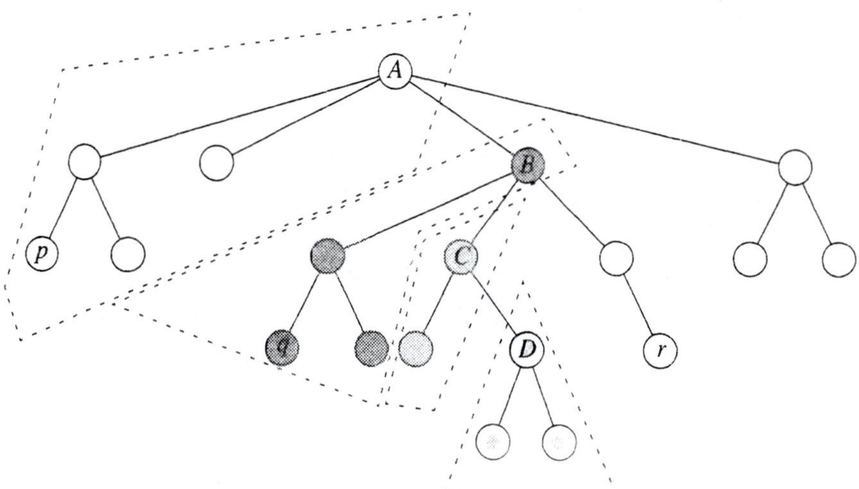

Figure 24.9 The sets immediately prior to the return from the recursive call to D; D is marked as visited and NCA(D, v) is v's anchor to the current path.

on the current access path that is closest to v. In Figure 24.9, p's anchor is A, q's anchor is B, and r is unanchored because it has yet to be visited; we can argue that r's anchor is r at the point that r is first visited. Each node on the current access path is an anchor (of at least itself). Furthermore, the visited nodes form equivalence classes: Two nodes are related if they have the same anchor, and we can regard each unvisited node as being in its own class.

Now, suppose once again that (D, v) is in the pair list. Then we have three cases.

1. v is unmarked, so we have no information to compute NCA(D, v). However, when v is marked, we are able to determine NCA(v, D).
2. v is marked but not in D's subtree, so NCA(D, v) is v's anchor.
3. v is in D's subtree, so NCA$(D, v) = D$. Note that this is not a special case because v's anchor is D.

The union/find algorithm is used to maintain the sets of nodes with common anchors.

All that remains to be done is to ensure that, at any instant, we can determine the anchor of any visited node. We can easily do so with the union/find algorithm. After a recursive call returns, we call `union`. For instance, after the recursive call to D in Figure 24.9 returns, all nodes in D have their anchor changed from D to C. The new situation is shown in Figure 24.10. Thus we need to merge the two equivalence classes into one. At any point, we can obtain the anchor for a vertex v by a call to a disjoint set `find`. Because `find` returns a set number, we use an array `anchor` to store the anchor node corresponding to a particular set.

The pseudocode is compact.

A pseudocode implementation of the NCA algorithm is shown in Figure 24.11. As mentioned earlier in the chapter, the `find` operation generally is based on the assumption that elements of the set are 0, 1, ..., $N - 1$, so we store a preorder number in each tree node in a preprocessing step that

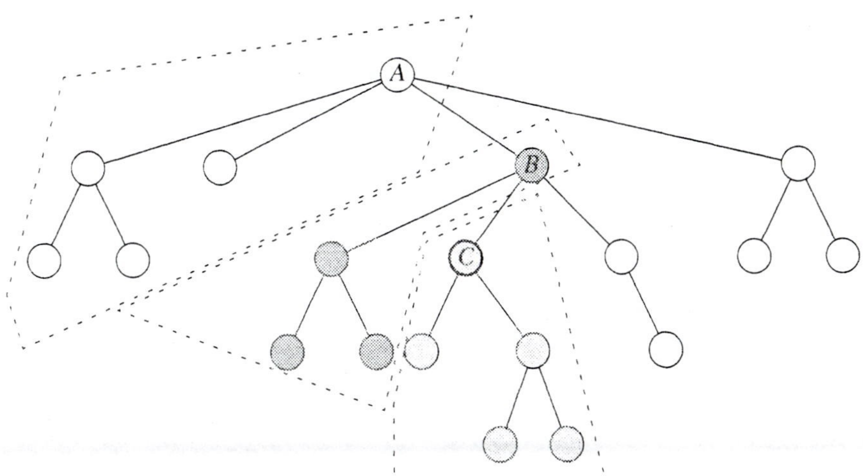

Figure 24.10 After the recursive call from *D* returns, we merge the set anchored by *D* into the set anchored by *C* and then compute all NCA(*C*, *v*) for nodes *v* marked prior to completing *C*'s recursive call.

```
1 // Nearest Common Ancestors algorithm.
2 //
3 // Preconditions (and global objects):
4 //     1. union/find structure is initialized
5 //     2. All nodes are initially unmarked
6 //     3. Preorder numbers are already assigned in num member
7 //     4. Each node can store its marked status
8 //     5. List of pairs is globally available
9
10 DisjSets s( treeSize );              // union/find
11 vector<Node *> anchor( treeSize ); // Anchor node for each set
12
13 // main makes the call NCA( root )
14 // after required initializations
15
16 NCA( Node *u )
17 {
18     anchor[ s.find( u->num ) ] = u;
19
20       // Do postorder calls
21     for( each child v of u )
22     {
23         NCA( v );
24         s.unionSets( s.find( u->num ), s.find( v->num ) );
25         anchor[ s.find( u->num ) ] = u;
26     }
27
28       // Do NCA calculation for pairs involving u
29     u->marked = true;
30     for( each v such that NCA( u, v ) is required )
31         if( v->marked )
32             cout << "NCA(" << u << ", " << v << ") is " <<
33                          anchor[ s.find( v->num ) ] << endl;
34 }
```

Figure 24.11 Pseudocode for the nearest common ancestors problem.

computes the size of the tree. An object-oriented approach might attempt to incorporate a mapping into the `find`, but we do not do so. We also assume that we have an array of lists in which to store the NCA requests; that is, list i stores the requests for tree node i. With those details taken care of, the code is remarkably short.

When a node u is first visited, it becomes the anchor of itself, as in line 18 of Figure 24.11. It then recursively processes its children v by making the call at line 23. After each recursive call returns, the subtree is combined into u's current equivalence class and we ensure that the anchor is updated at lines 24 and 25. When all the children have been processed recursively, we can mark u as processed at line 29 and finish by checking all NCA requests involving u at lines 30 to 33.[3]

24.3 The Quick-Find Algorithm

In this section and Section 24.4 we lay the groundwork for the efficient implementation of the union/find data structure. There are two basic strategies for solving the union/find problem. The first approach, the **quick-find algorithm,** ensures that the `find` instruction can be executed in constant worst-case time. The other approach, the **quick-union algorithm,** ensures that the `union` operation can be executed in constant worst-case time. It has been shown that both cannot be done simultaneously in constant worst-case (or even amortized) time.

For the `find` operation to be fast, in an array we could maintain the name of the equivalence class for each element. Then `find` is a simple constant time lookup. Suppose that we want to perform `union(`*a*, *b*`)`. Suppose, too, that a is in equivalence class i and that b is in equivalence class j. Then we can scan down the array, changing all i's to j's. Unfortunately, this scan takes linear time. Thus a sequence of $N - 1$ `union` operations (the maximum because then everything is in one set) would take quadratic time. In the typical case in which the number of `find`s is subquadratic, this time is clearly unacceptable.

One possibility is to keep all the elements that are in the same equivalence class in a linked list. This approach saves time when we are updating because we do not have to search the entire array. By itself that does not reduce the asymptotic running time, as performing $\Theta(N^2)$ equivalence class updates over the course of the algorithm is still possible.

The argument that an equivalence class can change at most log N times per item is also used in the quick-union algorithm. Quick-find is a simple algorithm, but quick-union is better.

If we also keep track of the size of the equivalence classes—and when performing a `union` change the name of the smaller class to the larger—the total time spent for N `union`s is $O(N \log N)$. The reason is that each element can have its equivalence class changed at most $\log N$ times because, every time its class is changed, its new equivalence class is at least twice as large as its old class (so the doubling principle applies).

This strategy provides that any sequence of at most M `find` and $N - 1$ `union` operations take at most $O(M + N \log N)$ time. If M is linear (or slightly nonlinear), this solution is still expensive. It also is a bit messy because we must maintain linked lists. In Section 24.4 we examine a solution to the union/find

3. Strictly speaking, u should be marked at the last statement, but marking it earlier handles the annoying request NCA(u, u).

problem that makes `union` easy but `find` hard—the quick-union algorithm. Even so, the running time for any sequence of at most M `find` and $N - 1$ `union` operations is only negligibly more than $O(M + N)$ time, and moreover, only a single array of integers is used.

24.4 The Quick-Union Algorithm

Recall that the union/find problem does not require a `find` operation to return any specific name, just that `find`s on two elements return the same answer if and only if they are in the same set. One possibility might be to use a tree to represent a set, as each element in a tree has the same root and the root can be used to name the set.

A tree is represented by an array of integers representing parent nodes. The set name of any node in a tree is the root of a tree.

Each set is represented by a tree (recall that a collection of trees is called a *forest*). The name of a set is given by the node at the root. Our trees are not necessarily binary trees, but their representation is easy because the only information we need is the parent. Thus we need only an array of integers: Each entry `p[i]` in the array represents the parent of element `i`, and we can use –1 as a parent to indicate a root. Figure 24.12 shows a forest and the array that represents it.

The `union` operation is constant time.

To perform a `union` of two sets, we merge the two trees by making the root of one tree a child of the root of the other. This operation clearly takes constant time. Figures 24.13–24.15 represent the forest after each of `union`(4, 5), `union`(6, 7), and `union`(4, 6), where we have adopted the convention that the new root after `union`(x, y) is x.

The cost of a `find` depends on the depth of the accessed node and could be linear.

A `find` operation on element x is performed by returning the root of the tree containing x. The time for performing this operation is proportional to the number of nodes on the path from x to the root. The `union` strategy outlined previously enables us to create a tree whose every node is on the path

0	–1
1	–1
2	–1
3	–1
4	–1
5	–1
6	–1
7	–1

Figure 24.12 A forest and its eight elements, initially in different sets.

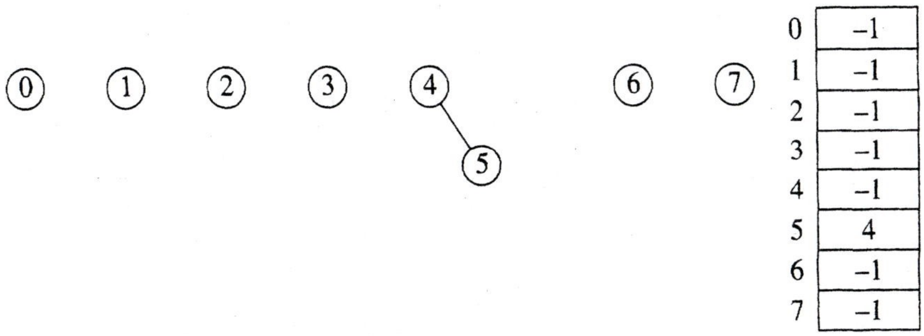

Figure 24.13 The forest after the `union` of trees with roots 4 and 5.

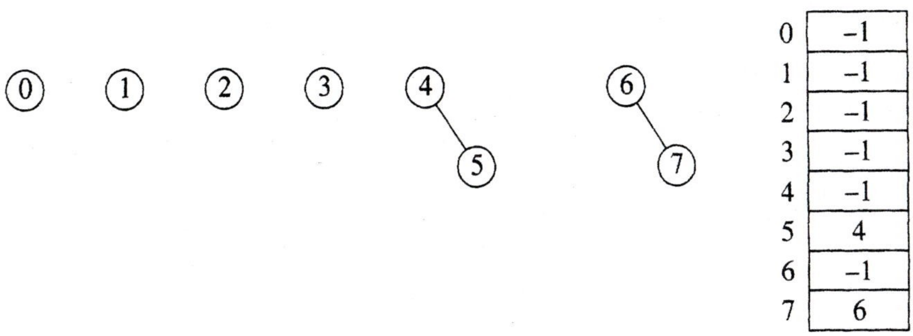

Figure 24.14 The forest after the `union` of trees with roots 6 and 7.

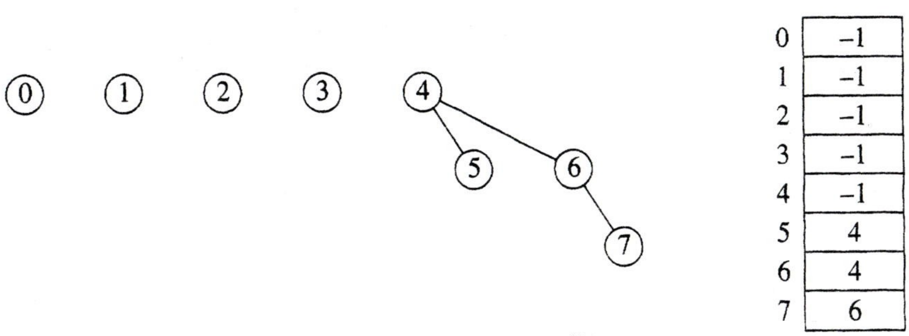

Figure 24.15 The forest after the `union` of trees with roots 4 and 6.

to x, resulting in a worst-case running time of $\Theta(N)$ per `find`. Typically (as shown in the preceding applications), the running time is computed for a sequence of M intermixed instructions. In the worst case, M consecutive operations could take $\Theta(MN)$ time.

Quadratic running time for a sequence of operations is generally unacceptable. Fortunately, there are several ways to easily ensure that this running time does not occur.

24.4.1 Smart Union Algorithms

We performed the previous `unions` rather arbitrarily by making the second tree a subtree of the first. A simple improvement is always to make the smaller tree a subtree of the larger, breaking ties by any method, an approach called **union-by-size.** The preceding three `union` operations were all ties, so we can consider that they were performed by size. If the next operation is `union`(3, 4), the forest shown in Figure 24.16 forms. Had the size heuristic not been used, a deeper forest would have been formed (three nodes rather than one would have been one level deeper).

Union-by-size guarantees logarithmic finds.

If the `union` operation is done by size, the depth of any node is never more than log N. A node is initially at depth 0, and when its depth increases as a result of a `union`, it is placed in a tree that is at least twice as large as before. Thus its depth can be increased at most log N times. (We used this argument in the quick-find algorithm in Section 24.3.) This outcome implies that the running time for a `find` operation is $O(\log N)$ and that a sequence of M operations takes at most $O(M \log N)$ time. The tree shown in Figure 24.17 illustrates the worst tree possible after 15 `union` operations and is obtained if all the `unions` are between trees of equal size. (The worst-case tree is called a *binomial tree*. Binomial trees have other applications in advanced data structures.)

Instead of –1 being stored for roots, the negative of the size is stored.

To implement this strategy, we need to keep track of the size of each tree. Since we are just using an array, we can have the array entry of the root contain the *negative* of the size of the tree, as shown in Figure 24.16. Thus the initial representation of the tree with all –1s is reasonable. When a

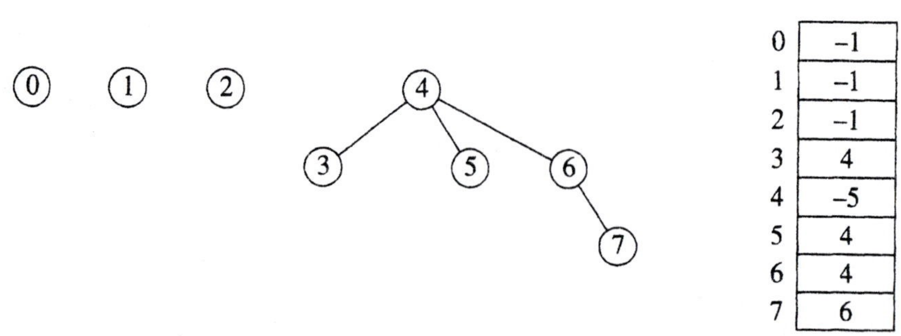

Figure 24.16 The forest formed by union-by-size, with the sizes encoded as negative numbers.

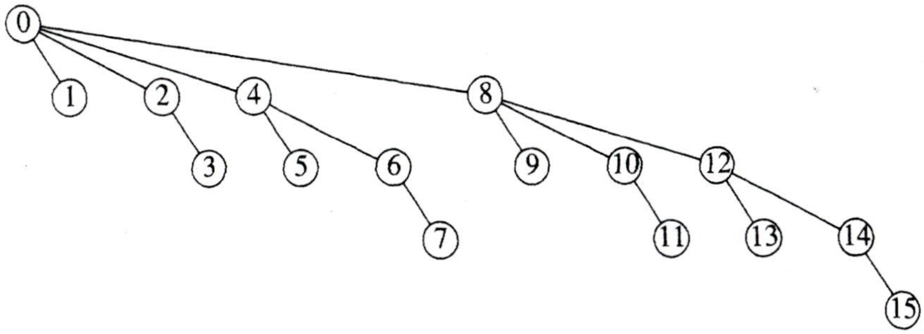

Figure 24.17 Worst-case tree for $N = 16$.

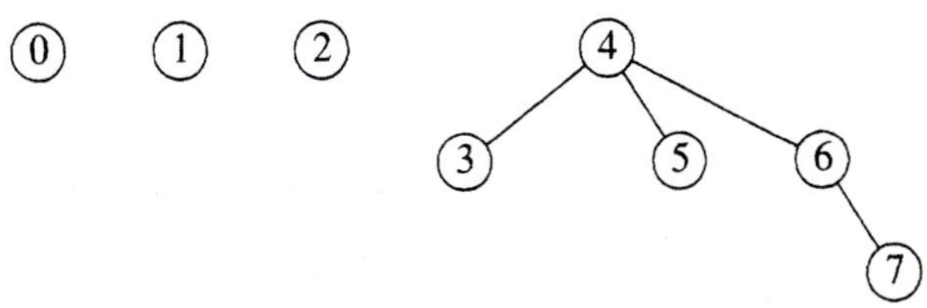

0	–1
1	–1
2	–1
3	4
4	–3
5	4
6	4
7	6

Figure 24.18 A forest formed by union-by-height, with the height encoded as a negative number.

`union` operation is performed, we check the sizes; the new size is the sum of the old. Thus union-by-size is not at all difficult to implement and requires no extra space. It is also fast on average because, when random `union` operations are performed, generally very small (usually one-element) sets are merged with large sets throughout the algorithm. Mathematical analysis of this process is quite complex; the references at the end of the chapter provide some pointers to the literature.

***Union-by-height* also guarantees logarithmic `find` operations.**

An alternative implementation that also guarantees logarithmic depth is **union-by-height** in which we keep track of the height of the trees instead of the size and perform `union` operations by making a shallower tree a subtree of the deeper tree. This algorithm is easy to write and use because the height of a tree increases only when two equally deep trees are joined (and then the height goes up by 1). Thus union-by-height is a trivial modification of union-by-size. As heights start at 0, we store the negative of the number of nodes rather than the height on the deepest path, as shown in Figure 24.18.

24.4.2 Path Compression

The union/find algorithm, as described so far, is quite acceptable for most cases. It is very simple and linear on average for a sequence of M instructions. However, the worst case is still unappealing. The reason is that a sequence of `union` operations occurring in some particular application (such as the NCA problem) is not obviously random (in fact, for certain trees, it is far from random). Hence we have to seek a better bound for the worst case of a sequence of M operations. Seemingly, no more improvements to the union algorithm are possible because the worst case is achievable when identical trees are merged. The only way to speed up the algorithm, without reworking the data structure entirely, then is to do something clever with the `find` operation.

***Path compression* makes every accessed node a child of the root until another `union` occurs.**

That something clever is **path compression.** Clearly, after we perform a `find` on x, changing x's parent to the root would make sense. In that way, a second `find` on x or any item in x's subtree becomes easier. There is no need to stop there, however. We might as well change the parents for all the nodes on the access path. In path compression *every* node on the path from x to the root has its parent changed to the root. Figure 24.19 shows the effect of path compression after `find(14)` on the generic worst tree shown in Figure 24.17. With an extra two parent changes, nodes 12 and 13 are now one position closer to the root and nodes 14 and 15 are now two positions closer. The fast future accesses on the nodes pay (we hope) for the extra work to do the path compression. Note that subsequent `union`s push the nodes deeper.

Path compression guarantees logarithmic amortized cost for the `find` operation.

When `union`s are done arbitrarily, path compression is a good idea because of the abundance of deep nodes; they are brought near the root by path compression. It has been proved that when path compression is done in this case, a sequence of M operations requires at most $O(M \log N)$ time, so path compression by itself guarantees logarithmic amortized cost for the `find` operation.

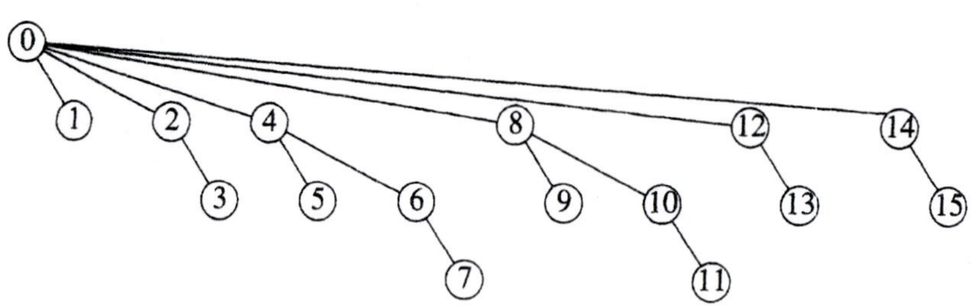

Figure 24.19 Path compression resulting from a `find(14)` on the tree shown in Figure 24.17.

Path compression is perfectly compatible with union-by-size. Thus both routines can be implemented at the same time. However, path compression is not entirely compatible with union-by-height because path compression can change the heights of the trees. We do not know how to recompute them efficiently, so we do not attempt to do so. Then the heights stored for each tree become estimated heights, called **ranks,** which is not a problem. The resulting algorithm, **union-by-rank,** is thus obtained from union-by-height when compression is performed. As we show in Section 24.6, the combination of a smart union rule and path compression gives an almost linear guarantee on the running time for a sequence of M operations.

Path compression and a smart union root guarantee essentially constant amortized cost per operation (i.e., a long sequence can be executed in almost linear time).

24.5 C++ Implementation

The class interface for a disjoint sets class is given in Figure 24.20, and the implementation is shown in Figure 24.21. We have omitted the trivial implementations of `assertIsRoot` and `assertIsItem`; these methods throw exceptions if the conditions they are asserting are false. The entire algorithm is amazingly short.

Disjoint sets are relatively simple to implement.

In our routine `unionSet` is performed on the roots of the trees. Sometimes the operation is implemented by passing any two elements and having `unionSet` perform the `find` operation to determine the roots.

```
// Disjoint set class.
// Use union by rank and path compression.
// Elements in the set are numbered starting at 0.
class DisjSets
{
  public:
    DisjSets( int numElements );

    int find( int x ) const;
    int find( int x );
    void unionSets( int root1, int root2 );

  private:
    vector<int> s;
    void assertIsRoot( int root ) const;
    void assertIsItem( int item ) const;
};
```

Figure 24.20 The disjoint sets class interface.

```
// Construct the disjoint sets object.
// numElements is the initial number of disjoint sets.
DisjSets::DisjSets( int numElements ) : s( numElements )
{
    for( int i = 0; i < s.size( ); i++ )
        s[ i ] = -1;
}

// Union two disjoint sets.
// root1 is the root of set 1. root2 is the root of set 2.
void DisjSets::unionSets( int root1, int root2 )
{
    assertIsRoot( root1 );
    assertIsRoot( root2 );
    if( s[ root2 ] < s[ root1 ] )  // root2 is deeper
        s[ root1 ] = root2;        // Make root2 new root
    else
    {
        if( s[ root1 ] == s[ root2 ] )
            s[ root1 ]--;          // Update height if same
        s[ root2 ] = root1;        // Make root1 new root
    }
}

// Perform a find without path compression.
int DisjSets::find( int x ) const
{
    assertIsItem( x );
    if( s[ x ] < 0 )
        return x;
    else
        return find( s[ x ] );
}

// Perform a find with path compression.
int DisjSets::find( int x )
{
    assertIsItem( x );
    if( s[ x ] < 0 )
        return x;
    else
        return s[ x ] = find( s[ x ] );
}
```

Figure 24.21 Implementation of a disjoint sets class.

The interesting procedure is `find`. The accessor cannot perform path compression, but the mutator can. For the mutator version, after the `find` has been performed recursively, `array[x]` is set to the root and then is returned. Because this procedure is recursive, all nodes on the path have their entries set to the root.

24.6 Worst Case for Union-by-Rank and Path Compression

When both heuristics are used, the algorithm is almost linear in the worst case. Specifically, the time required to process a sequence of at most $N - 1$ `union` operations and M `find` operations in the worst case is $\Theta(M\alpha(M, N))$ (provided that $M \geq N$), where $\alpha(M, N)$ is a functional inverse of **Ackermann's function,** which grows very quickly and is defined as follows:[4]

$$\begin{aligned} A(1, j) &= 2^j & j \geq 1; \\ A(i, 1) &= A(i-1, 2) & i \geq 2; \\ A(i, j) &= A(i-1, A(i, j-1)) & i, j \geq 2. \end{aligned}$$

From the preceding, we define

$$\alpha(M, N) = \min\{i \geq 1 | (A(i, \lfloor M/N \rfloor) > \log N)\}.$$

Ackermann's function grows very quickly, and its inverse is essentially at most 4.

You might want to compute some values, but for all practical purposes, $\alpha(M, N) \leq 4$, which is all that really matters here. For instance, for any $j > 1$, we have

$$\begin{aligned} A(2, j) &= A(1, A(2, j-1)) \\ &= 2^{A(2, j-1)} \\ &= 2^{2^{2^{2\cdots}}}, \end{aligned}$$

where the number of 2s in the exponent is j. The function $F(N) = A(2, N)$ is commonly called a single-variable Ackermann's function. The single-variable inverse of Ackermann's function, sometimes written as $\log^* N$, is the number of times the logarithm of N needs to be applied until $N \leq 1$. Thus $\log^* 65536 = 4$, because log log log log 65536 = 1, and $\log^* 2^{65536} = 5$. However, keep in mind that 2^{65536} has more than 20,000 digits. The function $\alpha(M, N)$

4. Ackermann's function is frequently defined with $A(1, j) = j + 1$ for $j \geq 1$. The form we use in this text grows faster; thus the inverse grows more slowly.

grows even slower than $\log^* N$. For instance, $A(3, 1) = A(2, 2) = 2^{2^2} = 16$. Thus for $N < 2^{16}$, $\alpha(M, N) \leq 3$. Further, because $A(4, 1) = A(3, 2) = A(2, A(3, 1)) = A(2, 16)$, which is 2 raised to a power of 16 stacked 2s, in practice, $\alpha(M, N) \leq 4$. However, $\alpha(M, N)$ is not a constant when M is slightly more than N, so the running time is not linear.[5]

In the remainder of this section, we prove a slightly weaker result. We show that any sequence of $M = \Omega(N)$ `union` and `find` operations takes a total of $O(M \log^* N)$ time. The same bound holds if we replace union-by-rank with union-by-size. This analysis is probably the most complex in this text and is one of the first truly complex analyses ever performed for an algorithm that is essentially trivial to implement. By extending this technique, we can show the stronger bound claimed previously.

24.6.1 Analysis of the Union/Find Algorithm

In this section, we establish a fairly tight bound on the running time of a sequence of $M = \Omega(N)$ `union` and `find` operations. The `union` and `find` operations may occur in any order, but `union` is done by rank and `find` is done with path compression.

We begin with some theorems concerning the number of nodes of rank r. Intuitively, because of the union-by-rank rule, there are many more nodes of small rank than of large rank. In particular, there can be at most one node of rank $\log N$. What we want to do is to produce as precise a bound as possible on the number of nodes of any particular rank r. Because ranks change only when `union` operations are performed (and then only when the two trees have the same rank), we can prove this bound by ignoring path compression. We do so in Theorem 24.1.

Theorem 24.1 *In the absence of path compression, when a sequence of* `union` *instructions is being executed, a node of rank r must have 2^r descendants (including itself).*

Proof *The proof is by induction. The basis $r = 0$ is clearly true. Let T be the tree of rank r with the fewest number of descendants and x be T's root. Suppose that the last* `union` *with which x was involved was between T_1 and T_2. Suppose that T_1's root was x. If T_1 had rank r, then T_1 would be a*

5. Note, however, that if $M = N \log^* N$, then $\alpha(M, N)$ is at most 2. Thus, so long as M is slightly more than linear, the running time is linear in M.

Proof (continued)

tree of rank r with fewer descendants than T. This condition contradicts the assumption that T is the tree with the smallest number of descendants. Hence the rank of T_1 is at most $r - 1$. The rank of T_2 is at most the rank of T_1 because of union-by-rank. As T has rank r and the rank could only increase because of T_2, it follows that the rank of T_2 is $r - 1$. Then the rank of T_1 is also $r - 1$. By the induction hypothesis, each tree has at least 2^{r-1} descendants, giving a total of 2^r and establishing the theorem.

Theorem 24.1 says that if no path compression is performed, any node of rank r must have at least 2^r descendants. Path compression can change this condition, of course, because it can remove descendants from a node. However, when `union` operations are performed—even with path compression—we are using ranks, or estimated heights. These ranks behave as if there is no path compression. Thus when the number of nodes of rank r are being bounded, path compression can be ignored, as in Theorem 24.2.

Theorem 24.2

The number of nodes of rank r is at most $N/2^r$.

Proof

Without path compression, each node of rank r is the root of a subtree of at least 2^r nodes. No other node in the subtree can have rank r. Thus all subtrees of nodes of rank r are disjoint. Therefore there are at most $N/2^r$ disjoint subtrees and hence $N/2^r$ nodes of rank r.

Theorem 24.3 seems somewhat obvious, but it is crucial to the analysis.

Theorem 24.3

At any point in the union/find algorithm, the ranks of the nodes on a path from a leaf to a root increase monotonically.

Proof

The theorem is obvious if there is no path compression. If after path compression, some node v is a descendant of w, then clearly v must have been a descendant of w when only `union` operations were considered. Hence the rank of v is strictly less than the rank of w.

There are not too many nodes of large rank, and the ranks increase on any path up toward a root.

The following is a summary of the preliminary results. Theorem 24.2 describes the number of nodes that can be assigned rank r. Because ranks are assigned only by `union` operations, which do not rely on path compression, Theorem 24.2 is valid at any stage of the union/find algorithm—even in the midst of path compression. Theorem 24.2 is tight in the sense that there can be $N/2^r$ nodes for any rank r. It also is slightly loose because the bound cannot hold for all ranks r simultaneously. While Theorem 24.2 describes the number of nodes in a rank r, Theorem 24.3 indicates the distribution of nodes in a rank r. As expected, the rank of nodes strictly increases along the path from a leaf to the root.

Pennies are used like a potential function. The total number of pennies is the total time.

We are now ready to prove the main theorem, and our basic plan is as follows. A `find` operation on any node v costs time proportional to the number of nodes on the path from v to the root. We charge 1 unit of cost for every node on the path from v to the root during each `find`. To help count the charges, we deposit an imaginary penny in each node on the path. This is strictly an accounting gimmick that is not part of the program. It is somewhat equivalent to the use of a potential function in the amortized analysis for splay trees and skew heaps. When the algorithm has finished, we collect all the coins that have been deposited to determine the total time.

We have both U.S. and Canadian pennies. Canadian pennies account for the first few times a node is compressed; U.S. pennies account for later compressions or noncompressions.

As a further accounting gimmick, we deposit both U.S. and Canadian pennies. We show that, during execution of the algorithm, we can deposit only a certain number of U.S. pennies during each `find` operation (regardless of how many nodes there are). We will also show that we can deposit only a certain number of Canadian pennies to each node (regardless of how many `finds` there are). Adding these two totals gives a bound on the total number of pennies that can be deposited.

We now sketch our accounting scheme in more detail. We begin by dividind the nodes by their ranks. We then divide the ranks into rank groups. On each `find`, we deposit some U.S. pennies in a general kitty and some Canadian pennies in specific nodes. To compute the total number of Canadian pennies deposited, we compute the deposits per node. By summing all the deposits for each node in rank r, we get the total deposits per rank r. Then we sum all the deposits for each rank r in group g and thereby obtain the total deposits for each rank group g. Finally, we sum all the deposits for each rank group g to obtain the total number of Canadian pennies deposited in the forest. Adding that total to the number of U.S. pennies in the kitty gives us the answer.

Ranks are partitioned into groups. The actual groups are determined at the end of the proof. Group 0 has only rank 0.

As mentioned previously, we partition the ranks into groups. Rank r goes into group $G(r)$, and G is to be determined later (to balance the U.S. and Canadian deposits). The largest rank in any rank group g is $F(g)$, where $F = G^{-1}$ is the *inverse* of G. The number of ranks in any rank group, $g > 0$, is thus $F(g) - F(g - 1)$. Clearly, $G(N)$ is a very loose upper bound on the largest

Group	Rank
0	0
1	1
2	2,3,4
3	5 through 9
4	10 through 16
i	$(i-1)^2$ through i^2

Figure 24.22 Possible partitioning of ranks into groups.

rank group. Suppose that we partitioned the ranks as shown in Figure 24.22. In this case, $G(r) = \lceil \sqrt{r} \rceil$. The largest rank in group g is $F(g) = g^2$. Also, observe that group $g > 0$ contains ranks $F(g-1) + 1$ through $F(g)$. This formula does not apply for rank group 0, so for convenience we ensure that rank group 0 contains only elements of rank 0. Note that the groups comprise consecutive ranks.

As mentioned earlier in the chapter, each `union` instruction takes constant time, so long as each root keeps track of its rank. Thus `union` operations are essentially free, as far as this proof goes.

When a node is compressed, its new parent will have a higher rank than its old parent.

Each `find` operation takes time proportional to the number of nodes on the path from the node representing the accessed item i to the root. We thus deposit one penny for each vertex on the path. If that is all we do, however, we cannot expect much of a bound because we are not taking advantage of path compression. Thus we must use some fact about path compression in our analysis. The key observation is that, as a result of path compression, a node obtains a new parent and the new parent is guaranteed to have a higher rank than the old parent.

Rules for U.S. and Canadian deposits.

To incorporate this fact into the proof, we use the following fancy accounting: For each node v on the path from the accessed node i to the root, we deposit one penny in one of two accounts.

1. If v is the root or if the parent of v is the root or if the parent of v is in a different rank group from v, then charge 1 unit under this rule and deposit a U.S. penny in the kitty.
2. Otherwise, deposit a Canadian penny in the node.

Theorem 24.4 states that the accounting is accurate.

Theorem 24.4 *For any `find` operation, the total number of pennies deposited, either in the kitty or in a node, is exactly equal to the number of nodes accessed during the `find`.*

Proof *Obvious.*

U.S. charges are limited by the number of different groups. Canadian charges are limited by the size of the groups. We eventually need to balance these costs.

Thus we need only sum all the U.S. pennies deposited under rule 1 and all the Canadian pennies deposited under rule 2. Before we go on with the proof, let us sketch the ideas. Canadian pennies are deposited in a node when it is compressed and its parent is in the same rank group as the node. Because the node gets a parent of higher rank after each path compression and because the size of a rank group is finite, eventually the node obtains a parent that is not in its rank group. Consequently, on the one hand, only a limited number of Canadian pennies can be placed in any node. This number is roughly the size of the node's rank group. On the other hand, the U.S. charges are also limited, essentially by the number of rank groups. Thus we want to choose both small rank groups (to limit the Canadian charges) and few rank groups (to limit the U.S. charges). We are now ready to fill in the details with a rapid-fire series of theorems, Theorems 24.5–24.10.

Theorem 24.5 *Over the entire algorithm, the total deposits of U.S. pennies under rule 1 amount to $M(G(N) + 2)$.*

Proof *For any `find` operation, at most two U.S. pennies are deposited because of the root and its child. By Theorem 24.3, the vertices going up the path are monotonically increasing in rank, and thus the rank group never decreases as we go up the path. Because there are at most $G(N)$ rank groups (besides group 0), only $G(N)$ other vertices can qualify as a rule 1 deposit for any particular `find`. Thus, during any `find`, at most $G(N) + 2$ U.S. pennies can be placed in the kitty. Thus at most $M(G(N) + 2)$ U.S. pennies can be deposited under rule 1 for a sequence of M `finds`.*

Theorem 24.6 *For any single node in rank group g, the total number of Canadian pennies deposited is at most $F(g)$.*

Proof

If a Canadian penny is deposited in a vertex v under rule 2, v will be moved by path compression and get a new parent of rank higher than its old parent. As the largest rank in its group is F(g), we are guaranteed that after F(g) coins are deposited, v's parent will no longer be in v's rank group.

The bound in Theorem 24.6 can be improved by using only the size of the rank group rather than its largest member. However, this modification does not improve the bound obtained for the union/find algorithm.

Theorem 24.7

The number of nodes, N(g), in rank group g > 0 is at most $N/2^{F(g-1)}$.

Proof

By Theorem 24.2, there are at most $N/2^r$ nodes of rank r. Summing over the ranks in group g, we obtain

$$
\begin{aligned}
N(g) &\le \sum_{r=F(g-1)+1}^{F(g)} \frac{N}{2^r} \\
&\le \sum_{r=F(g-1)+1}^{\infty} \frac{N}{2^r} \\
&\le N \sum_{r=F(g-1)+1}^{\infty} \frac{1}{2^r} \\
&\le \frac{N}{2^{F(g-1)+1}} \sum_{s=0}^{\infty} \frac{1}{2^s} \\
&\le \frac{2N}{2^{F(g-1)+1}} \\
&\le \frac{N}{2^{F(g-1)}}
\end{aligned}
$$

Theorem 24.8

The maximum number of Canadian pennies deposited in all vertices in rank group g is at most $NF(g)/2^{F(g-1)}$.

Proof

The result follows from a simple multiplication of the quantities obtained in Theorems 24.6 and 24.7.

Theorem 24.9 *The total deposit under rule 2 is at most $N\Sigma_{g=1}^{G(N)} F(g)/2^{F(g-1)}$ Canadian pennies.*

Proof *Because rank group 0 contains only elements of rank 0, it cannot contribute to rule 2 charges (it cannot have a parent in the same rank group). The bound is obtained by summing the other rank groups.*

Now we can specify the rank groups to minimize the bound. Our choice is not quite minimal, but it is close.

Thus we have the deposits under rules 1 and 2. The total is

$$M(G(N)+2) + N \sum_{g=1}^{G(N)} \frac{F(g)}{2^{F(g-1)}}. \qquad \textbf{(24.1)}$$

We still have not specified $G(N)$ or its inverse $F(N)$. Obviously, we are free to choose virtually anything we want, but choosing $G(N)$ to minimize the bound in Equation 24.1 makes sense. However, if $G(N)$ is too small, $F(N)$ will be large, thus hurting the bound. An apparently good choice is $F(i)$ to be the function recursively defined by $F(0)$ and $F(i) = 2^{F(i-1)}$, which gives $G(N) = 1 + \lfloor \log^* N \rfloor$. Figure 24.23 shows how this choice partitions the ranks. Note that group 0 contains only rank 0, which we required in the proof of Theorem 24.9. Note also that F is very similar to the single-variable Ackermann function, differing only in the definition of the base case. With this choice of F and G, we can complete the analysis in Theorem 24.10.

Theorem 24.10 *The running time of the union/find algorithm with $M = \Omega(N)$ `find` operations is $O(M \log^* N)$.*

Proof *Insert the definitions of F and G in Equation 24.1. The total number of U.S. pennies is $O(MG(N)) = O(M \log^* N)$. Because $F(g) = 2^{F(g-1)}$, the total number of Canadian pennies is $NG(N) = O(N \log^* N)$, and because $M = \Omega(N)$, the bound follows.*

Note that we have more U.S. pennies than Canadian pennies. The function $\alpha(M, N)$ balances things out, which is why it gives a better bound.

Group	Rank
0	0
1	1
2	2
3	3,4
4	5 through 6
5	17 through 65,536
6	65,537 through $2^{65,536}$
7	Truly huge ranks

Figure 24.23 Actual partitioning of ranks into groups used in the proof.

Summary

In this chapter we discussed a simple data structure for maintaining disjoint sets. When the `union` operation is performed, it does not matter, as far as correctness is concerned, which set retains its name. A valuable lesson that should be learned here is that considering the alternatives when a particular step is not totally specified can be very important. The `union` step is flexible. By taking advantage of this flexibility, we can get a much more efficient algorithm.

Path compression is one of the earliest forms of self-adjustment, which we have used elsewhere (splay trees and skew heaps). Its use here is extremely interesting from a theoretical point of view because it was one of the first examples of a simple algorithm with a not-so-simple worst-case analysis.

Objects of the Game

Ackermann's function A function that grows very quickly. Its inverse is essentially at most 4. (p. 865)

disjoint set class operations The two basic operations needed for disjoint set manipulation: They are `union` and `find`. (p. 846)

disjoint sets Sets having the property that each element appears in only one set. (p. 846)

equivalence class The equivalence class of an element *x* in set *S* is the subset of *S* that contains all the elements related to *x*. (p. 846)

equivalence relation A relation that is reflexive, symmetric, and transitive. (p. 845)

forest A collection of trees. (p. 853)

Kruskal's algorithm An algorithm used to select edges in increasing cost and that adds an edge to the tree if it does not create a cycle. (p. 851)

minimum spanning tree A connected subgraph of G that spans all vertices at minimum total cost. It is a fundamental graph theory problem. (p. 850)

nearest common ancestor problem Given a tree and a list of pairs of nodes in the tree, find the nearest common ancestor for each pair of nodes. Solution of this problem is important in graph algorithm and computational biology applications. (p. 853)

offline algorithm An algorithm in which the entire sequence of queries are made visible before the first answer is required. (p. 847)

online algorithm An algorithm in which an answer must be provided for each query before the next query can be viewed. (p. 847)

path compression Makes every accessed node a child of the root until another `union` occurs. (p. 862)

quick-find algorithm The union/find implementation in which `find` is a constant time operation. (p. 855)

quick-union algorithm The union/find implementation in which `union` is a constant time operation. (p. 857)

ranks In the disjoint set algorithm, the estimated heights of nodes. (p. 863)

relation Defined on a set if every pair of elements either is related or is not. (p. 845)

spanning tree A tree formed by graph edges that connect all the vertices of an undirected graph. (p. 850)

union-by-height Makes a shallower tree a child of the root of a deeper tree during a `union` operation. (p. 861)

union-by-rank Union-by-height when path compression is performed. (p. 863)

union-by-size Makes a smaller tree a child of the root of a larger tree during a `union` operation. (p. 860)

union/find algorithm An algorithm that is executed by processing `union` and `find` operations within a union/find data structure. (p. 847)

union/find data structure A method used to manipulate disjoint sets. (p. 846)

Common Errors

1. In using `union` we often assume that its parameters are tree roots. Havoc can result in code if we call such a `union` with non-roots as parameters.
2. Although not often used, `union` is a keyword in C++.

On the Internet

The disjoint sets class is available online. The following are the filenames.

DisjSets.h	Contains the disjoint sets class interface.
DisjSets.cpp	Contains the disjoint sets class implementation.
TestDisjSets.h	Contains a program to test the disjoint sets class.

Exercises

In Short

24.1. Show the result of the following sequence of instructions: *union* (1, 2), *union*(3, 4), *union*(3, 5), *union*(1, 7), *union*(3, 6), *union*(8, 9), *union*(1, 8), *union*(3, 10), *union*(3, 11), *union*(3, 12), *union*(3, 13), *union*(14, 15), *union*(16, 0), *union*(14, 16), *union*(1, 3), and *union*(1, 14) when the `union` operations are performed
   a. arbitrarily.
   b. by height.
   c. by size.

24.2. For each of the trees in Exercise 24.1, perform a `find` operation with path compression on the deepest node.

24.3. Find the minimum spanning tree for the graph shown in Figure 24.24.

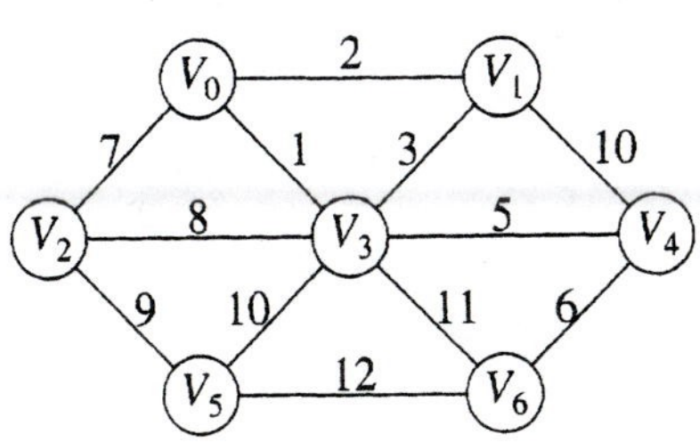

Figure 24.24 A graph *G* for Exercise 24.3

24.4. Show the operation of the NCA algorithm for the data given in Figure 24.8.

In Theory

24.5. Prove that for the mazes generated by the algorithm in Section 24.2.1 the path from the starting to ending points is unique.

24.6. Design an algorithm that generates a maze that contains no path from start to finish but has the property that the removal of a *prespecified* wall creates a unique path.

24.7. Prove that Kruskal's algorithm is correct. In your proof do you assume that the edge costs are nonnegative?

24.8. Show that, if a `union` operation is performed by height, the depth of any tree is logarithmic.

24.9. Show that, if all the `union` operations precede the `find` operations, then the disjoint set algorithm with path compression is linear, even if the `union`s are done arbitrarily. Note that the algorithm does not change; only the performance changes.

24.10. Suppose that you want to add an extra operation, `remove(x)`, which removes x from its current set and places it in its own. Show how to modify the union/find algorithm so that the running time of a sequence of M `union`, `find`, and `remove` operations is still $O(M\alpha(M, N))$.

24.11. Prove that, if `union` operations are done by size and path compression is performed, the worst-case running time is still $O(M \log^* N)$.

24.12. Suppose that you implement partial path compression on `find(i)` by changing the parent of every other node on the path from `i` to the root to its grandparent (where doing so makes sense). This process is called *path halving*. Prove that, if path halving is performed on the `find`s and either `union` heuristic is used, the worst-case running time is still $O(M \log^* N)$.

In Practice

24.13. Implement the `find` operation nonrecursively. Is there a noticeable difference in running time?

24.14. Suppose that you want to add an extra operation, `deunion`, which undoes the last `union` operation not already undone. One way to do so is to use union-by-rank—but a compressionless `find`—and use a stack to store the old state prior to a `union`. A `deunion` can be implemented by popping the stack to retrieve an old state.

a. Why can't we use path compression?

b. Implement the union/find/deunion algorithm.

Programming Problems

24.15. Write a program to determine the effects of path compression and the various union strategies. Your program should process a long sequence of equivalence operations, using all the strategies discussed (including path halving, introduced in Exercise 24.12).

24.16. Implement Kruskal's algorithm.

24.17. An alternative minimum spanning tree algorithm is due to Prim [12]. It works by growing a single tree in successive stages. Start by picking any node as the root. At the start of a stage, some nodes are part of the tree and the rest are not. In each stage, add the minimum-cost edge that connects a tree node with a nontree node. An implementation of Prim's algorithm is essentially identical to Dijkstra's shortest-path algorithm given in Section 15.3, with an update rule:

$$d_w = \min(d_w, c_{v,w})$$

(instead of $d_w = \min(d_w, d_v + c_{v,w})$). Also, as the graph is undirected, each edge appears in two adjacency lists. Implement Prim's algorithm and compare its performance to that of Kruskal's algorithm.

24.18. Write a program to solve the offline NCA problem for binary trees. Test its efficiency by constructing a random binary search tree of 10,000 elements and performing 10,000 ancestor queries.

References

Representation of each set by a tree was proposed in [8]. [1] attributes path compression to McIlroy and Morris and contains several applications of the union/find data structure. Kruskal's algorithm is presented in [11], and the alternative discussed in Exercise 24.17 is from [12]. The NCA algorithm is described in [2]. Other applications are described in [15].

The $O(M \log^* N)$ bound for the union/find problem is from [9]. Tarjan [13] obtained the $O(M\alpha(M, N))$ bound and showed that the bound is tight. That the bound is intrinsic to the general problem and cannot be improved by an alternative algorithm is demonstrated in [14]. A more precise bound for $M < N$ appears in [3] and [16]. Various other strategies for path compression and `union` achieve the same bounds; see [16] for details. If the sequence of `union` operations is known in advance, the union/find problem can be solved in $O(M)$ time [7]. This result can be used to show that the offline NCA problem is solvable in linear time.

Average-case results for the union/find problem appear in [6], [10], [17], and [4]. Results bounding the running time of any single operation (as opposed to the entire sequence) are given in [5].

1. A. V. Aho, J. E. Hopcroft, and J. D. Ullman, *The Design and Analysis of Computer Algorithms,* Addison-Wesley, Reading, Mass., 1974.
2. A. V. Aho, J. E. Hopcroft, and J. D. Ullman, "On Finding Lowest Common Ancestors in Trees," *SIAM Journal on Computing* **5** (1976), 115–132.
3. L. Banachowski, "A Complement to Tarjan's Result about the Lower Bound on the Set Union Problem," *Information Processing Letters* **11** (1980), 59–65.
4. B. Bollobas and I. Simon, "Probabilistic Analysis of Disjoint Set Union Algorithms," *SIAM Journal on Computing* **22** (1993), 1053–1086.
5. N. Blum, "On the Single-Operation Worst-Case Time Complexity of the Disjoint Set Union Problem," *SIAM Journal on Computing* **15** (1986), 1021–1024.
6. J. Doyle and R. L. Rivest, "Linear Expected Time of a Simple Union Find Algorithm," *Information Processing Letters* **5** (1976), 146–148.
7. H. N. Gabow and R. E. Tarjan, "A Linear-Time Algorithm for a Special Case of Disjoint Set Union," *Journal of Computer and System Sciences* **30** (1985), 209–221.
8. B. A. Galler and M. J. Fischer, "An Improved Equivalence Algorithm," *Communications of the ACM* **7** (1964), 301–303.
9. J. E. Hopcroft and J. D. Ullman, "Set Merging Algorithms," *SIAM Journal on Computing* **2** (1973), 294–303.
10. D. E. Knuth and A. Schonage, "The Expected Linearity of a Simple Equivalence Algorithm," *Theoretical Computer Science* **6** (1978), 281–315.

11. J. B. Kruskal, Jr., "On the Shortest Spanning Subtree of a Graph and the Traveling Salesman Problem," *Proceedings of the American Mathematical Society* **7** (1956), 48–50.

12. R. C. Prim, "Shortest Connection Networks and Some Generalizations," *Bell System Technical Journal* **36** (1957), 1389–1401.

13. R. E. Tarjan, "Efficiency of a Good but Not Linear Set Union Algorithm," *Journal of the ACM* **22** (1975), 215–225.

14. R. E. Tarjan, "A Class of Algorithms Which Require Nonlinear Time to Maintain Disjoint Sets," *Journal of Computer and System Sciences* **18** (1979), 110–127.

15. R. E. Tarjan, "Applications of Path Compression on Balanced Trees," *Journal of the ACM* **26** (1979), 690–715.

16. R. E. Tarjan and J. van Leeuwen, "Worst Case Analysis of Set Union Algorithms," *Journal of the ACM* **31** (1984), 245–281.

17. A. C. Yao, "On the Average Behavior of Set Merging Algorithms," *Proceedings of the Eighth Annual ACM Symposium on the Theory of Computation* (1976), 192–195.

Appendices

Appendix A

Miscellaneous C++ Details

In this appendix we briefly describe some features of C++ that are used in the text. We also detail some common C++ programming mistakes.

A.1 None of the Compilers Implement the Standard

Currently, all the compilers that we used have various bugs and fail to compile code that should be legal according to the Standard. We have attempted to program to the minimum common denominator and avoid features that do not work everywhere if a reasonable alternative is available. In some places that is impossible because the alternatives also expose compiler bugs (usually on different compilers). And in other cases, a recent compiler release may have a bug that generates compiler errors for (legal) code that previously compiled.

Listing specific compiler bugs is pointless, because many should be fixed in the next version (famous last words, indeed!), and others are bound to emerge. Instead, code in the text is written with the assumption of working compilers; the tinkering required for some compilers is described in the online `README` file and has been incorporated into the online code. The tinkering is usually minor, but you can waste hours (or even days) trying to do it on your own. Please examine the `README` file to find out about some of the known compiler bugs. This file is likely to remain current as newer versions of the compilers are released. The majority of problems stem from one of three sources: the Standard I/O Library, the introduction of namespaces (Section A.5), and templates (e.g., static members in class templates and function templates).

A.2 Unusual C++ Operators

In this section we describe four categories of C++ operators that occasionally cause confusion: the auto-increment/auto-decrement operators, the type conversion operator, the bitwise operators, and the ternary conditional operator.

A.2.1 Autoincrement and Autodecrement Operators

***Autoincrement* and *autodecrement* add and subtract 1, respectively. The operators are ++ and --. There are two forms, prefix and postfix.**

The C++ language provides operators to add and subtract 1 from an object. The ++ operator may appear either before or after the object upon which it is acting. In both cases the **autoincrement operator** ++ adds 1 to the value of the object. In C++, however, an operator applied to an object yields an expression that has a value. Although the object is guaranteed to be incremented before execution of the next statement, the following question arises: What is the value of the autoincrement expression if it is used in a larger expression?

In this case placement of the ++ is crucial. The semantics of ++x is that the value of the expression is the new value of x, whereas for x++ the value of the expression is the original value of x. For example, in

```
int x = 4, y = 7;
z = x++ + ++y;
```

after the assignment statement, the value of x is 5, the value of y is 8, and the value of z is the sum of the original value of x (4) and the new value of y (8), or 12.

The postfix form of autoincrement (x++) associates from left to right and has highest precedence; it is in a general group of postfix operators that includes the function call operator and a postfix autodecrement operator. The prefix form associates from right to left and is in the same group as the general class of unary operators that includes a prefix autodecrement and the unary plus and minus operators. These operators are immediately below postfix in strength of precedence.

Expressions such as x+x++ produce undefined results in C++ (because the compiler is free to adjust x at any point). Thus if the value of an object is altered in an expression, you must exercise some caution. With reasonable restraint, alteration is not a problem.

A.2.2 Type Conversions

The **type conversion operator** is used to generate a temporary object of a new type. Consider, for instance,

The ***type conversion operator*** **is used to generate a temporary object of a new type.**

```
double quotient;
int x = 6;
int y = 10;
quotient = x / y;      // Probably wrong!
```

In the division, since `x` and `y` are both integers, the result is integer division, and we obtain 0. Integer 0 is then implicitly converted to a `double` so it can be assigned to `quotient`. But we intended for `quotient` to be assigned 0.6. The solution is to generate a temporary object for either `x` or `y` so that the division is performed under the rules for `double`. On older compilers, that would be done in any of the following ways:

```
quotient = double( x ) / double( y ); // Best
quotient = double( x ) / y;           // OK
quotient = ( double ) x / y;          // C style -- avoid
```

Note that neither `x` nor `y` is changed. An unnamed temporary object is created, and its value is used for the division. The last form is the C style and is best avoided, although it works because the type conversion operator has precedence just below the unary operators.

One problem with the type conversions just shown is that they are hard to find in the code. The new standard adds several additional forms of type-conversion operators. The simplest form is the `static_cast`, which is used to perform a compile-time cast. For instance,

```
quotient = static_cast<double>( x ) / y; // New form
```

The newer form is much easier to search for; unfortunately, it takes more space to type. Other conversions are `const_cast`, `dynamic_cast`, and `reinterpret_cast`. The `const_cast` is used to cast away constness without creating a temporary. The `dynamic_cast` is used to perform a cast down an inheritance hierarchy at run time (with an error reported if the cast fails). The `reinterpret_cast` is used to cast between completely unrelated types.

A.2.3 Bitwise Operators

C++ provides *bitwise operators* for the bit-by-bit manipulation of integers. This process allows the packing of several Boolean objects into an integral type.

The C++ language provides **bitwise operators** for the bit-by-bit manipulation of integers. This process allows the packing of several Boolean objects into an integral type. The operators are ~ (unary complement), << and >> (left and right shift), & (bitwise AND), ^ (bitwise exclusive OR), | (bitwise OR), and assignment operators corresponding to all these operators except unary complement. Figure A.1 illustrates the result of applying these operators.[1] Note that the << and >> tokens used for input and output are the same as the bit shift operators. When the left side is a stream object, these operators have different meanings.

The precedence and associativity of the bitwise operators are somewhat arbitrary. When working with them, you should use parentheses.

Figure A.2 shows how the bitwise operators are used to pack information into a 16-bit integer. Such information is maintained by a typical university for a wide variety of reasons, including state and federal mandates. Many of the items require simple yes/no answers and are thus logically representable by a single bit. As Figure A.2 shows, 10 bits are used to represent 10 categories. A faculty member can have one of four possible ranks (assistant, associate, and full professor, as well as nontenure earning), and thus two bits are required. The remaining 4 bits are used to represent one of 16 possible colleges in the university.

Lines 26 and 27 show how `tim` is represented. Tim is a tenured associate professor in the College of Arts and Science. He holds a Ph.D., is a U.S. citizen, and works on the university's main campus. He is not a member of a minority group, disabled, or a veteran. He is on a 12-month contract. Thus `tim`'s bit pattern is given by

```
0011 10 1 0 1 1 1 1 0 0 0 0
```

```
// Assume ints are 16 bits
unsigned int a = 3737;        // 0000111010011001
unsigned int b = a << 1;      // 0001110100110010
unsigned int c = a >> 2;      // 0000001110100110
unsigned int d = 1 << 15;     // 1000000000000000
unsigned int e = a | b;       // 0001111110111011
unsigned int f = a & b;       // 0000110000010000
unsigned int g = a ^ b;       // 0001001110101011
unsigned int h = ~g;          // 1110110001010100
```

Figure A.1 Examples of bitwise operators.

1. Unsigned objects are best for bitwise operators because the results of the bit shifts can be machine dependent for signed objects.

```
1    // Faculty Profile Fields
2  enum
3  {
4       SEX          = 0x0001, // On if female
5       MINORITY     = 0x0002, // On if in a minority group
6       VETERAN      = 0x0004, // On if veteran
7       DISABLED     = 0x0008, // On if disabled
8       US_CITIZEN   = 0x0010, // On if citizen
9       DOCTORATE    = 0x0020, // On if holds a doctorate
10      TENURED      = 0x0040, // On if tenured
11      TWELVE_MON   = 0x0080, // On if on 12 month contract
12      VISITOR      = 0x0100, // On if not permanent faculty
13      CAMPUS       = 0x0200, // On if work is at main campus
14
15      RANK         = 0x0c00, // Two bits to represent rank
16      ASSISTANT    = 0x0400, // Assistant Professor
17      ASSOCIATE    = 0x0800, // Associate Professor
18      FULL         = 0x0c00, // Full Professor
19
20      COLLEGE      = 0xf000, // Represents 16 colleges
21         ...
22      ART_SCIENCE = 0x3000, // Arts and Science = College #3
23         ...
24  };
25      // Later in a function initialize appropriate fields
26      tim = ART_SCIENCE | ASSOCIATE | CAMPUS | TENURED |
27                  TWELVE_MON | DOCTORATE | US_CITIZEN;
28
29      // Promote tim To Full Professor
30      tim &= ~RANK;           // Turn all rank rields off
31      tim |= FULL;            // Turn rank fields on
```

Figure A.2 Packing bits for faculty profiles.

or `0x3af0`. This bit pattern is formed by applying the OR operator on the appropriate fields.

Lines 30 and 31 show the logic used when Tim is deservedly promoted to the rank of full professor. The RANK category has the two rank bits set to 1 and all the other bits set to 0; or

```
0000 11 0 0 0 0 0 0 0 0 0 0
```

The complement, ~RANK, is thus

```
1111 00 1 1 1 1 1 1 1 1 1 1
```

Applying a bitwise AND of this pattern and `tim`'s current setting turns off `tim`'s rank bits, giving

```
0011 00 1 0 1 1 1 1 0 0 0 0
```

The result of the bitwise OR operator at line 31 thus makes `tim` a full professor without altering any other bits, yielding

```
0011 11 1 0 1 1 1 1 0 0 0 0
```

We learn that Tim is tenured because `tim&TENURED` is a nonzero result. We can also find out that Tim is in College #3 by shifting to the right 12 bits and then looking at the resulting low 4 bits. Note that parentheses are required. The expression is `(tim>>12)&0xf`.

A.2.4 The Conditional Operator

The *conditional operator* `?:` is used as a shorthand for simple `if-else` statements.

The **conditional operator `?:`** is shorthand for simple `if-else` statements. The general form is

```
testExpr ? yesExpr : noExpr
```

We evaluate `testExpr` first; then we evaluate either `yesExpr` or `noExpr`, giving the result of the entire expression. We evaluate `yesExpr` if `testExpr` is true; otherwise, `noExpr` is evaluated. The precedence of the conditional operator is just above the assignment operators. This precedence allows us to avoid using parentheses when assigning the result of the conditional operator to an object. For example, the minimum of `x` and `y` is assigned to `minVal` as follows:

```
minVal = x <= y ? x : y;
```

A.3 Command-Line Arguments

Command-line arguments are available by declaring `main` with the signature

```
int main( int argc, char *argv[ ] )
```

Here `argc` is the number of command-line arguments (including the command name), and `argv` is an array of primitive strings (`char *` objects) that store the command-line arguments. As an example, the program shown in Figure A.3 implements the `echo` command.

```
#include <iostream>
using namespace std;

int main( int argc, char *argv[ ] )
{
    for( int i = 1; i < argc; i++ )
        cout << argv[ i ] << " ";
    cout << endl;

    return 0;
}
```

Figure A.3 The echo command.

A.4 Input and Output

Input and output (I/O) in C++ is achieved through the use of streams. The header file `iostream` is included for all basic I/O. Although the C library routines (e.g. `printf` and `scanf`) also work, their use is strongly discouraged. The iostream library is very sophisticated and has many options. We examine only the most basic ones used.

A.4.1 Basic Stream Operations

Four streams are predefined for terminal I/O: `cin`, `cout`, `cerr`, and `clog`; `cin` is the standard input, `cout` is the standard output, `cerr` is the standard error, and `clog` is also the standard error. The difference between `clog` and `cerr` is that writes to `clog` are unbuffered.

As we have shown, the stream extraction operator >> is used for formatted input, and the stream insertion operator << is used for formatted output, as in

```
int x;
int y;

cin >> x >> y;                      // Read x and then y
cout << x << " " << y << " "
     << ( x + y ) << endl;          // Output some stuff
```

Formally, the bit shift operators are overloaded to accept a stream and an object, and a function is present for each type of object; operator overloading guarantees that the correct function is matched. When a new class is built, the class designer can overload the bit shift operator so that objects of the new class can be output as though they were predefined types. Furthermore, because input streams and output streams are of different types, statements such as

```
cin << x;      // Attempt to output into cin
```

fail at compile time.

Input and output have their respective problems. For input, how do we detect errors? For output, how can we finely control the format?

Errors in the Input

In the preceding example, what happens if the user does not provide two integers but instead provides a sequence of letters? In that case we have an input error and two things happen. First, the result of the expression will be false, so we can run a test to determine if we do not get the input that we expect, as in

```
if( cin >> x >> y )
{
    // Read was ok
}
else
    // Error
```

Additionally, member functions can be applied to an input stream. For example, the expression

```
cin.eof( )
```

returns `true` if the end-of-file caused a read to fail. Be sure to remember that `eof` is true only after the fact. Thus the following code fragment is incorrect because it goes around the `while` loop once too often:

```
int x;
while( !cin.eof( ) )
{
    cin >> x;
    cout << "Read " << x << endl;
}
```

The expression

```
cin.fail( )
```

returns `true` if a format error has occurred. The expression

```
cin.good( )
```

returns `true` if all is well. Once an error has occurred, it should be cleared after recovery by a call to

```
cin.clear( );
```

However, if the same read is attempted, it will fail again because the same characters remain in the input stream unread. Typically a string or extra line will need to be read, and ignored, so that newly typed characters can be processed.

Manipulators

We have used `endl` in output, as in

```
cerr << "Format error" << endl;
```

A **manipulator,** `endl`'s function is to place a newline on the stream and then flush the stream buffer, forcing a write. Other manipulators, `dec`, `hex`, and `oct`, are used to change the output of integers to decimal, hexadecimal, and octal. Thus

```
cout << 37 << oct << 37 << hex << 37;
cout << 37;    // still hexadecimal
```

outputs 37, 45, 25, and 25. We can include the base (i.e., a leading `0` or `0x`) in the output by using

```
cout << setiosflags( ios::showbase );
```

The manipulator `setw( int tmpFieldWidth )` is used to set the field width for the next argument (only) placed on the output stream. If the actual width of an object is smaller than the field width allowed, it is right-justified (in that width) by default and filled with padding. We can control what is used as padding characters (the default is blank spaces). For instance, when writing amounts on checks, blank spaces are avoided to discourage fraud. Thus we might have

```
cout.setf( ios::fixed, ios::floatfield );
cout.fill( '*' );      // Pad with *
cout.precision( 2 );   // Two decimal places
cout << setw( 8 ) << 12.49 << endl;
```

which prints `***12.49`.

Instead of using `fill` and `precision` we can use their manipulators:

```
cout.setf( ios::fixed, ios::floatfield );
cout << setw( 8 ) << setprecision( 2 ) << setfill( '*' )
     << 12.49 << endl;
```

There are two important rules to keep in mind.

1. When using manipulators that do not take arguments (e.g., `endl`), do not add parentheses.
2. When using standard manipulators that do take arguments, include the standard header file `<iomanip>`.

A host of options are available. Check a current C++ reference manual for more details.

One-Character-at-a-Time Input and Output

The `put` member function can be used to output a single character. For instance,

```
cout.put( '\n' );
```

outputs a newline character. Similarly, the `get` member function can be used to read a single character (including a white-space character, if that is next in the input stream). It returns a logical false if the end-of-file causes a failure; otherwise, it returns a reference to the new input stream. Here is an example:

```
char ch;
if( cin.get( ch ) )
    cout << "Read " << ch << endl;
else
    cout << "End of file encountered" << endl;
```

Note that there are several versions of `get`. The `putback` member function is used to undo a `get`. The `peek` member function is used to examine the next character in the input stream without digesting it. Note that using `cin>>ch` in the preceding code gives different behavior because `operator>>` skips white space. Note also that in

```
int x;
cin >> x;
```

an immediate call to `cin.get(ch)` returns the character (possibly white space) that follows `x`.

Finally, the `getline` routine can be used to read a line of input. The declaration is

```
istream &
getline( istream & in, string & str, char delim = '\n' );
```

The `getline` routine reads characters from an input stream and forms a string `str`. Reading stops when either `delim` is encountered or the eof is reached. The `delim` character is not included in the string but is removed from the input stream.

The usual disclaimer applies: There are many more functions and options than discussed here.

A.4.2 Sequential Files

One basic rule of C++ is that everything that works for terminal I/O also works for files. To deal with a file, we associate either an `ifstream` (for input file) or `ofstream` (for output file) object with it.[2] We then use the same syntax as for terminal I/O. The header file `fstream` should be included. An example that illustrates the basic ideas is shown in Figure A.4.

Functions that deal with files but do not open them should have references to `ostream` and `istream` objects as parameters. An actual `ofstream` argument will match an `ostream &` formal parameter. Also, direct access files are supported, but we do not go into their details here.

A.4.3 String Streams

For many applications the `>>` operator is not sufficient. For instance, suppose that we are expecting to read two integers, `x` and `y`, repeatedly from an `istream f`. Initially, the following logic appears to work:

```
while( f >> x >> y )
{
    // process two integers
}
```

Unfortunately, this approach does not catch errors. For instance, files that contain only one integer per line are read without incident (because white space includes the newline character). If we want to insist that every line has at least two integers, we need to read a line at a time and then extract the integers from the line. We do so by using the `istringstream`; we must include the header file `sstream`. An example of typical use is the program fragment in Figure A.5.

On line 3 we read a single line of input from the file. A string stream is created at line 5. At lines 7 and 8 we read from the string stream. Note that the string stream has memory of previous reads. Supposedly we should be

2. To associate the stream to a file, we must provide a primitive string as a filename. Hence we usually include calls to `c_str` in the stream constructor.

```
#include <fstream>
#include <iostream>
using namespace std;

// Copy from inFile to outFile
void copy( const string & inFile, const string & outFile )
{
    // Cheap check for aliasing.
    if( inFile == outFile )
    {
        cerr << "Input and output files are identical\n";
        return;
    }

    // Open input stream.
    ifstream inStream( inFile.c_str( ) );
    if( !inStream )
    {
        cerr << "Can't open " << inFile << endl;
        return;
    }

    // Open output stream.
    ofstream outStream( outFile.c_str( ) );
    if( !outStream )
    {
        cerr << "Can't open " << outFile << endl;
        return;
    }
    // Do the copy.
    char ch;
    while( inStream.get( ch ) )
        if( !outStream.put( ch ) )
        {
            cerr << "Output error!" << endl;
            return;
        }
}
```

Figure A.4 A copy routine for files.

able to chain the extraction operators into one statement. However, this technique does not work on a few compilers, so instead we use separate extractions. After we have done the extractions, we test the stream state.

We do not need to reset the stream state because each iteration of the `while` loop generates a new string stream. To avoid the possibility of extraneous inputs, however, we might want to verify that nothing else is left in the string stream. The operations that can be performed on string streams are

```
string oneLine;

while( !getline( f, oneLine ).eof( ) )
{
    istringstream lineStr( oneLine );   // string stream

    lineStr >> x;           // Read first integer
    lineStr >> y;           // Read second integer

    if( !lineStr.fail( ) )
    {
        // Read two integers!!
    }
    else
    {
        // Error: but no need to issue reset
    }
}
```

Figure A.5 A program fragment that illustrates string streams.

identical to those that can be performed on general streams. We use `ostringstream` objects to compose character arrays; but using an `ostringstream` is a bit more complicated, so it is used less often.

A.5 Namespaces

The newly adopted C++ standard has added **namespaces.** In the original C++, once a class had been written and used in a library, its name could no longer be safely used for another class because of the possibility of a naming conflict. The use of namespaces solves this problem.

By default, functions and classes are declared in the global namespace, but a class or a set of functions can be declared in another namespace. In that case, a class or function in a different namespace can coexist without a naming conflict. To declare a namespace, we simply write

```
namespace NamespaceName
{
   ...
}
```

where `NamespaceName` is the name of the namespace. Inside the braces are the kinds of declarations and definitions that typically go in the global namespace. Inside `NamespaceName` we can access other parts of

NamespaceName without any special syntax. Outside NamespaceName, a ClassName class inside NamespaceName is accessed by NameSpace-Name::ClassName. Namespaces are open-ended, so additional classes can be part of the same namespace if we repeat the namespace declaration.

The entire standard library is declared in the namespace std. As a result, cout is properly referred to as std::cout. Using the full name all the time can be annoying and can lead to very long lines of code. As a result, the **using directive** has also been added to the Standard.

There are two forms of the using directive. In the first, we can write

```
using std::cout;
```

and have cout automatically recognized as shorthand for std::cout. In the second, we can write

```
using namespace std;
```

and have all symbols in the std namespace automatically known by their shorthands.

The second alternative—exposing the entire namespace—has a disadvantage: It is more likely to lead to ambiguities with classes that are visible from other namespaces (e.g., the global namespace). In that case, a compiler error results. Although the first alternative could lead to ambiguities, that is less likely (ambiguities are always avoidable by avoiding using directives entirely).

Currently, compilers do not correctly handle all aspects of namespaces. Good design would be to place all the text's code in a separate namespace. However, when we tried this approach, only one compiler handled the resulting code in an acceptable fashion. Thus all the text's code is in the global namespace (which occasionally conflicts with the STL library). The online code has preprocessor commands that make our classes appear to have a different name than the STL class (e.g., vector becomes Vector). See the online README file for details.

Additionally, we expose the entire std namespace in our code. Although this technique is less preferable than exposing it class by class (or symbol by symbol), we do so because at the present time, a wider set of compilers can (more or less) handle this technique better than any other. Again, this approach introduces some problems for some compilers, and you should consult the online README file for details.

A.6 New C++ Features

The newly adopted C++ standard has several new features. Some of them deprecate (i.e., make obsolete) old C++ code.[3] The following is a brief summary of the most important new features used in this text.

1. Old C++ programs were allowed to omit a return type from the function definition (and declaration), in which case the return type defaulted to `int`. This action is no longer legal. One consequence of this change is that `main` must have an explicit return type of `int`.
2. As we have shown, the standard I/O header file is now `iostream`, rather than `iostream.h`. Additionally, most of the standard library is now placed in a namespace named `std`. Consequently, symbols such as `cout` are no longer visible, unless they are specifically scoped as `std::cout` or unless a **using directive** is provided (as has been done throughout the text).
3. The string stream classes previously were `istrstream` and `ostrstream`, were found in `strstream.h`, and were constructed with primitive strings. The new form, detailed in Section A.4.3, is not available on older compilers.
4. The `bool` type and constants `true` and `false` are new.
5. The STL, including `vector`, is new and is not available on older compilers.
6. The `string` type is new.
7. The `explicit` keyword (see Section 2.2.2) is new.
8. `typename` is new.

Common C++ Errors

1. In C++, an `int` can be used instead of a `bool` in conditionals. In that case, 0 is false, nonzero is true, and thus –1 is true. (See error #2.)
2. The most common C++ error is using = instead of ==. Some programmers like to write conditional expressions with constants on the left-hand side (if possible), to get some compiler protection. In other words, instead of `if(x==4)`, it is not unusual to see `if(4==x)` so that an inadvertent = generates a compiler error. (See error #1.)

3. The online code contains options that allow it to compile on older systems. (Please read the online `README` file for more details.)

3. Adding unnecessary semicolons gives logical errors because the semicolon by itself is the `null` statement. Hence an unintended semicolon immediately following a `for`, `while`, or `if` statement is likely to go undetected and break your program.
4. Off-by-one errors are especially common in C++.
5. Local variables are not initialized by default. Do not attempt to use the value of an uninitialized variable. Be aware that 0 seems to be a common uninitialized value and occasionally gives the appearance of a working program.
6. At compile time, C++ detects some instances in which a function that is supposed to return a value fails to do so. But ultimately it is your responsibility to remember.
7. Arithmetic overflow is undetected in C++.
8. Mixing types can produce unexpected results, especially when unsigned quantities are involved. Do not overuse unsigned variables.
9. A leading `0` makes an integer constant octal when encountered as a token in source code, so, for example, `037` is decimal `31`.
10. Like all languages, floating point numbers are subject to rounding errors. Use `double` instead of `float` to make the effect less pronounced.
11. Multiple side effects in a single statement produce undefined results in some cases. There is a precise rule for this case, but in general keep the code simple, and you should not have any problems with it.
12. Division and mod operations can produce machine-dependent results when negative numbers are involved. Avoid this.
13. Precedence rules involving some operators (notably the bitwise operators) are counterintuitive. Many errors result from the wrong precedence. For instance, `?:` has lower precedence than `<<`.
14. Use `&&` and `||` for logical operations and `&` and `|` for bitwise operations. Do not mix them up.
15. The routines in `ctype.h` return 0 or nonzero, rather than true or false, or even 0 or 1.
16. The `else` clause matches the closest dangling `if`. A common error is to forget the braces needed to match the `else` to a distant dangling `if`.
17. When using a `switch` statement, a common error is to forget the `break` statement between logical cases. If it is forgotten, control passes through to the next case; generally this result is incorrect.

18. An object may be declared several times but must be defined only once. Otherwise, you get an error.
19. Escape sequences begin with the backslash character `\`, not the forward slash `/`.
20. The `eof` member function returns `true` only if a read has already failed because the end-of-file was reached. It cannot be used to test whether a read is about to fail.
21. If a stream read has failed, then you must call the `clear` member function to reset the stream's error state before attempting to read from the stream again. You will also need to read some characters to bypass the bad input.
22. Mismatched braces may give misleading answers. Use the balanced-symbol checker (see Section 12.1) to check whether that is the cause of a compiler error message.

Appendix B

Operators

Figure B.1 shows the precedence and associativity of the common C++ operators. It also indicates which operators are overloadable. The precedence of `throw` is just above the comma operator.

<table>
<tr><th>Category</th><th>Examples</th><th>Associativity</th><th>Overloadable</th></tr>
<tr><td>Scope resolution</td><td><code>::</code> (unary scope)
<code>::</code> (class scope)</td><td>Left to right</td><td>No</td></tr>
<tr><td>Postfix</td><td><code>function( ) []</code>
<code>-> . ++ --</code></td><td>Left to right</td><td>Yes, except .</td></tr>
<tr><td>Prefix and unary</td><td><code>sizeof * & ! ~ + -</code>
<code>++ -- new delete</code></td><td>Right to left</td><td>Yes, except <code>sizeof</code></td></tr>
<tr><td>Selector</td><td><code>->* .*</code></td><td>Left to right</td><td><code>->*</code> only</td></tr>
<tr><td>Multiplicative</td><td><code>* / %</code></td><td>Left to right</td><td>Yes</td></tr>
<tr><td>Additive</td><td><code>+ -</code></td><td>Left to right</td><td>Yes</td></tr>
<tr><td>Shift</td><td><code><< >></code></td><td>Left to right</td><td>Yes</td></tr>
<tr><td>Relational</td><td><code>< <= > >=</code></td><td>Left to right</td><td>Yes</td></tr>
<tr><td>Equality</td><td><code>== !=</code></td><td>Left to right</td><td>Yes</td></tr>
<tr><td>Boolean AND</td><td><code>&</code></td><td>Left to right</td><td>Yes</td></tr>
<tr><td>Boolean XOR</td><td><code>^</code></td><td>Left to right</td><td>Yes</td></tr>
<tr><td>Boolean OR</td><td><code>|</code></td><td>Left to right</td><td>Yes</td></tr>
<tr><td>Logical AND</td><td><code>&&</code></td><td>Left to right</td><td>Yes</td></tr>
<tr><td>Logical OR</td><td><code>||</code></td><td>Left to right</td><td>Yes</td></tr>
<tr><td>Conditional</td><td><code>?:</code></td><td>Right to left</td><td>No</td></tr>
<tr><td>Assignment</td><td><code>= *= /= %= += -=</code></td><td>Right to left</td><td>Yes</td></tr>
<tr><td>Comma</td><td><code>,</code></td><td>Left to right</td><td>Yes</td></tr>
</table>

Figure B.1 C++ operators listed from highest to lowest precedence.

Appendix C

Some Library Routines

In this appendix we list some of the library routines used in this text. Note that all these header files are inherited from C. The Standard specifies that alternate header files can be used. The alternates begin with an addition letter `c`, with the `.h` suffix removed.

C.1 Routines Declared in <ctype.h> and <cctype>

These routines test a character for various properties.

```
int isalnum( int ch );       // Nonzero if alphanumeric
int isalpha( int ch );       // Nonzero if alphabetic
int iscntrl( int ch );       // Nonzero if control character
int isdigit( int ch );       // Nonzero if 0-9
int isgraph( int ch );       // Nonzero if graphic
int islower( int ch );       // Nonzero if lower case
int isprint( int ch );       // Nonzero if printable
int ispunct( int ch );       // Nonzero if punctuation
int isspace( int ch );       // Nonzero if white space
int isupper( int ch );       // Nonzero if upper case
int isxdigit( int ch );      // Nonzero if 0-9 or a-f or A-F

int tolower( int ch );       // Return lower case equivalent
int toupper( int ch );       // Return upper case equivalent
```

C.2 Constants Declared in `<limits.h>` and `<climits>`

```
CHAR_BIT  // Bits per bytes

SCHAR_MIN // Smallest value, signed char
SCHAR_MAX // Largest value, signed char
UCHAR_MAX // Smallest value, unsigned char
CHAR_MIN  // Smallest value, char
CHAR_MAX  // Largest value, char

SHRT_MIN  // Smallest value, short
SHRT_MAX  // Largest value, short
USHRT_MAX // Largest value, unsigned short

INT_MIN   // Smallest value, int
INT_MAX   // Largest value, int
UINT_MAX  // Largest value, unsigned int

LONG_MIN  // Smallest value, long
LONG_MAX  // Largest value, long
ULONG_MAX // Largest value, unsigned long
```

C.3 Routines Declared in <math.h> and <cmath>

The <math.h> group provides routines for mathematical operations. On some Unix systems you must specify -lm as a last option to the compiler in order to load these routines. All angles are in radians.

```
  // Trigonometric functions -- all angles in radians
double sin( double theta );
double cos( double theta );
double tan( double theta );
double asin( double x );   // Result is between +/- PI/2
double acos( double x );   // Result is between 0 and PI
double atan( double x );   // Result is between +/- PI/2

  // Hyperbolic functions
double sinh( double theta );
double cosh( double theta );
double tanh( double theta );

  // Logarithms and exponents
double exp( double x );    // e to the x
double log( double x );    // log base e
double log10( double x ); // log base 10
double pow( double x, double y );  // x to the y
double sqrt( double x );   // Square root
  // Miscellaneous
double ceil( double x );   // Ceiling function
double floor( double x ); // Floor function
double fabs( double x );   // Absolute value
```

C.4 Routines Declared in `<stdlib.h>` and `<cstdlib>`

The `<stdlib.h>` group contains many routines, most of which are remnants of C and are best avoided. They include `malloc`, `free`, and some generic routines that use old style `void *` parameters instead of templates. Here we list only those that relate to either program termination or the environment.

```
  // Program termination
void abort( void );        // Terminate program with SIGABRT
int atexit( void ( *func )( void ) ); // See below
void exit( int status );   // Exit program, flush buffers

  // Spawn a command
int system( const char *command );

  // Get environment variable
char *getenv( const char *name );
```

The `abort` routine causes the program to terminate by sending signal `SIGABRT`. This action is not considered "normal termination."

The `exit` function terminates a program normally and is called implicitly when `main` returns. As a result, functions registered with `atexit` are called in reverse order of their registration. Output streams are then closed and flushed, and the program terminates with `status` passed back to the calling environment.

The result of `system` is to pass `command` to the operating system's *command processor* and run it. How that is done is highly system dependent.

The `getenv` routine is used to search for environment variables; again this routine is highly system dependent. For example, Unix users can try the statement

```
cout << "Terminal type is " << getenv( "TERM" ) << endl;
```

Appendix D

Primitive Arrays in C++

Throughout the text, we used the standard `vector` and `string` class to implement arrays and strings. These classes, which were recently added to the Standard Library, are implemented by using primitive arrays. We discussed the primitive arrays only briefly in the text because we believe that using them is generally a bad idea. However, there are cases when primitive arrays must be used. For instance, when you are using legacy code (i.e., old, already written code), you are likely to have to get your hands dirty and use primitive arrays. Also, using primitive arrays judiciously can make your program faster.

In this appendix we discuss primitive arrays in some detail. Our approach in the text made no use of this material; highlights of it were presented in the text only as needed. However, some students feel more comfortable starting with primitive arrays and working up to the STL `vector` and `string`; they are the target audience for this appendix.

We begin by describing the primitive arrays and the relationship of arrays and pointers in C++. We then cover primitive strings. Finally, we discuss the technique of pointer hopping, which revisits an old-style of C optimization. Although this technique is not as valuable as it used to be, it forms the basis of the STL interface and is of historical (and occasionally practical) interest.

D.1 Primitive Arrays

The *array indexing operator* `[]` provides access to any object in the array.

Just as a variable must be declared before it is used in an expression and initialized before its value is used, so must an array. An array is declared by giving it a name, in accordance with the usual identifier rules, and by telling the compiler what type the elements are. If we are defining an array, a size must also be provided. The size can be omitted if an initialization is present; the compiler then counts the number of initializers and takes that as the array size. Each object in the collection of objects that an array denotes can be accessed by use of the **array indexing operator `[]`**. We say that the `[]` operator **indexes** the array, meaning that it specifies which of the objects is to be accessed.

Arrays are indexed starting at zero.

In C++, arrays are always indexed starting at 0. Thus the declaration

```
int a[ 3 ];    // Three int objects: a[0], a[1], and a[2]
```

has the compiler allocate space to store three integers—namely, `a[0]`, `a[1]`, and `a[2]`. As we show later in this appendix, no index range checking is performed in C++, so an access out of the array index bounds is not caught by the compiler. No explicit run-time error is generated, but undefined and occasionally mysterious behavior occurs. Furthermore, if the array is passed as an actual argument to a function, the function has no idea how large the array is unless an additional parameter is passed. Finally, arrays cannot be copied by the = operator. In this section we stick with the core language features of arrays and pointers and discuss why these restrictions come into play.

D.1.1 The C++ Implementation: An Array Name Is a Pointer

The name of an array represents a pointer to the beginning of allocated memory for that array.

When a new array is allocated, the compiler multiplies the size in bytes of the type in the declaration by the array size (the integer constant between the `[]`) to decide how much memory to set aside. That is essentially the only use for the size component. In fact, after the array is allocated, with minor exceptions, the size is irrelevant because the name of the array represents a pointer to the beginning of allocated memory for that array, as illustrated in Figure D.1.

Suppose that we have the declarations

```
int a[ 3 ];
int i;
```

Array items are stored in contiguous, increasing memory locations.

The compiler allocates memory as follows. First, three integers are set aside for the array object and are referenced by `a[0]`, `a[1]`, and `a[2]`. The objects in the array are guaranteed to be stored in one contiguous block of memory. Thus if `a[0]` is stored at memory location 1000 and integers require 4 bytes, `a[1]` is guaranteed to be located at memory location 1004 and `a[2]` at memory location 1008. Finally, the compiler allocates storage for object `i`. One possibility is shown in Figure D.1, where `i` is allocated the next available memory slot.

For any `i`, we can deduce that `a[i]` would be stored at memory location 1000 + 4`i`. The value stored in `a` is `&a[0]`; this equivalence is always

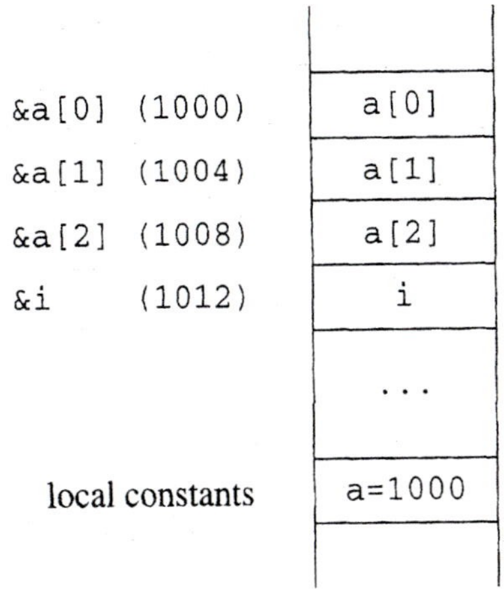

Figure D.1 Memory model for arrays (assumes 4-byte `int`); the declaration is `int a[3]; int i;`.

guaranteed and tells us that `a` is actually a pointer. Note that when an array 9
is allocated, the value of `a` is a constant; a pointer object is not created for it.[1] Now, to access the item `a[i]`, the compiler needs only to fetch the value of `a` and add `4i` to it.

Now that we have shown how arrays are manipulated in C++, you can see why some of the limitations discussed earlier occur. You can also see how arrays are passed as function parameters.

C++ has no built-in index range checking for arrays.

First, we have the problem of verifying that the index is in range. Performing the bounds check would require that we store the array size in an additional parameter. Certainly this approach is feasible, but it does incur both time and space overhead costs. In a common application of arrays (short strings), the overhead could be significant. As mentioned earlier, if the user wants to perform the range check, a class that performs bounds checks can be written and used as though it were a predefined array (this is the `vector` template). Thus we need not debate the wisdom of the language designer's decision not to mandate the range checks. However, the lack of range checking can cause serious problems. Consider the following code fragment that uses the previous declarations of `a` and `i`:

```
for( i = 0; i <= 3; i++ )
    a[ i ] = 0;
```

1. Because this case treats `a` as a constant rather than an object, `&a` is given a special meaning (constants do not normally have addresses) and in this case only, the value of `&a` is `a`.

The programmer has made the common error of referencing `a[3]`, forgetting that an array of size 3 represents indices 0 through 2 only. When `i` is 3, the compiler dutifully executes the statement `a[3]=0` without checking whether the index is valid. Suppose that memory is allocated as shown in Figure D.1. The effect is that memory location 1012 is overwritten with 0, thus demolishing `i`. The result—namely, resetting `i` to 0—creates an infinite loop. However, if the compiler decided (as some do) to leave memory location 1012 empty and place `i` elsewhere, the program appears to work. Thus off-by-one errors in array indexing can lead to bugs that are very difficult to spot. In our example the loop is infinite, but `i` was never directly changed.

Arrays cannot be copied or compared by using = and ==, respectively.

The second limitation of the basic array (which can also be fixed by a user-defined class) is array copying. Suppose that `a` and `b` are arrays of the same type. In many languages, if the arrays are also the same size, the statement `a=b` would perform an element-by-element copy of array `b` into array `a`. In C++ this statement is illegal because `a` and `b` represent constant pointers to the start of their respective arrays, specifically to `&a[0]` and `&b[0]`. Then `a=b` is an attempt to change where `a` points, rather than copying the contents of array `b` into array `a`. What makes the statement illegal, rather than legal but wrong, is that `a` cannot be reassigned to point somewhere else because it is essentially a constant object. The only way to copy two arrays is to do so element by element; there is no shorthand. A similar argument shows that the expression `a==b` does not evaluate to `true` if and only if each element of `a` matches the corresponding element of `b`. Instead, this expression is legal. It evaluates to `true` if and only if `a` and `b` represent the same memory location (i.e., they refer to the same array).

Finally, an array can be used as a parameter to a function, and the rules follow logically from our understanding that an array name is little more than a pointer. Suppose that we have a function `functionCall` that accepts one array of `int` as its parameter. The caller and callee views are

```
functionCall( actualArray );          // Function call
functionCall( int formalArray[ ] ) // Function declaration
```

The address of an array is passed by value. Consequently, the contents of an array are passed by reference.

Note that in the function declaration the brackets serve only as a type declaration, in the same way that `int` does. In the function call only the name of the array is passed; there are no brackets. In accordance with the call-by-value conventions of C++, the value of `actualArray` is copied into `formalArray`. Because `actualArray` represents the memory location where the entire array `actualArray` is stored, `formalArray[i]` accesses `actualArray[i]`. In other words, the variables represented by the indexed array are modifiable. Thus an array, *when considered as an aggregate*, is passed *by reference*. Moreover, any size component in the `formalArray` declaration is ignored, and the size of the actual array is unknown. If the size is needed, it must be passed as an additional parameter.

Note that passing the aggregate by reference means that `functionCall` can change elements in the array. We can use the `const` directive to attempt to disallow such changes (but this technique is not foolproof):

Use a `const` to disallow changes to the aggregate. The size of the formal array is unknown.

```
functionCall( const int formalArray[ ] );
```

D.1.2 Multidimensional Arrays

Sometimes an array access needs to be based on more than one index. A common example of this is a matrix. A **multidimensional array** is an array that is accessed by more than one index. It is allocated by specifying the size of its indices, and each element is accessed by placing each index in its own pair of brackets. For example, the declaration

A *multidimensional array* is an array that is accessed by more than one index.

```
int x[ 2 ][ 3 ];        // x has two rows and three columns
```

defines the two-dimensional array `x`, with the first index ranging from 0 to 1 and the second index ranging from 0 to 2 (for a total of six objects). The compiler sets aside six memory locations for these objects.

D.1.3 The `char *` Type, `const` Pointers, and Constant Strings

An important use of pointers and arrays is the C++ implementation of strings. The C++ base language provides some minimal support for strings, based entirely on the conventions of the C language and the C library. The result is too minimal to be useful in a modern language, so as they do with arrays, C++ programmers tend to rely on the `string` library class rather than the predefined language features. Nonetheless, you may want to know how strings are implemented in the basic C library because they form the basis for the `string` class.

In both C++ and C, a **string** is an array of characters. As a result, when it is passed to a function, the string has type `char *` or `const char *`. At first glance we might assume that the string `"Nina"` is an array of four characters: `'N'`, `'i'`, `'n'`, and `'a'`. The problem with this assumption is that if we pass this array to any routine, that routine would not know how many characters are in the array because, as we have shown, a function that receives an array receives only a pointer and thus has no idea how large the actual array is. One solution to this problem is to use a slightly larger array with an endmarker.

The *null terminator* is the special character that ends a string. It is represented by `'\0'`. You must allocate an extra spot for the null terminator.

For instance, we can declare an array of five elements, placing a blank in the last spot to signal that only the first four positions represent significant characters. If all routines are written to reflect this convention, we have a solution to our problem that requires little alteration of the language. Because we might actually want to use a blank in the string (e.g., to store a street address), we need to pick an endmarker that is not likely to appear elsewhere in the string. In C++ this special character is the **null terminator,** `'\0'`. The escape sequence indicates that the null terminator is always represented internally as zero, which leads to some shorthand when the controlling expression is written in an `if` statement or a loop. (A common error is to forget the \, leaving `'0'`, which is the character representation for the digit 0). Therefore, an array of six characters `'N'`, `'i'`, `'n'`, `'a'`, and `'\0'` represents the string `"Nina"`, no matter what is in the sixth character.

So far, what has C++ provided us in the way of string support? The answer is: absolutely nothing! Furthermore, it does not directly provide some things in the language. Suppose that we declare two strings, `str1` and `str2`, as in

```
char str1[ 10 ]; // Max length is nine
char str2[ 10 ]; // Max length is nine
```

Then the following statements cannot be correct:

```
str1 = str2;                    // Wrong!
cond = ( str1 == str2 );        // Wrong!
```

This failure follows directly from the facts that `str1` and `str2` are arrays and that array assignment and comparison are not supported directly by the language. Almost all the support, in fact, is provided by the C++ library, which specifies routines that work for null-terminated strings. The prototypes for these routines are given in the `<string.h>` include file. This file is replicated in `<cstring>`. Some routines of interest are shown in Figure D.2.

The `strcpy` routine does not verify that the target is large enough to store the copy.

The `strlen(str)` routine gives the length of the string represented by `str` (not including the null terminator); the length of `"Nina"` is 4. In this and all routines, if a `NULL` pointer is passed, you can expect a program crash. Note that this approach is different from passing a pointer to a memory cell

```
size_t strlen( const char *str );
char * strcpy(       char *lhs, const char *rhs );
char * strcat(       char *lhs, const char *rhs );
int    strcmp( const char *lhs, const char *rhs );
```

Figure D.2 Some of the string routines in `<string.h>`.

that contains the `'\0'` character, which represents the empty string of length 0. The `strcpy(lhs,rhs)` routine performs the assignment of strings; characters in the array given by `rhs` are copied into the array given by `lhs` until the null terminator is copied. If the string represented by `lhs` is not large enough to store the copy, another memory gets overwritten.

The abbreviations **`lhs`** and **`rhs`** stand for **left-hand side** and **right-hand side,** respectively. The order of parameters is easy to remember if you keep in mind that

The abbreviations `lhs` and `rhs` stand for *left-hand side* and *right-hand side,* respectively.

```
strcpy( lhs, rhs )
```

is meant to mimic the statement

```
lhs = rhs;
```

The return type `char *` allows `strcpy` calls to be chained in the same way as assignments: `strcpy(a,strcpy(b,c))` is much like `a=b=c`. The `strcat(lhs,rhs)` routine appends a copy of the string represented by `rhs` to the end of `lhs`. As with `strcpy`, it is the programmer's responsibility to ensure that `lhs` is pointing at sufficient memory to store the result. The `strcmp` routine compares two strings and returns a negative number, zero, or a positive number, depending on whether the first string is lexicographically less than, equal to, or greater than the second.

As described so far, C++ provides library routines for strings but no language support. In fact, the only language support is provided by a string constant. A **string constant** provides a shorthand mechanism for specifying a sequence of characters. It automatically includes the null terminator as an invisible last character. Any character (specified with an escape sequence, if necessary) may appear in the string constant, so `"Nina"` represents a five-character array. Additionally, a string constant can be used as an initializer for a character array. Thus

A *string constant* is a sequence of characters enclosed in double quotes. The null terminator is automatically included.

```
char name1[   ] = "Nina"; // name1 is an array of five chars
char name2[ 9 ] = "Nina"; // name2 is an array of nine chars
char name3[ 4 ] = "Nina"; // name3 is an array of four chars
```

In the first case the size of the array allocated for `name1` is determined implicitly. In the second case we have overallocated (which is necessary if we intend later to copy a longer string into `name2`). The third case is wrong because we have not allocated enough memory for the null terminator. Initialization by a string constant is a special exemption; we cannot say

```
char name4[ 8 ] = name1;    // ILLEGAL!
```

A string constant can be used in any place that both a string and a constant object can.

A string constant can be used any place that *both* a string and a constant object can. For instance, it may be used as the second parameter to `strcpy` but not as the first parameter. The reason is that the declaration for `strcpy` does not disallow the possibility that the first parameter might be altered (indeed, we know that it is). Because a string constant can be stored in read-only memory, allowing it to be used as a target of `strcpy` could result in a hardware error. Note that we can always send a nonconstant string to a parameter that expects a constant string. Thus we have

```
strcpy( name2, "Mark" );     // LEGAL
strcpy( "Mark", name2 );     // ILLEGAL!
strcpy( name2, name1 );      // LEGAL
```

The declarations for the string routines indicate that the parameters are pointers because the name of an array is a pointer. The second parameter to `strcpy` is a *constant string*, meaning that any string can be passed with a guarantee that it is to be unchanged. The first parameter is merely a *string* and might be changed. Consequently, a constant string, including string constants, cannot be passed.

Beginners tend to take the equivalence of arrays and pointers one step too far. Recall that the fundamental difference between an array and a pointer is that an array definition allocates enough memory to store the array, whereas a pointer points to memory that is allocated elsewhere. Because strings are arrays of characters, this distinction applies to strings. A common error is declaring a pointer when an array is needed. Consider the declarations

```
char name[ ] = "Nina";
char *name1  = "Nina";
char *name2;
```

The first declaration allocates five bytes for `name`, initializing it to a copy of the string constant `"Nina"` (including the null terminator). The second declaration states merely that `name1` points at the zeroth character of the string constant `"Nina"`. In fact, the declaration is wrong because we are mixing pointer types: The right side is a `const char *`, but the left side is merely a `char *`. Some compilers will complain. The reason is that a subsequent

```
name1[ 3 ] = 'e';
```

is an attempt to alter the string constant. A string constant is supposed to be *constant,* so this action should not be allowed. The easiest way for the compiler to disallow this action is to follow the convention that, if `a` is a constant array, then `a[i]` is a constant also and cannot be assigned to. If the statement

```
char *name1   = "Nina";
```

were allowed, name1[3] would be allowed. By enforcing constness at each assignment, the problem becomes manageable.[2] You can legally use

```
const char *name1 = "Nina";
```

but that is hardly the same as declaring an array to store a copy of the actual string; furthermore, name1[3]='e' is easily determined by the compiler to be illegal in this case. A common example where a const char * declaration would be used is

```
const char *message = "Welcome to FIU!";
```

Another common consequence of declaring a pointer instead of an array object is the following statement (in which we assume that name2 is declared as previously):

```
strcpy( name2, name );
```

Here the programmer expects to copy name into name2 but is fooled because the declaration for strcpy indicates that two pointers are to be passed. The call fails because name2 is just a pointer rather than a pointer to sufficient memory to hold a copy of name. If name2 is a NULL pointer, points at a string constant stored in read-only memory, or points at an illegal random location, strcpy is certain to attempt to dereference it, generating an error. If name2 points at a modifiable array (e.g., name2=name is executed), there is no problem.

Although all these procedures sound very restrictive and tricky, C++ provides a string type and makes it look just like any predefined type, such as an int. Consequently, we do not have to worry about the limitations implied in the C++ base language because they are hidden inside string.

D.2 Dynamic Allocation of Arrays: new [ ] and delete [ ]

Dynamic array allocation **allows us to allocate arbitrarily sized arrays and make them larger if needed.**

Suppose that we want to read a sequence of numbers and store them in an array for processing. The fundamental property of an array requires us to declare a size so that the compiler can allocate the correct amount of memory. We must make this declaration prior to the first access of the array. If we

2. We can type cast away the constness, but at this point the programmer is forfeiting the protection that C++ offers.

have no idea how many items to expect, making a reasonable choice for the array size is difficult. In this section we show how to allocate arrays dynamically and expand them if our initial estimate is too small. This technique, **dynamic array allocation,** allows us to allocate arbitrarily sized arrays and make them larger or smaller as the program runs.

The allocation method for arrays that we have used so far is

```
int a1[ SIZE ];        // SIZE is a compile-time constant
```

We also know that we can use

```
int *a2;
```

The *new operator* dynamically allocates memory.

like an array, except that no memory is allocated by the compiler for the array. The new operator allows us to obtain memory from the system as the program runs. We can use the expression

```
new int [ SIZE ]
```

to allocate enough memory to store SIZE int objects. The expression evaluates to the address where the start of that memory resides. It may be assigned only to an int * object, as in

```
int *a2 = new int [ SIZE ];
```

As a result, a2 is virtually indistinguishable from a1. The new operator is type-safe, meaning that

```
int *a2 = new char[ SIZE ];
```

would be detected at compile time as a type mismatch error.

So what is the difference, if any, between the two forms of array memory allocation? A technical difference is that the memory for a1 is taken from a different source than the memory for a2. However, this difference is transparent to the user. A second difference is that a1 cannot appear on the left-hand side of an assignment operator because the array name is a constant, whereas a2 can. This difference is also relatively minor, and if we declared

```
int * const a2 = new int [ SIZE ];
```

this difference would disappear. More important, SIZE does not have to be a compile-time constant when we use new.

```
void f( int i )
{
    int a1[ 10 ];
    int *a2 = new int [ 10 ];

    ...
    g( a1 );
    g( a2 );

    // On return, all memory associated with a1 is freed
    // On return, only the pointer a2 is freed;
    // 10 ints have leaked
    // delete [ ] a2;    // This would fix the leak
}
```

Figure D.3 Two ways to allocate arrays; one leaks memory.

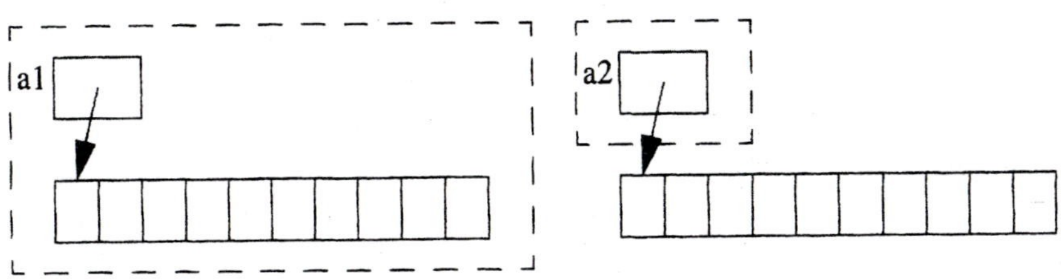

Figure D.4 Memory reclamation in Figure D.3.

A problem does occur when `a1` is a local variable. When the function in which it is declared returns (i.e., when `a1` exits scope), the memory associated with the array is reclaimed automatically by the system; `a1` exits scope when the block in which it is declared is exited. For example, in Figure D.3 `a1` is a local variable in a function `f`. When `f` returns, the entire contents of the `a1` object, including the memory associated with the array, is freed. In contrast, when `a2` exits scope only the memory associated with the pointer is freed; the memory allocated by `new` is now unreferenced, and we have a **memory leak.** The memory is claimed as used, but unreferenced, and is not used to satisfy future `new` requests. The situation is shown graphically in Figure D.4.

Memory allocated by `new` is not automatically recycled. Failure to recycle causes a *memory leak*.

To recycle the memory, we must use the **`delete` operator.** The syntax is

The *`delete`* operator recycles dynamically allocated memory that is no longer needed.

```
delete [ ] a2;
```

The [] is absolutely necessary here to ensure that all the objects in the allocated array are recycled. Without the []only a2[0] might be recycled, which is hardly what we intend. With new and delete we have to manage the memory ourselves rather than allow the compiler to do it for us. Why would we be interested in doing so? The answer is that, by managing memory ourselves, we can build expanding arrays. Suppose, for example, that in Figure D.3 we decide, after the declarations but before the calls to g at lines 7 and 8, that we really wanted 12 ints instead of 10. In the case of a1 we are stuck, and the call at line 7 cannot work. However, with a2 we have an alternative, as illustrated by the following maneuver:

```
int *original = a2;         // 1. Save pointer to the original
a2 = new int [ 12 ];        // 2. Have a2 point at more memory
for( int i = 0; i < 10; i++ ) // 3. Copy the old data over
    a2[ i ] = original[ i ];
delete [ ] original;        // 4. Recycle the original array
```

Always expand the array to a size that is some multiplicative constant times as large. Doubling is a good choice.

Figure D.5 shows the changes that result. A moment's thought should convince you that this operation is expensive because we copy all the elements from original to a2. If, for instance, this array expansion is in response to reading input, expanding an array every time we read a few elements would be inefficient. Thus when array expansion is implemented, we always make it some *multiplicative* constant times as large. For instance, we might expand it to make it twice as large. In this way, when we expand the array from N items to $2N$ items, the cost of the N copies can be apportioned over the next N items that can be inserted in the array without an expansion.

To make things more concrete, Figure D.6 shows a program that reads an unlimited number of integers from the standard input and stores the result in a dynamically expanding array. The function declaration for getInts tells us that it returns the address where the array will reside, and it sets the reference parameter itemsRead to indicate how many items were actually read. The & in the function declaration before itemsRead specifies that it is a reference to the actual parameter rather than a copy of it. Thus all changes in the formal parameter are reflected in the actual argument.

At the start of getInts, itemsRead is set to 0, as is the initial arraySize. We repeatedly read new items at line 15. If the array is full, as indicated by a successful test at line 17, the array is expanded. Lines 19–23 perform the array doubling. At line 19 we save a pointer to the currently allocated block of memory. We have to remember that the first time through the loop the pointer will be NULL. At line 20 we allocate a new block of

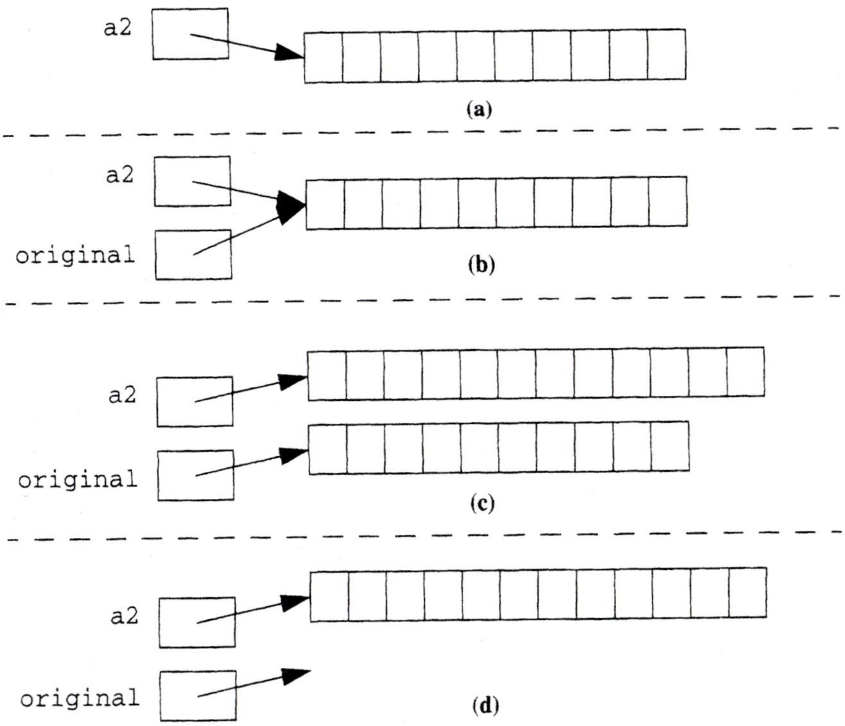

Figure D.5 Array expansion: (a) At the starting point, a2 points at 10 integers; (b) after step 1, `original` points at the 10 integers; (c) after steps 2 and 3, a2 points at 12 integers, the first 10 of which are copied from `original`; and (d) after step 4, the 10 integers are freed.

memory, roughly twice the size of the old. We add 1 so that the initial doubling converts a zero-sized array to an array of size 1. At line 24 we set the new array size. At line 26, the actual input item is assigned to the array, and the number of items read is incremented. When the input fails (for whatever reason), we merely return the pointer to the dynamically allocated memory. Note that

- we do not `delete` the array, and that
- the memory returned is somewhat larger than is actually needed, which can be easily fixed.

The `main` routine calls `getInts`, assigning the return value to a pointer.

```
#include <iostream>
#include <stdlib.h>
using namespace std;

// Read an unlimited number of ints with no attempts at error
// recovery; return a pointer to the data, and set itemsRead.
int * getInts( int & itemsRead )
{
    int arraySize = 0;
    int inputVal;
    int *array = NULL;    // Initialize to NULL pointer

    itemsRead = 0;
    cout << "Enter any number of integers: ";
    while( cin >> inputVal )
    {
        if( itemsRead == arraySize )
        {    // Array doubling code
            int *original = array;
            array = new int[ arraySize * 2 + 1 ];
            for( int i = 0; i < arraySize; i++ )
                array[ i ] = original[ i ];
            delete [ ] original; // Safe if original is NULL
            arraySize = arraySize * 2 + 1;
        }
        array[ itemsRead++ ] = inputVal;
    }
    return array;
}

int main( )
{
    int *array;
    int numItems;

    array = getInts( numItems );
    for( int i = 0; i < numItems; i++ )
        cout << array[ i ] << endl;

    return 0;
}
```

Figure D.6 Code for reading an unlimited number of `int`s and writing them out.

D.3 Pointer Arithmetic, Pointer Hopping, and Primitive Iteration

Many programmers spend lots of time attempting to hand-optimize their code. One common myth is that pointers can be used to access arrays more quickly than can the usual indexing method. That occasionally is true and sometimes leads to better or simpler code. However, in this section we show that this assertion is not universally true (and in fact is frequently false). This difference of opinion is interesting for two reasons. First, it illustrates that with modern compilers the speedups obtained by low-level optimizations often do not justify the effort put into them. Instead, we should concentrate on larger algorithmic optimization issues. Second, although the tricks that will be used reflect an old way of programming, that way is the basis for many constructs in the STL. So when we wonder why things in the STL are how they are, this section provides some of the answers.

We begin by looking at how arithmetic applies to pointers. We have two issues to consider. First, in an expression such as `*x+10` or `*x++`, is the operator (`+` or `++`) being applied to `x` or `*x`? The answer to this question is determined by normal precedence rules. In the first case 10 is added to `*x`, and in the second case the increment is applied to `x` (after the value of `*x` is used). The second issue, then, is to decide what incrementing or applying various operations to a pointer means. After considering this issue, we present an application that shows how pointer math is typically used and discuss whether using it is a good idea.

D.3.1 Implications of the Precedence of `*`, `&`, and `[ ]`

Postfix operators* have higher precedence than *prefix operators.

The dereferencing operator `*` and the address-of operator `&` are grouped in a class of **prefix operators.** These operators include the unary minus (`-`), the not operator (`!`), the bitwise complement operator (`~`), and the prefix increment and decrement operators (`++` and `--`), as well as `new`, `delete`, and `sizeof`. The prefix unary operators have higher precedence than almost all other operators; the exceptions are the scope operators and the **postfix operators,** such as the postfix increment and decrement operators (`++` and `--`), the function call operator `()`, and the array access operator `[]`. Consequently, the only arithmetic operators that have higher precedence than a dereferencing operator are the postfix increment and decrement operators. In the following expressions, the operator is applied to the dereferenced value:

```
*x + 5       // Adds 5 to *x
*x == 0      // True if *x is 0
*x / *y      // Divide *x by *y
```

Because of precedence rules, *x++ applies the ++ operator to x and then dereferences the original x.

Note that, because of precedence rules, `*x++` is interpreted as `*(x++)`, not `(*x)++`. The precedence of the array indexing operator tells us that if x is a pointer, the following operators are applied to the indexed value of x:

```
5 + x[ 0 ]     // Add x[0] and 5
0 == x[ 0 ]    // True if x[0] is 0
++x[ 0 ]       // Increment x[0]. Same as ++*x (why?)
x++[ 0 ]       // Same as *x++ (why?)
x == &x[ 0 ] // Always true
```

In the last example we reiterated that x always stores the memory location of `x[0]`. The precedence rules are convenient here because we do not need to use parentheses, as in `&(x[0])`.[3]

D.3.2 What Pointer Arithmetic Means

Suppose that x and y are pointer variables. Now that we have decided on precedence rules, we need to know their interpretation for arithmetic performed on pointers. For instance, what does multiply x by 2 mean? The answer in most cases is that arithmetic on pointers is totally meaningless and is therefore illegal. Most other languages allow only comparison, assignment, and dereferencing of pointers; C++ is somewhat more lenient.

Looking at the various operators, we see that none of the multiplicative operators make sense. Therefore a pointer may not be involved in a multiplication. The dereferenced value can, of course, be multiplied, so what we are restricting is computations involving addresses.

Two pointers are equal if they both point to NULL or they both point to the same address.

Equality and logical operators all make sense for pointers, so they are allowed and have obvious meanings. Two pointers are equal if they both point to NULL or they both point to the same address. Assignment by = is allowed, as we have shown, but `*=`, `/=`, and `%=` are disallowed. Therefore the questionable operators are the additive operators (including `+=`, `-=`, `++`, and `--`) and the relational operators (<, <=, >=, and >). To make sense, all these operators need to be viewed in the context of an array.

Figure D.7 shows an array a, a pointer ptr, and the assignment ptr=a. The diagram reinforces the idea that the value stored in a is just the memory location where the zeroth element of the array is stored and that elements of an array are guaranteed to be stored in consecutive and increasing memory locations. If a is an array of characters, `a[1]` is stored in memory location

3. Appendix B provides a table of C++ operators and their precedences.

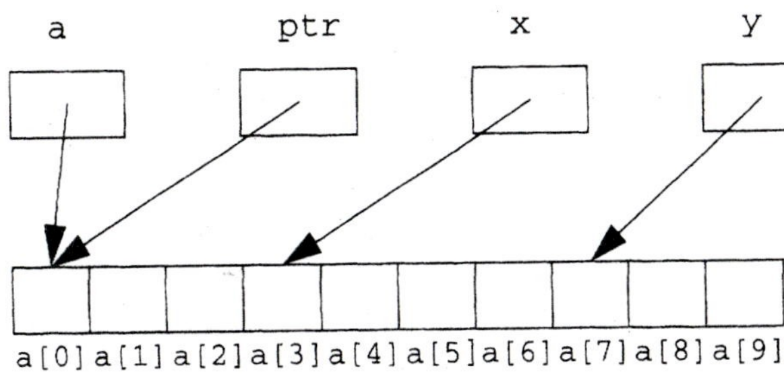

Figure D.7 Pointer arithmetic: `x=&a[3]; y=x+4;`.

`a+1` because characters use 1 byte. Thus the expression `++ptr` would increase `ptr` by 1, equalling the memory location of `a[1]`.

Therefore adding an integer to a pointer variable can make sense in an array of characters. If `a` was an array of 4-byte integers, adding 1 to `ptr` would make only partial sense under our current interpretation. The reason is that `ptr` would not actually be pointing at an integer but somewhere in the middle and would be misaligned, generally leading to a hardware fault. Because that interpretation would give erroneous results, in C++ we use the following interpretation: `++ptr` adds the size of the pointed at object to the address stored in `ptr`.

If `p` is a pointer and `x` is an integer type, `p+x` evaluates to an address `p` objects past `x`. This address is also the memory location of `p[x]`.

This interpretation carries over to other pointer operations. The expression `x=&a[3]` makes `x` point at `a[3]`. Parentheses are not needed, as mentioned earlier. The expression `y=x+4` makes `y` point at `a[7]`. We could thus use a pointer to traverse an array instead of using the usual index iteration method. We discuss this technique in Sections D.3.3 and D.3.4.

Although adding or subtracting an integer type from a pointer type makes sense, adding two pointers does not make sense. However, subtracting two pointers does make sense: `y-x` evaluates to 4 in the preceding example above (because subtraction is the inverse of addition). Thus pointers can be subtracted but not added.

For two pointers `x` and `y`, `x<y` is true if the object that `x` is pointed at is at a lower address than the object that `y` is pointing at. If we assume that neither is pointing at `NULL`, this expression is almost always meaningless unless both are pointing at elements in the same array. In that case `x<y` is true if `x` is pointing at a lower indexed element than `y` because, as we have indicated, the elements of an array are guaranteed to be stored in increasing and contiguous parts of memory. Comparing the values of pointers that point into the same array is the only legitimate use of the relational operator on pointers; all other uses should be avoided.

Do not use relational operators on pointers unless both pointers are pointing to parts of the same array.

To summarize, we have the following pointer operations:

- Pointers may be assigned, compared for equality (and inequality), and dereferenced in C++, as well as almost all other languages. The operators are `=`, `==`, `!=`, and `*`.
- We can apply the prefix or postfix increment operators to a pointer, add an integer, and subtract either an integer or pointer. The operators are `++`, `--`, `+`, `-`, `+=`, and `-=`.
- We can apply relational operators to pointers, but the result makes sense only if the pointers point to parts of the same array or at least one pointer points to `NULL`. The operators are `<`, `<=`, `>`, and `>=`.
- We can test against `NULL` by applying the `!` operator (because the `NULL` pointer has value 0).
- We can subscript and delete pointers via `[]` and `delete`.
- We can apply trivial operators, such as `&` and `sizeof`, to find out information about the pointer (not the object it is pointing at).
- We can apply some other operators, such as `->`.

D.3.3 A Pointer-Hopping Example

Figure D.8 illustrates how pointers can be used to traverse arrays. We have written two versions of `strlen`. Recall that a primitive string is simply an array of characters, with a null terminator signaling the end of the string (see Section D.1.3). The library routine `strlen` gives the length of a primitive string.

In the first version, `strlen1`, we use the normal indexing mechanism to step through the array of characters. When the `for` loop ends, the value of `i` is the index of the null terminator. But because the array starts at 0, this value equals the length of the string and can thus be used as the return value at line 9.

Pointers can be used to traverse arrays. This is called *pointer hopping*.

The *pointer-hopping* version is `strlen2`. At line 15, we declare a second pointer `sp` that is initialized to point at the start of the string. The `const` is necessary here because we have `sp` point where `str`, itself a `const`, points. We continually advance `sp`, breaking the loop only after it is pointing at the null terminator, which is written concisely at line 17. The value of `*sp++` is the character that `sp` points at, and immediately after the test is completed, `sp` is advanced to point at the next character in the string.

When the `while` loop terminates, `sp` is pointing at the position after the null terminator (because the `++` is applied even if the test indicates that a null terminator has been encountered). The length of the string is thus given by

```
1 // strlen implemented with usual indexing mechanism.
2 int strlen1( const char str[ ] )
3 {
4     int i;
5
6     for( i = 0; str[ i ] != '\0'; i++ )
7         ;
8
9     return i;
10 }
11
12 // strlen implemented with pointer hopping.
13 int strlen2( const char *str )
14 {
15     const char *sp = str;
16
17     while( *sp++ != '\0' )
18         ;
19
20     return sp - str - 1;
21 }
```

Figure D.8 The `strlen` routine coded two ways: (1) using indexing; and (2) using pointer hopping.

the formula at line 20 as 1 less than the difference between the final and initial positions of `sp`.[4]

A crucial observation with respect to the discussion of the STL in Chapter 7 is that, in `strlen1`, `i` is used to iterate over the collection of characters, and, in `strlen2`, `sp` is used to iterate over the collection of characters.

D.3.4 Is Pointer Hopping Worthwhile?

Why might a pointer implementation be faster than an array implementation? Let us consider a string of length 3. In array implementation we access the array via `s[0]`, `s[1]`, `s[2]`, and `s[3]`. Then `s[i]` is accessed by adding 1 to the previous value, `i-1`, and adding `s` and `i` to get the required memory location. In pointer implementation, `s[i]` is accessed by adding 1

4. It is tempting to initialize `sp` to `str-1` and use a prefix `++` operator in an attempt to simplify the return statement. This behavior is undefined in C++ because a pointer must point at `NULL`, an object, or (if an array) part of the array or perhaps one cell following the end of the array. It may not point to the cell prior to the start of the array. The resulting code runs correctly on almost all platforms but is nonetheless in technical violation of C++ rules.

Pointer hopping used to be an important technique. Optimizing compilers have made it generally unnecessary. Stick to algorithmic issues for speed improvements and leave code generation to the compiler.

to sp, and we do not keep a counter i. Thus we save an addition for each character, costing only an extra two subtractions during the return statement.

The next question is whether the trickier code is worth the time savings. The answer is that in most programs a few subroutines dominate the total running time. Historically, the use of trickier code for speed has been justified only for those routines that actually account for a significant portion of the program's running time or in routines used in enough different programs to make the optimization worthwhile. Thus in the old days C programs that used pointer hopping judiciously had a large speed advantage over programs written in other high-level languages. However, good modern compilers can, in many cases, perform this optimization. Thus the use of pointers to traverse arrays helps some compilers, is neutral for others, or may even generate slower code than the typical index addressing mechanism.

A *profiler* gives information about where a program is spending most of its running time.

The moral of the story is that, in many cases, the best approach is to leave minute coding details to the compiler and concentrate on the larger algorithmic issues and on writing the clearest code possible. Many systems have a **profiler** tool that allows you to decide where a program is spending most of its running time. This information will help you decide where to apply algorithmic improvements, so learning how to use the optimizer and profiler on your system is important.[5]

5. But be warned of optimizer horror stories: some overly aggressive optimizers have bugs in them and actually break working code.

Common C++ Errors

1. In the declaration `int *a = new int[100]`, the `sizeof` operator gives a misleading result. The size of `a` equals `sizeof(int*)`, and is typically four bytes.
2. To define an array, the array size must be a compile-time constant expression. Some compilers relax this rule, but this relaxation is not portable.
3. Two-dimensional arrays are indexed as `a[i][j]`, not `a[i,j]`.
4. When an array is deleted, you must use `delete[]`, not merely `delete`. Use the following general rules: Anything allocated by `new` requires `delete`, anything allocated by `new[]` requires `delete[]`, and anything else does not require `delete`.
5. Continuing the previous rule, the sequence `int a[10]; delete[] a;` is almost certain to cause problems because `a` was not allocated by `new[]`.

On the Internet

PointerHopping.cpp Shows the two `strlen` functions from Figure D.8.

Index

B

C

G

H

I

M

N

Q

S

T

U

V

W

X

Z